KU-282-164

wwnorton.com/naal

The StudySpace site that accompanies *The Norton Anthology of American Literature* is **FREE**, but you will need the code below to register for a password that will allow you to access the copyrighted materials on the site.

AMER-ICAN

THE NORTON ANTHOLOGY OF

AMERICAN

LITERATURE

EIGHTH EDITION

VOLUME E: LITERATURE SINCE 1945

INTERNATIONAL
EDITION

Wayne Franklin
PROFESSOR AND HEAD, ENGLISH
UNIVERSITY OF CONNECTICUT

Philip F. Gura
WILLIAM S. NEWMAN DISTINGUISHED PROFESSOR OF AMERICAN LITERATURE AND CULTURE
UNIVERSITY OF NORTH CAROLINA, CHAPEL HILL

Jerome Klinkowitz
UNIVERSITY DISTINGUISHED SCHOLAR AND PROFESSOR OF ENGLISH
UNIVERSITY OF NORTHERN IOWA

Arnold Krupat
PROFESSOR OF LITERATURE
SARAH LAWRENCE COLLEGE

Robert S. Levine
PROFESSOR OF ENGLISH AND DISTINGUISHED SCHOLAR-TEACHER
UNIVERSITY OF MARYLAND, COLLEGE PARK

Mary Loeffelholz
PROFESSOR OF ENGLISH
NORTHEASTERN UNIVERSITY

Jeanne Campbell Reesman
PROFESSOR OF ENGLISH
UNIVERSITY OF TEXAS AT SAN ANTONIO

Patricia B. Wallace
MARY AUGUSTA SCOTT PROFESSOR OF ENGLISH
VASSAR COLLEGE

THE NORTON ANTHOLOGY OF

AMERICAN
LITERATURE

EIGHTH EDITION

Nina Baym, *General Editor*

SWANLUND CHAIR AND CENTER FOR
ADVANCED STUDY PROFESSOR EMERITA OF ENGLISH
JUBILEE PROFESSOR OF LIBERAL ARTS AND SCIENCES
University of Illinois at Urbana-Champaign

Robert S. Levine, *Associate General Editor*

PROFESSOR OF ENGLISH AND DISTINGUISHED SCHOLAR–TEACHER
University of Maryland, College Park

VOLUME E: LITERATURE SINCE 1945

INTERNATIONAL EDITION

W · W · NORTON & COMPANY
NEW YORK · LONDON

W. W. Norton & Company has been independent since its founding in 1923, when William Warder Norton and Mary D. Herter Norton first published lectures delivered at the People's Institute, the adult education division of New York City's Cooper Union. The firm soon expanded its program beyond the Institute, publishing books by celebrated academics from America and abroad. By midcentury, the two major pillars of Norton's publishing program—trade books and college texts—were firmly established. In the 1950s, the Norton family transferred control of the company to its employees, and today—with a staff of four hundred and a comparable number of trade, college, and professional titles published each year—W. W. Norton & Company stands as the largest and oldest publishing house owned wholly by its employees.

Editor: Julia Reidhead
Associate Editor: Carly Fraser Doria
Managing Editor, College: Marian Johnson
Manuscript Editors: Michael Fleming, Katharine Ings,
Candace Levy, Susan Joseph, Pam Lawson
Electronic Media Editor: Eileen Connell
Production Manager: Benjamin Reynolds
Marketing Manager, Literature: Kimberly Bowers
Photo Editor: Stephanie Romeo
Photo Research: Jane Sanders Miller
Permissions Manager: Megan Jackson
Permissions Clearing: Margaret Gorenstein
Text Design: Jo Anne Metsch
Art Director: Rubina Yeh

Composition: The Westchester Book Group
Manufacturing: R. R. Donnelley & Sons—Crawfordsville, IN

The text of this book is composed in Fairfield Medium with the display set in Aperto.

Copyright © 2012, 2007, 2003, 1998, 1994, 1989, 1985, 1979
by W. W. Norton & Company, Inc.

Library of Congress Cataloging-in-Publication Data has been applied for.

ISBN 978-0-393-91256-2

W. W. Norton & Company, Inc., 500 Fifth Avenue, New York, NY 10110-0017
wwnorton.com

W. W. Norton & Company Ltd., Castle House, 75/76 Wells Street, London W1T 3QT
1 2 3 4 5 6 7 8 9 0

Contents

American Literature since 1945

Preface to the Eighth Edition

This edition of *The Norton Anthology of American Literature* is the last for me as General Editor, and I am delighted to announce that Robert S. Levine, the editor of Volume B, will take over as General Editor for the next and subsequent editions. Here he joins me as Associate Editor; together we have continued the work for which Norton has achieved its leading position among American literature anthologies. It has been a great pleasure to work on this anthology, to make contact with teachers and students around the country—indeed around the world. I know I leave *The Norton Anthology of American Literature* in immensely capable hands.

From the anthology's inception in 1979, the editors have had three main aims: first, to present a rich and substantial enough variety of works to enable teachers to build courses according to their own ideals (thus, teachers are offered more authors and more selections than they will probably use in any one course); second, to make the anthology self-sufficient by featuring many works in their entirety along with extensive selections for individual authors; third, to balance traditional interests with developing critical concerns in a way that points to a coherent American literary history. As early as 1979, we anthologized work by Anne Bradstreet, Mary Rowlandson, Sarah Kemble Knight, Phillis Wheatley, Margaret Fuller, Harriet Beecher Stowe, Frederick Douglass, Sarah Orne Jewett, Kate Chopin, Mary E. Wilkins Freeman, Booker T. Washington, Charles Chesnutt, Edith Wharton, W. E. B. Du Bois, and other writers who were not yet part of a standard canon. Yet we never shortchanged writers like Franklin, Emerson, Whitman, Hawthorne, Melville, Dickinson, Hemingway, Fitzgerald, and Faulkner, whose work students expected to read in their American literature courses, and whom teachers then and now would not think of doing without.

Although the so-called canon wars of the 1980s and 1990s have subsided, they initiated a review of our understanding of American literature that has enlarged the number and diversity of authors now recognized as contributors to the totality of American literature. The traditional writers, who look different in this expanded context, also appear different according to which of their works are selected. Teachers and students remain committed to the idea of the literary—that writers strive to produce artifacts that are both intellectually serious and formally skillful—but believe more than ever that writers should also be understood in relation to their cultural and historical situations. In endeavoring to do justice to these complex realities, we have worked, as in previous editions, with detailed suggestions from many teachers and, through those teachers, the students who use the anthology. Thanks to questionnaires, comment cards, face-to-face and phone discussions, letters, and email, we have been able to listen to those for whom this book is intended. For this Eighth Edition, we have drawn on the careful commentary of over 200 reviewers.

Our new materials continue the work of broadening the canon by representing 13 new writers in depth, without sacrificing widely assigned writers, many of whose selections have been reconsidered, reselected, and expanded. Our aim is always to provide extensive enough selections to do the writers justice, including complete works wherever possible. To the 34 complete longer texts already in the anthology—among them Hawthorne's *The Scarlet Letter* and Kate Chopin's *The Awakening*—we have added Margaret Fuller's "The Great Lawsuit," August Wilson's *Fences*, and Katherine Anne Porter's *Pale Horse, Pale Rider*. Two complete works—Eugene O'Neill's *Long Day's Journey into Night* and Tennessee Williams's *A Streetcar Named Desire*—are exclusive to *The Norton Anthology of American Literature*. Charles Brockden Brown, Louisa May Alcott, Upton Sinclair, Mourning Dove, Martin Luther King Jr., and Junot Díaz are among more than a dozen writers new to the Eighth Edition, which has expanded and in some cases reconfigured such central figures as Emerson, Hawthorne, Melville, Dickinson, and Twain, offering new approaches in the headnotes and section introductions. In fact, over the last two editions, the headnotes and, in many cases, selections for such frequently assigned authors as Benjamin Franklin, Washington Irving, James Fenimore Cooper, William Cullen Bryant, Lydia Maria Child, Henry Wadsworth Longfellow, Ralph Waldo Emerson, Harriet Beecher Stowe, Mark Twain, William Dean Howells, Henry James, Kate Chopin, W. E. B. Du Bois, Edith Wharton, Willa Cather, and William Faulkner have been revised, updated, and in some cases entirely rewritten in light of recent scholarship. The Eighth Edition further expands its selections of women writers and writers from diverse ethnic, racial, and regional backgrounds—always with attention to the critical acclaim that recognizes their contributions to the American literary record. New and recently added writers such as Sarah Winnemucca and Jane Johnston Schoolcraft, more selections from writers such as Zitkala Ša, and a cluster on "The Ghost Dance and Wounded Knee," all introduced and annotated by Native American specialist Arnold Krupat, enable teachers to bring early Native American writing and oratory into their syllabuses, or should they prefer, to focus on these selections as a free-standing unit leading toward the moment after 1945 when Native writers fully entered the mainstream of literary activity.

We are pleased to continue our popular innovation of topical gatherings of short texts that illuminate the cultural, historical, intellectual, and literary concerns of their respective periods. Designed to be taught in a class period or two, or used as background, each of the 14 clusters consists of brief, carefully excerpted primary and (in one case) secondary texts, about 6–10 per cluster, and an introduction. Diverse voices—many new to the anthology—highlight a range of views current when writers of a particular time period were active, and thus allow students better to understand some of the large issues that were being debated at particular historical moments. For example, in "Slavery, Race, and the Making of American Literature," texts by David Walker, William Lloyd Garrison, Angelina Grimké, Sojourner Truth, and Martin R. Delany speak to the great paradox of pre–Civil War

America, addressed by numerous authors of the period: the contradictory rupture between the realities of slavery and the nation's ideals of freedom.

The Eighth Edition strengthens this feature with six new and revised clusters attuned to the requests of teachers. To help students address the controversy over race and aesthetics in *Adventures of Huckleberry Finn*, we introduce a cluster in Volume C that shows what some of the leading critics of the past few decades have thought was at stake in reading and interpreting Twain's canonical novel. Entitled "Critical Controversy: Race and the Ending of *Adventures of Huckleberry Finn*," the cluster brings together selections by Toni Morrison, Jane Smiley, Leo Marx, Justin Kaplan, Julius Lester, Shelley Fisher Fishkin, and David L. Smith. For the contemporary period in Volume E, we print for the first time "Creative Nonfiction," a much-requested topic showcasing a newly important (and highly popular) literary genre, with selections by Edward Abbey, Barry Lopez, Jamaica Kincaid, Joan Didion, and Edwidge Danticat, among others. New to Volume A is a cluster on "First Encounters: Early European Accounts of Native Americans," while Volume B has a revised cluster, "Section, Region, Nation, Hemisphere," which puts new emphasis on U.S. imperial ambitions in the western hemisphere. Volume C also includes "Debates over 'Americanization,'" with selections by Theodore Roosevelt and others, and a new cluster on "The Ghost Dance and Wounded Knee."

The Eighth Edition of *The Norton Anthology of American Literature* features a dramatic expansion of our illustrations, including not only the color plates so popular in the last edition, but also over 120 black-and-white illustrations added throughout the volumes. In selecting color plates—from Juan de la Cosa's world map at the start of the sixteenth century to *The Gates* by Christo and Jeanne-Claude at the beginning of the twenty-first—the editors aimed to provide images relevant to literary works in the anthology while depicting arts and artifacts representative of each era. Throughout the five volumes of the Eighth Edition, we have similarly added visually striking black-and-white images that will provoke discussion. In addition, graphic works—segments from Art Spiegelman's canonical graphic novel *Maus* and from the colonial children's classic *The New-England Primer*, a facsimile page of Emily Dickinson manuscript, and an original illustration from Twain's *Roughing It*, along with the many new illustrations—open possibilities for teaching visual texts.

Period-by-Period Revisions

Volume A, Beginnings to 1820. "Beginnings to 1700," edited by Wayne Franklin, continues to feature narratives by early European explorers of the North American continent as they encountered and attempted to make sense of the diverse cultures they met, and as they attempted to justify their aim of claiming the territory for Europeans. These are precisely the issues foregrounded by the new cluster on "First Encounters," which gathers writings by Hernán Cortés, Samuel de Champlain, Robert Juet, and others. In addition to the recently added material from *The Bay Psalm Book*, Roger Williams, Edward Taylor, and *The New-England Primer*, we have added for this edition a contemporary telling by Navajo Irvin Morris of the Navajo Creation Story and Cotton Mather's "Bonifacius." We continue to offer the complete text of Rowlandson's enormously influential *A Narrative of the Captivity and Restoration of Mrs. Mary Rowlandson*. The heightened attention in this section to the combined religious and territorial aspirations of the Anglo settlers, which fail to take account of the perspectives of the Native American writers featured in Volume A, gives students a fuller sense of the inevitable conflicts ensuing from the European perception that North America was a "New World" rather than a long-settled world with its own history and traditions. We note, too, the important role of the experiences of, and narratives by, women in the early European settlement of the future United States.

In "American Literature 1700–1820," edited by Philip Gura, we approach the eighteenth century as a period of consolidation and development in an emergent American literature. The inclusion of a long excerpt from one of Charles Brockden Brown's major novels, *Edgar Huntly*, new to the Eighth Edition, calls attention to the Americanization of such important literary developments as the gothic. We have also added new selections by Benjamin Franklin and Thomas Jefferson. Understanding of the emergence of an "American" self is augmented by Franklin's *Autobiography*, included complete by teacher request, and Royall Tyler's popular play *The Contrast*. Recently added is the complete text of Hannah Foster's novel *The Coquette*, which uses a real-life tragedy to meditate on the proper role of well-bred women in the new republic and testifies to the existence of a female audience for the popular novels of the period. The cluster "Women's Poetry: From Manuscript to Print," with verse by six poets—among them Mercy Otis Warren, Sarah Wentworth Morton, and Annis Boudinot Stockton—indicates the importance of female literacy and the new sense among women that their writing could have political effect. A second cluster, edited by Arnold Krupat, "Native Americans: Contact and Conflict," collects speeches and accounts by Pontiac, Samson Occom, Chief Logan (as cited by Thomas Jefferson), Red Jacket, and Tecumseh, which, as a group, underscore a centuries-long pattern of initial friendly contact mutating into bitter and violent conflict between Native Americans and whites. This cluster, which focuses on Native Americans' points of view, wonderfully complements the new cluster on "First Encounters," which focuses on European colonizers' points of view.

Volume B, American Literature 1820–1865. Under the editorship of Robert S. Levine, this volume is now much more diverse. Emerson's *Nature*, Hawthorne's *Scarlet Letter*, Thoreau's *Walden*, Douglass's *Narrative*, and Whitman's *Song of Myself* are still complete in this volume, as well as novellas by Melville, Davis's *Life in the Iron Mills*, and other frequently assigned works. Aware of the important role of African American writers in the period, the omnipresence of race and slavery as literary and political themes, and the recognition of literary value in a previously ignored population, we have recently added two major African American writers, William Wells Brown and Frances E. W. Harper, as well as Douglass's complete novella, "The Heroic Slave." Thoreau's "Plea for Captain John Brown," more chapters from Stowe's *Uncle Tom's Cabin* (including a new chapter for the Eighth Edition), and the cluster "Slavery, Race, and the Making of American Literature" also help to remind students of how central slavery was to the literary and political life of the nation during this period. The volume also includes the newly revised cluster "Section, Region, Nation, Hemisphere," in which writers from various regions—such as the northerner Daniel Webster, the southerner William Gilmore Simms, and the Mexican Lorenzo de Zavala—convey their differing perspectives on a "national" literature while reflecting on the extraordinary enlargement of U.S. territory following the war with Mexico in 1846–48—land stretching to the Pacific Ocean that more than doubled the nation's size. The writings by Zavala, James Whitfield, and Julia Ward Howe in particular, added for this edition, offer new perspectives on expansionism and nation in a hemispheric context. "Native Americans: Resistance and Removal," edited by Arnold Krupat, gathers oratory and writings—by Native Americans such as Black Hawk, Petelasharo, Elias Boudinot, and the collective authors of the Cherokee Memorials as well as by whites such as Ralph Waldo Emerson—protesting Andrew Jackson's ruthless national policy of Indian removal. Political themes, far from diluting the literary imagination of American authors, served to inspire some of the most memorable writing of the day.

Women writers recently added to Volume B include Lydia Huntley Sigourney and the Native American writer Jane Johnston Schoolcraft. Recently added prose fiction includes chapters from Cooper's *Last of the Mohicans*, Sedgwick's *Hope Leslie*, and Melville's *Moby-Dick*, along with Poe's "The Black Cat" and Hawthorne's "Wakefield." By instructors' request, we increased the representation of poems by Longfellow and Whittier; poetry by Emily Dickinson is now presented in the texts recently established by R. W. Franklin (we retain the traditional Thomas Johnson numbers in brackets for reference) and includes a facsimile page from Fascicle 10. For the Eighth Edition there are a number of substantial additions: new poems and letters by Dickinson; the complete text of Margaret Fuller's important feminist essay "The Great Lawsuit"; a new section on Louisa May Alcott featuring her Civil War story "My Contraband" and a chapter from her best-selling *Little Women*. Other selections added to this edition include Washington Irving's "The Author's Account of Himself," a key chapter from Harriet Beecher Stowe's *Uncle Tom's Cabin* (on the death of Little Eva), Longfellow's poem "Hawthorne," Emerson's "Circles," Lydia Maria Child's influential antislavery story "The Quadroons," Fanny Fern's review of Whitman's *Leaves of Grass*, and Frances Harper's "Learning to Read."

Volume C, American Literature 1865–1914. Edited by Nina Baym, Robert S. Levine, and Jeanne Campbell Reesman, this volume over the last two editions has taken on a striking new look. To our well-received complete longer works—Twain's *Adventures of Huckleberry Finn*, Chopin's *The Awakening*, and James's *Daisy Miller*—we have added complete texts of Stephen Crane's *Maggie: A Girl of the Streets* and Abraham Cahan's *The Imported Bridegroom*, as well as chapters from Theodore Dreiser's *Sister Carrie* and Twain's *Roughing It*. Also recently added are selections from Twain's *Letters from the Earth*, Edith Wharton's "The Other Two" and "Roman Fever," and works by Sui Sin Far, Zitkala Ša, Joel Chandler Harris, and Ambrose Bierce. Along with additional writings by Walt Whitman and Emily Dickinson to help students bridge the years between the Civil War and the industrializing 1890s, we include James Weldon Johnson, Paul Laurence Dunbar, and Emma Lazarus. The recent additions of Maria Ruíz de Burton, Pauline Hopkins, Sarah Winnemucca, Mourning Dove, and Ida Wells-Barnett underscore the emergence of a literary culture in which women from diverse ethnic, racial, and regional backgrounds became part of American literary culture. Two clusters take up key political and literary disputes from the era: "Debates over 'Americanization,'" which has been newly revised for the Eighth Edition, addresses the sense of crisis engendered by the huge influx of immigrants in the century's last two decades, the relentless effort to deny Native Americans their rights unless they entirely abandoned their traditions, the debates over African American citizenship, and the question of national boundaries in an age of imperialist expansion that took the United States to far-flung places around the globe. Texts by Frederick Jackson Turner, Theodore Roosevelt, José Martí, Jane Addams, and Senator Albert Beveridge ask repeatedly, Who is an American? Literary movements attuned to these divisions are considered in "Realism and Naturalism," where critical writings by William Dean Howells, Henry James, Frank Norris, Theodore Dreiser, and Jack London illuminate the turn to realism and naturalism, styles developed to represent and deal with the rapidly changing character of the American nation as it entered the industrial era with a markedly more diverse and larger population.

We have added a number of new selections. For the first time, we include a chapter from Upton Sinclair's influential reformist novel *The Jungle* (a novel that continues to have a profound influence on how we think about the production and consumption of meat). We now include a complete short story by Pauline Hopkins, "A Dash for Liberty," which is based on the same slave rebellion that Frederick Douglass wrote about in "The Heroic Slave." By request of instructors and students, we have added two new stories by Kate Chopin, "Desiree's Baby" and "The Story of an Hour," and the volume also includes new selections by Sarah Orne Jewett, Sui Sin Far, Mary Austin, and Mourning Dove.

Volume D, American Literature 1914–1945. Edited by Mary Loeffelholz, Volume D offers a number of complete longer works—Eugene O'Neill's *Long Day's Journey into Night* (exclusive to the Norton Anthology), Nella Larsen's eminently teachable *Quicksand*, William Faulkner's *As I Lay Dying*, and Willa Cather's *My Ántonia*, which was returned by instructor request to the Seventh Edition and remains a popular work with instructors and students alike. The poet Mina Loy's experimental work and reconsidered selections by Ezra Pound, T. S. Eliot, Marianne Moore, Hart Crane, and Langston Hughes encourage students and teachers to contemplate the interrelation of modernist aesthetics with ethnic, regional, and popular writing. Two illuminating clusters address central events of the modern period. In "World War I and Its Aftermath," writings by Ernest Hemingway, Gertrude Stein, Jessie Redmon Fauset, and others explore sharply divided views on the U.S. role in World War I, as well as the radicalizing effect of modern warfare—with 365,000 American casualties—on contemporary writing. And in "Modernist Manifestos," F. T. Marinetti, Mina Loy, Ezra Pound, Willa Cather, William Carlos Williams, and Langston Hughes show how the manifesto as a form exerted a powerful influence on international modernism in all the arts. Additions to the Eighth Edition include Faulkner's popular "A Rose for Emily," Katherine Anne Porter's novella *Pale Horse, Pale Rider*, Gertrude Stein's "Objects," and Jean Toomer's "Blood

Burning Man." We also print for the first time Pietro Di Donato's "Christ in Concrete," one of the most popular works of the period, which helps to bring a new ethnic and class perspective into Volume D.

Volume E, American Literature since 1945. Volume E, jointly edited by Jerome Klinkowitz and Patricia B. Wallace, features a period introduction in which prose and poetry intermingle and for which "Postwar" no longer explains a period that grows longer with every edition. The result is a rich representation of the period's literary activity, and a more accurate presentation of the writers themselves, many of whom write in multiple genres. The volume continues to offer the complete texts of Tennessee Williams's *A Streetcar Named Desire* (exclusive to this anthology), Arthur Miller's *Death of a Salesman*, David Mamet's *Glengarry Glen Ross*, Allen Ginsberg's *Howl*, Sam Shepard's *True West*, and Louise Glück's long poem *October*, and we have added the complete text of August Wilson's play *Fences*. Introduced in the Seventh Edition, Art Spiegelman's prize-winning *Maus* opens possibilities for teaching the graphic novel. Another innovation from the Seventh Edition was the inclusion of teachable stand-alone segments from important novels by Saul Bellow (*The Adventures of Augie March*), Kurt Vonnegut (*Slaughterhouse-Five*), Rudolfo Anaya (*Bless Me, Ultima*), and Jack Kerouac (*Big Sur*), and we continue to print those chapters. Newly anthologized writers include Stephen Dixon, Martin Luther King, Jr., Thomas McGuane, Kay Ryan, and the Dominican-American fiction writer Junot Díaz, whose 2008 novel, *The Brief Wondrous Life of Oscar Wao*, won the Pulitzer Prize and was an international sensation. We have also added new selections for Elizabeth Bishop, Richard Powers, Grace Paley, Robert Haas, and a number of other writers. Two clusters, one entirely new, add literary and topical context to this diverse volume. "Postmodernist Manifestos," with texts by Ronald Sukenick, William H. Gass, Hunter S. Thompson, Charles Olson, Frank O'Hara, Elizabeth Bishop, A. R. Ammons, and Audre Lorde, shows how many literary artists saw experimentation in poetry and fiction as the best way to register politics and culture in the postwar era. The cluster pairs nicely with "Modernist Manifestos" in Volume D. New to the Eighth Edition is a cluster on "Creative Nonfiction." Here students are introduced to writers such as Joan Didion and Edward Abbey who self-consciously blend fiction and nonfiction, creating works that over the past few decades have become enormously popular and influential.

In all, we are delighted to offer this revised Eighth Edition to teachers and students, and we welcome your comments.

Additional Resources from the Publisher

The Eighth Edition retains the paperback splits format that has been welcomed by instructors and students for its flexibility and portability. This format accommodates the many instructors who use the anthology in a two-semester survey, but allows for mixing and matching the five volumes in a variety of courses organized by period or topic, at levels from introductory to advanced. To give instructors even more flexibility, the publisher is making available the full list of 220 Norton Critical Editions, including such frequently assigned novels as Harriet Beecher Stowe's *Uncle Tom's Cabin*, Herman Melville's *Moby-Dick*, Edith Wharton's *The House of Mirth*, and William Faulkner's *The Sound and the Fury*, among many others. A Norton Critical Edition can be included with either package or any individual paperback-split volume for free. Each Norton Critical Edition gives students an authoritative, carefully annotated text accompanied by rich contextual and critical materials prepared by an expert in the subject.

For students using *The Norton Anthology of American Literature*, the publisher provides a wealth of resources on the free StudySpace website (wwnorton.com/naal). Students who activate the password included in each new copy of the anthology gain access to more than 70 reading-comprehension quizzes with extensive feedback; bulleted period summaries and period review quizzes with feedback; timelines; maps; audio readings of public domain texts; Literary Workshops that show students step-by-step how to read, analyze, and respond in writing to a work of literature; and a new "Literary Places" feature that uses Google Tours tools to let students (virtually) visit Thoreau's Walden Pond, Faulkner's Oxford, Mississippi, home, Cather's Nebraska plains, and other literary places. The rich gathering of content on StudySpace is designed to help students understand individual works and appreciate the places, sounds, and sights of literature.

The publisher also provides extensive instructor-support materials. Designed to enhance large or small lecture environments, the Instructor Resource Disc, expanded for the Eighth Edition, features more than 300 images with explanatory captions; lecture PowerPoint slides for each period introduction and for most topic clusters; and audio recordings (MP3). Much praised by both new and experienced instructors, *Teaching with The Norton Anthology of American Literature: A Guide for Instructors* by Edward Whitley, Lehigh University, and Bruce Michelson, University of Illinois at Urbana-Champaign, provides detailed reading lists for a variety of approaches—the historical approach, the "major authors" approach, the literary traditions approach, and the approach by genre or theme. Each author/work entry offers teaching suggestions, discussion questions, and suggestions for incorporating multimedia from the Instructor Resource Disc, the *American Passages* website, as well as other outside resources. The Guide is available both in print and in a searchable online format. Finally, Norton Coursepacks bring high-quality digital media into a new or existing online course. The Coursepacks include all content from the StudySpace website, short-answer questions with suggested answers, and a bank of discussion questions adapted from the Guide. Norton's Coursepacks are available in a variety of formats, including Blackboard/WebCT, Desire2Learn, Angel, and Moodle, at no cost to instructors or students.

Instructors who adopt *The Norton Anthology of American Literature* have access to an extensive array of films and videos. In addition to videos of the plays by O'Neill, Williams, Miller, Mamet, and Shepard in the anthology, segments of the award-winning video series *American Passages: A Literary Survey* are available without charge on orders of specified quantities of the Norton Anthology. Funded by Annenberg/CPB, produced by Oregon Public Broadcasting, and developed with the Norton Anthology as its exclusive companion anthology, *American Passages* contains sixteen segments, each covering a literary movement or period by exploring two or three authors in depth. The videos are supported by the *American Passages* Archive, a searchable online archive of over 3,000 items, including visual art, audio files, primary-source materials, and additional texts, which may be accessed through the link on the StudySpace student website. A print instructor's guide and student guide are also available. For information about the videos, contact your Norton representative.

Editorial Procedures

As in past editions, editorial features—period introductions, headnotes, annotations, and bibliographies—are designed to be concise yet full and to give students necessary information without imposing an interpretation. The editors have updated all apparatus in response to new scholarship: period introductions have been entirely or substantially rewritten, as have many headnotes. All Selected Bibliographies and each period's general-resources bibliographies categorized by Reference Works, Histories, and Literary Criticism have been thoroughly updated. The Eighth Edition retains three editorial features that help students place their reading in historical and cultural context—a Texts/Contexts timeline following each period introduction, a map on the front endpaper of each volume, and a chronological chart, on the back endpaper, showing the lifespans of many of the writers anthologized.

Our policy has been to reprint each text in the form that accords, as far as it is possible to determine, to the intention of its author. There is one exception: we have modernized most spellings and (very sparingly) the punctuation in Volume A on the principle that archaic spellings and typography pose unnecessary problems for beginning students. We have used square brackets to indicate titles supplied by the editors for the convenience of students. Whenever a portion of a text has been omitted, we have indicated that omission with three asterisks. If the omitted portion is important for following the plot or argument, we give a brief summary within the text or in a footnote. After each work, we cite (when known) the date of composition on the left and the date of first publication on the right; in some instances, the latter is followed by the date of a revised edition for which the author was responsible.

The editors have benefited from commentary offered by hundreds of teachers throughout the country. Those teachers who prepared detailed critiques, or who offered special help in preparing texts, are listed under Acknowledgments, on a separate page. We also thank the many people at Norton who contributed to the Eighth Edition: Julia Reidhead, who supervised the Eighth Edition; Marian Johnson, managing editor, college; Carly Fraser Doria, associate editor; Eileen Connell, electronic media editor; Michael Fleming, Candace Levy, Katharine Ings, and Susan Joseph, manuscript editors; Pam Lawson, Jack Borrebach, Sophie Hagen, Diane Cipollone, project editors; Hannah Blaisdell, editorial assistant; Benjamin Reynolds, production manager; Jo Anne Metsch, designer; Trish Marx, manager, photo department; Stephanie Romeo, photo editor; Jane Sanders Miller, photo researcher Debra Morton Hoyt, art director; Megan Jackson, permissions manager; and

Margaret Gorenstein, who cleared permissions. We also wish to acknowledge our debt to the late George P. Brockway, former president and chairman at Norton, who invented this anthology, and to M. H. Abrams, Norton's advisor on English texts. All have helped us to create an anthology that, more than ever, is testimony to the continuing richness of American literary traditions.

NINA BAYM, General Editor
ROBERT S. LEVINE, Associate General Editor

Acknowledgments

Among our many critics, advisors, and friends, the following were of especial help toward the preparation of the Eighth Edition, either with advice or by providing critiques of particular periods of the anthology: David L. Anderson (Butler County Community College); Booker T. Anthony (Fayetteville State University); George Bailey (Northern Essex Community College); Anne Baker (North Carolina State University); Jack Barbera (University of Mississippi); Philip Barnard (University of Kansas); Brian Bartlett (Saint Mary's University); Richard Baskin (Gordon College); John Battenburg (California Polytechnic State University); Geraldine Cannon Becker (University of Maine–Fort Kent); Carolyn Bergonzo; Laura Bloxham (Whitworth College Spokane); Hester Blum (Penn State); Andrew Bodenrader (Manhattanville College); Constance Bracewell (University of Arizona); Norton Bradley Christie (Erskine College); David Brottman (Iowa State University); Adam Burkey (Miami University Oxford); Jill Hunter Burrill (Bunker Hill Community College); Dan Butcher (University of Alabama); Gina Caison (University of Alabama at Birmingham); Linda Camarasana (Queens College); Pat Campbell (Lake Sumter Community College); Marci Carrasquillo (Simpson College); Vincent Casaregola (Saint Louis University); Karen Chandler (University of Louisville); Wayne Chandler (Northwest Missouri State University); Chiung-huei Chang (National Taiwan Normal University); Kathryn Chittick (Trent University); Deborah Christie (University of Miama); Paul Colby (North Carolina State University); Brian Condrey (Yuba Community College); Ken Cox (Florence-Darlington Technical College); Kristine Dassinger (Genesee Community College); Clark David (University of Denver); Cynthia Davis (UCSB); Marybeth Davis (Liberty University); Laura Dawkins (Murray State University); Bruce Degi (Metropolitan State College of Denver); Regina Dilgen (Palm Beach Community College); Christine Doyle (Central Connecticut State University); Michael Drexler (Bucknell University); Robert Dunne (Central Connecticut State University); Gregory Eiselein (Kansas State University); Monika Elbert (Montclair State University); Hilary Emmett (University of Queensland, Australia); Lise Esch (Trident Technical College); Duncan Flaherty (Queens College); Seth Frechie (Cabrini College); Paul Gallipeo (Adirondack Community College); Granville Ganter (St. John's University); Jared Gardner (Ohio State University); Sarah Garland (University of East Anglia); Jerry Gibbens (Williams Baptist College); Marivel Gonzales-Herna (Del Mar College); Mary Goodwin (National Taiwan Normal University); Carey Goyette (Clinton Community College); Paul Grant (Sir Wilfred Grenfell College); Mark Graves (Morehead State

University); Beth Gray (Gadsden State Community College); Lashun Griffin (North Harris College); George Griffith (Chadron State College); Susan Hagen (Riverland Community College); Heidi Hanrahan (Shepherd University); Rabiul Hasan (Southern University of Baton Rouge); Thomas Heise (McGill University); Charles Hernandez (Gordon College); Carmine Hernwood (Gordon College); Avis Hewitt (Grand Valley State University); Elizabeth Hewitt (Ohio State University); Trent Hickman (Brigham Young University); Kathleen Hicks (Arizona State University); Marianna Hofer (University of Findlay); Melissa Homestead (University of Nebraska, Lincoln); Carl Horner (Flagler College); Brad Johnson (Palm Beach Community College); Gwendolyn Jones (Clayton State University); Daniel Kane (University of Sussex); Virginia M. Kennedy; Catherine Keohane (Bergen Community College); James Kirkpatrick (Central Piedmont Community College); Denise Knight (SUNY Cortland); Peter Kvidera (John Carroll University); Michael Latza (College of Lake County); William Lawton (James Madison University); Heidi Lee (Messiah College); Paul Lewis (Boston College); Gretchen Lieb (Vassar College); Sarah Locke (Weatherford College); Paul Long (Baltimore City Community College); Trish Loughran (University of Illinois); Scott Richard Lyons (University of Michigan); Jim Machor (Kansas State University); Paul Madachy (Prince George's Community College); D'Ann Madewell (North Lake College); Ursula McTaggart (Wilmington College); Phil Metres (John Carroll University); Shellie Michael (Volunteer State Community College); Wendy Pearce Miller (Marian College); Bob Morace (Daemen College); Thomas Morgan (University of Dayton); Bruce Michelson (University of Illinois at Urbana-Champaign); Irvin Morris; David Murdock (Gadsden State Community College); Axel Nissen (University of Oslo); John O'Brien (University of Virginia); Patrick O'Connell (Gannon University); Louis Oldani (Rockhurst University); Emily Orlando (Fairfield University); Amanda Page (University of North Carolina, Chapel Hill); Daniel Payne (SUNY Oneonta); H. Daniel Peck (Vassar College); Caesar Perkowski (Gordon College); Jeanne Phoenix Laurel (Niagara University); Albert Pionke (University of Alabama); Stephen Powers (Gordon College); Colin Ramsey (Appalachian State University); Elizabeth Renker (Ohio State University); John Ribar (Palm Beach Community College); Julien Rice; Sian Silyn Roberts (Queens College); Debra Rosenthal (John Carroll University); Dave Rota (University of Missouri St. Louis); Susan Ryan (University of Louisville); Charles Scarborough (Northern Virginia Community College); Jennifer Schell (Wichita State University); Carl Sederholm (Brigham Young University); Jessica Sellountos (Emory University); Linda Furg Selzer (Penn State University); Hal Shows (Keiser University); Cristobal Silva (Florida State University); Merrill Maguire Skaggs (Drew University); Derrick Spradlin (Freed Hardeman College); Roy Stamper (North Carolina State University); Jeffrey Steele (University of Wisconsin); Julia Stern (Northwestern University); Paul Strong (Alfred University); Brian Sweeney (Saint Joseph's University); Marcy Tanter (Tarleton State University); Erin Templeton (Converse College); Annette Trefzner (University of Mississippi); William Tucker (Olney Central College); April Van Camp (Indian River Community College); Adam Vines (University of Alabama at Birmingham); Pierre Walker (Salem State College); Laura Wallmenich (Alma College); Rick Walters (White Mountains Community College); Bill Ward (Appalachian State University); Robert West

(Mississippi State University); Stephen Whited (Piedmont College); Edward Whitelock (Gordon College); Edward Whitley (Lehigh University); Steve Whitton (Jacksonville State University); Lea Williamson (Blinn College); Kelly Wisecup (University of North Texas); Wesley Xi (National Taiwan University); Tamara Yohannes (University of Louisville); Elizabeth Young; Francis Zauhar (University of Pittsburgh at Johnstown).

THE NORTON ANTHOLOGY OF

AMERICAN LITERATURE

EIGHTH EDITION

VOLUME E: LITERATURE SINCE 1945

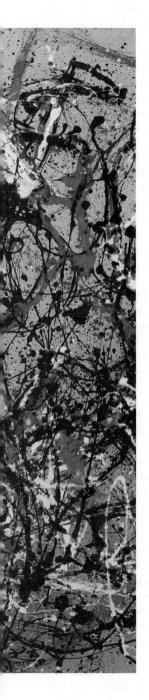

American Literature since 1945

THE UNITED STATES AND WORLD POWER

D istribution of power is a purpose of war, and the consequences of a world war are necessarily global. Having agreed to a policy of demanding unconditional surrender, the allied countries of Britain, the Soviet Union, and the United States positioned themselves to achieve nothing short of total victory over their enemies in World War II: Germany and Japan. Yet each country's contribution to victory made for startling contrasts in the following half century. Britain, beleaguered since the war's start in September 1939, fought against odds that depleted its resources and severely disrupted its traditional class structure. The Soviet Union, an amalgamation of nations under the central power of Russia, suffered the war's worst casualties when attacked by Germany in June 1941 and afterward, well into 1945, during the hideous contest of attrition along the war's bitter eastern front. Although newly established as a world power after the end of hostilities, the U.S.S.R. remained at an economic disadvantage and dissolved in 1991 after five decades of Cold War against its ideological adversaries in the West. It was the United States, entering the war after Japan's attack on Pearl Harbor on December 7, 1941, that emerged as the only world power in excellent economic shape. This new power, experienced both at home and abroad, became a major force in reshaping American culture for the balance of the twentieth century.

The great social effort involved in fighting World War II reorganized America's economy and altered its

---

Autumn Rhythms (detail), by Jackson Pollock. For more information about this painting, see the color insert in this volume.

people's lifestyles. Postwar existence revealed different kinds of men and women, with new aspirations among both majority and minority populations. New possibilities for action empowered individuals and groups in the pursuit of personal freedom and individual self-expression. During World War II American industry had expanded dramatically for military purposes; plants that had manufactured Chevrolets, Plymouths, Studebakers, Packards, and Fords now made B-24 Liberators and Grumman Avengers. With three million men in uniform, the vastly expanded workforce required increasing numbers of women. After hostilities were concluded many of these women were reluctant to return to homemaking; and then after a decade or so of domesticity, women emerged as a political force on behalf of their rights and opportunities in the workplace. This pattern extended to other groups as well. African Americans, whether they enlisted or were drafted, served in fighting units throughout the war and were unwilling to return to second-class status afterward; nor could a majority culture aware of their contribution continue to enforce segregation and other forms of prejudice so easily as before the war.

Economic power at the world level continued to influence American culture through the first two postwar decades. The first two—and only two—atomic bombs that have ever been used were exploded by the United States in Japan in August 1945; their effect was so horrific that geographical "containment" of America's nuclear-armed communist rivals emerged as the paramount American military policy. When Communist North Korea invaded American ally South Korea in 1950, therefore, the United States rejected responding with atomic weapons in favor of a United Nations–sponsored "police action" that followed a policy of using conventional weapons only and not pursuing enemy forces beyond specific boundaries. But if hot war was out, cold war was in, specifically the type of contest in which military strength was built up for deterrence rather than combat. Henceforth economic conduct would be a major factor in the American decision to contain the Soviet Union's attempt to expand its influence. In the years following World War II the U.S.S.R. had assumed a stance considered adversarial to Western interests. Ideologically, the opposition was between Western capitalism and Soviet state socialism; politically the contest exhibited itself in the West's rebuilding of Germany and the formation of the North Atlantic Treaty Organization (NATO) versus the Soviet Union's dominance over Eastern Europe by means of the Warsaw Pact. In Africa, where new nations gained independence from colonial rule, West and East competed for influence. Overall, the West perceived a threat in the U.S.S.R.'s 1948 attainment of nuclear weaponry and its maintenance of massive troop strength beyond its borders. When communist revolutionaries took control of mainland China in 1949, the Cold War moved beyond European boundaries to encompass the entire globe. Until the collapse of the Soviet Union in 1991, economic warfare motivated American activity as decisively as had the waging of World War II.

Throughout the 1950s and into the early 1960s, social critics perceived a stable conformity to American life, a dedication to an increasingly materialistic standard of living, whose ethical merit was ensured by a continuity with the prewar world—a continuity that proved to be delusory. In this initial postwar period white males benefited especially from the economy and saw the nature of their lives change. The G.I. Bill provided veterans with a college education; after World War II America would eventually have as much as 50 percent of its population college educated, a percentage unthinkable in prewar years and unmatched by any other nation. With world markets open to American goods, the expanded economy offered sophisticated technical and professional jobs for these college graduates; within a generation the alphabet soup of great corporations—IT&T, GE, RCA, IBM, and so forth—came to dominate employment patterns at home and around the globe. Higher incomes and demographic expansion created vast new suburbs beyond the limits of older cities, and the population of the United States began a westward shift. New roads accommodated this increasingly mobile society, including the interstate highway system begun in 1955. By 1960 the average American family was moving to a new place of residence at the rate of once every five years, as new opportunities beckoned and lifestyles expanded beyond the more traditional stability of "home." An age

The GI Bill of Rights (1944), which provided federal subsidies to support college education for returning World War II veterans, democratized American higher education. Shown here, veterans and other students at New York University in January 1945.

of plenty created a new managerial class, but also ensured an ample piece of the pie for workers protected by secure, well-organized unions.

But ways of life consonant with an isolated, stable economy could not survive in the new atmosphere of American power and wealth. The passage from the 1950s to the 1960s marks the great watershed of the postwar half-century. Conflicts between conformity and individuality, tradition and innovation, stability and disruption were announced and anticipated even before they materially influenced history and culture. The earliest harbinger was the 1960 election of John F. Kennedy as president. To a mainstream society that might have become complacent with the material success of the postwar years and had neglected the less fortunate, Kennedy offered an energetic program of involvement. Formally titled "The New Frontier," it reached from the participation of individual Americans in the Peace Corps (working to aid underdeveloped countries around the world) to the grand effort to conquer space. In the midst of his brief presidency, in October 1962, in what came to be known as the "Cuban Missile Crisis," the Soviet Union installed ballistic missiles in Cuba; when Kennedy protested this act

John F. Kennedy Jr. salutes at his father's funeral.

and began a naval blockade of the island nation, the possibility of nuclear warfare loomed closer than ever before, until the U.S.S.R. relented and withdrew its weapons. Domestic tensions also rose when Robert Kennedy, the president's brother and U.S. attorney general, took a newly activist approach toward desegregation, sending federal troops into the South to enforce the law. But there was a cultural grace to the Kennedy era as well, with the president's wife, Jacqueline, making involvement in the arts not just fashionable but also a matter of government policy.

The Sixties, as they are known, really began with the assassination of John F. Kennedy on November 22, 1963. The tumultuous dozen years of American history that followed represent a more combative period in civil rights, climaxing with the most sustained and effective attempts to remedy the evils of racial discrimination since the years of Reconstruction after the Civil War. For the first time since the suffrage movement following World War I, women organized to pursue their legal, ethical, and cultural interests, now defined as feminism. Active dissension within the culture emerged in response to military involvement in Vietnam, where in 1961 President Kennedy had sent small numbers of advisers to help the Republic of South Vietnam resist pressures from Communist North Vietnam. Presidents Lyndon Johnson and Richard Nixon expanded and continued the U.S. presence; and an increasingly strident opposition—fueled by protests on American college campuses and among the country's liberal intellectuals—turned into a much larger cultural revolution. Between 1967 and 1970 the nation experienced many outbreaks of violence, including political assassinations (of both presidential candidate Robert Kennedy and civil rights leader Dr. Martin Luther King Jr. in 1968), urban riots, and massive campus disruptions.

Torn apart by opposition to President Johnson and the climate of violence surrounding its national convention in Chicago in August 1968, the Democratic Party lost to Republican candidate Richard Nixon, who was then, like his predecessor, burdened with the Vietnam War and escalating dissent (leading to student deaths at Kent State and Jackson State universities in May 1970). By the time the Vietnam War ended in 1975 with the collapse of Saigon to North Vietnamese and Viet Cong forces, the United States had also been buffeted by transformative political trouble in the form of the Watergate scandal: a revelation of President Nixon's abuses of governmental privileges that led to his resignation in August 1974. These events mark the end of one of the more discomfortingly disruptive eras in American history.

By the end of the 1970s some characteristics of the previous decade's countercultural revolt had been accepted in the mainstream, including informalities of dress, relaxation of sexual codes of behavior, and an increased respect for individual rights. The 1980s witnessed a call for traditional values, interpreted as a return not to community and self-sacrifice but to the pursuit of wealth. During Ronald Reagan's presidency income disparities grew while taxes fell; the Sixties' distrust of government mutated into a defense of personal acquisition. Following the debacle in Vietnam, where more than fifty thousand Americans had died in a losing war, the military restricted itself in the 1980s and early 1990s to quick, sharply specified interventions (in Grenada, Panama, and most dramatically in the Gulf War of 1991), relying less on vague deterrence than on precise applications of technological expertise. Economically, America boomed, but in new ways: manufacturing dominance was replaced by service efficiency, massive workforces were downsized into more profitable units, while speculation and entrepreneurship replaced older modes of development.

As the twentieth century made its turn, global power experienced its greatest readjustment since World War II. American economic might had depleted the Soviet Union's ability to compete, and as that state's ethnic republics achieved independence and the old Warsaw Pact alliance of Eastern European nations collapsed, the European Union—once restricted to Western democracies—assumed even greater importance. With the attack on New York's World Trade Center and the Pentagon by terrorists on September 11, 2001, the third millennium threatened to echo the first, with religious forces setting political agendas and working to see those agendas fulfilled, beginning with a seemingly open-ended face-off between American and revolutionary Islamic forces in Afghanistan and Iraq.

LITERARY DEVELOPMENTS

In such a turbulent half century, literature also encompassed a great deal of change. Not surprisingly, during this period many important writers reexamined both what literature is meant to accomplish and how to accomplish it. Conflicts between conformity and individuality, tradition and innovation, stability and disruption characterized the literature of the period as they also shaped the historical and cultural milieu. Just as people in the first two decades following World War II addressed themselves to taking material advantage of the extensive gains won by the global victory, so writers

The Saturday Evening

POST

May 25, 1957 – *15¢*

"After the Prom." This 1957 *Saturday Evening Post* cover by
Norman Rockwell contrasts with the ominous headline, "How Will
America Behave IF H-BOMBS FALL?"

sought to capitalize on the successes of a previous literary generation. Cultural homogeneity was an ideal during the 1950s, patriotically so in terms of building up the foundations of American society to resist and contain Communism, materialistically so when it came to enjoying the benefits of capitalism. This ideal of homogeneity led many writers to assume that a single work—short story, novel, poem, or play—could represent the experiences of an entire people, that a common national essence lay beneath distinctions of gender, race, ethnicity, religion, or region. The literary world between 1945 and the Sixties often let readers believe that there could be such a thing as a representative American short story, nuanced for upper-middle-class patrons in the pages of the *New Yorker* magazine while slanted to more homely interests in *Collier's* and the *Saturday Evening Post*.

Novels of the immediate postwar period followed this trend in greater depth, in larger scale, and with more self-conscious justification. Ernest Hemingway, a master of the short story, had fostered the notion of novel writing as "going the distance," slugging it out all the way, as it were, in a fifteen-round championship prizefight. Publicized by others as one of the dominant literary figures of his day, Hemingway promoted his own example to influence a new generation of novelists who believed they had to act like him to be taken seriously. Hence the desire to write what was called "the great American novel"—a major work that would characterize the larger aspects of national experience. Ambitions were not simply to write a war novel, for example, but *the* war novel; not just a work about corporate big business, but something that encapsulated the subject for all times. Regionalism could remain an interest, but only if it provided broader meaning; here the example of William Faulkner encouraged the belief among younger writers that dealing with the American South meant grappling with monumental issues of guilt and the inexorable power of history. Major dramatists behaved the same way; if their immediate predecessors had drawn on classically tragic allusions in deepening their themes, postwar playwrights embraced otherwise mundane characters as universal types. The death of a salesman, for example, would be examined in the same spotlight once reserved for great people, for here indeed was a figure who stood for the postwar human being.

As a genre poetry was less tied to expectations about realism or national essence than was the novel or the short story. In the 1950s the poetic standard was the short lyric meditation, in which the poet, avoiding the first person, would find an object, a landscape, or an observed encounter that epitomized and clarified a feeling. A poem was the product of retrospection, a gesture of composure following the initial shock or stimulus that provided the occasion for writing. Some poets composed in intricate stanzas and skillful rhymes, deploying a mastery of verse form as one sign of the civilized mind's power to explore, tame, and distill raw experience. In the 1950s and 1960s poets acquired a new visibility in American life. After the war, writers' conferences and workshops, recordings, and published and broadcast interviews became common, and a network of poets traveling to give readings and to become poets-in-residence at universities began to form. Despite this increase in poetry's visibility, its marginal position in the nation's culture, when compared to that of prose fiction, may have allowed for more divergence from the ideal of homogeneity. The mid to late 1940s saw the publication of groundbreaking books as various as Gwendolyn Brooks's *A Street in Bronzeville* (1945), with its evocation of African American experience; Robert Duncan's *Heavenly City, Earthly City* (1947), with its mystical and homosexual themes; and Theodore Roethke's linguistically experimental sequence *The Lost Son* (1948). As early as 1950 Charles Olsen's manifesto, *Projective Verse*, called for a unit of poetic expression based not on predetermined metrical feet but on the poet's "breath" and the rhythms of the body. In the 1950s and 1960s a number of important poets displayed what the poet-critic Richard Howard called "the longing to lose the gift of order, despoiling the self of all that had been, merely, propriety." The poetry of Allen Ginsberg, Sylvia Plath, and John Berryman began as well mannered and formal, then turned to wilder and more disquieting forms of lyric exploration.

Like the notion of cultural conformity, the understanding of any single piece of literature as representing an entire people came under withering scrutiny during the 1960s. As the novelist Philip Roth remarked in 1960, "the American writer in the middle of the twentieth century has his hands full in trying to understand, describe, and then make credible much of American reality." Critical movements of the time articulated a new literary unease around the issue of realism, and writers responded to this unease by developing new literary strategies, new ways of dealing with a much more contentious, varied, and unstable sense of the era. Some writers felt that social reality had become too unstable to serve as a reliable anchor for their narratives, and some critics believed that fiction had exhausted its formal possibilities. A "Death of the Novel" controversy arose. Both the novel and the short story, some argued, demanded a set of fairly limited conventions; these conventions, such as characterization and development by means of dialogue, imagery, and symbolism, however, relied on a securely describable world to make sense.

In poetry, two important and transforming shocks were administered by Allen Ginsberg's *Howl* (1956) and Robert Lowell's *Life Studies* (1959). Ginsberg first delivered his poem aloud, during a reading at the Six Gallery in San Francisco in the fall of 1955; the following year it was published by Lawrence Ferlinghetti's City Lights Bookshop. In a single stroke, with the energy of a reborn Walt Whitman, Ginsberg made poetry one of the rallying points for underground protest and prophetic denunciation of the prosperous, complacent, gray-spirited Eisenhower years. The setting in which the poem appeared is also significant, for *Howl*, like other work associated with what came to be known as the San Francisco Renaissance, challenged the conventions of a literary tradition dominated by the East Coast. With its open, experimental form and strong oral emphasis, *Howl* sounded a departure from the well-shaped lyric. Lowell, a more "difficult," less popular poet, was rooted in the literary culture of Boston. But with *Life Studies*

City Lights Bookstore, in San Francisco, California, is a landmark to poetry and to freedom of speech. Owned by the poet Lawrence Ferlinghetti, City Lights published the work of Beat poets, most famously Allen Ginsberg's groundbreaking *Howl and Other Poems* (1956). Shown here outside the bookstore in 1956 are (left to right) Bob Donlin, Neal Cassady, Ginsberg, Robert LaVinge, and Ferlinghetti.

he too challenged the literary status quo, bringing a new directness and autobiographical intensity into American poetry as he exposed the psychological turbulence suffered by an inbred New Englander. Lowell's embrace of a more open, less heavily symbolic style was inspired, in part, by hearing the work of Ginsberg and others while on a reading tour of the West Coast.

The connection between these two volumes and the times in which they were written is direct and apparent. Their poems anticipated and explored the fissures in American social consensus that would erupt into the open conflicts of the 1960s and 1970s and shape American life for decades to come, with growing public unease concerning a broad range of issues: the uses of government and industrial power; the institutions of marriage and the family; the rights of racial minorities, women, and homosexuals; the use of drugs; alternative states of consciousness. Taken together, Ginsberg's and Lowell's books also suggested that the invigorating energies of postwar American poetry would arise from diverse regions of the country, their common aim being to restore poetry to a more vital relation with contemporary life.

Even as American life in the 1950s espoused conformity, technological advances in the exchange of information had made the particulars of that life ever harder to manage. As boundaries of time and space were eclipsed by television, air travel, and an accompanying global awareness, the once essential unities of representation (time, space, and action) no longer provided ground on which to build a work of literary art. As more became known about the world, the writer's ability to make sense of the whole was challenged. A culture that looked for all-encompassing expressions from its writers now seemed to demand the impossible. In the 1960s poets began to extend their subject matter to include more explicit and extreme areas of autobiographical revelation—sex, divorce, alcoholism, insanity. The convenient but not very precise label "confessional" came to be attached to certain books in which the intimate particulars of one person's life insisted on the distinctness of individual experience, not its representativeness. Other poets devised forms that reflected an understanding of poetry as provisional, as representing the changing flow of experience from moment to moment. Some poets began dating each of their poems, as though to suggest that the feelings involved belonged to the moment and were subject to change.

A parallel development in literary theory posed another great threat to conventional literature. Known as "Deconstruction" and brought to American shores from France by means of a series of university conferences and academic publications beginning in 1966, this style of criticism questioned the underlying assumptions behind any statement, exposing how what was accepted as absolute truth usually depended on rhetoric rather than fact, exposing indeed how "fact" itself was constructed by intellectual operations. This style of criticism became attractive to literary scholars who had been framing social and political questions in much the same terms—believing, for example, that the Vietnam War had been presented to the American people through slogans rather than realities. Many of the fiction writers, dramatists, and poets who sought stable employment in universities and colleges took part vigorously in these discussions. Deconstruction's preoccupation with language dismantled some of the boundaries between philosophy, poetry, psychology, and linguistics, and emphasized writing as a site of multiple "discourses." The idea of literature as self-expression was complicated by a focus on the social power of language and the constructed nature of subjectivity. The skepticism toward unity and coherence that marks the era extended to the very idea of the self. The Death of the Novel debates in prose fiction had an analogue in the intensified skepticism poets brought to the idea of narrative. Borrowing from the technologies of film and video (jump cuts, tracking shots, shifting camera angles, split screens), literature began to imagine a reader saturated with the sounds of contemporary discourse, a reader whose attention quickly shifts. All of these impulses converged to destabilize literary genres that were once thought to be reliable windows on the world.

Literature in the 1960s was often extreme in its methods and disruptive in its effects. Yet much like its social and political developments, the decade's literary trends remained influential beyond the Sixties. Writers continued to experiment with diverse practices with which to render a sense of contemporary reality, and they continued their artistic debates over how that reality was constituted and how it could be represented. Authors as diverse as John Updike, Bernard Malamud, and Ann Beattie continued to write realistic fiction, even in the heyday of Deconstruction, but in a style enriched by the rigorous cross-examination of its previously unquestioned methods. Even in a period at times overly conscious of self and world as fictional constructs, poets like Gwendolyn Brooks and Philip Levine engaged with history and politics, and others like Elizabeth Bishop and Stanley Kunitz remained committed to poetry's relation to a common world. In prose fiction a new group of realistic writers, called "Minimalists," made these challenges central to their work, crafting a manner of description that with great intensity limited itself to what could be most reliably accepted. What the Minimalists described was not endorsed by the authors as true; rather it consisted of signs that their characters accepted as truth, not objects from nature but conventions accepted by societies to go about the business of living. In a typical Minimalist story, although nothing sad is mentioned and no character grieves, someone makes a sign that she is saying something meant to be sad, and another character emits a perfect sign of being deeply unhappy in response. Objects that abound in such works are drawn from the consumer's world not for what they are but for what they signify, be it good taste or poor, wealth or deprivation. It is a workable way of writing realism in a world where philosophical definitions discourage such a term.

The social and political changes of the 1960s left a legacy even richer than those of critical and philosophical revolutions. Political dissent helped make available to literature a broad range of more insistent voices. Civil rights activism helped create the Black Arts Movement, which in turn replaced the notion of accepting only one token African American writer at a time with a much broader awareness of imaginative expression by a wide range of literary talent. A parallel movement saw Southern writers, like the poet Charles Wright and the fiction writer Barry Hannah, seeking modes of expression other than mourning the loss of the Civil War or feeling guilty about slavery. Jewish American writers, like the poet Stanley Kunitz and the fiction writers Philip Roth and Bernard Malamud, began moving beyond thematics of assimilation and identity to embrace subjects and techniques reaching from the deeply personal to the metapoetic or metafictive. Some women prose writers—Ursula LeGuin, for example—found that subgenres such as fantasy and science fiction could be useful in undermining long-held stereotypes of gender, while poets such as Adrienne Rich and Audre Lorde presented the experience of women hitherto silenced or unrepresented in literature. In both fiction and poetry, writers found that present-day life could be described with a new frankness and expanded awareness appropriate to women's wider and more egalitarian role in society. Native American writers received new respect from mainstream culture, initiated by attention to the land's ecology and recognition that the "Wild West" view of American history included a strategic stereotyping of Indian people. An important body of critical work helped create new contexts for thinking about Native American literature as both traditional and contemporary. In fact, in the 1970s and 1980s a fresh impetus of experimentation and literary commitment came from writers of minority traditions who gained access to presses and publishing venues. Available now were artistic expressions of the cultural complexity of the American population from Chinese Americans, Japanese Americans, Mexican Americans, and other groups previously excluded from the literary canon. These different traditions were not mutually exclusive; the work of many writers testified to an enlivening interaction between traditions, affirming the imagination's freedom to draw from many sources. As, earlier, the modernists had reached out to traditions beyond the Western— the poet Ezra Pound to the Chinese ideograph and the poet Charles Olson to Mayan Indian culture, for example—American writers of this period were redefining what constitutes America.

One of the most dramatic developments, during the 1970s and 1980s, one that indicated the broadening range of achievement among writers of many different backgrounds and persuasions, was the success of African American women—novelists, dramatists, and poets—in finding literary voices and making them heard as important articulations of experience. Here was a reminder of how so much of what passes for reality is nothing but artifice, fabrication, and convention—for here was a large group of people whose ancestors had been written out of history and who were still often denied speaking parts in national dialogues. Even with so much of a usable past effaced and identity repressed, these writers were able to find a means of expression that helped redefine readers' understanding of the world, whether in imaginative refigurings of the novel like Toni Morrison's, in book-length poetic sequences like Rita Dove's *Thomas and Beulah*, or in individual poems that gave voice to African American experience, like those of Lucille Clifton. By the close of the twentieth century other voices emerged that also had been written out of history, and many writers from minority traditions began to take their place at the center of American writing. "Realism," like "globalism," was now a much more expansive and inclusive term, from Sherman Alexie's Native Americans to Jhumpa Lahiri's international cosmopolites with their world-spanning technologies.

Another important development involved the increasing prominence of Latina/Latino writing in American literature. As the title of Dan Wakefield's 1959 nonfiction novel, *Island in the City*, suggests, communities of native Spanish speakers were once considered enclaves. Yet New York City's Puerto Rican Spanish Harlem not only spread, but was augumented by areas of Brooklyn and urban New Jersey being resettled by families from the Dominican Republic—families like those portrayed in the fiction of Julia Alvarez

Rita Dove served as Poet Laureate and Consultant in Poetry at the Library of Congress from 1993 to 1995. She was the youngest person—and first African American—to hold this appointment.

and Junot Díaz, whose lives were enriched by an interpolation of Anglo and Hispanic cultures, thanks to frequent travels between old and new homes. Such natural and spontaneous multiculturalism would make a work such as composer Leonard Bernstein's musical (and later film) *West Side Story* (1957) seem almost quaintly historical in its separation of societies. Elsewhere, persons of Hispanic heritage began rivaling in numbers their Anglo fellow citizens not just in Southern California's Orange County, which had once typified a Nixon–era style of white establishment values, but even in the small towns of Iowa and Nebraska, where their participation in agricultural industries such as meat-packing helped revive an endangered economy, not to mention their contributions to both popular entertainment and literary culture.

Contemporary literature values heterogeneity in its forms and pluralism in its cultural influences. This literature assumes a context wherein the nature of reality changes. Because contemporary culture appears so relentlessly artificial—political events, advertising, and television (including news programs) can all be seen as staged and packaged reforms of fiction—it is also increasingly a literature preoccupied with authenticity and a yearning for the real. Hence the appeal of documentary films, the popularity of the memoir, the attraction on DVDs of "outtakes" showing moments of disruption in the process of filmmaking. The burgeoning genre known as creative nonfiction—a term that first appeared officially in 1983 as a category for creative writing fellowships offered by the National Endowment of the Arts—reflects contemporary literature's impatience with the opposition between fact and fiction. Combining aspects of the essay, memoir, reportage, criticism, and autobiography, creative nonfiction uses the techniques of fiction to make a claim to the real. As represented in a cluster in this volume, creative nonfiction can be said to include some of the best environmental and travel writing, as well as hybrid forms of memoir that rely on the fiction of memory and factual research. *The Year of Magical Thinking* (2005), Joan Didion's account of the year following the sudden death of her husband, John Gregory Dunne, from cardiac arrest, is a case in point: it is part memoir, part medical research, part an almost clinical investigation of the phenomenon of grief.

Among contemporary literature's emblems is the Internet, and, in a digital age, reality is hybrid, with constant input from multiple sources and a proclivity for combining, editing, altering, and rearranging existing materials—processes analogous to DJ sampling in music. In such a culture, originality and plagiarism no longer seem necessarily opposing terms. As technology reshapes what we think about and how we experience contemporary literature, it is also reshaping how writers produce literature. Some contemporary writers edit online journals; they turn to hypertext to create computer-screen poems with simultaneous and open-ended possibilities, where the reader's choices shape poetic forms. Thanks to computer technology, novelists may include artificial intelligence among their casts of characters, as Richard Powers demonstrates in his novel *Galatea* 2.2 (1995). At the same time some contemporary writers continue to draft their work with pencil and paper, and some feel as much affinity with classical Chinese poets or the great nineteenth-century novelists as with computer technology.

It has been said that our contemporary culture provides the greatest variety of literary expression that has ever been available at any one time. From a war effort that demanded unity of purpose and a Cold War period that for a time encouraged conformity to a homogenous ideal, American writing has emerged in the twenty-first century to include a sophisticated mastery of technique broadened by an understanding of literature's role in characterizing reality, whether that reality is understood as transcendental and visionary or as rooted in the natural and material world. One thing distinguishing recent American works as contemporary is that the two different understandings of reality are not unified or reconciled; rather, as with the nuclei in Louise Glück's poem "Mitosis," "No one actually remembers them / as not divided."

A hallmark of the postwar period is its shift from unity to diversity as an ideal, and during this time American writing has been characterized by a great variety of styles employed simultaneously. If anything is common to the period, it is a self-conscious and experimental view of language as a tool of literary expression. In a wide variety of ways writers explore and test the ways language shapes our perceptions of reality, and their work moves in and out of various kinds of language, as if testing the limits and possibilities of the different discourses that make up contemporary life. This energetic investigation of language fuels a new inclusiveness and invigorates imaginative potential. Contemporary literature has survived the threats of its death to flourish in ways our writers are still imagining.

TEXTS	CONTEXTS
1941 Eudora Welty, "**Petrified Man**"	
1944 Stanley Kunitz, "**Father and Son**"	
1945 Randall Jarrell, "**The Death of the Ball Turret Gunner**"	1945 U.S. drops atomic bombs on Hiroshima and Nagasaki; Japan surrenders, ending World War II • Cold War begins
1947 Tennesse Williams, *A Streetcar Named Desire*	1947 Jackie Robinson becomes the first black Major League ballplayer
1948 Theodore Roethke, *The Lost Son*	
1949 Arthur Miller, *Death of a Salesman*	
1950 Richard Wilbur, "**A World without Objects Is a Sensible Emptiness**" • Charles Olson, "**Projective Verse**"	1950 Senator Joseph McCarthy begins attacks on communism
	1950–53 Korean War
1952 Ralph Ellison, *Invisible Man*	
1953 Saul Bellow, *The Adventures of Augie March* • Charles Olson, "**Maximus, to Himself**"	1953 House Concurrent Resolution 108 dictates government's intention to "terminate" its treaty relations with the Native American tribes
	1954 *Brown v. Board of Education* declares segregated schools unconstitutional • Beat Generation poets begin to gather at San Francisco's City Lights Bookshop
1955 Flannery O'Connor, "**Good Country People**"	
1955–68 John Berryman composes *The Dream Songs* (pub. 1964, 1968, 1977)	
1956 Allen Ginsberg, *Howl*	1956 Martin Luther King Jr. leads bus boycott in Montgomery, Alabama
1958 Bernard Malamud, "**The Magic Barrel**"	
1959 Philip Roth, "**Defender of the Faith**" • Robert Creeley, "**Kore**" • Robert Lowell, *Life Studies* • Frank O'Hara, "**Personism**"	1959 Fidel Castro becomes communist leader of Cuba
1960 Thomas Pynchon, "**Entropy**" • Gwendolyn Brooks, "**We Real Cool**" • Robert Duncan, "**Often I Am Permitted to Return to a Meadow**"	1960 Woolworth lunch counter sit-in in Greensboro, N.C., marks beginning of Civil Rights Movement
1961 Denise Levertov, "**The Jacob's Ladder**"	
1962 Jack Kerouac, *Big Sur* • Robert Hayden, "**Middle Passage**"	1962 United States and Soviet Union close to war over Russian missiles based in Cuba; missiles withdrawn
1963 James Wright, "**A Blessing**" • Martin Luther King Jr., "**I Have a Dream**"	1963 King delivers "I Have a Dream" speech • black church in Birmingham, Alabama, bombed, killing four girls • President John F. Kennedy assassinated

Boldface titles indicate works in the anthology.

TEXTS	CONTEXTS
1964 John Cheever, **"The Swimmer"** • Amiri Baraka (LeRoi Jones) **"An Agony. As Now."** • Frank O'Hara, **"A Step Away from Them"**	
1965 James Baldwin, **"Going to Meet the Man"** • A. R. Ammons, **"Corson's Inlet"**	1965 Riots break out in Watts section of Los Angeles • Malcolm X assassinated • hippie culture flourishes in San Francisco
	1965–73 Vietnam War
1966 James Merrill, **"The Broken Home"** • Sylvia Plath, *Ariel*	1966 National Organization for Women (NOW) founded • Hayden and Brooks criticized at Black Writers' Conference, Fisk University, for composing "academic" poetry
1967 A. R. Ammons, **"A Poem Is a Walk"** • W. S. Merwin, **"For a Coming Extinction"**	
1968 Donald Barthelme, **"The Balloon"** • Edward Abbey, **"Havasu"**	1968 King assassinated • Senator Robert F. Kennedy assassinated • photo of Earthrise by Apollo 8
1969 N. Scott Momaday, *The Way to Rainy Mountain* • Kurt Vonnegut, *Slaughterhouse-Five* • Galway Kinnell. **"The Porcupine"** • Robert Penn Warren, *Audubon*	1969 U.S. astronauts land on the moon • Stonewall riots in New York City initiate gay liberation movement • Woodstock Festival held near Bethel, New York
1970 Ishmael Reed, **"Neo-HooDoo Manifesto"**	1970 National Guard kills four students during antiwar demonstration at Kent State University, Ohio
1971 Audre Lorde, **"Black Mother Woman"**	
1972 Rudolfo A. Anaya, *Bless Me, Ultima* • Anne Sexton, *The Death of the Fathers* • Letter from Elizabeth Bishop to Robert Lowell objecting to use of personal letters in manuscript of *The Dolphin*	1972 Watergate Scandal • military draft ends
1973 Alice Walker, **"Everyday Use"** • Adrienne Rich, *Diving into the Wreck*	1973 *Roe v. Wade* legalizes abortion • American Indian Movement members occupy Wounded Knee, South Dakota
1974 Grace Paley, **"A Conversation with My Father"** • Annie Dillard, *Pilgrim at Tinker Creek*	1974 President Richard Nixon resigns in wake of Watergate, avoiding impeachment
1975 John Updike, **"Separating"** • John Ashbery, **"Self-Portrait in a Convex Mirror"** • Michael S. Harper, **"Nightmare Begins Responsibility"**	
1976 Elizabeth Bishop, *Geography III* • Maxine Hong Kingston, **"No Name Woman"** • Barry Lopez, **"The Raven"**	1976 U.S. bicentennial
1977 Audre Lorde, **"Poetry Is Not a Luxury"**	
1978 Ann Beattie, **"Weekend"** • Jamaica Kinkaid, **"Girl"**	
1979 Philip Levine, **"Starlight"** • Mary Oliver, **"The Black Snake"** • Robert Hass **"Meditation at Lagunitas"**	

TEXTS	CONTEXTS
1980 Toni Cade Bambara, **"Medley"** • Sam Shepard, *True West*	
1981 Leslie Marmon Silko, **"Lullaby"** • Lorna Dee Cervantes, **"The Body as Braille"** • James Dickey, **"Falling"** • Simon J. Ortiz, **"From Sand Creek"**	
1982 Raymond Carver, **"Cathedral"** • David Mamet, *Glengarry Glen Ross*	**1982** Equal Rights Amendment defeated • antinuclear movement protests manufacture of nuclear weapons • AIDS officially identified in the United States
1983 Toni Morrison, **"Recitatif"** • Joy Harjo, **"Call It Fear"**	
1984 Louise Erdrich, **"Dear John Wayne"**	
1985 Ursula K. Le Guin, **"She Unnames Them"** • Stanley Kunitz, **"The Wellfleet Whale"**	
1986 Louise Erdrich, **"Fleur"** • Art Spiegelman, *Maus I* • Rita Dove, *Thomas and Beulah* • Li-Young Lee, **"Eating Together"**	
1987 Gloria Anzaldúa, *Borderlands/La Frontera* • Sharon Olds, **"I Go Back to May 1937"**	
1988 Yusef Komunyakaa, **"Facing It"**	
1989 Amy Tan, *The Joy Luck Club*	**1989** Soviet Union collapses; Cold War ends • oil tanker *Exxon Valdez* runs aground in Alaska
1990 Robert Pinsky, **"The Want Bone"**	**1990** Congress passes Native American Graves Protection and Repatriation Act
1991 Sandra Cisneros, *Woman Hollering Creek*	**1991** United States enters Persian Gulf War • World Wide Web introduced
1993 Gary Snyder, **"Ripples on the Surface"** • A.R. Ammons, *Garbage* • Sherman Alexie, **"This Is What It Means to Say Phoenix, Arizona"**	
1994 Cathy Song, **"Lost Sister"** • Stephen Dixon, **"Flying"**	
1995 Jorie Graham, *The Dream of the Unified Field*	**1995** Federal building in Oklahoma City bombed in a terrorist attack
1996 W. S. Merwin, **"Lament for the Makers"** • Sherman Alexie, **"The Exaggeration of Despair"** • Junot Díaz, **"Drown"**	
1997 Julia Alvarez, *¡Yo!* • Fanny Howe, **"[Nobody wants crossed out girls around]"**	**1997** *Pathfinder* robot explores Mars

Boldface titles indicate works in the anthology.

TEXTS	CONTEXTS
1998 Billy Collins, "**I Chop Some Parsley While Listening to Art Blakey's Version of 'Three Blind Mice'**"	
1999 Jhumpa Lahiri, "**Sexy**" • Charles Simic, "**Arriving Celebrities**"	
2000 Charles Wright, "**North American Bear**" • Lucille Clifton, "**Moonchild**"	
2001 Charles Simic, "**Late September**"	2001 Execution of Timothy McVeigh, convicted of 1995 Oklahoma City bombing • September 11 terrorist attacks on Pentagon and World Trade Center
2002 Dorothy Allison, "**Stubborn Girls and Mean Stories**" • Alberto Ríos, "**Refugio's Hair**"	
	2003 United States and Great Britain invade Iraq
2004 Louise Glück, "**October**"	
2005 Kay Ryan, "**Home to Roost**" • Joan Didion, *The Year of Magical Thinking*	
2006 Thomas McGuane, "**Gallatin Canyon**" • Richard Powers, *The Echo Maker* • John Crawford, "**The Last True Story I'll Ever Tell**"	
2007 Edwidge Danticat, *Brother, I'm Dying*	2007 Advent of worst economic recession since the Great Depression.
	2009 Inauguration of Barack Obama as U.S. President
	2010 Massive oil spill in the Gulf of Mexico
	2011 Death of terrorist leader Osama bin Laden, architect of 9/11 attacks

STANLEY KUNITZ
1905-2006

For over thirty years at his home in Provincetown, Massachusetts, Stanley Kunitz tended a terraced hillside garden he created—"Stanley's folly," his wife, the painter Elise Asher, called it. To Kunitz the garden was an emblem for creativity and renewal much like poetry itself, and many of his poems draw images of plants and animals from this place. When Kunitz's 1995 collection, *Passing Through*, was published it coincided with his ninetieth birthday. The collection won the National Book Award and took its place in a poetic career that began sixty-five years earlier with his first book, *Intellectual Things* (1930). "Through the years I have found this gift of poetry to be life sustaining, life enhancing, and absolutely unpredictable," he said. It was a testament to the ongoing renewal of Kunitz's poetic gifts that in his eighties and nineties he wrote some of the finest poems of his career. For the period 2000–2001, at the age of ninety-five, he was named poet laureate of the United States.

Perhaps one reason Kunitz turned to the life-sustaining power of poetry was that his own life began in such painful circumstances. Six months before the poet's birth his father committed suicide, and throughout Kunitz's childhood his mother refused to let her husband's name be spoken in her presence: "She locked his name / in her deepest cabinet / and would not let him out / though I could hear him thumping" ("The Portrait"). Kunitz needed, he remarked, to find a way to transform his losses into creative experience. His early poetry, like the powerful "Father and Son," dramatizes that transformation and, with its dense syntax and hermetic imagery, suggests secret pain. Though Kunitz's tone ranges from wry playfulness in a love poem like "After the Last Dynasty" to elegiac lament in "The Wellfleet Whale," much of his work over the years has been an excavation of what he called, in the title of one poem, "The Thing That Eats the Heart."

A child of immigrants from a Lithuanian Jewish *shtetl*, Kunitz grew up in Worcester, Massachusetts, and revisits the surrounding landscape in a number of poems, like "Quinnapoxet," with its "abandoned reservoir" where "the snapping turtles cruised / and the bullheads swayed / in their bower of tree-stumps." An avid reader and a brilliant student, he earned a scholarship to Harvard University at a time when the university had a quota (2 percent) for Jewish students. He graduated summa cum laude, but, as Kunitz recounts it, when he continued his studies at Harvard and inquired about a teaching position, the university let it be known that his Jewish ancestry precluded an appointment. "It shattered me," he said. He then left academia for many years and worked as a reporter, an editor, and for a while as a small farmer. During World War II he served in the armed forces, and in 1946 he began a peripatetic teaching career that included Bennington College, the New School for Social Research, the University of Washington, and Brandeis University. In 1963 he took up a position at Columbia University, where he remained until 1985.

While *Intellectual Things* (the title comes from William Blake's "the tear is an intellectual thing") brought him attention, his next book, *Passport to War* (1944), went largely unnoticed. Yet he continued to write and publish poetry; and finally, when he was past fifty, he gained national recognition with his *Selected Poems 1928–1958* (1959), which won a Pulitzer Prize. Kunitz's early poems display his strong sense of drama. Tightly rhymed and metered, they often owe their startling images (for example, "The night nailed like an orange to my brow" from "Father and Son") to the influence of metaphysical poets like John Donne and George Herbert. But there is also something hidden about the early work, as if the complexity of the poet's language were a form of protection against the sources of his feeling. Then, with his important collection *The Testing-Tree* (1971), published when Kunitz was in his sixties ("my emancipation proclamation," he called it), his work became more open and relaxed. "My early writing was dense and convoluted," he said at the time, "so, I guess, was I. Now what I am seeking is a transparency of language and vision. Maybe age itself compels me to embrace the great simplicities." The transparency Kunitz sought revealed itself in a looser, two- to three-beat line, a more colloquial language. Most significant, after *The Testing-Tree*—whose title poem says, "the heart breaks and breaks / and lives by breaking"—Kunitz's work spoke its feeling more simply and directly. The poems of *Next-to-Last Things* (1985) and *Passing Through* (1995) continued this greater openness. One of these late poems, "The Wellfleet Whale," beautifully demonstrates Kunitz's distinctive idiom, combining precise observation of the natural world with a colloquial language that moves in the swells of ritual elegy and incantation.

Kunitz was notable as well for his generosity and commitment to other poets and artists; he was a close friend of the poet Theodore Roethke and the painter Mark Rothko. At Columbia, Kunitz helped shape the MFA program and served as a teacher and mentor to many younger writers. He supported a wider community of artists through his work as a founder of the residency program at the Fine Arts Work Center in Provincetown, Massachusetts; Louise Glück and Yosef Komunyakaa are among the many poets nurtured by this program at early stages of their careers. He also helped create Poets House, a literary center and library in New York City. For Kunitz, the sources of poetry were located beyond the individual self; in his words, "The poem comes in the form of a blessing—'like rapture breaking on the mind,' as I tried to phrase it in my youth." For more than seventy years Kunitz's work captured that sense of rapture and created a life-enhancing music of celebration and lament. His last book, *The Wild Braid: A Poet Reflects on a Century in the Garden* (2005), published in his one-hundredth year, united his loves for poetry and the garden.

Father and Son

Now in the suburbs and the falling light
I followed him, and now down sandy road
Whiter than bone-dust, through the sweet
Curdle of fields, where the plums
Dropped with their load of ripeness, one by one.[1]   5
Mile after mile I followed, with skimming feet,
After the secret master of my blood,
Him, steeped in the odor of ponds, whose indomitable love
Kept me in chains. Strode years; stretched into bird;
Raced through the sleeping country where I was young,   10
The silence unrolling before me as I came,
The night nailed like an orange to my brow.

How should I tell him my fable and the fears,
How bridge the chasm in a casual tone,
Saying, "The house, the stucco one you built,   15
We lost. Sister married and went from home,

---

1. Kunitz notes that these lines refer to rural Massachusetts as it was in his youth.

And nothing comes back, it's strange, from where she goes.
I lived on a hill that had too many rooms:
Light we could make, but not enough of warmth,
And when the light failed, I climbed under the hill.   20
The papers are delivered every day;
I am alone and never shed a tear."

At the water's edge, where the smothering ferns lifted
Their arms, "Father!" I cried, "Return! You know
The way. I'll wipe the mudstains from your clothes;   25
No trace, I promise, will remain. Instruct
Your son, whirling between two wars,
In the Gemara[2] of your gentleness,
For I would be a child to those who mourn
And brother to the foundlings of the field   30
And friend of innocence and all bright eyes.
O teach me how to work and keep me kind."

Among the turtles and the lilies he turned to me
The white ignorant hollow of his face.

1944

After the Last Dynasty[1]

Reading in Li Po[2]
how "the peach blossom follows the water"
I keep thinking of you
because you were so much like
Chairman Mao,[3]   5
naturally with the sex
transposed
and the figure slighter.
Loving you was a kind
of Chinese guerrilla war.   10
Thanks to your lightfoot genius
no Eighth Route Army[4]
kept its lines more fluid,
traveled with less baggage,
so nibbled the advantage.   15
Even with your small bad heart
you made a dance of departures.

2. The Gemara is the second and supplementary part of the Talmud, the oral law of the Jews, providing an extensive commentary by later rabbinical scholars on the traditional texts presented in the first part, the Mishna [Kunitz's note].
1. The Ch'ing Dynasty (1644–1912) was the last in a series of Chinese dynasties defined by rulers who came from the same family or line.
2. Chinese poet (701–762).

3. "Chairman Mao's summation of his strategy of guerilla warfare: 'Enemy advances, we retreat; enemy halts, we harass; enemy tires, we attack; enemy retreats, we pursue'" [Kunitz's note]. Mao Zedong (1893–1976), Communist leader of the People's Republic of China.
4. China's Red Army in the war of resistance against Japan.

In the cold spring rains
when last you failed me
I had nothing left to spend   20
but a red crayon language
on the character of the enemy
to break appointments,
to fight us not
with his strength   25
but with his weakness,
to kill us
not with his health
but with his sickness.
Pet, spitfire, blue-eyed pony,   30
here is a new note
I want to pin on your door,
though I am ten years late
and you are nowhere:
Tell me,   35
are you still mistress of the valley,
what trophies drift downriver,
why did you keep me waiting?

                                                      1971

Quinnapoxet[1]

I was fishing in the abandoned reservoir
back in Quinnapoxet,
where the snapping turtles cruised
and the bullheads swayed
in their bower of tree-stumps,   5
sleek as eels and pigeon-fat.
One of them gashed my thumb
with a flick of his razor fin
when I yanked the barb
out of his gullet.   10
The sun hung its terrible coals
over Buteau's farm: I saw
the treetops seething.

They came suddenly into view
on the Indian road,   15
evenly stepping
past the apple orchard,
commingling with the dust
they raised, their cloud of being,
against the dripping light   20

1. Quinnapoxet was a backwater village, no longer in existence, outside Worcester, Massachusetts, where I spent many of my childhood
summers as a boarder on the Buteau family farm.
The poem came to me in a dream [Kunitz's note].

looming larger and bolder.
She was wearing a mourning bonnet
and a wrap of shining taffeta.
"Why don't you write?" she cried
from the folds of her veil.   25
"We never hear from you."
I had nothing to say to her.
But for him who walked behind her
in his dark worsted suit,
with his face averted   30
as if to hide a scald,
deep in his other life,
I touched my forehead
with my swollen thumb
and splayed my fingers out—   35
in deaf-mute country
the sign for father.

1978

The Wellfleet Whale[1]

A few summers ago, on Cape Cod, a whale foundered on the beach,
a sixty-three-foot finback whale. When the tide went out, I
approached him. He was lying there, in monstrous desolation, making the most terrifying noises—rumbling—groaning. I put my
hands on his flanks and I could feel the life inside him. And while
I was standing there, suddenly he opened his eye. It was a big, red,
cold eye, and it was staring directly at me. A shudder of recognition
passed between us. Then the eye closed forever. I've been thinking
about whales ever since.

—Journal entry

1

You have your language too,
    an eerie medley of clicks
        and hoots and trills,
location-notes and love calls,
    whistles and grunts. Occasionally,   5
        it's like furniture being smashed,
or the creaking of a mossy door,
    sounds that all melt into a liquid
        song with endless variations,
as if to compensate   10
    for the vast loneliness of the sea.

1. Written in 1981 and first read at Harvard that year as the Phi Beta Kappa poem. The actual beaching of the whale in Wellfleet Harbor occurred September 12, 1966 [Kunitz's note]. Wellfleet is on Cape Cod, Massachusetts.

Sometimes a disembodied voice
breaks in as if from distant reefs,
    and it's as much as one can bear
        to listen to its long mournful cry,   15
a sorrow without name, both more
    and less than human. It drags
        across the ear like a record
running down.

2

No wind. No waves. No clouds.   20
    Only the whisper of the tide,
        as it withdrew, stroking the shore,
a lazy drift of gulls overhead,
    and tiny points of light
        bubbling in the channel.   25
It was the tag-end of summer.
    From the harbor's mouth
        you coasted into sight,
flashing news of your advent,
    the crescent of your dorsal fin   30
        clipping the diamonded surface.
We cheered at the sign of your greatness
    when the black barrel of your head
        erupted, ramming the water,
and you flowered for us   35
    in the jet of your spouting.

3

All afternoon you swam
    tirelessly round the bay,
        with such an easy motion,
the slightest downbeat of your tail,   40
    an almost imperceptible
        undulation of your flippers,
you seemed like something poured,
    not driven; you seemed
        to marry grace with power.   45
And when you bounded into air,
    slapping your flukes,
        we thrilled to look upon
pure energy incarnate
    as nobility of form.   50
        You seemed to ask of us
not sympathy, or love,
    or understanding,
        but awe and wonder.

That night we watched you   55
    swimming in the moon.

Your back was molten silver.
We guessed your silent passage
by the phosphorescence in your wake.
At dawn we found you stranded on the rocks. 60

4

There came a boy and a man
and yet other men running, and two
schoolgirls in yellow halters
and a housewife bedecked
with curlers, and whole families in beach 65
buggies with assorted yelping dogs.
The tide was almost out.
We could walk around you,
as you heaved deeper into the shoal,
crushed by your own weight, 70
collapsing into yourself,
your flippers and your flukes
quivering, your blowhole
spasmodically bubbling, roaring.
In the pit of your gaping mouth 75
you bared your fringework of baleen,[2]
a thicket of horned bristles.
When the Curator of Mammals
arrived from Boston
to take samples of your blood 80
you were already oozing from below.
Somebody had carved his initials
in your flank. Hunters of souvenirs
had peeled off strips of your skin,
a membrane thin as paper. 85
You were blistered and cracked by the sun.
The gulls had been pecking at you.
The sound you made was a hoarse and fitful bleating.
What drew us, like a magnet, to your dying?
You made a bond between us, 90
the keepers of the nightfall watch,
who gathered in a ring around you,
boozing in the bonfire light.
Toward dawn we shared with you
your hour of desolation, 95
the huge lingering passion
of your unearthly outcry,
as you swung your blind head
toward us and laboriously opened
a bloodshot, glistening eye, 100
in which we swam with terror and recognition.

---

2. Elastic, horny material forming the fringed plate that hangs, instead of teeth, from the upper jaw of baleen whales.

THE WELLFLEET WHALE | 27

5

Voyager, chief of the pelagic[3] world,
   you brought with you the myth
      of another country, dimly remembered,
where flying reptiles   105
   lumbered over the steaming marshes
      and trumpeting thunder lizards
wallowed in the reeds.
   While empires rose and fell on land,
      your nation breasted the open main,   110
rocked in the consoling rhythm
   of the tides. Which ancestor first plunged
      head-down through zones of colored twilight
to scour the bottom of the dark?
   You ranged the North Atlantic track   115
      from Port-of-Spain to Baffin Bay,[4]
edging between the ice-floes
   through the fat of summer,
      lob-tailing, breaching, sounding,
grazing in the pastures of the sea   120
   on krill[5]-rich orange plankton
      crackling with life.
You prowled down the continental shelf,
   guided by the sun and stars
      and the taste of alluvial[6] silt   125
on your way southward
   to the warm lagoons,
      the tropic of desire,
where the lovers lie belly to belly
   in the rub and nuzzle of their sporting;   130
      and you turned, like a god in exile,
out of your wide primeval element,
   delivered to the mercy of time.

   Master of the whale-roads,
let the white wings of the gulls   135
   spread out their cover.
      You have become like us,
disgraced and mortal.

                       1985

---

3. Living or occurring in the open ocean.
4. Inlet of the Atlantic Ocean between West Greenland and East Baffin Island. Port-of-Spain is the capital of Trinidad and Tobago.
5. Small marine crustaceans that are the principal food of baleen whales.
6. From sediment deposited by flowing water.

ROBERT PENN WARREN
1905–1989

I n 1969, with a long, distinguished career as a man of letters already behind him, Robert Penn Warren published his long poem *Audubon: A Vision*. Although Warren wrote many distinguished poems before the publication of the volume, until the 1960s he was best known for his fiction. In the six books of poetry that followed *Audubon*, Warren developed the claim he had begun earlier in his career to a powerful, distinctive, American voice. The mark of Warren's poetry, from early to late, is a passion directed toward the physical world and toward a knowledge of truth. As a poet he yearns for more than what life usually discloses, yet an intense love for the world accompanies this yearning.

Warren was born in Guthrie in southern Kentucky, and much of his writing reflects his engagement with the lessons of history as they can be read in the experience of the American South. He took this sense of history most immediately from his father, who read history and poetry aloud to the family, and from his maternal grandfather, Gabriel Telemachus Penn. Warren spent his boyhood summers on this grandfather's isolated tobacco farm. There the old man, who had fought on the Confederate side in the Civil War, told Warren tales of war while the two mapped out battles together, or the boy listened while his grandfather recited poetry "by the yard" (as Warren described it), especially Sir Walter Scott and Robert Burns. The memory of an idyllic boyhood spent dreaming amid the natural world informs many of Warren's poems, among them "American Portrait: Old Style," where he returns, in his seventies, to visit both the place of that boyhood and his childhood friend, K.

The decisive literary moment in Warren's life came when, at the age of sixteen, he enrolled at Vanderbilt University in Nashville. He had wanted to be a naval officer, but an eye injury prevented him from taking up his commission at Annapolis. Vanderbilt was enjoying a feverish interest in poetry at the time. (Even football players, Warren reported, seemed to be writing verse, and Warren remembers that people lined up for the latest issues of the *Dial* and other literary periodicals in which they might find new work by Yeats or Eliot or Hart Crane.) Part of the excitement was due to the presence of the poet John Crowe Ransom, who taught Warren's freshman composition class and soon involved him, even as an undergraduate, with the Fugitives, a group of faculty members and, according to Warren, "bookish, intelligent young businessmen" who met to discuss literature and philosophy. By the time Warren joined it was largely a poetry club at which Ransom and others read and criticized one another's work. Here Warren met Allen Tate, the gifted poet and critic, who found the redheaded undergraduate, five years his junior, "the most gifted person I have ever known." For years to come they constituted a kind of southern axis in American letters, and in 1930 they joined several other southern writers in a political manifesto, *I'll Take My Stand*. The collection of twelve essays envisioned an agrarian South with strong local cultures as the only humane alternative to an increasingly self-destructive industrialism centered in the North.

Warren attended graduate school at the University of California, at Yale, and then as a Rhodes Scholar at Oxford University in England. From 1935 to 1942 he was on the English faculty at Louisiana State University. There, along with Cleanth Brooks and Charles W. Pipkin, he founded the *Southern Review*, which for the seven years of their involvement was the most influential literary quarterly in the country. It was the principal forum for pioneering interpretative essays by "New

Critics" such as Ransom, Kenneth Burke, and R. P. Blackmur. (Brooks and Warren also edited *Understanding Poetry*, the important school anthology and text that introduced students to "close reading" on New Critical principles.) In addition, the *Southern Review* published the best fiction by emerging southern writers such as Katherine Anne Porter and Eudora Welty.

Warren's own fiction brought him wide critical attention in the 1940s. The novel *All the King's Men* (1946), which he conceived as a verse play, won the Pulitzer Prize and later became a film. It portrayed the rise and fall of a southern demagogue who closely resembled Huey Long, the Louisiana governor and senator who was assassinated in the rotunda of the Louisiana statehouse in 1935. Warren's interest was in showing the tangled motives of his protagonist, Willie Stark, a Depression-era governor who led a corrupt regime that was progressive in its social programs. In its focus on violent subjects with historical and psychological resonance, Warren's fiction anticipates his sequence *Audubon: A Vision*. Other novels, like *World Enough and Time* (1950), set in the Kentucky of the 1820s, are based on documents and grow out of his ongoing study of and response to southern history.

From 1944 to 1954 Warren was intensely active in fiction and published almost no poems. In 1952 he married the writer Eleanor Clark, his second wife, and, prompted by the landscapes where they lived in Europe and by the birth of a son and daughter in the mid 1950s, he returned to poetry with a new intimacy and autobiographical intensity. His earlier work, like "Bearded Oaks," had been strongly influenced by the formal control and the elegant, well-mannered rationality of John Crowe Ransom's verse. But beginning with the volume *Promises* (1957), and revealed fully in *Audubon*, Warren's poetic line loosened up, moved with vigor and raw energy. Although the tone of his poems sometimes grows too insistent or rhetorical, his muscular syntax and rhythm forged a "voice-instrument calibrated to experience," in the words of Dave Smith, a poet of a younger generation, indebted to Warren's work.

In *Democracy and Poetry* (1975), his Jefferson Lecture in the Humanities, Warren said, "What poetry most significantly celebrates is the capacity of man to face the deep, dark inwardness of his nature and fate." In *Audubon*, Warren's version of the historical John James Audubon must enter what Yeats once called "the abyss of the self" to create a heroic selfhood at the center of the poetry. Ornithologist and painter of *Birds of America*, Audubon (1785–1851) was artist and scientist, solitary searcher and classifier, consumed by his tasks. Basing part of his poem on Audubon's autobiographical account, Warren imagines a man launched into his true vision after an encounter with violence at the heart of experience: he narrowly escapes being robbed and murdered in the wilderness by a crone and her sons. In this incident Audubon must also confront the violent desire of his own "lust of the eye" and thereby reconcile in himself the need for both passion and reverence toward existence. Passion directs Warren's hero to slay the birds in order to paint them, to put them "In our imagination" (*Audubon* VI, "Love and Knowledge"). But reverence demands the heart's total response to the beauty of existence. This is why Warren commands his hero and himself: "Continue to walk in the world. Yes, love it!" While the most representative figure in Warren's poems is solitary—the individual, like Audubon, confronting versions of the American sublime—Warren also wrote a number of fine poems in other registers, among them some moving love poems. The sense of history that animates so much of his fiction becomes in his poems the persistent struggle of memory to overcome the passage of time, to make *then* into *now*, as reflected in the title of his volume *Now and Then: Poems 1976–1978* (1978). The struggle with time is one aspect of the heroic engagement with existence that was the dramatic center of Warren's work.

Bearded Oaks

The oaks, how subtle and marine,
Bearded, and all the layered light
Above them swims; and thus the scene,
Recessed, awaits the positive night.

So, waiting, we in the grass now lie   5
Beneath the languorous tread of light:
The grasses, kelp-like, satisfy
The nameless motions of the air.

Upon the floor of light, and time,
Unmurmuring, of polyp made,   10
We rest; we are, as light withdraws,
Twin atolls on a shelf of shade.

Ages to our construction went,
Dim architecture, hour by hour:
And violence, forgot now, lent   15
The present stillness all its power.

The storm of noon above us rolled,
Of light the fury, furious gold,
The long drag troubling us, the depth:
Dark is unrocking, unrippling, still.   20

Passion and slaughter, ruth, decay
Descend, minutely whispering down,
Silted down swaying streams, to lay
Foundation for our voicelessness.

All our debate is voiceless here,   25
As all our rage, the rage of stone
If hope is hopeless, then fearless is fear,
And history is thus undone.

Our feet once wrought the hollow street
With echo when the lamps were dead   30
At windows, once our headlight glare
Disturbed the doe that, leaping, fled.

I do not love you less that now
The caged heart makes iron stroke,
Or less that all that light once gave   35
The graduate dark should now revoke.

We live in time so little time
And we learn all so painfully,
That we may spare this hour's term
To practice for eternity.   40

1942

From Audubon[1]

I. Was Not the Lost Dauphin

[A]

Was not the lost dauphin, though handsome was only
Base-born and not even able
To make a decent living, was only
Himself, Jean Jacques, and his passion—what
Is man but his passion?   5

                 Saw,
Eastward and over the cypress swamp, the dawn,
Redder than meat, break;
And the large bird,
Long neck outthrust, wings crooked to scull air, moved   10
In a slow calligraphy, crank, flat, and black against
The color of God's blood spilt, as though
Pulled by a string.

                Saw
It proceed across the inflamed distance.   15

Moccasins set in hoar frost, eyes fixed on the bird,
Thought: "On that sky it is black."
Thought: "In my mind it is white."
Thinking: "*Ardea occidentalis*, heron the great one."

Dawn: his heart shook in the tension of the world.   20

Dawn: and what is your passion?

[B]

October: and the bear,
Daft in the honey-light, yawns.

The bear's tongue, pink as a baby's, out-crisps to the curled tip,
It bleeds the black blood of the blueberry.   25

The teeth are more importantly white
Than has ever been imagined.

The bear feels his own fat
Sweeten, like a drowse, deep to the bone.

1. John James Audubon (1785–1851), natural son of French parents (hence "Jean Jacques" in line 4), but later an American citizen. Painter, ornithologist, Kentucky settler, he dedicated his life to the pursuit, classification, and depiction of the *Birds of America* (first published in England, 1827). Among the stories told about his birth was one (false) that he was the Dauphin, the son of the dethroned and executed Louis XVI and Marie Antoinette of France.

Bemused, above the fume of ruined blueberries,   30
The last bee hums.

The wings, like mica, glint
In the sunlight.

He leans on his gun. Thinks
How thin is the membrane between himself and the world.   35

VI. *Love and Knowledge*

Their footless dance
Is of the beautiful liability of their nature.
Their eyes are round, boldly convex, bright as a jewel,
And merciless. They do not know
Compassion, and if they did,   5
We should not be worthy of it. They fly
In air that glitters like fluent crystal
And is hard as perfectly transparent iron, they cleave it
With no effort. They cry
In a tongue multitudinous, often like music.   10

He slew them, at surprising distances, with his gun.
Over a body held in his hand, his head was bowed low,
But not in grief.

He put them where they are, and there we see them:
In our imagination.   15

What is love?

Our name for it is knowledge.

VII. *Tell Me a Story*

[A]

Long ago, in Kentucky, I, a boy, stood
By a dirt road, in first dark, and heard
The great geese hoot northward.

I could not see them, there being no moon
And the stars sparse. I heard them.   5

I did not know what was happening in my heart.

It was the season before the elderberry blooms,
Therefore they were going north.

The sound was passing northward.

[B]

Tell me a story.   10

In this century, and moment, of mania,
Tell me a story.

Make it a story of great distances, and starlight.

The name of the story will be Time,
But you must not pronounce its name.   15

Tell me a story of deep delight.

1969

American Portrait: Old Style

I

Beyond the last house, where home was,
Past the marsh we found the old skull in, all nameless
And cracked in star-shape from a stone-smack,
Up the hill where the grass was tangled waist-high and wind-tousled,
To the single great oak that, in leaf-season, hung like   5
A thunderhead black against whatever blue the sky had,
And here, at the widest circumference of shade, when shade was,
Ran the trench, six feet long,
And wide enough for a man to lie down in,
In comfort, if comfort was still any object. No sign there   10
Of any ruined cabin or well, so Pap must have died of camp fever,
And the others pushed on, God knows where.

II

The Dark and Bloody Ground, so the teacher romantically said,
But one look out the window, and woods and ruined cornfields we saw:
A careless-flung corner of country, no hope and no history here. 15
No hope but the Pullman lights[1] that swept
Night-fields—glass-glint from some farmhouse and flicker of ditches—
Or the night freight's moan on the rise where
You might catch a ride on the rods,
Just for hell, or if need had arisen.   20
No history either—no Harrod or Finley or Booney,[2]
No tale how the Bluebellies[3] broke at the Rebel yell and cold steel.

---

1. Lights from the sleeping cars on trains.
2. James Harrod and Daniel Boone were pioneers and Indian scouts. Robert W. Finley was a pioneer and missionary. All three lived in Kentucky in the late 18th century.
3. Derogatory term for members of the Union Army in the Civil War.

So we had to invent it all, our Bloody Ground, K and I,
And him the best shot in ten counties and could call any bird-note back,
But school out, not big enough for the ballgame,   25
And in the full tide of summer, not ready
For the twelve-gauge yet, or even a job, so what

Can you do but pick up your BBs and Benjamin,
Stick corn pone in pocket, and head out
"To Rally in the Cane-Brake and Shoot the Buffalo"—   30
As my grandfather's cracked old voice would sing it
From days of his own grandfather—and often enough
It was only a Plymouth Rock or maybe a fat Dominecker
That fell to the crack of the unerring Decherd.[4]

III

Yes, imagination is strong. But not strong enough in the face of   35
The sticky feathers and BBs a mother's hand held out.
But no liberal concern was evinced for a Redskin,
As we trailed and out-tricked the sly Shawnees[5]
In a thicket of ironweed, and I wrestled one naked
And slick with his bear grease, till my hunting knife   40
Bit home, and the tomahawk
Slipped from his hand. And what mother cared about Bluebellies
Who came charging our trench? But we held
To pour the last volley at face-gape before
The tangle and clangor of bayonet.   45

Yes, a day is merely forever
In memory's shiningness,
And a year but a gust or a gasp
In the summer's heat of Time, and in that last summer
I was almost ready to learn   50
What imagination is—it is only
The lie we must learn to live by, if ever
We mean to live at all. Times change.
Things change. And K up and gone, and the summer
Gone, and I longed to know the world's name.   55

IV

Well, what I remember most
In a world long Time-pale and powdered
Like a vision still clinging to plaster
Set by Piero della Francesca[6]
Is how K, through lane-dust or meadow,   60
Seemed never to walk, but float
With a singular joy and silence,

4. A BB gun. "Plymouth Rock" and "Dominecker" are varieties of fowl.
5. Native Americans who lived mainly in the areas of Ohio and Indiana.
6. Early Renaissance painter whose frescoes, usually of religious subjects, are known for their clarity and idealization.

In his cloud of bird dogs, like angels,
With their eyes on his eyes like God,
And the sun on his uncut hair bright   65
As he passed through the ramshackle town and odd folks there
With coats on and vests and always soft gabble of money—
Polite in his smiling, but never much to say.

V

To pass through to what? No, not
To some wild white peak dreamed westward,   70
And each sunrise a promise to keep. No, only
The Big Leagues, not even a bird dog,
And girls that popped gum while they screwed.

Yes, this was his path, and no batter
Could do what booze finally did: 75
Just blow him off the mound—but anyway,
He had always called it a fool game, just something
For children who hadn't yet dreamed what
A man is, or barked a squirrel, or raised
A single dog from a pup.   80

VI

And I, too, went on my way, the winning and losing, or what
Is sometimes of all things the worst, the not knowing
One thing from the other, nor knowing
How the teeth in Time's jaw all snag backward
And whatever enters therein   85
Has less hope of remission than shark-meat,

And on Sunday afternoon, in the idleness of summer,
I found his farm, and him home there,
With the bird dogs crouched round in the grass
And their eyes on his eyes as he whispered   90
Whatever to bird dogs it was.
Then yelled: "Well, for Christ's sake—it's you!"

Yes, me, for Christ's sake, and some sixty
Years blown like a hurricane past! But what can you say—
Can you say—when *all-to-be-said* is the *done*?   95
So our talk ran to buffalo-hunting, and the look on his mother's face
When she held the BBs out.

And the sun sank slow as he stood there,
All Indian-brown from waist up, who never liked tops to his pants,
And standing nigh straight, but the arms and the pitcher's   100
Great shoulders, they were thinning to old-man thin.
Sun low, all silence, then sudden:
"But, Jesus," he cried, "what makes a man do what he does—
Him living until he dies!"

Sure, all of us live till we die, but bingo! 105
Like young David at brookside, he swooped down,
Snatched a stone, wound up, and let fly,[7]
And high on a pole over yonder the big brown insulator
Simply exploded. "See—I still got control!" he said.

VII

Late, late, toward sunset, I wandered 110
Where old dreams had once been Life's truth, and where
I saw the trench of our valor, now nothing
But a ditch full of late-season weed-growth,
Beyond the rim of shade.

There was nobody there, hence no shame to be saved from, so I 115
Just lie in the trench on my back and see high,
Beyond the tall ironweed stalks, or oak leaves
If I happened to look that way,
How the late summer's thinned-out sky moves,
Drifting on, drifting on, like forever, 120
From *where* on to *where*, and I wonder
What it would be like to die,
Like the nameless old skull in the swamp, lost,
And know yourself dead lying under
The infinite motion of sky. 125

VIII

But why should I lie here longer?
I am not dead yet, though in years,
And the world's way is yet long to go,
And I love the world even in my anger,
And that's a hard thing to outgrow. 130

1978

Mortal Limit

I saw the hawk ride updraft in the sunset over Wyoming.
It rose from coniferous darkness, past gray jags
Of mercilessness, past whiteness, into the gloaming
Of dream-spectral light above the last purity of snow-snags.

There—west—were the Tetons.[1] Snow-peaks would soon be 5
In dark profile to break constellations. Beyond what height
Hangs now the black speck? Beyond what range will gold eyes see
New ranges rise to mark a last scrawl of light?

7. I.e., as David overthrew the giant Goliath in 1
Samuel 17.

1. High mountain range in northwest Wyoming.

Or, having tasted that atmosphere's thinness, does it
Hang motionless in dying vision before   10
It knows it will accept the mortal limit,
And swing into the great circular downwardness that will restore

The breath of earth? Of rock? Of rot? Of other such
Items, and the darkness of whatever dream we clutch?

                                                                      1985

THEODORE ROETHKE
1908–1963

Theodore Roethke had the kind of childhood a poet might have invented. He was born in Saginaw, Michigan, where both his German grandfather and his father kept greenhouses for a living. The greenhouse world, he later said, represented for him "both heaven and hell, a kind of tropics created in the savage climate of Michigan, where austere German Americans turned their love of order and their terrifying efficiency into something truly beautiful." Throughout his life he was haunted both by the ordered, protected world of the greenhouse—the constant activity of growth, the cultivated flowers—and by the desolate landscape of his part of Michigan. "The marsh, the mire, the Void, is always there, immediate and terrifying. It is a splendid place for schooling the spirit. It is America."

Roethke's poetry often reenacted this "schooling" of the spirit by revisiting the landscapes of his childhood: the nature poems that make up the largest part of his early work try to bridge the distance between a child's consciousness and the adult mysteries presided over by his father. Roethke arranged and rearranged these poems to give the sense of a spiritual autobiography, especially in preparing the volumes *The Lost Son and Other Poems* (1948), *Praise to the End!* (1951), and *The Waking* (1953). In what are known as "the greenhouse poems," the greenhouse world emerged as a "reality harsher than reality," the cultivator's activity pulsating and threatening. Its overseers, like "Frau Bauman, Frau Schmidt, and Frau Schwartze" (the title of one poem) emerge as gods, fates, muses, and witches all in one. By focusing on the minute processes of botanical growth—the rooting, the budding—the poet found a way of participating in the mysteries of this once alien world, whether he was deep in the subterranean root cellar or, as a child, perched high on top of the greenhouse.

In his books *The Lost Son* and *Praise to the End!* Roethke explored the regenerative possibilities of prerational speech (like children's riddles) in which language as sound recaptures nonlogical states of being. In these poems, his most dazzling and original work, Roethke opened up the possibilities of language. The title of one section of the long poem *The Lost Son* is "The Gibber," a pun because the word means both a meaningless utterance and the pouch at the base of a flower's calyx. The pun identifies principles of growth with the possibilities of speech freed from logical meanings, and the sequence as a whole suggests the power of both nature and language to revive the spirit of an adult life: "A lively understandable spirit / Once entertained you. / It will come again. / Be still. / Wait."

If the nature poems of Roethke's first four books explore the anxieties within him since childhood, his later love poems show him in periods of release and momentary pleasure: "And I dance round and round, / A fond and foolish man, / And see and suffer myself / In another being at last." The love poems, many included in *Words for the Wind* (1958) and *The Far Field* (1964), are among the most appealing in modern American verse. His beautiful and tender "Elegy for Jane" should be included in this category. These poems stand in sharp relief to the suffering Roethke experienced in other areas of his personal life—several mental breakdowns and periods of alcoholism—which led to a premature death. *The Far Field*, a posthumous volume, includes fierce, strongly rhymed lyrics in which Roethke tried "bare, even terrible statement," pressing toward the threshold of spiritual insight: "A man goes far to find out what he is—/ Death of the self in a long, tearless night, / All natural shapes blazing unnatural light." The nature poems of this last volume, gathered as "The North American Sequence," use extended landscape to find natural analogies for the human passage toward the dark unknown, hoping "in their rhythms to catch the very movement of mind itself."

Roethke is remembered as one of the great teachers of poetry, especially by those young poets and critics who studied with him at the University of Washington from 1948 until the time of his death. James Wright, David Wagoner, and Richard Hugo, among others, attended his classes. He was noted for his mastery of sound and metrics. Although his own poetry was intensely personal, his starting advice to students always deemphasized undisciplined self-expression. "Write like someone else," he instructed beginners. In Roethke's own career, however, this advice had its costs. His apprenticeship to Yeats, in particular, endangered his own poetic voice; in some late poems the echo of this great predecessor makes Roethke all but inaudible.

Roethke was much honored later in his career: a Pulitzer Prize for *The Waking* (1953); a National Book Award and Bollingen Prize for the collected poems, *Words for the Wind* (1958); and a posthumous National Book Award for *The Far Field* (1964).

Cuttings

Sticks-in-a-drowse droop over sugary loam,
Their intricate stem-fur dries;
But still the delicate slips keep coaxing up water;
The small cells bulge;

One nub of growth   5
Nudges a sand-crumb loose,
Pokes through a musty sheath
Its pale tendrilous horn.

1948

Cuttings

(*later*)

This urge, wrestle, resurrection of dry sticks,
Cut stems struggling to put down feet,
What saint strained so much,
Rose on such lopped limbs to a new life?

I can hear, underground, that sucking and sobbing,   5
In my veins, in my bones I feel it,—
The small waters seeping upward,
The tight grains parting at last.
When sprouts break out,
Slippery as fish   10
I quail, lean to beginnings, sheath-wet.

1948

Root Cellar

Nothing would sleep in that cellar, dank as a ditch,
Bulbs broke out of boxes hunting for chinks in the dark,
Shoots dangled and drooped,
Lolling obscenely from mildewed crates,
Hung down long yellow evil necks, like tropical snakes.   5
And what a congress of stinks!—
Roots ripe as old bait,
Pulpy stems, rank, silo-rich,
Leaf-mold, manure, lime, piled against slippery planks.
Nothing would give up life: 10
Even the dirt kept breathing a small breath.

1948

Big Wind

Where were the greenhouses going,
Lunging into the lashing
Wind driving water
So far down the river
All the faucets stopped?—   5
So we drained the manure-machine
For the steam plant,
Pumping the stale mixture
Into the rusty boilers,
Watching the pressure gauge   10
Waver over to red,
As the seams hissed
And the live steam
Drove to the far
End of the rose-house,   15
Where the worst wind was,
Creaking the cypress window-frames,
Cracking so much thin glass
We stayed all night,
Stuffing the holes with burlap;   20

But she rode it out,
That old rose-house,
She hove into the teeth of it,
The core and pith of that ugly storm,
Ploughing with her stiff prow,   25
Bucking into the wind-waves
That broke over the whole of her,
Flailing her sides with spray,
Flinging long strings of wet across the roof-top,
Finally veering, wearing themselves out, merely   30
Whistling thinly under the wind-vents;
She sailed until the calm morning,
Carrying her full cargo of roses.

                                                                 1948

Weed Puller

Under the concrete benches,
Hacking at black hairy roots,—
Those lewd monkey-tails hanging from drainholes,—
Digging into the soft rubble underneath,
Webs and weeds,   5
Grubs and snails and sharp sticks,
Or yanking tough fern-shapes,
Coiled green and thick, like dripping smilax,[1]
Tugging all day at perverse life:
The indignity of it!—   10
With everything blooming above me,
Lilies, pale-pink cyclamen, roses,
Whole fields lovely and inviolate,—
Me down in that fetor of weeds,
Crawling on all fours,   15
Alive, in a slippery grave.

                                                                 1948

Frau Bauman, Frau Schmidt, and Frau Schwartze[1]

Gone the three ancient ladies
Who creaked on the greenhouse ladders,
Reaching up white strings
To wind, to wind
The sweet-pea tendrils, the smilax,[2]   5
Nasturtiums, the climbing

---

1. A type of fern.   by Roethke's father.
1. Women who worked in the greenhouse owned   2. A type of fern.

Roses, to straighten
Carnations, red
Chrysanthemums; the stiff
Stems, jointed like corn,   10
They tied and tucked,—
These nurses of nobody else.
Quicker than birds, they dipped
Up and sifted the dirt;
They sprinkled and shook;   15
They stood astride pipes,
Their skirts billowing out wide into tents,
Their hands twinkling with wet;
Like witches they flew along rows
Keeping creation at ease;   20
With a tendril for needle
They sewed up the air with a stem;
They teased out the seed that the cold kept asleep,—
All the coils, loops, and whorls.
They trellised the sun; they plotted for more than themselves.   25

I remember how they picked me up, a spindly kid,
Pinching and poking my thin ribs
Till I lay in their laps, laughing,
Weak as a whiffet;[3]
Now, when I'm alone and cold in my bed,   30
They still hover over me,
These ancient leathery crones,
With their bandannas stiffened with sweat,
And their thorn-bitten wrists,
And their snuff-laden breath blowing lightly over me in my first
    sleep.   35

                                                                         1948

Child on Top of a Greenhouse

The wind billowing out the seat of my britches,
My feet crackling splinters of glass and dried putty,
The half-grown chrysanthemums staring up like accusers,
Up through the streaked glass, flashing with sunlight,
A few white clouds all rushing eastward,   5
A line of elms plunging and tossing like horses,
And everyone, everyone pointing up and shouting!

                                                                         1948

---

3. A small, young, or unimportant person (probably from *whippet*, a small dog).

My Papa's Waltz

The whiskey on your breath
Could make a small boy dizzy;
But I hung on like death:
Such waltzing was not easy.

We romped until the pans   5
Slid from the kitchen shelf;
My mother's countenance
Could not unfrown itself.

The hand that held my wrist
Was battered on one knuckle;   10
At every step you missed
My right ear scraped a buckle.

You beat time on my head
With a palm caked hard by dirt,
Then waltzed me off to bed   15
Still clinging to your shirt.

1948

Dolor

I have known the inexorable sadness of pencils,
Neat in their boxes, dolor of pad and paper-weight,
All the misery of manilla folders and mucilage,
Desolation in immaculate public places,
Lonely reception room, lavatory, switchboard,   5
The unalterable pathos of basin and pitcher,
Ritual of multigraph, paper-clip, comma,
Endless duplication of lives and objects.
And I have seen dust from the walls of institutions,
Finer than flour, alive, more dangerous than silica,   10
Sift, almost invisible, through long afternoons of tedium,
Dropping a fine film on nails and delicate eyebrows,
Glazing the pale hair, the duplicate grey standard faces.

1948

Night Crow

When I saw that clumsy crow
Flap from a wasted tree,
A shape in the mind rose up:

Over the gulfs of dream
Flew a tremendous bird   5
Further and further away
Into a moonless black,
Deep in the brain, far back.

1948

The Lost Son

I. The Flight

At Woodlawn[1] I heard the dead cry:
I was lulled by the slamming of iron,
A slow drip over stones,
Toads brooding wells.
All the leaves stuck out their tongues;   5
I shook the softening chalk of my bones,
Saying,
Snail, snail, glister me forward,
Bird, soft-sigh me home,
Worm, be with me.   10
This is my hard time.

Fished in an old wound,
The soft pond of repose;
Nothing nibbled my line,
Not even the minnows came.   15

Sat in an empty house
Watching shadows crawl,
Scratching.
There was one fly.

Voice, come out of the silence.   20
Say something.
Appear in the form of a spider
Or a moth beating the curtain.

Tell me:
Which is the way I take;   25
Out of what door do I go,
Where and to whom?

Dark hollows said, lee to the wind,
The moon said, back of an eel,
The salt said, look by the sea,   30
Your tears are not enough praise,

---

1. A cemetery.

You will find no comfort here,
In the kingdom of bang and blab.

Running lightly over spongy ground,
Past the pasture of flat stones,   35
The three elms,
The sheep strewn on a field,
Over a rickety bridge
Toward the quick-water, wrinkling and rippling.

Hunting along the river,   40
Down among the rubbish, the bug-riddled foliage,
By the muddy pond-edge, by the bog-holes,
By the shrunken lake, hunting, in the heat of summer.

The shape of a rat?
It's bigger than that.   45
It's less than a leg
And more than a nose,
Just under the water
It usually goes.

Is it soft like a mouse?   50
Can it wrinkle its nose?
Could it come in the house
On the tips of its toes?

Take the skin of a cat
And the back of an eel,   55
Then roll them in grease,—
That's the way it would feel.

It's sleek as an otter
With wide webby toes
Just under the water   60
It usually goes.

2. *The Pit*

Where do the roots go?
    Look down under the leaves.
Who put the moss there?
    These stones have been here too long.   65
Who stunned the dirt into noise?
    Ask the mole, he knows.
I feel the slime of a wet nest.
    Beware Mother Mildew.
Nibble again, fish nerves.   70

3. *The Gibber*

At the wood's mouth,
By the cave's door,
I listened to something
I had heard before.

Dogs of the groin   75
Barked and howled,
The sun was against me,
The moon would not have me.

The weeds whined,
The snakes cried,   80
The cows and briars
Said to me: Die.

What a small song. What slow clouds. What dark water.
Hath the rain a father? All the caves are ice. Only the snow's here.
I'm cold. I'm cold all over. Rub me in father and mother.   85
Fear was my father, Father Fear.
His look drained the stones.

    What gliding shape
    Beckoning through halls,
    Stood poised on the stair,   90
    Fell dreamily down?

    From the mouths of jugs
    Perched on many shelves,
    I saw substance flowing
    That cold morning.   95

    Like a slither of eels
    That watery cheek
    As my own tongue kissed
    My lips awake.

Is this the storm's heart? The ground is unstilling itself.   100
My veins are running nowhere. Do the bones cast out their fire?
Is the seed leaving the old bed? These buds are live as birds.
Where, where are the tears of the world?
Let the kisses resound, flat like a butcher's palm;
Let the gestures freeze; our doom is already decided.   105
All the windows are burning! What's left of my life?
I want the old rage, the lash of primordial milk!
Goodbye, goodbye, old stones, the time-order is going,
I have married my hands to perpetual agitation,
I run, I run to the whistle of money.   110

    Money money money
    Water water water

How cool the grass is.
Has the bird left?
The stalk still sways.   115
Has the worm a shadow?
What do the clouds say?

These sweeps of light undo me.
Look, look, the ditch is running white!
I've more veins than a tree!   120
Kiss me, ashes, I'm falling through a dark swirl.

4. The Return

The way to the boiler was dark,
Dark all the way,
Over slippery cinders
Through the long greenhouse.   125

The roses kept breathing in the dark.
They had many mouths to breathe with.
My knees made little winds underneath
Where the weeds slept.

There was always a single light   130
Swinging by the fire-pit,
Where the fireman pulled out roses,
The big roses, the big bloody clinkers.[2]

Once I stayed all night.
The light in the morning came slowly over the white   135
Snow.
There were many kinds of cool
Air.
Then came steam.

Pipe-knock.   140

Scurry of warm over small plants.
Ordnung![3] ordnung!
Papa is coming!

A fine haze moved off the leaves;
Frost melted on far panes;   145
The rose, the chrysanthemum turned toward the light.
Even the hushed forms, the bent yellowy weeds
Moved in a slow up-sway.

2. Large cinders; the residue left in burning coal.   3. A call to order.

5. *"It was beginning winter"*

It was beginning winter,
An in-between time,   150
The landscape still partly brown:
The bones of weeds kept swinging in the wind,
Above the blue snow.

It was beginning winter,
The light moved slowly over the frozen field,   155
Over the dry seed-crowns,
The beautiful surviving bones
Swinging in the wind.

Light traveled over the wide field;
Stayed.   160
The weeds stopped swinging.
The mind moved, not alone,
Through the clear air, in the silence.

    Was it light?
    Was it light within?   165
    Was it light within light?
    Stillness becoming alive,
    Yet still?

A lively understandable spirit
Once entertained you.   170
It will come again.
Be still.
Wait.

                      1948

The Waking

    I wake to sleep, and take my waking slow.
    I feel my fate in what I cannot fear.
    I learn by going where I have to go.

    We think by feeling. What is there to know?
    I hear my being dance from ear to ear.   5
    I wake to sleep, and take my waking slow.

    Of those so close beside me, which are you?
    God bless the Ground! I shall walk softly there,
    And learn by going where I have to go.

    Light takes the Tree; but who can tell us how?   10
    The lowly worm climbs up a winding stair;
    I wake to sleep, and take my waking slow.

Great Nature has another thing to do
To you and me; so take the lively air,
And, lovely, learn by going where to go.   15

This shaking keeps me steady. I should know.
What falls away is always. And is near.
I wake to sleep, and take my waking slow.
I learn by going where I have to go.

1953

Elegy for Jane

My Student, Thrown by a Horse

I remember the neckcurls, limp and damp as tendrils;
And her quick look, a sidelong pickerel smile;
And how, once startled into talk, the light syllables leaped for her,
And she balanced in the delight of her thought,
A wren, happy, tail into the wind,   5
Her song trembling the twigs and small branches.
The shade sang with her;
The leaves, their whispers turned to kissing;
And the mold sang in the bleached valleys under the rose.

Oh, when she was sad, she cast herself down into such a pure depth,   10
Even a father could not find her:
Scraping her cheek against straw;
Stirring the clearest water.

My sparrow, you are not here,
Waiting like a fern, making a spiny shadow.   15
The sides of wet stones cannot console me,
Nor the moss, wound with the last light.

If only I could nudge you from this sleep,
My maimed darling, my skittery pigeon.
Over this damp grave I speak the words of my love: 20
I, with no rights in this matter,
Neither father nor lover.

1953

I Knew a Woman

I knew a woman, lovely in her bones,
When small birds sighed, she would sigh back at them;
Ah, when she moved, she moved more ways than one:
The shapes a bright container can contain!

Of her choice virtues only gods should speak,　　　　　5
Or English poets who grew up on Greek
(I'd have them sing in chorus, cheek to cheek).

How well her wishes went! She stroked my chin,
She taught me Turn, and Counter-turn, and Stand;[1]
She taught me Touch, that undulant white skin;　　　10
I nibbled meekly from her proffered hand;
She was the sickle; I, poor I, the rake,
Coming behind her for her pretty sake
(But what prodigious mowing we did make).

Love likes a gander, and adores a goose:　　　　　15
Her full lips pursed, the errant note to seize;
She played it quick, she played it light and loose;
My eyes, they dazzled at her flowing knees;
Her several parts could keep a pure repose,
Or one hip quiver with a mobile nose　　　　　　20
(She moved in circles, and those circles moved).

Let seed be grass, and grass turn into hay:
I'm martyr to a motion not my own;
What's freedom for? To know eternity.
I swear she cast a shadow white as stone.　　　　　25
But who would count eternity in days?
These old bones live to learn her wanton ways:
(I measure time by how a body sways).

　　　　　　　　　　　　　　　　　　　　　1958

Wish for a Young Wife

My lizard, my lively writher,
May your limbs never wither,
May the eyes in your face
Survive the green ice
Of envy's mean gaze;　　　　　　　　　　5
May you live out your life
Without hate, without grief,
And your hair ever blaze,
In the sun, in the sun,
When I am undone,　　　　　　　　　　10
When I am no one.

　　　　　　　　　　　　　　　　　　　　　1964

1. The triadic parts of a Pindaric ode, a ceremonious poem in the manner of the Greek lyric poet Pindar (c. 522–c. 438 B.C.E.).

In a Dark Time

In a dark time, the eye begins to see,
I meet my shadow in the deepening shade;
I hear my echo in the echoing wood—
A lord of nature weeping to a tree.
I live between the heron and the wren,   5
Beasts of the hill and serpents of the den.

What's madness but nobility of soul
At odds with circumstance? The day's on fire!
I know the purity of pure despair,
My shadow pinned against a sweating wall.   10
That place among the rocks—is it a cave,
Or winding path? The edge is what I have.

A steady storm of correspondences!
A night flowing with birds, a ragged moon,
And in broad day the midnight come again!   15
A man goes far to find out what he is—
Death of the self in a long, tearless night,
All natural shapes blazing unnatural light.

Dark, dark my light, and darker my desire.
My soul, like some heat-maddened summer fly,   20
Keeps buzzing at the sill. Which I is *I*?
A fallen man, I climb out of my fear.
The mind enters itself, and God the mind,
And one is One, free in the tearing wind.

1964

EUDORA WELTY
1909–2001

I n her essay "Place in Fiction," Eudora Welty spoke of her work as filled with the
spirit of place: "Location is the ground conductor of all the currents of emotion and
belief and moral conviction that charge out from the story in its course." Both her
outwardly uneventful life and her writing are most intimately connected to the topog-
raphy and atmosphere, the season and the soil of Mississippi, her lifelong home.

Born in Jackson to parents who came from the North, and raised in comfortable
circumstances (her father headed an insurance company), she attended Mississippi
State College for Women, then graduated from the University of Wisconsin in 1929.
After a course in advertising at the Columbia University School of Business, she
returned to Mississippi, working first as a radio writer and newspaper society editor,

Eudora Welty. A young Welty ponders the view from the
doorstep of a southern home.

then for the Depression-era Works Progress Administration, taking photographs of
and interviewing local residents. Those travels would be reflected in her fiction and
also in a book of her photographs, *One Time and Place*, published in 1971.

She began writing fiction after her return to Mississippi in 1931 and five years
later published her first story, "Death of a Traveling Salesman," in a small magazine.
Over the next two years six of her stories were published in the *Southern Review*, a
serious literary magazine one of whose editors was the poet and novelist Robert Penn
Warren. She also received strong support from Katherine Anne Porter, who contributed an introduction to Welty's first book of stories, *A Curtain of Green* (1941). That
introduction hailed the arrival of another gifted southern fiction writer, and in fact
the volume contained some of the best stories she ever wrote, such as "Petrified
Man." Her profusion of metaphor and the difficult surface of her narrative—often
oblique and indirect in its effect—were in part a mark of her admiration for modern writers like Virginia Woolf and (as with any young southern writer) William
Faulkner. Although Welty's stories were as shapely as that of her mentor, Porter,
they were more richly idiomatic and comic in their inclination. A second collection,
The Wide Net, appeared two years later; and her first novel, *The Robber Bridegroom*,
was published in 1942.

In that year and the next she was awarded the O. Henry Memorial Prize for the
best piece of short fiction, and from then on she received a steady stream of awards
and prizes, including the Pulitzer Prize for her novel *The Optimist's Daughter* (1972).
Her most ambitious and longest piece of fiction is *Losing Battles* (1970), in which she
aimed to compose a narrative made up almost wholly out of her characters' voices in
mainly humorous interplay. Like Robert Frost, Welty loved gossip in all its actuality
and intimacy, and if that love failed in the novels to produce compelling, extended
sequences, it did result in many lively and entertaining pages. Perhaps her finest
single book after *A Curtain of Green* was *The Golden Apples* (1949), a sequence of
tales about a fabulous, invented, small Mississippi community named Morgana. Her

characters appear and reappear in these related stories and come together most memorably in the brilliant "June Recital," perhaps her masterpiece.

Throughout her fiction Welty's wonderfully sharp sense of humor is strongly evident. Although her characters often consist of involuted southern families, physically handicapped, mentally retarded, or generally unstable kinfolk—and although her narratives are shot through with undercurrents of death, violence, and degradation—Welty transforms everything with an entertaining twist. No matter how desperate a situation may be, she makes us listen to the way a character talks about it; we pay attention to style rather than information. And although her attitude toward human folly is satiric, her satire is devoid of the wish to undermine and mock her characters. Instead, the vivid realizations of her prose give them irresistible life and a memorable expressiveness. Yet she remarked in an essay that "fine story writers seem to be in a sense obstructionists," and Welty's narratives unfold through varied repetitions or reiterations that have, she once claimed, the function of a deliberate double exposure in photography. By making us pay close attention to who is speaking and the implications of that speech, by asking us to imagine the way in which a silent character is responding to that speech, and by making us read behind the deceptively simple response she gives to that character, she makes us active readers, playfully engaged in a typically complicated scene. "Why I Live at the P.O.," "Keela, the Outcast Indian Maiden," "Powerhouse," "June Recital," "Petrified Man," and many others demonstrate the strength and the joy of her art. And although she has been called a "regional" writer, she has noted the condescending nature of that term, which she calls an "outsider's term; it has no meaning for the insider who is doing the writing, because as far as he knows he is simply writing about life" (*On Writing*). So it is with Eudora Welty's fiction.

The text is from *A Curtain of Green* (1941).

Petrified Man

"Reach in my purse and git me a cigarette without no powder in it if you kin, Mrs. Fletcher, honey," said Leota to her ten o'clock shampoo-and-set customer. "I don't like no perfumed cigarettes."

Mrs. Fletcher gladly reached over to the lavender shelf under the lavender-framed mirror, shook a hair net loose from the clasp of the patent-leather bag, and slapped her hand down quickly on a powder puff which burst out when the purse was opened.

"Why, look at the peanuts, Leota!" said Mrs. Fletcher in her marvelling voice.

"Honey, them goobers has been in my purse a week if they's been in it a day. Mrs. Pike bought them peanuts."

"Who's Mrs. Pike?" asked Mrs. Fletcher, settling back. Hidden in this den of curling fluid and henna[1] packs, separated by a lavender swing-door from the other customers, who were being gratified in other booths, she could give her curiosity its freedom. She looked expectantly at the black part in Leota's yellow curls as she bent to light the cigarette.

"Mrs. Pike is this lady from New Orleans," said Leota, puffing, and pressing into Mrs. Fletcher's scalp with strong red-nailed fingers. "A friend, not a customer. You see, like maybe I told you last time, me and Fred and Sal and

---

1. Reddish brown dye for tinting hair.

Joe all had us a fuss, so Sal and Joe up and moved out, so we didn't do a thing but rent out their room. So we rented it to Mrs. Pike. And Mr. Pike." She flicked an ash into the basket of dirty towels. "Mrs. Pike is a very decided blonde. *She* bought me the peanuts."

"She must be cute," said Mrs. Fletcher.

"Honey, 'cute' ain't the word for what she is. I'm tellin' you, Mrs. Pike is attractive. She has her a good time. She's got a sharp eye out, Mrs. Pike has."

She dashed the comb through the air, and paused dramatically as a cloud of Mrs. Fletcher's hennaed hair floated out of the lavender teeth like a small storm-cloud.

"Hair fallin'."

"Aw, Leota."

"Uh-huh, commencin' to fall out," said Leota, combing again, and letting fall another cloud.

"Is it any dandruff in it?" Mrs. Fletcher was frowning, her hair-line eyebrows diving down toward her nose, and her wrinkled, beady-lashed eyelids batting with concentration.

"Nope." She combed again. "Just fallin' out."

"Bet it was that last perm'nent you gave me that did it," Mrs. Fletcher said cruelly. "Remember you cooked me fourteen minutes."

"You had fourteen minutes comin' to you," said Leota with finality.

"Bound to be somethin'," persisted Mrs. Fletcher. "Dandruff, dandruff. I couldn't of caught a thing like that from Mr. Fletcher, could I?"

"Well," Leota answered at last, "you know what I heard in here yestiddy, one of Thelma's ladies was settin' over yonder in Thelma's booth gittin' a machineless, and I don't mean to insist or insinuate or anything, Mrs. Fletcher, but Thelma's lady just happ'med to throw out—I forgotten what she was talkin' about at the time—that you was p-r-e-g., and lots of times that'll make your hair do awful funny, fall out and God knows what all. It just ain't our fault, is the way I look at it."

There was a pause. The women stared at each other in the mirror.

"Who was it?" demanded Mrs. Fletcher.

"Honey, I really couldn't say," said Leota. "Not that you look it."

"Where's Thelma? I'll get it out of her," said Mrs. Fletcher.

"Now, honey, I wouldn't go and git mad over a little thing like that," Leota said, combing hastily, as though to hold Mrs. Fletcher down by the hair. "I'm sure it was somebody didn't mean no harm in the world. How far gone are you?"

"Just wait," said Mrs. Fletcher, and shrieked for Thelma, who came in and took a drag from Leota's cigarette.

"Thelma, honey, throw your mind back to yestiddy if you kin," said Leota, drenching Mrs. Fletcher's hair with a thick fluid and catching the overflow in a cold wet towel at her neck.

"Well, I got my lady half wound for a spiral," said Thelma doubtfully.

"This won't take but a minute," said Leota. "Who is it you got in there, old Horse Face? Just cast your mind back and try to remember who your lady was yestiddy who happ'm to mention that my customer was pregnant, that's all. She's dead to know."

Thelma drooped her blood-red lips and looked over Mrs. Fletcher's head into the mirror. "Why, honey, I ain't got the faintest," she breathed. "I really don't recollect the faintest. But I'm sure she meant no harm. I declare, I forgot my hair finally got combed and thought it was a stranger behind me."

"Was it that Mrs. Hutchinson?" Mrs. Fletcher was tensely polite.

"Mrs. Hutchinson? Oh, Mrs. Hutchinson." Thelma batted her eyes. "Naw, precious, she come on Thursday and didn't ev'm mention your name. I doubt if she ev'm knows you're on the way."

"Thelma!" cried Leota staunchly.

"All I know is, whoever it is 'll be sorry some day. Why, I just barely knew it myself!" cried Mrs. Fletcher. "Just let her wait!"

"Why? What're you gonna do to her?"

It was a child's voice, and the women looked down. A little boy was making tents with aluminum wave pinchers[2] on the floor under the sink.

"Billy Boy, hon, mustn't bother nice ladies," Leota smiled. She slapped him brightly and behind her back waved Thelma out of the booth. "Ain't Billy Boy a sight? Only three years old and already just nuts about the beauty-parlor business."

"I never saw him here before," said Mrs. Fletcher, still unmollified.

"He ain't been here before, that's how come," said Leota. "He belongs to Mrs. Pike. She got her a job but it was Fay's Millinery. He oughtn't to try on those ladies' hats, they come down over his eyes like I don't know what. They just git to look ridiculous, that's what, an' of course he's gonna put 'em on: hats. They tole Mrs. Pike they didn't appreciate him hangin' around there. Here, he couldn't hurt a thing."

"Well! I don't like children that much," said Mrs. Fletcher.

"Well!" said Leota moodily.

"Well! I'm almost tempted not to have this one," said Mrs. Fletcher. "That Mrs. Hutchinson! Just looks straight through you when she sees you on the street and then spits at you behind your back."

"Mr. Fletcher would beat you on the head if you didn't have it now," said Leota reasonably. "After going this far."

Mrs. Fletcher sat up straight. "Mr. Fletcher can't do a thing with me."

"He can't!" Leota winked at herself in the mirror.

"No, siree, he can't. If he so much as raises his voice against me, he knows good and well I'll have one of my sick headaches, and then I'm just not fit to live with. And if I really look that pregnant already—"

"Well, now, honey, I just want you to know—I habm't told any of my ladies and I ain't goin' to tell 'em—even that you're losin' your hair. You just get you one of those Stork-a-Lure dresses and stop worryin'. What people don't know don't hurt nobody, as Mrs. Pike says."

"Did you tell Mrs. Pike?" asked Mrs. Fletcher sulkily.

"Well, Mrs. Fletcher, look, you ain't ever goin' to lay eyes on Mrs. Pike or her lay eyes on you, so what diffunce does it make in the long run?"

"I knew it!" Mrs. Fletcher deliberately nodded her head so as to destroy a ringlet Leota was working on behind her ear. "Mrs. Pike!"

Leota sighed. "I reckon I might as well tell you. It wasn't any more Thelma's lady tole me you was pregnant than a bat."

"Not Mrs. Hutchinson?"

"Naw, Lord! It was Mrs. Pike."

---

2. Clips used to form and hold (or set) hair curl or wave.

"Mrs. Pike!" Mrs. Fletcher could only sputter and let curling fluid roll into her ear. "How could Mrs. Pike possibly know I was pregnant or otherwise, when she doesn't even know me? The nerve of some people!"

"Well, here's how it was. Remember Sunday?"

"Yes," said Mrs. Fletcher.

"Sunday, Mrs. Pike an' me was all by ourself. Mr. Pike and Fred had gone over to Eagle Lake, sayin' they was goin' to catch 'em some fish, but they didn't a course. So we was gettin' in Mrs. Pike's car, it's a 1939 Dodge—"

"1939, eh," said Mrs. Fletcher.

"—An' we was gettin' us a Jax beer apiece—that's the beer that Mrs. Pike says is made right in N.O., so she won't drink no other kind. So I seen you drive up to the drugstore an' run in for just a secont, leavin' I reckon Mr. Fletcher in the car, an' come runnin' out with looked like a perscription. So I says to Mrs. Pike, just to be makin' talk, 'Right yonder's Mrs. Fletcher, and I reckon that's Mr. Fletcher—she's one of my regular customers,' I says."

"I had on a figured print," said Mrs. Fletcher tentatively.

"You sure did," agreed Leota. "So Mrs. Pike, she give you a good look— she's very observant, a good judge of character, cute as a minute, you know— and she says, 'I bet you another Jax that lady's three months on the way.'"

"What gall!" said Mrs. Fletcher. "Mrs. Pike!"

"Mrs. Pike ain't goin' to bite you," said Leota. "Mrs. Pike is a lovely girl, you'd be crazy about her, Mrs. Fletcher. But she can't sit still a minute. We went to the travellin' freak show yestiddy after work. I got through early— nine o'clock. In the vacant store next door. What, you ain't been?"

"No, I despise freaks," declared Mrs. Fletcher.

"Aw. Well, honey, talkin' about bein' pregnant an' all, you ought to see those twins in a bottle, you really owe it to yourself."

"What twins?" asked Mrs. Fletcher out of the side of her mouth.

"Well, honey, they got these two twins in a bottle, see? Born joined plumb together—dead a course." Leota dropped her voice into a soft lyrical hum. "They was about this long—pardon—must of been full time, all right, wouldn't you say?—an' they had these two heads an' two faces an' four arms an' four legs, all kind of joined *here*. See, this face looked this-a-way, and the other face looked that-a-way, over their shoulder, see. Kinda pathetic."

"Glah!" said Mrs. Fletcher disapprovingly.

"Well, ugly? Honey, I mean to tell you—their parents was first cousins and all like that. Billy Boy, git me a fresh towel from off Teeny's stack—this 'n's wringin' wet—an' quit ticklin' my ankles with that curler. I declare! He don't miss nothin'."

"Me and Mr. Fletcher aren't one speck of kin, or he could never of had me," said Mrs. Fletcher placidly.

"Of course not!" protested Leota. "Neither is me an' Fred, not that we know of. Well, honey, what Mrs. Pike liked was the pygmies. They've got these pygmies down there, too, an' Mrs. Pike was just wild about 'em. You know, the teeniniest men in the universe? Well, honey, they can just rest back on their little bohunkus an' roll around an' you can't hardly tell if they're sittin' or standin'. That'll give you some idea. They're about forty-two years old. Just suppose it was your husband!"

"Well, Mr. Fletcher is five foot nine and one half," said Mrs. Fletcher quickly.

"Fred's five foot ten," said Leota, "but I tell him he's still a shrimp, account of I'm so tall." She made a deep wave over Mrs. Fletcher's other temple with the comb. "Well, these pygmies are a kind of a dark brown, Mrs. Fletcher. Not bad lookin' for what they are, you know."

"I wouldn't care for them," said Mrs. Fletcher. "What does that Mrs. Pike see in them?"

"Aw, I don't know," said Leota. "She's just cute, that's all. But they got this man, this petrified man, that ever'thing ever since he was nine years old, when it goes through his digestion, see, somehow Mrs. Pike says it goes to his joints and has been turning to stone."

"How awful!" said Mrs. Fletcher.

"He's forty-two too. That looks like a bad age."

"Who said so, that Mrs. Pike? I bet she's forty-two," said Mrs. Fletcher.

"Naw," said Leota, "Mrs. Pike's thirty-three, born in January, an Aquarian. He could move his head—like this. A course his head and mind ain't a joint, so to speak, and I guess his stomach ain't, either—not yet, anyways. But see—his food, he eats it, and it goes down, see, and then he digests it"— Leota rose on her toes for an instant—"and it goes out to his joints and before you can say 'Jack Robinson,' it's stone—pure stone. He's turning to stone. How'd you liked to be married to a guy like that? All he can do, he can move his head just a quarter of an inch. A course he *looks* just *terrible*."

"I should think he would," said Mrs. Fletcher frostily. "Mr. Fletcher takes bending exercises every night of the world. I make him."

"All Fred does is lay around the house like a rug. I wouldn't be surprised if he woke up some day and couldn't move. The petrified man just sat there moving his quarter of an inch though," said Leota reminiscently.

"Did Mrs. Pike like the petrified man?" asked Mrs. Fletcher.

"Not as much as she did the others," said Leota deprecatingly. "And then she likes a man to be a good dresser, and all that."

"Is Mr. Pike a good dresser?" asked Mrs. Fletcher sceptically.

"Oh, well, yeah," said Leota, "but he's twelve or fourteen years older'n her. She ast Lady Evangeline about him."

"Who's Lady Evangeline?" asked Mrs. Fletcher.

"Well, it's this mind reader they got in the freak show," said Leota. "Was real good. Lady Evangeline is her name, and if I had another dollar I wouldn't do a thing but have my other palm read. She had what Mrs. Pike said was the 'sixth mind' but she had the worst manicure I ever saw on a living person."

"What did she tell Mrs. Pike?" asked Mrs. Fletcher.

"She told her Mr. Pike was as true to her as he could be and besides, would come into some money."

"Humph!" said Mrs. Fletcher. "What does he do?"

"I can't tell," said Leota, "because he don't work. Lady Evangeline didn't tell me enough about my nature or anything. And I would like to go back and find out some more about this boy. Used to go with this boy until he got married to this girl. Oh, shoot, that was about three and a half years ago, when you was still goin' to the Robert E. Lee Beauty Shop in Jackson. He married her for her money. Another fortune-teller tole me that at the time. So I'm not in love with him anymore, anyway, besides being married to Fred, but Mrs. Pike thought, just for the hell of it, see, to ask Lady Evangeline was he happy."

"Does Mrs. Pike know everything about you already?" asked Mrs. Fletcher unbelievingly. "Mercy!"

"Oh, yeah, I tole her ever'thing about ever'thing, from now on back to I don't know when—to when I first started goin' out," said Leota. "So I ast Lady Evangeline for one of my questions, was he happily married, and she says, just like she was glad I ask her, 'Honey,' she says, 'naw, he idn't. You write down this day, March 8, 1941,' she says, 'and mock it down: three years from today him and her won't be occupyin' the same bed.' There it is, up on the wall with them other dates—see, Mrs. Fletcher? And she says, 'Child, you ought to be glad you didn't git him, because he's so mercenary.' So I'm glad I married Fred. He sure ain't mercenary, money don't mean a thing to him. But I sure would like to go back and have my other palm read."

"Did Mrs. Pike believe in what the fortune-teller said?" asked Mrs. Fletcher in a superior tone of voice.

"Lord, yes, she's from New Orleans. Ever'body in New Orleans believes ever'thing spooky. One of 'em in New Orleans before it was raided says to Mrs. Pike one summer she was goin' to go from State to State and meet some grey-headed men, and, sure enough, she says she went on a beautician convention up to Chicago. . . ."

"Oh!" said Mrs. Fletcher. "Oh, is Mrs. Pike a beautician too?"

"Sure she is," protested Leota. "She's a beautician. I'm goin' to git her in here if I can. Before she married. But it don't leave you. She says sure enough, there was three men who was a very large part of making her trip what it was, and they all three had grey in their hair and they went in six States. Got Christmas cards from 'em. Billy Boy, go see if Thelma's got any dry cotton. Look how Mrs. Fletcher's a-drippin'."

"Where did Mrs. Pike meet Mr. Pike?" asked Mrs. Fletcher primly.

"On another train," said Leota.

"I met Mr. Fletcher, or rather he met me, in a rental library," said Mrs. Fletcher with dignity, as she watched the net come down over her head.

"Honey, me an' Fred, we met in a rumble seat[3] eight months ago and we was practically on what you might call the way to the altar inside of half an hour," said Leota in a guttural voice, and bit a bobby pin open. "Course it don't last. Mrs. Pike says nothin' like that ever lasts."

"Mr. Fletcher and myself are as much in love as the day we married," said Mrs. Fletcher belligerently as Leota stuffed cotton into her ears.

"Mrs. Pike says it don't last," repeated Leota in a louder voice. "Now go git under the dryer. You can turn yourself on, can't you? I'll be back to comb you out. Durin' lunch I promised to give Mrs. Pike a facial. You know—free. Her bein' in the business, so to speak."

"I bet she needs one," said Mrs. Fletcher, letting the swing-door fly back against Leota. "Oh, pardon me."

A week later, on time for her appointment, Mrs. Fletcher sank heavily into Leota's chair after first removing a drug-store rental book, called *Life Is Like That*, from the seat. She stared in a discouraged way into the mirror.

"You can tell it when I'm sitting down, all right," she said.

3. Folding seat at the rear of an automobile.

Leota seemed preoccupied and stood shaking out a lavender cloth. She began to pin it around Mrs. Fletcher's neck in silence.

"I said you sure can tell it when I'm sitting straight on and coming at you this way," Mrs. Fletcher said.

"Why, honey, naw you can't," said Leota gloomily. "Why, I'd never know. If somebody was to come up to me on the street and say, 'Mrs. Fletcher is pregnant!' I'd say, 'Heck, she don't look it to me.'"

"If a certain party hadn't found it out and spread it around, it wouldn't be too late even now," said Mrs. Fletcher frostily, but Leota was almost choking her with the cloth, pinning it so tight, and she couldn't speak clearly. She paddled her hands in the air until Leota wearily loosened her.

"Listen, honey, you're just a virgin compared to Mrs. Montjoy," Leota was going on, still absent-minded. She bent Mrs. Fletcher back in the chair and, sighing, tossed liquid from a teacup on to her head and dug both hands into her scalp. "You know Mrs. Montjoy—her husband's that premature-greyheaded fella?"

"She's in the Trojan Garden Club, is all I know," said Mrs. Fletcher.

"Well, honey," said Leota, but in a weary voice, "she come in here not the week before and not the day before she had her baby—she come in here the very selfsame day, I mean to tell you. Child, we was all plumb scared to death. There she was! Come for her shampoo an' set. Why, Mrs. Fletcher, in an hour an' twenty minutes she was layin' up there in the Babtist Hospital with a seb'm-pound son. It was that close a shave. I declare, if I hadn't been so tired I would of drank up a bottle of gin that night."

"What gall," said Mrs. Fletcher. "I never knew her at all well."

"See, her husband was waitin' outside in the car, and her bags was all packed an' in the back seat, an' she was all ready, 'cept she wanted her shampoo an' set. An' havin' one pain right after another. Her husband kep' comin' in here, scared-like, but couldn't do nothin' with her a course. She yelled bloody murder, too, but she always yelled her head off when I give her a perm'nent."

"She must of been crazy," said Mrs. Fletcher. "How did she look?"

"Shoot!" said Leota.

"Well, I can guess," asid Mrs. Fletcher. "Awful."

"Just wanted to look pretty while she was havin' her baby, is all," said Leota airily. "Course, we was glad to give the lady what she was after—that's our motto—but I bet a hour later she wasn't payin' no mind to them little end curls. I bet she wasn't thinkin' about she ought to have on a net. It wouldn't of done her no good if she had."

"No, I don't suppose it would," said Mrs. Fletcher.

"Yeah man! She was a-yellin'. Just like when I give her perm'nent."

"Her husband ought to make her behave. Don't it seem that way to you?" asked Mrs. Fletcher. "He ought to put his foot down."

"Ha," said Leota. "A lot he could do. Maybe some women is soft."

"Oh, you mistake me, I don't mean for her to get soft—far from it! Women have to stand up for themselves, or there's just no telling. But now you take me—I ask Mr. Fletcher's advice now and then, and he appreciates it, especially on something important, like is it time for a permanent—not that I've told him about the baby. He says, 'Why, dear, go ahead!' Just ask their *advice*."

"Huh! If I ever ast Fred's advice we'd be floatin' down the Yazoo River on a houseboat or somethin' by this time," said Leota. "I'm sick of Fred. I told him to go over to Vicksburg."

"Is he going?" demanded Mrs. Fletcher.

"Sure. See, the fortune-teller—I went back and had my other palm read, since we've got to rent the room agin—said my lover was goin' to work in Vicksburg, so I don't know who she could mean, unless she meant Fred. And Fred ain't workin' here—that much is so."

"Is he going to work in Vicksburg?" asked Mrs. Fletcher. "And—"

"Sure. Lady Evangeline said so. Said the future is going to be brighter than the present. He don't want to go, but I ain't gonna put up with nothin' like that. Lays around the house an' bulls—did bull—with that good-for-nothin' Mr. Pike. He says if he goes who'll cook, but I says I never get to eat anyway—not meals. Billy Boy, take Mrs. Grover that *Screen Secrets* and leg it."

Mrs. Fletcher heard stamping feet go out the door.

"Is that that Mrs. Pike's little boy here again?" she asked, sitting up gingerly.

"Yeah, that's still him." Leota stuck out her tongue.

Mrs. Fletcher could hardly believe her eyes. "Well! How's Mrs. Pike, your attractive new friend with the sharp eyes who spreads it around town that perfect strangers are pregnant?" she asked in a sweetened tone.

"Oh, Mizziz Pike." Leota combed Mrs. Fletcher's hair with heavy strokes.

"You act like you're tired," said Mrs. Fletcher.

"Tired? Feel like it's four o'clock in the afternoon already," said Leota. "I ain't told you the awful luck we had, me and Fred? It's the worst thing you ever heard of. Maybe *you* think Mrs. Pike's got sharp eyes. Shoot, there's a limit! Well, you know, we rented out our room to this Mr. and Mrs. Pike from New Orleans when Sal an' Joe Fentress got mad at us 'cause they drank up some home-brew we had in the closet—Sal an' Joe did. So, a week ago Sat'-day Mr. and Mrs. Pike moved in. Well, I kinda fixed up the room, you know—put a sofa pillow on the couch and picked some ragged robbins and put in a vase, but they never did say they appreciated it. Anyway, then I put some old magazines on the table."

"I think that was lovely," said Mrs. Fletcher.

"Wait. So, come night 'fore last, Fred and this Mr. Pike, who Fred just took up with, was back from they said they was fishin', bein' as neither one of 'em has got a job to his name, and we was all settin' around their room. So Mrs. Pike was settin' there, readin' a old *Startling G-Man Tales* that was mine, mind you, I'd bought it myself, and all of a sudden she jumps!—into the air—you'd 'a' thought she'd set on a spider—an' says, 'Canfield'—ain't that silly, that's Mr. Pike—'Canfield, my God A'mighty,' she says, 'honey,' she says, 'we're rich, and you won't have to work.' Not that he turned one hand anyway. Well, me and Fred rushes over to her, and Mr. Pike, too, and there she sets, pointin' her finger at a photo in my copy of *Startling G-Man*. 'See that man?' yells Mrs. Pike. 'Remember him, Canfield?' 'Never forget a face,' says Mr. Pike. 'It's Mr. Petrie, that we stayed with him in the apartment next to ours in Toulouse Street in N.O. for six weeks. Mr. Petrie.' 'Well,' says Mrs. Pike, like she can't hold out one secont longer, 'Mr. Petrie is wanted for five hundred dollars cash, for rapin' four women in California, and I know where he is.'"

"Mercy!" said Mrs. Fletcher. "Where was he?"

At some time Leota had washed her hair and now she yanked her up by the back locks and sat her up.

"Know where he was?"

"I certainly don't," Mrs. Fletcher said. Her scalp hurt all over.

Leota flung a towel around the top of her customer's head. "Nowhere else but in that freak show! I saw him just as plain as Mrs. Pike. *He* was the petrified man!"

"Who would ever have thought that!" cried Mrs. Fletcher sympathetically.

"So Mr. Pike says, 'Well whatta you know about that', an' he looks real hard at the photo and whistles. And she starts dancin' and singin' about their good luck. She meant our bad luck! I made a point of tellin' that fortune-teller the next time I saw her. I said, 'Listen, that magazine was layin' around the house for a month, and there was the freak show runnin' night an' day, not two steps away from my own beauty parlor, with Mr. Petrie just settin' there waitin'. An' it had to be Mr. and Mrs. Pike, almost perfect strangers.'"

"What gall," said Mrs. Fletcher. She was only sitting there, wrapped in a turban, but she did not mind.

"Fortune-tellers don't care. And Mrs. Pike, she goes around actin' like she thinks she was Mrs. God," said Leota. "So they're goin' to leave tomorrow, Mr. and Mrs. Pike. And in the meantime I got to keep that mean, bad little ole kid here, gettin' under my feet ever' minute of the day an' talkin' back too."

"Have they gotten the five hundred dollars' reward already?" asked Mrs. Fletcher.

"Well," said Leota, "at first Mr. Pike didn't want to do anything about it. Can you feature that? Said he kinda liked that ole bird and said he was real nice to 'em, lent 'em money or somethin'. But Mrs. Pike simply tole him he could just go to hell, and I can see her point. She says, 'You ain't worked a lick in six months, and here I make five hundred dollars in two seconts, and what thanks do I get for it? You go to hell, Canfield,' she says. So," Leota went on in a despondent voice, "they called up the cops and they caught the ole bird, all right, right there in the freak show where I saw him with my own eyes, thinkin' he was petrified. He's the one. Did it under his real name—Mr. Petrie. Four women in California, all in the month of August. So Mrs. Pike gits five hundred dollars. And my magazine, and right next door to my beauty parlor. I cried all night, but Fred said it wasn't a bit of use and to go to sleep, because the whole thing was just a sort of coincidence—you know: can't do nothin' about it. He says it put him clean out of the notion of goin' to Vicksburg for a few days till we rent out the room agin—no tellin' who we'll git this time."

"But can you imagine anybody knowing this old man, that's raped four women?" persisted Mrs. Fletcher, and she shuddered audibly. "Did Mrs. Pike *speak* to him when she met him in the freak show?"

Leota had begun to comb Mrs. Fletcher's hair. "I says to her, I says, 'I didn't notice you fallin' on his neck when he was the petrified man—don't tell me you didn't recognize your fine friend?' And she says, 'I didn't recognize him with that white powder all over his face. He just looked familiar,' Mrs. Pike says, 'and lots of people look familiar.' But she says that ole petrified man did put her in mind of somebody. She wondered who it was! Kep' her awake, which man she'd ever knew it reminded her of. So when she seen the photo, it all come to her. Like a flash. Mr. Petrie. The way he'd turn his head and look at her when she took him in his breakfast."

"Took him in his breakfast!" shrieked Mrs. Fletcher. "Listen—don't tell me. I'd 'a' felt something."

"Four women. I guess those women didn't have the faintest notion at the time they'd be worth a hundred an' twenty-five bucks apiece some day to Mrs. Pike. We ast her how old the fella was then, an's she says he musta had one foot in the grave, at least. Can you beat it?"

"Not really petrified at all, of course," said Mrs. Fletcher meditatively. She drew herself up. "I'd 'a' felt something," she said proudly.

"Shoot! I did feel somethin'," said Leota. "I tole Fred when I got home I felt so funny. I said, 'Fred, that ole petrified man sure did leave me with a funny feelin'.' He says, 'Funny-haha or funny-peculiar?' and I says, 'Funny-peculiar.'" She pointed her comb into the air emphatically.

"I'll bet you did," said Mrs. Fletcher.

They both heard a crackling noise.

Leota screamed, "Billy Boy! What you doin' in my purse?"

"Aw, I'm just eatin' these ole stale peanuts up," said Billy Boy.

"You come here to me!" screamed Leota, recklessly flinging down the comb, which scattered a whole ashtray full of bobby pins and knocked down a row of Coca-Cola bottles. "This is the last straw!"

"I caught him! I caught him!" giggled Mrs. Fletcher. "I'll hold him on my lap. You bad, bad boy, you! I guess I better learn how to spank little old bad boys," she said.

Leota's eleven o'clock customer pushed open the swing-door upon Leota's paddling him heartily with the brush, while he gave angry but belittling screams which penetrated beyond the booth and filled the whole curious beauty parlor. From everywhere ladies began to gather round to watch the paddling. Billy Boy kicked both Leota and Mrs. Fletcher as hard as he could, Mrs. Fletcher with her new fixed smile.

Billy Boy stomped through the group of wild-haired ladies and went out the door, but flung back the words, "If you're so smart, why ain't you rich?"

1941

CHARLES OLSON
1910–1970

About the sense of place in Charles Olson's poems, Robert Creeley writes: "In short, the world is not separable, and we *are* in it." Being in the world, for Olson, meant experiencing it as present; for him, what happens in a poem happens now. Art, he said, "does not seek to describe but to enact." In the influential essay "Projective Verse" (1950)—a portion of which appears in the "Postmodern Manifestos" cluster of this anthology—he rejected the partitioning of reality that separates humanity from the natural world. His aim, he wrote, was to get "rid of the lyrical interference of the individual as ego, of the 'subject' and his soul, that peculiar presumption by which western man has interposed himself between what he is as a creature of nature . . . and those other creations of nature." To read Olson is to enter a critical and theoretical force field made up of his essays, lectures, and poems. His ultimate concern was reimagining the world, returning language (as Creeley writes) "to its place *in* experience." Although this ambition is inconsistently realized in Olson's poems, it directed his lifelong effort. And in this effort he was an extraordinarily influential figure for a group of poets whose work was beginning to be known in the 1950s, among them Creeley, Denise Levertov, and Robert Duncan.

Olson's influence grew out of his years at Black Mountain, an experimental college in North Carolina where he had served as an instructor and then as head or rector, succeeding the artist Josef Albers. In its flourishing years, under Olson's direction, the college included among its teachers and students key figures of the avant-garde: John Cage in music, Merce Cunningham in dance, Franz Kline and Robert Rauschenberg in painting. Just before going to Black Mountain, Olson published *Call Me Ishmael* (1947), a critical study of Herman Melville and *Moby-Dick* that declared his new independence of the formal academic systems. (He had been, as he put it, "uneducated" at Wesleyan, Yale, and Harvard, had taught at Clark University in Worcester, Massachusetts, and had taken an advanced degree in American civilization at Harvard.) *Call Me Ishmael*, unlike most literary studies, was fiercely personal and unorthodox—almost a prose poem proclaiming new bearings in American literature, especially the symbolic importance of the Pacific, the "unwarped primal world" that, according to the poet, was the true center of the American experience.

Olson claimed that "the substances of history now useful lie outside, under, right here, anywhere but in the direct continuum of society as we have had it." Therefore his own work, as he makes clear in his long poem *The Kingfishers* (1949, 1953) sharply cultivates the primitive sources of energy almost buried by civilized responses and instruments. As a sometime archaeologist, Olson "hunted among stones." He studied earlier North American cultures and worked among the Mayan ruins in the Yucatán, trying to recover the living elements of an archaic way of life. For Olson, the imagination of ancient cultures exists in the present as much as does a walk down the street in one's native town.

In his lifetime poetic project, the Maximus poems, Olson sought to do for his own life what the anthropologist does for a lost civilization; he aimed at recapturing or reinstating lost links to the unconscious sources of his being. Ezra Pound's *Cantos*, with their mosaic of disjointed and recurrent images, provided a formal model, but in Olson's eyes Pound was too devoted to reviving the values of European culture. The Maximus poems were designed to capture the mythical spirit of place—the fishing town of Gloucester, Massachusetts. There Olson grew up near a forested and swampy area called Dogtown, the site of rock debris deposited by glaciers, and a place that became a metaphor for primitive energies. Maximus is an enlarged version of its author. The facts of Olson's life in Gloucester (including perhaps even a joking allusion in the name Maximus to the fact that Olson was six-foot-eight) are used as a point of departure for an ambitious effort to project the entire historical, geological, and social presence of the town. Through the heightened awareness of Maximus, Olson tries to find the hidden energies that shape consciousness, "the primal features of those founders who lie buried in us." These features include the backgrounds and racial inheritance of his Swedish father and Irish-American mother. They also include the communal dependence on and subjection to the sea around the town.

So, for example, the opening Maximus poem, "I, Maximus of Gloucester, to You," renders the emergence of the central character out of the sea ("hot from boiling water"), identifying him with that element, and recalling Homer's identification of

Odysseus as seafarer. After establishing an offshore perspective, the poem moves to land, taking us into the harbor section of Gloucester and connecting the activity and skill of the poet to that of the fishermen, responsive to the natural world. Yet Olson knows that, even in Gloucester, the "mu-sick, mu-sick, mu-sick" of mass culture threatens this way of life. Later in the sequence he confronts his own difficulties in establishing the right relation to the world embodied in the fishermen; in "Maximus, to Himself," he writes, "The sea was not, finally, my trade / But even my trade, at it, I stood estranged / from that which was most familiar." The Maximus poems enact a quest to overcome such estrangement and to attain a wholeness celebrated in "Celestial Evening, October 1967," where the poet feels the "full volume of all which ever was" and the separation between inner and outer worlds dissolves.

In Olson's "open form," the theory of which he proposed the essay "Projective Verse," ordinary lineation, straight left-hand margin, regular meters, and verse forms are to be discarded in favor of a free placement of lines and phrases over the page. This "composition by field" would allow, through typographical adjustments, for something like a musical score in which the length of pauses, the degree of emphasis, even changes of speed could be indicated. The unit of poetic expression was not a predetermined metrical foot, but a particular poet's length of breath. The arrangement of words on the page would convey rhythms of thinking, breathing, and gesturing. Olson hoped to get closer to the poet's individuality by making the poem a graph of the process through which it was produced. "A poem is energy transferred from where the poet got it . . . by way of the poem itself to, all the way over to, the reader." The energetic movement of the opening Maximus poem is a fine example of Olson's theory turned to practice.

Like certain techniques of meditation and yoga, Olson's theory seems an effort to bring mental activity (here, writing) in touch with its instinctive physical origins. Although Olson extended many of Pound's notions of poetic immediacy, he transferred the authority for perceiving mythic truth from the mind dependent on European culture to the mind striving to get in touch with the instinctive roots of its own behavior. Throughout his life he sought the origins of things, and in the end the most memorable and accurate description of Olson is his own: "an archeologist of morning."

FROM THE MAXIMUS POEMS

I, Maximus of Gloucester,[1] to You

Off-shore, by islands hidden in the blood
jewels & miracles, I, Maximus
a metal hot from boiling water, tell you
what is a lance, who obeys the figures of
the present dance   5

---

1. A fishing town in Massachusetts where Olson grew up; it is surrounded on all sides by water and connected to the mainland by a bridge. Maximus is Olson's poetic persona, whose name suggests both Carl Jung's borrowed phrase "Homo maxi- mus" and the 2nd-century eclectic philosopher Maximus of Tyre. Tyre, also an island town, was one of the few cities in the ancient Middle East to maintain its culture in the face of Alexander the Great's Hellenizing influence.

1

the thing you're after
may lie around the bend
of the nest (second, time slain, the bird! the bird!

And there! (strong) thrust, the mast! flight
                          (of the bird   10
                          o kylix, o
                          Antony of Padua[2]
                          sweep low, o bless

the roofs, the old ones, the gentle steep ones
on whose ridge-poles the gulls sit, from which they depart,   15

                          And the flake-racks[3]
of my city!

2

love is form, and cannot be without
important substance (the weight
say, 58 carats each one of us, perforce   20
our goldsmith's scale

                   feather to feather added
                   (and what is mineral, what
                   is curling hair, the string
                   you carry in your nervous beak, these   25

                   make bulk these, in the end, are
                   the sum

                   (o my lady of good voyage
                   in whose arm, whose left arm rests
no boy but a carefully carved wood, a painted face, a schooner![4] 30
a delicate mast, as bow-sprit for

                          forwarding

3

the underpart is, though stemmed, uncertain
is, as sex is, as moneys are, facts!
facts, to be dealt with, as the sea is, the demand   35

---

2. Franciscan monk and teacher of the 13th
century, most famous for his "sermon to the
fishes." He is the patron saint of Gloucester's
Portuguese community. "Kylix": ancient Greek
drinking vessel.

3. For drying fish.
4. On the roof of the Our Lady of Good Voyage
Church in Gloucester's Portuguese quarter is a
statue of the Virgin Mary holding a schooner.

that they be played by, that they only can be, that they must
be played by, said he, coldly, the
ear!

By ear, he sd.
But that which matters, that which insists, that which will last,   40
that! o my people, where shall you find it, how, where, where shall you
listen
when all is become billboards, when, all, even silence, is spray-gunned?

when even our bird, my roofs,
cannot be heard

when even you, when sound itself is neoned in?   45

when, on the hill, over the water
where she who used to sing,
when the water glowed,
black, gold, the tide
outward, at evening   50

when bells came like boats
over the oil-slicks, milkweed
hulls

And a man slumped,
attentionless,   55
against pink shingles

o sea city)

4

one loves only form,
and form only comes
into existence when   60
the thing is born

       born of yourself, born
       of hay and cotton struts,
       of street-pickings, wharves, weeds
       you carry in, my bird   65
              of a bone of a fish
              of a straw, or will
              of a color, of a bell
              of yourself, torn

5

love is not easy   70
but how shall you know,
New England, now

that pejorocracy[5] is here, how
that street-cars, o Oregon, twitter
in the afternoon, offend[6]   75
a black-gold loin?
    how shall you strike,[7]
    o swordsman, the blue-red back
    when, last night, your aim
    was mu-sick, mu-sick, mu-sick   80
    And not the cribbage game?

       (o Gloucester-man,
       weave
       your birds and fingers
       new, your roof-tops,   85
       clean shit upon racks
       sunned on
       American
       braid
       with others like you, such   90
       extricable surface
       as faun and oral,
       satyr lesbos vase[8]

       o kill kill kill kill kill
       those   95
       who advertise you
       out)

       6

in! in! the bow-sprit, bird, the beak
in, the bend is, in, goes in, the form
that which you make, what holds, which is   100
the law of object, strut after strut, what you are, what you must be, what
the force can throw up, can, right now hereinafter erect,
the mast, the mast, the tender
mast!
    The nest, I say, to you, I Maximus, say   105
    under the hand, as I see it, over the waters
    from this place where I am, where I hear,
    can still hear

    from where I carry you a feather
    as though, sharp, I picked up,   110
    in the afternoon delivered you
    a jewel,

5. Word coined by Ezra Pound in *The Cantos*, meaning something like "rule by belittling" or "worsening rule."
6. Olson hated the recorded music piped into streetcars.
7. In Gloucester lingo a "striker" is a swordfish harpooner.
8. Lesbos was the home of Sappho, 6th-century B.C.E. lyric poet, one of the first Greeks to leave the oral tradition. The 6th century was also the height of archaic Greek vase painting.

        it flashing more than a wing,
than any old romantic thing,
than memory, than place,   115
than anything other than that which you carry

than that which is,
call it a nest, around the head of, call it
the next second

than that which you   120
can do!

                          1953

Maximus, to Himself

I have had to learn the simplest things
last. Which made for difficulties.
Even at sea I was slow, to get the hand out, or to cross
a wet deck.
        The sea was not, finally, my trade.   5
But even my trade, at it, I stood estranged
from that which was most familiar.[1] Was delayed,
and not content with the man's argument
that such postponement
is now the nature of   10
obedience,
            that we are all late
            in a slow time,
            that we grow up many
            And the single   15
            is not easily
            known

It could be, though the sharpness (the *achiote*[2])
I note in others,
makes more sense   20
than my own distances. The agilities

            they show daily
            who do the world's
            businesses
            And who do nature's   25
            as I have no sense
            I have done either

---

1. An echo of the ancient Greek philosopher Heraclitus: "We are estranged from that with which we are most familiar."

2. The seed of the annatto tree, which yields a reddish dye, resembling red (sharp) pepper.

I have made dialogues,
have discussed ancient texts,
have thrown what light I could, offered   30
what pleasures
doceat³ allows

But the known?
This, I have had to be given,
a life, love, and from one man   35
the world.

Tokens.
But sitting here
I look out as a wind
and water man, testing   40
And missing
some proof

I know the quarters
of the weather, where it comes from,
where it goes. But the stem of me,   45
this I took from their welcome,
or their rejection, of me

And my arrogance
was neither diminished
nor increased,   50
by the communication

2

It is undone business
I speak of, this morning,
with the sea
stretching out   55
from my feet

1953

[When do poppies bloom]

When do poppies bloom   I ask myself, stopping again
to look in Mrs. Frontiero's yard, beside her house on
this side from Birdseyes (or what was once Cunningham
& Thompson's and is now O'Donnell-Usen's) to see if
I have missed them, flaked out and dry-like like   5
Dennison's Crepe. And what I found was dark buds

---

3. That he teach (Latin)—one of the three functions of a poet, according to medieval theorists. Pound
modernized the concept in his essay "Make It New."

like cigars, and standing up   and my question is
when, then, will those blossoms more lotuses to the
West than lotuses wave like paper and petal by petal
seem more powerful than any thing except the Universe   10
itself, they are so animate-inanimate and dry-beauty not
any shove, or sit there poppies blow as crepe
paper. And in Mrs Frontiero's yard annually I
expect them as the King of the Earth must have
Penelope,[1] awaiting her return, love lies   15
so delicately on the pillow as this one flower,
petal and petal, carries nothing
into or out of the World   so threatening
were those cigar-stub cups just now, & I <u>know</u>
how quickly, and paper-like, absorbent   20
and krinkled paper, the poppy itself will, when here,
go again and the stalks stay like onion plants oh
come, poppy, when will you bloom?

                 The Fort[2]
                 June 15th [Wednesday]
                 XLVI

                             1975

Celestial Evening, October 1967

Advanced out toward the external from
the time I did actually lose space control,
here on the Fort[1] and kept turning left
like my star-nosed mole batted
on the head, not being able to   5
get home 50 yards as I was
from it. There is a vast

internal life, a sea or organism
full of sounds & memoried
objects swimming or sunk   10
in the great fall of it as,
when one further
ring of the 9 bounding
Earth & Heaven runs
into the daughter of God's   15
particular place, cave, palace—a tail

---

1. In Greek myth Odysseus's paradigmatically faithful wife. Olson, however, seems to be referring to the myth of Persephone, who reluctantly marries Hades, king of the Underworld. Persephone (to whom poppies are sacred) lives most of the time above ground but must return to Hades for some months every year because Hades tricked her into eating four pomegranate seeds.
2. A district in Gloucester, Massachusetts, where Olson settled after leaving Black Mountain in 1957. The brackets around "Wednesday" are Olson's.
1. See n. 2, above.

of Ocean whose waters then
are test if even a god
lies will tell & he or she spend
9 following years out of the company   20
of their own. The sounds

and objects of the great
10th within us are
what we hear see are motived by
dream belief care for discriminate   25
our loves & choices cares & failures unless
in this forbidding Earth & Heaven by

enclosure 9 times round plus
all that stream collecting as,
into her hands it comes: the   30

full volume of all which ever was which we
as such have that which is our part of it,
all history existence places splits of moon
& slightest oncoming smallest stars at
sunset, fears & horrors, grandparents'   35
lives as much as we have also features
and their forms, whatever grace or ugliness our legs
etc possess, it all

comes in as also outward leads
us after itself as though then   40
the horn of the nearest moon was
truth. I bend my ear, as,
if I were Amoghasiddi[2] and,
here on this plain where
like my mole I have   45
been knocked flat, attend,
to turn & turn within
the steady stream & collect which
within me ends as in her hall and I

hear all, the new moon new in all   50
the ancient sky

1967   1975

---

2. In Tibetan Buddhism one of the five Dhyana-Buddhas, or Buddhas of contemplation.

ELIZABETH BISHOP
1911–1979

"The enormous power of reticence," the poet Octavio Paz said in a tribute, "—that is the great lesson of Elizabeth Bishop." Bishop's reticence originates in a temperament indistinguishable from her style; her remarkable formal gifts allowed her to create ordered and lucid structures that hold strong feelings in place. Chief among these feelings was a powerful sense of loss. The crucial events of Bishop's life occurred within her first eight years. Born in Worcester, Massachusetts, she was eight months old when her father died. Her mother suffered a series of breakdowns and was permanently institutionalized when Elizabeth was five. "I've never concealed this," Bishop once wrote, "although I don't like to make too much of it. But of course it is an important fact, to me. I didn't see her again." The understatement in this remark is characteristic. When Bishop wrote about her early life—as she first did in several poems and stories in the 1950s and last did in her extraordinary final book, *Geography III* (1976)—she resisted sentimentality and self-pity. It was as if she could look at the events of her own life with the same unflinching gaze she turned on the landscapes that so consistently compelled her. The deep feeling in her poems rises out of direct and particular description, but Bishop does more than simply observe. Whether writing about her childhood landscape of Nova Scotia or her adopted Brazil, she often opens a poem with long perspectives on time, with landscapes that dwarf the merely human, emphasizing the dignified frailty of a human observer and the pervasive mysteries that surround her.

Examining her own case, she traces the observer's instinct to early childhood. "In the Waiting Room," a poem written in the early 1970s, probes the sources and motives behind her interest in details. Using an incident from when she was seven— a little girl waits for her aunt in the dentist's anteroom—Bishop shows how in the course of the episode she became aware, as if wounded, of the utter strangeness and engulfing power of the world. The spectator in that poem hangs on to details as a kind of life-jacket; she observes because she has to.

After her father's death Bishop and her mother lived with Bishop's maternal grandparents in Great Village, Nova Scotia. She remained there for several years after her mother was institutionalized, until she was removed ("kidnapped," she describes herself feeling in one of her stories) by her paternal grandparents and taken to live in Worcester, Massachusetts. This experience was followed by a series of illnesses (eczema, bronchitis, and asthma), which plagued her for many years. Bishop later lived with an aunt and attended Walnut Hill School, a private high school. In 1934 she graduated from Vassar College, where while a student she had been introduced to Marianne Moore. Moore's meticulous taste for fact was to influence Bishop's poetry, but more immediately Moore's independent life as a poet seemed an alternative to Bishop's vaguer intentions to attend medical school. Bishop lived in New York City and in Key West, Florida; a traveling fellowship took her to Brazil, which so appealed to her that she remained for more than sixteen years.

Exile and travel were at the heart of Bishop's poems from the start. The title of her first book, *North & South* (1946), looks backward to the northern seas of Nova Scotia and forward to the tropical worlds she was to choose so long as home. Her poems are set among these landscapes, where she can stress the sweep and violence of encircling and eroding geological powers or, in the case of Brazil, a bewildering botanical plenty. *Questions of Travel* (1965), her third volume, constitutes a sequence of poems initiating her, with her botanist-geologist-anthropologist's curiosity, into Brazilian life and the mysteries of what questions a traveler-exile should ask. In this series with its increasing penetration of a new country, a process is at work similar to one Bishop identifies in the great English naturalist Charles Darwin, of whom Bishop once said: "One admires the beautiful solid case being built up out of his endless, heroic observations, almost unconscious or automatic—and then comes a sudden relaxation, a forgetful phrase, and one feels the strangeness of his undertaking, sees the lonely young man, his eyes fixed on facts and minute details, sinking or sliding giddily off into the unknown."

In 1969 Bishop's *Complete Poems* appeared, an ironic title in light of the fact that she continued to write and publish new poetry. *Geography III* contains some of her best work, poems that, from the settled perspective of her return to the United States, look back and evaluate the appetite for exploration apparent in her earlier verse. The influence of her long friendship with the poet Robert Lowell, and their high regard for one another's work, may be felt in the way *Geography III* explores the terrain of memory and autobiography more powerfully and directly than does her earlier work. Bishop, however, believed that there were limits on the ways in which poems could use and reconfigure the materials of a life. Her 1972 letter to Lowell that discusses these limits appears in the "Postmodern Manifestos" cluster of this anthology. Having left Brazil, Bishop lived in Boston from 1970 and taught at Harvard University until 1977. She received the Pulitzer Prize for the combined volume *North & South and A Cold Spring* (1955) and the National Book Award for *The Complete Poems*, and in 1976 was the first woman and the first American to receive the Books Abroad Neustadt International Prize for Literature. Since Bishop's death, most of her published work has been gathered in two volumes: *The Complete Poems 1929–1979* and *The Collected Prose*. An edition of her unpublished poems and drafts, *Edgar Allen Poe & The Juke-Box*, was published to some controversy in 2006.

The Man-Moth[1]

Here, above,
cracks in the buildings are filled with battered moonlight.
The whole shadow of Man is only as big as his hat.
It lies at his feet like a circle for a doll to stand on,
and he makes an inverted pin, the point magnetized to the moon.   5
He does not see the moon; he observes only her vast properties,
feeling the queer light on his hands, neither warm nor cold,
of a temperature impossible to record in thermometers.

But when the Man-Moth
pays his rare, although occasional, visits to the surface,   10
the moon looks rather different to him. He emerges
from an opening under the edge of one of the sidewalks
and nervously begins to scale the faces of buildings.
He thinks the moon is a small hole at the top of the sky,
proving the sky quite useless for protection.   15
He trembles, but must investigate as high as he can climb.

---

1. Newspaper misprint for "mammoth" [Bishop's note]. Bishop explained that when she saw this misprint in the *New York Times* she took it as "an oracle . . . kindly explaining New York City to me, at least for a moment."

Up the façades,
his shadow dragging like a photographer's cloth behind him,
he climbs fearfully, thinking that this time he will manage
to push his small head through that round clean opening   20
and be forced through, as from a tube, in black scrolls on the
      light.
(Man, standing below him, has no such illusions.)
But what the Man-Moth fears most he must do, although
he fails, of course, and falls back scared but quite unhurt.

                  Then he returns   25
to the pale subways of cement he calls his home. He flits,
he flutters, and cannot get aboard the silent trains
fast enough to suit him. The doors close swiftly.
The Man-Moth always seats himself facing the wrong way
and the train starts at once at its full, terrible speed,   30
without a shift in gears or a gradation of any sort.
He cannot tell the rate at which he travels backwards.

                  Each night he must
be carried through artificial tunnels and dream recurrent dreams.
Just as the ties recur beneath his train, these underlie   35
his rushing brain. He does not dare look out the window,
for the third rail,[2] the unbroken draught of poison,
runs there beside him. He regards it as disease
he has inherited susceptibility to. He has to keep
his hands in pockets, as others must wear mufflers.   40

                  If you catch him,
hold up a flashlight to his eye. It's all dark pupil,
an entire night itself, whose haired horizon tightens
as he stares back, and closes up the eye. Then from the lids
one tear, his only possession, like the bee's sting, slips.   45
Slyly he palms it, and if you're not paying attention
he'll swallow it. However, if you watch, he'll hand it over,
cool as from underground springs and pure enough to drink.

                                                        1935

The Fish

I caught a tremendous fish
and held him beside the boat
half out of water, with my hook
fast in a corner of his mouth.
He didn't fight.   5
He hadn't fought at all.

---

2. The exposed electrical conductor of a railway that carries high voltage power and thus the threat of electrocution.

He hung a grunting weight,
battered and venerable
and homely. Here and there
his brown skin hung in strips   10
like ancient wallpaper,
and its pattern of darker brown
was like wallpaper:
shapes like full-blown roses
stained and lost through age.   15
He was speckled with barnacles,
fine rosettes of lime,
and infested
with tiny white sea-lice,
and underneath two or three   20
rags of green weed hung down.
While his gills were breathing in
the terrible oxygen
—the frightening gills,
fresh and crisp with blood,   25
that can cut so badly—
I thought of the coarse white flesh
packed in like feathers,
the big bones and the little bones,
the dramatic reds and blacks   30
of his shiny entrails,
and the pink swim-bladder
like a big peony.
I looked into his eyes
which were far larger than mine   35
but shallower, and yellowed,
the irises backed and packed
with tarnished tinfoil
seen through the lenses
of old scratched isinglass.[1]   40
They shifted a little, but not
to return my stare.
—It was more like the tipping
of an object toward the light.
I admired his sullen face,   45
the mechanism of his jaw,
and then I saw
that from his lower lip
—if you could call it a lip—
grim, wet, and weaponlike,   50
hung five old pieces of fish-line,
or four and a wire leader
with the swivel still attached,
with all their five big hooks
grown firmly in his mouth.   55

---

1. A whitish, semitransparent substance, originally obtained from the swim bladders of some freshwater fish and occasionally used for windows.

A green line, frayed at the end
where he broke it, two heavier lines,
and a fine black thread
still crimped from the strain and snap
when it broke and he got away.   60
Like medals with their ribbons
frayed and wavering,
a five-haired beard of wisdom
trailing from his aching jaw.
I stared and stared   65
and victory filled up
the little rented boat,
from the pool of bilge
where oil had spread a rainbow
around the rusted engine   70
to the bailer rusted orange,
the sun-cracked thwarts,
the oarlocks on their strings,
the gunnels—until everything
was rainbow, rainbow, rainbow!   75
And I let the fish go.

                                                              1946

Over 2,000 Illustrations and a Complete Concordance[1]

Thus should have been our travels:
serious, engravable.
The Seven Wonders of the World are tired
and a touch familiar, but the other scenes,
innumerable, though equally sad and still,   5
are foreign. Often the squatting Arab,
or group of Arabs, plotting, probably,
against our Christian Empire,
while one apart, with outstretched arm and hand
points to the Tomb, the Pit, the Sepulcher.[2]   10
The branches of the date-palms look like files.
The cobbled courtyard, where the Well is dry,
is like a diagram, the brickwork conduits
are vast and obvious, the human figure
far gone in history or theology,   15
gone with its camel or its faithful horse.
Always the silence, the gesture, the specks of birds
suspended on invisible threads above the Site,
or the smoke rising solemnly, pulled by threads.
Granted a page alone or a page made up   20

1. Part of the title of an old edition of the Bible described in the opening lines of the poem. A concordance is a guide to occurrences of words and proper names and places in a book.

2. Jesus's burial place, depicted (along with other places associated with his life, such as the Well and the Site) among the "2,000 illustrations" of the title.

of several scenes arranged in cattycornered rectangles
or circles set on stippled gray,
granted a grim lunette,[3]
caught in the toils of an initial letter,
when dwelt upon, they all resolve themselves.   25
The eye drops, weighted, through the lines
the burin[4] made, the lines that move apart
like ripples above sand,
dispersing storms, God's spreading fingerprint,
and painfully, finally, that ignite   30
in watery prismatic white-and-blue.

Entering the Narrows at St. Johns[5]
the touching bleat of goats reached to the ship.
We glimpsed them, reddish, leaping up the cliffs
among the fog-soaked weeds and butter-and-eggs.[6]   35
And at St. Peter's[7] the wind blew and the sun shone madly.
Rapidly, purposefully, the Collegians[8] marched in lines,
crisscrossing the great square with black, like ants.
In Mexico the dead man lay
in a blue arcade; the dead volcanoes   40
glistened like Easter lilies.
The jukebox went on playing "Ay, Jalisco!"
And at Volubilis[9] there were beautiful poppies
splitting the mosaics; the fat old guide made eyes.
In Dingle[1] harbor a golden length of evening   45
the rotting hulks held up their dripping plush.
The Englishwoman poured tea, informing us
that the Duchess was going to have a baby.
And in the brothels of Marrakesh[2]
the little pockmarked prostitutes   50
balanced their tea-trays on their heads
and did their belly-dances; flung themselves
naked and giggling against our knees,
asking for cigarettes. It was somewhere near there
I saw what frightened me most of all: 55
A holy grave, not looking particularly holy,
one of a group under a keyhole-arched stone baldaquin[3]
open to every wind from the pink desert.
An open, gritty, marble trough, carved solid
with exhortation, yellowed   60
as scattered cattle-teeth;
half-filled with dust, not even the dust
of the poor prophet paynim who once lay there.
In a smart burnoose[4] Khadour looked on amused.

---

3. An oval framing an illustration, often part of an enlarged initial letter.
4. An engraver's tool.
5. In Newfoundland.
6. A plant whose flowers are two shades of yellow.
7. The papal basilica in Rome.
8. Members of constituent orders of the Catholic Church.
9. A ruined Roman city in Morocco.
1. A town in southwest Ireland.
2. A city in Morocco.
3. Architectural canopy.
4. A long cloak with a hood. "Paynim": archaic literary word for pagan, especially Muslim.

Everything only connected by "and" and "and."   65
Open the book. (The gilt rubs off the edges
of the pages and pollinates the fingertips.)
Open the heavy book. Why couldn't we have seen
this old Nativity while we were at it?
—the dark ajar, the rocks breaking with light,   70
an undisturbed, unbreathing flame,
colorless, sparkless, freely fed on straw,
and, lulled within, a family with pets,
—and looked and looked our infant[5] sight away.

1955

The Bight[1]

On My Birthday

At low tide like this how sheer the water is.
White, crumbling ribs of marl protrude and glare
and the boats are dry, the pilings dry as matches.
Absorbing, rather than being absorbed,
the water in the bight doesn't wet anything,   5
the color of the gas flame turned as low as possible.
One can smell it turning to gas; if one were Baudelaire[2]
one could probably hear it turning to marimba music.
The little ocher dredge at work off the end of the dock
already plays the dry perfectly off-beat claves.   10
The birds are outsize. Pelicans crash
into this peculiar gas unnecessarily hard,
it seems to me, like pickaxes,
rarely coming up with anything to show for it,
and going off with humorous elbowings.   15
Black-and-white man-of-war birds soar
on impalpable drafts
and open their tails like scissors on the curves
or tense them like wishbones, till they tremble.
The frowsy sponge boats keep coming in   20
with the obliging air of retrievers,
bristling with jackstraw gaffs and hooks
and decorated with bobbles of sponges.
There is a fence of chicken wire along the dock
where, glinting like plowshares,   25
the blue-gray shark tails are hung up to dry
for the Chinese-restaurant trade.
Some of the little white boats are still piled up
against each other, or lie on their sides, stove in,
and not yet salvaged, if they ever will be, from the last bad storm,   30

5. Its Latin root (*infans*) means "speechless."
1. A bay or inlet.
2. French poet (1821–1867) whose theory of correspondences (see line 32) promised links, through poetry, between the physical and spiritual worlds.

like torn-open, unanswered letters.
The bight is littered with old correspondences.
Click. Click. Goes the dredge,
and brings up a dripping jawful of marl.
All the untidy activity continues,   35
awful but cheerful.

1955

At the Fishhouses

Although it is a cold evening,
down by one of the fishhouses
an old man sits netting,
his net, in the gloaming almost invisible
a dark purple-brown,   5
and his shuttle worn and polished.
The air smells so strong of codfish
it makes one's nose run and one's eyes water.
The five fishhouses have steeply peaked roofs
and narrow, cleated gangplanks slant up   10
to storerooms in the gables
for the wheelbarrows to be pushed up and down on.
All is silver: the heavy surface of the sea,
swelling slowly as if considering spilling over,
is opaque, but the silver of the benches,   15
the lobster pots, and masts, scattered
among the wild jagged rocks,
is of an apparent translucence
like the small old buildings with an emerald moss
growing on their shoreward walls.   20
The big fish tubs are completely lined
with layers of beautiful herring scales
and the wheelbarrows are similarly plastered
with creamy iridescent coats of mail,
with small iridescent flies crawling on them.   25
Up on the little slope behind the houses,
set in the sparse bright sprinkle of grass,
is an ancient wooden capstan,[1]
cracked, with two long bleached handles
and some melancholy stains, like dried blood,   30
where the ironwork has rusted.
The old man accepts a Lucky Strike.[2]
He was a friend of my grandfather.
We talk of the decline in the population
and of codfish and herring   35
while he waits for a herring boat to come in.
There are sequins on his vest and on his thumb.

1. Cylindrical drum around which rope is wound,   2. Brand of cigarettes.
used for winching.

He has scraped the scales, the principal beauty,
from unnumbered fish with that black old knife,
the blade of which is almost worn away.   40

Down at the water's edge, at the place
where they haul up the boats, up the long ramp
descending into the water, thin silver
tree trunks are laid horizontally
across the gray stones, down and down   45
at intervals of four or five feet.

Cold dark deep and absolutely clear,
element bearable to no mortal,
to fish and to seals . . . One seal particularly
I have seen here evening after evening.   50
He was curious about me. He was interested in music;
like me a believer in total immersion,[3]
so I used to sing him Baptist hymns.
I also sang "A Mighty Fortress Is Our God."
He stood up in the water and regarded me   55
steadily, moving his head a little.
Then he would disappear, then suddenly emerge
almost in the same spot, with a sort of shrug
as if it were against his better judgment.
Cold dark deep and absolutely clear,   60
the clear gray icy water . . . Back, behind us,
the dignified tall firs begin.
Bluish, associating with their shadows,
a million Christmas trees stand
waiting for Christmas. The water seems suspended   65
above the rounded gray and blue-gray stones.
I have seen it over and over, the same sea, the same,
slightly, indifferently swinging above the stones,
icily free above the stones,
above the stones and then the world.   70
If you should dip your hand in,
your wrist would ache immediately,
your bones would begin to ache and your hand would burn
as if the water were a transmutation of fire
that feeds on stones and burns with a dark gray flame.   75
If you tasted it, it would first taste bitter,
then briny, then surely burn your tongue.
It is like what we imagine knowledge to be:
dark, salt, clear, moving, utterly free,
drawn from the cold hard mouth   80
of the world, derived from the rocky breasts
forever, flowing and drawn, and since
our knowledge is historical, flowing, and flown.

1955

3. Form of baptism favored by Baptists.

Questions of Travel

There are too many waterfalls here; the crowded streams
hurry too rapidly down to the sea,
and the pressure of so many clouds on the mountaintops
makes them spill over the sides in soft slow-motion,
turning to waterfalls under our very eyes.   5
—For if those streaks, those mile-long, shiny, tearstains,
aren't waterfalls yet,
in a quick age or so, as ages go here,
they probably will be.
But if the streams and clouds keep travelling, travelling,   10
the mountains look like the hulls of capsized ships,
slime-hung and barnacled.

Think of the long trip home.
Should we have stayed at home and thought of here?
Where should we be today?   15
Is it right to be watching strangers in a play
in this strangest of theatres?
What childishness is it that while there's a breath of life
in our bodies, we are determined to rush
to see the sun the other way around?   20
The tiniest green hummingbird in the world?
To stare at some inexplicable old stonework,
inexplicable and impenetrable,
at any view,
instantly seen and always, always delightful?   25
Oh, must we dream our dreams
and have them, too?
And have we room
for one more folded sunset, still quite warm?

But surely it would have been a pity   30
not to have seen the trees along this road,
really exaggerated in their beauty,
not to have seen them gesturing
like noble pantomimists, robed in pink.
—Not to have had to stop for gas and heard   35
the sad, two-noted, wooden tune
of disparate wooden clogs
carelessly clacking over
a grease-stained filling-station floor.
(In another country the clogs would all be tested.   40
Each pair there would have identical pitch.)
—A pity not to have heard
the other, less primitive music of the fat brown bird
who sings above the broken gasoline pump
in a bamboo church of Jesuit baroque: 45
three towers, five silver crosses.
—Yes, a pity not to have pondered,

blurr'dly and inconclusively,
on what connection can exist for centuries
between the crudest wooden footwear   50
and, careful and finicky,
the whittled fantasies of wooden cages.
—Never to have studied history in
the weak calligraphy of songbirds' cages.
—And never to have had to listen to rain   55
so much like politicians' speeches:
two hours of unrelenting oratory
and then a sudden golden silence
in which the traveller takes a notebook, writes:

"Is it lack of imagination that makes us come   60
to imagined places, not just stay at home?
Or could Pascal[1] have been not entirely right
about just sitting quietly in one's room?

Continent, city, country, society:
the choice is never wide and never free.   65
And here, or there . . . No. Should we have stayed at home,
wherever that may be?"

                                                                    1965

The Armadillo

for Robert Lowell

This is the time of year
when almost every night
the frail, illegal fire balloons appear.
Climbing the mountain height,

rising toward a saint   5
still honored in these parts,
the paper chambers flush and fill with light
that comes and goes, like hearts.

Once up against the sky it's hard
to tell them from the stars—   10
planets, that is—the tinted ones:
Venus going down, or Mars,

or the pale green one. With a wind,
they flare and falter, wobble and toss;
but if it's still they steer between   15
the kite sticks of the Southern Cross,

---

1. French mathematician and philosopher (1623–1662) who said, "Men's misfortunes spring from the single cause that they are unable to stay quietly in one room" (*Pensées*, trans. J. M. Cohen).

receding, dwindling, solemnly
and steadily forsaking us,
or, in the downdraft from a peak,
suddenly turning dangerous.   20

Last night another big one fell.
It splattered like an egg of fire
against the cliff behind the house.
The flame ran down. We saw the pair

of owls who nest there flying up   25
and up, their whirling black-and-white
stained bright pink underneath, until
they shrieked up out of sight.

The ancient owls' nest must have burned.
Hastily, all alone,   30
a glistening armadillo left the scene,
rose-flecked, head down, tail down,

and then a baby rabbit jumped out,
short-eared, to our surprise.
So soft!—a handful of intangible ash   35
with fixed, ignited eyes.

Too pretty, dreamlike mimicry!
O falling fire and piercing cry
and panic, and a weak mailed fist[2]
clenched ignorant against the sky!   40

                                                                1965

Sestina[1]

September rain falls on the house.
In the failing light, the old grandmother
sits in the kitchen with the child
beside the Little Marvel Stove,
reading the jokes from the almanac,   5
laughing and talking to hide her tears.

She thinks that her equinoctial tears
and the rain that beats on the roof of the house
were both foretold by the almanac,
but only known to a grandmother.   10
The iron kettle sings on the stove.
She cuts some bread and says to the child,

---

2. The armadillo, curled tight and protected against everything but fire.

1. A fixed verse form in which the end words of the first six-line stanza must be used at the ends of the lines in the following stanzas in a rotating order; the final three lines must contain all six words.

It's time for tea now; but the child
is watching the teakettle's small hard tears
dance like mad on the hot black stove,   15
the way the rain must dance on the house.
Tidying up, the old grandmother
hangs up the clever almanac

on its string. Birdlike, the almanac
hovers half open above the child,   20
hovers above the old grandmother
and her teacup full of dark brown tears.
She shivers and says she thinks the house
feels chilly, and puts more wood in the stove.

It was to be, says the Marvel Stove.   25
I know what I know, says the almanac.
With crayons the child draws a rigid house
and a winding pathway. Then the child
puts in a man with buttons like tears
and shows it proudly to the grandmother.   30

But secretly, while the grandmother
busies herself about the stove,
the little moons fall down like tears
from between the pages of the almanac
into the flower bed the child   35
has carefully placed in the front of the house.

Time to plant tears, says the almanac.
The grandmother sings to the marvellous stove
and the child draws another inscrutable house.

                                                               1965

In the Waiting Room

In Worcester, Massachusetts,
I went with Aunt Consuelo
to keep her dentist's appointment
and sat and waited for her
in the dentist's waiting room.   5
It was winter. It got dark
early. The waiting room
was full of grown-up people,
arctics and overcoats,
lamps and magazines.   10
My aunt was inside
what seemed like a long time
and while I waited I read
the *National Geographic*

(I could read) and carefully   15
studied the photographs:
the inside of a volcano,
black, and full of ashes;
then it was spilling over
in rivulets of fire.   20
Osa and Martin Johnson[1]
dressed in riding breeches,
laced boots, and pith helmets.
A dead man slung on a pole
—"Long Pig,"[2] the caption said.   25
Babies with pointed heads
wound round and round with string;
black, naked women with necks
wound round and round with wire
like the necks of light bulbs.   30
Their breasts were horrifying.
I read it right straight through.
I was too shy to stop.
And then I looked at the cover:
the yellow margins, the date.   35

Suddenly, from inside,
came an *oh!* of pain
—Aunt Consuelo's voice—
not very loud or long.
I wasn't at all surprised;   40
even then I knew she was
a foolish, timid woman.
I might have been embarrassed,
but wasn't. What took me
completely by surprise   45
was that it was *me*:
my voice, in my mouth.
Without thinking at all
I was my foolish aunt,
I—we—were falling, falling,   50
our eyes glued to the cover
of the *National Geographic*,
February, 1918.

I said to myself: three days
and you'll be seven years old.   55
I was saying it to stop
the sensation of falling off
the round, turning world
into cold, blue-black space.
But I felt: you are an *I*,   60
you are an *Elizabeth*,

1. Famous explorers and travel writers.
2. Polynesian cannibals' name for the human carcass.

you are one of *them*.
Why should you be one, too?
I scarcely dared to look.
to see what it was I was.   65
I gave a sidelong glance
—I couldn't look any higher—
at shadowy gray knees,
trousers and skirts and boots
and different pairs of hands   70
lying under the lamps.
I knew that nothing stranger
had ever happened, that nothing
stranger could ever happen.
Why should I be my aunt,   75
or me, or anyone?
What similarities—
boots, hands, the family voice
I felt in my throat, or even
the *National Geographic*   80
and those awful hanging breasts—
held us all together
or made us all just one?
How—I didn't know any
word for it—how "unlikely" . . .   85
How had I come to be here,
like them, and overhear
a cry of pain that could have
got loud and worse but hadn't?

The waiting room was bright   90
and too hot. It was sliding
beneath a big black wave,
another, and another.

Then I was back in it.
The War was on. Outside,   95
in Worcester, Massachusetts,
were night and slush and cold,
and it was still the fifth
of February, 1918.

                                                        1976

The Moose

for Grace Bulmer Bowers

From narrow provinces
of fish and bread and tea,
home of the long tides

where the bay leaves the sea
twice a day and takes   5
the herrings long rides,

where if the river
enters or retreats
in a wall of brown foam
depends on if it meets   10
the bay coming in,
the bay not at home;

where, silted red,
sometimes the sun sets
facing a red sea,   15
and others, veins the flats'
lavender, rich mud
in burning rivulets;

on red, gravelly roads,
down rows of sugar maples,   20
past clapboard farmhouses
and neat, clapboard churches,
bleached, ridged as clamshells,
past twin silver birches,

through late afternoon   25
a bus journeys west,
the windshield flashing pink,
pink glancing off of metal,
brushing the dented flank
of blue, beat-up enamel;   30

down hollows, up rises,
and waits, patient, while
a lone traveller gives
kisses and embraces
to seven relatives   35
and a collie supervises.

Goodbye to the elms,
to the farm, to the dog.
The bus starts. The light
grows richer; the fog,   40
shifting, salty, thin,
comes closing in.

Its cold, round crystals
form and slide and settle
in the white hens' feathers,   45
in gray glazed cabbages,
on the cabbage roses
and lupins like apostles;

the sweet peas cling
to their wet white string   50
on the whitewashed fences;
bumblebees creep
inside the foxgloves,
and evening commences.

One stop at Bass River.   55
Then the Economies—
Lower, Middle, Upper;
Five Islands, Five Houses,[1]
where a woman shakes a tablecloth
out after supper.   60

A pale flickering. Gone.
The Tantramar marshes
and the smell of salt hay.
An iron bridge trembles
and a loose plank rattles   65
but doesn't give way.

On the left, a red light
swims through the dark:
a ship's port lantern.
Two rubber boots show,   70
illuminated, solemn.
A dog gives one bark.

A woman climbs in
with two market bags,
brisk, freckled, elderly.   75
"A grand night. Yes, sir,
all the way to Boston."
She regards us amicably.

Moonlight as we enter
the New Brunswick woods,   80
hairy, scratchy, splintery;
moonlight and mist
caught in them like lamb's wool
on bushes in a pasture.

The passengers lie back.   85
Snores. Some long sighs.
A dreamy divagation
begins in the night,
a gentle, auditory,
slow hallucination. . . .   90

1. These are small towns and villages in Nova Scotia, near Halifax.

In the creakings and noises,
an old conversation
—not concerning us,
but recognizable, somewhere,
back in the bus: 95
Grandparents' voices

uninterruptedly
talking, in Eternity:
names being mentioned,
things cleared up finally;   100
what he said, what she said,
who got pensioned;

deaths, deaths and sicknesses;
the year he remarried;
the year (something) happened.   105
She died in childbirth.
That was the son lost
when the schooner foundered.

He took to drink. Yes.
She went to the bad.   110
When Amos began to pray
even in the store and
finally the family had
to put him away.

"Yes . . ." that peculiar   115
affirmative. "Yes . . ."
A sharp, indrawn breath,
half groan, half acceptance,
that means "Life's like that.
We know *it* (also death)."   120

Talking the way they talked
in the old featherbed,
peacefully, on and on,
dim lamplight in the hall,
down in the kitchen, the dog   125
tucked in her shawl.

Now, it's all right now
even to fall asleep
just as on all those nights.
—Suddenly the bus driver   130
stops with a jolt,
turns off his lights.

A moose has come out of
the impenetrable wood
and stands there, looms, rather,   135

in the middle of the road.
It approaches; it sniffs at
the bus's hot hood.

Towering, antlerless,
high as a church,   140
homely as a house
(or, safe as houses).
A man's voice assures us
"Perfectly harmless . . ."

Some of the passengers   145
exclaim in whispers,
childishly, softly,
"Sure are big creatures."
"It's awful plain."
"Look! It's a she!"   150

Taking her time,
she looks the bus over,
grand, otherworldly.
Why, why do we feel
(we all feel) this sweet   155
sensation of joy?

"Curious creatures,"
says our quiet driver,
rolling his r's.
"Look at that, would you."   160
Then he shifts gears.
For a moment longer,

by craning backward,
the moose can be seen
on the moonlit macadam;   165
then there's a dim
smell of moose, an acrid
smell of gasoline.

                                          1976

One Art

The art of losing isn't hard to master;
so many things seem filled with the intent
to be lost that their loss is no disaster.

Lose something every day. Accept the fluster
of lost door keys, the hour badly spent.   5
The art of losing isn't hard to master.

Then practice losing farther, losing faster:
places, and names, and where it was you meant
to travel. None of these will bring disaster.

I lost my mother's watch. And look! my last, or
next-to-last, of three loved houses went.
The art of losing isn't hard to master.

I lost two cities, lovely ones. And, vaster,
some realms I owned, two rivers, a continent.
I miss them, but it wasn't a disaster.

—Even losing you (the joking voice, a gesture
I love) I shan't have lied. It's evident
the art of losing's not too hard to master
though it may look like (*Write* it!) like disaster.

1976

TENNESSEE WILLIAMS
1911–1983

S peaking of Blanche DuBois, the heroine of *A Streetcar Named Desire*, Tennessee
Williams once said, "She was a demonic creature; the size of her feeling was too
great for her to contain." In Williams's plays—he wrote and rewrote more than twenty
full-length dramas as well as screenplays and shorter works—his characters are driven
by the size of their feelings, much as Williams felt driven to write about them.

He was born Thomas Lanier Williams in Columbus, Mississippi. His mother,
"Miss Edwina," the daughter of an Episcopalian minister, was repressed and gen-
teel, very much the southern belle in her youth. His father, Cornelius, was a traveling salesman, often away from his family and often violent and drunk when at
home. As a child Williams was sickly and overly protected by his mother; he was
closely attached to his sister, Rose, repelled by the roughhouse world of boys, and
alienated from his father. The family's move from Mississippi to St. Louis, where
Cornelius became a sales manager of the shoe company he had traveled for, was
a shock to Mrs. Williams and her young children, used to living in small southern
towns where a minister's daughter was an important person. Yet Mrs. Williams could
take care of herself; she was a "survivor."

Williams went to the University of Missouri, but left after two years; his father
then found him a job in the shoe-factory warehouse. He worked there for nearly three
years, writing feverishly at night. (His closest friend at the time was a burly coworker,
easygoing and attractive to women, named Stanley Kowalski, whose name and characteristics Williams would borrow for *A Streetcar Named Desire*.) Williams found the
life so difficult, however, that he succumbed to a nervous breakdown. After recovering at the home of his beloved grandparents, he went on to further studies, finally
graduating at the age of twenty-seven. Earlier Rose had been suffering increasing
mental imbalance; the final trauma was apparently brought on by one of Cornelius's

alcoholic rages, in which he beat Edwina and, trying to calm Rose, made a gesture that she took to be sexual. Shortly thereafter Edwina signed the papers allowing Rose to be "tragically becalmed" by a prefrontal lobotomy. Rose spent most of her life in sanatoriums, except when Williams brought her out for visits.

The next year Williams left for New Orleans, the first of many temporary homes; it would provide the setting for *A Streetcar Named Desire*. In New Orleans he changed his name to "Tennessee," later giving—as often when discussing his life—various romantic reasons for doing so. There also he actively entered the homosexual world.

Williams had had plays produced at local theaters and in 1939 he won a prize for a collection of one-act plays, *American Blues*. The next year *Battle of Angels* failed (in 1957 he would rewrite it as *Orpheus Descending*). His first success was *The Glass Menagerie* (1945). Williams called it a "memory play," seen through the recollections of the writer, Tom, who talks to the audience about himself and about the scenes depicting his mother, Amanda, poverty-stricken but genteelly living on memories of her southern youth and her "gentlemen callers"; his crippled sister, Laura, who finds refuge in her "menagerie" of little glass animals; and the traumatic effect of a modern "gentleman caller" on them. While there are similarities between Edwina, Rose, and Tennessee on the one hand, and Amanda, Laura, and Tom on the other, there are also differences: the play is not literally autobiographical.

The financial success of *Menagerie* proved exhilarating, then debilitating. Williams fled to Mexico to work full-time on an earlier play, *The Poker Night*. It had begun as *The Moth*; its first image, as Williams's biographer, Donald Spoto, tells us, was "simply that of a woman, sitting with folded hands near a window, while moonlight streamed in and she awaited in vain the arrival of her boyfriend": named Blanche, she was at first intended as a young Amanda. During rehearsals of *Menagerie*, Williams had asked members of the stage crew to teach him to play poker, and he began to visualize his new play as a series of confrontations between working-class poker players and two refined southern women.

As the focus of his attention changed from Stanley to Blanche, *The Poker Night* turned into *A Streetcar Named Desire*. Upon opening in 1947, it was an even greater success than *The Glass Menagerie*, and it won the Pulitzer Prize. Williams was able to travel and to buy a home in Key West, Florida, where he did much of his ensuing work. At about this time his "transitory heart" found "a home at last" in a young man named Frank Merlo.

For more than a decade thereafter a new Williams play appeared almost every two years. Among the most successful were *The Rose Tattoo* (1950), in which the tempestuous heroine, Serafina, worshiping the memory of her dead husband, finds love again; the Pulitzer Prize–winning *Cat on a Hot Tin Roof* (1955), which portrays the conflict of the dying Big Daddy and his impotent son, Brick, watched and controlled by Brick's wife, "Maggie the Cat"; and *The Night of the Iguana* (1961), which brings a varied group of tormented people together at a rundown hotel on the Mexican coast. His plays were produced widely abroad and also became equally successful films. Yet some of the ones now regarded as the best of this period were commercial failures: *Summer and Smoke* (1948), for example, and the surrealistic and visionary *Camino Real* (1953).

For years Williams had depended on a wide variety of drugs, especially to help him sleep and to keep him awake in the early mornings, when he invariably worked. In the 1960s the drugs began to take a real toll. Other factors contributed to the decline of his later years: Frank Merlo's death, the emergence of younger playwrights of whom he felt blindly jealous, and the violent nature of the 1960s, which seemed both to mirror his inner chaos and to leave him behind.

Yet despite Broadway failures, critical disparagements, and a breakdown for which he was hospitalized, he valiantly kept working. Spoto notes that in Williams's late work, Rose was "the source and inspiration of everything he wrote, either directly—with a surrogate character representing her—or indirectly, in the situation of romanticized mental illness or unvarnished verisimilitude." This observation is

A game of seven-card stud poker continues as the action of *A Streetcar Named Desire* concludes. Original Broadway production, 1947.

certainly true of his last Broadway play, the failed *Clothes for a Summer Hotel* (1980), ostensibly about the ghosts of Scott and Zelda Fitzgerald, and of the play he obsessively wrote and rewrote, *The Two Character Play*, which chronicles the descent of a brother and sister, who are also lovers into madness and death.

Despite Williams's self-destructiveness, in his writing and in his social life, the work of his great years was now being seriously studied and often revived by regional and community theaters. Critics began to see that he was one of America's best and most dedicated playwrights. And he kept on working. He was collaborating on a film of two stories about Rose when he died, apparently having choked to death on the lid of a pill bottle.

Always reluctant to talk about his work (likening it to a "bird that will be startled away, as by a hawk's shadow"), Williams did not see himself in a tradition of American dramaturgy. He acknowledged the influence of Anton Chekhov, the nineteenth-century Russian writer of dramas with lonely, searching characters; of D. H. Lawrence, the British novelist who emphasized the theme of a sexual life force; and above all of the American Hart Crane, homosexual *poète maudit*, who, he said, "touched fire that burned [himself] alive," adding that "perhaps it is only through self-immolation of such a nature that we living beings can offer to you the entire truth of ourselves." Such a statement indicates the deeply confessional quality of Williams's writing, even in plays not directly autobiographical.

Although he never acknowledged any debt to the American playwright Eugene O'Neill, Williams shared with O'Neill an impatience over the theatrical conventions of realism. *The Glass Menagerie*, for example, uses screened projections, lighting effects, and music to emphasize that it takes place in Tom's memory. *A Streetcar Named Desire* moves in and out of the house on Elysian Fields, while music and lighting reinforce all the major themes. Williams also relies on the effects of language, especially of a vivid and colloquial Southern speech that may be compared with that of William Faulkner, Eudora Welty, or Flannery O'Connor. Rhythms of language become almost a musical indication of character, distinguishing Blanche from other characters. Reading or seeing his plays, we become aware of how symbolic repetitions—in Blanche's and Stanley's turns of phrase, the naked light bulb and the paper lantern, the Mexican woman selling flowers for the dead, the "Varsouviana" waltz and the reverberating voices—produce a heightening of reality: what Williams called "poetic realism."

More than a half century later does the destruction of Blanche, the "lady," still have the power to move us? Elia Kazan, in his director's notes, calls her "an outdated creature, approaching extinction . . . like a dinosaur." But Blythe Danner, who played Blanche in a 1988 revival, acutely observes that Williams "was attached to the things that were going to destroy him" and that Blanche, similarly, is attracted to and repelled by Stanley: "It's Tennessee fighting, fighting, fighting what he doesn't want to get into, what is very prevalent in his mind. That incredible contradiction in so many people is what he captures better than any other playwright."

Contemporary criticisms of Williams's plays focused on their violence and their obsession with sexuality, which in some of the later work struck some commentators as an almost morbid preoccupation with "perversion"—murder, rape, drugs, incest, nymphomania. The shriller voices making such accusations were attacking Williams for his homosexuality, which could not be publicly spoken of in this country until comparatively recently. These taboo topics, however, figure as instances of Williams's deeper subjects: desire and loneliness. As he said in an interview, "Desire is rooted in a longing for companionship, a release from the loneliness that haunts every individual." Loneliness and desire propel his characters into extreme behavior, no doubt, but such behavior literally dramatizes the plight that Williams saw as universal.

The following text is from *The Theatre of Tennessee Williams*, volume 1 (1971).

A Streetcar Named Desire

And so it was I entered the broken world
To trace the visionary company of love, its voice
An instant in the wind (I know not whither hurled)
But not for long to hold each desperate choice.
*   —"The Broken Tower" by Hart Crane[1]*

THE CHARACTERS

BLANCHE	PABLO
STELLA	A NEGRO WOMAN
STANLEY	A DOCTOR
MITCH	A NURSE
EUNICE	A YOUNG COLLECTOR
STEVE	A MEXICAN WOMAN

Scene One

The exterior of a two-story corner building on a street in New Orleans which is named Elysian Fields and runs between the L & N tracks and the river.[2] The section is poor but, unlike corresponding sections in other American cities, it has a

---

1. American poet (1899–1932).
2. Elysian Fields is a New Orleans street at the northern tip of the French Quarter, between the Louisville & Nashville railroad tracks and the Mississippi River. In Greek mythology the Elysian Fields are the abode of the blessed in the afterlife.

raffish charm. The houses are mostly white frame, weathered grey, with rickety outside stairs and galleries and quaintly ornamented gables. This building contains two flats, upstairs and down. Faded white stairs ascend to the entrances of both.

It is first dark of an evening early in May. The sky that shows around the dim white building is a peculiarly tender blue, almost a turquoise, which invests the scene with a kind of lyricism and gracefully attenuates the atmosphere of decay. You can almost feel the warm breath of the brown river beyond the river warehouses with their faint redolences of bananas and coffee. A corresponding air is evoked by the music of Negro entertainers at a barroom around the corner. In this part of New Orleans you are practically always just around the corner, or a few doors down the street, from a tinny piano being played with the infatuated fluency of brown fingers. This "Blue Piano" expresses the spirit of the life which goes on here.

Two women, one white and one colored, are taking the air on the steps of the building. The white woman is EUNICE, *who occupies the upstairs flat; the colored woman a neighbor, for New Orleans is a cosmopolitan city where there is a relatively warm and easy intermingling of races in the old part of town.*

Above the music of the "Blue Piano" the voices of people on the street can be heard overlapping.

> [*Two men come around the corner,* STANLEY KOWALSKI *and* MITCH. *They are about twenty-eight or thirty years old, roughly dressed in blue denim work clothes.* STANLEY *carries his bowling jacket and a red-stained package from a butcher's. They stop at the foot of the steps.*]

STANLEY [*bellowing*]   Hey there! Stella, baby!

> [STELLA *comes out on the first floor landing, a gentle young woman, about twenty-five, and of a background obviously quite different from her husband's.*]

STELLA [*mildly*]   Don't holler at me like that. Hi, Mitch.

STANLEY   Catch!

STELLA   What?

STANLEY   Meat!

> [*He heaves the package at her. She cries out in protest but manages to catch it: then she laughs breathlessly. Her husband and his companion have already started back around the corner.*]

STELLA [*calling after him*]   Stanley! Where are you going?

STANLEY   Bowling!

STELLA   Can I come watch?

STANLEY   Come on. [*He goes out.*]

STELLA   Be over soon. [*to the white woman*] Hello, Eunice. How are you?

EUNICE   I'm all right. Tell Steve to get him a poor boy's sandwich 'cause nothing's left here.

> [*They all laugh; the colored woman does not stop.* STELLA *goes out.*]

COLORED WOMAN   What was that package he th'ew at 'er? [*She rises from steps, laughing louder.*]

EUNICE   You hush, now!

NEGRO WOMAN   Catch *what!*

> [*She continues to laugh.* BLANCHE *comes around the corner, carrying a valise. She looks at a slip of paper, then at the building, then again at the slip and again at the building. Her expression is one of shocked disbelief. Her appearance is incongruous to this setting. She is daintily dressed in a white suit with a fluffy bodice, necklace and earrings of pearl, white*

gloves and hat, looking as if she were arriving at a summer tea or cocktail party in the garden district. She is about five years older than STELLA. *Her delicate beauty must avoid a strong light. There is something about her uncertain manner, as well as her white clothes, that suggests a moth.*]

EUNICE [*finally*]   What's the matter, honey? Are you lost?

BLANCHE [*with faintly hysterical humor*]   They told me to take a street-car named Desire, and then transfer to one called Cemeteries[3] and ride six blocks and get off at—Elysian Fields!

EUNICE   That's where you are now.

BLANCHE   At Elysian Fields?

EUNICE   This here is Elysian Fields.

BLANCHE   They mustn't have—understood—what number I wanted . . .

EUNICE   What number you lookin' for?

[BLANCHE *wearily refers to the slip of paper.*]

BLANCHE   Six thirty-two.

EUNICE   You don't have to look no further.

BLANCHE [*uncomprehendingly*]   I'm looking for my sister, Stella DuBois, I mean—Mrs. Stanley Kowalski.

EUNICE   That's the party.—You just did miss her, though.

BLANCHE   This—can this be—her home?

EUNICE   She's got the downstairs here and I got the up.

BLANCHE   Oh. She's—out?

EUNICE   You noticed that bowling alley around the corner?

BLANCHE   I'm—not sure I did.

EUNICE   Well, that's where she's at, watchin' her husband bowl. [*There is a pause.*] You want to leave your suitcase here an' go find her?

BLANCHE   No.

NEGRO WOMAN   I'll go tell her you come.

BLANCHE   Thanks.

NEGRO WOMAN   You welcome. [*She goes out.*]

EUNICE   She wasn't expecting you?

BLANCHE   No. No, not tonight.

EUNICE   Well, why don't you just go in and make yourself at home till they get back.

BLANCHE   How could I—do that?

EUNICE   We own this place so I can let you in.

[*She gets up and opens the downstairs door. A light goes on behind the blind, turning it light blue.* BLANCHE *slowly follows her into the downstairs flat. The surrounding areas dim out as the interior is lighted. Two rooms can be seen, not too clearly defined. The one first entered is primarily a kitchen but contains a folding bed to be used by* BLANCHE. *The room beyond this is a bedroom. Off this room is a narrow door to a bathroom.*]

EUNICE [*defensively, noticing* BLANCHE's *look*]   It's sort of messed up right now but when it's clean it's real sweet.

BLANCHE   Is it?

EUNICE   Uh-huh, I think so. So you're Stella's sister?

BLANCHE   Yes. [*wanting to get rid of her*] Thanks for letting me in.

EUNICE   *Por nada,*[4] as the Mexicans say, *por nada*! Stella spoke of you.

---

3. The end of a streetcar line that stopped at a cemetery. Desire is a New Orleans street.

4. It's nothing (Spanish).

BLANCHE Yes?

EUNICE I think she said you taught school.

BLANCHE Yes.

EUNICE And you're from Mississippi, huh?

BLANCHE Yes.

EUNICE She showed me a picture of your home-place, the plantation.

BLANCHE Belle Reve?[5]

EUNICE A great big place with white columns.

BLANCHE Yes . . .

EUNICE A place like that must be awful hard to keep up.

BLANCHE If you will excuse me, I'm just about to drop.

EUNICE Sure, honey. Why don't you set down?

BLANCHE What I meant was I'd like to be left alone.

EUNICE [offended] Aw. I'll make myself scarce, in that case.

BLANCHE I didn't meant to be rude, but—

EUNICE I'll drop by the bowling alley an' hustle her up. [She goes out the door.]

> [BLANCHE sits in a chair very stiffly with her shoulders slightly hunched and her legs pressed close together and her hands tightly clutching her purse as if she were quite cold. After a while the blind look goes out of her eyes and she begins to look slowly around. A cat screeches. She catches her breath with a startled gesture. Suddenly she notices something in a half opened closet. She springs up and crosses to it, and removes a whiskey bottle. She pours a half tumbler of whiskey and tosses it down. She carefully replaces the bottle and washes out the tumbler at the sink. Then she resumes her seat in front of the table.]

BLANCHE [faintly to herself] I've got to keep hold of myself! [STELLA comes quickly around the corner of the building and runs to the door of the downstairs flat.]

STELLA [calling out joyfully] Blanche!

> [For a moment they stare at each other. Then BLANCHE springs up and runs to her with a wild cry.]

BLANCHE Stella, oh, Stella, Stella! Stella for Star!

> [She begins to speak with feverish vivacity as if she feared for either of them to stop and think. They catch each other in a spasmodic embrace.]

BLANCHE Now, then, let me look at you. But don't you look at me, Stella, no, no, no, not till later, not till I've bathed and rested! And turn that over-light off! Turn that off! I won't be looked at in this merciles glare! [STELLA laughs and complies.] Come back here now! Oh, my baby! Stella! Stella for Star! [She embraces her again.] I thought you would never come back to this horrible place! What am I saying? I didn't mean to say that. I meant to be nice about it and say—Oh, what a convenient location and such—Ha-a-ha! Precious lamb! You haven't said a word to me.

STELLA You haven't given me a chance to, honey! [She laughs, but her glance at BLANCHE is a little anxious.]

BLANCHE Well, now you talk. Open your pretty mouth and talk while I look around for some liquor! I know you must have some liquor on the place! Where could it be, I wonder? Oh, I spy, I spy!

---

5. Beautiful Dream (French).

[*She rushes to the closet and removes the bottle; she is shaking all over and panting for breath as she tries to laugh. The bottle nearly slips from her grasp.*]

STELLA [*noticing*]   Blanche, you sit down and let me pour the drinks. I don't know what we've got to mix with. Maybe a coke's in the icebox. Look'n see, honey, while I'm—

BLANCHE   No coke, honey, not with my nerves tonight! Where—where—where is—?

STELLA   Stanley? Bowling! He loves it. They're having a—found some soda!—tournament . . .

BLANCHE   Just water, baby, to chase it! Now don't get worried, your sister hasn't turned into a drunkard, she's just all shaken up and hot and tired and dirty! You sit down, now, and explain this place to me! What are you doing in a place like this?

STELLA   Now, Blanche—

BLANCHE   Oh, I'm not going to be hypocritical, I'm going to be honestly critical about it! Never, never, never in my worst dreams could I picture— Only Poe! Only Mr. Edgar Allan Poe!—could do it justice! Out there I suppose is the ghoul-haunted woodland of Weir![6] [*She laughs.*]

STELLA   No, honey, those are the L & N tracks.

BLANCHE   No, now seriously, putting joking aside. Why didn't you tell me, why didn't you write me, honey, why didn't you let me know?

STELLA [*carefully, pouring herself a drink*]   Tell you what, Blanche?

BLANCHE   Why, that you had to live in these conditions!

STELLA   Aren't you being a little intense about it? It's not that bad at all! New Orleans isn't like other cities.

BLANCHE   This has got nothing to do with New Orleans. You might as well say—forgive me, blessed baby! [*She suddenly stops short.*] The subject is closed!

STELLA [*a little drily*]   Thanks.

[*During the pause,* BLANCHE *stares at her. She smiles at* BLANCHE.]

BLANCHE [*looking down at her glass, which shakes in her hand*]   You're all I've got in the world, and you're not glad to see me!

STELLA [*sincerely*]   Why, Blanche, you know that's not true.

BLANCHE   No?—I'd forgotten how quiet you were.

STELLA   You never did give me a chance to say much, Blanche. So I just got in the habit of being quiet around you.

BLANCHE [*vaguely*]   A good habit to get into . . . [*then, abruptly*] You haven't asked me how I happened to get away from the school before the spring term ended.

STELLA   Well, I thought you'd volunteer that information—if you wanted to tell me.

BLANCHE   You thought I'd been fired?

STELLA   No, I—thought you might have—resigned . . .

BLANCHE   I was so exhausted by all I'd been through my—nerves broke. [*nervously tamping cigarette*] I was on the verge of—lunacy, almost! So Mr. Graves—Mr. Graves is the high school superintendent—he suggested I take a leave of absence. I couldn't put all of those details into

---

6. From the refrain of Poe's gothic ballad "Ulalume" (1847).

the wire . . . [*She drinks quickly.*] Oh, this buzzes right through me and feels so *good!*

STELLA   Won't you have another?

BLANCHE   No, one's my limit.

STELLA   Sure?

BLANCHE   You haven't said a word about my appearance.

STELLA   You look just fine.

BLANCHE   God love you for a liar! Daylight never exposed so total a ruin! But you—you've put on some weight, yes, you're just as plump as a little partridge! And it's so becoming to you!

STELLA   Now, Blanche—

BLANCHE   Yes, it is, it is or I wouldn't say it! You just have to watch around the hips a little. Stand up.

STELLA   Not now.

BLANCHE   You hear me? I said stand up! [STELLA *complies reluctantly.*] You messy child, you, you've spilt something on that pretty white lace collar! About your hair—you ought to have it cut in a feather bob with your dainty features. Stella, you have a maid, don't you?

STELLA   No. With only two rooms it's—

BLANCHE   What? *Two* rooms, did you say?

STELLA   This one and— [*She is embarrassed.*]

BLANCHE   The other one? [*She laughs sharply. There is an embarrassed silence.*]

BLANCHE   I am going to take just one little tiny nip more, sort of to put the stopper on, so to speak. . . . Then put the bottle away so I won't be tempted. [*She rises.*] I want you to look at *my* figure! [*She turns around.*] You know I haven't put on one ounce in ten years, Stella? I weigh what I weighed the summer you left Belle Reve. The summer Dad died and you left us . . .

STELLA [*a little wearily*]   It's just incredible, Blanche, how well you're looking.

BLANCHE [*They both laugh uncomfortably.*]   But, Stella, there's only two rooms, I don't see where you're going to put me!

STELLA   We're going to put you in here.

BLANCHE   What kind of bed's this—one of those collapsible things? [*She sits on it.*]

STELLA   Does it feel all right?

BLANCHE [*dubiously*]   Wonderful, honey. I don't like a bed that gives much. But there's no door between the two rooms, and Stanley—will it be decent?

STELLA   Stanley is Polish, you know.

BLANCHE   Oh, yes. They're something like Irish, aren't they?

STELLA   Well—

BLANCHE   Only not so—highbrow? [*They both laugh again in the same way.*] I brought some nice clothes to meet all your lovely friends in.

STELLA   I'm afraid you won't think they are lovely.

BLANCHE   What are they like?

STELLA   They're Stanley's friends.

BLANCHE   Polacks?

STELLA   They're a mixed lot, Blanche.

BLANCHE Heterogeneous—types?

STELLA Oh, yes. Yes, types is right!

BLANCHE Well—anyhow—I brought nice clothes and I'll wear them. I guess you're hoping I'll say I'll put up at a hotel, but I'm not going to put up at a hotel. I want to be *near* you, got to be *with* somebody, I *can't* be *alone*! Because—as you must have noticed—I'm—*not* very *well*. . . . [*Her voice drops and her look is frightened.*]

STELLA You seem a little bit nervous or overwrought or something.

BLANCHE Will Stanley like me, or will I be just a visiting in-law, Stella? I couldn't stand that.

STELLA You'll get along fine together, if you'll just try not to—well—compare him with men that we went out with at home.

BLANCHE Is he so—different?

STELLA Yes. A different species.

BLANCHE In what way; what's he like?

STELLA Oh, you can't describe someone you're in love with! Here's a picture of him! [*She hands a photograph to* BLANCHE.]

BLANCHE An officer?

STELLA A Master Sergeant in the Engineers' Corps. Those are decorations!

BLANCHE He had those on when you met him?

STELLA I assure you I wasn't just blinded by all the brass.

BLANCHE That's not what I—

STELLA But of course there were things to adjust myself to later on.

BLANCHE Such as his civilian background! [STELLA *laughs uncertainly.*] How did he take it when you said I was coming?

STELLA Oh, Stanley doesn't know yet.

BLANCHE [*frightened*] You—haven't told him?

STELLA He's on the road a good deal.

BLANCHE Oh. Travels?

STELLA Yes.

BLANCHE Good. I mean—isn't it?

STELLA [*half to herself*] I can hardly stand it when he is away for a night . . .

BLANCHE Why, Stella!

STELLA When he's away for a week I nearly go wild!

BLANCHE Gracious!

STELLA And when he comes back I cry on his lap like a baby . . . [*She smiles to herself.*]

BLANCHE I guess that is what is meant by being in love . . . [STELLA *looks up with a radiant smile.*] Stella—

STELLA What?

BLANCHE [*in an uneasy rush*] I haven't asked you the things you probably thought I was going to ask. And so I'll expect you to be understanding about what *I* have to tell *you.*

STELLA What, Blanche? [*Her face turns anxious.*]

BLANCHE Well, Stella—you're going to reproach me, I know that you're bound to reproach me—but before you do—take into consideration—you left! I stayed and struggled! You came to New Orleans and looked out for yourself! *I* stayed at *Belle Reve* and tried to hold it together! I'm not meaning this in any reproachful way, but *all* the burden descended on *my* shoulders.

STELLA The best I could do was make my own living, Blanche.

[BLANCHE *begins to shake again with intensity.*]

BLANCHE I know, I know. But you are the one that abandoned Belle Reve, not I! I stayed and fought for it, bled for it, almost died for it!

STELLA Stop this hysterical outburst and tell me what's happened? What do you mean fought and bled? What kind of—

BLANCHE I knew you would, Stella. I knew you would take this attitude about it!

STELLA About—what?—please!

BLANCHE [*slowly*] The loss—the loss . . .

STELLA Belle Reve? Lost, is it? No!

BLANCHE Yes, Stella.

[*They stare at each other across the yellow-checked linoleum of the table.* BLANCHE *slowly nods her head and* STELLA *looks slowly down at her hands folded on the table. The music of the "Blue Piano" grows louder.* BLANCHE *touches her handkerchief to her forehead.*]

STELLA But how did it go? What happened?

BLANCHE [*springing up*] You're a fine one to ask me how it went!

STELLA Blanche!

BLANCHE You're a fine one to sit there *accusing me* of it!

STELLA *Blanche!*

BLANCHE I, I, I took the blows in my face and my body! All of those deaths! The long parade to the graveyard! Father, mother! Margaret, that dreadful way! So big with it, it couldn't be put in a coffin! But had to be burned like rubbish! You just came home in time for the funerals, Stella. And funerals are pretty compared to deaths. Funerals are quiet, but deaths—not always. Sometimes their breathing is hoarse, and sometimes it rattles, and sometimes they even cry out to you, "Don't let me go!" Even the old, sometimes, say, "Don't let me go." As if you were able to stop them! But funerals are quiet, with pretty flowers. And, oh, what gorgeous boxes they pack them away in! Unless you were there at the bed when they cried out, "Hold me!" you'd never suspect there was the struggle for breath and bleeding. You didn't dream, but I saw! *Saw! Saw!* And now you sit there telling me with your eyes that I let the place go! How in hell do you think all that sickness and dying was paid for? Death is expensive, Miss Stella! And old Cousin Jessie's right after Margaret's, hers! Why, the Grim Reaper had put up his tent on our doorstep! . . . Stella. Belle Reve was his headquarters! Honey—that's how it slipped through my fingers! Which of them left us a fortune? Which of them left a cent of insurance even? Only poor Jessie—one hundred to pay for her coffin. That was all, Stella! And I with my pitiful salary at the school. Yes, accuse me! Sit there and stare at me, thinking I let the place go! *I* let the place go? Where were *you!* In bed with your—Polack!

STELLA [*springing*] Blanche! You be still! That's enough! [*She starts out.*]

BLANCHE Where are you going?

STELLA I'm going into the bathroom to wash my face.

BLANCHE Oh, Stella, Stella, you're crying!

STELLA Does that surprise you?

BLANCHE Forgive me—I didn't mean to—

[*The sound of men's voices is heard.* STELLA *goes into the bathroom, closing the door behind her. When the men appear, and* BLANCHE *realizes it must be* STANLEY *returning, she moves uncertainly from the bathroom door to the dressing table, looking apprehensively toward the front door.* STANLEY *enters, followed by* STEVE *and* MITCH. STANLEY *pauses near his door,* STEVE *by the foot of the spiral stair, and* MITCH *is slightly above and to the right of them, about to go out. As the men enter, we hear some of the following dialogue.*]

STANLEY   Is that how he got it?

STEVE   Sure that's how he got it. He hit the old weather-bird for 300 bucks on a six-number-ticket.

MITCH   Don't tell him those things; he'll believe it.
[*Mitch starts out.*]

STANLEY [*restraining Mitch*]   Hey, Mitch—come back here.
[BLANCHE, *at the sound of voices, retires in the bedroom. She picks up* STANLEY'S *photo from dressing table, looks at it, puts it down. When* STANLEY *enters the apartment, she darts and hides behind the screen at the head of bed.*]

STEVE [*to* STANLEY *and* MITCH]   Hey, are we playin' poker tomorrow?

STANLEY   Sure—at Mitch's.

MITCH [*hearing this, returns quickly to the stair rail*]   No—not at my place. My mother's still sick!

STANLEY   Okay, at my place . . . [MITCH *starts out again.*] But you bring the beer!
[MITCH *pretends not to hear—calls out "Good night, all," and goes out, singing.* EUNICE'S *voice is heard, above.*]
Break it up down there! I made the spaghetti dish and ate it myself.

STEVE [*going upstairs*]   I told you and phoned you we was playing. [*to the men*] Jax beer![7]

EUNICE   You never phoned me once.

STEVE   I told you at breakfast—and phoned you at lunch . . .

EUNICE   Well, never mind about that. You just get yourself home here once in a while.

STEVE   You want it in the papers?
[*More laughter and shouts of parting come from the men.* STANLEY *throws the screen door of the kitchen open and comes in. He is of medium height, about five feet eight or nine, and strongly, compactly built. Animal joy in his being is implicit in all his movements and attitudes. Since earliest manhood the center of his life has been pleasure with women, the giving and taking of it, not with weak indulgence, dependently, but with the power and pride of a richly feathered male bird among hens. Branching out from this complete and satisfying center are all the auxiliary channels of his life, such as his heartiness with men, his appreciation of rough humor, his love of good drink and food and games, his car, his radio, everything that is his, that bears his emblem of the gaudy seed-bearer. He sizes women up at a glance, with sexual classifications, crude images flashing into his mind and determining the way he smiles at them.*]

BLANCHE [*drawing involuntarily back from his stare*]   You must be Stanley. I'm Blanche.

7. A local brand.

STANLEY Stella's sister?

BLANCHE Yes.

STANLEY H'lo. Where's the little woman?

BLANCHE In the bathroom.

STANLEY Oh. Didn't know you were coming in town.

BLANCHE I—uh—

STANLEY Where you from, Blanche?

BLANCHE Why, I—live in Laurel.

[*He has crossed to the closet and removed the whiskey bottle.*]

STANLEY In Laurel, huh? Oh, yeah. Yeah, in Laurel, that's right. Not in my territory. Liquor goes fast in hot weather. [*He holds the bottle to the light to observe its depletion.*] Have a shot?

BLANCHE No, I—rarely touch it.

STANLEY Some people rarely touch it, but it touches them often.

BLANCHE [*faintly*] Ha-ha.

STANLEY My clothes're stickin' to me. Do you mind if I make myself comfortable? [*He starts to remove his shirt.*]

BLANCHE Please, please do.

STANLEY Be comfortable is my motto.

BLANCHE It's mine, too. It's hard to stay looking fresh. I haven't washed or even powdered my face and—here you are!

STANLEY You know you can catch cold sitting around in damp things, especially when you been exercising hard like bowling is. You're a teacher, aren't you?

BLANCHE Yes.

STANLEY What do you teach, Blanche?

BLANCHE English.

STANLEY I never was a very good English student. How long you here for, Blanche?

BLANCHE I—don't know yet.

STANLEY You going to shack up here?

BLANCHE I thought I would if it's not inconvenient for you all.

STANLEY Good.

BLANCHE Traveling wears me out.

STANLEY Well, take it easy.

[*A cat screeches near the window,* BLANCHE *springs up.*]

BLANCHE What's that?

STANLEY Cats . . . Hey, Stella!

STELLA [*faintly, from the bathroom*] Yes, Stanley.

STANLEY Haven't fallen in, have you? [*He grins at* BLANCHE. *She tries unsuccessfully to smile back. There is a silence.*] I'm afraid I'll strike you as being the unrefined type. Stella's spoke of you a good deal. You were married once, weren't you?

[*The music of the polka rises up, faint in the distance.*]

BLANCHE Yes. When I was quite young.

STANLEY What happened?

BLANCHE The boy—the boy died. [*She sinks back down.*] I'm afraid I'm—going to be sick! [*Her head falls on her arms.*]

Scene Two

It is six o'clock the following evening. BLANCHE *is bathing.* STELLA *is completing her toilette.* BLANCHE's *dress, a flowered print, is laid out on* STELLA's *bed.*

STANLEY enters the kitchen from outside, leaving the door open on the perpetual "Blue Piano" around the corner.

STANLEY   What's all this monkey doings?

STELLA   Oh, Stan! [*She jumps up and kisses him, which he accepts with lordly composure.*] I'm taking Blanche to Galatoire's[8] for supper and then to a show, because it's your poker night.

STANLEY   How about my supper, huh? I'm not going to no Galatoire's for supper!

STELLA   I put you a cold plate on ice.

STANLEY   Well, isn't that just dandy!

STELLA   I'm going to try to keep Blanche out till the party breaks up because I don't know how she would take it. So we'll go to one of the little places in the Quarter afterward and you'd better give me some money.

STANLEY   Where is she?

STELLA   She's soaking in a hot tub to quiet her nerves. She's terribly upset.

STANLEY   Over what?

STELLA   She's been through such an ordeal.

STANLEY   Yeah?

STELLA   Stan, we've—lost Belle Reve!

STANLEY   The place in the country?

STELLA   Yes.

STANLEY   How?

STELLA [*vaguely*]   Oh, it had to be—sacrificed or something. [*There is a pause while* STANLEY *considers.* STELLA *is changing into her dress.*] When she comes in be sure to say something nice about her appearance. And, oh! Don't mention the baby. I haven't said anything yet, I'm waiting until she gets in a quieter condition.

STANLEY [*ominously*]   So?

STELLA   And try to understand her and be nice to her, Stan.

BLANCHE [*singing in the bathroom*]   "From the land of the sky blue water, They brought a captive maid!"

STELLA   She wasn't expecting to find us in such a small place. You see I'd tried to gloss things over a little in my letters.

STANLEY   So?

STELLA   And admire her dress and tell her she's looking wonderful. That's important with Blanche. Her little weakness!

STANLEY   Yeah. I get the idea. Now let's skip back a little to where you said the country place was disposed of.

STELLA   Oh!—yes . . .

STANLEY   How about that? Let's have a few more details on that subjeck.

STELLA   It's best not to talk much about it until she's calmed down.

STANLEY   So that's the deal, huh? Sister Blanche cannot be annoyed with business details right now!

---

8. Renowned fancy restaurant with traditional New Orleans cuisine.

STELLA You saw how she was last night.

STANLEY Uh-hum, I saw how she was. Now let's have a gander at the bill of sale.

STELLA I haven't seen any.

STANLEY She didn't show you no papers, no deed of sale or nothing like that, huh?

STELLA It seems like it wasn't sold.

STANLEY Well, what in hell was it then, give away? To charity?

STELLA Shhh! She'll hear you.

STANLEY I don't care if she hears me. Let's see the papers!

STELLA There weren't any papers, she didn't show any papers, I don't care about papers.

STANLEY Have you ever heard of the Napoleonic code?[9]

STELLA No, Stanley, I haven't heard of the Napoleonic code and if I have, I don't see what it—

STANLEY Let me enlighten you on a point or two, baby.

STELLA Yes?

STANLEY In the state of Louisiana we have the Napoleonic code according to which what belongs to the wife belongs to the husband and vice versa. For instance if I had a piece of property, or you had a piece of property—

STELLA My head is swimming!

STANLEY All right. I'll wait till she gets through soaking in a hot tub and then I'll inquire if *she* is acquainted with the Napoleonic code. It looks to me like you have been swindled, baby, and when you're swindled under the Napoleonic code I'm swindled *too*. And I don't like to be *swindled*.

STELLA There's plenty of time to ask her questions later but if you do now she'll go to pieces again. I don't understand what happened to Belle Reve but you don't know how ridiculous you are being when you suggest that my sister or I or anyone of our family could have perpetrated a swindle on anyone else.

STANLEY Then where's the money if the place was sold?

STELLA Not sold—*lost, lost!*

[*He stalks into bedroom, and she follows him.*]
Stanley!
[*He pulls open the wardrobe trunk standing in middle of room and jerks out an armful of dresses.*]

STANLEY Open your eyes to this stuff! You think she got them out of a teacher's pay?

STELLA Hush!

STANLEY Look at these feathers and furs that she come here to preen herself in! What's this here? A solid-gold dress, I believe! And this one! What is these here? Fox-pieces! [*He blows on them.*] Genuine fox fur-pieces, a half a mile long! Where are your fox-pieces, Stella? Bushy snow-white ones, no less! Where are your white fox-pieces?

STELLA Those are inexpensive summer furs that Blanche has had a long time.

---

9. This codification of French law (1802), made by Napoleon as emperor, is the basis for Louisiana's civil law.

STANLEY   I got an acquaintance who deals in this sort of merchandise. I'll have him in here to appraise it. I'm willing to bet you there's thousands of dollars invested in this stuff here!

STELLA   Don't be such an idiot, Stanley!
[*He hurls the furs to the day bed. Then he jerks open a small drawer in the trunk and pulls up a fistful of costume jewelry.*]

STANLEY   And what have we here? The treasure chest of a pirate!

STELLA   Oh, Stanley!

STANLEY   Pearls! Ropes of them! What is this sister of yours, a deep-sea diver? Bracelets of solid gold, too! Where are your pearls and gold bracelets?

STELLA   Shhh! Be still, Stanley!

STANLEY   And diamonds! A crown for an empress!

STELLA   A rhinestone tiara she wore to a costume ball.

STANLEY   What's rhinestone?

STELLA   Next door to glass.

STANLEY   Are you kidding? I have an acquaintance that works in a jewelry store. I'll have him in here to make an appraisal of this. Here's your plantation, or what was left of it, here!

STELLA   You have no idea how stupid and horrid you're being! Now close that trunk before she comes out of the bathroom!
[*He kicks the trunk partly closed and sits on the kitchen table.*]

STANLEY   The Kowalskis and the DuBoises have different notions.

STELLA   [*angrily*]   Indeed they have, thank heavens!—*I'm* going outside.
[*She snatches up her white hat and gloves and crosses to the outside door.*]
You come out with me while Blanche is getting dressed.

STANLEY   Since when do you give me orders?

STELLA   Are you going to stay here and insult her?

STANLEY   You're damn tootin' I'm going to stay here.
[STELLA *goes out to the porch.* BLANCHE *comes out of the bathroom in a red satin robe.*]

BLANCHE   [*airily*]   Hello, Stanley! Here I am, all freshly bathed and scented, and feeling like a brand new human being!
[*He lights a cigarette.*]

STANLEY   That's good.

BLANCHE   [*drawing the curtains at the windows*]   Excuse me while I slip on my pretty new dress!

STANLEY   Go right ahead, Blanche.
[*She closes the drapes between the rooms.*]

BLANCHE   I understand there's to be a little card party to which we ladies are cordially *not* invited!

STANLEY   [*ominously*]   Yeah?
[BLANCHE *throws off her robe and slips into a flowered print dress.*]

BLANCHE   Where's Stella?

STANLEY   Out on the porch.

BLANCHE   I'm going to ask a favor of you in a moment.

STANLEY   What could that be, I wonder?

BLANCHE   Some buttons in back! You may enter! [*He crosses through drapes with a smoldering look.*] How do I look?

STANLEY   You look all right.

BLANCHE   Many thanks! Now the buttons!

STANLEY   I can't do nothing with them.

BLANCHE   You men with your big clumsy fingers. May I have a drag on your cig?

STANLEY   Have one for yourself.

BLANCHE   Why, thanks! . . . It looks like my trunk has exploded.

STANLEY   Me an' Stella were helping you unpack.

BLANCHE   Well, you certainly did a fast and thorough job of it!

STANLEY   It looks like you raided some stylish shops in Paris.

BLANCHE   Ha-ha! Yes—clothes are my passion!

STANLEY   What does it cost for a string of fur-pieces like that?

BLANCHE   Why, those were a tribute from an admirer of mine!

STANLEY   He must have had a lot of—admiration!

BLANCHE   Oh, in my youth I excited some admiration. But look at me now! [*She smiles at him radiantly.*] Would you think it possible that I was once considered to be—attractive?

STANLEY   Your looks are okay.

BLANCHE   I was fishing for a compliment, Stanley.

STANLEY   I don't go in for that stuff.

BLANCHE   What—stuff?

STANLEY   Compliments to women about their looks. I never met a woman that didn't know if she was good-looking or not without being told, and some of them give themselves credit for more than they've got. I once went out with a doll who said to me, "I am the glamorous type, I am the glamorous type!" I said, "So what?"

BLANCHE   And what did she say then?

STANLEY   She didn't say nothing. That shut her up like a clam.

BLANCHE   Did it end the romance?

STANLEY   It ended the conversation—that was all. Some men are took in by this Hollywood glamor stuff and some men are not.

BLANCHE   I'm sure you belong in the second category.

STANLEY   That's right.

BLANCHE   I cannot imagine any witch of a woman casting a spell over you.

STANLEY   That's—right.

BLANCHE   You're simple, straightforward and honest, a little bit on the primitive side I should think. To interest you a woman would have to— [*She pauses with an indefinite gesture.*]

STANLEY   [*slowly*]   Lay . . . her cards on the table.

BLANCHE   [*smiling*]   Well, I never cared for wishy-washy people. That was why, when you walked in here last night, I said to myself—"My sister has married a man!"—Of course that was all that I could tell about you.

STANLEY   [*booming*]   Now let's cut the re-bop!¹

BLANCHE   [*pressing hands to her ears*]   Ouuuuu!

STELLA   [*calling from the steps*]   Stanley! You come out here and let Blanche finish dressing!

BLANCHE   I'm through dressing, honey.

---

1. Nonsense (from "bebop," a form of jazz).

STELLA Well, you come out, then.

STANLEY Your sister and I are having a little talk.

BLANCHE [*lightly*] Honey, do me a favor. Run to the drugstore and get me a lemon Coke with plenty of chipped ice in it!—Will you do that for me, sweetie?

STELLA [*uncertainly*] Yes. [*She goes around the corner of the building.*]

BLANCHE The poor little thing was out there listening to us, and I have an idea she doesn't understand you as well as I do. . . . All right; now, Mr. Kowalski, let us proceed without any more double-talk. I'm ready to answer all questions. I've nothing to hide. What is it?

STANLEY There is such a thing in this state of Louisiana as the Napoleonic code, according to which whatever belongs to my wife is also mine—and vice versa.

BLANCHE My, but you have an impressive judicial air!

[*She sprays herself with her atomizer; then playfully sprays him with it. He seizes the atomizer and slams it down on the dresser. She throws back her head and laughs.*]

STANLEY If I didn't know that you was my wife's sister I'd get ideas about you!

BLANCHE Such as what!

STANLEY Don't play so dumb. You know what!

BLANCHE [*she puts the atomizer on the table*] All right. Cards on the table. That suits me. [*She turns to* STANLEY.] I know I fib a good deal. After all, a woman's charm is fifty per cent illusion, but when a thing is important I tell the truth, and this is the truth: I haven't cheated my sister or you or anyone else as long as I have lived.

STANLEY Where's the papers? In the trunk?

BLANCHE Everything that I own is in that trunk.

[STANLEY *crosses to the trunk, shoves it roughly open and begins to open compartments.*]

BLANCHE What in the name of heaven are you thinking of! What's in the back of that little boy's mind of yours? That I am absconding with something, attempting some kind of treachery on my sister?—Let me do that! It will be faster and simpler . . . [*She crosses to the trunk and takes out a box.*] I keep my papers mostly in this tin box. [*She opens it.*]

STANLEY What's them underneath? [*He indicates another sheaf of paper.*]

BLANCHE These are love-letters, yellowing with antiquity, all from one boy. [*He snatches them up. She speaks fiercely.*] Give those back to me!

STANLEY I'll have a look at them first!

BLANCHE The touch of your hands insults them!

STANLEY Don't pull that stuff!

[*He rips off the ribbon and starts to examine them.* BLANCHE *snatches them from him, and they cascade to the floor.*]

BLANCHE Now that you've touched them I'll burn them!

STANLEY [*staring, baffled*] What in hell are they?

BLANCHE [*on the floor gathering them up*] Poems a dead boy wrote. I hurt him the way that you would like to hurt me, but you can't! I'm not young and vulnerable any more. But my young husband was and I—never mind about that! Just give them back to me!

STANLEY What do you mean by saying you'll have to burn them?

BLANCHE I'm sorry, I must have lost my head for a moment. Everyone has something he won't let others touch because of their—intimate nature . . .
> [*She now seems faint with exhaustion and she sits down with the strong box and puts on a pair of glasses and goes methodically through a large stack of papers.*]

Ambler & Ambler. Hmmmmm. . . . Crabtree. . . . More Ambler & Ambler.

STANLEY What is Ambler & Ambler?

BLANCHE A firm that made loans on the place.

STANLEY Then it *was* lost on a mortgage?

BLANCHE [*touching her forehead*] That must've been what happened.

STANLEY I don't want no ifs, ands or buts! What's all the rest of them papers?
> [*She hands him the entire box. He carries it to the table and starts to examine the paper.*]

BLANCHE [*picking up a large envelope containing more papers*] There are thousands of papers, stretching back over hundreds of years, affecting Belle Reve as, piece by piece, our improvident grandfathers and father and uncles and brothers exchanged the land for their epic fornications— to put it plainly! [*She removes her glasses with an exhausted laugh.*] The four-letter word deprived us of our plantation, till finally all that was left—and Stella can verify that!—was the house itself and about twenty acres of ground, including a graveyard, to which now all but Stella and I have retreated. [*She pours the contents of the envelope on the table.*] Here all of them are, all papers! I hereby endow you with them! Take them, peruse them—commit them to memory, even! I think it's wonderfully fitting that Belle Reve should finally be this bunch of old papers in your big, capable hands! . . . I wonder if Stella's come back with my lemon Coke . . . [*She leans back and closes her eyes.*]

STANLEY I have a lawyer acquaintance who will study these out.

BLANCHE Present them to him with a box of aspirin tablets.

STANLEY [*becoming somewhat sheepish*] You see, under the Napoleonic code—a man has to take an interest in his wife's affairs—especially now that she's going to have a baby.
> [BLANCHE *opens her eyes. The "Blue Piano" sounds louder.*]

BLANCHE Stella? Stella going to have a baby? [*dreamily*] I didn't know she was going to have a baby!
> [*She gets up and crosses to the outside door.* STELLA *appears around the corner with a carton from the drugstore.* STANLEY *goes into the bedroom with the envelope and the box. The inner rooms fade to darkness and the outside wall of the house is visible,* BLANCHE *meets* STELLA *at the foot of the steps to the sidewalk.*]

BLANCHE Stella, Stella for star! How lovely to have a baby! It's all right. Everything's all right.

STELLA I'm sorry he did that to you.

BLANCHE Oh, I guess he's just not the type that goes for jasmine perfume, but maybe he's what we need to mix with our blood now that we've lost Belle Reve. We thrashed it out. I feel a bit shaky, but I think I handled it nicely, I laughed and treated it all as a joke. [STEVE *and* PABLO *appear, carrying a case of beer.*] I called him a little boy and laughed and flirted. Yes, I was flirting with your husband! [*as the men approach*] The guests are gathering for the poker party. [*The two men pass between them, and enter the house.*] Which way do we go now, Stella—this way?

STELLA   No, this way. [*She leads* BLANCHE *away.*]

BLANCHE [*laughing*]   The blind are leading the blind!

    [*A tamale* VENDOR *is heard calling.*]

VENDOR'S VOICE   Red-hot!

Scene Three

THE POKER NIGHT[2]

*There is a picture of Van Gogh's[3] of a billiard-parlor at night. The kitchen now suggests that sort of lurid nocturnal brilliance, the raw colors of childhood's spectrum. Over the yellow linoleum of the kitchen table hangs an electric bulb with a vivid green glass shade. The poker players—*STANLEY, STEVE, MITCH *and* PABLO—*wear colored shirts, solid blues, a purple, a red-and-white check, a light green, and they are men at the peak of their physical manhood, as coarse and direct and powerful as the primary colors. There are vivid slices of watermelon on the table, whiskey bottles and glasses. The bedroom is relatively dim with only the light that spills between the portieres and through the wide window on the street.*

    For a moment, there is absorbed silence as a hand is dealt.

STEVE   Anything wild this deal?

PABLO   One-eyed jacks are wild.

STEVE   Give me two cards.

PABLO   You, Mitch?

MITCH   I'm out.

PABLO   One.

MITCH   Anyone want a shot?

STANLEY   Yeah. Me.

PABLO   Why don't somebody go to the Chinaman's and bring back a load of chop suey?

STANLEY   When I'm losing you want to eat! Ante up! Openers? Openers! Get y'r ass off the table, Mitch. Nothing belongs on a poker table but cards, chips and whiskey.

    [*He lurches up and tosses some watermelon rinds to the floor.*]

MITCH   Kind of on your high horse, ain't you?

STANLEY   How many?

STEVE   Give me three.

STANLEY   One.

MITCH   I'm out again. I oughta go home pretty soon.

STANLEY   Shut up.

MITCH   I gotta sick mother. She don't go to sleep until I come in at night.

STANLEY   Then why don't you stay home with her?

MITCH   She says to go out, so I go, but I don't enjoy it. All the while I keep wondering how she is.

STANLEY   Aw, for the sake of Jesus, go home, then!

PABLO   What've you got?

---

2. Williams's first title for *A Streetcar Named Desire* (see headnote).

3. *The Night Café*, by the Dutch Postimpressionist painter Vincent van Gogh (1853–1890).

STEVE   Spade flush.

MITCH   You all are married. But I'll be alone when she goes.—I'm going to the bathroom.

STANLEY   Hurry back and we'll fix you a sugar-tit.

MITCH   Aw, go rut. [*He crosses through the bedroom into the bathroom.*]

STEVE [*dealing a hand*]   Seven card stud.[4] [*telling his joke as he deals*] This ole farmer is out in back of his house sittin' down th'owing corn to the chickens when all at once he hears a loud cackle and this young hen comes lickety split around the side of the house with the rooster right behind her and gaining on her fast.

STANLEY [*impatient with the story*]   Deal!

STEVE   But when the rooster catches sight of the farmer th'owing the corn he puts on the brakes and lets the hen get away and starts pecking corn. And the old farmer says, "Lord God, I hopes I never gits *that* hongry!"

> [STEVE *and* PABLO *laugh. The sisters appear around the corner of the building.*]

STELLA   The game is still going on.

BLANCHE   How do I look?

STELLA   Lovely, Blanche.

BLANCHE   I feel so hot and frazzled. Wait till I powder before you open the door. Do I look done in?

STELLA   Why no. You are as fresh as a daisy.

BLANCHE   One that's been picked a few days.

> [STELLA *opens the door and they enter.*]

STELLA   Well, well, well. I see you boys are still at it?

STANLEY   Where you been?

STELLA   Blanche and I took in a show. Blanche, this is Mr. Gonzales and Mr. Hubbell.

BLANCHE   Please don't get up.

STANLEY   Nobody's going to get up, so don't be worried.

STELLA   How much longer is this game going to continue?

STANLEY   Till we get ready to quit.

BLANCHE   Poker is so fascinating. Could I kibitz?

STANLEY   You could not. Why don't you women go up and sit with Eunice?

STELLA   Because it is nearly two-thirty. [BLANCHE *crosses into the bedroom and partially closes the portieres.*] Couldn't you call it quits after one more hand?

> [*A chair scrapes.* STANLEY *gives a loud whack of his hand on her thigh.*]

STELLA [*sharply*]   That's not fun, Stanley.

> [*The men laugh,* STELLA *goes into the bedroom.*]

STELLA   It makes me so mad when he does that in front of people.

BLANCHE   I think I will bathe.

STELLA   Again?

BLANCHE   My nerves are in knots. Is the bathroom occupied?

STELLA   I don't know.

> [BLANCHE *knocks,* MITCH *opens the door and comes out, still wiping his hands on a towel.*]

---

4. An adventurous and risky variant of poker.

BLANCHE   Oh!—good evening.

MITCH   Hello. [*He stares at her.*]

STELLA   Blanche, this is Harold Mitchell. My sister, Blanche DuBois.

MITCH [*with awkward courtesy*]   How do you do, Miss DuBois.

STELLA   How is your mother now, Mitch?

MITCH   About the same, thanks. She appreciated your sending over that custard.—Excuse me, please.

> [*He crosses slowly back into the kitchen, glancing back at* BLANCHE *and coughing a little shyly. He realizes he still has the towel in his hands and with an embarrassed laugh hands it to* STELLA. BLANCHE *looks after him with a certain interest.*]

BLANCHE   That one seems—superior to the others.

STELLA   Yes, he is.

BLANCHE   I thought he had a sort of sensitive look.

STELLA   His mother is sick.

BLANCHE   Is he married?

STELLA   No.

BLANCHE   Is he a wolf?

STELLA   Why, Blanche! [BLANCHE *laughs.*] I don't think he would be.

BLANCHE   What does—what does he do? [*She is unbuttoning her blouse.*]

STELLA   He's on the precision bench in the spare parts department. At the plant Stanley travels for.

BLANCHE   Is that something much?

STELLA   No. Stanley's the only one of his crowd that's likely to get anywhere.

BLANCHE   What makes you think Stanley will?

STELLA   Look at him.

BLANCHE   I've looked at him.

STELLA   Then you should know.

BLANCHE   I'm sorry, but I haven't noticed the stamp of genius even on Stanley's forehead.

> [*She takes off the blouse and stands in her pink silk brassiere and white skirt in the light through the portieres. The game has continued in undertones.*]

STELLA   It isn't on his forehead and it isn't genius.

BLANCHE   Oh. Well, what is it, and where? I would like to know.

STELLA   It's a drive that he has. You're standing in the light, Blanche!

BLANCHE   Oh, am I!

> [*She moves out of the yellow streak of light.* STELLA *has removed her dress and put on a light blue satin kimona.*]

STELLA [*with girlish laughter*]   You ought to see their wives.

BLANCHE [*laughingly*]   I can imagine. Big, beefy things, I suppose.

STELLA   You know that one upstairs? [*more laughter*] One time [*laughing*] the plaster— [*laughing*] cracked—

STANLEY   You hens cut out that conversation in there!

STELLA   You can't hear us.

STANLEY   Well, you can hear me and I said to hush up!

STELLA   This is my house and I'll talk as much as I want to!

BLANCHE   Stella, don't start a row.

STELLA   He's half drunk!—I'll be out in a minute.

[*She goes into the bathroom,* BLANCHE *rises and crosses leisurely to a small white radio and turns it on.*]

STANLEY Awright, Mitch, you in?

MITCH What? Oh!—No, I'm out!

[BLANCHE *moves back into the streak of light. She raises her arms and stretches, as she moves indolently back to the chair. Rhumba music comes over the radio.* MITCH *rises at the table.*]

STANLEY Who turned that on in there?

BLANCHE I did. Do you mind?

STANLEY Turn it off!

STEVE Aw, let the girls have their music.

PABLO Sure, that's good, leave it on!

STEVE Sounds like Xavier Cugat![5]

[STANLEY *jumps up and, crossing to the radio, turns it off. He stops short at the sight of* BLANCHE *in the chair. She returns his look without flinching. Then he sits again at the poker table. Two of the men have started arguing hotly.*]

STEVE I didn't hear you name it.

PABLO Didn't I name it, Mitch?

MITCH I wasn't listenin'.

PABLO What were you doing, then?

STANLEY He was looking through them drapes. [*He jumps up and jerks roughly at curtains to close them.*] Now deal the hand over again and let's play cards or quit. Some people get ants when they win.

[MITCH *rises as* STANLEY *returns to his seat.*]

STANLEY [*yelling*] Sit down!

MITCH I'm going to the "head." Deal me out.

PABLO Sure he's got ants now. Seven five-dollar bills in his pants pocket folded up tight as spitballs.

STEVE Tomorrow you'll see him at the cashier's window getting them changed into quarters.

STANLEY And when he goes home he'll deposit them one by one in a piggy bank his mother give him for Christmas. [*dealing*] This game is Spit in the Ocean.[6]

[MITCH *laughs uncomfortably and continues through the portieres. He stops just inside.*]

BLANCHE [*softly*] Hello! The Little Boys' Room is busy right now.

MITCH We've—been drinking beer.

BLANCHE I hate beer.

MITCH It's—a hot weather drink.

BLANCHE Oh, I don't think so; it always makes me warmer. Have you got any cigs? [*She has slipped on the dark red satin wrapper.*]

MITCH Sure.

BLANCHE What kind are they?

MITCH Luckies.

BLANCHE Oh, good. What a pretty case. Silver?

MITCH Yes. Yes; read the inscription.

---

5. Cuban bandleader (1900–1990), well known for composing and playing rhumbas.

6. Another variant of poker.

BLANCHE   Oh, is there an inscription? I can't make it out. [*He strikes a match and moves closer.*] Oh! [*reading with feigned difficulty*] "And if God choose, / I shall but love thee better—after—death!" Why, that's from my favorite sonnet by Mrs. Browning.[7]

MITCH   You know it?

BLANCHE   Certainly I do!

MITCH   There's a story connected with that inscription.

BLANCHE   It sounds like a romance.

MITCH   A pretty sad one.

BLANCHE   Oh?

MITCH   The girl's dead now.

BLANCHE   [*in a tone of deep sympathy*]   Oh!

MITCH   She knew she was dying when she give me this. A very strange girl, very sweet—very!

BLANCHE   She must have been fond of you. Sick people have such deep, sincere attachments.

MITCH   That's right, they certainly do.

BLANCHE   Sorrow makes for sincerity, I think.

MITCH   It sure brings it out in people.

BLANCHE   The little there is belongs to people who have experienced some sorrow.

MITCH   I believe you are right about that.

BLANCHE   I'm positive that I am. Show me a person who hasn't known any sorrow and I'll show you a shuperficial—Listen to me! My tongue is a little—thick! You boys are responsible for it. The show let out at eleven and we couldn't come home on account of the poker game so we had to go somewhere and drink. I'm not accustomed to having more than one drink. Two is the limit—and *three*! [*She laughs.*] Tonight I had three.

STANLEY   Mitch!

MITCH   Deal me out. I'm talking to Miss—

BLANCHE   DuBois.

MITCH   Miss DuBois?

BLANCHE   It's a French name. It means woods and Blanche means white, so the two together mean white woods. Like an orchard in spring! You can remember it by that.

MITCH   You're French?

BLANCHE   We are French by extraction. Our first American ancestors were French Huguenots.

MITCH   You are Stella's sister, are you not?

BLANCHE   Yes, Stella is my precious little sister. I call her little in spite of the fact she's somewhat older than I. Just slightly. Less than a year. Will you do something for me?

MITCH   Sure. What?

BLANCHE   I bought this adorable little colored paper lantern at a Chinese shop on Bourbon. Put it over the light bulb! Will you, please?

MITCH   Be glad to.

---

7. Elizabeth Barrett Browning (1806–1861), British poet, most famous for her sequence of love poems, *Sonnets from the Portuguese.* The quota-tion here is from sonnet 43, better known by its first line, "How do I love thee?"

BLANCHE I can't stand a naked light bulb, any more than I can a rude remark or a vulgar action.

MITCH [*adjusting the lantern*] I guess we strike you as being a pretty rough bunch.

BLANCHE I'm very adaptable—to circumstances.

MITCH Well, that's a good thing to be. You are visiting Stanley and Stella?

BLANCHE Stella hasn't been so well lately, and I came down to help her for a while. She's very run down.

MITCH You're not—?

BLANCHE Married? No, no. I'm an old maid schoolteacher!

MITCH You may teach school but you're certainly not an old maid.

BLANCHE Thank you, sir! I appreciate your gallantry!

MITCH So you are in the teaching profession?

BLANCHE Yes. Ah, yes . . .

MITCH Grade school or high school or—

STANLEY [*bellowing*] Mitch!

MITCH Coming!

BLANCHE Gracious, what lung-power! . . . I teach high school. In Laurel.

MITCH What do you teach? What subject?

BLANCHE Guess!

MITCH I bet you teach art or music? [BLANCHE *laughs delicately.*] Of course I could be wrong. You might teach arithmetic.

BLANCHE Never arithmetic, sir; never arithmetic! [*with a laugh*] I don't even know my multiplication tables! No, I have the misfortune of being an English instructor. I attempt to instill a bunch of bobby-soxers and drugstore Romeos with reverence for Hawthorne and Whitman and Poe!

MITCH I guess that some of them are more interested in other things.

BLANCHE How very right you are! Their literary heritage is not what most of them treasure above all else! But they're sweet things! And in the spring, it's touching to notice them making their first discovery of love! As if nobody had ever known it before!

[*The bathroom door opens and* STELLA *comes out.* BLANCHE *continues talking to* MITCH.]

Oh! Have you finished? Wait—I'll turn on the radio.

[*She turns the knobs on the radio and it begins to play "Wien, Wien, nur du allein."*[8] BLANCHE *waltzes to the music with romantic gestures,* MITCH *is delighted and moves in awkward imitation like a dancing bear.* STANLEY *stalks fiercely through the portieres into the bedroom. He crosses to the small white radio and snatches it off the table. With a shouted oath, he tosses the instrument out the window.*]

STELLA Drunk—drunk—animal thing, you! [*She rushes through to the poker table.*] All of you—please go home! If any of you have one spark of decency in you—

BLANCHE [*wildly*] Stella, watch out, he's—

[STANLEY *charges after* STELLA.]

MEN [*feebly*] Take it easy, Stanley. Easy, fellow.—Let's all—

STELLA You lay your hands on me and I'll—

[*She backs out of sight. He advances and disappears. There is the sound of a blow.* STELLA *cries out.* BLANCHE *screams and runs into the kitchen.*

8. Vienna, Vienna, you are my only (German); a waltz from an operetta by Franz Lehár (1870–1948).

The men rush forward and there is grappling and cursing. Something is overturned with a crash.]

BLANCHE [*shrilly*]   My sister is going to have a baby!

MITCH   This is terrible.

BLANCHE   Lunacy, absolute lunacy!

MITCH   Get him in here, men.

[STANLEY *is forced, pinioned by the two men, into the bedroom. He nearly throws them off. Then all at once he subsides and is limp in their grasp. They speak quietly and lovingly to him and he leans his face on one of their shoulders.*]

STELLA [*in a high, unnatural voice, out of sight*]   I want to go away, I want to go away!

MITCH   Poker shouldn't be played in a house with women.

[BLANCHE *rushes into the bedroom.*]

BLANCHE   I want my sister's clothes! We'll go to that woman's upstairs!

MITCH   Where is the clothes?

BLANCHE [*opening the closet*]   I've got them! [*She rushes through to* STELLA.] Stella, Stella, precious! Dear, dear little sister, don't be afraid!

[*With her arm around* STELLA, BLANCHE *guides her to the outside door and upstairs.*]

STANLEY [*dully*]   What's the matter; what's happened?

MITCH   You just blew your top, Stan.

PABLO   He's okay, now.

STEVE   Sure, my boy's okay!

MITCH   Put him on the bed and get a wet towel.

PABLO   I think coffee would do him a world of good, now.

STANLEY [*thickly*]   I want water.

MITCH   Put him under the shower!

[*The men talk quietly as they lead him to the bathroom.*]

STANLEY   Let the rut go of me, you sons of bitches!

[*Sounds of blows are heard. The water goes on full tilt.*]

STEVE   Let's get quick out of here!

[*They rush to the poker table and sweep up their winnings on their way out.*]

MITCH [*sadly but firmly*]   Poker should not be played in a house with women.

[*The door closes on them and the place is still. The Negro entertainers in the bar around the corner play "Paper Doll"[9] slow and blue. After a moment* STANLEY *comes out of the bathroom dripping water and still in his clinging wet polka dot drawers.*]

STANLEY   Stella! [*There is a pause.*] My baby doll's left me!

[*He breaks into sobs. Then he goes to the phone and dials, still shuddering with sobs.*]

Eunice? I want my baby! [*He waits a moment; then he hangs up and dials again.*] Eunice! I'll keep on ringin' until I talk with my baby!

[*An indistinguishable shrill voice is heard. He hurls phone to floor. Dissonant brass and piano sounds as the rooms dim out to darkness and the outer walls appear in the night light. The "Blue Piano" plays for a brief interval. Finally,* STANLEY *stumbles half-dressed out to the porch and*

---

9. Popular song of the early 1940s by Johnny Black.

down the wooden steps to the pavement before the building. There he throws back his head like a baying hound and bellows his wife's name: "Stella! Stella, sweetheart! Stella!"]

STANLEY   Stell-*lahhhhh!*

EUNICE [*calling down from the door of her upper apartment*]   Quit that howling out there an' go back to bed!

STANLEY   I want my baby down here. Stella, Stella!

EUNICE   She ain't comin' down so you quit! Or you'll git th' law on you!

STANLEY   Stella!

EUNICE   You can't beat on a woman an' then call 'er back! She won't come! And her goin' t' have a baby! . . . You stinker! You whelp of a Polack, you! I hope they do haul you in and turn the fire hose on you, same as the last time!

STANLEY [*humbly*]   Eunice, I want my girl to come down with me!

EUNICE   Hah! [*She slams her door.*]

STANLEY [*with heaven-splitting violence*]   STELL-LAHHHHH!

[*The low-tone clarinet moans. The door upstairs opens again.* STELLA *slips down the rickety stairs in her robe. Her eyes are glistening with tears and her hair loose about her throat and shoulders. They stare at each other. Then they come together with low, animal moans. He falls to his knees on the steps and presses his face to her belly, curving a little with maternity. Her eyes go blind with tenderness as she catches his head and raises him level with her. He snatches the screen door open and lifts her off her feet and bears her into the dark flat.* BLANCHE *comes out the upper landing in her robe and slips fearfully down the steps.*]

BLANCHE   Where is my little sister? Stella? Stella?

[*She stops before the dark entrance of her sister's flat. Then catches her breath as if struck. She rushes down to the walk before the house. She looks right and left as if for a sanctuary. The music fades away,* MITCH *appears from around the corner.*]

MITCH   Miss DuBois?

BLANCHE   Oh!

MITCH   All quiet on the Potomac now?

BLANCHE   She ran downstairs and went back in there with him.

MITCH   Sure she did.

BLANCHE   I'm terrified!

MITCH   Ho-ho! There's nothing to be scared of. They're crazy about each other.

BLANCHE   I'm not used to such—

MITCH   Naw, it's a shame this had to happen when you just got here. But don't take it serious.

BLANCHE   Violence! Is so—

MITCH   Set down on the steps and have a cigarette with me.

BLANCHE   I'm not properly dressed.

MITCH   That don't make no difference in the Quarter.

BLANCHE   Such a pretty silver case.

MITCH   I showed you the inscription, didn't I?

BLANCHE   Yes. [*During the pause, she looks up at the sky.*] There's so much— so much confusion in the world . . . [*He coughs diffidently.*] Thank you for being so kind! I need kindness now.

Scene Four

It is early the following morning. There is a confusion of street cries like a choral chant.

STELLA *is lying down in the bedroom. Her face is serene in the early morning sunlight. One hand rests on her belly, rounding slightly with new maternity. From the other dangles a book of colored comics. Her eyes and lips have that almost narcotized tranquility that is in the faces of Eastern idols.*

The table is sloppy with remains of breakfast and the debris of the preceding night, and STANLEY'S *gaudy pyjamas lie across the threshold of the bathroom. The outside door is slightly ajar on a sky of summer brilliance.*

BLANCHE *appears at this door. She has spent a sleepless night and her appearance entirely contrasts with* STELLA'S. *She presses her knuckles nervously to her lips as she looks through the door, before entering.*

BLANCHE   Stella?

STELLA [*stirring lazily*]   Hmmh?
> [BLANCHE *utters a moaning cry and runs into the bedroom, throwing herself down beside* STELLA *in a rush of hysterical tenderness.*]

BLANCHE   Baby, my baby sister!

STELLA [*drawing away from her*]   Blanche, what is the matter with you?
> [BLANCHE *straightens up slowly and stands beside the bed looking down at her sister with knuckles pressed to her lips.*]

BLANCHE   He's left?

STELLA   Stan? Yes.

BLANCHE   Will he be back?

STELLA   He's gone to get the car greased. Why?

BLANCHE   Why! I've been half crazy, Stella! When I found out you'd been insane enough to come back in here after what happened—I started to rush in after you!

STELLA   I'm glad you didn't.

BLANCHE   What were you thinking of? [STELLA *makes an indefinite gesture.*] Answer me! What? What?

STELLA   Please, Blanche! Sit down and stop yelling.

BLANCHE   All right, Stella. I will repeat the question quietly now. How could you come back in this place last night? Why, you must have slept with him!
> [STELLA *gets up in a calm and leisurely way.*]

STELLA   Blanche, I'd forgotten how excitable you are. You're making much too much fuss about this.

BLANCHE   Am I?

STELLA   Yes, you are, Blanche. I know how it must have seemed to you and I'm awful sorry it had to happen, but it wasn't anything as serious as you seem to take it. In the first place, when men are drinking and playing poker anything can happen. It's always a powder-keg. He didn't know what he was doing. . . . He was as good as a lamb when I came back and he's really very, very ashamed of himself.

BLANCHE   And that—that makes it all right?

STELLA   No, it isn't all right for anybody to make such a terrible row, but—people do sometimes. Stanley's always smashed things. Why, on our wedding night—soon as we came in here—he snatched off one of my slippers and rushed about the place smashing light bulbs with it.

BLANCHE He did—*what?*

STELLA He smashed all the light bulbs with the heel of my slipper! [*She laughs.*]

BLANCHE And you—you *let* him? Didn't *run,* didn't *scream?*

STELLA I was—sort of—thrilled by it. [*She waits for a moment.*] Eunice and you had breakfast?

BLANCHE Do you suppose I wanted any breakfast?

STELLA There's some coffee left on the stove.

BLANCHE You're so—matter of fact about it, Stella.

STELLA What other can I be? He's taken the radio to get it fixed. It didn't land on the pavement so only one tube was smashed.

BLANCHE And you are standing there smiling!

STELLA What do you want me to do?

BLANCHE Pull yourself together and face the facts.

STELLA What are they, in your opinion?

BLANCHE In my opinion? You're married to a madman!

STELLA No!

BLANCHE Yes, you are, your fix is worse than mine is! Only you're not being sensible about it. I'm going to *do* something. Get hold of myself and make myself a new life!

STELLA Yes?

BLANCHE But you've given in. And that isn't right, you're not old! You can get out.

STELLA [*slowly and emphatically*] I'm not in anything I want to get out of.

BLANCHE [*incredulously*] What—Stella?

STELLA I said I am not in anything that I have a desire to get out of. Look at the mess in this room! And those empty bottles! They went through two cases last night! He promised this morning that he was going to quit having these poker parties, but you know how long such a promise is going to keep. Oh, well, it's his pleasure, like mine is movies and bridge. People have got to tolerate each other's habits, I guess.

BLANCHE I don't understand you. [STELLA *turns toward her.*] I don't understand your indifference. Is this a Chinese philosophy you've—cultivated?

STELLA Is what—what?

BLANCHE This—shuffling about and mumbling—'One tube smashed—beer bottles—mess in the kitchen!'—as if nothing out of the ordinary has happened! [STELLA *laughs uncertainly and picking up the broom, twirls it in her hands.*]

BLANCHE Are you deliberately shaking that thing in my face?

STELLA No.

BLANCHE Stop it. Let go of that broom. I won't have you cleaning up for him!

STELLA Then who's going to do it? Are you?

BLANCHE I? I!

STELLA No, I didn't think so.

BLANCHE Oh, let me think, if only my mind would function! We've got to get hold of some money, that's the way out!

STELLA I guess that money is always nice to get hold of.

BLANCHE   Listen to me. I have an idea of some kind. [*Shakily she twists a cigarette into her holder.*] Do you remember Shep Huntleigh? [STELLA *shakes her head.*] Of course you remember Shep Huntleigh. I went out with him at college and wore his pin for a while. Well—

STELLA   Well?

BLANCHE   I ran into him last winter. You know I went to Miami during the Christmas holidays?

STELLA   No.

BLANCHE   Well, I did. I took the trip as an investment, thinking I'd meet someone with a million dollars.

STELLA   Did you?

BLANCHE   Yes. I ran into Shep Huntleigh—I ran into him on Biscayne Boulevard, on Christmas Eve, about dusk . . . getting into his car—Cadillac convertible; must have been a block long!

STELLA   I should think it would have been—inconvenient in traffic!

BLANCHE   You've heard of oil wells?

STELLA   Yes—remotely.

BLANCHE   He has them, all over Texas. Texas is literally spouting gold in his pockets.

STELLA   My, my.

BLANCHE   Y'know how indifferent I am to money. I think of money in terms of what it does for you. But he could do it, he could certainly do it!

STELLA   Do what, Blanche?

BLANCHE   Why—set us up in a—shop!

STELLA   What kind of a shop?

BLANCHE   Oh, a—shop of some kind! He could do it with half what his wife throws away at the races.

STELLA   He's married?

BLANCHE   Honey, would I be here if the man weren't married? [STELLA *laughs a little.* BLANCHE *suddenly springs up and crosses to phone. She speaks shrilly.*] How do I get Western Union?—Operator! Western Union!

STELLA   That's a dial phone, honey.

BLANCHE   I can't dial, I'm too—

STELLA   Just dial O.

BLANCHE   O?

STELLA   Yes, "O" for Operator! [BLANCHE *considers a moment; then she puts the phone down.*]

BLANCHE   Give me a pencil. Where is a slip of paper? I've got to write it down first—the message, I mean . . . [*She goes to the dressing table, and grabs up a sheet of Kleenex and an eyebrow pencil for writing equipment.*] Let me see now . . . [*She bites the pencil.*] 'Darling Shep. Sister and I in desperate situation.'

STELLA   I beg your pardon!

BLANCHE   'Sister and I in desperate situation. Will explain details later. Would you be interested in—?' [*She bites the pencil again.*] 'Would you be—interested—in . . .' [*She smashes the pencil on the table and springs up.*] You never get anywhere with direct appeals!

STELLA   [*with a laugh*]   Don't be so ridiculous, darling!

BLANCHE   But I'll think of something, I've *got* to think of—*some*thing! Don't laugh at me, Stella! Please, please don't—I—I want you to look at the contents of my purse! Here's what's in it! [*She snatches her purse open.*] Sixty-five measly cents in coin of the realm!

STELLA [*crossing to bureau*]   Stanley doesn't give me a regular allowance, he likes to pay bills himself, but—this morning he gave me ten dollars to smooth things over. You take five of it, Blanche, and I'll keep the rest.

BLANCHE   Oh, no. No, Stella.

STELLA [*insisting*]   I know how it helps your morale just having a little pocket-money on you.

BLANCHE   No, thank you—I'll take to the streets!

STELLA   Talk sense! How did you happen to get so low on funds?

BLANCHE   Money just goes—it goes places. [*She rubs her forehead.*] Sometime today I've got to get hold of a Bromo!¹

STELLA   I'll fix you one now.

BLANCHE   Not yet—I've got to keep thinking!

STELLA   I wish you'd just let things go, at least for a—while . . .

BLANCHE   Stella, I can't live with him! You can, he's your husband. But how could I stay here with him, after last night, with just those curtains between us?

STELLA   Blanche, you saw him at his worst last night.

BLANCHE   On the contrary, I saw him at his best! What such a man has to offer is animal force and he gave a wonderful exhibition of that! But the only way to live with such a man is to—go to bed with him! And that's your job—not mine!

STELLA   After you've rested a little, you'll see it's going to work out. You don't have to worry about anything while you're here. I mean—expenses . . .

BLANCHE   I have to plan for us both, to get us both—out!

STELLA   You take it for granted that I am in something that I want to get out of.

BLANCHE   I take it for granted that you still have sufficient memory of Belle Reve to find this place and these poker players impossible to live with.

STELLA   Well, you're taking entirely too much for granted.

BLANCHE   I can't believe you're in earnest.

STELLA   No?

BLANCHE   I understand how it happened—a little. You saw him in uniform, an officer, not here but—

STELLA   I'm not sure it would have made any difference where I saw him.

BLANCHE   Now don't say it was one of those mysterious electric things between people! If you do I'll laugh in your face.

STELLA   I am not going to say anything more at all about it!

BLANCHE   All right, then, don't!

STELLA   But there are things that happen between a man and a woman in the dark—that sort of make everything else seem—unimportant. [*Pause.*]

BLANCHE   What you are talking about is brutal desire—just—Desire!— the name of that rattle-trap streetcar that bangs through the Quarter, up one old narrow street and down another . . .

STELLA   Haven't you ever ridden on that streetcar?

---

1. Short for Bromo-seltzer, a headache remedy.

BLANCHE   It brought me here.—Where I'm not wanted and where I'm ashamed to be . . .

STELLA   Then don't you think your superior attitude is a bit out of place?

BLANCHE   I am not being or feeling at all superior, Stella. Believe me I'm not! It's just this. This is how I look at it. A man like that is someone to go out with—once—twice—three times when the devil is in you. But live with? Have a child by?

STELLA   I have told you I love him.

BLANCHE   Then I *tremble* for you! I just—*tremble* for you. . . .

STELLA   I can't help your trembling if you insist on trembling!

[*There is a pause.*]

BLANCHE   May I—speak—*plainly?*

STELLA   Yes, do. Go ahead. As plainly as you want to.

[*Outside, a train approaches. They are silent till the noise subsides. They are both in the bedroom. Under cover of the train's noise* STANLEY *enters from outside. He stands unseen by the women, holding some packages in his arms, and overhears their following conversation. He wears an undershirt and grease-stained seersucker pants.*]

BLANCHE   Well—if you'll forgive me—he's *common!*

STELLA   Why, yes, I suppose he is.

BLANCHE   Suppose! You can't have forgotten that much of our bringing up, Stella, that you just *suppose* that any part of a gentleman's in his nature! *Not one particle, no!* Oh, if he was just—*ordinary!* Just *plain*— but good and wholesome, but—*no.* There's something downright—*bestial*—about him! You're hating me saying this, aren't you?

STELLA [*coldly*]   Go on and say it all, Blanche.

BLANCHE   He acts like an animal, has an animal's habits! Eats like one, moves like one, talks like one! There's even something—sub-human— something not quite to the stage of humanity yet! Yes, something—ape-like about him, like one of those pictures I've seen in—anthropological studies! Thousands and thousands of years have passed him right by, and there he is—Stanley Kowalski—survivor of the Stone Age! Bearing the raw meat home from the kill in the jungle! And you—*you* here— *waiting* for him! Maybe he'll strike you or maybe grunt and kiss you! That is, if kisses have been discovered yet! Night falls and the other apes gather! There in the front of the cave, all grunting like him, and swilling and gnawing and hulking! His poker night! you call it—this party of apes! Somebody growls—some creature snatches at something—the fight is on! *God!* Maybe we are a long way from being made in God's image, but Stella—my sister—there has been *some* progress since then! Such things as art—as poetry and music—such kinds of new light have come into the world since then! In some kinds of people some tenderer feelings have had some little beginning! That we have got to make *grow!* And *cling* to, and hold as our flag! In this dark march toward whatever it is we're approaching. . . . *Don't—don't hang back with the brutes!*

[*Another train passes outside.* STANLEY *hesitates, licking his lips. Then suddenly he turns stealthily about and withdraws through front door. The women are still unaware of his presence. When the train has passed he calls through the closed front door.*]

STANLEY   Hey! Hey, Stella!

STELLA [*who has listened gravely to* BLANCHE]   Stanley!

BLANCHE   Stell, I—

[*But* STELLA *has gone to the front door.* STANLEY *enters casually with his packages.*]

STANLEY   Hiyuh, Stella. Blanche back?

STELLA   Yes, she's back.

STANLEY   Hiyuh, Blanche. [*He grins at her.*]

STELLA   You must've got under the car.

STANLEY   Them darn mechanics at Fritz's don't know their ass fr'm—Hey!

[STELLA *has embraced him with both arms, fiercely, and full in the view of* BLANCHE. *He laughs and clasps her head to him. Over her head he grins through the curtains at* BLANCHE. *As the lights fade away, with a lingering brightness on their embrace, the music of the "Blue Piano" and trumpet and drums is heard.*]

Scene Five

BLANCHE *is seated in the bedroom fanning herself with a palm leaf as she reads over a just-completed letter. Suddenly she bursts into a peal of laughter.* STELLA *is dressing in the bedroom.*

STELLA   What are you laughing at, honey?

BLANCHE   Myself, myself, for being such a liar! I'm writing a letter to Shep. [*She picks up the letter.*] "Darling Shep. I am spending the summer on the wing, making flying visits here and there. And who knows, perhaps I shall take a sudden notion to *swoop* down on *Dallas!* How would you feel about that? Ha-ha! [*She laughs nervously and brightly, touching her throat as if actually talking to* SHEP.] Forewarned is forearmed, as they say!"— How does that sound?

STELLA   Uh-huh . . .

BLANCHE [*going on nervously*]   "Most of my sister's friends go north in the summer but some have homes on the Gulf and there has been a continued round of entertainments, teas, cocktails, and luncheons—"

[*A disturbance is heard upstairs at the Hubbells' apartment.*]

STELLA   Eunice seems to be having some trouble with Steve.

[EUNICE'*s voice shouts in terrible wrath.*]

EUNICE   I heard about you and that blonde!

STEVE   That's a damn lie!

EUNICE   You ain't pulling the wool over my eyes! I wouldn't mind if you'd stay down at the Four Deuces, but you always going up.

STEVE   Who ever seen me up?

EUNICE   I seen you chasing her 'round the balcony—I'm gonna call the vice squad!

STEVE   Don't you throw that at me!

EUNICE [*shrieking*]   You hit me! I'm gonna call the police!

[*A clatter of aluminum striking a wall is heard, followed by a man's angry roar, shouts and overturned furniture. There is a crash; then a relative hush.*]

BLANCHE [*brightly*]   Did he *kill* her?

[EUNICE *appears on the steps in daemonic disorder.*]

STELLA   No! She's coming downstairs.

EUNICE   Call the police, I'm going to call the police! [*She rushes around the corner.*]

> [*They laugh lightly.* STANLEY *comes around the corner in his green and scarlet silk bowling shirt. He trots up the steps and bangs into the kitchen.* BLANCHE *registers his entrance with nervous gestures.*]

STANLEY   What's a matter with Eun-uss?

STELLA   She and Steve had a row. Has she got the police?

STANLEY   Naw. She's gettin' a drink.

STELLA   That's much more practical!

> [STEVE *comes down nursing a bruise on his forehead and looks in the door.*]

STEVE   She here?

STANLEY   Naw, naw. At the Four Deuces.

STEVE   That rutting hunk! [*He looks around the corner a bit timidly, then turns with affected boldness and runs after her.*]

BLANCHE   I must jot that down in my notebook. Ha-ha! I'm compiling a notebook of quaint little words and phrases I've picked up here.

STANLEY   You won't pick up nothing here you ain't heard before.

BLANCHE   Can I count on that?

STANLEY   You can count on it up to five hundred.

BLANCHE   That's a mighty high number. [*He jerks open the bureau drawer, slams it shut and throws shoes in a corner. At each noise* BLANCHE *winces slightly. Finally she speaks.*] What sign were you born under?

STANLEY   [*while he is dressing*]   Sign?

BLANCHE   Astrological sign. I bet you were born under Aries. Aries people are forceful and dynamic. They dote on noise! They love to bang things around! You must have had lots of banging around in the army and now that you're out, you make up for it by treating inanimate objects with such a fury!

> [STELLA *has been going in and out of closet during this scene. Now she pops her head out of the closet.*]

STELLA   Stanley was born just five minutes after Christmas.

BLANCHE   Capricorn—the Goat!

STANLEY   What sign were *you* born under?

BLANCHE   Oh, my birthday's next month, the fifteenth of September; that's under Virgo.

STANLEY   What's Virgo?

BLANCHE   Virgo is the Virgin.

STANLEY   [*contemptuously*]   Hah! [*He advances a little as he knots his tie.*] Say, do you happen to know somebody named Shaw?

> [*Her face expresses a faint shock. She reaches for the cologne bottle and dampens her handkerchief as she answers carefully.*]

BLANCHE   Why, everybody knows somebody named Shaw!

STANLEY   Well, this somebody named Shaw is under the impression he met you in Laurel, but I figure he must have got you mixed up with some other party because this other party is someone he met at a hotel called the Flamingo.

> [BLANCHE *laughs breathlessly as she touches the cologne-dampened handkerchief to her temples.*]

BLANCHE   I'm afraid he does have me mixed up with this "other party."
  The Hotel Flamingo is not the sort of establishment I would dare to be
  seen in!

STANLEY   You know of it?

BLANCHE   Yes, I've seen it and smelled it.

STANLEY   You must've got pretty close if you could smell it.

BLANCHE   The odor of cheap perfume is penetrating.

STANLEY   That stuff you use is expensive?

BLANCHE   Twenty-five dollars an ounce! I'm nearly out. That's just a hint
  if you want to remember my birthday! [*She speaks lightly but her voice
  has a note of fear.*]

STANLEY   Shaw must've got you mixed up. He goes in and out of Laurel
  all the time so he can check on it and clear up any mistake.

  [*He turns away and crosses to the portieres.* BLANCHE *closes her eyes as if
  faint. Her hand trembles as she lifts the handkerchief again to her forehead.* STEVE *and* EUNICE *come around corner.* STEVE'S *arm is around*
  EUNICE'S *shoulder and she is sobbing luxuriously and he is cooing love-
  words. There is a murmur of thunder as they go slowly upstairs in a tight
  embrace.*]

STANLEY [*to* STELLA]   I'll wait for you at the Four Deuces!

STELLA   Hey! Don't I rate one kiss?

STANLEY   Not in front of your sister.

  [*He goes out.* BLANCHE *rises from her chair. She seems faint; looks
  about her with an expression of almost panic.*]

BLANCHE   Stella! What have you heard about me?

STELLA   Huh?

BLANCHE   What have people been telling you about me?

STELLA   Telling?

BLANCHE   You haven't heard any—unkind—gossip about me?

STELLA   Why, no, Blanche, of course not!

BLANCHE   Honey, there was—a good deal of talk in Laurel.

STELLA   About *you*, Blanche?

BLANCHE   I wasn't so good the last two years or so, after Belle Reve had
  started to slip through my fingers.

STELLA   All of us do things we—

BLANCHE   I never was hard or self-sufficient enough. When people are
  soft—soft people have got to shimmer and glow—they've got to put on
  soft colors, the colors of butterfly wings, and put a—paper lantern over
  the light. . . . It isn't enough to be soft. You've got to be soft *and attractive.* And I—I'm fading now! I don't know how much longer I can turn
  the trick.

  [*The afternoon has faded to dusk.* STELLA *goes into the bedroom and
  turns on the light under the paper lantern. She holds a bottled soft
  drink in her hand.*]

BLANCHE   Have you been listening to me?

STELLA   I don't listen to you when you are being morbid! [*She advances
  with the bottled Coke.*]

BLANCHE [*with abrupt change to gaiety*]   Is that Coke for me?

STELLA   Not for anyone else!

BLANCHE   Why, you precious thing, you! Is it just Coke?

STELLA [*turning*]   You mean you want a shot in it!

BLANCHE   Well, honey, a shot never does a Coke any harm! Let me! You mustn't wait on me!

STELLA   I like to wait on you, Blanche. It makes it seem more like home. [*She goes into the kitchen, finds a glass and pours a shot of whiskey into it.*]

BLANCHE   I have to admit I love to be waited on . . . [*She rushes into the bedroom.* STELLA *goes to her with the glass.* BLANCHE *suddenly clutches* STELLA'S *free hand with a moaning sound and presses the hand to her lips.* STELLA *is embarrassed by her show of emotion.* BLANCHE *speaks in a choked voice.*] You're—you're—so *good* to me! And I—

STELLA   Blanche.

BLANCHE   I know, I won't! You hate me to talk sentimental! But honey, *believe* I feel things more than I *tell* you! I *won't* stay long! I won't, I *promise* I—

STELLA   Blanche!

BLANCHE [*hysterically*]   I won't, I promise, *I'll* go! Go *soon*! I will *really*! I *won't* hang around until he—throws me out . . .

STELLA   Now will you stop talking foolish?

BLANCHE   Yes, honey. Watch how you pour—that fizzy stuff foams over! [BLANCHE *laughs shrilly and grabs the glass, but her hand shakes so it almost slips from her grasp.* STELLA *pours the Coke into the glass. It foams over and spills.* BLANCHE *gives a piercing cry.*]

STELLA [*shocked by the cry*]   Heavens!

BLANCHE   Right on my pretty white skirt!

STELLA   Oh . . . Use my hanky. Blot gently.

BLANCHE [*slowly recovering*]   I know—gently—gently . . .

STELLA   Did it stain?

BLANCHE   Not a bit. Ha-ha! Isn't that lucky? [*She sits down shakily, taking a grateful drink. She holds the glass in both hands and continues to laugh a little.*]

STELLA   Why did you scream like that?

BLANCHE   I don't know why I screamed! [*continuing nervously*] Mitch— Mitch is coming at seven. I guess I am just feeling nervous about our relations. [*She begins to talk rapidly and breathlessly.*] He hasn't gotten a thing but a good-night kiss, that's all I have given him, Stella. I want his respect. And men don't want anything they get too easy. But on the other hand men lose interest quickly. Especially when the girl is over—thirty. They think a girl over thirty ought to—the vulgar term is—"put out." . . . And I—I'm not "putting out." Of course he—he doesn't know—I mean I haven't informed him—of my real age!

STELLA   Why are you sensitive about your age?

BLANCHE   Because of hard knocks my vanity's been given. What I mean is—he thinks I'm sort of—prim and proper, you know! [*She laughs out sharply.*] I want to *deceive* him enough to make him—want me . . .

STELLA   Blanche, do you want *him*?

BLANCHE   I want to *rest*! I want to breathe quietly again! Yes—I *want* Mitch . . . *very badly*! Just think! If it happens! I can leave here and not be anyone's problem . . .

[STANLEY *comes around the corner with a drink under his belt.*]

STANLEY [*bawling*]   Hey, Steve! Hey, Eunice! Hey, Stella!
[*There are joyous calls from above. Trumpet and drums are heard from around the corner.*]

STELLA [*kissing* BLANCHE *impulsively*]   It *will* happen!

BLANCHE [*doubtfully*]   It will?

STELLA   It *will*! [*She goes across into the kitchen, looking back at* BLANCHE.]
It will, honey, *it will.* . . . But don't take another drink! [*Her voice catches as she goes out the door to meet her husband.*]

[BLANCHE *sinks faintly back in her chair with her drink.* EUNICE *shrieks with laughter and runs down the steps.* STEVE *bounds after her with goatlike screeches and chases her around corner.* STANLEY *and* STELLA *twine arms as they follow, laughing. Dusk settles deeper. The music from the Four Deuces is slow and blue.*]

BLANCHE   Ah, me, ah, me, ah, me . . .
[*Her eyes fall shut and the palm leaf fan drops from her fingers. She slaps her hand on the chair arm a couple of times. There is a little glimmer of lightning about the building.* A YOUNG MAN *comes along the street and rings the bell.*]

BLANCHE   Come in.
[*The* YOUNG MAN *appears through the portieres. She regards him with interest.*]

BLANCHE   Well, well! What can I do for *you*?

YOUNG MAN   I'm collecting for *The Evening Star.*

BLANCHE   I didn't know that stars took up collections.

YOUNG MAN   It's the paper.

BLANCHE   I know, I was joking—feebly! Will you—have a drink?

YOUNG MAN   No, ma'am. No, thank you. I can't drink on the job.

BLANCHE   Oh, well, now, let's see. . . . No, I don't have a dime! I'm not the lady of the house. I'm her sister from Mississippi. I'm one of those poor relations you've heard about.

YOUNG MAN   That's all right. I'll drop by later. [*He starts to go out. She approaches a little.*]

BLANCHE   Hey! [*He turns back shyly. She puts a cigarette in a long holder.*] Could you give me a light? [*She crosses toward him. They meet at the door between the two rooms.*]

YOUNG MAN   Sure. [*He takes out a lighter.*] This doesn't always work.

BLANCHE   It's temperamental? [*It flares.*] Ah!—thank you. [*He starts away again.*] Hey! [*He turns again, still more uncertainly. She goes close to him.*] Uh—what time is it?

YOUNG MAN   Fifteen of seven, ma'am.

BLANCHE   So late? Don't you just love these long rainy afternoons in New Orleans when an hour isn't just an hour—but a little piece of eternity dropped into your hands—and who knows what to do with it? [*She touches his shoulders.*] You—uh—didn't get wet in the rain?

YOUNG MAN   No, ma'am. I stepped inside.

BLANCHE   In a drugstore? And had a soda?

YOUNG MAN   Uh-huh.

BLANCHE   Chocolate?

YOUNG MAN   No, ma'am. Cherry.

BLANCHE [*laughing*]   Cherry!

YOUNG MAN   A cherry soda.

BLANCHE   You make my mouth water. [*She touches his cheek lightly, and smiles. Then she goes to the trunk.*]

YOUNG MAN   Well, I'd better be going—

BLANCHE [*stopping him*]   Young man!

> [*He turns. She takes a large, gossamer scarf from the trunk and drapes it about her shoulders. In the ensuing pause, the "Blue Piano" is heard. It continues through the rest of this scene and the opening of the next. The young man clears his throat and looks yearningly at the door.*]

Young man! Young, young, young man! Has anyone ever told you that you look like a young Prince out of the Arabian Nights?

> [*The* YOUNG MAN *laughs uncomfortably and stands like a bashful kid.* BLANCHE *speaks softly to him.*]

Well, you do, honey lamb! Come here. I want to kiss you, just once, softly and sweetly on your mouth!

> [*Without waiting for him to accept, she crosses quickly to him and presses her lips to his.*]

Now run along, now, quickly! It would be nice to keep you, but I've got to be good—and keep my hands off children.

> [*He stares at her a moment. She opens the door for him and blows a kiss at him as he goes down the steps with a dazed look. She stands there a little dreamily after he has disappeared. Then* MITCH *appears around the corner with a bunch of roses.*]

BLANCHE [*gaily*]   Look who's coming! My Rosenkavalier! Bow to me first . . . now present them! *Ahhhh—Merciiii!*[2]

> [*She looks at him over them, coquettishly pressing them to her lips. He beams at her self-consciously.*]

Scene Six

It is about two A.M on the same evening. The outer wall of the building is visible. BLANCHE *and* MITCH *come in. The utter exhaustion which only a neurasthenic personality can know is evident in* BLANCHE'S *voice and manner.* MITCH *is stolid but depressed. They have probably been out to the amusement park on Lake Pontchartrain, for* MITCH *is bearing, upside down, a plaster statuette of Mae West, the sort of prize won at shooting galleries and carnival games of chance.*

BLANCHE [*stopping lifelessly at the steps*]   Well— [MITCH *laughs uneasily.*] Well . . .

MITCH   I guess it must be pretty late—and you're tired.

BLANCHE   Even the hot tamale man has deserted the street, and he hangs on till the end. [MITCH *laughs uneasily again.*] How will you get home?

MITCH   I'll walk over to Bourbon and catch an owl-car.

BLANCHE [*laughing grimly*]   Is that streetcar named Desire still grinding along the tracks at this hour?

MITCH [*heavily*]   I'm afraid you haven't gotten much fun out of this evening, Blanche.

BLANCHE   I spoiled it for *you.*

---

2. "Merci": thank you (French). "My Rosenkavalier": Knight of the Rose (German); title of a romantic opera (1911) by Richard Strauss.

MITCH   No, you didn't, but I felt all the time that I wasn't giving you much—entertainment.

BLANCHE   I simply couldn't rise to the occasion. That was all. I don't think I've ever tried so hard to be gay and made such a dismal mess of it. I get ten points for trying!—I *did* try.

MITCH   Why did you try if you didn't feel like it, Blanche?

BLANCHE   I was just obeying the law of nature.

MITCH   Which law is that?

BLANCHE   The one that says the lady must entertain the gentleman—or no dice! See if you can locate my door key in this purse. When I'm so tired my fingers are all thumbs!

MITCH [*rooting in her purse*]   This it?

BLANCHE   No, honey, that's the key to my trunk which I must soon be packing.

MITCH   You mean you are leaving here soon?

BLANCHE   I've outstayed my welcome.

MITCH   This it?

[*The music fades away.*]

BLANCHE   Eureka! Honey, you open the door while I take a last look at the sky. [*She leans on the porch rail. He opens the door and stands awkwardly behind her.*] I'm looking for the Pleiades, the Seven Sisters, but these girls are not out tonight. Oh, yes they are, there they are! God bless them! All in a bunch going home from their little bridge party. . . . Y' get the door open? Good boy! I guess you—want to go now . . .

[*He shuffles and coughs a little.*]

MITCH   Can I—uh—kiss you—good night?

BLANCHE   Why do you always ask me if you may?

MITCH   I don't know whether you want me to or not.

BLANCHE   Why should you be so doubtful?

MITCH   That night when we parked by the lake and I kissed you, you—

BLANCHE   Honey, it wasn't the kiss I objected to. I liked the kiss very much. It was the other little—familiarity—that I—felt obliged to—discourage. . . . I didn't resent it! Not a bit in the world! In fact, I was somewhat flattered that you—desired me! But, honey, you know as well as I do that a single girl, a girl alone in the world, has got to keep a firm hold on her emotions or she'll be lost!

MITCH [*solemnly*]   Lost?

BLANCHE   I guess you are used to girls that like to be lost. The kind that get lost immediately, on the first date!

MITCH   I like you to be exactly the way that you are, because in all my—experience—I have never known anyone like you.

[BLANCHE *looks at him gravely; then she bursts into laughter and then claps a hand to her mouth.*]

MITCH   Are you laughing at me?

BLANCHE   No, honey. The lord and lady of the house have not yet returned, so come in. We'll have a nightcap. Let's leave the lights off. Shall we?

MITCH   You just—do what you want to.

[BLANCHE *precedes him into the kitchen. The outer wall of the building disappears and the interiors of the two rooms can be dimly seen.*]

BLANCHE [*remaining in the first room*] The other room's more comfortable—go on in. This crashing around in the dark is my search for some liquor.

MITCH You want a drink?

BLANCHE I want *you* to have a drink! You have been so anxious and solemn all evening, and so have I; we have both been anxious and solemn and now for these few last remaining moments of our lives together—I want to create—*joie de vivre*! I'm lighting a candle.

MITCH That's good.

BLANCHE We are going to be very Bohemian. We are going to pretend that we are sitting in a little artists' cafe on the Left Bank in Paris! [*She lights a candle stub and puts it in a bottle.*] *Je suis la Dame aux Camellias! Vous êtes—Armand!*[3] Understand French?

MITCH [*heavily*] Naw. Naw, I—

BLANCHE *Voulez-vous couchez avec moi ce soir? Vous ne comprenez pas? Ah, quelle dommage!*[4]—I mean it's a damned good thing. . . . I've found some liquor! Just enough for two shots without any dividends, honey . . .

MITCH [*heavily*] That's—good.

[*She enters the bedroom with the drinks and the candle.*]

BLANCHE Sit down! Why don't you take off your coat and loosen your collar?

MITCH I better leave it on.

BLANCHE No. I want you to be comfortable.

MITCH I am ashamed of the way I perspire. My shirt is sticking to me.

BLANCHE Perspiration is healthy. If people didn't perspire they would die in five minutes. [*She takes his coat from him.*] This is a nice coat. What kind of material is it?

MITCH They call that stuff alpaca.

BLANCHE Oh. Alpaca.

MITCH It's very light-weight alpaca.

BLANCHE Oh. Light-weight alpaca.

MITCH I don't like to wear a wash-coat even in summer because I sweat through it.

BLANCHE Oh.

MITCH And it don't look neat on me. A man with a heavy build has got to be careful of what he puts on him so he don't look too clumsy.

BLANCHE You are not too heavy.

MITCH You don't think I am?

BLANCHE You are not the delicate type. You have a massive bone-structure and a very imposing physique.

MITCH Thank you. Last Christmas I was given a membership to the New Orleans Athletic Club.

BLANCHE Oh, good.

MITCH It was the finest present I ever was given. I work out there with the weights and I swim and I keep myself fit. When I started there, I was

3. I am the Lady of the Camellias! You are— Armand! (French). Both are characters in the popular romantic play *La Dame aux Camélias* (1852), by the French author Alexandre Dumas *fils*; she is a courtesan who gives up her true love, Armand.

4. Would you like to sleep with me this evening? You don't understand? Ah, what a pity! (French).

getting soft in the belly but now my belly is hard. It is so hard now that a man can punch me in the belly and it don't hurt me. Punch me! Go on! See?

[*She pokes lightly at him.*]

BLANCHE   Gracious. [*Her hand touches her chest.*]

MITCH   Guess how much I weigh, Blanche?

BLANCHE   Oh, I'd say in the vicinity of—one hundred and eighty?

MITCH   Guess again.

BLANCHE   Not that much?

MITCH   No. More.

BLANCHE   Well, you're a tall man and you can carry a good deal of weight without looking awkward.

MITCH   I weigh two hundred and seven pounds and I'm six feet one and one half inches tall in my bare feet—without shoes on. And that is what I weigh stripped.

BLANCHE   Oh, my goodness, me! It's awe-inspiring.

MITCH   [*embarrassed*]   My weight is not a very interesting subject to talk about. [*He hesitates for a moment.*] What's yours?

BLANCHE   My weight?

MITCH   Yes.

BLANCHE   Guess!

MITCH   Let me lift you.

BLANCHE   Samson![5] Go on, lift me. [*He comes behind her and puts his hands on her waist and raises her lightly off the ground.*] Well?

MITCH   You are light as a feather.

BLANCHE   Ha-ha! [*He lowers her but keeps his hands on her waist.* BLANCHE *speaks with an affectation of demureness.*] You may release me now.

MITCH   Huh?

BLANCHE   [*gaily*]   I said unhand me, sir. [*He fumblingly embraces her. Her voice sounds gently reproving.*] Now, Mitch. Just because Stanley and Stella aren't at home is no reason why you shouldn't behave like a gentleman.

MITCH   Just give me a slap whenever I step out of bounds.

BLANCHE   That won't be necessary. You're a natural gentleman, one of the very few that are left in the world. I don't want you to think that I am severe and old maid school-teacherish or anything like that. It's just—well—

MITCH   Huh?

BLANCHE   I guess it is just that I have—old-fashioned ideals! [*She rolls her eyes, knowing he cannot see her face.* MITCH *goes to the front door. There is a considerable silence between them.* BLANCHE *sighs and* MITCH *coughs self-consciously.*]

MITCH   [*finally*]   Where's Stanley and Stella tonight?

BLANCHE   They have gone out. With Mr. and Mrs. Hubbell upstairs.

MITCH   Where did they go?

BLANCHE   I think they were planning to go to a midnight prevue at Loew's State.

MITCH   We should all go out together some night.

---

5. Legendary strong man in the Old Testament.

BLANCHE   No. That wouldn't be a good plan.

MITCH   Why not?

BLANCHE   You are an old friend of Stanley's?

MITCH   We was together in the Two-forty-first.[6]

BLANCHE   I guess he talks to you frankly?

MITCH   Sure.

BLANCHE   Has he talked to you about me?

BLANCHE   Oh—not very much.

BLANCHE   The way you say that, I suspect that he has.

MITCH   No, he hasn't said much.

BLANCHE   But what he *has* said. What would you say his attitude toward me was?

MITCH   Why do you want to ask that?

BLANCHE   Well—

MITCH   Don't you get along with him?

BLANCHE   What do you think?

MITCH   I don't think he understands you.

BLANCHE   That is putting it mildly. If it weren't for Stella about to have a baby, I wouldn't be able to endure things here.

MITCH   He isn't—nice to you?

BLANCHE   He is insufferably rude. Goes out of his way to offend me.

MITCH   In what way, Blanche?

BLANCHE   Why, in every conceivable way.

MITCH   I'm surprised to hear that.

BLANCHE   Are you?

MITCH   Well, I—don't see how anybody could be rude to you.

BLANCHE   It's really a pretty frightful situation. You see, there's no privacy here. There's just these portieres between the two rooms at night. He stalks through the rooms in his underwear at night. And I have to ask him to close the bathroom door. That sort of commonness isn't necessary. You probably wonder why I don't move out. Well, I'll tell you frankly. A teacher's salary is barely sufficient for her living expenses. I didn't save a penny last year and so I had to come here for the summer. That's why I have to put up with my sister's husband. And he has to put up with me, apparently so much against his wishes. . . . Surely he must have told you how much he hates me!

MITCH   I don't think he hates you.

BLANCHE   He hates me. Or why would he insult me? The first time I laid eyes on him I thought to myself, that man is my executioner! That man will destroy me, unless——

MITCH   Blanche—

BLANCHE   Yes, honey?

MITCH   Can I ask you a question?

BLANCHE   Yes. What?

MITCH   How old are you?

[*She makes a nervous gesture.*]

BLANCHE   Why do you want to know?

---

6. Engineering battalion in World War II.

MITCH   I talked to my mother about you and she said, "How old is Blanche?"
And I wasn't able to tell her. [*There is another pause.*]

BLANCHE   You talked to your mother about me?

MITCH   Yes.

BLANCHE   Why?

MITCH   I told my mother how nice you were, and I liked you.

BLANCHE   Were you sincere about that?

MITCH   You know I was.

BLANCHE   Why did your mother want to know my age?

MITCH   Mother is sick.

BLANCHE   I'm sorry to hear it. Badly?

MITCH   She won't live long. Maybe just a few months.

BLANCHE   Oh.

MITCH   She worries because I'm not settled.

BLANCHE   Oh.

MITCH   She wants me to be settled down before she— [*His voice is hoarse and he clears his throat twice, shuffling nervously around with his hands in and out of his pockets.*]

BLANCHE   You love her very much, don't you?

MITCH   Yes.

BLANCHE   I think you have a great capacity for devotion. You will be lonely when she passes on, won't you? [MITCH *clears his throat and nods.*] I understand what that is.

MITCH   To be lonely?

BLANCHE   I loved someone, too, and the person I loved I lost.

MITCH   Dead? [*She crosses to the window and sits on the sill, looking out. She pours herself another drink.*] A man?

BLANCHE   He was a boy, just a boy, when I was a very young girl. When I was sixteen, I made the discovery—love. All at once and much, much too completely. It was like you suddenly turned a blinding light on something that had always been half in shadow, that's how it struck the world for me. But I was unlucky. Deluded. There was something different about the boy, a nervousness, a softness and tenderness which wasn't like a man's, although he wasn't the least bit effeminate looking—still—that thing was there. . . . He came to me for help. I didn't know that. I didn't find out anything till after our marriage when we'd run away and come back and all I knew was I'd failed him in some mysterious way and wasn't able to give the help he needed but couldn't speak of! He was in the quicksands and clutching at me—but I wasn't holding him out, I was slipping in with him! I didn't know that. I didn't know anything except I loved him unendurably but without being able to help him or help myself. Then I found out. In the worst of all possible ways. By coming suddenly into a room that I thought was empty—which wasn't empty, but had two people in it . . . the boy I had married and an older man who had been his friend for years . . .

[*A locomotive is heard approaching outside. She claps her hands to her ears and crouches over. The headlight of the locomotive glares into the room as it thunders past. As the noise recedes she straightens slowly and continues speaking.*]

Afterward we pretended that nothing had been discovered. Yes, the three of us drove out to Moon Lake Casino, very drunk and laughing all the way.

[*Polka music sounds, in a minor key faint with distance.*]

We danced the Varsouviana![7] Suddenly in the middle of the dance the boy I had married broke away from me and ran out of the casino. A few moments later—a shot!

[*The polka stops abruptly.* BLANCHE *rises stiffly. Then, the polka resumes in a major key.*]

I ran out—all did!—all ran and gathered about the terrible thing at the edge of the lake! I couldn't get near for the crowding. Then somebody caught my arm. "Don't go any closer! Come back! You don't want to see!" See? See what! Then I heard voices say—Allan! Allan! The Grey boy! He'd stuck the revolver into his mouth, and fired—so that the back of his head had been—blown away!

[*She sways and covers her face.*]

It was because—on the dance floor—unable to stop myself—I'd suddenly said—"I saw! I know! You disgust me . . ." And then the searchlight which had been turned on the world was turned off again and never for one moment since has there been any light that's stronger than this—kitchen—candle . . .

[MITCH *gets up awkwardly and moves toward her a little. The polka music increases.* MITCH *stands beside her.*]

MITCH [*drawing her slowly into his arms*] You need somebody. And I need somebody, too. Could it be—you and me, Blanche?

[*She stares at him vacantly for a moment. Then with a soft cry huddles in his embrace. She makes a sobbing effort to speak but the words won't come. He kisses her forehead and her eyes and finally her lips. The Polka tune fades out. Her breath is drawn and released in long, grateful sobs.*]

BLANCHE Sometimes—there's God—so quickly!

Scene Seven

It is late afternoon in mid-September.

The portieres are open and a table is set for a birthday supper, with cake and flowers.

STELLA *is completing the decorations as* STANLEY *comes in.*

STANLEY What's all this stuff for?

STELLA Honey, it's Blanche's birthday.

STANLEY She here?

STELLA In the bathroom.

STANLEY [*mimicking*] "Washing out some things"?

STELLA I reckon so.

STANLEY How long she been in there?

STELLA All afternoon.

STANLEY [*mimicking*] "Soaking in a hot tub"?

STELLA Yes.

STANLEY Temperature 100 on the nose, and she soaks herself in a hot tub.

---

7. Fast Polish waltz, similar to the polka.

STELLA   She says it cools her off for the evening.

STANLEY   And you run out an' get her cokes, I suppose? And serve 'em to Her Majesty in the tub? [STELLA *shrugs.*] Set down here a minute.

STELLA   Stanley, I've got things to do.

STANLEY   Set down! I've got th' dope on your big sister, Stella.

STELLA   Stanley, stop picking on Blanche.

STANLEY   That girl calls *me* common!

STELLA   Lately you been doing all you can think of to rub her the wrong way, Stanley, and Blanche is sensitive and you've got to realize that Blanche and I grew up under very different circumstances than you did.

STANLEY   So I been told. And told and told and told! You know she's been feeding us a pack of lies here?

STELLA   No, I don't, and—

STANLEY   Well, she has, however. But now the cat's out of the bag! I found out some things!

STELLA   What—things?

STANLEY   Things I already suspected. But now I got proof from the most reliable sources—which I have checked on!

    [BLANCHE *is singing in the bathroom a saccharine popular ballad which is used contrapuntally with* STANLEY's *speech.*]

STELLA   [*to* STANLEY]   Lower your voice!

STANLEY   Some canary bird, huh!

STELLA   Now please tell me quietly what you think you've found out about my sister.

STANLEY   Lie Number One: All this squeamishness she puts on! You should just know the line she's been feeding to Mitch. He thought she had never been more than kissed by a fellow! But Sister Blanche is no lily! Ha-ha! Some lily she is!

STELLA   What have you heard and who from?

STANLEY   Our supply-man down at the plant has been going through Laurel for years and he knows all about her and everybody else in the town of Laurel knows all about her. She is as famous in Laurel as if she was the President of the United States, only she is not respected by any party! This supply-man stops at a hotel called the Flamingo.

BLANCHE   [*singing blithely*]   "Say, it's only a paper moon, Sailing over a cardboard sea—But it wouldn't be make-believe If you believed in me!"[8]

STELLA   What about the—Flamingo?

STANLEY   She stayed there, too.

STELLA   My sister lived at Belle Reve.

STANLEY   This is after the home-place had slipped through her lily-white fingers! She moved to the Flamingo! A second-class hotel which has the advantage of not interfering in the private social life of the personalities there! The Flamingo is used to all kinds of goings-on. But even the management of the Flamingo was impressed by Dame Blanche! In fact they was so impressed by Dame Blanche that they requested her to turn in her room key—for permanently! This happened a couple of weeks before she showed here.

---

8. From "It's Only a Paper Moon" (1933), a popular song by Harold Arlen.

BLANCHE [*singing*]   "It's a Barnum and Bailey world, Just as phony as it can be—But it wouldn't be make-believe If you believed in me!"

STELLA   What—contemptible—lies!

STANLEY   Sure, I can see how you would be upset by this. She pulled the wool over your eyes as much as Mitch's!

STELLA   It's pure invention! There's not a word of truth in it and if if I were a man and this creature had dared to invent such things in my presence—

BLANCHE [*singing*]   "Without your love, It's a honky-tonk parade! Without your love, It's a melody played In a penny arcade . . ."

STANLEY   Honey, I told you I thoroughly checked on these stories! Now wait till I finished. The trouble with Dame Blanche was that she couldn't put on her act any more in Laurel! They got wised up after two or three dates with her and then they quit, and she goes on to another, the same old line, same old act, same old hooey! But the town was too small for this to go on forever! And as time went by she became a town character. Regarded as not just different but downright loco—nuts. [STELLA *draws back.*] And for the last year or two she has been washed up like poison. That's why she's here this summer, visiting royalty, putting on all this act—because she's practically told by the mayor to get out of town! Yes, did you know there was an army camp near Laurel and your sister's was one of the places called "Out-of-Bounds"?

BLANCHE   "It's only a paper moon, Just as phony as it can be—But it wouldn't be make-believe If you believed in me!"

STANLEY   Well, so much for her being such a refined and particular type of girl. Which brings us to Lie Number Two.

STELLA   I don't want to hear any more!

STANLEY   She's not going back to teach school! In fact I am willing to bet you that she never had no idea of returning to Laurel! She didn't resign temporarily from the high school because of her nerves! No, siree, Bob! She didn't. They kicked her out of that high school before the spring term ended—and I hate to tell you the reason that step was taken! A seventeen-year-old boy—she'd gotten mixed up with!

BLANCHE   "It's a Barnum and Bailey world, Just as phony as it can be—"
   [*In the bathroom the water goes on loud; little breathless cries and peals of laughter are heard as if a child were frolicking in the tub.*]

STELLA   This is making me—sick!

STANLEY   The boy's dad learned about it and got in touch with the high school superintendent. Boy, oh, boy, I'd like to have been in that office when Dame Blanche was called on the carpet! I'd like to have seen her trying to squirm out of that one! But they had her on the hook good and proper that time and she knew that the jig was all up! They told her she better move on to some fresh territory. Yep, it was practickly a town ordinance passed against her!
   [*The bathroom door is opened and* BLANCHE *thrusts her head out, holding a towel about her hair.*]

BLANCHE   Stella!

STELLA [*faintly*]   Yes, Blanche?

BLANCHE   Give me another bath-towel to dry my hair with. I've just washed it.

STELLA   Yes, Blanche. [*She crosses in a dazed way from the kitchen to the bathroom door with a towel.*]

BLANCHE   What's the matter, honey?

STELLA   Matter? Why?

BLANCHE   You have such a strange expression on your face!

STELLA   Oh— [*she tries to laugh*] I guess I'm a little tired!

BLANCHE   Why don't you bathe, too, soon as I get out?

STANLEY [*calling from the kitchen*]   How soon is that going to be?

BLANCHE   Not so terribly long! Possess your soul in patience!

STANLEY   It's not my soul, it's my kidneys I'm worried about!

[BLANCHE *slams the door.* STANLEY *laughs harshly.* STELLA *comes slowly back into the kitchen.*]

STANLEY   Well, what do you think of it?

STELLA   I don't believe all of those stories and I think your supply-man was mean and rotten to tell them. It's possible that some of the things he said are partly true. There are things about my sister I don't approve of—things that caused sorrow at home. She was always—flighty!

STANLEY   Flighty!

STELLA   But when she was young, very young, she married a boy who wrote poetry. . . . He was extremely good-looking. I think Blanche didn't just love him but worshipped the ground he walked on! Adored him and thought him almost too fine to be human! But then she found out—

STANLEY   What?

STELLA   This beautiful and talented young man was a degenerate. Didn't your supply-man give you that information?

STANLEY   All we discussed was recent history. That must have been a pretty long time ago.

STELLA   Yes, it was—a pretty long time ago . . .

[STANLEY *comes up and takes her by the shoulders rather gently. She gently withdraws from him. Automatically she starts sticking little pink candles in the birthday cake.*]

STANLEY   How many candles you putting in that cake?

STELLA   I'll stop at twenty-five.

STANLEY   Is company expected?

STELLA   We asked Mitch to come over for cake and ice-cream.

[STANLEY *looks a little uncomfortable. He lights a cigarette from the one he has just finished.*]

STANLEY   I wouldn't be expecting Mitch over tonight.

[STELLA *pauses in her occupation with candles and looks slowly around at* STANLEY.]

STELLA   Why?

STANLEY   Mitch is a buddy of mine. We were in the same outfit together—Two-forty-first Engineers. We work in the same plant and now on the same bowling team. You think I could face him if—

STELLA   Stanley Kowalski, did you—did you repeat what that—?

STANLEY   You're goddam right I told him! I'd have that on my conscience the rest of my life if I knew all that stuff and let my best friend get caught!

STELLA   Is Mitch through with her?

STANLEY   Wouldn't you be if—?

STELLA   I said, *Is Mitch through with her?*

[BLANCHE's *voice is lifted again, serenely as a bell. She sings* "But it wouldn't be make-believe If you believed in me."]

STANLEY   No, I don't think he's necessarily through with her—just wised up!

STELLA   Stanley, she thought Mitch was—going to—going to marry her. I was hoping so, too.

STANLEY   Well, he's not going to marry her. Maybe he *was*, but he's not going to jump in a tank with a school of sharks—now! [*He rises.*] Blanche! Oh, Blanche! Can I please get in my bathroom? [*There is a pause.*]

BLANCHE   Yes, indeed, sir! Can you wait one second while I dry?

STANLEY   Having waited one hour I guess one second ought to pass in a hurry.

STELLA   And she hasn't got her job? Well, what will she do!

STANLEY   She's not stayin' here after Tuesday. You know that, don't you? Just to make sure I bought her ticket myself. A bus ticket.

STELLA   In the first place, Blanche wouldn't go on a bus.

STANLEY   She'll go on a bus and like it.

STELLA   No, she won't, no, she won't, Stanley!

STANLEY   *She'll go!* Period. P.S. She'll go *Tuesday*!

STELLA [*slowly*]   What'll—she—do? What on earth will she—*do*!

STANLEY   Her future is mapped out for her.

STELLA   What do you mean?

   [BLANCHE *sings.*]

STANLEY   Hey, canary bird! Toots! Get *OUT* of the *BATHROOM*!

   [*The bathroom door flies open and* BLANCHE *emerges with a gay peal of laughter, but as* STANLEY *crosses past her, a frightened look appears in her face, almost a look of panic. He doesn't look at her but slams the bathroom door shut as he goes in.*]

BLANCHE [*snatching up a hairbrush*]   Oh, I feel so good after my long, hot bath, I feel so good and cool and—rested!

STELLA [*sadly and doubtfully from the kitchen*]   Do you, Blanche?

BLANCHE [*snatching up a hairbrush*]   Yes, I do, so refreshed! [*She tinkles her highball glass.*] A hot bath and a long, cold drink always give me a brand new outlook on life! [*She looks through the portieres at* STELLA, *standing between them, and slowly stops brushing.*] Something has happened!—What is it?

STELLA [*turning away quickly*]   Why, nothing has happened, Blanche.

BLANCHE   You're lying! Something has!

   [*She stares fearfully at* STELLA, *who pretends to be busy at the table. The distant piano goes into a hectic breakdown.*]

Scene Eight

Three quarters of an hour later.

The view through the big windows is fading gradually into a still-golden dusk. A torch of sunlight blazes on the side of a big water-tank or oil-drum across the empty lot toward the business district which is now pierced by pinpoints of lighted windows or windows reflecting the sunset.

The three people are completing a dismal birthday supper. STANLEY *looks sullen.* STELLA *is embarrassed and sad.*

BLANCHE *has a tight, artificial smile on her drawn face. There is a fourth place at the table which is left vacant.*

BLANCHE [*suddenly*]   Stanley, tell us a joke, tell us a funny story to make us all laugh. I don't know what's the matter, we're all so solemn. Is it because I've been stood up by my beau?
    [STELLA *laughs feebly.*]
    It's the first time in my entire experience with men, and I've had a good deal of all sorts, that I've actually been stood up by anybody! Ha-ha! I don't know how to take it. . . . Tell us a funny little story, Stanley! Something to help us out.
STANLEY   I didn't think you liked my stories, Blanche.
BLANCHE   I like them when they're amusing but not indecent.
STANLEY   I don't know any refined enough for your taste.
BLANCHE   Then let me tell one.
STELLA   Yes, you tell one, Blanche. You used to know lots of good stories.
    [*The music fades.*]
BLANCHE   Let me see, now. . . . I must run through my repertoire! Oh, yes—I love parrot stories! Do you all like parrot stories? Well, this one's about the old maid and the parrot. This old maid, she had a parrot that cursed a blue streak and knew more vulgar expressions than Mr. Kowalski!
STANLEY   Huh.
BLANCHE   And the only way to hush the parrot up was to put the cover back on its cage so it would think it was night and go back to sleep. Well, one morning the old maid had just uncovered the parrot for the day—when who should she see coming up the front walk but the preacher! Well, she rushed back to the parrot and slipped the cover back on the cage and then she let in the preacher. And the parrot was perfectly still, just as quiet as a mouse, but just as she was asking the preacher how much sugar he wanted in his coffee—the parrot broke the silence with a loud—[*She whistles.*]—and said—"God *damn*, but that was a short day!"
    [*She throws back her head and laughs.* STELLA *also makes an ineffectual effort to seem amused.* STANLEY *pays no attention to the story but reaches way over the table to spear his fork into the remaining chop which he eats with his fingers.*]
BLANCHE   Apparently Mr. Kowalski was not amused.
STELLA   Mr. Kowalski is too busy making a pig of himself to think of anything else!
STANLEY   That's right, baby.
STELLA   Your face and your fingers are disgustingly greasy. Go and wash up and then help me clear the table.
    [*He hurls a plate to the floor.*]
STANLEY   That's how I'll clear the table! [*He seizes her arm.*] Don't ever talk that way to me! "Pig—Polack—disgusting—vulgar—greasy!"—them kind of words have been on your tongue and your sister's too much around here! What do you two think you are? A pair of queens? Remember what Huey Long[9] said—"Every Man is a King!" And I am the king

9. Demagogic Louisiana political leader, governor, and senator (1893–1935).

around here, so don't forget it! [*He hurls a cup and saucer to the floor.*]
My place is cleared! You want me to clear your places?

    [STELLA *begins to cry weakly.* STANLEY *stalks out on the porch and lights a cigarette. The Negro entertainers around the corner are heard.*]

BLANCHE What happened while I was bathing? What did he tell you, Stella?

STELLA Nothing, nothing, nothing!

BLANCHE I think he told you something about Mitch and me! You know why Mitch didn't come but you won't tell me! [STELLA *shakes her head helplessly.*] I'm going to call him!

STELLA I wouldn't call him, Blanche.

BLANCHE I am, I'm going to call him on the phone.

STELLA [*miserably*] I wish you wouldn't.

BLANCHE I intend to be given some explanation from someone!

    [*She rushes to the phone in the bedroom.* STELLA *goes out on the porch and stares reproachfully at her husband. He grunts and turns away from her.*]

STELLA I hope you're pleased with your doings. I never had so much trouble swallowing food in my life, looking at that girl's face and the empty chair! [*She cries quietly.*]

BLANCHE [*at the phone*] Hello. Mr. Mitchell, please. . . . Oh. . . . I would like to leave a number if I may. Magnolia 9047. And say it's important to call. . . . Yes, very important. . . . Thank you.

    [*She remains by the phone with a lost, frightened look.* STANLEY *turns slowly back toward his wife and takes her clumsily in his arms.*]

STANLEY Stell, it's gonna be all right after she goes and after you've had the baby. It's gonna be all right again between you and me the way that it was. You remember the way that it was? Them nights we had together? God, honey, it's gonna be sweet when we can make noise in the night the way that we used to and get the colored lights going with nobody's sister behind the curtains to hear us!

    [*Their upstairs neighbors are heard in bellowing laughter at something.* STANLEY *chuckles.*]

Steve an' Eunice . . .

STELLA Come on back in. [*She returns to the kitchen and starts lighting the candles on the white cake.*] Blanche?

BLANCHE Yes. [*She returns from the bedroom to the table in the kitchen.*] Oh, those pretty, pretty little candles! Oh, don't burn them, Stella.

STELLA I certainly will.

    [STANLEY *comes back in.*]

BLANCHE You ought to save them for baby's birthdays. Oh, I hope candles are going to glow in his life and I hope that his eyes are going to be like candles, like two blue candles lighted in a white cake!

STANLEY [*sitting down*] What poetry!

BLANCHE [*she pauses reflectively for a moment*] I shouldn't have called him.

STELLA There's lots of things could have happened.

BLANCHE There's no excuse for it, Stella. I don't have to put up with insults. I won't be taken for granted.

STANLEY Goddamn, it's hot in here with the steam from the bathroom.

BLANCHE   I've said I was sorry three times. [*The piano fades out.*] I take hot baths for my nerves. Hydrotherapy, they call it. You healthy Polack, without a nerve in your body, of course you don't know what anxiety feels like!

STANLEY   I am not a Polack. People from Poland are Poles, not Polacks. But what I am is a one-hundred-per-cent American, born and raised in the greatest country on earth and proud as hell of it, so don't ever call me a Polack.

[*The phone rings.* BLANCHE *rises expectantly.*]

BLANCHE   Oh, that's for me, I'm sure.

STANLEY   *I'm* not sure. Keep your seat. [*He crosses leisurely to phone.*] H'lo. Aw, yeh, hello, Mac.

[*He leans against wall, staring insultingly in at* BLANCHE. *She sinks back in her chair with a frightened look.* STELLA *leans over and touches her shoulder.*]

BLANCHE   Oh, keep your hands off me, Stella. What is the matter with you? Why do you look at me with that pitying look?

STANLEY [*bawling*]   QUIET IN THERE!—We've got a noisy woman on the place.—Go on, Mac. At Riley's? No, I don't wanta bowl at Riley's. I had a little trouble with Riley last week. I'm the team captain, ain't I? All right, then, we're not gonna bowl at Riley's, we're gonna bowl at the West Side or the Gala! All right, Mac. See you!

[*He hangs up and returns to the table.* BLANCHE *fiercely controls herself, drinking quickly from her tumbler of water. He doesn't look at her but reaches in a pocket. Then he speaks slowly and with false amiability.*]

Sister Blanche, I've got a little birthday remembrance for you.

BLANCHE   Oh, have you, Stanley? I wasn't expecting any, I—I don't know why Stella wants to observe my birthday! I'd much rather forget it—when you—reach twenty-seven! Well—age is a subject that you'd prefer to— ignore!

STANLEY   Twenty-seven?

BLANCHE [*quickly*]   What is it? Is it for *me*?

[*He is holding a little envelope toward her.*]

STANLEY   Yes, I hope you like it!

BLANCHE   Why, why—Why, it's a—

STANLEY   Ticket! Back to Laurel! On the Greyhound! Tuesday!

[*The Varsouviana music steals in softly and continues playing.* STELLA *rises abruptly and turns her back.* BLANCHE *tries to smile. Then she tries to laugh. Then she gives both up and springs from the table and runs into the next room. She clutches her throat and then runs into the bathroom. Coughing, gagging sounds are heard.*]

Well!

STELLA   You didn't need to do that.

STANLEY   Don't forget all that I took off her.

STELLA   You needn't have been so cruel to someone alone as she is.

STANLEY   Delicate piece she is.

STELLA   She is. She was. You didn't know Blanche as a girl. Nobody, nobody, was tender and trusting as she was. But people like you abused her, and forced her to change.

[*He crosses into the bedroom, ripping off his shirt, and changes into a brilliant silk bowling shirt. She follows him.*]

Do you think you're going bowling now?

STANLEY Sure.

STELLA You're not going bowling. [*She catches hold of his shirt.*] Why did you do this to her?

STANLEY I done nothing to no one. Let go of my shirt. You've torn it.

STELLA I want to know why. Tell me why.

STANLEY When we first met, me and you, you thought I was common. How right you was, baby. I was common as dirt. You showed me the snap-shot of the place with the columns. I pulled you down off them columns and how you loved it, having them colored lights going! And wasn't we happy together, wasn't it all okay till she showed here?

> [STELLA *makes a slight movement. Her look goes suddenly inward as if some interior voice had called her name. She begins a slow, shuffling progress from the bedroom to the kitchen, leaning and resting on the back of the chair and then on the edge of a table with a blind look and listening expression.* STANLEY, *finishing with his shirt, is unaware of her reaction.*]

And wasn't we happy together? Wasn't it all okay? Till she showed here. Hoity-Toity, describing me as an ape. [*He suddenly notices the change in* STELLA.] Hey, what is it, Stel? [*He crosses to her.*]

STELLA [*quietly*] Take me to the hospital.

> [*He is with her now, supporting her with his arm, murmuring indistinguishably as they go outside.*]

Scene Nine

A while later that evening. BLANCHE *is seated in a tense hunched position in a bedroom chair that she has recovered with diagonal green and white stripes. She has on her scarlet satin robe. On the table beside chair is a bottle of liquor and a glass. The rapid, feverish polka tune, the "Varsouviana," is heard. The music is in her mind; she is drinking to escape it and the sense of disaster closing in on her, and she seems to whisper the words of the song. An electric fan is turning back and forth across her.*

MITCH comes around the corner in work clothes: blue denim shirt and pants. He is unshaven. He climbs the steps to the door and rings. BLANCHE *is startled.*

BLANCHE Who is it, please?

MITCH [*hoarsely*] Me. Mitch.

> [*The polka tune stops.*]

BLANCHE Mitch!—Just a minute.

> [*She rushes about frantically, hiding the bottle in a closet, crouching at the mirror and dabbing her face with cologne and powder. She is so excited that her breath is audible as she dashes about. At last she rushes to the door in the kitchen and lets him in.*]

Mitch!—Y'know, I really shouldn't let you in after the treatment I have received from you this evening! So utterly uncavalier! But hello, beautiful!

> [*She offers him her lips. He ignores it and pushes past her into the flat. She looks fearfully after him as he stalks into the bedroom.*]

My, my, what a cold shoulder! And such uncouth apparel! Why, you haven't even shaved! The unforgivable insult to a lady! But I forgive you. I forgive you because it's such a relief to see you. You've stopped that polka tune that I had caught in my head. Have you ever had anything caught in your head? No, of course you haven't, you dumb angel-puss, you'd never get anything awful caught in your head!

[*He stares at her while she follows him while she talks. It is obvious that he has had a few drinks on the way over.*]

MITCH   Do we have to have that fan on?

BLANCHE   No!

MITCH   I don't like fans.

BLANCHE   Then let's turn it off, honey. I'm not partial to them!

[*She presses the switch and the fan nods slowly off. She clears her throat uneasily as* MITCH *plumps himself down on the bed in the bedroom and lights a cigarette.*]

I don't know what there is to drink. I—haven't investigated.

MITCH   I don't want Stan's liquor.

BLANCHE   It isn't Stan's. Everything here isn't Stan's. Some things on the premises are actually mine! How is your mother? Isn't your mother well?

MITCH   Why?

BLANCHE   Something's the matter tonight, but never mind. I won't cross-examine the witness. I'll just—[*She touches her forehead vaguely. The polka tune starts up again.*]—pretend I don't notice anything different about you! That—music again . . .

MITCH   What music?

BLANCHE   The "Varsourviana"! The polka tune they were playing when Allan—Wait!

[*A distant revolver shot is heard.* BLANCHE *seems relieved.*]

There now, the shot! It always stops after that.

[*The polka music dies out again.*]

Yes, now it's stopped.

MITCH   Are you boxed out of your mind?

BLANCHE   I'll go and see what I can find in the way of— [*She crosses into the closet, pretending to search for the bottle.*] Oh, by the way, excuse me for not being dressed. But I'd practically given you up! Had you forgotten your invitation to supper?

MITCH   I wasn't going to see you any more.

BLANCHE   Wait a minute. I can't hear what you're saying and you talk so little that when you do say something, I don't want to miss a single syllable of it. . . . What am I looking around here for? Oh, yes—liquor! We've had so much excitement around here this evening that I *am* boxed out of my mind! [*She pretends suddenly to find the bottle. He draws his foot up on the bed and stares at her contemptuously.*] Here's something. Southern Comfort! What is that, I wonder?

MITCH   If you don't know, it must belong to Stan.

BLANCHE   Take your foot off the bed. It has a light cover on it. Of course you boys don't notice things like that. I've done so much with this place since I've been here.

MITCH   I bet you have.

BLANCHE   You saw it before I came. Well, look at it now! This room is almost—dainty! I want to keep it that way. I wonder if this stuff ought to be mixed with something? Ummm, it's sweet, so sweet! It's terribly, terribly sweet! Why, it's a *liqueur*, I believe! Yes, that's what it *is*, a liqueur!

[MITCH *grunts.*] I'm afraid you won't like it, but try it, and maybe you will.

MITCH   I told you already I don't want none of his liquor and I mean it. You ought to lay off his liquor. He says you been lapping it up all summer like a wild cat!

BLANCHE   What a fantastic statement! Fantastic of him to say it, fantastic of you to repeat it! I won't descend to the level of such cheap accusations to answer them, even!

MITCH   Huh.

BLANCHE   What's in your mind? I see something in your eyes!

MITCH [*getting up*]   It's dark in here.

BLANCHE   I like it dark. The dark is comforting to me.

MITCH   I don't think I ever seen you in the light. [BLANCHE *laughs breathlessly.*] That's a fact!

BLANCHE   Is it?

MITCH   I've never seen you in the afternoon.

BLANCHE   Whose fault is that?

MITCH   You never want to go out in the afternoon.

BLANCHE   Why, Mitch, you're at the plant in the afternoon!

MITCH   Not Sunday afternoon. I've asked you to go out with me sometimes on Sundays but you always make an excuse. You never want to go out till after six and then it's always some place that's not lighted much.

BLANCHE   There is some obscure meaning in this but I fail to catch it.

MITCH   What it means is I've never had a real good look at you, Blanche. Let's turn the light on here.

BLANCHE [*fearfully*]   Light? Which light? What for?

MITCH   This one with the paper thing on it. [*He tears the paper lantern off the light bulb. She utters a frightened gasp.*]

BLANCHE   What did you do that for?

MITCH   So I can take a look at you good and plain!

BLANCHE   Of course you don't really mean to be insulting!

MITCH   No, just realistic.

BLANCHE   I don't want realism. I want magic! [MITCH *laughs.*] Yes, yes, magic! I try to give that to people. I misrepresent things to them. I don't tell truth, I tell what *ought* to be truth. And if that is sinful, then let me be damned for it!—*Don't turn the light on!*

[MITCH *crosses to the switch. He turns the light on and stares at her. She cries out and covers her face. He turns the lights off again.*]

MITCH [*slowly and bitterly*]   I don't mind you being older than what I thought. But all the rest of it—Christ! That pitch about your ideals being so old-fashioned and all the malarkey that you've dished out all summer. Oh, I knew you weren't sixteen any more. But I was a fool enough to believe you was straight.

BLANCHE   Who told you I wasn't—"straight"? My loving brother-in-law. And you believed him.

MITCH   I called him a liar at first. And then I checked on the story. First I asked our supply-man who travels through Laurel. And then I talked directly over long-distance to this merchant.

BLANCHE   Who is this merchant?

MITCH   Kiefaber.

BLANCHE   The merchant Kiefaber of Laurel! I know the man. He whistled at me. I put him in his place. So now for revenge he makes up stories about me.

MITCH   Three people, Kiefaber, Stanley and Shaw, swore to them!

BLANCHE   Rub-a-dub-dub, three men in a tub! And such a filthy tub!

MITCH   Didn't you stay at a hotel called The Flamingo?

BLANCHE   Flamingo? No! Tarantula was the name of it! I stayed at a hotel called The Tarantula Arms!

MITCH [*stupidly*]   Tarantula?

BLANCHE   Yes, a big spider! That's where I brought my victims. [*She pours herself another drink.*] Yes, I had many intimacies with strangers. After the death of Allan—intimacies with strangers was all I seemed able to fill my empty heart with. . . . I think it was panic, just panic, that drove me from one to another, hunting for some protection—here and there, in the most—unlikely places—even, at last, in a seventeen-year-old boy but—somebody wrote the superintendent about it—"This woman is morally unfit for her position!"

   [*She throws back her head with convulsive, sobbing laughter. Then she repeats the statement, gasps, and drinks.*]

True? Yes, I suppose—unfit somehow—anyway. . . . So I came here. There was nowhere else I could go. I was played out. You know what played out is? My youth was suddenly gone up the water-spout, and—I met you. You said you needed somebody. Well, I needed somebody, too. I thanked God for you, because you seemed to be gentle—a cleft in the rock of the world that I could hide in! But I guess I was asking, hoping—too much! Kiefaber, Stanley and Shaw have tied an old tin can to the tail of the kite.

   [*There is a pause. MITCH stares at her dumbly.*]

MITCH   You lied to me, Blanche.

BLANCHE   Don't say I lied to you.

MITCH   Lies, lies, inside and out, all lies.

BLANCHE   Never inside, I didn't lie in my heart . . .

   [*A VENDOR comes around the corner. She is a blind MEXICAN WOMAN in a dark shawl, carrying bunches of those gaudy tin flowers that lower-class Mexicans display at funerals and other festive occasions. She is calling barely audibly. Her figure is only faintly visible outside the building.*]

MEXICAN WOMAN   Flores. Flores, Flores para los muertos.[1] Flores. Flores.

BLANCHE   What? Oh! Somebody outside . . . [*She goes to the door, opens it and stares at the MEXICAN WOMAN.*]

MEXICAN WOMAN [*she is at the door and offers BLANCHE some of her flowers*]   Flores? Flores para los muertos?

BLANCHE [*frightened*]   No, no! Not now! Not now!

   [*She darts back into the apartment, slamming the door.*]

MEXICAN WOMAN [*she turns away and starts to move down the street*]   Flores para los muertos.

   [*The polka tune fades in.*]

BLANCHE [*as if to herself*]   Crumble and fade and—regrets—recriminations . . . "If you'd done this, it wouldn't've cost me that!"

---

1. Flowers for the dead (Spanish).

MEXICAN WOMAN   Corones[2] para los muertos. Corones . . .

BLANCHE   Legacies! Huh. . . . And other things such as bloodstained pillow-slips—"Her linen needs changing"—"Yes, Mother. But couldn't we get a colored girl to do it?" No, we couldn't of course. Everything gone but the—

MEXICAN WOMAN   Flores.

BLANCHE   Death—I used to sit here and she used to sit over there and death was as close as you are. . . . We didn't dare even admit we had ever heard of it!

MEXICAN WOMAN   Flores para los muertos, flores—flores . . .

BLANCHE   The opposite is desire. So do you wonder? How could you possibly wonder! Not far from Belle Reve, before we had lost Belle Reve, was a camp where they trained young soldiers. On Sunday nights they would go in town to get drunk—

MEXICAN WOMAN [softly]   Corones . . .

BLANCHE   —and on the way back they would stagger onto my lawn and call—"Blanche! Blanche!"—the deaf old lady remaining suspected nothing. But sometimes I slipped outside to answer their calls. . . . Later the paddy-wagon would gather them up like daisies . . . the long way home . . .
[The MEXICAN WOMAN turns slowly and drifts back off with her soft mournful cries. BLANCHE goes to the dresser and leans forward on it. After a moment, MITCH rises and follows her purposefully. The polka music fades away. He places his hands on her waist and tries to turn her about.]

BLANCHE   What do you want?

MITCH [fumbling to embrace her]   What I been missing all summer.

BLANCHE   Then marry me, Mitch!

MITCH   I don't think I want to marry you anymore.

BLANCHE   No?

MITCH [dropping his hands from her waist]   You're not clean enough to bring in the house with my mother.

BLANCHE   Go away, then. [He stares at her.] Get out of here quick before I start screaming fire! [Her throat is tightening with hysteria.] Get out of here quick before I start screaming fire.
[He still remains staring. She suddenly rushes to the big window with its pale blue square of the soft summer light and cries wildly.]
Fire! Fire! Fire!
[With a startled gasp, MITCH turns and goes out the outer door, clatters awkwardly down the steps and around the corner of the building. BLANCHE staggers back from the window and falls to her knees. The distant piano is slow and blue.]

Scene Ten

It is a few hours later that night.

BLANCHE has been drinking fairly steadily since MITCH left. She has dragged her wardrobe trunk into the center of the bedroom. It hangs open with flowery dresses thrown across it. As the drinking and packing went on, a mood of hysterical exhilaration came into her and she has decked herself out in a somewhat

---

2. Wreaths (Spanish).

soiled and crumpled white satin evening gown and a pair of scuffed silver slippers with brilliants set in their heels.

Now she is placing the rhinestone tiara on her head before the mirror of the dressing-table and murmuring excitedly as if to a group of spectral admirers.

BLANCHE How about taking a swim, a moonlight swim at the old rock-quarry? If anyone's sober enough to drive a car! Ha-ha! Best way in the world to stop your head buzzing! Only you've got to be careful to dive where the deep pool is—if you hit a rock you don't come up till tomorrow . . .

> [*Tremblingly she lifts the hand mirror for a closer inspection. She catches her breath and slams the mirror face down with such violence that the glass cracks. She moans a little and attempts to rise.* STANLEY *appears around the corner of the building. He still has on the vivid green silk bowling shirt. As he rounds the corner the honky-tonk music is heard. It continues softly throughout the scene. He enters the kitchen, slamming the door. As he peers in at* BLANCHE *he gives a low whistle. He has had a few drinks on the way and has brought some quart beer bottles home with him.*]

BLANCHE How is my sister?

STANLEY She is doing okay.

BLANCHE And how is the baby?

STANLEY [*grinning amiably*] The baby won't come before morning so they told me to go home and get a little shut-eye.

BLANCHE Does that mean we are to be alone in here?

STANLEY Yep. Just me and you, Blanche. Unless you got somebody hid under the bed. What've you got on those fine feathers for?

BLANCHE Oh, that's right. You left before my wire came.

STANLEY You got a wire?

BLANCHE I received a telegram from an old admirer of mine.

STANLEY Anything good?

BLANCHE I think so. An invitation.

STANLEY What to? A fireman's ball?

BLANCHE [*throwing back her head*] A cruise of the Caribbean on a yacht!

STANLEY Well, well. What do you know?

BLANCHE I have never been so surprised in my life.

STANLEY I guess not.

BLANCHE It came like a bolt from the blue!

STANLEY Who did you say it was from?

BLANCHE An old beau of mine.

STANLEY The one that give you the white fox-pieces?

BLANCHE Mr. Shep Huntleigh. I wore his ATO pin my last year at college. I hadn't seen him again until last Christmas. I ran in to him on Biscayne Boulevard. Then—just now—this wire—inviting me on a cruise of the Caribbean! The problem is clothes. I tore into my trunk to see what I have that's suitable for the tropics!

STANLEY And come up with that—gorgeous—diamond—tiara?

BLANCHE This old relic? Ha-ha! It's only rhinestones.

STANLEY Gosh. I thought it was Tiffany diamonds. [*He unbuttons his shirt.*]

BLANCHE Well, anyhow, I shall be entertained in style.

STANLEY Uh-huh. It goes to show, you never know what is coming.

BLANCHE   Just when I thought my luck had begun to fail me—

STANLEY   Into the picture pops this Miami millionaire.

BLANCHE   This man is not from Miami. This man is from Dallas.

STANLEY   This man is from Dallas?

BLANCHE   Yes, this man is from Dallas where gold spouts out of the ground!

STANLEY   Well, just so he's from somewhere! [*He starts removing his shirt.*]

BLANCHE   Close the curtains before you undress any further.

STANLEY [*amiably*]   This is all I'm going to undress right now. [*He rips the sack off a quart beer bottle*] Seen a bottle-opener?

> [*She moves slowly toward the dresser, where she stands with her hands knotted together.*]

I used to have a cousin who could open a beer bottle with his teeth. [*pounding the bottle cap on the corner of table*] That was his only accomplishment, all he could do—he was just a human bottle-opener. And then one time, at a wedding party, he broke his front teeth off! After that he was so ashamed of himself he used t' sneak out of the house when company came . . .

> [*The bottle cap pops off and a geyser of foam shoots up. Stanley laughs happily, holding up the bottle over his head.*]

Ha-ha! Rain from heaven! [*He extends the bottle toward her*] Shall we bury the hatchet and make it a loving-cup? Huh?

BLANCHE   No, thank you.

STANLEY   Well, it's a red-letter night for us both. You having an oil millionaire and me having a baby.

> [*He goes to the bureau in the bedroom and crouches to remove something from the bottom drawer.*]

BLANCHE [*drawing back*]   What are you doing in here?

STANLEY   Here's something I always break out on special occasions like this. The silk pyjamas I wore on my wedding night!

BLANCHE   Oh.

STANLEY   When the telephone rings and they say, "You've got a son!" I'll tear this off and wave it like a flag! [*He shakes out a brilliant pyjama coat.*] I guess we are both entitled to put on the dog. [*He goes back to the kitchen with the coat over his arm.*]

BLANCHE   When I think of how divine it is going to be to have such a thing as privacy once more—I could weep with joy!

STANLEY   This millionaire from Dallas is not going to interfere with your privacy any?

BLANCHE   It won't be the sort of thing you have in mind. This man is a gentleman and he respects me. [*improvising feverishly*] What he wants is my companionship. Having great wealth sometimes makes people lonely! A cultivated woman, a woman of intelligence and breeding, can enrich a man's life—immeasurably! I have those things to offer, and this doesn't take them away. Physical beauty is passing. A transitory possession. But beauty of the mind and richness of the spirit and tenderness of the heart—and I have all of those things—aren't taken away, but grow! Increase with the years! How strange that I should be called a destitute woman! When I have all of these treasures locked in my heart. [*A choked sob comes from her.*] I think of myself as a very, very rich woman! But I have been foolish—casting my pearls before swine!

STANLEY Swine, huh?

BLANCHE Yes, swine! Swine! And I'm thinking not only of you but of your friend, Mr. Mitchell. He came to see me tonight. He dared to come here in his work clothes! And to repeat slander to me, vicious stories that he had gotten from you! I gave him his walking papers . . .

STANLEY You did, huh?

BLANCHE But then he came back. He returned with a box of roses to beg my forgiveness! He implored my forgiveness. But some things are not forgivable. Deliberate cruelty is not forgivable. It is the one unforgivable thing in my opinion and it is the one thing of which I have never, never been guilty. And so I told him, I said to him, "Thank you," but it was foolish of me to think that we could ever adapt ourselves to each other. Our ways of life are too different. Our attitudes and our backgrounds are incompatible. We have to be realistic about such things. So farewell, my friend! And let there be no hard feelings . . .

STANLEY Was this before or after the telegram came from the Texas oil millionaire?

BLANCHE What telegram? No! No, after! As a matter of fact, the wire came just as—

STANLEY As a matter of fact there wasn't no wire at all!

BLANCHE Oh, oh!

STANLEY There isn't no millionaire! And Mitch didn't come back with roses 'cause I know where he is—

BLANCHE Oh!

STANLEY There isn't a goddam thing but imagination!

BLANCHE Oh!

STANLEY And lies and conceit and tricks!

BLANCHE Oh!

STANLEY And look at yourself! Take a look at yourself in that worn-out Mardi Gras outfit, rented for fifty cents from some rag-picker! And with the crazy crown on! What queen do you think you are?

BLANCHE Oh—God . . .

STANLEY I've been on to you from the start! Not once did you pull any wool over this boy's eyes! You come in here and sprinkle the place with powder and spray perfume and cover the light-bulb with a paper lantern, and lo and behold the place has turned into Egypt and you are the Queen of the Nile! Sitting on your throne and swilling down my liquor! I say—Ha!—Ha! Do you hear me? Ha—ha—ha! [He walks into the bedroom.]

BLANCHE Don't come in here!

[Lurid reflections appear on the walls around BLANCHE. The shadows are of a grotesque and menacing form. She catches her breath, crosses to the phone and jiggles the hook. STANLEY goes into the bathroom and closes the door.]

Operator, operator! Give me long-distance, please. . . . I want to get in touch with Mr. Shep Huntleigh of Dallas. He's so well known he doesn't require any address. Just ask anybody who—Wait!!—No, I couldn't find it right now. . . . Please understand, I—No! No, wait!. . . . One moment! Someone is—Nothing! Hold on, please!

[She sets the phone down and crosses warily into the kitchen. The night is filled with inhuman voices like cries in a jungle. The shadows and *lurid reflections move sinuously as flames along the wall spaces. Through the back wall of the rooms, which have become transparent, can be seen the sidewalk. A prostitute has rolled a drunkard. He pursues her along the walk, overtakes her and there is a struggle. A policeman's whistle breaks it up. The figures disappear. Some moments later the Negro Woman appears around the corner with a sequined bag which the prostitute had dropped on the walk. She is rooting excitedly through it.* BLANCHE *presses her knuckles to her lips and returns slowly to the phone. She speaks in a hoarse whisper.*]

BLANCHE Operator! Operator! Never mind long-distance. Get Western Union. There isn't time to be—Western—Western Union!

[*She waits anxiously.*]

Western Union? Yes! I—want to—Take down this message! "In desperate, desperate circumstances! Help me! Caught in a trap. Caught in—" Oh!

[*The bathroom door is thrown open and* STANLEY *comes out in the brilliant silk pyjamas. He grins at her as he knots the tasseled sash about his waist. She gasps and backs away from the phone. He stares at her for a count of ten. Then a clicking becomes audible from the telephone, steady and rasping.*]

STANLEY You left th' phone off th' hook.

[*He crosses to it deliberately and sets it back on the hook. After he has replaced it, he stares at her again, his mouth slowly curving into a grin, as he weaves between* BLANCHE *and the outer door. The barely audible "Blue Piano" begins to drum up louder. The sound of it turns into the roar of an approaching locomotive.* BLANCHE *crouches, pressing her fists to her ears until it has gone by.*]

BLANCHE [*finally straightening*] Let me—let me get by you!

STANLEY Get by me? Sure. Go ahead. [*He moves back a pace in the doorway.*]

BLANCHE You—you stand over there! [*She indicates a further position.*]

STANLEY [*grinning*] You got plenty of room to walk by me now.

BLANCHE Not with you there! But I've got to get out somehow!

STANLEY You think I'll interfere with you? Ha-ha!

[*The "Blue Piano" goes softly. She turns confusedly and makes a faint gesture. The inhuman jungle voices rise up. He takes a step toward her, biting his tongue which protrudes between his lips.*]

STANLEY [*softly*] Come to think of it—maybe you wouldn't be bad to—interfere with . . .

[BLANCHE *moves backward through the door into the bedroom.*]

BLANCHE Stay back! Don't you come toward me another step or I'll—

STANLEY What?

BLANCHE Some awful thing will happen! It will!

STANLEY What are you putting on now?

[*They are now both inside the bedroom.*]

BLANCHE I warn you, don't, I'm in danger!

[*He takes another step. She smashes a bottle on the table and faces him, clutching the broken top.*]

STANLEY What did you do that for?

BLANCHE So I could twist the broken end in your face!

STANLEY I bet you would do that!

BLANCHE I would! I will if you—

STANLEY Oh! So you want some roughhouse! All right, let's have some roughhouse!

> [*He springs toward her, overturning the table. She cries out and strikes at him with the bottle top but he catches her wrist.*]

Tiger—tiger! Drop the bottle-top! Drop it! We've had this date with each other from the beginning!

> [*She moans. The bottle-top falls. She sinks to her knees: He picks up her inert figure and carries her to the bed. The hot trumpet and drums from the Four Deuces sound loudly.*]

Scene Eleven

It is some weeks later. STELLA *is packing* BLANCHE's *things. Sounds of water can be heard running in the bathroom.*

*The portieres are partly open on the poker players—*STANLEY, STEVE, MITCH *and* PABLO—*who sit around the table in the kitchen. The atmosphere of the kitchen is now the same raw, lurid one of the disastrous poker night.*

The building is framed by the sky of turquoise. STELLA *has been crying as she arranges the flowery dresses in the open trunk.*

EUNICE *comes down the steps from her flat above and enters the kitchen. There is an outburst from the poker table.*

STANLEY Drew to an inside straight and made it, by God.

PABLO *Maldita sea tu suerto!*

STANLEY Put it in English, greaseball.

PABLO I am cursing your rutting luck.

STANLEY [*prodigiously elated*] You know what luck is? Luck is believing you're lucky. Take at Salerno.[3] I believed I was lucky. I figured that 4 out of 5 would not come through but I would . . . and I did. I put that down as a rule. To hold front position in this rat-race you've got to believe you are lucky.

MITCH You . . . you . . . you . . . Brag . . . brag . . . bull . . . bull.

> [STELLA *goes into the bedroom and starts folding a dress.*]

STANLEY What's the matter with him?

EUNICE [*walking past the table*] I always did say that men are callous things with no feelings, but this does beat anything. Making pigs of yourselves. [*She comes through the portieres into the bedroom.*]

STANLEY What's the matter with her?

STELLA How is my baby?

EUNICE Sleeping like a little angel. Brought you some grapes. [*She puts them on a stool and lowers her voice.*] Blanche?

STELLA Bathing.

EUNICE How is she?

STELLA She wouldn't eat anything but asked for a drink.

EUNICE What did you tell her?

STELLA I—just told her that—we'd made arrangements for her to rest in the country. She's got it mixed in her mind with Shep Huntleigh.

> [BLANCHE *opens the bathroom door slightly.*]

BLANCHE Stella.

---

3. Important beachhead in the Allied invasion of Italy in World War II.

STELLA Yes, Blanche.

BLANCHE If anyone calls while I'm bathing take the number and tell them I'll call right back.

STELLA Yes.

BLANCHE That cool yellow silk—the bouclé. See if it's crushed. If it's not too crushed I'll wear it and on the lapel that silver and turquoise pin in the shape of a seahorse. You will find them in the heart-shaped box I keep my accessories in. And Stella . . . Try and locate a bunch of artificial violets in that box, too, to pin with the seahorse on the lapel of the jacket.

[*She closes the door.* STELLA *turns to* EUNICE.]

STELLA I don't know if I did the right thing.

EUNICE What else could you do?

STELLA I couldn't believe her story and go on living with Stanley.

EUNICE Don't ever believe it. Life has got to go on. No matter what happens, you've got to keep on going.

[*The bathroom door opens a little.*]

BLANCHE [*looking out*] Is the coast clear?

STELLA Yes, Blanche. [*to* EUNICE] Tell her how well she's looking.

BLANCHE Please close the curtains before I come out.

STELLA They're closed.

STANLEY —How many for you?

PABLO Two.

STEVE Three.

[BLANCHE *appears in the amber light of the door. She has a tragic radiance in her red satin robe following the sculptural lines of her body. The "Varsouviana" rises audibly as* BLANCHE *enters the bedroom.*]

BLANCHE [*with faintly hysterical vivacity*] I have just washed my hair.

STELLA Did you?

BLANCHE I'm not sure I got the soap out.

EUNICE Such fine hair!

BLANCHE [*accepting the compliment*] It's a problem. Didn't I get a call?

STELLA Who from, Blanche?

BLANCHE Shep Huntleigh . . .

STELLA Why, not yet, honey!

BLANCHE How strange! I—

[*At the sound of* BLANCHE's *voice* MITCH's *arm supporting his cards has sagged and his gaze is dissolved into space.* STANLEY *slaps him on the shoulder.*]

STANLEY Hey, Mitch, come to!

[*The sound of this new voice shocks* BLANCHE. *She makes a shocked gesture, forming his name with her lips.* STELLA *nods and looks quickly away.* BLANCHE *stands quite still for some moments—the silver-backed mirror in her hand and a look of sorrowful perplexity as though all human experience shows on her face.* BLANCHE *finally speaks but with sudden hysteria.*]

BLANCHE What's going on here?

[*She turns from* STELLA *to* EUNICE *and back to* STELLA. *Her rising voice penetrates the concentration of the game.* MITCH *ducks his head lower but* STANLEY *shoves back his chair as if to rise.* STEVE *places a restraining hand on his arm.*]

BLANCHE [*continuing*]   What's happened here? I want an explanation of what's happened here.

STELLA [*agonizingly*]   Hush! Hush!

EUNICE   Hush! Hush! Honey.

STELLA   Please, Blanche.

BLANCHE   Why are you looking at me like that? Is something wrong with me?

EUNICE   You look wonderful, Blanche. Don't she look wonderful?

STELLA   Yes.

EUNICE   I understand you are going on a trip.

STELLA   Yes, Blanche *is*. She's going on a vacation.

EUNICE   I'm green with envy.

BLANCHE   Help me, help me get dressed!

STELLA [*handing her dress*]   Is this what you—

BLANCHE   Yes, it will do! I'm anxious to get out of here—this place is a trap!

EUNICE   What a pretty blue jacket.

STELLA   It's lilac colored.

BLANCHE   You're both mistaken. It's Della Robbia blue.[4] The blue of the robe in the old Madonna pictures. Are these grapes washed?

[*She fingers the bunch of grapes which* EUNICE *had brought in.*]

EUNICE   Huh?

BLANCHE   Washed, I said. Are they washed?

EUNICE   They're from the French Market.

BLANCHE   That doesn't mean they've been washed. [*The cathedral bells chime.*] Those cathedral bells—they're the only clean thing in the Quarter. Well, I'm going now. I'm ready to go.

EUNICE [*whispering*]   She's going to walk out before they get here.

STELLA   Wait, Blanche.

BLANCHE   I don't want to pass in front of those men.

EUNICE   Then wait'll the game breaks up.

STELLA   Sit down and . . .

[BLANCHE *turns weakly, hesitantly about. She lets them push her into a chair.*]

BLANCHE   I can smell the sea air. The rest of my time I'm going to spend on the sea. And when I die, I'm going to die on the sea. You know what I shall die of [*She plucks a grape.*] I shall die of eating an unwashed grape one day out on the ocean. I will die—with my hand in the hand of some nice-looking ship's doctor, a very young one with a small blond mustache and a big silver watch. "Poor lady," they'll say, "the quinine did her no good. That unwashed grape has transported her soul to heaven." [*The cathedral chimes are heard.*] And I'll be buried at sea sewn up in a clean white sack and dropped overboard—at noon—in the blaze of summer—and into an ocean as blue as [*chimes again*] my first lover's eyes!

[*A* DOCTOR *and a* MATRON *have appeared around the corner of the building and climbed the steps to the porch. The gravity of their profession is exaggerated—the unmistakable aura of the state institution with its cynical detachment. The* DOCTOR *rings the doorbell. The murmur of the game is interrupted.*]

---

4. A shade of light blue seen in terra cottas made by the Della Robbia family in the Italian Renaissance.

EUNICE [*whispering to* STELLA] That must be them.

[STELLA *presses her fists to her lips.*]

BLANCHE [*rising slowly*] What is it?

EUNICE [*affectedly casual*] Excuse me while I see who's at the door.

STELLA Yes.

[EUNICE *goes into the kitchen.*]

BLANCHE [*tensely*] I wonder if it's for me.

[*A whispered colloquy takes place at the door.*]

EUNICE [*returning, brightly*] Someone is calling for Blanche.

BLANCHE It *is* for me, then! [*She looks fearfully from one to the other and then to the portieres. The "Varsouviana" faintly plays.*] Is it the gentleman I was expecting from Dallas?

EUNICE I think it is, Blanche.

BLANCHE I'm not quite ready.

STELLA Ask him to wait outside.

BLANCHE I . . .

[EUNICE *goes back to the portieres. Drums sound very softly.*]

STELLA Everything packed?

BLANCHE My silver toilet articles are still out.

STELLA Ah!

EUNICE [*returning*] They're waiting in front of the house.

BLANCHE They! Who's "they"?

EUNICE There's a lady with him.

BLANCHE I cannot imagine who this "lady" could be! How is she dressed?

EUNICE Just—just a sort of a—plain-tailored outfit.

BLANCHE Possibly she's— [*Her voice dies out nervously.*]

STELLA Shall we go, Blanche?

BLANCHE Must we go through that room?

STELLA I will go with you.

BLANCHE How do I look?

STELLA Lovely.

EUNICE [*echoing*] Lovely.

[BLANCHE *moves fearfully to the portieres.* EUNICE *draws them open for her.* BLANCHE *goes into the kitchen.*]

BLANCHE [*to the men*] Please don't get up. I'm only passing through.

[*She crosses quickly to outside door.* STELLA *and* EUNICE *follow. The poker players stand awkwardly at the table—all except* MITCH *who remains seated, looking down at the table.* BLANCHE *steps out on a small porch at the side of the door. She stops short and catches her breath.*]

DOCTOR How do you do?

BLANCHE You are not the gentleman I was expecting. [*She suddenly gasps and starts back up the steps. She stops by* STELLA, *who stands just outside the door, and speaks in a frightening whisper.*] That man isn't Shep Hunt-leigh.

[*The "Varsouviana" is playing distantly.* STELLA *stares back at* BLANCHE. EUNICE *is holding* STELLA's *arm. There is a moment of silence—no sound but that of* STANLEY *steadily shuffling the cards.* BLANCHE *catches her breath again and slips back into the flat. She enters the flat with a peculiar smile, her eyes wide and brilliant. As soon as her sister goes past her,* STELLA *closes her eyes and clenches her hands.* EUNICE *throws her arms comfortingly about her. Then she starts up to her flat.* BLANCHE *stops just inside the door.* MITCH *keeps staring down at his hands on the table, but the other men look at her curiously. At last she starts around the table toward the bedroom. As she does,* STANLEY *suddenly pushes back his chair and rises as if to block her way. The* MATRON *follows her into the flat.*]

STANLEY   Did you forget something?

BLANCHE [*shrilly*]   Yes! Yes, I forgot something!
[*She rushes past him into the bedroom. Lurid reflections appear on the walls in odd, sinuous shapes. The "Varsouviana" is filtered into a weird distortion, accompanied by the cries and noises of the jungle.* BLANCHE *seizes the back of a chair as if to defend herself.*]

STANLEY [*sotto voce*][5]   Doc, you better go in.

DOCTOR [*sotto voce, motioning to the* MATRON]   Nurse, bring her out.
[*The* MATRON *advances on one side,* STANLEY *on the other. Divested of all the softer properties of womanhood, the* MATRON *is a peculiarly sinister figure in her severe dress. Her voice is bold and toneless as a firebell.*]

MATRON   Hello, Blanche.
[*The greeting is echoed and re-echoed by other mysterious voices behind the walls, as if reverberated through a canyon of rock.*]

STANLEY   She says that she forgot something.
[*The echo sounds in threatening whispers.*]

MATRON   That's all right.

STANLEY   What did you forget, Blanche?

BLANCHE   I—I—

MATRON   It don't matter. We can pick it up later.

STANLEY   Sure. We can send it along with the trunk.

BLANCHE [*retreating in panic*]   I don't know you—I don't know you. I want to be—left alone—please!

MATRON   Now, Blanche!

ECHOES [*rising and falling*]   Now, Blanche—now, Blanche—now, Blanche!

STANLEY   You left nothing here but spilt talcum and old empty perfume bottles—unless it's the paper lantern you want to take with you. You want the lantern?
[*He crosses to dressing table and seizes the paper lantern, tearing it off the light bulb, and extends it toward her. She cries out as if the lantern was herself. The* MATRON *steps boldly toward her. She screams and tries to break past the* MATRON. *All the men spring to their feet.* STELLA *runs out to the porch, with* EUNICE *following to comfort her, simultaneously with the confused voices of the men in the kitchen.* STELLA *rushes into* EUNICE's *embrace on the porch.*]

STELLA   Oh, my God, Eunice help me! Don't let them do that to her, don't let them hurt her! Oh, God, oh, please God, don't hurt her! What are they doing to her? What are they doing? [*She tries to break from* EUNICE's *arms.*]

EUNICE   No, honey, no, no, honey. Stay here. Don't go back in there. Stay with me and don't look.

STELLA   What have I done to my sister? Oh, God, what have I done to my sister?

EUNICE   You done the right thing, the only thing you could do. She couldn't stay here; there wasn't no other place for her to go.

---

5. In an undertone [Italian].

[*While* STELLA *and* EUNICE *are speaking on the porch the voices of the men in the kitchen overlap them.* MITCH *has started toward the bedroom.* STANLEY *crosses to block him.* STANLEY *pushes him aside.* MITCH *lunges and strikes at* STANLEY. STANLEY *pushes* MITCH *back.* MITCH *collapses at the table, sobbing. During the preceding scenes, the* MATRON *catches hold of* BLANCHE's *arm and prevents her flight.* BLANCHE *turns wildly and scratches at the* MATRON. *The heavy woman pinions her arms.* BLANCHE *cries out hoarsely and slips to her knees.*]

MATRON   These fingernails have to be trimmed. [*The* DOCTOR *comes into the room and she looks at him.*] Jacket, Doctor?

DOCTOR   Not unless necessary.

[*He takes off his hat and now he becomes personalized. The unhuman quality goes. His voice is gentle and reassuring as he crosses to* BLANCHE *and crouches in front of her. As he speaks her name, her terror subsides a little. The lurid reflections fade from the walls, the inhuman cries and noises die out and her own hoarse crying is calmed.*]

DOCTOR   Miss DuBois.

[*She turns her face to him and stares at him with desperate pleading. He smiles; then he speaks to the* MATRON.]

It won't be necessary.

BLANCHE [*faintly*]   Ask her to let go of me.

DOCTOR [*to the* MATRON]   Let go.

[*The* MATRON *releases her.* BLANCHE *extends her hands toward the* DOCTOR. *He draws her up gently and supports her with his arm and leads her through the portieres.*]

BLANCHE [*holding tight to his arm*]   Whoever you are—I have always depended on the kindness of strangers.

[*The poker players stand back as* BLANCHE *and the* DOCTOR *cross the kitchen to the front door. She allows him to lead her as if she were blind. As they go out on the porch,* STELLA *cries out her sister's name from where she is crouched a few steps up on the stairs.*]

STELLA   Blanche! Blanche, Blanche!

[BLANCHE *walks on without turning, followed by the* DOCTOR *and the* MATRON. *They go around the corner of the building.* EUNICE *descends to* STELLA *and places the child in her arms. It is wrapped in a pale blue blanket.* STELLA *accepts the child, sobbingly.* EUNICE *continues downstairs and enters the kitchen where the men, except for* STANLEY, *are returning silently to their places about the table.* STANLEY *has gone out on the porch and stands at the foot of the steps looking at* STELLA.]

STANLEY [*a bit uncertainly*]   Stella?

[*She sobs with inhuman abandon. There is something luxurious in her complete surrender to crying now that her sister is gone.*]

STANLEY [*voluptuously, soothingly*]   Now, honey. Now, love. Now, now, love. [*He kneels beside her and his fingers find the opening of her blouse.*] Now, now, love, Now, love. . . .

[*The luxurious sobbing, the sensual murmur fade away under the swelling music of the "Blue Piano" and the muted trumpet.*]

STEVE   This game is seven-card stud.

CURTAIN

1947

JOHN CHEEVER
1912–1982

" **I** t seems to me that man's inclination toward light, toward brightness, is very nearly botanical—and I mean spiritual light. One not only needs it, one struggles for it." These sentences from an interview with John Cheever, conducted by the novelist John Hersey, at first glance look strange coming from a *"New Yorker* writer" of entertaining stories in which harried, well-to-do, white middle-class suburbanites conduct their lives. "Our Chekhov of the exurbs," he was dubbed by the reviewer John Leonard, with reference to the mythical community of Shady Hill (which Cheever created along the lines of existing ones in Fairfield, Connecticut, or Westchester County, New York). Yet Chekhov's own characters, living in darkness, aspire toward "spiritual fight," with a similarly "botanical" inclination. Trapped in their beautifully appointed houses and neighborhoods but carried along by the cool, effortless prose of their creator, Cheever's characters are viewed with a sympathetic irony, well-seasoned by sadness.

Cheever's early years were not notably idyllic, and he reveals little nostalgia for a lost childhood. Born in Quincy, Massachusetts, he grew up in what he describes as shabby gentility, with his father departing the family when his son was fifteen. (Cheever had an older brother, Fred, with whom he formed a strong but troubled relationship.) Two years later his father lost the family's money in the crash of 1929, and by that time Cheever had been expelled from Thayer Academy, in Braintree. The expulsion marked the end of his formal education and the beginning of his career as a writer; for, remarkably, he wrote a short story about the experience, titled it "Expelled," and sent it to the *New Republic,* where Malcolm Cowley (who would become a lifelong friend) published it.

During the 1930s Cheever lived in New York City, in impoverished circumstances, taking odd jobs to support himself and winning a fellowship to the writer's colony at Yaddo, in Saratoga Springs. His New York life would provide the material for many of his early stories, whose protagonists are rather frequently in desperate economic situations. With the coming of World War II, Cheever joined the armed forces and served in the Pacific theater but saw no combat. In 1941 he married Mary Winternitz. About the marriage, which produced three children and lasted through four decades, Cheever said, "That two people—both of us tempermental, quarrelsome, and intensely ambitious—could have gotten along for such a vast period of time is for me a very good example of the boundlessness of human nature." Meanwhile, with the help of Malcolm Cowley, he began to publish in the *New Yorker* and in 1943, while he was serving in the military, his first book of stories (*The Way Some People Live*) was published to favorable reviews. Over the decades to follow the stories continued to appear, largely in the *New Yorker,* where he became—along with J. D. Salinger and John Updike—a recurrent phenomenon. Five further volumes of short fiction were published, and in 1978 *The Stories of John Cheever* gathered those he wished to be remembered for.

Although he is praised for his skill as a realist depictor of suburban manners and morals, Cheever's art cannot be adequately understood in such terms. As Stephen C. Moore has usefully pointed out, "His best stories move from a base in a mimetic presentation of surface reality—the *scenery* of apparently successful American middle class life—to fables of heroism." Cheever's embattled heroes express themselves in taking up challenges that are essentially fabulous, and foolhardy: swimming home across the backyard pools of Westchester ("The Swimmer," printed here); performing feats of physical daredeviltry in suburban living rooms ("O Youth and Beauty"); or dealing with the myriad demands and temptations that beset the hero who, having escaped death in an airplane, returns home to more severe trials ("The Country Husband"). Whatever the specific narrative, we are always aware of the storyteller's art, shaping ordinary life into the odder, more willful figures of fantasy and romance.

While Cheever will be remembered primarily as a short-story writer, his output includes a respectable number of novels. In 1957 he won a National Book Award for his first one, *The Wapshot Chronicle* (it was followed by *The Wapshot Scandal*, in 1964), notable for its New England seacoast setting and domestic flavor, if less so for a continuously engaging narrative line. Perhaps his most gripping novel is *Bullet Park* (1969), which, like the best of the stories, is both realistic and fabulous. The suburban milieu, seen from the 5:42 train from New York, has never been depicted more accurately, even lovingly, by Cheever. And as is to be expected, his protagonist's carefully built, pious suburban existence turns out to be a mess. The novel provoked interesting disagreement about its merits (some critics felt the narrative manipulations both ruthless and sentimental), but there was no disagreement about the vivid quality of its represented life, on the commuter train or at the cocktail party. In the years just previous to his death, and after a bout with alcohol and drug addiction, Cheever published his two final novels, *Falconer* (1978) and *Oh What a Paradise It Seems* (1980), the former receiving much praise for its harrowing rendering of prison life. (Farragut, the novel's hero, is sent to Falconer Prison for killing his brother; Cheever lived in Ossining, New York, home of Sing Sing Prison, during his later years.)

From the beginning to the end of his career he was and remained a thoroughly professional writer, wary of pronouncing on the world at large (there is a noticeable absence of politics and ideology in his work) or on the meaning and significance of his own art. As one sees from his *Journals* (1991), he agonized over the disruptive facts of his alcoholism and his homosexuality. But he remained a private man, seemingly untouched by experiments—or fads—in fiction writing. Whether or not, as T. S. Eliot said about Henry James, he had a mind so fine that no idea could violate it, Cheever remained firmly resistant to ideas of all sorts. This insular tendency is probably a reason why his work makes less than a "major" claim on us, but it is also the condition responsible for his devoted and scrupulous attention to the particularities of middle-class life at the far edge of its promised dream.

This text of "The Swimmer" is from *The Brigadier and the Golf Widow* (1964).

The Swimmer

It was one of those midsummer Sundays when everyone sits around saying: "I *drank* too much last night." You might have heard it whispered by the parishioners leaving church, heard it from the lips of the priest himself, struggling with his cassock in the *vestiarium*,[1] heard it from the golf links and the tennis courts, heard it from the wildlife preserve where the leader of the Audubon group was suffering from a terrible hangover. "I *drank* too much," said Donald Westerhazy. "We all *drank* too much," said Lucinda Merrill. "It must have been the wine," said Helen Westerhazy. "I *drank* too much of that claret."

This was at the edge of the Westerhazys' pool. The pool, fed by an artesian well with a high iron content, was a pale shade of green. It was a fine

---

1. Cloakroom for religious vestments adjacent to a church's sanctuary.

day. In the west there was a massive stand of cumulus cloud so like a city seen from a distance—from the bow of an approaching ship—that it might have had a name. Lisbon. Hackensack.[2] The sun was hot. Neddy Merrill sat by the green water, one hand in it, one around a glass of gin. He was a slender man—he seemed to have the especial slenderness of youth—and while he was far from young he had slid down his banister that morning and given the bronze backside of Aphrodite[3] on the hall table a smack, as he jogged toward the smell of coffee in his dining room. He might have been compared to a summer's day, particularly the last hours of one, and while he lacked a tennis racket or a sail bag the impression was definitely one of youth, sport, and clement weather. He had been swimming and now he was breathing deeply, stertorously as if he could gulp into his lungs the components of that moment, the heat of the sun, the intenseness of his pleasure. It all seemed to flow into his chest. His own house stood in Bullet Park,[4] eight miles to the south, where his four beautiful daughters would have had their lunch and might be playing tennis. Then it occurred to him that by taking a dogleg to the southwest he could reach his home by water.

His life was not confining and the delight he took in this observation could not be explained by its suggestion of escape. He seemed to see, with a cartographer's eye, that string of swimming pools, that quasi-subterranean stream that curved across the county. He had made a discovery, a contribution to modern geography; he would name the stream Lucinda after his wife. He was not a practical joker nor was he a fool but he was determinedly original and had a vague and modest idea of himself as a legendary figure. The day was beautiful and it seemed to him that a long swim might enlarge and celebrate its beauty.

He took off a sweater that was hung over his shoulders and dove in. He had an inexplicable contempt for men who did not hurl themselves into pools. He swam a choppy crawl, breathing either with every stroke or every fourth stroke and counting somewhere well in the back of his mind the one-two one-two of a flutter kick. It was not a serviceable stroke for long distances but the domestication of swimming had saddled the sport with some customs and in his part of the world a crawl was customary. To be embraced and sustained by the light green water was less a pleasure, it seemed, than the resumption of a natural condition, and he would have liked to swim without trunks, but this was not possible, considering his project. He hoisted himself up on the far curb—he never used the ladder—and started across the lawn. When Lucinda asked where he was going he said he was going to swim home.

The only maps and charts he had to go by were remembered or imaginary but these were clear enough. First there were the Grahams, the Hammers, the Lears, the Howlands, and the Crosscups. He would cross Ditmar Street to the Bunkers and come, after a short portage, to the Levys, the Welchers, and the public pool in Lancaster. Then there were the Hallorans, the Sachses, the Biswangers, Shirley Adams, the Gilmartins, and the Clydes. The day was lovely, and that he lived in a world so generously supplied with water seemed like a clemency, a beneficence. His heart was high and he ran across the grass. Making his way home by an uncommon route gave him

2. A town in New Jersey. Lisbon is the capital of Portugal.
3. Greek goddess of love and beauty.

4. Fictive suburb used as a location for many of Cheever's stories and novels.

the feeling that he was a pilgrim, an explorer, a man with a destiny, and he knew that he would find friends all along the way; friends would line the banks of the Lucinda River.

He went through a hedge that separated the Westerhazys' land from the Grahams', walked under some flowering apple trees, passed the shed that housed their pump and filter, and came out at the Grahams' pool. "Why, Neddy," Mrs. Graham said, "what a marvelous surprise. I've been trying to get you on the phone all morning. Here, let me get you a drink." He saw then, like any explorer, that the hospitable customs and traditions of the natives would have to be handled with diplomacy if he was ever going to reach his destination. He did not want to mystify or seem rude to the Grahams nor did he have the time to linger there. He swam the length of their pool and joined them in the sun and was rescued, a few minutes later, by the arrival of two carloads of friends from Connecticut. During the uproarious reunions he was able to slip away. He went down by the front of the Grahams' house, stepped over a thorny hedge, and crossed a vacant lot to the Hammers'. Mrs. Hammer, looking up from her roses, saw him swim by although she wasn't quite sure who it was. The Lears heard him splashing past the open windows of their living room. The Howlands and the Crosscups were away. After leaving the Howlands' he crossed Ditmar Street and started for the Bunkers', where he could hear, even at that distance, the noise of a party.

The water refracted the sound of voices and laughter and seemed to suspend it in midair. The Bunkers' pool was on a rise and he climbed some stairs to a terrace where twenty-five or thirty men and women were drinking. The only person in the water was Rusty Towers, who floated there on a rubber raft. Oh how bonny and lush were the banks of the Lucinda River! Prosperous men and women gathered by the sapphire-colored waters while caterer's men in white coats passed them cold gin. Overhead a red de Haviland trainer was circling around and around and around in the sky with something like the glee of a child in a swing. Ned felt a passing affection for the scene, a tenderness for the gathering, as if it was something he might touch. In the distance he heard thunder. As soon as Enid Bunker saw him she began to scream: "Oh look who's here! What a marvelous surprise! When Lucinda said that you couldn't come I thought I'd *die*." She made her way to him through the crowd, and when they had finished kissing she led him to the bar, a progress that was slowed by the fact that he stopped to kiss eight or ten other women and shake the hands of as many men. A smiling bartender he had seen at a hundred parties gave him a gin and tonic and he stood by the bar for a moment, anxious not to get stuck in any conversation that would delay his voyage. When he seemed about to be surrounded he dove in and swam close to the side to avoid colliding with Rusty's raft. At the far end of the pool he bypassed the Tomlinsons with a broad smile and jogged up the garden path. The gravel cut his feet but this was the only unpleasantness. The party was confined to the pool, and as he went toward the house he heard the brilliant, watery sound of voices fade, heard the noise of a radio from the Bunkers' kitchen, where someone was listening to a ballgame. Sunday afternoon. He made his way through the parked cars and down the grassy border of their driveway to Alewives' Lane. He did not want to be seen on the road in his bathing trunks but there was no traffic and he made the short distance to the Levys' driveway, marked with a private property sign and a green tube for the *New York Times.* All the doors and windows of the big house were open but there were no signs of life; not even a dog barked. He went around the side of the house to the pool and saw that the Levys had only recently left. Glasses and bottles and dishes of nuts were on a table at the deep end, where there was a bathhouse or gazebo, hung with Japanese lanterns. After swimming the pool he got himself a glass and poured a drink. It was his fourth or fifth drink and he had swum nearly half the length of the Lucinda River. He felt tired, clean, and pleased at that moment to be alone; pleased with everything.

It would storm. The stand of cumulus cloud—that city—had risen and darkened, and while he sat there he heard the percussiveness of thunder again. The de Haviland trainer was still circling overhead and it seemed to Ned that he could almost hear the pilot laugh with pleasure in the afternoon; but when there was another peal of thunder he took off for home. A train whistle blew and he wondered what time it had gotten to be. Four? Five? He thought of the provincial station at that hour, where a waiter, his tuxedo concealed by a raincoat, a dwarf with some flowers wrapped in newspaper, and a woman who had been crying would be waiting for the local. It was suddenly growing dark; it was that moment when the pin-headed birds seem to organize their song into some acute and knowledgeable recognition of the storm's approach. Then there was a fine noise of rushing water from the crown of an oak at his back, as if a spigot there had been turned. Then the noise of fountains came from the crowns of all the tall trees. Why did he love storms, what was the meaning of his excitement when the door sprang open and the rain wind fled rudely up the stairs, why had the simple task of shutting the windows of an old house seemed fitting and urgent, why did the first watery notes of a storm wind have for him the unmistakable sound of good news, cheer, glad tidings? Then there was an explosion, a smell of cordite, and rain lashed the Japanese lanterns that Mrs. Levy had bought in Kyoto the year before last, or was it the year before that?

He stayed in the Levys' gazebo until the storm had passed. The rain had cooled the air and he shivered. The force of the wind had stripped a maple of its red and yellow leaves and scattered them over the grass and the water. Since it was midsummer the tree must be blighted, and yet he felt a peculiar sadness at this sign of autumn. He braced his shoulders, emptied his glass, and started for the Welchers' pool. This meant crossing the Lindleys' riding ring and he was surprised to find it overgrown with grass and all the jumps dismantled. He wondered if the Lindleys had sold their horses or gone away for the summer and put them out to board. He seemed to remember having heard something about the Lindleys and their horses but the memory was unclear. On he went, barefoot through the wet grass, to the Welchers', where he found their pool was dry.

This breach in his chain of water disappointed him absurdly, and he felt like some explorer who seeks a torrential headwater and finds a dead stream. He was disappointed and mystified. It was common enough to go away for the summer but no one ever drained his pool. The Welchers had definitely gone away. The pool furniture was folded, stacked, and covered with a tarpaulin. The bathhouse was locked. All the windows of the house were shut, and when he went around to the driveway in front he saw a for-sale sign nailed to a tree. When had he last heard from the Welchers—when, that is, had he and Lucinda last regretted an invitation to dine with them? It seemed only a week or so ago. Was his memory failing or had he so disciplined it in the repression of unpleasant facts that he had damaged his sense of the truth? Then in the distance he heard the sound of a tennis game. This cheered him, cleared away all his apprehensions and let him regard the overcast sky and the cold air with indifference. This was the day that Neddy Merrill swam across the county. That was the day! He started off then for his most difficult portage.

Had you gone for a Sunday afternoon ride that day you might have seen him, close to naked, standing on the shoulders of route 424, waiting for a chance to cross. You might have wondered if he was the victim of foul play, had his car broken down, or was he merely a fool. Standing barefoot in the deposits of the highway—beer cans, rags, and blowout patches—exposed to all kinds of ridicule, he seemed pitiful. He had known when he started that this was a part of his journey—it had been on his maps—but confronted with the lines of traffic, worming through the summery light, he found himself unprepared. He was laughed at, jeered at, a beer can was thrown at him, and he had no dignity or humor to bring to the situation. He could have gone back, back to the Westerhazys', where Lucinda would still be sitting in the sun. He had signed nothing, vowed nothing, pledged nothing, not even to himself. Why, believing as he did, that all human obduracy was susceptible to common sense, was he unable to turn back? Why was he determined to complete his journey even if it meant putting his life in danger? At what point had this prank, this joke, this piece of horseplay become serious? He could not go back, he could not even recall with any clearness the green water at the Westerhazys', the sense of inhaling the day's components, the friendly and relaxed voices saying that they had *drunk* too much. In the space of an hour, more or less, he had covered a distance that made his return impossible.

An old man, tooling down the highway at fifteen miles an hour, let him get to the middle of the road, where there was a grass divider. Here he was exposed to the ridicule of the northbound traffic, but after ten or fifteen minutes he was able to cross. From here he had only a short walk to the Recreation Center at the edge of the Village of Lancaster, where there were some handball courts and a public pool.

The effect of the water on voices, the illusion of brilliance and suspense, was the same here as it had been at the Bunkers' but the sounds here were louder, harsher, and more shrill, and as soon as he entered the crowded enclosure he was confronted with regimentation. "ALL SWIMMERS MUST TAKE A SHOWER BEFORE USING THE POOL. ALL SWIMMERS MUST USE THE FOOTBATH. ALL SWIMMERS MUST WEAR THEIR IDENTIFICATION DISKS." He took a shower, washed his feet in a cloudy and bitter solution and made his way to the edge of the water. It stank of chlorine and looked to him like a sink. A pair of lifeguards in a pair of towers blew police whistles at what seemed to be regular intervals and abused the swimmers through a public address system. Neddy remembered the sapphire water at the Bunkers' with longing and thought that he might contaminate himself—damage his own prosperousness and charm—by swimming in this murk, but he reminded himself that he was an explorer, a pilgrim, and that this was merely a stagnant bend in the Lucinda River. He dove, scowling with distaste, into the chlorine and had to swim with his head above water to avoid collisions, but even so he was bumped into, splashed and jostled. When he got to the shallow end both lifeguards were shouting at him: "Hey, you, you without the identification disk, get outa the water." He did, but they had no way of pursuing him and he went through the reek of suntan oil and chlorine out through the hurricane fence and passed the handball courts. By crossing the road he entered the wooded part of the Halloran estate. The woods were not cleared and the footing was treacherous and difficult until he reached the lawn and the clipped beech hedge that encircled their pool.

The Hallorans were friends, an elderly couple of enormous wealth who seemed to bask in the suspicion that they might be Communists. They were zealous reformers but they were not Communists, and yet when they were accused, as they sometimes were, of subversion, it seemed to gratify and excite them. Their beech hedge was yellow and he guessed this had been blighted like the Levys' maple. He called hullo, hullo, to warn the Hallorans of his approach, to palliate his invasion of their privacy. The Hallorans, for reasons that had never been explained to him, did not wear bathing suits. No explanations were in order, really. Their nakedness was a detail in their uncompromising zeal for reform and he stepped politely out of his trunks before he went through the opening in the hedge.

Mrs. Halloran, a stout woman with white hair and a serene face, was reading the *Times*. Mr. Halloran was taking beech leaves out of the water with a scoop. They seemed not surprised or displeased to see him. Their pool was perhaps the oldest in the county, a fieldstone rectangle, fed by a brook. It had no filter or pump and its waters were the opaque gold of the stream.

"I'm swimming across the county," Ned said.

"Why, I didn't know one could," exclaimed Mrs. Halloran.

"Well, I've made it from the Westerhazys'," Ned said. "That must be about four miles."

He left his trunks at the deep end, walked to the shallow end, and swam this stretch. As he was pulling himself out of the water he heard Mrs. Halloran say: "We've been *terribly* sorry to hear about all your misfortunes, Neddy."

"My misfortunes?" Ned asked. "I don't know what you mean."

"Why, we heard that you'd sold the house and that your poor children . . ."

"I don't recall having sold the house," Ned said, "and the girls are at home."

"Yes," Mrs. Halloran sighed. "Yes . . ." Her voice filled the air with an unseasonable melancholy and Ned spoke briskly. "Thank you for the swim."

"Well, have a nice trip," said Mrs. Halloran.

Beyond the hedge he pulled on his trunks and fastened them. They were loose and he wondered if, during the space of an afternoon, he could have lost some weight. He was cold and he was tired and the naked Hallorans and their dark water had depressed him. The swim was too much for his strength but how could he have guessed this, sliding down the banister that morning and sitting in the Westerhazys' sun? His arms were lame. His legs felt rubbery and ached at the joints. The worst of it was the cold in his bones and the feeling that he might never be warm again. Leaves were falling down around him and he smelled woodsmoke on the wind. Who would be burning wood at this time of year?

He needed a drink. Whiskey would warm him, pick him up, carry him through the last of his journey, refresh his feeling that it was original and valorous to swim across the county. Channel swimmers took brandy. He needed a stimulant. He crossed the lawn in front of the Hallorans' house and went down a little path to where they had built a house for their only daughter Helen and her husband Eric Sachs. The Sachses' pool was small and he found Helen and her husband there.

"Oh, *Neddy*," Helen said. "Did you lunch at Mother's?"

"Not *really*," Ned said. "I *did* stop to see your parents." This seemed to be explanation enough. "I'm terribly sorry to break in on you like this but I've taken a chill and I wonder if you'd give me a drink."

"Why, I'd *love* to," Helen said, "but there hasn't been anything in this house to drink since Eric's operation. That was three years ago."

Was he losing his memory, had his gift for concealing painful facts let him forget that he had sold his house, that his children were in trouble, and that his friend had been ill? His eyes slipped from Eric's face to his abdomen, where he saw three pale, sutured scars, two of them at least a foot long. Gone was his navel, and what, Neddy thought, would the roving hand, bed-checking one's gifts at 3 A.M. make of a belly with no navel, no link to birth, this breach in the succession?

"I'm sure you can get a drink at the Biswangers'," Helen said. "They're having an enormous do. You can hear it from here. Listen!"

She raised her head and from across the road, the lawns, the gardens, the woods, the fields, he heard again the brilliant noise of voices over water. "Well, I'll get wet," he said, still feeling that he had no freedom of choice about his means of travel. He dove into the Sachses' cold water and, gasping, close to drowning, made his way from one end of the pool to the other. "Lucinda and I want *terribly* to see you," he said over his shoulder, his face set toward the Biswangers'. "We're sorry it's been so long and we'll call you *very* soon."

He crossed some fields to the Biswangers' and the sounds of revelry there. They would be honored to give him a drink, they would be happy to give him a drink, they would in fact be lucky to give him a drink. The Biswangers invited him and Lucinda for dinner four times a year, six weeks in advance. They were always rebuffed and yet they continued to send out their invitations, unwilling to comprehend the rigid and undemocratic realities of their society. They were the sort of people who discussed the price of things at cocktails, exchanged market tips during dinner, and after dinner told dirty stories to mixed company. They did not belong to Neddy's set—they were not even on Lucinda's Christmas card list. He went toward their pool with feelings of indifference, charity, and some unease, since it seemed to be getting dark and these were the longest days of the year. The party when he joined it was noisy and large. Grace Biswanger was the kind of hostess who asked the optometrist, the veterinarian, the real-estate dealer and the dentist. No one was swimming and the twilight, reflected on the water of the pool, had a wintry gleam. There was a bar and he started for this. When Grace Biswanger saw him she came toward him, not affectionately as he had every right to expect, but bellicosely.

"Why, this party has everything," she said loudly, "including a gate crasher."

She could not deal him a social blow—there was no question about this and he did not flinch. "As a gate crasher," he asked politely, "do I rate a drink?"

"Suit yourself," she said. "You don't seem to pay much attention to invitations."

She turned her back on him and joined some guests, and he went to the bar and ordered a whiskey. The bartender served him but he served him rudely. His was a world in which the caterer's men kept the social score, and to be rebuffed by a part-time barkeep meant that he had suffered some loss of social esteem. Or perhaps the man was new and uninformed. Then he heard Grace at his back say: "They went for broke overnight—nothing but income—and he showed up drunk one Sunday and asked us to loan him five thousand dollars. . . ." She was always talking about money. It was worse than eating your peas off a knife. He dove into the pool, swam its length and went away.

The next pool on his list, the last but two, belonged to his old mistress, Shirley Adams. If he had suffered any injuries at the Biswangers' they would be cured here. Love—sexual roughhouse in fact—was the supreme elixir, the painkiller, the brightly colored pill that would put the spring back into his step, the joy of life in his heart. They had had an affair last week, last month, last year. He couldn't remember. It was he who had broken it off, his was the upper hand, and he stepped through the gate of the wall that surrounded her pool with nothing so considered as self-confidence. It seemed in a way to be his pool as the lover, particularly the illicit lover, enjoys the possessions of his mistress with an authority unknown to holy matrimony. She was there, her hair the color of brass, but her figure, at the edge of the lighted, cerulean water, excited in him no profound memories. It had been, he thought, a light-hearted affair, although she had wept when he broke it off. She seemed confused to see him and he wondered if she was still wounded. Would she, God forbid, weep again?

"What do you want?" she asked.

"I'm swimming across the county."

"Good Christ. Will you ever grow up?"

"What's the matter?"

"If you've come here for money," she said, "I won't give you another cent."

"You could give me a drink."

"I could but I won't. I'm not alone."

"Well, I'm on my way."

He dove in and swam the pool, but when he tried to haul himself up onto the curb he found that the strength in his arms and his shoulders had gone, and he paddled to the ladder and climbed out. Looking over his shoulder he saw, in the lighted bathhouse, a young man. Going out onto the dark lawn he smelled chrysanthemums or marigolds—some stubborn autumnal fragrance—on the night air, strong as gas. Looking overhead he saw that the stars had come out, but why should he seem to see Andromeda, Cepheus, and Cassiopeia? What had become of the constellations of midsummer? He began to cry.

It was probably the first time in his adult life that he had ever cried, certainly the first time in his life that he had ever felt so miserable, cold, tired, and bewildered. He could not understand the rudeness of the caterer's barkeep or the rudeness of a mistress who had come to him on her knees and showered his trousers with tears. He had swum too long, he had been immersed too long, and his nose and his throat were sore from the water. What he needed then was a drink, some company, and some clean dry clothes, and while he could have cut directly across the road to his home he went on to the Gilmartins' pool. Here, for the first time in his life, he did not dive but went down the steps into the icy water and swam a hobbled side stroke that he might have learned as a youth. He staggered with fatigue on his way to the Clydes' and paddled the length of their pool, stopping again and again with his hand on the curb to rest. He climbed up the ladder and wondered if he had the strength to get home. He had done what he wanted, he had swum the county, but he was so stupefied with exhaustion that his triumph seemed vague. Stooped, holding onto the gateposts for support, he turned up the driveway of his house.

The place was dark. Was it so late that they had all gone to bed? Had Lucinda stayed at the Westerhazys' for supper? Had the girls joined her there or gone someplace else? Hadn't they agreed, as they usually did on Sunday, to regret all their invitations and stay at home? He tried the garage doors to see what cars were in but the doors were locked and rust came off the handles onto his hands. Going toward the house, he saw that the force of the thunderstorm had knocked one of the rain gutters loose. It hung down over the front door like an umbrella rib, but it could be fixed in the morning. The house was locked, and he thought that the stupid cook or the stupid maid must have locked the place up until he remembered that it had been some time since they had employed a maid or a cook. He shouted, pounded on the door, tried to force it with his shoulder, and then, looking in at the windows, saw that the place was empty.

1964

ROBERT HAYDEN
1913–1980

" Hayden is by far the best chronicler and rememberer of the African American heritage in these Americas that I know of," the poet Michael Harper, whose own sense of history is indebted to Robert Hayden's work, has said. Hayden's poems save what has vanished, what has been lost to standard histories, like a 1920s prizefighter from the Midwest ("Free Fantasia: Tiger Flowers") or a miner trapped in Crystal Cave ("Beginnings, V"). He records the loss of what others never noticed as missing, and in their recovery he discovers a significance in the passing moment, the passed-over figure, the inarticulate gesture, which lasts through time. Always, in his words, "opposed to the chauvinistic and the doctrinaire" in art, he cherished the freedom of the poet to write about whatever seized the imagination. But his imagination was in its nature elegiac and historical. As he remembers and re-creates the African American heritage, he speaks to the struggles of the individual spirit for freedom and to painful self-divisions known to the people of many times and places. But if the circumstances he confronts in his poems are often harsh, his work captures the energy and joyfulness that make survival possible.

Born in Detroit, Michigan, Hayden grew up in a poor neighborhood called by its inhabitants, with affectionate irony, "Paradise Valley." His powerful sequence *Elegies for Paradise Valley* (1978) resurrects the neighborhood in its racial and ethnic mix. Memory for Hayden is an act of love that leads to self-awareness; in this sequence and in poems like "Those Winter Sundays," he writes about his own past, confronts its pain, and preserves its sustaining moments of happiness.

Hayden had a deep understanding of the conflicts that divide the self. His family history gave him an early acquaintance with such self-division: his parents' marriage ended when he was young, and his mother left him in the care of foster parents (whose surname he adopted) when she left Detroit to look for work. He remained with the Haydens even after his mother returned to Detroit when he was a teenager and lived for a period with his foster family until conflict arose between her and his foster mother. "I lived in the midst of so much turmoil all the time I didn't know if I loved or hated," he once said. As an African American and as a poet Hayden also lived between worlds. He courageously maintained his sense of vocation through years of critical neglect and amid the demands of full-time teaching at Fisk University from 1946 to 1968. He published his first book, *Heart-Shape in the Dust*, in 1940, but his mature work did not appear in quantity until his volume *Ballad of Remembrance* (1962). At the same time his belief that the poet should not be restricted by any set of themes, racial or otherwise, and the highly formal quality of his work led to criticism by some young African American writers in the 1960s. But Hayden never abandoned his belief in the power of art to speak universally. In a 1974 interview he told Dennis Gendron of rereading Yeats's poem "Easter 1916" in the wake of the riots in Detroit— "that is the kind of poetry I want to write," he said, in admiration of the ways Yeats conceived a particular historical and political moment so that it speaks across time and place.

In fact, Hayden did himself write that kind of poetry. His most famous poem, "Middle Passage," demonstrates his transfiguring imagination and the knowledge of historical documents, which began early in his career. In 1936, after leaving college because of increasingly difficult economic conditions, Hayden joined the Federal Writers Project of the Works Progress Administration, and for two years he researched the history of abolition movements and the Underground Railroad in Michigan. "Middle Passage" is a collage of accounts of the slave ships that transported men and women from Africa into slavery in the New World. Through the multiple voices in the poem, Hayden lets the accounts of those who participated in (and profited from) the slave trade reveal the evidence of their own damnation. The blindness that attacks one of the ships becomes a symbol of the devastating suffering of those transported into slavery and of the moral blindness everywhere evident in the traders' accounts. The collage technique allows Hayden to suggest the fragmentation of the story; the silences in the poem evoke the missing voices of those who suffered and died on the voyages or in the intolerable conditions of slavery. At the heart of the poem is the account of a rebellion led by one of the slaves (Cinquez) on the ship *Amistad*. Cinquez is one of several figures in Hayden's poems who dramatize "The deep immortal human wish / the timeless will" ("Middle Passage") that for Hayden is the indomitable yearning for freedom. This "timeless will" and struggle also appear in his poems about Harriet Tubman ("Runagate Runagate"), Nat Turner, Frederick Douglass, Phillis Wheatley, and the later figures Paul Robeson and Bessie Smith.

Hayden's experiment with collage technique in "Middle Passage" connects him to modernist poets like T. S. Eliot and William Carlos Williams and to an African American tradition acutely aware of the power of voice. He continued to experiment with poetic form and with the creation of different voices, always testing the possibilities of craft and forging a language to express what he knew and felt. His sequences *Beginnings* and *Elegies for Paradise Valley* demonstrate his formal originality, as does his late poem "American Journal," with its long lines and its approximation to prose. Hayden loved language and was unafraid to be lushly descriptive as well as to be precisely imagistic. His work summons us to notice the world as we had not before and offers us candor, clearsightedness, and a transforming gaiety.

From 1968 until his death Hayden was professor of English at the University of Michigan at Ann Arbor. In 1976 he became the first African American to be appointed poetry consultant to the Library of Congress, the position now known as poet laureate of the United States.

Middle Passage[1]

I

Jesús, Estrella, Esperanza, Mercy[2]

> Sails flashing to the wind like weapons,
> sharks following the moans the fever and the dying;
> horror the corposant and compass rose.[3]

Middle Passage: 5
>   voyage through death
>   to life upon these shores.

> "10 April 1800—
> Blacks rebellious. Crew uneasy. Our linguist says
> their moaning is a prayer for death,   10
> ours and their own. Some try to starve themselves.
> Lost three this morning leaped with crazy laughter
> to the waiting sharks, sang as they went under."

Desire, Adventure, Tartar, Ann:

> Standing to America, bringing home   15
> black gold, black ivory, black seed.

>> *Deep in the festering hold thy father lies,*
>> *of his bones New England pews are made,*
>> *those are altar lights that were his eyes.*[4]

Jesus   Saviour   Pilot   Me   20
Over   Life's   Tempestuous   Sea[5]

> We pray that Thou wilt grant, O Lord,
> safe passage to our vessels bringing
> heathen souls unto Thy chastening.

1. Main route for the slave trade in the Atlantic between Africa and the West Indies.
2. Names of slave ships. (*Estrella* and *Esperanza* are Spanish for "Star" and "Hope," respectively.)
3. Circle printed on a map showing compass directions. "Corposant": a fiery luminousness that can appear on the decks of ships during electrical storms.
4. "Full fathom five thy father lies; / Of his bones are coral made; / Those are pearls that were his eyes" (Shakespeare's *Tempest* 1.2.400–02). The sprite Ariel is singing about the supposed death by drowning of the king of Naples.
5. Words from a Protestant hymn.

Jesus   Saviour   25

    "8 bells. I cannot sleep, for I am sick
    with fear, but writing eases fear a little
    since still my eyes can see these words take shape
    upon the page & so I write, as one
    would turn to exorcism. 4 days scudding,   30
    but now the sea is calm again. Misfortune
    follows in our wake like sharks (our grinning
    tutelary gods). Which one of us
    has killed an albatross?[6] A plague among
    our blacks—Ophthalmia: blindness—& we   35
    have jettisoned the blind to no avail.
    It spreads, the terrifying sickness spreads.
    Its claws have scratched sight from the Capt.'s eyes
    & there is blindness in the fo'c'sle[7]
    & we must sail 3 weeks before we come   40
    to port."

        What port awaits us, Davy Jones'
        or home? I've heard of slavers drifting, drifting,
        playthings of wind and storm and chance, their crews
        gone blind, the jungle hatred   45
        crawling up on deck.

Thou   Who   Walked   On   Galilee

    "Deponent further sayeth *The Bella J*
    left the Guinea Coast
    with cargo of five hundred blacks and odd   50
    for the barracoons[8] of Florida:

    "That there was hardly room 'tween-decks for half
    the sweltering cattle stowed spoon-fashion there;
    that some went mad of thirst and tore their flesh
    and sucked the blood: 55

    "That Crew and Captain lusted with the comeliest
    of the savage girls kept naked in the cabins;
    that there was one they called The Guinea Rose
    and they cast lots and fought to lie with her:

    "That when the Bo's'n piped all hands,[9] the flames   60
    spreading from starboard already were beyond
    control, the negroes howling and their chains
    entangled with the flames:

---

6. A bird of good omen; to kill one is an unlucky
and impious act (as in Samuel Taylor Coleridge's
Rime of the Ancient Mariner).
7. Short for forecastle, the place in a ship where
sailors are quartered.
8. Barracks or enclosures for slaves.
9. I.e., when the boatswain (petty officer aboard
a ship) signaled to summon all the crew on deck.

"That the burning blacks could not be reached,
that the Crew abandoned ship,   65
leaving their shrieking negresses behind,
that the Captain perished drunken with the wenches:

"Further Deponent sayeth not."

Pilot   Oh   Pilot   Me

II

Aye, lad, and I have seen those factories,   70
Gambia, Rio Pongo, Calabar;[1]
have watched the artful mongos[2] baiting traps
of war wherein the victor and the vanquished

Were caught as prizes for our barracoons.
Have seen the nigger kings whose vanity   75
and greed turned wild black hides of Fellatah,
Mandingo, Ibo, Kru[3] to gold for us.

And there was one—King Anthracite we named him—
fetish face beneath French parasols
of brass and orange velvet, impudent mouth   80
whose cups were carven skulls of enemies:

He'd honor us with drum and feast and conjo[4]
and palm-oil-glistening wenches deft in love,
and for tin crowns that shone with paste,
red calico and German-silver trinkets   85

Would have the drums talk war and send
his warriors to burn the sleeping villages
and kill the sick and old and lead the young
in coffles[5] to our factories.

Twenty years a trader, twenty years,   90
for there was wealth aplenty to be harvested
from those black fields, and I'd be trading still
but for the fevers melting down my bones.

III

Shuttles in the rocking loom of history,
the dark ships move, the dark ships move,   95
their bright ironical names
like jests of kindness on a murderer's mouth;

---

1. A city in southeast Nigeria. Gambia is a river
and nation in West Africa. Rio Pongo is a water-
course, dry for most of the year, in East Africa.
2. I.e., Africans.

3. African tribes.
4. Dance.
5. Train of slaves fastened together.

plough through thrashing glister toward
fata morgana's lucent melting shore,
weave toward New World littorals[6] that are   100
mirage and myth and actual shore.

Voyage through death,
                    voyage whose chartings are unlove.

A charnel stench, effluvium of living death
spreads outward from the hold,   105
where the living and the dead, the horribly dying,
lie interlocked, lie foul with blood and excrement.

> *Deep in the festering hold thy father lies,*
> *the corpse of mercy rots with him,*
> *rats eat love's rotten gelid eyes.*   110

But, oh, the living look at you
with human eyes whose suffering accuses you,
whose hatred reaches through the swill of dark
to strike you like a leper's claw.

You cannot stare that hatred down   115
or chain the fear that stalks the watches
and breathes on you its fetid scorching breath;
cannot kill the deep immortal human wish,
the timeless will.

> "But for the storm that flung up barriers   120
> of wind and wave, *The Amistad,*[7] señores,
> would have reached the port or Príncipe in two,
> three days at most; but for the storm we should
> have been prepared for what befell.
> Swift as the puma's leap it came. There was   125
> that interval of moonless calm filled only
> with the water's and the rigging's usual sounds,
> then sudden movement, blows and snarling cries
> and they had fallen on us with machete
> and marlinspike. It was as though the very   130
> air, the night itself were striking us.
> Exhausted by the rigors of the storm,
> we were no match for them. Our men went down
> before the murderous Africans. Our loyal
> Celestino ran from below with gun   135
> and lantern and I saw, before the cane-
> knife's wounding flash, Cinquez,
> that surly brute who calls himself a prince,

6. Coastal regions. "Fata morgana": mirage.
7. A Spanish ship—the name means "Friendship"—that carried fifty-three illegally obtained
slaves out of Havana, Cuba, in July 1839. The
slaves revolted and seized the ship.

directing, urging on the ghastly work.[8]
He hacked the poor mulatto down, and then   140
he turned on me. The decks were slippery
when daylight finally came. It sickens me
to think of what I saw, of how these apes
threw overboard the butchered bodies of
our men, true Christians all, like so much jetsam.   145
Enough, enough. The rest is quickly told:
Cinquez was forced to spare the two of us
you see to steer the ship to Africa,
and we like phantoms doomed to rove the sea
voyaged east by day and west by night,   150
deceiving them, hoping for rescue,
prisoners on our own vessel, till
at length we drifted to the shores of this
your land, America, where we were freed
from our unspeakable misery. Now we   155
demand, good sirs, the extradition of
Cinquez and his accomplices to La
Havana.[9] And it distresses us to know
there are so many here who seem inclined
to justify the mutiny of these blacks.   160
We find it paradoxical indeed
that you whose wealth, whose tree of liberty
are rooted in the labor of your slaves
should suffer the august John Quincy Adams
to speak with so much passion of the right   165
of chattel slaves to kill their lawful masters
and with his Roman rhetoric weave a hero's
garland for Cinquez.[1] I tell you that
we are determined to return to Cuba
with our slaves and there see justice done. Cinquez—   170
or let us say 'the Prince'—Cinquez shall die."

The deep immortal human wish,
the timeless will:

Cinquez its deathless primaveral image,
life that transfigures many lives.   175

Voyage through death
            to life upon these shores.

                                                1962

___

8. During the mutiny the Africans, led by a man called Cinqué, or Cinquez, killed the captain, his slave Celestino, and the mate, but spared the two slave owners.
9. After two months the *Amistad* reached Long Island Sound, where it was detained by the American ship *Washington*, the slaves were imprisoned, and the owners were freed. The owners began litigation to return the slaves to Havana to be tried for murder.
1. The case reached the Supreme Court in 1841; the Africans were defended by former president John Quincy Adams, and the court released the thirty-seven survivors to return to Africa.

Homage to the Empress of the Blues[1]

Because there was a man somewhere in a candystripe silk shirt,
gracile and dangerous as a jaguar and because a woman moaned for him
in sixty-watt gloom and mourned him Faithless Love
Twotiming Love Oh Love Oh Careless Aggravating Love,

> She came out on the stage in yards of pearls, emerging like   5
> a favorite scenic view, flashed her golden smile and sang.

Because grey laths began somewhere to show from underneath
torn hurdygurdy[2] lithographs of dollfaced heaven;
and because there were those who feared alarming fists of snow
on the door and those who feared the riot-squad of statistics,   10

> She came out on the stage in ostrich feathers, beaded satin,
> and shone that smile on us and sang.

        1962

Those Winter Sundays

> Sundays too my father got up early
> and put his clothes on in the blueblack cold,
> then with cracked hands that ached
> from labor in the weekday weather made
> banked fires blaze. No one ever thanked him.   5
>
> I'd wake and hear the cold splintering, breaking.
> When the rooms were warm, he'd call,
> and slowly I would rise and dress,
> fearing the chronic angers of that house,
>
> Speaking indifferently to him,   10
> who had driven out the cold
> and polished my good shoes as well.
> What did I know, what did I know
> of love's austere and lonely offices?

        1962

---

1. Bessie Smith (1895–1937), one of the greatest American blues singers. Her flamboyant style, which grew out of the black vaudeville tradition, made her popular in the 1920s.

2. A disreputable kind of dance hall. "Laths": the strips of wood that form a backing for wall plaster.

Free Fantasia: Tiger Flowers[1]

for Michael

The sporting people
along St. Antoine—[2]
that scufflers'
paradise of ironies—
   bet salty money   5
on his righteous
   hook and jab.

I was a boy then, running
(unbeknownst to Pa)
errands for Miss Jackie   10
and Stack-o'-Diamonds' Eula Mae.
. . . Their perfumes,
rouged Egyptian faces.
   Their pianolas jazzing.

O Creole babies,   15
Dixie odalisques,[3]
speeding through cutglass
dark to see the macho angel
   trick you'd never
turn, his bluesteel prowess   20
   in the ring.

Hardshell believers
amen'd the wreck
as God A'mighty's
will. I'd thought   25
   such gaiety could not
die. Nor could our
   elegant avenger.

The Virgin Forest
by Rousseau[4]—   30
its psychedelic flowers
towering, its deathless
   dark dream figure
death the leopard
   claws—I choose it   35
now as elegy
   for Tiger Flowers.

1975

---

1. A midwestern boxer (1895–1927) who in 1926 became the first African American middleweight champion.
2. Street in Detroit, Michigan.
3. Female slaves or concubines in a harem.
4. Henri Rousseau (1844–1910), French painter known for jungle scenes and exotic colors.

RANDALL JARRELL
1914–1965

" **M**onstrously knowing and monstrously innocent. . . . A Wordsworth with the obsession of a Lewis Carroll"—so Robert Lowell once described his friend and fellow poet Randall Jarrell. Jarrell was a teacher and a critic as well as a poet, and for many writers of his generation—Lowell, Delmore Schwartz, and John Berryman among them—he was the critic whose taste was most unerring, who seemed to know instantly what was genuine and what was not. An extraordinary teacher, he loved the activity of teaching, both in and out of the classroom; "the gods who had taken away the poet's audience had given him students," he once said. The novelist Peter Taylor recalls that when he came to Vanderbilt University as a freshman in the mid-1930s, Jarrell, then a graduate student, had already turned the literary students into disciples; he held court discussing Chekhov on the sidelines of touch football games. For all his brilliance Jarrell was, at heart, democratic. Believing that poetry belongs to every life, his teaching, his literary criticism, and his poetry aimed to recapture and reeducate a general audience lost to poetry in an age of specialization. Jarrell's interests were democratic as well, and he had a lifelong fascination with popular culture. Witty and incisive, Jarrell could be intimidating; at the same time he remained deeply in touch with childhood's mystery and enchantment. It was as if, his close friend the philosopher Hannah Arendt once said, he "had emerged from the enchanted forests." He loved fairy tales, translated a number of them, and wrote several books for children, among them *The Bat-Poet* (1964). The childlike quality of the person informs Jarrell's poems as well; he is unembarrassed by the adult heart still in thrall to childhood's wishes.

Jarrell was born in Nashville, Tennessee, but spent much of his childhood in Long Beach, California. When his parents divorced, he, then eleven, remained for a year with his grandparents in Hollywood, then returned to live with his mother in Nashville. He majored in psychology at Vanderbilt and stayed on there to do graduate work in English. In 1937 he left Nashville to teach at Kenyon College (Gambier, Ohio) at the invitation of his old Vanderbilt professor John Crowe Ransom, the New Critic and Fugitive poet. From that time on Jarrell almost always had some connection with a university: after Kenyon, the University of Texas, Sarah Lawrence College, and from 1947 until his death, the Women's College of the University of North Carolina at Greensboro. But, as his novel *Pictures from an Institution* (1954) with its mixed satiric and tender views of academic life suggests, he was never satisfied with a cloistered education. As poetry editor of *The Nation* (1946), and then in a series of essays and reviews collected as *Poetry and the Age* (1953), he introduced readers to the work of his contemporaries—Elizabeth Bishop, Robert Lowell, John Berryman, the William Carlos Williams of *Paterson*—and influentially reassessed the reputations of Whitman and Robert Frost.

Among the poets who emerged after World War II, Jarrell stands out for his colloquial plainness. While others—Richard Wilbur and the early Robert Lowell, for example—were writing highly structured poems with complicated imagery, Jarrell's work feels and sounds close to what he calls in one poem the "dailiness of life" ("Well Water"). He is master of the everyday heartbreak and identifies with ordinary forms of loneliness. Jarrell's gift of imaginative sympathy appears in the treatment of soldiers in his war poems, the strongest to come out of World War II. He had been trained as an Army Air Force pilot and after that as a control operator,

The Gotham Book Mart. This midtown Manhattan store was famous for its literary eminences. A December 1948 party drew a roomful of midcentury writers, including, clockwise, W. H. Auden on the ladder, Elizabeth Bishop, Delmore Schwartz, Randall Jarrell, Charles Henri Ford, William Rose Benét, Stephen Spender, Marya Zaturenska, Horace Gregory, Tennessee Williams, Richard Eberhart, Gore Vidal, and José Garcia Villa.

and he had a sense of the war's special casualties. With their understanding of soldiers as both destructive and innocent at the same time, these poems make his volumes *Little Friend, Little Friend* (1945) and *Losses* (1948) powerful and moving. Jarrell also empathized with the dreams, loneliness, and disappointments of women, whose perspective he often adopted, as in the title poem of his collection *The Woman at the Washington Zoo* (1960) and his poem "Next Day."

Against the blasted or unrealized possibilities of adult life Jarrell often poised the rich mysteries of childhood. The title poem of his last book, *The Lost World* (1965), looks back to his Los Angeles playtime, the movie sets and plaster dinosaurs and pterodactyls against whose eternal light-hearted presence he measures his own aging. The poem has Jarrell's characteristic sense or loss but also his capacity for a mysterious happiness, which animates the poem even as he holds "nothing" in his hands.

Jarrell suffered a nervous breakdown in February 1965, but returned to teaching that fall. In October he was struck down by a car and died. His *Complete Poems* were published posthumously (1969), as were a translation of Goethe's *Faust*, Part I, in preparation at his death, and two books of essays, *The Third Book of Criticism* (1969) and *Kipling, Auden & Co.* (1980).

90 North[1]

At home, in my flannel gown, like a bear to its floe,
I clambered to bed; up the globe's impossible sides
I sailed all night—till at last, with my black beard,
My furs and my dogs, I stood at the northern pole.

There in the childish night my companions lay frozen,   5
The stiff furs knocked at my starveling throat,
And I gave my great sigh: the flakes came huddling,
Were they really my end? In the darkness I turned to my rest.

—Here, the flag snaps in the glare and silence
Of the unbroken ice. I stand here,   10
The dogs bark, my beard is black, and I stare
At the North Pole . . .
          And now what? Why, go back.

Turn as I please, my step is to the south.
The world—my world spins on this final point
Of cold and wretchedness: all lines, all winds   15
End in this whirlpool I at last discover.

And it is meaningless. In the child's bed
After the night's voyage, in that warm world
Where people work and suffer for the end
That crowns the pain—in that Cloud-Cuckoo-Land[2]   20

I reached my North and it had meaning.
Here at the actual pole of my existence,
Where all that I have done is meaningless,
Where I die or live by accident alone—

Where, living or dying, I am still alone;   25
Here where North, the night, the berg of death
Crowd me out of the ignorant darkness,
I see at last that all the knowledge

I wrung from the darkness—that the darkness flung me—
Is worthless as ignorance: nothing comes from nothing,   30
The darkness from the darkness. Pain comes from the darkness
And we call it wisdom. It is pain.

                                  1942

---

1. The latitude of the North Pole.
2. A fantasy world; in Aristophanes' comedy *The*   *Birds* (414 B.C.E.), an imaginary city the cuckoos build in the sky.

The Death of the Ball Turret Gunner[1]

From my mother's sleep I fell into the State,
And I hunched in its belly till my wet fur froze.
Six miles from earth, loosed from its dream of life,
I woke to black flak[2] and the nightmare fighters.
When I died they washed me out of the turret with a hose.   5

                                                        1945

Second Air Force

Far off, above the plain the summer dries,
The great loops of the hangars sway like hills.
Buses and weariness and loss, the nodding soldiers
Are wire, the bare frame building, and a pass
To what was hers; her head hides his square patch   5
And she thinks heavily: My son is grown.
She sees a world: sand roads, tar-paper barracks,
The bubbling asphalt of the runways, sage,
The dunes rising to the interminable ranges,
The dim flights moving over clouds like clouds.   10
The armorers in their patched faded green,
Sweat-stiffened, banded with brass cartridges,
Walk to the line; their Fortresses,[1] all tail,
Stand wrong and flimsy on their skinny legs,
And the crews climb to them clumsily as bears.   15
The head withdraws into its hatch (a boy's),
The engines rise to their blind laboring roar,
And the green, made beasts run home to air.
Now in each aspect death is pure.
(At twilight they wink over men like stars   20
And hour by hour, through the night, some see
The great lights floating in—from Mars, from Mars.)
How emptily the watchers see them gone.

They go, there is silence; the woman and her son
Stand in the forest of the shadows, and the light   25
Washes them like water. In the long-sunken city
Of evening, the sunlight stills like sleep
The faint wonder of the drowned; in the evening,
In the last dreaming light, so fresh, so old,

---

1. A ball turret was a plexiglass sphere set into the belly of a B-17 or B-24 [bomber], and inhabited by two .50 caliber machine-guns and one man, a short, small man. When this gunner tracked with his machine-guns a fighter attacking his bomber from below, he revolved with the turret; hunched upside-down in his little sphere, he looked like the foetus in the womb. The fighters which attacked him were armed with cannon firing explosive shells. The hose was a steam hose [Jarrell's note].
2. Antiaircraft fire.
1. Flying Fortresses, a type of bomber in World War II.

The soldiers pass like beasts, unquestioning,   30
And the watcher for an instant understands
What there is then no need to understand;
But she wakes from her knowledge, and her stare,
A shadow now, moves emptily among
The shadows learning in their shadowy fields   35
The empty missions.
                    Remembering,
She hears the bomber calling, *Little Friend!*[2]
To the fighter hanging in the hostile sky,
And sees the ragged flame eat, rib by rib,   40
Along the metal of the wing into her heart:
The lives stream out, blossom, and float steadily
To the flames of the earth, the flames
That burn like stars above the lands of men.

She saves from the twilight that takes everything   45
A squadron shipping, in its last parade—
Its dogs run by it, barking at the band—
A gunner walking to his barracks, half-asleep,
Starting at something, stumbling (above, invisible,
The crews in the steady winter of the sky   50
Tremble in their wired fur); and feels for them
The love of life for life. The hopeful cells
Heavy with someone else's death, cold carriers
Of someone else's victory, grope past their lives
Into her own bewilderment: The years meant *this*?   55

But for them the bombers answer everything.

                                                1945

Next Day

Moving from Cheer to Joy, from Joy to All,
I take a box
And add it to my wild rice, my Cornish game hens.
The slacked or shorted, basketed, identical
Food-gathering flocks   5
Are selves I overlook. Wisdom, said William James,[1]

Is learning what to overlook. And I am wise
If that is wisdom.
Yet somehow, as I buy All from these shelves

2. In "Second Air Force" the woman visiting her son remembers what she has read on the front page of her newspaper the week before, a conversation between a bomber, in flames over Germany, and one of the fighters protecting it: "Then I heard the bomber call me in: 'Little Friend, Little Friend, I got two engines on fire. Can you see me, Little Friend?' I said, 'I'm crossing right over you. Let's go home'" [Jarrell's note].
1. From *Principles of Psycholog*, by the American philosopher William James (1842–1910).

And the boy takes it to my station wagon,   10
What I've become
Troubles me even if I shut my eyes.

When I was young and miserable and pretty
And poor, I'd wish
What all girls wish: to have a husband,   15
A house and children. Now that I'm old, my wish
Is womanish:
That the boy putting groceries in my car

See me. It bewilders me he doesn't see me.
For so many years   20
I was good enough to eat: the world looked at me
And its mouth watered. How often they have undressed me,
The eyes of strangers!
And, holding their flesh within my flesh, their vile

Imaginings within my imagining,   25
I too have taken
The chance of life. Now the boy pats my dog
And we start home. Now I am good.
The last mistaken,
Ecstatic, accidental bliss, the blind   30

Happiness that, bursting, leaves upon the palm
Some soap and water—
It was so long ago, back in some Gay
Twenties, Nineties, I don't know . . . Today I miss
My lovely daughter   35
Away at school, my sons away at school,

My husband away at work—I wish for them.
The dog, the maid,
And I go through the sure unvarying days
At home in them. As I look at my life,   40
I am afraid
Only that it will change, as I am changing:

I am afraid, this morning, of my face.
It looks at me
From the rear-view mirror, with the eyes I hate,   45
The smile I hate. Its plain, lined look
Of gray discovery
Repeats to me: "You're old." That's all, I'm old.

And yet I'm afraid, as I was at the funeral
I went to yesterday.   50
My friend's cold made-up face, granite among its flowers,
Her undressed, operated-on, dressed body
Were my face and body.
As I think of her I hear her telling me

How young I seem; I *am* exceptional;   55
I think of all I have.
But really no one is exceptional,
No one has anything, I'm anybody,
I stand beside my grave
Confused with my life, that is commonplace and solitary.   60

1965

Well Water

What a girl called "the dailiness of life"
(Adding an errand to your errand. Saying,
"Since you're up . . ." Making you a means to
A means to a means to) is well water
Pumped from an old well at the bottom of the world.   5
The pump you pump the water from is rusty
And hard to move and absurd, a squirrel-wheel
A sick squirrel turns slowly, through the sunny
Inexorable hours. And yet sometimes
The wheel turns of its own weight, the rusty   10
Pump pumps over your sweating face the clear
Water, cold, so cold! you cup your hands
And gulp from them the dailiness of life.

1965

Thinking of the Lost World

This spoonful of chocolate tapioca
Tastes like—like peanut butter, like the vanilla
Extract Mama told me not to drink.
Swallowing the spoonful, I have already traveled
Through time to my childhood. It puzzles me   5
That age is like it.
                    Come back to that calm country
Through which the stream of my life first meandered,
My wife, our cat, and I sit here and see
Squirrels quarreling in the feeder, a mockingbird   10
Copying our chipmunk, as our end copies
Its beginning.
                    Back in Los Angeles, we missed
Los Angeles. The sunshine of the Land
Of Sunshine is a gray mist now, the atmosphere   15
Of some factory planet: when you stand and look
You see a block or two, and your eyes water.
The orange groves are all cut down . . . My bow
Is lost, all my arrows are lost or broken,
My knife is sunk in the eucalyptus tree   20

Too far for even Pop to get it out,
And the tree's sawed down. It and the stair-sticks
And the planks of the tree house are all firewood
Burned long ago; its gray smoke smells of Vicks.[1]

Twenty Years After, thirty-five years after,   25
Is as good as ever—better than ever,
Now that D'Artagnan[2] is no longer old—
Except that it is unbelievable.
I say to my old self: "I believe. Help thou
Mine unbelief."   30
          I believe the dinosaur
Or pterodactyl's married the pink sphinx
And lives with those Indians in the undiscovered
Country between California and Arizona
That the mad girl told me she was princess of—   35
Looking at me with the eyes of a lion,
Big, golden, without human understanding,
As she threw paper-wads from the back seat
Of the car in which I drove her with her mother
From the jail in Waycross to the hospital   40
In Daytona. If I took my eyes from the road
And looked back into her eyes, the car would—I'd be—

Or if only I could find a crystal set[3]
Sometimes, surely, I could still hear their chief
Reading to them from Dumas or *Amazing Stories*;   45
If I could find in some Museum of Cars
Mama's dark blue Buick, Lucky's electric,
Couldn't I be driven there? Hold out to them,
The paraffin half picked out, Tawny's dewclaw—
And have walk to me from among their wigwams   50
My tall brown aunt, to whisper to me: "Dead?
They told you I was dead?"
                As if you could die!
If I never saw you, never again
Wrote to you, even, after a few years,   55
How often you've visited me, having put on,
As a mermaid puts on her sealskin, another face
And voice, that don't fool me for a minute—
That are yours for good . . . All of them are gone
Except for me; and for me nothing is gone—   60
The chicken's body is still going round
And round in widening circles, a satellite
From which, as the sun sets, the scientist bends
A look of evil on the unsuspecting earth.
Mama and Pop and Dandeen are still there   65
In the Gay Twenties.
          The Gay Twenties! You say

1. A remedy for colds.
2. Hero of *The Three Musketeers* (1844), by Alexandre Dumas *père*; its sequel was *Twenty Years*
After (1845).
3. Old-fashioned radio receiver.

The Gay Nineties . . . But it's all right: they *were* gay,
O so gay! A certain number of years after,
Any time is Gay, to the new ones who ask: 70
"Was that the first World War or the second?"
Moving between the first world and the second,
I hear a boy call, now that my beard's gray:
"Santa Claus! Hi, Santa Claus!" It *is* miraculous
To have the children call you Santa Claus. 75
I wave back. When my hand drops to the wheel,
It is brown and spotted, and its nails are ridged
Like Mama's. Where's my own hand? My smooth
White bitten-fingernailed one? I seem to see
A shape in tennis shoes and khaki riding-pants 80
Standing there empty-handed; I reach out to it
Empty-handed, my hand comes back empty,
And yet my emptiness is traded for its emptiness,
I have found that Lost World in the Lost and Found
Columns whose gray illegible advertisements 85
My soul has memorized world after world:
LOST—NOTHING. STRAYED FROM NOWHERE. NO REWARD.
I hold in my own hands, in happiness,
Nothing: the nothing for which there's no reward.

1965

JOHN BERRYMAN
1914–1972

From a generation whose ideal poem was short, self-contained, and ironic, John
Berryman emerged as the author of two extended and passionate works: "Homage to Mistress Bradstreet" and the lyric sequence *The Dream Songs*. It was as if
Berryman needed more space than the single lyric provided—a larger theater in
which to play out an unrelenting psychic drama. He had written shorter poems—
songs and sonnets—but his discovery of large-scale dramatic situations and strange
new voices astonished his contemporaries.

Berryman seemed fated to intense suffering and self-preoccupation. His father, a
banker, shot himself outside his son's window when the boy was twelve. The suicide
haunted Berryman to the end of his own life, which also came by suicide. Berryman,
who was born John Smith, took a new name from his stepfather, also a banker. His
childhood was a series of displacements: ten years near McAlester, Oklahoma, then
Tampa, Florida, and after his father's suicide, Gloucester, Massachusetts, and New
York City. His mother's second marriage ended in divorce, but his stepfather sent
him to private school in Connecticut. Berryman graduated from Columbia College
in 1936 and won a fellowship to Clare College, Cambridge, England.

He was later to say of himself, "I masquerade as a writer. Actually I am a scholar."
However misleading this may be about his poetry, it reminds us that all his life Berryman drew nourishment from teaching—at Wayne State, at Harvard (1940–43),

then off and on at Princeton, and from 1955 until his death, at the University of Minnesota. He chose to teach not creative writing but literature and the "history of civilization," and he claimed that such teaching forced him into areas in which he would not otherwise have done detailed work. A mixture of bookishness and wildness characterizes all his writing: five years of research lay behind the intensities of "Homage to Mistress Bradstreet," while an important constituent of "huffy Henry's" personality in *The Dream Songs* is his professorial awkwardness and exhibitionism.

Berryman seemed drawn to borrowing identities in his poetry. In his first important volume, *The Dispossessed* (1948), he had experimented with various dramatic voices in the short poems "Nervous Songs: The Song of the Demented Priest," "A Professor's Song," "The Song of the Tortured Girl," and "The Song of the Man Forsaken and Obsessed." The *dispossession* of the book's title had two opposite and urgent meanings for him: "the miserable, *put out of one's own*, and the relieved, saved, undevilled, de-spelled." Taking on such roles was for Berryman both a revelation of his castout, fatherless state and an exorcism of it. It was perhaps in that spirit that he entered into an imaginary dialogue with what he felt as the kindred nature of the Puritan poet Anne Bradstreet. "Both of our worlds unhanded us." What started out to be a poem of fifty lines emerged as the fifty-seven stanzas of "Homage to Mistress Bradstreet" (1956), a work so absorbing that after completing it Berryman claimed to be "a ruin for two years." It was not Bradstreet's poetry that engaged him. Quite the contrary: he was fascinated by the contrast between her "bald abstract rime" and her life of passionate suffering. The poem explores the kinship between Bradstreet and Berryman as figures of turbulence and rebellion.

Berryman took literary encouragement from another American poet of the past, Stephen Crane, about whom he wrote a book-length critical study in 1950. Crane's poems, he said, have "the character of a 'dream,' something seen naively in a new relation." Berryman's attraction to a poetry that accommodated the nightmare antics of the dream world became apparent in his own long work, *The Dream Songs*. It was modeled, he claimed, on "the greatest American poem," Whitman's "Song of Myself," in which the speaker assumes a fluid, ever-changing persona. 77 *Dream Songs* was published in 1964. Additional poems, to a total of 385, appeared in *His Toy, His Dream, His Rest* (1968). (Some uncollected dream songs were published posthumously in *Henry's Fate*, 1977, and drafts of others remained in manuscript.) Obvious links exist between Berryman and other so-called confessional writers such as Robert Lowell, Sylvia Plath, and Anne Sexton. But the special autobiographical flavor of *The Dream Songs* is that of a psychic vaudeville; as in dreams, the poet represents himself through a fluid series of *alter egos*, whose voices often flow into one another in single poems. One of these voices is that of a blackface minstrel, and Berryman's appropriation of this dialect prompted Michael Harper's poem "Tongue-Tied in Black and White," written both as homage to Berryman and as part of Harper's quarrel with the use of "that needful black idiom offending me" ("Tongue-Tied in Black and White"). Despite the suffering that these poems enact, Berryman seemed to find a secret strength through the staginess, variety, resourcefulness, and renewals of these poems.

The Dream Songs brought Berryman a success that was not entirely beneficial. The collection *Love and Fame* (1970) shows him beguiled by his own celebrity and wrestling with some of its temptations. In an unfinished, posthumously published novel, *Recovery*, he portrays himself as increasingly prey to alcoholism. Berryman had been married twice before, and his hospitalization for drinking and for periods of insanity had put a strain on his third marriage. He came to distrust his poetry as a form of exhibitionism and was clearly, in his use of the discipline of prose and in the prayers that crowd his last two volumes of poetry (*Delusions, Etc.* appeared posthumously), in search of some new and humbling style. Having been raised a strict Catholic and fallen away from the church, he tried to return to it in his last years, speaking of his need for a "God of rescue." On January 7, 1972, Berryman committed suicide by leaping from a Minneapolis bridge.

Homage to Mistress Bradstreet Anne Bradstreet ("Born 1612 Anne Dudley, married at 16 Simon Bradstreet, a Cambridge man, steward to the Countess of Warwick and protege of her father Thomas Dudley secretary to the Earl of Lincoln. Crossed in the *Arbella*, 1630, under Governor Winthrop" [Berryman's note]) came to the Massachusetts Bay Colony when she was eighteen years old. She was one of the first poets on American soil. Of this poem, Berryman says:

> An American historian somewhere observes that all colonial settlements are intensely conservative, *except* in the initial break-off point (whether religious, political, legal, or whatever). Trying to do justice to both parts of this obvious truth—which I came upon only after the poem was finished—I concentrated upon the second and the poem laid itself out in a series of rebellions. I had her rebel first against the new environment and above all against her barrenness (which in fact lasted for years), then against her marriage (which in fact seems to have been brilliantly happy), and finally against her continuing life of illness, loss, and age. These are the three large sections of the poem; they are preceded and followed by an exordium and coda, of four stanzas each, spoken by the "I" of the twentieth-century poet, which modulates into her voice, who speaks most of the poem. Such is the plan. Each rebellion, of course, is succeeded by submission, although even in the moment of the poem's supreme triumph—the presentment, too long to quote now, of the birth of her first child—rebellion survives.

Berryman wrote two stanzas of the poem and found himself stalled for five years, during which he gathered material, until he discovered the strategy of dialogue and inserted himself in the poem. "Homage to Mistress Bradstreet" was first published in *Partisan Review* in 1953, but did not appear as a book until 1956.

In his exordium (stanzas 1–4), the poet makes an intense identification between himself and Bradstreet, both of them alienated by hardship or circumstance from those around them: "We are on each other's hands / who care. Both of our worlds unhanded us." The identification is so complete that in the subsequent stanzas he hears her voice recounting the tribulations of life in a new country, her yearnings for the England she left behind, her lonely dedication to her poetry, and the personal suffering in her early barrenness and miscarriages. Stanza 17 continues in Bradstreet's voice.

From Homage to Mistress Bradstreet

* * *

17

The winters close, Springs open, no child stirs
under my withering heart, O seasoned heart   130
God grudged his aid.
All things else soil like a shirt.
Simon is much away. My executive[1] stales.
The town came through for the cartway by the pales,[2]
but my patience is short,   135
I revolt from, I am like, these savage foresters

---

1. Power to act.   2. Stockade fence.

18

whose passionless dicker in the shade, whose glance
impassive & scant, belie their murderous cries
when quarry seems to show.
Again I must have been wrong, twice.[3]   140
Unwell in a new way. Can that begin?
God brandishes. O love, O I love. Kin,
gather. My world is strange
and merciful, ingrown months, blessing a swelling trance.[4]

19

So squeezed, wince you I scream? I love you & hate   145
off with you. Ages! *Useless.* Below my waist
he has me in Hell's vise.
Stalling. He let go. Come back: brace
me somewhere. No. No. Yes! everything down
hardens I press with horrible joy down   150
my back cracks like a wrist
shame I am voiding oh behind it is too late

20

hide me forever I work thrust I must free
now I all muscles & bones concentrate
what is living from dying?   155
Simon I must leave you so untidy
Monster you are killing me Be sure
I'll have you later Women do endure
I can *can* no longer
and it passes the wretched trap whelming and I am me   160

21

drencht & powerful, I did it with my body!
One proud tug greens Heaven. Marvellous,
unforbidding Majesty.
Swell, imperious bells. I fly.
Mountainous, woman not breaks and will bend: 165
sways God nearby: anguish comes to an end.
Blossomed Sarah,[5] and I
blossom. Is that thing alive? I hear a famisht howl.

22

Beloved household, I am Simon's wife,
and the mother of Samuel—whom greedy yet I miss   170
out of his kicking place.

3. One of the several allusions to her failure to become pregnant.
4. Her first child was not born until about 1633

[Berryman's note].
5. Wife of Abraham, barren until old age, when she gave birth to Isaac (Genesis 17.19).

More in some ways I feel at a loss,
freer. Cantabanks & mummers,[6] nears
longing for you. Our chopping[7] scores my ears,
our costume bores my eyes.   175
St. George[8] to the good sword, rise! chop-logic's rife

23

& fever & Satan & Satan's ancient fere.[9]
Pioneering is not feeling well,
not Indians, beasts.
Not all their riddling can forestall   180
one leaving. Sam, your uncle has had to
go from us to live with God. 'Then Aunt went too?'
Dear, she does wait still.
Stricken: 'Oh. Then he takes us one by one.' My dear.

24

Forswearing it otherwise, they starch their minds.   185
Folkmoots, & blether, blether. John Cotton rakes[1]
to the synod of Cambridge.[2]
Down from my body my legs flow,
out from it arms wave, on it my head shakes.
Now Mistress Hutchinson rings forth a call—   190
should she? many creep out a broken wall—
affirming the Holy Ghost
dwells in one justified. Factioning passion blinds

25

all to all her good, all—can she be exiled?
Bitter sister, victim! I miss you.   195
—I miss you, Anne,[3]
day or night weak as a child,
tender & empty, doomed, quick to no tryst.
—I hear you. Be kind, you who leaguer[4]
my image in the mist.   200
—Be kind you, to one unchained eager far & wild

6. Ballad singers and mimes.
7. *Chopping:* disputing, snapping, haggling; axing [Berryman's note].
8. Patron saint of England; the slayer of dragons.
9. *Fere:* his friend Death [Berryman's note].
1. *"Rakes:* inclines, as a mast; bows" [Berryman's note]. "Folkmoots": a town assembly for debate. "Blether": nonsense.
2. In the first synod (a body for religious debate), Cotton agreed to the condemnation and banishment of his follower Anne Hutchinson. Her heresies included a deemphasis of perfect moral conduct as evidence of the justification for Christian salvation.

3. One might say: He [the poet] is enabled to speak, at last, in the fortune of an echo of her—and when she is loneliest (her former spiritual adviser [John Cotton] having deserted Anne Hutchinson, and this her [Bradstreet's] closest friend banished), as if she had summoned him; and only thus, perhaps, is she enabled to hear him. This second section of the poem is a dialogue, his voice however ceasing well before it ends at [line] 307, and hers continuing for the whole third part until the coda ([stanzas] 54–57) [Berryman's note].
4. Beleaguer, besiege.

26

and if, O my love, my heart is breaking, please
neglect my cries and I will spare you. Deep
in Time's grave, Love's, you lie still.
Lie still.—Now? That happy shape   205
my forehead had under my most long, rare,
ravendark, hidden, soft bodiless hair
you award me still.
You must not love me, but I do not bid you cease.

27

Veiled my eyes, attending. How can it be I?   210
Moist, with parted lips, I listen, wicked.
I shake in the morning & retch.
Brood I do on myself naked.
A fading world I dust, with fingers new.
—I have earned the right to be alone with you.   215
—What right can that be?
Convulsing, if you love, enough, like a sweet lie.

28

Not that, I know, you can. This cratered skin,
like the crabs & shells of my Palissy[5] ewer, touch!
Oh, you do, you do?   220
Falls on me what I like a witch,
for lawless holds, annihilations of law
which Time and he and man abhor, foresaw:
sharper than what my Friend[6]
brought me for my revolt when I moved smooth & thin,   225

29

faintings black, rigour, chilling, brown
parching, back, brain burning, the grey pocks
itch, a manic stench
of pustules snapping, pain floods the palm,
sleepless, or a red shaft with a dreadful start   230
rides at the chapel, like a slipping heart.
My soul strains in one qualm
ah but *this* is not to save me but to throw me down.

30

And out of this I lull. It lessens. Kiss me.
That once. As sings out up in sparkling dark   235
a trail of a star & dies,
while the breath flutters, sounding, mark,

5. Bernard Palissy (1510–1590), French Protestant ceramicist noted for special glazes and highly
ornamented pieces.

6. Allusion to the punishments of God visited on
those who rebel against him (cf. Isaiah 1.6).

so shorn ought such caresses to us be
who, deserving nothing, flush and flee
the darkness of that light,   240
a lurching frozen from a warm dream. Talk to me.

31[7]

—It is Spring's New England. Pussy willows wedge
up in the wet. Milky crestings, fringed
yellow, in heaven, eyed
by the melting hand-in-hand or mere   245
desirers single, heavy-footed, rapt,
make surge poor human hearts. Venus is trapt—
the hefty pike shifts, sheer[8]—
in Orion blazing. Warblings, odours, nudge to an edge—

32

—Ravishing, ha, what crouches outside ought,   250
flamboyant, ill, angelic. Often, now,
I am afraid of you.
I am a sobersides; I know.
I *want* to take you for my lover.—Do.
—I hear a madness. Harmless I to you   255
am not, not I?—No.
—I cannot but be. Sing a concord of our thought.

33

—Wan dolls in indigo on gold:[9] refrain
my western lust. I am drowning in this past.
I lose sight of you   260
who mistress me from air. Unbraced
in delirium of the grand depths,[1] giving away
haunters what kept me, I breathe solid spray.
—I am losing you!
Straiten me on.[2]—I suffered living like a stain: 265

34

I trundle the bodies, on the iron bars,
over that fire backward & forth; they burn;

---

7. Berryman (in *Poets on Poetry*) called this
speech of the poet to Bradstreet "an only half-
subdued aria-stanza."
8. Lines 246–47 are opposed images of the bottom of the sea against the summit of the sky, as
imaged by the planet Venus and the constellation
Orion. "Sheer" in the sense of "invisible" (quoted
from comments by Berryman in the Italian translation of "Mistress Bradstreet" by Sergio Perosa).
9. Cf., on Byzantine icons [here, the impassive
Madonnas painted against gold backgrounds in
medieval altarpieces of the Eastern Church],
Frederick Rolfe ("Baron Corvo"): "Who ever
dreams of praying (with expectation of response)

for the prayer of a Tintoretto or a Titian, or a
Bellini, or a Botticelli? But who can refrain from
crying 'O Mother!' to these unruffleable wan dolls
in indigo on gold?" (quoted from *The Desire and
Pursuit of the Whole* by Graham Greene in *The
Last Childhood*) [Berryman's note].
1. "Délires des grandes profoundeurs," described
by [the twentieth-century French marine explorer
Jacques-Yves] Cousteau and others; a euphoria,
sometimes fatal, in which the hallucinated diver
offers passing fish his line, helmet, anything [Ber-
ryman's note; he translates the French phrase in
line 262].
2. I.e., tighten your embrace.

bits fall. I wonder if
I killed them. Women serve my turn.
—Dreams! You are good.—No.—Dense with hardihood   270
the wicked are dislodged, and lodged the good.
In green space we are safe.
God awaits us (but I am yielding) who Hell wars.

35

—I cannot feel myself God waits. He flies
nearer a kindly world; or he is flown.   275
One Saturday's rescue[3]
won't show. Man is entirely alone
may be. I am a man of griefs & fits
trying to be my friend. And the brown smock splits,
down the pale flesh a gash   280
broadens and Time holds up your heart against my eyes.

36

—Hard and divided heaven! creases me. Shame
is failing. My breath is scented, and I throw
hostile glances towards God.
Crumpling plunge of a pestle, bray:[4]   285
sin cross & opposite, wherein I survive
nightmares of Eden. Reaches foul & live
he for me, this soul
to crunch, a minute tangle of eternal flame.

37

I fear Hell's hammer-wind. But fear does wane.   290
Death's blossoms grain my hair; I cannot live.
A black joy clashes
joy, in twilight. The Devil said
'I will deal toward her softly, and her enchanting cries
will fool the horns of Adam.'[5] Father of lies,   295
a male great pestle smashes
small women swarming towards the mortar's rim in vain.

38

I see the cruel spread Wings black with saints!
Silky my breasts not his, mine, mine to withhold
or tender, tender.   300
I am sifting, nervous, and bold.
The light is changing. Surrender this loveliness

---

3. As of cliffhangers, movie serials wherein each week's episode ends with a train bearing down on the strapped heroine or with the hero dangling over an abyss into which Indians above him peer with satisfaction before they hatchet the rope; *rescue*: forcible recovery (by the owner) of goods distrained [Berryman's note].

4. Punning (according to Berryman's notes) on (1) the pulverizing action of a mortar and pestle and (2) the strident noise of a donkey.
5. Referring to Satan's temptation of Eve, who was to eat the apple from the Tree of Knowledge and then convince Adam to do so (cf. Genesis 3).

you cannot make me do. *But* I will. Yes.
What horror, down stormy air,
warps towards me? My threatening promise faints   305

39[6]

torture me, Father, lest not I be thine!
Tribunal terrible & pure, my God,
mercy for him and me.
Faces half-fanged, Christ drives abroad,
and though the crop hopes, Jane[7] is so slipshod   310
I cry. Evil dissolves, & love, like foam;
that love. Prattle of children powers me home,
my heart claps like the swan's
under a frenzy of *who* love me & who shine.[8]

* * *

1953, 1956

From The Dream Songs[1]

1

Huffy Henry hid   the day,
unappeasable Henry sulked.
I see his point,—a trying to put things over.
It was the thought that they thought
they could *do* it made Henry wicked & away.   5
But he should have come out and talked.

All the world like a woolen lover
once did seem on Henry's side.
Then came a departure.
Thereafter nothing fell out as it might or ought.   10
I don't see how Henry, pried
open for all the world to see, survived.

6. The stanza is unsettled, like [stanza] 24, by a middle line, signaling a broad transition [Berryman's note].
7. A servant.
8. The final stanzas present Bradstreet's intensified vision of death and damnation and include the death of her father, blaspheming. But in the last four stanzas the poem modulates back into the poet's voice and his vow to keep Bradstreet alive in his loving memory and in his writing. "Hover, utter, still, a sourcing whom my lost candle like the firefly loves."
1. These poems were written over a period of thirteen years. (77 *Dream Songs* was published in 1964, and the remaining poems appeared in *His Toy, His Dream, His Rest* in 1968. Some uncollected dream songs were included in the volume *Henry's Fate*, which appeared five years after Berryman committed suicide in 1972.) Berryman placed an introductory note at the head of *His Toy, His Dream, His Rest*: "The poem then, whatever its wide cast of characters, is essentially about an imaginary character (not the poet, not me) named Henry, a white American in early middle age sometimes in blackface, who has suffered an irreversible loss and talks about himself sometimes in the first person, sometimes in the third, sometimes even in the second; he has a friend, never named, who addresses him as Mr. Bones and variants thereof. Requiescant in pace."

What he has now to say is a long
wonder the world can bear & be.
Once in a sycamore I was glad   15
all at the top, and I sang.
Hard on the land wears the strong sea
and empty grows every bed.

14

Life, friends, is boring. We must not say so.
After all, the sky flashes, the great sea yearns,
we ourselves flash and yearn,
and moreover my mother told me as a boy
(repeatedly) 'Ever to confess you're bored   5
means you have no

Inner Resources.' I conclude now I have no
inner resources, because I am heavy bored.
Peoples bore me,
literature bores me, especially great literature,   10
Henry bores me, with his plights & gripes
as bad as achilles,[2]

who loves people and valiant art, which bores me.
And the tranquil hills, & gin, look like a drag
and somehow a dog   15
has taken itself & its tail considerably away
into mountains or sea or sky, leaving
behind: me, wag.

29

There sat down, once, a thing on Henry's heart
so heavy, if he had a hundred years
& more, & weeping, sleepless, in all them time
Henry could not make good.
Starts again always in Henry's ears   5
the little cough somewhere, an odour, a chime.

And there is another thing he has in mind
like a grave Sienese face[3] a thousand years
would fail to blur the still profiled reproach of. Ghastly,
with open eyes, he attends, blind.   10
All the bells say: too late. This is not for tears;
thinking.

2. Greek hero of Homer's *Iliad*, who, angry at slights against his honor, sulked in his tent and refused to fight against the Trojans.

3. Allusion to the somber, austere mosaiclike religious portraits by the Italian painters who worked in Siena during the 13th and 14th centuries.

But never did Henry, as he thought he did,
end anyone and hacks her body up
and hide the pieces, where they may be found.   15
He knows: he went over everyone, & nobody's missing.
Often he reckons, in the dawn, them up.
Nobody is ever missing.

40

I'm scared a lonely. Never see my son,
easy be not to see anyone,
combers[4] out to sea
know they're goin somewhere but not me.
Got a little poison, got a little gun.   5
I'm scared a lonely.

I'm scared a only one thing, which is me,
from othering I don't take nothin, see,
for any hound dog's sake.
But this is where I livin, where I rake   10
my leaves and cop my promise,[5] this' where we
cry oursel's awake.

Wishin was dyin but I gotta make
it all this way to that bed on these feet
where peoples said to meet.   15
Maybe but even if I see my son
forever never, get back on the take,
free, black & forty-one.[6]

45

He stared at ruin. Ruin stared straight back.
He thought they was old friends. He felt on the stair
where her papa found them bare
they became familiar. When the papers were lost
rich with pals' secrets, he thought he had the knack   5
of ruin. Their paths crossed

and once they crossed in jail; they crossed in bed;
and over an unsigned letter their eyes met,
and in an Asian city
directionless & lurchy at two & three,   10

---

4. Waves that roll over and break with a foamy
crest.
5. Slang for "pile up potential."

6. Playing on "free, white, and twenty-one," colloquial for legally independent.

or trembling to a telephone's fresh threat,
and when some wired his head

to reach a wrong opinion, 'Epileptic'.
But he noted now that: they were not old friends.
He did not know this one.   15
This one was a stranger, come to make amends
for all the imposters, and to make it stick.
Henry nodded, un-.

384

The marker slants, flowerless, day's almost done,
I stand above my father's grave with rage,
often, often before
I've made this awful pilgrimage to one
who cannot visit me, who tore his page   5
out: I come back for more,

I spit upon this dreadful banker's grave
who shot his heart out in a Florida dawn
O ho alas alas
When will indifference come, I moan & rave   10
I'd like to scrabble till I got right down
away down under the grass

and ax the casket open ha to see
just how he's taking it, which he sought so hard
we'll tear apart   15
the mouldering grave clothes ha & then Henry
will heft the ax once more, his final card,
and fell it on the start.

1968

BERNARD MALAMUD
1914–1986

B ernard Malamud began late as a writer, publishing his first novel at age thirty-
eight and reaching a wider audience about a decade later. It is his second novel
(*The Assistant*, 1957) that most readers, rightly, consider his best. Malamud knew
well the urban life he wrote about in that book. He was born in Brooklyn, graduated
from Erasmus Hall High School in Brooklyn and the City College of New York, then

earned a master's degree at Columbia. During the 1940s he taught evening classes at Erasmus Hall and Harlem Evening High School, while writing short stories that by 1950 had begun to appear in such magazines as *Partisan Review* and *Commentary*. Along with Saul Bellow, he was an important member of the group of Jewish novelists who flourished in the 1950s and beyond, but unlike Bellow, his stories were usually notable for the way they captured the speech and manners of working-class, recently immigrated Jews.

That urban Jewish milieu was absent from his first novel, *The Natural* (1952), which tells of an injured Major League pitcher reborn into a splendid outfielder. (Malamud may have been influenced by John R. Tunis's popular boy's book, *The Kid from Tompkinsville*, 1939.) The book contains much allegorical play with the Grail legend and other myths, but it held at arm's length Malamud's deeper concerns, which came to full expression in *The Assistant*, with its vivid but depressing rendering of a grocer's day-to-day existence. Rejecting the frenetic verbal energy of his first novel, Malamud wrote *The Assistant* in a low-key, rather toneless style, just right for catching the drab solemnities of his characters' lives. Like Bellow's *The Victim*, published a few years previously, the novel is about human responsibility and the possibilities for conversion, seen through the conflict between Jew and gentile. This conflict is given life through faithfully rendered speech and the patient yet always surprising turns of event with which the story unfolds. If the allegorical twist at its end is too ingenious for belief, still *The Assistant* remains unforgettable.

In subsequent novels Malamud extended and relaxed his style. The comic *A New Life* (1962) is about a hapless college professor at a West Coast university (Malamud taught at Oregon State for a time). *The Fixer* (1966) is a parable-history of the ritual murder of a Christian child. *The Tenants* (1971) attempted, in eventually violent, sensationalistic terms, to portray one minority's experience confronting another's—Jew against African American. *Dubin's Lives* (1979) is a slightly conventional tale of a writer of biographies who is suddenly overtaken by life, in the form of a desirable young woman (the novel is set in Vermont, where Malamud lived for years, teaching at Bennington College from 1961 until he retired). *God's Grace* (1982), by contrast, is a parable or fable, set in a post-thermonuclear future.

While these later novels seem sometimes abstract and often willed, *The Assistant* and Malamud's short fiction present memorable portraits of embattled Jews in grotesque circumstances. At times these figures resemble heroes of folklore; at other times they threaten to collapse into caricatures. In a story such as "The Lady in the Lake," the pathetic-comic hero becomes both. At his best, in that story or ones such as "The Magic Barrel" (printed here), "Idiots First," and "The Last Mohican," Malamud imagines, intensely and purely, his lonely questers for perfection as they become entangled in the imperfections of a social world. Such occasions of tragicomic humiliation sound the deeper note that was Malamud's trademark.

The following text is from the short-story collection *The Magic Barrel* (1958).

The Magic Barrel

Not long ago there lived in uptown New York, in a small, almost meager room, though crowded with books, Leo Finkle, a rabbinical student at the Yeshiva University.[1] Finkle, after six years of study, was to be ordained in June and had been advised by an acquaintance that he might find it easier to win himself a congregation if he were married. Since he had no present

1. In New York City; it offers courses in theological as well as secular disciplines. Generically, "yeshiva" is a term for a Jewish seminary.

prospects of marriage, after two tormented days of turning it over in his mind, he called in Pinye Salzman, a marriage broker whose two-line advertisement he had read in the *Forward*.[2]

The matchmaker appeared one night out of the dark fourth-floor hallway of the graystone rooming house where Finkle lived, grasping a black, strapped portfolio that had been worn thin with use. Salzman, who had been long in the business, was of slight but dignified build, wearing an old hat, and an overcoat too short and tight for him. He smelled frankly of fish, which he loved to eat, and although he was missing a few teeth, his presence was not displeasing, because of an amiable manner curiously contrasted with mournful eyes. His voice, his lips, his wisp of beard, his bony fingers were animated, but give him a moment of repose and his mild blue eyes revealed a depth of sadness, a characteristic that put Leo a little at ease although the situation, for him, was inherently tense.

He at once informed Salzman why he had asked him to come, explaining that his home was in Cleveland, and that but for his parents, who had married comparatively late in life, he was alone in the world. He had for six years devoted himself almost entirely to his studies, as a result of which, understandably, he had found himself without time for a social life and the company of young women. Therefore he thought it the better part of trial and error—of embarrassing fumbling—to call in an experienced person to advise him on these matters. He remarked in passing that the function of the marriage broker was ancient and honorable, highly approved in the Jewish community, because it made practical the necessary without hindering joy. Moreover, his own parents had been brought together by a matchmaker. They had made, if not a financially profitable marriage—since neither had possessed any worldly goods to speak of—at least a successful one in the sense of their everlasting devotion to each other. Salzman listened in embarrassed surprise, sensing a sort of apology. Later, however, he experienced a glow of pride in his work, an emotion that had left him years ago, and he heartily approved of Finkle.

The two went to their business. Leo had led Salzman to the only clear place in the room, a table near a window that overlooked the lamp-lit city. He seated himself at the matchmaker's side but facing him, attempting by an act of will to suppress the unpleasant tickle in his throat. Salzman eagerly unstrapped his portfolio and removed a loose rubber band from a thin packet of much-handled cards. As he flipped through them, a gesture and sound that physically hurt Leo, the student pretended not to see and gazed steadfastly out the window. Although it was still February, winter was on its last legs, signs of which he had for the first time in years begun to notice. He now observed the round white moon, moving high in the sky through a cloud menagerie, and watched with half-open mouth as it penetrated a huge hen, and dropped out of her like an egg laying itself. Salzman, though pretending through eyeglasses he had just slipped on, to be engaged in scanning the writing on the cards, stole occasional glances at the young man's distinguished face, noting with pleasure the long, severe scholar's nose, brown eyes heavy with learning, sensitive yet ascetic lips, and a certain, almost hollow

2. *The Jewish Daily Forward*, a Yiddish-language daily newspaper published in New York City.

quality of the dark cheeks. He gazed around at shelves upon shelves of books and let out a soft, contented sigh.

When Leo's eyes fell upon the cards, he counted six spread out in Salzman's hand.

"So few?" he asked in disappointment.

"You wouldn't believe me how much cards I got in my office," Salzman replied. "The drawers are already filled to the top, so I keep them now in a barrel, but is every girl good for a new rabbi?"

Leo blushed at this, regretting all he had revealed of himself in a curriculum vitae he had sent to Salzman. He had thought it best to acquaint him with his strict standards and specifications, but in having done so, he felt he had told the marriage broker more than was absolutely necessary.

He hesitantly inquired, "Do you keep photographs of your clients on file?"

"First comes family, amount of dowry, also what kind promises," Salzman replied, unbuttoning his tight coat and settling himself in the chair. "After come pictures, rabbi."

"Call me Mr. Finkle. I'm not yet a rabbi."

Salzman said he would, but instead called him doctor, which he changed to rabbi when Leo was not listening too attentively.

Salzman adjusted his horn-rimmed spectacles, gently cleared his throat and read in an eager voice the contents of the top card:

"Sophie P. Twenty four years. Widow one year. No children. Educated high school and two years college. Father promises eight thousand dollars. Has wonderful wholesale business. Also real estate. On the mother's side comes teachers, also one actor. Well known on Second Avenue."

Leo gazed up in surprise. "Did you say a widow?"

"A widow don't mean spoiled, rabbi. She lived with her husband maybe four months. He was a sick boy she made a mistake to marry him."

"Marrying a widow has never entered my mind."

"This is because you have no experience. A widow, especially if she is young and healthy like this girl, is a wonderful person to marry. She will be thankful to you the rest of her life. Believe me, if I was looking now for a bride, I would marry a widow."

Leo reflected, then shook his head.

Salzman hunched his shoulders in an almost imperceptible gesture of disappointment. He placed the card down on the wooden table and began to read another:

"Lily H. High school teacher. Regular. Not a substitute. Has savings and new Dodge car. Lived in Paris one year. Father is successful dentist thirty-five years. Interested in professional man. Well Americanized family. Wonderful opportunity."

"I knew her personally," said Salzman. "I wish you could see this girl. She is a doll. Also very intelligent. All day you could talk to her about books and theater and what not. She also knows current events."

"I don't believe you mentioned her age?"

"Her age?" Salzman said, raising his brows. "Her age is thirty-two years."

Leo said after a while, "I'm afraid that seems a little too old."

Salzman let out a laugh. "So how old are you, rabbi?"

"Twenty-seven."

"So what is the difference, tell me, between twenty-seven and thirty-two? My own wife is seven years older than me. So what did I suffer?—Nothing. If Rothschild's[3] daughter wants to marry you, would you say on account her age, no?"

"Yes," Leo said dryly.

Salzman shook off the no in the yes. "Five years don't mean a thing. I give you my word that when you will live with her for one week you will forget her age. What does it mean five years—that she lived more and knows more than somebody who is younger? On this girl, God bless her, years are not wasted. Each one that it comes makes better the bargain."

"What subjects does she teach in high school?"

"Languages. If you heard the way she speaks French, you will think it is music. I am in the business twenty-five years, and I recommend her with my whole heart. Believe me, I know what I'm talking, rabbi."

"What's on the next card?" Leo said abruptly.

Salzman reluctantly turned up the third card:

"Ruth K. Nineteen years. Honor student. Father offers thirteen thousand cash to the right bridegroom. He is a medical doctor. Stomach specialist with marvelous practice. Brother in law owns own garment business. Particular people."

Salzman looked as if he had read his trump card.

"Did you say nineteen?" Leo asked with interest.

"On the dot."

"Is she attractive?" He blushed. "Pretty?"

Salzman kissed his finger tips. "A little doll. On this I give you my word. Let me call the father tonight and you will see what means pretty."

But Leo was troubled. "You're sure she's that young?"

"This I am positive. The father will show you the birth certificate."

"Are you positive there isn't something wrong with her?" Leo insisted.

"Who says there is wrong?"

"I don't understand why an American girl her age should go to a marriage broker."

A smile spread over Salzman's face.

"So for the same reason you went, she comes."

Leo flushed. "I am pressed for time."

Salzman, realizing he had been tactless, quickly explained. "The father came, not her. He wants she should have the best, so he looks around himself. When we will locate the right boy he will introduce him and encourage. This makes a better marriage than if a young girl without experience takes for herself. I don't have to tell you this."

"But don't you think this young girl believes in love?" Leo spoke uneasily.

Salzman was about to guffaw but caught himself and said soberly, "Love comes with the right person, not before."

Leo parted dry lips but did not speak. Noticing that Salzman had snatched a glance at the next card, he cleverly asked, "How is her health?"

"Perfect," Salzman said, breathing with difficulty. "Of course, she is a little lame on her right foot from an auto accident that it happened to her

---

3. Once prominent, enormously wealthy family of Jewish international bankers and business leaders.

when she was twelve years, but nobody notices on account she is so brilliant and also beautiful."

Leo got up heavily and went to the window. He felt curiously bitter and upbraided himself for having called in the marriage broker. Finally, he shook his head.

"Why not?" Salzman persisted, the pitch of his voice rising.

"Because I detest stomach specialists."

"So what do you care what is his business? After you marry her do you need him? Who says he must come every Friday night in your house?"

Ashamed of the way the talk was going, Leo dismissed Salzman, who went home with heavy, melancholy eyes.

Though he had felt only relief at the marriage broker's departure, Leo was in low spirits the next day. He explained it as arising from Salzman's failure to produce a suitable bride for him. He did not care for his type of clientele. But when Leo found himself hesitating whether to seek out another matchmaker, one more polished than Pinye, he wondered if it could be— his protestations to the contrary, and although he honored his father and mother—that he did not, in essence, care for the matchmaking institution? This thought he quickly put out of mind yet found himself still upset. All day he ran around in the woods—missed an important appointment, forgot to give out his laundry, walked out of a Broadway cafeteria without paying and had to run back with the ticket in his hand; had even not recognized his land-lady in the street when she passed with a friend and courteously called out, "A good evening to you, Doctor Finkle." By nightfall, however, he had regained sufficient calm to sink his nose into a book and there found peace from his thoughts.

Almost at once there came a knock on the door. Before Leo could say enter, Salzman, commercial cupid, was standing in the room. His face was gray and meager, his expression hungry, and he looked as if he would expire on his feet. Yet the marriage broker managed, by some trick of the muscles, to display a broad smile.

"So good evening. I am invited?"

Leo nodded, disturbed to see him again, yet unwilling to ask the man to leave.

Beaming still, Salzman laid his portfolio on the table. "Rabbi, I got for you tonight good news."

"I've asked you not to call me rabbi. I'm still a student."

"Your worries are finished. I have for you a first-class bride."

"Leave me in peace concerning this subject," Leo pretended lack of interest.

"The world will dance at your wedding."

"Please, Mr. Salzman, no more."

"But first must come back my strength," Salzman said weakly. He fum-bled with the portfolio straps and took out of the leather case an oily paper bag, from which he extracted a hard, seeded roll and a small, smoked white fish. With a quick motion of his hand he stripped the fish out of its skin and began ravenously to chew. "All day in a rush," he muttered.

Leo watched him eat.

"A sliced tomato you have maybe?" Salzman hesitantly inquired.

"No."

The marriage broker shut his eyes and ate. When he had finished he carefully cleaned up the crumbs and rolled up the remains of the fish, in the paper bag. His spectacled eyes roamed the room until he discovered, amid some piles of books, a one-burner gas stove. Lifting his hat he humbly asked, "A glass tea you got, rabbi?"

Conscience-stricken, Leo rose and brewed the tea. He served it with a chunk of lemon and two cubes of lump sugar, delighting Salzman.

After he had drunk his tea, Salzman's strength and good spirits were restored.

"So tell me, rabbi," he said amiably, "you considered some more the three clients I mentioned yesterday?"

"There was no need to consider."

"Why not?"

"None of them suits me."

"What then suits you?"

Leo let it pass because he could give only a confused answer.

Without waiting for a reply, Salzman asked, "You remember this girl I talked to you—the high school teacher?"

"Age thirty-two?"

But, surprisingly, Salzman's face lit in a smile. "Age twenty-nine."

Leo shot him a look. "Reduced from thirty-two?"

"A mistake," Salzman avowed. "I talked today with the dentist. He took me to his safety deposit box and showed me the birth certificate. She was twenty-nine years last August. They made her a party in the mountains where she went for her vacation. When her father spoke to me the first time I forgot to write the age and I told you thirty-two, but now I remember this was a different client, a widow."

"The same one you told me about? I thought she was twenty-four?"

"A different. Am I responsible that the world is filled with widows?"

"No, but I'm not interested in them, nor for that matter, in school teachers."

Salzman pulled his clasped hands to his breast. Looking at the ceiling he devoutly exclaimed, "Yiddishe kinder,[4] what can I say to somebody that he is not interested in high school teachers? So what then you are interested?"

Leo flushed but controlled himself.

"In what else will you be interested," Salzman went on, "if you not interested in this fine girl that she speaks four languages and has personally in the bank ten thousand dollars? Also her father guarantees further twelve thousand. Also she has a new car, wonderful clothes, talks on all subjects, and she will give you a first-class home and children. How near do we come in our life to paradise?"

"If she's so wonderful, why wasn't she married ten years ago?"

"Why?" said Salzman with a heavy laugh. "—Why? Because she is *partikiler*.[5] This is why. She wants the *best*."

Leo was silent, amused at how he had entangled himself. But Salzman had aroused his interest in Lily H., and he began seriously to consider calling on her. When the marriage broker observed how intently Leo's mind

4. Jewish children (Yiddish); the sense is, what do these children know of the world as their parents knew it.
5. Yiddish corruption of "particular."

was at work on the facts he had supplied, he felt certain they would soon come to an agreement.

Late Saturday afternoon, conscious of Salzman, Leo Finkle walked with Lily Hirschorn along Riverside Drive. He walked briskly and erectly, wearing with distinction the black fedora he had that morning taken with trepidation out of the dusty hat box on his closet shelf, and the heavy black Saturday coat he had thoroughly whisked clean. Leo also owned a walking stick, a present from a distant relative, but quickly put temptation aside and did not use it. Lily, petite and not unpretty, had on something signifying the approach of spring. She was au courant,[6] animatedly, with all sorts of subjects, and he weighed her words and found her surprisingly sound—score another for Salzman, whom he uneasily sensed to be somewhere around, hiding perhaps high in a tree along the street, flashing the lady signals with a pocket mirror; or perhaps a cloven-hoofed Pan,[7] piping nuptial ditties as he danced his invisible way before them, strewing wild buds on the walk and purple grapes in their path, symbolizing fruit of a union, though there was of course still none.

Lily startled Leo by remarking, "I was thinking of Mr. Salzman, a curious figure, wouldn't you say?"

Not certain what to answer, he nodded.

She bravely went on, blushing, "I for one am grateful for his introducing us. Aren't you?"

He courteously replied, "I am."

"I mean," she said with a little laugh—and it was all in good taste, or at least gave the effect of being not in bad—"do you mind that we came together so?"

He was not displeased with her honesty, recognizing that she meant to set the relationship aright, and understanding that it took a certain amount of experience in life, and courage, to want to do it quite that way. One had to have some sort of past to make that kind of beginning.

He said that he did not mind. Salzman's function was traditional and honorable—valuable for what it might achieve, which, he pointed out, was frequently nothing.

Lily agreed with a sigh. They walked on for a while and she said after a long silence, again with a nervous laugh, "Would you mind if I asked you something a little bit personal? Frankly, I find the subject fascinating." Although Leo shrugged, she went on half embarrassedly, "How was it that you came to your calling? I mean was it a sudden passionate inspiration?"

Leo, after a time, slowly replied, "I was always interested in the Law."[8]

"You saw revealed in it the presence of the Highest?"

He nodded and changed the subject. "I understand that you spent a little time in Paris, Miss Hirschorn?"

"Oh, did Mr. Salzman tell you, Rabbi Finkle?" Leo winced but she went on, "It was ages ago and almost forgotten. I remember I had to return for my sister's wedding."

And Lily would not be put off. "When," she asked in a trembly voice, "did you become enamored of God?"

---

6. In keeping with the times (French).
7. Ancient Greek rural deity, part man and part goat, who presided over shepherds and flocks.
8. The "Law," or Torah, consists of Genesis, Exo-
dus, Leviticus, Numbers, and Deuteronomy—that part of Old Testament Scripture called the Pentateuch (Five Books of Moses).

He stared at her. Then it came to him that she was talking not about Leo Finkle, but of a total stranger, some mystical figure, perhaps even passionate prophet that Salzman had dreamed up for her—no relation to the living or dead. Leo trembled with rage and weakness. The trickster had obviously sold her a bill of goods, just as he had him, who'd expected to become acquainted with a young lady of twenty-nine, only to behold, the moment he laid eyes upon her strained and anxious face, a woman past thirty-five and aging rapidly. Only his self control had kept him this long in her presence.

"I am not," he said gravely, "a talented religious person," and in seeking words to go on, found himself possessed by shame and fear. "I think," he said in a strained manner, "that I came to God not because I loved Him, but because I did not."

This confession he spoke harshly because its unexpectedness shook him.

Lily wilted. Leo saw a profusion of loaves of bread go flying like ducks high over his head, not unlike the winged loaves by which he had counted himself to sleep last night. Mercifully, then, it snowed, which he would not put past Salzman's machinations.

He was infuriated with the marriage broker and swore he would throw him out of the room the minute he reappeared. But Salzman did not come that night, and when Leo's anger had subsided, an unaccountable despair grew in its place. At first he thought this was caused by his disappointment in Lily, but before long it became evident that he had involved himself with Salzman without a true knowledge of his own intent. He gradually realized—with an emptiness that seized him with six hands—that he had called in the broker to find him a bride because he was incapable of doing it himself. This terrifying insight he had derived as a result of his meeting and conversation with Lily Hirschorn. Her probing questions had somehow irritated him into revealing—to himself more than her—the true nature of his relationship to God, and from that it had come upon him, with shocking force, that apart from his parents, he had never loved anyone. Or perhaps it went the other way, that he did not love God so well as he might, because he had not loved man. It seemed to Leo that his whole life stood starkly revealed and he saw himself for the first time as he truly was—unloved and loveless. This bitter but somehow not fully unexpected revelation brought him to a point of panic, controlled only by extraordinary effort. He covered his face with his hands and cried.

The week that followed was the worst of his life. He did not eat and lost weight. His beard darkened and grew ragged. He stopped attending seminars and almost never opened a book. He seriously considered leaving the Yeshiva, although he was deeply troubled at the thought of the loss of all his years of study—saw them like pages torn from a book, strewn over the city—and at the devastating effect of this decision upon his parents. But he had lived without knowledge of himself, and never in the Five Books and all the Commentaries—mea culpa[9]—had the truth been revealed to him. He did not know where to turn, and in all this desolating loneliness there was no *to whom*, although he often thought of Lily but not once could bring himself to go downstairs and make the call. He became touchy and irritable,

9. Literally, "through my fault" (Latin), an admission of error. "Commentaries": explanatory written commentaries on the Pentateuch.

especially with his landlady, who asked him all manner of personal questions; on the other hand, sensing his own disagreeableness, he waylaid her on the stairs and apologized abjectly, until mortified, she ran from him. Out of this, however, he drew the consolation that he was a Jew and that a Jew suffered. But gradually, as the long and terrible week drew to a close, he regained his composure and some idea of purpose in life: to go on as planned. Although he was imperfect, the ideal was not. As for his quest of a bride, the thought of continuing afflicted him with anxiety and heartburn, yet perhaps with this new knowledge of himself he would be more successful than in the past. Perhaps love would now come to him and a bride to that love. And for this sanctified seeking who needed a Salzman?

The marriage broker, a skeleton with haunted eyes, returned that very night. He looked, withal, the picture of frustrated expectancy—as if he had steadfastly waited the week at Miss Lily Hirschorn's side for a telephone call that never came.

Casually coughing, Salzman came immediately to the point: "So how did you like her?"

Leo's anger rose and he could not refrain from chiding the matchmaker: "Why did you lie to me, Salzman?"

Salzman's pale face went dead white, the world had snowed on him.

"Did you not state that she was twenty-nine?" Leo insisted.

"I gave you my word—"

"She was thirty-five, if a day. *At least* thirty-five."

"Of this don't be too sure. Her father told me—"

"Never mind. The worst of it was that you lied to her."

"How did I lie to her, tell me?"

"You told her things about me that weren't true. You made me out to be more, consequently less than I am. She had in mind a totally different person, a sort of semimystical Wonder Rabbi."

"All I said, you was a religious man."

"I can imagine."

Salzman sighed. "This is my weakness that I have," he confessed. "My wife says to me I shouldn't be a salesman, but when I have two fine people that they would be wonderful to be married, I am so happy that I talk too much." He smiled wanly. "This is why Salzman is a poor man."

Leo's anger left him. "Well, Salzman, I'm afraid that's all."

The marriage broker fastened hungry eyes on him.

"You don't want anymore a bride?"

"I do," said Leo, "but I have decided to seek her in a different way. I am no longer interested in an arranged marriage. To be frank, I now admit the necessity of premarital love. That is, I want to be in love with the one I marry."

"Love?" said Salzman, astounded. After a moment he remarked, "For us, our love is our life, not for the ladies. In the ghetto they—"

"I know, I know," said Leo. "I've thought of it often. Love, I have said to myself, should be a by-product of living and worship rather than its own end. Yet for myself I find it necessary to establish the level of my need and fulfill it."

Salzman shrugged but answered, "Listen, rabbi, if you want love, this I can find for you also. I have such beautiful clients that you will love them the minute your eyes will see them."

Leo smiled unhappily. "I'm afraid you don't understand."

But Salzman hastily unstrapped his portfolio and withdrew a manila packet from it.

"Pictures," he said, quickly laying the envelope on the table.

Leo called after him to take the pictures away, but as if on the wings of the wind, Salzman had disappeared.

March came. Leo had returned to his regular routine. Although he felt not quite himself yet—lacked energy—he was making plans for a more active social life. Of course it would cost something, but he was an expert in cutting corners; and when there were no corners left he would make circles rounder. All the while Salzman's pictures had lain on the table, gathering dust. Occasionally as Leo sat studying, or enjoying a cup of tea, his eyes fell on the manila envelope, but he never opened it.

The days went by and no social life to speak of developed with a member of the opposite sex—it was difficult, given the circumstances of his situation. One morning Leo toiled up the stairs to his room and stared out the window at the city. Although the day was bright his view of it was dark. For some time he watched people in the street below hurrying along and then turned with a heavy heart to his little room. On the table was the packet. With a sudden relentless gesture he tore it open. For a half-hour he stood by the table in a state of excitement, examining the photographs of the ladies Salzman had included. Finally, with a deep sigh he put them down. There were six, of varying degrees of attractiveness, but look at them long enough and they all became Lily Hirschorn: all past their prime, all starved behind bright smiles, not a true personality in the lot. Life, despite their frantic yoohooings, had passed them by; they were pictures in a brief case that stank of fish. After a while, however, as Leo attempted to return the photographs into the envelope, he found in it another, a snapshot of the type taken by a machine for a quarter. He gazed at it a moment and let out a cry.

Her face deeply moved him. Why, he could at first not say. It gave him the impression of youth—spring flowers, yet age—a sense of having been used to the bone, wasted; this came from the eyes, which were hauntingly familiar, yet absolutely strange. He had a vivid impression that he had met her before, but try as he might he could not place her although he could almost recall her name, as if he had read it in her own handwriting. No, this couldn't be; he would have remembered her. It was not, he affirmed, that she had an extraordinary beauty—no, though her face was attractive enough; it was that *something* about her moved him. Feature for feature, even some of the ladies of the photographs could do better; but she leaped forth to his heart—had *lived*, or wanted to—more than just wanted, perhaps regretted how she had lived—had somehow deeply suffered: it could be seen in the depths of those reluctant eyes, and from the way the light enclosed and shone from her, and within her, opening realms of possibility: this was her own. Her he desired. His head ached and eyes narrowed with the intensity of his gazing, then as if an obscure fog had blown up in the mind, he experienced fear of her and was aware that he had received an impression, somehow, of evil. He shuddered, saying softly, it is thus with us all. Leo brewed some tea in a small pot and sat sipping it without sugar, to calm himself. But before he had finished drinking, again with excitement he examined the face and found it good: good for Leo Finkle. Only such a one could understand him and help him seek whatever he was seeking. She might, perhaps, love him. How she had happened to be among the discards in Salzman's barrel he could never guess, but he knew he must urgently go find her.

Leo rushed downstairs, grabbed up the Bronx telephone book, and searched for Salzman's home address. He was not listed, nor was his office. Neither was he in the Manhattan book. But Leo remembered having written down the address on a slip of paper after he had read Salzman's advertisement in the "personals" column of the *Forward*. He ran up to his room and tore through his papers, without luck. It was exasperating. Just when he needed the matchmaker he was nowhere to be found. Fortunately Leo remembered to look in his wallet. There on a card he found his name written and a Bronx address. No phone number was listed, the reason—Leo now recalled—he had originally communicated with Salzman by letter. He got on his coat, put a hat on over his skull cap and hurried to the subway station. All the way to the far end of the Bronx he sat on the edge of his seat. He was more than once tempted to take out the picture and see if the girl's face was as he remembered it, but he refrained, allowing the snapshot to remain in his inside coat pocket, content to have her so close. When the train pulled into the station he was waiting at the door and bolted out. He quickly located the street Salzman had advertised.

The building he sought was less than a block from the subway, but it was not an office building, nor even a loft, nor a store in which one could rent office space. It was a very old tenement house. Leo found Salzman's name in pencil on a soiled tag under the bell and climbed three dark flights to his apartment. When he knocked, the door was opened by a thin, asthmatic, gray-haired woman, in felt slippers.

"Yes?" she said, expecting nothing. She listened without listening. He could have sworn he had seen her, too, before but knew it was an illusion.

"Salzman—does he live here? Pinye Salzman," he said, "the matchmaker?"

She stared at him a long minute. "Of course."

He felt embarrassed. "Is he in?"

"No." Her mouth, though left open, offered nothing more.

"The matter is urgent. Can you tell me where his office is?"

"In the air." She pointed upward.

"You mean he has no office?" Leo asked.

"In his socks."

He peered into the apartment. It was sunless and dingy, one large room divided by a half-open curtain, beyond which he could see a sagging metal bed. The near side of a room was crowded with rickety chairs, old bureaus, a three-legged table, racks of cooking utensils, and all the apparatus of a kitchen. But there was no sign of Salzman or his magic barrel, probably also a figment of the imagination. An odor of frying fish made Leo weak to the knees.

"Where is he?" he insisted. "I've got to see your husband."

At length she answered, "So who knows where he is? Every time he thinks a new thought he runs to a different place. Go home, he will find you."

"Tell him Leo Finkle."

She gave no sign she had heard.

He walked downstairs, depressed.

But Salzman, breathless, stood waiting at his door.

Leo was astounded and overjoyed. "How did you get here before me?"

"I rushed."

"Come inside."

They entered. Leo fixed tea, and a sardine sandwich for Salzman. As they were drinking he reached behind him for the packet of pictures and handed them to the marriage broker.

Salzman put down his glass and said expectantly, "You found somebody you like?"

"Not among these."

The marriage broker turned away.

"Here is the one I want." Leo held forth the snapshot.

Salzman slipped on his glasses and took the picture into his trembling hand. He turned ghastly and let out a groan.

"What's the matter?" cried Leo.

"Excuse me. Was an accident this picture. She isn't for you."

Salzman frantically shoved the manila packet into his portfolio. He thrust the snapshot into his pocket and fled down the stairs.

Leo, after momentary paralysis, gave chase and cornered the marriage broker in the vestibule. The landlady made hysterical outcries but neither of them listened.

"Give me back the picture, Salzman."

"No." The pain in his eyes was terrible.

"Tell me who she is then."

"This I can't tell you. Excuse me."

He made to depart, but Leo, forgetting himself, seized the matchmaker by his tight coat and shook him frenziedly.

"Please," sighed Salzman. *"Please."*

Leo ashamedly let him go. "Tell me who she is," he begged. "It's very important for me to know."

"She is not for you. She is a wild one—wild, without shame. This is not a bride for a rabbi."

"What do you mean wild?"

"Like an animal. Like a dog. For her to be poor was a sin. This is why to me she is dead now."

"In God's name, what do you mean?"

"Her I can't introduce to you," Salzman said.

"Why are you so excited?"

"Why, he asks," Salzman said, bursting into tears. "This is my baby, my Stella, she should burn in hell."

Leo hurried up to bed and hid under the covers. Under the covers he thought his life through. Although he soon fell asleep he could not sleep her out of his mind. He woke, beating his breast. Though he prayed to be rid of her, his prayers went unanswered. Through days of torment he endlessly struggled not to love her; fearing success, he escaped it. He then concluded to convert her to goodness, himself to God. The idea alternately nauseated and exalted him.

He perhaps did not know that he had come to a final decision until he encountered Salzman in a Broadway cafeteria. He was sitting alone at a rear table, sucking the bony remains of a fish. The marriage broker appeared haggard, and transparent to the point of vanishing.

Salzman looked up at first without recognizing him. Leo had grown a pointed beard and his eyes were weighted with wisdom.

"Salzman," he said, "love has at last come to my heart."

"Who can love from a picture?" mocked the marriage broker.

"It is not impossible."

"If you can love her, then you can love anybody. Let me show you some new clients that they just sent me their photographs. One is a little doll."

"Just her I want," Leo murmured.

"Don't be a fool, doctor. Don't bother with her."

"Put me in touch with her, Salzman," Leo said humbly. "Perhaps I can be of service."

Salzman had stopped eating and Leo understood with emotion that it was now arranged.

Leaving the cafeteria, he was, however, afflicted by a tormenting suspicion that Salzman had planned it all to happen this way.

Leo was informed by letter that she would meet him on a certain corner, and she was there one spring night, waiting under a street lamp. He appeared, carrying a small bouquet of violets and rosebuds. Stella stood by the lamp post, smoking. She wore white with red shoes, which fitted his expectations, although in a troubled moment he had imagined the dress red, and only the shoes white. She waited uneasily and shyly. From afar he saw that her eyes—clearly her father's—were filled with desperate innocence. He pictured, in her, his own redemption. Violins and lit candles revolved in the sky. Leo ran forward with flowers outthrust.

Around the corner, Salzman, leaning against a wall, chanted prayers for the dead.

1958

RALPH ELLISON
1914–1994

66 **I** f the Negro, or any other writer, is going to do what's expected of him, he's lost the battle before he takes the field." This remark of Ralph Ellison's, taken from his *Paris Review* interview of 1953, serves in more than one sense as an appropriate motto for his own career. He did not do what his critics, literary or political, suggested that he ought to, but insisted on being a writer rather than a spokesman for a cause or a representative figure. His importance to American letters is partly due to this independence. He also did the unexpected, however, in not following his fine first novel with the others that were predicted. While maintaining a strong presence on the literary scene by writing essays on a wide variety of social and cultural issues, Ellison published only excerpts from his work in progress: a massive novel that may well have run to three volumes, a single book of which was assem-

Ellison, Langston Hughes, and James Baldwin at the Newport Jazz Festival in 1958.

bled after his death and published as *Juneteenth* (1999), later expanded as *Three Days Before the Shooting . . .* (2010).

Ellison was born in Oklahoma; grew up in Oklahoma City; won a state scholarship; and attended the Tuskegee Institute, where he was a music major, his instrument the trumpet. His musical life was wide enough to embrace both "serious music" and the world of Southwest–Kansas City jazz just reaching its heyday when Ellison was a young man. He became friends with the blues singer Jimmy Rushing and was acquainted with other members of what would be the great Count Basie band of the 1930s; this "deep, rowdy stream of jazz" figured for him as an image of the power and control that constituted art. Although he was a serious student of music and composition, his literary inclinations eventually dominated his musical ones; but testimony to his abiding knowledge and love of music may be found in some of the essays in his collection *Shadow and Act* (1964).

Ellison left Tuskegee and went north to New York City. There, in 1936, he met the novelist Richard Wright, who encouraged him as a writer, and Ellison began to publish reviews and short stories. *Invisible Man*, begun in 1945, was published seven years later and won the National Book Award. Ellison subsequently received a number of awards and lectureships; taught at the Salzburg Seminar, at Bard College, and at the University of Chicago; and in 1970 was named Albert Schweitzer Professor of the Humanities at New York University, where he taught until his retirement. Yet he admitted to being troubled by the terms in which *Invisible Man's* success—and perhaps his own career as well—were defined. In the *Paris Review* interview he deprecatingly referred to his novel as largely a failure, wished that rather than a "statement" about the American Negro it could be read "simply as a novel," and hoped that in twenty years it would be so read, casually adding, "if it's around that long."

Invisible Man may have outlived Ellison's expectations, but not without suffering attacks from critics. The most powerful of these, Irving Howe, took the author to task for not following Richard Wright's lead and devoting his fiction to the Negro cause. Howe believed that African Americans should write social protest novels about the tragedy of black ghetto life. *Invisible Man* had used its protagonist's "invisibility" to entertain a much broader range of possibilities; and though by no means socially irresponsible, the novel is dedicated to the richness of life and art that becomes possible when the imagination is liberated from close realism.

From Invisible Man

Prologue[1]

I am an invisible man. No, I am not a spook like those who haunted Edgar Allan Poe; nor am I one of your Hollywood-movie ectoplasms. I am a man of substance, of flesh and bone, fiber and liquids—and I might even be said to possess a mind. I am invisible, understand, simply because people refuse to see me. Like the bodiless heads you see sometimes in circus sideshows, it is as though I have been surrounded by mirrors of hard, distorting glass. When they approach me they see only my surroundings, themselves, or figments of their imagination—indeed, everything and anything except me.

Nor is my invisibility exactly a matter of a bio-chemical accident to my epidermis. That invisibility to which I refer occurs because of a peculiar disposition in the eyes of those with whom I come in contact. A matter of the construction of their *inner* eyes, those eyes with which they look through their physical eyes upon reality. I am not complaining, nor am I protesting either. It is sometimes advantageous to be unseen, although it is most often rather wearing on the nerves. Then too, you're constantly being bumped against by those of poor vision. Or again, you often doubt if you really exist. You wonder whether you aren't simply a phantom in other people's minds. Say, a figure in a nightmare which the sleeper tries with all his strength to destroy. It's when you feel like this that, out of resentment, you begin to bump people back. And, let me confess, you feel that way most of the time. You ache with the need to convince yourself that you do exist in the real world, that you're a part of all the sound and anguish, and you strike out with your fists, you curse and you swear to make them recognize you. And, alas, it's seldom successful.

One night I accidentally bumped into a man, and perhaps because of the near darkness he saw me and called me an insulting name. I sprang at him, seized his coat lapels and demanded that he apologize. He was a tall blond man, and as my face came close to his he looked insolently out of his blue eyes and cursed me, his breath hot in my face as he struggled. I pulled his chin down sharp upon the crown of my head, butting him as I had seen the West Indians do, and felt his flesh tear and the blood gush out, and I yelled, "Apologize! Apologize!" But he continued to curse and struggle, and I butted him again and again until he went down heavily, on his knees, profusely bleeding. I kicked him repeatedly, in a frenzy because he still uttered insults though his lips were frothy with blood. Oh yes, I kicked him! And in my outrage I got out my knife and prepared to slit his throat, right there beneath the lamplight in the deserted street, holding him in the collar with one hand, and opening the knife with my teeth—when it occurred to me that the man had

---

1. Ras the Destroyer, Rinehart, and Brother Jack, mentioned in the prologue, are characters who will appear later in the novel.

not *seen* me, actually; that he, as far as he knew, was in the midst of a walking nightmare! And I stopped the blade, slicing the air as I pushed him away, letting him fall back to the street. I stared at him hard as the lights of a car stabbed through the darkness. He lay there, moaning on the asphalt; a man almost killed by a phantom. It unnerved me. I was both disgusted and ashamed. I was like a drunken man myself, wavering about on weakened legs. Then I was amused: Something in this man's thick head had sprung out and beaten him within an inch of his life. I began to laugh at this crazy discovery. Would he have awakened at the point of death? Would Death himself have freed him for wakeful living? But I didn't linger. I ran away into the dark, laughing so hard I feared I might rupture myself. The next day I saw his picture in the *Daily News*, beneath a caption stating that he had been "mugged." Poor fool, poor blind fool, I thought with sincere compassion, mugged by an invisible man!

Most of the time (although I do not choose as I once did to deny the violence of my days by ignoring it) I am not so overtly violent. I remember that I am invisible and walk softly so as not to awaken the sleeping ones. Sometimes it is best not to awaken them; there are few things in the world as dangerous as sleepwalkers. I learned in time though that it is possible to carry on a fight against them without their realizing it. For instance, I have been carrying on a fight with Monopolated Light & Power for some time now. I use their service and pay them nothing at all, and they don't know it. Oh, they suspect that power is being drained off, but they don't know where. All they know is that according to the master meter back there in their power station a hell of a lot of free current is disappearing somewhere into the jungle of Harlem. The joke, of course, is that I don't live in Harlem but in a border area. Several years ago (before I discovered the advantages of being invisible) I went through the routine process of buying service and paying their outrageous rates. But no more. I gave up all that, along with my apartment, and my old way of life: That way based upon the fallacious assumption that I, like other men, was visible. Now, aware of my invisibility, I live rent-free in a building rented strictly to whites, in a section of the basement that was shut off and forgotten during the nineteenth century, which I discovered when I was trying to escape in the night from Ras the Destroyer. But that's getting too far ahead of the story, almost to the end, although the end is in the beginning and lies far ahead.

The point now is that I found a home—or a hole in the ground, as you will. Now don't jump to the conclusion that because I call my home a "hole" it is damp and cold like a grave; there are cold holes and warm holes. Mine is a warm hole. And remember, a bear retires to his hole for the winter and lives until spring; then he comes strolling out like the Easter chick breaking from its shell. I say all this to assure you that it is incorrect to assume that, because I'm invisible and live in a hole, I am dead. I am neither dead nor in a state of suspended animation. Call me Jack-the-Bear,[2] for I am in a state of hibernation.

My hole is warm and full of light. Yes, *full* of light. I doubt if there is a brighter spot in all New York than this hole of mine, and I do not exclude Broadway. Or the Empire State Building on a photographer's dream night.

2. Also the title of a 1940 jazz recording by Duke Ellington and his orchestra.

But that is taking advantage of you. Those two spots are among the darkest of our whole civilization—pardon me, our whole *culture* (an important distinction, I've heard)—which might sound like a hoax, or a contradiction, but that (by contradiction, I mean) is how the world moves: Not like an arrow, but a boomerang. (Beware of those who speak of the *spiral* of history; they are preparing a boomerang. Keep a steel helmet handy.) I know; I have been boomeranged across my head so much that I now can see the darkness of lightness. And I love light. Perhaps you'll think it strange that an invisible man should need light, desire light, love light. But maybe it is exactly because I *am* invisible. Light confirms my reality, gives birth to my form. A beautiful girl once told me of a recurring nightmare in which she lay in the center of a large dark room and felt her face expand until it filled the whole room, becoming a formless mass while her eyes ran in bilious jelly up the chimney. And so it is with me. Without light I am not only invisible, but formless as well; and to be unaware of one's form is to live a death. I myself, after existing some twenty years, did not become alive until I discovered my invisibility.

That is why I fight my battle with Monopolated Light & Power. The deeper reason, I mean: It allows me to feel my vital aliveness. I also fight them for taking so much of my money before I learned to protect myself. In my hole in the basement there are exactly 1,369 lights. I've wired the entire ceiling, every inch of it. And not with fluorescent bulbs, but with the older, more-expensive-to-operate kind, the filament type. An act of sabotage, you know. I've already begun to wire the wall. A junk man I know, a man of vision, has supplied me with wire and sockets. Nothing, storm or flood, must get in the way of our need for light and ever more and brighter light. The truth is the light and light is the truth. When I finish all four walls, then I'll start on the floor. Just how that will go, I don't know. Yet when you have lived invisible as long as I have you develop a certain ingenuity. I'll solve the problem. And maybe I'll invent a gadget to place my coffee pot on the fire while I lie in bed, and even invent a gadget to warm my bed—like the fellow I saw in one of the picture magazines who made himself a gadget to warm his shoes! Though invisible, I am in the great American tradition of tinkers. That makes me kin to Ford, Edison and Franklin. Call me, since I have a theory and a concept, a "thinker-tinker." Yes, I'll warm my shoes; they need it, they're usually full of holes. I'll do that and more.

Now I have one radio-phonograph; I plan to have five. There is a certain acoustical deadness in my hole, and when I have music I want to *feel* its vibration, not only with my ear but with my whole body. I'd like to hear five recordings of Louis Armstrong playing and singing "What Did I Do to Be So Black and Blue"—all at the same time. Sometimes now I listen to Louis while I have my favorite dessert of vanilla ice cream and sloe gin. I pour the red liquid over the white mound, watching it glisten and the vapor rising as Louis bends that military instrument into a beam of lyrical sound. Perhaps I like Louis Armstrong because he's made poetry out of being invisible. I think it must be because he's unaware that he *is* invisible. And my own grasp of invisibility aids me to understand his music. Once when I asked for a cigarette, some jokers gave me a reefer, which I lighted when I got home and sat listening to my phonograph. It was a strange evening. Invisibility, let me explain, gives one a slightly different sense of time, you're never quite on the beat. Sometimes you're ahead and sometimes behind. Instead of the swift and imperceptible flowing of time, you are aware of its nodes, those points where time stands still or from which it leaps ahead. And you slip into the breaks and look around. That's what you hear vaguely in Louis' music.

Once I saw a prizefighter boxing a yokel. The fighter was swift and amazingly scientific. His body was one violent flow of rapid rhythmic action. He hit the yokel a hundred times when the yokel held up his arms in stunned surprise. But suddenly the yokel, rolling about in the gale of boxing gloves, struck one blow and knocked science, speed and footwork as cold as a well-digger's posterior. The smart money hit the canvas. The long shot got the nod. The yokel had simply stepped inside of his opponent's sense of time. So under the spell of the reefer I discovered a new analytical way of listening to music. The unheard sounds came through, and each melodic line existed of itself, stood out clearly from all the rest, said its piece, and waited patiently for the other voices to speak. That night I found myself hearing not only in time, but in space as well. I not only entered the music but descended, like Dante, into its depths. *And beneath the swiftness of the hot tempo there was a slower tempo and a cave and I entered it and looked around and heard an old woman singing a spiritual as full of Weltschmerz as flamenco, and beneath that lay a still lower level on which I saw a beautiful girl the color of ivory pleading in a voice like my mother's as she stood before a group of slaveowners who bid for her naked body, and below that I found a lower level and a more rapid tempo and I heard someone shout:*

"Brothers and sisters, my text this morning is the 'Blackness of Blackness.'"

And a congregation of voices answered: "That blackness is most black, brother, most black . . ."

"In the beginning . . ."

"At the very start," they cried.

". . . there was blackness . . ."

"Preach it . . ."

". . . and the sun . . ."

"The sun, Lawd . . ."

". . . was blood red . . ."

"Red . . ."

"Now black is . . ." the preacher shouted.

"Bloody . . ."

"I said black is . . ."

"Preach it, brother . . ."

". . . an' black ain't . . ."

"Red, Lawd, red: He said it's red!"

"Amen, brother . . ."

"Black will git you . . ."

"Yes, it will . . ."

". . . an' black won't . . ."

"Now, it won't!"

"It do . . ."

"It do, Lawd . . ."

". . . an' it don't."

"Halleluiah . . ."

". . . It'll put you, glory, glory, Oh my Lawd, in the WHALE'S BELLY."

"Preach it, dear brother . . ."

"... an' make you tempt ..."

"Good God a-mighty!"

"Old Aunt Nelly!"

"Black will make you ..."

"Black ..."

"... or black will un-make you."

"Ain't it the truth, Lawd?"

And at that point a voice of trombone timbre screamed at me, "Git out of here, you fool! Is you ready to commit treason?"

And I tore myself away, hearing the old singer of spirituals moaning, "Go curse your God, boy, and die."

I stopped and questioned her, asked her what was wrong.

"I dearly loved my master, son," she said.

"You should have hated him," I said.

"He gave me several sons," she said, "and because I loved my sons I learned to love their father though I hated him too."

"I too have become acquainted with ambivalence," I said. "That's why I'm here."

"What's that?"

"Nothing, a word that doesn't explain it. Why do you moan?"

"I moan this way 'cause he's dead," she said.

"Then tell me, who is that laughing upstairs?"

"Them's my sons. They glad."

"Yes, I can understand that too," I said.

"I laughs too, but I moans too. He promised to set us free but he never could bring hisself to do it. Still I loved him ..."

"Loved him? You mean ... ?"

"Oh, yes, but I loved something else even more."

"What more?"

"Freedom."

"Freedom," I said. "Maybe freedom lies in hating."

"Naw, son, it's in loving. I loved him and give him the poison and he withered away like a frost-bit apple. Them boys woulda tore him to pieces with they homemade knives."

"A mistake was made somewhere," I said, "I'm confused." And I wished to say other things, but the laughter upstairs became too loud and moan-like for me and I tried to break out of it, but I couldn't. Just as I was leaving I felt an urgent desire to ask her what freedom was and went back. She sat with her head in her hands, moaning softly; her leather-brown face was filled with sadness.

"Old woman, what is this freedom you love so well?" I asked around a corner of my mind.

She looked surprised, then thoughtful, then baffled. "I done forgot, son. It's all mixed up. First I think it's one thing, then I think it's another. It gits my head to spinning. I guess now it ain't nothing but knowing how to say what I got up in my head. But it's a hard job, son. Too much is done happen to me in too short a time. Hit's like I have a fever. Ever'time I starts to walk my head gits to swirling and I falls down. Or if it ain't that, it's the boys; they gits to laughing and wants to kill up the white folks. They's bitter, that's what they is ..."

"But what about freedom?"

"Leave me 'lone, boy; my head aches!"

I left her, feeling dizzy myself. I didn't get far.

Suddenly one of the sons, a big fellow six feet tall, appeared out of nowhere and struck me with his fist.

"What's the matter, man?" I cried.

"You made Ma cry!"

"But how?" I said, dodging a blow.

"Askin' her them questions, that's how. Git outa here and stay, and next time you got questions like that, ask yourself!"

He held me in a grip like cold stone, his fingers fastening upon my windpipe until I thought I would suffocate before he finally allowed me to go. I stumbled about dazed, the music beating hysterically in my ears. It was dark. My head cleared and I wandered down a dark narrow passage, thinking I heard his foot-steps hurrying behind me. I was sore, and into my being had come a profound craving for tranquillity, for peace and quiet, a state I felt I could never achieve. For one thing, the trumpet was blaring and the rhythm was too hectic. A tom-tom beating like heart-thuds began drowning out the trumpet, filling my ears. I longed for water and I heard it rushing through the cold mains my fingers touched as I felt my way, but I couldn't stop to search because of the footsteps behind me.

"Hey, Ras," I called. "Is it you, Destroyer? Rinehart?"

No answer, only the rhythmic footsteps behind me. Once I tried crossing the road, but a speeding machine struck me, scraping the skin from my leg as it roared past.

Then somehow I came out of it, ascending hastily from this underworld of sound to hear Louis Armstrong innocently asking,

> *What did I do*
> *To be so black*
> *And blue?*

At first I was afraid; this familiar music had demanded action, the kind of which I was incapable, and yet had I lingered there beneath the surface I might have attempted to act. Nevertheless, I know now that few really listen to this music. I sat on the chair's edge in a soaking sweat, as though each of my 1,369 bulbs had everyone become a klieg light[3] in an individual setting for a third degree with Ras and Rinehart in charge. It was exhausting—as though I had held my breath continuously for an hour under the terrifying serenity that comes from days of intense hunger. And yet, it was a strangely satisfying experience for an invisible man to hear the silence of sound. I had discovered unrecognized compulsions of my being—even though I could not answer "yes" to their promptings. I haven't smoked a reefer since, however; not because they're illegal, but because to *see* around corners is enough (that is not unusual when you are invisible). But to hear around them is too much; it inhibits action. And despite Brother Jack and all that sad, lost period of the Brotherhood, I believe in nothing if not in action.

Please, a definition: A hibernation is a covert preparation for a more overt action.

Besides, the drug destroys one's sense of time completely. If that hap-pened, I might forget to dodge some bright morning and some cluck would

3. Powerful arc light used in making movies.

run me down with an orange and yellow street car, or a bilious bus! Or I might forget to leave my hole when the moment for action presents itself.

Meanwhile I enjoy my life with the compliments of Monopolated Light & Power. Since you never recognize me even when in closest contact with me, and since, no doubt, you'll hardly believe that I exist, it won't matter if you know that I tapped a power line leading into the building and ran it into my hole in the ground. Before that I lived in the darkness into which I was chased, but now I see. I've illuminated the blackness of my invisibility—and vice versa. And so I play the invisible music of my isolation. The last statement doesn't seem just right, does it? But it is; you hear this music simply because music is heard and seldom seen, except by musicians. Could this compulsion to put invisibility down in black and white be thus an urge to make music of invisibility? But I am an orator, a rabble rouser—Am? I *was*, and perhaps shall be again. Who knows? All sickness is not unto death, neither is invisibility.

I can hear you say, "What a horrible, irresponsible bastard!" And you're right. I leap to agree with you. I am one of the most irresponsible beings that ever lived. Irresponsibility is part of my invisibility; any way you face it, it is a denial. But to whom can I be responsible, and why should I be, when you refuse to see me? And wait until I reveal how truly irresponsible I am. Responsibility rests upon recognition, and recognition is a form of agreement. Take the man whom I almost killed: Who was responsible for that near murder—I? I don't think so, and I refuse it. I won't buy it. You can't give it to me. *He* bumped *me, he* insulted *me.* Shouldn't he, for his own personal safety, have recognized my hysteria, my "danger potential"? He, let us say, was lost in a dream world. But didn't *he* control that dream world—which, alas, is only too real!—and didn't *he* rule me out of it? And if he had yelled for a policeman, wouldn't *I* have been taken for the offending one? Yes, yes, yes! Let me agree with you, I was the irresponsible one; for I should have used my knife to protect the higher interests of society. Some day that kind of foolishness will cause us tragic trouble. All dreamers and sleepwalkers must pay the price, and even the invisible victim is responsible for the fate of all. But I shirked that responsibility; I became too snarled in the incompatible notions that buzzed within my brain. I was a coward . . .

But what did *I* do to be so blue? Bear with me.

Chapter I

[BATTLE ROYAL]

It goes a long way back, some twenty years. All my life I had been looking for something, and everywhere I turned someone tried to tell me what it was. I accepted their answers too, though they were often in contradiction and even self-contradictory. I was naïve. I was looking for myself and asking everyone except myself questions which I, and only I, could answer. It took me a long time and much painful boomeranging of my expectations to achieve a realization everyone else appears to have been born with: That I am nobody but myself. But first I had to discover that I am an invisible man!

And yet I am no freak of nature, nor of history. I was in the cards, other things having been equal (or unequal) eighty-five years ago. I am not ashamed of my grandparents for having been slaves. I am only ashamed of myself for having at one time been ashamed. About eighty-five years ago they were told that they were free, united with others of our country in everything pertaining to the common good, and, in everything social, separate like the fingers of the hand. And they believed it. They exulted in it. They stayed in their place, worked hard, and brought up my father to do the same. But my grandfather is the one. He was an odd old guy, my grandfather, and I am told I take after him. It was he who caused the trouble. On his deathbed he called my father to him and said, "Son, after I'm gone I want you to keep up the good fight. I never told you, but our life is a war and I have been a traitor all my born days, a spy in the enemy's country ever since I give up my gun back in the Reconstruction. Live with your head in the lion's mouth. I want you to overcome 'em with yeses, undermine 'em with grins, agree 'em to death and destruction, let 'em swoller you till they vomit or bust wide open." They thought the old man had gone out of his mind. He had been the meekest of men. The younger children were rushed from the room, the shades drawn and the flame of the lamp turned so low that it sputtered on the wick like the old man's breathing. "Learn it to the younguns," he whispered fiercely; then he died.

But my folks were more alarmed over his last words than over his dying. It was as though he had not died at all, his words caused so much anxiety. I was warned emphatically to forget what he had said and, indeed, this is the first time it has been mentioned outside the family circle. It had a tremendous effect upon me, however. I could never be sure of what he meant. Grandfather had been a quiet old man who never made any trouble, yet on his deathbed he had called himself a traitor and a spy, and he had spoken of his meekness as a dangerous activity. It became a constant puzzle which lay unanswered in the back of my mind. And whenever things went well for me I remembered my grandfather and felt guilty and uncomfortable. It was as though I was carrying out his advice in spite of myself. And to make it worse, everyone loved me for it. I was praised by the most lily-white men of the town. I was considered an example of desirable conduct—just as my grandfather had been. And what puzzled me was that the old man had defined it as *treachery*. When I was praised for my conduct I felt a guilt that in some way I was doing something that was really against the wishes of the white folks, that if they had understood they would have desired me to act just the opposite, that I should have been sulky and mean, and that that really would have been what they wanted, even though they were fooled and thought they wanted me to act as I did. It made me afraid that some day they would look upon me as a traitor and I would be lost. Still I was more afraid to act any other way because they didn't like that at all. The old man's words were like a curse. On my graduation day I delivered an oration in which I showed that humility was the secret, indeed, the very essence of progress. (Not that I believed this—how could I, remembering my grandfather?—I only believed that it worked.) It was a great success. Everyone praised me and I was invited to give the speech at a gathering of the town's leading white citizens. It was a triumph for our whole community.

It was in the main ballroom of the leading hotel. When I got there I discovered that it was on the occasion of a smoker, and I was told that since I was to be there anyway I might as well take part in the battle royal to be fought by some of my schoolmates as part of the entertainment. The battle royal came first.

All of the town's big shots were there in their tuxedoes, wolfing down the buffet foods, drinking beer and whiskey and smoking black cigars. It was a large room with a high ceiling. Chairs were arranged in neat rows around three sides of a portable boxing ring. The fourth side was clear, revealing a gleaming space of polished floor. I had some misgivings over the battle royal, by the way. Not from a distaste for fighting, but because I didn't care too much for the other fellows who were to take part. They were tough guys who seemed to have no grandfather's curse worrying their minds. No one could mistake their toughness. And besides, I suspected that fighting a battle royal might detract from the dignity of my speech. In those pre-invisible days I visualized myself as a potential Booker T. Washington.[4] But the other fellows didn't care too much for me either, and there were nine of them. I felt superior to them in my way, and I didn't like the manner in which we were all crowded together into the servants' elevator. Nor did they like my being there. In fact, as the warmly lighted floors flashed past the elevator we had words over the fact that I, by taking part in the fight, had knocked one of their friends out of a night's work.

We were led out of the elevator through a rococo hall into an anteroom and told to get into our fighting togs. Each of us was issued a pair of boxing gloves and ushered out into the big mirrored hall, which we entered looking cautiously about us and whispering, lest we might accidentally be heard above the noise of the room. It was foggy with cigar smoke. And already the whiskey was taking effect. I was shocked to see some of the most important men of the town quite tipsy. They were all there—bankers, lawyers, judges, doctors, fire chiefs, teachers, merchants. Even one of the more fashionable pastors. Something we could not see was going on up front. A clarinet was vibrating sensuously and the men were standing up and moving eagerly forward. We were a small tight group, clustered together, our bare upper bodies touching and shining with anticipatory sweat; while up front the big shots were becoming increasingly excited over something we still could not see. Suddenly I heard the school superintendent, who had told me to come, yell, "Bring up the shines, gentlemen! Bring up the little shines!"

We were rushed up to the front of the ballroom, where it smelled even more strongly of tobacco and whiskey. Then we were pushed into place. I almost wet my pants. A sea of faces, some hostile, some amused, ringed around us, and in the center, facing us, stood a magnificent blonde—stark naked. There was dead silence. I felt a blast of cold air chill me. I tried to back away, but they were behind me and around me. Some of the boys stood with lowered heads, trembling. I felt a wave of irrational guilt and fear. My teeth chattered, my skin turned to goose flesh, my knees knocked. Yet I was strongly attracted and looked in spite of myself. Had the price of looking been blindness, I would have looked. The hair was yellow like that of a circus kewpie doll, the face heavily powdered and rouged, as though to form an abstract mask, the eyes hollow and smeared a cool blue, the color of a baboon's butt. I felt a desire to spit upon her as my eyes brushed slowly over her body. Her breasts were firm and round as the domes of East Indian temples, and I stood so

---

4. African American author and educator (1856–1915).

close as to see the fine skin texture and beads of pearly perspiration glistening like dew around the pink and erected buds of her nipples. I wanted at one
and the same time to run from the room, to sink through the floor, or go to
her and cover her from my eyes and the eyes of the others with my body; to
feel the soft thighs, to caress her and destroy her, to love her and murder her,
to hide from her, and yet to stroke where below the small American flag tat-
tooed upon her belly her thighs formed a capital V. I had a notion that of all
in the room she saw only me with her impersonal eyes.

And then she began to dance, a slow sensuous movement; the smoke
of a hundred cigars clinging to her like the thinnest of veils. She seemed
like a fair bird-girl girdled in veils calling to me from the angry surface of
some gray and threatening sea. I was transported. Then I became aware of
the clarinet playing and the big shots yelling at us. Some threatened us if we
looked and others if we did not. On my right I saw one boy faint. And now
a man grabbed a silver pitcher from a table and stepped close as he dashed
ice water upon him and stood him up and forced two of us to support him
as his head hung and moans issued from his thick bluish lips. Another boy
began to plead to go home. He was the largest of the group, wearing dark
red fighting trunks much too small to conceal the erection which projected
from him as though in answer to the insinuating low-registered moaning of
the clarinet. He tried to hide himself with his boxing gloves.

And all the while the blonde continued dancing, smiling faintly at the big
shots who watched her with fascination, and faintly smiling at our fear. I
noticed a certain merchant who followed her hungrily, his lips loose and
drooling. He was a large man who wore diamond studs in a shirtfront which
swelled with the ample paunch underneath, and each time the blonde swayed
her undulating hips he ran his hand through the thin hair of his bald head and,
with his arms upheld, his posture clumsy like that of an intoxicated panda,
wound his belly in a slow and obscene grind. This creature was completely
hypnotized. The music had quickened. As the dancer flung herself about
with a detached expression on her face, the men began reaching out to touch
her. I could see their beefy fingers sink into the soft flesh. Some of the others
tried to stop them and she began to move around the floor in graceful circles,
as they gave chase, slipping and sliding over the polished floor. It was mad.
Chairs went crashing, drinks were spilt, as they ran laughing and howling
after her. They caught her just as she reached a door, raised her from the
floor, and tossed her as college boys are tossed at a hazing, and above her red,
fixed-smiling lips I saw the terror and disgust in her eyes, almost like my own
terror and that which I saw in some of the other boys. As I watched, they
tossed her twice and her soft breasts seem to flatten against the air and her
legs flung wildly as she spun. Some of the more sober ones helped her to
escape. And I started off the floor, heading for the anteroom with the rest of
the boys.

Some were still crying and in hysteria. But as we tried to leave we were
stopped and ordered to get into the ring. There was nothing to do but what
we were told. All ten of us climbed under the ropes and allowed ourselves
to be blindfolded with broad bands of white cloth. One of the men seemed
to feel a bit sympathetic and tried to cheer us up as we stood with our backs
against the ropes. Some of us tried to grin. "See that boy over there?" one of
the men said. "I want you to run across at the bell and give it to him right in

the belly. If you don't get him, I'm going to get you. I don't like his looks."
Each of us was told the same. The blindfolds were put on. Yet even then I
had been going over my speech. In my mind each word was as bright as
flame. I felt the cloth pressed into place, and frowned so that it would be
loosened when I relaxed.

But now I felt a sudden fit of blind terror. I was unused to darkness. It
was as though I had suddenly found myself in a dark room filled with poisonous cottonmouths. I could hear the bleary voices yelling insistently for
the battle royal to begin.

"Get going in there!"

"Let me at that big nigger!"

I strained to pick up the school superintendent's voice, as though to
squeeze some security out of that slightly more familiar sound.

"Let me at those black sonsabitches!" someone yelled.

"No, Jackson, no!" another voice yelled. "Here, somebody, help me hold
Jack."

"I want to get at that ginger-colored nigger. Tear him limb from limb," the
first voice yelled.

I stood against the ropes trembling. For in those days I was what they called
ginger-colored, and he sounded as though he might crunch me between his
teeth like a crisp ginger cookie.

Quite a struggle was going on. Chairs were being kicked about and I
could hear voices grunting as with a terrific effort. I wanted to see, to see
more desperately than ever before. But the blindfold was tight as a thick
skin-puckering scab and when I raised my gloved hands to push the layers
of white aside a voice yelled, "Oh, no you don't, black bastard! Leave that
alone!"

"Ring the bell before Jackson kills him a coon!" someone boomed in the
sudden silence. And I heard the bell clang and the sound of the feet scuffling forward.

A glove smacked against my head. I pivoted, striking out stiffly as someone went past, and felt the jar ripple along the length of my arm to my shoulder. Then it seemed as though all nine of the boys had turned upon me at
once. Blows pounded me from all sides while I struck out as best I could. So
many blows landed upon me that I wondered if I were not the only blindfolded fighter in the ring, or if the man called Jackson hadn't succeeded in
getting me after all.

Blindfolded, I could no longer control my motions. I had no dignity. I
stumbled about like a baby or a drunken man. The smoke had become
thicker and with each new blow it seemed to sear and further restrict my
lungs. My saliva became like hot bitter glue. A glove connected with my head,
filling my mouth with warm blood. It was everywhere. I could not tell if the
moisture I felt upon my body was sweat or blood. A blow landed hard against
the nape of my neck. I felt myself going over, my head hitting the floor.
Streaks of blue light filled the black world behind the blindfold. I lay prone,
pretending that I was knocked out, but felt myself seized by hands and
yanked to my feet. "Get going, black boy! Mix it up!" My arms were like lead,
my head smarting from blows. I managed to feel my way to the ropes and
held on, trying to catch my breath. A glove landed in my mid-section and I

went over again, feeling as though the smoke had become a knife jabbed into my guts. Pushed this way and that by the legs milling around me, I finally pulled erect and discovered that I could see the black, sweat-washed forms weaving in the smoky-blue atmosphere like drunken dancers weaving to the rapid drum-like thuds of blows.

Everyone fought hysterically. It was complete anarchy. Everybody fought everybody else. No group fought together for long. Two, three, four, fought one, then turned to fight each other, were themselves attacked. Blows landed below the belt and in the kidney, with the gloves open as well as closed, and with my eye partly opened now there was not so much terror. I moved carefully, avoiding blows, although not too many to attract attention, fighting from group to group. The boys groped about like blind, cautious crabs crouching to protect their mid-sections, their heads pulled in short against their shoulders, their arms stretched nervously before them, with their fists testing the smoke-filled air like the knobbed feelers of hypersensitive snails. In one corner I glimpsed a boy violently punching the air and heard him scream in pain as he smashed his hand against a ring post. For a second I saw him bent over holding his hand, then going down as a blow caught his unprotected head. I played one group against the other, slipping in and throwing a punch then stepping out of range while pushing the others into the melee to take the blows blindly aimed at me. The smoke was agonizing and there were no rounds, no bells at three minute intervals to relieve our exhaustion. The room spun around me, a swirl of lights, smoke, sweating bodies surrounded by tense white faces. I bled from both nose and mouth, the blood spattering upon my chest.

The men kept yelling, "Slug him, black boy! Knock his guts out!"

"Uppercut him! Kill him! Kill that big boy!"

Taking a fake fall, I saw a boy going down heavily beside me as though we were felled by a single blow, saw a sneaker-clad foot shoot into his groin as the two who had knocked him down stumbled upon him. I rolled out of range, feeling a twinge of nausea.

The harder we fought the more threatening the men became. And yet, I had begun to worry about my speech again. How would it go? Would they recognize my ability? What would they give me?

I was fighting automatically when suddenly I noticed that one after another of the boys was leaving the ring. I was surprised, filled with panic, as though I had been left alone with an unknown danger. Then I understood. The boys had arranged it among themselves. It was the custom for the two men left in the ring to slug it out for the winner's prize. I discovered this too late. When the bell sounded two men in tuxedoes leaped into the ring and removed the blindfold. I found myself facing Tatlock, the biggest of the gang. I felt sick at my stomach. Hardly had the bell stopped ringing in my ears than it clanged again and I saw him moving swiftly toward me. Thinking of nothing else to do I hit him smash on the nose. He kept coming, bringing the rank sharp violence of stale sweat. His face was a black blank of a face, only his eyes alive—with hate of me and aglow with a feverish terror from what had happened to us all. I became anxious. I wanted to deliver my speech and he came at me as though he meant to beat it out of me. I smashed him again and again, taking his blows as they came. Then on a sudden impulse I struck him lightly and as we clinched, I whispered, "Fake like I knocked you out, you can have the prize."

"I'll break your behind," he whispered hoarsely.

"For *them?*"

"For *me*, sonofabitch!"

They were yelling for us to break it up and Tatlock spun me half around with a blow, and as a joggled camera sweeps in a reeling scene, I saw the howling red faces crouching tense beneath the cloud of blue-gray smoke. For a moment the world wavered, unraveled, flowed, then my head cleared and Tatlock bounced before me. That fluttering shadow before my eyes was his jabbing left hand. Then falling forward, my head against his damp shoulder, I whispered,

"I'll make it five dollars more."

"Go to hell!"

But his muscles relaxed a trifle beneath my pressure and I breathed, "Seven?"

"Give it to your ma," he said, ripping me beneath the heart.

And while I still held him I butted him and moved away. I felt myself bombarded with punches. I fought back with hopeless desperation. I wanted to deliver my speech more than anything else in the world, because I felt that only these men could judge truly my ability, and now this stupid clown was ruining my chances. I began fighting carefully now, moving in to punch him and out again with my greater speed. A lucky blow to his chin and I had him going too—until I heard a loud voice yell, "I got my money on the big boy."

Hearing this, I almost dropped my guard. I was confused: Should I try to win against the voice out there? Would not this go against my speech, and was not this a moment for humility, for nonresistance? A blow to my head as I danced about sent my right eye popping like a jack-in-the-box and settled my dilemma. The room went red as I fell. It was a dream fall, my body languid and fastidious as to where to land, until the floor became impatient and smashed up to meet me. A moment later I came to. An hypnotic voice said FIVE emphatically. And I lay there, hazily watching a dark red spot of my own blood shaping itself into a butterfly, glistening and soaking into the soiled gray world of the canvas.

When the voice drawled TEN I was lifted up and dragged to a chair. I sat dazed. My eye pained and swelled with each throb of my pounding heart and I wondered if now I would be allowed to speak. I was wringing wet, my mouth still bleeding. We were grouped along the wall now. The other boys ignored me as they congratulated Tatlock and speculated as to how much they would be paid. One boy whimpered over his smashed hand. Looking up front, I saw attendants in white jackets rolling the portable ring away and placing a small square rug in the vacant space surrounded by chairs. Perhaps, I thought, I will stand on the rug to deliver my speech.

Then the M.C. called to us, "Come on up here boys and get your money."

We ran forward to where the men laughed and talked in their chairs, waiting. Everyone seemed friendly now.

"There it is on the rug," the man said. I saw the rug covered with coins of all dimensions and a few crumpled bills. But what excited me, scattered here and there, were the gold pieces.

"Boys, it's all yours," the man said. "You get all you grab."

"That's right, Sambo," a blond man said, winking at me confidentially.

I trembled with excitement, forgetting my pain. I would get the gold and the bills, I thought. I would use both hands. I would throw my body against the boys nearest me to block them from the gold.

"Get down around the rug now," the man commanded, "and don't anyone touch it until I give the signal."

"This ought to be good," I heard.

As told, we got around the square rug on our knees. Slowly the man raised his freckled hand as we followed it upward with our eyes.

I heard, "These niggers look like they're about to pray!"

Then, "Ready," the man said. "Go!"

I lunged for a yellow coin lying on the blue design of the carpet, touching it and sending a surprised shriek to join those rising around me. I tried frantically to remove my hand but could not let go. A hot, violent force tore through my body, shaking me like a wet rat. The rug was electrified. The hair bristled up on my head as I shook myself free. My muscles jumped, my nerves jangled, writhed. But I saw that this was not stopping the other boys. Laughing in fear and embarrassment, some were holding back and scooping up the coins knocked off by the painful contortions of the others. The men roared above us as we struggled.

"Pick it up, goddamnit, pick it up!" someone called like a bass-voiced parrot. "Go on, get it!"

I crawled rapidly around the floor, picking up the coins, trying to avoid the coppers and to get greenbacks and the gold. Ignoring the shock by laughing, as I brushed the coins off quickly, I discovered that I could contain the electricity—a contradiction, but it works. Then the men began to push us onto the rug. Laughing embarrassedly, we struggled out of their hands and kept after the coins. We were all wet and slippery and hard to hold. Suddenly I saw a boy lifted into the air, glistening with sweat like a circus seal, and dropped, his wet back landing flush upon the charged rug, heard him yell and saw him literally dance upon his back, his elbows beating a frenzied tattoo upon the floor, his muscles twitching like the flesh of a horse stung by many flies. When he finally rolled off, his face was gray and no one stopped him when he ran from the floor amid booming laughter.

"Get the money," the M.C. called. "That's good hard American cash!"

And we snatched and grabbed, snatched and grabbed. I was careful not to come too close to the rug now, and when I felt the hot whiskey breath descend upon me like a cloud of foul air I reached out and grabbed the leg of a chair. It was occupied and I held on desperately.

"Leggo, nigger! Leggo!"

The huge face wavered down to mine as he tried to push me free. But my body was slippery and he was too drunk. It was Mr. Colcord, who owned a chain of movie houses and "entertainment palaces." Each time he grabbed me I slipped out of his hands. It became a real struggle. I feared the rug more than I did the drunk, so I held on, surprising myself for a moment by trying to topple *him* upon the rug. It was such an enormous idea that I found myself actually carrying it out. I tried not to be obvious, yet when I grabbed his leg, trying to tumble him out of the chair, he raised up roaring with laughter, and, looking at me with soberness dead in the eye, kicked me viciously in the chest. The chair leg flew out of my hand and I felt myself going and rolled. It was as though I had rolled through a bed of hot coals. It seemed a whole century would pass before I would roll free, a century in which I was seared through the deepest levels of my body to the fearful breath within me and the breath seared and heated to the point of explosion. It'll all be over in a flash, I thought as I rolled clear. It'll all be over in a flash.

But not yet, the men on the other side were waiting, red faces swollen as though from apoplexy as they bent forward in their chairs. Seeing their fingers coming toward me I rolled away as a fumbled football rolls off the receiver's fingertips, back into the coals. That time I luckily sent the rug sliding out of place and heard the coins ringing against the floor and the boys scuffling to pick them up and the M.C. calling, "All right, boys, that's all. Go get dressed and get your money."

I was limp as a dish rag. My back felt as though it had been beaten with wires.

When we had dressed the M.C. came in and gave us each five dollars, except Tatlock, who got ten for being last in the ring. Then he told us to leave. I was not to get a chance to deliver my speech, I thought. I was going out into the dim alley in despair when I was stopped and told to go back. I returned to the ballroom, where the men were pushing back their chairs and gathering in groups to talk.

The M.C. knocked on a table for quiet. "Gentlemen," he said, "we almost forgot an important part of the program. A most serious part, gentlemen. This boy was brought here to deliver a speech which he made at his graduation yesterday . . ."

"Bravo!"

"I'm told that he is the smartest boy we've got out there in Greenwood. I'm told that he knows more big words than a pocket-sized dictionary."

Much applause and laughter.

"So now, gentlemen, I want you to give him your attention."

There was still laughter as I faced them, my mouth dry, my eye throbbing. I began slowly, but evidently my throat was tense, because they began shouting, "Louder! Louder!"

"We of the younger generation extol the wisdom of that great leader and educator," I shouted, "who first spoke these flaming words of wisdom: 'A ship lost at sea for many days suddenly sighted a friendly vessel. From the mast of the unfortunate vessel was seen a signal: "Water, water; we die of thirst!" The answer from the friendly vessel came back: "Cast down your bucket where you are." The captain of the distressed vessel, at last heeding the injunction, cast down his bucket, and it came up full of fresh sparkling water from the mouth of the Amazon River.' And like him I say, and in his words, 'To those of my race who depend upon bettering their condition in a foreign land, or who underestimate the importance of cultivating friendly relations with the Southern white man, who is his next-door neighbor, I would say: "Cast down your bucket where you are"—cast it down in making friends in every manly way of the people of all races by whom we are surrounded . . .'"

I spoke automatically and with such fervor that I did not realize that the men were still talking and laughing until my dry mouth, filling up with blood from the cut, almost strangled me. I coughed, wanting to stop and go to one of the tall brass, sand-filled spittoons to relieve myself, but a few of the men, especially the superintendent, were listening and I was afraid. So I gulped it down, blood, saliva and all, and continued. (What powers of endurance I had during those days! What enthusiasm! What a belief in the lightness of things!) I spoke even louder in spite of the pain. But still they talked and still they laughed, as though deaf with cotton in dirty ears. So I spoke with greater emotional emphasis. I closed my ears and swallowed blood until I was nauseated. The speech seemed a hundred times as long as before, but I could not leave out a single word. All had to be said, each memorized nuance considered, rendered. Nor was that all. Whenever I uttered a word of three or more syllables a group of voices would yell for me to repeat it. I used the phrase "social responsibility," and they yelled:

"What's that word you say, boy?"

"Social responsibility," I said.

"What?"

"Social . . ."

"Louder."

". . . responsibility."

"More!"

"Respon—"

"Repeat!"

"—sibility."

The room filled with the uproar of laughter until, no doubt, distracted by having to gulp down my blood, I made a mistake and yelled a phrase I had often seen denounced in newspaper editorials, heard debated in private.

"Social . . ."

"What?" they yelled.

". . . equality—"

The laughter hung smokelike in the sudden stillness. I opened my eyes, puzzled. Sounds of displeasure filled the room. The M.C. rushed forward. They shouted hostile phrases at me. But I did not understand.

A small dry mustached man in the front row blared out, "Say that slowly, son!"

"What, sir?"

"What you just said!"

"Social responsibility, sir," I said.

"You weren't being smart, were you, boy?" he said, not unkindly.

"No, sir!"

"You sure that about 'equality' was a mistake?"

"Oh, yes, sir," I said. "I was swallowing blood."

"Well, you had better speak more slowly so we can understand. We mean to do right by you, but you've got to know your place at all times. All right, now, go on with your speech."

I was afraid. I wanted to leave but I wanted also to speak and I was afraid they'd snatch me down.

"Thank you, sir," I said, beginning where I had left off, and having them ignore me as before.

Yet when I finished there was a thunderous applause. I was surprised to see the superintendent come forth with a package wrapped in white tissue paper, and, gesturing for quiet, address the men.

"Gentlemen, you see that I did not overpraise the boy. He makes a good speech and some day he'll lead his people in the proper paths. And I don't have to tell you that that is important in these days and times. This is a good, smart boy, and so to encourage him in the right direction, in the name of the Board of Education I wish to present him a prize in the form of this . . ."

He paused, removing the tissue paper and revealing a gleaming calfskin brief case.

". . . in the form of this first-class article from Shad Whitmore's shop."

"Boy," he said, addressing me, "take this prize and keep it well. Consider it a badge of office. Prize it. Keep developing as you are and some day it will be filled with important papers that will help shape the destiny of your people."

I was so moved that I could hardly express my thanks. A rope of bloody saliva forming a shape like an undiscovered continent drooled upon the leather and I wiped it quickly away. I felt an importance that I had never dreamed.

"Open it and see what's inside," I was told.

My fingers a-tremble, I complied, smelling the fresh leather and finding an official-looking document inside. It was a scholarship to the state college for Negroes. My eyes filled with tears and I ran awkwardly off the floor.

I was overjoyed; I did not even mind when I discovered that the gold pieces I had scrambled for were brass pocket tokens advertising a certain make of automobile.

When I reached home everyone was excited. Next day the neighbors came to congratulate me. I even felt safe from grandfather, whose deathbed curse usually spoiled my triumphs. I stood beneath his photograph with my brief case in hand and smiled triumphantly into his stolid black peasant's face. It was a face that fascinated me. The eyes seemed to follow everywhere I went.

That night I dreamed I was at a circus with him and that he refused to laugh at the clowns no matter what they did. Then later he told me to open my brief case and read what was inside and I did, finding an official envelope stamped with the state seal; and inside the envelope I found another and another, endlessly, and I thought I would fall of weariness. "Them's years," he said. "Now open that one." And I did and in it I found an engraved document containing a short message in letters of gold. "Read it," my grandfather said. "Out loud!"

"To Whom It May Concern," I intoned. "Keep This Nigger-Boy Running."

I awoke with the old man's laughter ringing in my ears.

(It was a dream I was to remember and dream again for many years after. But at that time I had no insight into its meaning. First I had to attend college.)

1952

SAUL BELLOW
1915–2005

Winner of the Nobel Prize in Literature in 1976, Saul Bellow distinguished himself through a writing career that spanned nearly two-thirds of a century. Bellow, the child of Russian Jewish immigrants, was born in Lachine, Quebec, a suburb of Montreal, and spent nine years there before moving with his family to Chicago. While relishing the style of big-city life typical of the 1920s and 1930s, he pursued an increasingly intellectual track through Tuley High School, the University of Chicago, and Northwestern University. Literature was always Bellow's great love, but as his biographer James Atlas explains, the antisemitic establishment was unreceptive to his ambitions. "In search of career advice," Atlas notes, Bellow sought counsel from the chair of Northwestern's English Department, William Frank Bryan, who warned him against postgraduate study in the field, because "no Jew could really grasp the tradition of English literature. . . . No Jew would ever have the right *feeling* for it." Bellow therefore began work toward a master's degree in sociology and anthropology at the University of Wisconsin. Discouraged by the technical work required and chided by his new advisor for being too literary, he dropped out after just one semester, returning to Chicago and a lifelong career in literature that involved teaching (initially at a downtown teachers college, later most prestigiously as a member of the University of Chicago's Committee on Social Thought), editing (first for the *Encyclopaedia Britannica*, then for his own journal, *The Noble Savage*), and writing fiction. Except for brief service in the bureaucracy of the merchant marine during World War II, a Guggenheim Fellowship year in Paris (1948–49), and some time living in New York City and the New England countryside, Bellow made Chicago his primary residence and the setting for his most characteristic work, most famously *The Adventures of Augie March* (1953). In finding a voice for the protagonist of this novel Bellow discovered his own style, a mix of the urban colloquial and the erudite.

Bellow's first novel, *Dangling Man*, was not published until he was nearly thirty. It is a short series of elegantly morose meditations, told through the journal of a young man waiting to be inducted into the army and with the "freedom" of having nothing to do but wait. Eventually he is drafted: "Long live regimentation," he sardonically exults. His second novel, *The Victim* (1947), continues the investigation of ways people strive to be relieved of self-determination. This book concerns a week in the life of Asa Leventhal, alone in New York City while his wife visits a relative, who is suddenly confronted by a figure from the past (Kirby Allbee, a Gentile) who succeeds in implicating Leventhal with the past and its present manifestations. *The Victim* is Bellow's most somberly naturalistic depiction of a man brought up against forces larger than himself, yet from the opening sentence ("On some nights New York is as hot as Bangkok") a poetic dimension appears and helps create the sense of mystery and disturbance felt by both the main character and the reader.

Dangling Man and *The Victim* are highly wrought, mainly humorless books; in two long novels published in the 1950s Bellow opened up into new ranges of aspiration and situational zaniness, which brought him respectful admiration from many critics. *The Adventures of Augie March* and *Henderson the Rain King* (1959) are each narrated by an "I" who, like his predecessor Huck Finn, is good at lighting out for the territory ahead of whoever means to tie him down. The hero's adventures, whether occurring in Chicago, Mexico, or Africa, are exuberantly delivered in an always stimulating and sometimes overactive prose. *Augie* is filled with sights and sounds, colors and surfaces; its tone is self-involved, affectionate, and affirmative; *Henderson*, Bellow's most extravagant narrative, has the even more fabulous air of a quest-romance, in which the hero returns home from Africa at peace with the world he had been warring against.

The ironic motto for Bellow's novels of the 1950s may well be "Seize the Day," as in the title of perhaps his most sharply defined piece of fiction. This short novel (1956) is both painful and exhilarating because it so fully exposes its hero (Tommy Wilhelm, an aging out-of-work ex-actor) to the insults of other people who don't understand him, to a city (New York, particularly its Upper West Side) impervious to his needs, and to a narrative prose that mixes ridicule and affection so thoroughly as to make them scarcely distinguishable. *Seize the Day* combines, within Tommy's monologues, a wildness and pathos of bitter comedy that was a powerful new element in Bellow's work.

In "Where Do We Go from Here?: The Future of Fiction," an essay published in 1965, Bellow pointed out that nineteenth-century American literature—Emerson, Thoreau, Whitman, Melville—was highly didactic in its efforts to "instruct a young and raw nation." Bellow sees himself in this instructive tradition and in the international company of "didactic" novelists like Dostoyevsky, D. H. Lawrence, and Joseph Conrad; he believes also that "the imagination is looking for new ways to express virtue . . . we have barely begun to comprehend what a human being is." These concerns animate the novels Bellow wrote in the years since *Henderson*. In *Herzog* (1964) the hero is another down-and-outer, a professor-intellectual, a student of Romanticism and of the glorification of Self, which Herzog believes both modern life and modernist literature have been undercutting. At the same time he is a comic and pathetic victim of marital disorder; like all Bellow's heroes, Herzog has a terrible time with women, yet cannot live without them. In *Mr. Sammler's Planet* (1970), written out of the disorders of the late 1960s, the atmosphere is grimmer. Sammler, an aging Jew living (again) on New York's Upper West Side, analyzes and judges but cannot understand the young or blacks, or the mass of people gathered at Broadway and Ninety-sixth Street. He sees about him everywhere "poverty of soul" but admits that he too has "a touch of the same disease—the disease of the single self explaining what was what and who was who."

These novels, as well as *Humboldt's Gift* (1975), have been accused of parading too single-handedly attitudes toward which their author is sympathetic, whereas *The Dean's December* (1982) was criticized by John Updike, in a review, for being too much *"about* Saul Bellow," even though indirectly. Subsequently, a collection of shorter fiction, *Him with His Foot in His Mouth* (1984); the novels *More Die of Heartbreak* (1987) and *Ravelstein* (2000); three novellas, *The Bellarosa Connection* (1989), *A Theft* (1989), and *The Actual* (1997); and three stories collected as *Something to Remember Me By* (1991) exhibit various talky, informal protagonists and narrators with a lot on their minds. Matters of form and plot in these works seem less important than the ideas and active energy struck off by human beings in turmoil— usually comic turmoil. What Bellow finds moving in Theodore Dreiser's work, "his balkiness and sullenness, and then his allegiance to life," is still found in his own: complaint and weariness, fault-finding, accusation of self and others—these gestures directed at "life" also make up the stuff of life and the "allegiance" out of which Bellow's heroes are made. We read him for this range of interest; for flexibility and diversity of style and idiom; and for the eloquences of nostalgia, invective, and lamentation that make up his intensely imagined world.

Married five times, he ended his academic career with a brief residency at Boston University, afterward retiring to rural Vermont, where he died two months short of his ninetieth birthday and five years after publishing *Ravelstein*, his nineteenth book and a work indicative of the conservative, traditionalist posture of his later career.

From The Adventures of Augie March

Chapter One

I am an American, Chicago born—Chicago, that somber city—and go at things as I have taught myself, free-style, and will make the record in my own way: first to knock, first admitted; sometimes an innocent knock, sometimes a not so innocent. But a man's character is his fate, says Heraclitus,[1] and in the end there isn't any way to disguise the nature of the knocks by acoustical work on the door or gloving the knuckles.

Everybody knows there is no fineness or accuracy of suppression; if you hold down one thing you hold down the adjoining.

My own parents were not much to me, though I cared for my mother. She was simple-minded, and what I learned from her was not what she taught, but on the order of object lessons. She didn't have much to teach, poor woman. My brothers and I loved her. I speak for them both; for the elder it is safe enough; for the younger one, Georgie, I have to answer—he was born an idiot—but I'm in no need to guess, for he had a song he sang as he ran drag-footed with his stiff idiot's trot, up and down along the curl-wired fence in the backyard:

> Georgie Mahchy, Augie, Simey
> Winnie Mahchy, evwy, evwy love Mama.

He was right about everyone save Winnie, Grandma Lausch's poodle, a pursy old overfed dog. Mama was Winnie's servant, as she was Grandma Lausch's. Loud-breathing and wind-breaking, she lay near the old lady's stool on a cushion embroidered with a Berber[2] aiming a rifle at a lion. She was personally Grandma's, belonged to her suite; the rest of us were the governed, and especially Mama. Mama passed the dog's dish to Grandma, and Winnie received her food at the old lady's feet from the old lady's hands. These hands and feet were small; she wore a shriveled sort of lisle on her legs and her slippers were gray—ah, the gray of that felt, the gray despotic to souls—with pink ribbons. Mama, however, had large feet, and around the house she wore men's shoes, usually without strings, and a dusting or mobcap like somebody's fanciful cotton effigy of the form of the brain. She was meek and long, round-eyed like Georgie—gentle green round eyes and a gentle freshness of color in her long face. Her hands were work-reddened, she had very few of her teeth left—to heed the knocks as they come—and she and Simon wore the same ravelly coat-sweaters. Besides having round eyes, Mama had circular glasses that I went with her to the free dispensary on Harrison Street[3] to get. Coached by Grandma Lausch, I went to do the lying. Now I know it wasn't so necessary to lie, but then everyone thought so, and Grandma Lausch especially, who was one of those Machiavellis of small street and neighborhood that my young years were full of. So Grandma, who had it all ready before we left the house and must have put in hours plotting it out in thought and phrase, lying small in her chilly small room under the featherbed, gave it to

---

1. Early Greek philosopher (fl. c. 480 B.C.E.) famous for his cryptic aphorisms and for positing the existence of the human soul.

2. Non-Arabic North African tribesman.
3. Downtown location of Chicago's social welfare agency.

me at breakfast. The idea was that Mama wasn't keen enough to do it right. That maybe one didn't need to be keen didn't occur to us; it was a contest. The dispensary would want to know why the Charities didn't pay for the glasses. So you must say nothing about the Charities, but that sometimes money from my father came and sometimes it didn't, and that Mama took boarders. This was, in a delicate and choosy way, by ignoring and omitting certain large facts, true. It was true enough for *them*, and at the age of nine I could appreciate this perfectly. Better than my brother Simon, who was too blunt for this kind of maneuver and, anyway, from books, had gotten hold of some English schoolboy notions of honor. *Tom Brown's Schooldays*[4] for many years had an influence we were not in a position to afford.

Simon was a blond boy with big cheekbones and wide gray eyes and had the arms of a cricketer—I go by the illustrations; we never played anything but softball. Opposed to his British style was his patriotic anger at George III.[5] The mayor was at that time ordering the schoolboard to get history books that dealt more harshly with the king, and Simon was very hot at Cornwallis.[6] I admired this patriotic flash, his terrific personal wrath at the general, and his satisfaction over his surrender at Yorktown,[7] which would often come over him at lunch while we ate our bologna sandwiches. Grandma had a piece of boiled chicken at noon, and sometimes there was the gizzard for bristle-headed little Georgie, who loved it and blew at the ridgy thing more to cherish than to cool it. But this martial true-blood pride of Simon's disqualified him for the crafty task to be done at the dispensary; he was too disdainful to lie and might denounce everybody instead. I could be counted on to do the job, because I enjoyed it. I loved a piece of strategy. I had enthusiasms too; I had Simon's, though there was never much meat in Cornwallis for me, and I had Grandma Lausch's as well. As for the truth of these statements I was instructed to make—well, it was a fact that we had a boarder. Grandma Lausch was our boarder, not a relation at all. She was supported by two sons, one from Cincinnati and one from Racine, Wisconsin. The daughters-in-law did not want her, and she, the widow of a powerful Odessa[8] businessman—a divinity over us, bald, whiskery, with a fat nose, greatly armored in a cutaway, a double-breasted vest, powerfully buttoned (his blue photo, enlarged and retouched by Mr. Lulov, hung in the parlor, doubled back between the portico columns of the full-length mirror, the dome of the stove beginning where his trunk ended)—she preferred to live with us, because for so many years she was used to direct a house, to command, to govern, to manage, scheme, devise, and intrigue in all her languages. She boasted French and German besides Russian, Polish, and Yiddish; and who but Mr. Lulov, the retouch artist from Division Street,[9] could have tested her claim to French? And he was a serene bogus too, that triple-backboned gallant tea-drinker. Except that he had been a hackie in

4. Novel (1857) based on experiences at Rugby School, by the English jurist and religious reformer Thomas Hughes (1822–1896).
5. King (1738–1820) of England, Scotland, and Ireland during a period (r. 1760–1820) that included the American Revolution.
6. Charles Cornwallis (1738–1805), British general who made the final surrender in the American Revolution.
7. Village in southeast Virginia where in 1781

British forces surrendered to George Washington's Continental Army, effectively ending the American Revolution.
8. City in the Ukraine on the Black Sea, departure point for many Russian Jews who emigrated to North America in the late 19th and early 20th centuries.
9. Commercial and shopping street on Chicago's North Side.

Paris, once, and if he told the truth about that might have known French among other things, like playing tunes on his teeth with a pencil or singing and keeping time with a handful of coins that he rattled by jigging his thumb along the table, and how to play chess.

Grandma Lausch played like Timur, whether chess or klabyasch,[1] with palatal catty harshness and sharp gold in her eyes. Klabyasch she played with Mr. Kreindl, a neighbor of ours who had taught her the game. A powerful stub-handed man with a large belly, he swatted the table with those hard hands of his, flinging down his cards and shouting "*Shtoch! Yasch! Menél! Klabyasch!*"[2] Grandma looked sardonically at him. She often said, after he left, "If you've got a Hungarian friend you don't need an enemy." But there was nothing of the enemy about Mr. Kreindl. He merely, sometimes, sounded menacing because of his drill-sergeant's bark. He was an old-time Austro-Hungarian[3] conscript, and there was something soldierly about him: a neck that had strained with pushing artillery wheels, a campaigner's red in the face, a powerful bite in his jaw and gold-crowned teeth, green cockeyes and soft short hair, altogether Napoleonic.[4] His feet slanted out on the ideal of Frederick the Great,[5] but he was about a foot under the required height for guardsmen. He had a masterly look of independence. He and his wife—a woman quiet and modest to the neighbors and violently quarrelsome at home—and his son, a dental student, lived in what was called the English basement at the front of the house. The son, Kotzie, worked evenings in the corner drugstore and went to school in the neighborhood of County Hospital, and it was he who told Grandma about the free dispensary. Or rather, the old woman sent for him to find out what one could get from those state and county places. She was always sending for people, the butcher, the grocer, the fruit peddler, and received them in the kitchen to explain that the Marches had to have discounts. Mama usually had to stand by. The old woman would tell them, "You see how it is—do I have to say more? There's no man in the house and children to bring up." This was her most frequent argument. When Lubin, the caseworker, came around and sat in the kitchen, familiar, bald-headed, in his gold glasses, his weight comfortable, his mouth patient, she shot it at him: "How do you expect children to be brought up?" While he listened, trying to remain comfortable but gradually becoming like a man determined not to let a grasshopper escape from his hand. "Well, my dear, Mrs. March could raise your rent," he said. She must often have answered—for there were times when she sent us all out to be alone with him—"Do you know what things would be like without me? You ought to be grateful for the way I hold them together." I'm sure she even said, "And when I die, Mr. Lubin, you'll see what you've got on your hands." I'm one hundred per cent sure of it. To us nothing was ever said that might weaken her rule by suggesting it would ever end. Besides, it would have shocked us to hear it, and she, in her miraculous knowledge of us, able to be extremely close to our

---

1. Card game taking its name from the Yiddish verb for "to gather." "Timur": also Tamerlane, Mongol warrior (1336–1405) whose conquests stretched from the Ukraine to northern India.
2. Successive winning tricks.
3. The dual monarchy of Austria and Hungary (1867–1918) encompassed Austria, Hungary, Bohemia, and parts of Poland, Romania, Italy, and the Balkans.
4. Era and style of Napoléon Bonaparte's (1769–1821) rule as Napoléon I, emperor of the French (1804–15).
5. Frederick II (1712–1786), called "the Great," king of Prussia (r. 1740–86), patron of the arts and philosophy.

thoughts—she was one sovereign who knew exactly the proportions of love, respect, and fear of power in her subjects—understood how we would have been shocked. But to Lubin, for reasons of policy and also because she had to express feelings she certainly had, she must have said it. He had a harassed patience with her of "deliver me from such clients," though he tried to appear master of the situation. He held his derby between his thighs (his suits, always too scanty in the pants, exposed white socks and bulldog shoes, crinkled, black, and bulging with toes), and he looked into the hat as though debating whether it was wise to release his grasshopper on the lining for a while.

"I pay as much as I can afford," she would say.

She took her cigarette case out from under her shawl, she cut a Murad[6] in half with her sewing scissors and picked up the holder. This was still at a time when women did not smoke. Save the intelligentsia—the term she applied to herself. With the holder in her dark little gums between which all her guile, malice, and command issued, she had her best inspirations of strategy. She was as wrinkled as an old paper bag, an autocrat, hard-shelled and jesuitical,[7] a pouncy old hawk of a Bolshevik,[8] her small ribboned gray feet immobile on the shoekit and stool Simon had made in the manual-training class, dingy old wool Winnie whose bad smell filled the flat on the cushion beside her. If wit and discontent don't necessarily go together, it wasn't from the old woman that I learned it. She was impossible to satisfy. Kreindl, for example, on whom we could depend, Kreindl who carried up the coal when Mama was sick and who instructed Kotzie to make up our prescriptions for nothing, she called "that trashy Hungarian," or "Hungarian pig." She called Kotzie "the baked apple"; she called Mrs. Kreindl "the secret goose," Lubin "the shoemaker's son," the dentist "the butcher," the butcher "the timid swindler." She detested the dentist, who had several times unsuccessfully tried to fit her with false teeth. She accused him of burning her gums when taking the impressions. But then she tried to pull his hands away from her mouth. I saw that happen: the stolid, square-framed Dr. Wernick, whose compact forearms could have held off a bear, painfully careful with her, determined, concerned at her choked screams, and enduring her scratches. To see her struggle like that was no easy thing for me, and Dr. Wernick was sorry to see me there too, I know, but either Simon or I had to squire her wherever she went. Here particularly she needed a witness to Wernick's cruelty and clumsiness as well as a shoulder to lean on when she went weakly home. Already at ten I was only a little shorter than she and big enough to hold her small weight.

"You saw how he put his paws over my face so I couldn't breathe?" she said. "God made him to be a butcher. Why did he become a dentist? His hands are too heavy. The touch is everything to a dentist. If his hands aren't right he shouldn't be let practice. But his wife worked hard to send him through school and make a dentist of him. And I must go to him and be burned because of it."

The rest of us had to go to the dispensary—which was like the dream of a multitude of dentists' chairs, hundreds of them in a space as enormous as

<hr/>

6. A Turkish cigarette, named for the Murad River.

7. Reference to the Society of Jesus, commonly called Jesuits, a Catholic religious order famous for its intellectual rigor, founded in 1540 by the Spanish priest Ignatius of Loyola (1491–1556).

8. Left-wing political party allied with other Communist forces in the Russian Revolution (1917).

an armory, and green bowls with designs of glass grapes, drills lifted zigzag as insects' legs, and gas flames on the porcelain swivel trays—a thundery gloom in Harrison Street of limestone county buildings and cumbersome red streetcars with metal grillwork on their windows and monarchical iron whiskers of cowcatchers front and rear. They lumbered and clanged, and their brake tanks panted in the slushy brown of a winter afternoon or the bare stone brown of a summer's, salted with ash, smoke, and prairie dust, with long stops at the clinics to let off dumpers, cripples, hunchbacks, brace-legs, crutch-wielders, tooth and eye sufferers, and all the rest.

So before going with my mother for the glasses I was always instructed by the old woman and had to sit and listen with profound care. My mother too had to be present, for there must be no slip-up. She must be coached to say nothing. "Remember, Rebecca," Grandma would rerepeat, "let him answer everything." To which Mama was too obedient even to say yes, but only sat and kept her long hands folded on the bottle-fly iridescence of the dress the old woman had picked for her to wear. Very healthy and smooth, her color; none of us inherited this high a color from her, or the form of her nose with nostrils turned back and showing a little of the partition. "You keep out of it. If they ask you something, you look at Augie like this." And she illustrated how Mama was to turn to me, terribly exact, if she had only been able to drop her habitual grandeur. "Don't tell anything. Only answer questions," she said to me. My mother was anxious that I should be worthy and faithful. Simon and I were her miracles or accidents; Georgie was her own true work in which she returned to her fate after blessed and undeserved success. "Augie, listen to Grandma. Hear what she says," was all she ever dared when the old woman unfolded her plan.

"When they ask you, 'Where is your father?' you say, 'I don't know where, miss.' No matter how old she is, you shouldn't forget to say 'miss.' If she wants to know where he was the last time you heard from him, you must tell her that the last time he sent a money order was about two years ago from Buffalo, New York. Never say a word about the Charity. The Charity you should never mention, you hear that? Never. When she asks you how much the rent is, tell her eighteen dollars. When she asks where the money comes from, say you have boarders. How many? Two boarders. Now, say to me, how much rent?"

"Eighteen dollars."

"And how many boarders?"

"Two."

"And how much do they pay?"

"How much should I say?"

"Eight dollars each a week."

"Eight dollars."

"So you can't go to a private doctor, if you get sixty-four dollars a month. The eyedrops alone cost me five when I went, and he scalded my eyes. And these specs"—she tapped the case—"cost ten dollars the frames and fifteen the glasses."

Never but at such times, by necessity, was my father mentioned. I claimed to remember him; Simon denied that I did, and Simon was right. I liked to imagine it.

"He wore a uniform," I said. "Sure I remember. He was a soldier."

"Like hell he was. You don't know anything about it."

"Maybe a sailor."

"Like hell. He drove a truck for Hall Brothers laundry on Marshfield,[9] that's what he did. *I* said he used to wear a uniform. Monkey sees, monkey does; monkey hears, monkey says." Monkey was the basis of much thought with us. On the sideboard, on the Turkestan runner, with their eyes, ears, and mouth covered, we had see-no-evil, speak-no-evil, hear-no-evil, a lower trinity of the house. The advantage of lesser gods is that you can take their names any way you like. "Silence in the courthouse, monkey wants to speak; speak, monkey, speak." "The monkey and the bamboo were playing in the grass . . ." Still the monkeys could be potent, and awesome besides, and deep social critics when the old woman, like a great lama—for she is Eastern to me, in the end—would point to the squatting brown three, whose mouths and nostrils were drawn in sharp blood-red, and with profound wit, her unkindness finally touching greatness, say, "Nobody asks you to love the whole world, only to be honest, *ehrlich*.[1] Don't have a loud mouth. The more you love people the more they'll mix you up. A child loves, a person respects. Respect is better than love. And that's respect, the middle monkey." It never occurred to us that she sinned mischievously herself against that convulsed speak-no-evil who hugged his lips with his hands; but no criticism of her came near our minds at any time, much less when the resonance of a great principle filled the whole kitchen.

She used to read us lessons off poor Georgie's head. He would kiss the dog. This bickering handmaiden of the old lady, at one time. Now a dozy, long-sighing crank and proper object of respect for her years of right-minded but not exactly lovable busyness. But Georgie loved her—and Grandma, whom he would kiss on the sleeve, on the knee, taking knee or arm in both hands and putting his underlip forward, chaste, lummoxy, caressing, gentle and diligent when he bent his narrow back, blouse bagging all over it, whitish hair pointy and close as a burr or sunflower when the seeds have been picked out of it. The old lady let him embrace her and spoke to him in the following way: "Hey, you, boy, clever *junge*,[2] you like the old Grandma, my minister, my *cavalyer*?[3] That's-a-boy. You know who's good to you, who gives you gizzards and necks? Who? Who makes noodles for you? Yes. Noodles are slippery, hard to pick up with a fork and hard to pick up with the fingers. You see how the little bird pulls the worm? The little worm wants to stay in the ground. The little worm doesn't want to come out. Enough, you're making my dress wet." And she'd sharply push his forehead off with her old prim hand, having fired off for Simon and me, mindful always of her duty to wise us up, one more animadversion on the trustful, loving, and simple surrounded by the cunning-hearted and tough, a fighting nature of birds and worms, and a desperate mankind without feelings. Illustrated by Georgie. But the principal illustration was not Georgie but Mama, in her love-originated servitude, simpleminded, abandoned with three children. This was what old lady Lausch was driving at, now, in the later wisdom of her life, that she had a second family to lead.

---

9. Commercial avenue on Chicago's North Side.
1. Sincere (German).
2. Young man (German).

3. Yiddish borrowing from the German *kavalier* (gentleman) and Polish *kawaler* (bachelor, gallant).

And what must Mama have thought when in any necessary connection my father was brought into the conversation? She sat docile. I conceive that she thought of some detail about him—a dish he liked, perhaps meat and potatoes, perhaps cabbage or cranberry sauce; perhaps that he disliked a starched collar, or a soft collar; that he brought home the *Evening American* or the *Journal.*[4] She thought this because her thoughts were always simple; but she felt abandonment, and greater pains than conscious mental ones put a dark streak to her simplicity. I don't know how she made out before, when we were alone after the desertion, but Grandma came and put a regulating hand on the family life. Mama surrendered powers to her that maybe she had never known she had and took her punishment in drudgery; occupied a place, I suppose, among women conquered by a superior force of love, like those women whom Zeus got the better of in animal form and who next had to take cover from his furious wife. Not that I can see my big, gentle, dilapidated, scrubbing, and lugging mother as a fugitive of immense beauty from such classy wrath, or our father as a marble-legged Olympian. She had sewed buttonholes in a coat factory in a Wells Street[5] loft and he was a laundry driver—there wasn't even so much as a picture of him left when he blew. But she does have a place among such women by the deeper right of continual payment. And as for vengeance from a woman, Grandma Lausch was there to administer the penalties under the standards of legitimacy, representing the main body of married womankind.

Still the old lady had a heart. I don't mean to say she didn't. She was tyrannical and a snob about her Odessa luster and her servants and governesses, but though she had been a success herself she knew what it was to fall through susceptibility. I began to realize this when I afterward read some of the novels she used to send me to the library for. She taught me the Russian alphabet so that I could make out the titles. Once a year she read *Anna Karenina* and *Eugene Onegin.*[6] Occasionally I got into hot water by bringing a book she didn't want. "How many times do I have to tell you if it doesn't say *roman* I don't want it? You didn't look inside. Are your fingers too weak to open the book? Then they should be too weak to play ball or pick your nose. For that you've got strength! *Bozhe moy!*[7] God in Heaven! You haven't got the brains of a cat, to walk two miles and bring me a book about religion because it says Tolstoi on the cover."

The old *grande dame*, I don't want to be misrepresenting her. She was suspicious of what could have been, given one wrong stitch of heredity, a family vice by which we could have been exploited. She didn't want to read Tolstoi on religion. She didn't trust him as a family man because the countess had had such trouble with him. But although she never went to the synagogue, ate bread on Passover, sent Mama to the pork butcher where meat was cheaper, loved canned lobster and other forbidden food, she was not an atheist and free-thinker. Mr. Anticol, the old junky she called (search me why) "Rameses"—after the city named with Pithom in the Scriptures maybe;[8] no

---

4. Chicago newpapers of the era.
5. Light-industrial street immediately north of Chicago's downtown area.
6. Verse narrative (1823–31) by the Russian poet Aleksandr Pushkin (1799–1837). "*Anna Karenina*": novel (1875–77) by the Russian novelist Leo

Tolstoy (1828–1910).
7. Oh, my God (Russian).
8. *Exodus* 1.11: "Therefore they set taskmasters over them to afflict them with heavy burdens; and they built for Pharoah store-cities, Pithom and Raamses."

telling what her inspirations were—was that. A real rebel to God. Icy and canny, she would listen to what he had to say and wouldn't declare herself. He was ruddy, and gloomy; his leathery serge cap made him flat-headed, and his alley calls for rags, old iron—"recks aline," he sung it—made him gravel-voiced and gruff. He had tough hair and brows and despising brown eyes; he was a studious, shaggy, meaty old man. Grandma bought a set of the *Encyclopedia Americana*—edition of 1892, I think—from him and saw to it that Simon and I read it; and he too, whenever he met us, asked, "How's the set?" believing, I reckon, that it taught irreverence to religion. What had made him an atheist was a massacre of Jews in his town. From the cellar where he was hidden he saw a laborer pissing on the body of his wife's younger brother, just killed. "So don't talk to me about God," he said. But it was he that talked about God, all the time. And while Mrs. Anticol stayed pious, it was his idea of grand apostasy to drive to the reform synagogue on the high holidays and park his pink-eye nag among the luxurious, whirl-wired touring cars of the rich Jews who bared their heads inside as if they were attending a theater, a kind of abjectness in them that gave him grim entertainment to the end of his life. He caught a cold in the rain and died of pneumonia.

Grandma, all the same, burned a candle on the anniversary of Mr. Lausch's death, threw a lump of dough on the coals when she was baking, as a kind of offering, had incantations over baby teeth and stunts against the evil eye. It was kitchen religion and had nothing to do with the giant God of the Creation who turned back the waters and exploded Gomorrah, but it was on the side of religion at that. And while we're on that side I'll mention the Poles—we were just a handful of Jews among them in the neighborhood—and the swollen, bleeding hearts on every kitchen wall, the pictures of saints, baskets of death flowers tied at the door, communions, Easters, and Christmases. And sometimes we were chased, stoned, bitten, and beat up for Christ-killers, all of us, even Georgie, articled, whether we liked it or not, to this mysterious trade. But I never had any special grief from it, or brooded, being by and large too larky and boisterous to take it to heart, and looked at it as needing no more special explanation than the stone-and-bat wars of the street gangs or the swarming on a fall evening of parish punks to rip up fences, screech and bawl at girls, and beat up strangers. It wasn't in my nature to fatigue myself with worry over being born to this occult work, even though some of my friends and playmates would turn up in the middle of these mobs to trap you between houses from both ends of a passageway. Simon had less truck with them. School absorbed him more, and he had his sentiments anyway, a mixed extract from Natty Bumppo, Quentin Durward, Tom Brown, Clark at Kaskaskia, the messenger who brought the good news from Ratisbon,[9] and so on, that kept him more to himself. I was just a slow understudy to this, just as he never got me to put in hours on his Sandow muscle builder[1] and the gimmick for developing the sinews of the wrist. I

9. The French name for the German city of Regensburg, which was captured by Napoleon's armies in 1809. "Natty Bumppo": protagonist of the Leatherstocking novels by the American novelist James Fenimore Cooper (1789–1851). "Quentin Durward": eponymous hero in the novel (1823) by the Scottish poet and novelist Sir Walter Scott (1771–1832). "Tom Brown": see n. 4, p. 228.

"Clark at Kaskasia": the American military leader George Rogers Clark (1752–1818) captured the British frontier fort at Kaskaskia, Illinois, in 1778. 1. Device named after Eugen Sandow (1867–1925), American physical culturist born in Germany, famous for his performances as a body-builder and for advocacy of physical education.

was an easy touch for friendships, and most of the time they were cut short by older loyalties. I was pals longest with Stashu Kopecs, whose mother was a midwife graduated from the Aesculapian School of Midwifery on Milwaukee Avenue.[2] Well to do, the Kopecses had an electric player piano and linoleums in all the rooms, but Stashu was a thief, and to run with him I stole too: coal off the cars, clothes from the lines, rubber balls from the dime store, and pennies off the newsstands. Mostly for the satisfaction of dexterity, though Stashu invented the game of stripping in the cellar and putting on girls' things swiped from the clotheslines. Then he too showed up in a gang that caught me one cold afternoon of very little snow while I was sitting on a crate frozen into the mud, eating Nabisco[3] wafers, my throat full of the sweet dust. Foremost, there was a thug of a kid, about thirteen but undersized, hard and grieved-looking. He came up to accuse me, and big Moonya Staplanski, just out of the St. Charles Reformatory[4] and headed next for the one at Pontiac,[5] backed him up.

"You little Jew bastard, you hit my brother," Moonya said.

"I never did. I never even saw him before."

"You took away a nickel from him. How did you buy them biscuits else, you?"

"I got them at home."

Then I caught sight of Stashu, hayheaded and jeering, pleased to sickness with his deceit and his new-revealed brotherhood with the others, and I said, "Hey, you lousy bed-wetter, Stashu, you know Moon ain't even got a brother."

Here the kid hit me and the gang jumped me, Stashu with the rest, tearing the buckles from my sheepskin coat and bloodying my nose.

"Who is to blame?" said Grandma Lausch when I came home. "You know who? You are, Augie, because that's all the brains you have to go with that piss-in-bed *accoucherka's*[6] son. Does Simon hang around with them? Not Simon. He has too much sense." I thanked God she didn't know about the stealing. And in a way, because that was her schooling temperament, I suspect she was pleased that I should see where it led to give your affections too easily. But Mama, the prime example of this weakness, was horrified. Against the old lady's authority she didn't dare to introduce her feelings during the hearing, but when she took me into the kitchen to put a compress on me she nearsightedly pored over my scratches, whispering and sighing to me, while Georgie tottered around behind her, long and white, and Winnie lapped water under the sink.

1953

2. Commercial and shopping street on Chicago's North Side, at this time a Polish-American neighborhood.
3. Brand name of the National Biscuit Company.
4. Site of the Illinois State Reformatory for Boys.
5. Site of the Illinois Correctional Center.
6. Yiddish borrowing from the Polish *akuszerka* (midwife).

ARTHUR MILLER
1915-2005

For much modern American drama the family is the central subject, as the anthology selections show. In *Long Day's Journey into Night* Eugene O'Neill studied his own family through the Tyrones; in Tennessee Williams's *A Streetcar Named Desire* the Kowalskis are one family, which Blanche invades, while Blanche and Stella, as sisters, are another. Most of Arthur Miller's plays, as well, concentrate on the family and envision an ideal world as, perhaps, an enlarged family. Often the protagonist's sense of family draws him into conflict with—and eventual doom in—the outside world. Yet Miller recognized that an ideal is sometimes a rationalization. Joe Keller insists in *All My Sons* (1947) that during the war he shipped damaged airplane parts to support his family, but a desire for commercial success was part of his motive. Eddie Carbone in *A View from the Bridge* (1955) accepts death because of his sense of responsibility to his niece, but married man though he is, he may also be in love with that same niece. In *Death of a Salesman* (1949) Willy Loman's delusions and self-deceptions derive from, and return to, his image of himself as family provider, an image he cannot live up to; driven by his desire to be "well liked," a successful social personality, he fails to connect with either of his sons and neglects his wife. Thus Miller's treatment of the family leads to a treatment both of personal ideals and of the society within which families have to operate.

Miller was born into a German Jewish family in Manhattan; his father was a well-to-do but almost illiterate clothing manufacturer, his mother an avid reader. When his father's business collapsed after the stock market crash in 1929, the family moved to Brooklyn, where Miller graduated from high school. His subsequent two years of work in an automobile-parts warehouse to earn money for college tuition are warmly recalled in his play *A Memory of Two Mondays* (1955). At the University of Michigan he enrolled as a journalism student. These were the years of the Spanish Civil War, the rise of fascism, and the attraction of Marxism as a way out of the Depression, and here Miller formed his political views. He also began to write plays, which won prizes at the university and in New York. He then went to work for the Federal Theater Project, wrote radio plays, toured army camps to gather material for a film, and married Mary Slattery, the first of his three wives.

In 1947 Miller enjoyed his first Broadway success, *All My Sons*. (*The Man Who Had All the Luck* had failed in 1944.) This strongly realistic portrayal of a family divided because of the father's insistence on business as usual during World War II drew the attention of audiences and theater critics. *Death of a Salesman*, his masterpiece, was produced two years later and won the Pulitzer Prize. An adaptation of Ibsen's *An Enemy of the People* followed in 1951. It was suggested to him by the actors Fredric March and Florence Eldridge, but Miller was clearly drawn by Ibsen's hero, Dr. Stockmann, who leads a fight against pollution with strong but confused idealism.

In the 1950s the hysterical search for supposed communist infiltration of American life reached its height, as Senator Joseph McCarthy summoned suspect after suspect to hearings in Washington. Miller later said that at this time he was reading a book about the Salem witch trials and saw that "the main point of the hearings, precisely as in seventeenth-century Salem, was that the accused make public confession, damn his confederates as well as his Devil master, and guarantee his sterling new allegiance by breaking disgusting old vows—whereupon he was let loose to rejoin the society of extremely decent people." Out of this came *The Crucible* (1953), in which the hero, John Proctor, allows himself to be executed rather than sign away his name and his children's respect. Hysteria touched Miller personally when he was denied a passport and in 1957 was convicted of contempt of Congress for refusing to name suspected communists (this conviction was unanimously overturned by the Supreme Court the following year).

Miller had long been looking for a way to dramatize what he had earlier learned about mob control of the Brooklyn waterfront and finally did so in the one-act play *A View from the Bridge*, produced with *A Memory of Two Mondays* in 1955; later he would rework *View* into a full-length play. Meanwhile, he had met the glamorous movie actress Marilyn Monroe; they married in 1956, after he divorced his first wife. He wrote the screenplay *The Misfits* for Monroe, but in their private life, their complex natures were ill-sorted. The marriage ended in divorce in 1961, and a year later he married the photographer Ingeborg Morath, with whom he collaborated on several books of photographs and essays.

In 1964 two plays opened: *After the Fall* (in which the protagonist is a thinly disguised Miller investigating his family, his responsibilities, and his wives) and *Incident at Vichy* (about Jews and Nazis in Vichy, France). While these were by no means as successful as *Salesman*, they returned him seriously to the stage. Among

Actor Lee J. Cobb as Willy Loman being restrained by actors Arthur Kennedy (left) and Cameron Mitchell (right) as his sons Biff and Hap respectively in the 1949 original Broadway production of ***Death of a Salesman***.

later plays are *The Price* (1968), *The Creation of the World and Other Business* (1972), *The Archbishop's Ceiling* (1977), and two one-act plays under the title *Danger: Memory!* (1986). These last fared poorly in New York, but found successful productions elsewhere in the world.

Miller in his later years was something of an activist. In the late 1960s he was asked to become president of PEN (Poets, Essayists, Novelists), the international writers' group. By opening this organization to writers in what were then Iron Curtain countries and speaking out for those repressed by totalitarian regimes, he became a respected champion of human rights.

Like his contemporary Tennessee Williams, Miller rejected the influence of "mawkish twenties slang" and "deadly repetitiveness." Again like Williams, Miller was impatient with prosy dialogue and well-made structures. As he explained, the success of *A Streetcar Named Desire* in 1947 helped him write *Death of a Salesman*:

> With *Streetcar*, Tennessee had printed a license to speak at full throat, and it helped strengthen me as I turned to Willy Loman, a salesman always full of words, and better yet, a man who could never cease trying, like Adam, to name himself and the world's wonders. I had known all along that this play could not be encompassed by conventional realism, and for one integral reason: in Willy the past was as alive as what was happening at the moment, sometimes even crashing in to completely overwhelm his mind. I wanted precisely the same fluidity of form.

In *Salesman* the action moves effortlessly from the present—the last twenty-four hours of Willy's life—into moments in his memory, symbolized in the stage setting by the idyllic leaves around his house that, in these past moments, block out the threatening apartment houses. The successful realization of this fluidity on the stage was greatly aided by Miller's director, Elia Kazan, and his stage designer, Jo Mielziner, both of whom had worked with Williams two years earlier on *Streetcar*. A striking difference between Williams and Miller, however, is the latter's overt moralizing, which adds a didactic element to his plays not to be found in those of Williams.

The text is from *Arthur Miller's Collected Plays* (1957).

Death of a Salesman

Certain Private Conversations in Two Acts and a Requiem

THE CHARACTERS

WILLY LOMAN	THE WOMAN	JENNY
LINDA	CHARLEY	STANLEY
BIFF	UNCLE BEN	MISS FORSYTHE
HAPPY	HOWARD WAGNER	LETTA
BERNARD		

The action takes place in WILLY LOMAN's *house and yard and in various places he visits in the New York and Boston of today.*

Act One

A melody is heard, playing upon a flute. It is small and fine, telling of grass and trees and the horizon. The curtain rises.

Before us is the Salesman's house. We are aware of towering, angular shapes behind it, surrounding it on all sides. Only the blue light of the sky falls upon the house and forestage; the surrounding area shows an angry flow of orange. As more light appears, we see a solid vault of apartment houses around the small, fragile-seeming home. An air of the dream clings to the place, a dream rising out of reality. The kitchen at center seems actual enough, for there is a kitchen table with three chairs, and a refrigerator. But no other fixtures are seen. At the back of the kitchen there is a draped entrance, which leads to the living-room. To the right of the kitchen, on a level raised two feet, is a bedroom furnished only with a brass bedstead and a straight chair. On a shelf over the bed a silver athletic trophy stands. A window opens onto the apartment house at the side.

Behind the kitchen, on a level raised six and a half feet, is the boys' bedroom, at present barely visible. Two beds are dimly seen, and at the back of the room a dormer window. (This bedroom is above the unseen living-room.) At the left a stairway curves up to it from the kitchen.

The entire setting is wholly or, in some places, partially transparent. The roofline of the house is one-dimensional; under and over it we see the apartment buildings. Before the house lies an apron, curving beyond the forestage into the orchestra. This forward area serves as the back yard as well as the locale of all WILLY's *imaginings and of his city scenes. Whenever the action is in the present the actors observe the imaginary wall-lines, entering the house only through its door at the left. But in the scenes of the past these boundaries are broken, and characters enter or leave a room by stepping "through" a wall onto the forestage.*

From the right, WILLY LOMAN, *the Salesman, enters, carrying two large sample cases. The flute plays on. He hears but is not aware of it. He is past sixty years of age, dressed quietly. Even as he crosses the stage to the doorway of the house, his exhaustion is apparent. He unlocks the door, comes into the kitchen, and thankfully lets his burden down, feeling the soreness of his palms. A word-sigh escapes his lips—it might be "Oh, boy, oh, boy." He closes the door, then carries his cases out into the living-room, through the draped kitchen doorway.*

LINDA, *his wife, has stirred in her bed at the right. She gets out and puts on a robe, listening. Most often jovial, she has developed an iron repression of her exceptions to* WILLY's *behavior—she more than loves him, she admires him, as though his mercurial nature, his temper, his massive dreams and little cruelties, served her only as sharp reminders of the turbulent longings within him, longings which she shares but lacks the temperament to utter and follow to their end.*

LINDA [*hearing* WILLY *outside the bedroom, calls with some trepidation*] Willy!

WILLY   It's all right. I came back.

LINDA   Why? What happened? [*slight pause*] Did something happen, Willy?

WILLY   No, nothing happened.

LINDA   You didn't smash the car, did you?

WILLY [*with casual irritation*]   I said nothing happened. Didn't you hear me?

LINDA   Don't you feel well?

WILLY   I'm tired to the death. [*The flute has faded away. He sits on the bed beside her, a little numb.*] I couldn't make it. I just couldn't make it, Linda.

LINDA [*very carefully, delicately*]   Where were you all day? You look terrible.

WILLY   I got as far as a little above Yonkers. I stopped for a cup of coffee. Maybe it was the coffee.

LINDA   What?

WILLY [*after a pause*]   I suddenly couldn't drive any more. The car kept going off onto the shoulder, y'know?

LINDA [*helpfully*]   Oh. Maybe it was the steering again. I don't think Angelo knows the Studebaker.

WILLY   No, it's me, it's me. Suddenly I realize I'm goin' sixty miles an hour and I don't remember the last five minutes. I'm—I can't seem to—keep my mind to it.

LINDA   Maybe it's your glasses. You never went for your new glasses.

WILLY   No, I see everything. I came back ten miles an hour. It took me nearly four hours from Yonkers.

LINDA [*resigned*]   Well, you'll just have to take a rest, Willy, you can't continue this way.

WILLY   I just got back from Florida.

LINDA   But you didn't rest your mind. Your mind is overactive, and the mind is what counts, dear.

WILLY   I'll start out in the morning. Maybe I'll feel better in the morning. [*She is taking off his shoes.*] These goddam arch supports are killing me.

LINDA   Take an aspirin. Should I get you an aspirin? It'll soothe you.

WILLY [*with wonder*]   I was driving along, you understand? And I was fine. I was even observing the scenery. You can imagine, me looking at scenery, on the road every week of my life. But it's so beautiful up there, Linda, the trees are so thick, and the sun is warm. I opened the windshield and just let the warm air bathe over me. And then all of a sudden I'm goin' off the road! I'm tellin' ya, I absolutely forgot I was driving. If I'd've gone the other way over the white line I might've killed somebody. So I went on again—and five minutes later I'm dreamin' again, and I nearly— [*He presses two fingers against his eyes.*] I have such thoughts, I have such strange thoughts.

LINDA   Willy, dear. Talk to them again. There's no reason why you can't work in New York.

WILLY   They don't need me in New York. I'm the New England man. I'm vital in New England.

LINDA   But you're sixty years old. They can't expect you to keep traveling every week.

WILLY   I'll have to send a wire to Portland. I'm supposed to see Brown and Morrison tomorrow morning at ten o'clock to show the line. Goddammit, I could sell them! [*He starts putting on his jacket.*]

LINDA [*taking the jacket from him*]   Why don't you go down to the place tomorrow and tell Howard you've simply got to work in New York? You're too accommodating, dear.

WILLY   If old man Wagner was alive I'd a been in charge of New York now! That man was a prince, he was a masterful man. But that boy of his, that Howard, he don't appreciate. When I went north the first time, the Wagner Company didn't know where New England was!

LINDA   Why don't you tell those things to Howard, dear?

WILLY [*encouraged*]   I will, I definitely will. Is there any cheese?

LINDA   I'll make you a sandwich.

WILLY   No, go to sleep. I'll take some milk. I'll be up right away. The boys in?

LINDA   They're sleeping. Happy took Biff on a date tonight.

WILLY [*interested*]   That so?

LINDA   It was so nice to see them shaving together, one behind the other, in the bathroom. And going out together. You notice? The whole house smells of shaving lotion.

WILLY   Figure it out. Work a lifetime to pay off a house. You finally own it, and there's nobody to live in it.

LINDA   Well, dear, life is a casting off. It's always that way.

WILLY   No, no, some people—some people accomplish something. Did Biff say anything after I went this morning?

LINDA   You shouldn't have criticized him, Willy, especially after he just got off the train. You mustn't lose your temper with him.

WILLY   When the hell did I lose my temper? I simply asked him if he was making any money. Is that a criticism?

LINDA   But, dear, how could he make any money?

WILLY [*worried and angered*]   There's such an undercurrent in him. He became a moody man. Did he apologize when I left this morning?

LINDA   He was crestfallen, Willy. You know how he admires you. I think if he finds himself, then you'll both be happier and not fight any more.

WILLY   How can he find himself on a farm? Is that a life? A farmhand? In the beginning, when he was young, I thought, well, a young man, it's good for him to tramp around, take a lot of different jobs. But it's more than ten years now and he has yet to make thirty-five dollars a week?

LINDA   He's finding himself, Willy.

WILLY   Not finding yourself at the age of thirty-four is a disgrace!

LINDA   Shh!

WILLY   The trouble is he's lazy, goddammit!

LINDA   Willy, please!

WILLY   Biff is a lazy bum!

LINDA   They're sleeping. Get something to eat. Go on down.

WILLY   Why did he come home? I would like to know what brought him home.

LINDA   I don't know. I think he's still lost, Willy. I think he's very lost.

WILLY   Biff Loman is lost. In the greatest country in the world a young man with such—personal attractiveness, gets lost. And such a hard worker. There's one thing about Biff—he's not lazy.

LINDA   Never.

WILLY [*with pity and resolve*]   I'll see him in the morning; I'll have a nice talk with him. I'll get him a job selling. He could be big in no time. My God! Remember how they used to follow him around in high school? When he smiled at one of them their faces lit up. When he walked down the street . . . [*He loses himself in reminiscences.*]

LINDA [*trying to bring him out of it*]   Willy, dear, I got a new kind of American-type cheese today. It's whipped.

WILLY   Why do you get American when I like Swiss?

LINDA   I just thought you'd like a change—

WILLY   I don't want a change! I want Swiss cheese. Why am I always being contradicted?

LINDA [*with a covering laugh*]   I thought it would be a surprise.

WILLY   Why don't you open a window in here, for God's sake?

LINDA [*with infinite patience*]   They're all open, dear.

WILLY   The way they boxed us in here. Bricks and windows, windows and bricks.

LINDA   We should've bought the land next door.

WILLY   The street is lined with cars. There's not a breath of fresh air in the neighborhood. The grass don't grow any more, you can't raise a carrot in the back yard. They should've had a law against apartment houses. Remember those two beautiful elm trees out there? When I and Biff hung the swing between them?

LINDA   Yeah, like being a million miles from the city.

WILLY   They should've arrested the builder for cutting those down. They massacred the neighborhood. [*lost*] More and more I think of those days, Linda. This time of year it was lilac and wisteria. And then the peonies would come out, and the daffodils. What fragrance in this room!

LINDA   Well, after all, people had to move somewhere.

WILLY   No, there's more people now.

LINDA   I don't think there's more people. I think—

WILLY   There's more people! That's what's ruining this country! Population is getting out of control. The competition is maddening! Smell the stink from that apartment house! And another one on the other side . . . How can they whip cheese?

        [*On* WILLY's *last line,* BIFF *and* HAPPY *raise themselves up in their beds, listening.*]

LINDA   Go down, try it. And be quiet.

WILLY   [*turning to* LINDA, *guiltily*]   You're not worried about me, are you, sweetheart?

BIFF   What's the matter?

HAPPY   Listen!

LINDA   You've got too much on the ball to worry about.

WILLY   You're my foundation and my support, Linda.

LINDA   Just try to relax, dear. You make mountains out of molehills.

WILLY   I won't fight with him any more. If he wants to go back to Texas, let him go.

LINDA   He'll find his way.

WILLY   Sure. Certain men just don't get started till later in life. Like Thomas Edison, I think. Or B. F. Goodrich. One of them was deaf. [*He starts for the bedroom doorway.*] I'll put my money on Biff.

LINDA   And Willy—if it's warm Sunday we'll drive in the country. And we'll open the windshield, and take lunch.

WILLY   No, the windshields don't open on the new cars.

LINDA   But you opened it today.

WILLY   Me? I didn't. [*He stops.*] Now isn't that peculiar! Isn't that a remarkable—[*He breaks off in amazement and fright as the flute is heard distantly.*]

LINDA   What, darling?

WILLY   That is the most remarkable thing.

LINDA   What, dear?

WILLY   I was thinking of the Chevvy. [*slight pause*] Nineteen twenty-eight . . . when I had that red Chevvy—[*breaks off*] That funny? I coulda sworn I was driving that Chevvy today.

LINDA   Well, that's nothing. Something must've reminded you.

WILLY Remarkable. Ts. Remember those days? The way Biff used to simo-
nize that car? The dealer refused to believe there was eighty thousand
miles on it. [*He shakes his head.*] Heh! [*to* LINDA] Close your eyes, I'll be
right up. [*He walks out of the bedroom.*]

HAPPY [*to* BIFF] Jesus, maybe he smashed up the car again!

LINDA [*calling after* WILLY] Be careful on the stairs, dear! The cheese is
on the middle shelf! [*She turns, goes over to the bed, takes his jacket, and
goes out of the bedroom.*]

> [*Light has risen on the boys' room. Unseen,* WILLY *is heard talking to
> himself, "Eighty thousand miles," and a little laugh.* BIFF *gets out of bed,
> comes downstage a bit, and stands attentively.* BIFF *is two years older
> than his brother* HAPPY, *well built, but in these days bears a worn air and
> seems less self-assured. He has succeeded less, and his dreams are stron-
> ger and less acceptable than* HAPPY'S. HAPPY *is tall, powerfully made.
> Sexuality is like a visible color on him, or a scent that many women have
> discovered. He, like his brother, is lost, but in a different way, for he has
> never allowed himself to turn his face toward defeat and is thus more
> confused and hard-skinned, although seemingly more content.*]

HAPPY [*getting out of bed*] He's going to get his license taken away if he
keeps that up. I'm getting nervous about him, y'know, Biff?

BIFF His eyes are going.

HAPPY No, I've driven with him. He sees all right. He just doesn't keep
his mind on it. I drove into the city with him last week. He stops at a
green light and then it turns red and he goes. [*He laughs.*]

BIFF Maybe he's color-blind.

HAPPY Pop? Why he's got the finest eye for color in the business. You know
that.

BIFF [*sitting down on his bed*] I'm going to sleep.

HAPPY You're not still sour on Dad, are you Biff?

BIFF He's all right, I guess.

WILLY [*underneath them, in the living-room*] Yes, sir, eighty thousand
miles—eighty-two thousand!

BIFF You smoking?

HAPPY [*holding out a pack of cigarettes*] Want one?

BIFF [*taking a cigarette*] I can never sleep when I smell it.

WILLY What a simonizing job, heh!

HAPPY [*with deep sentiment*] Funny, Biff, y'know? Us sleeping in here
again? The old beds. [*He pats his bed affectionately.*] All the talk that
went across those two beds, huh? Our whole lives.

BIFF Yeah. Lotta dreams and plans.

HAPPY [*with a deep and masculine laugh*] About five hundred women
would like to know what was said in this room.

> [*They share a soft laugh.*]

BIFF Remember that big Betsy something—what the hell was her name—
over on Bushwick Avenue?

HAPPY [*combing his hair*] With the collie dog!

BIFF That's the one. I got you in there, remember?

HAPPY Yeah, that was my first time—I think. Boy, there was a pig! [*They
laugh, almost crudely.*] You taught me everything I know about women.
Don't forget that.

BIFF   I bet you forgot how bashful you used to be. Especially with girls.

HAPPY   Oh, I still am, Biff.

BIFF   Oh, go on.

HAPPY   I just control it, that's all. I think I got less bashful and you got more so. What happened, Biff? Where's the old humor, the old confidence? [*He shakes* BIFF's *knee.* BIFF *gets up and moves restlessly about the room.*] What's the matter?

BIFF   Why does Dad mock me all the time?

HAPPY   He's not mocking you, he—

BIFF   Everything I say there's a twist of mockery on his face. I can't get near him.

HAPPY   He just wants you to make good, that's all. I wanted to talk to you about Dad for a long time, Biff. Something's—happening to him. He—talks to himself.

BIFF   I noticed that this morning. But he always mumbled.

HAPPY   But not so noticeable. It got so embarrassing I sent him to Florida. And you know something? Most of the time he's talking to you.

BIFF   What's he say about me?

HAPPY   I can't make it out.

BIFF   What's he say about me?

HAPPY   I think the fact that you're not settled, that you're still kind of up in the air . . .

BIFF   There's one or two other things depressing him, Happy.

HAPPY   What do you mean?

BIFF   Never mind. Just don't lay it all to me.

HAPPY   But I think if you just got started—I mean—is there any future for you out there?

BIFF   I tell ya, Hap, I don't know what the future is. I don't know—what I'm supposed to want.

HAPPY   What do you mean?

BIFF   Well, I spent six or seven years after high school trying to work myself up. Shipping clerk, salesman, business of one kind or another. And it's a measly manner of existence. To get on that subway on the hot mornings in summer. To devote your whole life to keeping stock, or making phone calls, or selling or buying. To suffer fifty weeks of the year for the sake of a two-week vacation, when all you really desire is to be outdoors, with your shirt off. And always to have to get ahead of the next fella. And still—that's how you build a future.

HAPPY   Well, you really enjoy it on a farm? Are you content out there?

BIFF [*with rising agitation*]   Hap, I've had twenty or thirty different kinds of jobs since I left home before the war, and it always turns out the same. I just realized it lately. In Nebraska when I herded cattle, and the Dakotas, and Arizona, and now in Texas. It's why I came home now, I guess, because I realized it. This farm I work on, it's spring there now, see? And they've got about fifteen new colts. There's nothing more inspiring or—beautiful than the sight of a mare and a new colt. And it's cool there now, see? Texas is cool now, and it's spring. And whenever spring comes to where I am, I suddenly get the feeling, my God, I'm not gettin' anywhere! What the hell am I doing, playing around with horses, twenty-eight dollars a week! I'm thirty-four years old. I oughta be makin' my future. That's when I come running home. And now, I get here, and I don't know what to do with myself. [*after a pause*] I've always made a point of not wasting my life, and everytime I come back here I know that all I've done is to waste my life.

HAPPY   You're a poet, you know that, Biff? You're a—you're an idealist!

BIFF   No, I'm mixed up very bad. Maybe I oughta get married. Maybe I oughta get stuck into something. Maybe that's my trouble. I'm like a boy. I'm not married. I'm not in business, I just—I'm like a boy. Are you content, Hap? You're a success, aren't you? Are you content?

HAPPY   Hell, no!

BIFF   Why? You're making money, aren't you?

HAPPY   [*moving about with energy, expressiveness*]   All I can do now is wait for the merchandise manager to die. And suppose I get to be merchandise manager? He's a good friend of mine, and he just built a terrific estate on Long Island. And he lived there about two months and sold it, and now he's building another one. He can't enjoy it once it's finished. And I know that's just what I would do. I don't know what the hell I'm workin' for. Sometimes I sit in my apartment—all alone. And I think of the rent I'm paying. And it's crazy. But then, it's what I always wanted. My own apartment, a car, and plenty of women. And still, goddammit, I'm lonely.

BIFF   [*with enthusiasm*]   Listen why don't you come out West with me?

HAPPY   You and I, heh?

BIFF   Sure, maybe we could buy a ranch. Raise cattle, use our muscles. Men built like we are should be working out in the open.

HAPPY   [*avidly*]   The Loman Brothers, heh?

BIFF   [*with vast affection*]   Sure, we'd be known all over the counties!

HAPPY   [*enthralled*]   That's what I dream about, Biff. Sometimes I want to just rip my clothes off in the middle of the store and outbox that goddam merchandise manager. I mean I can outbox, outrun, and outlift anybody in that store, and I have to take orders from those common, petty sons-of-bitches till I can't stand it any more.

BIFF   I'm tellin' you, kid, if you were with me I'd be happy out there.

HAPPY   [*enthused*]   See, Biff, everybody around me is so false that I'm constantly lowering my ideals . . .

BIFF   Baby, together we'd stand up for one another, we'd have someone to trust.

HAPPY   If I were around you—

BIFF   Hap, the trouble is we weren't brought up to grub for money. I don't know how to do it.

HAPPY   Neither can I!

BIFF   Then let's go!

HAPPY   The only thing is—what can you make out there?

BIFF   But look at your friend. Builds an estate and then hasn't the peace of mind to live in it.

HAPPY   Yeah, but when he walks into the store the waves part in front of him. That's fifty-two thousand dollars a year coming through the revolving door, and I got more in my pinky finger than he's got in his head.

BIFF   Yeah, but you just said—

HAPPY   I gotta show some of those pompous, self-important executives over there that Hap Loman can make the grade. I want to walk into the store the way he walks in. Then I'll go with you, Biff. We'll be together yet, I swear. But take those two we had tonight. Now weren't they gorgeous creatures?

BIFF Yeah, yeah, most gorgeous I've had in years.

HAPPY I get that any time I want, Biff. Whenever I feel disgusted. The only trouble is, it gets like bowling or something. I just keep knockin' them over and it doesn't mean anything. You still run around a lot?

BIFF Naa. I'd like to find a girl—steady, somebody with substance.

HAPPY That's what I long for.

BIFF Go on! You'd never come home.

HAPPY I would! Somebody with character, with resistance! Like Mom, y'know? You're gonna call me a bastard when I tell you this. That girl Charlotte I was with tonight is engaged to be married in five weeks. [*He tries on his new hat.*]

BIFF No kiddin'!

HAPPY Sure, the guy's in line for the vice-presidency of the store. I don't know what gets into me, maybe I just have an overdeveloped sense of competition or something, but I went and ruined her, and furthermore I can't get rid of her. And he's the third executive I've done that to. Isn't that a crummy characteristic? And to top it all, I go to their weddings! [*indignantly, but laughing*] Like I'm not supposed to take bribes. Manufacturers offer me a hundred-dollar bill now and then to throw an order their way. You know how honest I am, but it's like this girl, see. I hate myself for it. Because I don't want the girl, and, still, I take it and—I love it!

BIFF Let's go to sleep.

HAPPY I guess we didn't settle anything, heh?

BIFF I just got one idea that I think I'm going to try.

HAPPY What's that?

BIFF Remember Bill Oliver?

HAPPY Sure, Oliver is very big now. You want to work for him again?

BIFF No, but when I quit he said something to me. He put his arm on my shoulder, and he said, "Biff, if you ever need anything, come to me."

HAPPY I remember that. That sounds good.

BIFF I think I'll go to see him. If I could get ten thousand or even seven or eight thousand dollars I could buy a beautiful ranch.

HAPPY I bet he'd back you. 'Cause he thought highly of you, Biff. I mean, they all do. You're well liked, Biff. That's why I say to come back here, and we both have the apartment. And I'm tellin' you, Biff, any babe you want . . .

BIFF No, with a ranch I could do the work I like and still be something. I just wonder though. I wonder if Oliver still thinks I stole that carton of basketballs.

HAPPY Oh, he probably forgot that long ago. It's almost ten years. You're too sensitive. Anyway, he didn't really fire you.

BIFF Well, I think he was going to. I think that's why I quit. I was never sure whether he knew or not. I know he thought the world of me, though. I was the only one he'd let lock up the place.

WILLY [*below*] You gonna wash the engine, Biff?

HAPPY Shh!

[BIFF *looks at* HAPPY, *who is gazing down, listening.* WILLY *is mumbling in the parlor.*]

HAPPY   You hear that?

[*They listen.* WILLY *laughs warmly.*]

BIFF [*growing angry*]   Doesn't he know Mom can hear that?

WILLY   Don't get your sweater dirty, Biff!

[*A look of pain crosses* BIFF's *face.*]

HAPPY   Isn't that terrible? Don't leave again, will you? You'll find a job here. You gotta stick around. I don't know what to do about him, it's getting embarrassing.

WILLY   What a simonizing job!

BIFF   Mom's hearing that!

WILLY   No kiddin', Biff, you got a date? Wonderful!

HAPPY   Go on to sleep. But talk to him in the morning, will you?

BIFF [*reluctantly getting into bed*]   With her in the house. Brother!

HAPPY [*getting into bed*]   I wish you'd have a good talk with him.

[*The light on their room begins to fade.*]

BIFF [*to himself in bed*]   That selfish, stupid . . .

HAPPY   Sh . . . Sleep, Biff.

[*Their light is out. Well before they have finished speaking,* WILLY's *form is dimly seen below in the darkened kitchen. He opens the refrigerator, searches in there, and takes out a bottle of milk. The apartment houses are fading out, and the entire house and surroundings become covered with leaves. Music insinuates itself as the leaves appear.*]

WILLY   Just wanna be careful with those girls, Biff, that's all. Don't make any promises. No promises of any kind. Because a girl, y'know, they always believe what you tell 'em, and you're very young, Biff, you're too young to be talking seriously to girls.

[*Light rises on the kitchen.* WILLY, *talking, shuts the refrigerator door and comes downstage to the kitchen table. He pours milk into a glass. He is totally immersed in himself, smiling faintly.*]

WILLY   Too young entirely, Biff. You want to watch your schooling first. Then when you're all set, there'll be plenty of girls for a boy like you. [*He smiles broadly at a kitchen chair.*] That so? The girls pay for you? [*He laughs.*] Boy, you must really be makin' a hit.

[WILLY *is gradually addressing—physically—a point offstage, speaking through the wall of the kitchen, and his voice has been rising in volume to that of a normal conversation.*]

WILLY   I been wondering why you polish the car so careful. Ha! Don't leave the hubcaps, boys. Get the chamois to the hubcaps. Happy, use newspaper on the windows, it's the easiest thing. Show him how to do it, Biff! You see, Happy? Pad it up, use it like a pad. That's it, that's it, good work. You're doin' all right, Hap. [*He pauses, then nods in approbation for a few seconds, then looks upward.*] Biff, first thing we gotta do when we get time is clip that big branch over the house. Afraid it's gonna fall in a storm and hit the roof. Tell you what. We get a rope and sling her around, and then we climb up there with a couple of saws and take her down. Soon as you finish the car, boys, I wanna see ya. I got a surprise for you, boys.

BIFF [*offstage*]   Whatta ya got, Dad?

WILLY   No, you finish first. Never leave a job till you're finished—remember that, [*looking toward the "big trees"*] Biff, up in Albany I saw a beautiful hammock. I think I'll buy it next trip, and we'll hang it right between those two elms. Wouldn't that be something? Just swingin' there under those branches. Boy, that would be . . .

[YOUNG BIFF and YOUNG HAPPY *appear from the direction* WILLY *was addressing.* HAPPY *carries rags and a pail of water.* BIFF, *wearing a sweater with a block "S," carries a football.*]

BIFF [*pointing in the direction of the car offstage*] How's that, Pop, professional?

WILLY Terrific. Terrific job, boys. Good work, Biff.

HAPPY Where's the surprise, Pop?

WILLY In the back seat of the car.

HAPPY Boy! [*He runs off.*]

BIFF What is it, Dad? Tell me, what'd you buy?

WILLY [*laughing, cuffs him*] Never mind, something I want you to have.

BIFF [*turns and starts off*] What is it, Hap?

HAPPY [*offstage*] It's a punching bag!

BIFF Oh, Pop!

WILLY It's got Gene Tunney's[1] signature on it!

[HAPPY *runs onstage with a punching bag.*]

BIFF Gee, how'd you know we wanted a punching bag?

WILLY Well, it's the finest thing for the timing.

HAPPY [*lies down on his back and pedals with his feet*] I'm losing weight, you notice, Pop?

WILLY [*to* HAPPY] Jumping rope is good too.

BIFF Did you see the new football I got?

WILLY [*examining the ball*] Where'd you get a new ball?

BIFF The coach told me to practice my passing.

WILLY That so? And he gave you the ball, heh?

BIFF Well, I borrowed it from the locker room. [*He laughs confidentially.*]

WILLY [*laughing with him at the left*] I want you to return that.

HAPPY I told you he wouldn't like it!

BIFF [*angrily*] Well, I'm bringing it back!

WILLY [*stopping the incipient argument, to* HAPPY] Sure, he's gotta practice with a regulation ball, doesn't he? [*to* BIFF] Coach'll probably congratulate you on your initiative!

BIFF Oh, he keeps congratulating my initiative all the time, Pop.

WILLY That's because he likes you. If somebody else took that ball there'd be an uproar. So what's the report, boys, what's the report?

BIFF Where'd you go this time, Dad? Gee we were lonesome for you.

WILLY [*pleased, puts an arm around each boy and they come down to the apron*] Lonesome, heh?

BIFF Missed you every minute.

WILLY Don't say? Tell you a secret, boys. Don't breathe it to a soul. Someday I'll have my own business, and I'll never have to leave home any more.

HAPPY Like Uncle Charley, heh?

WILLY Bigger than Uncle Charley! Because Charley is not—liked. He's liked, but he's not—well liked.

BIFF Where'd you go this time, Dad?

---

1. World heavyweight boxing champion from 1926 to 1928.

WILLY Well, I got on the road, and I went north to Providence. Met the Mayor.

BIFF The Mayor of Providence!

WILLY He was sitting in the hotel lobby.

BIFF What'd he say?

WILLY He said, "Morning!" And I said, "You got a fine city here, Mayor." And then he had coffee with me. And then I went to Waterbury. Waterbury is a fine city. Big clock city, the famous Waterbury clock. Sold a nice bill there. And then Boston—Boston is the cradle of the Revolution. A fine city. And a couple of other towns in Mass., and on to Portland and Bangor and straight home!

BIFF Gee, I'd love to go with you sometime, Dad.

WILLY Soon as summer comes.

HAPPY Promise?

WILLY You and Hap and I, and I'll show you all the towns. America is full of beautiful towns and fine, upstanding people. And they know me, boys, they know me up and down New England. The finest people. And when I bring you fellas up, there'll be open sesame for all of us, 'cause one thing, boys: I have friends. I can park my car in any street in New England, and the cops protect it like their own. This summer, heh?

BIFF and HAPPY [together] Yeah! You bet!

WILLY We'll take our bathing suits.

HAPPY We'll carry your bags, Pop!

WILLY Oh, won't that be something! Me comin' into the Boston stores with you boys carryin' my bags. What a sensation!

[BIFF is prancing around, practicing passing the ball.]

WILLY You nervous, Biff, about the game?

BIFF Not if you're gonna be there.

WILLY What do they say about you in school, now that they made you captain?

HAPPY There's a crowd of girls behind him everytime the classes change.

BIFF [taking WILLY's hand] This Saturday, Pop, this Saturday—just for you, I'm going to break through for a touchdown.

HAPPY You're supposed to pass.

BIFF I'm takin' one play for Pop. You watch me, Pop, and when I take off my helmet, that means I'm breakin' out. Then you watch me crash through that line!

WILLY [kisses BIFF] Oh, wait'll I tell this in Boston!

[BERNARD enters in knickers. He is younger than BIFF, earnest and loyal, a worried boy.]

BERNARD Biff, where are you? You're supposed to study with me today.

WILLY Hey, looka Bernard. What're you lookin' so anemic about, Bernard?

BERNARD He's gotta study, Uncle Willy. He's got Regents[2] next week.

HAPPY [tauntingly, spinning BERNARD around] Let's box, Bernard!

BERNARD Biff! [He gets away from HAPPY.] Listen, Biff, I heard Mr. Birnbaum say that if you don't start studyin' math he's gonna flunk you, and you won't graduate. I heard him!

WILLY You better study with him, Biff. Go ahead now.

2. Compulsory statewide high school examinations in New York.

BERNARD   I heard him!

BIFF   Oh, Pop, you didn't see my sneakers! [*He holds up a foot for* WILLY *to look at.*]

WILLY   Hey, that's a beautiful job of printing!

BERNARD [*wiping his glasses*]   Just because he printed University of Virginia on his sneakers doesn't mean they've got to graduate him, Uncle Willy!

WILLY [*angrily*]   What're you talking about? With scholarships to three universities they're gonna flunk him?

BERNARD   But I heard Mr. Birnbaum say—

WILLY   Don't be a pest, Bernard! [*to his boys*] What an anemic!

BERNARD   Okay, I'm waiting for you in my house, Biff.
     [BERNARD *goes off. The Lomans laugh.*]

WILLY   Bernard is not well liked, is he?

BIFF   He's liked, but he's not well liked.

HAPPY   That's right, Pop.

WILLY   That's just what I mean. Bernard can get the best marks in school, y'understand, but when he gets out in the business world, y'understand, you are going to be five times ahead of him. That's why I thank Almighty God you're both built like Adonises.[3] Because the man who makes an appearance in the business world, the man who creates personal interest, is the man who gets ahead. Be liked and you will never want. You take me, for instance. I never have to wait in line to see a buyer. "Willy Loman is here!" That's all they have to know, and I go right through.

BIFF   Did you knock them dead, Pop?

WILLY   Knocked 'em cold in Providence, slaughtered 'em in Boston.

HAPPY [*on his back, pedaling again*]   I'm losing weight, you notice, Pop?
     [LINDA *enters, as of old, a ribbon in her hair, carrying a basket of washing.*]

LINDA [*with youthful energy*]   Hello, dear!

WILLY   Sweetheart!

LINDA   How'd the Chevvy run?

WILLY   Chevrolet, Linda, is the greatest car ever built. [*to the boys*] Since when do you let your mother carry wash up the stairs?

BIFF   Grab hold there, boy!

HAPPY   Where to, Mom?

LINDA   Hang them up on the line. And you better go down to your friends, Biff. The cellar is full of boys. They don't know what to do with themselves.

BIFF   Ah, when Pop comes home they can wait!

WILLY [*laughs appreciatively*]   You better go down and tell them what to do, Biff.

BIFF   I think I'll have them sweep out the furnace room.

WILLY   Good work, Biff.

BIFF [*goes through wall-line of kitchen to doorway at back and calls down*]   Fellas! Everybody sweep out the furnace room! I'll be right down!

VOICES   All right! Okay, Biff.

BIFF   George and Sam and Frank, come out back! We're hangin' up the wash! Come on, Hap, on the double!
     [*He and* HAPPY *carry out the basket.*]

---

3. In Greek mythology Adonis was a beautiful youth favored by Aphrodite, the goddess of love.

LINDA   The way they obey him!

WILLY   Well, that training, the training. I'm tellin' you, I was sellin' thousands and thousands, but I had to come home.

LINDA   Oh, the whole block'll be at that game. Did you sell anything?

WILLY   I did five hundred gross in Providence and seven hundred gross in Boston.

LINDA   No! Wait a minute, I've got a pencil. [*She pulls pencil and paper out of her apron pocket.*] That makes your commission . . . Two hundred—my God! Two hundred and twelve dollars!

WILLY   Well, I didn't figure it yet, but . . .

LINDA   How much did you do?

WILLY   Well, I—I did—about a hundred and eighty gross in Providence. Well, no—it came to—roughly two hundred gross on the whole trip.

LINDA   [*without hesitation*]   Two hundred gross. That's . . . [*She figures.*]

WILLY   The trouble was that three of the stores were half closed for inventory in Boston. Otherwise I woulda broke records.

LINDA   Well, it makes seventy dollars and some pennies. That's very good.

WILLY   What do we owe?

LINDA   Well, on the first there's sixteen dollars on the refrigerator—

WILLY   Why sixteen?

LINDA   Well, the fan belt broke, so it was a dollar eighty.

WILLY   But it's brand new.

LINDA   Well, the man said that's the way it is. Till they work themselves in, y'know.

[*They move through the wall-line into the kitchen.*]

WILLY   I hope we didn't get stuck on that machine.

LINDA   They got the biggest ads of any of them!

WILLY   I know, it's a fine machine. What else?

LINDA   Well, there's nine-sixty for the washing machine. And for the vacuum cleaner there's three and a half due on the fifteenth. Then the roof, you got twenty-one dollars remaining.

WILLY   It don't leak, does it?

LINDA   No, they did a wonderful job. Then you owe Frank for the carburetor.

WILLY   I'm not going to pay that man! That goddam Chevrolet, they ought to prohibit the manufacture of that car!

LINDA   Well, you owe him three and a half. And odds and ends, comes to around a hundred and twenty dollars by the fifteenth.

WILLY   A hundred and twenty dollars! My God, if business don't pick up I don't know what I'm gonna do!

LINDA   Well, next week you'll do better.

WILLY   Oh, I'll knock 'em dead next week. I'll go to Hartford. I'm very well liked in Hartford. You know, the trouble is, Linda, people don't seem to take to me.

[*They move onto the forestage.*]

LINDA   Oh, don't be foolish.

WILLY   I know it when I walk in. They seem to laugh at me.

LINDA   Why? Why would they laugh at you? Don't talk that way, Willy.

[WILLY *moves to the edge of the stage.* LINDA *goes into the kitchen and starts to darn stockings.*]

WILLY   I don't know the reason for it, but they just pass me by. I'm not noticed.

LINDA   But you're doing wonderful, dear. You're making seventy to a hundred dollars a week.

WILLY   But I gotta be at it ten, twelve hours a day. Other men—I don't know—they do it easier. I don't know why—I can't stop myself—I talk too much. A man oughta come in with a few words. One thing about Charley. He's a man of few words, and they respect him.

LINDA   You don't talk too much, you're just lively.

WILLY [*smiling*]   Well, I figure, what the hell, life is short, a couple of jokes. [*to himself*] I joke too much! [*The smiles goes.*]

LINDA   Why? You're—

WILLY   I'm fat. I'm very—foolish to look at, Linda. I didn't tell you, but Christmas time I happened to be calling on F. H. Stewarts, and a salesman I know, as I was going in to see the buyer I heard him say something about—walrus. And I—I cracked him right across the face. I won't take that. I simply will not take that. But they do laugh at me. I know that.

LINDA   Darling . . .

WILLY   I gotta overcome it. I know I gotta overcome it. I'm not dressing to advantage, maybe.

LINDA   Willy, darling, you're the handsomest man in the world—

WILLY   Oh, no, Linda.

LINDA   To me you are. [*slight pause*] The handsomest.
        [*From the darkness is heard the laughter of a woman.* WILLY *doesn't turn to it, but it continues through* LINDA's *lines.*]

LINDA   And the boys, Willy. Few men are idolized by their children the way you are.
        [*Music is heard as behind a scrim,*[4] *to the left of the house,* THE WOMAN, *dimly seen, is dressing.*]

WILLY [*with great feeling*]   You're the best there is, Linda, you're a pal, you know that? On the road—on the road I want to grab you sometimes and just kiss the life outa you.
        [*The laughter is loud now, and he moves into a brightening area at the left, where* THE WOMAN *has come from behind the scrim and is standing, putting on her hat, looking into a "mirror" and laughing.*]

WILLY   'Cause I get so lonely—especially when business is bad and there's nobody to talk to. I get the feeling that I'll never sell anything again, that I won't make a living for you, or a business, a business for the boys. [*He talks through* THE WOMAN's *subsiding laughter;* THE WOMAN *primps at the "mirror."*] There's so much I want to make for—

THE WOMAN   Me? You didn't make me, Willy. I picked you.

WILLY [*pleased*]   You picked me?

THE WOMAN [*who is quite proper-looking,* WILLY's *age*]   I did. I've been sitting at that desk watching all the salesmen go by, day in, day out. But you've got such a sense of humor, and we do have such a good time together, don't we?

WILLY   Sure, sure. [*He takes her in his arms.*] Why do you have to go now?

4. Part of a stage set; a painted gauze curtain that becomes transparent when lighted from the back.

THE WOMAN   It's two o'clock . . .

WILLY   No, come on in! [*He pulls her.*]

THE WOMAN   . . . my sisters'll be scandalized. When'll you be back?

WILLY   Oh, two weeks about. Will you come up again?

THE WOMAN   Sure thing. You do make me laugh. It's good for me. [*She squeezes his arm, kisses him.*] And I think you're a wonderful man.

WILLY   You picked me, heh?

THE WOMAN   Sure. Because you're so sweet. And such a kidder.

WILLY   Well, I'll see you next time I'm in Boston.

THE WOMAN   I'll put you right through to the buyers.

WILLY [*slapping her bottom*]   Right. Well, bottoms up!

THE WOMAN [*slaps him gently and laughs*]   You just kill me, Willy. [*He suddenly grabs her and kisses her roughly.*] You kill me. And thanks for the stockings. I love a lot of stockings. Well, good night.

WILLY   Good night. And keep your pores open!

THE WOMAN   Oh, Willy!

> [THE WOMAN *bursts out laughing, and* LINDA's *laughter blends in.* THE WOMAN *disappears into the dark. Now the area at the kitchen table brightens.* LINDA *is sitting where she was at the kitchen table, but now is mending a pair of her silk stockings.*]

LINDA   You are, Willy. The handsomest man. You've got no reason to feel that—

WILLY [*coming out of* THE WOMAN's *dimming area and going over to* LINDA] I'll make it all up to you, Linda. I'll—

LINDA   There's nothing to make up, dear. You're doing fine, better than—

WILLY [*noticing her mending*]   What's that?

LINDA   Just mending my stockings. They're so expensive—

WILLY [*angrily, taking them from her*]   I won't have you mending stockings in this house! Now throw them out!

> [LINDA *puts the stockings in her pocket.*]

BERNARD [*entering on the run*]   Where is he? If he doesn't study!

WILLY [*moving to the forestage, with great agitation*]   You'll give him the answers!

BERNARD   I do, but I can't on a Regents! That's a state exam! They're liable to arrest me!

WILLY   Where is he? I'll whip him, I'll whip him!

LINDA   And he'd better give back that football, Willy, it's not nice.

WILLY   Biff! Where is he? Why is he taking everything?

LINDA   He's too rough with the girls, Willy. All the mothers are afraid of him!

WILLY   I'll whip him!

BERNARD   He's driving the car without a license!

> [THE WOMAN's *laugh is heard.*]

WILLY   Shut up!

LINDA   All the mothers—

WILLY   Shut up!

BERNARD [*backing quietly away and out*]   Mr. Birnbaum says he's stuck up.

WILLY   Get outa here!

BERNARD   If he doesn't buckle down he'll flunk math! [*He goes off.*]

LINDA   He's right, Willy, you've gotta—

WILLY [*exploding at her*] There's nothing the matter with him! You want him to be a worm like Bernard? He's got spirit, personality . . .

[*As he speaks,* LINDA, *almost in tears, exist into the living-room.* WILLY *is alone in the kitchen, wilting and staring. The leaves are gone. It is night again, and the apartment houses look down from behind.*]

WILLY Loaded with it. Loaded! What is he stealing? He's giving it back, isn't he? Why is he stealing? What did I tell him? I never in my life told him anything but decent things.

[HAPPY *in pajamas has come down the stairs;* WILLY *suddenly becomes aware of* HAPPY's *presence.*]

HAPPY Let's go now, come on.

WILLY [*sitting down at the kitchen table*] Huh! Why did she have to wax the floors herself? Everytime she waxes the floors she keels over. She knows that!

HAPPY Shh! Take it easy. What brought you back tonight?

WILLY I got an awful scare. Nearly hit a kid in Yonkers. God! Why didn't I go to Alaska with my brother Ben that time! Ben! That man was a genius, that man was success incarnate! What a mistake! He begged me to go.

HAPPY Well, there's no use in—

WILLY You guys! There was a man started with the clothes on his back and ended up with diamond mines!

HAPPY Boy, someday I'd like to know how he did it.

WILLY What's the mystery? The man knew what he wanted and went out and got it! Walked into a jungle, and comes out, the age of twenty-one, and he's rich! The world is an oyster, but you don't crack it open on a mattress!

HAPPY Pop, I told you I'm gonna retire you for life.

WILLY You'll retire me for life on seventy goddam dollars a week? And your women and your car and your apartment, and you'll retire me for life! Christ's sake, I couldn't get past Yonkers today! Where are you guys, where are you? The woods are burning! I can't drive a car!

[CHARLEY *has appeared in the doorway. He is a large man, slow of speech, laconic, immovable. In all he says, despite what he says, there is pity, and, now, trepidation. He has a robe over pajamas, slippers on his feet. He enters the kitchen.*]

CHARLEY Everything all right?

HAPPY Yeah, Charley, everything's . . .

WILLY What's the matter?

CHARLEY I heard some noise. I thought something happened. Can't we do something about the walls? You sneeze in here, and in my house hats blow off.

HAPPY Let's go to bed, Dad. Come on.

[CHARLEY *signals to* HAPPY *to go.*]

WILLY You go ahead, I'm not tired at the moment.

HAPPY [*to* WILLY] Take it easy, huh? [*He exits.*]

WILLY What're you doin' up?

CHARLEY [*sitting down at the kitchen table opposite* WILLY] Couldn't sleep good. I had a heartburn.

WILLY Well, you don't know how to eat.

CHARLEY I eat with my mouth.

WILLY   No, you're ignorant. You gotta know about vitamins and things like that.

CHARLEY   Come on, let's shoot. Tire you out a little.

WILLY [*hesitantly*]   All right. You got cards?

CHARLEY [*taking a deck from his pocket*]   Yeah, I got them. Someplace. What is it with those vitamins?

WILLY [*dealing*]   They build up your bones. Chemistry.

CHARLEY   Yeah, but there's no bones in a heartburn.

WILLY   What are you talkin' about? Do you know the first thing about it?

CHARLEY   Don't get insulted.

WILLY   Don't talk about something you don't know anything about.
   [*They are playing. Pause.*]

CHARLEY   What're you doin' home?

WILLY   A little trouble with the car.

CHARLEY   Oh. [*pause*] I'd like to take a trip to California.

WILLY   Don't say.

CHARLEY   You want a job?

WILLY   I got a job, I told you that. [*after a slight pause*] What the hell are you offering me a job for?

CHARLEY   Don't get insulted.

WILLY   Don't insult me.

CHARLEY   I don't see no sense in it. You don't have to go on this way.

WILLY   I got a good job. [*slight pause*] What do you keep comin' in here for?

CHARLEY   You want me to go?

WILLY [*after a pause, withering*]   I can't understand it. He's going back to Texas again. What the hell is that?

CHARLEY   Let him go.

WILLY   I got nothin' to give him, Charley, I'm clean, I'm clean.

CHARLEY   He won't starve. None a them starve. Forget about him.

WILLY   Then what have I got to remember?

CHARLEY   You take it too hard. To hell with it. When a deposit bottle is broken you don't get your nickel back.

WILLY   That's easy enough for you to say.

CHARLEY   That ain't easy for me to say.

WILLY   Did you see the ceiling I put up in the living-room?

CHARLEY   Yeah, that's a piece of work. To put up a ceiling is a mystery to me. How do you do it?

WILLY   What's the difference?

CHARLEY   Well, talk about it.

WILLY   You gonna put up a ceiling?

CHARLEY   How could I put up a ceiling?

WILLY   Then what the hell are you bothering me for?

CHARLEY   You're insulted again.

WILLY   A man who can't handle tools is not a man. You're disgusting.

CHARLEY   Don't call me disgusting, Willy.
   [UNCLE BEN, *carrying a valise and an umbrella, enters the forestage from around the right corner of the house. He is a stolid man, in his sixties, with a mustache and an authoritative air. He is utterly certain of his destiny, and there is an aura of far places about him. He enters exactly as* WILLY *speaks.*]

WILLY I'm getting awfully tired, Ben.
  [BEN's *music is heard.* BEN *looks around at everything.*]
CHARLEY Good, keep playing; you'll sleep better. Did you call me Ben?
  [BEN *looks at his watch.*]
WILLY That's funny. For a second there you reminded me of my brother Ben.
BEN I only have a few minutes. [*He strolls, inspecting the place.* WILLY *and* CHARLEY *continue playing.*]
CHARLEY You never heard from him again, heh? Since that time?
WILLY Didn't Linda tell you? Couple of weeks ago we got a letter from his wife in Africa. He died.
CHARLEY That so.
BEN [*chuckling*] So this is Brooklyn, eh?
CHARLEY Maybe you're in for some of his money.
WILLY Naa, he had seven sons. There's just one opportunity I had with that man . . .
BEN I must make a train, William. There are several properties I'm looking at in Alaska.
WILLY Sure, sure! If I'd gone with him to Alaska that time, everything would've been totally different.
CHARLEY Go on, you'd froze to death up there.
WILLY What're you talking about?
BEN Opportunity is tremendous in Alaska, William. Surprised you're not up there.
WILLY Sure, tremendous.
CHARLEY Heh?
WILLY There was the only man I ever met who knew the answers.
CHARLEY Who?
BEN How are you all?
WILLY [*taking a pot, smiling*] Fine, fine.
CHARLEY Pretty sharp tonight.
BEN Is Mother living with you?
WILLY No, she died a long time ago.
CHARLEY Who?
BEN That's too bad. Fine specimen of a lady, Mother.
WILLY [*to* CHARLEY] Heh?
BEN I'd hoped to see the old girl.
CHARLEY Who died?
BEN Heard anything from Father, have you?
WILLY [*unnerved*] What do you mean, who died?
CHARLEY [*taking a pot*] What're you talkin' about?
BEN [*looking at his watch*] William, it's half-past eight!
WILLY [*as though to dispel his confusion he angrily stops* CHARLEY's *hand*] That's my build!
CHARLEY I put the ace—
WILLY If you don't know how to play the game I'm not gonna throw my money away on you!
CHARLEY [*rising*] It was my ace, for God's sake!
WILLY I'm through, I'm through!
BEN When did Mother die?

WILLY   Long ago. Since the beginning you never knew how to play cards.

CHARLEY [*picks up the cards and goes to the door*]   All right! Next time I'll bring a deck with five aces.

WILLY   I don't play that kind of game!

CHARLEY [*turning to him*]   You ought to be ashamed of yourself!

WILLY   Yeah?

CHARLEY   Yeah! [*He goes out.*]

WILLY [*slamming the door after him*]   Ignoramus!

BEN [*as* WILLY *comes toward him through the wall-line of the kitchen*]   So you're William.

WILLY [*shaking* BEN'*s hand*]   Ben! I've been waiting for you so long! What's the answer? How did you do it?

BEN   Oh, there's a story in that.

[LINDA *enters the forestage, as of old, carrying the wash basket.*]

LINDA   Is this Ben?

BEN [*gallantly*]   How do you do, my dear.

LINDA   Where've you been all these years? Willy's always wondered why you—

WILLY [*pulling* BEN *away from her impatiently*]   Where is Dad? Didn't you follow him? How did you get started?

BEN   Well, I don't know how much you remember.

WILLY   Well, I was just a baby, of course, only three or four years old—

BEN   Three years and eleven months.

WILLY   What a memory, Ben!

BEN   I have many enterprises, William, and I have never kept books.

WILLY   I remember I was sitting under the wagon in—was it Nebraska?

BEN   It was South Dakota, and I gave you a bunch of wild flowers.

WILLY   I remember you walking away down some open road.

BEN [*laughing*]   I was going to find Father in Alaska.

WILLY   Where is he?

BEN   At that age I had a very faulty view of geography, William. I discovered after a few days that I was heading due south, so instead of Alaska, I ended up in Africa.

LINDA   Africa!

WILLY   The Gold Coast!

BEN   Principally diamond mines.

LINDA   Diamond mines!

BEN   Yes, my dear. But I've only a few minutes—

WILLY   No! Boys! Boys! [YOUNG BIFF *and* HAPPY *appear.*] Listen to this. This is your Uncle Ben, a great man! Tell my boys, Ben!

BEN   Why, boys, when I was seventeen I walked into the jungle, and when I was twenty-one I walked out. [*He laughs.*] And by God I was rich.

WILLY [*to the boys*]   You see what I been talking about? The greatest things can happen!

BEN [*glancing at his watch*]   I have an appointment in Ketchikan Tuesday week.

WILLY   No, Ben! Please tell about Dad. I want my boys to hear. I want them to know the kind of stock they spring from. All I remember is a man with a big beard, and I was in Mamma's lap, sitting around a fire, and some kind of high music.

BEN His flute. He played the flute.

WILLY Sure, the flute, that's right!

[*New music is heard, a high, rollicking tune.*]

BEN Father was a very great and a very wild-hearted man. We would start in Boston, and he'd toss the whole family into the wagon, and then he'd drive the team right across the country; through Ohio, and Indiana, Michigan, Illinois, and all the Western states. And we'd stop in the towns and sell the flutes that he'd made on the way. Great inventor, Father. With one gadget he made more in a week than a man like you could make in a lifetime.

WILLY That's just the way I'm bringing them up, Ben—rugged, well liked, all-around.

BEN Yeah? [*to* BIFF] Hit that, boy—hard as you can. [*He pounds his stomach.*]

BIFF Oh, no, sir!

BEN [*taking boxing stance*] Come on, get to me! [*He laughs.*]

WILLY Go to it, Biff! Go ahead, show him!

BIFF Okay! [*He cocks his fist and starts in.*]

LINDA [*to* WILLY] Why must he fight, dear?

BEN [*sparring with* BIFF] Good boy! Good boy!

WILLY How's that, Ben, heh?

HAPPY Give him the left, Biff!

LINDA Why are you fighting?

BEN Good boy! [*Suddenly comes in, trips* BIFF, *and stands over him, the point of his umbrella poised over* BIFF's *eye.*]

LINDA Look out, Biff!

BIFF Gee!

BEN [*patting* BIFF's *knee*] Never fight fair with a stranger, boy. You'll never get out of the jungle that way. [*taking* LINDA's *hand and bowing*] It was an honor and a pleasure to meet you, Linda.

LINDA [*withdrawing her hand coldly, frightened*] Have a nice—trip.

BEN [*to* WILLY] And good luck with your—what do you do?

WILLY Selling.

BEN Yes. Well . . . [*He raises his hand in farewell to all.*]

WILLY No, Ben, I don't want you to think . . . [*He takes* BEN's *arm to show him.*] It's Brooklyn, I know, but we hunt too.

BEN Really, now.

WILLY Oh, sure, there's snakes and rabbits and—that's why I moved out here. Why, Biff can fell any one of these trees in no time! Boys! Go right over to where they're building the apartment house and get some sand. We're gonna rebuild the entire front stoop right now! Watch this, Ben!

BIFF Yes, sir! On the double, Hap!

HAPPY [*as he and* BIFF *run off*] I lost weight, Pop, you notice?

[CHARLEY *enters in knickers, even before the boys are gone.*]

CHARLEY Listen, if they steal any more from that building the watchman'll put the cops on them!

LINDA [*to* WILLY] Don't let Biff . . .

[BEN *laughs lustily.*]

WILLY You shoulda seen the lumber they brought home last week. At least a dozen six-by-tens worth all kinds a money.

CHARLEY   Listen, if that watchman—

WILLY   I gave them hell, understand. But I got a couple of fearless characters there.

CHARLEY   Willy, the jails are full of fearless characters.

BEN [*clapping* WILLY *on the back, with a laugh at* CHARLEY]   And the stock exchange, friend!

WILLY [*joining in* BEN's *laughter*]   Where are the rest of your pants?

CHARLEY   My wife bought them.

WILLY   Now all you need is a golf club and you can go upstairs and go to sleep, [*to* BEN] Great athlete! Between him and his son Bernard they can't hammer a nail!

BERNARD [*rushing in*]   The watchman's chasing Biff!

WILLY [*angrily*]   Shut up! He's not stealing anything!

LINDA [*alarmed, hurrying off left*]   Where is he? Biff, dear! [*She exits.*]

WILLY [*moving toward the left, away from* BEN]   There's nothing wrong. What's the matter with you?

BEN   Nervy boy. Good!

WILLY [*laughing*]   Oh, nerves of iron, that Biff!

CHARLEY   Don't know what it is. My New England man comes back and he's bleedin', they murdered him up there.

WILLY   It's contacts, Charley, I got important contacts!

CHARLEY [*sarcastically*]   Glad to hear it, Willy. Come in later, we'll shoot a little casino. I'll take some of your Portland money. [*He laughs at* WILLY *and exits.*]

WILLY [*turning to* BEN]   Business is bad, it's murderous. But not for me, of course.

BEN   I'll stop by on my way back to Africa.

WILLY [*longingly*]   Can't you stay a few days? You're just what I need, Ben, because I—I have a fine position here, but I—well, Dad left when I was such a baby and I never had a chance to talk to him and I still feel—kind of temporary about myself.

BEN   I'll be late for my train.

[*They are at opposite ends of the stage.*]

WILLY   Ben, my boys—can't we talk? They'd go into the jaws of hell for me, see, but I—

BEN   William, you're being first-rate with your boys. Outstanding, manly chaps!

WILLY [*hanging on to his words*]   Oh, Ben, that's good to hear! Because sometimes I'm afraid that I'm not teaching them the right kind of—Ben, how should I teach them?

BEN [*giving great weight to each word, and with a certain vicious audacity*]   William, when I walked into the jungle, I was seventeen. When I walked out I was twenty-one. And, by God, I was rich! [*He goes off into darkness around the right corner of the house.*]

WILLY   . . . was rich! That's just the spirit I want to imbue them with! To walk into a jungle! I was right! I was right! I was right!

[BEN *is gone, but* WILLY *is still speaking to him as* LINDA, *in nightgown and robe, enters the kitchen, glances around for* WILLY, *then goes to the door of the house, looks out and sees him. Comes down to his left. He looks at her.*]

LINDA   Willy, dear? Willy?

WILLY   I was right!

LINDA   Did you have some cheese? [*He can't answer.*] It's very late, darling. Come to bed, heh?

WILLY [*looking straight up*]   Gotta break your neck to see a star in this yard.

LINDA   You coming in?

WILLY   Whatever happened to that diamond watch fob? Remember? When Ben came from Africa that time? Didn't he give me a watch fob with a diamond in it?

LINDA   You pawned it, dear. Twelve, thirteen years ago. For Biff's radio correspondence course.

WILLY   Gee, that was a beautiful thing. I'll take a walk.

LINDA   But you're in your slippers.

WILLY [*starting to go around the house at the left*]   I was right! I was! [*half to* LINDA, *as he goes, shaking his head*] What a man! There was a man worth talking to. I was right!

LINDA [*calling after* WILLY]   But in your slippers, Willy!
       [WILLY *is almost gone when* BIFF, *in his pajamas, comes down the stairs and enters the kitchen.*]

BIFF   What is he doing out there?

LINDA   Sh!

BIFF   God Almighty, Mom, how long has he been doing this?

LINDA   Don't, he'll hear you.

BIFF   What the hell is the matter with him?

LINDA   It'll pass by morning.

BIFF   Shouldn't we do anything?

LINDA   Oh, my dear, you should do a lot of things, but there's nothing to do so go to sleep.
       [HAPPY *comes down the stairs and sits on the steps.*]

HAPPY   I never heard him so loud, Mom.

LINDA   Well, come around more often; you'll hear him. [*She sits down at the table and mends the lining of* WILLY'*s jacket.*]

BIFF   Why didn't you ever write me about this, Mom?

LINDA   How would I write to you? For over three months you had no address.

BIFF   I was on the move. But you know I thought of you all the time. You know that, don't you, pal?

LINDA   I know, dear, I know. But he likes to have a letter. Just to know that there's still a possibility for better things.

BIFF   He's not like this all the time, is he?

LINDA   It's when you come home he's always the worst.

BIFF   When I come home?

LINDA   When you write you're coming, he's all smiles, and talks about the future, and—he's just wonderful. And then the closer you seem to come, the more shaky he gets, and then, by the time you get here, he's arguing, and he seems angry at you. I think it's just that maybe he can't bring himself to—to open up to you. Why are you so hateful to each other? Why is that?

BIFF [*evasively*]   I'm not hateful, Mom.

LINDA   But you no sooner come in the door than you're fighting!

BIFF I don't know why. I mean to change. I'm tryin', Mom, you understand?

LINDA Are you home to stay now?

BIFF I don't know. I want to look around, see what's doin'.

LINDA Biff, you can't look around all your life, can you?

BIFF I just can't take hold, Mom. I can't take hold of some kind of a life.

LINDA Biff, a man is not a bird, to come and go with the springtime.

BIFF Your hair . . . [*He touches her hair.*] Your hair got so gray.

LINDA Oh, it's been gray since you were in high school. I just stopped dyeing it, that's all.

BIFF Dye it again, will ya? I don't want my pal looking old. [*He smiles.*]

LINDA You're such a boy! You think you can go away for a year and . . . You've got to get it into your head now that one day you'll knock on this door and there'll be strange people here—

BIFF What are you talking about? You're not even sixty, Mom.

LINDA But what about your father?

BIFF [*lamely*] Well, I meant him too.

HAPPY He admires Pop.

LINDA Biff, dear, if you don't have any feeling for him, then you can't have any feeling for me.

BIFF Sure I can, Mom.

LINDA No. You can't just come to see me, because I love him. [*with a threat, but only a threat, of tears*] He's the dearest man in the world to me, and I won't have anyone making him feel unwanted and low and blue. You've got to make up your mind now, darling, there's no leeway any more. Either he's your father and you pay him that respect, or else you're not to come here. I know he's not easy to get along with—nobody knows that better than me—but . . .

WILLY [*from the left, with a laugh*] Hey, hey, Biffo!

BIFF [*starting to go out after* WILLY] What the hell is the matter with him? [HAPPY *stops him.*]

LINDA Don't—don't go near him!

BIFF Stop making excuses for him! He always, always wiped the floor with you. Never had an ounce of respect for you.

HAPPY He's always had respect for—

BIFF What the hell do you know about it?

HAPPY [*surlily*] Just don't call him crazy!

BIFF He's got no character—Charley wouldn't do this. Not in his own house—spewing out that vomit from his mind.

HAPPY Charley never had to cope with what he's got to.

BIFF People are worse off than Willy Loman. Believe me, I've seen them!

LINDA Then make Charley your father, Biff. You can't do that, can you? I don't say he's a great man. Willy Loman never made a lot of money. His name was never in the paper. He's not the finest character that ever lived. But he's a human being, and a terrible thing is happening to him. So attention must be paid. He's not to be allowed to fall into his grave like an old dog. Attention, attention must be finally paid to such a person. You called him crazy—

BIFF I didn't mean—

LINDA No, a lot of people think he's lost his—balance. But you don't have to be very smart to know what his trouble is. The man is exhausted.

HAPPY   Sure!

LINDA   A small man can be just as exhausted as a great man. He works for a company thirty-six years this March, opens up unheard-of territories to their trademark, and now in his old age they take his salary away.

HAPPY [*indignantly*]   I didn't know that, Mom.

LINDA   You never asked, my dear! Now that you get your spending money someplace else you don't trouble your mind with him.

HAPPY   But I gave you money last—

LINDA   Christmas time, fifty dollars! To fix the hot water it cost ninety-seven fifty! For five weeks he's been on straight commission, like a beginner, an unknown!

BIFF   Those ungrateful bastards!

LINDA   Are they any worse than his sons? When he brought them business, when he was young, they were glad to see him. But now his old friends, the old buyers that loved him so and always found some order to hand him in a pinch—they're all dead, retired. He used to be able to make six, seven calls a day in Boston. Now he takes his valises out of the car and puts them back and takes them out again and he's exhausted. Instead of walking he talks now. He drives seven hundred miles, and when he gets there no one knows him any more, no one welcomes him. And what goes through a man's mind, driving seven hundred miles home without having earned a cent? Why shouldn't he talk to himself? Why? When he has to go to Charley and borrow fifty dollars a week and pretend to me that it's his pay? How long can that go on? How long? You see what I'm sitting here and waiting for? And you tell me he has no character? The man who never worked a day but for your benefit? When does he get the medal for that? Is this his reward—to turn around at the age of sixty-three and find his sons, who he loved better than his life, one a philandering bum—

HAPPY   Mom!

LINDA   That's all you are, my baby! [*to* BIFF] And you! What happened to the love you had for him? You were such pals! How you used to talk to him on the phone every night! How lonely he was till he could come home to you!

BIFF   All right, Mom. I'll live here in my room, and I'll get a job. I'll keep away from him, that's all.

LINDA   No, Biff. You can't stay here and fight all the time.

BIFF   He threw me out of this house, remember that.

LINDA   Why did he do that? I never knew why.

BIFF   Because I know he's a fake and he doesn't like anybody around who knows!

LINDA   Why a fake? In what way? What do you mean?

BIFF   Just don't lay it all at my feet. It's between me and him—that's all I have to say. I'll chip in from now on. He'll settle for half my pay check. He'll be all right. I'm going to bed. [*He starts for the stairs.*]

LINDA   He won't be all right.

BIFF [*turning on the stairs, furiously*]   I hate this city and I'll stay here. Now what do you want?

LINDA   He's dying, Biff.

   [HAPPY *turns quickly to her, shocked.*]

BIFF [*after a pause*] Why is he dying?

LINDA He's been trying to kill himself.

BIFF [*with great horror*] How?

LINDA I live from day to day.

BIFF What're you talking about?

LINDA Remember I wrote you that he smashed up the car again? In February?

BIFF Well?

LINDA The insurance inspector came. He said that they have evidence. That all these accidents in the last year—weren't—weren't—accidents.

HAPPY How can they tell that? That's a lie.

LINDA It seems there's a woman . . . [*she takes a breath as*]

⎰BIFF [*sharply but contained*] What woman?
⎱LINDA [*simultaneously*]   . . . and this woman . . .

LINDA What?

BIFF Nothing. Go ahead.

LINDA What did you say?

BIFF Nothing. I just said what woman?

HAPPY What about her?

LINDA Well, it seems she was walking down the road and saw his car. She says that he wasn't driving fast at all, and that he didn't skid. She says he came to that little bridge, and then deliberately smashed into the railing, and it was only the shallowness of the water that saved him.

BIFF Oh, no, he probably just fell asleep again.

LINDA I don't think he fell asleep.

BIFF Why not?

LINDA Last month . . . [*with great difficulty*] Oh, boys, it's so hard to say a thing like this! He's just a big stupid man to you, but I tell you there's more good in him than in many other people. [*She chokes, wipes her eyes.*] I was looking for a fuse. The lights blew out, and I went down the cellar. And behind the fuse box—it happened to fall out—was a length of rubber pipe—just short.

HAPPY No kidding?

LINDA There's a little attachment on the end of it. I knew right away. And sure enough, on the bottom of the water heater there's a new little nipple on the gas pipe.

HAPPY [*angrily*] That—jerk.

BIFF Did you have it taken off?

LINDA I'm—I'm ashamed to. How can I mention it to him? Every day I go down and take away that little rubber pipe. But, when he comes home, I put it back where it was. How can I insult him that way? I don't know what to do. I live from day to day, boys. I tell you, I know every thought in his mind. It sounds so old-fashioned and silly, but I tell you he put his whole life into you and you've turned your backs on him. [*She is bent over in the chair, weeping, her face in her hands.*] Biff, I swear to God! Biff, his life is in your hands!

HAPPY [*to* BIFF] How do you like that damned fool!

BIFF [*kissing her*] All right, pal, all right. It's all settled now. I've been remiss. I know that, Mom. But now I'll stay, and I swear to you, I'll apply myself, [*kneeling in front of her, in a fever of self-reproach*] It's just—you see, Mom, I don't fit in business. Not that I won't try. I'll try, and I'll make good.

HAPPY   Sure you will. The trouble with you in business was you never tried to please people.

BIFF   I know, I—

HAPPY   Like when you worked for Harrison's. Bob Harrison said you were tops, and then you go and do some damn fool, thing like whistling whole songs in the elevator like a comedian.

BIFF [*against* HAPPY]   So what? I like to whistle sometimes.

HAPPY   You don't raise a guy to a responsible job who whistles in the elevator!

LINDA   Well, don't argue about it now.

HAPPY   Like when you'd go off and swim in the middle of the day instead of taking the line around.

BIFF [*his resentment rising*]   Well, don't you run off? You take off sometimes, don't you? On a nice summer day?

HAPPY   Yeah, but I cover myself!

LINDA   Boys!

HAPPY   If I'm going to take a fade the boss can call any number where I'm supposed to be and they'll swear to him that I just left. I'll tell you something that I hate to say, Biff, but in the business world some of them think you're crazy.

BIFF [*angered*]   Screw the business world!

HAPPY   All right, screw it! Great, but cover yourself!

LINDA   Hap, Hap!

BIFF   I don't care what they think! They've laughed at Dad for years, and you know why? Because we don't belong in this nuthouse of a city! We should be mixing cement on some open plain, or—or carpenters. A carpenter is allowed to whistle!

[WILLY *walks in from the entrance of the house, at left.*]

WILLY   Even your grandfather was better than a carpenter. [*Pause. They watch him.*] You never grew up. Bernard does not whistle in the elevator, I assure you.

BIFF [*as though to laugh* WILLY *out of it*]   Yeah, but you do, Pop.

WILLY   I never in my life whistled in an elevator! And who in the business world thinks I'm crazy?

BIFF   I didn't mean it like that, Pop. Now don't make a whole thing out of it, will ya?

WILLY   Go back to the West! Be a carpenter, a cowboy, enjoy yourself!

LINDA   Willy, he was just saying—

WILLY   I heard what he said!

HAPPY [*trying to quiet* WILLY]   Hey, Pop, come on now . . .

WILLY [*continuing over* HAPPY's *line*]   They laugh at me, heh? Go to Filene's, go to the Hub, go to Slattery's, Boston. Call out the name Willy Loman and see what happens! Big Shot!

BIFF   All right, Pop.

WILLY   Big!

BIFF   All right!

WILLY   Why do you always insult me?

BIFF I didn't say a word. [*to* LINDA] Did I say a word?

LINDA He didn't say anything, Willy.

WILLY [*going to the doorway of the living-room*] All right, good night, good night.

LINDA Willy, dear, he just decided . . .

WILLY [*to* BIFF] If you get tired hanging around tomorrow, paint the ceiling I put up in the living-room.

BIFF I'm leaving early tomorrow.

HAPPY He's going to see Bill Oliver, Pop.

WILLY [*interestedly*] Oliver? For what?

BIFF [*with reserve, but trying, trying*] He always said he'd stake me. I'd like to go into business, so maybe I can take him up on it.

LINDA Isn't that wonderful?

WILLY Don't interrupt. What's wonderful about it? There's fifty men in the City of New York who'd stake him. [*to* BIFF] Sporting goods?

BIFF I guess so. I know something about it and—

WILLY He knows something about it! You know sporting goods better than Spalding, for God's sake! How much is he giving you?

BIFF I don't know, I didn't even see him yet, but—

WILLY Then what're you talkin' about?

BIFF [*getting angry*] Well, all I said was I'm gonna see him, that's all!

WILLY [*turning away*] Ah, you're counting your chickens again.

BIFF [*starting left for the stairs*] Oh, Jesus, I'm going to sleep!

WILLY [*calling after him*] Don't curse in this house!

BIFF [*turning*] Since when did you get so clean?

HAPPY [*trying to stop them*] Wait a . . .

WILLY Don't use that language to me! I won't have it!

HAPPY [*grabbing* BIFF, *shouts*] Wait a minute! I got an idea. I got a feasible idea. Come here, Biff, let's talk this over now, let's talk some sense here. When I was down in Florida last time, I thought of a great idea to sell sporting goods. It just came back to me. You and I, Biff—we have a line, the Loman Line. We train a couple of weeks, and put on a couple of exhibitions, see?

WILLY That's an idea!

HAPPY Wait! We form two basketball teams, see? Two water-polo teams. We play each other. It's a million dollars' worth of publicity. Two brothers, see? The Loman Brothers. Displays in the Royal Palms—all the hotels. And banners over the ring and the basketball court: "Loman Brothers." Baby, we could sell sporting goods!

WILLY That is a one-million-dollar idea!

LINDA Marvelous!

BIFF I'm in great shape as far as that's concerned.

HAPPY And the beauty of it is, Biff, it wouldn't be like a business. We'd be out playin' ball again . . .

BIFF [*enthused*] Yeah, that's . . .

WILLY Million-dollar . . .

HAPPY And you wouldn't get fed up with it, Biff. It'd be the family again. There'd be the old honor, and comradeship, and if you wanted to go off for a swim or somethin'—well, you'd do it! Without some smart cooky gettin' up ahead of you!

WILLY   Lick the world! You guys together could absolutely lick the civilized world.

BIFF   I'll see Oliver tomorrow. Hap, if we could work that out . . .

LINDA   Maybe things are beginning to—

WILLY [*wildly enthused, to* LINDA]   Stop interrupting! [*to* BIFF] But don't wear sport jacket and slacks when you see Oliver.

BIFF   No, I'll—

WILLY   A business suit, and talk as little as possible, and don't crack any jokes.

BIFF   He did like me. Always liked me.

LINDA   He loved you!

WILLY [*to* LINDA]   Will you stop! [*to* BIFF] Walk in very serious. You are not applying for a boy's job. Money is to pass. Be quiet, fine, and serious. Everybody likes a kidder, but nobody lends him money.

HAPPY   I'll try to get some myself, Biff. I'm sure I can.

WILLY   I see great things for you kids, I think your troubles are over. But remember, start big and you'll end big. Ask for fifteen. How much you gonna ask for?

BIFF   Gee, I don't know—

WILLY   And don't say "Gee." "Gee" is a boy's word. A man walking in for fifteen thousand dollars does not say "Gee!"

BIFF   Ten, I think, would be top though.

WILLY   Don't be so modest. You always started too low. Walk in with a big laugh. Don't look worried. Start off with a couple of your good stories to lighten things up. It's not what you say, it's how you say it—because personality always wins the day.

LINDA   Oliver always thought the highest of him—

WILLY   Will you let me talk?

BIFF   Don't yell at her, Pop, will ya?

WILLY [*angrily*]   I was talking, wasn't I?

BIFF   I don't like you yelling at her all the time, and I'm tellin' you, that's all.

WILLY   What're you, takin' over this house?

LINDA   Willy—

WILLY [*turning on her*]   Don't take his side all the time, goddammit!

BIFF [*furiously*]   Stop yelling at her!

WILLY [*suddenly pulling on his cheek, beaten down, guilt ridden*]   Give my best to Bill Oliver—he may remember me. [*He exits through the living-room doorway.*]

LINDA [*her voice subdued*]   What'd you have to start that for? [BIFF *turns away.*] You see how sweet he was as soon as you talked hopefully? [*She goes over to* BIFF.] Come up and say good night to him. Don't let him go to bed that way.

HAPPY   Come on, Biff, let's buck him up.

LINDA   Please, dear. Just say good night. It takes so little to make him happy. Come. [*She goes through the living-room doorway, calling upstairs from within the living-room*] Your pajamas are hanging in the bathroom, Willy!

HAPPY [*looking toward where* LINDA *went out*]   What a woman! They broke the mold when they made her. You know that, Biff?

BIFF   He's off salary. My God, working on commission!

HAPPY   Well, let's face it: he's no hot-shot selling man. Except that sometimes, you have to admit, he's a sweet personality.

BIFF [*deciding*]   Lend me ten bucks, will ya? I want to buy some new ties.

HAPPY   I'll take you to a place I know. Beautiful stuff. Wear one of my
striped shirts tomorrow.

BIFF   She got gray. Mom got awful old. Gee, I'm gonna go in to Oliver
tomorrow and knock him for a—

HAPPY   Come on up. Tell that to Dad. Let's give him a whirl. Come on.

BIFF [*steamed up*]   You know, with ten thousand bucks, boy!

HAPPY [*as they go into the living-room*]   That's the talk, Biff, that's the first
time I've heard the old confidence out of you! [*from within the living-
room, fading off*] You're gonna live with me, kid, and any babe you want
just say the word . . . [*The last lines are hardly heard. They are mounting
the stairs to their parents' bedroom.*]

LINDA [*entering her bedroom and addressing* WILLY, *who is in the bathroom.
She is straightening the bed for him.*]   Can you do anything about the
shower? It drips.

WILLY [*from the bathroom*]   All of a sudden everything falls to pieces!
Goddam plumbing, oughta be sued, those people. I hardly finished putting it in and the thing . . . [*His words rumble off.*]

LINDA   I'm just wondering if Oliver will remember him. You think he
might?

WILLY [*coming out of the bathroom in his pajamas*]   Remember him?
What's the matter with you, you crazy? If he'd've stayed with Oliver he'd
be on top by now! Wait'll Oliver gets a look at him. You don't know the
average caliber any more. The average young man today—[*he is getting
into bed*]—is got a caliber of zero. Greatest thing in the world for him
was to bum around.

[BIFF *and* HAPPY *enter the bedroom. Slight pause.*]

WILLY [*stops short, looking at* BIFF]   Glad to hear it, boy.

HAPPY   He wanted to say good night to you, sport.

WILLY [*to* BIFF]   Yeah. Knock him dead, boy. What'd you want to tell me?

BIFF   Just take it easy, Pop. Good night. [*He turns to go.*]

WILLY [*unable to resist*]   And if anything falls off the desk while you're talking to him—like a package or something—don't you pick it up. They have
office boys for that.

LINDA   I'll make a big breakfast—

WILLY   Will you let me finish? [*to* BIFF] Tell him you were in the business
in the West. Not farm work.

BIFF   All right, Dad.

LINDA   I think everything—

WILLY [*going right through her speech*]   And don't undersell yourself. No
less than fifteen thousand dollars.

BIFF [*unable to bear him*]   Okay. Good night, Mom. [*He starts moving.*]

WILLY   Because you got a greatness in you, Biff, remember that. You got all
kinds a greatness . . . [*He lies back, exhausted.* BIFF *walks out.*]

LINDA [*calling after* BIFF]   Sleep well, darling!

HAPPY   I'm gonna get married, Mom. I wanted to tell you.

LINDA   Go to sleep, dear.

HAPPY [*going*]   I just wanted to tell you.

WILLY   Keep up the good work. [HAPPY *exits.*] God . . . remember that
Ebbets Field[5] game? The championship of the city?

LINDA   Just rest. Should I sing to you?

WILLY   Yeah. Sing to me. [LINDA *hums a soft lullaby.*] When that team came
out—he was the tallest, remember?

LINDA   Oh, yes. And in gold.

[BIFF *enters the darkened kitchen, takes a cigarette, and leaves the house.
He comes downstage into a golden pool of light. He smokes, staring at the
night.*]

WILLY   Like a young god. Hercules[6]—something like that. And the sun,
the sun all around him. Remember how he waved to me? Right up from
the field, with the representatives of three colleges standing by? And the
buyers I brought, and the cheers when he came out—Loman, Loman,
Loman! God Almighty, he'll be great yet. A star like that, magnificent,
can never really fade away!

[*The light on* WILLY *is fading. The gas heater begins to glow through the
kitchen wall, near the stairs, a blue flame beneath red coils.*]

LINDA [*timidly*]   Willy dear, what has he got against you?

WILLY   I'm so tired. Don't talk any more.

[BIFF *slowly returns to the kitchen. He stops, stares toward the heater.*]

LINDA   Will you ask Howard to let you work in New York?

WILLY   First thing in the morning. Everything'll be all right.

[BIFF *reaches behind the heater and draws out a length of rubber tubing. He is horrified and turns his head toward* WILLY's *room, still dimly
lit, from which the strains of* LINDA's *desperate but monotonous humming rise.*]

WILLY [*staring through the window into the moonlight*]   Gee, look at the
moon moving between the buildings!

[BIFF *wraps the tubing around his hand and quickly goes up the stairs.*]

CURTAIN

Act Two

Music is heard, gay and bright. The curtain rises as the music fades away. WILLY,
in shirt sleeves, is sitting at the kitchen table, sipping coffee, his hat in his lap.
LINDA *is filling his cup when she can.*

WILLY   Wonderful coffee. Meal in itself.

LINDA   Can I make you some eggs?

WILLY   No. Take a breath.

LINDA   You look so rested, dear.

WILLY   I slept like a dead one. First time in months. Imagine, sleeping till
ten on a Tuesday morning. Boys left nice and early, heh?

LINDA   They were out of here by eight o'clock.

WILLY   Good work!

LINDA   It was so thrilling to see them leaving together. I can't get over the
shaving lotion in this house!

WILLY [*smiling*]   Mmm—

5. Brooklyn sports stadium.
6. In Greek and Roman mythology the son of

the chief god (Zeus, Jupiter), famous for his great
strength.

LINDA Biff was very changed this morning. His whole attitude seemed to be hopeful. He couldn't wait to get downtown to see Oliver.

WILLY He's heading for a change. There's no question, there simply are certain men that take longer to get—solidified. How did he dress?

LINDA His blue suit. He's so handsome in that suit. He could be a—anything in that suit!

[WILLY *gets up from the table.* LINDA *holds his jacket for him.*]

WILLY There's no question, no question at all. Gee, on the way home tonight I'd like to buy some seeds.

LINDA [*laughing*] That'd be wonderful. But not enough sun gets back there. Nothing'll grow any more.

WILLY You wait, kid, before it's all over we're gonna get a little place out in the country, and I'll raise some vegetables, a couple of chickens . . .

LINDA You'll do it yet, dear.

[WILLY *walks out of his jacket.* LINDA *follows him.*]

WILLY And they'll get married, and come for a weekend. I'd build a little guest house. 'Cause I got so many fine tools, all I'd need would be a little lumber and some peace of mind.

LINDA [*joyfully*] I sewed the lining . . .

WILLY I could build two guest houses, so they'd both come. Did he decide how much he's going to ask Oliver for?

LINDA [*getting him into the jacket*] He didn't mention it, but I imagine ten or fifteen thousand. You going to talk to Howard today?

WILLY Yeah. I'll put it to him straight and simple. He'll just have to take me off the road.

LINDA And Willy, don't forget to ask for a little advance, because we've got the insurance premium. It's the grace period now.

WILLY That's a hundred . . . ?

LINDA A hundred and eight, sixty-eight. Because we're a little short again.

WILLY Why are we short?

LINDA Well, you had the motor job on the car . . .

WILLY That goddam Studebaker!

LINDA And you got one more payment on the refrigerator . . .

WILLY But it just broke again!

LINDA Well, it's old, dear.

WILLY I told you we should've bought a well-advertised machine. Charley bought a General Electric and it's twenty years old and it's still good, that son-of-a-bitch.

LINDA But, Willy—

WILLY Whoever heard of a Hastings refrigerator? Once in my life I would like to own something outright before it's broken! I'm always in a race with the junkyard! I just finished paying for the car and it's on its last legs. The refrigerator consumes belts like a goddam maniac. They time those things. They time them so when you finally paid for them, they're used up.

LINDA [*buttoning up his jacket as he unbuttons it*] All told, about two hundred dollars would carry us, dear. But that includes the last payment on the mortgage. After this payment, Willy, the house belongs to us.

WILLY It's twenty-five years!

LINDA Biff was nine years old when we bought it.

WILLY   Well, that's a great thing. To weather a twenty-five year mortgage is—

LINDA   It's an accomplishment.

WILLY   All the cement, the lumber, the reconstruction I put in this house! There ain't a crack to be found in it anymore.

LINDA   Well, it served its purpose.

WILLY   What purpose? Some stranger'll come along, move in, and that's that. If only Biff would take this house, and raise a family . . . [*He starts to go.*] Good-by, I'm late.

LINDA [*suddenly remembering*]   Oh, I forgot! You're supposed to meet them for dinner.

WILLY   Me?

LINDA   At Frank's Chop House on Forty-eighth near Sixth Avenue.

WILLY   Is that so! How about you?

LINDA   No, just the three of you. They're gonna blow you to a big meal!

WILLY   Don't say! Who thought of that?

LINDA   Biff came to me this morning, Willy, and he said, "Tell Dad, we want to blow him to a big meal." Be there six o'clock. You and your two boys are going to have dinner.

WILLY   Gee whiz! That's really somethin'. I'm gonna knock Howard for a loop, kid. I'll get an advance, and I'll come home with a New York job. Goddammit, now I'm gonna do it!

LINDA   Oh, that's the spirit, Willy!

WILLY   I will never get behind a wheel the rest of my life!

LINDA   It's changing, Willy, I can feel it changing!

WILLY   Beyond a question. G'by, I'm late. [*He starts to go again.*]

LINDA [*calling after him as she runs to the kitchen table for a handkerchief*]   You got your glasses?

WILLY [*feels for them, then comes back in*]   Yeah, yeah, got my glasses.

LINDA [*giving him the handkerchief*]   And a handkerchief.

WILLY   Yeah, handkerchief.

LINDA   And your saccharine?

WILLY   Yeah, my saccharine.

LINDA   Be careful on the subway stairs.
  [*She kisses him, and a silk stocking is seen hanging from her hand.* WILLY *notices it.*]

WILLY   Will you stop mending stockings? At least while I'm in the house. It gets me nervous. I can't tell you. Please.
  [LINDA *hides the stocking in her hand as she follows* WILLY *across the forestage in front of the house.*]

LINDA   Remember, Frank's Chop House.

WILLY [*passing the apron*]   Maybe beets would grow out there.

LINDA [*laughing*]   But you tried so many times.

WILLY   Yeah. Well, don't work hard today. [*He disappears around the right corner of the house.*]

LINDA   Be careful!
  [*As* WILLY *vanishes,* LINDA *waves to him. Suddenly the phone rings. She runs across the stage and into the kitchen and lifts it.*]

LINDA   Hello? Oh, Biff! I'm so glad you called, I just . . . Yes, sure, I just told him. Yes, he'll be there for dinner at six o'clock, I didn't forget. Listen,

I was just dying to tell you. You know that little rubber pipe I told you about? That he connected to the gas heater? I finally decided to go down the cellar this morning and take it away and destroy it. But it's gone! Imagine? He took it away himself, it isn't there! [*She listens.*] When? Oh, then you took it. Oh—nothing, it's just that I'd hoped he'd taken it away himself. Oh, I'm not worried, darling, because this morning he left in such high spirits, it was like the old days! I'm not afraid any more. Did Mr. Oliver see you? . . . Well, you wait there then. And make a nice impression on him, darling. Just don't perspire too much before you see him. And have a nice time with Dad. He may have big news too! . . . That's right, a New York job. And be sweet to him tonight, dear. Be loving to him. Because he's only a little boat looking for a harbor. [*She is trembling with sorrow and joy.*] Oh, that's wonderful, Biff, you'll save his life. Thanks, darling. Just put your arm around him when he comes into the restaurant. Give him a smile. That's the boy . . . Good-by, dear. . . . You got your comb? . . . That's fine. Good-by, Biff dear.

> [*In the middle of her speech,* HOWARD WAGNER, *thirty-six, wheels in a small typewriter table on which is a wire-recording machine and proceeds to plug it in. This is on the left forestage. Light slowly fades on* LINDA *as it rises on* HOWARD. HOWARD *is intent on threading the machine and only glances over his shoulder as* WILLY *appears.*]

WILLY   Pst! Pst!

HOWARD   Hello, Willy, come in.

WILLY   Like to have a little talk with you, Howard.

HOWARD   Sorry to keep you waiting. I'll be with you in a minute.

WILLY   What's that, Howard?

HOWARD   Didn't you ever see one of these? Wire recorder.

WILLY   Oh. Can we talk a minute?

HOWARD   Records things. Just got delivery yesterday. Been driving me crazy, the most terrific machine I ever saw in my life. I was up all night with it.

WILLY   What do you do with it?

HOWARD   I bought it for dictation, but you can do anything with it. Listen to this. I had it home last night. Listen to what I picked up. The first one is my daughter. Get this. [*He flicks the switch and "Roll out the Barrel" is heard being whistled.*] Listen to that kid whistle.

WILLY   That is lifelike, isn't it?

HOWARD   Seven years old. Get that tone.

WILLY   Ts, ts. Like to ask a little favor if you . . .

> [*The whistling breaks off, and the voice of* HOWARD's *daughter is heard.*]

HIS DAUGHTER   "Now you, Daddy."

HOWARD   She's crazy for me! [*Again the same song is whistled.*] That's me! Ha! [*He winks.*]

WILLY   You're very good!

> [*The whistling breaks off again. The machine runs silent for a moment.*]

HOWARD   Sh! Get this now, this is my son.

HIS SON   "The capital of Alabama is Montgomery; the capital of Arizona is Phoenix; the capital of Arkansas is Little Rock; the capital of California is Sacramento . . ." [*and on, and on*]

HOWARD   [*holding up five fingers*]   Five years old, Willy!

WILLY   He'll make an announcer some day!

HIS SON [*continuing*]   "The capital . . ."

HOWARD   Get that—alphabetical order! [*The machine breaks off suddenly.*] Wait a minute. The maid kicked the plug out.

WILLY   It certainly is a—

HOWARD   Sh, for God's sake!

HIS SON   "It's nine o'clock, Bulova watch time. So I have to go to sleep."

WILLY   That really is—

HOWARD   Wait a minute! The next is my wife.
   [*They wait.*]

HOWARD'S VOICE   "Go on, say something." [*pause*] "Well, you gonna talk?"

HIS WIFE   "I can't think of anything."

HOWARD'S VOICE   "Well, talk—it's turning."

HIS WIFE [*shyly, beaten*]   "Hello." [*silence*] "Oh, Howard, I can't talk into this . . ."

HOWARD [*snapping the machine off*]   That was my wife.

WILLY   That is a wonderful machine. Can we—

HOWARD   I tell you, Willy, I'm gonna take my camera, and my handsaw, and all my hobbies, and out they go. This is the most fascinating relaxation I ever found.

WILLY   I think I'll get one myself.

HOWARD   Sure, they're only a hundred and a half. You can't do without it. Supposing you wanna hear Jack Benny,[7] see? But you can't be at home at that hour. So you tell the maid to turn the radio on when Jack Benny comes on, and this automatically goes on with the radio . . .

WILLY   And when you come home you . . .

HOWARD   You can come home twelve o'clock, one o'clock, any time you like, and you get yourself a Coke and sit yourself down, throw the switch, and there's Jack Benny's program in the middle of the night!

WILLY   I'm definitely going to get one. Because lots of time I'm on the road, and I think to myself, what I must be missing on the radio!

HOWARD   Don't you have a radio in the car?

WILLY   Well, yeah, but who ever thinks of turning it on?

HOWARD   Say, aren't you supposed to be in Boston?

WILLY   That's what I want to talk to you about, Howard. You got a minute? [*He draws a chair in from the wing.*]

HOWARD   What happened? What're you doing here?

WILLY   Well . . .

HOWARD   You didn't crack up again, did you?

WILLY   Oh, no. No . . .

HOWARD   Geez, you had me worried there for a minute. What's the trouble?

WILLY   Well, tell you the truth, Howard. I've come to the decision that I'd rather not travel any more.

HOWARD   Not travel! Well, what'll you do?

WILLY   Remember, Christmas time, when you had the party here? You said you'd try to think of some spot for me here in town.

HOWARD   With us?

WILLY   Well, sure.

---

7. Vastly popular radio comedian of the 1930s and 1940s.

HOWARD Oh, yeah, yeah. I remember. Well, I couldn't think of anything for you, Willy.

WILLY I tell ya, Howard. The kids are all grown up, y'know. I don't need much any more. If I could take home—well, sixty-five dollars a week, I could swing it.

HOWARD Yeah, but Willy, see I—

WILLY I tell ya why, Howard. Speaking frankly and between the two of us, y'know—I'm just a little tired.

HOWARD Oh, I could understand that, Willy. But you're a road man, Willy, and we do a road business. We've only got a half-dozen salesmen on the floor here.

WILLY God knows, Howard, I never asked a favor of any man. But I was with the firm when your father used to carry you in here in his arms.

HOWARD I know that, Willy, but—

WILLY Your father came to me the day you were born and asked me what I thought of the name of Howard, may he rest in peace.

HOWARD I appreciate that, Willy, but there just is no spot here for you. If I had a spot I'd slam you right in, but I just don't have a single solitary spot.

[*He looks for his lighter.* WILLY *has picked it up and gives it to him. Pause.*]

WILLY [*with increasing anger*] Howard, all I need to set my table is fifty dollars a week.

HOWARD But where am I going to put you, kid?

WILLY Look, it isn't a question of whether I can sell merchandise, is it?

HOWARD No, but it's a business, kid, and everybody's gotta pull his own weight.

WILLY [*desperately*] Just let me tell you a story, Howard—

HOWARD 'Cause you gotta admit, business is business.

WILLY [*angrily*] Business is definitely business, but just listen for a minute. You don't understand this. When I was a boy—eighteen, nineteen—I was already on the road. And there was a question in my mind as to whether selling had a future for me. Because in those days I had a yearning to go to Alaska. See, there were three gold strikes in one month in Alaska, and I felt like going out. Just for the ride, you might say.

HOWARD [*barely interested*] Don't say.

WILLY Oh, yeah, my father lived many years in Alaska. He was an adventurous man. We've got quite a little streak of self-reliance in our family. I thought I'd go out with my older brother and try to locate him, and maybe settle in the North with the old man. And I was almost decided to go, when I met a salesman in the Parker House. His name was Dave Singleman. And he was eighty-four years old, and he'd drummed merchandise in thirty-one states. And old Dave, he'd go up to his room, y'understand, put on his green velvet slippers—I'll never forget—and pick up his phone and call the buyers, and without ever leaving his room, at the age of eighty-four, he made a living. And when I saw that, I realized that selling was the greatest career a man could want. 'Cause what could be more satisfying than to be able to go, at the age of eighty-four, into twenty or thirty different cities, and pick up a phone, and be remembered and loved and helped by so many different people? Do you know? when he died—and by the way he died the death of a salesman, in his green velvet slippers in the smoker of the New York, New Haven and Hartford, going into Boston—when he died, hundreds of salesmen and buyers were at his funeral. Things were sad on a lotta trains for months after that. [*He stands up.* HOWARD *has not looked at him.*] In those days there was personality in it, Howard. There was respect, and comradeship, and gratitude in it. Today, it's all cut and dried, and there's no chance for bringing friendship to bear—or personality. You see what I mean? They don't know me anymore.

HOWARD [*moving away, toward the right*]   That's just the thing, Willy.

WILLY   If I had forty dollars a week—that's all I'd need. Forty dollars, Howard.

HOWARD   Kid, I can't take blood from a stone, I—

WILLY [*desperation is on him now*]   Howard, the year Al Smith[8] was nominated, your father came to me and—

HOWARD [*starting to go off*]   I've got to see some people, kid.

WILLY [*stopping him*]   I'm talking about your father! There were promises made across this desk! You mustn't tell me you've got people to see—I put thirty-four years into this firm, Howard, and now I can't pay my insurance! You can't eat the orange and throw the peel away—a man is not a piece of fruit! [*after a pause*] Now pay attention. Your father—in 1928 I had a big year. I averaged a hundred and seventy dollars a week in commissions.

HOWARD [*impatiently*]   Now, Willy, you never averaged—

WILLY [*banging his hand on the desk*]   I averaged a hundred and seventy dollars a week in the year of 1928! And your father came to me—or rather, I was in the office here—it was right over this desk—and he put his hand on my shoulder—

HOWARD [*getting up*]   You'll have to excuse me, Willy, I gotta see some people. Pull yourself together. [*going out*] I'll be back in a little while.

[*On* HOWARD's *exit, the light on his chair grows very bright and strange.*]

WILLY   Pull myself together! What the hell did I say to him? My God, I was yelling at him! How could I! [WILLY *breaks off, staring at the light, which occupies the chair, animating it. He approaches this chair, standing across the desk from it.*] Frank, Frank, don't you remember what you told me that time? How you put your hand on my shoulder, and Frank . . . [*He leans on the desk and as he speaks the dead man's name he accidentally switches on the recorder, and instantly*]

HOWARD's SON   ". . . of New York is Albany. The capital of Ohio is Cincinnati, the capital of Rhode Island is . . ." [*The recitation continues.*]

WILLY [*leaping away with fright, shouting*]   Ha! Howard! Howard! Howard!

HOWARD [*rushing in*]   What happened?

WILLY [*pointing at the machine, which continues nasally, childishly, with the capital cities*]   Shut it off! Shut it off!

HOWARD [*pulling the plug out*]   Look, Willy . . .

WILLY [*pressing his hands to his eyes*]   I gotta get myself some coffee. I'll get some coffee . . .

[WILLY *starts to walk out.* HOWARD *stops him.*]

---

8. Democratic candidate for president in 1928.

HOWARD [*rolling up the cord*]   Willy, look . . .

WILLY   I'll go to Boston.

HOWARD   Willy, you can't go to Boston for us.

WILLY   Why can't I go?

HOWARD   I don't want you to represent us. I've been meaning to tell you for a long time now.

WILLY   Howard, are you firing me?

HOWARD   I think you need a good long rest, Willy.

WILLY   Howard—

HOWARD   And when you feel better, come back, and we'll see if we can work something out.

WILLY   But I gotta earn money, Howard. I'm in no position to—

HOWARD   Where are your sons? Why don't your sons give you a hand?

WILLY   They're working on a very big deal.

HOWARD   This is no time for false pride, Willy. You go to your sons and you tell them that you're tired. You've got two great boys, haven't you?

WILLY   Oh, no question, no question, but in the meantime . . .

HOWARD   Then that's that, heh?

WILLY   All right, I'll go to Boston tomorrow.

HOWARD   No, no.

WILLY   I can't throw myself on my sons. I'm not a cripple!

HOWARD   Look, kid, I'm busy, I'm busy this morning.

WILLY [*grasping* HOWARD's *arm*]   Howard, you've got to let me go to Boston!

HOWARD [*hard, keeping himself under control*]   I've got a line of people to see this morning. Sit down, take five minutes, and pull yourself together, and then go home, will ya? I need the office, Willy. [*He starts to go, turns, remembering the recorder, starts to push off the table holding the recorder.*] Oh, yeah. Whenever you can this week, stop by and drop off the samples. You'll feel better, Willy, and then come back and we'll talk. Pull yourself together, kid, there's people outside.

> [HOWARD *exits, pushing the table off left.* WILLY *stares into space, exhausted. Now the music is heard*—BEN's *music*—*first distantly, then closer, closer. As* WILLY *speaks,* BEN *enters from the right. He carries valise and umbrella.*]

WILLY   Oh, Ben, how did you do it? What is the answer? Did you wind up the Alaska deal already?

BEN   Doesn't take much time if you know what you're doing. Just a short business trip. Boarding ship in an hour. Wanted to say good-by.

WILLY   Ben, I've got to talk to you.

BEN [*glancing at his watch*]   Haven't the time, William.

WILLY [*crossing the apron to* BEN]   Ben, nothing's working out. I don't know what to do.

BEN   Now, look here, William. I've bought timberland in Alaska and I need a man to look after things for me.

WILLY   God, timberland! Me and my boys in those grand outdoors!

BEN   You've a new continent at your doorstep, William. Get out of these cities, they're full of talk and time payments and courts of law. Screw on your fists and you can fight for a fortune up there.

WILLY Yes, yes! Linda, Linda!

[LINDA *enters as of old, with the wash.*]

LINDA Oh, you're back?

BEN I haven't much time.

WILLY No, wait! Linda, he's got a proposition for me in Alaska.

LINDA But you've got— [*to* BEN] He's got a beautiful job here.

WILLY But in Alaska, kid, I could—

LINDA You're doing well enough, Willy!

BEN [*to* LINDA] Enough for what, my dear?

LINDA [*frightened of* BEN *and angry at him*] Don't say those things to him! Enough to be happy right here, right now. [*to* WILLY, *while* BEN *laughs*] Why must everybody conquer the world? You're well liked, and the boys love you, and someday—[*to* BEN]—why, old man Wagner told him just the other day that if he keeps it up he'll be a member of the firm, didn't he, Willy?

WILLY Sure, sure. I am building something with this firm, Ben, and if a man is building something he must be on the right track, mustn't he?

BEN What are you building? Lay your hand on it. Where is it?

WILLY [*hesitantly*] That's true, Linda, there's nothing.

LINDA Why? [*to* BEN] There's a man eighty-four years old—

WILLY That's right, Ben, that's right. When I look at that man I say, what is there to worry about?

BEN Bah!

WILLY It's true, Ben. All he has to do is go into any city, pick up the phone, and he's making his living and you know why?

BEN [*picking up his valise*] I've got to go.

WILLY [*holding* BEN *back*] Look at this boy!

[BIFF, *in his high school sweater, enters carrying suitcase.* HAPPY *carries* BIFF's *shoulder guards, gold helmet, and football pants.*]

WILLY Without a penny to his name, three great universities are begging for him, and from there the sky's the limit, because it's not what you do, Ben. It's who you know and the smile on your face! It's contacts, Ben, contacts! The whole wealth of Alaska passes over the lunch table at the Commodore Hotel, and that's the wonder, the wonder of this country, that a man can end with diamonds here on the basis of being liked! [*He turns to* BIFF.] And that's why when you get out on that field today it's important. Because thousands of people will be rooting for you and loving you. [*to* BEN, *who has again begun to leave*] And Ben! when he walks into a business office his name will sound out like a bell and all the doors will open to him! I've seen it, Ben, I've seen it a thousand times! You can't feel it with your hand like timber, but it's there!

BEN Good-by, William.

WILLY Ben, am I right? Don't you think I'm right? I value your advice.

BEN There's a new continent at your doorstep, William. You could walk out rich. Rich! [*He is gone.*]

WILLY We'll do it here, Ben! You hear me? We're gonna do it here!

[*Young* BERNARD *rushes in. The gay music of the Boys is heard.*]

BERNARD Oh, gee, I was afraid you left already!

WILLY Why? What time is it?

BERNARD It's half-past one!

WILLY   Well, come on, everybody! Ebbets Field next stop! Where's the pennants? [*He rushes through the wall-line of the kitchen and out into the living-room.*]

LINDA [*to* BIFF]   Did you pack fresh underwear?

BIFF [*who has been limbering up*]   I want to go!

BERNARD   Biff, I'm carrying your helmet, ain't I?

HAPPY   No, I'm carrying the helmet.

BERNARD   Oh, Biff, you promised me.

HAPPY   I'm carrying the helmet.

BERNARD   How am I going to get in the locker room?

LINDA   Let him carry the shoulder guards. [*She puts her coat and hat on in the kitchen.*]

BERNARD   Can I, Biff? 'Cause I told everybody I'm going to be in the locker room.

HAPPY   In Ebbets Field it's the clubhouse.

BERNARD   I meant the clubhouse. Biff!

HAPPY   Biff!

BIFF [*grandly, after a slight pause*]   Let him carry the shoulder guards.

HAPPY [*as he gives* BERNARD *the shoulder guards*]   Stay close to us now.
     [WILLY *rushes in with the pennants.*]

WILLY [*handing them out*]   Everybody wave when Biff comes out on the field. [HAPPY *and* BERNARD *run off.*] You set now, boy?
     [*The music has died away.*]

BIFF   Ready to go, Pop. Every muscle is ready.

WILLY [*at the edge of the apron*]   You realize what this means?

BIFF   That's right, Pop.

WILLY [*feeling* BIFF's *muscles*]   You're comin' home this afternoon captain of the All-Scholastic Championship Team of the City of New York.

BIFF   I got it, Pop. And remember, pal, when I take off my helmet, that touchdown is for you.

WILLY   Let's go! [*He is starting out, with his arm around* BIFF, *when* CHAR-LEY *enters, as of old, in knickers.*] I got no room for you, Charley.

CHARLEY   Room? For what?

WILLY   In the car.

CHARLEY   You goin' for a ride? I wanted to shoot some casino.

WILLY [*furiously*]   Casino! [*incredulously*] Don't you realize what today is?

LINDA   Oh, he knows, Willy. He's just kidding you.

WILLY   That's nothing to kid about!

CHARLEY   No, Linda, what's goin' on?

LINDA   He's playing in Ebbets Field.

CHARLEY   Baseball in this weather?

WILLY   Don't talk to him. Come on, come on! [*He is pushing them out.*]

CHARLEY   Wait a minute, didn't you hear the news?

WILLY   What?

CHARLEY   Don't you listen to the radio? Ebbets Field just blew up.

WILLY   You go to hell! [CHARLEY *laughs. Pushing them out*] Come on, come on! We're late.

CHARLEY [*as they go*]   Knock a homer, Biff, knock a homer!

WILLY [*the last to leave, turning to* CHARLEY]   I don't think that was funny, Charley. This is the greatest day of his life.

CHARLEY Willy, when are you going to grow up?

WILLY Yeah, heh? When this game is over, Charley, you'll be laughing out of the other side of your face. They'll be calling him another Red Grange.⁹ Twenty-five thousand a year.

CHARLEY [*kidding*] Is that so?

WILLY Yeah, that's so.

CHARLEY Well, then, I'm sorry, Willy. But tell me something.

WILLY What?

CHARLEY Who is Red Grange?

WILLY Put up your hands. Goddam you, put up your hands!
[CHARLEY, *chuckling, shakes his head and walks away, around the left corner of the stage.* WILLY *follows him. The music rises to a mocking frenzy.*]

WILLY Who the hell do you think you are, better than everybody else? You don't know everything, you big, ignorant, stupid . . . Put up your hands!
[*Light rises, on the right side of the forestage, on a small table in the reception room of* CHARLEY'S *office. Traffic sounds are heard.* BERNARD, *now mature, sits whistling to himself. A pair of tennis rackets and an overnight bag are on the floor beside him.*]

WILLY [*offstage*] What are you walking away for? Don't walk away! If you're going to say something say it to my face! I know you laugh at me behind my back. You'll laugh out of the other side of your goddam face after this game. Touchdown! Touchdown! Eighty thousand people! Touchdown! Right between the goal posts.
[BERNARD *is a quiet, earnest, but self-assured young man.* WILLY'S *voice is coming from right upstage now.* BERNARD *lowers his feet off the table and listens.* JENNY, *his father's secretary, enters.*]

JENNY [*distressed*] Say, Bernard, will you go out in the hall?

BERNARD What is that noise? Who is it?

JENNY Mr. Loman. He just got off the elevator.

BERNARD [*getting up*] Who's he arguing with?

JENNY Nobody. There's nobody with him. I can't deal with him any more, and your father gets all upset everytime he comes. I've got a lot of typing to do, and your father's waiting to sign it. Will you see him?

WILLY [*entering*] Touchdown! Touch— [*He sees* JENNY.] Jenny, Jenny, good to see you. How're ya? Workin'? Or still honest?

JENNY Fine. How've you been feeling?

WILLY Not much any more, Jenny. Ha, ha! [*He is surprised to see the rackets.*]

BERNARD Hello, Uncle Willy.

WILLY [*almost shocked*] Bernard! Well, look who's here! [*He comes quickly, guiltily to* BERNARD *and warmly shakes his hand.*]

BERNARD How are you? Good to see you.

WILLY What are you doing here?

BERNARD Oh, just stopped by to see Pop. Get off my feet till my train leaves. I'm going to Washington in a few minutes.

WILLY Is he in?

---

9. Harold Edward Grange (1903–1991), all-American halfback at the University of Illinois from 1923 to 1925, then played professionally for the Chicago Bears.

BERNARD   Yes, he's in his office with the accountant. Sit down.

WILLY [*sitting down*]   What're you going to do in Washington?

BERNARD   Oh, just a case I've got there, Willy.

WILLY   That so? [*indicating the rackets*]   You going to play tennis there?

BERNARD   I'm staying with a friend who's got a court.

WILLY   Don't say. His own tennis court. Must be fine people, I bet.

BERNARD   They are, very nice. Dad tells me Biff's in town.

WILLY [*with a big smile*]   Yeah, Biff's in. Working on a very big deal, Bernard.

BERNARD   What's Biff doing?

WILLY   Well, he's been doing very big things in the West. But he decided to establish himself here. Very big. We're having dinner. Did I hear your wife had a boy?

BERNARD   That's right. Our second.

WILLY   Two boys! What do you know!

BERNARD   What kind of a deal has Biff got?

WILLY   Well, Bill Oliver—very big sporting-goods man—he wants Biff very badly. Called him in from the West. Long distance, carte blanche, special deliveries. Your friends have their own private tennis court?

BERNARD   You still with the old firm, Willy?

WILLY [*after a pause*]   I'm—I'm overjoyed to see how you made the grade, Bernard, overjoyed. It's an encouraging thing to see a young man really—really—Looks very good for Biff—very—[*He breaks off, then*] Bernard—[*He is so full of emotion, he breaks off again.*]

BERNARD   What is it, Willy?

WILLY [*small and alone*]   What—what's the secret?

BERNARD   What secret?

WILLY   How—how did you? Why didn't he ever catch on?

BERNARD   I wouldn't know that, Willy.

WILLY [*confidentially, desperately*]   You were his friend, his boyhood friend. There's something I don't understand about it. His life ended after that Ebbets Field game. From the age of seventeen nothing good ever happened to him.

BERNARD   He never trained himself for anything.

WILLY   But he did, he did. After high school he took so many correspondence courses. Radio mechanics; television; God knows what, and never made the slightest mark.

BERNARD [*taking off his glasses*]   Willy, do you want to talk candidly?

WILLY [*rising, faces BERNARD*]   I regard you as a very brilliant man, Bernard. I value your advice.

BERNARD   Oh, the hell with the advice, Willy. I couldn't advise you. There's just one thing I've always wanted to ask you. When he was supposed to graduate, and the math teacher flunked him—

WILLY   Oh, that son-of-a-bitch ruined his life.

BERNARD   Yeah, but, Willy, all he had to do was go to summer school and make up that subject.

WILLY   That's right, that's right.

BERNARD   Did you tell him not to go to summer school?

WILLY   Me? I begged him to go. I ordered him to go!

BERNARD   Then why wouldn't he go?

WILLY Why? Why! Bernard, that question has been trailing me like a ghost for the last fifteen years. He flunked the subject, and laid down and died like a hammer hit him!

BERNARD Take it easy, kid.

WILLY Let me talk to you—I got nobody to talk to. Bernard, Bernard, was it my fault? Y'see? It keeps going around in my mind, maybe I did something to him. I got nothing to give him.

BERNARD Don't take it so hard.

WILLY Why did he lay down? What is the story there? You were his friend!

BERNARD Willy, I remember, it was June, and our grades came out. And he'd flunked math.

WILLY That son-of-a-bitch!

BERNARD No, it wasn't right then. Biff just got very angry, I remember, and he was ready to enroll in summer school.

WILLY [surprised] He was?

BERNARD He wasn't beaten by it at all. But then, Willy, he disappeared from the block for almost a month. And I got the idea that he'd gone up to New England to see you. Did he have a talk with you then?

[WILLY stares in silence.]

BERNARD Willy?

WILLY [with a strong edge of resentment in his voice] Yeah, he came to Boston. What about it?

BERNARD Well, just that when he came back—I'll never forget this, it always mystifies me. Because I'd thought so well of Biff, even though he'd always taken advantage of me. I loved him, Willy, y'know? And he came back after that month and took his sneakers—remember those sneakers with "University of Virginia" printed on them? He was so proud of those, wore them every day. And he took them down in the cellar, and burned them up in the furnace. We had a fist fight. It lasted at least half an hour. Just the two of us, punching each other down the cellar, and crying right through it. I've often thought of how strange it was that I knew he'd given up his life. What happened in Boston, Willy?

[WILLY looks at him as at an intruder.]

BERNARD I just bring it up because you asked me.

WILLY [angrily] Nothing. What do you mean, "What happened?" What's that got to do with anything?

BERNARD Well, don't get sore.

WILLY What are you trying to do, blame it on me? If a boy lays down is that my fault?

BERNARD Now, Willy, don't get—

WILLY Well, don't—don't talk to me that way! What does that mean, "What happened?"

[CHARLEY enters. He is in his vest, and he carries a bottle of bourbon.]

CHARLEY Hey, you're going to miss that train. [He waves the bottle.]

BERNARD Yeah, I'm going. [He takes the bottle.] Thanks, Pop. [He picks up his rackets and bag.] Good-by, Willy, and don't worry about it. You know, "If at first you don't succeed . . ."

WILLY Yes, I believe in that.

BERNARD But sometimes, Willy, it's better for a man just to walk away.

WILLY Walk away?

BERNARD That's right.

WILLY But if you can't walk away?

BERNARD [*after a slight pause*] I guess that's when it's tough. [*extending his hand*] Good-by, Willy.

WILLY [*shaking* BERNARD'S *hand*] Good-by, boy.

CHARLEY [*an arm on* BERNARD'S *shoulder*] How do you like this kid? Gonna argue a case in front of the Supreme Court.

BERNARD [*protesting*] Pop!

WILLY [*genuinely shocked, pained, and happy*] No! The Supreme Court!

BERNARD I gotta run. 'By, Dad!

CHARLEY Knock 'em dead, Bernard!

[BERNARD *goes off.*]

WILLY [*as* CHARLEY *takes out his wallet*] The Supreme Court! And he didn't even mention it!

CHARLEY [*counting out money on the desk*] He don't have to—he's gonna do it.

WILLY And you never told him what to do, did you? You never took any interest in him.

CHARLEY My salvation is that I never took any interest in anything. There's some money—fifty dollars. I got an accountant inside.

WILLY Charley, look . . . [*with difficulty*] I got my insurance to pay. If you can manage it—I need a hundred and ten dollars.

[CHARLEY *doesn't reply for a moment; merely stops moving.*]

WILLY I'd draw it from my bank but Linda would know, and I . . .

CHARLEY Sit down, Willy.

WILLY [*moving toward the chair*] I'm keeping an account of everything, remember. I'll pay every penny back. [*He sits.*]

CHARLEY Now listen to me, Willy.

WILLY I want you to know I appreciate . . .

CHARLEY [*sitting down on the table*] Willy, what're you doin'? What the hell is goin' on in your head?

WILLY Why? I'm simply . . .

CHARLEY I offered you a job. You can make fifty dollars a week. And I won't send you on the road.

WILLY I've got a job.

CHARLEY Without pay? What kind of job is a job without pay? [*He rises.*] Now, look kid, enough is enough. I'm no genius but I know when I'm being insulted.

WILLY Insulted!

CHARLEY Why don't you want to work for me?

WILLY What's the matter with you? I've got a job.

CHARLEY Then what're you walkin' in here every week for?

WILLY [*getting up*] Well, if you don't want me to walk in here—

CHARLEY I am offering you a job!

WILLY I don't want your goddam job!

CHARLEY When the hell are you going to grow up?

WILLY [*furiously*] You big ignoramus, if you say that to me again I'll rap you one! I don't care how big you are! [*He's ready to fight. Pause.*]

CHARLEY [*kindly, going to him*] How much do you need, Willy?

WILLY Charley, I'm strapped, I'm strapped. I don't know what to do. I was just fired.

CHARLEY Howard fired you?

WILLY That snotnose. Imagine that? I named him. I named him Howard.

CHARLEY Willy, when're you gonna realize that them things don't mean anything? You named him Howard, but you can't sell that. The only thing you got in this world is what you can sell. And the funny thing is that you're a salesman, and you don't know that.

WILLY I've always tried to think otherwise. I guess. I always felt that if a man was impressive, and well liked, that nothing—

CHARLEY Why must everybody like you? Who liked J. P. Morgan?[1] Was he impressive? In a Turkish bath he'd look like a butcher. But with his pockets on he was very well liked. Now listen, Willy, I know you don't like me, and nobody can say I'm in love with you, but I'll give you a job because—just for the hell of it, put it that way. Now what do you say?

WILLY I—I just can't work for you, Charley.

CHARLEY What're you, jealous of me?

WILLY I can't work for you, that's all, don't ask me why.

CHARLEY [angered, takes out more bills] You been jealous of me all your life, you damned fool! Here, pay your insurance. [He puts the money in WILLY's hand.]

WILLY I'm keeping strict accounts.

CHARLEY I've got some work to do. Take care of yourself. And pay your insurance.

WILLY [moving to the right] Funny, y'know? After all the highways, and the trains, and the appointments, and the years, you end up worth more dead than alive.

CHARLEY Willy, nobody's worth nothin' dead. [after a slight pause] Did you hear what I said?

[WILLY stands still, dreaming.]

CHARLEY Willy!

WILLY Apologize to Bernard for me when you see him. I didn't mean to argue with him. He's a fine boy. They're all fine boys, and they'll end up big—all of them. Someday they'll all play tennis together. Wish me luck, Charley. He saw Bill Oliver today.

CHARLEY Good luck.

WILLY [on the verge of tears] Charley, you're the only friend I got. Isn't that a remarkable thing? [He goes out.]

CHARLEY Jesus!

[CHARLEY stares after him a moment and follows. All light blacks out. Suddenly raucous music is heard, and a red glow rises behind the screen at right. STANLEY, a young waiter, appears, carrying a table, followed by HAPPY, who is carrying two chairs.]

STANLEY [putting the table down] That's all right, Mr. Loman, I can handle it myself. [He turns and takes the chairs from HAPPY and places them at the table.]

HAPPY [glancing around] Oh, this is better.

1. John Pierpont Morgan (1837–1913), American banker and philanthropist famed for his enormous wealth.

STANLEY   Sure, in the front there you're in the middle of all kinds a noise. Whenever you got a party. Mr. Loman, you just tell me and I'll put you back here. Y'know, there's a lotta people they don't like it private, because when they go out they like to see a lotta action around them because they're sick and tired to stay in the house by theirself. But I know you, you ain't from Hackensack. You know what I mean?

HAPPY [*sitting down*]   So how's it coming, Stanley?

STANLEY   Ah, it's a dog life. I only wish during the war they'd a took me in the Army. I coulda been dead by now.

HAPPY   My brother's back, Stanley.

STANLEY   Oh, he come back, heh? From the Far West.

HAPPY   Yeah, big cattle man, my brother, so treat him right. And my father's coming too.

STANLEY   Oh, your father too!

HAPPY   You got a couple of nice lobsters?

STANLEY   Hundred per cent, big.

HAPPY   I want them with the claws.

STANLEY   Don't worry, I don't give you no mice. [HAPPY *laughs*.] How about some wine? It'll put a head on the meal.

HAPPY   No. You remember, Stanley, that recipe I brought you from overseas? With the champagne in it?

STANLEY   Oh, yeah, sure. I still got it tacked up yet in the kitchen. But that'll have to cost a buck apiece anyways.

HAPPY   That's all right.

STANLEY   What'd you, hit a number or somethin'?

HAPPY   No, it's a little celebration. My brother is—I think he pulled off a big deal today. I think we're going into business together.

STANLEY   Great! That's the best for you. Because a family business, you know what I mean?—that's the best.

HAPPY   That's what I think.

STANLEY   'Cause what's the difference? Somebody steals? It's in the family. Know what I mean? [*sotto voce*][2] Like this bartender here. The boss is goin' crazy what kinda leak he's got in the cash register. You put it in but it don't come out.

HAPPY [*raising his head*]   Sh!

STANLEY   What?

HAPPY   You notice I wasn't lookin' right or left, was I?

STANLEY   No.

HAPPY   And my eyes are closed.

STANLEY   So what's the—?

HAPPY   Strudel's comin'.

STANLEY [*catching on, looks around*]   Ah, no, there's no—
[*He breaks off as a furred, lavishly dressed girl enters and sits at the next table. Both follow her with their eyes.*]

STANLEY   Geez, how'd ya know?

HAPPY   I got radar or something. [*staring directly at her profile*] Oooooooo . . . Stanley.

STANLEY   I think that's for you, Mr. Loman.

2. In an undertone [Italian].

HAPPY Look at that mouth. Oh, God. And the binoculars.

STANLEY Geez, you got a life, Mr. Loman.

HAPPY Wait on her.

STANLEY [*going to the girl's table*] Would you like a menu, ma'am?

GIRL I'm expecting someone, but I'd like a—

HAPPY Why don't you bring her—excuse me, miss, do you mind? I sell champagne, and I'd like you to try my brand. Bring her a champagne, Stanley.

GIRL That's awfully nice of you.

HAPPY Don't mention it. It's all company money. [*He laughs.*]

GIRL That's a charming product to be selling, isn't it?

HAPPY Oh, gets to be like everything else. Selling is selling, y'know.

GIRL I suppose.

HAPPY You don't happen to sell, do you?

GIRL No, I don't sell.

HAPPY Would you object to a compliment from a stranger? You ought to be on a magazine cover.

GIRL [*looking at him a little archly*] I have been.
     [STANLEY *comes in with a glass of champagne.*]

HAPPY What'd I say before, Stanley? You see? She's a cover girl.

STANLEY Oh, I could see, I could see.

HAPPY [*to the* GIRL] What magazine?

GIRL Oh, a lot of them. [*She takes the drink.*] Thank you.

HAPPY You know what they say in France, don't you? "Champagne is the drink of the complexion"—Hya, Biff!
     [BIFF *has entered and sits with* HAPPY.]

BIFF Hello, kid. Sorry I'm late.

HAPPY I just got here. Uh, Miss—?

GIRL Forsythe.

HAPPY Miss Forsythe, this is my brother.

BIFF Is Dad here?

HAPPY His name is Biff. You might've heard of him. Great football player.

GIRL Really? What team?

HAPPY Are you familiar with football?

GIRL No, I'm afraid I'm not.

HAPPY Biff is quarterback with the New York Giants.

GIRL Well, that's nice, isn't it? [*She drinks.*]

HAPPY Good health.

GIRL I'm happy to meet you.

HAPPY That's my name. Hap. It's really Harold, but at West Point they called me Happy.

GIRL [*now really impressed*] Oh, I see. How do you do? [*She turns her profile.*]

BIFF Isn't Dad coming?

HAPPY You want her?

BIFF Oh, I could never make that.

HAPPY I remember the time that idea would never come into your head. Where's the old confidence, Biff?

BIFF I just saw Oliver—

HAPPY   Wait a minute. I've got to see that old confidence again. Do you want her? She's on call.

BIFF   Oh, no. [*He turns to look at the* GIRL.]

HAPPY   I'm telling you. Watch this. [*turning to the* GIRL] Honey? [*She turns to him.*] Are you busy?

GIRL   Well, I am . . . but I could make a phone call.

HAPPY   Do that, will you, honey? And see if you can get a friend. We'll be here for a while. Biff is one of the greatest football players in the country.

GIRL [*standing up*]   Well, I'm certainly happy to meet you.

HAPPY   Come back soon.

GIRL   I'll try.

HAPPY   Don't try, honey, try hard.
        [*The* GIRL *exits.* STANLEY *follows, shaking his head in bewildered admiration.*]

HAPPY   Isn't that a shame now? A beautiful girl like that? That's why I can't get married. There's not a good woman in a thousand. New York is loaded with them, kid!

BIFF   Hap, look—

HAPPY   I told you she was on call!

BIFF [*strangely unnerved*]   Cut it out, will ya? I want to say something to you.

HAPPY   Did you see Oliver?

BIFF   I saw him all right. Now look, I want to tell Dad a couple of things and I want you to help me.

HAPPY   What? Is he going to back you?

BIFF   Are you crazy? You're out of your goddam head, you know that?

HAPPY   Why? What happened?

BIFF [*breathlessly*]   I did a terrible thing today, Hap. It's been the strangest day I ever went through. I'm all numb, I swear.

HAPPY   You mean he wouldn't see you?

BIFF   Well, I waited six hours for him, see? All day. Kept sending my name in. Even tried to date his secretary so she'd get me to him, but no soap.

HAPPY   Because you're not showin' the old confidence, Biff. He remembered you, didn't he?

BIFF [*stopping* HAPPY *with a gesture*]   Finally, about five o'clock, he comes out. Didn't remember who I was or anything. I felt like such an idiot, Hap.

HAPPY   Did you tell him my Florida idea?

BIFF   He walked away. I saw him for one minute. I got so mad I could've torn the walls down! How the hell did I ever get the idea I was a salesman there? I even believed myself that I'd been a salesman for him! And then he gave me one look and—I realized what a ridiculous lie my whole life has been! We've been talking in a dream for fifteen years. I was a shipping clerk.

HAPPY   What'd you do?

BIFF [*with great tension and wonder*]   Well, he left, see. And the secretary went out. I was all alone in the waiting-room. I don't know what came over me, Hap. The next thing I know I'm in his office—paneled walls, everything. I can't explain it. I—Hap, I took his fountain pen.

HAPPY   Geez, did he catch you?

BIFF   I ran out. I ran down all eleven flights. I ran and ran and ran.

HAPPY   That was an awful dumb—what'd you do that for?

BIFF   [*agonized*]   I don't know, I just—wanted to take something, I don't know. You gotta help me, Hap, I'm gonna tell Pop.

HAPPY   You crazy? What for?

BIFF   Hap, he's got to understand that I'm not the man somebody lends that kind of money to. He thinks I've been spiting him all these years and it's eating him up.

HAPPY   That's just it. You tell him something nice.

BIFF   I can't.

HAPPY   Say you got a lunch date with Oliver tomorrow.

BIFF   So what do I do tomorrow?

HAPPY   You leave the house tomorrow and come back at night and say Oliver is thinking it over. And he thinks it over for a couple of weeks, and gradually it fades away and nobody's the worse.

BIFF   But it'll go on forever!

HAPPY   Dad is never so happy as when he's looking forward to something! [WILLY *enters.*]

HAPPY   Hello, scout!

WILLY   Gee, I haven't been here in years! [STANLEY *has followed* WILLY *in and sets a chair for him.* STANLEY *starts off but* HAPPY *stops him.*]

HAPPY   Stanley! [STANLEY *stands by, waiting for an order.*]

BIFF   [*going to* WILLY *with guilt, as to an invalid*]   Sit down, Pop. You want a drink?

WILLY   Sure, I don't mind.

BIFF   Let's get a load on.

WILLY   You look worried.

BIFF   N-no. [*to* STANLEY] Scotch all around. Make it doubles.

STANLEY   Doubles, right. [*He goes.*]

WILLY   You had a couple already, didn't you?

BIFF   Just a couple, yeah.

WILLY   Well, what happened, boy? [*nodding affirmatively, with a smile*] Everything go all right?

BIFF   [*takes a breath, then reaches out and grasps* WILLY'S *hand*]   Pal . . . [*He is smiling bravely, and* WILLY *is smiling too.*] I had an experience today.

HAPPY   Terrific, Pop.

WILLY   That so? What happened?

BIFF   [*high, slightly alcoholic, above the earth*]   I'm going to tell you everything from first to last. It's been a strange day. [*Silence. He looks around, composes himself as best he can, but his breath keeps breaking the rhythm of his voice.*] I had to wait quite a while for him, and—

WILLY   Oliver?

BIFF   Yeah, Oliver. All day, as a matter of cold fact. And a lot of—instances—facts, Pop, facts about my life came back to me. Who was it, Pop? Who ever said I was a salesman with Oliver?

WILLY   Well, you were.

BIFF   No, Dad, I was a shipping clerk.

WILLY But you were practically—

BIFF [*with determination*] Dad, I don't know who said it first, but I was never a salesman for Bill Oliver.

WILLY What're you talking about?

BIFF Let's hold on to the facts tonight, Pop. We're not going to get anywhere bullin' around. I was a shipping clerk.

WILLY [*angrily*] All right, now listen to me—

BIFF Why don't you let me finish?

WILLY I'm not interested in stories about the past or any crap of that kind because the woods are burning, boys, you understand? There's a big blaze going on all around. I was fired today.

BIFF [*shocked*] How could you be?

WILLY I was fired, and I'm looking for a little good news to tell your mother, because the woman has waited and the woman has suffered. The gist of it is that I haven't got a story left in my head, Biff. So don't give me a lecture about facts and aspects. I am not interested. Now what've you got to say to me?

    [STANLEY *enters with three drinks. They wait until he leaves.*]

WILLY Did you see Oliver?

BIFF Jesus, Dad!

WILLY You mean you didn't go up there?

HAPPY Sure he went up there.

BIFF I did. I—saw him. How could they fire you?

WILLY [*on the edge of his chair*] What kind of a welcome did he give you?

BIFF He won't even let you work on commission?

WILLY I'm out! [*driving*] So tell me, he gave you a warm welcome?

HAPPY Sure, Pop, sure!

BIFF [*driven*] Well, it was kind of—

WILLY I was wondering if he'd remember you. [*to* HAPPY] Imagine, man doesn't see him for ten, twelve years and gives him that kind of a welcome!

HAPPY Damn right!

BIFF [*trying to return to the offensive*] Pop, look—

WILLY You know why he remembered you, don't you? Because you impressed him in those days.

BIFF Let's talk quietly and get this down to the facts, huh?

WILLY [*as though* BIFF *had been interrupting*] Well, what happened? It's great news, Biff. Did he take you into his office or'd you talk in the waiting-room?

BIFF Well, he came in, see, and—

WILLY [*with a big smile*] What'd he say? Betcha he threw his arm around you.

BIFF Well, he kinda—

WILLY He's a fine man. [*to* HAPPY] Very hard man to see, y'know.

HAPPY [*agreeing*] Oh, I know.

WILLY [*to* BIFF] Is that where you had the drinks?

BIFF Yeah, he gave me a couple of—no, no!

HAPPY [*cutting in*] He told him my Florida idea.

WILLY Don't interrupt. [*to* BIFF] How'd he react to the Florida idea?

BIFF Dad, will you give me a minute to explain?

WILLY I've been waiting for you to explain since I sat down here! What happened? He took you into his office and what?

BIFF Well—I talked. And—he listened, see.

WILLY Famous for the way he listens, y'know. What was his answer?

BIFF His answer was— [*He breaks off, suddenly angry.*] Dad, you're not letting me tell you what I want to tell you!

WILLY [*accusing, angered*] You didn't see him, did you?

BIFF I did see him!

WILLY What'd you insult him or something? You insulted him, didn't you?

BIFF Listen, will you let me out of it, will you just let me out of it!

HAPPY What the hell!

WILLY Tell me what happened!

BIFF [*to* HAPPY] I can't talk to him!

> [*A single trumpet note jars the ear. The light of green leaves stains the house, which holds the air of night and a dream.* YOUNG BERNARD *enters and knocks on the door of the house.*]

YOUNG BERNARD [*frantically*] Mrs. Loman, Mrs. Loman!

HAPPY Tell him what happened!

BIFF [*to* HAPPY] Shut up and leave me alone!

WILLY No, no. You had to go and flunk math!

BIFF What math? What're you talking about?

YOUNG BERNARD Mrs. Loman, Mrs. Loman!

> [LINDA *appears in the house, as of old.*]

WILLY [*wildly*] Math, math, math!

BIFF Take it easy, Pop!

YOUNG BERNARD Mrs. Loman!

WILLY [*furiously*] If you hadn't flunked you'd've been set by now!

BIFF Now, look, I'm gonna tell you what happened, and you're going to listen to me.

YOUNG BERNARD Mrs. Loman!

BIFF I waited six hours—

HAPPY What the hell are you saying?

BIFF I kept sending in my name but he wouldn't see me. So finally he . . .

> [*He continues unheard as light fades low on the restaurant.*]

YOUNG BERNARD Biff flunked math!

LINDA No!

YOUNG BERNARD Birnbaum flunked him! They won't graduate him!

LINDA But they have to. He's gotta go to the university. Where is he? Biff! Biff!

YOUNG BERNARD No, he left. He went to Grand Central.

LINDA Grand—You mean he went to Boston!

YOUNG BERNARD Is Uncle Willy in Boston?

LINDA Oh, maybe Willy can talk to the teacher. Oh, the poor, poor boy!

> [*Light on house area snaps out.*]

BIFF [*at the table, now audible, holding up a gold fountain pen*] . . . so I'm washed up with Oliver, you understand? Are you listening to me?

WILLY [*at a loss*] Yeah, sure. If you hadn't flunked—

BIFF Flunked what? What're you talking about?

WILLY Don't blame everything on me! I didn't flunk math—you did! What pen?

HAPPY   That was awful dumb, Biff, a pen like that is worth—

WILLY [*seeing the pen for the first time*]   You took Oliver's pen?

BIFF [*weakening*]   Dad, I just explained it to you.

WILLY   You stole Bill Oliver's fountain pen!

BIFF   I didn't exactly steal it! That's just what I've been explaining to you!

HAPPY   He had it in his hand and just then Oliver walked in, so he got nervous and stuck it in his pocket!

WILLY   My God, Biff!

BIFF   I never intended to do it, Dad!

OPERATOR'S VOICE   Standish Arms, good evening!

WILLY [*shouting*]   I'm not in my room!

BIFF [*frightened*]   Dad, what's the matter? [*He and* HAPPY *stand up.*]

OPERATOR   Ringing Mr. Loman for you!

WILLY   I'm not there, stop it!

BIFF [*horrified, gets down on one knee before* WILLY]   Dad, I'll make good, I'll make good. [WILLY *tries to get to his feet.* BIFF *holds him down.*] Sit down now.

WILLY   No, you're no good, you're no good for anything.

BIFF   I am, Dad, I'll find something else, you understand? Now don't worry about anything. [*He holds up* WILLY's *face.*] Talk to me, Dad.

OPERATOR   Mr. Loman does not answer. Shall I page him?

WILLY [*attempting to stand, as though to rush and silence the* OPERATOR]   No, no, no!

HAPPY   He'll strike something, Pop.

WILLY   No, no . . .

BIFF [*desperately, standing over* WILLY]   Pop, listen! Listen to me! I'm telling you something good. Oliver talked to his partner about the Florida idea. You listening? He—he talked to his partner, and he came to me . . . I'm going to be all right, you hear? Dad, listen to me, he said it was just a question of the amount!

WILLY   Then you . . . got it?

HAPPY   He's gonna be terrific, Pop!

WILLY [*trying to stand*]   Then you got it, haven't you? You got it! You got it!

BIFF [*agonized, holds* WILLY *down*]   No, no. Look, Pop. I'm supposed to have lunch with them tomorrow. I'm just telling you this so you'll know that I can still make an impression, Pop. And I'll make good somewhere, but I can't go tomorrow, see?

WILLY   Why not? You simply—

BIFF   But the pen, Pop!

WILLY   You give it to him and tell him it was an oversight!

HAPPY   Sure, have lunch tomorrow!

BIFF   I can't say that—

WILLY   You were doing a crossword puzzle and accidentally used his pen!

BIFF   Listen, kid, I took those balls years ago, now I walk in with his fountain pen? That clinches it, don't you see? I can't face him like that! I'll try elsewhere.

PAGE'S VOICE   Paging Mr. Loman!

WILLY   Don't you want to be anything?

BIFF   Pop, how can I go back?

WILLY   You don't want to be anything, is that what's behind it?

BIFF [*now angry at* WILLY *for not crediting his sympathy*] Don't take it that way! You think it was easy walking into that office after what I'd done to him? A team of horses couldn't have dragged me back to Bill Oliver!

WILLY Then why'd you go?

BIFF Why did I go? Why did I go! Look at you! Look at what's become of you!

[*Off left,* THE WOMAN *laughs.*]

WILLY Biff, you're going to go to that lunch tomorrow, or—

BIFF I can't go. I've got no appointment!

HAPPY Biff for . . . !

WILLY Are you spiting me?

BIFF Don't take it that way! Goddammit!

WILLY [*strikes* BIFF *and falters away from the table*] You rotten little louse! Are you spiting me?

THE WOMAN Someone's at the door, Willy!

BIFF I'm no good, can't you see what I am?

HAPPY [*separating them*] Hey, you're in a restaurant! Now cut it out, both of you? [*The girls enter.*] Hello, girls, sit down.

[THE WOMAN *laughs, off left.*]

MISS FORSYTHE I guess we might as well. This is Letta.

THE WOMAN Willy, are you going to wake up?

BIFF [*ignoring* WILLY] How're ya, miss, sit down. What do you drink?

MISS FORSYTHE Letta might not be able to stay long.

LETTA I gotta get up early tomorrow. I got jury duty. I'm so excited! Were you fellows ever on a jury?

BIFF No, but I been in front of them! [*The girls laugh.*] This is my father.

LETTA Isn't he cute? Sit down with us, Pop.

HAPPY Sit him down, Biff!

BIFF [*going to him*] Come on, slugger, drink us under the table. To hell with it! Come on, sit down, pal.

[*On* BIFF's *last insistence,* WILLY *is about to sit.*]

THE WOMAN [*now urgently*] Willy, are you going to answer the door!

[THE WOMAN's *call pulls* WILLY *back. He starts right, befuddled.*]

BIFF Hey, where are you going?

WILLY Open the door.

BIFF The door?

WILLY The washroom . . . the door . . . where's the door?

BIFF [*leading* WILLY *to the left*] Just go straight down.

[WILLY *moves left.*]

THE WOMAN Willy, Willy, are you going to get up, get up, get up, get up?

[WILLY *exits left.*]

LETTA I think it's sweet you bring your daddy along.

MISS FORSYTHE Oh, he isn't really your father!

BIFF [*at left, turning to her resentfully*] Miss Forsythe, you've just seen a prince walk by. A fine, troubled prince. A hard-working, unappreciated prince. A pal, you understand? A good companion. Always for his boys.

LETTA That's so sweet.

HAPPY Well, girls, what's the program? We're wasting time. Come on, Biff. Gather round. Where would you like to go?

BIFF Why don't you do something for him?

HAPPY Me!

BIFF Don't you give a damn for him, Hap?

HAPPY What're you talking about? I'm the one who—

BIFF I sense it, you don't give a good goddam about him. [*He takes the rolled-up hose from his pocket and puts it on the table in front of* HAPPY.] Look what I found in the cellar, for Christ's sake. How can you bear to let it go on?

HAPPY Me? Who goes away? Who runs off and—

BIFF Yeah, but he doesn't mean anything to you. You could help him—I can't! Don't you understand what I'm talking about? He's going to kill himself, don't you know that?

HAPPY Don't I know it! Me!

BIFF Hap, help him! Jesus . . . help him . . . Help me, help me, I can't bear to look at his face! [*Ready to weep, he hurries out, up right.*]

HAPPY [*starting after him*] Where are you going?

MISS FORSYTHE What's he so mad about?

HAPPY Come on, girls, we'll catch up with him.

MISS FORSYTHE [*as* HAPPY *pushes her out*] Say, I don't like that temper of his!

HAPPY He's just a little overstrung, he'll be all right!

WILLY [*off left, as* THE WOMAN *laughs*] Don't answer! Don't answer!

LETTA Don't you want to tell your father—

HAPPY No, that's not my father. He's just a guy. Come on, we'll catch Biff, and, honey, we're going to paint this town! Stanley, where's the check! Hey, Stanley!

[*They exit.* STANLEY *looks toward left.*]

STANLEY [*calling to* HAPPY *indignantly*] Mr. Loman! Mr. Loman!

[STANLEY *picks up a chair and follows them off. Knocking is heard off left.* THE WOMAN *enters, laughing.* WILLY *follows her. She is in a black slip; he is buttoning his shirt. Raw, sensuous music accompanies their speech.*]

WILLY Will you stop laughing? Will you stop?

THE WOMAN Aren't you going to answer the door? He'll wake the whole hotel.

WILLY I'm not expecting anybody.

THE WOMAN Whyn't you have another drink, honey, and stop being so damn self-centered?

WILLY I'm so lonely.

THE WOMAN You know you ruined me, Willy? From now on, whenever you come to the office, I'll see that you go right through to the buyers. No waiting at my desk any more, Willy. You ruined me.

WILLY That's nice of you to say that.

THE WOMAN Gee, you are self-centered! Why so sad? You are the saddest, self-centeredest soul I ever did see-saw. [*She laughs. He kisses her.*] Come on inside, drummer boy. It's silly to be dressing in the middle of the night. [*As knocking is heard*] Aren't you going to answer the door?

WILLY They're knocking on the wrong door.

THE WOMAN But I felt the knocking. And he heard us talking in here. Maybe the hotel's on fire!

WILLY [*his terror rising*] It's a mistake.

THE WOMAN Then tell them to go away!

WILLY There's nobody there.

THE WOMAN It's getting on my nerves, Willy. There's somebody standing out there and it's getting on my nerves!

WILLY [*pushing her away from him*] All right, stay in the bathroom here, and don't come out. I think there's a law in Massachusetts about it, so don't come out. It may be that new room clerk. He looked very mean. So don't come out. It's a mistake, there's no fire.

> [*The knocking is heard again. He takes a few steps away from her, and she vanishes into the wing. The light follows him, and now he is facing* YOUNG BIFF, *who carries a suitcase.* BIFF *steps toward him. The music is gone.*]

BIFF Why didn't you answer?

WILLY Biff! What are you doing in Boston?

BIFF Why didn't you answer? I've been knocking for five minutes, I called you on the phone—

WILLY I just heard you. I was in the bathroom and had the door shut. Did anything happen home?

BIFF Dad—I let you down.

WILLY What do you mean?

BIFF Dad . . .

WILLY Biffo, what's this about? [*putting his arm around* BIFF] Come on, let's go downstairs and get you a malted.

BIFF Dad, I flunked math.

WILLY Not for the term?

BIFF The term. I haven't got enough credits to graduate.

WILLY You mean to say Bernard wouldn't give you the answers?

BIFF He did, he tried, but I only got a sixty-one.

WILLY And they wouldn't give you four points?

BIFF Birnbaum refused absolutely. I begged him, Pop, but he won't give me those points. You gotta talk to him before they close the school. Because if he saw the kind of man you are, and you just talked to him in your way, I'm sure he'd come through for me. The class came right before practice, see, and I didn't go enough. Would you talk to him? He'd like you, Pop. You know the way you could talk.

WILLY You're on. We'll drive right back.

BIFF Oh, Dad, good work! I'm sure he'll change for you!

WILLY Go downstairs and tell the clerk I'm checkin' out. Go right down.

BIFF Yes, sir! See, the reason he hates me, Pop—one day he was late for class so I got up at the blackboard and imitated him. I crossed my eyes and talked with a lithp.

WILLY [*laughing*] You did? The kids like it?

BIFF They nearly died laughing!

WILLY Yeah? What'd you do?

BIFF The thquare root of thixthy twee is . . . [WILLY *bursts out laughing;* BIFF *joins him.*] And in the middle of it he walked in!

> [WILLY *laughs and* THE WOMAN *joins in offstage.*]

WILLY [*without hesitation*] Hurry downstairs and—

BIFF Somebody in there?

WILLY No, that was next door.

[THE WOMAN *laughs offstage.*]

BIFF   Somebody got in your bathroom!

WILLY   No, it's the next room, there's a party—

THE WOMAN [*enters laughing. She lisps this*]   Can I come in? There's something in the bathtub, Willy, and it's moving!

   [WILLY *looks at* BIFF, *who is staring open-mouthed and horrified at* THE WOMAN.]

WILLY   Ah—you better go back to your room. They must be finished painting by now. They're painting her room so I let her take a shower here. Go back, go back . . . [*He pushes her.*]

THE WOMAN [*resisting*]   But I've got to get dressed, Willy, I can't—

WILLY   Get out of here! Go back, go back . . . [*suddenly striving for the ordinary*] This is Miss Francis, Biff, she's a buyer. They're painting her room. Go back, Miss Francis, go back . . .

THE WOMAN   But my clothes, I can't go out naked in the hall!

WILLY [*pushing her offstage*]   Get outa here! Go back, go back!

   [BIFF *slowly sits down on his suitcase as the argument continues offstage.*]

THE WOMAN   Where's my stockings? You promised me stockings, Willy!

WILLY   I have no stockings here!

THE WOMAN   You had two boxes of size nine sheers for me, and I want them!

WILLY   Here, for God's sake, will you get outa here!

THE WOMAN [*enters holding a box of stockings*]   I just hope there's nobody in the hall. That's all I hope. [*to* BIFF] Are you football or baseball?

BIFF   Football.

THE WOMAN [*angry, humiliated*]   That's me too. G'night. [*She snatches her clothes from* WILLY, *and walks out.*]

WILLY [*after a pause*]   Well, better get going. I want to get to the school first thing in the morning. Get my suits out of the closet. I'll get my valise. [BIFF *doesn't move.*] What's the matter? [BIFF *remains motionless, tears falling.*] She's a buyer. Buys for J. H. Simmons. She lives down the hall—they're painting. You don't imagine— [*He breaks off. After a pause*] Now listen, pal, she's just a buyer. She sees merchandise in her room and they have to keep it looking just so . . . [*Pause. Assuming command*] All right, get my suits. [BIFF *doesn't move.*] Now stop crying and do as I say. I gave you an order. Biff, I gave you an order! Is that what you do when I give you an order? How dare you cry! [*putting his arm around* BIFF] Now look, Biff, when you grow up you'll understand about these things. You mustn't—you mustn't overemphasize a thing like this. I'll see Birnbaum first thing in the morning.

BIFF   Never mind.

WILLY [*getting down beside* BIFF]   Never mind! He's going to give you those points. I'll see to it.

BIFF   He wouldn't listen to you.

WILLY   He certainly will listen to me. You need those points for the U. of Virginia.

BIFF   I'm not going there.

WILLY   Heh? If I can't get him to change that mark you'll make it up in summer school. You've got all summer to—

BIFF [*his weeping breaking from him*]   Dad . . .

WILLY [*infected by it*]   Oh, my boy . . .

BIFF   Dad . . .

WILLY   She's nothing to me, Biff. I was lonely, I was terribly lonely.

BIFF   You—you gave her Mama's stockings! [*His tears break through and he rises to go.*]

WILLY [*grabbing for* BIFF]   I gave you an order!

BIFF   Don't touch me, you—liar!

WILLY   Apologize for that!

BIFF   You fake! You phony little fake! You fake! [*Overcome, he turns quickly and weeping fully goes out with his suitcase,* WILLY *is left on the floor on his knees.*]

WILLY   I gave you an order! Biff, come back here or I'll beat you! Come back here! I'll whip you!

[STANLEY *comes quickly in from the right and stands in front of* WILLY.]

WILLY [*shouts at* STANLEY]   I gave you an order . . .

STANLEY   Hey, let's pick it up, pick it up, Mr. Loman. [*He helps* WILLY *to his feet.*] Your boys left with the chippies. They said they'll see you home.

[*A second waiter watches some distance away.*]

WILLY   But we were supposed to have dinner together.

[*Music is heard,* WILLY's *theme.*]

STANLEY   Can you make it?

WILLY   I'll—sure, I can make it. [*suddenly concerned about his clothes*] Do I—I look all right?

STANLEY   Sure, you look all right. [*He flicks a speck off* WILLY's *lapel.*]

WILLY   Here—here's a dollar.

STANLEY   Oh, your son paid me. It's all right.

WILLY [*putting it in* STANLEY's *hand*]   No, take it. You're a good boy.

STANLEY   Oh, no, you don't have to . . .

WILLY   Here—here's some more, I don't need it any more, [*after a slight pause*] Tell me—is there a seed store in the neighborhood?

STANLEY   Seeds? You mean like to plant?

[*As* WILLY *turns,* STANLEY *slips the money back into his jacket pocket.*]

WILLY   Yes. Carrots, peas . . .

STANLEY   Well, there's hardware stores on Sixth Avenue, but it may be too late now.

WILLY [*anxiously*]   Oh, I'd better hurry. I've got to get some seeds. [*He starts off to the right.*] I've got to get some seeds, right away. Nothing's planted. I don't have a thing in the ground.

[WILLY *hurries out as the light goes down.* STANLEY *moves over to the right after him, watches him off. The other waiter has been staring at* WILLY.]

STANLEY [*to the waiter*]   Well, whatta you looking at?

[*The waiter picks up the chairs and moves off right.* STANLEY *takes the table and follows him. The light fades on this area. There is a long pause, the sound of the flute coming over. The light gradually rises on the kitchen, which is empty.* HAPPY *appears at the door of the house, followed by* BIFF. HAPPY *is carrying a large bunch of long-stemmed roses. He enters the kitchen, looks around for* LINDA. *Not seeing her, he turns to* BIFF, *who is just outside the house door, and makes a gesture with his hands, indicating "Not here, I guess." He looks into the living-room and freezes. Inside,* LINDA, *unseen, is seated,* WILLY's *coat on her lap. She rises omi-*

nously and quietly and moves toward HAPPY, *who backs up into the kitchen, afraid.*]

HAPPY Hey, what're you doing up? [LINDA *says nothing but moves toward him implacably.*] Where's Pop? [*He keeps backing to the right, and now* LINDA *is in full view in the doorway to the living-room.*] Is he sleeping?

LINDA Where were you?

HAPPY [*trying to laugh it off*] We met two girls, Mom, very fine types. Here, we brought you some flowers. [*offering them to her*] Put them in your room, Ma.

[*She knocks them to the floor at* BIFF'*s feet. He has now come inside and closed the door behind him. She stares at* BIFF, *silent.*]

HAPPY Now what'd you do that for? Mom, I want you to have some flowers—

LINDA [*cutting* HAPPY *off, violently to* BIFF] Don't you care whether he lives or dies?

HAPPY [*going to the stairs*] Come upstairs, Biff.

BIFF [*with a flare of disgust, to* HAPPY] Go away from me! [*to* LINDA] What do you mean, lives or dies? Nobody's dying around here, pal.

LINDA Get out of my sight! Get out of here!

BIFF I wanna see the boss.

LINDA You're not going near him!

BIFF Where is he? [*He moves into the living-room and* LINDA *follows.*]

LINDA [*shouting after* BIFF] You invite him for dinner. He looks forward to it all day—[BIFF *appears in his parents' bedroom, looks around and exits*]— and then you desert him there. There's no stranger you'd do that to!

HAPPY Why? He had a swell time with us. Listen, when I—[LINDA *comes back into the kitchen*]—desert him I hope I don't outlive the day!

LINDA Get out of here!

HAPPY Now look, Mom . . .

LINDA Did you have to go to women tonight? You and your lousy rotten whores!

[BIFF *re-enters the kitchen.*]

HAPPY Mom, all we did was follow Biff around trying to cheer him up! [*to* BIFF] Boy, what a night you gave me!

LINDA Get out of here, both of you, and don't come back! I don't want you tormenting him any more. Go on now, get your things together! [*to* BIFF] You can sleep in his apartment. [*She starts to pick up the flowers and stops herself.*] Pick up this stuff, I'm not your maid any more. Pick it up, you bum, you!

[HAPPY *turns his back to her in refusal.* BIFF *slowly moves over and gets down on his knees, picking up the flowers.*]

LINDA You're a pair of animals! Not one, not another living soul would have had the cruelty to walk out on that man in a restaurant!

BIFF [*not looking at her*] Is that what he said?

LINDA He didn't have to say anything. He was so humiliated he nearly limped when he came in.

HAPPY But, Mom, he had a great time with us—

BIFF [*cutting him off violently*] Shut up!

[*Without another word,* HAPPY *goes upstairs.*]

LINDA You! You didn't even go in to see if he was all right!

BIFF [*still on the floor in front of* LINDA, *the flowers in his hand; with self-loathing*]   No. Didn't. Didn't do a damned thing. How do you like that, heh? Left him babbling in a toilet.

LINDA   You louse. You . . .

BIFF   Now you hit it on the nose! [*He gets up, throws the flowers in the waste-basket.*] The scum of the earth, and you're looking at him!

LINDA   Get out of here!

BIFF   I gotta talk to the boss, Mom. Where is he?

LINDA   You're not going near him. Get out of this house!

BIFF   [*with absolute assurance, determination*]   No. We're gonna have an abrupt conversation, him and me.

LINDA   You're not talking to him!
[*Hammering is heard from outside the house, off right.* BIFF *turns toward the noise.*]

LINDA [*suddenly pleading*]   Will you please leave him alone?

BIFF   What's he doing out there?

LINDA   He's planting the garden!

BIFF [*quietly*]   Now? Oh, my God!
[BIFF *moves outside,* LINDA *following. The light dies down on them and comes up on the center of the apron as* WILLY *walks into it. He is carrying a flashlight, a hoe, and a handful of seed packets. He raps the top of the hoe sharply to fix it firmly, and then moves to the left, measuring off the distance with his foot. He holds the flashlight to look at the seed packets, reading off the instructions. He is in the blue of night.*]

WILLY   Carrots . . . quarter-inch apart. Rows . . . one-foot rows. [*He measures it off.*] One foot. [*He puts down a package and measures off.*] Beets. [*He puts down another package and measures again.*] Lettuce. [*He reads the package, puts it down.*] One foot— [*He breaks off as* BEN *appears at the right and moves slowly down to him.*] What a proposition, ts, ts. Terrific, terrific. 'Cause she's suffered, Ben, the woman has suffered. You understand me? A man can't go out the way he came in, Ben, a man has got to add up to something. You can't, you can't— [BEN *moves toward him as though to interrupt.*] You gotta consider, now. Don't answer so quick. Remember, it's a guaranteed twenty-thousand-dollar proposition. Now look, Ben, I want you to go through the ins and outs of this thing with me. I've got nobody to talk to, Ben, and the woman has suffered, you hear me?

BEN [*standing still, considering*]   What's the proposition?

WILLY   It's twenty thousand dollars on the barrelhead. Guaranteed, gilt-edged, you understand?

BEN   You don't want to make a fool of yourself. They might not honor the policy.

WILLY   How can they dare refuse? Didn't I work like a coolie to meet every premium on the nose? And now they don't pay off! Impossible!

BEN   It's called a cowardly thing, William.

WILLY   Why? Does it take more guts to stand here the rest of my life ringing up a zero?

BEN [*yielding*]   That's a point, William. [*He moves, thinking, turns.*] And twenty thousand—that *is* something one can feel with the hand, it is there.

WILLY [*now assured, with rising power*]   Oh, Ben, that's the whole beauty
of it! I see it like a diamond, shining in the dark, hard and rough, that I
can pick up and touch in my hand. Not like—like an appointment! This
would not be another damned-fool appointment, Ben, and it changes all
the aspects. Because he thinks I'm nothing, see, and so he spites me.
But the funeral— [*straightening up*] Ben, that funeral will be massive!
They'll come from Maine, Massachusetts, Vermont, New Hampshire! All
the old-timers with the strange license plates—that boy will be thunder-
struck, Ben, because he never realized—I am known! Rhode Island, New
York, New Jersey—I am known, Ben, and he'll see it with his eyes once
and for all. He'll see what I am, Ben! He's in for a shock, that boy!
BEN [*coming down to the edge of the garden*]   He'll call you a coward.
WILLY [*suddenly fearful*]   No, that would be terrible.
BEN   Yes. And a damned fool.
WILLY   No, no, he mustn't, I won't have that! [*He is broken and desperate.*]
BEN   He'll hate you, William.
  [*The gay music of the Boys is heard.*]
WILLY   Oh, Ben, how do we get back to all the great times? Used to be so
full of light, and comradeship, the sleigh-riding in winter, and the rud-
diness on his cheeks. And always some kind of good news coming up,
always something nice coming up ahead. And never even let me carry
the valises in the house, and simonizing, simonizing that little red car!
Why, why can't I give him something and not have him hate me?
BEN   Let me think about it. [*He glances at his watch.*] I still have a little
time. Remarkable proposition, but you've got to be sure you're not making a fool of yourself.
  [BEN *drifts off upstage and goes out of sight.* BIFF *comes down from the
  left.*]
WILLY [*suddenly conscious of* BIFF, *turns and looks up at him, then begins
picking up the packages of seeds in confusion*]   Where the hell is that
seed? [*indignantly*] You can't see nothing out here! They boxed in the
whole goddam neighborhood!
BIFF   There are people all around here. Don't you realize that?
WILLY   I'm busy. Don't bother me.
BIFF [*taking the hoe from* WILLY]   I'm saying good-by to you, Pop. [WILLY
looks at him, silent, unable to move.] I'm not coming back any more.
WILLY   You're not going to see Oliver tomorrow?
BIFF   I've got no appointment, Dad.
WILLY   He put his arm around you, and you've got no appointment?
BIFF   Pop, get this now, will you? Everytime I've left it's been a fight that
sent me out of here. Today I realized something about myself and I tried
to explain it to you and I—I think I'm just not smart enough to make any
sense out of it for you. To hell with whose fault it is or anything like that.
[*He takes* WILLY's *arm.*] Let's just wrap it up, heh? Come on in, we'll tell
Mom. [*He gently tries to pull* WILLY *to left.*]
WILLY [*frozen, immobile, with guilt in his voice*]   No, I don't want to see her.
BIFF   Come on! [*He pulls again, and* WILLY *tries to pull away.*]
WILLY [*highly nervous*]   No, no, I don't want to see her.
BIFF [*tries to look into* WILLY's *face, as if to find the answer there*]   Why
don't you want to see her?

WILLY [*more harshly now*]   Don't bother me, will you?

BIFF   What do you mean, you don't want to see her? You don't want them calling you yellow, do you? This isn't your fault; it's me, I'm a bum. Now come inside! [WILLY *strains to get away.*] Did you hear what I said to you?

>   [WILLY *pulls away and quickly goes by himself into the house.* BIFF *follows.*]

LINDA [*to* WILLY]   Did you plant, dear?

BIFF [*at the door, to* LINDA]   All right, we had it out. I'm going and I'm not writing any more.

LINDA [*going to* WILLY *in the kitchen*]   I think that's the best way, dear. 'Cause there's no use drawing it out, you'll just never get along.

>   [WILLY *doesn't respond.*]

BIFF   People ask where I am and what I'm doing, you don't know, and you don't care. That way it'll be off your mind and you can start brightening up again. All right? That clears it, doesn't it? [WILLY *is silent, and* BIFF *goes to him.*] You gonna wish me luck, scout? [*He extends his hand.*] What do you say?

LINDA   Shake his hand, Willy.

WILLY [*turning to her, seething with hurt*]   There's no necessity to mention the pen at all, y'know.

BIFF [*gently*]   I've got no appointment, Dad.

WILLY [*erupting fiercely*]   He put his arm around . . . ?

BIFF   Dad, you're never going to see what I am, so what's the use of arguing? If I strike oil I'll send you a check. Meantime forget I'm alive.

WILLY [*to* LINDA]   Spite, see?

BIFF   Shake hands, Dad.

WILLY   Not my hand.

BIFF   I was hoping not to go this way.

WILLY   Well, this is the way you're going. Good-by.

>   [BIFF *looks at him a moment, then turns sharply and goes to the stairs.*]

WILLY [*stops him with*]   May you rot in hell if you leave this house!

BIFF [*turning*]   Exactly what is it that you want from me?

WILLY   I want you to know, on the train, in the mountains, in the valleys, wherever you go, that you cut down your life for spite!

BIFF   No, no.

WILLY   Spite, spite, is the word of your undoing! And when you're down and out, remember what did it. When you're rotting somewhere beside the railroad tracks, remember, and don't you dare blame it on me!

BIFF   I'm not blaming it on you!

WILLY   I won't take the rap for this, you hear?

>   [HAPPY *comes down the stairs and stands on the bottom step, watching.*]

BIFF   That's just what I'm telling you!

WILLY [*sinking into a chair at the table, with full accusation*]   You're trying to put a knife in me—don't think I don't know what you're doing!

BIFF   All right, phony! Then let's lay it on the line. [*He whips the rubber tube out of his pocket and puts it on the table.*]

HAPPY   You crazy—

LINDA   Biff! [*She moves to grab the hose, but* BIFF *holds it down with his hand.*]

BIFF   Leave it there! Don't move it!

WILLY [*not looking at it*]   What is that?

BIFF   You know goddam well what that is.

WILLY [*caged, wanting to escape*]   I never saw that.

BIFF   You saw it. The mice didn't bring it into the cellar! What is this supposed to do, make a hero out of you? This supposed to make me sorry for you?

WILLY   Never heard of it.

BIFF   There'll be no pity for you, you hear it? No pity!

WILLY [*to* LINDA]   You hear the spite!

BIFF   No, you're going to hear the truth—what you are and what I am!

LINDA   Stop it!

WILLY   Spite!

HAPPY [*coming down toward* BIFF]   You cut it now!

BIFF [*to* HAPPY]   The man don't know who we are! The man is gonna know! [*to* WILLY] We never told the truth for ten minutes in this house!

HAPPY   We always told the truth!

BIFF [*turning on him*]   You big blow, are you the assistant buyer? You're one of the two assistants to the assistant, aren't you?

HAPPY   Well, I'm practically—

BIFF   You're practically full of it! We all are! And I'm through with it. [*to* WILLY] Now hear this, Willy, this is me.

WILLY   I know you!

BIFF   You know why I had no address for three months? I stole a suit in Kansas City and I was in jail. [*to* LINDA, *who is sobbing*] Stop crying. I'm through with it.

[LINDA *turns away from them, her hands covering her face.*]

WILLY   I suppose that's my fault!

BIFF   I stole myself out of every good job since high school!

WILLY   And whose fault is that?

BIFF   And I never got anywhere because you blew me so full of hot air I could never stand taking orders from anybody! That's whose fault it is!

WILLY   I hear that!

LINDA   Don't, Biff!

BIFF   It's goddam time you heard that! I had to be boss big shot in two weeks, and I'm through with it!

WILLY   Then hang yourself! For spite, hang yourself!

BIFF   No! Nobody's hanging himself, Willy! I ran down eleven flights with a pen in my hand today. And suddenly I stopped, you hear me? And in the middle of that office building, do you hear this? I stopped in the middle of that building and I saw—the sky. I saw the things that I love in this world. The work and the food and time to sit and smoke. And I looked at the pen and said to myself, what the hell am I grabbing this for? Why am I trying to become what I don't want to be? What am I doing in an office, making a contemptuous, begging fool of myself, when all I want is out there, waiting for me the minute I say I know who I am! Why can't I say that, Willy? [*He tries to make* WILLY *face him, but* WILLY *pulls away and moves to the left.*]

WILLY [*with hatred, threateningly*]   The door of your life is wide open!

BIFF   Pop! I'm a dime a dozen, and so are you!

WILLY [*turning on him now in an uncontrolled outburst*] I am not a dime a dozen! I am Willy Loman, and you are Biff Loman!

[BIFF *starts for* WILLY, *but is blocked by* HAPPY. *In his fury,* BIFF *seems on the verge of attacking his father.*]

BIFF I am not a leader of men, Willy, and neither are you. You were never anything but a hard-working drummer who landed in the ash can like all the rest of them! I'm one dollar an hour, Willy! I tried seven states and couldn't raise it. A buck an hour! Do you gather my meaning? I'm not bringing home any prizes any more, and you're going to stop waiting for me to bring them home!

WILLY [*directly to* BIFF] You vengeful, spiteful mut!

[BIFF *breaks from* HAPPY. WILLY, *in fright, starts up the stairs.* BIFF *grabs him.*]

BIFF [*at the peak of his fury*] Pop, I'm nothing! I'm nothing, Pop. Can't you understand that? There's no spite in it any more. I'm just what I am, that's all.

[BIFF's *fury has spent itself, and he breaks down, sobbing, holding on to* WILLY, *who dumbly fumbles for* BIFF's *face.*]

WILLY [*astonished*] What're you doing? What're you doing? [*to* LINDA] Why is he crying?

BIFF [*crying, broken*] Will you let me go, for Christ's sake? Will you take that phony dream and burn it before something happens? [*Struggling to contain himself, he pulls away and moves to the stairs.*] I'll go in the morning. Put him—put him to bed. [*Exhausted,* BIFF *moves up the stairs to his room.*]

WILLY [*after a long pause, astonished, elevated*] Isn't that—isn't that remarkable? Biff—he likes me!

LINDA He loves you, Willy!

HAPPY [*deeply moved*] Always did, Pop.

WILLY Oh, Biff! [*staring wildly*] He cried! Cried to me. [*He is choking with his love, and now cries out his promise.*] That boy—that boy is going to be magnificent!

[BEN *appears in the light just outside the kitchen.*]

BEN Yes, outstanding, with twenty thousand behind him.

LINDA [*sensing the racing of his mind, fearfully, carefully*] Now come to bed, Willy. It's all settled now.

WILLY [*finding it difficult not to rush out of the house*] Yes, we'll sleep. Come on. Go to sleep, Hap.

BEN And it does take a great kind of a man to crack the jungle.

[*In accents of dread,* BEN's *idyllic music starts up.*]

HAPPY [*his arm around* LINDA] I'm getting married, Pop, don't forget it. I'm changing everything. I'm gonna run that department before the year is up. You'll see, Mom. [*He kisses her.*]

BEN The jungle is dark but full of diamonds, Willy.

[WILLY *turns, moves, listening to* BEN.]

LINDA Be good. You're both good boys, just act that way, that's all.

HAPPY 'Night, Pop. [*He goes upstairs.*]

LINDA [*to* WILLY] Come, dear.

BEN [*with greater force*] One must go in to fetch a diamond out.

WILLY [*to* LINDA, *as he moves slowly along the edge of the kitchen, toward the door*] I just want to get settled down, Linda. Let me sit alone for a little.

LINDA [*almost uttering her fear*]   I want you upstairs.

WILLY [*taking her in his arms*]   In a few minutes, Linda. I couldn't sleep right now. Go on, you look awful tired. [*He kisses her.*]

BEN   Not like an appointment at all. A diamond is rough and hard to the touch.

WILLY   Go on now. I'll be right up.

LINDA   I think this is the only way, Willy.

WILLY   Sure, it's the best thing.

BEN   Best thing!

WILLY   The only way. Everything is gonna be—go on, kid, get to bed. You look so tired.

LINDA   Come right up.

WILLY   Two minutes.

[LINDA *goes into the living-room, then reappears in her bedroom.* WILLY *moves just outside the kitchen door.*]

WILLY   Loves me. [*wonderingly*]   Always loved me. Isn't that a remarkable thing? Ben, he'll worship me for it!

BEN [*with promise*]   It's dark there, but full of diamonds.

WILLY   Can you imagine that magnificence with twenty thousand dollars in his pocket?

LINDA [*calling from her room*]   Willy! Come up!

WILLY [*calling into the kitchen*]   Yes! Yes. Coming! It's very smart, you realize that, don't you, sweetheart? Even Ben sees it. I gotta go, baby. 'By! 'By! [*going over to* BEN, *almost dancing*] Imagine? When the mail comes he'll be ahead of Bernard again!

BEN   A perfect proposition all around.

WILLY   Did you see how he cried to me? Oh, if I could kiss him, Ben!

BEN   Time, William, time!

WILLY   Oh, Ben, I always knew one way or another we were gonna make it, Biff and I!

BEN [*looking at his watch*]   The boat. We'll be late. [*He moves slowly off into the darkness.*]

WILLY [*elegiacally, turning to the house*]   Now when you kick off, boy, I want a seventy-yard boot, and get right down the field under the ball, and when you hit, hit low and hit hard, because it's important, boy. [*He swings around and faces the audience.*] There's all kinds of important people in the stands, and the first thing you know . . . [*suddenly realizing he is alone*] Ben! Ben, where do I . . . ? [*He makes a sudden movement of search.*] Ben, how do I . . . ?

LINDA [*calling*]   Willy, you coming up?

WILLY [*uttering a gasp of fear, whirling about as if to quiet her*]   Sh! [*He turns around as if to find his way; sounds, faces, voices, seem to be swarming in upon him and he flicks at them, crying,*] Sh! Sh! [*Suddenly music, faint and high, stops him. It rises in intensity, almost to an unbearable scream. He goes up and down on his toes, and rushes off around the house.*] Shhh!

LINDA   Willy?

[*There is no answer.* LINDA *waits.* BIFF *gets up off his bed. He is still in his clothes.* HAPPY *sits up.* BIFF *stands listening.*]

LINDA [*with real fear*]   Willy, answer me! Willy!

[*There is the sound of a car starting and moving away at full speed.*]

LINDA No!

BIFF [*rushing down the stairs*] Pop!

>[*As the car speeds off, the music crashes down in a frenzy of sound, which becomes the soft pulsation of a single cello string.* BIFF *slowly returns to his bedroom. He and* HAPPY *gravely don their jackets.* LINDA *slowly walks out of her room. The music has developed into a dead march. The leaves of day are appearing over everything.* CHARLEY *and* BERNARD *somberly dressed, appear and knock on the kitchen door.* BIFF *and* HAPPY *slowly descend the stairs to the kitchen as* CHARLEY *and* BERNARD *enter. All stop a moment when* LINDA, *in clothes of mourning, bearing a little bunch of roses, comes through the draped doorway into the kitchen. She goes to* CHARLEY *and takes his arm. Now all move toward the audience, through the wall-line of the kitchen. At the limit of the apron,* LINDA *lays down the flowers, kneels, and sits back on her heels. All stare down at the grave.*]

Requiem

CHARLEY It's getting dark, Linda.

>[LINDA *doesn't react. She stares at the grave.*]

BIFF How about it, Mom? Better get some rest, heh? They'll be closing the gate soon.

>[LINDA *makes no move. Pause.*]

HAPPY [*deeply angered*] He had no right to do that. There was no necessity for it. We would've helped him.

CHARLEY [*grunting*] Hmmm.

BIFF Come along, Mom.

LINDA Why didn't anybody come?

CHARLEY It was a very nice funeral.

LINDA But where are all the people he knew? Maybe they blame him.

CHARLEY Naa. It's a rough world, Linda. They wouldn't blame him.

LINDA I can't understand it. At this time especially. First time in thirty-five years we were just about free and clear. He only needed a little salary. He was even finished with the dentist.

CHARLEY No man only needs a little salary.

LINDA I can't understand it.

BIFF There were a lot of nice days. When he'd come home from a trip; or on Sundays, making the stoop; finishing the cellar; putting on the new porch; when he built the extra bathroom; and put up the garage. You know something, Charley, there's more of him in that front stoop than in all the sales he ever made.

CHARLEY Yeah. He was a happy man with a batch of cement.

LINDA He was so wonderful with his hands.

BIFF He had the wrong dreams. All, all, wrong.

HAPPY [*almost ready to fight* BIFF] Don't say that!

BIFF He never knew who he was.

CHARLEY [*stopping* HAPPY'S *movement and reply. To* BIFF] Nobody dast blame this man. You don't understand: Willy was a salesman. And for a salesman, there is no rock bottom to the life. He don't put a bolt to a nut, he don't tell you the law or give you medicine. He's a man way out there in the blue, riding on a smile and a shoeshine. And when they start not smiling back—that's an earthquake. And then you get yourself a couple of spots on your hat, and you're finished. Nobody dast blame this man. A salesman is got to dream, boy. It comes with the territory.

BIFF   Charley, the man didn't know who he was.

HAPPY [*infuriated*]   Don't say that!

BIFF   Why don't you come with me, Happy?

HAPPY   I'm not licked that easily. I'm staying right in this city, and I'm gonna beat this racket! [*He looks at* BIFF, *his chin set.*] The Loman Brothers!

BIFF   I know who I am, kid.

HAPPY   All right, boy. I'm gonna show you and everybody else that Willy Loman did not die in vain. He had a good dream. It's the only dream you can have—to come out number-one man. He fought it out here, and this is where I'm gonna win it for him.

BIFF [*with a hopeless glance at* HAPPY, *bends toward his mother*]   Let's go, Mom.

LINDA   I'll be with you in a minute. Go on, Charley. [*He hesitates.*]   I want to, just for a minute. I never had a chance to say good-by.

[CHARLEY *moves away, followed by* HAPPY. BIFF *remains a slight distance up and left of* LINDA. *She sits there, summoning herself. The flute begins, not far away, playing behind her speech.*]

LINDA   Forgive me, dear. I can't cry. I don't know what it is, but I can't cry. I don't understand it. Why did you ever do that? Help me, Willy, I can't cry. It seems to me that you're just on another trip. I keep expecting you. Willy, dear, I can't cry. Why did you do it? I search and search and I search, and I can't understand it, Willy. I made the last payment on the house today. Today, dear. And there'll be nobody home. [*A sob rises in her throat.*] We're free and clear. [*Sobbing more fully, released*] We're free. [BIFF *comes slowly toward her.*] We're free . . . We're free . . .

[BIFF *lifts her to her feet and moves out up right with her in his arms.* LINDA *sobs quietly.* BERNARD *and* CHARLEY *come together and follow them, followed by* HAPPY. *Only the music of the flute is left on the darkening stage as over the house the hard towers of the apartment buildings rise into sharp focus, and*]

CURTAIN

1949

ROBERT LOWELL
1917–1977

I n "North Haven," her poem in memory of Robert Lowell, Elizabeth Bishop translates the bird song as Lowell seemed to hear it: "repeat, repeat, repeat, revise, revise, revise." Repeatedly, even obsessively, Lowell returned to certain subjects in his poems. Each return confirmed an existing pattern even as it opened the possibility for revision. In fact, Lowell's life was full of revision. Descended from Protestant New Englanders, he converted to Catholicism, then fell away from it; he married three times; and he changed his poetic style more than once. In the later part of his career Lowell revised even his published poems and did so repeatedly. "Revision is inspiration," he once said, "no reading of the finished work as exciting as writing the last changes." Revision allowed for Lowell's love of stray events, his attraction to the fluidity of life (in this, he resembles Wallace Stevens). But Lowell also wanted to organize life into formal patterns, to locate the random moment in the design of an epic history (his Catholicism can be seen, in part, as an expression of this desire). History offered plot and repetition: just as patterns of his childhood recurred in adult life, the sins of his New England ancestors were reenacted by contemporary America. Lowell's vision of history leaned toward apocalypse, toward the revelation of a prior meaning that the poet agonized to determine, and yet he cherished the freedom of "human chances," with all their indeterminacy. His poems had to accommodate these opposing impulses. Concerning the sequence of poems in *Notebook 1967–1968*, begun as a poetic diary, he said: "Accident threw up the subject and the plot swallowed them—famished for human chances." If Lowell often swallowed up the casual, the random, the ordinary, and the domestic into the forms of his poems, his best plots have a spontaneity whose meanings cannot be fixed.

The burden of family history was substantial for Lowell, whose ancestors included members of Boston's patrician families. His grandfather was a well-known Episcopal minister and head of the fashionable St. Mark's School, which the poet was later to attend. His great-granduncle James Russell Lowell had been a poet and ambassador to England. The family's light note was provided by the poet Amy Lowell, "big and a scandal, as if Mae West were a cousin." In the context of this history Lowell's father, who fared badly in business after his retirement from service as a naval officer, appeared as a diminished figure.

Lowell's first act of revising family history was to leave the East after two years at Harvard (1935–37) in order to study at Kenyon College with John Crowe Ransom, the poet and critic. The move brought him in closer touch with the New Criticism and its predilections for "formal difficult poems," the wit and irony of English Metaphysical writers such as John Donne. He also, through Ransom and the poet Allen Tate, came into contact with (although never formally joined) the Fugitive movement, whose members were southern agrarians opposed to what they regarded as the corrupting values of northern industrialism.

Two of the acts that most decisively separated Lowell from family history were his conversion to Roman Catholicism (1940) and his resistance to American policies in World War II. Although he tried to enlist in the navy, he refused to be drafted into the army. He opposed the saturation bombing of Hamburg and the Allied policy of unconditional surrender and was as a result sentenced to a year's confinement in New York City's West Street jail. The presiding judge at his hearing admonished him for "marring" his family traditions. In his first book, *Lord Weary's Castle* (1946), his Catholicism provided a set of symbols and a distanced platform from which to express his violent antagonism to Protestant mercantile Boston. The stunning, apocalyptic conclusions of these early poems ("the Lord survives the rainbow of his will" or "The blue kingfisher dives on you in fire") render the devastating judgment of the eternal on the fallen history of the individual and the nation.

Alongside these poems drawing on Old Testament anger were poems in *Lord Weary's Castle*, such as "Mr. Edwards and the Spider," that explored from within the nervous intensity that underlay Puritan revivalism. Later dramatic narratives with modern settings, such as "The Mills of the Kavanaghs" and "Falling Asleep over the Aeneid," reveal his psychological interest in and obsession with ruined New England families.

In *Life Studies* (1959) Lowell changed his style dramatically. His subjects became explicitly autobiographical, his language more open and direct. In 1957 he gave readings in California, where Allen Ginsberg and the other Beats had just made their strongest impact in San Francisco. In contrast to their candid, breezy writing, Lowell felt his own seemed "distant, symbol-ridden, and willfully difficult. . . . I felt my old poems hid what they were really about, and many times offered a stiff, humorless, and even impenetrable surface." Although more controlled and severe than Beat writers, he was stimulated by Ginsberg's self-revelations to write more openly than he had about his parents and grandparents, about the mental breakdowns he suffered in the 1950s, and about the difficulties of marriage. (Lowell divorced his first wife, the novelist Jean Stafford, and married the critic Elizabeth Hardwick in 1949).

Life Studies, by and large, records his ambivalence toward the New England where he resettled after the war, on Boston's "hardly passionate Marlborough Street." Revising his stance toward New England and family history, he no longer denounces the city of his fathers as if he were a privileged outsider. In complicated psychological portraits of his childhood, his relation to his parents and his wives, he assumes a portion of the weakness and vulnerability for himself.

In 1960 Lowell left Boston to live in New York City. *For the Union Dead* (1964), the book that followed, continued the autobiographical vein of *Life Studies*. Lowell called it a book about "witheredness . . . lemony, soured and dry, the drouth I had touched with my own hands." These poems seem more carefully controlled than his earlier *Life Studies*. Often they organize key images from the past into a pattern that illuminates the present. The book includes a number of poems that fuse private and public themes, such as "Fall 1961" and the volume's title poem.

In 1969 Lowell published *Notebook 1967–1968* and then revised these poems for a second, augmented edition, called simply *Notebook* (1970). In 1973, in a characteristic act, he once more revised, rearranged, and expanded *Notebook*'s poems and published them in two separate books. The more personal poems, recording the breakup of his second marriage and his separation from his wife and daughter, were published as *For Lizzie and Harriet*. Those dealing more with public subjects, past and present, were published as *History*. These two books show Lowell once again engaged with the relations between the random event, or the moment out of a personal life, and an epic design. In these unrhymed, loosely blank-verse revisions of the sonnet, Lowell responded to the books he was reading, to the events of his personal life, and to the Vietnam War, of which he was an outspoken critic. "Things I felt or saw, or read were drift in the whirlpool."

At the same time a new collection of sonnets, *The Dolphin* (1973), appeared, recording his marriage to Lady Caroline Blackwood. (Lowell's friend the poet Elizabeth Bishop objected to his use of Blackwood's letters in the volume, and her letter to Lowell on this subject appears in the "Postmodern Manifestos" cluster of this anthology.) He divided his time between her home in England and periods of teaching writing and literature at Harvard—a familiar pattern for him, in which the old tensions between New England and "elsewhere" were being constantly explored and renewed. His last book, *Day by Day* (1977), records those stresses as well as new marital difficulties. It also contains some of his most powerful poems about his childhood.

For those who cherish the work of the early Lowell, with its manic, rhythmic energy and its enjambed lines building to fierce power, or those who admire the passionate engagement of *Life Studies* or *For the Union Dead*, the poems of his last four books can be disappointing. At times flat and dispirited, they can seem worked up rather than fully imagined. Yet the later Lowell demonstrates his substantial gifts in a quieter mode.

Lowell's career included an interest in the theater, for which he wrote a version of *Prometheus Bound*, a translation of Racine's *Phaedra*, and adaptations of Melville and Hawthorne stories gathered as *The Old Glory*. He also translated from modern European poetry and the classics, often freely as "imitations," which brought important poetic voices into English currency. His *Selected Poems* (his own choices) appeared in

1976. When he died suddenly at the age of sixty, he was the dominant and most honored poet of his generation—not only for his ten volumes of verse but for his broad activity as a man of letters. He took upon himself the role of poet as public figure, sometimes at great personal cost. He was with the group of writers who led Vietnam War protesters against the Pentagon in 1967, where Norman Mailer, a fellow protester, observed that "Lowell gave off at times the unwilling haunted saintliness of a man who was repaying the moral debts of ten generations of ancestors."

Colloquy in Black Rock[1]

Here the jack-hammer jabs into the ocean;
My heart, you race and stagger and demand
More blood-gangs for your nigger-brass percussions,
Till I, the stunned machine of your devotion,
Clanging upon this cymbal of a hand,   5
Am rattled screw and footloose. All discussions

End in the mud-flat detritus of death.
My heart, beat faster, faster. In Black Mud[2]
Hungarian workmen give their blood
For the martyre Stephen,[3] who was stoned to death.   10

Black Mud, a name to conjure with: O mud
For watermelons gutted to the crust,
Mud for the mole-tide[4] harbor, mud for mouse,
Mud for the armored Diesel fishing tubs that thud
A year and a day[5] to wind and tide; the dust   15
Is on this skipping heart that shakes my house,

House of our Savior who was hanged till death.
My heart, beat faster, faster. In Black Mud
Stephen the martyre was broken down to blood:
Our ransom is the rubble of his death.   20
Christ walks on the black water. In Black Mud
Darts the kingfisher. On Corpus Christi, heart,
Over the drum-beat of St. Stephen's choir
I hear him, *Stupor Mundi*,[6] and the mud
Flies from his hunching wings and beak—my heart,   25
The blue kingfisher dives on you in fire.

1946

1. A section of Bridgeport, Connecticut, where Lowell went to live in 1944 after serving his jail term as a conscientious objector. It had a large Hungarian population.
2. The speaker's name for mud flats near Black Rock.
3. A reference to the wartime blood donations of the workers; the patron saint of Hungary, King Stephen I (977–1038); and St. Stephen Promartyr, the first Christian to be killed for his faith.

4. Special currents produced by a mole (breakwater).
5. Perhaps the "year and a day" of Lowell's prison sentence.
6. Marvel of the world. "Kingfisher": a short-tailed bird that dives for fish; associated in the poem's last line with Christ, the "fisher of men." "Corpus Christi": a Catholic feast day, celebrating the transformation of the communion wafer into the body of Christ.

The Quaker Graveyard in Nantucket

[*For Warren Winslow*,[1] *Dead at Sea*]

Let man have dominion over the fishes of the sea and the fowls of
the air and the beasts of the whole earth, and every creeping creature that moveth upon the earth.[2]

I

A brackish reach of shoal off Madaket[3]—
The sea was still breaking violently and night
Had steamed into our North Atlantic Fleet,
When the drowned sailor clutched the drag-net. Light
Flashed from his matted head and marble feet,   5
He grappled at the net
With the coiled, hurdling muscles of his thighs:
The corpse was bloodless, a botch of reds and whites,
Its open, staring eyes
Were lustreless dead-lights[4]   10
Or cabin-windows on a stranded hulk
Heavy with sand. We weight the body, close
Its eyes and heave it seaward whence it came,
Where the heel-headed dogfish barks its nose
On Ahab's[5] void and forehead; and the name   15
Is blocked in yellow chalk.
Sailors, who pitch this portent at the sea
Where dreadnaughts shall confess
Its hell-bent deity,
When you are powerless   20
To sand-bag this Atlantic bulwark, faced
By the earth-shaker, green, unwearied, chaste
In his steel scales: ask for no Orphean lute
To pluck life back.[6] The guns of the steeled fleet
Recoil and then repeat   25
The hoarse salute.

II

Whenever winds are moving and their breath
Heaves at the roped-in bulwarks of this pier,
The terns and sea-gulls tremble at your death
In these home waters. Sailor, can you hear   30
The Pequod's[7] sea wings, beating landward, fall
Headlong and break on our Atlantic wall

1. A cousin of Lowell's who died in the sinking
of a naval vessel during World War II.
2. From Genesis 1.26, the account of the creation of humankind.
3. On Nantucket Island.
4. Shutters over portholes to keep out water in a
storm. The images in lines 4–11 come from "The
Shipwreck," the opening chapter of *Cape Cod*,
by Henry David Thoreau (1817–1862).
5. Protagonist of the novel *Moby-Dick*, by Herman Melville (1819–1891); he drowns as the culmination of his obsessive hunt for the white
whale. Melville uses Ahab's forehead as an
emblem of his monomaniac passion.
6. In Greek mythology Orpheus, through his
music, tried to win the freedom of his bride,
Eurydice, from the Underworld. "Earth-shaker":
an epithet for Poseidon, the Greek god of the
oceans and of earthquakes.
7. Ahab's ship, destroyed by Moby-Dick.

Off 'Sconset, where the yawing S-boats[8] splash
The bellbuoy, with ballooning spinnakers,
As the entangled, screeching mainsheet clears   35
The blocks: off Madaket, where lubbers[9] lash
The heavy surf and throw their long lead squids
For blue-fish? Sea-gulls blink their heavy lids
Seaward. The winds' wings beat upon the stones,
Cousin, and scream for you and the claws rush   40
At the sea's throat and wring it in the slush
Of this old Quaker graveyard where the bones
Cry out in the long night for the hurt beast
Bobbing by Ahab's whaleboats in the East.

III

All you recovered from Poseidon died   45
With you, my cousin, and the harrowed brine
Is fruitless on the blue beard of the god,
Stretching beyond us to the castles in Spain,
Nantucket's westward haven. To Cape Cod
Guns, cradled on the tide,   50
Blast the eelgrass about a waterclock
Of bilge and backwash, roil the salt and sand
Lashing earth's scaffold, rock
Our warships in the hand
Of the great God, where time's contrition blues   55
Whatever it was these Quaker[1] sailors lost
In the mad scramble of their lives. They died
When time was open-eyed,
Wooden and childish; only bones abide
There, in the nowhere, where their boats were tossed   60
Sky-high, where mariners had fabled news
Of IS,[2] the whited monster. What it cost
Them is their secret. In the sperm-whale's slick
I see the Quakers drown and hear their cry:
"If God himself had not been on our side,   65
If God himself had not been on our side,
When the Atlantic rose against us, why,
Then it had swallowed us up quick."

IV

This is the end of the whaleroad[3] and the whale
Who spewed Nantucket bones on the thrashed swell   70
And stirred the troubled waters to whirlpools
To send the Pequod packing off to hell:
This is the end of them, three-quarters fools,
Snatching at straws to sail

8. Type of large racing sailboats. "Yawing": steering wildly in heavy seas.
9. Sailor's term for awkward crew members.
1. The whaling population of Nantucket included many Quakers.
2. The white whale is here imagined as a force like the God of Exodus 3.14, who, when asked his name by Moses, replies, "I AM THAT I AM." Also an abbreviation of Iesu Salvator, Latin for Jesus, savior of men.
3. An Anglo-Saxon epithet for the sea.

Seaward and seaward on the turntail whale,   75
Spouting out blood and water as it rolls,
Sick as a dog to these Atlantic shoals:
Clamavimus,[4] O depths. Let the sea-gulls wail

For water, for the deep where the high tide
Mutters to its hurt self, mutters and ebbs.   80
Waves wallow in their wash, go out and out,
Leave only the death-rattle of the crabs,
The beach increasing, its enormous snout
Sucking the ocean's side.
This is the end of running on the waves;   85
We are poured out like water. Who will dance
The mast-lashed master of Leviathans
Up from this field of Quakers in their unstoned graves?

                               V

When the whale's viscera go and the roll
Of its corruption overruns this world   90
Beyond tree-swept Nantucket and Woods Hole[5]
And Martha's Vineyard, Sailor, will your sword
Whistle and fall and sink into the fat?
In the great ash-pit of Jehoshaphat[6]
The bones cry for the blood of the white whale,   95
The fat flukes arch and whack about its ears,
The death-lance churns into the sanctuary, tears
The gun-blue swingle,[7] heaving like a flail,
And hacks the coiling life out: it works and drags
And rips the sperm-whale's midriff into rags,   100
Gobbets of blubber spill to wind and weather,
Sailor, and gulls go round the stoven timbers
Where the morning stars sing out together
And thunder shakes the white surf and dismembers
The red flag hammered in the mast-head.[8] Hide,   105
Our steel, Jonas Messias, in Thy side.[9]

              VI. OUR LADY OF WALSINGHAM[1]

There once the penitents took off their shoes
And then walked barefoot the remaining mile;
And the small trees, a stream and hedgerows file
Slowly along the munching English lane,   110
Like cows to the old shrine, until you lose

---

4. We have called (Latin), adapting the opening
of Psalm 130: "Out of the depths have I cried unto
thee, O Lord."
5. On the coast of Massachusetts, near the
island of Martha's Vineyard.
6. "The day of judgment. The world, according to
some prophets, will end in fire" [Lowell's note]. In
Joel 3, the Last Judgment takes place in the valley
of Jehoshaphat.
7. Knifelike wooden instrument for beating flax
(info fiber for spinning).

8. At the end of Moby-Dick, the arm of the American Indian Tashtego appears from the waves and
nails Ahab's flag to the sinking mast.
9. Because he emerged alive from the belly of a
whale, the prophet Jonah is often linked with the
messiah as a figure of salvation.
1. Lowell took these details from E. I. Watkin's
Catholic Art and Culture (1942), which includes
a description of the medieval shrine of the Virgin
at Walsingham.

Track of your dragging pain.
The stream flows down under the druid tree,
Shiloah's² whirlpools gurgle and make glad
The castle of God. Sailor, you were glad   115
And whistled Sion by that stream. But see:

Our Lady, too small for her canopy,
Sits near the altar. There's no comeliness
At all or charm in that expressionless
Face with its heavy eyelids. As before,   120
This face, for centuries a memory,
*Non est species, neque decor,*³
Expressionless, expresses God: it goes
Past castled Sion. She knows what God knows,
Not Calvary's Cross nor crib at Bethlehem   125
Now, and the world shall come to Walsingham.

VII

The empty winds are creaking and the oak
Splatters and splatters on the cenotaph,
The boughs are trembling and a gaff
Bobs on the untimely stroke   130
Of the greased wash exploding on a shoal-bell
In the old mouth of the Atlantic. It's well;
Atlantic, you are fouled with the blue sailors,
Sea-monsters, upward angel, downward fish:
Unmarried and corroding, spare of flesh   135
Mart once of supercilious, wing'd clippers,
Atlantic, where your bell-trap guts its spoil
You could cut the brackish winds with a knife
Here in Nantucket, and cast up the time
When the Lord God formed man from the sea's slime   140
And breathed into his face the breath of life,
And blue-lung'd combers lumbered to the kill.
The Lord survives the rainbow⁴ of His will.

1946

Mr. Edwards and the Spider¹

I saw the spiders marching through the air,
Swimming from tree to tree that mildewed day
In latter August when the hay
Came creaking to the barn. But where

2. The stream that flows past God's Temple on Mount Sion (Isaiah 8.6). In Isaiah 51.11 the redeemed come "singing into Zion."
3. There is no ostentation or elegance (Latin).
4. Alluding to God's covenant with Noah after the Flood. The rainbow symbolized the fact that humanity would never again be destroyed by flood

(Genesis 9.11).
1. Jonathan Edwards (1703–1758), Puritan preacher and theologian. Lowell quotes his writings throughout. The details of the first stanza come from his youthful essay "Of Insects" ("The Habits of Spiders").

The wind is westerly,   5
Where gnarled November makes the spiders fly
Into the apparitions of the sky,
They purpose nothing but their ease and die
Urgently beating east to sunrise and the sea;

What are we in the hands of the great God?   10
It was in vain you set up thorn and briar
    In battle array against the fire
    And treason crackling in your blood;
        For the wild thorns grow tame
And will do nothing to oppose the flame;   15
Your lacerations tell the losing game
You play against a sickness past your cure.
How will the hands be strong? How will the heart endure?[2]

A very little thing, a little worm,
Or hourglass-blazoned spider,[3] it is said,   20
    Can kill a tiger. Will the dead
    Hold up his mirror and affirm
        To the four winds the smell
And flash of his authority? It's well
If God who holds you to the pit of hell,   25
Much as one holds a spider, will destroy,
Baffle and dissipate your soul. As a small boy

On Windsor Marsh,[4] I saw the spider die
When thrown into the bowels of fierce fire:
    There's no long struggle, no desire   30
    To get up on its feet and fly—
        It stretches out its feet
And dies. This is the sinner's last retreat;
Yes, and no strength exerted on the heat
Then sinews the abolished will, when sick   35
And full of burning, it will whistle on a brick.

But who can plumb the sinking of that soul?
Josiah Hawley,[5] picture yourself cast
    Into a brick-kiln where the blast
    Fans your quick vitals to a coal—   40
        If measured by a glass,
How long would it seem burning! Let there pass
A minute, ten, ten trillion; but the blaze
Is infinite, eternal: this is death,
To die and know it. This is the Black Widow, death.   45

1946

2. This stanza draws on Edwards's sermon "Sinners in the Hands of an Angry God," whose point of departure is Ezekiel 22.14: "Can thine heart endure or can thine hands be strong in the days that I shall deal with thee?" (cf. line 18).
3. The poisonous black widow spider has, on the underside of its abdomen, a red marking that resembles an hourglass.
4. East Windsor, Connecticut, Edwards's childhood home.
5. Edwards's uncle, Joseph Hawley.

My Last Afternoon with Uncle Devereux Winslow

1922: the stone porch of my grandfather's summer house

I

"I won't go with you. I want to stay with Grandpa!"
That's how I threw cold water
on my Mother and Father's
watery martini pipe dreams at Sunday dinner.
. . . Fontainebleau, Mattapoisett, Puget Sound. . . .[1]   5
Nowhere was anywhere after a summer
at my Grandfather's farm.
Diamond-pointed, athirst and Norman,[2]
its alley of poplars
paraded from Grandmother's rose garden   10
to a scary stand of virgin pine,
scrub, and paths forever pioneering.

One afternoon in 1922,
I sat on the stone porch, looking through
screens as black-grained as drifting coal.   15
Tockytock, tockytock
clumped our Alpine, Edwardian cuckoo clock,
slung with strangled, wooden game.
Our farmer was cementing a root-house[3] under the hill.
One of my hands was cool on a pile   20
of black earth, the other warm
on a pile of lime. All about me
were the works of my Grandfather's hands:
snapshots of his *Liberty Bell* silver mine;
his high school at *Stuttgart am Neckar*,[4]   25
stogie-brown beams; fools'-gold nuggets;
octagonal red tiles,
sweaty with a secret dank, crummy with ant-stale;
a Rocky Mountain chaise longue,
its legs, shellacked saplings.   30
A pastel-pale Huckleberry Finn
fished with a broom straw in a basin
hollowed out of a millstone.
Like my Grandfather, the décor
was manly, comfortable,   35
overbearing, disproportioned.

What were those sunflowers? Pumpkins floating shoulder-high?
It was sunset, Sadie and Nellie
bearing pitchers of ice-tea,

1. Sound connected to the Pacific Ocean via the Strait of Juan de Fuca, in the Pacific Northwest. "Fontainebleau": rich pastoral suburb of Paris, site of one of the royal châteaux. "Mattapoisett": town in Plymouth County, Massachusetts, first settled in the 1750s.

2. A stage of Romanesque architecture developed in the French province of Normandy.
3. For storing bulbs, root vegetables, etc.
4. City in Germany, on the Neckar River. "*Liberty Bell* silver mine": located near Telluride, Colorado; it boomed in the 1890s.

oranges, lemons, mint, and peppermints,   40
and the jug of shandygaff,
which Grandpa made by blending half and half
yeasty, wheezing homemade sarsaparilla with beer.
The farm, entitled *Char-de-sa*
in the Social Register,   45
was named for my Grandfather's children:
Charlotte, Devereux, and Sarah.
No one had died there in my lifetime . . .
Only Cinder, our Scottie puppy
paralyzed from gobbling toads.   50
I sat mixing black earth and lime.

II

I was five and a half.
My formal pearl gray shorts
had been worn for three minutes.
My perfection was the Olympian   55
poise of my models in the imperishable autumn
display windows
of Rogers Peet's boys' store below the State House
in Boston. Distorting drops of water
pinpricked my face in the basin's mirror.   60
I was a stuffed toucan
with a bibulous, multicolored beak.

III

Up in the air
by the lakeview window in the billards-room,
lurid in the doldrums of the sunset hour,   65
my Great Aunt Sarah
was learning *Samson and Delilah*.[5]
She thundered on the keyboard of her dummy piano,
with gauze curtains like a boudoir table,
accordionlike yet soundless.   70
It had been bought to spare the nerves
of my Grandmother,
tone-deaf, quick as a cricket,
now needing a fourth for "Auction,"[6]
and casting a thirsty eye   75
on Aunt Sarah, risen like the phoenix
from her bed of troublesome snacks and Tauchnitz classics.[7]

Forty years earlier,
twenty, auburn headed,
grasshopper notes of genius!   80
Family gossip says Aunt Sarah

---

5. A piano version of the opera by Camille Saint-
Saëns (1835–1921).
6. Auction bridge.

7. German paperback editions that included standard English and American works (in English).

tilted her archaic Athenian nose
and jilted an Astor.[8]
Each morning she practiced
on the grand piano at Symphony Hall,   85
deathlike in the off-season summer—
its naked Greek statues draped with purple
like the saints in Holy Week. . . .
On the recital day, she failed to appear.

IV

I picked with a clean finger nail at the blue anchor   90
on my sailor blouse washed white as a spinnaker.
What in the world was I wishing?
. . . A sail-colored horse browsing in the bullrushes . . .
A fluff of the west wind puffing
my blouse, kiting me over our seven chimneys,   95
troubling the waters. . . .
As small as sapphires were the ponds: *Quittacus, Snippituit,*
and *Assawompses,* halved by "the Island,"
where my Uncle's duck blind
floated in a barrage of smoke-clouds.   100
Double-barreled shotguns
stuck out like bundles of baby crow-bars.
A single sculler in a camouflaged kayak
was quacking to the decoys. . . .

At the cabin between the waters,   105
the nearest windows were already boarded.
Uncle Devereux was closing camp for the winter.
As if posed for "the engagement photograph,"
he was wearing his severe
war-uniform of a volunteer Canadian officer.   110
Daylight from the doorway riddled his student posters,
tacked helter-skelter on walls as raw as a boardwalk.
Mr. Punch,[9] a water melon in hockey tights,
was tossing off a decanter of Scotch.
La Belle France in a red, white and blue toga   115
was accepting the arm of her "protector,"
the ingenu and porcine Edward VII.[1]
The pre-war music hall belles
had goose necks, glorious signatures, beauty-moles,
and coils of hair like rooster tails.   120
The finest poster was two or three young men in khaki kilts
being bushwhacked on the veldt[2]—
They were almost life-size. . . .

---

8. A member of the wealthiest family in the United States during the 19th century.
9. A plump cartoon-figure emblem of the English humor magazine *Punch*, founded in 1841.
1. Edward VII (1841–1910), king of England, famous as a ladies' man, is depicted with his arm around the female emblem of France in a poster celebrating the Entente Cordiale, a rapprochement between England and France.
2. Open country in South Africa. The Boer War (1899–1902) was fought by the English against descendants of Dutch settlers there.

My Uncle was dying at twenty-nine.
"You are behaving like children,"   125
said my Grandfather,
when my Uncle and Aunt left their three baby daughters,
and sailed for Europe on a last honeymoon . . .
I cowered in terror.
I wasn't a child at all—   130
unseen and all-seeing, I was Agrippina[3]
in the Golden House of Nero. . . .
Near me was the white measuring-door
my Grandfather had penciled with my Uncle's heights.
In 1911, he had stopped growing at just six feet.   135
While I sat on the tiles,
and dug at the anchor on my sailor blouse,
Uncle Devereux stood behind me.
He was as brushed as Bayard, our riding horse.
His face was putty.   140
His blue coat and white trousers
grew sharper and straighter.
His coat was a blue jay's tail,
his trousers were solid cream from the top of the bottle.
He was animated, hierarchical,   145
like a ginger snap man in a clothes-press.
He was dying of the incurable Hodgkin's disease. . . .
My hands were warm, then cool, on the piles
of earth and lime,
a black pile and a white pile. . . .   150
Come winter,
Uncle Devereux would blend to the one color.

1959

Home after Three Months Away[1]

Gone now the baby's nurse,
a lioness who ruled the roost
and made the Mother cry.
She used to tie
gobbets of porkrind[2] in bowknots of gauze—   5
three months they hung like soggy toast
on our eight foot magnolia tree,
and helped the English sparrows
weather a Boston winter.

3. Mother of the Roman emperor Nero. Involved in court intrigue and affairs of state, she poisoned her second husband and was later murdered by her son.

1. This poem was written following one of Lowell's hospitalizations at McLean Psychiatric Hospital in Belmont, Boston.
2. Small chunks of fried or roasted skin of a pig.

Three months, three months!   10
Is Richard now himself again?[3]
Dimpled with exaltation,
my daughter holds her levee in the tub.
Our noses rub,
each of us pats a stringy lock of hair—   15
they tell me nothing's gone.
Though I am forty-one,
not forty now, the time I put away
was child's-play. After thirteen weeks
my child still dabs her cheeks   20
to start me shaving. When
we dress her in her sky-blue corduroy,
she changes to a boy,
and floats my shaving brush
and washcloth in the flush. . . .   25
Dearest, I cannot loiter here
in lather like a polar bear.

Recuperating, I neither spin nor toil.[4]
Three stories down below,
a choreman tends our coffin's length of soil,   30
and seven horizontal tulips blow.
Just twelve months ago,
these flowers were pedigreed
imported Dutchmen; now no one need
distinguish them from weed.   35
Bushed by the late spring snow,
they cannot meet
another year's snowballing enervation.

I keep no rank nor station.
Cured, I am frizzled, stale and small.   40

                                                              1958

Memories of West Street and Lepke[1]

Only teaching on Tuesdays, book-worming
in pajamas fresh from the washer each morning,
I hog a whole house on Boston's
"hardly passionate Marlborough Street,"[2]

---

3. Variation of "Richard's himself again," a line spoken by Richard III before the battle of Bosworth in a 1700 adaptation of Shakespeare's *Richard III* (1591?) by English actor-manager and playwright Colley Cibber (1671–1757).
4. Allusion to Matthew 6.28: "Consider the lilies of the field, how they grow: they neither toil nor spin."
1. In 1943 Lowell was sentenced to a year in New York City's West Street jail for his refusal to serve in the armed forces. Among the prisoners was Lepke Buchalter, head of the organized crime syndicate Murder Incorporated, who had been convicted of murder.
2. William James's phrase for a street in the elegant Back Bay section of Boston, where Lowell lived in the 1950s.

where even the man   5
scavenging filth in the back alley trash cans,
has two children, a beach wagon, a helpmate,
and is a "young Republican."
I have a nine months' daughter,
young enough to be my granddaughter.   10
Like the sun she rises in her flame-flamingo infants' wear.

These are the tranquillized *Fifties*,
and I am forty. Ought I to regret my seedtime?
I was a fire-breathing Catholic C.O.,[3]
and made my manic statement,   15
telling off the state and president, and then
sat waiting sentence in the bull pen
beside a Negro boy with curlicues
of marijuana in his hair.

Given a year.   20
I walked on the roof of the West Street Jail, a short
enclosure like my school soccer court,
and saw the Hudson River once a day
through sooty clothesline entanglements
and bleaching khaki tenements.   25
Strolling, I yammered metaphysics with Abramowitz,
a jaundice-yellow ("it's really tan")
and fly-weight pacifist,
so vegetarian,
he wore rope shoes and preferred fallen fruit.   30
He tried to convert Bioff and Brown,
the Hollywood pimps, to his diet.
Hairy, muscular, suburban,
wearing chocolate double-breasted suits,
they blew their tops and beat him black and blue.   35

I was so out of things, I'd never heard
of the Jehovah's Witnesses.[4]
"Are you a C.O.?" I asked a fellow jailbird.
"No," he answered, "I'm a J.W."
He taught me the "hospital tuck,"[5]   40
and pointed out the T-shirted back
of *Murder Incorporated*'s Czar Lepke,
there piling towels on a rack,
or dawdling off to his little segregated cell full
of things forbidden the common man: 45
a portable radio, a dresser, two toy American
flags tied together with a ribbon of Easter palm.
Flabby, bald, lobotomized,
he drifted in a sheepish calm,
where no agonizing reappraisal   50

3. Conscientious objector (to war).
4. A Christian revivalist sect that strongly opposes
war and denies the power of the state in matters

of conscience.
5. The authorized, efficient way of making beds
in a hospital.

jarred his concentration on the electric chair—
hanging like an oasis in his air
of lost connections. . . .

1959

Skunk Hour

for Elizabeth Bishop

Nautilus Island's[1] hermit
heiress still lives through winter in her Spartan cottage;
her sheep still graze above the sea.
Her son's a bishop. Her farmer
is first selectman in our village;   5
she's in her dotage.

Thirsting for
the hierarchic privacy
of Queen Victoria's century,
she buys up all   10
the eyesores facing her shore,
and lets them fall.

The season's ill—
we've lost our summer millionaire,
who seemed to leap from an L. L. Bean   15
catalogue.[2] His nine-knot yawl
was auctioned off to lobstermen.
A red fox stain covers Blue Hill.

And now our fairy
decorator brightens his shop for fall;   20
his fishnet's filled with orange cork,
orange, his cobbler's bench and awl;
there is no money in his work,
he'd rather marry.

One dark night,   25
my Tudor Ford climbed the hill's skull;
I watched for love-cars. Lights turned down,
they lay together, hull to hull,
where the graveyard shelves on the town. . . .
My mind's not right.   30

A car radio bleats,
"Love, O careless Love. . . ." I hear

---

1. The poem is set in Castine, Maine, where
Lowell had a summer house.
2. From a mail-order house in Maine that primarily sells sporting goods and clothing to the
wealthy and upper middle class.

my ill-spirit sob in each blood cell,
as if my hand were at its throat. . . .
I myself am hell;[3]   35
nobody's here—

only skunks, that search
in the moonlight for a bite to eat.
They march on their soles up Main Street:
white stripes, moonstruck eyes' red fire   40
under the chalk-dry and spar spire
of the Trinitarian Church.

I stand on top
of our back steps and breathe the rich air—
a mother skunk with her column of kittens swills the garbage pail. 45
She jabs her wedge-head in a cup
of spur cream, drops her ostrich tail,
and will not scare.

                                                            1959

Night Sweat

Work-table, litter, books and standing lamp,
plain things, my stalled equipment, the old broom—
but I am living in a tidied room,
for ten nights now I've felt the creeping damp
float over my pajamas' wilted white . . .   5
Sweet salt embalms me and my head is wet,
everything streams and tells me this is right;
my life's fever is soaking in night sweat—
one life, one writing! But the downward glide
and bias of existing wrings us dry—   10
always inside me is the child who died,
always inside me is his will to die—
one universe, one body . . . in this urn
the animal night sweats of the spirit burn.
Behind me! You! Again I feel the light   15
lighten my leaded eyelids, while the gray
skulled horses whinny for the soot of night.
I dabble in the dapple of the day,
a heap of wet clothes, seamy, shivering,
I see my flesh and bedding washed with light,   20
my child exploding into dynamite,
my wife . . . your lightness alters everything,
and tears the black web from the spider's sack,
as your heart hops and flutters like a hare.
Poor turtle, tortoise, if I cannot clear   25

---

3. "Which way I fly is Hell, myself am Hell" (Satan in Milton's *Paradise Lost* 4.75).

the surface of these troubled waters here,
absolve me, help me, Dear Heart, as you bear
this world's dead weight and cycle on your back.

                                                    1964

For the Union Dead[1]

"Relinquunt Omnia Servare Rem Publicam."[2]

The old South Boston Aquarium stands
in a Sahara of snow now. Its broken windows are boarded.
The bronze weathervane cod has lost half its scales.
The airy tanks are dry.

Once my nose crawled like a snail on the glass;   5
my hand tingled
to burst the bubbles
drifting from the noses of the cowed, compliant fish.

My hand draws back. I often sigh still
for the dark downward and vegetating kingdom   10
of the fish and reptile. One morning last March,
I pressed against the new barbed and galvanized

fence on the Boston Common. Behind their cage,
yellow dinosaur steamshovels were grunting
as they cropped up tons of mush and grass   15
to gouge their underworld garage.

Parking spaces luxuriate like civic
sandpiles in the heart of Boston.
A girdle of orange, Puritan-pumpkin colored girders
braces the tingling Statehouse,   20

shaking over the excavations, as it faces Colonel Shaw
and his bell-cheeked Negro infantry
on St. Gaudens' shaking Civil War relief,
propped by a plank splint against the garage's earthquake.

Two months after marching through Boston,   25
half the regiment was dead;

---

1. First published as "Colonel Shaw and the Massachusetts' 54th" in a paperback edition of *Life Studies* (1960). It became the title poem of *For the Union Dead* (1964).
2. Robert Gould Shaw (1837–1863) led the first all–African American regiment in the Union army during the Civil War. He was killed in the attack against Fort Wagner, South Carolina. A bronze relief by the sculptor Augustus Saint-Gaudens (1848–1897), dedicated in 1897, standing opposite the Massachusetts State House on Boston Common, commemorates the deaths. A Latin inscription on the monument reads *Omnia Reliquit Servare Rem Publicam* ("He leaves all behind to save the Republic"). Lowell's epigraph alters the inscription slightly, changing the third-person singular (*he*) to the third-person plural: "*They* give up everything to save the Republic."

at the dedication
William James[3] could almost hear the bronze Negroes breathe.

Their monument sticks like a fishbone
in the city's throat.   30
Its Colonel is as lean
as a compass-needle.

He has an angry wrenlike vigilance,
a greyhound's gentle tautness;
he seems to wince at pleasure,   35
and suffocate for privacy.

He is out of bounds now. He rejoices in man's lovely,
peculiar power to choose life and die—
when he leads his black soldiers to death,
he cannot bend his back.   40

On a thousand small town New England greens,
the old white churches hold their air
of sparse, sincere rebellion; frayed flags
quilt the graveyards of the Grand Army of the Republic.

The stone statues of the abstract Union Soldier   45
grow slimmer and younger each year—
wasp-waisted, they doze over muskets
and muse through their sideburns . . .

Shaw's father wanted no monument
except the ditch,   50
where his son's body was thrown[4]
and lost with his "niggers."

The ditch is nearer.
There are no statues for the last war[5] here;
on Boylston Street,[6] a commercial photograph   55
shows Hiroshima boiling[7]

over a Mosler Safe, the "Rock of Ages"[8]
that survived the blast. Space is nearer.
When I crouch to my television set,
the drained faces of Negro school-children rise like balloons.[9]   60

Colonel Shaw
is riding on his bubble,
he waits
for the blessed break.

3. Philosopher and psychologist (1842–1910) who taught at Harvard.
4. By the Confederate soldiers at Fort Wagner.
5. World War II.
6. In Boston, where the poem is set.
7. On August 6, 1945, the United States dropped an atomic bomb on this Japanese city.
8. Biblical reference to an indestructible and supernatural rock, the foundation of an everlasting kingdom. Used as an advertising slogan by Mosler Safes.
9. Probably news photographs connected with contemporary civil rights demonstrations to secure desegregation of schools in the South.

The Aquarium is gone. Everywhere,   65
giant finned cars nose forward like fish;
a savage servility
slides by on grease.

1960, 1964

GWENDOLYN BROOKS
1917–2000

66 **I**f there was ever a born poet," the writer Alice Walker once said in an interview,
"I think it is Brooks." A passionate sense of language and an often daring use of
formal structures are hallmarks of Gwendolyn Brooks's poetry. She used these gifts
in a career characterized by dramatic evolution, a career that linked two very different generations of African American poets. "Until 1967," Brooks said, "my own Blackness did not confront me with a shrill spelling of itself." She then grouped herself
with militant black writers and defined her work as belonging primarily to the African American community. In her earlier work, however, Brooks followed the example
of the older writers of the Harlem Renaissance, Langston Hughes and Countee Cullen among them, who honored the ideal of an integrated society. In that period her
work received support largely from white audiences. But Brooks's changing sense of
her commitments should not obscure her persistent, underlying concerns. She never
lacked political awareness, and in remarkably versatile poems, both early and late,
she wrote about black experience and black rage, with a particular awareness of the
complex lives of black women.

Brooks was born in Topeka, Kansas; she grew up in Chicago and is closely identified with the energies and problems of its black community. She went to Chicago's Englewood High School and graduated from Wilson Junior College. Brooks
remembered writing poetry from the time she was seven and keeping poetry notebooks from the time she was eleven. She got her education in the moderns—poets
such as Pound and Eliot—under the guidance of a rich Chicago socialite, Inez
Cunningham Stark, who was a reader for *Poetry* magazine and taught a poetry
class at the Southside Community Art Center. Her first book, *A Street in Bronzeville*
(1945), took its title from the name journalists gave to Chicago's black ghetto. Her
poems portrayed the waste and loss that are the inevitable result of what Langston
Hughes called the "dream deferred." With her second book of poems, *Annie Allen*
(1949), Brooks became the first African American to receive the Pulitzer Prize for
poetry.

In *Annie Allen* and in her Bronzeville poems (*Bronzeville Boys and Girls*, 1956,
continued the work begun in *A Street in Bronzeville*), Brooks concentrated on portraits of what Hughes called "the ordinary aspects of black life," stressing the vitality and the often subversive morality of ghetto figures. She portrayed the good girls
who want to be bad; the bored children of hardworking, pious mothers; the laments
of women, some of them mothers, abandoned by their men. Brooks's diction was
a combination of the florid biblical speech of black Protestant preachers, street
talk, and the traditional vocabulary of English and American verse. She wrote vigorous, strongly accented, and strongly rhymed lines with a great deal of alliteration.

She also cultivated traditional lyric forms; for example, she was one of the few modern poets to write extensively in the sonnet form.

A great change in Brooks's life came at Fisk University in 1967 with the Second Black Writers' Conference, in whose charged activist atmosphere she encountered many of the new young black poets. After this Brooks tested the possibility of writing poetry exclusively for black audiences. She drew closer to militant political groups as a result of conducting poetry workshops for some members of the Blackstone Rangers, a teenage gang in Chicago. In autobiographical writings such as her prose *Report from Part One* (1972), Brooks became more self-conscious about her own potential role as a leader of black feminists. She left her New York publisher to have her work printed by African American publishers, especially the Broadside Press. Brooks's poetry, too, changed, in both its focus and its technique. Her subjects tended to be more explicitly political and to deal with questions of revolutionary violence and issues of African American identity. Stylistically, her work evolved out of the concentrated imagery and narratives of her earlier writing, with its often formal diction, and moved toward an increased use of the energetic, improvisatory rhythms of jazz, the combinations of African chants, and an emphatically spoken language. The resulting poetry constantly revises itself and its sense of the world, open to change but evoking history. "How does one convey the influence Gwendolyn Brooks has had on generations—not only writers but people from all walks of life?" the poet Rita Dove has remarked, remembering how, as a young woman, she was "struck by these poems . . . that weren't afraid to take language and swamp it, twist it, and engage it so that it shimmered and dashed and lingered."

From A Street in Bronzeville

to David and Keziah Brooks

kitchenette building

We are things of dry hours and the involuntary plan,
Grayed in, and gray. "Dream" makes a giddy sound, not strong
Like "rent," "feeding a wife," "satisfying a man."

But could a dream send up through onion fumes
Its white and violet, fight with fried potatoes   5
And yesterday's garbage ripening in the hall,
Flutter, or sing an aria down these rooms

Even if we were willing to let it in,
Had time to warm it, keep it very clean,
Anticipate a message, let it begin?   10

We wonder. But not well! not for a minute!
Since Number Five is out of the bathroom now,
We think of lukewarm water, hope to get in it.

1945

the mother

Abortions will not let you forget.
You remember the children you got that you did not get,
The damp small pulps with a little or with no hair,
The singers and workers that never handled the air.
You will never neglect or beat   5
Them, or silence or buy with a sweet.
You will never wind up the sucking-thumb
Or scuttle off ghosts that come.
You will never leave them, controlling your luscious sigh,
Return for a snack of them, with gobbling mother-eye.   10

I have heard in the voices of the wind the voices of my dim
        killed children.
I have contracted. I have eased
My dim dears at the breasts they could never suck.
I have said, Sweets, if I sinned, if I seized
Your luck   15
And your lives from your unfinished reach,
If I stole your births and your names,
Your straight baby tears and your games,
Your stilted or lovely loves, your tumults, your marriages, aches,
        and your deaths,
If I poisoned the beginnings of your breaths,   20
Believe that even in my deliberateness I was not deliberate.
Though why should I whine,
Whine that the crime was other than mine?—
Since anyhow you are dead.
Or rather, or instead,   25
You were never made.

But that too, I am afraid,
Is faulty: oh, what shall I say, how is the truth to be said?
You were born, you had body, you died.
It is just that you never giggled or planned or cried.   30

Believe me, I loved you all.
Believe me, I knew you, though faintly, and I loved, I loved you
All.

                                                                      1945

a song in the front yard

I've stayed in the front yard all my life.
I want a peek at the back
Where it's rough and untended and hungry weed grows.
A girl gets sick of a rose.

I want to go in the back yard now 5
And maybe down the alley,
To where the charity children play.
I want a good time today.

They do some wonderful things.
They have some wonderful fun. 10
My mother sneers, but I say it's fine
How they don't have to go in at quarter to nine.
My mother, she tells me that Johnnie Mae
Will grow up to be a bad woman.
That George'll be taken to Jail soon or late 15
(On account of last winter he sold our back gate.)

But I say it's fine. Honest, I do.
And I'd like to be a bad woman, too,
And wear the brave stockings of night-black lace
And strut down the streets with paint on my face. 20

1945

The White Troops Had Their Orders But the Negroes Looked Like Men

They had supposed their formula was fixed.
They had obeyed instructions to devise
A type of cold, a type of hooded gaze.
But when the Negroes came they were perplexed.
These Negroes looked like men. Besides, it taxed 5
Time and the temper to remember those
Congenital iniquities that cause
Disfavor of the darkness. Such as boxed
Their feelings properly, complete to tags—
A box for dark men and a box for Other— 10
Would often find the contents had been scrambled.
Or even switched. Who really gave two figs?
Neither the earth nor heaven ever trembled.
And there was nothing startling in the weather.

1945

From The Womanhood

The Children of the Poor

II

What shall I give my children? who are poor,
Who are adjudged the leastwise of the land,
Who are my sweetest lepers, who demand

No velvet and no velvety velour;
But who have begged me for a brisk contour,   5
Crying that they are quasi, contraband
Because unfinished, graven by a hand
Less than angelic, admirable or sure.
My hand is stuffed with mode, design, device.
But I lack access to my proper stone.   10
And plenitude of plan shall not suffice
Nor grief nor love shall be enough alone
To ratify my little halves who bear
Across an autumn freezing everywhere.

                                                     1949

We Real Cool

THE POOL PLAYERS.
SEVEN AT THE GOLDEN SHOVEL.

We real cool. We
Left school. We

Lurk late. We
Strike straight. We

Sing sin. We   5
Thin gin. We

Jazz June. We
Die soon.

                                                     1960

The Bean Eaters

They eat beans mostly, this old yellow pair.
Dinner is a casual affair.
Plain chipware on a plain and creaking wood,
Tin flatware.

Two who are Mostly Good.   5
Two who have lived their day,
But keep on putting on their clothes
And putting things away.

And remembering . . .
Remembering, with twinklings and twinges,   10
As they lean over the beans in their rented back room that is full of beads
    and receipts and dolls and cloths, tobacco crumbs, vases and fringes.

                                                     1960

A Bronzeville Mother Loiters in Mississippi. Meanwhile a Mississippi Mother Burns Bacon

From the first it had been like a
Ballad. It had the beat inevitable. It had the blood.
A wildness cut up, and tied in little bunches,
Like the four-line stanzas of the ballads she had never quite
Understood—the ballads they had set her to, in school.   5

Herself: the milk-white maid, the "maid mild"
Of the ballad. Pursued
By the Dark Villain. Rescued by the Fine Prince.
The Happiness-Ever-After.
That was worth anything.   10
It was good to be a "maid mild."
That made the breath go fast.

Her bacon burned. She
Hastened to hide it in the step-on can, and
Drew more strips from the meat case. The eggs and sour-milk biscuits   15
Did well. She set out a jar
Of her new quince preserve.

. . . But there was a something about the matter of the Dark Villain.
He should have been older, perhaps.
The hacking down of a villain was more fun to think about   20
When his menace possessed undisputed breadth, undisputed height,
And a harsh kind of vice.
And best of all, when his history was cluttered
With the bones of many eaten knights and princesses.

The fun was disturbed, then all but nullified   25
When the Dark Villain was a blackish child
Of fourteen, with eyes still too young to be dirty,
And a mouth too young to have lost every reminder
Of its infant softness.

That boy must have been surprised! For   30
These were grown-ups. Grown-ups were supposed to be wise.
And the Fine Prince—and that other—so tall, so broad, so
Grown! Perhaps the boy had never guessed
That the trouble with grown-ups was that under the magnificent shell of
    adulthood, just under,
Waited the baby full of tantrums.   35

It occurred to her that there may have been something
Ridiculous in the picture of the Fine Prince
Rushing (rich with the breadth and height and
Mature solidness whose lack, in the Dark Villain, was impressing her,
Confronting her more and more as this first day after the trial   40
And acquittal wore on) rushing

With his heavy companion to hack down (unhorsed)
That little foe.
So much had happened, she could not remember now what that foe had done
Against her, or if anything had been done.   45
The one thing in the world that she did know and knew
With terrifying clarity was that her composition
Had disintegrated. That, although the pattern prevailed,
The breaks were everywhere. That she could think
Of no thread capable of the necessary   50
Sew-work.

She made the babies sit in their places at the table.
Then, before calling Him, she hurried
To the mirror with her comb and lipstick. It was necessary
To be more beautiful than ever.   55
The beautiful wife.
For sometimes she fancied he looked at her as though
Measuring her. As if he considered, Had she been worth It?

Had *she* been worth the blood, the cramped cries, the little stuttering
      bravado,
The gradual dulling of those Negro eyes,   60
The sudden, overwhelming *little-boyness* in that barn?
Whatever she might feel or half-feel, the lipstick necessity was something
      apart. He must never conclude
That she had not been worth It.

He sat down, the Fine Prince, and
Began buttering a biscuit. He looked at his hands.   65
He twisted in his chair, he scratched his nose.
He glanced again, almost secretly, at his hands.
More papers were in from the North, he mumbled. More meddling
      headlines.
With their pepper-words, "bestiality," and "barbarism," and
"Shocking."   70
The half-sneers he had mastered for the trial worked across
His sweet and pretty face.

What he'd like to do, he explained, was kill them all.
The time lost. The unwanted fame.
Still, it had been fun to show those intruders   75
A thing or two. To show that snappy-eyed mother,
That sassy, Northern, brown-black——

Nothing could stop Mississippi.
He knew that. Big Fella
Knew that.   80
And, what was so good, Mississippi knew that.
Nothing and nothing could stop Mississippi.
They could send in their petitions, and scar
Their newspapers with bleeding headlines. Their governors
Could appeal to Washington. . . .   85

"What I want," the older baby said, "is 'lasses on my jam."
Whereupon the younger baby
Picked up the molasses pitcher and threw
The molasses in his brother's face. Instantly
The Fine Prince leaned across the table and slapped   90
The small and smiling criminal.

She did not speak. When the Hand
Came down and away, and she could look at her child,
At her baby-child,
She could think only of blood.   95
Surely her baby's cheek
Had disappeared, and in its place, surely,
Hung a heaviness, a lengthening red, a red that had no end.
She shook her head. It was not true, of course.
It was not true at all. The   100
Child's face was as always, the
Color of the paste in her paste-jar.

She left the table, to the tune of the children's lamentations, which were
     shriller
Than ever. She
Looked out of a window. She said not a word. *That*   105
Was one of the new Somethings—
The fear,
Tying her as with iron.

Suddenly she felt his hands upon her. He had followed her
To the window. The children were whimpering now.   110
Such bits of tots. And she, their mother,
Could not protect them. She looked at her shoulders, still
Gripped in the claim of his hands. She tried, but could not resist the idea
That a red ooze was seeping, spreading darkly, thickly, slowly,
Over her white shoulders, her own shoulders,   115
And over all of Earth and Mars.

He whispered something to her, did the Fine Prince, something
About love, something about love and night and intention.

She heard no hoof-beat of the horse and saw no flash of the shining steel.
He pulled her face around to meet   120
His, and there it was, close close,
For the first time in all those days and nights,
His mouth, wet and red,
So very, very, very red,
Closed over hers.   125

Then a sickness heaved within her. The courtroom Coca-Cola,
The courtroom beer and hate and sweat and drone,
Pushed like a wall against her. She wanted to bear it.
But his mouth would not go away and neither would the
Decapitated exclamation points in that Other Woman's eyes.   130

She did not scream.
She stood there.
But a hatred for him burst into glorious flower,
And its perfume enclasped them—big,
Bigger than all magnolias.   135

The last bleak news of the ballad.
The rest of the rugged music.
The last quatrain.

1960

The Last Quatrain of the Ballad of Emmett Till[1]

after the murder,
after the burial

Emmett's mother is a pretty-faced thing;
    the tint of pulled taffy.
She sits in a red room,   5
    drinking black coffee.
She kisses her killed boy.
    And she is sorry.
Chaos in windy grays
    through a red prairie.   10

1960

The Blackstone Rangers[1]

I. As Seen by Disciplines[2]

There they are.
Thirty at the corner.
Black, raw, ready.
Sores in the city
that do not want to heal.   5

II. The Leaders

Jeff. Gene. Geronimo. And Bop.
They cancel, cure and curry.
Hardly the dupes of the downtown thing
the cold bonbon,
the rhinestone thing. And hardly   10
in a hurry.

---

1. A fourteen-year-old African American boy lynched in Mississippi in 1955 for allegedly "leering" at a white woman.

1. A tough Chicago street gang. Blackstone Street is the eastern boundary of Chicago's black ghetto.
2. I.e., law enforcers.

Hardly Belafonte, King,
Black Jesus, Stokely, Malcolm X or Rap.[3]
Bungled trophies.
Their country is a Nation on no map.   15

Jeff, Gene, Geronimo and Bop
in the passionate noon,
in bewitching night
are the detailed men, the copious men.
They curry, cure,   20
they cancel, cancelled images whose Concerts
are not divine, vivacious; the different tins
are intense last entries; pagan argument;
translations of the night.

The Blackstone bitter bureaus   25
(bureaucracy is footloose) edit, fuse
unfashionable damnations and descent;
and exulting, monstrous hand on monstrous hand,
construct, strangely, a monstrous pearl or grace.

III. Gang Girls

A RANGERETTE

Gang Girls are sweet exotics.   30
Mary Ann
uses the nutrients of her orient,
but sometimes sighs for Cities of blue and jewel
beyond her Ranger rim of Cottage Grove.[4]
(Bowery Boys, Disciples, Whip-Birds will   35
dissolve no margins, stop no savory sanctities.)

Mary is
a rose in a whiskey glass.

Mary's
Februaries shudder and are gone. Aprils   40
fret frankly, lilac hurries on.
Summer is a hard irregular ridge.
October looks away.
And that's the Year!

3. Belafonte: Harold George Belafonte (b. 1927), Jamaican-American musician, actor, and social activist, who popularized the Caribbean musical style and has advocated for civil rights and humanitarian causes throughout his career. King: Martin Luther King Jr. (1929–1968), Baptist pastor, one of the most prominent civil rights activists of the 1950s and 1960s. He followed a philosophy of nonviolence and led nonviolent demonstrations against segregation and injustice. He was also a gifted and eloquent orator on the subject of civil rights. "Black Jesus": One representation of Jesus, generally accepted by the black Christian community in Africa. Stokely Carmi-chael (1941–1998), Trinidadian-American black activist, leader of the Student Nonviolent Coordinating Committee (SNCC) and the Black Panthers. He urged African Americans to form and lead their own organizations and to reject the values and cultural mores of American society. Malcolm X: b. Malcolm Little (1925–1965), also known as Malik El-Shabazz, a black Muslim Minister, a national spokesman for the National of Islam, and one of the most prominent black nationalist leaders in the United States. He advocated black pride, economic self-reliance, and identity politics.
4. Street of overcrowded tenements in the ghetto.

Save for her bugle-love.   45
Save for the bleat of not-obese devotion.
Save for Somebody Terribly Dying, under
the philanthropy of robins. Save for her Ranger
bringing
an amount of rainbow in a string-drawn bag.   50
"Where did you get the diamond?" Do not ask:
but swallow, straight, the spirals of his flask
and assist him at your zipper; pet his lips
and help him clutch you.

Love's another departure.   55
Will there be any arrivals, confirmations?
Will there be gleaning?

Mary, the Shakedancer's child
from the rooming-flat, pants carefully, peers at
her laboring lover. . . .   60
                    Mary! Mary Ann!
Settle for sandwiches! settle for stocking caps!
for sudden blood, aborted carnival,
the props and niceties of non-loneliness—
the rhymes of Leaning.   65

                                                    1968

To the Diaspora[1]

you did not know you were Afrika

When you set out for Afrika
you did not know you were going.
Because
you did not know you were Afrika.
You did not know the Black continent   5
that had to be reached
was you.

I could not have told you then that some sun
would come,
somewhere over the road,   10
would come evoking the diamonds
of you, the Black continent—
somewhere over the road.
You would not have believed my mouth.

When I told you, meeting you somewhere close   15
to the heat and youth of the road,
liking my loyalty, liking belief,
you smiled and you thanked me but very little believed me.

---

1. People settled far from their ancestral homelands.

Here is some sun. Some.
Now off into the places rough to reach.   20
Though dry, though drowsy, all unwillingly a-wobble,
into the dissonant and dangerous crescendo.
Your work, that was done, to be done to be done to be done.

1981

ROBERT DUNCAN
1919–1988

In *The Truth & Life of Myth: An Essay in Essential Autobiography* (1968) Robert Duncan writes: "In the very beginning, in the awakening of childhood back of this later awakening of the man I was to be, there had been my mother's voice reading the fairy tales and myths that were to remain the charged ground of my poetic reality." Myth remained for Duncan the ground of poetic reality throughout his life, expressing for him the relation between the individual life and the life of the universe. Duncan believed in the enduring truth of myth as a story of soul making, which was for him, as for Keats, the poet's primary activity. Learned and widely read, Duncan used myths from many traditions (in this, he reminds us of Ezra Pound), including those of Christianity, Jewish mysticism, and classical and Egyptian mythology.

Duncan's deepest concerns as a poet are expressed in the myth of Eros and Psyche, which he retells in "A Poem Beginning with a Line by Pindar." He once wrote, "Psyche must doubt and seek to know; reading must become life and writing; and all go wrong. There is no way then but Psyche's search, the creative work of a union in knowledge and experience." This description of Psyche's work might serve to describe his own: in "A Poem Beginning with a Line by Pindar" Duncan carries out the work of poets before him (Pound, William Carlos Williams, and especially Walt Whitman): the creative work of understanding experience (both the individual's and the nation's) and of recovering lost possibility. As Psyche's task is the recovery of Eros, Duncan is a love poet in the fullest sense. Love, for him, necessarily involves loss and recovery, death and life. In his work the recurring image of Atlantis, the fabled sunken island, reinforces this sense of a paradise lost through catastrophe, to be recovered by the poet, as by Psyche, through trial and through the effort of imagination.

Duncan's life began with loss: his mother died at his birth, in Oakland, California, and he connected this birth memory to his fascination with "the mother-country that has been lost in legend." He was adopted at six months by Edwin and Minnehaha Symmes, from whose engagement in Hermetic and Rosicrucian studies he took his continuing interest in the magical and the occult. Duncan grew to his early manhood and to his vocation as a poet during World War II, and he linked his understanding of his personal strife to a sense of national strife, as in "A Poem Beginning with a Line by Pindar." In 1936 he entered the University of California at Berkeley, where he found the first of several artistic and social communities that would always be an important part of his life. In 1938 he moved east and during the early 1940s lived in New York City, where he was part of a group of writers that included Anaïs Nin, Henry Miller, Kenneth Patchen, and George Barker. (The poems of his book *Caesar's Gate*, published in 1955, describe what he has called the "adolescent dismay" of this period.) In New York he also came in contact with the abstract expressionist painters, and he brought with him the excitement of what he had seen when he returned to Berkeley in 1946. There, under the mentorship of Kenneth Rexroth, Duncan along with the poets Jack Spicer and Robin Blaser began a "renaissance," which he has described as "a reinterpretation of the work of Stein, Joyce, Pound, H.D., Williams, D. H. Lawrence, not as 'we moderns' but as links in a spiritual tradition."

Heavenly City Earthly City, Duncan's first book, appeared in 1947. In the 1950s he encountered the poetics of Charles Olson, whose understanding of the poem as "a field of action" confirmed and invigorated Duncan's thinking about poetic forms. In 1956 he taught for several months at Black Mountain College in North Carolina, where Olson was rector. Also in the 1950s he began a domestic life with the painter Jess Collins, which was to inform his work for the rest of his life. The household they created together existed, for Duncan, in vital relation to his sense of place in the universe as a whole ("The imagination of this cosmos is as immediate to me as the imagination of my household or myself," he wrote in his essay "Toward an Open Universe"). Both hearth and cosmos are governed by love, for Duncan the creator of growth and harmony but also the source of fury and suffering. Since his essay "The Homosexual in Society" (1944), Duncan had openly declared his homosexuality, and his work gives powerful expression to the struggles of the passional self.

The publication of *The Opening of the Field* (1960) marked, Duncan said, the beginning of his mature work as a poet, and the poems of this book remain some of his finest. Close to this time he also began his important prose work *The H.D. Book*, a work-in-progress of which more than ten chapters appeared in little magazines during his life. Duncan first read H.D.'s *Trilogy* in the 1940s, and her poems were relatively unknown when he began his study of her. In what may be one of the most important works of criticism by an American poet in the twentieth century, he explores the connections between his work and H.D.'s and in various chapters comments brilliantly and provocatively on modernism more generally. Duncan was drawn to H.D. by a desire to reclaim the poetic ground from which mythology arises, a place (like the meadow in "Often I Am Permitted to Return to a Meadow") that permits return to the "first feeling" of childhood. Like William Blake, whom he began to study in 1950, Duncan is a poet of mythopoetic imagination, one for whom poetry is a form of spiritual testimony.

Duncan used "traditional" as an adjective of praise and understood his work as recovering the past in present meanings. His models included not only H.D. and Blake but also the major figures of Whitman and Dante. He was drawn toward Whitman and Dante, he wrote, as each "projected a poem central to his civilization and his vision of ultimate reality—*Leaves of Grass*, like *The Divina Commedia*, being not an epic narrative but the spiritual testament of self-realization." In the work of H.D., Whitman, and Dante, Duncan found the wholeness for which his Psyche searched.

Given that, for Duncan, everything in the universe is related, it is not surprising that his personal sense of apocalpyse extended into explicitly political poems. In his introduction to *Bending the Bow* (1971) he wrote, "We enter again and again the last days of our own history, for everywhere living productive forms in the evolution of forms fail, weaken or grow monstrous, destroying the terms of their existence." Duncan felt history grow monstrous especially during the events of the Vietnam War, and he struggled in his work to confront the meanings of that experience. One sign of the seriousness and difficulty of his struggle was his decision, in the 1970s, not to publish another book for at least ten years. The work gestating during that time emerged in two volumes: *Ground Work: Before the War* (1983) and *Ground Work II: In the Dark* (1987). Together the collections represent the culmination of Duncan's years of effort as a poet. What sets Duncan apart from many other poets who addressed the Vietnam War is that he does not separate himself from "the nation's store of crimes long / unacknowledged, unrepented" ("From Robert Southwell's 'The Burning Babe'"). In this and other poems Duncan confronts his own implication in the evils of war, in the nation's crimes, and he understands the task of self-restoration as a personal and political act.

Duncan's spiritual vision, which he distinguished from any religious orthodoxy, and his serious interest in mysticism set him apart from the mainstreams of contemporary American poetry. This, combined with fifteen years in which he chose to publish relatively little until his last books appeared, led to a neglect of his astonishing achievement as a poet. For Duncan, poetry has a generative function that is at the heart of life, and this makes his poems ambitious. If his work does not always achieve the wholeness to which it aspires, this may be, in part, because he aspires to so much. He believed that no single poem is ever complete in its meaning; each poem awakens the possibility of a new beginning. Although his range of reference can sometimes leave the reader behind, Duncan's best work reaches beyond itself, stirring the reader into just such an awakened sense of life.

Often I Am Permitted to Return to a Meadow

as if it were a scene made-up by the mind,
that is not mine, but is a made place,

that is mine, it is so near to the heart,
an eternal pasture folded in all thought
so that there is a hall therein   5

that is a made place, created by light
wherefrom the shadows that are forms fall.

Wherefrom fall all architectures I am
I say are likenesses of the First Beloved
whose flowers are flames lit to the Lady.   10

She it is Queen Under The Hill[1]
whose hosts are a disturbance of words within words
that is a field folded.

It is only a dream of the grass blowing
east against the source of the sun   15
in an hour before the sun's going down

whose secret we see in a children's game
of ring a round of roses told.

Often I am permitted to return to a meadow
as if it were a given property of the mind   20
that certain bounds hold against chaos,

that is a place of first permission,
everlasting omen of what is.

1960

1. I.e., Persephone, or Kora, queen of life and death. The daughter of Demeter, the Greek goddess of fruitfulness and harvest, she was kidnapped by Hades and became his queen in the Underworld, where she lived several months of the year. The remaining months she spent with her mother in the upper world.

A Poem Beginning with a Line by Pindar[1]

I

The light foot hears you and the brightness begins[2]
god-step at the margins of thought,
    quick adulterous tread at the heart.
Who is it that goes there?
    Where I see your quick face   5
notes of an old music pace the air,
torse-reverberations[3] of a Grecian lyre.

In Goya's canvas Cupid and Psyche[4]
have a hurt voluptuous grace
bruised by redemption. The copper light   10
falling upon the brown boy's slight body
is carnal fate that sends the soul wailing
up from blind innocence, ensnared
    by dimness
into the deprivations of desiring sight.   15

But the eyes in Goya's painting are soft,
diffuse with rapture absorb the flame.
Their bodies yield out of strength.
    Waves of visual pleasure
wrap them in a sorrow previous to their impatience.   20

A bronze of yearning, a rose that burns
    the tips of their bodies, lips,
ends of fingers, nipples. He is not wingd.
His thighs are flesh, are clouds
    lit by the sun in its going down,   25
Hot luminescence at the loins of the visible.

1. Greek lyric poet (c. 522–c. 438 B.C.E.), author of celebratory odes. "When in the inception of a 'Poem Beginning with a Line by Pindar,' reading late at night the third line of the first Pythian Ode in the translation by Wade-Gery and Bowra, my mind lost hold of Pindar's sense and was faced with certain puns in that the words *light, foot, hears, you, brightness, begins* moved in a world beyond my reading; these were no longer words alone but powers in a theogony, having resonances in Hesiodic and Orphic cosmogonies where the foot that moves in the dance of the poem appears as the pulse of measures in first things. Immediately, sight of Goya's great canvas, once seen in the Marquis deCambo's collection in Barcelona, came to me like a wave carrying the vision—out of the evocation of the fragment from Pindar and out of Goya's pictorial evocation, to add to the masterly powers of my own—the living vision, Cupid and Psyche were there; then the power of a third master, not a master of poetry or of picture but of storytelling, the power of Lucius Apuleius was there too . . . the living genius of these three stood as my masters, and I stood in the very presence of the story of Cupid and Psyche" (Duncan, *The Truth and Life of Myth*). A "theogony" is an account of the origin and descent of the gods; a "cosmogony," an account of the origin of the world or universe. Hesiod was a Greek poet (fl. 800 B.C.E.), among whose works was a *Theogony*. "Orphic" has to do with the legendary Greek poet-musician Orpheus or the rites ascribed to him. For Goya, Cupid and Psyche, and Apuleius, see n. 4, below.
2. The third line of Pindar's Pythian Ode.
3. "Torse": twisted or wreathed.
4. The Spanish artist Francisco José de Goya (1746–1828) painted a canvas called *Cupid and Psyche*. The story of Cupid and Psyche is told by the Latin writer Lucius Apuleius (fl. c. 155 C.E.) in *The Golden Ass*. Psyche (the Greek personification of the soul) marries Cupid, or Eros (the god of love). As a condition of their union Cupid forbids her to look at him and comes to her only in darkness, leaving before dawn. Prompted by her sisters, Psyche disobeys, and Cupid flees. Through a series of trials, however, she becomes immortal and is reunited with Cupid forever.

But they are not in a landscape.
They exist in an obscurity.

The wind spreading the sail serves them.
The two jealous sisters eager for her ruin   30
    serve them.
That she is ignorant, ignorant of what Love will be,
    serves them.
The dark serves them.
The oil scalding his shoulder serves them,[5]   35
serves their story. Fate, spinning,
    knots the threads for Love.

Jealousy, ignorance, the hurt . . . serve them.

II

This is magic. It is passionate dispersion.
What if they grow old? The gods   40
    would not allow it.
      Psyche is preserved.

In time we see a tragedy, a loss of beauty
    the glittering youth
of the god retains—but from this threshold   45
    it is age
that is beautiful. It is toward the old poets
    we go, to their faltering,
their unaltering wrongness that has style,
    their variable truth,   50
    the old faces,
words shed like tears from
a plenitude of powers time stores.

A stroke.   These little strokes.   A chill.
    The old man, feeble, does not recoil[6]   55
Recall. A phase so minute,
    only a part of the word in- jerrd.

    The Thundermakers descend,

damerging a nuv. A nerb.
    The present dented of the U   60
nighted stayd.   States.   The heavy clod?
    Cloud.   Invades the brain.   What
    if lilacs last in *this* dooryard bloomd?[7]

---

5. In the story Psyche holds an oil lamp above the sleeping Cupid to see him, but a drop of oil spills onto his shoulder. He wakes and flees.
6. A reference to the American poet William Carlos Williams (1883–1963), who suffered a series of strokes that injured his capacity for speech. Duncan phonetically presents this damage.
7. "When Lilacs Last in the Dooryard Bloom'd," Walt Whitman's elegy for Abraham Lincoln, was published in 1866.

Hoover, Roosevelt, Truman, Eisenhower[8]—
where among these did the power reside   65
that moves the heart? What flower of the nation
bride-sweet broke to the whole rapture?
Hoover, Coolidge, Harding, Wilson[9]
hear the factories of human misery turning out commodities.
For whom are the holy matins of the heart ringing?   70
Noble men in the quiet of morning hear
Indians singing the continent's violent requiem.
Harding, Wilson, Taft, Roosevelt,[1]
idiots fumbling at the bride's door,
hear the cries of men in meaningless debt and war.   75
Where among these did the spirit reside
that restores the land to productive order?
McKinley, Cleveland, Harrison, Arthur,
Garfield, Hayes, Grant, Johnson,[2]
dwell in the roots of the heart's rancor.   80
How sad "amid lanes and through old woods"[3]
    echoes Whitman's love for Lincoln!

There is no continuity then.   Only a few
        posts of the good remain.   I too
that am a nation sustain the damage   85
        where smokes of continual ravage
obscure the flame.
                    It is across great scars of wrong
        I reach toward the song of kindred men
        and strike again the naked string   90
old Whitman sang from. Glorious mistake!
        that cried:

    "The theme is creative and has vista."
    "He is the president of regulation."[4]

    I see always the under side turning,   95
fumes that injure the tender landscape.
        From which up break
lilac blossoms of courage in daily act
        striving to meet a natural measure.

---

8. U.S. presidents (terms of office follow): Herbert Hoover (1929–33), Franklin Roosevelt (1933–45), Harry Truman (1945–52), and Dwight Eisenhower (1953–61).
9. U.S. presidents: Calvin Coolidge (1923–29), Warren Harding (1921–23), and Woodrow Wilson (1913–21).
1. U.S. presidents: William Taft (1909–13), Theodore Roosevelt (1901–09).
2. U.S. presidents: William McKinley (1897–1901), Grover Cleveland (1885–89; 1893–97), Benjamin Harrison (1889–93), Chester Arthur (1881–85), James Garfield (March–September 1881; assassinated), Rutherford Hayes (1869–77), and Andrew Johnson (1865–69).
3. From Whitman's "When Lilacs Last in the Dooryard Bloom'd."
4. From Whitman's "Preface" to the 1855 edition of Leaves of Grass; in it he declares the great, creative theme of the American republic and the role of the poet in the United States: "Their Presidents shall not be their common referee so much as their poets shall."

III   (*for Charles Olson*)[5]

                Psyche's tasks—the sorting of seeds   100

wheat   barley   oats   poppy   coriander
anise   beans   lentils   peas   —every grain
            in its right place
                       before nightfall;
gathering the gold wool from the cannibal sheep   105
(for the soul must weep
      and come near upon death);

harrowing Hell for a casket Proserpina keeps
                      that must not
be opend . . . containing beauty?   110

no!   Melancholy coild like a serpent
                 that is deadly sleep
     we are not permitted
          to succumb to.
These are the old tasks.[6]   115
You've heard them before.

     They must be impossible. Psyche
must despair, be brought to her
                 insect instructor;
must obey the counsels of the green reed;   120
saved from suicide by a tower speaking,
     must follow to the letter
     freakish instructions.[7]

In the story the ants help. The old man at Pisa[8]
     mixd in whose mind   125
(to draw the sorts) are all seeds
     as a lone ant from a broken ant-hill[9]
had part restored by an insect, was
     upheld by a lizard

             (to draw the sorts)   130
the wind is part of the process[1]
         defines a nation of the wind—

5. American poet and friend of Duncan's (1910–1970). His essay "Projective Verse" (see the "Postmodern Manifestos" cluster of this anthology) encouraged Duncan's sense of the poem as a "field."

6. To be reunited with Cupid, Psyche must accomplish a series of tasks set by Venus (Cupid's mother): she must separate and sort a storehouse of seeds, she must bring Venus some of the gold fleece from a flock of cannibal sheep, and she must descend to Hell to bring back to Venus a measure of the beauty of Proserpina, queen of the Underworld.

7. In these tasks Psyche is aided by ants, who help sort the grain; by the river god, who instructs her in how to gather fleece; and by a voice from a tower, which instructs her in how to reach Hell safely and what she must do on return.

8. The American poet Ezra Pound (1885–1972), from whose *Pisan Cantos* (part of his long poem *The Cantos*) Duncan quotes. Pound wrote these cantos while imprisoned for treason by American forces in Italy during World War II.

9. Pound, "Canto LXXVI." "Draw the sorts": draw lots, cast fortunes.

1. Pound, "Canto LXXIV."

father of many notions,
                               Who?
let the light into the dark?   began   135
the many movements of the passion?
                                       West
from east   men push.
                         The islands are blessd
(cursed)   that swim below the sun,   140

   man upon whom the sun has gone down![2]

There is the hero who struggles east
widdershins[3] to free the dawn   and must
                     woo Night's daughter,
sorcery, black passionate rage, covetous queens,   145
so that the fleecy sun go   back from Troy,
        Colchis,[4] India . . . all the blazing armies
spent, he must struggle alone toward the pyres of Day.

                     The light that is Love
rushes on toward passion. It verges upon dark.   150
        Roses and blood flood the clouds.
        Solitary first riders advance into legend.

   This land, where I stand, was all legend
in my grandfathers' time: cattle raiders,
        animal tribes, priests, gold.   155
It was the West.[5] Its vistas painters saw
        in diffuse light, in melancholy,
in abysses left by glaciers as if they had been the sun
        primordial carving empty enormities
                     out of the rock.   160

                  Snakes lurk
guarding secrets.   Those first ones
                     survived solitude.

        Scientia
holding the lamp, driven by doubt;[6]   165
Eros naked in foreknowledge
smiling in his sleep;   and the light
spilld, burning his shoulder—the outrage
        that conquers legend—
passion, dismay, longing, search   170
        flooding up where

2. A reference to Odysseus, hero of Homer's *Odyssey*. Duncan here quotes Pound's epithet for the hero, whose movement is toward home, in his "Canto LXXIV." In this section of the poem Duncan fuses several mythic questors, among them Psyche, Odysseus, and Jason.
3. In a contrary direction; here, opposite to the usual course of the sun.
4. An ancient country on the eastern shore of the Black Sea, the land where Jason and the Argonauts sought a golden fleece. "Fleecy sun": i.e., the golden fleece Psyche must bring to Venus. The ancient city of Troy was the site of the Trojan War, after which Odysseus began his journey home.
5. The American West.
6. The desire to know what Cupid looks like drives Psyche to her mistake. "Scientia": knowledge.

the Beloved is lost.   Psyche travels
life after life, my life, station
        after station,
to be tried   175
        without break, without
news, knowing only—but what did she know?
    The oracle at Miletus had spoken
truth surely: that he was Serpent-Desire
        that flies thru the air,   180
a monster-husband.[7] But she saw him fair

whom Apollo's mouthpiece said spread
        pain
beyond cure   to those
        wounded by his arrows.   185

Rilke torn by a rose thorn[8]
blackend toward Eros.   Cupidinous Death!
    that will not take no for an answer.

IV

    Oh yes!   Bless the footfall where
step by step   the boundary walker   190
(in Maverick Road   the snow
thud by thud   from the roof
circling the house—another tread)

    that foot   informd
by the weight of all things   195
        that can be elusive
no more than a nearness to the mind
        of a single image

            Oh yes!   this
most dear   200
        the catalyst force that renders clear
the days of a life from the surrounding medium!
        Yes, beautiful rare wilderness!
wildness that verifies strength of my tame mind,
        clearing held against indians,   205
health that prepared to meet death,
        the stubborn hymns going up
into the ramifications of the hostile air

    that, deceptive, gives way.

7. In Apuleius's story Psyche's parents consult
the oracle (shrine from which a god reveals the
future) of Apollo at Miletus before her marriage
to Eros. The oracle responds that Psyche is destined for no mortal lover and that her husband
will be a monster "whom neither gods nor men
can resist."
8. Rainer Maria Rilke (1875–1926), German lyric
poet whose work expresses the interconnections
of life, death, and love; he died from a rose-thorn
scratch.

Who is there?   O, light the light!   210
        The Indians give way,   the clearing falls.
Great Death gives way   and unprepares us.
        Lust gives way.   The Moon gives way.
Night gives way.   Minutely,   the Day gains.

She saw the body of her beloved   215
        dismemberd in waking . . . or was it
in sight?   *Finders Keepers* we sang
        when we were children   or were taught to sing
before our histories began   and we began
        who were beloved   our animal life   220
toward the Beloved,   sworn to be Keepers.

        On the hill before the wind came
the grass moved toward the one sea,
        blade after blade dancing in waves.

There the children turn the ring to the left.   225
There the children turn the ring to the right.
        Dancing . . . Dancing . . .

And the lonely psyche goes up thru the boy to the king
        that in the caves of history dreams.
Round and round the children turn.   230
        London Bridge that is a kingdom falls.[9]

We have come so far that all the old stories
whisper once more.
Mount Segur, Mount Victoire, Mount Tamalpais[1] . . .
        rise to adore the mystery of Love!   235

(An ode? Pindar's art, the editors tell us, was not a statue but a mosaic,
an accumulation of metaphor. But if he was archaic, not classic, a survival of obsolete mode, there may have been old voices in the survival
that directed the heart. So, a line from a hymn came in a novel I was
reading to help me. Psyche, poised to leap—and Pindar too, the editors   240
write, goes too far, topples over—listend to a tower that said, *Listen to
me!* The oracle[2] had said, *Despair! The Gods themselves abhor his power.*
And then the virgin flower of the dark falls back flesh of our flesh from
which everywhere . . .

                the information flows   245
                    that is yearning. A line of Pindar
                moves from the area of my lamp
                    toward morning.

---

9. Reference to the children's song "London
Bridge Is Falling Down."
1. Duncan's list of mountains moves from east
to west; to Mount Tamalpais, in western California, across the Golden Gate from San Francisco,
where Duncan lived.
2. I.e., the tower that spoke to Psyche on her
quest and the oracle of Apollo that warned
Psyche's parents.

In the dawn that is nowhere
   I have seen the willful children   250

clockwise and counter-clockwise turning.

                                    1960

Interrupted Forms

Long slumbering, often coming forward,
haunting the house I am the house I live in
resembles so, does he recall me or I
recall him?   Seeing you the other day
long I lookt to see your face his, longing   5
without reason.   I meant to tell
or spell your name, to dwell in the charm
I almost felt in the stone,   the impassive
weight of old feeling, the cold awakening
I meant to tell you of, as if telling could reach you,   10
at last come into your embrace again, my arms
hold you, mounting, coming into your life
my life and interruption of all long lasting
              inertia in feeling,
arousal.   15

         In dreams
insubstantially you have come before my eyes'
expectations, and, even in waking,
taking over the field of sight   fleetingly
stronger than what my eyes see,   20
the thought of you thought has eyes to see
has eyes to meet your answering eyes
thought raises.   I am speaking of a ghost
the heart is glad to have return,   of a room
I have often been lonely in,   of a desertion   25
that remains even where I am most cherisht
and surrounded by Love's company,   of a form,
wholly fulfilling the course of my life, interrupted,
of a cold in the full warmth of the sunlight
that seeks to come in close to your heart   30
              for warmth.

                                    1984

RICHARD WILBUR
b. 1921

Richard Wilbur was born in New York City and grew up in the country in New Jersey. His father was a painter, and his mother came from a family prominent in journalism. He was educated at Amherst College, where Robert Frost was a frequent guest and teacher, and Wilbur's remarkable gifts as a prosodist often remind us of the older poet. Of the effects of his college years Wilbur says: "Most American poets of my generation were taught to admire the English metaphysical poets of the seventeenth century and such contemporary masters of irony as John Crowe Ransom. We were led by our teachers and by the critics whom we read to feel that the most adequate and convincing poetry is that which accommodates mixed feelings, clashing ideas, and incongruous images." Nevertheless, over his long and varied career he has written in a wide range of forms, including the dramatic monologue (represented here by "The Mind-Reader").

After graduation and service in the infantry in Italy and France (1943–45), Wilbur returned to study for an M.A. at Harvard, with a firm notion of what he expected to get out of poetry. "My first poems were written in answer to the inner and outer disorders of the Second World War and they helped me . . . to take ahold of raw events and convert them, provisionally, into experience." He reasserted the balance of mind against instinct and violence: "The praiseful, graceful soldier/Shouldn't be fired by his gun." The poised lyrics in *The Beautiful Changes* (1947), including the lovely title poem of that volume, and *Ceremony* (1950) also reclaimed the value of pleasure, defined as an interplay of intelligence with sensuous enjoyment. Whether looking at a real French landscape, as in "Grasse: The Olive Trees," or a French landscape painting, as in "Ceremony," the point was to show the witty shaping power of the mind in nature.

Wilbur prefers strict stanzaic forms and meters; "limitation makes for power: the strength of the genie comes of his being confined in a bottle." In individual lines and the structure of an entire poem, his emphasis is on a civilized balancing of perceptions. "A World without Objects Is a Sensible Emptiness" begins with the "tall camels of the spirit" but qualifies our views of lonely spiritual impulses. The poem summons us back to find visionary truth grasped through sensual experience. "All shining things need to be shaped and borne." Wilbur favors what he has called "a spirituality which is not abstracted, not dissociated and world-renouncing," as is clear from "Love Calls Us to the Things of This World," a hymn of praise to clothes hanging on a laundry line ("Oh, let there be nothing on earth but laundry"). "A good part of my work could, I suppose, be understood as a public quarrel with the aesthetics of Edgar Allan Poe"—presumably with Poe's notion that poetry provided *indefinite* sensations and aspired to the abstract condition of music.

Wilbur was among the first of the younger postwar poets to adopt a style of living and working different from the masters of an earlier generation—from Eliot, an ironic priestlike modernist who lived as a publisher-poet in England, or William Carlos Williams, a doctor in New Jersey, or Wallace Stevens, a remote insurance executive in Connecticut. Wilbur was a teacher-poet and gave frequent readings. Instead of thinking of himself as an alienated artist, he came to characterize himself as a "poet-citizen," part of what he judged a widening community of poets addressing themselves to an audience increasingly responsive to poetry. Wilbur's taste for civilized wit and his metrical skill made him an ideal translator of the seventeenth-century satirical comedies of Molière, *The Misanthrope* (1955) and *Tartuffe* (1963). They are frequently staged, as is the musical version of Voltaire's *Candide* for which Wilbur was one of the collaborating lyricists. Wilbur received the Pulitzer Prize for his volume *Things of This World* (1956) and served as the second poet laureate of the United States in 1987–88. His *Collected Poems 1943–2004* appeared in 2004.

The Beautiful Changes

One wading a Fall meadow finds on all sides
The Queen Anne's Lace lying like lilies
On water; it glides
So from the walker, it turns
Dry grass to a lake, as the slightest shade of you   5
Valleys my mind in fabulous blue Lucernes.[1]

The beautiful changes as a forest is changed
By a chameleon's tuning his skin to it;
As a mantis, arranged
On a green leaf, grows   10
Into it, makes the leaf leafier, and proves
Any greenness is deeper than anyone knows.

Your hands hold roses always in a way that says
They are not only yours; the beautiful changes
In such kind ways,   15
Wishing ever to sunder
Things and things' selves for a second finding, to lose
For a moment all that it touches back to wonder.

1947

The Death of a Toad

A toad the power mower caught,
Chewed and clipped of a leg, with a hobbling hop has got
    To the garden verge, and sanctuaried him
    Under the cineraria leaves, in the shade
        Of the ashen heartshaped leaves, in a dim,   5
            Low, and a final glade.

    The rare original heartsblood goes,
Spends on the earthen hide, in the folds and wizenings, flows
    In the gutters of the banked and staring eyes. He lies
    As still as if he would return to stone,   10
        And soundlessly attending, dies
            Toward some deep monotone,

---

1. Lakes having the quality of Switzerland's Lake Lucerne, known for its beauty.

Toward misted and ebullient seas
And cooling shores, toward lost Amphibia's emperies.[1]
Day dwindles, drowning, and at length is gone   15
In the wide and antique eyes, which still appear
To watch, across the castrate lawn,
The haggard daylight steer.

1950

"A World without Objects Is a Sensible Emptiness"[1]

The tall camels of the spirit
Steer for their deserts, passing the last groves loud
With the sawmill shrill of the locust, to the whole honey of the arid
Sun. They are slow, proud,

And move with a stilted stride   5
To the land of sheer horizon, hunting Traherne's
Sensible emptiness, there where the brain's lantern-slide
Revels in vast returns.

O connoisseurs of thirst,
Beasts of my soul who long to learn to drink   10
Of pure mirage, those prosperous islands are accurst
That shimmer on the brink

Of absence; auras, lustres,
And all shinings need to be shaped and borne.
Think of those painted saints, capped by the early masters   15
With bright, jauntily-worn

Aureate plates, or even
Merry-go-round rings. Turn, O turn
From the fine sleights of the sand, from the long empty oven
Where flames in flamings burn   20

Back to the trees arrayed
In bursts of glare, to the halo-dialing run
Of the country creeks, and the hills' bracken tiaras made
Gold in the sunken sun,

Wisely watch for the sight   25
Of the supernova[2] burgeoning over the barn,
Lampshine blurred in the stream of beasts, the spirit's right
Oasis, light incarnate.

1950

1. Archaic for "empires." "Amphibia" refers to "double life" and animals who live on water or land.
1. From "Meditation 65," by the English Metaphysical poet Thomas Traherne (c. 1638–1674):
"Life without objects is sensible emptiness, and that is a greater misery than death or nothing." ("Sensible" = "palpable to the senses.")
2. A scientific term for an exploding star, here associated with the Star of Bethlehem.

Love Calls Us to the Things of This World

The eyes open to a cry of pulleys,
And spirited from sleep, the astounded soul
Hangs for a moment bodiless and simple
As false dawn.
                Outside the open window   5
The morning air is all awash with angels.

Some are in bed-sheets, some are in blouses,
Some are in smocks: but truly there they are.
Now they are rising together in calm swells
Of halcyon[1] feeling, filling whatever they wear   10
With the deep joy of their impersonal breathing;

Now they are flying in place, conveying
The terrible speed of their omnipresence, moving
And staying like white water; and now of a sudden
They swoon down into so rapt a quiet   15
That nobody seems to be there.
                   The soul shrinks

From all that it is about to remember,
From the punctual rape of every blessèd day,
And cries,   20
        "Oh, let there be nothing on earth but laundry,
Nothing but rosy hands in the rising steam
And clear dances done in the sight of heaven."

Yet, as the sun acknowledges
With a warm look the world's hunks and colors,   25
The soul descends once more in bitter love
To accept the waking body, saying now
In a changed voice as the man yawns and rises,

"Bring them down from their ruddy gallows;
Let there be clean linen for the backs of thieves;   30
Let lovers go fresh and sweet to be undone,
And the heaviest nuns walk in a pure floating
Of dark habits,
            keeping their difficult balance."

1956

---

1. Calm, peaceful. The word originated as the name of a mythological bird anciently fabled to breed at about the time of the winter solstice in a nest floating on the sea, and then to charm the wind and waves so that the sea became especially calm.

The Mind-Reader

Lui parla.[1]

for Charles and Eula

Some things are truly lost. Think of a sun-hat
Laid for the moment on a parapet
While three young women—one, perhaps, in mourning—
Talk in the crenellate shade.[2] A slight wind plucks
And budges it; it scuffs to the edge and cartwheels   5
Into a giant view of some description:
Haggard escarpments,[3] if you like, plunge down
Through mica shimmer to a moss of pines
Amidst which, here or there, a half-seen river
Lobs up a blink of light. The sun-hat falls,   10
With what free flirts and stoops you can imagine,
Down through that reeling vista or another,
Unseen by any, even by you or me.
It is as when a pipe-wrench, catapulted
From the jounced back of a pick-up truck, dives headlong   15
Into a bushy culvert;[4] or a book
Whose reader is asleep, garbling the story,
Glides from beneath a steamer chair and yields
Its flurried pages to the printless sea.

It is one thing to escape from consciousness   20
As such things do, another to be pent
In the dream-cache or stony oubliette[5]
Of someone's head.

           They found, when I was little,
That I could tell the place of missing objects.   25
I stood by the bed of a girl, or the frayed knee
Of an old man whose face was lost in shadow.
When did you miss it?, people would be saying,
Where did you see it last? And then those voices,
Querying or replying, came to sound   30
Like cries of birds when the leaves race and whiten
And a black overcast is shelving over.
The mind is not a landscape, but if it were
There would in such case be a tilted moon
Wheeling beyond the wood through which you groped,   35
Its fine spokes breaking in the tangled thickets.
There would be obfuscations, paths which turned
To dried-up stream-beds, hemlocks which invited
Through shiny clearings to a groundless shade;   .
And yet in a sure stupor you would come   40
At once upon dilapidated cairns,

---

1. He [the mind-reader, an Italian] speaks.
2. I.e., the shade provided by battlements.
3. Worn cliffs.

4. Drain under a road. "Pipe-wrench": wrench
for gripping and turning metal pipe.
5. Dungeon pit (French *oublie*, "to forget").

Abraded moss, and half-healed blazes[6] leading
To where, around the turning of a fear,
The lost thing shone.

                    Imagine a railway platform—   45
The long cars come to a cloudy halt beside it,
And the fogged windows offering a view
Neither to those within nor those without,
Now, in the crowd—forgive my predilection—
Is a young woman standing amidst her luggage,   50
Expecting to be met by you, a stranger.
See how she turns her head, the eyes engaging
And disengaging, pausing and shying away.
It is like that with things put out of mind,
As the queer saying goes: a lost key hangs   55
Trammeled by threads in what you come to see
As the webbed darkness of a sewing-basket,
Flashing a little; or a photograph,
Misplaced in an old ledger, turns its bled
Oblivious profile to rebuff your vision,   60
Yet glistens with the fixative of thought.
What can be wiped from memory? Not the least
Meanness, obscenity, humiliation,
Terror which made you clench your eyes, or pulse
Of happiness which quickened your despair.   65
Nothing can be forgotten, as I am not
Permitted to forget.

                    It was not far
From that to this—this corner café table
Where, with my lank grey hair and vatic gaze,[7]   70
I sit and drink at the receipt of custom.
They come here, day and night, so many people:
Sad women of the quarter, dressed in black,
As to a black confession; blinking clerks
Who half-suppose that Taurus ruminates   75
Upon their destinies;[8] men of affairs
Down from Milan to clear it with the magus[9]
Before they buy or sell some stock or other;
My fellow-drunkards; fashionable folk,
Mocking and ravenously credulous,   80
And skeptics bent on proving me a fraud
For fear that some small wonder, unexplained,
Should leave a fissure in the world, and all
Saint Michael's host[1] come flapping back.

---

6. Cuts on trees to mark a path in a forest. "Cairns" (piles of stones) and rubbed-away moss would serve the same purpose.
7. I.e., a gaze like that of a prophet.
8. I.e., that they are influenced by astrological signs (of which Taurus, the bull, is one).
9. Expert in the occult.
1. St. Michael the archangel and his host of angels, whose war in heaven is predicted in Revelation 12.7–9.

                                        I give them   85
Paper and pencil, turn away and light
A cigarette, as you have seen me do;
They write their questions; fold them up; I lay
My hand on theirs and go into my frenzy,
Raising my eyes to heaven, snorting smoke,   90
Lolling my head as in the fumes of Delphi;[2]
And then, with shaken, spirit-guided fingers,
Set down the oracle. All that, of course,
Is trumpery,[3] since nine times out of ten
What words float up within another's thought   95
Surface as soon as mine, unfolding there
Like paper flowers in a water-glass.
In the tenth case, I sometimes cheat a little.
That shocks you? But consider: what I do
Cannot, so most conceive, be done at all,   100
And when I fail, I am a charlatan
Even to such as I have once astounded—
Whereas a tailor can mis-cut my coat
And be a tailor still. I tell you this
Because you know that I have the gift, the burden.   105
Whether or not I put my mind to it,
The world usurps me ceaselessly; my sixth
And never-resting sense is a cheap room
Black with the anger of insomnia,
Whose wall-boards vibrate with the mutters, plaints,   110
And flushings of the race.[4]

                            What should I tell them?
I have no answers. *Set your fears at rest,*
I scribble when I must. *Your paramour*
Is faithful, and your spouse is unsuspecting.   115
You were not seen, that day, beneath the fig-tree.
Still, be more cautious. When the time is ripe,
Expect promotion. I foresee a message
From a far person who is rich and dying.
You are admired in secret. If, in your judgment,   120
Profit is in it, you should take the gamble.
As for these fits of weeping, they will pass.

It makes no difference that my lies are bald
And my evasions casual. It contents them
Not to have spoken, yet to have been heard.   125
What more do they deserve, if I could give it,
Mute breathers as they are of selfish hopes
And small anxieties? Faith, justice, valor,
All those reputed rarities of soul
Confirmed in marble by our public statues—   130
You may be sure that they are rare indeed

---

2. Site of the most famous Greek oracle, at which, for a fee, seekers could have their questions answered by a priestess possessed by the "fumes."

3. Worthless nonsense.
4. I.e., the human race. "Plaints, / And flushings": complaints and sudden rushes of emotion.

Where the soul mopes in private, and I listen.
Sometimes I wonder if the blame is mine,
If through a sullen fault of the mind's ear
I miss a resonance in all their fretting.   135
Is there some huge attention, do you think,
Which suffers us and is inviolate,
To which all hearts are open, which remarks
The sparrow's weighty fall,[5] and overhears
In the worst rancor a deflected sweetness?   140
I should be glad to know it.

                              Meanwhile, saved
By the shrewd habit of concupiscence,
which, like a visor, narrows my regard,
And drinking studiously until my thought   145
Is a blind lowered almost to the sill,
I hanker for that place beyond the sparrow
Where the wrench beds in mud, the sun-hat hangs
In densest branches, and the book is drowned.[6]
Ah, you have read my mind. One more, perhaps . . .   150
A mezzo-litro. Grazie, professore.[7]

                                                                    1976

5. Shakespeare's Hamlet, just before his death, speaks of the "special providence in the fall of a sparrow" (5.2.157–58).
6. At the end of Shakespeare's *Tempest*, the magician Prospero renounces his island and his magic, saying, "Deeper than did ever plummet sound / I'll drown my book" (5.1.56–57).
7. The speaker thanks the listening "professore" for the offer of another half-liter of wine.

JACK KEROUAC
1922–1969

Like the lives of many trailblazing writers, Jack Kerouac's life was filled with contradictions. Regarded as a liberator of prose and champion of idiomatic American expression, he did not start learning English until grade school and never felt comfortable speaking it until he finished high school (his parents were of French-Canadian background, and French was the family's language at home in Lowell, Massachusetts; his given name was "Jean-Louis"). Having won a football scholarship to Columbia University, he rejected the athletic crowd to join the literary innovators gathering at the college neighborhood's popular West End Bar, among them Allen Ginsberg and William S. Burroughs, who would achieve fame as poet and novelist, respectively. Not famous himself until the late 1950s, when a wave of interest in the self-proclaimed Beat Movement installed him as its unwilling leader, he rode the crest of the counterculture's growing fascination with Eastern religions, most notably Zen Buddhism, while never rejecting the Catholicism of his childhood. Even adulatory responses to his work risked contradiction. For example, critics praised his most famous novel, *On the Road* (1957), for its expansiveness and movement reminiscent of America's Manifest Destiny myth, although the book's narrative progress is in fact from the West Coast to the East.

Kerouac's ambitions were monumental, but a lifetime of heavy drinking killed him by age forty-seven. His several marriages, until his last one, ended with annulment, desertion, or divorce. His greatest loyalty as an adult was to his widowed mother, in later years an invalid, whom he cared for until his death. Wartime service in the merchant marine had given Kerouac manual skills useful for employment during the wanderings that characterized his life; railroad brakeman and forest-fire lookout were among the jobs he took throughout the late 1940s and into the 1950s until royalties from *On the Road* could sustain a pattern of bumming around, visiting friends, and writing as inspiration struck. "Home" was a series of addresses in Massachusetts, New York (on Long Island), and Florida, most of them chosen for his mother's convenience.

Two favorite hangouts were the San Francisco Bay Area and the coastal wilderness of California's Big Sur, an area running south from Carmel-by-the-Sea to San Luis Obispo. This is the setting for the novel most typical of Kerouac's problematic career. Composed quickly (he usually took just three days to six weeks to write a novel), on a roll of teletype paper similar to the one that aided his almost nonstop production of *On the Road, Big Sur* (1962) draws on a visit to the poet Lawrence Ferlinghetti and other Bay Area friends and a solitary stay in Ferlinghetti's isolated cabin in Bixby Canyon (here called the Raton Canyon, with Ferlinghetti taking the name "Louis [also Lorenzo] Monsanto"). Its form, shared by all but the first of Kerouac's novels (*The Town and the City*, 1950, a social novel in the realistic mode), is what the author called "spontaneous prose," equivalent to jazz improvisation in its emphasis on rhythms and inflections and the freewheeling nature of its references. Those references include Buddhism (which he had studied for its literary properties but finally rejected as a religion), Catholicism, books and authors, popular culture, friends and family, all propelled by the writer's exuberance, a momentum that exceeds conventional limits of narrative order.

"My work comprises one vast book like [the early twentieth-century French novelist Marcel] Proust's except that my remembrances are written on the run instead of afterwards in a sick bed," Kerouac observes in the headnote preceding the first chapter of *Big Sur*. Though his canon consists of more than a dozen novels published during his lifetime and others recovered from manuscript and issued after his death, the author had seen them as one grand project, the parts of which he intended to revise, integrate, and present to readers as one massive narrative when done. Neither writing nor publishing them in the order in which he had experienced their action, Kerouac did not live long enough to even begin his intended synthesis. But he named the project "the Duluoz Legend," from the name of his protagonist in *Big Sur* and other works. Central to the legend is Kerouac's close friendship with Neal Cassady (fictionalized as Dean Moriarity in *On the Road* and as Cody Pomeray in *Visions of Cody*, 1972). Their relationship had been the motivation for both the author's wanderings and his impulsive, sometimes explosive manner of writing. (Reacting to the confinements of postwar commercial culture, the Beat Movement took its name in part from the term "beatific," or blissful, and celebrated free-form narration and a matching lifestyle.) But according to critic Warren French, this relationship also marked the limits of Kerouac's literary vision: his concern for human freedom tended toward the "elegaic and defeatist," whereas Cassady moved on from the Beat Movement to the "heroic account of the triumph of the individual over the system" that a new 1960s counterculture was finding in such works as novelist Ken Kesey's *One Flew Over the Cuckoo's Nest* (1962) and *Sometimes a Great Notion* (1964).

Though not published until after Kerouac's death, *Visions of Cody* had been written in 1959. *Big Sur* was composed in 1960 and is considered the formal conclusion to the Duluoz legend, the scope of which covered the author's lifetime and filled such novels as *The Subterraneans* (1958), *The Dharma Bums* (1958), and *Desolation Angels* (1965, covering earlier experiences). It begins with the narrator fleeing fame and seeking recovery from the nervous breakdown that fame has induced.

From Big Sur

8

But there's moonlit fognight, the blossoms of the fire flames in the stove——There's giving an apple to the mule, the big lips taking hold——There's the bluejay drinking my canned milk by throwing his head back with a miffle of milk on his beak——There's the scratching of the raccoon or of the rat out there, at night——There's the poor little mouse eating her nightly supper in the humble corner where I've put out a little delight-plate full of cheese and chocolate candy (for my days of killing mice are over)——There's the raccoon in his fog, there the man to his fireside, and both are lonesome for God——There's me coming back from seaside nightsittings like a muttering old Bhikku[1] stumbling down the path——There's me throwing my spotlight on a sudden raccoon who clambers up a tree his little heart beating with fear but I yell in French "Hello there little man" (*allo ti bonhomme*)[2]—— There's the bottle of olives, 49¢, imported, pimentos, I eat them one by one wondering about the late afternoon hillsides of Greece——And there's my spaghetti with tomato sauce and my oil and vinegar salad and my applesauce *relishe*[3] my dear and my black coffee and Roquefort cheese and afterdinner nuts, my dear, all in the woods——(Ten delicate olives slowly chewed at midnight is something no one's ever done in luxurious restaurants)—— There's the present moment fraught with tangled woods——There's the bird suddenly quiet on his branch while his wife glances at him——There's the grace of an axe handle as good as an Eglevsky[4] ballet——There's "Mien Mo Mountain"[5] in the fog illumined August moon mist among other heights gorgeous and misty rising in dimmer tiers somehow rosy in the night like the classic silk paintings of China and Japan——There's a bug, a helpless little wingless crawler, drowning in a water can, I get it out and it wanders and goofs on the porch till I get sick of watching——There's the spider in the outhouse minding his own business——There's my side of bacon hanging from a hook on the ceiling of the shack——There's the laughter of the loon in the shadow of the moon——There's an owl hooting in weird Bodhidharma trees[6]——There's flowers and redwood logs——There's the simple woodfire and the careful yet absentminded feeding of it which is an activity that like all activities is no-activity (*Wu Wei*)[7] yet it is a meditation in itself especially because all wood-fires, like snowflakes, are different every time——Yes,

---

1. One who has renounced worldly life and joined the mendicant and contemplative Theravada Buddhist community as a monk.
2. *"Ti"* is slang for "little" in French-Canadian French, taken from *"petit"*; *"Bon homme"* is standard French for "good natured fellow."
3. Slang borrowing from French for "relish."
4. André Eglevsky (1917–1977), Russian-born American ballet dancer and teacher, premier dancer in George Balanchine's New York City Ballet and founder of the Eglevsky Ballet (1961).

5. Hozomeen Mountain, near Desolation Peak in the North Cascade Range in Mount Baker National Forest, Washington State.
6. A Bodhi (fig) tree shaded the Buddha when he attained enlightenment. "Bodhidharma": 6th-century Indian Buddhist monk who traveled to China and founded Zen (Ch'an) Buddhism.
7. Chinese for "non-action," a principle in Chinese Taoism by which yielding to others is often the most effective response to a problem.

there's the resinous purge of a flame-enveloped redwood log——Yes the cross-sawed redwood log turns into a coal and looks like a City of the Gand-harvas[8] or like a western butte at sunset——There's the bhikku's broom, the kettle——There's the laced soft fud over the sand, the sea——There's all these avid preparations for decent sleep like the night I'm looking for my sleeping socks (so's not to dirty the sleepingbag inside) and find myself sing-ing "A donde es me sockiboos?"[9]——Yes, and down in the valley there's my burro, Alf, the only living being in sight——There's in mid of sleep the moon appearing——There's universal substance which is divine substance because where else can it be?——There's the family of deer on the dirt road at dusk——There's the creek coughing down the glade——There's the fly on my thumb rubbing its nose then stepping to the page of my book——There's the hummingbird swinging his head from side to side like a hoodlum—— There's all that, and all my fine thoughts, even unto my ditty written to the sea "I took a pee, into the sea, acid to acid, and me to ye" yet I went crazy inside three weeks.

For who could go crazy that could be so relaxed as that: but wait: there are the signposts of something wrong.

9

The first signpost came after that marvelous day I went hiking up the canyon road again to the highway at the bridge where there was a rancher mailbox where I could dump mail (a letter to my mother and saying in it give a kiss to Tyke, my cat, and a letter to old buddy Julien addressed to Coaly Rustnut from Runty Onenut) and as I walked way up there I could see the peaceful roof of my cabin way below and half mile away in the old trees, could see the porch, the cot where I slept, and my red handkerchief on the bench beside the cot (a simple little sight: of my handkerchief a half mile away making me unaccountably happy)——And on the way back pausing to meditate in the grove of trees where Alf the Sacred Burro slept and seeing the roses of the unborn in my closed eyelids just as clearly as I had seen the red handkerchief and also my own footsteps in the seaside sand from way up on the bridge, saw, or heard, the words "Roses of the Unborn"[1] as I sat crosslegged in soft meadow sand, heard that awful stillness at the heart of life, but felt strangely low, as tho premonition of the next day——When I went to the sea in the afternoon and suddenly took a huge deep Yogic breath to get all that good sea air in me but somehow just got an overdose of iodine, or of evil, maybe the sea caves, maybe the seaweed cities, something, my heart suddenly beating—— Thinking I'm gonna get the local vibrations instead here I am almost fainting only it isnt an ecstatic swoon by St. Francis,[2] it comes over me in the form of horror of an eternal condition of sick mortality in me——In me and in everyone——I felt completely nude of all poor protective devices like thoughts about life or meditations under trees and the "ultimate" and all that shit, in fact the other pitiful devices of making supper or saying "What I do now next? chop wood?"——I see myself as just doomed, pitiful——An awful real-

8. Hindu male nature spirits of the air, of forests, and of mountains.
9. Nonstandard Spanish for "Where is my . . . ?"
1. Statement used by Kerouac as dedication in

his *Book of Dreams* (1961), a set of autobiograph-ical transcriptions.
2. Francis of Assisi (1181/1182–1226), Italian founder of the Franciscan religious order.

ization that I have been fooling myself all my life thinking there was a next thing to do to keep the show going and actually I'm just a sick clown and so is everybody else——All all of it, pitiful as it is, not even really any kind of commonsense animate effort to ease the soul in this horrible sinister condition (of mortal hopelessness) so I'm left sitting there in the sand after having almost fainted and stare at the waves which suddenly are not waves at all, with I guess what must have been the goopiest downtrodden expression God if He exists must've ever seen in His movie career——*Éh vache*,[3] I hate to write——All my tricks laid bare, even the realization that they're laid bare itself laid bare as a lotta bunk——The sea seems to yell to me GO TO YOUR DESIRE DONT HANG AROUND HERE——For after all the sea must be like God, God isnt asking us to mope and suffer and sit by the sea in the cold at midnight for the sake of writing down useless sounds, he gave us the tools of self reliance after all to make it straight thru bad life mortality towards Paradise maybe I hope——But some miserables like me dont even know it, when it comes to us we're amazed——Ah, life is a gate, a way, a path to Paradise anyway, why not live for fun and joy and love or some sort of girl by a fireside, why not go to your desire and LAUGH . . . but I ran away from that seashore and never came back again without that secret knowledge: that it didnt want me there, that I was a fool to sit there in the first place, the sea has its waves, the man has his fireside, period.

That being the first indication of my later flip——But also on the day of leaving the cabin to hitch hike back to Frisco[4] and see everybody and by now I'm tired of my food (forgot to bring jello, you need jello after all that bacon fat and cornmeal in the woods, every woodsman needs jello) (or cokes) (or something)——But it's time to leave, I'm now so scared by that iodine blast by the sea and by the boredom of the cabin I take 20 dollars worth of perishable food left and spread it out on a big board below the cabin porch for the bluejays and the raccoon and the mouse and the whole lot, pack up, and go——But before I go I realize this isnt my own cabin (here's the second sign-post of my madness), I have no right to hide Monsanto's[5] rat poison, as I've been doing, feeding the mouse instead, as I said——So like a dutiful guest in another man's cabin I take the cover off the rat poison but compromise by simply leaving the box on the top shelf, so nobody can complain—— And go off like that——But during my absence, but——You'll see.

10

With my mind even and upright and abiding nowhere, as Hui Neng[6] would say, I go dancing off like a fool from my sweet retreat, rucksack on back, after only three weeks and really after only 3 or 4 days of boredom, and go hankering back for the city——"You go out in joy and in sadness you return," says Thomas à Kempis[7] talking about all the fools who go forth for pleasure like high school boys on Saturday night hurrying clacking down the sidewalk to the car adjusting their ties and rubbing their hands with anticipatory zeal,

---

3. Hey cow (French; "*éh*" is slang).
4. Slang for "San Francisco."
5. The character Lorenzo Monsanto, based on the America poet Lawrence Ferlinghetti (b. 1919); "Monsanto" also evokes the Monsanto Chemical Company, whose products include rodent poison.
6. Chinese monastic patriarch (638–713) of Zen (Ch'an) Buddhism.
7. Dutch ecclesiastic (c. 1380–1471) and spiritual writer.

only to end up Sunday morning groaning in bleary beds that Mother has to make anyway——It's a beautiful day as I come out of that ghostly canyon road and step out on the coast highway,[8] just this side of Raton Canyon bridge, and there they are, thousands and thousands of tourists driving by slowly on the high curves all oo ing and aa ing at all that vast blue panorama of seas washing and raiding at the coast of California——I figure I'll get a ride into Monterey real easy and take the bus there and be in Frisco by night-fall for a big ball of wino yelling with the gang, I feel in fact Dave Wain oughta be back by now, or Cody will be ready for a ball, and there'll be girls, and such and such, forgetting entirely that only three weeks previous I'd been sent fleeing from that gooky city by the horrors——But hadnt the sea told me to flee back to my own reality?

But it is beautiful especially to see up ahead north a vast expanse of curving seacoast with inland mountains dreaming under slow clouds, like a scene of ancient Spain, or properly really like a scene of the real essentially Spanish California, the old Monterey pirate coast right there, you can see what the Spaniards must've thought when they came around the bend in their magnificent sloopies and saw all that dreaming fatland beyond the seashore whitecap doormat——Like the land of gold——The old Monterey and Big Sur and Santa Cruz[9] magic——So I confidently adjust my pack straps and start trudging down the road looking back over my shoulder to thumb.

This is the first time I've hitch hiked in years and I soon begin to see that things have changed in America, you cant get a ride any more (but of course especially on a strictly tourist road like this coast highway with no trucks or business)——Sleek long stationwagon after wagon comes sleering by smoothly, all colors of the rainbow and pastel at that, pink, blue, white, the husband is in the driver's seat with a long ridiculous vacationist hat with a long baseball visor making him look witless and idiot——Beside him sits wifey, the boss of America, wearing dark glasses and sneering, even if he wanted to pick me up or anybody up she wouldn't let him——But in the two deep backseats are children, children, millions of children, all ages, they're fighting and screaming over ice cream, they're spilling vanilla all over the Tartan[1] seatcovers——There's no room anymore anyway for a hitch hiker, tho conceivably the poor bastard might be allowed to ride like a meek gun-man or silent murderer in the very back platform of the wagon, but here no, alas! here is ten thousand racks of drycleaned and perfectly pressed suits and dresses of all sizes for the family to look like millionaires every time they stop at a roadside dive for bacon and eggs——Every time the old man's trousers start to get creased a little in the front he's made to take down a fresh pair of slacks from the back rack and go on, like that, bleakly, tho he might have secretly wished just a good oldtime fishing trip alone or with his buddies for this year's vacation——But the P.T.A. has prevailed over every one of his desires by now, 1960's, it's no time for him to yearn for Big Two Hearted River[2] and the old sloppy pants and the string of fish in the tent, or the woodfire with Bourbon at night——It's time for motels, roadside driveins,

---

8. The Pacific Coast Highway, here taking the protagonist from the Big Sur region through the city of Monterey, south of San Francisco.
9. California city immediately north of Monterey and south of San Francisco.

1. Scottish plaid, common in the era's commercial design.
2. Featured in a story by the American fiction writer Ernest Hemingway (1899–1961) included in his collection *In Our Time* (1925).

bringing napkins to the gang in the car, having the car washed before the return trip——And if he thinks he wants to explore any of the silent secret roads of America it's no go, the lady in the sneering dark glasses has now become the navigator and sits there sneering over her previously printed blue-lined roadmap distributed by happy executives in neckties to the vacationists of America who would also wear neckties (after having come along so far) but the vacation fashion is sports shirts, long visored hats, dark glasses, pressed slacks and baby's first shoes dipped in gold oil dangling from the dashboard——So here I am standing in that road with that big woeful rucksack but also probably with that expression of horror on my face after all those nights sitting in the seashore under giant black cliffs, they see in me the very apotheosical[3] opposite of their every vacation dream and of course drive on——That afternoon I say about 5 thousand cars or probably 3 thousand passed me not one of them ever dreamed of stopping——Which didnt bother me anyway because at first seeing that gorgeous long coast up to Monterey I thought "Well I'll just hike right in, it's only 14 miles, I oughta do that easy"——And on the way there's all kindsa interesting things to see anyway like the seals barking on rocks below, or quiet old farms made of logs on the hills across the highway, or sudden upstretches that go along dreamy seaside meadows where cows grace and graze in full sight of endless blue Pacific——But because I'm wearing desert boots with their fairly thin soles, and the sun is beating hot on the tar road, the heat finally gets through the soles and I begin to deliver heat blisters in my sockiboos——I'm limping along wondering what's the matter with me when I realize I've got blisters——I sit by the side of the road and look——I take out my first aid kit from the pack and apply unguents and put on corn-pads and carry on——But the combination of the heavy pack and the heat of the road increases the pain of the blisters until finally I realize I've got to hitch hike a ride or never make it to Monterey at all.

But the tourists bless their hearts after all, they couldnt know, only think I'm having a big happy hike with my rucksack and they drive on, even tho I stick out my thumb——I'm in despair because I'm really stranded now, and by the time I've walked seven miles I still have seven to go but I cant go on another step——I'm also thirsty and there are absolutely no filling stations or anything along the way——My feet are ruined and burned, it develops now into a day of complete torture, from nine o'clock in the morning till four in the afternoon I negotiate those nine or so miles when I finally have to stop and sit down and wipe the blood off my feet——And then when I fix the feet and put the shoes on again, to hike on, I can only do it mincingly with little twinkletoe steps like Babe Ruth,[4] twisting footsteps every way I can think of not to press too hard on any particular blister——So that the tourists (lessening now as the sun starts to go down) can now plainly see that there's a man on the highway limping under a huge pack and asking for a ride, but still they're afraid he may be the Hollywood hitch hiker[5] with the hidden gun and besides he's got a rucksack on his back as tho he'd just

---

3. Raised to the status of a god.
4. George Herman Ruth (1895–1948), famous home-run-hitting American baseball player whose nimble stance and baserunning technique con-

trasted with his girth and power.
5. In *The Hitch-Hiker* (1956), an American film directed by Ida Lupino, a hitchhiker becomes a serial murderer.

escaped from the war in Cuba[6]——Or's got dismembered bodies in the bag anyway——But as I say I dont blame them.

The only car that passes that might have given me a ride is going in the wrong direction, down to Sur, and it's a rattly old car of some kind with a big bearded "South Coast Is the Lonely Coast"[7] folksinger in it waving at me but finally a little truck pulls up and waits for me 50 yards ahead and I limprun that distance on daggers in my feet——It's a guy with a dog——He'll drive me to the next gas station, then he turns off——But when he learns about my feet he takes me clear to the bus station in Monterey——Just as a gesture of kindness——No particular reason, and I've made no particular plea about my feet, just mentioned it.

I offer to buy him a beer but he's going on home for supper so I go into the bus station and clean up and change and pack things away, stow the bag in the locker, buy the bus ticket, and go limping quietly in the blue fog streets of Monterey evening feeling light as feather and happy as a million-aire——The last time I ever hitch hiked——And NO RIDES a sign.

11

The next sign is in Frisco itself where after a night of perfect sleep in an old skid row hotel room I go to see Monsanto at his City Lights bookstore[8] and he's smiling and glad to see me, says "We were coming out to see you next weekend you should have waited," but there's something else in his expres-sion——When we're alone he says "Your mother wrote and said your cat is dead."

Ordinarily the death of a cat means little to most men, a lot to fewer men, but to me, and that cat, it was exactly and no lie and sincerely like the death of my little brother——I loved Tyke with all my heart, he was my baby who as a kitten just slept in the palm of my hand with his little head hanging down, or just purring, for hours, just as long as I held him that way, walking or sitting——He was like a floppy fur wrap around my wrist, I just twist him around my wrist or drape him and he just purred and purred and even when he got big I still held him that way, I could even hold this big cat in both hands with my arms outstretched right over my head and he'd just purr, he had complete confidence in me——And when I'd left New York to come to my retreat in the woods I'd carefully kissed him and instructed him to wait for me, *"Attends pour mué kitigingoo"*[9]——But my mother said in the letter he had died the NIGHT AFTER I LEFT!——But maybe you'll understand me by seeing for yourself by reading the letter:

"Sunday July 20, 1960, Dear Son, I'm afraid you wont like my letter because I only have sad news for you right now. I really dont know how to tell you this but Brace up Honey. I'm going through hell myself. Little Tyke is *gone.* Saturday all day he was fine and seemed to pick up strength, but late at night I was watching T.V. a late movie. Just about 1:30 A.M. when he started

6. The Cuban Revolution (1956–59), led by Fidel Castro (b. 1926).
7. Traditional folk song modified and performed by various folksingers of the period. "South Coast" properly refers to the seascape south of Los Angeles in Orange County, California, but the song is associated with the Big Sur region in Monterey County, south of San Francisco.
8. San Francisco bookstore and publishing house operated (beginning in 1955) by Lawrence Fer-linghetti; a gathering place for Beat writers (see headnote), it is still in existence.
9. "Wait for me . . ." (nonstandard French).

belching and throwing up. I went to him and tried to fix him up but to no *availe.*[1] He was shivering like he was cold so I rapped him up in a Blanket then he started to throw up all over me. And that was the last of him. Needless to say how I feel and what I went through. I stayed up till 'day *Break*' and did all I could to revive him but it was useless. I realized at 4 A.M. he was gone so at six I wrapped him up good in a clean blanket——and at 7 A.M. went out to dig his grave. I never did anything in my whole life so heart breaking as to bury my beloved little Tyke who was as human as you and I. I buried him under the Honeysuckle vines, the corner, of the fence. I just cant sleep or eat. I keep looking and hoping to see him come through the cellar door calling *Ma Wow.* I'm just plain sick and the weirdest thing happened when I buried Tyke, all the black Birds I fed all Winter seemed to have known what was going on. Honest Son this is no lies. There was lots and lots of *em* flying over my head and chirping, and settling on the fence, for a whole hour after Tyke was laid to rest——that's something I'll never forget——I wish I had a camera at the time but God and Me knows it and saw it. Now Honey I know this is going to hurt you but I had to tell you somehow . . . I'm so sick not physically but heart sick . . . I just cant believe or realize that my Beautiful little Tyke is no more——and that I wont be seeing him come through his little "Shanty" or Walking through the green grass. . . . P.S. I've got to dismantle Tyke's shanty, I just cant go out there and see it empty——as is. Well Honey, write soon again and be kind to yourself. Pray the real "God"—— Your old Mom XXXXXX."

So when Monsanto told me the news and I was sitting there *smiling* with happiness the way all people feel when they come out of a long solitude either in the woods or in a hospital bed, bang, my heart sank, it sank in fact with the same strange idiotic helplessness as when I took the unfortunate deep breath on the seashore——All the premonitions tying in together.

Monsanto sees that I'm terribly sad, he sees my little smile (the smile that came over me in Monterey just so glad to be back in the world after the solitudes and I'd walked around the streets just bemusedly Mona Lisa'ing[2] at the sight of everything)——He sees now how that smile has slowly melted away into a mawk of chagrin——Of course he cant know since I didnt tell him and hardly wanta tell it now, that my relationship with my cat and the other previous cats has always been a little dotty: some kind of psychological identification of the cats with my dead brother Gerard who'd taught me to love cats when I was 3 and 4 and we used to lie on the floor on our bellies and watch them lap up milk——The death of "little brother" Tyke indeed—— Monsanto seeing me so downcast says "Maybe you oughta go back to the cabin for a few more weeks——or are you just gonna get drunk again"—— "I'm gonna get drunk yes"——Because anyway there are so many things brewing, everybody's waiting, I've been daydreaming a thousand wild parties in the woods——In fact it's fortunate I've heard of the death of Tyke in my favorite exciting city of San Francisco, if I had been home when he died I might have gone mad in a different way but tho I now ran out to get drunk with the boys and still once in a while that funny little smile of joy came back as I drank, and melted away again because now the smile itself was a

1. Avail (nonstandard French borrowing from English).
2. Smiling; from the painting properly called *La*

Gioconda, by the Italian artist Leonardo da Vinci (1452–1519), famous for its subject's elusive smile.

reminder of death, the news made me go mad anyway at the end of the three week binge, creeping up on me finally on that terrible day of St. Carolyn By The Sea[3] as I can also call it——All, all confusing till I explain.

Meanwhile anyway poor Monsanto a man of letters wants to enjoy big news swappings with me about writing and what everybody's doing, and then Fagan comes into the store (downstairs to Monsanto's old rolltop desk making me also feel chagrin because it always was the ambition of my youth to end up a kind of literary businessman with a rolltop desk, combining my father image with the image of myself as a writer, which Monsanto without even thinking about it has accomplished at the drop of a hat)——Monsanto with his husky shoulders, big blue eyes, twinkling rosy skin, that perpetual smile of his that earned him the name Smiler in college and a smile you often wondered "Is it real?" until you realized if Monsanto should ever stop using that smile how could the world go on anyway——It was that kind of smile too inseparable from him to be believably allowed to disappear——Words words words but he is a grand guy as I'll show and now with real manly sympathy he really felt I should not go on big binges if I felt so bad, "At any rate," sez he, "you can go back a little later huh"——"Okay Lorry"——"Did you write anything?"——"I wrote the sounds of the sea, I'll tell you all about it——It was the most happy three weeks of my life dammit and now this has to happen, poor little Tyke——You should have seen him a big beautiful yellow Persian the kind they call calico"——"Well you still have my dog Homer, and how was Alf out there?"——"Alf the Sacred Burro, he ha, he stands in groves of trees in the afternoon suddenly you see him it's almost scarey, but I fed him apples and shredded wheat and everything" (and animals are so sad and patient I thought as I remembered Tyke's eyes and Alf's eyes, ah death, and to think this strange scandalous death comes also to human beings, yea to Smiler even, poor Smiler, and poor Homer his dog, and all of us)——I'm also depressed because I know how horrible my mother now feels all alone without her little chum in the house back there 3 thousand miles (and indeed by Jesus it turns out later some silly beatniks[4] trying to see me broke the windowpane in the front door trying to get in and scared her so much she barricaded the door with furniture all the rest of that summer).

But there's old Ben Fagan puffing and chuckling over his pipe so what the hell, why bother grownup men and poets at that with your own troubles—— So Ben and I and his chum Jonesy also a chuckly pipesmoker go out to the bar (Mike's Place) and sip a few beers, at first I vow I'm not going to get drunk after all, we even go out to the park to have a long talk in the warm sun that always turns to delightful cool foggy dusk in that town of towns—— We're sitting in the park of the big Italian white church watching kids play and people go by, for some reason I'm bemused by the sight of a blonde woman hurrying somewhere "Where's she going? does she have a secret sailor lover? is she only going to finish her typing afterhours in the office? what if we knew Ben what every one of these people goin by is headed for, some door, some restaurant, some secret romance"——"You sound like you stored up a lot of energy and innerest in life in those woods"——And Ben knows that for sure because he's been months in the wilderness too,

3. Narrator's nickname for a friend appearing in chapter 34.

4. Followers of the Beat Movement.

alone——Old Ben, much thinner than he used to be in our madder Dharma Bum[5] days of 5 years ago, a little gaunt in fact, but still the same old Ben who stays up late at night chuckling over the Lankavatara Scripture[6] and writing poems about raindrops——And he knows me very well, he knows I'll get drunk tonight and for weeks on end just on general principles and that a day will come in a few weeks when I'll be so exhausted I wont be able to talk to anybody and he'll come and visit me and just silently at my side be puffing his pipe, as I sleep——The kind of guy he is——I trying to explain about Tyke to him but some people are cat lovers and some aint, tho Ben always has a little kitty around his pad——His pad usually has a straw rug on the floor, with a pillow 'pon which he sits crosslegged, by a smoking teapot, his bookshelves full of Stein and Pound and Wallace Stevens[7]——A strange quiet poet who was only beginning to be recognized as a big rosy secret sage (one of his lines "When I leave town all my friends go back on the sauce")——And I'm on my way to the sauce right now.

Because anyway old Dave Wain is back and Dave I can see him rubbing his hands in anticipation of another big wild binge with me like we had the year before when he drove me back to New York from the west coast, with George Baso the little Japanese Zen master hepcat sitting crosslegged on the back mattress of Dave's jeepster[8] (Willie the Jeep), a terrific trip through Las Vegas, St. Louis, stopping off at expensive motels and drinking nothing but the best Scotch out of the bottle all the way——And what better way to go back to New York, I could have blown 190 dollars on an airplane——And Dave's never met the great Cody and will be looking forward to that——So me and Ben leave the park and slowly walk to the bar on Columbus Street[9] and I order my first double bourbon and gingerale.

The lights are twinkling on outside in that fantastic toy street, I can feel the joy rise in my soul——I now remember Big Sur with a clear piercing love and agony and even the death of Tyke fits in with everything but I dont realize the enormity of what's yet to come——We call up Dave Wain who's back from Reno[1] and he comes blattin down to the bar in his jeepster driving that marvelous way he does (once he was a cab-driver) talking all the time and never making a mistake, in fact as good a driver as Cody altho I cant imagine anybody being that good and asked Cody about it the next day——But old jealous drivers always point out faults and complain, "Ah well that Dave Wain of yours doesnt takes his curves right, he eases up and sometimes even pokes the brake a little instead of just ridin that old curve around on increased power, man you gotta *work* those curves"——Obvious at this time now, by the way and parenthetically, that there's so much to tell about the fateful following three weeks it's hardly possible to find anyplace to begin.

Like life, actually——And how multiple it all is!——"And what happened to little old George Baso, boy?"——"Little old George Baso is probably dyin of T.B. in a hospital outsida Tulare"[2]——"Gee, Dave, we gotta go see him"——

5. "Dharma": the concept of truth or right in Hinduism and Buddhism, elevated to the status of universal truth in the latter. *The Dharma Bums* (1958) is Kerouac's novel based on his experiences as a fire watcher in Washington State.
6. The sacred text of Mahayana Buddhism.
7. Prominent American modernists: fiction writer Gertrude Stein (1874–1946), poet Ezra

Pound (1885–1972), and poet Wallace Stevens (1879–1955).
8. Sport model of the Willys Jeep.
9. Working-class entertainment street in San Francisco.
1. Nevada city near the border with California on the major highway route to San Francisco.
2. City in central California south of Fresno.

"Yessir, let's do that tomorrow"——As usual Dave has no money whatever but that doesnt bother me at all, I've got plenty, I go out the following day and cash 500 dollars worth of travelers checks just so's me and old Dave can really have a good time——Dave likes good food and drink and so do I—— But he's got this young kid he brought back from Reno called Ron Blake who is a good-looking teenager with blond hair who wants to be a sensational new Chet Baker[3] singer and comes on with that tiresome hipster approach that was natural 5 or 10 and even 25 years ago but now in 1960 is a pose, in fact I dug him as a con man conning Dave (tho for what, I dont know)—— But Dave Wain that lean rangy red head Welchman with his penchant for going off in Willie to fish in the Rogue River up in Oregon where he knows an abandoned mining camp, or for blattin around the desert roads, for suddenly reappearing in town to get drunk, and a marvelous poet himself, has that certain something that young hip teenagers probably wanta imitate—— For one thing is one of the world's best talkers, and funny too——As I'll show——It was he and George Baso who hit on the fantastically simple truth that everybody in America was walking around with a dirty behind, but everybody, because the ancient ritual of washing with water after the toilet had not occurred in all the modern antisepticsm——Says Dave "People in America have all these racks of drycleaned clothes like you say on their trips, they spatter Eau de Cologne all over themselves, they wear Ban and Aid or whatever it is under their armpits, they get aghast to see a spot on a shirt or a dress, they probably change underwear and socks maybe even twice a day, they go around all puffed up and insolent thinking themselves the cleanest people on earth and they're walkin around with dirty azzoles——Isnt that amazing? give me a little nip on that tit" he says reaching for my drink so I order two more, I've been engrossed, Dave can order all the drinks he wants anytime, "The President of the United States, the big ministers of state, the great bishops and shmishops and big shots everywhere, down to the lowest factory worker with all his fierce pride, movie stars, executives and great engineers and presidents of law firms and advertising firms with silk shirts and neckties and great expensive traveling cases in which they place these various expensive English imported hair brushes and shaving gear and pomades and perfumes are all walkin around with dirty azzoles! All you gotta do is simply wash yourself with soap and water! it hasnt occurred to anybody in America at all it's one of the funniest things I've ever heard of! dont you think it's marvelous that we're being called filthy unwashed beatniks but we're the only ones walkin around with clean azzoles?"——The whole azzole shot in fact had spread swiftly and everybody I knew and Dave knew from coast to coast had embarked on this great crusade which I must say is a good one——In fact in Big Sur I'd instituted a shelf in Monsanto's outhouse where the soap must be kept and everyone had to bring a can of water there on each trip——Monsanto hadnt heard about it yet, "Do you realize that until we tell poor Lorenzo Monsanto the famous writer that he is walking around with a dirty azzole he will be doing just that?"——"Let's go tell him right now!"——"Why of course if we wait another minute . . . and besides do you know what it *does* to people to walk around with a dirty azzole? it leaves a great yawning guilt that they cant understand all day, they go to

3. Chesney Henry Baker (1929–1988), American jazz trumpeter and singer.

work all cleaned up in the morning and you can smell all that freshly laundered clothes and Eau de Cologne in the commute train yet there's something gnawing at them, something's wrong, they know something's wrong they dont know just what!"——We rush to tell Monsanto at once in the bookstore around the corner.

By now we're beginning to feel great——Fagan has retired saying typically "Okay you guys go ahead and get drunk, I'm goin home and spend a quiet evening in a hot bath with a book"——"Home" is also where Dave Wain and Ron Blake live——It's an old roominghouse of four stories on the edge of the Negro district of San Francisco where Dave, Ben, Jonesy, a painter called Lanny Meadows, a mad French Canadian drinker called Pascal and a Negro called Johnson all live in different rooms with their clutter of rucksacks and floor mattresses and books and gear, each one taking turns one day a week to go out and do all the shopping and come back and cook up a big communal dinner in the kitchen——All ten or twelve of them sharing the rent, and with that rotation of dinner, they end up living comfortable lives with wild parties and girls rushing in, people bringing bottles, all at about a minimum of seven dollars a week say——It's a wonderful place but at the same time a little maddening, in fact a whole lot maddening because the painter Lanny Meadows loves music and has installed his Hi Fi speaker in the kitchen altho he applies the records in a back room so the daily cook may be concentrating on his Mulligan stew and all of a sudden Stravinski's[4] dinosaurs start dinning overhead——And at night there are bottlecrashing parties usually supervised by wild Pascal who is a sweet kid but crazy when he drinks——A regular nuthouse actually and just exactly the image of what the journalists want to say about the Beat Generation nevertheless a harmless and pleasant arrangement for young bachelors and a good idea in the long run——Because you can rush into any room and find the expert, like say Ben's room and ask "Hey what did Bodhidharma say to the Second Patriarch?"[5]——"He said go fuck yourself, make your mind like a wall, dont pant after outside activities and dont bug me with your outside plans"——"So the guy goes out and stands on his head in the snow?"——"No that was Fubar"[6]——Or you go runnin into Dave Wain's room and there he is sitting crosslegged on his mattress on the floor reading Jane Austen,[7] you ask "What's the best way to make beef Stroganoff?"——"Beef Stroganoff is very simple, 't'aint nothin but a good well cooked beef and onion stew that you let cool afterwards then you throw in mushrooms and lotsa sour cream, I'll come down and show way soon's I finish this chapter in this marvelous novel, I wanta find out what happens next"——Or you go into the Negro's room and ask if you can borrow his tape recorder because right at the moment some funny things are being said in the kitchen by Duluoz and McLear and Monsanto and some newspaperman——Because the kitchen was also the main talking room where everybody sat in a clutter of dishes and ashtrays and all kinds of visitors came——The year before a beautiful 16 year old Japanese girl had come there just to interview

4. Igor Stravinsky (1882–1971), Russian composer of *The Rite of Spring* (1913), a ballet received by audiences as cacophonous; in the 1940 Walt Disney movie *Fantasia*, *The Rite of Spring* serves as the soundtrack to an animation depicting the rise and decline of the dinosaurs.
5. The first Zen patriarch of China conveyed the Twelve Nirdanas (principles of consciousness) to Huike, the second Zen patriarch.
6. U.S. military slang anagram for "Fucked Up Beyond All Recognition."
7. English author (1775–1817) of novels including *Pride and Prejudice* (1813).

me, for instance, but chaperoned by a Chinese painter——The phone rang consistently——Even wild Negro hepcats from around the corner came in with bottles (Edward Kool and several others)——There was Zen, jazz, booze, pot and all the works but it was somehow obviated (as a supposedly degenerate idea) by the sight of a 'beatnik' carefully painting the wall of his room and clean white with nice little red borders around the door and window-frames——Or someone is sweeping out the livingroom. Itinerant visitors like me or Ron Blake always had an extra mattress to sleep on.

12

But Dave is anxious and so am I to see great Cody who is always the major part of my reason for journeying to the west coast so we call him up at Los Gatos 50 miles away down the Santa Clara Valley and I hear his dear sad voice saying "Been waitin for ya old buddy, come on down right away, but I'll be goin to work at midnight so hurry up and you can visit me at work soon's the boss leaves round two and I'll show you my new job of tire recappin and see if you cant bring a little somethin like a girl or sumptin, just kiddin, come on down pal——"

So there's old Willie waiting for us down on the street parked across from the little pleasant Japanese liquor store where as usual, according to our ritual, I run and get Pernod[8] or Scotch or anything good while Dave wheels around to pick me up at the store door, and I get in the front seat right at Dave's right where I belong all the time like old Honored Samuel Johnson[9] while everybody else that wants to come along has to scramble back there on the mattress (a full mattress, the seats are out) and squat there or lie down there and also generally keep silent because when Dave's got the wheel of Willie in his hand and I've got the bottle in mine and we're off on a trip the talking all comes from the front seat——"By God" yells Dave all glad again "it's just like old times Jack, gee old Willie's been sad for ya, waitin for ya to come back——So now I'm gonna show ya how old Willie's even improved with age, had him reconditioned in Reno last month, here he goes, are you ready Willie?" and off we go and the beauty of it all this particular summer is that the front right seat is broken and just rocks back and forth gently to every one of Dave's driving moves——It's like sitting in a rocking chair on a porch only this is a moving porch and a porch to talk on at that——And insteada watching old men pitch horseshoes from this here talking porch it's all that fine white clean line in the middle of the road as we go flying like birds over the Harrison ramps and whatnot Dave always uses to sneak out of Frisco real fast and avoid all the traffic——Soon we're set straight and pointed head on down beautiful fourlane Bayshore Highway to that lovely Santa Clara Valley——But I'm amazed that after only a few years the damn thing no longer has prune fields and vast beet fields like at Lawrence[1] when I was a brakeman on the Southern Pacific[2] and even after, it's one long row of houses right down the line 50 miles to San Jose like a great monstrous Los Angeles beginning to grow south of Frisco.

8. Trademarked French anise-flavored liquer used in cocktails.
9. English poet, essayist, critic, and lexicographer (1709–1784).

1. Area in Santa Clara County south of San Francisco, by 1960 engulfed in the metropolitan sprawl of San Jose, part of the San Francisco Bay Area.
2. Major railroad.

At first it's beautiful to just watch that white line reel in to Willie's snout but when I start looking around out the window there's just endless housing tracts and new blue factories everywhere——Sez Dave "Yes that's right, the population explosion is gonna cover every bit of backyard dirt in America someday in fact they'll even have to start piling up friggin levels of houses and others over that like your cityCityCITY till the houses reach a hundred miles in the air in all directions of the map and people looking at the earth from another planet with super telescopes will see a prickly ball hangin in space——It's like real horrible when you come to think of it, even us with all our fancy talks, shit man it's all millions of people and events piling up almost unimaginable now, like raving babboons we'll all be piled on top of each other or one another or whatever you're sposed to say——Hundreds of millions of hungry mouths raving for more more more——And the sadness of it all is that the world hasnt any chance to produce say a writer whose life could really actually touch all this life in every detail like you always say, some writer who could bring you sobbing thru the bed fuckin bedcribs of the moon to see it all even unto the goddamned last gory detail of some dismal robbery of the heart at dawn when no one cares like Sinatra sings" ("When no one cares," he sings in his low baritone but resumes):—"Some strict sweeper sweeping it all up, I mean the incredible helplessness I felt Jack when Céline ended his Journey To The End Of The Night[3] by pissing in the Seine River at dawn there I am thinkin my God there's probably somebody pissing in the Trenton River at dawn right now, the Danube, the Ganges, the frozen Obi, the Yellow, the Paraña, the Willamette, the Merrimac in Missouri too, the Missouri itself, the Yuma, the Amazon, the Thames, the Po;[4] the so and so, it's so friggin endless it's like poems endless everywhere and no one knows any bettern old Buddha you know where he says it's like 'There are immeasurable star misty aeons of universes more numerous than the sands in all the galaxies, multiplied by a billion lightyears of multiplication, in fact if I were to go on you'd be scared and couldnt comprehend and you'd despair so much you'd drop dead,' that's what he just about said in one of those sutras——Macrocosms and microcosms and chillicosms and microbes and finally you got all these marvelous books a man aint even got time to read em all, what you gonna do in this already piled up multiple world when you have to think of the Book of Songs, Faulkner, César Birotteau, Shakespeare, Satyricons, Dantes, in fact long stories guys tell you in bars, in fact the sutras themselves, Sir Philip Sidney, Sterne, Ibn El Arabi, the copious Lope de Vega and the uncopious goddamn Cervantes, shoo, then there's all those Catulluses and Davids[5] and radio listening skid row sages to contend with because they've all got a million stories too and you too Ron Blake in the backseat

---

3. Novel (1932) by Louis-Ferdinand Céline, pen name of the French novelist Louis-Ferdinand Destouches (1894–1961).
4. Rivers in France, Central Europe, Massachusetts, the U.S. Great Plains, California, South America, England, and Italy.
5. King David (fl. 970 B.C.E.) of ancient Israel, credited with writing many of the Psalms; *Book of Songs*, a translation of Chinese poems published in 1937; William Faulkner (1897–1962), American novelist; Cesar Birotteau, principal character in *Histoire de la grandeur et la décadence de César Birotteau* (1838), by the French novelist Honoré de Balzac (1799–1850); William Shakespeare (1564–1616), English dramatist and poet; *Satyricon* (c. 60 C.E.), comic picaresque narrative written in prose and poetry by the Roman author Gaius Petronius Arbiter (c. 27–66 C.E.); Dante Alighieri (1265–1321), Italian poet; Sir Philip Sidney (1554–1586), English poet; Laurence Sterne (1713–1768), British novelist; Ibn al-'Arabi (1165–1240), Muslim mystic philosopher; Lope Felix de Vega Carpio (1562–1635), Spanish dramatist; Miguel de Cervantes Saavedra (1547–1616), Spanish novelist; Gaius Valerius Catullus (c. 84–54 B.C.E.), Roman poet.

shut up! down to everything which is so much that it is of necessity dont you think NOthing anyway, huh?" (expressing exactly the way I feel, of course).

And to corroborate all that about the too-much-ness of the world, in fact, there's Stanley Popovich also in the back mattress next to Ron, Stanley Popovich of New York suddenly arrived in San Francisco with Jamie his Italian beauty girl but's going to leave her in a few days to go work for the circus, a big tough Yugoslav kid who ran the Seven Arts Gallery in New York with big bearded beatnik readings but now comes the circus and a whole big on-the-road of his own——It's too much, in fact right this minute he's started telling us about circus work——On top of all that old Cody is up ahead with HIS thousand stories——We all agree it's too big to keep up with, that we're surrounded by life, that we'll never understand it, so we center it all in by swigging Scotch from the bottle and when it's empty I run out of the car and buy another one, period.

13

But on the way to Cody's my madness already began to manifest itself in a stranger way, another one of those signposts of something wrong I mentioned a ways back: I thought I saw a flying saucer in the sky over Los Gatos—— From five miles away——I look and I see this thing flying along and mention it to Dave who takes one brief look and says "Ah it's only the top of a radio tower"——It reminds me of the time I took a mescaline pill[6] and thought an airplane was a flying saucer (a strange story this, a man has to be crazy to write it anyway).

But there's old Cody in the livingroom of his fine ranchito[7] home sittin over his chess set pondering a problem and right by the fresh woodfire in the fireplace his wife's set out because she knows I love fireplaces——She a good friend of mine too——The kids are sleeping in the back, it's about eleven, and good old Cody shakes my hand again——Havent seen him for several years because mainly he's just spent two years in San Quentin[8] on a stupid charge of possession of marijuana————He was on his way to work on the railroad one night and was short on time and his driving license had been already revoked for speeding so he saw two bearded bluejeaned beatniks parked, asked them to trade a quick ride to work at the railroad station for two sticks of tea,[9] they complied and arrested him——They were disguised policemen——For this great crime he spent two years in San Quentin in the same cell with a murderous gunman——His job was sweeping out the cotton mill room——I expect him to be all bitter and out of his head because of this but strangely and magnificently he's become quieter, more radiant, more patient, manly, more friendly even——And tho the wild frenzies of his old road days with me have banked down he still has the same taut eager face and supple muscles and looks like he's ready to go anytime——But actually loves his home (paid for by railroad insurance when he broke his leg trying to stop a boxcar from crashing), loves his wife in a way tho they fight

6. Psychedelic drug obtained from buttonlike tops of the mescal cactus, used in some Native American ceremonies and popular with the beatnik subculture.
7. Small ranch (Mexican Spanish).
8. California State prison for serious offenders located on Point Quentin, Marin County, north of San Francisco Bay.
9. Slang for marijuana; two sticks would be two marijuana cigarettes.

some, loves his kids and especially his little son Timmy John partly named after me——Poor old, good old Cody sittin there with his chess set, wants immediately to challenge somebody to a chess game but only has an hour to talk to us before he goes to work supporting the family by rushing out and pushing his Nash Rambler[1] down the quiet Los Gatos suburb street, jumping in, starting the motor, in fact his only complaint is that the Nash wont start without a push——No bitter complaints about society whatever from this grand and ideal man who really loves me moreover as if I deserved it, but I'm bursting to explain everything to him, not even Big Sur but the past several years, but there's no chance with everybody yakking——And in fact I can see in Cody's eyes that he can see in my own eyes the regret we both feel that recently we havent had chances to talk whatever, like we used to do driving across America and back in the old road days, too many people now want to talk to us and tell us *their* stories, we've been hemmed in and surrounded and outnumbered——The circle's closed in on the old heroes of the night——But he says "However you guys, come on down round 'bout one when the boss leaves and watch me work and keep me company awhile before you go back to the City"——I can see Dave Wain really loves him at once, and Stanley Popovich too who's come along on this trip just to meet the fabled "Dean Moriarty"——The name I give Cody in "On the Road"[2]—— But O, it breaks my heart to see he's lost his beloved job on the railroad and after all the seniority he'd piled up since 1948 and now is reduced to tire recapping and dreary parole visits——All for two sticks of wild loco weed that grows by itself in Texas because God wanted it——

And there over the bookshelf is the old photo of me and Cody arm in arm in the early days on a sunny street——

I rush to explain to Cody what happened the year before when his religious advisor at the prison had invited me to come to San Quentin to lecture the religious class——Dave Wain was supposed to drive me and wait outside the prison walls as I'd go in there alone, probably with a pepup nip bottle hidden in my coat (I hoped) and I'd be led by big guards to the lecture room of the prison and there would be sitting a hundred or so cons including Cody probably all proud in the front row——And I would begin by telling them I had been in jail myself once and that I had no right nevertheless to lecture them on religion——But they're all lonely prisoners and dont care what I talk about——The whole thing arranged, in any case, and on the big morning I wake up instead dead drunk on a floor, it's already noon and too late, Dave Wain is on the floor also, Willie's parked outside to take us to Quentin for the lecture but it's too late——But now Cody says "It's alright old buddy I understand"——Altho our friend Irwin had done it, lectured there, but Irwin can do all sorta things like that being more social than I am and capable of going in there as he did and reading his wildest poems which set the prison yard humming with excitement tho I think he shouldna done it after all because I say just to show up for any reason except visiting inside a prison is still SIGNIFYING[3]——And I tell this to

1. Popular American automobile, a family sedan.
2. *On the Road* (1957), Kerouac's only best-selling novel. (Cody Pomeray and Dean Moriarty are both Kerouac's fictional names for his friend Neal Cassady.)

3. African American verbal rhetorical device for creating new, often ironic or obscure, meanings for old words and signs, a tradition reaching from slave days to contemporary rap and hip-hop music.

Cody who ponders a chess problem and says "Drinkin again, hey?" (if there's anything he hates is to see me drink).

We help him push his Nash down the street, then drink awhile and talk with Evelyn a beautiful blonde woman that young Ron Blake wants and even Dave Wain wants but she's got her mind on other things and taking care of the children who have to go to school and dancing classes in the morning and hardly gets a word in edgewise anyway as we all yak and yell like fools to impress her tho all she really wants is to be alone with me to talk about Cody and his latest soul.

Which includes the fact of Billie Dabney his mistress who has threatened to take Cody away completely from Evelyn, as I'll show later.

So we do go out to the San Jose highway to watch Cody recap tires——There he is wearing goggles working like Vulcan[4] at his forge, throwing tires all over the place with fantastic strength, the good ones high up on a pile, "This one's no good" down on another, bing, bang, talking all the time a long fantastic lecture on tire recapping which has Dave Wain marvel with amazement——("My God he can do all that and even explain while he's doing it")——But I just mention in connection with the fact that Dave Wain now realizes why I've always loved Cody——Expecting to see a bitter ex con he sees instead a martyr of the American Night in goggles in some dreary tire shop at 2 A.M. making fellows laugh with joy with his funny explanations yet at the same time to a T performing every bit of the work he's being paid for——Rushing up and ripping tires off car wheels with a jicklo,[5] clang, throwing it on the machine, starting up big roaring steams but yelling explanations over that, darting, bending, flinging, flaying, till Dave Wain said he thought he was going to die laughing or crying right there on the spot.

So we drive back to town and go to the mad boardinghouse to drink some more and I pass out dead drunk on the floor as usual in that house, waking up in the morning groaning far from my clean cot on the porch in Big Sur——No bluejays yakking for me to wake up any more, no gurgling creek, I'm back in the grooky city and I'm trapped.

14

Instead there's the sound of bottles crashing in the livingroom where poor Lex Pascal is holding forth yelling, it reminds of the time a year ago when Jarry Wagner's future wife got sore at Lex and threw a half gallonfull of tokay[6] across the room and hooked him right across the eye, thereupon sailing to Japan to marry Jarry in a big Zen ceremony that made coast to coast papers but all old Lex's got is a cut which I try to fix in the bathroom upstairs saying "Hey, that cut's already stopped bleeding, you'll be alright Lex"——"I'm French Canadian too" he says proudly and when Dave and I and George Baso get ready to drive back to New York he gives me a St. Christopher medal[7] as a goingaway gift——Lex the kind of guy shouldnt really be living in this wild beat boardinghouse, should hide on a ranch somewhere, powerful, good-looking, full of crazy desire for women and booze and never enough

---

4. Roman god of fire and volcanoes, often pictured at a blacksmith's forge.
5. Tool used for separating rubber tires from metal wheels.

6. Inexpensive wine.
7. Medal commemorating St. Christopher, a martyred 3rd-century Catholic saint, patron and protector of travelers.

of either——So as the bottles crash again and the Hi Fi's playing Beethoven's Solemn Mass[8] I fall asleep on the floor.

Waking up the next morning groaning of course, but this is the big day when we're going to go visit poor George Baso at the TB hospital in the Valley——Dave perks me up right away bringing coffee or wine optional—— I'm on Ben Pagan's floor somehow, apparently I've harangued him till dawn about Buddhism—some Buddhist.

Complicated already but now suddenly appears Joey Rosenberg a strange young kid from Oregon with a full beard and his hair growing right down to his neck like Raul Castro,[9] once the California High School high jump champ who was only about 5 foot 6 but had made the incredible leap of six foot nine over the bar! and shows his highjump ability too by the way he dances around on light feet——A strange athlete who's suddenly decided instead to become some sort of beat Jesus and in fact you see perfect purity and sincerity in his young blue eyes——In fact his eyes are so pure you dont notice the crazy hair and beard, and also he's wearing ragged but strangely elegant clothing ("One of the first of the new Beat Dandies," McLear told me a few days later, "did you hear about that? there's a new strange underground group of beatniks or whatever who wear special smooth dandy clothes even tho it may just be a jean jacket with shino slacks[1] they'll always have strange beautiful shoes or shirts, or turn around and wear fancy pants unpressed acourse but with torn sneakers")——Joey is wearing something like brown soft garments like a tunic or something and his shoes look like Las Vegas sports shoes——The moment he sees my battered blue little sneakers that I'd used at Big Sur when my feet go sore, that is in case my feet got sore on a rocky hike, he wants them for himself, he wants to swap the snazzy Las Vegas sports shoes (pale leather, untooled) for my silly little tightfitting tho perfect sneakers that in fact I was wearing because the Monterey hike blisters were still hurting me——So we swap——And I ask Dave Wain about him: Dave says: "He's one of the really strangest sweetest guys I've ever known, showed up about a week ago I hear tell, they asked him what he wanted to do and never answers, just smiles——He just sorta wants to dig everything and just watch and enjoy and say nothing particular about it——If someone's to ask him 'Let's drive to New York' he'd jump right for it without a word——On a sort of a pilgrimage, see, with all that youth, us old fucks oughta take a lesson from him, in faith too, he has faith, I can see it in his eyes, he has faith in any direction he may take with anyone just like Christ I guess."

It's strange that in a later revery I imagined myself walking across a field to find the strange gang of pilgrims in Arkansas and Dave Wain was sitting there saying "Shhh, He's sleeping," "He" being Joey and all the disciples are following him on a march to New York after which they expect to keep going walking on water to the other shore——But of course (in my revery even) I scoff and dont believe it (a kind of story daydreaming I often do) but in the morning when I look into Joey Rosenberg's eyes I instantly realize it IS Him, Jesus, because anyone (according to the rules of my revery) who looks into those eyes is instantly convinced and converted——So the revery continues into a long farfetched story ending with thinking I.B.M. machines

---

8. *Missa Solemnis* in D Major, Opus 123 (1817–23), by the German composer Ludwig van Beethoven (1770–1827), is playing on the stereo.

9. Raul Castro Ruz (b. 1931), brother of Fidel (see n. 6, p. 358).

1. Slang for polished cotton chino.

trying to destroy this "Second Coming" etc. (but also, in reality, a few months later I threw away his shoes in the ashcan back home because I felt they had brought me bad luck and wishing I'd kept my blue sneakers with the little holes in the toes!)

So anyway we get Joey and Ron Blake who's always following Dave and go off to see Monsanto at the store, our usual ritual, then across the corner to Mike's Place where we start off the 10 A.M. with food, drink and a few games of pool at the tables along the bar——Joey winning the game and a stranger poolshark you never saw with his long Biblical hair bending to slide the cue stick smoothly through completely professionally competent fingerstance and smashing home long straight drives, like seeing Jesus shoot pool of course—— And meanwhile all the food these poor starved kids all three of them do pack in and eat!——It's not every day they're with a drunken novelist with hundreds of dollars to splurge on them, they order everything, spaghetti, follow that up with Jumbo Hamburgers, follow that up with ice cream and pie and puddings, Dave Wain has a huge appetite anyway but adds Manhattans and Martinis to the side of his plate——I'm just wailing away on my old fatal double bourbons and gingerale and I'll be sorry in a few days.

Any drinker knows how the process works: the first day you get drunk is okay, the morning after means a big head but so you can kill that easy with a few more drinks and a meal, but if you pass up the meal and go on to another night's drunk, and wake up to keep the toot going, and continue on to the fourth day, there'll come one day when the drinks wont take effect because you're chemically overloaded and you'll have to sleep it off but cant sleep any more because it was alcohol itself that made you sleep those last five nights, so delirium sets in——Sleeplessness, sweat, trembling, a groaning feeling of weakness where your arms are numb and useless, nightmares, (nightmares of death) . . . well, there's more of that up later.

About noon which is now the peak of a golden blurry new day for me we pick up Dave's girl Romana Swartz a big Rumanian monster beauty of some kind (I mean with big purple eyes and very tall and big but Mae West[2] big), Dave whispers in my ear "You oughta see her walking around that Zen-East House in those purple panties of hers, nothing else on, there's one married guy lives there who goes crazy every time she goes down the hall tho I dont blame him, would you? she's not trying to entice him or anybody she's just a nudist, she believe in nudism and bygod she's going to practice it!" (the Zen-East house being another sort of boardinghouse but this one for all kinds of married people and single and some small bohemian type families all races studying Subud or something, I never was there)——She's a big beautiful brunette anyway in the line of taste you might attribute to every slaky hungry sex slave in the world but also intelligent, well read, writes poetry, is a Zen student, knows everything, is in fact just simply a big healthy Rumanian Jewess who wants to marry a good hardy man and go live on a farm in the valley, that's it——

The T.B. hospital is about two hours away through Tracy and down the San Joaquin Valley, Dave drives beautiful with Romana between us and me holding the bottle again, it's bright beautiful California sunshine and prune orchards out there zipping by——It's always fun to have a good driver

2. Stage name of actress Mary Jane West (1893–1980), famous for her buxom figure and bawdy humor.

and a bottle and dark glasses on a fine sunny afternoon going somewhere interesting, and all the good conversation as I said——Ron and Joey are on the back mattress sitting crosslegged just like poor George Baso had sat on that trip last year from Frisco to New York.

But the main thing I'd liked at once about that Japanese kid was what he told me the first night I met him in that crazy kitchen of the Buchanan Street house: from midnight to 6 A.M. in his slow methodical voice he gave me his own tremendous version of the Life of Buddha beginning with infancy and right down to the end——George's theory (he has many theories and has actually run meditation classes with bells, just really a serious young lay priest of Japanese Buddhism when all is said and done) is that Buddha did not reject amorous love life with his wife and with his harem girls because he was sexually disinterested but on the contrary had been taught in the highest arts of lovemaking and eroticism possible in the India of that time, when great tomes like the Kama Sutra were in the process of being developed, tomes that give you instructions on every act, facet, approach, moment, trick, lick, lock, bing and bang and slurp of how to make love with another human being "male or female" insisted George: "He knew everything there is to know about all kinds of sex so that when he abandoned the world of pleasure to go be an ascetic in the forest everybody of course knew that he wasnt putting it all down out of ignorance——It served to make people of those times feel a marvelous respect for all his words——And he was just no simple Casanova[3] with a few frigid affairs across the years, man he went all the way, he had ministers and special eunuchs and special women who taught him love, special virgins were brought to him, he was acquainted with every aspect of perversity and non perversity and as you know he was also a great archer, horseman, he was just completely trained in all the arts of living by his father's orders because his father wanted to make sure he'd NEVER leave the palace——They used every trick in the books to entice him to a life of pleasure and as you know they even had him happily married to a beautiful girl called Yasodhara and he had a son with her Rahula and he also had his harem which included dancing boys and everything in the books" then George would go into every detail of this knowledge, like "He knew that the phallus is held with the hand and moved inside the vagina with a rotary movement, but this was only the first of several variations where there is also the lowering down of the gal's hips so that the vulva you see recedes and the phallus is introduced with a fast quick movement like stinging of a wasp, or else the vulva is protruded by means of lifting up the hips high so that the member is buried with a sudden rush right to the basis, or then he can withdraw real teasing like, or concentrate on right or left side——And then he knew all the gestures, words, expressions, what to do with a flower, what not to do with a flower, how to drink the lip in all kinds of kissing or how to crush kiss or soft kiss, man he was a *genius* in the beginning" . . . and so on, George went all the way telling me this till 6 A.M. it being one of the most fantastic *Buddha Charitas*[4] I'd ever heard ending with George's own perfect enunciation of the law of the Twelve Nirdanas whereby Buddha just logically disconnected all creation and laid it bare for what it was, under the Bo Tree, a chain

3. Giovanni Giacomo Casanova de Seingalt (1725–1798), Italian libertine and adventurer.

4. Properly *Buddha caritas*, a state of unconditional openness, generosity, and patience.

of illusions——And on the trip to New York with Dave and me up front talking all the way poor George just sat there on the mattress for the most part very quiet and told us he was taking this trip to find out if HE was traveling to New York or just the CAR (Willie the Jeep) was traveling to New York or was it just the WHEELS were rolling, or the tires, or what——A Zen problem of some kind——So that when we'd see grain elevators on the Plains of Oklahoma George would say quietly "Well it seems to me that grain elevator is sorta waitin for the road to approach it" or he'd say suddenly "While you guys was talkin just then about how to mix a good Pernod Martini I just saw a white horse standing in an abandoned storefront"——In Las Vegas we'd taken a good motel room and gone out to play a little roulette, in St. Louis we'd gone to see the great bellies of the East St. Louis[5] hootchy kootchy joints where three of the most marvelous young girls performed smiling directly at us as tho they knew all about George and his theories about erogenous Buddha (there sits the monarch observing the donzinggerls) and as tho they knew anyway all about Dave Wain who whenever he sees a beautiful girls says licking his lips "Yum Yum." . . .

But now George has T.B. and they tell me he may even die——Which adds to that darkness in my mind, all these DEATH things piling up suddenly—— But I cant believe old Zen Master George is going to allow his body to die just now tho it looks like it when we pass through the lawn and come to a ward of beds and see him sitting dejected on the edge of his bed with his hair hanging over his brow where before it was always combed back——He's in a bathrobe and looks up at us almost displeased (but everybody is displeased by unexpected visits from friends or relatives in a hospital)——Nobody wants to be surprised on their hospital bad——He sighs and comes out to the warm lawn with us and the expression on his face says "Well ah so you've come to see me because I'm sick but what do you really want?" as tho all the old humorous courage of the year before has now given way to a profoundly deep Japanese skepticism like that of a Samurai warrior in a fit of suicidal depression (surprising me by its abject gloomy fearful frown).

1962

5. Working-class city in Illinois across the Mississippi River from St. Louis, Missouri.

KURT VONNEGUT
1922–2007

A s a counterculture hero of the turbulent 1960s and a best-selling author among readers of popular fiction in the four decades afterward, Kurt Vonnegut was at once more traditional and more complicated than his enthusiasts might believe. To a generation of young people who felt their country had forsaken them, he offered examples of common decency and cultural idealism as basic as a grade-school civics

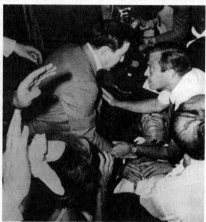

At left, **Dresden in 1945,** following the Allied firebombing. At right, **Senator Robert F. Kennedy** lies mortally wounded by an assassin's bullet on June 4, 1968. These two events bookend Vonnegut's *Slaughterhouse Five.*

lesson. For a broader readership who felt conventional fiction was inadequate to express the way their lives had been disrupted by the era's radical social changes, he wrote novels structured in more pertinently contemporary terms, bereft of such unifying devices as conclusive characterization and chronologically organized plots. His most famous novel, *Slaughterhouse-Five* (1969), takes as its organizing incident the Allied firebombing of the German city of Dresden late in World War II, as witnessed by the American prisoner of war Billy Pilgrim. Yet despite its origins in the 1940s, the manner of its telling is much more akin to the writing of Americans of the 1960s, who were coming to terms with the Vietnam War. Like the war in Southeast Asia, *Slaughterhouse-Five* abjured the certainties of an identifiable beginning, middle, and end; both presented a mesmerizing sense of confused, apparently directionless present, with no sense of totalization or conclusiveness. Together, this World War II novel and the later war during which it was written speak for the unsettling nature of the American 1960s; the assassination of presidential candidate Robert F. Kennedy figures in the book's concluding chapter. Yet this unconventional structure is paired with the language of American vernacular (much in the manner of Vonnegut's hero, Mark Twain). Where more elevated speech would obscure his point, this author speaks plainly and simply, drawing his words, phrases, and inflections from the American middle class and its common experiences of life.

Vonnegut was born in Indianapolis, Indiana, to a family prominent in business and the arts. During the Great Depression of the 1930s, the sensitive, well-read teenager saw his mother's inherited wealth dissipate, his father's career as an architect crumble for lack of work, and his extended family scatter around the country in search of new careers. Service as a World War II infantryman taught him not only how politics reshapes the world but also how science (Vonnegut had been studying biochemistry in college before enlistment) could be used to create effects as destructive to humankind as the Dresden firestorm. Working as a publicist for the General Electric Corporation after the war, the author learned firsthand about the strategies for managing the lifestyles of millions. In short, before writing his first story in 1950 Kurt Vonnegut had shared many formative experiences of his generation. Reworking those experiences would yield fictions and a public stance that helped his fellow Americans adjust to a reinvented postwar world.

Vonnegut's advice, like Mark Twain's, would be unapologetically lowbrow. Part of each writer's appeal is that he pokes holes in the pseudo-sophistications of supposedly more serious approaches. In a 1982 lecture, "Fates Worse Than Death," Vonnegut noted that the self-consciously highbrow *New Yorker* magazine had never published his work. Indeed, he wrote his short stories of the 1950s for the immensely more general readership of *Collier's* and *The Saturday Evening Post.* These stories (collected in 1968 as *Welcome to the Monkey House*) deflate the pretentions of wealth, expertise, and influence with demonstrations of middle-class values and common sense. At the same time Vonnegut was writing novels in formats borrowed from popular subgenres: science fiction dystopia for *Player Piano* (1952), space opera for *The Sirens of Titan* (1959), spy thriller for *Mother Night* (1961), scientific apocalypse and intrigue for *Cat's Cradle* (1963), and prince-and-the-pauper critique of riches for *God Bless You, Mr. Rosewater* (1965). Each work challenges the technical and thematic conventions of the novel, yet each time within the familiarity of a commonly available form.

In the middle 1960s, with his family-magazine markets having gone out of business, Vonnegut began writing essays for popular magazines such as *Esquire, McCall's,* and the *Ladies Home Journal.* Reviewing *The Random House Dictionary* for the *New York Times Book Review* (October 30, 1966), he contrasted the assignment's linguistic complexity with his own shuffling, hands-in-pockets approach. As lexographers debated theories like prescriptive versus descriptive standards of language, for example, Vonnegut could just shrug and say that the former, "as nearly as I could tell, was like an honest cop, while descriptive was like a boozed-up war buddy from Mobile, Alabama." In other essays the author's similarly self-effacing humor undermined positions that used intellectual pretensions to support their points. To the overenthusiasts for science fiction who try to include writers like Leo Tolstoy and Franz Kafka in their brotherhood, he objects that "it is as though I were to claim everybody of note belonged fundamentally to Delta Upsilon, my own lodge, incidentally, whether he knew it or not. Kafka would have made a desperately unhappy D.U." Thus a false analogy is transformed into a logical fallacy: that of the excluded middle, here saying Kakfa is to science fiction not as science fiction is to Delta Upsilon, but as Kafka is to D.U. The argument is thus won by playing with the unquestioned standards of logic, overturning intellectual pretentions by the silliness of their own deductions.

With the success of *Slaughterhouse-Five* and the widespread appreciation of his essays and personal appearances, Kurt Vonnegut became much more publically outspoken about major issues. From his new home in New York City (where he moved in 1970 following nearly two decades of writing in obscurity on Cape Cod, Massachusetts) the author wrote novels such as *Galápagos* (1985), *Hocus Pocus* (1990), and *Timequake* (1997), works treating such topics as the evolution and possible devolution of humankind and America's economic and social role at the end of the twentieth century. Vonnegut's challenges to the conventions of traditional fiction make him as innovative as any of the literary disruptionists of the postmodern era, yet he trusts in the honesty of plain and accurate statement. His last book was a series of sociopolitical essays collected as *A Man without a Country* (2005). Two years before his death, the author found himself once more embraced by a new young audience seeking an explanation for their era's woes. Hence his advice in "How to Write with Style," from his 1981 collection, *Palm Sunday:* "I myself find that I trust my writing most, and others seem to trust it most, when I sound like a person from Indianapolis, which I am."

From Slaughterhouse-Five

Chapter One[1]

All this happened, more or less. The war parts, anyway, are pretty much true. One guy I knew really *was* shot in Dresden[2] for taking a teapot that wasn't his. Another guy I knew really *did* threaten to have his personal enemies killed by hired gunmen after the war. And so on. I've changed all the names.

I really *did* go back to. Dresden with Guggenheim money[3] (God love it) in 1967. It looked a lot like Dayton, Ohio, more open spaces than Dayton has. There must be tons of human bone meal in the ground.

I went back there with an old war buddy, Bernard V. O'Hare, and we made friends with a cab driver, who took us to the slaughterhouse where we had been locked up at night as prisoners of war. His name was Gerhard Müller. He told us that he was a prisoner of the Americans for a while. We asked him how it was to live under Communism, and he said that it was terrible at first, because everybody had to work so hard, and because there wasn't much shelter or food or clothing. But things were much better now. He had a pleasant little apartment, and his daughter was getting an excellent education. His mother was incinerated in the Dresden fire-storm. So it goes.

He sent O'Hare a postcard at Christmastime, and here is what it said:

"I wish you and your family also as to your friend Merry Christmas and a happy New Year and I hope that we'll meet again in a world of peace and freedom in the taxi cab if the accident will."

I like that very much: "If the accident will."

I would hate to tell you what this lousy little book cost me in money and anxiety and time. When I got home from the Second World War twenty-three years ago, I thought it would be easy for me to write about the destruction of Dresden, since all I would have to do would be to report what I had seen. And I thought, too, that it would be a masterpiece or at least make me a lot of money, since the subject was so big.

But not many words about Dresden came from my mind then—not enough of them to make a book, anyway. And not many words come now, either, when I have become an old fart with his memories and his Pall Malls,[4] with his sons full grown.

I think of how useless the Dresden part of my memory has been, and yet how tempting Dresden has been to write about, and I am reminded of the famous limerick:

> There was a young man from Stamboul,
> Who soliloquized thus to his tool:
> "You took all my wealth

---

1. In conventional terms an autobiographical preface. Vonnegut's innovation is to format it as indistinguishable from the eight chapters of fictive narrative that follow (in which he identifies himself as a participant three times), before a final chapter that in conventional terms would be an autobiographical epilogue.

2. City in southeastern Germany destroyed in a bombing raid by the British Royal Air Force on the night of February 13–14, 1945.
3. Fellowship funded by the Guggenheim Foundation, New York City.
4. Popular brand of cigarettes.

> And you ruined my health,
> And now you won't *pee*, you old fool."

And I'm reminded, too, of the song that goes:

> My name is Yon Yonson,
> I work in Wisconsin,
> I work in a lumbermill there.
> The people I meet when I walk down the street,
>
> They say, "What's your name?"
> And I say,
> "My name is Yon Yonson,
> I work in Wisconsin . . ."

And so on to infinity.

Over the years, people I've met have often asked me what I'm working on, and I've usually replied that the main thing was a book about Dresden.

I said that to Harrison Starr,[5] the movie-maker, one time, and he raised his eyebrows and inquired, "Is it an anti-war book?"

"Yes," I said. "I guess."

"You know what I say to people when I hear they're writing anti-war books?"

"No. What *do* you say, Harrison Starr?"

"I say, 'Why don't you write an anti-*glacier* book instead?'"

What he meant, of course, was that there would always be wars, that they were as easy to stop as glaciers. I believe that, too.

And, even if wars didn't keep coming like glaciers, there would still be plain old death.

When I was somewhat younger, working on my famous Dresden book, I asked an old war buddy named Bernard V. O'Hare if I could come to see him. He was a district attorney in Pennsylvania. I was a writer on Cape Cod.[6] We had been privates in the war, infantry scouts. We had never expected to make any money after the war, but we were doing quite well.

I had the Bell Telephone Company find him for me. They are wonderful that way. I have this disease late at night sometimes, involving alcohol and the telephone. I get drunk, and I drive my wife away with a breath like mustard gas and roses. And then, speaking gravely and elegantly into the telephone, I ask the telephone operators to connect me with this friend or that one, from whom I have not heard in years.

I got O'Hare on the line in this way. He is short and I am tall. We were Mutt and Jeff in the war. We were captured together in the war. I told him who I was on the telephone. He had no trouble believing it. He was up. He was reading. Everybody else in his house was asleep.

"Listen—" I said, "I'm writing this book about Dresden. I'd like some help remembering stuff. I wonder if I could come down and see you, and we could drink and talk and remember."

5. American filmmaker (b. 1937).
6. Peninsula in eastern Massachusetts; Vonnegut's residence from 1952 to 1970.

He was unenthusiastic. He said he couldn't remember much. He told me, though, to come ahead.

"I think the climax of the book will be the execution of poor old Edgar Derby," I said. "The irony is *so* great. A whole city gets burned down, and thousands and thousands of people are killed. And then this one American foot soldier is arrested in the ruins for taking a teapot. And he's given a regular trial, and then he's shot by a firing squad."

"Um," said O'Hare.

"Don't you think that's really where the climax should come?"

"I don't know anything about it," he said. "That's your trade, not mine."

As a trafficker in climaxes and thrills and characterization and wonderful dialogue and suspense and confrontations, I had outlined the Dresden story many times. The best outline I ever made, or anyway the prettiest one, was on the back of a roll of wallpaper.

I used my daughter's crayons, a different color for each main character. One end of the wallpaper was the beginning of the story, and the other end was the end, and then there was all that middle part, which was the middle. And the blue line met the red line and then the yellow line, and the yellow line stopped because the character represented by the yellow line was dead. And so on. The destruction of Dresden was represented by a vertical band of orange cross-hatching, and all the lines that were still alive passed through it, came out the other side.

The end, where all the lines stopped, was a beetfield on the Elbe, outside of Halle.[7] The rain was coming down. The war in Europe had been over for a couple of weeks. We were formed in ranks, with Russian soldiers guarding us—Englishmen, Americans, Dutchmen, Belgians, Frenchmen, Canadians, South Africans, New Zealanders, Australians, thousands of us about to stop being prisoners of war.

And on the other side of the field were thousands of Russians and Poles and Yugoslavians and so on guarded by American soldiers. An exchange was made there in the rain—one for one. O'Hare and I climbed into the back of an American truck with a lot of others. O'Hare didn't have any souvenirs. Almost everybody else did. I had a ceremonial Luftwaffe[8] saber, still do. The rabid little American I call Paul Lazzaro in this book had about a quart of diamonds and emeralds and rubies and so on. He had taken these from dead people in the cellars of Dresden. So it goes.

An idiotic Englishman, who had lost all his teeth somewhere, had his souvenir in a canvas bag. The bag was resting on my insteps. He would peek into the bag every now and then, and he would roll his eyes and swivel his scrawny neck, trying to catch people looking covetously at his bag. And he would bounce the bag on my insteps.

I thought this bouncing was a accidental. But I was mistaken. He *had* to show somebody what was in the bag, and he had decided he could trust me. He caught my eye, winked, opened the bag. There was a plaster model of the Eiffel Tower in there. It was painted gold. It had a clock in it.

"There's a smashin' thing," he said.

7. The River Elbe flows through Germany; Halle is a German city located on the River Saale, a   tributary of the Elbe.
8. German Air Force.

And we were flown to a rest camp in France, where we were fed chocolate malted milkshakes and other rich foods until we were all covered with baby fat. Then we were sent home, and I married a pretty girl who was covered with baby fat, too.

And we had babies.

And they're all grown up now, and I'm an old fart with his memories and his Pall Malls. My name is Yon Yonson, I work in Wisconsin, I work in a lumbermill there.

Sometimes I try to call up old girl friends on the telephone late at night, after my wife has gone to bed. "Operator, I wonder if you could give me the number of a Mrs. So-and-So. I think she lives at such-and-such."

"I'm sorry, sir. There is no such listing."

"Thanks, Operator. Thanks just the same."

And I let the dog out, or I let him in, and we talk some. I let him know I like him, and he lets me know he likes me. He doesn't mind the smell of mustard gas and roses.

"You're all right, Sandy," I'll say to the dog. "You know that, Sandy? You're O.K."

Sometimes I'll turn on the radio and listen to a talk program from Boston or New York. I can't stand recorded music if I've been drinking a good deal.

Sooner or later I go to bed, and my wife asks me what time it is. She always has to know the time. Sometimes I don't know, and I say, "Search *me.*"

I think about my education sometimes. I went to the University of Chicago for a while after the Second World War. I was a student in the Department of Anthropology. At that time, they were teaching that there was absolutely no difference between anybody. They may be teaching that still.

Another thing they taught was that nobody was ridiculous or bad or disgusting. Shortly before my father died, he said to me, "You know—you never wrote a story with a villain in it."

I told him that was one of the things I learned in college after the war.

While I was studying to be an anthropologist, I was also working as a police reporter for the famous Chicago City News Bureau for twenty-eight dollars a week. One time they switched me from the night shift to the day shift, so I worked sixteen hours straight. We were supported by all the newspapers in town, and the AP and the UP[9] and all that. And we would cover the courts and the police stations and the Fire Department and the Coast Guard out on Lake Michigan and all that. We were connected to the institutions that supported us by means of pneumatic tubes which ran under the streets of Chicago.

Reporters would telephone in stories to writers wearing headphones, and the writers would stencil the stories on mimeograph sheets. The stories were mimeographed and stuffed into the brass and velvet cartridges which the pneumatic tubes ate. The very toughest reporters and writers were women who had taken over the jobs of men who'd gone to war.

And the first story I covered I had to dictate over the telephone to one of those beastly girls. It was about a young veteran who had taken a job running an old-fashioned elevator in an office building. The elevator door on

9. Associated Press and United Press, rival wire news services subscribed to by various newspapers.

the first floor was ornamental iron lace. Iron ivy snaked in and out of the holes. There was an iron twig with two iron lovebirds perched upon it.

This veteran decided to take his car into the basement, and he closed the door and started down, but his wedding ring was caught in all the ornaments. So he was hoisted into the air and the floor of the car went down, dropped out from under him, and the top of the car squashed him. So it goes.

So I phoned this in, and the woman who was going to cut the stencil asked me, "What did his wife say?"

"She doesn't know yet," I said. "It just happened."

"Call her up and get a statement."

"What?"

"Tell her you're Captain Finn of the Police Department. Say you have some sad news. Give her the news, and see what she says."

So I did. She said about what you would expect her to say. There was a baby. And so on.

When I got back to the office, the woman writer asked me, just for her own information, what the squashed guy had looked like when he was squashed.

I told her.

"Did it bother you?" she said. She was eating a Three Musketeers Candy Bar.

"Heck no, Nancy," I said. "I've seen lots worse than that in the war."

Even then I was supposedly writing a book about Dresden. It wasn't a famous air raid back then in America. Not many Americans knew how much worse it had been than Hiroshima,[1] for instance. I didn't know that, either. There hadn't been much publicity.

I happened to tell a University of Chicago professor at a cocktail party about the raid as I had seen it, about the book I would write. He was a member of a thing called The Committee on Social Thought.[2] And he told me about the concentration camps, and about how the Germans had made soap and candles out of the fat of dead Jews and so on.

All I could say was, "I know, I know. I *know*."

World War Two had certainly made everybody very tough. And I became a public relations man for General Electric in Schenectady, New York, and a volunteer fireman in the village of Alplaus, where I bought my first home. My boss there was one of the toughest guys I ever hope to meet. He had been a lieutenant colonel in public relations in Baltimore. While I was in Schenectady he joined the Dutch Reformed Church, which is a very tough church, indeed.

He used to ask me sneeringly sometimes why I hadn't been an officer, as though I'd done something wrong.

My wife and I had lost our baby fat. Those were our scrawny years. We had a lot of scrawny veterans and their scrawny wives for friends. The nicest veterans in Schenectady, I thought, the kindest and funniest ones, the ones who hated war the most, were the ones who'd really fought.

---

1. City in southwestern Japan destroyed on August 6, 1945, in the first atomic bombing, by the United States Army Air Force.

2. Prestigious interdisciplinary committee that includes the University of Chicago's most eminent professors.

I wrote the Air Force back then, asking for details about the raid on Dresden, who ordered it, how many planes did it, why they did it, what desirable results there had been and so on. I was answered by a man who, like myself, was in public relations. He said that he was sorry, but that the information was top secret still.

I read the letter out loud to my wife, and I said, "Secret? My God—from *whom?*"

We were United World Federalists back then. I don't know what we are now. Telephoners, I guess. We telephone a lot—or *I* do, anyway, late at night.

A couple of weeks after I telephoned my old war buddy, Bernard V. O'Hare, I really *did* go to see him. That must have been in 1964 or so—whatever the last year was for the New York World's Fair.[3] *Eheu, fugaces labuntur anni.*[4] My name is Yon Yonson. There was a young man from Stamboul.

I took two little girls with me, my daughter, Nanny, and her best friend, Allison Mitchell. They had never been off Cape Cod before. When we saw a river, we had to stop so they could stand by it and think about it for a while. They had never seen water in that long and narrow, unsalted form before. The river was the Hudson. There were carp in there and we saw them. They were as big as atomic submarines.

We saw waterfalls, too, streams jumping off cliffs into the valley of the Delaware. There were lots of things to stop and see—and then it was time to go, always time to go. The little girls were wearing white party dresses and black party shoes, so strangers would know at once how nice they were. "Time to go, girls," I'd say. And we would go.

And the sun went down, and we had supper in an Italian place, and then I knocked on the front door of the beautiful stone house of Bernard V. O'Hare. I was carrying a bottle of Irish whiskey like a dinner bell.

I met his nice wife, Mary, to whom I dedicate this book. I dedicate it to Gerhard Müller, the Dresden taxi driver, too. Mary O'Hare is a trained nurse, which is a lovely thing for a woman to be.

Mary admired the two little girls I'd brought, mixed them in with her own children, sent them all upstairs to play games and watch television. It was only after the children were gone that I sensed that Mary didn't like me or didn't like *something* about the night. She was polite but chilly.

"It's a nice cozy house you have here," I said, and it really was.

"I've fixed up a place where you can talk and not be bothered," she said.

"Good," I said, and I imagined two leather chairs near a fire in a paneled room, where two old soldiers could drink and talk. But she took us into the kitchen. She had put two straight-backed chairs at a kitchen table with a white porcelain top. That table top was screaming with reflected light from a two-hundred-watt bulb overhead. Mary had prepared an operating room. She put only one glass on it, which was for me. She explained that O'Hare couldn't drink the hard stuff since the war.

---

3. The 1964 World's Fair was held at Flushing Meadows, Queens, New York City, from April 22, 1964, to October 18, 1964, and again from April 21, 1965, to October 17, 1965.

4. Alas, the fleeting years are slipping by (Latin); from Ode 2.14 by the Roman poet Horace (65–8 B.C.E.).

So we sat down. O'Hare was embarrassed, but he wouldn't tell me what was wrong. I couldn't imagine what it was about me that could burn up Mary so. I was a family man. I'd been married only once. I wasn't a drunk. I hadn't done her husband any dirt in the war.

She fixed herself a Coca-Cola, made a lot of noise banging the ice-cube tray in the stainless steel sink. Then she went into another part of the house. But she wouldn't sit still. She was moving all over the house, opening and shutting doors, even moving furniture around to work off anger.

I asked O'Hare what I'd said or done to make her act that way.

"It's all right," he said. "Don't worry about it. It doesn't have anything to do with you." That was kind of him. He was lying. It had everything to do with me.

So we tried to ignore Mary and remember the war. I took a couple of belts of the booze I'd brought. We would chuckle or grin sometimes, as though war stories were coming back, but neither one of us could remember anything good. O'Hare remembered one guy who got into a lot of wine in Dresden, before it was bombed, and we had to take him home in a wheelbarrow. It wasn't much to write a book about. I remembered two Russian soldiers who had looted a clock factory. They had a horse-drawn wagon full of clocks. They were happy and drunk. They were smoking huge cigarettes they had rolled in newspaper.

That was about *it* for memories, and Mary was still making noise. She finally came out in the kitchen again for another Coke. She took another tray of ice cubes from the refrigerator, banged it in the sink, even though there was already plenty of ice out.

Then she turned to me, let me see how angry she was, and that the anger was for me. She had been talking to herself, so what she said was a fragment of a much larger conversation. "You were just *babies* then!" she said.

"What?" I said.

"You were just babies in the war—like the ones upstairs!"

I nodded that this was true. We *had* been foolish virgins in the war, right at the end of childhood.

"But you're not going to write it that way, are you." This wasn't a question. It was an accusation.

"I—I don't know," I said.

"Well, *I* know," she said. "You'll pretend you were men instead of babies, and you'll be played in the movies by Frank Sinatra and John Wayne or some of those other glamorous, war-loving, dirty old men. And war will look just wonderful, so we'll have a lot more of them. And they'll be fought by babies like the babies upstairs."

So then I understood. It was war that made her so angry. She didn't want her babies or anybody else's babies killed in wars. And she thought wars were partly encouraged by books and movies.

So I held up my right hand and I made her a promise: "Mary," I said, "I don't think this book of mine is ever going to be finished. I must have written five thousand pages by now, and thrown them all away. If I ever do finish it, though, I give you my word of honor: there won't be a part for Frank Sinatra or John Wayne.

"I tell you what," I said, "I'll call it 'The Children's Crusade.'"

She was my friend after that.

O'Hare and I gave up on remembering, went into the living room, talked about other things. We became curious about the real Children's Crusade, so O'Hare looked it up in a book he had, *Extraordinary Popular Delusions and the Madness of Crowds*, by Charles Mackay, LL. D.[5] It was first published in London in 1841.

Mackay had a low opinion of *all* Crusades. The Children's Crusade struck him as only slightly more sordid than the ten Crusades for grown-ups. O'Hare read this handsome passage out loud:

History in her solemn page informs us that the crusaders were but ignorant and savage men, that their motives were those of bigotry unmitigated, and that their pathway was one of blood and tears. Romance, on the other hand, dilates upon their piety and heroism, and portrays, in her most glowing and impassioned hues, their virtue and magnanimity, the imperishable honor they acquired for themselves, and the great services they rendered to Christianity.

And then O'Hare read this: *Now what was the grand result of all these struggles? Europe expended millions of her treasures, and the blood of two million of her people; and a handful of quarrelsome knights retained possession of Palestine for about one hundred years!*

Mackay told us that the Children's Crusade started in 1213, when two monks got the idea of raising armies of children in Germany and France, and selling them in North Africa as slaves. Thirty thousand children volunteered, thinking they were going to Palestine. *They were no doubt idle and deserted children who generally swarm in great cities, nurtured on vice and daring*, said Mackay, *and ready for anything.*

Pope Innocent the Third[6] thought they were going to Palestine, too, and he was thrilled. "These children are awake while we are asleep!" he said.

Most of the children were shipped out of Marseilles,[7] and about half of them drowned in shipwrecks. The other half got to North Africa where they were sold.

Through a misunderstanding, some children reported for duty at Genoa,[8] where no slave ships were waiting. They were fed and sheltered and questioned kindly by good people there—then given a little money and a lot of advice and sent back home.

"Hooray for the good people of Genoa," said Mary O'Hare.

I slept that night in one of the children's bedrooms. O'Hare had put a book for me on the bedside table. It was *Dresden, History, Stage and Gallery*, by Mary Endell.[9] It was published in 1908, and its introduction began:

It is hoped that this little book will make itself useful. It attempts to give to an English-reading public a bird's-eye view of how Dresden came to look as it does, architecturally; of how it expanded musically, through the genius of a few men,

---

5. British poet (1814–1889), journalist, and editor (most famously of the *Glasgow Argus* from 1844 to 1848).
6. (c. 1160–1216).
7. Seaport in southern France.

8. Seaport in northwest Italy.
9. Dates and nationality unknown; writer of the introduction to this book, by the German illustrator Fritz August Gottfried Endell (1873–1955).

to its present bloom; and it calls attention to certain permanent landmarks in art that make its Gallery the resort of those seeking lasting impressions.

I read some history further on:

Now, in 1760, Dresden underwent siege by the Prussians.[1] *On the fifteenth of July began the cannonade. The Picture-Gallery took fire. Many of the paintings had been transported to the Königstein,*[2] *but some were seriously injured by splinters of bombshells,—notably Francia's "Baptism of Christ."*[3] *Furthermore, the stately Kreuzkirche*[4] *tower, from which the enemy's movements had been watched day and night, stood in flames. It later succumbed. In sturdy contrast with the pitiful fate of the Kreuzkirche, stood the Frauenkirche,*[5] *from the curves of whose stone dome the Prussian bombs rebounded like rain. Friederich*[6] *was obliged finally to give up the siege, because he learned of the fall of Glatz,*[7] *the critical point of his new conquests. "We must be off to Silesia, so that we do not lose everything."*

The devastation of Dresden was boundless. When Goethe[8] *as a young student visited the city, he still found sad ruins: "Von der Kuppel der Frauenkirche sah ich diese leidigen Trümmer zwischen die schöne städtische Ordnung hineingesät, da rühmte mir der Küster die Kunst des Baumeisters, welcher Kirche und Kuppel auf einen so unerwünschten Fall schon eingerichtet und bombenfest erbaut hatte. Der gute Sakristan deutete mir alsdann auf Ruinene nach allen Seiten und sagte bedenklich lakonisch: Das hat der Feind gethan!"*[9]

The two little girls and I crossed the Delaware River where George Washington had crossed it,[1] the next morning. We went to the New York World's Fair, saw what the past had been like, according to the Ford Motor Car Company and Walt Disney, saw what the future would be like, according to General Motors.

And I asked myself about the present: how wide it was, how deep it was, how much was mine to keep.

I taught creative writing in the famous Writers Workshop at the University of Iowa[2] for a couple of years after that. I got into some perfectly beautiful trouble, got out of it again. I taught in the afternoons. In the mornings I wrote. I was not to be disturbed. I was working on my famous book about Dresden.

---

1. The Seven Years' War (1756–63), in which England and Prussia defeated Austria, France, Russia, Sweden, and Saxony.
2. Fortress overlooking the town of the same name, on the Elbe's left bank.
3. Painting (1509) by the Italian artist Francesco Raibolini (c. 1450–1517).
4. Church of the Cross (German).
5. Church of Our Lady (German).
6. Frederick II (1712–1786), known as the Great, ruler of Prussia (1740–86).
7. German name for the Polish city Kłodzko in Lower Silesia, the southwestern region of today's Poland.
8. Johann Wolfgang von Goethe (1749–1832), German poet and dramatist.
9. From the dome of the Church of Our Lady I saw those sad ruins strewn amidst the city's lovely orderliness; at that point the sacrist praised the skill of the architect, who had seen to it that church and dome would withstand bombing should such an unfortunate situation occur. Then the good sacristan pointed out ruins in all directions and said in a pensive and laconic way: "The enemy did this!" (German).
1. Commanding the Continental Army during the American Revolution, George Washington (1732–1799) crossed the Delaware River with his troops on December 25, 1776, an event depicted by the German-born American artist Emanuel Gottlieb Leutze (1816–1868) in his painting *George Washington Crossing the Delaware* (1851).
2. Creative writing program founded in 1936; the Famous Writers School of Greenwich, Connecticut, was a mail-order school in the 1960s.

And somewhere in there a nice man named Seymour Lawrence[3] gave me a three-book contract, and I said, "O.K., the first of the three will be my famous book about Dresden."

The friends of Seymour Lawrence call him "Sam." And I say to Sam now: "Sam—here's the book."

It is so short and jumbled and jangled, Sam, because there is nothing intelligent to say about a massacre. Everybody is supposed to be dead, to never say anything or want anything ever again. Everything is supposed to be very quiet after a massacre, and it always is, except for the birds.

And what do the birds say? All there is to say about a massacre, things like "Poo-tee-weet?"

I have told my sons that they are not under any circumstances to take part in massacres, and that the news of massacres of enemies is not to fill them with satisfaction or glee.

I have also told them not to work for companies which make massacre machinery, and to express contempt for people who think we need machinery like that.

As I've said: I recently went back to Dresden with my friend O'Hare. We had a million laughs in Hamburg and West Berlin and East Berlin and Vienna and Salzburg and Helsinki, and in Leningrad, too. It was very good for me, because I saw a lot of authentic backgrounds for made-up stories which I will write later on. One of them will be "Russian Baroque" and another will be "No Kissing" and another will be "Dollar Bar" and another will be "If the Accident Will," and so on.

And so on.

There was a Lufthansa[4] plane that was supposed to fly from Philadelphia to Boston to Frankfurt. O'Hare was supposed to get on in Philadelphia and I was supposed to get on in Boston, and off we'd go. But Boston was socked in, so the plane flew straight to Frankfurt from Philadelphia. And I became a non-person in the Boston fog, and Lufthansa put me in a limousine with some other non-persons and sent us to a motel for a non-night.

The time would not pass. Somebody was playing with the clocks, and not only with the electric clocks, but the wind-up kind, too. The second hand on my watch would twitch once, and a year would pass, and then it would twitch again.

There was nothing I could do about it. As an Earthling, I had to believe whatever clocks said—and calendars.

I had two books with me, which I'd meant to read on the plane. One was *Words for the Wind*, by Theodore Roethke,[5] and this is what I found in there:

---

3. American publisher (1926–1994) whose imprint was with the Delacorte Press.
4. German national airline.

5. A 1957 collection by the American poet (1908–1963).

I wake to sleep, and take my waking slow.
I feel my fate in what I cannot fear.
I learn by going where I have to go.

My other book was Erika Ostrovsky's *Céline and His Vision.*[6] Céline was a brave French soldier in the First World War—until his skull was cracked. After that he couldn't sleep, and there were noises in his head. He became a doctor, and he treated poor people in the daytime, and he wrote grotesque novels all night. No art is possible without a dance with death, he wrote.

The truth is death, he wrote. *I've fought nicely against it as long as I could . . . danced with it, festooned it, waltzed it around . . . decorated it with streamers, titillated it . . .*

Time obsessed him. Miss Ostrovsky reminded me of the amazing scene in *Death on the Installment Plan*[7] where Céline wants to stop the bustling of a street crowd. He screams on paper, *Make them stop . . . don't let them move anymore at all . . . There, make them freeze . . . once and for all! . . . So that they won't disappear anymore!*

I looked through the Gideon Bible in my motel room[8] for tales of great destruction. *The sun was risen upon the Earth when Lot entered into Zo-ar,* I read. *Then the Lord rained upon Sodom and upon Gomorrah brimstone and fire from the Lord out of Heaven; and He overthrew those cities, and all the plain, and all the inhabitants of the cities, and that which grew upon the ground.*

So it goes.

Those were vile people in both those cities, as is well known. The world was better off without them.

And Lot's wife, of course, was told not to look back where all those people and their homes had been. But she *did* look back, and I love her for that, because it was so human.

So she was turned to a pillar of salt. So it goes.

People aren't supposed to look back. I'm certainly not going to do it anymore.

I've finished my war book now. The next one I write is going to be fun.

This one is a failure, and had to be, since it was written by a pillar of salt. It begins like this:

Listen:

Billy Pilgrim has come unstuck in time.

It ends like this:

Poo-tee-weet?

1969

---

6. A 1967 study, by the Austrian-born American critic (b. c. 1927) of modern French literature, of Louis-Ferdinand Destouches (1894–1961), French novelist writing under the pen name Louis-Ferdinand Céline.

7. Published in 1936.
8. The Gideons are a Christian traveling men's association established in 1899 and active since 1908 in publishing Bibles and placing them in all hotel and motel rooms.

GRACE PALEY
1922–2007

"A Conversation with My Father" is not Grace Paley's only story about a daughter's visit with an elderly, terminally ill father. Like other repeated situations in her work, such visits enable Paley to explore nontraditional matters through traditional means, such as dialogue. Unlike her contemporaries whose concern with fiction making overshadows the situations their stories would otherwise convey, Paley directs her imaginative explanations to realistic events, in which larger social and moral issues reinforce her literary innovations. Her ability to adapt nontraditional techniques into realistic short stories makes her accessible to a readership otherwise unfriendly to the aesthetic solipsism of self-exploratory fiction (or "metafiction" as it has come to be called).

That Paley's protagonist talks with her father rather than simply writing about him indicates an important characteristic: in such narratives the author wishes not to present a lecture (though figures in her stories sometimes give them) but rather to achieve an understanding through dialogue. This dialectic quality is evident in the stories in her first collection, *The Little Disturbances of Man* (1959), some of which draw on situations first encountered when adapting to marriage and family life in the difficult circumstances of an army camp. By the time of *Enormous Changes at the Last Minute* (1974) Paley develops her most noteworthy theme, that of women (often single mothers) building satisfactory relationships with the world around them by talking with each other (and sometimes to themselves). The title story from this second collection also shows Paley expanding her language to include an almost poetic phraseology whose facility with metaphors and similes makes much of her narrative action happen directly on the page. Here a father, the same father, is recalled as a child first seeing the American flag, then as a young immigrant taking advantage of what that symbol represents: "Under its protection and working like a horse, he'd read Dickens, gone to medical school, and shot like a surface-to-air missile right into the middle class." By making a comparison to current military technology erupt from the sentence's quainter, almost century-old references, Paley startles her reader and employs a kind of alternative narrative action.

Grace Paley was born in New York City, the child of Russian Jewish immigrants from Ukraine. She attended Hunter College, but graduated from the Merchants and Bankers Business and Secretarial School. Married during college, she had two children and was later divorced, not remarrying until 1972. During the 1950s she became an activist for social issues, first working to close Washington Square (in her Greenwich Village neighborhood) to traffic, later protesting the Vietnam War; in 1978 she was arrested on the White House lawn in a demonstration against nuclear weapons. The success of *Enormous Changes at the Last Minute* drew the attention of other writers to her, and throughout the 1970s and 1980s she was a regular participant on literary panels with innovative fictionalists such as Donald Barthelme and William H. Gass. Her third collection, *Later the Same Day* (1985), continued her method of using metafictive techniques for writing otherwise realistic short stories. In the front matter of *Enormous Changes at the Last Minute*, where a disclaimer about correspondences between fact and fiction would customarily appear, she posted this warning: "Everyone in this book is imagined into life except the father. No matter what story he has to live in, he's my father, I. Goodside, M.D., artist, and storyteller."

Paley also published several volumes of poetry; like her short stories, Paley's poems are marked by their humor, observations of life, and humanity of voice. "Here" is a late, lovely example of her gifts as a poet. In addition Paley wrote direct social commentary. Especially noteworthy was her essay in the September 1975 issue of *Ms.* magazine, "Other People's Children," objecting to the massive and hurried evacuation of South Vietnamese children during the Vietnam War's last days on the grounds that mothers' rights and interests were grossly violated.

The text below is from *Enormous Changes at the Last Minute* (1974).

A Conversation with My Father

My father is eighty-six years old and in bed. His heart, that bloody motor, is equally old and will not do certain jobs any more. It still floods his head with brainy light. But it won't let his legs carry the weight of his body around the house. Despite my metaphors, his muscle failure is not due to his old heart, he says, but to a potassium shortage. Sitting on one pillow, leaning on three, he offers last-minute advice and makes a request.

"I would like you to write a simple story just once more," he says, "the kind de Maupassant wrote, or Chekhov,[1] the kind you used to write. Just recognizable people and then write down what happened to them next."

I say, "Yes, why not? That's possible." I want to please him, though I don't remember writing that way. I *would* like to try to tell such a story, if he means the kind that begins: "There was a woman . . ." followed by plot, the absolute line between two points which I've always despised. Not for literary reasons, but because it takes all hope away. Everyone, real or invented, deserves the open destiny of life.

Finally I thought of a story that had been happening for a couple of years right across the street. I wrote it down, then read it aloud. "Pa," I said, "how about this? Do you mean something like this?"

> Once in my time there was a woman and she had a son. They lived nicely, in a small apartment in Manhattan. This boy at about fifteen became a junkie, which is not unusual in our neighborhood. In order to maintain her close friendship with him, she became a junkie too. She said it was part of the youth culture, with which she felt very much at home. After a while, for a number of reasons, the boy gave it all up and left the city and his mother in disgust. Hopeless and alone, she grieved. We all visit her.

"O.K., Pa, that's it," I said, "an unadorned and miserable tale."

"But that's not what I mean," my father said. "You misunderstood me on purpose. You know there's a lot more to it. You know that. You left everything out. Turgenev[2] wouldn't do that. Chekhov wouldn't do that. There are in fact Russian writers you never heard of, you don't have an inkling of, as

1. Anton Chekhov (1860–1904), Russian dramatist and story writer, whose characters often discuss moral nuances at length. Guy de Maupassant (1850–1893), French author of well-made sentimental stories and novels.
2. Ivan Turgenev (1818–1883), Russian novelist noted for his tragic vision.

good as anyone, who can write a plain ordinary story, who would not leave out what you have left out. I object not to facts but to people sitting in trees talking senselessly, voices from who knows where . . ."

"Forget that one, Pa, what have I left out now? In this one?"

"Her looks, for instance."

"Oh. Quite handsome, I think. Yes."

"Her hair?"

"Dark, with heavy braids, as though she were a girl or a foreigner."

"What were her parents like, her stock? That she became such a person. It's interesting, you know."

"From out of town. Professional people. The first to be divorced in their county. How's that? Enough?" I asked.

"With you, it's all a joke," he said. "What about the boy's father? Why didn't you mention him? Who was he? Or was the boy born out of wedlock?"

"Yes," I said. "He was born out of wedlock."

"For Godsakes, doesn't anyone in your stories get married? Doesn't anyone have the time to run down to City Hall before they jump into bed?"

"No," I said. "In real life, yes. But in my stories, no."

"Why do you answer me like that?"

"Oh, Pa, this is a simple story about a smart woman who came to N.Y.C. full of interest love trust excitement very up to date, and about her son, what a hard time she had in this world. Married or not, it's of small consequence."

"It is of great consequence," he said.

"O.K.," I said.

"O.K. O.K. yourself," he said, "but listen. I believe you that she's good-looking, but I don't think she was so smart."

"That's true," I said. "Actually that's the trouble with stories. People start out fantastic. You think they are extraordinary, but it turns out as the work goes along, they're just average with a good education. Sometimes the other way around, the person's a kind of dumb innocent, but he outwits you and you can't even think of an ending good enough."

"What do you do then?" he asked. He had been a doctor for a couple of decades and then an artist for a couple of decades and he's still interested in details, craft, technique.

"Well, you just have to let the story lie around till some agreement can be reached between you and the stubborn hero."

"Aren't you talking silly, now?" he asked. "Start again," he said. "It so happens I'm not going out this evening. Tell the story again. See what you can do this time."

"O.K.," I said. "But it's not a five-minute job." Second attempt:

Once, across the street from us, there was a fine handsome woman, our neighbor. She had a son whom she loved because she'd known him since birth (in helpless chubby infancy, and in the wrestling, hugging ages, seven to ten, as well as earlier and later). This boy, when he fell into the fist of adolescence, became a junkie. He was not a hopeless one. He was in fact hopeful, an ideologue and successful converter. With his busy brilliance, he wrote persuasive articles for his high-school newspaper. Seeking a wider audience, using important connections, he drummed into Lower Manhattan newsstand distribution a periodical called *Oh! Golden Horse!*[3]

In order to keep him from feeling guilty (because guilt is the stony heart of nine tenths of all clinically diagnosed cancers in America today, she said), and because she had always believed in giving bad habits room at home where one could keep an eye on them, she too became a junkie. Her kitchen was famous for a while—a center for intellectual addicts who knew what they were doing. A few felt artistic like Coleridge and others were scientific and revolutionary like Leary.[4] Although she was often high herself, certain good mothering reflexes remained, and she saw to it that there was lots of orange juice around and honey and milk and vitamin pills. However, she never cooked anything but chili, and that no more than once a week. She explained, when we talked to her, seriously, with neighborly concern, that it was her part in the youth culture and she would rather be with the young, it was an honor, than with her own generation.

One week, while nodding through an Antonioni film,[5] this boy was severely jabbed by the elbow of a stern and proselytizing girl, sitting beside him. She offered immediate apricots and nuts for his sugar level, spoke to him sharply, and took him home.

She had heard of him and his work and she herself published, edited, and wrote a competitive journal called *Man Does Live By Bread Alone.* In the organic heat of her continuous presence he could not help but become interested once more in his muscles, his arteries, and nerve connections. In fact he began to love them, treasure them, praise them with funny little songs in *Man Does Live* . . .

> *the fingers of my flesh transcend*
> *my transcendental soul*
> *the tightness in my shoulders end*
> *my teeth have made me whole*

To the mouth of his head (that glory of will and determination) he brought hard apples, nuts, wheat germ, and soybean oil. He said to his old friends, from now on, I guess I'll keep my wits about me. I'm going on the natch. He said he was about to begin a spiritual deep-breathing journey. How about you too, Mom? he asked kindly.

His conversion was so radiant, splendid, that neighborhood kids his age began to say that he had never been a real addict at all, only a journalist along for the smell of the story. The mother tried several times to give up what had become without her son and his friends a lonely habit. This effort only brought it to supportable levels. The boy and his girl took their electronic mimeograph and moved to the bushy edge of another borough. They were very strict. They said they would not see her again until she had been off drugs for sixty days.

---

3. "Horse" is slang for heroin.
4. Timothy Leary (1920–1996), American psychologist who in the 1960s encouraged experimentation with hallucinogenic drugs. Samuel Taylor Coleridge (1772–1834), English poet who wrote "Kubla Khan" under the influence of opium.
5. Michelangelo Antonioni (1912–2007), Italian filmmaker known for his intellectual style. The boy could be "nodding" in response to the film or the heroin.

At home alone in the evening, weeping, the mother read and reread the seven issues of *Oh! Golden Horse!* They seemed to her as truthful as ever. We often crossed the street to visit and console. But if we mentioned any of our children who were at college or in the hospital or dropouts at home, she would cry out, My baby! My baby! and burst into terrible, face-scarring, time-consuming tears. The End.

First my father was silent, then he said, "Number One: You have a nice sense of humor. Number Two: I see you can't tell a plain story. So don't waste time." Then he said sadly, "Number Three: I suppose that means she was alone, she was left like that, his mother. Alone. Probably sick?"

I said, "Yes."

"Poor woman. Poor girl, to be born in a time of fools to live among fools. The end. The end. You were right to put that down. The end."

I didn't want to argue, but I had to say, "Well, it is not necessarily the end, Pa."

"Yes," he said, "what a tragedy. The end of a person."

"No, Pa," I begged him. "It doesn't have to be. She's only about forty. She could be a hundred different things in this world as time goes on. A teacher or a social worker. An ex-junkie! Sometimes it's better than having a master's in education."

"Jokes," he said. "As a writer that's your main trouble. You don't want to recognize it. Tragedy! Plain tragedy! Historical tragedy! No hope. The end."

"Oh, Pa," I said. "She could change."

"In your own life, too, you have to look it in the face."

He took a couple of nitroglycerin. "Turn to five," he said, pointing to the dial on the oxygen tank. He inserted the tubes into his nostrils and breathed deep. He closed his eyes and said, "No."

I had promised the family to always let him have the last word when arguing, but in this case I had a different responsibility. That woman lives across the street. She's my knowledge and my invention. I'm sorry for her. I'm not going to leave her there in that house crying. (Actually neither would Life, which unlike me has no pity.)

Therefore: She did change. Of course her son never came home again. But right now, she's the receptionist in a storefront community clinic in the East Village.[6] Most of the customers are young people, some old friends. The head doctor has said to her, "If we only had three people in this clinic with your experiences . . ."

"The doctor said that?" My father took the oxygen tubes out of his nostrils and said, "Jokes. Jokes again."

"No, Pa, it could really happen that way, it's a funny world nowadays."

"No," he said. "Truth first. She will slide back. A person must have character. She does not."

"No, Pa," I said. "That's it. She's got a job. Forget it. She's in that storefront working."

---

6. Immigrant neighborhood east of Greenwich Village in lower Manhattan that in the 1960s became home to an antiestablishment youth counterculture.

"How long will it be?" he asked. "Tragedy! You too. When will you look it in the face?"

1974

Here

Here I am in the garden laughing
an old woman with heavy breasts
and a nicely mapped face

how did this happen
well that's who I wanted to be   5

at last   a woman
in the old style   sitting
stout thighs apart under
a big skirt   grandchild sliding
on   off my lap   a pleasant   10
summer perspiration

that's my old man across the yard
he's talking to the meter reader[1]
he's telling him the world's sad story
how electricity is oil or uranium   15
and so forth   I tell my grandson
run over to your grandpa   ask him
to sit beside me for a minute   I
am suddenly exhausted by my desire
to kiss his sweet explaining lips   20

2000

1. A utilities worker who reads electric, gas, water, or steam consumption meters and records the volume used.

JAMES DICKEY
1923–1997

J ames Dickey was born in Atlanta, Georgia, and grew up in one of its suburbs, where he was a high school football star and a self-professed "wild motorcycle rider." After a year (1942) at Clemson College in South Carolina, he enlisted in the air force. As a young man he had admired the English Romantic poet Byron, largely for what he symbolized: bold, masculine swagger and a love of martial and sexual adventure. During off-hours from combat missions in the South Pacific, Dickey began to frequent wartime libraries, where he read writers like Herman Melville and James Agee and explored anthologies of modern poetry. After the war, at Vanderbilt University and through the encouragement of one of his professors, Dickey seriously began writing poetry.

His first published poem appeared in *Sewanee Review* while he was still a college senior; his first book of verse, *Into the Stone*, appeared in 1960. From that time Dickey consistently regarded poetry as the center of his career, although he was at different periods an advertising man for Coca-Cola in New York and Atlanta, a college teacher, a training officer for pilots during the Korean War, a best-selling novelist (*Deliverance*, 1970), and a screenwriter (adapting *Deliverance* for Hollywood).

Dickey's work examines the heroic and sometimes excessive figure of the self in moments of crisis or danger. It shows a desire to ascend beyond the human world, to resist the downward pull of mortality in ways that may remind us of the modern American poet Hart Crane. In the title poem of his volume *Drowning with Others* (1962), for example, the speaker imagines the moment when a man feels "my own wingblades spring," and finds himself "rising and singing / With my last breath," free of the "down-soaring dead." *Helmets* (1964) includes a powerful group of war poems in which Dickey struggles for a vision that will allow him to transcend death. In other earlier work he often explores the instinctual and unconscious aspect of experience and sometimes identifies with totemic animals, as in "The Heaven of Animals," where he envisions a world in which "Their instincts wholly bloom / And they rise. / The soft eyes open."

In Dickey's earlier poems the speaker was primarily an observer, describing as if from outside these states of animal and instinctual grace. The poet tended to write in short lines—three accents or beats per line. With *Buckdancer's Choice* (1965) Dickey became interested in longer "split lines," which he used from then on. The line of verse is splintered into phrases, each group of words separated from the next by spaces designed to take the place of punctuation. The purpose is to approximate the way the mind "associates in bursts of words, in jumps." Instead of being spoken by a distanced observer, the poem is placed within the mind of someone caught in a moment of crisis or excitement.

One of his most central later poems written in the longer line is "Falling," with its rendering of the consciousness of a stewardess who falls from an airplane into space. Like the earlier "Drowning with Others," this poem confirms the importance in Dickey's work of flight, that figure for the self's transcendence of mortality. In "Falling" he gives us the woman's "superhuman act" as she drifts above the tiny human world and possesses, for those moments, a godlike vision. Yet even as Dickey's poem suspends the moment of falling, it admits the pull of gravity that brings the woman closer and closer to the ground and to her death. "Falling" expresses Dickey's enduring interest in danger and in the immortal longings of the titanic self.

Dickey's interest in violence and power as subjects is suggested by the apocalyptic title of his 1970 volume *The Eye Beaters, Blood, Victory, Madness, Buckhead and Mercy*, and many of his later poems are designed to administer shocks to the reader's system. Dickey enjoyed cutting a flamboyant public figure with a reputation for hard drinking and fast motorcycles. He also enjoyed being a publicist for the life of the poet, as if he were a latter-day Byron, sometimes situating himself in a paradoxical cross between serious literary criticism and advertisements for himself. He published the series *Self-Interviews* as well as a penetrating collection of reviews of other poets, *Babel to Byzantium* (1968). In 1966–68 he was consultant in poetry at the Library of Congress, the position later known as poet laureate of the United States.

Drowning with Others

There are moments a man turns from us
Whom we have all known until now.
Upgathered, we watch him grow,
Unshipping his shoulder bones

Like human, everyday wings   5
That he has not ever used,
Releasing his hair from his brain,
A kingfisher's crest, confused

By the God-tilted light of Heaven.
His deep, window-watching smile   10
Comes closely upon us in waves,
And spreads, and now we are

At last within it, dancing.
Slowly we turn and shine
Upon what is holding us,   15
As under our feet he soars,

Struck dumb as the angel of Eden,[1]
In wide, eye-opening rings.
Yet the hand on my shoulder fears
To feel my own wingblades spring,   20

To feel me sink slowly away
In my hair turned loose like a thought
Of a fisherbird dying in flight.
If I opened my arms, I could hear

Every shell in the sea find the word   25
It has tried to put into my mouth.
Broad flight would become of my dancing,
And I would obsess the whole sea,

But I keep rising and singing
With my last breath. Upon my back,   30
With his hand on my unborn wing,
A man rests easy as sunlight

Who has kept himself free of the forms
Of the deaf, down-soaring dead,
And me laid out and alive   35
For nothing at all, in his arms.

                                                        1962

---

1. Very probably the cherubim who guard the entrance to the Garden of Eden after Adam and Eve have
been banished (Genesis 3.24).

The Heaven of Animals

Here they are. The soft eyes open.
If they have lived in a wood
It is a wood.
If they have lived on plains
It is grass rolling   5
Under their feet forever.

Having no souls, they have come,
Anyway, beyond their knowing.
Their instincts wholly bloom
And they rise.   10
The soft eyes open.

To match them, the landscape flowers,
Outdoing, desperately
Outdoing what is required:
The richest wood,   15
The deepest field.

For some of these,
It could not be the place
It is, without blood.
These hunt, as they have done,   20
But with claws and teeth grown perfect,

More deadly than they can believe.
They stalk more silently,
And crouch on the limbs of trees,
And their descent   25
Upon the bright backs of their prey

May take years
In a sovereign floating of joy.
And those that are hunted
Know this as their life,   30
Their reward: to walk

Under such trees in full knowledge
Of what is in glory above them,
And to feel no fear,
But acceptance, compliance.   35
Fulfilling themselves without pain

At the cycle's center,
They tremble, they walk
Under the tree,
They fall, they are torn,   40
They rise, they walk again.

1962

Falling

"A 29-year-old stewardess fell . . . to her death tonight when she
was swept through an emergency door that suddenly sprang
open. . . . The body . . . was found . . . three hours after the accident."

—*New York Times*

The states when they black out and lie there rolling   when they turn
To something transcontinental   move by   drawing moonlight out of the
   great
One-sided stone hung off the starboard wingtip   some sleeper next to
An engine is groaning for coffee   and there is faintly coming in
Somewhere the vast beast-whistle of space. In the galley with its racks   5
Of trays   she rummages for a blanket   and moves in her slim tailored
Uniform to pin it over the cry at the top of the door. As though she blew

The door down with a silent blast from her lungs   frozen   she is black
Out finding herself   with the plane nowhere and her body taking by the
   throat
The undying cry of the void   falling   living   beginning to be
   something   10
That no one has ever been and lived through   screaming without enough
   air
Still neat   lipsticked   stockinged   girdled by regulation   her hat
Still on   her arms and legs in no world   and yet spaced also strangely
With utter placid rightness on thin air   taking her time   she holds it
In many places   and now, still thousands of feet from her death she seems   15
To slow   she develops interest   she turns in her maneuverable body

To watch it. She is hung high up in the overwhelming middle of things in
   her
Self   in low body-whistling wrapped intensely   in all her dark dance-
   weight
Coming down from a marvelous leap   with the delaying, dumfounding
   ease
Of a dream of being drawn   like endless moonlight to the harvest soil   20
Of a central state of one's country   with a great gradual warmth coming
Over her   floating   finding more and more breath in what she has been
   using
For breath   as the levels become more human   seeing clouds placed
   honestly
Below her left and right   riding slowly toward them   she clasps it all
To her and can hang her hands and feet in it in peculiar ways   and   25
Her eyes opened wide by wind, can open her mouth as wide   wider and
   suck
All the heat from the cornfields   can go down on her back with a feeling
Of stupendous pillows stacked under her   and can turn   turn as to
   someone
In bed   smile, understood in darkness   can go away   slant   slide
Off tumbling   into the emblem of a bird with its wings half-spread   30
Or whirl madly on herself   in endless gymnastics in the growing warmth

Of wheatfields rising toward the harvest moon.   There is time to live
In superhuman health   seeing mortal unreachable lights far down seeing
An ultimate highway with one late priceless car probing it   arriving
In a square town   and off her starboard arm the glitter of water catches 35
The moon by its own shaken side   scaled, roaming silver   My God it is
    good
And evil   lying in one after another of all the positions for love
Making   dancing   sleeping   and now cloud wisps at her no
Raincoat   no matter   all small towns brokenly brighter from inside
Cloud   she walks over them like rain   bursts out to behold a Greyhound   40
Bus shooting light through its sides   it is the signal to go straight
Down like a glorious diver   then feet first   her skirt stripped beautifully
Up   her face in fear-scented cloths   her legs deliriously bare   then
Arms out   she slow-rolls over   steadies out   waits for something great
To take control of her   trembles near feathers   planes head-down   45
The quick movements of bird-necks turning her head   gold eyes the
    insight-
eyesight of owls blazing into the hencoops   a taste for chicken
    overwhelming
Her   the long-range vision of hawks enlarging all human lights of cars
Freight trains   looped bridges   enlarging the moon racing slowly
Through all the curves of a river   all the darks of the midwest blazing   50
From above. A rabbit in a bush turns white   the smothering chickens
Huddle   for over them there is still time for something to live
With the streaming half-idea of a long stoop   a hurtling   a fall
That is controlled   that plummets as it wills   turns gravity
Into a new condition, showing its other side like a moon   shining   55
New Powers   there is still time to live on a breath made of nothing
But the whole night   time for her to remember to arrange her skirt
Like a diagram of a bat   tightly it guides her   she has this flying-skin
Made of garments   and there are also those sky-divers on TV   sailing
In sunlight   smiling under their goggles   swapping batons back and
    forth   60
And He who jumped without a chute and was handed one by a diving
Buddy. She looks for her grinning companion   white teeth   nowhere
She is screaming   singing hymns   her thin human wings spread out
From her neat shoulders   the air beast-crooning to her   warbling
And she can no longer behold the huge partial form of the world   now   65
She is watching her country lose its evoked master shape   watching it lose
And gain   get back its houses and peoples   watching it bring up
Its local lights   single homes   lamps on barn roofs   if she fell
Into water she might live   like a diver   cleaving   perfect   plunge

Into another   heavy silver   unbreathable   slowing   saving   70
Element: there is water   there is time to perfect all the fine
Points of diving   feet together   toes pointed   hands shaped right
To insert her into water like a needle   to come out healthily dripping
And be handed a Coca-Cola   there they are   there are the waters
Of life   the moon packed and coiled in a reservoir   so let me begin   75
To plane across the night air of Kansas   opening my eyes superhumanly
Bright   to the damned moon   opening the natural wings of my jacket

By Don Loper[1] *moving like a hunting owl toward the glitter of water*
One cannot just *fall   just tumble screaming all that time   one must* use
It   she is now through with all   through all   clouds   damp   hair   80
Straightened   the last wisp of fog pulled apart on her face like wool
      revealing
New darks   new progressions of headlights along dirt roads from chaos

And night   a gradual warming   a new-made, inevitable world of one's
      own
Country   a great stone of light in its waiting waters   hold   hold out
For water: who knows when what correct young woman must take up her
      body   85
And fly   and head for the moon-crazed inner eye of midwest imprisoned
Water   stored up for her for years   the arms of her jacket slipping
Air up her sleeves to go   all over her? What final things can be said
Of one who starts out sheerly in her body in the high middle of night
Air   to track down water like a rabbit where it lies like life itself   90
Off to the right in Kansas? She goes toward   the blazing-bare lake
Her skirts neat   her hands and face warmed more and more by the air
Rising from pastures of beans   and under her   under chenille bedspreads
The farm girls are feeling the goddess in them struggle and rise brooding
On the scratch-shining posts of the bed   dreaming of female signs   95
Of the moon   male blood like iron   of what is really said by the moan
Of airliners passing over them at dead of midwest midnight   passing
Over brush fires   burning out in silence on little hills   and will wake
To see the woman they should be   struggling on the rooftree to become
Stars: for her the ground is closer   water is nearer   she passes   100
It   then banks   turns   her sleeves fluttering differently as she rolls
Out to face the east, where the sun shall come up from wheatfields she
      must
Do something with water   fly to it   fall in it   drink it   rise
From it   but there is none left upon earth   the clouds have drunk it back
The plants have sucked it down   there are standing toward her only   105
The common fields of death   she comes back from flying to falling
Returns to a powerful cry   the silent scream with which she blew down
The coupled door of the airliner   nearly   nearly losing hold
Of what she has done   remembers   remembers the shape at the heart
Of cloud   fashionably swirling   remembers she still has time to die   110
Beyond explanation. Let her now take off her hat in summer air the
      coutour
Of cornfields   and have enough time to kick off her one remaining
Shoe with the toes   of the other foot   to unhook her stockings
With calm fingers, noting how fatally easy it is to undress in midair
Near death   when the body will assume without effort any position   115
Except the one that will sustain it   enable it to rise   live
Not die   nine farms hover close   widen   eight of them separate, leaving
One in the middle   then the fields of that farm do the same   there is no
Way to back off   from her chosen ground   but she sheds the jacket
With its silver sad impotent wings   sheds the bat's guiding tailpiece   120

1. Hollywood costume and clothing designer (1906–1972).

Of her skirt   the lightning-charged clinging of her blouse   the intimate
Inner flying-garment of her slip in which she rides like the holy ghost
Of a virgin   sheds the long windsocks of her stockings   absurd
Brassiere   then feels the girdle required by regulations squirming
Off her: no longer monobuttocked   she feels the girdle flutter   shake   125
In her hand   and float   upward   her clothes rising off her ascending
Into cloud   and fights away from her head the last sharp dangerous shoe
Like a dumb bird   and now will drop in   SOON   now will drop

In like this   the greatest thing that ever came to Kansas   down from all
Heights   all levels of American breath   layered in the lungs from the
      frail   130
Chill of space to the loam where extinction slumbers in corn tassels thickly
And breathes like rich farmers counting: will come among them after
Her last superhuman act   the last slow careful passing of her hands
All over her unharmed body   desired by every sleeper in his dream:
Boys finding for the first time their loins filled with heart's blood   135
Widowed farmers whose hands float under light covers to find themselves
Arisen at sunrise   the splendid position of blood unearthly drawn
Toward clouds   all feel something   pass over them as she passes
Her palms over *her* long legs   *her* small breasts   and deeply between
Her thighs   her hair shot loose from all pins   streaming in the wind   140
Of her body   let her come openly   trying at the last second to land
On her back   This is it   THIS
                              All those who find her impressed
In the soft loam   gone down   driven well into the image of her body
The furrows for miles flowing in upon her where she lies very deep   145
In her mortal outline   in the earth as it is in cloud   can tell nothing
But that she is there   inexplicable   unquestionable   and remember
That something broke in them as well   and began to live and die more
When they walked for no reason into their fields to where the whole earth
Caught her   interrupted her maiden flight   told her how to lie   she
      cannot   150
Turn   go away   cannot move   cannot slide off it and assume another
Position   no sky-diver with any grin could save her   hold her in his arms
Plummet with her   unfold above her his wedding silks   she can no longer
Mark the rain with whirling women that take the place of a dead wife
Or the goddess in Norwegian farm girls   or all the back-breaking whores   155
Of Wichita. All the known air above her is not giving up quite one
Breath   it is all gone   and yet not dead   not anywhere else
Quite   lying still in the field on her back   sensing the smells
Of incessant growth try to lift her   a little sight left in the corner
Of one eye   fading   seeing something wave   lies believing   160
That she could have made it   at the best part of her brief goddess
State   to water   gone in headfirst   come out smiling   invulnerable
Girl in a bathing-suit ad   but she is lying like a sunbather at the last
Of moonlight   half-buried in her impact on the earth   not far
From a railroad trestle   a water tank   she could see if she could   165
Raise her head from her modest hole   with her clothes beginning
To come down all over Kansas   into bushes   on the dewy sixth green
Of a golf course   one shoe   her girdle coming down fantastically
On a clothesline, where it belongs   her blouse on a lightning rod:

Lies in the fields   in *this* field   on her broken back as though on   170
A cloud she cannot drop through   while farmers sleepwalk without
Their women from houses   a walk like falling toward the far waters
Of life   in moonlight   toward the dreamed eternal meaning of their farms
Toward the flowering of the harvest in their hands   that tragic cost
Feels herself go   go toward   go outward   breathes at last fully   175
Not   and tries   less   once   tries   tries   AH, GOD—

1981

Postmodern Manifestos

olitical and cultural manifestos, as public declarations of motives and intents,
inevitably signal change rather than stasis. Such statements of purpose—the
Communist Manifesto (1848) by Marx and Engels, for example, or the Preface
added by Wordsworth to the second edition (1800) of his and Coleridge's *Lyrical
Ballads*—say as much about what their writers do not want as about what they do.
When the transition from modernism to postmodernism overlapped with larger
political and cultural issues of the American 1950s and 1960s, poets and fiction
writers issued outspoken manifestos about the need for a new literary aesthetic.

Feeling stifled under modernist formalism and the mainstream culture of the
1950s, many poets sought a return to the "unstructured places of being" that A. R.
Ammons has called poetry's true source. After several decades in which impersonality and objectivity were the key values in poetry criticism, poets shifted the focus
from the poem as artifact (the "well-wrought urn," in the critic Cleanth Brooks's
phrase) to the poem as open-ended process. The unconscious began to take up a
larger place in poetry, and accident and chance became, at times, structuring principles, as we see in some of Ammons's poems. A similar emphasis on process informed
the work of the abstract expressionist painters and the improvisatory group of jazz
musicians, like Charlie "Bird" Parker, whose kinetic musical explorations became
for many writers emblems of artistic activity. When the poet Charles Olson, in his
manifesto "Projective Verse," described poetry as a "transfer of energy" he revealed
the implicit physiology underlying this new paradigm; the shift from artifact to process relocated poetry in the body, with its breath, movement, and changes. For
some poets a focus on the body brought attention to issues of gender and the ways
in which the particularity of a woman's embodied experiences had been silenced in
poetry. In many cases tapping into the energy of the body led directly to the erotic,
as is clear in Frank O'Hara's remark that the appeal of poetic measure is like buying
a "pair of pants . . . tight enough so everyone will want to go to bed with you." A
poetry open to the unconscious and centered in the body became more personal,
inviting into the poem the particulars of a poet's life.

Envisioning poetry as an embodied process was both liberating and confusing.
For some, such a vision erased distinctions important to many readers and writers,
blurring the boundaries between open-ended form and the absence of form, or
between the writer's work and life. In a letter to her fellow poet Robert Lowell,
Elizabeth Bishop expresses her deep concern about the "infinite mischief" created
by an absence of distinctions, and she quotes English poet and novelist Thomas
Hardy to warn of the dangers of "mixing of fact and fiction in unknown proportions." Although written in 1972, Bishop's words have a startling relevance for the
impassioned contemporary debates over a writer's obligation to distinguish fact
from fiction in his or her work.

In fiction, too, the issue under debate was realism. Whether grounded in sociological observation (as some later nineteenth-century writers would have it) or in
psychology and myth (the favorite of some twentieth-century moderns), such representation had become, by 1960, an orientation harder and harder to defend. That
was the year the novelist Philip Roth famously despaired of it. "The American writer
in the middle of the twentieth century has his hands full in trying to understand,
describe, and then make credible much of the American reality," he noted in a symposium on culture and the novel. Reviewing the antics of the previous decade—
whose historical moments had included anticommunist witchhunts and political

scandals bordering on the absurd—Roth concluded that "it stupifies, it sickens, it infuriates, and finally it is even a kind of embarrassment to one's own meager imagination. The actuality is continually outdoing our talents, and the culture tosses up figures almost daily that are the envy of any novelist." One response by subsequent writers would be to write what the critic Linda Hutcheon has called "historiographic metafiction," in which the novelist treats actual events and fantasized material on an equal basis, with an emphasis on how history and fiction are events created by the imagination; Robert Coover's *The Public Burning* (1977), for example, handles the execution of convicted spies Julius and Ethel Rosenberg and Richard Nixon's conduct in the 1950s just this way. Other writers chose to question the very presumption of representational literary art. Fiction is not about experience, it is *more* experience, went this argument. As an object made and placed in the world, its constituent elements are not persons, places, or things but rather words. Like the action painting of the abstract expressionist Jackson Pollock, whose canvas was not a surface upon which to represent but an arena within which to act, the novels and short stories thus produced were more about the author's self-apparent act of writing and the reader's conscious involvement as a receptor of the work. Literary journalism, as always influenced by its fictive cousin, now centered less on presumed objectivity than on the experience of the journalist encountering that object.

RONALD SUKENICK

R onald Sukenick (1932–2004) was an innovative fictionist, beginning with his novel *Up* (1968). As the title of his collection *The Death of the Novel and Other Stories* (1969) suggests, he viewed critical theory about fiction as just one more story, with neither more nor less credibility than any other work of the imagination. As he argues in the text reprinted here, adapted from a publicity release he prepared for his second novel, *Out* (1973), and collected in his *In Form: Digressions on the Act of Fiction* (1985), fictive narrative was not *about* something but *was* something—not a representation of the world but something added to that world as another object to be encountered. This approach not only stood traditional mimesis on its head but argued that representation in fiction was fundamentally dishonest—a fraudulent totalization that misrepresented reality. What was reality? For Sukenick, in his story collections and novels that reached through the 1980s and 1990s to conclude with the posthumously published *Last Fall* (2005), fiction was above all an activity, a self-conscious act of creating a literary work with no illusions about the nature of its making. All aspects of his career focused on this purpose, including his teaching of creative writing (at the University of Colorado), his encouragement of independent publishing through the Coordinating Council of Literary Magazines, and his founding of the *American Book Review* in 1977 as an alternative to establishment journalism.

Innovative Fiction/Innovative Criteria

It seems strange to have to talk about innovation in fiction, but the American novel until the end of the sixties was so static that we have not yet fully understood how parochial and narrow the accepted literary norm for fiction had become.

Properly speaking, there is no such thing as "innovative fiction." The novel *is* innovation—it is not called the "novel" for nothing. Fiction is the most fluid and changing of literary forms, the one that most immediately reflects the changes in our collective consciousness, and in fact that is one of its great virtues. As soon as fiction gets frozen into one particular model, it loses that responsiveness to our immediate experience that is its hallmark. It becomes literary. It seems to me that this is one of the major factors contributing to the recent decline in the popularity of fiction: people no longer believe in the novel as a medium that gets at the truth of their lives.

The form of fiction that comes down to us through Jane Austen, George Eliot, and Hemingway[1] is no longer adequate to capture our experience. Either the novel will change, or it will die. Today's money-making novels are those that sell to the movies—in other words, they are essentially written for another medium. No one takes novels seriously until they become movies, which is to say that no one takes novels seriously.

Perhaps I exaggerate slightly, but not much. If we are going to have a wide and serious audience for fiction again we are going to have to re-examine the source of the novel's power beyond the particular forms of fiction that have become so dull to so many.

And first of all we will have to make a fundamental distinction between fiction and data. The great advantage of fiction over history, journalism, or any other supposedly "factual" kind of writing is that it is an expressive medium. It transmits feeling, energy, excitement. Television can give us the news, but fiction can best express our response to the news. No other medium—especially not film—can so well deal with our strongest and often most intimate responses to the large and small facts of our daily lives. No other medium, in other words, can so well keep track of the reality of our experience. But to do this successfully the novel must continually reinvent itself to remain in touch with the texture of our lives. It must make maximum expressive use of all elements of the printed page, including the relation of print to blank space. It must break through the literary formulas when necessary while at the same time preserving what is essential to fiction: incident, feeling, power, scope, and the sense of consciousness struggling with circumstance.

There is not one new fiction, but many. Novelists today have an unprecedented number of stylistic options, a range of choice involving not so much a struggle of an old form with a new, but an opening out, a broader awareness of the possibilities of the medium. Perhaps the most sensible working definition for what is new in fiction is simply what is not old, what lies outside the literary clichés of the formula of plot, character, and social realism. But this situation also creates problems of judgment: novelty does not guarantee quality, and it becomes crucial to distinguish the superficial from the substantial, regardless of form. To make such distinctions we must go back to the sources of fiction, stripped of inessentials and historical trappings, so that we can recognize the fundamental virtues of the novel though they

---

1. Ernest Hemingway (1899–1961), American novelist and short-story writer. Jane Austen (1775–1817), English novelist George Eliot, pen name of Mary Ann Evans (1819–1880), English novelist and essayist.

may appear in odd recombinations and unaccustomed forms. New fiction requires new criteria, but such criteria will be rooted in the essentials of the medium: not plot, but ongoing incident; not characterization, but consciousness struggling with circumstance; not social realism, but a sense of situation; and so on. Innovative fiction, when successful by these criteria, is not "experimental" but represents the progressive struggle of art to rescue the truth of our experience.

1974

WILLIAM H. GASS

William H. Gass (b. 1924) earned a Ph.D. in philosophy and taught the subject for his full academic career, beginning at Purdue University and continuing at Washington University in St. Louis, Missouri. Yet his major interests have been literary. His early work, the novel *Omensetter's Luck* (1966) and the story collection *In the Heart of the Heart of the Country* (1968), identified him as a proponent of serious fiction, but it was his novella, *Willie Masters' Lonesome Wife* (1968), and his first book of essays, *Fiction and the Figures of Life* (1970, from which the piece reprinted here is taken), that established his credentials as a radical innovator. The novella is as anti-illusionistic as anything Ronald Sukenick might conceive: printed in several different typefaces on four different colors of paper with various graphic devices coursing through the text, including coffee-cup stains and a cascade of footnotes that at one point chase the narrative off the page, it speaks boldly for a fiction that seeks to be nothing more than its own obvious self. In his one other novel, *The Tunnel* (1995), Gass examines historical ideas in a similarly self-conscious manner. His most frequent venues, however, have been books of essays, in which he uses philosophical principles as argumentative support for innovative fiction. Gass's essays, like his literary debates with the realist John Gardner, make eloquent arguments for the worth of such fiction, on ethical and aesthetic grounds.

The Medium of Fiction

It seems a country-headed thing to say: that literature is language, that stories and the places and the people in them[1] are merely made of words as chairs are made of smoothed sticks and sometimes of cloth or metal tubes. Still, we cannot be too simple at the start, since the obvious is often the unobserved. Occasionally we should allow the trite to tease us into thought, for such old friends, the clichés in our life, are the only strangers we can know. It seems incredible, the ease with which we sink through books quite out of sight,[2] pass clamorous pages into soundless dreams. That novels should be made of words, and merely words, is shocking, really. It's as

1. For the people, see "The Concept of Character in Fiction" [Gass's note; this essay, appears later in his collection].
2. This, as well as the comparison with mathe-

matics, is returned to in "In Terms of the Toenail: Fiction and the Figures of Life" [Gass's note; this essay appears later in his collection].

though you had discovered that your wife were made of rubber: the bliss of all those years, the fears . . . from sponge.

Like the mathematician, like the philosopher, the novelist makes things out of concepts. Concepts, consequently, must be his critical concern: not the defects of his person, the crimes on his conscience, other men's morals, or their kindness or cruelty. The painter squeezes space through his pigments. Paint stains his fingers. How can he forget the color he has loaded on his brush or that blank canvas audience before him? Yet the novelist frequently behaves as if his work were all heart, character, and story; he professes to hate abstraction, mathematics, and the pure works of mind. Of course, unlike poetry, and despite its distinguished figures, for a long time now the novel has been an amateur's affair, an open field for anybody's running, and it has drawn the idle, sick, and gossipaceous, the vaguely artistic—prophets, teachers, muckrakers—all the fanatical explainers, those dreamily scientific, and those anally pedantic.

Paint stains the fingers; the sculptor's hair is white with dust; but concepts have no physical properties; they do not permit smell or reflect light; they do not fill space or contain it; they do not age. "Five" is no wider, older, or fatter than "four"; "apple" isn't sweeter than "quince," rounder than "pear," smoother than "peach." To say, then, that literature is language is to say that literature is made of meanings, concepts, ideas, forms (please yourself with the term), and that these are so static and eternal as to shame the stars.

Like the mathematician. For the novelist to be at all, in any way, like a mathematician is shocking. It's worse than discovering your privates are plastic. Because there's no narration among numbers. It is logically impossible. Time's lacking.

When David Hilbert,[3] the great logician, heard that a student had given up mathematics to write novels, he is supposed to have said: "It was just as well; he did not have enough imagination to become a first-rate mathematician."

The yammer of thought, the constant one-after-another of sounds, the shapes of words, the terrible specter of spelling, are each due to this fact that meanings are heavenly bodies which, to our senses, must somehow announce themselves. A word is a concept made flesh, if you like—the eternal presented as noise. When I spell, then, let's say, "avoirdupois,"[4] I am forming our name for that meaning, but it might, just as well, be written down "dozzo," or still more at length, with the same lack of logic, "typary," "snoddle," or "willmullynull." "Avoirdupois." An unreasonable body. Nonetheless lovely. "Avoirdupois."

There is a fundamental contradiction in our medium.[5] We work with a marble of flaws. My mind is utterly unlike my body,[6] and unless you're an angel, so, I am certain, is yours. Poor Descartes[7] really wrote on the problems of poets: word sense and word sound, math and mechanics, the mind and its body, can they touch? And how, pray God, can they resemble? In the

---

3. Russian-born German mathematician (1862–1943).
4. Weight measure based on sixteen ounces to a pound.
5. See "Gertrude Stein: Her Escape from Protective Language" [Gass's note; this essay appears later in his collection; Stein (1874–1946) was an American poet and novelist active in France].

6. The contrast which is meant here is not that often alleged to exist between thought and feeling, but that between consciousness and things [Gass's note].
7. René Descartes (1596–1650), French philosopher and mathematician best known for the formulation "Cogito ergo sum," Latin for "I think, therefore I am."

act of love, as in all the arts, the soul should be felt by the tongue and the fingers, felt in the skin. So should our sounds come to color up the surface of our stories like a blush. This adventitious music is the only sensory quality our books can have. As Frost[8] observed, even the empty sentence has a sound, or rather—I should say—*is* a series of nervous tensions and resolves. No artist dares neglect his own world's body, for *nothing else*, nothing else about his book is physical.

In the hollow of a jaw, the ear, upon the page, concepts now begin to move: they appear, accelerate, they race, they hesitate a moment, slow, turn, break, join, modify, and it becomes reasonable to speak of the problems of narration for the first time. Truly (that is to say, technically), narration is that part of the art of fiction concerned with the coming on and passing off of words—not the familiar arrangement of words in dry strings like so many shriveled worms, but their formal direction and rapidity. But this is not what's usually meant.

For most people, fiction is history; fiction is history without tables, graphs, dates, imports, edicts, evidence, laws; history without hiatus—intelligible, simple, smooth. Fiction is sociology freed of statistics, politics with no real party in the opposition; it's a world where play money buys you cardboard squares of colored country; a world where everyone is obediently psychological, economic, ethnic, geographical—framed in a keyhole and always nude, each figure fashioned from the latest thing in cello-see-through, so we may observe our hero's guts, too, if we choose: ah, they're blue, and squirming like a tickled river. For truth without effort, thought without rigor, feeling without form, existence without commitment: what will you give? for a wind-up world, a toy life? . . . six bits?[9] for a book with a thicker skin? . . . six bucks? I am a man, myself, intemperately mild, and though it seems to me as much deserved as it's desired, I have no wish to steeple quires of paper passion up so many sad unelevating rears.

Nay, not *seems*, it *is* a stubborn, country-headed thing to say: that there are no events but words in fiction. Words mean things. Thus we use them every day: make love, buy bread, and blow up bridges. But the use of language in fiction only mimics its use in life. A sign like GENTS, for instance, tells me where to pee. It conveys information; it produces feelings of glad relief. I use the sign, but I dare not dawdle under it. It might have read MEN or borne a moustache. This kind of sign passes out of consciousness, is extinguished by its use. In literature, however, the sign remains; it sings; and we return to it again and again.

In contrast, the composer's medium is pure; that is, the tones he uses exist for music, and are made by instruments especially designed. Imagine his feelings, then, if he were forced to employ the meaningful noises of every day: bird calls, sirens, screams, alarm bells, whistles, ticks, and human chatter. He could plead all he liked that his music was pure, but we would know that he'd written down sounds from a play unseen, and we would insist that it told a story. Critics would describe the characters (one wears a goatee) and quarrel over their motives, marriages, or mothers, all their dark genes. Although no one wonders, of a painted peach, whether the tree it grew on was watered properly, we are happily witness, week after week, to further

---

8. Robert Frost (1874–1963), American poet.   9. Slang for seventy-five cents.

examination of Hamlet or Madame Bovary,[1] quite as if they were real. And they are so serious, so learned, so certain—so laughable—these ladies and gentlemen. Ah well, it's merely energy which might otherwise elucidate the Trinity.[2]

So the novelist makes his book from boards which say LADIES and GENTS. Every scrap has been worn, every item handled; most of the pieces are dented or split. The writer may choose to be heroic—poets often are—he may strive to purify his diction and achieve an exclusively literary language. He may pretend that every syllable he speaks hasn't been spit, sometimes, in someone else's mouth. Such poets scrub, they clean, they smooth, they polish, until we can scarcely recognize their words on the page. "A star glide, a single frantic sullenness, a single financial grass greediness," wrote Gertrude Stein. *"Toute Pensée émet un Coup de Dés,"* wrote Mallarmé.[3] Most novelists, however (it is one of the things that make them one), try to turn the tattering to account— incorporate it cleverly—as the painter does when he pastes up a collage of newspaper, tin foil, and postage stamps. He will recognize, for example, that stories are wonderful devices for controlling the speed of the mind, for resting it after hard climbs; they give a reassuring light to a dark place, and help the reader hold, like handsome handles, heavy luggage on long trips.

A dedicated storyteller, though—a true lie-minded man—will serve his history best, and guarantee its popularity, not by imitating nature, since nature's no source of verisimilitude, but by following as closely as he can our simplest, most direct and unaffected forms of daily talk, for we report real things, things which intrigue and worry us, and such resembling gossip in a book allows us to believe in figures and events we cannot see, shall never touch, with an assurance of safety which sets our passions free. He will avoid recording consciousness since consciousness is private—we do not normally "take it down"—and because no one really believes in any other feelings than his own. However, the moment our writer concentrates on sound, the moment he formalizes his sentences, the moment he puts in a figure of speech or turns a phrase, shifts a tense or alters tone, the moment he carries description, or any account, beyond need, he begins to turn his reader's interest away from the world which lies among his words like a beautiful woman among her slaves, and directs him toward the slaves themselves. This illustrates a basic principle: if I describe my peach too perfectly, it's the poem which will make my mouth water . . . while the real peach spoils.

Sculptures take up space and gather dust. Concepts do not. They take up us. They invade us as we read, and they achieve, as our resistance and their forces vary, every conceivable degree of occupation. Imagine a worry or a pain, an obsessive thought, a jealousy or hate so strong it renders you insensible to all else. Then while it lasts, you are that fear, that ache, for consciousness is always smaller than its opportunities, and can contract around a kernel like a shell. A piece of music can drive you out and take your place. The purpose of a literary work is the capture of consciousness, and the consequent creation, in you, of an imagined sensibility, so that while you read you are that patient pool or cataract of concepts which the author has con-

1. Protagonists, respectively, of Shakespeare's play (1602) and of the novel (1857) by the French writer Gustave Flaubert (1821–1880).
2. Christian conception of a three-person God (Father, Son, and Holy Spirit).
3. Every thought is a chance you take (French). Stéphane Mallarmé (1842–1898), French poet.

structed; and though at first it might seem as if the richness of life had been replaced by something less so—senseless noises, abstract meanings, mere shadows of worldly employment—yet the new self with which fine fiction and good poetry should provide you is as wide as the mind is, and musicked deep with feeling. While listening to such symbols sounding, the blind perceive; thought seems to grow a body; and the will is at rest amid that moving like a gull asleep on the sea. Perhaps we'll be forgiven, then, if we fret about our words and continue country-headed. It is not a refusal to please. There's no willfulness, disdain, exile . . . no anger. Because a consciousness electrified by beauty—is that not the aim and emblem and the ending of all finely made love?

Are you afraid?

1970

HUNTER S. THOMPSON

Hunter S. Thompson (1937–2005) was born in Louisville, Kentucky. He was a gifted student in literature, but misbehavior at the end of his senior year of high school earned him thirty days in juvenile detention, which prevented his graduation. Joining the air force as a way of getting out of town led to more trouble but also introduced him to the pleasures of life in the Caribbean, where he found work as a newspaper reporter. From there he moved on to feature journalism for such new countercultural magazines as *Scanlan's*, *Ramparts*, and *Rolling Stone*. Early attempts at fiction proved unpublishable until much later in his career, which he fashioned as an extreme style of literary journalism, his method focusing more on the observer's reaction to events than on events themselves (and using the techniques of fiction, such as characterization, imagery, and symbolism, to express those reactions). His most famous books remain his earliest ones: *Hell's Angels* (1967), covering a year he spent riding with this motorcycle gang; *Fear and Loathing in Las Vegas* (1971), an account of his failure to cover a dirt-bike race and a narcotics-law-enforcement convention; and *Fear and Loathing on the Campaign Trail '72* (1973), collecting his presidential campaign reporting as a correspondent for *Rolling Stone*. A self-styled Doctor of Gonzo Journalism, Thompson continued to publish personal reporting about the excesses of American culture until his death from a self-inflicted gunshot.

From Fear and Loathing in Las Vegas

The Circus-Circus[1] is what the whole hep world would be doing on Saturday night if the Nazis had won the war. This is the Sixth Reich.[2] The ground floor is full of gambling tables, like all the other casinos . . . but the place is about four stories high, in the style of a circus tent, and all manner

---

1. Casino and entertainment center opened in Las Vegas, Nevada, in 1968.
2. The Nazi government in Germany (1933–45)

declared itself the Third Reich; there were no Fourth and Fifth Reichs.

of strange County-Fair/Polish Carnival madness is going on up in this space. Right above the gambling tables the Forty Flying Carazito Brothers are doing a high-wire trapeze act, along with four muzzled Wolverines and the Six Nymphet Sisters from San Diego . . . so you're down on the main floor playing blackjack, and the stakes are getting high when suddenly you chance to look up, and there, right smack above your head is a half-naked fourteen-year-old girl being chased through the air by a snarling wolverine, which is suddenly locked in a death battle with two silver-painted Polacks who come swinging down from opposite balconies and meet in mid-air on the wolverine's neck . . . both Polacks seize the animal as they fall straight down towards the crap tables—but they bounce off the net; they separate and spring back up towards the roof in three different directions, and just as they're about to fall again they are grabbed out of the air by three Korean Kittens and trapezed off to one of the balconies.

This madness goes on and on, but nobody seems to notice. The gambling action runs twenty-four hours a day on the main floor, and the circus never ends. Meanwhile, on all the upstairs balconies, the customers are being hustled by every conceivable kind of bizarre shuck. All kinds of funhouse-type booths. Shoot the pasties off the nipples of a ten-foot bull-dyke and win a cotton-candy goat. Stand in front of this fantastic machine, my friend, and for just 99¢ your likeness will appear, two hundred feet tall, on a screen above downtown Las Vegas. Ninety-nine cents more for a voice message. "Say whatever you want, fella. They'll hear you, don't worry about that. Remember you'll be two hundred feet tall."

Jesus Christ. I could see myself lying in bed in the Mint Hotel, half-asleep and staring idly out the window, when suddenly a vicious nazi drunkard appears two hundred feet tall in the midnight sky, screaming gibberish at the world: "Woodstock Über Alles!"[3]

We will close the drapes tonight. A thing like that could send a drug person careening around the room like a ping-pong ball. Hallucinations are bad enough. But after a while you learn to cope with things like seeing your dead grandmother crawling up your leg with a knife in her teeth. Most acid fanciers can handle this sort of thing.

But *nobody* can handle that other trip—the possibility that any freak with $1.98 can walk into the Circus-Circus and suddenly appear in the sky over downtown Las Vegas twelve times the size of God, howling anything that comes into his head. No, this is not a good town for psychedelic drugs. Reality itself is too twisted.

1971

---

3. Woodstock Over Everything (German); a play on the German National Anthem ("*Das Lied der Deutschen,*" popularly known as "*Deutschland, Deutschland, Über Alles*"), with a reference to Woodstock, the rock festival held August 15–17, 1969, outside Bethel, an area southwest of Woodstock, New York, an event considered the high point of 1960s counterculture.

CHARLES OLSON

Charles Olson (1910–1970), represented elsewhere in this anthology by a selection of his poems, first published "Projective Verse" in a pamphlet, *Poetry New York*, in 1950. Two years earlier he had joined the faculty of North Carolina's Black Mountain College, where his colleagues included the choreographer Merce Cunningham (1919–2009), the painter Josef Albers (1888–1976), and the poet Robert Creeley (1926–2005), whose poetry is selected elsewhere in this anthology and from whom Olson borrowed the statement "FORM IS NEVER MORE THAN AN EXTENSION OF CONTENT." By advocating a set of formal principles based on the breath as a unit of measure, Olson described a new form of poetic measure unfolding on the "open field" of the page. His essay became a manifesto for poets reacting against the strictures of traditional forms.

From Projective Verse

(projectile   (percussive   (prospective

vs.

The NON-Projective

* * *

I

First, some simplicities that a man learns, if he works in OPEN, or what can also be called COMPOSITION BY FIELD, as opposed to inherited line, stanza, over-all form, what is the "old" base of the non-projective.

(1) the *kinetics* of the thing. A poem is energy transferred from where the poet got it (he will have some several causations), by way of the poem itself to, all the way over to, the reader. Okay. Then the poem itself must, at all points, be a high energy-construct and, at all points, an energy-discharge. So: how is the poet to accomplish same energy, how is he, what is the process by which a poet gets in, at all points energy at least the equivalent of the energy which propelled him in the first place, yet an energy which is peculiar to verse alone and which will be, obviously, also different from the energy which the reader, because he is a third term, will take away?

This is the problem which any poet who departs from closed form is specially confronted by. And it involves a whole series of new recognitions. From the moment he ventures into FIELD COMPOSITION—puts himself in the open—he can go by no track other than the one the poem under hand declares, for itself. Thus he has to behave, and be, instant by instant, aware of some several forces just now beginning to be examined. (It is much more, for example, this push, than simply such a one as Pound[1] put, so wisely, to get us started: "the musical phrase," go by it, boys, rather than by the metronome.)

---

1. Ezra Pound (1885–1972), American poet and critic, a major figure of the modernist movement in early 20th-century poetry.

(2) is the *principle*, the law which presides conspicuously over such composition, and, when obeyed, is the reason why a projective poem can come into being. It is this: FORM IS NEVER MORE THAN AN EXTENSION OF CONTENT. (Or so it got phrased by one, R. Creeley, and it makes absolute sense to me, with this possible corollary, that right form, in any given poem, is the only and exclusively possible extension of content under hand.) There it is, brothers, sitting there, for USE.

Now (3) the *process* of the thing, how the principle can be made so to shape the energies that the form is accomplished. And I think it can be boiled down to one statement (first pounded into my head by Edward Dahlberg)[2]: ONE PERCEPTION MUST IMMEDIATELY AND DIRECTLY LEAD TO A FURTHER PERCEPTION. It means exactly what it says, is a matter of, at *all* points (even, I should say, of our management of daily reality as of the daily work) get on with it, keep moving, keep in, speed, the nerves, their speed, the perceptions, theirs, the acts, the split second acts, the whole business, keep it moving as fast as you can, citizen. And if you also set up as a poet, USE USE USE the process at all points, in any given poem always, always one perception must must must MOVE, INSTANTER, ON ANOTHER!

So there we are, fast, there's the dogma. And its excuse, its usableness, in practice. Which gets us, it ought to get us, inside the machinery, now, 1950, of how projective verse is made.

If I hammer, if I recall in, and keep calling in, the breath, the breathing as distinguished from the hearing, it is for cause, it is to insist upon a part that breath plays in verse which has not (due, I think, to the smothering of the power of the line by too set a concept of foot) has not been sufficiently observed or practiced, but which has to be if verse is to advance to its proper force and place in the day, now, and ahead. I take it that PROJECTIVE VERSE teaches, is, this lesson, that that verse will only do in which a poet manages to register both the acquisitions of his ear *and* the pressures of his breath.

1950

2. Edward Dahlberg (1900–1977), American novelist and essayist.

FRANK O'HARA

On August 27, 1959, the poet Frank O'Hara (1926–1966) had a lunchtime conversation with the poet and playwright then known as LeRoi Jones, now Amiri Baraka (b. 1934). (Selections from the work of both these writers appear elsewhere in this anthology.) It was a heady period of multiplying literary "movements," and the two decided, as a joke, to invent their own movement. A week later O'Hara wrote "Personism," which presents "a movement I recently founded and which nobody yet knows about," and sent it as a letter to Donald Allen (1912–2004), who published it in the anthology *The New American Poetry 1945–1960* (1960). Allen's anthology, a kind of midcentury avant-garde cultural manifesto, became one of the most influential collections of poetry and poetics published since World War II. O'Hara's contribution retains the original mocking spirit of his lunchtime conversation, but it also offers a lively description of poetry as an address from one person to another. "In all modesty, I confess it may be the death of literature as we know it," O'Hara jokes, but his effort to loosen poetry from the academic debates about meaning and from an elite idea of "literature," and to restore it to the immediacy of one person speaking to another, was serious and proved influential.

From Personism: A Manifesto

Everything is in the poems, but at the risk of sounding like the poor wealthy man's Allen Ginsberg[1] I will write to you because I just heard that one of my fellow poets thinks that a poem of mine that can't be got at one reading is because I was confused too. Now, come on. I don't believe in god, so I don't have to make elaborately sounded structures. I hate Vachel Lindsay,[2] always have, I don't even like rhythm, assonance, all that stuff. You just go on your nerve. If someone's chasing you down the street with a knife you just run, you don't turn around and shout, "Give it up! I was a track star for Mineola Prep."

That's for the writing poems part. As for their reception, suppose you're in love and someone's mistreating (*mal aimé*)[3] you, you don't say, "Hey, you can't hurt me this way, I *care*!" you just let all the different bodies fall where they may, and they always do may after a few months. But that's not why you fell in love in the first place, just to hang onto life, so you have to take your chances and try to avoid being logical. Pain always produces logic, which is very bad for you.

I'm not saying that I don't have practically the most lofty ideas of anyone writing today, but what difference does that make? they're just ideas. The only good thing about it is that when I get lofty enough I've stopped thinking and that's when refreshment arrives.

But how can you really care if anybody gets it, or gets what it means, or if it improves them. Improves them for what? for death? Why hurry them along? Too many poets act like a middle-aged mother trying to get her kids to eat too much cooked meat, and potatoes with drippings (tears). I don't give a damn whether they eat or not. Forced feeding leads to excessive thinness (effete). Nobody should experience anything they don't need to, if they don't need poetry bully for them, I like the movies too. And after all, only Whitman and Crane and Williams,[4] of the American poets, are better than the movies. As for measure and other technical apparatus, that's just common sense: if you're going to buy a pair of pants you want them to be tight enough so everyone will want to go to bed with you. There's nothing metaphysical about it. Unless, of course, you flatter yourself into thinking that what you're experiencing is "yearning."

---

1. American poet (1926–1997) and member of the Beat generation.
2. American poet (1879–1931) famous for his emphatic use of sound and rhythm.
3. Poorly loved (French). *La Chanson du mal-aimé* (The Song of the Poorly Loved) is a poem by the French Symbolist poet Guillaume Apollinaire (1880–1918).
4. Walt Whitman (1819–1892), Hart Crane (1899–1932), and William Carlos Williams (1883–1963).

Abstraction in poetry, which Allen recently commented on in It is, is intriguing.[5] I think it appears mostly in the minute particulars where decision is necessary. Abstraction (in poetry, not in painting) involves personal removal by the poet. For instance, the decision involved in the choice between "the nostalgia of the infinite" and "the nostalgia for the infinite" defines an attitude towards degree of abstraction. The nostalgia of the infinite representing the greater degree of abstraction, removal, and negative capability (as in Keats and Mallarmé).[6] Personism, a movement which I recently founded and which nobody yet knows about, interests me a great deal, being so totally opposed to this kind of abstract removal that it is verging on a true abstraction for the first time, really, in the history of poetry. Personism is to Wallace Stevens what la poésie pure was to Béranger.[7] Personism has nothing to do with philosophy, it's all art. It does not have to do with personality or intimacy, far from it! But to give you a vague idea, one of its minimal aspects is to address itself to one person (other than the poet himself), thus evoking overtones of love without destroying love's life-giving vulgarity, and sustaining the poet's feelings towards the poem while preventing love from distracting him into feeling about the person. That's part of personism. It was founded by me after lunch with LeRoi Jones on August 27, 1959, a day in which I was in love with someone (not Roi, by the way, a blond). I went back to work and wrote a poem for this person. While I was writing it I was realizing that if I wanted to I could use the telephone instead of writing the poem, and so Personism was born. It's a very exciting movement which will undoubtedly have lots of adherents. It puts the poem squarely between the poet and the person, Lucky Pierre style,[8] and the poem is correspondingly gratified. The poem is at last between two persons instead of two pages. In all modesty, I confess that it may be the death of literature as we know it. * * *

September 3, 1959

1960

5. Donald Allen (1912–2004), a poet and the editor of the anthology in which O'Hara's essay appeared, wrote frequently about abstraction in poetry.
6. John Keats (1795–1821), English Romantic poet. Stéphane Mallarmé (1842–1898), French Symbolist poet and critic.
7. Wallace Stevens (1879–1955), American poet.

Pierre-Jean de Béranger (1780–1857), French poet and songwriter who became determined to sing for the people.
8. "Lucky Pierre": slang phrase for either a man in a sexual threesome of two women and one man or the middle man in a threesome of sexually entwined men.

ELIZABETH BISHOP

The following letter is from an extensive correspondence between Elizabeth Bishop (1911–1979) and Robert Lowell (1917–1977), both of whom are represented elsewhere in this anthology by a selection of their respective poems. The two writers were friends for many years and often exchanged their work. In March 1972 Bishop had been reading the manuscript of Lowell's latest book, The Dolphin (published in 1974). The Dolphin includes a number of poems about Lowell's love for Caroline Blackwood. While Bishop admired the poetry in the manuscript, she objected to *The Dolphin's* use of excerpts from the letters of Lowell's second wife, Elizabeth Hardwick, whom he divorced in 1972, the same year in which he married Blackwood. In Bishop's view, Lowell's use of Hardwick's letters violated a trust and mixed fact with fiction in unclear and inappropriate ways.

From Letter to Robert Lowell

March 21, 1972

* * * It's hell to write this, so please first do believe I think *Dolphin* is magnificent poetry. It is also honest poetry—*almost.* You probably know already what my reactions are. I have one tremendous and awful BUT.

If you were any other poet I can think of I certainly wouldn't attempt to say anything at all; I wouldn't think it was worth it. But because it is you, and a great poem (I've never used the word "great" before, that I remember), and I love you a lot—I feel I must tell you what I really think. There are several reasons for this—some are worldly ones, and therefore secondary . . . but the primary reason is because I love you so much I can't bear to have you publish something that I regret and that you might live to regret, too. The worldly part of it is that it—the poem—parts of it—may well be taken up and used against you by all the wrong people—who are just waiting in the wings to attack you.—One shouldn't consider them, perhaps. But it seems wrong to play right into their hands, too.

(Don't be alarmed. I'm not talking about the whole poem—just one aspect of it.)

Here is a quotation from dear little Hardy[1] that I copied out years ago—long before *Dolphin*, or even the *Notebooks*, were thought of. It's from a letter written in 1911, referring to "an abuse which was said to have occurred—that of publishing details of a lately deceased man's life under the guise of a novel, with assurances of truth scattered in the newspapers." (Not exactly the same situation as *Dolphin*, but fairly close.)

"What should certainly be protested against, in cases where there is no authorization, is the mixing of fact and fiction in unknown proportions. Infinite mischief would lie in that. If any statements in the dress of fiction are covertly hinted to be fact, all must be fact, and nothing else but fact, for obvious reasons. The power of getting lies

Robert Lowell and Elizabeth Bishop (shown here in Brazil, summer 1962) shared a friendship that Lowell once described as "together, till life's end." They met in 1947 and were friends and correspondents until Lowell died in 1977. Bishop died two years later.

believed about people through that channel after they are dead, by stirring in a few truths, is a horror to contemplate."

I'm sure my point is only too plain. Lizzie is not dead, etc.—but there is a "mixture of fact & fiction," and you have *changed* her letters. That is "infinite mischief," I think. The first one, page 10, is so shocking—well, I don't know what to say. And page 47 . . . and a few after that. One can use one's life as material—one does, anyway—but these letters—aren't you violating a trust? IF you were given permission—IF you hadn't changed them . . . etc. But *art just isn't worth that much.* I keep remembering Hopkins's marvelous letter to Bridges[2] about the idea of a "gentleman" being the highest thing ever conceived—higher than a "Christian," even, certainly than a poet. It is not being "gentle" to use personal, tragic, anguished letters that way—it's cruel.

* * *

* * * In general, I deplore the "confessional"—however, when you wrote *Life Studies* perhaps it was a necessary movement, and it helped make poetry more real, fresh and immediate. But now—ye gods—anything goes, and I am so sick of poems about the students' mothers & fathers and sex lives and so on. All that *can* be done—but at the same time one surely should have a feeling that one can trust the writer—not to distort, tell lies, etc.

The letters, as you have used them, present fearful problems: what's true, what isn't; how one can bear to witness such suffering and yet not know how much of it one *needn't* suffer with, how much has been "made up," and so on.

I don't give a damn what someone like Mailer[3] writes about his wives & marriages—I just hate the level we seem to live and think and feel on at present—but I do give a damn about what you write! * * * This counts and I can't bear to have anything you write tell—perhaps—what we're really like in 1972—perhaps it's as simple as that. But are we? * * *

April 10, 1972   1994

---

1. Thomas Hardy (1840–1928), English poet and novelist.
2. The English poet and Jesuit priest Gerard Manley Hopkins (1844–1889) corresponded with the English poet and critic Robert Bridges (1844–1930).
3. Norman Mailer (1923–2007), American novelist and nonfiction writer.

A. R. AMMONS

A mmons (1926–2001), represented elsewhere in this anthology by a selection of his poems, delivered "A Poem Is a Walk" as a lecture for teachers at the International Poetry Forum in Pittsburgh, Pennsylvania, in April 1967. It was published in 1968 in Cornell University's literary journal, *Epoch*. By 1964 Ammons had joined the English faculty at Cornell (in Ithaca, New York), where he was a much-loved teacher. His concerns as a poet and as a teacher of poetry are evident in this essay, which provides an account of poetry as an "interior seeking," its shape unfolding through a process of discovery. In the essay Ammons locates the essential rhythms of poetry in the motions of the body as it moves through the world. A peripatetic writer and theorist, Ammons employs this essay's principles in his poetry. "A Poem Is a Walk" also connects Ammons to the American Transcendentalist tradition. It recalls the famous essay "Walking" (1862), by Henry David Thoreau (1817–1862), in which this activity is figured as inward exploration, and the poems of Robert Frost (1874–1963), many of which are structured as a walk. A similar impulse can be found in such poets as Robert Creeley, Frank O'Hara, and Jorie Graham. Selections from each of these writers appear elsewhere in this anthology.

From A Poem Is a Walk

What justification is there for comparing a poem with a walk rather than with something else? I take the walk to be the externalization of an interior seeking so that the analogy is first of all between the external and the internal. Poets not only do a lot of walking but talk about it in their poems: "I wandered lonely as a cloud," "Now I out walking," and "Out walking in the frozen swamp one gray day." There are countless examples, and many of them suggest that both the real and the fictive walk are externalizations of an inward seeking. The walk magnified is the journey, and probably no figure has been used more often than the journey for both the structure and concern of an interior seeking.

How does a poem resemble a walk? First, each makes use of the whole body, involvement is total, both mind and body. You can't take a walk without feet and legs, without a circulatory system, a guidance and coordinating system, without eyes, ears, desire, will, need: the total person. This observation is important not only for what it includes but for what it rules out: as with a walk, a poem is not simply a mental activity: it has body, rhythm, feeling, sound, and mind, conscious and subconscious. The pace at which a poet walks (and thinks), his natural breath-length, the line he pursues, whether forthright and straight or weaving and meditative, his whole "air," whether of aimlessness or purpose—all these things and many more figure into the "physiology" of the poem he writes.

A second resemblance is that every walk is unreproducible, as is every poem. Even if you walk exactly the same route each time—as with a sonnet— the events along the route cannot be imagined to be the same from day to day, as the poet's health, sight, his anticipations, moods, fears, thoughts cannot be the same. There are no two identical sonnets or villanelles. If there were, we would not know how to keep the extra one: it would have no separate existence. If a poem is each time new, then it is necessarily an act of discovery, a chance taken, a chance that may lead to fulfillment or disaster. The poet exposes himself to the risk. All that has been said about poetry, all that he has learned about poetry, is only a partial assurance.

The third resemblance between a poem and a walk is that each turns, one or more times, and eventually returns. It's conceivable that a poem could rake out and go through incident after incident without ever returning, merely ending in the poet's return to dust. But most poems and most walks return. I have already quoted the first line from Frost's "The Wood-Pile." Now, here are the first three lines:

> Out walking in the frozen swamp one gray day,
> I paused and said, 'I will turn back from here.
> No, I will go on farther—and we shall see.'

The poet is moving outward seeking the point from which he will turn back. In "The Wood-Pile" there is no return: return is implied. The poet goes farther and farther into the swamp until he finds by accident the point of illumination with which he closes the poem.

But the turns and returns or implied returns give shape to the walk and to the poem. With the first step, the number of shapes the walk might take is infinite, but then the walk begins to "define" itself as it goes along, though freedom remains total with each step: any tempting side road can be turned into on impulse, or any wild patch of woods can be explored. The pattern of the walk is to come true, is to be recognized, discovered. The pattern, when discovered, may be found to apply to the whole walk, or only a segment of the walk may prove to have contour and therefore suggestion and shape. From previous knowledge of the terrain, inner and outer, the poet may have before the walk an inkling of a possible contour. Taking the walk would then be searching out or confirming, giving actuality to, a previous intuition.

The fourth resemblance has to do with the motion common to poems and walks. The motion may be lumbering clipped, wavering, tripping, mechanical, dance-like, awkward, staggering, slow, etc. But the motion occurs only in the body of the walker or in the body of the words. It can't be extracted and contemplated. It is nonreproducible and nonlogical. It can't be translated into another body. There is only one way to know it and that is to enter into it.

To summarize, a walk involves the whole person; it is not reproducible: its shape occurs, unfolds: it has a motion characteristic of the walker.

* * *

There is no ideal walk, then, though I haven't taken the time to prove it out completely, except the useless, meaningless walk. Only uselessness is empty enough for the presence of so many uses, and only through uselessness can the ideal walk come into the sum total of its uses. Only uselessness can allow the walk to be totally itself.

I hope you are, now, if you were not before, ready to agree with me that the greatest wrong that can be done a poem is to substitute a known part for an unknown whole and that the choice to be made is the freedom of nothingness: that our experience of poetry is least injured when we accept it as useless, meaningless, and nonrational.

* * * Poetry is a mode of discourse that differs from logical exposition. It is the mode I spoke of earlier, that can reconcile opposites into a "real" world both concrete and universal. Teach that. Teach the distinction.

Second, I would suggest you teach that poetry leads us to the unstructured sources of our beings, to the unknown, and returns us to our rational, structured selves refreshed. Having once experienced the mystery, plenitude, contradiction, and composure of a work of art, we afterward have a built-in resistance to the slogans and propaganda of oversimplification that have often contributed to the destruction of human life. Poetry is a verbal means to a nonverbal source. It is a motion to no-motion, to the still point of contemplation and deep realization. Its knowledges are all negative and, therefore, more positive than any knowledge. Nothing that can be said about it in words is worth saying.

April 1967   1968

AUDRE LORDE

As a black feminist, lesbian, poet, cancer survivor, and social activist, Audre Lorde (1934–1992) felt compelled to respond to the frequent assertion among activists that writing poetry is a luxury. Her essay "Poetry Is Not a Luxury" originally appeared in *Chrysalis: A Magazine of Female Culture* in 1977 and was reprinted in her well-known collection of essays, *Sister, Outsider* (1989). Lorde argued that, rather than being a luxury, poetry is "a vital necessity" because it creates a language in which to express women's hopes and dreams. The writing process, as she describes it, gives life and voice to what is unnamed and as yet unthought, and thus overcomes the forces in society that silence women's experiences. In this sense poetry articulates the vision necessary for social change to occur. Lorde's life and work reflected her belief that poetry is a form of empowerment and a tool for survival. A selection of her poems can be found elsewhere in this anthology.

From Poetry Is Not a Luxury

For women, then, poetry is not a luxury. It is a vital necessity of our existence. It forms the quality of the light within which we predicate our hopes and dreams toward survival and change, first made into language, then into idea, then into more tangible action. Poetry is the way we help give name to the nameless so it can be thought. The farthest external horizons of our hopes and fears are cobbled by our poems, carved from the rock experiences of our daily lives.

As they become known and accepted to ourselves, our feelings, and the honest exploration of them, become sanctuaries and fortresses and spawning grounds for the most radical and daring of ideas, the house of difference so necessary to change and the conceptualization of any meaningful action. Right now, I could name at least ten ideas I would once have found intolerable or incomprehensible and frightening, except as they came after dreams and poems. This is not idle fantasy, but the true meaning of "It feels right to me." We can train ourselves to respect our feelings and to discipline (transpose) them into a language that catches those feelings so they can be shared. And where that language does not yet exist, it is our poetry which helps to fashion it. Poetry is not only dream or vision, it is the skeleton architecture of our lives.

1977   1978

DENISE LEVERTOV
1923–1997

Denise Levertov once wrote of her predecessor, the poet H.D.: "She showed a way to penetrate mystery; which means, not to flood darkness with light so that darkness is destroyed, but to *enter into* darkness, mystery, so that it is experienced." Along with Robert Duncan, Levertov carried out in her own distinctive way H. D.'s tradition of visionary poetry. More grounded than her predecessor in observing the natural world and in appreciating daily life, Levertov connected the concrete to the invisible, as suggested by the image of *The Jacob's Ladder* (1961), the title of her fifth book. She desired that a poem be "hard as a floor, sound as a bench" but also that it be "mysterious" ("Illustrious Ancestors"), and in her poems ordinary events open into the unknown. The origins of Levertov's magical sense of the world are not difficult to trace. She was born in England and wrote of her parents: "My mother was descended from the Welsh Tailor and mystic Angel Jones of Mold, my father from the noted Hasid, Schneour Zaiman (d. 1831), the 'Rav of Northern White Russia.'" In "Illustrious Ancestors" Levertov claimed a connection to her forefathers, both mystical and Hasidic: "some line still taut between me and them." Hasidism, a sect of Judaism that emphasizes the soul's communion with God rather than formal religious observance and encourages what Levertov called "a wonder at creation," was an important influence on her father, Paul Philip Levertoff. He had converted to Christianity as a student and later became an Anglican priest, but he retained his interest in Judaism and told Hasidic legends to Levertov and her older sister, Olga, throughout their childhoods. From her mother, Beatrice Spooner-Jones, Levertov learned to look closely at the world around her, and we might say of her work what she said of her mother: "with how much gazing / her life had paid tribute to the world's body" ("The 90th Year").

In 1947 Levertov married an American, Mitchell Goodman (they later divorced), and moved to the United States. She described this move as crucial to her development as a poet; it "necessitated the finding of new rhythms in which to write, in accordance with new rhythms of life and speech." In this discovery of a new idiom the stylistic influence of William Carlos Williams was especially important to her; without it, she said, "I could not have developed from a British Romantic with an almost Victorian background to an American poet of any vitality." Levertov embraced Williams's interest in an organic poetic form, growing out of the poet's relation to her subject, and like Duncan and Robert Creeley, she actively explored the relations between the line and the unit of breath as they control rhythm, melody, and stress.

But if Levertov became the poet she was by becoming an American poet, her European heritage also enriched her sense of influence. Although her poem "September 1961" acknowledges her link to "the old great ones" (Ezra Pound, Williams, and H. D.), she was as at home with the German lyric poet Rainer Maria Rilke as with the American Transcendentalist Ralph Waldo Emerson. And in the United States she discovered the work of the Jewish theologian and philosopher Martin Buber, which renewed her interest "in the Hasidic ideas with which I was dimly acquainted as a child." Her eclecticism let her move easily between plain and richly descriptive language, between a vivid perception of the "thing itself" and the often radiant mystery that, for Levertov, arose from such seeing.

From 1956 to 1959 Levertov lived with her husband and son in Mexico. They were joined there by her mother, who, after her daughter's departure, remained in Mexico for the final eighteen years of her life (she died in 1977). Several moving poems in Levertov's collection *Life in the Forest* (1978), among them "The 90th Year" and "Death in Mexico," address her mother's last years. In the late 1960s the political crisis prompted by the Vietnam War turned Levertov's work more directly to public woes, as reflected in her following four books. Not all the poems in these books explicitly concern political issues ("The Sorrow Dance," for example, contains her sequence in memory of her sister, Olga, one of her finest, most powerful poems); nonetheless, many poems originated in a need for public testimony. Her overtly political poems are not often among her best, however; their very explicitness restricted her distinctive strengths as a poet, which included a feeling for the inexplicable, a language lyrical enough to express wish and desire, and a capacity for playfulness. But it is a mistake to separate too rigidly the political concerns in her work from a larger engagement with the world. As she wrote: "If a degree of intimacy is a condition of lyric expression, surely—at times when events make feelings run high—that intimacy between writer and political belief does exist, and is as intense as other emotions."

The power of Levertov's poems depends on her capacity to balance, however precariously, her two-sided vision, to keep alive both terms of what one critic called her "magical realism." At its best her work seems to spring from experience deep within her, stirred into being by a source beyond herself (as "Caedmon" is suddenly "affrighted" by an angel, or the poet at the age of sixteen dreams deeply, "sunk in the well"). Her finest poems render the inexplicable nature of our ordinary lives and their capacity for unexpected beauty. But Levertov's capacity for pleasure in the world never strays too far from the knowledge that the very landscapes that delight us contain places "that can pull you / down" ("Zeroing In"), as our inner landscapes also contain places "'that are bruised forever, that time / never assuages, never.'"

Levertov published several collections of prose, including *The Poet in the World* (1973), *Light Up the Cave* (1981), and *New and Selected Essays* (1992). In 1987 she published her fifteenth book of poems, *Breathing the Water*. This book contains a long sequence, *The Showings: Lady Julian of Norwich, 1342–1416*, which continues the link between Levertov's work and a visionary tradition. She published three subsequent collections: *A Door in the Hive* (1989), *Evening Train* (1992), and *Tesserae* (1995). Levertov taught widely and from 1982 until her death was professor of English at Stanford University, where she was an important teacher for a younger generation of writers.

To the Snake

Green Snake, when I hung you round my neck
and stroked your cold, pulsing throat
as you hissed to me, glinting

arrowy gold scales, and I felt
        the weight of you on my shoulders,   5
and the whispering silver of your dryness
        sounded close at my ears—
Green Snake—I swore to my companions that certainly
        you were harmless! But truly
I had no certainty, and no hope, only desiring   10
        to hold you, for that joy,
                    which left
a long wake of pleasure, as the leaves moved
and you faded into the pattern
of grass and shadows, and I returned   15
smiling and haunted, to a dark morning.

                                   1960

The Jacob's Ladder[1]

The stairway is not
a thing of gleaming strands
a radiant evanescence
for angels' feet that only glance in their tread, and need not
touch the stone.   5

It is of stone.
A rosy stone that takes
a glowing tone of softness
only because behind it the sky is a doubtful, a doubting
night gray.   10

A stairway of sharp
angles, solidly built.
One sees that the angels must spring
down from one step to the next, giving a little
lift of the wings: 15

and a man climbing
must scrape his knees, and bring
the grip of his hands into play. The cut stone
consoles his groping feet. Wings brush past him.
The poem ascends.   20

                                   1961

In Mind

There's in my mind a woman
of innocence, unadorned but

---

1. Jacob dreamed of "a ladder set up on the earth, and the top of it reached to heaven: and behold the angels of God ascending and descending on it" (Genesis 28.12).

fair-featured, and smelling of
apples or grass. She wears

a utopian smock or shift, her hair   5
is light brown and smooth, and she

is kind and very clean without
ostentation—
               but she has
no imagination.   10
               And there's a
turbulent moon-ridden girl

or old woman, or both,
dressed in opals and rags, feathers

and torn taffeta,   15
who knows strange songs—

but she is not kind.

                                 1964

Souvenir d'amitié[1]

Two fading red spots mark on my thighs
where a flea from the fur of a black, curly, yearning dog
bit me, casually, and returned into the fur.

Melanie was the dog's name. That afternoon
she had torn the screen from a door and littered fragments   5
of screen everywhere, and of chewed-up paper,

stars, whole constellations of paper, glimmered
in shadowy floor corners. She had been punished, adequately;
this was not a first offense. And forgiven,

but sadly: her master knew she would soon discover
other ways to show forth her discontent, her black humor.   10
Meanwhile, standing on hind legs like a human child,

she came to lean her body, her arms and head,
in my lap. I was a friendly stranger. She gave me
a share of her loneliness, her warmth, her flea.   15

                                 1970

---

1. Memory of friendship (French).

What Were They Like?

1) Did the people of Vietnam
   use lanterns of stone?
2) Did they hold ceremonies
   to reverence the opening of buds?
3) Were they inclined to quiet laughter?
4) Did they use bone and ivory,
   jade and silver, for ornament?
5) Had they an epic poem?
6) Did they distinguish between speech and singing?

1) Sir, their light hearts turned to stone.
   It is hot remembered whether in gardens
   stone lanterns illumined pleasant ways.
2) Perhaps they gathered once to delight in blossom,
   but after the children were killed
   there were no more buds.
3) Sir, laughter is bitter to the burned mouth.
4) A dream ago, perhaps. Ornament is for joy.
   All the bones were charred.
5) It is not remembered. Remember,
   most were peasants; their life
   was in rice and bamboo.
   When peaceful clouds were reflected in the paddies
   and the water buffalo stepped surely along terraces,
   maybe fathers told their sons old tales.
   When bombs smashed those mirrors
   there was time only to scream.
6) There is an echo yet
   of their speech which was like a song.
   It was reported their singing resembled
   the flight of moths in moonlight.
   Who can say? It is silent now.

1971

Caedmon[1]

All others talked as if
talk were a dance.
Clodhopper I, with clumsy feet
would break the gliding ring.
Early I learned to

---

1. "The story comes, of course, from the Venerable Bede's *History of the English Church and People*, but I first read it as a child in John Richard Green's *History of the English People*, 1855" [Levertov's note]. Caedmon (fl. 658–680) was, according to the story, an illiterate cowherd employed by a monastery; one night he received a divine call to sing verses in praise of God. He is the earliest known Christian poet in English.

hunch myself
close by the door:
then when the talk began
I'd wipe my
mouth and wend   10
unnoticed back to the barn
to be with the warm beasts,
dumb among body sounds
of the simple ones.
I'd see by a twist   15
of lit rush[2] the motes
of gold moving
from shadow to shadow
slow in the wake
of deep untroubled sighs.   20
The cows
munched or stirred or were still. I
was at home and lonely,
both in good measure. Until
the sudden angel affrighted me—light effacing   25
my feeble beam,
a forest of torches, feathers of flame, sparks upflying:
but the cows as before
were calm, and nothing was burning,
        nothing but I, as that hand of fire   30
touched my lips and scorched my tongue
and pulled my voice
           into the ring of the dance.

1987

---

2. The piths of rush plants were used for candlewicks.

JAMES BALDWIN
1924–1987

James Baldwin was born in Harlem, the first of nine children. From his novel *Go Tell It on the Mountain* (1953) and his story "The Rockpile," we learn about the extremely painful relationship he had with his father (actually his stepfather). David Baldwin, son of a slave, was a lay preacher rigidly committed to a vengeful God who would eventually judge white people as they deserved; in the meantime much of the vengeance was taken out on James. His father's "unlimited capacity for introspection and rancor," as the son later put it, must have had a profound effect on the sermonizing style Baldwin developed. Just as important was Baldwin's conversion and resulting service as a preacher in his father's church, as we can see from both the rhythm and the message of his prose—which is very much a *spoken* prose.

Baldwin did well in school and, having received a hardship deferment from military service because his father was dying, attached himself to Greenwich Village, where he concentrated on becoming a writer. In 1944 he met Richard Wright, at that time "the greatest black writer in the world for me," in whose early books Baldwin "found expressed, for the first time in my life, the sorrow, the rage, and the murderous bitterness which was eating up my life and the lives of those about me." Wright helped him win a Eugene Saxton fellowship, and in 1948, when Baldwin went to live in Paris, he was following in Wright's footsteps (Wright had become an expatriate to the same city a year earlier). It is perhaps for this reason that in his early essays written for *Partisan Review* and published in 1955 as *Notes of a Native Son* (with the title's explicit reference to Wright's 1940 novel, *Native Son*) Baldwin dissociated himself from the image of American life found in Wright's "protest work" and, like the novelist Ralph Ellison, went about protesting in his own way.

As far as his novels are concerned, Baldwin's way involved a preoccupation with the intertwining of sexual with racial concerns, particularly in America. His interest in what it means to be black and homosexual in relation to mainstream white society is most fully and interestingly expressed in his third novel, *Another Country* (1962). (He had previously written *Go Tell It on the Mountain*, and a second novel, *Giovanni's Room*, 1955, about a white expatriate in Paris and his male lover.) *Another Country* contains scenes full of lively detail and intelligent reflection, expressed in a manner that takes advantage of the novel's expansive form. In his short stories collected in *Going to Meet the Man* (1965), the racial terrorism of America as he perceived it made its own grotesque stylistic statement. The writer's challenge was to maintain steady control in the face of atrocities that might otherwise disrupt the narrative's ability to contain such events.

His later novels, *Tell Me How Long the Train's Been Gone* (1968) and *Just Above My Head* (1979), were more polemical. Like his fellow novelist Norman Mailer, Baldwin risked advertising himself too strenuously and sometimes let spokesmanship become a primary motivator. Like Ellison, he experienced many pressures to be more than just a writer, but he nevertheless produced artistically significant novels and stories. No black writer has been better able to imagine white experience, to speak in various tones of different kinds and behaviors of people or places other than his own. In its sensitivity to shades of discrimination and moral shape, and in its commitment—despite everything—to America, his voice was comparable in importance to that of any person of letters from recent decades, as tributes paid to him at his death agreed.

The following text is from *Going to Meet the Man* (1965).

Going to Meet the Man

"What's the matter?" she asked.

"I don't know," he said, trying to laugh, "I guess I'm tired."

"You've been working too hard," she said. "I keep telling you."

"Well, goddammit, woman," he said, "it's not my fault!" He tried again; he wretchedly failed again. Then he just lay there, silent, angry, and helpless. Excitement filled him like a toothache, but it refused to enter his flesh. He stroked her breast. This was his wife. He could not ask her to do just a little thing for him, just to help him out, just for a little while, the way he could ask a nigger girl to do it. He lay there, and he sighed. The image of a black girl caused a distant excitement in him, like a far-away light; but, again, the excitement was more like pain; instead of forcing him to act, it made action impossible.

"Go to sleep," she said, gently, "you got a hard day tomorrow."

"Yeah," he said, and rolled over on his side, facing her, one hand still on one breast. "Goddamn the niggers. The black stinking coons. You'd think they'd learn. Wouldn't you think they'd learn? I mean, *wouldn't* you?"

"They going to be out there tomorrow," she said, and took his hand away, "get some sleep."

He lay there, one hand between his legs, staring at the frail sanctuary of his wife. A faint light came from the shutters; the moon was full. Two dogs, far away, were barking at each other, back and forth, insistently, as though they were agreeing to make an appointment. He heard a car coming north on the road and he half sat up, his hand reaching for his holster, which was on a chair near the bed, on top of his pants. The lights hit the shutters and seemed to travel across the room and then went out. The sound of the car slipped away, he heard it hit gravel, then heard it no more. Some liver-lipped students, probably, heading back to that college—but coming from where? His watch said it was two in the morning. They could be coming from anywhere, from out of state most likely, and they would be at the court-house tomorrow. The niggers were getting ready. Well, they would be ready, too.

He moaned. He wanted to let whatever was in him out; but it wouldn't come out. Goddamn! he said aloud, and turned again, on his side, away from Grace, staring at the shutters. He was a big, healthy man and he had never had any trouble sleeping. And he wasn't old enough yet to have any trouble getting it up—he was only forty-two. And he was a good man, a God-fearing man, he had tried to do his duty all his life, and he had been a deputy sheriff for several years. Nothing had ever bothered him before, certainly not getting it up. Sometimes, sure, like any other man, he knew that he wanted a little more spice than Grace could give him and he would drive over yonder and pick up a black piece or arrest her, it came to the same thing, but he couldn't do that now, no more. There was no telling what might happen once your ass was in the air. And they were low enough to kill a man then, too, every one of them, or the girl herself might do it, right while she was making believe you made her feel so good. The niggers. What had the good Lord Almighty had in mind when he made the niggers? Well. They were pretty good at that, all right. Damn. Damn. Goddamn.

This wasn't helping him to sleep. He turned again, toward Grace again, and moved close to her warm body. He felt something he had never felt before. He felt that he would like to hold her, hold her, hold her, and be buried in her like a child and never have to get up in the morning again and go downtown to face those faces, good Christ, they were ugly! and never have to enter that jailhouse again and smell that smell and hear that singing; never again feel that filthy, kinky, greasy hair under his hand, never again watch those black breasts leap against the leaping cattle prod, never hear those moans again or watch that blood run down or the fat lips split or the sealed eyes struggle open. They were animals, they were no better than animals, what could be done with people like that? Here they had been in a civilized country for years and they still lived like animals. Their houses were dark, with oil cloth or cardboard in the windows, the smell was enough to make you puke your guts out, and there they sat, a whole tribe, pumping out kids, it looked like, every damn five minutes, and laughing and talking and playing music like they didn't have a care in the world, and he reckoned they didn't, neither, and coming to the door, into the sunlight, just standing there, just looking foolish, not thinking of anything but just getting back to what they were doing, saying, Yes suh, Mr. Jesse. I surely will, Mr. Jesse. Fine weather, Mr. Jesse. Why, I thank you, Mr. Jesse. He had worked for a mail-order house for a while and it had been his job to collect the payments for the stuff they bought. They were too dumb to know that they were being cheated blind, but that was no skin off his ass—he was just supposed to do his job. They would be late—they didn't have the sense to put money aside; but it was easy to scare them, and he never really had any trouble. Hell, they all liked him, the kids used to smile when he came to the door. He gave them candy, sometimes, or chewing gum, and rubbed their rough bullet heads— maybe the candy should have been poisoned. Those kids were grown now. He had had trouble with one of them today.

"There was this nigger today," he said; and stopped; his voice sounded peculiar. He touched Grace. "You awake?" he asked. She mumbled something, impatiently, she was probably telling him to go to sleep. It was all right. He knew that he was not alone.

"What a funny time," he said, "to be thinking about a thing like that—you listening?" She mumbled something again. He rolled over on his back. "This nigger's one of the ringleaders. We had trouble with him before. We must have had him out there at the work farm three or four times. Well, Big Jim C. and some of the boys really had to whip that nigger's ass today." He looked over at Grace; he could not tell whether she was listening or not; and he was afraid to ask again. "They had this line you know, to register"—he laughed, but she did not—"and they wouldn't stay where Big Jim C. wanted them, no, they had to start blocking traffic all around the court house so couldn't nothing or nobody get through, and Big Jim C. told them to disperse and they wouldn't move, they just kept up that singing, and Big Jim C. figured that the others would move if this nigger would move, him being the ringleader, but he wouldn't move and he wouldn't let the others move, so they had to beat him and a couple of the others and they threw them in the wagon—but I didn't see this nigger till I got to the jail. They were still singing and I was supposed to make them stop. Well, I couldn't make them stop for me but I knew he could make them stop. He was lying on the ground jerking and moaning, they had threw him in a cell by himself, and blood was coming out his ears from where Big Jim C. and his boys had whipped him. Wouldn't you think they'd learn? I put the prod to him and he jerked some more and he kind of screamed—but he didn't have much voice left. "You make them stop that singing," I said to him, "you hear me? You make them stop that singing." He acted like he didn't hear me and I put it to him again, under his arms, and he just rolled around on the floor and blood started coming from his mouth. He'd pissed his pants already." He paused. His mouth felt dry and his throat was as rough as sandpaper; as he talked, he began to hurt all over with that peculiar excitement which refused to be released. "You all are going to stop your singing, I said to him, and you are going to stop coming down to the court house and disrupting traffic and molesting the people and keeping us from our duties and keeping doctors from getting to sick white women and getting all them Northerners in this town to give our town a bad name—!" As he said this, he kept prodding the boy, sweat pouring from beneath the helmet he had not yet taken off. The boy rolled around in his own dirt and water and blood and tried to scream again as the prod hit his testicles, but the scream did not come out, only a kind of rattle and a moan. He stopped. He was not supposed to kill the nigger. The cell was filled with a terrible odor. The boy was still. "You hear me?" he called. "You had enough?" The singing went on. "You had enough?" His foot leapt out, he had not known it was going to, and caught the boy flush on the jaw. *Jesus,* he thought, *this ain't no nigger, this is a goddamn bull,* and he screamed again, "You had enough? You going to make them stop that singing now?"

But the boy was out. And now he was shaking worse than the boy had been shaking. He was glad no one could see him. At the same time, he felt very close to a very peculiar, particular joy; something deep in him and deep in his memory was stirred, but whatever was in his memory eluded him. He took off his helmet. He walked to the cell door.

"White man," said the boy, from the floor, behind him.

He stopped. For some reason, he grabbed his privates.

"You remember Old Julia?"

The boy said, from the floor, with his mouth full of blood, and one eye, barely open, glaring like the eye of a cat in the dark, "My grandmother's name was Mrs. Julia Blossom. *Mrs.* Julia Blossom. You going to call our women by their right names yet.—And those kids ain't going to stop singing. We going to keep on singing until every one of you miserable white mothers go stark raving out of your minds." Then he closed the one eye; he spat blood; his head fell back against the floor.

He looked down at the boy, whom he had been seeing, off and on, for more than a year, and suddenly remembered him: Old Julia had been one of his mail-order customers, a nice old woman. He had not seen her for years, he supposed that she must be dead.

He had walked into the yard, the boy had been sitting in a swing. He had smiled at the boy, and asked, "Old Julia home?"

The boy looked at him for a long time before he answered. "Don't no Old Julia live here."

"This is her house. I know her. She's lived here for years."

The boy shook his head. "You might know a Old Julia someplace else, white man. But don't nobody by that name live here."

He watched the boy; the boy watched him. The boy certainly wasn't more than ten. *White man.* He didn't have time to be fooling around with some crazy kid. He yelled, "Hey! Old Julia!"

But only silence answered him. The expression on the boy's face did not change. The sun beat down on them both, still and silent; he had the feeling that he had been caught up in a nightmare, a nightmare dreamed by a child; perhaps one of the nightmares he himself had dreamed as a child. It had that feeling—everything familiar, without undergoing any other change—had been subtly and hideously displaced: the trees, the sun, the patches of grass in the yard, the leaning porch and the weary porch steps and the card-board in the windows and the black hole of the door which looked like the entrance to a cave, and the eyes of the pickaninny, all, all, were charged with malevolence. *White man.* He looked at the boy. "She's gone out?"

The boy said nothing.

"Well," he said, "tell her I passed by and I'll pass by next week." He started to go; he stopped. "You want some chewing gum?"

The boy got down from the swing and started for the house. He said, "I don't want nothing you got, white man." He walked into the house and closed the door behind him.

Now the boy looked as though he were dead. Jesse wanted to go over to him and pick him up and pistol whip him until the boy's head burst open like a melon. He began to tremble with what he believed was rage, sweat, both cold and hot, raced down his body, the singing filled him as though it were a weird, uncontrollable, monstrous howling rumbling up from the depths of his own belly, he felt an icy fear rise in him and raise him up, and he shouted, he howled, "You lucky we *pump* some white blood into you every once in a while—your women! Here's what I got for all the black bitches in the world—!" Then he was, abruptly, almost too weak to stand; to his bewilderment, his horror, beneath his own fingers, he felt himself violently stiffen—with no warning at all; he dropped his hands and he stared at the boy and he left the cell.

"All that singing they do," he said. "All that singing." He could not remember the first time he had heard it; he had been hearing it all his life. It was the sound with which he was most familiar—though it was also the sound of which he had been least conscious—and it had always contained an obscure comfort. They were singing to God. They were singing for mercy and they hoped to go to heaven, and he had even sometimes felt, when looking into the eyes of some of the old women, a few of the very old men, that they were singing for mercy for his soul, too. Of course he had never thought of their heaven or of what God was, or could be, for them; God was the same for everyone, he supposed, and heaven was where good people went—he supposed. He had never thought much about what it meant to be a good person. He tried to be a good person and treat everybody right: it wasn't his fault if the niggers had taken it into their heads to fight against God and go against the rules laid down in the Bible for everyone to read! Any preacher would tell you that. He was only doing his duty: protecting white people from the niggers and the niggers from themselves. And there were still lots of good niggers around—he had to remember that; they weren't all like that boy this afternoon; and the good niggers must be mighty sad to see what was happening to their people. They would thank him when this was over. In that way they had, the best of them, not quite looking him in the eye, in a low voice, with a little smile: We surely thanks you, Mr. Jesse. From the bottom of our hearts, we thanks you. He smiled. They hadn't all gone crazy. This trouble would pass.—He knew that the young people had changed some of the words to the songs. He had scarcely listened to the words before and he did not listen to them now; but he knew that the words were different; he could hear that much. He did not know if the faces were different, he had never, before this trouble began, watched them as they sang, but he certainly did not like what he saw now. They hated him, and this hatred was blacker than their hearts, blacker than their skins, redder than their blood, and harder, by far, than his club. Each day, each night, he felt worn out, aching, with their smell in his nostrils and filling his lungs, as though he were drowning—drowning in niggers; and it was all to be done again when he awoke. It would never end. It would never end. Perhaps this was what the singing had meant all along. They had not been singing black folks into heaven, they had been singing white folks into hell.

Everyone felt this black suspicion in many ways, but no one knew how to express it. Men much older than he, who had been responsible for law and order much longer than he, were now much quieter than they had been, and the tone of their jokes, in a way that he could not quite put his finger on, had changed. These men were his models, they had been friends to his father, and they had taught him what it meant to be a man. He looked to them for courage now. It wasn't that he didn't know that what he was doing was right—he knew that, nobody had to tell him that; it was only that he missed the ease of former years. But they didn't have much time to hang out with each other these days. They tended to stay close to their families every free minute because nobody knew what might happen next. Explosions rocked the night of their tranquil town. Each time each man wondered silently if perhaps this time the dynamite had not fallen into the wrong hands. They thought that they knew where all the guns were; but they could not possibly know every move that was made in that secret place where the darkies lived. From time to time it was suggested that they form a posse and search the home of every nigger, but they hadn't done it yet. For one thing, this might have brought the bastards from the North down on their backs; for another, although the niggers were scattered throughout the town— down in the hollow near the railroad tracks, way west near the mills, up on the hill, the well-off ones, and some out near the college—nothing seemed to happen in one part of town without the niggers immediately knowing it in the other. This meant that they could not take them by surprise. They rarely mentioned it, but they *knew* that some of the niggers had guns. It stood to reason, as they said, since, after all, some of them had been in the Army. There were niggers in the Army right now and God knows they wouldn't have had any trouble stealing this half-assed government blind—the whole world was doing it, look at the European countries and all those countries in Africa. They made jokes about it—bitter jokes; and they cursed the government in Washington, which had betrayed them; but they had not yet formed a posse. Now, if their town had been laid out like some towns in the North, where all the niggers lived together in one locality, they could have gone down and set fire to the houses and brought about peace that way. If the niggers had all lived in one place, they could have kept the fire in one place. But the way this town was laid out, the fire could hardly be controlled. It would spread all over town—and the niggers would probably be helping it to spread. Still, from time to time, they spoke of doing it, anyway; so that now there was a real fear among them that somebody might go crazy and light the match.

They rarely mentioned anything not directly related to the war that they were fighting, but this had failed to establish between them the unspoken communication of soldiers during a war. Each man, in the thrilling silence which sped outward from their exchanges, their laughter, and their anecdotes, seemed wrestling, in various degrees of darkness, with a secret which he could not articulate to himself, and which, however directly it related to the war, related yet more surely to his privacy and his past. They could no longer be sure, after all, that they had all done the same things. They had never dreamed that their privacy could contain any element of terror, could threaten, that is, to reveal itself, to the scrutiny of a judgment day, while remaining unreadable and inaccessible to themselves; nor had they dreamed that the past, while certainly refusing to be forgotten, could yet so stubbornly refuse to be remembered. They felt themselves mysteriously set at naught, as no longer entering into the real concerns of other people—while here they were, out-numbered, fighting to save the civilized world. They had thought that people would care—people didn't care; not enough, anyway, to help them. It would have been a help, really, or at least a relief, even to have been forced to surrender. Thus they had lost, probably forever, their old and easy connection with each other. They were forced to depend on each other more and, at the same time, to trust each other less. Who could tell when one of them might not betray them all, for money, or for the ease of confession? But no one dared imagine what there might be to confess. They were soldiers fighting a war, but their relationship to each other was that of accomplices in a crime. They all had to keep their mouths shut.

I stepped in the river at Jordan.

Out of the darkness of the room, out of nowhere, the line came flying up at him, with the melody and the beat. He turned wordlessly toward his sleeping wife. *I stepped in the river at Jordan.* Where had he heard that song?

"Grace," he whispered. "You awake?"

She did not answer. If she was awake, she wanted him to sleep. Her breathing was slow and easy, her body slowly rose and fell.

I stepped in the river at Jordan.
The water came to my knees.

He began to sweat. He felt an overwhelming fear, which yet contained a curious and dreadful pleasure.

I stepped in the river at Jordan.
The water came to my waist.

It had been night, as it was now, he was in the car between his mother and his father, sleepy, his head in his mother's lap, sleepy, and yet full of excitement. The singing came from far away, across the dark fields. There were no lights anywhere. They had said good-bye to all the others and turned off on this dark dirt road. They were almost home.

I stepped in the river at Jordan,
The water came over my head,
I looked way over to the other side,
He was making up my dying bed!

"I guess they singing for him," his father said, seeming very weary and subdued now. "Even when they're sad, they sound like they just about to go and tear off a piece." He yawned and leaned across the boy and slapped his wife lightly on the shoulder, allowing his hand to rest there for a moment. "Don't they?"

"Don't talk that way," she said.

"Well, that's what we going to do," he said, "you can make up your mind to that." He started whistling. "You see? When I begin to feel it, I gets kind of musical, too."

Oh, Lord! Come on and ease my troubling mind!

He had a black friend, his age, eight, who lived nearby. His name was Otis. They wrestled together in the dirt. Now the thought of Otis made him sick. He began to shiver. His mother put her arm around him.

"He's tired," she said.

"We'll be home soon," said his father. He began to whistle again.

"We didn't see Otis this morning," Jesse said. He did not know why he said this. His voice, in the darkness of the car, sounded small and accusing.

"You haven't seen Otis for a couple of mornings," his mother said.

That was true. But he was only concerned about *this* morning.

"No," said his father, "I reckon Otis's folks was afraid to let him show himself this morning."

"But Otis didn't do nothing!" Now his voice sounded questioning.

"Otis *can't* do nothing," said his father, "he's too little." The car lights picked up their wooden house, which now solemnly approached them, the lights falling around it like yellow dust. Their dog, chained to a tree, began to bark.

"We just want to make sure Otis *don't* do nothing," said his father, and stopped the car. He looked down at Jesse. "And you tell him what your Daddy said, you hear?"

"Yes sir," he said.

His father switched off the lights. The dog moaned and pranced, but they ignored him and went inside. He could not sleep. He lay awake, hearing the night sounds, the dog yawning and moaning outside, the sawing of the crickets, the cry of the owl, dogs barking far away, then no sounds at all, just the heavy, endless buzzing of the night. The darkness pressed on his eyelids like a scratchy blanket. He turned, he turned again. He wanted to call his mother, but he knew his father would not like this. He was terribly afraid. Then he heard his father's voice in the other room, low, with a joke in it; but this did not help him, it frightened him more, he knew what was going to happen. He put his head under the blanket, then pushed his head out again, for fear, staring at the dark window. He heard his mother's moan, his father's sigh; he gritted his teeth. Then their bed began to rock. His father's breathing seemed to fill the world.

That morning, before the sun had gathered all its strength, men and women, some flushed and some pale with excitement, came with news. Jesse's father seemed to know what the news was before the first jalopy stopped in the yard, and he ran out, crying, "They got him, then? They got him?"

The first jalopy held eight people, three men and two women and three children. The children were sitting on the laps of the grown-ups. Jesse knew two of them, the two boys; they shyly and uncomfortably greeted each other. He did not know the girl.

"Yes, they got him," said one of the women, the older one, who wore a wide hat and a fancy, faded blue dress. "They found him early this morning."

"How far had he got?" Jesse's father asked.

"He hadn't got no further than Harkness," one of the men said. "Look like he got lost up there in all them trees—or maybe he just got so scared he couldn't move." They all laughed.

"Yes, and you know it's near a graveyard, too," said the younger woman, and they laughed again.

"Is that where they got him now?" asked Jesse's father.

By this time there were three cars piled behind the first one, with everyone looking excited and shining, and Jesse noticed that they were carrying food. It was like a Fourth of July picnic.

"Yeah, that's where he is," said one of the men, "declare, Jesse, you going to keep us here all day long, answering your damn fool questions. Come on, we ain't got no time to waste."

"Don't bother putting up no food," cried a woman from one of the other cars, "we got enough. Just come on."

"Why, thank you," said Jesse's father, "we be right along, then."

"I better get a sweater for the boy," said his mother, "in case it turns cold."

Jesse watched his mother's thin legs cross the yard. He knew that she also wanted to comb her hair a little and maybe put on a better dress, the dress she wore to church. His father guessed this, too, for he yelled behind her, "Now don't you go trying to turn yourself into no movie star. You just come on." But he laughed as he said this, and winked at the men; his wife was younger and prettier than most of the other women. He clapped Jesse on the head and started pulling him toward the car. "You all go on," he said, "I'll be right behind you. Jesse, you go tie up that there dog while I get this car started."

The cars sputtered and coughed and shook; the caravan began to move; bright dust filled the air. As soon as he was tied up, the dog began to bark. Jesse's mother came out of the house, carrying a jacket for his father and a sweater for Jesse. She had put a ribbon in her hair and had an old shawl around her shoulders.

"Put these in the car, son," she said, and handed everything to him. She bent down and stroked the dog, looked to see if there was water in his bowl, then went back up the three porch steps and closed the door.

"Come on," said his father, "ain't nothing in there for nobody to steal." He was sitting in the car, which trembled and belched. The last car of the caravan had disappeared but the sound of singing floated behind them.

Jesse got into the car, sitting close to his father, loving the smell of the car, and the trembling, and the bright day, and the sense of going on a great and unexpected journey. His mother got in and closed the door and the car began to move. Not until then did he ask, "Where are we going? Are we going on a picnic?"

He had a feeling that he knew where they were going, but he was not sure.

"That's right," his father said, "we're going on a picnic. You won't ever forget *this* picnic—!"

"Are we," he asked, after a moment, "going to see the bad nigger—the one that knocked down old Miss Standish?"

"Well, I reckon," said his mother, "that we *might* see him."

He started to ask, *Will a lot of niggers be there? Will Otis be there?*—but he did not ask his question, to which, in a strange and uncomfortable way, he already knew the answer. Their friends, in the other cars, stretched up the road as far as he could see; other cars had joined them; there were cars behind them. They were singing. The sun seemed suddenly very hot, and he was at once very happy and a little afraid. He did not quite understand what was happening, and he did not know what to ask—he had no one to ask. He had grown accustomed, for the solution of such mysteries, to go to Otis. He felt that Otis knew everything. But he could not ask Otis about this. Anyway, he had not seen Otis for two days; he had not seen a black face anywhere for more than two days; and he now realized, as they began chugging up the long hill which eventually led to Harkness, that there were no black faces on the road this morning, no black people anywhere. From the houses in which they lived, all along the road, no smoke curled, no life stirred—maybe one or two chickens were to be seen, that was all. There was no one at the windows, no one in the yard, no one sitting on the porches, and the doors were closed. He had come this road many a time and seen women washing in the yard (there were no clothes on the clotheslines), men working in the fields, children playing in the dust; black men passed them on the road other mornings, other days, on foot, or in wagons, sometimes in cars, tipping their hats, smiling, joking, their teeth a solid white against their skin, their eyes as warm as the sun, the blackness of their skin like dull fire against the white or the blue or the grey of their torn clothes. They passed the nigger church—dead-white, desolate, locked up; and the graveyard, where no one knelt or walked, and he saw no flowers. He wanted to ask, *Where are they? Where are they all?* But he did not dare. As the hill grew steeper, the sun grew colder. He looked at his mother and his father. They looked straight ahead, seeming to be listening to the singing which echoed and echoed in this graveyard silence. They were strangers to him now. They were looking at something he could not see. His father's lips had a strange, cruel curve, he wet his lips from time to time, and swallowed. He was terribly aware of his father's tongue, it was as though he had never seen it before. And his father's body suddenly seemed immense, bigger than a mountain. His eyes, which were grey-green, looked yellow in the sunlight; or at least there was a light in them which he had never seen before. His mother patted her hair and adjusted the ribbon, leaning forward to look into the car mirror. "You look all right," said his father, and laughed. "When that nigger looks at you, he's going to swear he throwed his life away for nothing. Wouldn't be surprised if he don't come back to haunt you." And he laughed again.

The singing now slowly began to cease; and he realized that they were nearing their destination. They had reached a straight, narrow, pebbly road, with trees on either side. The sunlight filtered down on them from a great height, as though they were underwater; and the branches of the trees scraped against the cars with a tearing sound. To the right of them, and beneath them, invisible now, lay the town; and to the left, miles of trees which led to the high mountain range which his ancestors had crossed in order to settle in this valley. Now, all was silent, except for the bumping of the tires against the rocky road, the sputtering of motors, and the sound of a crying child. And they seemed to move more slowly. They were beginning to climb again. He watched the cars ahead as they toiled patiently upward, disappearing into the sunlight of the clearing. Presently, he felt their vehicle also rise, heard his father's changed breathing, the sunlight hit his face, the trees moved away from them, and they were there. As their car crossed the clearing, he looked around. There seemed to be millions, there were certainly hundreds of people in the clearing, staring toward something he could not see. There was a fire. He could not see the flames, but he smelled the smoke. Then they were on the other side of the clearing, among the trees again. His father drove off the road and parked the car behind a great many other cars. He looked down at Jesse.

"You all right?" he asked.

"Yes sir," he said.

"Well, come on, then," his father said. He reached over and opened the door on his mother's side. His mother stepped out first. They followed her into the clearing. At first he was aware only of confusion, of his mother and father greeting and being greeted, himself being handled, hugged, and patted, and told how much he had grown. The wind blew the smoke from the fire across the clearing into his eyes and nose. He could not see over the backs of the people in front of him. The sounds of laughing and cursing and wrath—and something else—rolled in waves from the front of the mob to the back. Those in front expressed their delight at what they saw, and this delight rolled backward, wave upon wave, across the clearing, more acrid than the smoke. His father reached down suddenly and sat Jesse on his shoulders.

Now he saw the fire—of twigs and boxes, piled high; flames made pale orange and yellow and thin as a veil under the steadier light of the sun; grey-blue smoke rolled upward and poured over their heads. Beyond the shifting curtain of fire and smoke, he made out first only a length of gleaming chain, attached to a great limb of the tree; then he saw that this chain bound two black hands together at the wrist, dirty yellow palm facing dirty yellow palm. The smoke poured up; the hands dropped out of sight; a cry went up from the crowd. Then the hands slowly came into view again, pulled upward by the chain. This time he saw the kinky, sweating, bloody head—he had never before seen a head with so much hair on it, hair so black and so tangled that it seemed like another jungle. The head was hanging. He saw the forehead, flat and high, with a kind of arrow of hair in the center, like he had, like his father had; they called it a widow's peak; and the mangled eyebrows, the wide nose, the closed eyes, and the glinting eyelashes and the hanging lips, all streaming with blood and sweat. His hands were straight above his head. All his weight pulled downward from his hands; and he was a big man, a bigger man than his father, and black as an African jungle cat, and naked. Jesse pulled upward; his father's hands held him firmly by the ankles. He wanted to say something, he did not know what, but nothing he said could have been heard, for now the crowd roared again as a man stepped forward and put more wood on the fire. The flames leapt up. He thought he heard the hanging man scream, but he was not sure. Sweat was pouring from the hair in his armpits, poured down his sides, over his chest, into his navel and his groin. He was lowered again; he was raised again. Now Jesse knew that he heard him scream. The head went back, the mouth wide open, blood bubbling from the mouth; the veins of the neck jumped out; Jesse clung to his father's neck in terror as the cry rolled over the crowd. The cry of all the people rose to answer the dying man's cry. He wanted death to come quickly. They wanted to make death wait: and it was they who held death, now, on a leash which they lengthened little by little. *What did he do?* Jesse wondered. *What did the man do? What did he do?*—but he could not ask his father. He was seated on his father's shoulders, but his father was far away. There were two older men, friends of his father's, raising and lowering the chain; everyone, indiscriminately, seemed to be responsible for the fire. There was no hair left on the nigger's privates, and the eyes, now, were wide open, as white as the eyes of a clown or a doll. The smoke now carried a terrible odor across the clearing, the odor of something burning which was both sweet and rotten.

He turned his head a little and saw the field of faces. He watched his mother's face. Her eyes were very bright, her mouth was open: she was more beautiful than he had ever seen her, and more strange. He began to feel a joy he had never felt before. He watched the hanging, gleaming body, the most beautiful and terrible object he had ever seen till then. One of his father's friends reached up and in his hands he held a knife: and Jesse wished that he had been that man. It was a long, bright knife and the sun seemed to catch it, to play with it, to caress it—it was brighter than the fire. And a wave of laughter swept the crowd. Jesse felt his father's hands on his ankles slip and tighten. The man with the knife walked toward the crowd, smiling slightly; as though this were a signal, silence fell; he heard his mother cough. Then the man with the knife walked up to the hanging body. He turned and smiled again. Now there was a silence all over the field. The hanging head looked up. It seemed fully conscious now, as though the fire had burned out terror and pain. The man with the knife took the nigger's privates in his hand, one hand, still smiling, as though he were weighing them. In the cradle of the one white hand, the nigger's privates seemed as remote as meat being weighed in the scales; but seemed heavier, too, much heavier, and Jesse felt his scrotum tighten; and huge, huge, much bigger than his father's, flaccid, hairless, the largest thing he had ever seen till then, and the blackest. The white hand stretched them, cradled them, caressed them. Then the dying man's eyes looked straight into Jesse's eyes—it could not have been as long as a second, but it seemed longer than a year. Then Jesse screamed, and the crowd screamed as the knife flashed, first up, then down, cutting the dreadful thing away, and the blood came roaring down. Then the crowd rushed forward, tearing at the body with their hands, with knives, with rocks, with stones, howling and cursing. Jesse's head, of its own weight, fell downward toward his father's head. Someone stepped forward and drenched the body with kerosene. Where the man had been, a great sheet of flame appeared. Jesse's father lowered him to the ground.

"Well, I told you," said his father, "you wasn't never going to forget *this* picnic." His father's face was full of sweat, his eyes were very peaceful. At that moment Jesse loved his father more than he had ever loved him. He felt that his father had carried him through a mighty test, had revealed to him a great secret which would be the key to his life forever.

"I reckon," he said. "I reckon."

Jesse's father took him by the hand and, with his mother a little behind them, talking and laughing with the other women, they walked through the crowd, across the clearing. The black body was on the ground, the chain which had held it was being rolled up by one of his father's friends. Whatever the fire had left undone, the hands and the knives and the stones of the people had accomplished. The head was caved in, one eye was torn out, one ear was hanging. But one had to look carefully to realize this, for it was, now, merely a black charred object on the black, charred ground. He lay spread-eagled with what had been a wound between what had been his legs.

"They going to leave him here, then?" Jesse whispered.

"Yeah," said his father, "they'll come and get him by and by. I reckon we better get over there and get some of that food before it's all gone."

"I reckon," he muttered now to himself, "I reckon." Grace stirred and touched him on the thigh: the moonlight covered her like glory. Something bubbled up in him, his nature again returned to him. He thought of the boy in the cell; he thought of the man in the fire; he thought of the knife and grabbed himself and stroked himself and a terrible sound, something between a high laugh and a howl, came out of him and dragged his sleeping wife up on one elbow. She stared at him in a moonlight which had now grown cold as ice. He thought of the morning and grabbed her, laughing and crying, crying and laughing, and he whispered, as he stroked her, as he took her, "Come on, sugar, I'm going to do you like a nigger, just like a nigger, come on, sugar, and love me just like you'd love a nigger." He thought of the morning as he labored and she moaned, thought of morning as he labored harder than he ever had before, and before his labors had ended, he heard the first cock crow and the dogs begin to bark, and the sound of tires on the gravel road.

1965

FLANNERY O'CONNOR
1925–1964

Flannery O'Connor, one of the twentieth century's finest short story writers, was born in Savannah; lived with her mother in Milledgeville, Georgia, for much of her life; and died before her fortieth birthday—a victim like her father of disseminated lupus. She was stricken with this incurable disease in 1950 while at work on her first novel; injections of a cortisone derivative arrested it, but the cortisone weakened her bones to the extent that from 1955 on she could get around only on crutches. She was able to write, travel, and lecture until 1964, when the lupus reactivated itself and killed her. A Roman Catholic throughout her life, she is quoted as having remarked, apropos of a trip to Lourdes, "I had the best-looking crutches in Europe." This remark suggests the kind of hair-raising jokes that centrally inform her writing as well as a refusal to indulge in self-pity over her fate.

She published two novels, *Wise Blood* (1952) and *The Violent Bear It Away* (1960), both weighty with symbolic and religious concerns and ingeniously contrived in the black-humored manner of Nathanael West, her American predecessor in this mode. But her really memorable creations of characters and actions take place in the stories, which are extremely funny, sometimes unbearably so, and finally we may wonder just what we are laughing at. Upon consideration the jokes appear dreadful, as with Manley Pointer's treatment of Joy Hopewell's artificial leg in "Good Country People" or Mr. Shiftlet's of his bride in "The Life You Save May Be Your Own."

Another American "regionalist," the poet Robert Frost, whose work contains its own share of dreadful jokes, once confessed to being more interested in people's speech than in the people themselves. A typical Flannery O'Connor story consists at its most vital level of people talking, clucking their endless reiterations of clichés about life, death, and the universe. These clichés are captured with beautiful accuracy by an artist who had spent her life listening to them, lovingly and maliciously keeping track until she could put them to use. Early in her life she hoped to be a cartoonist, and there is cartoonlike mastery in her vivid renderings of character through speech and other gesture. Critics have called her a maker of grotesques, a label that like other ones—regionalist, Southern lady, or Roman Catholic novelist—might have annoyed if it didn't obviously amuse her too. She once remarked tartly that "anything that comes out of the South is going to be called grotesque by the Northern reader, unless it is grotesque, in which case it is going to be called realistic."

Of course, this capacity for mockery, along with a facility in portraying perverse behavior, may work against other demands we make of the fiction writer, and O'Connor seldom suggests that her characters have inner lives that are imaginable, let alone worth respect. Instead she emphasizes her sharp eye and her ability to tell a tale and keep it moving inevitably toward completion. These completions are usually violent, occurring when the character—in many cases a woman—must confront an experience that she cannot handle by her old trustworthy language and habit-hardened responses. O'Connor's art lies partly in making it impossible for us merely to scorn the banalities of expression and behavior by which these people get through their lives. However dark the comedy, it keeps in touch with the things of this world, even when some force from another world threatens to annihilate the embattled protagonist. And although the stories are filled with religious allusions and parodies, they do not try to inculcate a doctrine. One of her best ones is titled "Revelation," but we seldom finish an O'Connor story with a simple, unambiguous sense of what has been revealed. Instead we trust that the tale's internal fun and richness reveal what it has to reveal. We can agree also, in sadness, with the critic Irving Howe's conclusion to his review of her posthumous collection of stories that it is intolerable for such a writer to have died at the age of thirty-nine.

The following texts are from *A Good Man Is Hard to Find* (1955).

The Life You Save May Be Your Own

The old woman and her daughter were sitting on their porch when Mr. Shiftlet came up their road for the first time. The old woman slid to the edge of her chair and leaned forward, shading her eyes from the piercing sunset with her hand. The daughter could not see far in front of her and continued to play with her fingers. Although the old woman lived in this desolate spot with only her daughter and she had never seen Mr. Shiftlet before, she could tell, even from a distance, that he was a tramp and no one to be afraid of. His left coat sleeve was folded up to show there was only half an arm in it and his gaunt figure listed slightly to the side as if the breeze were pushing him. He had on a black town suit and a brown felt hat that was turned up in the front and down in the back and he carried a tin tool box by a handle. He came on, at an amble, up her road, his face turned toward the sun which appeared to be balancing itself on the peak of a small mountain.

The old woman didn't change her position until he was almost into her yard; then she rose with one hand fisted on her hip. The daughter, a large girl in a short blue organdy dress, saw him all at once and jumped up and began to stamp and point and make excited speechless sounds.

Mr. Shiftlet stopped just inside the yard and set his box on the ground and tipped his hat at her as if she were not in the least afflicted; then he turned toward the old woman and swung the hat all the way off. He had long black slick hair that hung flat from a part in the middle to beyond the tips of his ears on either side. His face descended in forehead for more than half its length and ended suddenly with his features just balanced over a jutting steel-trap jaw. He seemed to be a young man but he had a look of composed dissatisfaction as if he understood life thoroughly.

"Good evening," the old woman said. She was about the size of a cedar fence post and she had a man's gray hat pulled down low over her head.

The tramp stood looking at her and didn't answer. He turned his back and faced the sunset. He swung both his whole and his short arm up slowly so that they indicated an expanse of sky and his figure formed a crooked cross. The old woman watched him with her arms folded across her chest as if she were the owner of the sun, and the daughter watched, her head thrust forward and her fat helpless hands hanging at the wrists. She had long pink-gold hair and eyes as blue as a peacock's neck.

He held the pose for almost fifty seconds and then he picked up his box and came on to the porch and dropped down on the bottom step. "Lady," he said in a firm nasal voice, "I'd give a fortune to live where I could see me a sun do that every evening."

"Does it every evening," the old woman said and sat back down. The daughter sat down too and watched him with a cautious sly look as if he were a bird that had come up very close. He leaned to one side, rooting in his pants pocket, and in a second he brought out a package of chewing gum and offered her a piece. She took it and unpeeled it and began to chew without taking her eyes off him. He offered the old woman a piece but she only raised her upper lip to indicate she had no teeth.

Mr. Shiftlet's pale sharp glance had already passed over everything in the yard—the pump near the corner of the house and the big fig tree that three or four chickens were preparing to roost in—and had moved to a shed where he saw the square rusted back of an automobile. "You ladies drive?" he asked.

"That car ain't run in fifteen year," the old woman said. "The day my husband died, it quit running."

"Nothing is like it used to be, lady," he said. "The world is almost rotten."

"That's right," the old woman said. "You from around here?"

"Name Tom T. Shiftlet," he murmured, looking at the tires.

"I'm pleased to meet you," the old woman said. "Name Lucynell Crater and daughter Lucynell Crater. What you doing around here, Mr. Shiftlet?"

He judged the car to be about a 1928 or '29 Ford. "Lady," he said, and turned and gave her his full attention, "lemme tell you something. There's one of these doctors in Atlanta that's taken a knife and cut the human heart—the human heart," he repeated, leaning forward, "out of a man's chest and held it in his hand," and he held his hand out, palm up, as if it were slightly weighted with the human heart, "and studied it like it was a day-old chicken, and lady," he said, allowing a long significant pause in which his head slid forward and his clay-colored eyes brightened, "he don't know no more about it than you or me."

"That's right," the old woman said.

"Why, if he was to take that knife and cut into every corner of it, he still wouldn't know no more than you or me. What you want to bet?"

"Nothing," the old woman said wisely. "Where you come from, Mr. Shiftlet?"

He didn't answer. He reached into his pocket and brought out a sack of tobacco and a package of cigarette papers and rolled himself a cigarette, expertly with one hand, and attached it in a hanging position to his upper lip. Then he took a box of wooden matches from his pocket and struck one on his shoe. He held the burning match as if he were studying the mystery of flame while it traveled dangerously toward his skin. The daughter began to make loud noises and to point to his hand and shake her finger at him, but when the flame was just before touching him, he leaned down with his hand cupped over it as if he were going to set fire to his nose and lit the cigarette.

He flipped away the dead match and blew a stream of gray into the evening. A sly look came over his face. "Lady," he said, "nowadays, people'll do anything anyways. I can tell you my name is Tom T. Shiftlet and I come from Tarwater, Tennessee, but you never have seen me before: how you know I ain't lying? How you know my name ain't Aaron Sparks, lady, and I come from Singleberry, Georgia, or how you know it's not George Speeds and I come from Lucy, Alabama, or how you know I ain't Thompson Bright from Toolafalls, Mississippi?"

"I don't know nothing about you," the old woman muttered, irked.

"Lady," he said, "people don't care how they lie. Maybe the best I can tell you is, I'm a man; but listen lady," he said and paused and made his tone more ominous still, "what is a man?"

The old woman began to gum a seed. "What you carry in that tin box, Mr. Shiftlet?" she asked.

"Tools," he said, put back. "I'm a carpenter."

"Well, if you come out here to work, I'll be able to feed you and give you a place to sleep but I can't pay. I'll tell you that before you begin," she said.

There was no answer at once and no particular expression on his face. He leaned back against the two-by-four that helped support the porch roof. "Lady," he said slowly, "there's some men that some things mean more to them than money." The old woman rocked without comment and the daughter watched the trigger that moved up and down in his neck. He told the old woman then that all most people were interested in was money, but he asked what a man was made for. He asked her if a man was made for money, or what. He asked her what she thought she was made for but she didn't answer, she only sat rocking and wondered if a one-armed man could put a new roof on her garden house. He asked a lot of questions that she didn't answer. He told her that he was twenty-eight years old and had lived a varied life. He had been a gospel singer, a foreman on the railroad, an assistant in an undertaking parlor, and he come over the radio for three months with Uncle Roy and his Red Creek Wranglers. He said he had fought and bled in the Arm Service of his country and visited every foreign land and that everywhere he had seen people that didn't care if they did a thing one way or another. He said he hadn't been raised thataway.

A fat yellow moon appeared in the branches of the fig tree as if it were going to roost there with the chickens. He said that a man had to escape to the country to see the world whole and that he wished he lived in a desolate place like this where he could see the sun go down every evening like God made it to do.

"Are you married or are you single?" the old woman asked.

There was a long silence. "Lady," he asked finally, "where would you find you an innocent woman today? I wouldn't have any of this trash I could just pick up."

The daughter was leaning very far down, hanging her head almost between her knees watching him through a triangular door she had made in her overturned hair; and she suddenly fell in a heap on the floor and began to whimper. Mr. Shiftlet straightened her out and helped her get back in the chair.

"Is she your baby girl?" he asked.

"My only," the old woman said "and she's the sweetest girl in the world. I would give her up for nothing on earth. She's smart too. She can sweep the floor, cook, wash, feed the chickens, and hoe. I wouldn't give her up for a casket of jewels."

"No," he said kindly, "don't ever let any man take her away from you."

"Any man come after her," the old woman said, "'ll have to stay around the place."

Mr. Shiftlet's eye in the darkness was focused on a part of the automobile bumper that glittered in the distance. "Lady," he said, jerking his short arm up as if he could point with it to her house and yard and pump, "there ain't a broken thing on this plantation that I couldn't fix for you, one-arm jackleg or not. I'm a man," he said with a sullen dignity, "even if I ain't a whole one. I got," he said, tapping his knuckles on the floor to emphasize the immensity of what he was going to say, "a moral intelligence!" and his face pierced out of the darkness into a shaft of doorlight and he stared at her as if he were astonished himself at this impossible truth.

The old woman was not impressed with the phrase. "I told you you could hang around and work for food," she said, "if you don't mind sleeping in that car yonder."

"Why listen, lady," he said with a grin of delight, "the monks of old slept in their coffins!"

"They wasn't as advanced as we are," the old woman said.

The next morning he began on the roof of the garden house while Lucynell, the daughter, sat on a rock and watched him work. He had not been around a week before the change he had made in the place was apparent. He had patched the front and back steps, built a new hog pen, restored a fence, and taught Lucynell, who was completely deaf and had never said a word in her life, to say the word "bird." The big rosy-faced girl followed him everywhere, saying "Burrttddt ddbirrrttdt," and clapping her hands. The old woman watched from a distance, secretly pleased. She was ravenous for a son-in-law.

Mr. Shiftlet slept on the hard narrow back seat of the car with his feet out the side window. He had his razor and a can of water on a crate that served him as a bedside table and he put up a piece of mirror against the back glass and kept his coat neatly on a hanger that he hung over one of the windows.

In the evenings he sat on the steps and talked while the old woman and Lucynell rocked violently in their chairs on either side of him. The old woman's three mountains were black against the dark blue sky and were visited off and on by various planets and by the moon after it had left the chickens. Mr. Shiftlet pointed out that the reason he had improved this plantation was because he had taken a personal interest in it. He said he was even going to make the automobile run.

He had raised the hood and studied the mechanism and he said he could tell that the car had been built in the days when cars were really built. You take now, he said, one man puts in one bolt and another man puts in another bolt and another man puts in another bolt so that it's a man for a bolt. That's why you have to pay so much for a car: you're paying all those men. Now if you didn't have to pay but one man, you could get you a cheaper car and one that had had a personal interest taken in it, and it would be a better car. The old woman agreed with him that this was so.

Mr. Shiftlet said that the trouble with the world was that nobody cared, or stopped and took any trouble. He said he never would have been able to teach Lucynell to say a word if he hadn't cared and stopped long enough.

"Teach her to say something else," the old woman said.

"What you want her to say next?" Mr. Shiftlet asked.

The old woman's smile was broad and toothless and suggestive. "Teach her to say 'sugarpie,'" she said.

Mr. Shiftlet already knew what was on her mind.

The next day he began to tinker with the automobile and that evening he told her that if she would buy a fan belt, he would be able to make the car run.

The old woman said she would give him the money. "You see that girl yonder?" she asked, pointing to Lucynell who was sitting on the floor a foot away, watching him, her eyes blue even in the dark. "If it was ever a man wanted to take her away, I would say, 'No man on earth is going to take that sweet girl of mine away from me!' but if he was to say, 'Lady, I don't want to take her away, I want her right here,' I would say, 'Mister, I don't blame you none. I wouldn't pass up a chance to live in a permanent place and get the sweetest girl in the world myself. You ain't no fool,' I would say."

"How old is she?" Mr. Shiftlet asked casually.

"Fifteen, sixteen," the old woman said. The girl was nearly thirty but because of her innocence it was impossible to guess.

"It would be a good idea to paint it too," Mr. Shiftlet remarked. "You don't want it to rust out."

"We'll see about that later," the old woman said.

The next day he walked into town and returned with the parts he needed and a can of gasoline. Late in the afternoon, terrible noises issued from the shed and the old woman rushed out of the house, thinking Lucynell was somewhere having a fit. Lucynell was sitting on a chicken crate, stamping her feet and screaming, "Burrddttt! bddurrddtttt!" but her fuss was drowned out by the car. With a volley of blasts it emerged from the shed, moving in a fierce and stately way. Mr. Shiftlet was in the driver's seat, sitting very erect. He had an expression of serious modesty on his face as if he had just raised the dead.

That night, rocking on the porch, the old woman began her business, at once. "You want you an innocent woman, don't you," she asked sympathetically. "You don't want none of this trash."

"No'm, I don't," Mr. Shiftlet said.

"One that can't talk," she continued, "can't sass you back or use foul language. That's the kind for you to have. Right there," and she pointed to Lucynell sitting cross-legged in her chair, holding both feet in her hands.

"That's right," he admitted. "She wouldn't give me any trouble."

"Saturday," the old woman said, "you and her and me can drive into town and get married."

Mr. Shiftlet eased his position on the steps.

"I can't get married right now," he said. "Everything you want to do takes money and I ain't got any."

"What you need with money?" she asked.

"It takes money," he said. "Some people'll do anything anyhow these days, but the way I think, I wouldn't marry no woman that I couldn't take on a trip like she was somebody. I mean take her to a hotel and treat her. I wouldn't marry the Duchesser Windsor,"[1] he said firmly, "unless I could take her to a hotel and giver something good to eat."

---

1. I.e., the Duchess of Windsor, Wallis Warfield Simpson (1896–1986), American-born wife of the British King Edward VIII.

"I was raised thataway and there ain't a thing I can do about it. My old mother taught me how to do."

"Lucynell don't even know what a hotel is," the old woman muttered. "Listen here, Mr. Shiftlet," she said, sliding forward in her chair, "you'd be getting a permanent house and a deep well and the most innocent girl in the world. You don't need no money. Lemme tell you something: there ain't any place in the world for a poor disabled friendless drifting man."

The ugly words settled in Mr. Shiftlet's head like a group of buzzards in the top of a tree. He didn't answer at once. He rolled himself a cigarette and lit it and then he said in an even voice, "Lady, a man is divided into two parts, body and spirit."

The old woman clamped her gums together.

"A body and a spirit," he repeated. "The body, lady, is like a house: it don't go anywhere; but the spirit, lady, is like a automobile: always on the move, always . . ."

"Listen, Mr. Shiftlet," she said, "my well never goes dry and my house is always warm in the winter and there's no mortgage on a thing about this place. You can go to the courthouse and see for yourself. And yonder under that shed is a fine automobile." She laid the bait carefully. "You can have it painted by Saturday. I'll pay for the paint."

In the darkness, Mr. Shiftlet's smile stretched like a weary snake waking up by a fire. After a second he recalled himself and said, "I'm only saying a man's spirit means more to him than anything else. I would have to take my wife off for the weekend without no regards at all for cost. I got to follow where my spirit says to go."

"I'll give you fifteen dollars for a weekend trip," the old woman said in a crabbed voice. "That's the best I can do."

"That wouldn't hardly pay for more than the gas and the hotel," he said. "It wouldn't feed her."

"Seventeen-fifty," the old woman said. "That's all I got so it isn't any use you trying to milk me. You can take a lunch."

Mr. Shiftlet was deeply hurt by the word "milk." He didn't doubt that she had more money sewed up in her mattress but he had already told her he was not interested in her money. "I'll make that do," he said and rose and walked off without treating with her further.

On Saturday the three of them drove into town in the car that the paint had barely dried on and Mr. Shiftlet and Lucynell were married in the Ordinary's office[2] while the old woman witnessed. As they came out of the courthouse, Mr. Shiftlet began twisting his neck in his collar. He looked morose and bitter as if he had been insulted while someone held him. "That didn't satisfy me none," he said. "That was just something a woman in an office did, nothing but paper work and blood tests. What do they know about my blood? If they was to take my heart and cut it out," he said, "they wouldn't know a thing about me. It didn't satisfy me at all."

"It satisfied the law," the old woman said sharply.

"The law," Mr. Shiftlet said and spit. "It's the law that don't satisfy me."

He had painted the car dark green with a yellow band around it just under the windows. The three of them climbed in the front seat and the old

---

2. Chambers in which this justice of the peace performs the marriage ceremony.

woman said, "Don't Lucynell look pretty? Looks like a baby doll." Lucynell was dressed up in a white dress that her mother had uprooted from a trunk and there was a Panama hat on her head with a bunch of red wooden cherries on the brim. Every now and then her placid expression was changed by a sly isolated little thought like a shoot of green in the desert. "You got a prize!" the old woman said.

Mr. Shiftlet didn't even look at her.

They drove back to the house to let the old woman off and pick up the lunch. When they were ready to leave, she stood staring in the window of the car, with her fingers clenched around the glass. Tears began to seep sideways out of her eyes and ran along the dirty creases in her face. "I ain't ever been parted with her for two days before," she said.

Mr. Shiftlet started the motor.

"And I wouldn't let no man have her but you because I seen you would do right. Good-bye, Sugarbaby," she said, clutching at the sleeve of the white dress. Lucynell looked straight at her and didn't seem to see her there at all. Mr. Shiftlet eased the car forward so that she had to move her hands.

The early afternoon was clear and open and surrounded by pale blue sky. Although the car would go only thirty miles an hour, Mr. Shiftlet imagined a terrific climb and dip and swerve that went entirely to his head so that he forgot his morning bitterness. He had always wanted an automobile but he had never been able to afford one before. He drove very fast because he wanted to make Mobile by nightfall.

Occasionally he stopped his thoughts long enough to look at Lucynell in the seat beside him. She had eaten the lunch as soon as they were out of the yard and now she was pulling the cherries off the hat one by one and throwing them out the window. He became depressed in spite of the car. He had driven about a hundred miles when he decided that she must be hungry again and at the next small town they came to, he stopped in front of an aluminum-painted eating place called The Hot Spot and took her in and ordered her a plate of ham and grits. The ride had made her sleepy and as soon as she got up on the stool, she rested her head on the counter and shut her eyes. There was no one in The Hot Spot but Mr. Shiftlet and the boy behind the counter, a pale youth with a greasy rag hung over his shoulder. Before he could dish up the food, she was snoring gently.

"Give it to her when she wakes up," Mr. Shiftlet said. "I'll pay for it now."

The boy bent over her and stared at the long pink-gold hair and the half-shut sleeping eyes. Then he looked up and stared at Mr. Shiftlet. "She looks like an angel of Gawd," he murmured.

"Hitchhiker," Mr. Shiftlet explained. "I can't wait. I got to make Tuscaloosa."

The boy bent over again and very carefully touched his finger to a strand of the golden hair and Mr. Shiftlet left.

He was more depressed than ever as he drove on by himself. The late afternoon had grown hot and sultry and the country had flattened out. Deep in the sky a storm was preparing very slowly and without thunder as if it meant to drain every drop of air from the earth before it broke. There were times when Mr. Shiftlet preferred not to be alone. He felt too that a man with a car had a responsibility to others and he kept his eye out for a hitchhiker. Occasionally he saw a sign that warned: "Drive carefully. The life you save may be your own."

The narrow road dropped off on either side into dry fields and here and there a shack or a filling station stood in a clearing. The sun began to set directly in front of the automobile. It was a reddening ball that through his windshield was slightly flat on the bottom and top. He saw a boy in overalls and a gray hat standing on the edge of the road and he slowed the car down and stopped in front of him. The boy didn't have his hand raised to thumb the ride, he was only standing there, but he had a small cardboard suitcase and his hat was set on his head in a way to indicate that he had left somewhere for good. "Son," Mr. Shiftlet said, "I see you want a ride."

The boy didn't say he did or he didn't but he opened the door of the car and got in, and Mr. Shiftlet started driving again. The child held the suitcase on his lap and folded his arms on top of it. He turned his head and looked out the window away from Mr. Shiftlet. Mr. Shiftlet felt oppressed. "Son," he said after a minute, "I got the best old mother in the world so I reckon you only got the second best."

The boy gave him a quick dark glance and then turned his face back out the window.

"It's nothing so sweet," Mr. Shiftlet continued, "as a boy's mother. She taught him his first prayers at her knee, she give him love when no other would, she told him what was right and what wasn't, and she seen that he done the right thing. Son," he said, "I never rued a day in my life like the one I rued when I left that old mother of mine."

The boy shifted in his seat but he didn't look at Mr. Shiftlet. He unfolded his arms and put one hand on the door handle.

"My mother was a angel of Gawd," Mr. Shiftlet said in a very strained voice. "He took her from heaven and giver to me and I left her." His eyes were instantly clouded over with a mist of tears. The car was barely moving.

The boy turned angrily in the seat. "You go to the devil!" he cried. "My old woman is a flea bag and yours is a stinking pole cat!" and with that he flung the door open and jumped out with his suitcase into the ditch.

Mr. Shiftlet was so shocked that for about a hundred feet he drove along slowly with the door still open. A cloud, the exact color of the boy's hat and shaped like a turnip, had descended over the sun, and another, worse looking, crouched behind the car. Mr. Shiftlet felt that the rottenness of the world was about to engulf him. He raised his arm and let it fall again to his breast. "Oh Lord!" he prayed. "Break forth and wash the slime from this earth!"

The turnip continued slowly to descend. After a few minutes there was a guffawing peal of thunder from behind and fantastic raindrops, like tin-can tops, crashed over the rear of Mr. Shiftlet's car. Very quickly he stepped on the gas and with his stump sticking out the window he raced the galloping shower into Mobile.

1955

Good Country People

Besides the neutral expression that she wore when she was alone, Mrs. Freeman had two others, forward and reverse, that she used for all her human dealings. Her forward expression was steady and driving like the advance of a heavy truck. Her eyes never swerved to left or right but turned as the story turned as if they followed a yellow line down the center of it. She seldom used the other expression because it was not often necessary for her to retract a statement, but when she did, her face came to a complete stop, there was an almost imperceptible movement of her black eyes, during which they seemed to be receding, and then the observer would see that Mrs. Freeman, though she might stand there as real as several grain sacks thrown on top of each other, was no longer there in spirit. As for getting anything across to her when this was the case, Mrs. Hopewell had given it up. She might talk her head off. Mrs. Freeman could never be brought to admit herself wrong on any point. She would stand there and if she could be brought to say anything, it was something like, "Well, I wouldn't of said it was and I wouldn't of said it wasn't," or letting her gaze range over the top kitchen shelf where there was an assortment of dusty bottles, she might remark, "I see you ain't ate many of them figs you put up last summer."

They carried on their important business in the kitchen at breakfast. Every morning Mrs. Hopewell got up at seven o'clock and lit her gas heater and Joy's. Joy was her daughter, a large blonde girl who had an artificial leg. Mrs. Hopewell thought of her as a child though she was thirty-two years old and highly educated. Joy would get up while her mother was eating and lumber into the bathroom and slam the door, and before long, Mrs. Freeman would arrive at the back door. Joy would hear her mother call, "Come on in," and then they would talk for a while in low voices that were indistinguishable in the bathroom. By the time Joy came in, they had usually finished the weather report and were on one or the other of Mrs. Freeman's daughters, Glynese or Carramae. Joy called them Glycerin and Caramel. Glynese, a redhead, was eighteen and had many admirers; Carramae, a blonde, was only fifteen but already married and pregnant. She could not keep anything on her stomach. Every morning Mrs. Freeman told Mrs. Hopewell how many times she had vomited since the last report.

Mrs. Hopewell liked to tell people that Glynese and Carramae were two of the finest girls she knew and that Mrs. Freeman was a *lady* and that she was never ashamed to take her anywhere or introduce her to anybody they might meet. Then she would tell how she had happened to hire the Freemans in the first place and how they were a godsend to her and how she had had them four years. The reason for her keeping them so long was that they were not trash. They were good country people. She had telephoned the man whose name they had given as a reference and he had told her that Mr. Freeman was a good farmer but that his wife was the nosiest woman ever to walk the earth. "She's got to be into everything," the man said. "If she don't get there before the dust settles, you can bet she's dead, that's all. She'll want to know all your business. I can stand him real good," he had said, "but me nor my wife neither could have stood that woman one more minute on this place." That had put Mrs. Hopewell off for a few days.

She had hired them in the end because there were no other applicants but she had made up her mind beforehand exactly how she would handle the woman. Since she was the type who had to be into everything, then, Mrs. Hopewell had decided, she would not only let her be into everything, she would *see to it* that she was into everything—she would give her the responsibility of everything, she would put her in charge. Mrs. Hopewell had no bad qualities of her own but she was able to use other people's in such a constructive way that she never felt the lack. She had hired the Freemans and she had kept them four years.

Nothing is perfect. This was one of Mrs. Hopewell's favorite sayings. Another was: that is life! And still another, the most important, was: well, other people have their opinions too. She would make these statements, usually at the table, in a tone of gentle insistence as if no one held them but her, and the large hulking Joy, whose constant outrage had obliterated every expression from her face, would stare just a little to the side of her, her eyes icy blue, with the look of someone who has achieved blindness by an act of will and means to keep it.

When Mrs. Hopewell said to Mrs. Freeman that life was like that, Mrs. Freeman would say, "I always said so myself." Nothing had been arrived at by anyone that had not first been arrived at by her. She was quicker than Mr. Freeman. When Mrs. Hopewell said to her after they had been on the place a while, "You know, you're the wheel behind the wheel," and winked, Mrs. Freeman had said, "I know it. I've always been quick. It's some that are quicker than others."

"Everybody is different," Mrs. Hopewell said.

"Yes, most people is," Mrs. Freeman said.

"It takes all kinds to make the world."

"I always said it did myself."

The girl was used to this kind of dialogue for breakfast and more of it for dinner; sometimes they had it for supper too. When they had no guest they ate in the kitchen because that was easier. Mrs. Freeman always managed to arrive at some point during the meal and to watch them finish it. She would stand in the doorway if it were summer but in the winter she would stand with one elbow on top of the refrigerator and look down on them, or she would stand by the gas heater, lifting the back of her skirt slightly. Occasionally she would stand against the wall and roll her head from side to side. At no time was she in any hurry to leave. All this was very trying on Mrs. Hopewell but she was a woman of great patience. She realized that nothing is perfect and that in the Freemans she had good country people and that if, in this day and age, you get good country people, you had better hang onto them.

She had had plenty of experience with trash. Before the Freemans she had averaged one tenant family a year. The wives of these farmers were not the kind you would want to be around you for very long. Mrs. Hopewell, who had divorced her husband long ago, needed someone to walk over the fields with her; and when Joy had to be impressed for these services, her remarks were usually so ugly and her face so glum that Mrs. Hopewell would say, "If you can't come pleasantly, I don't want you at all," to which the girl, standing square and rigid-shouldered with her neck thrust slightly forward, would reply, "If you want me, here I am—LIKE I AM."

Mrs. Hopewell excused this attitude because of the leg (which had been shot off in a hunting accident when Joy was ten). It was hard for Mrs. Hopewell to realize that her child was thirty-two now and that for more than twenty years she had had only one leg. She thought of her still as a child because it tore her heart to think instead of the poor stout girl in her thirties who had never danced a step or had any *normal* good times. Her name was really Joy but as soon as she was twenty-one and away from home, she had had it legally changed. Mrs. Hopewell was certain that she had thought and thought until she had hit upon the ugliest name in any language. Then she had gone and had the beautiful name, Joy, changed without telling her mother until after she had done it. Her legal name was Hulga.

When Mrs. Hopewell thought the name, Hulga, she thought of the broad blank hull of a battleship. She would not use it. She continued to call her Joy to which the girl responded but in a purely mechanical way.

Hulga had learned to tolerate Mrs. Freeman who saved her from taking walks with her mother. Even Glynese and Carramae were useful when they occupied attention that might otherwise have been directed at her. At first she had thought she could not stand Mrs. Freeman for she had found that it was not possible to be rude to her. Mrs. Freeman would take on strange resentments and for days together she would be sullen but the source of her displeasure was always obscure; a direct attack, a positive leer, blatant ugliness to her face—these never touched her. And without warning one day, she began calling her Hulga.

She did not call her that in front of Mrs. Hopewell who would have been incensed but when she and the girl happened to be out of the house together, she would say something and add the name Hulga to the end of it, and the big spectacled Joy-Hulga would scowl and redden as if her privacy had been intruded upon. She considered the name her personal affair. She had arrived at it first purely on the basis of its ugly sound and then the full genius of its fitness had struck her. She had a vision of the name working like the ugly sweating Vulcan who stayed in the furnace and to whom, presumably, the goddess had to come when called.[1] She saw it as the name of her highest creative act. One of her major triumphs was that her mother had not been able to turn her dust into Joy, but the greater one was that she had been able to turn it herself into Hulga. However, Mrs. Freeman's relish for using the name only irritated her. It was as if Mrs. Freeman's beady steel-pointed eyes had penetrated far enough behind her face to reach some secret fact. Something about her seemed to fascinate Mrs. Freeman and then one day Hulga realized that it was the artificial leg. Mrs. Freeman had a special fondness for the details of secret infections, hidden deformities, assaults upon children. Of diseases, she preferred the lingering or incurable. Hulga had heard Mrs. Hopewell give her the details of the hunting accident, how the leg had been literally blasted off, how she had never lost consciousness. Mrs. Freeman could listen to it any time as if it had happened an hour ago.

When Hulga stumped into the kitchen in the morning (she could walk without making the awful noise but she made it—Mrs. Hopewell was certain—because it was ugly-sounding), she glanced at them and did not speak. Mrs. Hopewell would be in her red kimono with her hair tied around

---

1. Vulcan was the Greek god of fire, whom Venus, goddess of love, "presumably" obeyed as her consort.

her head in rags. She would be sitting at the table, finishing her breakfast and Mrs. Freeman would be hanging by her elbow outward from the refrigerator, looking down at the table. Hulga always put her eggs on the stove to boil and then stood over them with her arms folded, and Mrs. Hopewell would look at her—a kind of indirect gaze divided between her and Mrs. Freeman—and would think that if she would only keep herself up a little, she wouldn't be so bad looking. There was nothing wrong with her face that a pleasant expression wouldn't help. Mrs. Hopewell said that people who looked on the bright side of things would be beautiful even if they were not.

Whenever she looked at Joy this way, she could not help but feel that it would have been better if the child had not taken the Ph.D. It had certainly not brought her out any and now that she had it, there was no more excuse for her to go to school again. Mrs. Hopewell thought it was nice for girls to go to school to have a good time but Joy had "gone through." Anyhow, she would not have been strong enough to go again. The doctors had told Mrs. Hopewell that with the best of care, Joy might see forty-five. She had a weak heart. Joy had made it plain that if it had not been for this condition, she would be far from these red hills and good country people. She would be in a university lecturing to people who knew what she was talking about. And Mrs. Hopewell could very well picture her there, looking like a scarecrow and lecturing to more of the same. Here she went about all day in a six-year-old skirt and a yellow sweat shirt with a faded cowboy on a horse embossed on it. She thought this was funny; Mrs. Hopewell thought it was idiotic and showed simply that she was still a child. She was brilliant but she didn't have a grain of sense. It seemed to Mrs. Hopewell that every year she grew less like other people and more like herself—bloated, rude, and squint-eyed. And she said such strange things! To her own mother she had said—without warning, without excuse, standing up in the middle of a meal with her face purple and her mouth half full—"Woman! do you ever look inside? Do you ever look inside and see what you are *not*? God!" she had cried sinking down again and staring at her plate, "Malebranche[2] was right: we are not our own light. We are not our own light!" Mrs. Hopewell had no idea to this day what brought that on. She had only made the remark, hoping Joy would take it in, that a smile never hurt anyone.

The girl had taken the Ph.D. in philosophy and this left Mrs. Hopewell at a complete loss. You could say, "My daughter is a nurse," or "My daughter is a school teacher," or even, "My daughter is a chemical engineer." You could not say, "My daughter is a philosopher." That was something that had ended with the Greeks and Romans. All day Joy sat on her neck in a deep chair, reading. Sometimes she went for walks but she didn't like dogs or cats or birds or flowers or nature or nice young men. She looked at nice young men as if she could smell their stupidity.

One day Mrs. Hopewell had picked up one of the books the girl had just put down and opening it at random, she read, "Science, on the other hand, has to assert its soberness and seriousness afresh and declare that it is concerned solely with what-is. Nothing—how can it be for science anything but a horror and a phantasm? If science is right, then one thing stands firm: science wishes to know nothing of nothing. Such is after all the strictly

2. Nicolas Malebranche (1638–1715), French philosopher.

scientific approach to Nothing. We know it by wishing to know nothing of Nothing." These words had been underlined with a blue pencil and they worked on Mrs. Hopewell like some evil incantation in gibberish. She shut the book quickly and went out of the room as if she were having a chill.

This morning when the girl came in, Mrs. Freeman was on Carramae. "She thrown up four times after supper," she said, "and was up twict in the night after three o'clock. Yesterday she didn't do nothing but ramble in the bureau drawer. All she did. Stand up there and see what she could run up on."

"She's got to eat," Mrs. Hopewell muttered, sipping her coffee, while she watched Joy's back at the stove. She was wondering what the child had said to the Bible salesman. She could not imagine what kind of a conversation she could possibly have had with him.

He was a tall gaunt hatless youth who had called yesterday to sell them a Bible. He had appeared at the door, carrying a large black suitcase that weighted him so heavily on one side that he had to brace himself against the door facing. He seemed on the point of collapse but he said in a cheerful voice, "Good morning, Mrs. Cedars!" and set the suitcase down on the mat. He was not a bad-looking young man though he had on a bright blue suit and yellow socks that were not pulled up far enough. He had prominent face bones and a streak of sticky-looking brown hair falling across his forehead.

"I'm Mrs. Hopewell," she said.

"Oh!" he said, pretending to look puzzled but with his eyes sparkling, "I saw it said 'The Cedars' on the mailbox so I thought you was Mrs. Cedars!" and he burst out in a pleasant laugh. He picked up the satchel and under cover of a pant, he fell forward into her hall. It was rather as if the suitcase had moved first, jerking him after it. "Mrs. Hopewell!" he said and grabbed her hand. "I hope you are well!" and he laughed again and then all at once his face sobered completely. He paused and gave her a straight earnest look and said, "Lady, I've come to speak of serious things."

"Well, come in," she muttered, none too pleased because her dinner was almost ready. He came into the parlor and sat down on the edge of a straight chair and put the suitcase between his feet and glanced around the room as if he were sizing her up by it. Her silver gleamed on the two sideboards; she decided he had never been in a room as elegant as this.

"Mrs. Hopewell," he began, using her name in a way that sounded almost intimate, "I know you believe in Chrustian service."

"Well yes," she murmured.

"I know," he said and paused, looking very wise with his head cocked on one side, "that you're a good woman. Friends have told me."

Mrs. Hopewell never liked to be taken for a fool. "What are you selling?" she asked.

"Bibles," the young man said and his eye raced around the room before he added, "I see you have no family Bible in your parlor, I see that is the one lack you got!"

Mrs. Hopewell could not say, "My daughter is an atheist and won't let me keep the Bible in the parlor." She said, stiffening slightly, "I keep my Bible by my bedside." This was not the truth. It was in the attic somewhere.

"Lady," he said, "the word of God ought to be in the parlor."

"Well, I think that's a matter of taste," she began. "I think . . ."

"Lady," he said, "for a Chrustian, the word of God ought to be in every room in the house besides in his heart. I know you're a Chrustian because I can see it in every line of your face."

She stood up and said, "Well, young man, I don't want to buy a Bible and I smell my dinner burning."

He didn't get up. He began to twist his hands and looking down at them, he said softly, "Well lady, I'll tell you the truth—not many people want to buy one nowadays and besides, I know I'm real simple. I don't know how to say a thing but to say it. I'm just a country boy." He glanced up into her unfriendly face. "People like you don't like to fool with country people like me!"

"Why!" she cried, "good country people are the salt of the earth! Besides, we all have different ways of doing, it takes all kinds to make the world go 'round. That's life!"

"You said a mouthful," he said.

"Why, I think there aren't enough good country people in the world!" she said, stirred. "I think that's what's wrong with it!"

His face had brightened. "I didn't inraduce myself," he said. "I'm Manley Pointer from out in the country around Willohobie, not even from a place, just from near a place."

"You wait a minute," she said. "I have to see about my dinner." She went out to the kitchen and found Joy standing near the door where she had been listening.

"Get rid of the salt of the earth," she said, "and let's eat."

Mrs. Hopewell gave her a pained look and turned the heat down under the vegetables. "I can't be rude to anybody," she murmured and went back into the parlor.

He had opened the suitcase and was sitting with a Bible on each knee.

"You might as well put those up," she told him. "I don't want one."

"I appreciate your honesty," he said. "You don't see any more real honest people unless you go way out in the country."

"I know," she said, "real genuine folks!" Through the crack in the door she heard a groan.

"I guess a lot of boys come telling you they're working their way through college," he said, "but I'm not going to tell you that. Somehow," he said, "I don't want to go to college. I want to devote my life to Chrustian service. See," he said, lowering his voice, "I got this heart condition. I may not live long. When you know it's something wrong with you and you may not live long, well then, lady . . ." He paused, with his mouth open, and stared at her.

He and Joy had the same condition! She knew that her eyes were filling with tears but she collected herself quickly and murmured, "Won't you stay for dinner? We'd love to have you!" and was sorry the instant she heard herself say it.

"Yes mam," he said in an abashed voice, "I would sher love to do that!"

Joy had given him one look on being introduced to him and then throughout the meal had not glanced at him again. He had addressed several remarks to her, which she had pretended not to hear. Mrs. Hopewell could not understand deliberate rudeness, although she lived with it, and she felt she had always to overflow with hospitality to make up for Joy's lack of courtesy. She urged him to talk about himself and he did. He said he was the seventh child of twelve and that his father had been crushed under a tree when he himself was eight years old. He had been crushed very badly, in fact, almost cut in two and was practically not recognizable. His mother had got along the best she could by hard working and she had always seen that her children went to Sunday School and that they read the Bible every evening. He was now nineteen years old and he had been selling Bibles for four months. In that time he had sold seventy-seven Bibles and had the promise of two more sales. He wanted to become a missionary because he thought that was the way you could do most for people. "He who losest his life shall find it," he said simply and he was so sincere, so genuine and earnest that Mrs. Hopewell would not for the world have smiled. He prevented his peas from sliding onto the table by blocking them with a piece of bread which he later cleaned his plate with. She could see Joy observing sidewise how he handled his knife and fork and she saw too that every few minutes, the boy would dart a keen appraising glance at the girl as if he were trying to attract her attention.

After dinner Joy cleared the dishes off the table and disappeared and Mrs. Hopewell was left to talk with him. He told her again about his childhood and his father's accident and about various things that had happened to him. Every five minutes or so she would stifle a yawn. He sat for two hours until finally she told him she must go because she had an appointment in town. He packed his Bibles and thanked her and prepared to leave, but in the doorway he stopped and wrung her hand and said that not on any of his trips had he met a lady as nice as her and he asked if he could come again. She had said she would always be happy to see him.

Joy had been standing in the road, apparently looking at something in the distance, when he came down the steps toward her, bent to the side with his heavy valise. He stopped where she was standing and confronted her directly. Mrs. Hopewell could not hear what he said but she trembled to think what Joy would say to him. She could see that after a minute Joy said something and that then the boy began to speak again, making an excited gesture with his free hand. After a minute Joy said something else at which the boy began to speak once more. Then to her amazement, Mrs. Hopewell saw the two of them walk off together, toward the gate. Joy had walked all the way to the gate with him and Mrs. Hopewell could not imagine what they had said to each other, and she had not yet dared to ask.

Mrs. Freeman was insisting upon her attention. She had moved from the refrigerator to the heater so that Mrs. Hopewell had to turn and face her in order to seem to be listening. "Glynese gone out with Harvey Hill again last night," she said. "She had this sty."

"Hill," Mrs. Hopewell said absently, "is that the one who works in the garage?"

"Nome, he's the one that goes to chiropracter school," Mrs. Freeman said. "She had this sty. Been had it two days. So she says when he brought her in the other night he says, 'Lemme get rid of that sty for you,' and she says, 'How?' and he says, 'You just lay yourself down acrost the seat of that car and I'll show you.' So she done it and he popped her neck. Kept on a-popping it several times until she made him quit. This morning," Mrs. Freeman said, "she ain't got no sty. She ain't got no traces of a sty."

"I never heard of that before," Mrs. Hopewell said.

"He ast her to marry him before the Ordinary,"[3] Mrs. Freeman went on, "and she told him she wasn't going to be married in no *office*."

"Well, Glynese is a fine girl," Mrs. Hopewell said. "Glynese and Carramae are both fine girls."

"Carramae said when her and Lyman was married Lyman said it sure felt sacred to him. She said he said he wouldn't take five hundred dollars for being married by a preacher."

"How much would he take?" the girl asked from the stove.

"He said he wouldn't take five hundred dollars," Mrs. Freeman repeated.

"Well we all have work to do," Mrs. Hopewell said.

"Lyman said it just felt more sacred to him," Mrs. Freeman said. "The doctor wants Carramae to eat prunes. Says instead of medicine. Says them cramps is coming from pressure. You know where I think it is?"

"She'll be better in a few weeks," Mrs. Hopewell said.

"In the tube," Mrs. Freeman said. "Else she wouldn't be as sick as she is."

Hulga had cracked her two eggs into a saucer and was bringing them to the table along with a cup of coffee that she had filled too full. She sat down carefully and began to eat, meaning to keep Mrs. Freeman there by questions if for any reason she showed an inclination to leave. She could perceive her mother's eye on her. The first round-about question would be about the Bible salesman and she did not wish to bring it on. "How did he pop her neck?" she asked.

Mrs. Freeman went into a description of how he had popped her neck. She said he owned a '55 Mercury but that Glynese said she would rather marry a man with only a '36 Plymouth who would be married by a preacher. The girl asked what if he had a '32 Plymouth and Mrs. Freeman said what Glynese had said was a '36 Plymouth.

Mrs. Hopewell said there were not many girls with Glynese's common sense. She said what she admired in those girls was their common sense. She said that reminded her that they had had a nice visitor yesterday, a young man selling Bibles. "Lord," she said, "he bored me to death but he was so sincere and genuine I couldn't be rude to him. He was just good country people, you know," she said, "—just the salt of the earth."

"I seen him walk up," Mrs. Freeman said, "and then later—I seen him walk off," and Hulga could feel the slight shift in her voice, the slight insinuation, that he had not walked off alone, had he? Her face remained expressionless but the color rose into her neck and she seemed to swallow it down with the next spoonful of egg. Mrs. Freeman was looking at her as if they had a secret together.

"Well, it takes all kinds of people to make the world go 'round," Mrs. Hopewell said. "It's very good we aren't all alike."

"Some people are more alike than others," Mrs. Freeman said.

Hulga got up and stumped, with about twice the noise that was necessary, into her room and locked the door. She was to meet the Bible salesman at ten o'clock at the gate. She had thought about it half the night. She had started thinking of it as a great joke and then she had begun to see profound implications in it. She had lain in bed imagining dialogues for them that were insane

3. Justice of the peace who performs the marriage ceremony in chambers rather than in public.

on the surface but that reached below to depths that no Bible salesman would be aware of. Their conversation yesterday had been of this kind.

He had stopped in front of her and had simply stood there. His face was bony and sweaty and bright, with a little pointed nose in the center of it, and his look was different from what it had been at the dinner table. He was gazing at her with open curiosity, with fascination, like a child watching a new fantastic animal at the zoo, and he was breathing as if he had run a great distance to reach her. His gaze seemed somehow familiar but she could not think where she had been regarded with it before. For almost a minute he didn't say anything. Then on what seemed an insuck of breath, he whispered, "You ever ate a chicken that was two days old?"

The girl looked at him stonily. He might have just put this question up for consideration at the meeting of a philosophical association. "Yes," she presently replied as if she had considered it from all angles.

"It must have been mighty small!" he said triumphantly and shook all over with little nervous giggles, getting very red in the face, and subsiding finally into his gaze of complete admiration, while the girl's expression remained exactly the same.

"How old are you?" he asked softly.

She waited some time before she answered. Then in a flat voice she said, "Seventeen."

His smiles came in succession like waves breaking on the surface of a little lake. "I see you got a wooden leg," he said. "I think you're brave. I think you're real sweet."

The girl stood blank and solid and silent.

"Walk to the gate with me," he said. "You're a brave sweet little thing and I liked you the minute I seen you walk in the door."

Hulga began to move forward.

"What's your name?" he asked, smiling down on the top of her head.

"Hulga," she said.

"Hulga," he murmured, "Hulga. Hulga. I never heard of anybody name Hulga before. You're shy, aren't you, Hulga?" he asked.

She nodded, watching his large red hand on the handle of the giant valise.

"I like girls that wear glasses," he said. "I think a lot. I'm not like these people that a serious thought don't ever enter their heads. It's because I may die."

"I may die too," she said suddenly and looked up at him. His eyes were very small and brown, glittering feverishly.

"Listen," he said, "don't you think some people was meant to meet on account of what all they got in common and all? Like they both think serious thoughts and all?" He shifted the valise to his other hand so that the hand nearest her was free. He caught hold of her elbow and shook it a little. "I don't work on Saturday," he said. "I like to walk in the woods and see what Mother Nature is wearing. O'er the hills and far away. Pic-nics and things. Couldn't we go on a pic-nic tomorrow? Say yes, Hulga," he said and gave her a dying look as if he felt his insides about to drop out of him. He had even seemed to sway slightly toward her.

During the night she had imagined that she seduced him. She imagined that the two of them walked on the place until they came to the storage barn beyond the two back fields and there, she imagined, that things came to such a pass that she very easily seduced him and that then, of course, she had to reckon with his remorse. True genius can get an idea across even to an inferior mind. She imagined that she took his remorse in hand and changed it into a deeper understanding of life. She took all his shame away and turned it into something useful.

She set off for the gate at exactly ten o'clock, escaping without drawing Mrs. Hopewell's attention. She didn't take anything to eat, forgetting that food is usually taken on a picnic. She wore a pair of slacks and a dirty white shirt, and as an afterthought, she had put some Vapex on the collar of it since she did not own any perfume. When she reached the gate no one was there.

She looked up and down the empty highway and had the furious feeling that she had been tricked, that he had only meant to make her walk to the gate after the idea of him. Then suddenly he stood up, very tall, from behind a bush on the opposite embankment. Smiling, he lifted his hat which was new and wide-brimmed. He had not worn it yesterday and she wondered if he had bought it for the occasion. It was toast-colored with a red and white band around it and was slightly too large for him. He stepped from behind the bush still carrying the black valise. He had on the same suit and the same yellow socks sucked down in his shoes from walking. He crossed the highway and said, "I knew you'd come!"

The girl wondered acidly how he had known this. She pointed to the valise and asked, "Why did you bring your Bibles?"

He took her elbow, smiling down on her as if he could not stop. "You can never tell when you'll need the word of God, Hulga," he said. She had a moment in which she doubted that this was actually happening and then they began to climb the embankment. They went down into the pasture toward the woods. The boy walked lightly by her side, bouncing on his toes. The valise did not seem to be heavy today; he even swung it. They crossed half the pasture without saying anything and then, putting his hand easily on the small of her back, he asked softly, "Where does your wooden leg join on?"

She turned an ugly red and glared at him and for an instant the boy looked abashed. "I didn't mean you no harm," he said. "I only meant you're so brave and all. I guess God takes care of you."

"No," she said, looking forward and walking fast, "I don't even believe in God."

At this he stopped and whistled. "No!" he exclaimed as if he were too astonished to say anything else.

She walked on and in a second he was bouncing at her side, fanning with his hat. "That's very unusual for a girl," he remarked, watching her out of the corner of his eye. When they reached the edge of the wood, he put his hand on her back again and drew her against him without a word and kissed her heavily.

The kiss, which had more pressure than feeling behind it, produced that extra surge of adrenalin in the girl that enables one to carry a packed trunk out of a burning house, but in her, the power went at once to the brain. Even before he released her, her mind, clear and detached and ironic anyway, was regarding him from a great distance, with amusement but with pity. She had never been kissed before and she was pleased to discover that it was an unexceptional experience and all a matter of the mind's control. Some people might enjoy drain water if they were told it was vodka. When the boy, looking expectant but uncertain, pushed her gently away, she turned and walked on, saying nothing as if such business, for her, were common enough.

He came along panting at her side, trying to help her when he saw a root that she might trip over. He caught and held back the long swaying blades of thorn vine until she had passed beyond them. She led the way and he came breathing heavily behind her. Then they came out on a sunlit hillside, sloping softly into another one a little smaller. Beyond, they could see the rusted top of the old barn where the extra hay was stored.

The hill was sprinkled with small pink weeds. "Then you ain't saved?" he asked suddenly, stopping.

The girl smiled. It was the first time she had smiled at him at all. "In my economy," she said, "I'm saved and you are damned but I told you I didn't believe in God."

Nothing seemed to destroy the boy's look of admiration. He gazed at her now as if the fantastic animal at the zoo had put its paw through the bars and given him a loving poke. She thought he looked as if he wanted to kiss her again and she walked on before he had the chance.

"Ain't there somewheres we can sit down sometime?" he murmured, his voice softening toward the end of the sentence.

"In that barn," she said.

They made for it rapidly as if it might slide away like a train. It was a large two-story barn, cool and dark inside. The boy pointed up the ladder that led into the loft and said, "It's too bad we can't go up there."

"Why can't we?" she asked.

"Yer leg," he said reverently.

The girl gave him a contemptuous look and putting both hands on the ladder, she climbed it while he stood below, apparently awestruck. She pulled herself expertly through the opening and then looked down at him and said, "Well, come on if you're coming," and he began to climb the ladder, awkwardly bringing the suitcase with him.

"We won't need the Bible," she observed.

"You never can tell," he said, panting. After he had got into the loft, he was a few seconds catching his breath. She had sat down in a pile of straw. A wide sheath of sunlight, filled with dust particles, slanted over her. She lay back against a bale, her face turned away, looking out the front opening of the barn where hay was thrown from a wagon into the loft. The two pink-speckled hillsides lay back against a dark ridge of woods. The sky was cloudless and cold blue. The boy dropped down by her side and put one arm under her and the other over her and began methodically kissing her face, making little noises like a fish. He did not remove his hat but it was pushed far enough back not to interfere. When her glasses got in his way, he took them off of her and slipped them into his pocket.

The girl at first did not return any of the kisses but presently she began to and after she had put several on his cheek, she reached his lips and remained there, kissing him again and again as if she were trying to draw all the breath out of him. His breath was clear and sweet like a child's and the kisses were sticky like a child's. He mumbled about loving her and about knowing when he first seen her that he loved her, but the mumbling was like the sleepy fretting of a child being put to sleep by his mother. Her mind, throughout this, never stopped or lost itself for a second to her feelings. "You ain't said you loved me none," he whispered finally, pulling back from her. "You got to say that."

She looked away from him off into the hollow sky and then down at a black ridge and then down farther into what appeared to be two green swelling lakes. She didn't realize he had taken her glasses but this landscape could not seem exceptional to her for she seldom paid any close attention to her surroundings.

"You got to say it," he repeated. "You got to say you love me."

She was always careful how she committed herself. "In a sense," she began, "if you use the word loosely, you might say that. But it's not a word I use. I don't have illusions. I'm one of those people who see *through* to nothing."

The boy was frowning. "You got to say it. I said it and you got to say it," he said.

The girl looked at him almost tenderly. "You poor baby," she murmured. "It's just as well you don't understand," and she pulled him by the neck, facedown against her. "We are all damned," she said, "but some of us have taken off our blindfolds and see that there's nothing to see. It's a kind of salvation."

The boy's astonished eyes looked blankly through the ends of her hair. "Okay," he almost whined, "but do you love me or don'tcher?"

"Yes," she said and added, "in a sense. But I must tell you something. There mustn't be anything dishonest between us." She lifted his head and looked him in the eye. "I am thirty years old," she said. "I have a number of degrees."

The boy's look was irritated but dogged. "I don't care," he said. "I don't care a thing about what all you done. I just want to know if you love me or don'tcher?" and he caught her to him and wildly planted her face with kisses until she said, "Yes, yes."

"Okay then," he said, letting her go. "Prove it."

She smiled, looking dreamily out on the shifty landscape. She had seduced him without even making up her mind to try. "How?" she asked, feeling that he should be delayed a little.

He leaned over and put his lips to her ear. "Show me where your wooden leg joins on," he whispered.

The girl uttered a sharp little cry and her face instantly drained of color. The obscenity of the suggestion was not what shocked her. As a child she had sometimes been subject to feelings of shame but education had removed the last traces of that as a good surgeon scrapes for cancer; she would no more have felt it over what he was asking than she would have believed in his Bible. But she was as sensitive about the artificial leg as a peacock about his tail. No one ever touched it but her. She took care of it as someone else would his soul, in private and almost with her own eyes turned away. "No," she said.

"I known it," he muttered, sitting up. "You're just playing me for a sucker."

"Oh no no!" she cried. "It joins on at the knee. Only at the knee. Why do you want to see it?"

The boy gave her a long penetrating look. "Because," he said, "it's what makes you different. You ain't like anybody else."

She sat staring at him. There was nothing about her face or her round freezing-blue eyes to indicate that this had moved her; but she felt as if her heart had stopped and left her mind to pump her blood. She decided that for the first time in her life she was face to face with real innocence. This boy, with an instinct that came from beyond wisdom, had touched the truth about her. When after a minute, she said in a hoarse high voice, "All right," it was like surrendering to him completely. It was like losing her own life and finding it again, miraculously, in his.

Very gently he began to roll the slack leg up. The artificial limb, in a white sock and brown flat shoe, was bound in a heavy material like canvas and ended in an ugly jointure where it was attached to the stump. The boy's face and his voice were entirely reverent as he uncovered it and said, "Now show me how to take it off and on."

She took it off for him and put it back on again and then he took it off himself, handling it as tenderly as if it were a real one. "See!" he said with a delighted child's face. "Now I can do it myself!"

"Put it back on," she said. She was thinking that she would run away with him and that every night he would take the leg off and every morning put it back on again. "Put it back on," she said.

"Not yet," he murmured, setting it on its foot out of her reach. "Leave it off for a while. You got me instead."

She gave a cry of alarm but he pushed her down and began to kiss her again. Without the leg she felt entirely dependent on him. Her brain seemed to have stopped thinking altogether and to be about some other function that it was not very good at. Different expressions raced back and forth over her face. Every now and then the boy, his eyes like two steel spikes, would glance behind him where the leg stood. Finally she pushed him off and said, "Put it back on me now."

"Wait," he said. He leaned the other way and pulled the valise toward him and opened it. It had a pale blue spotted lining and there were only two Bibles in it. He took one of these out and opened the cover of it. It was hollow and contained a pocket flask of whiskey, a pack of cards, and a small blue box with printing on it. He laid these out in front of her one at a time in an evenly-spaced row, like one presenting offerings at the shrine of a goddess. He put the blue box in her hand. THIS PRODUCT TO BE USED ONLY FOR THE PREVENTION OF DISEASE, she read, and dropped it. The boy was unscrewing the top of the flask. He stopped and pointed, with a smile, to the deck of cards. It was not an ordinary deck but one with an obscene picture on the back of each card. "Take a swig," he said, offering her the bottle first. He held it in front of her, but like one mesmerized, she did not move.

Her voice when she spoke had an almost pleading sound. "Aren't you," she murmured, "aren't you just good country people?"

The boy cocked his head. He looked as if he were just beginning to understand that she might be trying to insult him. "Yeah," he said, curling his lip slightly, "but it ain't held me back none. I'm as good as you any day in the week."

"Give me my leg," she said.

He pushed it farther away with his foot. "Come on now, let's begin to have us a good time," he said coaxingly. "We ain't got to know one another good yet."

"Give me my leg!" she screamed and tried to lunge for it but he pushed her down easily.

"What's the matter with you all of a sudden?" he asked, frowning as he screwed the top on the flask and put it quickly back inside the Bible. "You just a while ago said you didn't believe in nothing. I thought you was some girl!"

Her face was almost purple. "You're a Christian!" she hissed. "You're a fine Christian! You're just like them all—say one thing and do another. You're a perfect Christian, you're . . ."

The boy's mouth was set angrily. "I hope you don't think," he said in a lofty indignant tone, "that I believe in that crap! I may sell Bibles but I know which end is up and I wasn't born yesterday and I know where I'm going!"

"Give me my leg!" she screeched. He jumped up so quickly that she barely saw him sweep the cards and the blue box into the Bible and throw the Bible into the valise. She saw him grab the leg and then she saw it for an instant slanted forlornly across the inside of the suitcase with a Bible at either side of its opposite ends. He slammed the lid shut and snatched up the valise and swung it down the hole and then stepped through himself.

When all of him had passed but his head, he turned and regarded her with a look that no longer had any admiration in it. "I've gotten a lot of interesting things," he said. "One time I got a woman's glass eye this way. And you needn't to think you'll catch me because Pointer ain't really my name. I use a different name at every house I call at and don't stay nowhere long. And I'll tell you another thing, Hulga," he said, using the name as if he didn't think much of it, "you ain't so smart. I been believing in nothing every since I was born!" and then the toast-colored hat disappeared down the hole and the girl was left, sitting on the straw in the dusty sunlight. When she turned her churning face toward the opening, she saw his blue figure struggling successfully over the green speckled lake.

Mrs. Hopewell and Mrs. Freeman, who were in the back pasture, digging up onions, saw him emerge a little later from the woods and head across the meadow toward the highway. "Why, that looks like that nice dull young man that tried to sell me a Bible yesterday," Mrs. Hopewell said, squinting. "He must have been selling them to the Negroes back in there. He was so simple," she said, "but I guess the world would be better off if we were all that simple."

Mrs. Freeman's gaze drove forward and just touched him before he disappeared under the hill. Then she returned her attention to the evil-smelling onion shoot she was lifting from the ground. "Some can't be that simple," she said. "I know I never could."

1955

A. R. AMMONS
1926–2001

Ammons wrote that he "was born big and jaundiced (and ugly) on February 18, 1926, in a farmhouse 4 miles southwest of Whiteville, North Carolina, and 2 miles northwest of New Hope Elementary School and New Hope Baptist Church." It was characteristic of Ammons to be laconic, self-deprecating, unfailingly local, and unfailingly exact. He belonged to the homemade strain of American writers rather than the Europeanized or cosmopolitan breed. His poems are filled with the landscapes in which he lived: North Carolina, the southern coast of New Jersey, and the surroundings of Ithaca, New York, where he was a member of the English department of Cornell University.

Ammons's career did not start out with a traditional literary education. At Wake Forest College in North Carolina he studied mostly science, especially biology and chemistry, and that scientific training strongly colored his poems. In 1951–52, after working briefly as a high school principal in North Carolina, he studied English literature for three semesters at the University of California at Berkeley. When he returned from Berkeley he spent twelve years as an executive for a biological-glass manufacturer in New Jersey.

In 1955, his thirtieth year, Ammons published his first book of poems, *Ommateum*. The title refers to the compound structure of an insect's eye and foreshadows a twofold impulse in Ammons's work. On the one hand he is involved in the minute observation of natural phenomena; on the other hand he is frustrated by the physical limitations analogous to those of the insects' vision. We see the world as insects do, in small portions and in impulses that take in but do not totally resolve the many images we receive. "Overall is beyond me," Ammons says in "Corsons Inlet," in which the shifting details of shoreline and dunes represent a severe challenge to the poet-observer. There are no straight lines. The contours differ every day, every hour, and they teach the poet the endless adjustments he must make to nature's fluidity.

"A poem is a walk," Ammons said (his essay of that title is excerpted in the "Post-modern Manifestos" cluster of this anthology). His work is characterized by the motion he found everywhere in nature, a motion answered by his mental activity. Both nearsighted and farsighted, he looks closely at vegetation, small animals, the minute shifts of wind and weather and light, yet over and over again seems drawn to the American Transcendentalist Ralph Waldo Emerson's visionary aspirations for poetry. "Poetry," Emerson remarked, "was all written before time was, and whenever we are so finely organized that we can penetrate into that region where the air is music, we hear those primal warnings and attempt to write them down." Much of Ammons's poetry tests this promise to see if it yields a glimpse of supernatural order.

The self in Ammons's poems is a far more modest presence than in the work of many other American writers. Sometimes he is a "surrendered self among unwelcoming forms" (as he writes in the conclusion of "Gravelly Run"); in many other poems he is at home in a universe, both human and natural, whose variety delights him. He is that rare thing, a contemporary poet of praise, one who says "I can find nothing lowly / in the universe" ("Still") and convinces us he speaks the truth.

Ammons began his career writing short lyrics, almost journal entries in an unending career of observation. But the laconic notations—of a landslide, a shift in the shoreline from one day to the next—often bore abstract titles ("Clarity," "Saliences") as if to suggest the connections he felt between concrete experience and speculative thought. Ammons often experimented with poetic form in his effort to make his verse responsive to the engaging but evasive particularity of natural process. This formal inventiveness is part of his work's appeal. "Stop on any word and language gives way: / the blades of reason, unlightened by motion, sink in," he remarks in his "Essay on Poetics." To create *Tape for the Turn of the Year* (1965) he typed a book-length day-to-day verse diary on a roll of adding-machine tape. The poem ended when the tape did. This was his first and most flamboyant attempt to turn his verse into something beyond mere gatherings. He then discovered that the long poem was the form best adapted to his continuing dialogue between the specific and the general. The appearance in 1993 of *Garbage*, a National Book Award winner, confirmed Ammons's gift for creating a book-length, immensely readable, moving, and funny poem, structured around a recurring set of images and ideas but full of digressions.

Ammons tended to use the colon—what one critic calls "the most democratic punctuation," suggesting as it does equivalence on both sides. Used in place of the period, it keeps a line from coming to a halt or stopping the flow in which the mind feverishly suggests analogies among its minutely perceived experiences. Many notable examples of Ammons's extended forms are gathered in *The Selected Longer Poems* (1980), although that book does not include his remarkable *Sphere: The Form of a Motion* (1974). A book-length poem with no full stops, 155 sections of four tercets each, it aspires to be what Ammons's predecessor Wallace Stevens called "the poem of the act of the mind." The only unity in *Sphere* is the mind's power to make analogies between the world's constant "diversifications." Ammons was committed to the provisional, the self-revising, and this commitment kept his poetry fresh over a long career. Writing of his sense of the world in "The Dwelling," from *Sumerian Vistas* (1987), Ammons says, "here the plainest / majesty gave us what it could." The same might be said of his wonderfully generous and witty poems, which constitute a distinctive and invaluable legacy for American poetry.

So I Said I Am Ezra

So I said I am Ezra
and the wind whipped my throat
gaming for the sounds of my voice
   I listened to the wind
go over my head and up into the night   5
Turning to the sea I said
        I am Ezra
but there were no echoes from the waves
The words were swallowed up
   in the voice of the surf   10
or leaping over the swells
lost themselves oceanward
   Over the bleached and broken fields
I moved my feet and turning from the wind
   that ripped sheets of sand   15
   from the beach and threw them
   like seamists across the dunes
swayed as if the wind were taking me away
and said
        I am Ezra   20
As a word too much repeated
falls out of being
so I Ezra went out into the night
like a drift of sand
and splashed among the windy oats   25
that clutch the dunes
of unremembered seas

1955

Corsons Inlet

I went for a walk over the dunes again this morning
to the sea,
then turned right along
   the surf
           rounded a naked headland   5
           and returned

   along the inlet shore:

it was muggy sunny, the wind from the sea steady and high,
crisp in the running sand,
    some breakthroughs of sun   10
   but after a bit

continuous overcast:

the walk liberating, I was released from forms,
from the perpendiculars,
    straight lines, blocks, boxes, binds   15
of thought
into the hues, shadings, rises, flowing bends and blends
       of sight:

            I allow myself eddies of meaning:
yield to a direction of significance   20
running
like a stream through the geography of my work:
   you can find
in my sayings
        swerves of action   25
        like the inlet's cutting edge:
     there are dunes of motion,
organizations of grass, white sandy paths of remembrance
in the overall wandering of mirroring mind:

but Overall is beyond me: is the sum of these events   30
I cannot draw, the ledger I cannot keep, the accounting
beyond the account:

in nature there are few sharp lines: there are areas of
primrose
   more or less dispersed;   35
disorderly orders of bayberry; between the rows
of dunes,
irregular swamps of reeds,
though not reeds alone, but grass, bayberry, yarrow, all . . .
predominantly reeds: 40

I have reached no conclusions, have erected no boundaries,
shutting out and shutting in, separating inside
        from outside: I have
        drawn no lines:
        as   45

manifold events of sand
change the dune's shape that will not be the same shape
tomorrow,

so I am willing to go along, to accept
the becoming   50
thought, to stake off no beginnings or ends, establish
        no walls:

by transitions the land falls from grassy dunes to creek
to undercreek: but there are no lines, though
        change in that transition is clear   55
        as any sharpness: but "sharpness" spread out,
allowed to occur over a wider range
than mental lines can keep:

the moon was full last night: today, low tide was low:
black shoals of mussels exposed to the risk   60
of air
and, earlier, of sun,
waved in and out with the waterline, waterline inexact,
caught always in the event of change:
        a young mottled gull stood free on the shoals   65
        and ate
to vomiting: another gull, squawking possession, cracked a crab,
picked out the entrails, swallowed the soft-shelled legs, a ruddy
turnstone[1] running in to snatch leftover bits:

risk is full: every living thing in   70
siege: the demand is life, to keep life: the small
white blacklegged egret, how beautiful, quietly stalks and spears
        the shallows, darts to shore
            to stab—what? I couldn't
        see against the black mudflats—a frightened   75
        fiddler crab?

        the news to my left over the dunes and
reeds and bayberry clumps was
        fall: thousands of tree swallows
        gathering for flight: 80
        an order held
        in constant change: a congregation
rich with entropy: nevertheless, separable, noticeable
        as one event,

---

1. A ploverlike migratory bird.

                    not chaos: preparations for   85
flight from winter,
cheet, cheet, cheet, cheet, wings rifling the green clumps,
beaks
at the bayberries
      a perception full of wind, flight, curve,   90
      sound:
      the possibility of rule as the sum of rulelessness:
the "field" of action
with moving, incalculable center:

in the smaller view, order tight with shape: 95
blue tiny flowers on a leafless weed: carapace of crab:
snail shell:
              pulsations of order
              in the bellies of minnows: orders swallowed,
broken down, transferred through membranes   100
to strengthen larger orders: but in the large view, no
lines or changeless shapes: the working in and out, together
              and against, of millions of events: this,
                    so that I make
                    no form of   105
                    formlessness:

orders as summaries, as outcomes of actions override
or in some way result, not predictably (seeing me gain
the top of a dune,
the swallows   110
could take flight—some other fields of bayberry
              could enter fall
              berryless) and there is serenity:

              no arranged terror: no forcing of image, plan,
or thought: 115
no propaganda, no humbling of reality to precept:

terror pervades but is not arranged, all possibilities
of escape open: no route shut, except in
      the sudden loss of all routes:

              I see narrow orders, limited tightness, but will   120
not run to that easy victory:
              still around the looser, wider forces work:
              I will try
      to fasten into order enlarging grasps of disorder, widening
scope, but enjoying the freedom that   125
Scope eludes my grasp, that there is no finality of vision,
that I have perceived nothing completely,
              that tomorrow a new walk is a new walk.

                                                            1965

Easter Morning

I have a life that did not become,
that turned aside and stopped,
astonished:
I hold it in me like a pregnancy or
as on my lap a child   5
not to grow or grow old but dwell on

it is to his grave I most
frequently return and return
to ask what is wrong, what was
wrong, to see it all by   10
the light of a different necessity
but the grave will not heal
and the child,
stirring, must share my grave
with me, an old man having   15
gotten by on what was left

when I go back to my home country in these
fresh far-away days, it's convenient to visit
everybody, aunts and uncles, those who used to say,
look how he's shooting up, and the   20
trinket aunts who always had a little
something in their pocketbooks, cinnamon bark
or a penny or nickel, and uncles who
were the rumored fathers of cousins
who whispered of them as of great, if   25
troubled, presences, and school
teachers, just about everybody older
(and some younger) collected in one place
waiting, particularly, but not for
me, mother and father there, too, and others   30
close, close as burrowing
under skin, all in the graveyard
assembled, done for, the world they
used to wield, have trouble and joy
in, gone   35

the child in me that could not become
was not ready for others to go,
to go on into change, blessings and
horrors, but stands there by the road
where the mishap occurred, crying out for   40
help, come and fix this or we
can't get by, but the great ones who
were to return, they could not or did
not hear and went on in a flurry and
now, I say in the graveyard, here   45
lies the flurry, now it can't come

back with help or helpful asides, now
we all buy the bitter
incompletions, pick up the knots of
horror, silently raving, and go on   50
crashing into empty ends not
completions, not rondures the fullness
has come into and spent itself from
I stand on the stump
of a child, whether myself   55
or my little brother who died, and
yell as far as I can, I cannot leave this place, for
for me it is the dearest and the worst,
it is life nearest to life which is
life lost: it is my place where   60
I must stand and fail,
calling attention with tears
to the branches not lofting
boughs into space, to the barren
air that holds the world that was my world   65

though the incompletions
(& completions) burn out
standing in the flash high-burn
momentary structure of ash, still it
is a picture-book, letter-perfect   70
Easter morning: I have been for a
walk: the wind is tranquil: the brook
works without flashing in an abundant
tranquility: the birds are lively with
voice: I saw something I had   75
never seen before: two great birds,
maybe eagles, blackwinged, whitenecked
and -headed, came from the south oaring
the great wings steadily; they went
directly over me, high up, and kept on   80
due north: but then one bird,
the one behind, veered a little to the
left and the other bird kept on seeming
not to notice for a minute: the first
began to circle as if looking for   85
something, coasting, resting its wings
on the down side of some of the circles:
the other bird came back and they both
circled, looking perhaps for a draft;
they turned a few more times, possibly   90
rising—at least, clearly resting—
then flew on falling into distance till
they broke across the local bush and
trees: it was a sight of bountiful
majesty and integrity: the having   95
patterns and routes, breaking
from them to explore other patterns or

better way to routes, and then the
return: a dance sacred as the sap in
the trees, permanent in its descriptions   100
as the ripples round the brook's
ripplestone: fresh as this particular
flood of burn breaking across us now
from the sun.

1981

Singling & Doubling Together

My nature singing in me is your nature singing:
you have means to veer down, filter through,
and, coming in,
harden into vines that break back with leaves,
so that when the wind stirs   5
I know you are there and I hear you in leafspeech,

though of course back into your heightenings I
can never follow: you are there beyond
tracings flesh can take,
and farther away surrounding and informing the systems,   10
you are as if nothing, and
where you are least knowable I celebrate you most

or here most when near dusk the pheasant squawks and
lofts at a sharp angle to the roost cedar,
I catch in the angle of that ascent,   15
in the justness of that event your pheasant nature,
and when dusk settles, the bushes creak and
snap in their natures with your creaking

and snapping nature: I catch the impact and turn
it back: cut the grass and pick up branches   20
under the elm, rise to the several tendernesses
and griefs, and you will fail me only as from the still
of your great high otherness you fail all things,
somewhere to lift things up, if not those things again:

even you risked all the way into the taking on of shape   25
and time fail and fail with me, as me,
and going hence with me know the going hence
and in the cries of that pain it is you crying and
you know of it and it is my pain, my tears, my loss—
what but grace   30

have I to bear in every motion,
embracing or turning away, staggering or standing still,
while your settled kingdom sways in the distillations of light

and plunders down into the darkness with me
and comes nowhere up again but changed into your   35
singing nature when I need sing my nature nevermore.

1983

From Garbage

2

garbage has to be the poem of our time because
garbage is spiritual, believable enough

to get our attention, getting in the way, piling
up, stinking, turning brooks brownish and

creamy white: what else deflects us from the   5
errors of our illusionary ways, not a temptation

to trashlessness, that is too far off, and,
anyway, unimaginable, unrealistic: I'm a

hole puncher or hole plugger: stick a finger
in the dame (*dam*, damn, dike), hold back the issue   10

of creativity's floor, the forthcoming, futuristic,
the origins feeding trash: down by I-95 in

Florida where flatland's ocean- and gulf-flat,
mounds of disposal rise (for if you dug

something up to make room for something to put   15
in, what about the something dug up, as with graves:)

the garbage trucks crawl as if in obeisance,
as if up ziggurats[1] toward the high places gulls

and garbage keep alive, offerings to the gods
of garbage, or retribution, of realistic   20

expectation, the deities of unpleasant
necessities: refined, young earthworms,

drowned up in macadam pools by spring rains, moisten
out white in a day or so and, round spots,

look like sputum or creamy-rich, broken-up cold   25
clams: if this is not the best poem of the

---

1. The temple towers of the Babylonians, which consisted of a lofty pyramidal structure, built in successive stages, with outside staircases and a religious shrine on top.

century, can it be about the worst poem of the
century: it comes, at least, toward the end,

so a long tracing of bad stuff can swell
under its measure: but there on the heights   30

a small smoke wafts the sacrificial bounty
day and night to layer the sky brown, shut us

in as into a lidded kettle, the everlasting
flame these acres-deep of tendance keep: a

free offering of a crippled plastic chair: 35
a played-out sports outfit: a hill-myna

print stained with jelly: how to write this
poem, should it be short, a small popping of

duplexes, or long, hunting wide, coming home
late, losing the trail and recovering it: 40

should it act itself out, illustrations,
examples, colors, clothes or intensify

reductively into statement, bones any corpus
would do to surround, or should it be nothing

at all unless it finds itself: the poem,   45
which is about the pre-socratic idea of the

dispositional axis from stone to wind, wind
to stone (with my elaborations, if any)

is complete before it begins, so I needn't
myself hurry into brevity, though a weary reader   50

might briefly be done: the axis will be clear
enough daubed here and there with a little ink

or fined out into every shade and form of its
revelation: this is a scientific poem,

asserting that nature models values, that we   55
have invented little (copied), reflections of

possibilities already here, this where we came
to and how we came: a priestly director behind the

black-chuffing dozer leans the gleanings and
reads the birds, millions of loners circling   60

a common height, alighting to the meaty streaks
and puffy muffins (puffins?): there is a mound,

too, in the poet's mind dead language is hauled
off to and burned down on, the energy held and

shaped into new turns and clusters, the mind   65
strengthened by what it strengthens: for

where but in the very asshole of comedown is
redemption: as where but brought low, where

but in the grief of failure, loss, error do we
discern the savage afflictions that turn us around: 70

where but in the arrangements love crawls us
through, not a thing left in our self-display

unhumiliated, do we find the sweet seed of
new routes; but we are natural: nature, not

we, gave rise to us; we are not, though, though   75
natural, divorced from higher, finer configurations:

tissues and holograms of energy circulate in
us and seek and find representations of themselves

outside us, so that we can participate in
celebrations high and know reaches of feeling   80

and sight and thought that penetrate (really
penetrate) far, far beyond these our wet cells,

right on up past our stories, the planets, moons,
and other bodies locally to the other end of

the pole where matter's forms diffuse and   85
energy loses all means to express itself except

as spirit, there, oh, yes, in the abiding where
mind but nothing else abides, the eternal,

until it turns into another pear or sunfish,
that momentary glint in the fisheye having   90

been there so long, coming and going, it's
eternity's glint: it all wraps back round,

into and out of form, palpable and impalpable,
and in one phase, the one of grief and love,

we know the other, where everlastingness comes to   95
sway, okay and smooth: the heaven we mostly

want, though, is this jet-hoveled hell back,
heaven's daunting asshole: one must write and

rewrite till one writes it right: if I'm in
touch, she said, then I've got an edge: what   100

the hell kind of talk is that: I can't believe
I'm merely an old person: whose mother is dead,

whose father is gone and many of whose
friends and associates have wended away to the

ground, which is only heavy wind, or to ashes,   105
a lighter breeze: but it was all quite frankly

to be expected and not looked forward to: even
old trees, I remember some of them, where they

used to stand: pictures taken by some of them:
and old dogs, specially one imperial black one,   110

quad dogs with their hier*archies* (another *archie*)[2]
one succeeding another, the barking and romping

sliding away like slides from a projector: what
were they then that are what they are now:

1993

2. The A. R. in Ammons's name stands for Archie Randolph.

JAMES MERRILL
1926–1995

When James Merrill's *First Poems* was published in 1950, he was immediately recognized as one of the most gifted and polished poets of his generation. But not until *Water Street* (1962), his third volume of poems, did Merrill begin to enlist his brilliant technique and sophisticated tone in developing a poetic autobiography. The book takes its title from the street where he lived in the seaside village of Stonington, Connecticut. The opening poem, "An Urban Convalescence," explores his decision to leave New York, which he sees as a distracting city that destroys its past. He portrays his move as a rededication to his past and an attempt through poetry "to make some kind of house / Out of the life lived, out of the love spent."

The metaphor of "home" is an emotional center to which Merrill's writing often returns, as in "The Broken Home," which recalls elements of Merrill's experience as the son of parents who divorced when he was young. He had been born to the second marriage of Charles E. Merrill, financier and founder of the best-known brokerage firm in America. "The Broken Home" shows how memory and writing have the power to reshape boyhood pain and conflict so as to achieve "the unstiflement of the entire story." Such an attitude distinguishes Merrill from his contemporaries (Robert Lowell, Anne Sexton, Sylvia Plath) whose autobiographical impulse expresses itself primarily in the present tense and the use of poems as an urgent journal true to the moment.

As an undergraduate at Amherst College, Merrill had written an honors thesis on the French novelist Marcel Proust (1871–1922). His poetry was clearly affected by Proust's notion that the literary exercise of memory slowly discloses the patterns of childhood experience that we are destined to relive. Proust showed in his *In Search of Lost Time* (1913–27) how such power over chaotic past material is often triggered involuntarily by an object or an episode in the present whose associations reach back into formative childhood encounters. The questions he asked were asked by Sigmund Freud (1856–1939), the founder of psychoanalysis, as well: What animates certain scenes—and not others—for us? To answer such questions Merrill presents some of his poems from the viewpoint of an observant child. In other poems the poet is explicitly present, at his desk, trying to incorporate into his adult understanding of the contours of his life the pain and freshness of childhood memories. The poems are narrative (one of his early books was called *Short Stories*) as often as lyric, in the hope that dramatic *action* will reveal the meanings with which certain objects have become charged. As Merrill sees it, "You hardly ever need to *state* your feelings. The point is to feel and keep the eyes open. Then what you feel is expressed, is mimed back at you by the scene. A room, a landscape. I'd go a step further. We don't *know* what we feel until we see it distanced by this kind of translation."

Merrill traveled extensively and presented landscapes from his travels as ways of exploring alternative or buried states of his own mind, the "translations" of which he speaks. Poems such as "Days of 1964" and "After the Fire" reflect his experiences in Greece, where he spent a portion of each year. They respectively anticipate and comment on *The Fire Screen* (1969), a sequence describing the rising and falling curve of a love affair partly in terms of an initiation into Greece with its power to strip away urban sophistication. The books that followed served as initiations into other psychic territories. Problems of family relationships and the erotic entanglements of homosexual love previously seen on an intimate scale were in *Braving the Elements* (1972) acted out against a wider backdrop: the long landscapes, primitive geological perspectives, and erosions of the American Far West. Here human experience, examined in his earlier work in close-up, is seen as part of a longer process of evolution comprehensible in terms of enduring nonhuman patterns.

In *Divine Comedies* (which received the Pulitzer Prize in 1977) Merrill began his most ambitious work: two-thirds of it is devoted to "The Book of Ephraim," a long narrative. It not only recapitulates his career but also attempts to locate individual psychic energies as part of a larger series of nourishing influences: friends living and dead, literary predecessors, scientific theories of the growth of the universe and the mind, the life of other periods and even other universes—all conducted through a set of encounters with the "other world" in séances at the Ouija board. It is a witty and original and assured attempt to take the intimate material of the short lyric that characterized his earlier work and cast it onto an epic scale. The second and third volumes of the trilogy, *Mirabell: Books of Number* and *Scripts for the Pageant*, appeared in 1978 and 1980, respectively; the entire work was collected in 1982 under the title *The Changing Light at Sandover*. By the time of his death, Merrill had established himself as an American formal master, one whose grace and wit made his remarkable variations on traditional forms seem as easy as casual speech. This mastery is evident in his sequence "Family Week at Oracle Ranch" (from his last book, *A Scattering of Salts*, 1995), where Merrill's formal daring is matched by an equally remarkable emotional daring. An edition of his *Collected Prose* (2004) further confirmed his stature in American letters.

An Urban Convalescence

Out for a walk, after a week in bed,
I find them tearing up part of my block
And, chilled through, dazed and lonely, join the dozen
In meek attitudes, watching a huge crane
Fumble luxuriously in the filth of years.   5
Her jaws dribble rubble. An old man
Laughs and curses in her brain,
Bringing to mind the close of *The White Goddess*.[1]

As usual in New York, everything is torn down
Before you have had time to care for it.   10
Head bowed, at the shrine of noise, let me try to recall
What building stood here. Was there a building at all?
I have lived on this same street for a decade.

Wait. Yes. Vaguely a presence rises
Some five floors high, of shabby stone   15
—Or am I confusing it with another one
In another part of town, or of the world?—
And over its lintel into focus vaguely
Misted with blood (my eyes are shut)
A single garland sways, stone fruit, stone leaves,   20
Which years of grit had etched until it thrust
Roots down, even into the poor soil of my seeing.
When did the garland become part of me?
I ask myself, amused almost,
Then shiver once from head to toe,   25
Transfixed by a particular cheap engraving of garlands
Bought for a few francs long ago,
All calligraphic tendril and cross-hatched rondure,
Ten years ago, and crumpled up to stanch
Boughs dripping, whose white gestures filled a cab,   30
And thought of neither then nor since.
Also, to clasp them, the small, red-nailed hand
Of no one I can place. Wait. No. Her name, her features
Lie toppled underneath that year's fashions.
The words she must have spoken, setting her face   35
To fluttering like a veil, I cannot hear now,
Let alone understand.

So that I am already on the stair,
As it were, of where I lived,
When the whole structure shudders at my tread   40
And soundlessly collapses, filling
The air with motes of stone.

---

1. The book (1948) in which the English poet
Robert Graves sets forth the theory that authentic poetry is inspired by a primitive goddess who
is both creative and destructive. The crane is her
sacred bird, which through a pun Merrill here
associates with the mechanical crane. Its operator seems like a crazed parody poet, committed
only to demolition.

Onto the still erect building next door
Are pressed levels and hues—
Pocked rose, streaked greens, brown whites.   45
Who drained the pousse-café?[2]
Wires and pipes, snapped off at the roots, quiver.

Well, that is what life does. I stare
A moment longer, so. And presently
The massive volume of the world   50
Closes again.

Upon that book I swear
To abide by what it teaches:
Gospels of ugliness and waste,
Of towering voids, of soiled gusts,   55
Of a shrieking to be faced
Full into, eyes astream with cold—

With cold?
All right then. With self-knowledge.

Indoors at last, the pages of *Time* are apt   60
To open, and the illustrated mayor of New York,
Given a glimpse of how and where I work,
To note yet one more house that can be scrapped.

Unwillingly I picture
My walls weathering in the general view.   65
It is not even as though the new
Buildings did very much for architecture.

Suppose they did. The sickness of our time requires
That these as well be blasted in their prime.
You would think the simple fact of having lasted   70
Threatened our cities like mysterious fires.

There are certain phrases which to use in a poem
Is like rubbing silver with quicksilver. Bright
But facile, the glamour deadens overnight.
For instance, how "the sickness of our time"   75

Enhances, then debases, what I feel.
At my desk I swallow in a glass of water
No longer cordial, scarcely wet, a pill
They had told me not to take until much later.

With the result that back into my imagination   80
The city glides, like cities seen from the air,
Mere smoke and sparkle to the passenger
Having in mind another destination

2. An after-dinner drink made up of layers of different-colored cordials.

Which now is not that honey-slow descent
Of the Champs-Elysées,[3] her hand in his,   85
But the dull need to make some kind of house
Out of the life lived, out of the love spent.

                                                        1962

The Broken Home

Crossing the street,
I saw the parents and the child
At their window, gleaming like fruit
With evening's mild gold leaf.

In a room on the floor below,   5
Sunless, cooler—a brimming
Saucer of wax, marbly and dim—
I have lit what's left of my life.

I have thrown out yesterday's milk
And opened a book of maxims.   10
The flame quickens. The word stirs.

Tell me, tongue of fire,
That you and I are as real
At least as the people upstairs.

                    •

My father, who had flown in World War I,   15
Might have continued to invest his life
In cloud banks well above Wall Street and wife.
But the race was run below, and the point was to win.

Too late now, I make out in his blue gaze
(Through the smoked glass of being thirty-six)   20
The soul eclipsed by twin black pupils, sex
And business; time was money in those days.

Each thirteenth year he married. When he died
There were already several chilled wives
In sable orbit—rings, cars, permanent waves.   25
We'd felt him warming up for a green bride.

He could afford it. He was "in his prime"
At three score ten. But money was not time.

                    •

When my parents were younger this was a popular act:
A veiled woman would leap from an electric, wine-dark car   30

_____

3. A stylish boulevard in Paris.

To the steps of no matter what—the Senate or the Ritz Bar—
And bodily, at newsreel speed, attack

No matter whom—Al Smith or José Maria Sert
Or Clemenceau[1]—veins standing out on her throat
As she yelled *War mongerer! Pig! Give us the vote!*,   35
And would have to be hauled away in her hobble skirt.

What had the man done? Oh, made history.
Her business (he had implied) was giving birth,
Tending the house, mending the socks.

Always that same old story—   40
Father Time and Mother Earth,[2]
A marriage on the rocks.

                              •

One afternoon, red, satyr-thighed
Michael, the Irish setter, head
Passionately lowered, led   45
The child I was to a shut door. Inside,

Blinds beat sun from the bed.
The green-gold room throbbed like a bruise.
Under a sheet, clad in taboos
Lay whom we sought, her hair undone, outspread,   50

And of a blackness found, if ever now, in old
Engravings where the acid bit.
I must have needed to touch it
Or the whiteness—was she dead?
Her eyes flew open, startled strange and cold.   55
The dog slumped to the floor. She reached for me. I fled.

                              •

Tonight they have stepped out onto the gravel.
The party is over. It's the fall
Of 1931. They love each other still.

She: Charlie, I can't stand the pace.   60
He: Come on, honey—why, you'll bury us all!

A lead soldier guards my windowsill:
Khaki rifle, uniform, and face.
Something in me grows heavy, silvery, pliable.

How intensely people used to feel!   65
Like metal poured at the close of a proletarian novel,[3]

---

1. Georges Clemenceau (1841–1929), premier of France during World War I, visited the United States in 1922. Alfred E. Smith (1873–1944), a governor of New York and in 1928 candidate for the presidency. Sert (1876–1945), a Spanish painter who in 1930 decorated the lobby of the Waldorf-Astoria Hotel in New York.

2. A reference to Cronus (Greek for "Time"), ruler of the ancient Titans, and to his wife, Rhea, an earth deity known as Mother of the Gods. Because Cronus ate their children as soon as they were born, Rhea plotted his overthrow.

3. Socialist novel that romanticized laborers.

Refined and glowing from the crucible,
I see those two hearts, I'm afraid,
Still. Cool here in the graveyard of good and evil,
They are even so to be honored and obeyed.   70

                                       •

. . . Obeyed, at least, inversely. Thus
I rarely buy a newspaper, or vote.
To do so, I have learned, is to invite
The tread of a stone guest[4] within my house.

Shooting this rusted bolt, though, against him,   75
I trust I am no less time's child than some
Who on the heath impersonate Poor Tom[5]
Or on the barricades risk life and limb.

Nor do I try to keep a garden, only
An avocado in a glass of water—   80
Roots pallid, gemmed with air. And later,

When the small gilt leaves have grown
Fleshy and green, I let them die, yes, yes,
And start another. I am earth's no less.

                                       •

A child, a red dog roam the corridors,   85
Still, of the broken home. No sound. The brilliant
Rag runners halt before wide-open doors.
My old room! Its wallpaper—cream, medallioned
With pink and brown—brings back the first nightmares,
Long summer colds, and Emma, sepia-faced,   90
Perspiring over broth carried upstairs
Aswim with golden fats I could not taste.

The real house became a boarding-school.
Under the ballroom ceiling's allegory
Someone at last may actually be allowed   95
To learn something; or, from my window, cool
With the unstiflement of the entire story,
Watch a red setter stretch and sink in cloud.

                                              1966

Dead Center

Upon reflection, as I dip my pen
Tonight, forth ripple messages in code.
In Now's black waters burn the stars of Then.

---

4. The *commendatore* in Mozart's *Don Giovanni* (1787) returns as a statue to get his revenge.
5. In Shakespeare's *King Lear*, Edgar, disowned by his father, wanders the heath disguised as a madman.

Seen from the embankment, marble men
Sleep upside down, bat-wise, the sleep bestowed 5
Upon reflection. As I dip my pen

Thinking how others, deeper into Zen,
Blew on immediacy until it glowed,
In Now's black waters burn the stars of Then.

Or else I'm back at Grandmother's. I'm ten, 10
Dust hides my parents' roadster from the road
Which dips—*into* reflection, with my pen.

Breath after breath, harsh O's of oxygen—
Never deciphered, what do they forebode?
In Now's black waters burn the stars. Ah then 15

Leap, Memory, supreme equestrienne,
Through hoops of fire, circuits you overload!
Beyond reflection, as I dip my pen
In Now's black waters, burn the stars of Then.

1984

Family Week at Oracle Ranch

1 The Brochure

The world outstrips us. In my day,
Had such a place existed,
It would have been advertised with photographs
Of doctors—silver hair, pince-nez—

Above detailed credentials, 5
Not this wide-angle moonscape, lawns and pool,
Patients sharing pain like fudge from home—
As if these were the essentials,

As if a month at what it invites us to think
Is little more than a fat farm for Anorexics, 10
Substance Abusers, Love & Relationship Addicts
Could help *you*, light of my life, when even your shrink . . .

The message, then? That costly folderol,
Underwear made to order in Vienna,
Who needs it! Let the soul hang out 15
At Benetton[1]—stone-washed, one size fits all.

1. A chain of clothing stores featuring T-shirts, jeans, sweaters.

2 *Instead of Complexes*

Simplicities. Just seven words—AFRAID,
HURT, LONELY, etc.—to say it with.
Shades of the first watercolor box
(I "felt blue," I "saw red").   20

Also some tips on brushwork. Not to say
"Your silence hurt me,"
Rather, "When you said nothing I felt hurt."
No blame, that way.

Dysfunctionals like us fail to distinguish   25
Between the two modes at first.
While the connoisseur of feeling throws up his hands:
Used to depicting personal anguish

With a full palette—hues, oils, glazes, thinner—
He stares into these withered wells and feels,   30
Well . . . SAD and ANGRY? Future lavender!
An infant Monet[2] blinks beneath his skin.

3 *The Counsellors*

They're in recovery, too, and tell us from what,
And that's as far as it goes.
Like the sun-priests' in *The Magic Flute*[3]   35
Their ritualized responses serve the plot.

Ken, for example, blond brows knitted: "When
James told the group he worried about dying
Without his lover beside him, I felt SAD."
Thank you for sharing, Ken,   40

I keep from saying; it would come out snide.
Better to view them as deadpan panels
Storing up sunlight for the woebegone,
Prompting from us lines electrified

By buried switches flipped (after how long!) . . .   45
But speak in private meanwhile? We may not
Until a voice within the temple lifts
Bans yet unfathomed into song.

---

2. Claude Monet (1840–1926), French impressionist painter.
3. One of the most famous of Wolfgang Amadeus
Mozart's works, *The Magic Flute* is a *singspiel*—i.e., a combination of songs and dialogue.

4 Gestalt[4]

Little Aileen is a gray plush bear
With button eyes and nose.   50
Perky in flowered smock and clean white collar,
She occupies the chair

Across from the middleaged Big Aileen, face hid
In hands and hands on knees.
Her sobs break. In great waves it's coming back.   55
The uncle. What he did.

Little Aileen is her Inner Child
Who didn't . . . who didn't deserve. . . .
The horror kissed asleep, round Big Aileen
Fairytale thorns grow wild.   60

SADNESS and GUILT entitle us to watch
The survivor compose herself,
Smoothing the flowered stuff, which has ridden up,
Over an innocent gray crotch.

5 Effects of Early "Religious Abuse"

The great recurrent "sinner" found   65
In Dostoevsky[5]—twisted mouth,
Stormlit eyes—before whose irresistible
Unworthiness the pure in heart bow down . . .

Cockcrow. Back across the frozen Neva
To samovar and warm, untubercular bed,   70
Far from the dens of vodka, mucus and semen,
They dream. I woke, the fever

Dripping insight, a spring thaw.
You and the others, wrestling with your demons,
Christs of self-hatred, Livingstones[6] of pain,   75
Had drawn the lightning. In a flash I saw

My future: medic at some Armageddon
Neither side wins. I burned with SHAME for the years
You'd spent among sufferings uncharted—
Not even my barren love to rest your head on.   80

---

4. A configuration or pattern having specific properties that cannot be derived from the sum of its component parts (German): in psychology, the name for a theory that physiological or psychological phenomena do not occur through the summation of individual elements but through gestalts functioning separately or interrelatedly.

5. Fyodor Dostoyevsky (1821–1881), Russian novelist whose work probes the religious questions of sin and redemption.
6. Those resembling David Livingstone (1813–1873), a Scottish missionary and explorer in Africa who sought the source of the Nile River.

6 The Panic

Except that Oracle has maps
Of all those badlands. Just now, when you lashed out,
"There's a lot of disease in this room!"
And we felt our faith in one another lapse,

Ken had us break the circle and repair   85
To "a safe place in the room." Faster than fish
We scattered—Randy ducking as from a sniper,
Aileen, wedged in a corner, cradling her bear.

You and I stood flanking the blackboard,
Words as usual between us,   90
But backs to the same wall, for solidarity.
This magical sureness of movement no doubt scored

Points for all concerned, yet the only
Child each had become trembled for you
Thundering forth into the corridors,   95
Decibels measuring how HURT, how LONELY—

7 Tunnel Vision

New Age music. "Close your eyes now. You
Are standing," says the lecturer on Grief,
"At a tunnel's mouth. There's light at the end.
The walls, as you walk through   100

Are hung with images: who you loved that year,
An island holiday, a highschool friend.
Younger and younger, step by step—
And suddenly you're here,

At home. Go in. It's your whole life ago."   105
A pink eye-level sun flows through the hall.
"Smell the smells. It's supper time.
Go to the table." Years have begun to flow

Unhindered down my face. Why?
Because nobody's there. The grown-ups? Shadows.   110
The meal? A mirror. Reflect upon it. Before
Reentering the tunnel say goodbye,

8 Time Recaptured[7]

Goodbye to childhood, that unhappy haven.
It's over, weep your fill. Let go

---

7. The title evokes Marcel Proust's novel, whose title is sometimes translated as *The Past Recaptured*,
sometimes as *Time Regained*.

Of the dead dog, the lost toy. Practise grieving   115
At funerals—anybody's. Let go even

Of those first ninety seconds missed,
Fifty-three years ago, of a third-rate opera
Never revived since then. The GUILT you felt,
Adding it all the same to your master list!   120

Which is why, this last morning, when I switch
The FM on, halfway to Oracle,
And hear the announcer say
(Invisibly reweaving the dropped stitch),

"We bring you now the Overture   125
To Ambroise Thomas's seldom-heard *Mignon*,"[8]
Joy (word rusty with disuse)
Flashes up, deserved and pure.

9 Leading the Blind

Is this you—smiling helplessly? Pinned to your chest,
A sign: *Confront Me If I Take Control*.   130
Plus you must wear (till sundown) a black eyeshade.
All day you've been the littlest, the clumsiest.

We're seated face to face. Take off your mask,
Ken says. Now look into each other deeply. Speak,
As far as you can trust, the words of healing.   135
Your pardon for my own blindness I ask;

You mine, for all you hid from me. Two old
Crackpot hearts once more aswim with color,
Our Higher Power has but to dip his brush—
Lo and behold!   140

The group approves. The ban lifts. Let me guide you,
Helpless but voluble, into a dripping music.
The rainbow brightens with each step. Go on,
Take a peek. This once, no one will chide you.

10 The Desert Museum

—Or, as the fat, nearsighted kid ahead   145
Construes his ticket, "Wow, Dessert Museum!"
I leave tomorrow, so you get a pass.
Safer, both feel, instead

Of checking into the No-Tell Motel,
To check it out—our brave new dried-out world.   150

8. An opera by French operatic composer Ambroise Thomas (1811–1896).

Exhibits: crystals that for eons glinted
Before the wits did; fossil shells

From when this overlook lay safely drowned;
Whole spiny families repelled by sex,
Whom dying men have drunk from (Randy, frightened,   155
Hugging Little Randy, a red hound). . . .

At length behind a wall of glass, in shade,
The mountain lioness too indolent
To train them upon us unlids her gems
Set in the saddest face Love ever made.   160

11 The Twofold Message

(a) You are a brave and special person, (b)
There are far too many people in the world
For this to still matter for very long.
But (Ken goes on) since you obviously

Made the effort to attend Family Week,   165
We hope that we have shown you just how much
You have in common with everybody else.
Not to be "terminally unique"

Will be the consolation you take home.
Remember, Oracle is only the first step   170
In your recovery. The rest is up to you
And the twelve-step program you become

Involved in. An amazing forty per cent
Of our graduates are still clean after two years.
The rest? Well. . . . Given our society,   175
Sobriety is hard to implement.

12 And If

And if it were all like the moon?
Full this evening, bewitchingly
Glowing in a dark not yet complete
Above the world, explicit rune   180

Of change. Change is the "feeling" that dilutes
Those seven others to uncertain washes
Of soot and silver, inks unknown in my kit.
Change sends out shoots

Of FEAR and LONELINESS; of GUILT, as well,   185
Towards the old, abandoned patterns;
Of joy eventually, and self-forgiveness—
Colors few of us brought to Oracle . . .

And if the old patterns recur?
Ask how the co-dependent moon, another night,   190
Feels when the light drains wholly from her face.
Ask what that cold comfort means to her.

                                                              1995

ROBERT CREELEY
1926-2005

" I was shy of the word 'poet,'" Robert Creeley once said, "and all its associations in a world I was then intimate with. It was not, in short, a fit attention for a young man raised in the New England manner, compact of Puritanically deprived senses of speech and sensuality. Life was real and life was earnest, and one had best get on with it." Despite the "constant, restless moving" that Creeley called a pattern in his life, his work retained its connections to his New England background (he was born in Massachusetts), with its economy of speech and natural resources, and with the lingering heritage of its Puritanism. His chosen vocabulary is spare (someone once noted that 80 percent of his volume *Words*, 1967, consists of monosyllables), but his work is, in part, a reaction against the strictures of his background, as seen most clearly in his explicit treatment of the erotic and sensual. Like William Carlos Williams, he sees the poet's role as overthrowing repression and creating the possibility for contact. But Creeley's poems are especially interesting for the ways they conduct a struggle between the self-conscious mind and the instincts of the body, for their exposure of the mind's relentless self-regard. The effort of the poet is to break through the mind's enclosures and to enter fully into the world. Such a breakthrough is evident in a poem like "The Birds," which captures the poet's desire to give himself over to the world in the way the birds "ride the air," and its rhythms and language enact a realization of this desire. Other poems, however, are grounded in the difficulty of release from a painful self-consciousness. Whether joyful or agonized, Creeley's work as a whole is characterized by an awareness of his own act of thinking about what he feels. He may have been the most self-conscious passionate poet in the American canon.

After the death of his father, a doctor, when Creeley was four, he was brought up in a family of five women. He began his life of restless motion in 1944, when he dropped out of Harvard after a year and joined the American Field Service in India and Burma. He returned to Harvard a year later, but left again in 1947 without receiving a degree. In 1946 he married for the first time, and he and his wife lived for a period on Cape Cod (commuting by boat to his classes at Harvard), then on a farm in New Hampshire. Early in 1950, with his friend Jacob Leed, Creeley attempted to publish an alternative literary magazine and wrote to every writer he knew, and some he did not, soliciting contributions. One of his correspondents sent him several of Charles Olson's poems. Although the magazine never happened, in 1950 Creeley and Olson began a correspondence that would run to thousands of letters (the correspondence at one point, according to Creeley, took up eight hours of each day). After a period in Aix-en-Provence and then in Mallorca, where he founded the Divers Press, he accepted Olson's invitation to join the faculty at Black Mountain College, where he founded and edited the *Black Mountain Review* (Olson solved the problem of Creeley's never having graduated from Harvard by having Black Mountain grant him a degree). Olson, Creeley said, "taught me how to write. Not how to write poems that he wrote, but how to write poems that I write. This is a very curious and specific difference." The richly reciprocal nature of the friendship between the two poets led Olson to quote Creeley's now famous statement on organic form, "Form is never more than an extension of content," in bold print in his essay on "Projective Verse" (a selection from which appears in the "Postmodern Manifestos" cluster of this anthology) and to dedicate *The Maximus Poems* to him.

In the company of poets to whom Creeley felt most indebted—Whitman, Hart Crane, Olson, and Williams—Williams was the one with whom he shared most (epigraphs from Williams's poems open several of Creeley's books). In the work of Creeley, as in the work of Williams, women are a recurrent presence: wife, mother, daughter, queen, or muse, the figure of the woman is composite. Her presence in his poems expresses Creeley's need for contact with what he called "the most persistent *other* of our existence, eschewing male order, allowing us to live at last." For Creeley this contact was invigorating, erotic, difficult, and confusing, and his frequent poems about marriage, such as "For Love," dedicated to his second wife, Bobbie Louise Hall, render "tedium / despair, a painful / sense of isolation" even as they celebrate "the company of love." "He continues the art of the troubadours with its themes of love and trial," Robert Duncan once wrote of him. While Creeley wrote often of love's trials (he was married three times) he remained a poet in its service. Visited by the muse in "Kore" (as happens also in "The Door" and "The Finger"), the poet hears her ask a question he also shares: "O love, / where are you / leading / me now?"

The question Creeley asks in "Kore" suggests that for him the poem was a discovery of what might be said, an activity or a form of wandering ("life tracking itself," as he called it) in which the destination or subject is not known beforehand. His poems often enact a walk, where the poet's particular form of walking is presented as stumbling (as in "The Door," where he writes, "The Lady has always moved to the next town / and you stumble on after Her"). The stumbling walk is, of course, open to error, and the form of Creeley's poems presents a wandering that at times missteps in search of its true form or subject. His presentation of himself as a stumbler also suggests his humorous self-awareness. The playfulness of some of his poems, like "The Messengers," contrasts with their sometimes agonized uncertainty. "I am *given* to write poems," Creeley said. "I cannot anticipate their occasion. I have used all the intelligence I can muster to follow the possibilities that the poem . . . is declaring, but I cannot anticipate the necessary conclusion in the activity." As this comment suggests, Creeley emphasized process and discovery in pursuit of "the particular instance." Such an emphasis necessarily makes his work uneven—some poems wander without discovery, others capture an instant that may not be worth capturing. But in his best poems Creeley measured thinking and feeling, measured out the uncertain pursuit of an instant's possibility. His poetic form was shaped by an acute awareness of himself, the moment, and the line as a rhythmic unit, and the pleasures of his poems lie in this awareness and in their openness to discovery. If he was a wanderer in the poems as he was in his life, his wandering repeatedly takes him home: to domesticity, to love, to the work of memory, and, most characteristically, to a fresh sense of the present, as when he sees "the light then / of the sun coming / for another morning / in the world" ("The World").

Kore[1]

As I was walking
   I came upon
chance walking
   the same road upon.

As I sat down   5
   by chance to move
later
   if and as I might,

light the wood was,
   light and green,   10
and what I saw
   before I had not seen.

It was a lady
   accompanied
by goat men[2]   15
   leading her.

Her hair held earth.
   Her eyes were dark.
A double flute[3]
   made her move.   20

"O love,
   where are you
leading
   me now?"

                        1959

I Know a Man

As I sd to my
friend, because I am
always talking,—John, I

sd, which was not his
name, the darkness sur-   5
rounds us, what

---

1. Kore, literally "maiden," is an epithet for the Greek earth goddess Persephone. While picking flowers with some companions, she was kidnapped by Hades (who had been struck by an arrow from Eros, the god of love) and taken to the Underworld. There she spends part of the year as queen of the dead; part of the time she lives aboveground with her mother, Demeter. Her annual reemergence is linked with the reemergence of Earth's fertility in spring and summer.
2. Or satyrs, Greek mythological creatures, with the upper bodies of men and the legs of goats.
3. Ancient Greek musical instrument.

can we do against
it, or else, shall we &
why not, buy a goddamn big car,

drive, he sd, for   10
christ's sake, look
out where yr going.

1962

For Love

for Bobbie

Yesterday I wanted to
speak of it, that sense above
the others to me
important because all

that I know derives   5
from what it teaches me.
Today, what is it that
is finally so helpless,

different, despairs of its own
statement, wants to   10
turn away, endlessly
to turn away.

If the moon did not . . .
no, if you did not
I wouldn't either, but   15
what would I not

do, what prevention, what
thing so quickly stopped.
That is love yesterday
or tomorrow, not   20

now. Can I eat
what you give me. I
have not earned it. Must
I think of everything

as earned. Now love also   25
becomes a reward so
remote from me I have
only made it with my mind.

Here is tedium,
despair, a painful   30

sense of isolation and
whimsical if pompous

self-regard. But that image
is only of the mind's
vague structure, vague to me   35
because it is my own.

Love, what do I think
to say. I cannot say it.
What have you become to ask,
what have I made you into,   40

companion, good company,
crossed legs with skirt, or
soft body under
the bones of the bed.

Nothing says anything   45
but that which it wishes
would come true, fears
what else might happen in

some other place, some
other time not this one.   50
A voice in my place, an
echo of that only in yours.

Let me stumble into
not the confession but
the obsession I begin with   55
now. For you

also (also)
some time beyond place, or
place beyond time, no
mind left to   60

say anything at all,
that face gone, now.
Into the company of love
it all returns.

1962

The Messengers

for Allen Ginsberg

The huge dog, Broderick, and
the smile of the quick eyes
of Allen light a kind world.

Their feelings, under some distance
of remote skin, must touch, 5
wondering at what impatience does

block them. So little love
to share among so many, so much
yellow-orange hair, on the one,

and on the other, such a darkness 10
of long hanging hair now, such
slightness of body, and a voice that

rises on the sounds of feeling.
Aie! It raises the world, lifts,
falls, like a sudden sunlight, like 15

that edge of the black night sweeps
the low lying fields, of soft grasses,
bodies, fills them with quiet longing.

1967

The Birds

for Jane and Stan Brakhage

I'll miss the small birds that come
for the sugar you put out
and the bread crumbs. They've

made the edge of the sea domestic
and, as I am, I welcome that. 5
Nights my head seemed twisted

with dreams and the sea wash,
I let it all come quiet, waking,
counting familiar thoughts and objects.

Here to rest, like they say, I best 10
liked walking along the beach
past the town till one reached

the other one, around the corner
of rock and small trees. It was
clear, and often empty, and   15

peaceful. Those lovely ungainly
pelicans fished there, dropping
like rocks, with grace, from the air,

headfirst, then sat on the water,
letting the pouch of their beaks   20
grow thin again, then swallowing

whatever they'd caught. The birds,
no matter they're not of our kind,
seem most like us here. I want

to go where they go, in a way, if   25
a small and common one. I want
to ride that air which makes the sea

seem down there, not the element
in which one thrashes to come up.
I love water, I *love* water—   30

but I also love air, and fire.

                                                            1972

Fathers

Scattered, aslant
faded faces a column
a rise of the packed
peculiar place to a
modest height makes   5
a view of common lots
in winter then, a ground
of battered snow crusted
at the edges under
it all, there under   10
my fathers their
faded women, friends,
the family all echoed,
names trees more tangible
physical place more tangible   15
the air of this place the road
going past to Watertown[1]

1. Town in Massachusetts, just west of Boston.

or down to my mother's
grave, my father's grave, not
now this resonance of   20
each other one was his, his
survival only, his curious
reticence, his dead state,
his emptiness, his acerbic
edge cuts the hands to   25
hold him, hold on, wants
the ground, *wants* this frozen ground.

1986

ALLEN GINSBERG
1926–1997

" Hold back the edges of your gowns, Ladies, we are going through hell." William
Carlos Williams's introduction to Allen Ginsberg's *Howl* (1956) was probably
the most auspicious public welcome from one poet to another since, one hundred
years before, the American Transcendentalist Ralph Waldo Emerson had hailed the
unknown Walt Whitman in a letter that Whitman used as a preface to the second
edition of *Leaves of Grass*. *Howl* combined apocalyptic criticism of the dull, prosperous Eisenhower years with exuberant celebration of an emerging counterculture. It
was the best-known and most widely circulated book of poems of its time, and with its
appearance Ginsberg became part of the history of publicity as well as the history of
poetry. *Howl* and Jack Kerouac's novel *On the Road* (1957) were the pocket Bibles of
the generation whose name Kerouac had coined—"Beat," with its punning overtones
of "beaten down" and "beatified."

Ginsberg was the son of Louis Ginsberg, a poet and schoolteacher in New Jersey,
and of Naomi Ginsberg, a Russian émigré, whose madness and eventual death her
son memorialized in "Kaddish" (1959). His official education took place at Columbia
University, but for him as for Kerouac the presence of William Burroughs in New
York was equally influential. Burroughs (1914–1997), later the author of *Naked Lunch*
(1959), one of the most inventive experiments in American prose, was at that time a
drug addict about to embark on an expatriate life in Mexico and Tangier. He helped
Ginsberg discover modern writers: Kafka, Yeats, Céline, Rimbaud. Ginsberg responded
to Burroughs's liberated kind of life, to his comic-apocalyptic view of American society, and to his bold literary use of autobiography, as when writing about his own
experience with addicts and addiction in *Junkie*, whose chapters Ginsberg was reading in manuscript form in 1950.

Ginsberg's New York career has passed into mythology for a generation of poets
and readers. In 1945, his sophomore year, he was expelled from Columbia: he had
sketched some obscene drawings and phrases in the dust of his dormitory window
to draw the attention of a neglectful cleaning woman to the grimy state of his room.
Then, living periodically with Burroughs and Kerouac, he shipped out for short
trips as a messman on merchant tankers and worked in addition as a welder, a night
porter, and a dishwasher.

One summer, in a Harlem apartment, Ginsberg underwent what he always represented as the central conversion experience of his life. He had an "auditory vision" of the English poet William Blake reciting his poems: first "Ah! Sunflower," and then a few minutes later the same oracular voice intoning "The Sick Rose." It was "like hearing the doom of the whole universe, and at the same time the inevitable beauty of that doom." Ginsberg was convinced that the presence of "this big god over all . . . and that the whole purpose of being born was to wake up to Him."

Ginsberg eventually finished Columbia in 1948 with high grades but under a legal cloud. Herbert Huncke, a colorful but irresponsible addict friend, had been using Ginsberg's apartment as a storage depot for the goods he stole to support his drug habit. To avoid prosecution as an accomplice, Ginsberg had to plead insanity and spent eight months in the Columbia Psychiatric Institute.

After more odd jobs and considerable success as a market researcher in San Francisco, Ginsberg left the straight, nine-to-five world for good. He was drawn to San Francisco, he said, by its "long honorable . . . tradition of Bohemian—Buddhist—Wobbly [the I.W.W., an early radical labor movement]—mystical—anarchist social involvement." In the years after 1954 he met San Francisco poets such as Robert Duncan, Kenneth Rexroth, Gary Snyder (who was studying Chinese and Japanese at Berkeley), and Lawrence Ferlinghetti, whose City Lights Bookshop became the publisher of *Howl*. The night Ginsberg read the new poem aloud at the Six Gallery has been called "the birth trauma of the Beat Generation."

The spontaneity of surface in *Howl* conceals but grows out of Ginsberg's care and self-consciousness about rhythm and meter. Under the influence of William Carlos Williams, who had befriended him in Paterson after he left the mental hospital, Ginsberg had started carrying around a notebook to record the rhythms of voices around him. Kerouac's *On the Road* gave him further examples of "frank talk" and, in addition, of an "oceanic" prose "sometimes as sublime as epic line." Under Kerouac's influence Ginsberg began the long tumbling lines that were to become his trademark. He carefully explained that all of *Howl and Other Poems* was an experiment in what

Ginsberg reading *Howl* in New York City in 1966, nine years after the court ruling finding it of redeeming social value and declaring it not obscene.

could be done with the long line, the longer unit of breath that seemed natural for him. "My feeling is for a big long clanky statement," one that accommodates "not the way you would *say* it, a thought, but the way you would think it—i.e., we think rapidly, in visual images as well as words, and if each successive thought were transcribed in its confusion . . . you get a slightly different prosody than if you were talking slowly."

Ginsberg learned the long line as well from biblical rhetoric, from the eighteenth-century English poet Christopher Smart, and above all, from Whitman and Blake. His first book pays tribute to both of these latter poets. "A Supermarket in California," with its movement from exclamations to sad questioning, is Ginsberg's melancholy reminder of what has become, after a century, of Whitman's vision of American plenty. In "Sunflower Sutra" he celebrates the battered nobility beneath our industrial "skin of grime." Ginsberg at his best gives a sense of doom and beauty, whether in the denunciatory impatient prophecies of *Howl* or in the catalog of suffering in "Kaddish." His disconnected phrases can accumulate as narrative shrieks or, at other moments, can build as a litany of praise.

By the end of the 1960s Ginsberg was widely known and widely traveled. He had conducted publicly his own pursuit of inner peace during a long stay with Buddhist instructors in India and at home served as a kind of guru for many young people disoriented by the Vietnam War. Ginsberg read his poetry and held "office hours" in universities all over America, a presence at everything from "be-ins"—mass outdoor festivals of chanting, costumes, and music—to antiwar protests. He was a gentle and persuasive presence at hearings for many kinds of reform: revision of severe drug laws and laws against homosexuality. Ginsberg had lived for years with the poet Peter Orlovsky and wrote frankly about their relationship. His poems record his drug experiences as well, and "The Change," written in Japan in 1963, marks his decision to keep away from what he considered the nonhuman domination of drugs and to lay new stress on "living in and inhabiting the human form."

In "The Fall of America" (1972) Ginsberg turned to "epic," a poem including history and registering the ups and downs of his travels across the United States. These "transit" poems sometimes seem like tape-recorded random lists of sights, sounds, and names, but at their best they give a sense of how far America has fallen, by measuring the provisional and changing world of nuclear America against the traces of nature still visible in our landscape and place-names. With Ginsberg's death, contemporary American poetry lost one of its most definitive and revolutionary figures. Happily, the poems endure.

Howl

for Carl Solomon[1]

I

I saw the best minds of my generation destroyed by madness, starving
    hysterical naked,
dragging themselves through the negro streets at dawn looking for an angry
    fix,

1. Ginsberg met Solomon (b. 1928) while both were patients in the Columbia Psychiatric Institute in 1949 and called him "an intuitive Bronx Dadaist and prose-poet." Many details in "Howl" come from the "apocryphal history" that Solomon told Ginsberg in 1949. In "More Mishaps" (1968) Solomon admits that these adventures were "compounded partly of truth, but for the most [of] raving self-justification, crypto-bohemian boasting . . . effeminate prancing and esoteric aphorisms."

angelheaded hipsters burning for the ancient heavenly connection[2] to the
    starry dynamo in the machinery of night,
who poverty and tatters and hollow-eyed and high sat up smoking in the
    supernatural darkness of cold-water flats floating across the tops of
    cities contemplating jazz,
who bared their brains to Heaven under the El and saw Mohammedan[3]
    angels staggering on tenement roofs illuminated,   5
who passed through universities with radiant cool eyes hallucinating
    Arkansas and Blake-light[4] tragedy among the scholars of war,
who were expelled from the academies for crazy & publishing obscene odes
    on the windows of the skull,
who cowered in unshaven rooms in underwear, burning their money in
    wastebaskets and listening to the Terror through the wall,
who got busted in their pubic beards returning through Laredo with a belt
    of marijuana for New York,
who ate fire in paint hotels or drank turpentine in Paradise Alley,[5] death, or
    purgatoried their torsos night after night   10
with dreams, with drugs, with waking nightmares, alcohol and cock and
    endless balls,
incomparable blind streets of shuddering cloud and lightning in the mind
    leaping toward poles of Canada & Paterson,[6] illuminating all the
    motionless world of Time between,
Peyote solidities of halls, backyard green tree cemetery dawns, wine
    drunkenness over the rooftops, storefront boroughs of teahead joyride
    neon blinking traffic light, sun and moon and tree vibrations in the
    roaring winter dusks of Brooklyn, ashcan rantings and kind king light
    of mind,
who chained themselves to subways for the endless ride from Battery to
    holy Bronx[7] on benzedrine until the noise of wheels and children
    brought them down shuddering mouth-wracked and battered bleak of
    brain all drained of brilliance in the drear light of Zoo,
who sank all night in submarine light of Bickford's floated out and sat
    through the stale beer afternoon in desolate Fugazzi's,[8] listening to the
    crack of doom on the hydrogen jukebox,   15
who talked continuously seventy hours from park to pad to bar to Bellevue[9]
    to museum to the Brooklyn Bridge,
a lost battalion of platonic conversationalists jumping down the stoops off
    fire escapes off windowsills off Empire State out of the moon,
yacketayakking screaming vomiting whispering facts and memories and
    anecdotes and eyeball kicks and shocks of hospitals and jails and wars,

---

2. In one sense a person who can supply drugs.
3. An English term for a Muslim, commonly used in Western literature until the mid-twentieth century; now considered offensive by many Muslims because it implies that they worship the prophet Mohammed (or Muhammad) in the same way that Christians worship Christ. "The El": the elevated railway in New York City; also a Hebrew word for God.
4. Refers to Ginsberg's apocalyptic vision of the English poet William Blake (1757–1827).
5. A tenement courtyard in New York's East Village; setting of Kerouac's *The Subterraneans* (1958).

6. Ginsberg's hometown; also the town celebrated by William Carlos Williams in his long poem *Paterson* (1946–58).
7. Opposite ends of a New York subway line running from the Battery (the southern tip of Manhattan) to the Bronx Zoo as its northern terminus.
8. New York bar that was a hipster hangout in the 1950s and 1960s. "Bickford's": a line of restaurants and cafeterias in the New York area from the 1920s to the 1960s.
9. New York public hospital to which psychiatric patients may be committed.

whole intellects disgorged in total recall for seven days and nights with
   brilliant eyes, meat for the Synagogue cast on the pavement,
who vanished into nowhere Zen New Jersey leaving a trail of ambiguous
   picture postcards of Atlantic City Hall,   20
suffering Eastern sweats and Tangerian bone-grindings and migraines of
   China[1] under junk-withdrawal in Newark's bleak furnished room,
who wandered around and around at midnight in the railroad yard
   wondering where to go, and went, leaving no broken hearts,
who lit cigarettes in boxcars boxcars boxcars racketing through snow
   toward lonesome farms in grandfather night,
who studied Plotinus Poe St. John of the Cross[2] telepathy and bop kaballah[3]
   because the cosmos instinctively vibrated at their feet in Kansas,
who loned it through the streets of Idaho seeking visionary indian angels
   who were visionary indian angels,   25
who thought they were only mad when Baltimore gleamed in supernatural
   ecstasy,
who jumped in limousines with the Chinaman of Oklahoma on the impulse
   of winter midnight streetlight smalltown rain,
who lounged hungry and lonesome through Houston seeking jazz or sex or
   soup, and followed the brilliant Spaniard to converse about America
   and Eternity, a hopeless task, and so took ship to Africa,
who disappeared into the volcanoes of Mexico leaving behind nothing but
   the shadow of dungarees and the lava and ash of poetry scattered in
   fireplace Chicago,
who reappeared on the West Coast investigating the FBI in beards and
   shorts with big pacifist eyes sexy in their dark skin passing out
   incomprehensible leaflets,   30
who burned cigarette holes in their arms protesting the narcotic tobacco
   haze of Capitalism,
who distributed Supercommunist pamphlets in Union Square weeping and
   undressing while the sirens of Los Alamos[4] wailed them down, and
   wailed down Wall,[5] and the Staten Island ferry also wailed,
who broke down crying in white gymnasiums naked and trembling before
   the machinery of other skeletons,
who bit detectives in the neck and shrieked with delight in policecars for
   committing no crime but their own wild cooking pederasty and
   intoxication,
who howled on their knees in the subway and were dragged off the roof
   waving genitals and manuscripts,   35
who let themselves be fucked in the ass by saintly motorcyclists, and
   screamed with joy,
who blew and were blown by those human seraphim, the sailors, caresses
   of Atlantic and Caribbean love,
who balled in the morning in the evenings in rosegardens and the grass of
   public parks and cemeteries scattering their semen freely to whomever
   come who may,

1. African and Asian sources of drugs.
2. Spanish visionary and poet (1542–1591), author of *The Dark Night of the Soul*. Plotinus (205–270), visionary Roman philosopher. Edgar Allan Poe (1809–1849), American poet and author of supernatural tales.
3. A mystical tradition of interpreting Hebrew scripture. "Bop": jazz style of the 1940s.
4. New Mexico center for the development of the atomic bomb. In New York in the 1930s Union Square was a gathering place for radical speakers.
5. Wall Street; but also alludes to the Wailing Wall, a place of public lamentation in Jerusalem.

who hiccupped endlessly trying to giggle but wound up with a sob behind a
    partition in a Turkish Bath when the blonde & naked angel came to
    pierce them with a sword,[6]
who lost their loveboys to the three old shrews of fate[7] the one eyed shrew
    of the heterosexual dollar the one eyed shrew that winks out of the
    womb and the one eyed shrew that does nothing but sit on her ass and
    snip the intellectual golden threads of the craftsman's loom,   40
who copulated ecstatic and insatiate with a bottle of beer a sweetheart a
    package of cigarettes a candle and fell off the bed, and continued
    along the floor and down the hall and ended fainting on the wall with
    a vision of ultimate cunt and come eluding the last gyzym of
    consciousness,
who sweetened the snatches of a million girls trembling in the sunset, and
    were red eyed in the morning but prepared to sweeten the snatch of
    the sunrise, flashing buttocks under barns and naked in the lake,
who went out whoring through Colorado in myriad stolen nightcars, N.C.,[8]
    secret hero of these poems, cocksman and Adonis of Denver—joy to
    the memory of his innumerable lays of girls in empty lots & diner
    backyards, moviehouses' rickety rows, on mountaintops in caves or
    with gaunt waitresses in familiar roadside lonely petticoat upliftings &
    especially secret gas-station solipsisms of johns, & hometown alleys
    too,
who faded out in vast sordid movies, were shifted in dreams, woke on a
    sudden Manhattan, and picked themselves up out of basements
    hungover with heartless Tokay[9] and horrors of Third Avenue iron
    dreams & stumbled to unemployment offices,
who walked all night with their shoes full of blood on the snowbank docks
    waiting for a door in the East River to open to a room full of steamheat
    and opium,   45
who created great suicidal dramas on the apartment cliff-banks of the
    Hudson under the wartime blue floodlight of the moon & their heads
    shall be crowned with laurel in oblivion,
who ate the lamb stew of the imagination or digested the crab at the muddy
    bottom of the rivers of Bowery,[1]
who wept at the romance of the streets with their pushcarts full of onions
    and bad music,
who sat in boxes breathing in the darkness under the bridge, and rose up to
    build harpsichords in their lofts,
who coughed on the sixth floor of Harlem crowned with flame under the
    tubercular sky surrounded by orange crates of theology,   50
who scribbled all night rocking and rolling over lofty incantations which
    in the yellow morning were stanzas of gibberish,
who cooked rotten animals lung heart feet tail borsht & tortillas dreaming
    of the pure vegetable kingdom,
who plunged themselves under meat trucks looking for an egg,

6. An allusion to *The Ecstasy of St. Teresa*, a sculpture by Lorenzo Bernini (1598–1680) based on St. Teresa of Ávila's (1515–1582) distinctly erotic description of a religious vision.
7. In Greek mythology goddesses who determine a mortal's life by spinning out a length of thread and cutting it at the time of death.
8. Neal Cassady, hip companion of Jack Kerouac and the original Dean Moriarty, one of the leading figures in *On the Road*.
9. A naturally sweet wine made in Hungary.
1. Southern extension of Third Avenue in New York City; traditional haunt of derelicts and alcoholics.

who threw their watches off the roof to cast their ballot for Eternity outside
    of Time, & alarm clocks fell on their heads every day for the next
    decade,
who cut their wrists three times successively unsuccessfully, gave up and
    were forced to open antique stores where they thought they were
    growing old and cried,   55
who were burned alive in their innocent flannel suits on Madison Avenue[2]
    amid blasts of leaden verse & the tanked-up clatter of the iron
    regiments of fashion & the nitroglycerine shrieks of the fairies of
    advertising & the mustard gas of sinister intelligent editors, or were
    run down by the drunken taxicabs of Absolute Reality,
who jumped off the Brooklyn Bridge this actually happened and walked
    away unknown and forgotten into the ghostly daze of Chinatown soup
    alleyways & firetrucks, not even one free beer,
who sang out of their windows in despair, fell out of the subway window,
    jumped in the filthy Passaic,[3] leaped on negroes, cried all over the
    street, danced on broken wineglasses barefoot smashed phonograph
    records of nostalgic European 1930's German jazz finished the
    whiskey and threw up groaning into the bloody toilet, moans in their
    ears and the blast of colossal steamwhistles,
who barreled down the highways of the past journeying to each other's
    hotrod-Golgotha[4] jail-solitude watch or Birmingham jazz incarnation,
who drove crosscountry seventytwo hours to find out if I had a vision or you
    had a vision or he had a vision to find out Eternity,   60
who journeyed to Denver, who died in Denver, who came back to Denver &
    waited in vain, who watched over Denver & brooded & loned in
    Denver and finally went away to find out the Time, & now Denver is
    lonesome for her heroes,
who fell on their knees in hopeless cathedrals praying for each other's
    salvation and light and breasts, until the soul illuminated its hair for a
    second,
who crashed through their minds in jail waiting for impossible criminals
    with golden heads and the charm of reality in their hearts who sang
    sweet blues to Alcatraz,
who retired to Mexico to cultivate a habit, or Rocky Mount to tender
    Buddha or Tangiers to boys or Southern Pacific to the black
    locomotive or Harvard to Narcissus to Woodlawn[5] to the daisychain or
    grave,
who demanded sanity trials accusing the radio of hypnotism & were left
    with their insanity & their hands & a hung jury,   65
who threw potato salad at CCNY lecturers on Dadaism[6] and subsequently
    presented themselves on the granite steps of the madhouse with
    shaven heads and harlequin speech of suicide, demanding
    instantaneous lobotomy,

---

2. Center of New York advertising agencies.
3. River flowing past Paterson, New Jersey.
4. The place in ancient Judea where Jesus was
believed to have been crucified; also known as
Calvary.
5. A cemetery in the Bronx. The Southern
Pacific is a railroad company. The references in
this line are to the lives of Kerouac, Cassidy, and
William Burroughs (an author and fellow Beat).
6. Artistic cult of absurdity (c. 1916–20).
"CCNY": City College of New York. This and the
following incidents probably derived from the
"apocryphal history of my adventures" related by
Solomon to Ginsberg.

and who were given instead the concrete void of insulin metrasol electricity
   hydrotherapy psychotherapy occupational therapy pingpong &
   amnesia,
who in humorless protest overturned only one symbolic pingpong table,
   resting briefly in catatonia,
returning years later truly bald except for a wig of blood, and tears and
   fingers, to the visible madman doom of the wards of the madtowns of
   the East,
Pilgrim State's Rockland's and Greystone's[7] foetid halls, bickering with the
   echoes of the soul, rocking and rolling in the midnight solitude-bench
   dolmen-realms of love, dream of life a nightmare, bodies turned to
   stone as heavy as the moon,   70
with mother finally*******, and the last fantastic book flung out of the
   tenement window, and the last door closed at 4 AM and the last
   telephone slammed at the wall in reply and the last furnished room
   emptied down to the last piece of mental furniture, a yellow paper rose
   twisted on a wire hanger in the closet, and even that imaginary,
   nothing but a hopeful little bit of hallucination—
ah, Carl,[8] while you are not safe I am not safe, and now you're really in the
   total animal soup of time—
and who therefore ran through the icy streets obsessed with a sudden flash
   of the alchemy of the use of the ellipse the catalog the meter & the
   vibrating plane,
who dreamt and made incarnate gaps in Time & Space through images
   juxtaposed, and trapped the archangel of the soul between 2 visual
   images and joined the elemental verbs and set the noun and dash of
   consciousness together jumping with sensation of Pater Omnipotens
   Aeterna Deus[9]
to recreate the syntax and measure of poor human prose and stand before
   you speechless and intelligent and shaking with shame, rejected yet
   confessing out the soul to conform to the rhythm of thought in his
   naked and endless head,   75
the madman bum and angel beat in Time, unknown, yet putting down
   here what might be left to say in time come after death,
and rose reincarnate in the ghostly clothes of jazz in the goldhorn shadow
   of the band and blew the suffering of America's naked mind for love
   into an eli eli lamma lamma sabacthani[1] saxophone cry that shivered
   the cities down to the last radio
with the absolute heart of the poem of life butchered out of their own
   bodies good to eat a thousand years.

II

What sphinx of cement and aluminum bashed open their skulls and ate up
   their brains and imagination?

7. Three psychiatric hospitals near New York.
Solomon was institutionalized at Pilgrim State
and Rockland; Ginsberg's mother, Naomi, was
permanently institutionalized at Greystone after
years of suffering hallucinations and paranoid
attacks. She died there in 1956, the year after
"Howl" was written.
8. Solomon.
9. All-Powerful Father, Eternal God (Latin). An
allusion to a phrase used by the French painter
Paul Cézanne (1839–1906), in a 1904 letter
describing the effects of nature. In an interview,
Ginsberg compared his own method of sharply
juxtaposed images with Cézanne's foreshorten-
ing of perspective in landscape painting.
1. Christ's last words on the Cross: My God, my
God, why have you forsaken me? (Aramaic).

Moloch![2] Solitude! Filth! Ugliness! Ashcans and unobtainable dollars!
    Children screaming under the stairways! Boys sobbing in armies! Old
    men weeping in the parks!   80
Moloch! Moloch! Nightmare of Moloch! Moloch the loveless! Mental
    Moloch! Moloch the heavy judger of men!
Moloch the incomprehensible prison! Moloch the crossbone soulless
    jailhouse and Congress of sorrows! Moloch whose buildings are
    judgment! Moloch the vast stone of war! Moloch the stunned
    governments!
Moloch whose mind is pure machinery! Moloch whose blood is running
    money! Moloch whose fingers are ten armies! Moloch whose breast is
    a cannibal dynamo! Moloch whose ear is a smoking tomb!
Moloch whose eyes are a thousand blind windows! Moloch whose
    skyscrapers stand in the long streets like endless Jehovahs! Moloch
    whose factories dream and croak in the fog! Moloch whose
    smokestacks and antennae crown the cities!
Moloch whose love is endless oil and stone! Moloch whose soul is
    electricity and banks! Moloch whose poverty is the specter of genius!
    Moloch whose fate is a cloud of sexless hydrogen! Moloch whose
    name is the Mind!   85
Moloch in whom I sit lonely! Moloch in whom I dream Angels! Crazy in
    Moloch! Cocksucker in Moloch! Lacklove and manless in Moloch!
Moloch who entered my soul early! Moloch in whom I am a consciousness
    without a body! Moloch who frightened me out of my natural ecstasy!
    Moloch whom I abandon! Wake up in Moloch! Light streaming out of
    the sky!
Moloch! Moloch! Robot apartments! invisible suburbs! skeleton treasuries!
    blind capitals! demonic industries! spectral nations! invincible
    madhouses! granite cocks! monstrous bombs!
They broke their backs lifting Moloch to Heaven! Pavements, trees, radios,
    tons! lifting the city to Heaven which exists and is everywhere about
    us!
Visions! omens! hallucinations! miracles! ecstasies! gone down the Ameri-
    can river!   90
Dreams! adorations! illuminations! religions! the whole boatload of
    sensitive bullshit!
Breakthroughs! over the river! flips and crucifixions! gone down the flood!
    Highs! Epiphanies! Despairs! Ten years' animal screams and suicides!
    Minds! New loves! Mad generation! down on the rocks of Time!
Real holy laughter in the river! They saw it all! the wild eyes! the holy yells!
    They bade farewell! They jumped off the roof! to solitude! waving!
    carrying flowers! Down to the river! into the street!

III

Carl Solomon! I'm with you in Rockland
    where you're madder than I am   95
I'm with you in Rockland
    where you must feel very strange

---

2. Ginsberg's own annotation in the facsimile edition of the poem reads: "'Moloch': or Molech, the
Canaanite fire god, whose worship was marked by
parents' burning their children as proprietary sacrifice. 'And thou shalt not let any of thy seed pass
through the fire to Molech' [Leviticus 18:21]."

I'm with you in Rockland
>where you imitate the shade of my mother
I'm with you in Rockland   100
>where you've murdered your twelve secretaries
I'm with you in Rockland
>where you laugh at this invisible humor
I'm with you in Rockland
>where we are great writers on the same dreadful typewriter   105
I'm with you in Rockland
>where your condition has become serious and is reported on the radio
I'm with you in Rockland
>where the faculties of the skull no longer admit the worms of the
>senses
I'm with you in Rockland   110
>where you drink the tea of the breasts of the spinsters of Utica[3]
I'm with you in Rockland
>where you pun on the bodies of your nurses the harpies of the Bronx
I'm with you in Rockland
>where you scream in a straightjacket that you're losing the game of
>the actual pingpong of the abyss   115
I'm with you in Rockland
>where you bang on the catatonic piano the soul is innocent and
>immortal it should never die ungodly in an armed madhouse
I'm with you in Rockland
>where fifty more shocks will never return your soul to its body again
>from its pilgrimage to a cross in the void
I'm with you in Rockland   120
>where you accuse your doctors of insanity and plot the Hebrew
>socialist revolution against the fascist national Golgotha
I'm with you in Rockland
>where you will split the heavens of Long Island and resurrect your
>living human Jesus from the superhuman tomb
I'm with you in Rockland
>where there are twenty five thousand mad comrades all together
>singing the final stanzas of the Internationale[4]   125
I'm with you in Rockland
>where we hug and kiss the United States under our bedsheets the
>United States that coughs all night and won't let us sleep
I'm with you in Rockland
>where we wake up electrified out of the coma by our own souls'
>airplanes roaring over the roof they've come to drop angelic bombs
>the hospital illuminates itself   imaginary walls collapse   O skinny
>legions run outside   O starry-spangled shock of mercy the eternal
>war is here   O victory forget your underwear we're free
I'm with you in Rockland   130
>in my dreams you walk dripping from a sea-journey on the highway
>across America in tears to the door of my cottage in the Western night

San Francisco, 1955–56   1956

---

3. Town in central New York.
4. Former socialist and communist song; the official Soviet anthem until 1944.

Footnote to Howl

Holy ! Holy ! Holy ! Holy ! Holy ! Holy ! Holy ! Holy ! Holy ! Holy ! Holy !
    Holy ! Holy ! Holy ! Holy !
The world is holy ! The soul is holy ! The skin is holy ! The nose is holy !
    The tongue and cock and hand and asshole holy !
Everything is holy ! everybody's holy ! everywhere is holy ! everyday is in
    eternity ! Everyman's an angel !
The bum's as holy as the seraphim ! the madman is holy as you my soul are
    holy !
The typewriter is holy the poem is holy the voice is holy the hearers are
    holy the ecstasy is holy !   5
Holy Peter holy Allen holy Solomon holy Lucien holy Kerouac holy Huncke
    holy Burroughs holy Gassady[1] holy the unknown buggered and
    suffering beggars holy the hideous human angels !
Holy my mother in the insane asylum ! Holy the cocks of the grandfathers
    of Kansas !
Holy the groaning saxophone ! Holy the bop apocalypse ! Holy the
    jazzbands marijuana hipsters peace & junk & drums !
Holy the solitudes of skyscrapers and pavements ! Holy the cafeterias filled
    with the millions ! Holy the mysterious rivers of tears under the
    streets !
Holy the lone juggernaut ! Holy the vast lamb of the middle-class ! Holy the
    crazy shepherds of rebellion ! Who digs Los Angeles IS Los Angeles ! 10
Holy New York Holy San Francisco Holy Peoria & Seattle Holy Paris Holy
    Tangiers Holy Moscow Holy Istanbul !
Holy time in eternity holy eternity in time holy the clocks in space holy the
    fourth dimension holy the fifth International holy the Angel in
    Moloch !

1955–56   1956, 1959

A Supermarket in California

What thoughts I have of you tonight, Walt Whitman,[1] for I walked down
the sidestreets under the trees with a headache self-conscious looking at
the full moon.
    In my hungry fatigue, and shopping for images, I went into the neon
fruit supermarket, dreaming of your enumerations!

1. All the figures mentioned here are Americans who shared or inspired a literary bohemia of the time. "Peter": Peter Orlovsky (1933–2010), Beat poet and Ginsberg's lover for four decades. "Allen": Ginsberg. "Solomon": Carl Solomon (1928–1993), whom Ginsberg met at the psychiatric hospital where Ginsberg's mother was being treated and to whom Ginsberg dedicated "Howl." "Lucien": Lucien Carr (1923–2005), one of the Beats and Ginsberg's roommate at Columbia University in the 1940s. "Kerouac": Jack Kerouac (1922–1969), novelist and founding figure of the Beat generation. "Huncke": Herbert Huncke (1915–1996), writer who influenced Ginsberg and who introduced Ginsberg and Kerouac to the term "beat." "Burroughs": William Burroughs (1914–1997), writer, spoken-word performer, and social critic most famous for the novel *Naked Lunch* (1959). "Cassady": Neal Cassady (1926–1968), an icon of the Beat generation and the inspiration for the character Dean Moriarty in Kerouac's best-known work, *On the Road* (1957).
1. American poet (1819–1892), author of *Leaves of Grass*, against whose homosexuality and vision of American plenty Ginsberg measures himself.

What peaches and what penumbras![2] Whole families shopping at night!
Aisles full of husbands! Wives in the avocados, babies in the tomatoes!—
and you, Garcia Lorca,[3] what were you doing down by the watermelons?

I saw you, Walt Whitman, childless, lonely old grubber, poking among
the meats in the refrigerator and eyeing the grocery boys.
I heard you asking questions of each: Who killed the pork chops? What
price bananas? Are you my Angel?   5
I wandered in and out of the brilliant stacks of cans following you, and
followed in my imagination by the store detective.
We strode down the open corridors together in our solitary fancy tasting
artichokes, possessing every frozen delicacy, and never passing the cashier.

Where are we going, Walt Whitman? The doors close in an hour. Which
way does your beard point tonight?
(I touch your book and dream of our odyssey in the supermarket and
feel absurd.)
Will we walk all night through solitary streets? The trees add shade to
shade, lights out in the houses, we'll both be lonely.   10

Will we stroll dreaming of the lost America of love past blue automobiles in driveways, home to our silent cottage?
Ah, dear father, graybeard, lonely old courage-teacher, what America
did you have when Charon quit poling his ferry and you got out on a
smoking bank and stood watching the boat disappear on the black waters
of Lethe?[4]

Berkeley, 1955   1956

Sunflower Sutra[1]

I walked on the banks of the tincan banana dock and sat down under the
    huge shade of a Southern Pacific locomotive to look at the sunset over
    the box house hills and cry.
Jack Kerouac[2] sat beside me on a busted rusty iron pole, companion, we
    thought the same thoughts of the soul, bleak and blue and sad-eyed,
    surrounded by the gnarled steel roots of trees of machinery.
The oily water on the river mirrored the red sky, sun sank on top of final
    Frisco[3] peaks, no fish in that stream, no hermit in those mounts, just
    ourselves rheumy-eyed and hung-over like old bums on the riverbank,
    tired and wily.
Look at the Sunflower, he said, there was a dead gray shadow against the
    sky, big as a man, sitting dry on top of a pile of ancient sawdust—

2. Partial shadows.
3. Federico García Lorca (1898–1936), Spanish
poet and dramatist and author of "A Poet in New
York," whose work is characterized by surrealist
and homoerotic inspiration.
4. Forgetfulness. In Greek mythology, one of the
rivers of Hades, the Underworld. Charon was

the boatman who ferried the dead to Hades.
1. Sanskrit for "thread"; the word refers to Brah-
min or Buddhist religious texts of ritual instruction.
2. Fellow Beat (1922–1969), author of *On the
Road* (1957).
3. San Francisco.

—I rushed up enchanted—it was my first sunflower, memories of
    Blake[4]—my visions—Harlem   5
and Hells of the Eastern rivers, bridges clanking Joes Greasy Sandwiches,
    dead baby carriages, black treadless tires forgotten and unretreaded,
    the poem of the riverbank, condoms & pots, steel knives, nothing
    stainless, only the dank muck and the razor sharp artifacts passing into
    the past—
and the gray Sunflower poised against the sunset, crackly bleak and dusty
    with the smut and smog and smoke of olden locomotives in its eye—
corolla[5] of bleary spikes pushed down and broken like a battered crown,
    seeds fallen out of its face, soon-to-be-toothless mouth of sunny air,
    sunrays obliterated on its hairy head like a dried wire spiderweb,
leaves stuck out like arms out of the stem, gestures from the sawdust root,
    broke pieces of plaster fallen out of the black twigs, a dead fly in its
    ear,
Unholy battered old thing you were, my sunflower O my soul, I loved you
    then!   10
The grime was no man's grime but death and human locomotives,
all that dress of dust, that veil of darkened railroad skin, that smog of
    cheek, that eyelid of black mis'ry, that sooty hand or phallus or
    protuberance of artificial worse-than-dirt—industrial—modern—all
    that civilization spotting your crazy golden crown—
and those blear thoughts of death and dusty loveless eyes and ends and
    withered roots below, in the home-pile of sand and sawdust, rubber
    dollar bills, skin of machinery, the guts and innards of the weeping
    coughing car, the empty lonely tincans with their rusty tongues alack,
    what more could I name, the smoked ashes of some cock cigar, the
    cunts of wheelbarrows and the milky breasts of cars, wornout asses out
    of chairs & sphincters of dynamos—all these
entangled in your mummied roots—and you there standing before me in
    the sunset, all your glory in your form!
A perfect beauty of a sunflower! a perfect excellent lovely sunflower
    existence! a sweet natural eye to the new hip moon, woke up alive
    and excited grasping in the sunset shadow sunrise golden monthly
    breeze!   15
How many flies buzzed round you innocent of your grime, while you
    cursed the heavens of the railroad and your flower soul?
Poor dead flower? when did you forget you were a flower? when did you
    look at your skin and decide you were an impotent dirty old
    locomotive? the ghost of a locomotive? the specter and shade of a once
    powerful mad American locomotive?
You were never no locomotive, Sunflower, you were a sunflower!
And you Locomotive, you are a locomotive, forget me not!
So I grabbed up the skeleton thick sunflower and stuck it at my side like a
    scepter,   20
and deliver my sermon to my soul, and Jack's soul too, and anyone who'll
    listen,

---

4. In Harlem in 1948 Ginsberg had a hallucinatory revelation in which he heard the English
poet William Blake (1757–1827) reciting Blake's
poems "Ah! Sunflower" and "The Sick Rose."
5. Petals forming the inner envelope of a flower.

—We're not our skin of grime, we're not our dread bleak dusty imageless
   locomotive, we're all golden sunflowers inside, blessed by our own
   seed & hairy naked accomplishment-bodies growing into mad black
   formal sunflowers in the sunset, spied on by our eyes under the
   shadow of the mad locomotive riverbank sunset Frisco hilly tincan
   evening sitdown vision.

Berkeley, 1955   1956

To Aunt Rose

Aunt Rose—now—might I see you
with your thin face and buck tooth smile and pain
       of rheumatism—and a long black heavy shoe
          for your bony left leg
limping down the long hall in Newark on the running carpet   5
       past the black grand piano
          in the day room
             where the parties were
and I sang Spanish loyalist[1] songs
       in a high squeaky voice   10
          (hysterical) the committee listening
       while you limped around the room
          collected the money—
Aunt Honey, Uncle Sam, a stranger with a cloth arm
       in his pocket   15
          and huge young bald head
             of Abraham Lincoln Brigade[2]

—your long sad face
       your tears of sexual frustration
          (what smothered sobs and bony hips   20
             under the pillows of Osborne Terrace)
—the time I stood on the toilet seat naked
       and you powdered my thighs with Calomine
          against the poison ivy—my tender
             and shamed first black curled hairs   25
what were you thinking in secret heart then
       knowing me a man already—
and I an ignorant girl of family silence on the thin pedestal
       of my legs in the bathroom—Museum of Newark.
          Aunt Rose   30
Hitler is dead, Hitler is in Eternity; Hitler is with
       Tamburlane and Emily Brontë[3]

---

1. During the Spanish Civil War (1936–39) many
left-wing Americans—among them Ginsberg's
relatives in Newark—sympathized with the Spanish loyalists who were resisting Francisco Franco's
(1892–1975) efforts to become Fascist dictator of
Spain.

2. American volunteers who fought against the
Fascists in the Spanish Civil War.
3. English poet and novelist (1818–1848), author
of *Wuthering Heights*. Tamburlane was a Mideast-
ern "scourge" and conqueror (hero of Christopher
Marlowe's *Tamburlane*, 1588).

Though I see you walking still, a ghost on Osborne Terrace
    down the long dark hall to the front door
      limping a little with a pinched smile   35
      in what must have been a silken
          flower dress
welcoming my father, the Poet, on his visit to Newark
    —see you arriving in the living room
      dancing on your crippled leg   40
      and clapping hands his book
      had been accepted by Liveright[4]

Hitler is dead and Liveright's gone out of business
The Attic of the Past and *Everlasting Minute* are out of print
    Uncle Harry sold his last silk stocking   45
    Claire quit interpretive dancing school
    Buba sits a wrinkled monument in Old
      Ladies Home blinking at hew babies

last time I saw you was the hospital
    pale skull protruding under ashen skin   50
      blue veined unconscious girl
      in an oxygen tent
the war in Spain has ended long ago
    Aunt Rose

Paris, 1958   1961

On Burroughs' Work[1]

The method must be purest meat
    and no symbolic dressing,
actual visions & actual prisons
    as seen then and now.

Prisons and visions presented   5
    with rare descriptions
corresponding exactly to those
    of Alcatraz and Rose.[2]

A naked lunch is natural to us,
    we eat reality sandwiches.   10
But allegories are so much lettuce.
    Don't hide the madness.

San Jose, 1954   1963

---

4. Leading American publisher of the 1920s and 1930s (now a subsidiary of W. W. Norton); published *The Everlasting Minute* (1937), poems by Allen Ginsberg's father, Louis, whose first book was *The Attic of the Past* (1920).
1. William Burroughs (1914–1997), a senior member of the Beat generation, homosexual, former heroin addict, author of the novels *Junkie* (1953, 1964) and *Naked Lunch* (1959).
2. In 1948 Ginsberg had a hallucinatory vision of the English poet William Blake (1757–1827) reciting Blake's poem "The Sick Rose." Alcatraz was the island prison in San Francisco Bay.

Ego Confession

I want to be known as the most brilliant man in America
Introduced to Gyalwa Karmapa heir of the Whispered Transmission Crazy
    Wisdom Practice Lineage[1]
as the secret young wise man who visited him and winked anonymously
    decade ago in Gangtok[2]
Prepared the way for Dharma in America without mentioning Dharma—
    scribbled laughter
Who saw Blake[3] and abandoned God   5
To whom the Messianic Fink sent messages darkest hour sleeping on steel
    sheets "somewhere in the Federal Prison system" Weathermen[4] got no
    Moscow Gold
who went backstage to Cecil Taylor[5] serious chat chord structure & Time
    in a nightclub
who fucked a rose-lipped rock star in a tiny bedroom slum watched by a
    statue of Vajrasattva—[6]
and overthrew the CIA with a silent thought—
Old Bohemians many years hence in Viennese beergardens'll recall   10
his many young lovers with astonishing faces and iron breasts
gnostic apparatus and magical observation of rainbow-lit spiderwebs
extraordinary cooking, lung stew & Spaghetti a la Vongole and recipe for
    salad dressing 3 parts oil one part vinegar much garlic and honey a
    spoonful
his extraordinary ego, at service of Dharma and completely empty
unafraid of its own self's spectre   15
parroting gossip of gurus and geniuses famous for their reticence—
Who sang a blues made rock stars weep and moved an old black guitarist
    to laughter in Memphis—
I want to be the spectacle of Poesy triumphant over trickery of the world
Omniscient breathing its own breath thru War tear gas spy hallucination
whose common sense astonished gaga Gurus and rich Artistes—   20
who called the Justice department & threaten'd to Blow the Whistle
Stopt Wars, turned back petrochemical Industries' Captains to grieve &
    groan in bed
Chopped wood, built forest houses & established farms
distributed monies to poor poets & nourished imaginative genius of the land
Sat silent in jazz roar writing poetry with an ink pen—   25
wasn't afraid of God or Death after his 48th year—
let his brains turn to water under Laughing Gas his gold molar pulled by
    futuristic dentists
Seaman knew ocean's surface a year
carpenter late learned bevel and mattock

1. I.e., spiritual head of the Karma Kagyu tradition of Tibetan Buddhism. The Tibetan yogi and saint Milarepa (1052–1136?) once said that his lineage was "crazed with devotion, crazed by truth, crazy for Dharma! [in Buddhism, divine law]."
2. Capitol of the Indian state of Sikkim and the site of one of the most sacred monasteries of Buddhism.
3. William Blake (1757–1827), English poet and mystic, whom Ginsberg had seen in a hallucinatory vision.
4. Revolutionary terrorist student group of the 1960s.
5. American pianist and poet (b. 1929), one of the most important innovators in jazz improvisation.
6. A figure of Tantric iconography, depicted holding the vajra (Sanskrit, "thunderbolt" and "diamond"). The vajra destroys ignorance, is indestructible, and symbolizes the male principle.

son, conversed with elder Pound[7] & treated his father gently   30
—All empty all for show, all for the sake of Poesy
to set surpassing example of sanity as measure for late generations
Exemplify Muse Power to the young avert future suicide
accepting his own lie & the gaps between lies with equal good humor
Solitary in worlds full of insects & singing birds all solitary   35
—who had no subject but himself in many disguises
some outside his own body including empty air-filled space forests & cities—
Even climbed mountains to create his mountain, with ice ax & crampons &
    ropes, over Glaciers—

San Francisco, October 1974   1977

7. Ezra Pound (1885–1972), American poet and critic who was a leader of the modernist movement in early 20th-century poetry.

FRANK O'HARA
1926–1966

After Frank O'Hara's death, the critic Donald Allen gathered O'Hara's *Collected Poems* and was surprised to discover that there were more than five hundred, many not published before. Some had to be retrieved from letters or from scraps of paper in boxes and trunks. O'Hara's poems were often spontaneous acts, revised minimally or not at all, then scattered generously, half forgotten. His work was published not by large commercial presses but by small presses and by art galleries such as Tibor de Nagy. These influential but fugitive paperbacks—*A City Winter* (1952), *Meditations in an Emergency* (1956), *Lunch Poems* (1964), and *Second Avenue* (1960)—included love poems, "letter" poems, "postcards," and odes, each bearing the mark of its occasion: a birthday, a thank-you, memories of a lunch hour, or simply "Having a Coke with You." They are filled, like diaries, with the names of Manhattan streets, writers, artists, restaurants, cafés, and films. O'Hara practiced what he once called, in mockery of pompous poetic manifestos, "personism." The term came to him one day at the office when he was writing a poem for someone he loved. "While I was writing it I was realizing that if I wanted to I could use the telephone instead of writing the poem, and so Personism was born. . . . It puts the poem squarely between the poet and the person, Lucky Pierre style, and the poem is correspondingly gratified. The poem is at last between two persons instead of two pages." (O'Hara's essay "Personism" is excerpted in the "Postmodern Manifestos" cluster of this anthology.)

O'Hara moved to New York City in 1951. He was born in Baltimore and grew up in Worcester, Massachusetts. He had served in the navy for two years (and been stationed in the South Pacific and Japan), then studied at Harvard, where he majored in music and English. In New York he became involved in the art world, working at different times as an editor and critic for *Art News* and a curator for the Museum of Modern Art. But he was not simply making a living; he was also making a life. In these years abstract expressionism—nonrepresentational painting—flourished, and New York replaced Paris as the art capital of the world. O'Hara met and wrote about painters such as Willem de Kooning, Franz Kline, and Jackson Pollock, then producing their most brilliant work. After 1955, as a special assistant in the International Program of the Museum of Modern Art, O'Hara helped organize important traveling exhibitions that introduced the new American painting to the art world abroad.

As friends, many of these painters (and sculptors) were the occasions for and recipients of O'Hara's poems. Even more important, their way of working served as a model for his own style of writing. As the poet John Ashbery puts it, "The poem [is] the chronicle of the creative act that produces it." At the simplest level this means including the random jumps, distractions, and loose associations involved in writing about a particular moment, and sometimes recording the pauses in the writing of the poem ("And now that I have finished dinner I can continue"). In O'Hara's work the casual is often, unexpectedly, the launching point for the visionary. The offhand chronicle of a lunch-hour walk can suddenly crystallize around a thunderclap memory of three friends, artists who died young: "First / Bunny died, then John Latouche, / then Jackson Pollock. But is the / earth as full as life was full, of them?"

O'Hara was indisputably, for his generation, *the* poet of New York; the city was for him what pastoral or rural worlds were for other writers, a source of refreshment and fantasy. But behind the exultation of O'Hara's cityscapes, a reader can often sense the melancholy that is made explicit in poems such as "A Step Away from Them." Part of the city's allure was that it answered O'Hara's driving need to reach out for friends, events, animation. His eagerness is balanced on "the wilderness wish / of wanting to be everything to everybody everywhere." O'Hara's poetry also displays an understanding of the intersections between the fast-paced energy of urban life and the world of machines.

O'Hara's example of a resonant casualness encouraged other poets—Ashbery, Kenneth Koch, and James Schuyler. Loosely known as the "New York school" of poets, they occasionally collaborated on poems, plays, and happenings. O'Hara's bravado was a rallying point for these writers outside the more traditional and historically conscious modernism of Ezra Pound and T. S. Eliot. His poems were like "inspired rambling," open to all levels and areas of experience, expressed in a colloquial tone that could easily shade into surrealistic dream. "I'm too blue, / An elephant takes up his trumpet, / money flutters from the windows of cries." More recently the influence of O'Hara's casual and often comic voice makes itself felt in the work of Billy Collins.

A few days after his fortieth birthday, in 1966, O'Hara was struck down at night by a beach buggy on Fire Island, New York, and died a few hours later. Despite his premature death he enabled a nourishing interaction of painting, writing, dance, and theater.

To the Harbormaster

I wanted to be sure to reach you;
though my ship was on the way it got caught
in some moorings. I am always tying up
and then deciding to depart. In storms and
at sunset, with the metallic coils of the tide   5
around my fathomless arms, I am unable
to understand the forms of my vanity
or I am hard alee with my Polish rudder[1]

---

1. Probably a submerged comic reference to *The Polish Rider*, by the Dutch painter Rembrandt Harmensz van Rijn (1606–1669). O'Hara said this poem was about his friend the painter Larry Rivers (1923–2002), who expressed a continuing fascination with Rembrandt's painting of a knight on horseback. "Hard alee": a movement toward the lee, or sheltered side, of a sailboat, i.e., away from the wind.

in my hand and the sun sinking. To
you I offer my hull and the tattered cordage   10
of my will. The terrible channels where
the wind drives me against the brown lips
of the reeds are not all behind me. Yet
I trust the sanity of my vessel; and
if it sinks, it may well be in answer   15
to the reasoning of the eternal voices,
the waves which have kept me from reaching you.

1954?   1957

Why I Am Not a Painter

I am not a painter, I am a poet.
Why? I think I would rather be
a painter, but I am not. Well,

for instance, Mike Goldberg
is starting a painting. I drop in.   5
"Sit down and have a drink" he
says. I drink; we drink. I look
up. "You have SARDINES in it."
"Yes, it needed something there."
"Oh." I go and the days go by   10
and I drop in again. The painting
is going on, and I go, and the days
go by. I drop in. The painting is
finished. "Where's SARDINES?"
All that's left is just   15
letters, "It was too much," Mike says.

But me? One day I am thinking of
a color: orange. I write a line
about orange. Pretty soon it is a
whole page of words, not lines.   20
Then another page. There should be
so much more, not of orange, of
words, of how terrible orange is
and life. Days go by. It is even in
prose, I am a real poet. My poem   25
is finished and I haven't mentioned
orange yet. It's twelve poems, I call
it ORANGES. And one day in a gallery
I see Mike's painting, called SARDINES.

1957

A Step Away from Them

It's my lunch hour, so I go
for a walk among the hum-colored
cabs. First, down the sidewalk
where laborers feed their dirty
glistening torsos sandwiches   5
and Coca-Cola, with yellow helmets
on. They protect them from falling
bricks, I guess. Then onto the
avenue where skirts are flipping
above heels and blow up over   10
grates. The sun is hot, but the
cabs stir up the air. I look
at bargains in wristwatches. There
are cats playing in sawdust.
              On   15
to Times Square, where the sign
blows smoke over my head,[1] and higher
the waterfall pours lightly. A
Negro stands in a doorway with a
toothpick, languorously agitating.   20
A blonde chorus girl clicks: he
smiles and rubs his chin. Everything
suddenly honks: it is 12:40 of
a Thursday.
              Neon in daylight is a   25
great pleasure, as Edwin Denby[2] would
write, as are light bulbs in daylight.
I stop for a cheeseburger at JULIET's
CORNER. Giulietta Masina, wife of
Federico Fellini, è bell' attrice.[3]   30
And chocolate malted. A lady in
foxes on such a day puts her poodle
in a cab.
              There are several Puerto
Ricans on the avenue today, which   35
makes it beautiful and warm. First
Bunny died, then John Latouche,
then Jackson Pollock.[4] But is the
earth as full as life was full, of them?
And one has eaten and one walks,   40
past the magazines with nudes

1. Famous steam-puffing billboard, advertising cigarettes.
2. Fellow poet (1903–1983) and influential ballet critic.
3. Is [a] beautiful actress (Italian). Masina (1921–1994), Italian film actress, starred in many films by her husband, the Italian filmmaker Fellini (1920–1993), including *Juliet of the Spirits* (1965).
4. Abstract expressionist painter (1912–1956), considered the originator of "action" painting. "Bunny": V. R. Lang (1924–1956), poet and director of The Poet's Theater in Cambridge, Massachusetts, where she produced several of O'Hara's plays. Latouche (1917–1956), lyricist for several New York musicals, such as *The Golden Apple*. All three were gifted friends of the poet who met tragic deaths.

and the posters for bullfight and
the Manhattan Storage Warehouse,
which they'll soon tear down. I
used to think they had the Armory   45
Show[5] there.
        A glass of papaya juice
and back to work. My heart is in my
pocket, it is Poems by Pierre Reverdy.[6]

1956   1964

The Day Lady[1] Died

It is 12:20 in New York a Friday
three days after Bastille day,[2] yes
it is 1959 and I go get a shoeshine
because I will get off the 4:19 in Easthampton[3]
at 7:15 and then go straight to dinner   5
and I don't know the people who will feed me

I walk up the muggy street beginning to sun
and have a hamburger and a malted and buy
an ugly new world writing to see what the poets
in Ghana are doing these days   10
                I go on to the bank
and Miss Stillwagon (first name Linda I once heard)
doesn't even look up my balance for once in her life
and in the GOLDEN GRIFFIN I get a little Verlaine
for Patsy[4] with drawings by Bonnard although I do   15
think of Hesiod, trans. Richmond Lattimore or
Brendan Behan's new play or Le Balcon or Les Nègres
of Genet,[5] but I don't, I stick with Verlaine
after practically going to sleep with quandariness

and for Mike I just stroll into the PARK LANE   20
Liquor Store and ask for a bottle of Strega and
then I go back where I came from to 6th Avenue
and the tobacconist in the Ziegfeld Theatre and
casually ask for a carton of Gauloises and a carton
of Picayunes, and a NEW YORK POST with her face on it   25

---

5. Site in 1913 of the influential and controversial first American showing of European postimpressionist painters.
6. French poet (1899–1960) whose work strongly influenced O'Hara's writing.
1. Billie Holiday (1915–1959), also known as Lady Day, classic blues and jazz singer.
2. July 14, the French national holiday.
3. Town in eastern Long Island, a summer resort then popular among New York artists.
4. Patsy Southgate, an artist and friend of the poet. "Golden Griffin": a bookstore that was

located close to the Museum of Modern Art. "Verlaine": Paul Verlaine (1844–1896), French poet.
5. Plays (The Balcony and The Blacks, both 1955) by the French writer Jean Genet (1910–1986?), whose subjects were often the homosexual world and the lives of the dispossessed. "Bonnard": Pierre Bonnard (1867–1947), French painter and printmaker. "Hesiod": early Greek poet (c. 700 B.C.E.) and author of Works and Days, translated by the American poet Richmond Lattimore (1906–1984). Brendan Behan (1923–1964), Irish writer and dramatist.

and I am sweating a lot by now and thinking of
leaning on the john door in the 5 SPOT
while she whispered a song along the keyboard
to Mal Waldron[6] and everyone and I stopped breathing

1959   1960

A True Account of Talking to the Sun at Fire Island

The Sun woke me this morning loud
and clear, saying "Hey! I've been
trying to wake you up for fifteen
minutes. Don't be so rude, you are
only the second poet I've ever chosen   5
to speak to personally
                        so why
aren't you more attentive? If I could
burn you through the window I would
to wake you up. I can't hang around   10
here all day."
                "Sorry, Sun, I stayed
up late last night talking to Hal."

"When I woke up Mayakovsky[1] he was
a lot more prompt" the Sun said   15
petulantly. "Most people are up
already waiting to see if I'm going
to put in an appearance."
                        I tried
to apologize "I missed you yesterday."   20
"That's better" he said. "I didn't
know you'd come out." "You may be
wondering why I've come so close?"
"Yes" I said beginning to feel hot
wondering if maybe he wasn't burning me   25
anyway.
            "Frankly I wanted to tell you
I like your poetry. I see a lot
on my rounds and you're okay. You may
not be the greatest thing on earth, but   30
you're different. Now, I've heard some
say you're crazy, they being excessively
calm themselves to my mind, and other
crazy poets think that you're a boring
reactionary. Not me.   35
                    Just keep on
like I do and pay no attention. You'll

6. Billie Holiday's accompanist (1926–2002).   poet and representative of early 20th-century
1. Vladimir Mayakovsky (1893–1930), Russian   Futurism.

find that people always will complain
about the atmosphere, either too hot
or too cold too bright or too dark, days   40
too short or too long.
                    If you don't appear
at all one day they think you're lazy
or dead. Just keep right on, I like it.

And don't worry about your lineage   45
poetic or natural. The Sun shines on
the jungle, you know, on the tundra
the sea, the ghetto. Wherever you were
I knew it and saw you moving. I was waiting
for you to get to work.   50

                    And now that you
are making your own days, so to speak,
even if no one reads you but me
you won't be depressed. Not
everyone can look up, even at me. It   55
hurts their eyes."
                    "Oh Sun, I'm so grateful to you!"

"Thanks and remember I'm watching. It's
easier for me to speak to you out
here. I don't have to slide down   60
between buildings to get your ear.
I know you love Manhattan, but
you ought to look up more often.
                    And
always embrace things, people earth   65
sky stars, as I do, freely and with
the appropriate sense of space. That
is your inclination, known in the heavens
and you should follow it to hell, if
necessary, which I doubt.   70
                    Maybe we'll
speak again in Africa, of which I too
am specially fond. Go back to sleep now
Frank, and I may leave a tiny poem
in that brain of yours as my farewell."   75

"Sun, don't go!" I was awake
at last. "No, go I must, they're calling
me."
          "Who are they?"
                    Rising he said "Some   80
day you'll know. They're calling to you
too." Darkly he rose, and then I slept.

                                        1971

GALWAY KINNELL
b. 1927

I n a 1971 interview Galway Kinnell praised Walt Whitman's *Song of Myself*: "The final action of the poem where Whitman dissolves into the air and into the ground, is for me one of the great moments of self-transcendence in poetry. In one way or another, consciously or not, all poems try to pass beyond the self." This capacity for self-transcendence is dramatized in Kinnell's work, where he enters the lives of animals ("The Porcupine," "The Bear") and experiences himself as part of the natural world, like the flower he speaks for in "Flower Herding on Mount Monadnock." "Part of poetry's usefulness in the world," he has said, "is that it pays some of our huge unpaid tribute to the things and creatures that share the earth with us." His work moves between a vivid sense of the world's physical actuality and an equally vivid sense of its dissolution, for mortality is Kinnell's great theme. It appears in his work both as extinction and as "the flowing away into the universe which we desire." This theme is worked out at length in his sequence *The Book of Nightmares* (1978).

Kinnell grew up in Providence, Rhode Island, and attended Princeton University, where he and a classmate, W. S. Merwin, sometimes read each other their poems. He has written continuously since that time, combining his life of poetry with political commitments. Kinnell has been director of an adult-education program in Chicago, a journalist in Iran, and a field-worker for the Congress of Racial Equality in Louisiana. More recently, he has taught at a large number of colleges and universities.

Kinnell's experiences working for voter registration in the South in the 1960s make their way into his long poem "The Last River" (*Body Rags*, 1969). Over the years Kinnell has frequently written poems that unite personal life with the events of the nation. His work includes powerful war poems such as "Vapor Trail Reflected in the Frog Pond" and "The Dead Shall Be Raised Incorruptible," and in "The Past" (1985) he meditates on, and imagines his way into, the consequences of the dropping of the atomic bombs on Hiroshima and Nagasaki. Elsewhere he has suggested that poetry is an alternative to a technological world in which domination of nature represses the knowledge of death. In 1994 his collection *Imperfect Thirst* extended his meditation on mortality into the arena of family history and personal memory. In a moving poem, "Neverland," on his sister's confrontation with death's agony and mystery, the last words she speaks are, "Now is when the point of the story changes."

Kinnell's earliest work, as seen in *What a Kingdom It Was* (1960) and *First Poems 1946–1954* (1970), is formally intricate. The course of his career has been a movement to a looser line, a more uncluttered diction. His sense of form arises from what he calls the "inner shape" of the poem: "saying in its own music what matters most." Over the years he has come to write poems that maintain musicality and a richness of language while never departing too far from the speaking voice. Kinnell's attraction to the nonhuman world, which may remind us of Theodore Roethke and Gary Snyder, gives his work a vivid sense of life's diversity. But he has sometimes elevated the instinctual at the expense of a shaping, conscious awareness and has written as if the very need for poetic form were, in and of itself, repressive. The finest of Kinnell's poems combine self-transcendence with self-awareness in rhythms that convey a powerful physical energy and an empathetic imagination. His description of Whitman can serve as a description of Kinnell's best work: "All his feelings for existence, for himself, for his own place, come out in what he says about them. . . . He rescues these things from death and lets them live in his poems and, in turn, they save him from incoherence and silence."

The Porcupine

1

Fatted
on herbs, swollen on crabapples,
puffed up on bast and phloem,[1] ballooned
on willow flowers, poplar catkins, first
leafs of aspen and larch,   5
the porcupine
drags and bounces his last meal through ice,
mud, roses and goldenrod, into the stubbly high fields.

2

In character
he resembles us in seven ways: 10
he puts his mark on outhouses,
he alchemizes by moonlight,
he shits on the run,
he uses his tail for climbing,
he chuckles softly to himself when scared,   15
he's overcrowded if there's more than one of him per five acres,
his eyes have their own inner redness.

3

Digger of
goings across floors, of hesitations
at thresholds, of   20
handprints of dread
at doorpost or window jamb, he would
gouge the world
empty of us, hack and crater
it   25
until it is nothing, if that
could rinse it of all our sweat and pathos.

Adorer of ax
handles aflow with grain, of arms
of Morris chairs,[2] of hand   30
crafted objects
steeped in the juice of fingertips,
of surfaces wetted down
with fist grease and elbow oil,
of clothespins that have   35
grabbed our body-rags by underarm and crotch . . .

1. I.e., on plant tissues.   2. Easy chairs.

Unimpressed—bored—
by the whirl of the stars, by *these*
he's astonished, ultra-
Rilkean[3] angel!   40

for whom the true
portion of the sweetness of earth
is one of-those bottom-heavy, glittering, saccadic
bits
of salt water that splash down   45
the haunted ravines of a human face.

4

A farmer shot a porcupine three times
as it dozed on a tree limb. On
the way down it tore open its belly
on a broken   50
branch, hooked its gut,
and went on falling. On the ground
it sprang to its feet, and
paying out gut heaved
and spartled[4] through a hundred feet of goldenrod   55
before
the abrupt emptiness.

5

The Avesta[5]
puts porcupine killers
into hell for nine generations, sentencing them   60
to gnaw out
each other's hearts for the
salts of desire.

I roll
this way and that in the great bed, under   65
the quilt
that mimics this country of broken farms and woods,
the fatty sheath of the man
melting off,
the self-stabbing coil   70
of bristles reversing, blossoming outward—
a red-eyed, hard-toothed, arrow-stuck urchin
tossing up mattress feathers,
pricking the
woman beside me until she cries.   75

---

3. The German poet Rainer Maria Rilke (1875–
1926) wrote in a letter that "the 'angel' of [Rilke's
Duino] Elegies has nothing to do with the angel of
the Christian heaven. . . . The angel of the Elegies
is that being which stands for the idea of recognizing a higher order of reality in invisibility."
4. Variant of "sprottle," to sprawl or struggle
helplessly.
5. Book of the sacred writings of Zoroastrian-
ism, a Persian religion.

6

In my time I have
crouched, quills erected,
Saint
Sebastian[6] of the
scared heart, and been
beat dead with a locust club   80
on the bare snout.
And fallen from high places
I have fled, have
jogged   85
over fields of goldenrod,
terrified, seeking home,
and among flowers
I have come to myself empty, the rope
strung out behind me   90
in the fall sun
suddenly glorified with all my blood.

7

And tonight I think I prowl broken
skulled or vacant as a
sucked egg in the wintry meadow, softly chuckling, blank   95
template of myself, dragging
a starved belly through the lichflowered acres,
where
burdock looses the ark of its seed
and thistle holds up its lost blooms   100
and rosebushes in the wind scrape their dead limbs
for the forced-fire
of roses.

                                                                              1969

Blackberry Eating

I love to go out in late September
among the fat, overripe, icy, black blackberries
to eat blackberries for breakfast,
the stalks very prickly, a penalty
they earn for knowing the black art   5
of blackberry-making; and as I stand among them
lifting the stalks to my mouth, the ripest berries
fall almost unbidden to my tongue,
as words sometimes do, certain peculiar words

---

6. Early Christian saint and martyr (d. 288); he was shot full of arrows by an execution squad and miraculously survived, only to be beaten to death later.

like *strengths* or *squinched*,   10
many-lettered, one-syllabled lumps,
which I squeeze, squinch open, and splurge well
in the silent, startled, icy, black language
of blackberry-eating in late September.

                                                                   1980

After Making Love We Hear Footsteps

For I can snore like a bullhorn
or play loud music
or sit up talking with any reasonably sober Irishman
and Fergus will only sink deeper
into his dreamless sleep, which goes by all in one flash,   5
but let there be that heavy breathing
or a stifled come-cry anywhere in the house
and he will wrench himself awake
and make for it on the run—as now, we lie together,
after making love, quiet, touching along the length of our bodies,   10
familiar touch of the long-married,
and he appears—in his baseball pajamas, it happens,
the neck opening so small he has to screw them on—
and flops down between us and hugs us and snuggles himself to sleep,
his face gleaming with satisfaction at being this very child.   15

In the half darkness we look at each other
and smile
and touch arms across this little, startlingly muscled body—
this one whom habit of memory propels to the ground of his making,
sleeper only the mortal sounds can sing awake,   20
this blessing love gives again into our arms.

                                                                   1980

Cemetery Angels

On these cold days
they stand over
our dead, who will
erupt into flower as soon
as memory and human shape   5
rot out of them, each bent
forward and with wings
partly opened as though
warming itself at a fire.

                                                                   1985

Neverland[1]

Bending over her bed, I saw the smile
I must have seen when gaping up from the crib.
Knowing death comes, imagining it,
may be a fair price for consciousness.
But looking at my sister, I wished   5
she could have been snatched up
to die by surprise, without ever knowing about death.
Too late. Wendy said, "I am in three parts.
Here on the left is red. That is pain.
On the right is yellow. That is exhaustion.   10
The rest is white. I don't know yet what white is."
For most people, one day everything is all right.
The next, the limbic node[2] catches fire. The day after,
the malleus in one ear starts missing the incus.[3]
Then the arthritic opposable thumb no longer opposes   15
whoever screwed the top onto the jam jar.
Then the coraco-humeral ligament[4] frizzles apart,
the liver speckles, the kidneys dent,
two toes lose their souls. Of course,
before things get worse, a person could run.   20
I could take off right now, climb the pure forms
that surmount time and death, follow a line
down Avenue D, make a 90° turn right on 8th Street,
90° left on C, right on 7th, left on B, then cross
to Sixth Avenue, catch the A train to Nassau,   25
the station where the A pulls up beside the Z,[5]
get off, hop on the Z, hurtle under the river
and rise on Euclid under the stars and taste,
with my sweetheart, in perfectly circular kisses,
the actual saliva of paradise.   30
Then, as if Wendy suddenly understood
this flaw in me, that I could die
still wanting what is not to be had here, drink
and drink and yet have most of my thirst
intact for the water table, she opened her eyes.   35
"I want you to know I'm not afraid of dying,"
she said. "I just wish it didn't take so long."
Seeing her look so young and begin to die
all on her own, I wanted to whisk her off.
Quickly she said, "Let's go home." From outside   40
in the driveway came the gargling noise
of a starter motor, and a low steady rumbling, as if
my car had turned itself on and was warming up the engine.
She said this as if we had gone over to visit

1. A fictional island associated with immortality
and eternal childhood in the play *Peter Pan*, by
the Scottish writer J. M. Barrie (1860–1937).
One of the play's central characters, Wendy,
bears the same name as Kinnell's sister.
2. Brain structure responsible for emotion and
motivation.
3. Middle bone of the middle ear, also called the
anvil. "Malleus": outermost bone of the middle
ear.
4. Shoulder ligament.
5. New York City streets and subway trains.

a friend, to sign our names on the cast   45
on the leg she broke swinging on our swing,
and some awful indoor game had gone wrong,
and Wendy had turned to me and said, "Let's go home."
She had closed her eyes. She looked entirely white.
Her hair had been white for years; in her illness   50
her skin became as if powdered with twice-bleached flour;
now her lips seemed to have lost their blood.
Color flashed only when she opened her eyes.
Snow will come down next winter, in the woods;
the fallen trees will have that flesh on their bones.   55
When the eye of the woods opens, a bluejay shuttles.
Outside, suddenly, all was quiet, and
I realized my car had shut off its engine.
Now a spot of rosiness showed in each of her cheeks:
blushes, perhaps, at a joy she had kept from us,   60
from somewhere in her life, perhaps two mouths,
hers and a beloved's, near each other, like roses
sticking out of a bottle of invisible water.
She was losing the half-given, half-learned
art of speech, and it became for her a struggle   65
to find words, form them, position them,
then quickly utter them. After much effort
she said, "Now is when the point of the story changes."
After that, one eye at a time, the left listened,
and drifted, the right focused, gleamed   70
meanings at me, drifted. Stalwart,
the halves of the brain, especially the right.
Now, as they ratchet the box holding
her body into the earth, a voice calls
back across the region she passes through,   75
in prolonged, even notes that swell and diminish.
Now it sounds from under the farthest horizon,
and now it grows faint, and now I cannot hear it.

                                                               1994

JOHN ASHBERY
b. 1927

John Ashbery has described his writing this way: "I think that any one of my poems might be considered to be a snapshot of whatever is going on in my mind at the time—first of all the desire to write a poem, after that wondering if I've left the oven on or thinking about where I must be in the next hour." Ashbery has developed a style hospitable to quicksilver changes in tone and attention. His work often moves freely between different modes of discourse, between a language of popular culture and commonplace experience and a heightened rhetoric often associated with poetic vision. Ashbery's poems show an awareness of the various linguistic codes (including clichés and conventional public speech) by which we live and through which we define ourselves. This awareness includes an interest in what he has called "prose voices," and he has often written in a way that challenges the supposed boundaries between poetry and prose.

Ashbery's poetry was not always so open to contradictory notions and impulses. His early books rejected the mere surfaces of realism and the momentary in order to get at "remoter areas of consciousness." The protagonist of "Illustration" (from his first book, *Some Trees*) is a cheerful nun about to leave behind the irrelevancies of the world by leaping from a skyscraper. Her act implies "Much that is beautiful must be discarded / So that we may resemble a taller / impression of ourselves." To reach the "remoter areas of consciousness," Ashbery tried various technical experiments. He used highly patterned forms such as the sestina in "Some Trees" and "The Tennis Court Oath" (1962) not with any show of mechanical brilliance but to explore: "I once told somebody that writing a sestina was rather like riding downhill on a bicycle and having the pedals push your feet. I wanted my feet to be pushed into places they wouldn't normally have taken."

Ashbery was born in Rochester, New York. He attended Deerfield Academy and Harvard, from which he graduated in 1949. He received an M.A. in English from Columbia in 1951. After a preliminary stay in France as a Fulbright scholar, he returned in 1958 for eight years and was art critic for the European edition of the *New York Herald Tribune* and reported the European shows and exhibitions for *Art News* and *Arts International*. He returned to New York in 1965 to be executive editor of *Art News*, a position he held until 1972. Since then he has been professor of English in the creative writing program of Brooklyn College and art critic for *Newsweek* magazine.

Ashbery's interest in art played a formative role in his poetry. He is often associated with Frank O'Hara, James Schuyler, and Kenneth Koch as part of the "New York school" of poets. The name refers to their common interest in the New York school of abstract painters of the 1940s and 1950s, some of whose techniques they wished to adapt to poetry. These painters avoided realism in order to stress the work of art as a representation of the creative act that produced it—as in the action paintings of Jackson Pollock. Ashbery's long poem *Self-Portrait in a Convex Mirror* gives as much attention to the rapidly changing feelings of the poet in the act of writing his poem as it does to the Renaissance painting that inspired him. The poem moves back and forth between the distracted energies that feed a work of art and the completed composition, which the artist feels as both a triumph and a falsification of complex feelings. Ashbery shares with O'Hara a sense of the colloquial brilliance of daily life in New York and sets this in tension with the concentration and stasis of art.

Self-Portrait in a Convex Mirror (1975) was followed by *Houseboat Days* (1977), *As We Know* (1979), *Shadow Train* (1981), and *A Wave* (1984). His important book-length poem, *Flow Chart*, appeared in 1991 followed by collections of shorter poems, *And the Stars Were Shining* (1995), *Your Name Here* (2000) and *A Worldly Country* (2007). *Notes From the Air* (2007) is a collection of his later poems. His entertaining and provocative *Other Traditions* (2000) is a collection of his Norton Lectures on poetry at Harvard. Ashbery's work, especially his earlier, more highly experimental poems, has become particularly influential for a younger generation identified as "Language" poets, such as Charles Bernstein, Lyn Hejinian, Michael Palmer, and Susan Howe. They have been attracted to the linguistic playfulness of Ashbery's poetry and to its resistance to being read as a single, personal voice. Exposing and sometimes breaking through the world's dominant uses of language, Ashbery's poems open new possibilities of meaning: "We are all talkers / It is true, but underneath the talk lies / The moving and not wanting to be moved, the loose / Meaning, untidy and simple like the threshing floor" ("Soonest Mended").

Illustration

I

A novice[1] was sitting on a cornice
High over the city. Angels

Combined their prayers with those
Of the police, begging her to come off it.

One lady promised to be her friend.   5
"I do not want a friend," she said.

A mother offered her some nylons
Stripped from her very legs. Others brought

Little offerings of fruit and candy,
The blind man all his flowers. If any   10

Could be called successful, these were,
For that the scene should be a ceremony

Was what she wanted. "I desire
Monuments," she said. "I want to move

Figuratively, as waves caress   15
The thoughtless shore. You people I know

Will offer me every good thing
I do not want. But please remember

I died accepting them." With that, the wind
Unpinned her bulky robes, and naked   20

As a roc's[2] egg, she drifted softly downward
Out of the angels' tenderness and the minds of men.

II

Much that is beautiful must be discarded
So that we may resemble a taller

Impression of ourselves. Moths climb in the flame,   25
Alas, that wish only to be the flame:

They do not lessen our stature.
We twinkle under the weight

---

1. Student in the first stage of instruction to be a
nun.

2. Legendary bird of prey.

Of indiscretions. But how could we tell
That of the truth we know, she was   30

The somber vestment? For that night, rockets sighed
Elegantly over the city, and there was feasting:

There is so much in that moment!
So many attitudes toward that flame,

We might have soared from earth, watching her glide   35
Aloft, in her peplum³ of bright leaves.

But she, of course, was only an effigy
Of indifference, a miracle

Not meant for us, as the leaves are not
Winter's because it is the end.   40

                                                                      1956

Soonest Mended

Barely tolerated, living on the margin
In our technological society, we were always having to be rescued
On the brink of destruction, like heroines in *Orlando Furioso*¹
Before it was time to start all over again.
There would be thunder in the bushes, a rustling of coils,   5
And Angelica, in the Ingres painting,² was considering
The colorful but small monster near her toe, as though wondering
      whether forgetting
The whole thing might not, in the end, be the only solution.
And then there always came a time when
Happy Hooligan³ in his rusted green automobile   10
Came plowing down the course, just to make sure everything was O.K.,
Only by that time we were in another chapter and confused
About how to receive this latest piece of information.
Was it information? Weren't we rather acting this out
For someone else's benefit, thoughts in a mind   15
With room enough and to spare for our little problems (so they began
      to seem),
Our daily quandary about food and the rent and bills to be paid?
To reduce all this to a small variant,
To step free at last, minuscule on the gigantic plateau—
This was our ambition: to be small and clear and free.   20

3. In ancient Greece a drapery about the upper part of the body.
1. Fantastical epic poem by Ludovico Ariosto (1474–1533), whose romantic heroine Angelica is constantly being rescued from imminent perils such as monsters and storms at sea.

2. *Roger Delivering Angelica* (1819), a painting based on a scene from Ariosto, by French artist Jean-Auguste-Dominique Ingres (1780–1867).
3. The good-natured, simple title character of a popular comic strip of the 1920s and 1930s.

Alas, the summer's energy wanes quickly.
A moment and it is gone. And no longer
May we make the necessary arrangements, simple as they are.
Our star was brighter perhaps when it had water in it.
Now there is no question even of that, but only   25
Of holding on to the hard earth so as not to get thrown off,
With an occasional dream, a vision: a robin flies across
The upper corner of the window, you brush your hair away
And cannot quite see, or a wound will flash
Against the sweet faces of the others, something like: 30
This is what you wanted to hear, so why
Did you think of listening to something else? We are all talkers
It is true, but underneath the talk lies
The moving and not wanting to be moved, the loose
Meaning, untidy and simple like a threshing floor.[4]   35

These then were some hazards of the course,
Yet though we knew the course *was* hazards and nothing else
It was still a shock when, almost a quarter of a century later,
The clarity of the rules dawned on you for the first time.
They were the players, and we who had struggled at the game   40
Were merely spectators, though subject to its vicissitudes
And moving with it out of the tearful stadium, borne on shoulders,
    at last.
Night after night this message returns, repeated
In the flickering bulbs of the sky, raised past us, taken away from us,
Yet ours over and over until the end that is past truth,   45
The being of our sentences, in the climate that fostered them,
Not ours to own, like a book, but to be with, and sometimes
To be without, alone and desperate.
But the fantasy makes it ours, a kind of fence-sitting
Raised to the level of an esthetic ideal. These were moments, years,   50
Solid with reality, faces, namable events, kisses, heroic acts,
But like the friendly beginning of a geometrical progression
Not too reassuring, as though meaning could be cast aside some day
When it had been outgrown. Better, you said, to stay cowering
Like this in the early lessons, since the promise of learning   55
Is a delusion, and I agreed, adding that
Tomorrow would alter the sense of what had already been learned,
That the learning process is extended in this way, so that from this
    standpoint
None of us ever graduates from college,
For time is an emulsion,[5] and probably thinking not to grow up   60
Is the brightest kind of maturity for us, right now at any rate.
And you see, both of us were right, though nothing
Has somehow come to nothing; the avatars[6]
Of our conforming to the rules and living
Around the home have made—well, in a sense, "good citizens" of us,   65
Brushing the teeth and all that, and learning to accept

4. Used at harvest time to separate the wheat from the chaff, which is to be discarded.
5. A chemical solution in which the particles of one liquid are suspended in another.
6. Incarnations.

The charity of the hard moments as they are doled out,
For this is action, this not being sure, this careless
Preparing, sowing the seeds crooked in the furrow,
Making ready to forget, and always coming back   70
To the mooring of starting out, that day so long ago.

1970

Self-Portrait in a Convex Mirror[1]

As Parmigianino did it, the right hand
Bigger than the head, thrust at the viewer
And swerving easily away, as though to protect
What it advertises. A few leaded panes, old beams,
Fur, pleated muslin, a coral ring run together   5
In a movement supporting the face, which swims
Toward and away like the hand
Except that it is in repose. It is what is
Sequestered. Vasari[2] says, "Francesco one day set himself
To take his own portrait, looking at himself for that purpose   10
In a convex mirror, such as is used by barbers . . .
He accordingly caused a ball of wood to be made
By a turner, and having divided it in half and
Brought it to the size of the mirror, he set himself
With great art to copy all that he saw in the glass,"   15
Chiefly his reflection, of which the portrait
Is the reflection once removed.
The glass chose to reflect only what he saw
Which was enough for his purpose: his image
Glazed, embalmed, projected at a 180-degree angle.   20
The time of day or the density of the light
Adhering to the face keeps it
Lively and intact in a recurring wave
Of arrival. The soul establishes itself.
But how far can it swim out through the eyes   25
And still return safely to its nest? The surface
Of the mirror being convex, the distance increases
Significantly; that is, enough to make the point
That the soul is a captive, treated humanely, kept
In suspension, unable to advance much farther   30
Than your look as it intercepts the picture.
Pope Clement and his court were "stupefied"
By it,[3] according to Vasari, and promised a commission
That never materialized. The soul has to stay where it is,

---

1. This self-portrait, by the Italian Mannerist Parmigianino (Girolamo Francesco Mazzola, 1503–1540) on a convex piece of poplar wood, hangs in the Kunsthistorisches Museum in Vienna.
2. Giorgio Vasari (1511–1574), Italian architect, painter, and art historian whose *Lives of the Most*

Eminent Italian Painters, Sculptors, and Architects is the principal source of information about those artists.
3. When Parmigianino moved from his native Parma to Rome in 1524, he presented the self-portrait to Pope Clement VII as a credential for papal patronage.

Even though restless, hearing raindrops at the pane,   35
The sighing of autumn leaves thrashed by the wind,
Longing to be free, outside, but it must stay
Posing in this place. It must move
As little as possible. This is what the portrait says.
But there is in that gaze a combination   40
Of tenderness, amusement and regret, so powerful
In its restraint that one cannot look for long.
The secret is too plain. The pity of it smarts,
Makes hot tears spurt: that the soul is not a soul,
Has no secret, is small, and it fits   45
Its hollow perfectly: its room, our moment of attention.
That is the tune but there are no words.
The words are only speculation
(From the Latin *speculum*, mirror):
They seek and cannot find the meaning of the music.   50
We see only postures of the dream,
Riders of the motion that swings the face
Into view under evening skies, with no
False disarray as proof of authenticity.
But it is life englobed.   55
One would like to stick one's hand
Out of the globe, but its dimension,
What carries it, will not allow it.
No doubt it is this, not the reflex
To hide something, which makes the hand loom large   60
As it retreats slightly. There is no way
To build it flat like a section of wall:
It must join the segment of a circle,
Roving back to the body of which it seems
So unlikely a part, to fence in and shore up the face   65
On which the effort of this condition reads
Like a pinpoint of a smile, a spark
Or star one is not sure of having seen
As darkness resumes. A perverse light whose
Imperative of subtlety dooms in advance its   70
Conceit to light up: unimportant but meant.
Francesco, your hand is big enough
To wreck the sphere, and too big,
One would think, to weave delicate meshes
That only argue its further detention.   75
(Big, but not coarse, merely on another scale,
Like a dozing whale on the sea bottom
In relation to the tiny, self-important ship
On the surface.) But your eyes proclaim
That everything is surface. The surface is what's there   80
And nothing can exist except what's there.
There are no recesses in the room, only alcoves,
And the window doesn't matter much, or that
Sliver of window or mirror on the right, even
As a gauge of the weather, which in French is   85
Le temps, the word for time, and which

Follows a course wherein changes are merely
Features of the whole. The whole is stable within
Instability, a globe like ours, resting
On a pedestal of vacuum, a ping-pong ball   90
Secure on its jet of water.
And just as there are no words for the surface, that is,
No words to say what it really is, that it is not
Superficial but a visible core, then there is
No way out of the problem of pathos vs. experience.   95
You will stay on, restive, serene in
Your gesture which is neither embrace nor warning
But which holds something of both in pure
Affirmation that doesn't affirm anything.

The balloon pops, the attention   100
Turns dully away. Clouds
In the puddle stir up into sawtoothed fragments.
I think of the friends
Who came to see me, of what yesterday
Was like. A peculiar slant   105
Of memory that intrudes on the dreaming model
In the silence of the studio as he considers
Lifting the pencil to the self-portrait.
How many people came and stayed a certain time,
Uttered light or dark speech that became part of you   110
Like light behind windblown fog and sand,
Filtered and influenced by it, until no part
Remains that is surely you. Those voices in the dusk
Have told you all and still the tale goes on
In the form of memories deposited in irregular   115
Clumps of crystals. Whose curved hand controls,
Francesco, the turning seasons and the thoughts
That peel off and fly away at breathless speeds
Like the last stubborn leaves ripped
From wet branches? I see in this only the chaos   120
Of your round mirror which organizes everything
Around the polestar[4] of your eyes which are empty,
Know nothing, dream but reveal nothing.
I feel the carousel starting slowly
And going faster and faster: desk, papers, books,   125
Photographs of friends, the window and the trees
Merging in one neutral band that surrounds
Me on all sides, everywhere I look.
And I cannot explain the action of leveling,
Why it should all boil down to one   130
Uniform substance, a magma[5] of interiors.
My guide in these matters is your self,
Firm, oblique, accepting everything with the same
Wraith of a smile, and as time speeds up so that it is soon
Much later, I can know only the straight way out,   135

---

4. The North Star, hence the magnetic center.   5. Soft mixture of organic or mineral materials.

The distance between us. Long ago
The strewn evidence meant something,
The small accidents and pleasures
Of the day as it moved gracelessly on,
A housewife doing chores. Impossible now   140
To restore those properties in the silver blur that is
The record of what you accomplished by sitting down
"With great art to copy all that you saw in the glass"
So as to perfect and rule out the extraneous
Forever. In the circle of your intentions certain spars[6]   145
Remain that perpetuate the enchantment of self with self:
Eyebeams, muslin, coral. It doesn't matter
Because these are things as they are today
Before one's shadow ever grew
Out of the field into thoughts of tomorrow.   150

Tomorrow is easy, but today is uncharted,
Desolate, reluctant as any landscape
To yield what are laws of perspective
After all only to the painter's deep
Mistrust, a weak instrument though   155
Necessary. Of course some things
Are possible, it knows, but it doesn't know
Which ones. Some day we will try
To do as many things as are possible
And perhaps we shall succeed at a handful   160
Of them, but this will not have anything
To do with what is promised today, our
Landscape sweeping out from us to disappear
On the horizon. Today enough of a cover burnishes
To keep the supposition of promises together   165
In one piece of surface, letting one ramble
Back home from them so that these
Even stronger possibilities can remain
Whole without being tested. Actually
The skin of the bubble-chamber's as tough as   170
Reptile eggs; everything gets "programmed" there
In due course: more keeps getting included
Without adding to the sum, and just as one
Gets accustomed to a noise that
Kept one awake but now no longer does,   175
So the room contains this flow like an hourglass
Without varying in climate or quality
(Except perhaps to brighten bleakly and almost
Invisibly, in a focus sharpening toward death—more
Of this later). What should be the vacuum of a dream   180
Becomes continually replete as the source of dreams
Is being tapped so that this one dream
May wax, flourish like a cabbage rose,

6. Pieces of lustrous mineral; also, round timbers used to extend a sail.

Defying sumptuary laws,[7] leaving us
To awake and try to begin living in what   185
Has now become a slum. Sydney Freedberg in his
Parmigianino says of it: "Realism in this portrait
No longer produces an objective truth, but a *bizarria*[8] . . .
However its distortion does not create
A feeling of disharmony. . . . The forms retain   190
A strong measure of ideal beauty," because
Fed by our dreams, so inconsequential until one day
We notice the hole they left. Now their importance
If not their meaning is plain. They were to nourish
A dream which includes them all, as they are   195
Finally reversed in the accumulating mirror.
They seemed strange because we couldn't actually see them.
And we realize this only at a point where they lapse
Like a wave breaking on a rock, giving up
Its shape in a gesture which expresses that shape.   200
The forms retain a strong measure of ideal beauty
As they forage in secret on our idea of distortion.
Why be unhappy with this arrangement, since
Dreams prolong us as they are absorbed?
Something like living occurs, a movement   205
Out of the dream into its codification.

As I start to forget it
It presents its stereotype again
But it is an unfamiliar stereotype, the face
Riding at anchor, issued from hazards, soon   210
To accost others, "rather angel than man" (Vasari).
Perhaps an angel looks like everything
We have forgotten, I mean forgotten
Things that don't seem familiar when
We meet them again, lost beyond telling,   215
Which were ours once. This would be the point
Of invading the privacy of this man who
"Dabbled in alchemy, but whose wish
Here was not to examine the subtleties of art
In a detached, scientific spirit: he wished through them   220
To impart the sense of novelty and amazement to the spectator"
(Freedberg). Later portraits such as the Uffizi
"Gentleman," the Borghese "Young Prelate" and
The Naples "Antea" issue from Mannerist
Tensions,[9] but here, as Freedberg points out,   225
The surprise, the tension are in the concept
Rather than its realization.
The consonance of the High Renaissance[1]

7. Laws regulating private behavior, in this case mode of dress.
8. Distortion. Sydney J. Freedberg, *Parmigianino: His Works in Painting* (1950).
9. Mannerism was a style of painting in 16th-century Italy in which proportions or the laws of perspective were distorted to produce effects of tension or disturbance. "Uffizi" and "Borghese": galleries in Florence and Rome, respectively.
1. In Italian painting and architecture the period in the late 15th and early 16th centuries in which the harmonious proportions ("consonance") of classical art were emulated and honored.

Is present, though distorted by the mirror.
What is novel is the extreme care in rendering   230
The velleities[2] of the rounded reflecting surface
(It is the first mirror portrait),
So that you could be fooled for a moment
Before you realize the reflection
Isn't yours. You feel then like one of those   235
Hoffmann[3] characters who have been deprived
Of a reflection, except that the whole of me
Is seen to be supplanted by the strict
Otherness of the painter in his
Other room. We have surprised him   240
At work, but no, he has surprised us
As he works. The picture is almost finished,
The surprise almost over, as when one looks out,
Startled by a snowfall which even now is
Ending in specks and sparkles of snow.   245
It happened while you were inside, asleep,
And there is no reason why you should have
Been awake for it, except that the day
Is ending and it will be hard for you
To get to sleep tonight, at least until late.   250

The shadow of the city injects its own
Urgency: Rome where Francesco
Was at work during the Sack:[4] his inventions
Amazed the soldiers who burst in on him;
They decided to spare his life, but he left soon after;   255
Vienna where the painting is today, where
I saw it with Pierre in the summer of 1959; New York
Where I am now, which is a logarithm[5]
Of other cities. Our landscape
Is alive with filiations, shuttlings;   260
Business is carried on by look, gesture,
Hearsay. It is another life to the city,
The backing of the looking glass of the
Unidentified but precisely sketched studio. It wants
To siphon off the life of the studio, deflate   265
Its mapped space to enactments, island it.
That operation has been temporarily stalled
But something new is on the way, a new preciosity
In the wind. Can you stand it,
Francesco? Are you strong enough for it?   270
This wind brings what it knows not, is
Self-propelled, blind, has no notion

---

2. Subtle tendencies.
3. E. T. A. Hoffman (1776–1822), German author known for his tales of the supernatural.
4. In 1527 the Hapsburg emperor Charles V sacked Rome in an assertion of power against Pope Clement VII.

5. Mathematical term referring to the power to which a fixed number (the base) must be raised to obtain a given number or variable. In Ashbery's work this is less a mathematical concept than an image of the way an apparently fixed concept can multiply or divide into other forms.

Of itself. It is inertia that once
Acknowledged saps all activity, secret or public:
Whispers of the word that can't be understood   275
But can be felt, a chill, a blight
Moving outward along the capes and peninsulas
Of your nervures and so to the archipelagoes
And to the bathed, aired secrecy of the open sea.
This is its negative side. Its positive side is   280
Making you notice life and the stresses
That only seemed to go away, but now,
As this new mode questions, are seen to be
Hastening out of style. If they are to become classics
They must decide which side they are on.   285
Their reticence has undermined
The urban scenery, made its ambiguities
Look willful and tired, the games of an old man.
What we need now is this unlikely
Challenger pounding on the gates of an amazed   290
Castle. Your argument, Francesco,
Had begun to grow stale as no answer
Or answers were forthcoming. If it dissolves now
Into dust, that only means its time had come
Some time ago, but look now, and listen: 295
It may be that another life is stocked there
In recesses no one knew of; that it,
Not we, are the change; that we are in fact it
If we could get back to it, relive some of the way
It looked, turn our faces to the globe as it sets   300
And still be coming out all right:
Nerves normal, breath normal. Since it is a metaphor
Made to include us, we are a part of it and
Can live in it as in fact we have done,
Only leaving our minds bare for questioning   305
We now see will not take place at random
But in an orderly way that means to menace
Nobody—the normal way things are done,
Like the concentric growing up of days
Around a life: correctly, if you think about it.   310

A breeze like the turning of a page
Brings back your face: the moment
Takes such a big bite out of the haze
Of pleasant intuition it comes after.
The locking into place is "death itself,"   315
As Berg said of a phrase in Mahler's Ninth,[6]
Or, to quote Imogen in *Cymbeline*, "There cannot
Be a pinch in death more sharp than this,"[7] for,
Though only exercise or tactic, it carries
The momentum of a conviction that had been building.   320

---

6. Alban Berg (1885–1935), Viennese composer of twelve-tone music, speaking of the Ninth Symphony of his predecessor the Austrian com- poser Gustav Mahler (1860–1911).
7. Shakespeare, *Cymbeline* 1.1.131–32.

Mere forgetfulness cannot remove it
Nor wishing bring it back, as long as it remains
The white precipitate[8] of its dream
In the climate of sighs flung across our world,
A cloth over a birdcage. But it is certain that   325
What is beautiful seems so only in relation to a specific
Life, experienced or not, channeled into some form
Steeped in the nostalgia of a collective past.
The light sinks today with an enthusiasm
I have known elsewhere, and known why   330
It seemed meaningful, that others felt this way
Years ago. I go on consulting
This mirror that is no longer mine
For as much brisk vacancy as is to be
My portion this time. And the vase is always full   335
Because there is only just so much room
And it accommodates everything. The sample
One sees is not to be taken as
Merely that, but as everything as it
May be imagined outside time—not as a gesture   340
But as all, in the refined, assimilable state.
But what is this universe the porch of
As it veers in and out, back and forth,
Refusing to surround, us and still the only
Thing we can see? Love once   345
Tipped the scales but now is shadowed, invisible,
Though mysteriously present, around somewhere.
But we know it cannot be sandwiched
Between two adjacent moments, that its windings
Lead nowhere except to further tributaries   350
And that these empty themselves into a vague
Sense of something that can never be known
Even though it seems likely that each of us
Knows what it is and is capable of
Communicating it to the other. But the look   355
Some wear as a sign makes one want to
Push forward ignoring the apparent
Naïveté of the attempt, not caring
That no one is listening, since the light
Has been lit once and for all in their eyes   360
And is present, unimpaired, a permanent anomaly,
Awake and silent. On the surface of it
There seems no special reason why that light
Should be focused by love, or why
The city falling with its beautiful suburbs   365
Into space always less clear, less defined,
Should read as the support of its progress,
The easel upon which the drama unfolded
To its own satisfaction and to the end
Of our dreaming, as we had never imagined   370

8. In chemistry a solid deposit separated from a solution.

It would end, in worn daylight with the painted
Promise showing through as a gage, a bond.
This nondescript, never-to-be defined daytime is
The secret of where it takes place
And we can no longer return to the various   375
Conflicting statements gathered, lapses of memory
Of the principal witnesses. All we know
Is that we are a little early, that
Today has that special, lapidary[9]
Todayness that the sunlight reproduces   380
Faithfully in casting twig-shadows on blithe
Sidewalks. No previous day would have been like this.
I used to think they were all alike,
That the present always looked the same to everybody
But this confusion drains away as one   385
Is always cresting into one's present.
Yet the "poetic," straw-colored space
Of the long corridor that leads back to the painting,
Its darkening opposite—is this
Some figment of "art," not to be imagined   390
As real, let alone special? Hasn't it too its lair
In the present we are always escaping from
And falling back into, as the waterwheel of days
Pursues its uneventful, even serene course?
I think it is trying to say it is today   395
And we must get out of it even as the public
Is pushing through the museum now so as to
Be out by closing time. You can't live there.
The gray glaze of the past attacks all know-how:
Secrets of wash and finish that took a lifetime   400
To learn and are reduced to the status of
Black-and-white illustrations in a book where colorplates
Are rare. That is, all time
Reduces to no special time. No one
Alludes to the change; to do so might   405
Involve calling attention to oneself
Which would augment the dread of not getting out
Before having seen the whole collection
(Except for the sculptures in the basement:
They are where they belong).   410
Our time gets to be veiled, compromised
By the portrait's will to endure. It hints at
Our own, which we were hoping to keep hidden.
We don't need paintings or
Doggerel written by mature poets when   415
The explosion is so precise, so fine.
Is there any point even in acknowledging
The existence of all that? Does it
Exist? Certainly the leisure to
Indulge stately pastimes doesn't,   420

---

9. Gemlike, precisely cut.

Any more. Today has no margins, the event arrives
Flush with its edges, is of the same substance,
Indistinguishable. "Play" is something else;
It exists, in a society specifically
Organized as a demonstration of itself. 425
There is no other way, and those assholes
Who would confuse everything with their mirror games
Which seem to multiply stakes and possibilities, or
At least confuse issues by means of an investing
Aura that would corrode the architecture 430
Of the whole in a haze of suppressed mockery,
Are beside the point. They are out of the game,
Which doesn't exist until they are out of it.
It seems like a very hostile universe
But as the principle of each individual thing is 435
Hostile to, exists at the expense of all the others
As philosophers have often pointed out, at least
This thing, the mute, undivided present,
Has the justification of logic, which
In this instance isn't a bad thing 440
Or wouldn't be, if the way of telling
Didn't somehow intrude, twisting the end result
Into a caricature of itself. This always
Happens, as in the game where
A whispered phrase passed around the room 445
Ends up as something completely different.
It is the principle that makes works of art so unlike
What the artist intended. Often he finds
He has omitted the thing he started out to say
In the first place. Seduced by flowers, 450
Explicit pleasures, he blames himself (though
Secretly satisfied with the result), imagining
He had a say in the matter and exercised
An option of which he was hardly conscious,
Unaware that necessity circumvents such resolutions 455
So as to create something new
For itself, that there is no other way,
That the history of creation proceeds according to
Stringent laws, and that things
Do get done in this way, but never the things 460
We set out to accomplish and wanted so desperately
To see come into being. Parmigianino
Must have realized this as he worked at his
Life-obstructing task. One is forced to read
The perfectly plausible accomplishment of a purpose 465
Into the smooth, perhaps even bland (but so
Enigmatic) finish. Is there anything
To be serious about beyond this otherness
That gets included in the most ordinary
Forms of daily activity, changing everything 470
Slightly and profoundly, and tearing the matter
Of creation, any creation, not just artistic creation

Out of our hands, to install it on some monstrous, near
Peak, too close to ignore, too far
For one to intervene? This otherness, this   475
"Not-being-us" is all there is to look at
In the mirror, though no one can say
How it came to be this way. A ship
Flying unknown colors has entered the harbor.
You are allowing extraneous matters   480
To break up your day, cloud the focus
Of the crystal ball. Its scene drifts away
Like vapor scattered on the wind. The fertile
Thought-associations that until now came
So easily, appear no more, or rarely. Their   485
Colorings are less intense, washed out
By autumn rains and winds, spoiled, muddied,
Given back to you because they are worthless.
Yet we are such creatures of habit that their
Implications are still around *en permanence*, confusing   490
Issues. To be serious only about sex
Is perhaps one way, but the sands are hissing
As they approach the beginning of the big slide
Into what happened. This past
Is now here: the painter's   495
Reflected face, in which we linger, receiving
Dreams and inspirations on an unassigned
Frequency, but the hues have turned metallic,
The curves and edges are not so rich. Each person
Has one big theory to explain the universe   500
But it doesn't tell the whole story
And in the end it is what is outside him
That matters, to him and especially to us
Who have been given no help whatever
In decoding our own man-size quotient and must rely   505
On second-hand knowledge. Yet I know
That no one else's taste is going to be
Any help, and might as well be ignored.
Once it seemed so perfect—gloss on the fine
Freckled skin, lips moistened as though about to part   510
Releasing speech, and the familiar look
Of clothes and furniture that one forgets.
This could have been our paradise: exotic
Refuge within an exhausted world, but that wasn't
In the cards, because it couldn't have been   515
The point. Aping naturalness may be the first step
Toward achieving an inner calm
But it is the first step only, and often
Remains a frozen gesture of welcome etched
On the air materializing behind it,   520
A convention. And we have really
No time for these, except to use them
For kindling. The sooner they are burnt up
The better for the roles we have to play.

Therefore I beseech you, withdraw that hand,   525
Offer it no longer as shield or greeting,
The shield of a greeting, Francesco:
There is room for one bullet in the chamber:
Our looking through the wrong end
Of the telescope as you fall back at a speed   530
Faster than that of light to flatten ultimately
Among the features of the room, an invitation
Never mailed, the "it was all a dream"
Syndrome, though the "all" tells tersely
Enough how it wasn't. Its existence   535
Was real, though troubled, and the ache
Of this waking dream can never drown out
The diagram still sketched on the wind,
Chosen, meant for me and materialized
In the disguising radiance of my room.   540
We have seen the city; it is the gibbous[1]
Mirrored eye of an insect. All things happen
On its balcony and are resumed within,
But the action is the cold, syrupy flow
Of a pageant. One feels too confined,   545
Sifting the April sunlight for clues,
In the mere stillness of the ease of its
Parameter.[2] The hand holds no chalk
And each part of the whole falls off
And cannot know it knew, except   550
Here and there, in cold pockets
Of remembrance, whispers out of time.

                                                         1975

Myrtle

How funny your name would be
if you could follow it back to where
the first person thought of saying it,
naming himself that, or maybe
some other persons thought of it   5
and named that person. It would
be like following a river to its source,
which would be impossible. Rivers have no source.
They just automatically appear at a place
where they get wider, and soon a real   10
river comes along, with fish and debris,
regal as you please, and someone
has already given it a name: St. Benno[1]

1. Irregularly rounded or convex (for example, the form of the moon between half moon and full moon).
2. A constant whose values characterize the variables in a system.
1. St. Benno of Meissen (1010–1106), patron of angling.

> (saints are popular for this purpose) or, or
> some other name, the name of his   15
> long-lost girlfriend, who comes
> at long last to impersonate that river,
> on a stage, her voice clanking
> like its bed, her clothing of sand
> and pasted paper, a piece of real technology,   20
> while all along she is thinking, I can
> do what I want to do. But I want to stay here.

1996

W. S. MERWIN
b. 1927

" I started writing hymns for my father almost as soon as I could write at all, illustrating them," W. S. Merwin has said. "I recall some rather stern little pieces addressed . . . to backsliders, but I can remember too wondering whether there might not be some liberating mode." Merwin's father was a Presbyterian minister in Union, New Jersey, and Scranton, Pennsylvania, where Merwin grew up. Apart from hymn writing Merwin had almost no acquaintance with poetry until, on a scholarship, he entered Princeton University. There he read verse steadily and began to write with the encouragement of the poet John Berryman and the critic R. P. Blackmur. Then Merwin's extensive study of foreign languages and literatures enabled him to find work as a tutor abroad. He remained, like Ezra Pound, apart from American literary institutions and became a translator of European literature, especially medieval romance and modern Symbolist poetry.

Merwin's continuing activity as a translator has been a resource and stimulus for his own poetry. In translating two great medieval epics, the French *Song of Roland* (1963) and the Spanish *The Poem of the Cid* (1959), his object was to bring into English a diction "rough, spare, sinewy, rapid" that would transmit the directness and energy of the world of chivalric imagination. His first book, *A Masque for Janus* (1952), includes ballads, songs, and carols—often based on medieval verse forms—the slightly antique diction of which gives an air of simple mystery to poems about love, inner heroism, and death.

In later books Merwin drew his subjects from a more clearly contemporary context. Many of the poems in *The Drunk in the Furnace* (1960) and *The Moving Target* (1963) are about members of his family and memories of his boyhood in Scranton. A further change came with *The Lice* (1967), a volume whose brief, prophetic poems reflect Merwin's despair at that time: he believed "the future was so bleak that there was no point in writing anything at all"; what happened was that "the poems kind of pushed their way upon me when I wasn't thinking about writing." This despair and an accompanying anger are palpable in a poem like "For a Coming Extinction." In many of these poems and those of volumes immediately following, Merwin tries to reach below the surface of urban American experience but without the benefit of narrative or preestablished metrical forms. He speaks through humble figures, as in "Peasant: His Prayer to the Powers of This World." Or he uses the most commonplace occurrences as a point of departure for meditation: "Evening, or Daybreak." His poems quickly become parables, spoken in a voice concerned less with descriptive detail than with archetypal elements: the ways in which each evening prefigures death, each dawn the passing of time.

Of these short poems Merwin says: "What is needed for any particular nebulous unwritten hope that may become a poem is not a manipulable, more or less predictable recurring pattern, but an unduplicatable resonance, something that would be like an echo except that it is repeating no sound." Hence his unpunctuated lines of varying lengths, which seem a series of related oracular phrases, each corresponding to a breath. The poems frequently use the metaphor of a threshold or door, locating the reader at a moment between life and death or between life and a visionary afterlife. The poet is stationed at that imagined spot between the past and the present or between the present and the future. In 1973 he prepared *Asian Figures*, a series of adaptations of Asian proverbs, that reflect his continuing interest in compact meditative forms such as rituals and prayers.

Merwin has always been concerned with absence, with what is silent, vanished, invisible, yet real. In many of the poems gathered in his *Selected Poems* (1988) and *The Rain in the Trees* (1988), this concern focuses on forms of life endangered by ecological destruction. Merwin resides primarily in Hawaii, and his book-length narrative poem *The Folding Cliffs* (1998) explores Hawaiian history while gathering together, in his description, "almost all of my interests—interests in nonliterate peoples, in their and our relation to the earth, to the primal sources of things, our relation to the natural world, . . . the destruction of the earth for abstract and greedy reasons." Merwin's singular power in both shorter and longer poems is beautifully evident in his collection *The River Sound* (1999). His *Migration: New and Selected Poems* (2005), which gathers work from the 1960s through 2005, received the National Book Award for poetry. He has since published *Present Company* (2005) and *The Shadow of Sirius* (2008). In 2010 Merwin was appointed the seventeenth Poet Laureate Consultant in Poetry to the Library of Congress.

The Drunk in the Furnace

For a good decade
The furnace stood in the naked gully, fireless
And vacant as any hat. Then when it was
No more to them than a hulking black fossil
To erode unnoticed with the rest of the junk-hill   5
By the poisonous creek, and rapidly to be added
    To their ignorance.

They were afterwards astonished
To confirm, one morning, a twist of smoke like a pale
Resurrection, staggering out of its chewed hole,   10
And to remark then other tokens that someone,
Cosily bolted behind the eye-holed iron
Door of the drafty burner, had there established
    His bad castle.

Where he gets his spirits   15
It's a mystery. But the stuff keeps him musical:

Hammer-and-anvilling with poker and bottle
To his jugged bellowings, till the last groaning clang
As he collapses onto the rioting
Springs of a litter of car-seats ranged on the grates,   20
       To sleep like an iron pig.

       In their tar-paper church
On a text about stoke-holes that are sated never
Their Reverend lingers. They nod and hate trespassers.
When the furnace wakes, though, all afternoon   25
Their witless offspring flock like piped rats[1] to its siren
Crescendo, and agape on the crumbling ridge
       Stand in a row and learn.

                                                        1960

For the Anniversary of My Death

Every year without knowing it I have passed the day
When the last fires will wave to me
And the silence will set out
Tireless traveller
Like the beam of a lightless star   5

Then I will no longer
Find myself in life as in a strange garment
Surprised at the earth
And the love of one woman
And then shamelessness of men   10
As today writing after three days of rain
Hearing the wren sing and the falling cease
And bowing not knowing to what

                                                        1967

For a Coming Extinction

Gray whale
Now that we are sending you to The End
That great god
Tell him
That we who follow you invented forgiveness   5
And forgive nothing

I write as though you could understand
And I could say it

---

1. Allusion to the Pied Piper of Hamelin, whose piping lured the rats from the town; when he was not paid, he lured away the children as well.

One must always pretend something
Among the dying   10
When you have left the seas nodding on their stalks
Empty of you

Tell him that we were made
On another day[1]

The bewilderment will diminish like an echo   15
Winding along your inner mountains
Unheard by us
And find its way out
Leaving behind it the future
Dead   20
And ours

When you will not see again
The whale calves trying the light
Consider what you will find in the black garden
And its court   25
The sea cows the Great Auks the gorillas[2]
The irreplaceable hosts ranged countless
And fore-ordaining as stars
Our sacrifices
Join your word to theirs   30
Tell him
That it is we who are important

1967

Losing a Language

A breath leaves the sentences and does not come back
yet the old still remember something that they could say

but they know now that such things are no longer believed
and the young have fewer words

many of the things the words were about   5
no longer exist

the noun for standing in mist by a haunted tree
the verb for I

the children will not repeat
the phrases their parents speak   10

---

1. In Genesis 1 God creates humans on the sixth day and gives them dominion over all other creatures in the world. The animals had been created on the fifth and sixth days.

2. Animals extinct or endangered. Sea cows are large walruslike animals. The great auks were large flightless sea birds.

somebody has persuaded them
that it is better to say everything differently

so that they can be admired somewhere
farther and farther away

where nothing that is here is known   15
we have little to say to each other

we are wrong and dark
in the eyes of the new owners

the radio is incomprehensible
the day is glass   20

when there is a voice at the door it is foreign
everywhere instead of a name there is a lie

nobody has seen it happening
nobody remembers

this is what the words were made   25
to prophesy

here are the extinct feathers
here is the rain we saw

                                                                    1988

Lament for the Makers[1]

I that all through my early days
I remember well was always
    the youngest of the company
    save for one sister after me

from the time when I was able   5
to walk under the dinner table
    and be punished for that promptly
    because its leaves could fall on me

father and mother overhead
who they talked with and what they said   10
    were mostly clouds that knew already
    directions far too old for me

---

1. The title and stanza form of this poem are taken from the Scots poet William Dunbar (c. 1460–c. 1520), whose "Lament for the Makers" mourns the passing of fellow poets and confesses the poet's fear of mortality. Merwin's poem like- wise commemorates the passing of fellow poets, a number of whom are represented in this anthology and can be found by consulting the index. Only the names of those poets not repre- sented in this volume are annotated here.

at school I skipped a grade so that
whatever I did after that
 each year everyone would be   15
 older and hold it up to me

at college many of my friends
were returning veterans
 equipped with an authority
 I admired and they treated me   20

as the kid some years below them
so I married half to show them
 and listened with new vanity
 when I heard it said to me

how young I was and what a shock   25
I was the youngest on the block
 I thought I had it coming to me
 and I believe it mattered to me

and seemed my own and there to stay
for a while then came the day   30
 I was in another country
 other older friends around me

my youth by then taken for granted
and found that it had been supplanted
 the notes in some anthology   35
 listed persons born after me

how long had that been going on
how could I be not quite so young
 and not notice and nobody
 even bother to inform me   40

though my fond hopes were taking longer
than I had hoped when I was younger
 a phrase that came more frequently
 to suggest itself to me

but the secret was still there   45
safe in the unprotected air
 that breath that in its own words only
 sang when I was a child to me

and caught me helpless to convey it
with nothing but the words to say it   50
 though it was those words completely
 and they rang it was clear to me

with a changeless overtone
I have listened for since then

hearing that note endlessly   55
vary every time beyond me

trying to find where it comes from
and to what words it may come
    and forever after be
    present for the thought kept at me   60

that my mother and every day
of our lives would slip away
    like the summer and suddenly
    all would have been taken from me

but that presence I had known   65
sometimes in words would not be gone
    and if it spoke even once for me
    it would stay there and be me

however few might choose those words
for listening to afterwards   70
    there I would be awake to see
    a world that looked unchanged to me

I suppose that was what I thought
young as I was then and that note
    sang from the words of somebody   75
    in my twenties I looked around me

to all the poets who were then
living and whose lines had been
    sustenance and company
    and a light for years to me   80

I found the portraits of their faces
first in the rows of oval spaces
    in Oscar Williams' *Treasury*[2]
    so they were settled long before me

and they would always be the same   85
in that distance of their fame
    affixed in immortality
    during their lifetimes while around me

all was woods seen from a train
no sooner glimpsed than gone again   90
    but those immortals constantly
    in some measure reassured me

2. Oscar Williams's *A Little Treasury of Modern Poetry* (1950), an anthology containing some of the major English and American modernists, featured on its cover oval portraits of the poets represented.

then first there was Dylan Thomas
from the White Horse[3] taken from us
　　to the brick wall I woke to see　　　　　　　95
　　for years across the street from me

then word of the death of Stevens
brought a new knowledge of silence
　　the nothing but there finally
　　the sparrow saying *Be thou me*　　　　　　100

how long his long auroras had
played on the darkness overhead
　　since I looked up from my Shelley
　　and Arrowsmith[4] first showed him to me

and not long from his death until　　　　　　　105
Edwin Muir[5] had fallen still
　　that fine bell of the latter day
　　not well heard yet it seems to me

Sylvia Plath then took her own
direction into the unknown　　　　　　　　　110
　　from her last stars and poetry
　　in the house a few blocks from me

Williams[6] a little afterwards
was carried off by the black rapids
　　that flowed through Paterson as he　　　　　115
　　said and their rushing sound is in me

that was the time that gathered Frost[7]
into the dark where he was lost
　　to us but from too far to see
　　his voice keeps coming back to me　　　　　120

at the number he had uttered
to the driver a last word
　　then that watchful and most lonely
　　wanderer whose words went with me

　　　　everywhere Elizabeth　　　　　　　125
　　　　Bishop lay alone in death

3. Thomas (1914–1953), a Welsh poet, collapsed at the White Horse Tavern in Greenwich Village, and subsequently died, after drinking heavily while in New York City to take part in a reading of his play, *Under Milk Wood* (1954).
4. William Arrowsmith (1924–1992), scholar and translator, was a classmate and friend of Merwin's when they were undergraduates at Princeton University. "Be Thou Me" appears in canto VI of "It Must Change," from Wallace Stevens's long poem *Notes Toward a Supreme Fiction*: "Bethou me, said sparrow, to the crackled blade, / And you, and you, bethou me as you blow, / When in my coppice you behold me be." Stevens (1879–1955) is echoing canto V of Percy Bysshe Shelley (1792–1822), "Ode to the West Wind": "Be thou, Spirit Fierce, / My spirit. Be thou me, impetuous one!" Another of Stevens's long poems is titled "The Auroras of Autumn."
5. Scottish poet (1887–1963).
6. William Carlos Williams (1883–1963), American modernist poet whose work includes the long autobiographical poem *Paterson*.
7. Robert Frost (1874–1963), American poet whose works include "Stopping by Woods on a Snowy Evening."

they were leaving the party early
our elders it came home to me

but the needle moved among us
taking always by surprise   130
   flicking by too fast to see
   to touch a friend born after me

and James Wright by his darkened river
heard the night heron pass over
   took his candle down the frosty   135
   road and disappeared before me

Howard Moss[8] had felt the gnawing
at his name and found that nothing
   made it better he was funny
   even so about it to me   140

Graves[9] in his nineties lost the score
forgot that he had died before
   found his way back innocently
   who once had been a guide to me

Nemerov[1] sadder than his verse   145
said a new year could not be worse
   then the black flukes of agony
   went down leaving the words with me

Stafford[2] watched his hand catch the light
seeing that it was time to write   150
   a memento of their story
   signed and is a plain before me

then the sudden news that Ted
Roethke had been found floating dead
   in someone's pool at night but he   155
   still rises from his lines for me

and on the rimless wheel in turn
Eliot[3] spun and Jarrell was borne
   off by a car who had loved to see
   the racetrack then there came to me   160

one day the knocking at the garden
door and the news that Berryman
   from the bridge had leapt who twenty
   years before had quoted to me

8. American poet (1922–1987).
9. Robert Graves (1895–1985), poet and translator whose work includes *The White Goddess*
(1944). As a young man Merwin worked for a
short time as a tutor for Graves's children.

1. Howard Nemerov (1920–1991), American poet.
2. William Stafford (1914–1993), American poet.
3. T. S. Eliot (1888–1965), Anglo-American modernist poet.

the passage where *a jest* wrote Crane   165
falls from the speechless caravan[4]
 with a wave to bones and Henry[5]
 and to all that he had told me

I dreamed that Auden[6] sat up in bed
but I could not catch what he said   170
 by the time he was already
 dead someone next morning told me

and Marianne Moore entered the ark
Pound[7] would say no more from the dark
 who once had helped to set me free 175
 I thought of the prose around me

and David Jones[8] would rest until
the turn of time under the hill
 but from the sleep of Arthur[9] he
 wakes an echo that follows me   180

Lowell thought the shadow skyline
coming toward him was Manhattan
 but it blacked out in the taxi
 once he read his *Notebook* to me

now Jimmy Merrill's voice is heard 185
like an aria afterward
 and we know he will never be
 old after all who spoke to me

on the cold street that last evening
of his heart that leapt at finding   190
 some yet unknown poetry
 then waved through the window to me

in that city we were born in
one by one they have all gone
 out of the time and language we 195
 had in common which have brought me

to this season after them
the best words did not keep them from
 leaving themselves finally
 as this day is going from me   200

---

4. Hart Crane (1899–1952), American poet, author of the poetic sequence *The Bridge* (1930), from which the lines in italics are taken.
5. Characters in John Berryman's *Dream Songs*, selections from which appear in this volume.
6. W. H. Auden (1907–1973), Anglo-American poet.

7. Marianne Moore (1887–1972) and Ezra Pound (1885–1972), American modernist poets.
8. Anglo-Welsh artist and poet (1895–1974).
9. The legendary King Arthur, who ruled over the Knights of the Round Table, figures in several of David Jones's poems and essays.

and the clear note they were hearing
never promised anything
   but the true sound of brevity
   that will go on after me

1996

Ceremony after an Amputation

Spirits of the place who were here before I saw it
   to whom I have made such offerings as I have known how to make
   wanting from the first to approach you with recognition
   bringing for your swept ridge trees lining the wind with seedlings
   that have grown now to become these long wings in chorus   5
   where the birds assemble and settle their flying lives
   you have taught me without meaning and have lifted me up
   without talk or promise and again and again reappeared to me
   unmistakable and changing and unpronounceable as a face

dust of the time a day in late spring after the silk of rain   10
   had fallen softly through the night and after the green morning
   the afternoon floating brushed with gold and then the sounds
   of machines erupting across the valley and elbowing up the slopes
   pushing themselves forward to occupy you to be more of you
   who remain the untouched silence through which they are passing   15
   I try to hear you remembering that we are not separate
   to find you who cannot be lost or elsewhere or incomplete

nature of the solitary machine coming into the story
   from the minds that conceived you and the hands that first
      conjured up
   the phantom of you in fine lines on the drawing board   20
   you for whom function is all the good that exists
   you to whom I have come with nothing but purpose
   a purpose of my own as though it was something we shared
   you that were pried from the earth without anyone
   consulting you and were carried off burned beaten metamorphosed 25
   according to plans and lives to which you owed nothing

let us be at peace with each other let peace be what is between us
   and you now single vanished part of my left hand bit of bone
      finger-end index
   who began with me in the dark that was already my mother
   you who touched whatever I could touch of the beginning   30
   and were how I touched and who remembered the sense of it
   when I thought I had forgotten it you in whom it waited
   under your only map of one untrodden mountain
   you who did as well as we could through all the hours at the piano
   and who helped undo the bras and found our way to the treasure   35

and who held the fruit and the pages and knew how to button
    my right cuff and to wash my left ear and had taken in
    heart beats of birds and beloved faces and hair by day and by night
    fur of dogs ears of horses tongues and the latches of doors
    so that I still feel them clearly long after they are gone   40
    and lake water beside the boat one evening of an ancient summer
    and the vibration of a string over which a bow was moving
    as though the sound of the note were still playing
    and the hand of my wife found in the shallows of waking

you who in a flicker of my inattention   45
    signalled to me once only my error telling me
    of the sudden blow from the side so that I looked down
    to see not you any longer but instead a mouth
    full of blood calling after you who had already gone gone
    gone ahead into what I cannot know or reach or touch   50
    leaving in your place only the cloud of pain rising
    into the day filling the light possessing every sound
    becoming the single color and taste and direction

yet as the pain recedes and the moment of it
    you remain with me even in the missing of you   55
    small boat moving before me on the current under the daylight
    whatever you had touched and had known and took with you
    is with me now as you are when you are already there
    unseen part of me reminding me warning me
    pointing to what I cannot see never letting me forget   60
    you are my own speaking only to me going with me
    all the rest of the way telling me what is still here

2000

JAMES WRIGHT
1927–1980

" My name is James A. Wright, and I was born / Twenty-five miles from this infected grave, / In Martins Ferry, Ohio, where one slave / To Hazel-Atlas Glass became my father"; so James Wright introduced himself in an early poem, "At the Executed Murderer's Grave." The angry assertiveness in these lines suggests his embattled relations with an America he loves and hates. This America is symbolized for him by the landscape of Ohio, in particular by Martins Ferry, just across the Ohio River from Wheeling, West Virginia, the home of Wheeling Steel and of the glass factory where his father worked for fifty years. In Wright's work this landscape is harsh evidence of the way the social world has contaminated a natural world infinitely more beautiful and self-restoring. The same social world that destroys the landscape also turns its back on those whose lives meet failure or defeat, and Wright's deep knowledge of defeat and his anger at this exclusion lead him to the murderer's grave. It is not simply that Wright sympathizes with social outcasts, but rather, as Robert Hass acutely pointed out, "the suffering of other people, particularly the lost and the derelict, is actually a part of his own emotional life. It is what he writes from, not what he writes about." As a poet who writes out of loss, Wright is elegiac, memorializing a vanished beauty and lost hopes. So deep is his sense of loss that he will sometimes identify with anyone and anything that is scarred or wounded ("I am not a happy man by talent," he once said. "Sometimes I have been very happy, but characteristically I'm a miserable son of a bitch"). Any serious reading of his work has to contend with sorting out those poems in which this identification is unthinking and sentimental, poems where Wright suggests that all forms of suffering and defeat are equal and alike. What remains in some of his best work is a curiously tough-minded tenderness at work in his exploration of despair. He admires, for example, the sumac flourishing in the Ohio landscape, its bark so tough it "will turn aside hatchets and knife blades" ("The Sumac in Ohio").

When Wright finished high school, he joined the army. In 1948 he left the military to attend Kenyon College in Ohio on the G.I. Bill ("I applied to several schools in Ohio," he once said, "and they all said no except Kenyon College. So I went there"). He was lucky in his teachers; at Kenyon he studied with John Crowe Ransom and, after a Fulbright scholarship to the University of Vienna, he went to the University of Washington, where he studied with the poet Theodore Roethke and also became a close friend of Richard Hugo's. At Washington he wrote a Ph.D. dissertation on Charles Dickens and received the degree in 1959. Thereafter he became a teacher, first at the University of Minnesota, Minneapolis (1957–64), and later at Hunter College, New York (1966–80).

From both Ransom and Roethke, Wright learned poetic form. From Ransom in particular he took what he called "the Horatian ideal" of the carefully made, unified poem. Wright would later say that were he to choose a master, he would choose the Latin poet Horace, "who was able to write humorously and kindly in flawless verse." The Horatian impulse in Wright—restrained, formal, sometimes satirical—helps hold in check a deep-seated romanticism that idealizes nature and the unconscious. His first two books, *The Green Wall* (1957), chosen to appear in the Yale Younger Poets series, and *Saint Judas* (1959), are formal and literary in style although much of their subject matter (the murderer, the lunatic, a deaf child) might be called Romantic. Wright seems in these books closest to Thomas Hardy, Robert Frost, and Edwin Arlington Robinson. But in the 1960s, like a great many other American poets, he moved away from traditional forms, explored more open and improvisatory poetic structures, and began to depend heavily on what his fellow poet Robert Bly called "the deep image." Wright had been translating the work of Spanish poets often associated with surrealism—Pablo Neruda, César Vallejo, and Juan Ramón Jiménez—as well as the German Georg Trakl (whom he translated in collaboration with Bly), and he took from them, in part, a reliance on the power of a poetic image to evoke association deep within the unconscious. He followed his volume *The Branch Will Not Break* (1963) with two books, *Shall We Gather at the River* (1968) and *Two Citizens* (1974), in which he began to overwork certain images ("stone," "dark"), as if repetition were a substitute for clarity. Some of the poems in these books succeed in carrying us into areas of experience that resist the discursive, but the effect of a number of poems is to exclude conscious intelligence, to celebrate "whatever is not mind," as Robert Hass has pointed out. It is as if Wright responded to the scarred landscape outside (and inside) him by fleeing to an inwardness so deep it could not partake of thought or expression.

But Wright's love of clarity and form and his ability to see through pretensions (including his own) resurface in *Moments of the Italian Summer* (1976), *To a Blos-*

soming Pear Tree (1977), and his posthumous last collection, *This Journey* (1982). Restored to a unity of thinking and feeling, many of the poems in these books convey the flawed beauty of the world with a loving and witty tenderness. He often writes with particular feeling about creatures—finches, lizards, hermit crabs—whose liveliness and fragility touch him (in this and other regards his work has been important to the poet Mary Oliver). In "A Finch Sitting Out a Windstorm," his final portrait of the finch suggests admiration of its stubborness in the face of loss: "But his face is as battered / As Carmen Basilio's. / He never listens / To me."

Though the poems of his final book do not abandon the anger he feels thinking of the ruined landscapes of Ohio, the European setting of many of the poems extends his sense of ruin into a knowledge of how time chips away at all human creation, with or without the help of men and women. Although he had claimed to be constitutionally unhappy, the poems of *This Journey* suggest that before his death from cancer a deep happiness took him by surprise. We turn to Wright's work for its fierce understanding of defeat, for its blend of American speech rhythms with the formal music of poetry, and for the loveliness he finds in the imperfect and neglected. Accustomed to expect the worst, he had an enduring capacity to be astonished by this loveliness, as in this childhood memory of a trip to the icehouse with his father: "We stood and breathed the rising steam of that amazing winter, and carried away in our wagon the immense fifty-pound diamond, while the old man chipped us each a jagged little chunk and then walked behind us, his hands so calm they were trembling for us, trembling with exquisite care" ("The Ice House").

Autumn Begins in Martins Ferry, Ohio

In the Shreve High football stadium,
I think of Polacks nursing long beers in Tiltonsville,
And gray faces of Negroes in the blast furnace at Benwood,[1]
And the ruptured night watchman of Wheeling Steel,
Dreaming of heroes.   5

All the proud fathers are ashamed to go home.
Their women cluck like starved pullets,
Dying for love.

Therefore,
Their sons grow suicidally beautiful   10
At the beginning of October,
And gallop terribly against each other's bodies.

1963

---

1. A town south of Martins Ferry, where the Wheeling Steel Works are located. Tiltonsville is a town in easternmost Ohio, north of Martins Ferry.

To the Evening Star: Central Minnesota

Under the water tower at the edge of town
A huge Airedale ponders a long ripple
In the grass fields beyond.
Miles off, a whole grove silently
Flies up into the darkness.   5
One light comes on in the sky,
One lamp on the prairie.

Beautiful daylight of the body, your hands carry seashells.
West of this wide plain,
Animals wilder than ours   10
Come down from the green mountains in the darkness.
Now they can see you, they know
The open meadows are safe.

1963

A Blessing

Just off the highway to Rochester, Minnesota,
Twilight bounds softly forth on the grass.
And the eyes of those two Indian ponies
Darken with kindness.
They have come gladly out of the willows   5
To welcome my friend and me.
We step over the barbed wire into the pasture
Where they have been grazing all day, alone.
They ripple tensely, they can hardly contain their happiness
That we have come.   10
They bow shyly as wet swans. They love each other.
There is no loneliness like theirs.
At home once more,
They begin munching the young tufts of spring in the darkness.
I would like to hold the slenderer one in my arms,   15
For she has walked over to me
And nuzzled my left hand.
She is black and white,
Her mane falls wild on her forehead,
And the light breeze moves me to caress her long ear   20
That is delicate as the skin over a girl's wrist.
Suddenly I realize
That if I stepped out of my body I would break
Into blossom.

1963

A Centenary Ode: Inscribed to Little Crow,
Leader of the Sioux Rebellion in Minnesota, 1862[1]

I had nothing to do with it. I was not here.
I was not born.
In 1862, when your hotheads
Raised hell from here to South Dakota,
My own fathers scattered into West Virginia   5
And southern Ohio.
My family fought the Confederacy
And fought the Union.[2]
None of them got killed.
But for all that, it was not my fathers   10
Who murdered you.
Not much.

I don't know
Where the fathers of Minneapolis finalized
Your flayed carcass.   15
Little Crow, true father
Of my dark America.
When I close my eyes I lose you among
Old loneliness.
My family were a lot of singing drunks and good carpenters.   20
We had brothers who loved one another no matter what they did.
And they did plenty.

I think they would have run like hell from your Sioux.
And when you caught them you all would have run like hell
From the Confederacy and from the Union   25
Into the hills and hunted for a few things,
Some bull-cat under the stones, a gar[3] maybe,
If you were hungry, and if you were happy,
Sunfish and corn.

If only I knew where to mourn you,   30
I would surely mourn.

But I don't know.

I did not come here only to grieve
For my people's defeat.
The troops of the Union, who won,   35
Still outnumber us.
Old Paddy Beck, my great-uncle, is dead
At the old soldiers' home near Tiffen, Ohio.

---

1. Under Little Crow a group of Sioux attacked
and killed more than eight hundred settlers and
soldiers in Minnesota. They were eventually
routed by federal troops. About a month later
Little Crow, while foraging for food, was shot by
white farmers.
2. During the Civil War members of Wright's
family fought on both sides of the conflict.
3. Long pikelike freshwater fish. "Bull-cat":
catfish.

He got away with every last stitch
Of his uniform, save only   40
The dress trousers.

Oh all around us,
The hobo jungles of America grow wild again.
The pick handles bloom like your skinned spine.
I don't even know where   45
My own grave is.

                                                              1971

With the Shell of a Hermit Crab

Lugete, O Veneres Cupidinesque[1]
—Catullus

This lovely little life whose toes
Touched the white sand from side to side,
How delicately no one knows,
Crept from his loneliness, and died.

From deep waters long miles away   5
He wandered, looking for his name,
And all he found was you and me,
A quick life and a candle flame.

Today, you happen to be gone.
I sit here in the raging hell,   10
The city of the dead, alone,
Holding a little empty shell.

I peer into his tiny face.
It looms too huge for me to bear.
Two blocks away the sea gives place   15
To river. Both are everywhere.

I reach out and flick out the light.
Darkly I touch his fragile scars,
So far away, so delicate,
Stars in a wilderness of stars.   20

                                                              1977

---

1. Mourn, O Venuses and Cupids (Latin). The opening line of the ancient Roman poet Catullus's "Poem 3," a mock-elegy on the death of his mistress's bird.

PHILIP LEVINE
b. 1928

In one of his poems Philip Levine imagines a former life "as a small, quick fox," who stands "in the pathway shouting and refusing / to budge, feeling the dignity / of the small creature menaced / by the many and larger" ("The Fox"). This self-portrait has Levine's characteristic humor, but it aptly renders his deep, even stubborn, sympathy with ordinary men and women and his equally stubborn antipathy toward those who look down on ordinary life. Levine shares the faith of his favorite poet, Walt Whitman, in an inclusive, democratic poetry, and, with Whitman, he might boast he is "one of the roughs."

Levine was born to a Jewish family in Detroit, Michigan, and began factory work at fourteen, during the war years. He continued to work while he attended Wayne (now Wayne State) University in Detroit and has held what he calls "a succession of stupid jobs"—working in a bottling corporation, for Cadillac, for Chevrolet Gear and Axle, and for Wyandotte Chemical Company. At one point in his life he also trained as a boxer. In 1957 he received an MFA from the University of Iowa, where the poets John Berryman and Robert Lowell were his teachers. In 1958 he moved to California and taught for many years at California State University at Fresno, where his students included Sherley Ann Williams, David St. John, Luis Omar Salinas, and Gary Soto. In the mid-1960s he went to Spain for the first time and felt "when I looked at the Spanish landscape I was looking at a part of myself. . . . In a year I began to become Catalan in a small way." He has since edited and translated the work of some Spanish poets. He teaches at New York University.

His fellow poet Galway Kinnell once suggested that Levine "used to hold something back as if for fear poetry would betray him into tenderness. In his recent poems, it has done exactly that." Although an anger at society energizes many Levine poems—including the title poem of his book *They Feed They Lion* (1972), a response to the 1967 riots in his native Detroit—his twenty-some volumes of poetry demonstrate a wide range of feeling. At heart he is a narrative poet, even in his brief lyrics, like Thomas Hardy or Robert Penn Warren—both of whom he admires. His stories most often tell of loss and remembrance, and Levine's elegiac strain is one source of his tenderness. Feeling himself in a world where "No One Remembers" (the title of one of his poems), where life is characterized by impermanence, his poems re-create the people, landscapes, and events that make up—as the title of his 1976 collection puts it—*The Names of the Lost*. His books, *What Work Is* (1991), *The Simple Truth* (1994), *The Mercy* (1999), *Breath* (2004), and *News of the World* (2007), show Levine using several of his gifts—his narrative skill, his affection and respect for the ordinary person, his acute sense of place—with increased ambition and rhythmic power.

With its rapid motion between the colloquial and the lyrical, Levine's best work has a distinctively gritty radiance. A strong, physical sense grounds his powerful nostalgia, giving us a world we can see and touch. Levine calls himself a Romantic, and one of the dangers in his work is its tendency to inflate experience. Saving him from such inflation, though, is a lively, subversive, comic sense often directed at himself. His memorable poems are energetic; they vary the stresses of syntax against the short, trimeter line in which he often composes and accumulate power as they move along. But Levine's lines can sometimes seem arbitrary, as if what we really had was prose broken into pieces. In the work of the poets he most admires, Levine argues, the failures do not matter—all that matters is the genuine poems. His own best poems rise out of a world we inhabit in common, where the experiences of ordinary life and work are transfused with energy and feeling. On Levine's appointment as Poet Laureate for 2011–12, he was called a laureate "of the industrial heartland."

Animals Are Passing from Our Lives

It's wonderful how I jog
on four honed-down ivory toes
my massive buttocks slipping
like oiled parts with each light step.

I'm to market. I can smell   5
the sour, grooved block, I can smell
the blade that opens the hole
and the pudgy white fingers

that shake out the intestines
like a hankie. In my dreams   10
the snouts drool on the marble,
suffering children, suffering flies,

suffering the consumers
who won't meet their steady eyes
for fear they could see. The boy   15
who drives me along believes

that any moment I'll fall
on my side and drum my toes
like a typewriter or squeal
and shit like a new housewife   20

discovering television,
or that I'll turn like a beast
cleverly to hook his teeth
with my teeth. No. Not this pig.

1968

Detroit Grease Shop Poem

Four bright steel crosses,
universal joints,[1] plucked
out of the burlap sack—
"the heart of the drive train,"
the book says. Stars   5
on Lemon's wooden palm,
stars that must be capped,

---

1. Shaft couplings designed to transmit rotation from one shaft to another.

rolled, and annointed,
that have their orders
and their commands as he   10
has his.
                    Under the blue
hesitant light another day
at Automotive
in the city of dreams.   15
We're all here to count
and be counted, Lemon,
Rosie, Eugene, Luis,
and me, too young to know
this is for keeps, pinning   20
on my apron, rolling up
my sleeves.
                    The roof leaks
from yesterday's rain,
the waters gather above us   25
waiting for one mistake.
When a drop falls on Lemon's
corded arm, he looks at it
as though it were something
rare or mysterious   30
like a drop of water or
a single lucid meteor
fallen slowly from
nowhere and burning on
his skin like a tear.   35

                                                          1972

Starlight

My father stands in the warm evening
on the porch of my first house.
I am four years old and growing tired.
I see his head among the stars,
the glow of his cigarette, redder   5
than the summer moon riding
low over the old neighborhood: We
are alone, and he asks me if I am happy.
"Are you happy?" I cannot answer.
I do not really understand the word,   10
and the voice, my father's voice, is not
his voice, but somehow thick and choked,
a voice I have not heard before, but
heard often since. He bends and passes
a thumb beneath each of my eyes.   15
The cigarette is gone, but I can smell
the tiredness that hangs on his breath.

He has found nothing, and he smiles
and holds my head with both his hands.
Then he lifts me to his shoulder,   20
and now I too am there among the stars,
as tall as he. Are you happy? I say.
He nods in answer, Yes! oh yes! oh yes!
And in that new voice he says nothing,
holding my head tight against his head,   25
his eyes closed up against the starlight,
as though those tiny blinking eyes
of light might find a tall, gaunt child
holding his child against the promises
of autumn, until the boy slept   30
never to waken in that world again.

1979

Fear and Fame

Half an hour to dress, wide rubber hip boots,
gauntlets to the elbow, a plastic helmet
like a knight's but with a little glass window
that kept steaming over, and a respirator
to save my smoke-stained lungs. I would descend   5
step by slow step into the dim world
of the pickling tank and there prepare
the new solutions from the great carboys
of acids lowered to me on ropes—all from a recipe
I shared with nobody and learned from Frank O'Mera   10
before he went off to the bars on Vernor Highway
to drink himself to death. A gallon of hydrochloric
steaming from the wide glass mouth, a dash
of pale nitric to bubble up, sulphuric to calm,
metals for sweeteners, cleansers for salts,   15
until I knew the burning stew was done.
Then to climb back, step by stately step, the adventurer
returned to the ordinary blinking lights
of the swingshift at Feinberg and Breslin's
First-Rate Plumbing and Plating with a message   20
from the kingdom of fire. Oddly enough
no one welcomed me back, and I'd stand
fully armored as the downpour of cold water
rained down on me and the smoking traces puddled
at my feet like so much milk and melting snow.   25
Then to disrobe down to my work pants and shirt,
my black street shoes and white cotton socks,
to reassume my nickname, strap on my Bulova,
screw back my wedding ring, and with tap water
gargle away the bitterness as best I could.   30
For fifteen minutes or more I'd sit quietly

off to the side of the world as the women
polished the tubes and fixtures to a burnished purity
hung like Christmas ornaments on the racks
pulled steadily toward the tanks I'd cooked.   35
Ahead lay the second cigarette, held in a shaking hand,
as I took into myself the sickening heat to quell heat,
a lunch of two Genoa salami sandwiches and Swiss cheese
on heavy peasant bread baked by my Aunt Tsipie,
and a third cigarette to kill the taste of the others.   40
Then to arise and dress again in the costume
of my trade for the second time that night, stiffened
by the knowledge that to descend and rise up
from the other world merely once in eight hours is half
what it takes to be known among women and men.   45

                                                               1991

The Simple Truth

I bought a dollar and a half's worth of small red potatoes,
took them home, boiled them in their jackets
and ate them for dinner with a little butter and salt.
Then I walked through the dried fields
on the edge of town. In middle June the light   5
hung on in the dark furrows at my feet,
and in the mountain oaks overhead the birds
were gathering for the night, the jays and mockers
squawking back and forth, the finches still darting
into the dusty light. The woman who sold me   10
the potatoes was from Poland; she was someone
out of my childhood in a pink spangled sweater and sunglasses
praising the perfection of all her fruits and vegetables
at the road-side stand and urging me to taste
even the pale, raw sweet corn trucked all the way,   15
she swore, from New Jersey. "Eat, eat," she said,
"Even if you don't I'll say you did."
                                        Some things
you know all your life. They are so simple and true
they must be said without elegance, meter and rhyme,   20
they must be laid on the table beside the salt shaker,
the glass of water, the absence of light gathering
in the shadows of picture frames, they must be
naked and alone, they must stand for themselves.
My friend Henri and I arrived at this together in 1965   25
before I went away, before he began to kill himself,
and the two of us to betray our love. Can you taste
what I'm saying? It is onions or potatoes, a pinch
of simple salt, the wealth of melting butter, it is obvious,
it stays in the back of your throat like a truth   30
you never uttered because the time was always wrong,

it stays there for the rest of your life, unspoken,
made of that dirt we call earth, the metal we call salt,
in a form we have no words for, and you live on it.

1996

ANNE SEXTON
1928–1974

Anne Sexton's first book of poems, *To Bedlam and Part Way Back* (1960), was published at a time when the label "confessional" came to be attached to poems more frankly autobiographical than had been usual in American verse. For Sexton the term is particularly apt. Although she had abandoned the Roman Catholicism into which she was born, her poems enact something analogous to preparing for and receiving religious absolution.

Sexton's confessions were to be made in terms more startling than the traditional Catholic images of her childhood. The purpose of her poems was not to analyze or explain behavior but to make it palpable in all its ferocity of feeling. Poetry "should be a shock to the senses. It should also hurt." This is apparent in both her themes and the ways in which she exhibits her subjects. Sexton writes about sex, illegitimacy, guilt, madness, and suicide. *To Bedlam* portrays her breakdown, her time in a mental hospital, her efforts at reconciliation with her daughter and husband when she returns. Her second book, *All My Pretty Ones* (1962), takes its title from Shakespeare's *Macbeth* and refers to the deaths of both her parents within three months of one another. Later books—*Live or Die* (1966), *The Death Notebooks* (1974), and *The Awful Rowing toward God* (1975; posthumous)—act out a debate about suicide and prefigure Sexton's taking of her own life. And yet, as the poet's tender address to her daughter in "Little Girl, My String Bean, My Lovely Woman" suggests, Sexton's work ranges beyond an obsession with death.

Sexton spoke of images as "the heart of poetry. Images come from the unconscious. Imagination and the unconscious are one and the same." Powerful images substantiate the strangeness of feelings and through them the poet attempts to redefine experiences so as to gain understanding, absolution, or revenge. Sexton's poems, poised between, as her titles suggest, life and death or "bedlam and part way back," are efforts at establishing a middle ground of self-assertion, substituting surreal images for the reductive versions of life visible to the exterior eye.

Sexton was born in 1928 in Newton, Massachusetts, and attended Garland Junior College. She came to poetry fairly late—when she was twenty-eight, after seeing the critic I. A. Richards lecturing about the sonnet on television. In the late 1950s she attended poetry workshops in the Boston area, including Robert Lowell's poetry seminars at Boston University. One of her fellow students was Sylvia Plath, whose suicide she commemorated in a poem, "Sylvia's Death." Sexton claimed that she was less influenced by Lowell's *Life Studies* than by W. D. Snodgrass's autobiographical *Heart's Needle* (1959), but certainly Lowell's support and the association with Plath left their mark on her and made it possible for her to publish. Although her career was relatively brief, she received several major literary prizes, including the Pulitzer Prize for *Live or Die* and an American Academy of Arts and Letters traveling fellowship. Her suicide came after a series of mental breakdowns.

The Truth the Dead Know

For My Mother, Born March 1902, Died March 1959
and My Father, Born February 1900, Died June 1959

Gone, I say and walk from church,
refusing the stiff procession to the grave,
letting the dead ride alone in the hearse.
It is June. I am tired of being brave.

We drive to the Cape. I cultivate   5
myself where the sun gutters from the sky,
where the sea swings in like an iron gate
and we touch. In another country people die.

My darling, the wind falls in like stones
from the whitehearted water and when we touch   10
we enter touch entirely. No one's alone.
Men kill for this, or for as much.

And what of the dead? They lie without shoes
in their stone boats. They are more like stone
than the sea would be if it stopped. They refuse   15
to be blessed, throat, eye and knucklebone.

                                                     1962

The Starry Night

That does not keep me from having a terrible
need of—shall I say the word—religion.
Then I go out at night to paint the stars.
—Vincent Van Gogh[1]
in a letter to his brother

The town does not exist
except where one black-haired tree slips
up like a drowned woman into the hot sky.
The town is silent. The night boils with eleven stars.
Oh starry starry night! This is how   5
I want to die.

It moves. They are all alive.
Even the moon bulges in its orange irons
to push children, like a god, from its eye.
The old unseen serpent swallows up the stars.   10

---

1. Dutch painter (1853–1890) who in his thirties became insane and committed suicide. This letter to his brother—his only confidant—was written in September 1888. At the time he was painting *Starry Night on the Rhône*.

Oh starry starry night! This is how
I want to die:

into that rushing beast of the night,
sucked up by that great dragon, to split
from my life with no flag,   15
no belly,
no cry.

                                                                    1962

Sylvia's Death

for Sylvia Plath[1]

Oh Sylvia, Sylvia,
with a dead box of stones and spoons,

with two children, two meteors
wandering loose in the tiny playroom,

with your mouth into the sheet,   5
into the roofbeam, into the dumb prayer,

(Sylvia, Sylvia,
where did you go
after you wrote me
from Devonshire   10
about raising potatoes
and keeping bees?)

what did you stand by,
just how did you lie down into?

Thief!—   15
how did you crawl into,

crawl down alone
into the death I wanted so badly and for so long,

the death we said we both outgrew,
the one we wore on our skinny breasts,   20

the one we talked of so often each time
we downed three extra dry martinis in Boston,

---

1. American poet (1932–1963) and friend of Sexton's who committed suicide. Plath was living in London with her two children, having separated from her husband, the poet Ted Hughes, the previous year.

the death that talked of analysts and cures,
the death that talked like brides with plots,

the death we drank to,
the motives and then the quiet deed? 25

(In Boston
the dying
ride in cabs,
yes death again, 30
that ride home
with *our* boy.)

O Sylvia, I remember the sleepy drummer
who beat on our eyes with an old story,

how we wanted to let him come 35
like a sadist or a New York fairy

to do his job,
a necessity, a window in a wall or a crib,

and since that time he waited
under our heart, our cupboard, 40

and I see now that we store him up
year after year, old suicides

and I know at the news of your death,
a terrible taste for it, like salt.

(And me, 45
me too.
And now, Sylvia,
you again
with death again,
that ride home 50
with *our* boy.)

And I say only
with my arms stretched out into that stone place,

what is your death
but an old belonging, 55

a mole that fell out
of one of your poems?

(O friend,
while the moon's bad,
and the king's gone, 60

and the queen's at her wit's end
the bar fly ought to sing!)

O tiny mother,
you too!
O funny duchess!   65
O blonde thing!

February 17, 1963   1966

Little Girl, My String Bean, My Lovely Woman

My daughter, at eleven
(almost twelve), is like a garden.

Oh darling! Born in that sweet birthday suit
and having owned it and known it for so long,
now you must watch high noon enter—   5
noon, that ghost hour.
Oh, funny little girl—this one under a blueberry sky,
this one! How can I say that I've known
just what you know and just where you are?

It's not a strange place, this odd home   10
where your face sits in my hand
so full of distance,
so full of its immediate fever.
The summer has seized you,
as when, last month in Amalfi,[1] I saw   15
lemons as large as your desk-side globe—
that miniature map of the world—
and I could mention, too,
the market stalls of mushrooms
and garlic buds all engorged.   20
Or I think even of the orchard next door,
where the berries are done
and the apples are beginning to swell.
And once, with our first backyard,
I remember I planted an acre of yellow beans   25
we couldn't eat.

Oh, little girl,
my stringbean,
how do you grow?
You grow this way.   30
You are too many to eat.

---

1. A seaport town in Campania, Italy.

I hear
as in a dream
the conversation of the old wives
speaking of *womanhood.*   35
I remember that I heard nothing myself.
I was alone.
I waited like a target.

Let high noon enter—
the hour of the ghosts.   40
Once the Romans believed
that noon was the ghost hour,
and I can believe it, too,
under that startling sun,
and someday they will come to you,   45
someday, men bare to the waist, young Romans
at noon where they belong,
with ladders and hammers
while no one sleeps.

But before they enter   50
I will have said,
Your bones are lovely,
and before their strange hands
there was always this hand that formed.

Oh, darling, let your body in,   55
let it tie you in,
in comfort.
What I want to say, Linda,
is that women are born twice.

If I could have watched you grow   60
as a magical mother might,
if I could have seen through my magical transparent belly,
there would have been such ripening within:
your embryo,
the seed taking on its own,   65
life clapping the bedpost,
bones from the pond,
thumbs and two mysterious eyes,
the awfully human head,
the heart jumping like a puppy,   70
the important lungs,
the becoming—
while it becomes!
as it does now,
a world of its own,   75
a delicate place.

I say hello
to such shakes and knockings and high jinks,

such music, such sprouts,
such dancing-mad-bears of music,   80
such necessary sugar,
such goings-on!

Oh, little girl,
my stringbean,
how do you grow?   85
You grow this way.
You are too many to eat.

What I want to say, Linda,
is that there is nothing in your body that lies.
All that is new is telling the truth.   90
I'm here, that somebody else,
an old tree in the background.

Darling,
stand still at your door,
sure of yourself, a white stone, a good stone—   95
as exceptional as laughter
you will strike fire,
that new thing!

July 14, 1964   1966

From The Death of the Fathers[1]

2. How We Danced

The night of my cousin's wedding
I wore blue.   25
I was nineteen
and we danced, Father, we orbited.
We moved like angels washing themselves.
We moved like two birds on fire.
Then we moved like the sea in a jar,   30
slower and slower.
The orchestra played
"Oh how we danced on the night we were wed."
And you waltzed me like a lazy Susan
and we were dear,   35
very dear.
Now that you are laid out,
useless as a blind dog,
now that you no longer lurk,
the song rings in my head.   40
Pure oxygen was the champagne we drank
and clicked our glasses, one to one.

---

1. Printed here are parts 2 and 3 of a six-part sequence.

The champagne breathed like a skin diver
and the glasses were crystal and the bride
and groom gripped each other in sleep   45
like nineteen-thirty marathon dancers.
Mother was a belle and danced with twenty men.
You danced with me never saying a word.
Instead the serpent spoke as you held me close.
The serpent, that mocker, woke up and pressed against me   50
like a great god and we bent together
like two lonely swans.

3. The Boat

Father
(he calls himself
"old sea dog"),   55
in his yachting cap
at the wheel of the Christ-Craft,
a mahogany speedboat
named *Go Too III*,
speeds out past Cuckold's Light[2]   60
over the dark brainy blue.
I in the very back
with an orange life jacket on.
I in the dare seat.
Mother up front.   65
Her kerchief flapping.
The waves deep as whales.
(Whales in fact have been sighted.
A school two miles out of Boothbay Harbor.)[3]
It is bumpy and we are going too fast.   70
The waves are boulders that we ride upon.
I am seen and we are riding
to Pemaquid[4] or Spain.
Now the waves are higher;
they are round buildings.   75
We start to go through them
and the boat shudders.
Father is going faster.
I am wet.
I am tumbling on my seat   80
like a loose kumquat.
Suddenly
a wave that we go under.
Under. Under. Under.
We are daring the sea.   85
We have parted it.
We are scissors.
Here in the green room

2. A Maine lighthouse.   4. A village near the sea in Maine.
3. A coastal town in Maine.

the dead are very close.
Here in the pitiless green   90
where there are no keepsakes
or cathedrals an angel spoke:
You have no business.
No business here.
Give me a sign,   95
cried Father,
and the sky breaks over us.
There is air to have.
There are gulls kissing the boat.
There is the sun as big as a nose.   100
And here are the three of us
dividing our deaths,
bailing the boat
and closing out
the cold wing that has clasped us   105
this bright August day.

1972

ADRIENNE RICH
b. 1929

A childhood of reading and hearing poems taught Adrienne Rich to love the
sound of words; her adult life taught her that poetry must "consciously situate
itself amid political conditions." Over the years she has conducted a passionate
struggle to honor these parts of herself, in her best poems brilliantly mixing what
she calls "the poetry of the actual world with the poetry of sound." Extending a
dialogue—between art and politics—that she first discovered in W. B. Yeats, whose
poems she read as an undergraduate at Radcliffe, her work addresses with particular power the experiences of women, experiences often omitted from history and
misrepresented in literature. Our culture, she believes, is "split at the root" (to adapt
the title of one of her essays); art is separated from politics, and the poet's identity as
a woman is separated from her art. Rich's work seeks a language that will expose
and integrate these divisions in the self and in the world. To do this she has written
"directly and overtly as a woman, out of a woman's body and experience," for "to take
women's existence seriously as theme and source for art, was something I had been
hungering to do, needing to do, all my writing life."

Rich's first book was published in the Yale Younger Poets series, a prize particularly important for poets of her generation (others in the series have included James
Wright, John Ashbery, and W. S. Merwin). W. H. Auden, the judge for the series in
the 1950s, said of Rich's volume *A Change of World* (1951) that her poems "were
neatly and modestly dressed . . . respect their elders, but are not cowed by them and
do not tell fibs." Rich, looking back at that period from the vantage point of 1972,
renders a more complicated sense of things. In an influential essay, "When We

Dead Awaken," she recalls this period as one in which the chief models for poetry were men; from those models she first learned her craft. Even in reading the poetry of older women writers she found herself "looking . . . for the same things I found in the poetry of men . . . , to be equal was still confused with sounding the same." Twenty years and five volumes after *A Change of World* she published *The Will to Change*, taking its title from the opening line of Charles Olson's *The Kingfishers*: "What does not change / is the will to change." The shift of emphasis in Rich's titles signals an important turn in her work—from acceptance of change as a way of the world to an active sense of change as willed or desired.

In 1953 Rich married and in her twenties gave birth to three children within four years, "a radicalizing experience," she said. It was during this time that Rich experienced most severely that gap between what she calls the "energy of creation" and the "energy of relation. . . . In those early years I always felt the conflict as a failure of love in myself." In her later work Rich came to identify the source of that conflict not as individual but as social, and in 1976 she published a book of prose, *Of Woman Born: Motherhood as Experience and Institution*, in which she contrasts the actual experience of bearing and raising children with the myths fostered by our medical, social, and political institutions.

With her third and fourth books, *Snapshots of a Daughter-in-Law* (1963) and *Necessities of Life* (1966), Rich began explicitly to treat problems that have engaged her ever since. The title poem of *Snapshots* exposes the gap between literary versions of women's experience and the day-to-day truths of their lives.

Rich's poems aim at self-definition, at establishing boundaries of the self, but they also fight off the notion that insights remain solitary and unshared. Many of her poems proceed by means of intimate argument, sometimes with externalized parts of herself, as if to dramatize the way identity forms from the self's movement beyond fixed boundaries. In some of her most powerful later poems she pushes her imagination to recognize the multiple aspects of the self ("My selves," she calls them in her poem "Integrity"); in "Transcendental Etude," she writes: *"I am the lover and the loved, / home and wanderer, she who splits / firewood and she who knocks, a stranger / in the storm."* In other important later poems she has carried out a dialogue with lives similar to and different from her own, as in the generous and powerful title poem of her collection *An Atlas of the Difficult World*. As she writes in the essay "Blood, Bread, and Poetry," in her development as a poet she came to feel "more and more urgently the dynamic between poetry as language and poetry as a kind of action, probing, burning, stripping, placing itself in dialogue with others."

After Rich and her husband moved to New York City in 1966 they became increasingly involved in radical politics, especially in the opposition to the Vietnam War. These concerns are reflected in the poems of *Leaflets* (1969) and *The Will to Change* (1971). Along with new subject matter came equally important changes in style. Rich's poems throughout the 1960s moved away from formal verse patterns to more jagged utterance. Devices such as sentence fragments, lines of varying length, irregular spacing to mark off phrases emphasized a voice of greater urgency. Ever since "Snapshots of a Daughter-in-Law" Rich had been dating her poems, as if to mark each one as provisional, true to the moment but an instrument of passage, like an entry in a journal in which feelings are subject to continual revision.

In the 1970s Rich dedicated herself increasingly to feminism. Her work as a poet, a prose writer, and a public speaker took on a new unity and intensity. The continuing task was to see herself—as she put it in 1984—as neither "unique nor universal, but a person in history, a woman and not a man, a white and also Jewish inheritor of a particular Western consciousness, from the making of which most women have been excluded." She says in "Planetarium": "I am an instrument in the shape / of a woman trying to translate pulsations / into images for the relief of the body / and the reconstruction of the mind."

Rich's collections of prose—*Of Woman Born*; *On Lies, Secrets, and Silences: Selected Prose 1966–1978*; *Blood, Bread, and Poetry: Selected Prose 1979–1985*, *What Is Found There: Notebooks on Poetry and Politics* (1993), and *Arts of the Possible* (2001)—provide an important context for her poems. In these works she addresses issues of women's education and their literary traditions, Jewish identity, the relations between poetry and politics, and what she has called "the erasure of lesbian existence." As a young woman Rich had been stirred by James Baldwin's comment that "any real change implies the breakup of the world as one has always known it, the loss of all that gave one an identity, the end of safety." In many ways her essays, like her poems, track the forces that resist such change and the human conditions that require it. Her essay "Compulsory Heterosexuality and Lesbian Existence" is an important example of such an examination.

Although Rich's individual poems do not consistently succeed in expressing a political vision without sacrificing "intensity of language," her work is best read as a continuous process. The books have an air of ongoing, pained investigation, almost scientific in intention but with an ardor suggested by their titles: *The Dream of a Common Language* (1977), *A Wild Patience Has Taken Me Thus Far* (1981), *The Fact of a Doorframe* (1984), and *Your Native Land, Your Life* (1986). Rich's more recent books, *Time's Power* (1989), *An Atlas of the Difficult World* (1991), *Dark Fields of the Republic: Poems 1991–1995* (1995), *Midnight Salvage: Poems 1995–1998* (1999), *Fox* (2001), and *The School Among the Ruins* (2004), demonstrate an ongoing power of language and deepening poetic vision. *Telephone Ringing in the Labyrinth* (2007) collects poems from 2004–2006. Most recently, Rich has published *A Human Eye: Essays on Art in Society, 1997–2008* and *Tonight No Poetry Will Serve: Poems 2007–2010*. Reading through her poems we may sometimes wish for more relaxation and playfulness, for a liberating comic sense of self almost never present in her work. What we find, however, is invaluable—a poet whose imagination confronts and resists the harsh necessities of our times and keeps alive a vision of what is possible: "a whole new poetry beginning here" ("Transcendental Etude").

Snapshots of a Daughter-in-Law

1

You, once a belle in Shreveport,
with henna-colored hair, skin like a peachbud,
still have your dresses copied from that time,
and play a Chopin prelude
called by Cortot: "*Delicious recollections*   5
float like perfume through the memory."[1]

Your mind now, moldering like wedding-cake,
heavy with useless experience, rich
with suspicion, rumor, fantasy,
crumbling to pieces under the knife-edge   10
of mere fact. In the prime of your life.

Nervy, glowering, your daughter
wipes the teaspoons, grows another way.

---

1. A remark made by Alfred Cortot (1877–1962), a well-known French pianist, in his *Chopin: 24 Preludes* (1930); he is referring specifically to Chopin's Prelude No. 7, Andantino, A Major.

2

Banging the coffee-pot into the sink
she hears the angels chiding, and looks out   15
past the raked gardens to the sloppy sky.
Only a week since They said: *Have no patience.*

The next time it was: *Be insatiable.*
Then: *Save yourself; others you cannot save.*
Sometimes she's let the tapstream scald her arm,   20
a match burn to her thumbnail,

or held her hand above the kettle's snout
right in the woolly steam. They are probably angels,
since nothing hurts her anymore, except
each morning's grit blowing into her eyes.   25

3

A thinking woman sleeps with monsters.[2]
The beak that grips her, she becomes. And Nature,
that sprung-lidded, still commodious
steamer-trunk of *tempora* and *mores*[3]
gets stuffed with it all: the mildewed orange-flowers,   30
the female pills, the terrible breasts
of Boadicea[4] beneath flat foxes' heads and orchids.

Two handsome women, gripped in argument,
each proud, acute, subtle, I hear scream
across the cut glass and majolica   35
like Furies[5] cornered from their prey:
The argument *ad feminam*,[6] all the old knives
that have rusted in my back, I drive in yours,
ma semblable, ma soeur![7]

4

Knowing themselves too well in one another: 40
their gifts no pure fruition, but a thorn,
the prick filed sharp against a hint of scorn . . .

2. A reference to W. B. Yeats's "Leda and the Swan," a poem about the rape of a maiden by Zeus in the form of a giant bird. The poem ends: "Did she put on his knowledge with his power / Before the indifferent beak could let her drop?"
3. Times and customs (Latin, literal trans.). This alludes perhaps to the Roman orator Cicero's famous phrase "O Tempora! O Mores!" ("Alas for the degeneracy of our times and the low standard of our morals!").
4. British queen in the time of the Emperor Nero; she led her people in a large, ultimately unsuccessful revolt against Roman rule. "Female pills": remedies for menstrual pain.
5. Greek goddesses of vengeance. "Majolica": a kind of earthenware with a richly colored glaze.
6. Feminine version of the Latin phrase *ad hominem* (literally, "to the man"), referring to an argument directed not to reason but to personal prejudices and emotions.
7. The last line of Charles Baudelaire's French poem "Au Lecteur" addresses *"Hypocrite lecteur!—mon semblable—mon frère!"* (Hypocrite reader, like me, my brother!); Rich here instead addresses *"ma soeur"* (my sister). See also T. S. Eliot, "The Waste Land," line 76.

Reading while waiting
for the iron to heat,
writing, *My Life had stood—a Loaded Gun*[8]—   45
in that Amherst pantry while the jellies boil and scum,
or, more often,
iron-eyed and beaked and purposed as a bird,
dusting everything on the whatnot every day of life.

5

Dulce ridens, dulce loquens,[9]   50
she shaves her legs until they gleam
like petrified mammoth-tusk.

6

When to her lute Corinna sings[1]
neither words nor music are her own;
only the long hair dipping   55
over her cheek, only the song
of silk against her knees
and these
adjusted in reflections of an eye.

Poised, trembling and unsatisfied, before   60
an unlocked door, that cage of cages,
tell us, you bird, you tragical machine—
is this *fertilisante douleur*?[2] Pinned down
by love, for you the only natural action,
are you edged more keen   65
to prise the secrets of the vault? has Nature shown
her household books to you, daughter-in-law,
that her sons never saw?

7

"To have in this uncertain world some stay
which cannot be undermined, is   70
of the utmost consequence."[3]
              Thus wrote
a woman, partly brave and partly good,
who fought with what she partly understood.
Few men about her would or could do more,   75
hence she was labeled harpy, shrew and whore.

8. *"Emily Dickinson, Complete Poems*, ed. T. H. Johnson, 1960, p. 369" [Rich's note]; this is the poem numbered 754 in the Johnson edition. Amherst, Massachusetts, is the town where Dickinson lived her entire life (1830–1886).
9. Sweetly laughing, sweetly speaking (Latin, from Horace, *Odes*, 22.23–24).
1. First line of a lyric poem by Thomas Campion (1567–1620) about the extent to which a courtier is moved by Corinna's beautiful music.
2. Fertilizing (or life-giving) sorrow (French).
3. "From Mary Wollstonecraft, *Thoughts on the Education of Daughters*, London, 1787" [Rich's note]. Wollstonecraft (1759–1797), one of the first feminist thinkers, is best-known for her "Vindication of the Rights of Woman."

8

"You all die at fifteen," said Diderot,[4]
and turn part legend, part convention.
Still, eyes inaccurately dream
behind closed windows blankening with steam.   80
Deliciously, all that we might have been,
all that we were—fire, tears,
wit, taste, martyred ambition—
stirs like the memory of refused adultery
the drained and flagging bosom of our middle years.   85

9

*Not that it is done well, but
that it is done at all?*[5] Yes, think
of the odds! or shrug them off forever.
This luxury of the precocious child,
Time's precious chronic invalid,—   90
would we, darlings, resign it if we could?
Our blight has been our sinecure:
mere talent was enough for us—
glitter in fragments and rough drafts.

Sigh no more, ladies.   95
　　　　　　　Time is male
and in his cups drinks to the fair.
Bemused by gallantry, we hear
our mediocrities over-praised,
indolence read as abnegation,   100
slattern thought styled intuition,
every lapse forgiven, our crime
only to cast too bold a shadow
or smash the mold straight off.

For that, solitary confinement,   105
tear gas, attrition shelling.
Few applicants for that honor.

10

　　　　　　　　Well,
she's long about her coming, who must be
more merciless to herself than history.   110
Her mind full to the wind, I see her plunge
breasted and glancing through the currents,

---

4. Denis Diderot (1713–1784), French philosopher, encyclopedist, playwright, and critic. "'You all die at fifteen': '*Vous mourez toutes à quinze ans,*' from the *Lettres à Sophie Volland,* quoted by Simone de Beauvoir in *Le Deuxième Sexe,* Vol. II, pp. 123–24" [Rich's note].

5. An allusion to Samuel Johnson's remark to James Boswell: "Sir, a woman's preaching is like a dog's walking on his hinder legs. It is not done well; but you are surprised to find it done at all" (July 31, 1763).

taking the light upon her
at least as beautiful as any boy
or helicopter,[6]   115
        poised, still coming,
her fine blades making the air wince

but her cargo
no promise then:
delivered   120
palpable
ours.

1958–60   1963

"I Am in Danger—Sir—"[1]

"Half-cracked" to Higginson,[2] living,
afterward famous in garbled versions,
your hoard of dazzling scraps a battlefield,
now your old snood

mothballed at Harvard   5
and you in your variorum monument[3]
equivocal to the end—
who are you?

Gardening the day-lily,
wiping the wine-glass stems,   10
your thought pulsed on behind
a forehead battered paper-thin,

you, woman, masculine
in single-mindedness,
for whom the word was more   15
than a symptom—

a condition of being.
Till the air buzzing with spoiled language

6. "She comes down from the remoteness of ages, from Thebes, from Crete, from Chichén-Itzá; and she is also the totem set deep in the African jungle; she is a helicopter and she is a bird; and there is this, the greatest wonder of all: under her tinted hair the forest murmur becomes a thought, and words issue from her breasts" (Simone de Beauvoir, The Second Sex, trans. H. M. Parshley [New York, 1953], 729). (A translation of the passage from Le Deuxième Sexe, Vol. II, 574, cited in French by Rich.)
1. A sentence in a letter from Emily Dickinson to Thomas Wentworth Higginson (1823–1911), a critic and editor with whom she opened corre-
spondence in 1862 and to whom she sent some of her poems. She writes: "You think my gait 'spasmodic'—I am in danger—Sir—You think me 'uncontrolled'—I have no Tribunal."
2. In a letter Higginson described Dickinson as "my partially cracked Poetess at Amherst."
3. The Poems of Emily Dickinson, ed. Thomas H. Johnson, 3 vols. (Cambridge, Mass., 1955) is a "variorum" in that it contains all the variant readings in her manuscripts. "Mothballed at Harvard": the Houghton Rare Books Library at Harvard University has a collection of Emily Dickinson manuscripts and memorabilia.

sang in your ears
of Perjury   20

and in your half-cracked way you chose
silence for entertainment,
chose to have it out at last
on your own premises.

1964   1966

A Valediction Forbidding Mourning[1]

My swirling wants. Your frozen lips.
The grammar turned and attacked me.
Themes, written under duress.
Emptiness of the notations.

They gave me a drug that slowed the healing of wounds.   5

I want you to see this before I leave:
the experience of repetition as death
the failure of criticism to locate the pain
the poster in the bus that said:
my bleeding is under control.   10

A red plant in a cemetery of plastic wreaths.

A last attempt: the language is a dialect called metaphor.
These images go unglossed: hair, glacier, flashlight.
When I think of a landscape I am thinking of a time.
When I talk of taking a trip I mean forever.   15
I could say: those mountains have a meaning
but further than that I could not say.

To do something very common, in my own way.

1970   1971

Diving into the Wreck

First having read the book of myths,
and loaded the camera,
and checked the edge of the knife-blade,
I put on
the body-armor of black rubber   5

---

1. Title of a famous poem by John Donne (1572–1631) in which the English poet forbids his wife to lament his departure for a trip to the Continent.

the absurd flippers
the grave and awkward mask.
I am having to do this
not like Cousteau[1] with his
assiduous team   10
aboard the sun-flooded schooner
but here alone.

There is a ladder.
The ladder is always there
hanging innocently   15
close to the side of the schooner.
We know what it is for,
we who have used it.
Otherwise
it's a piece of maritime floss   20
some sundry equipment.

I go down.
Rung after rung and still
the oxygen immerses me
the blue light   25
the clear atoms
of our human air.
I go down.
My flippers cripple me,
I crawl like an insect down the ladder   30
and there is no one
to tell me when the ocean
will begin.

First the air is blue and then
it is bluer and then green and then   35
black I am blacking out and yet
my mask is powerful
it pumps my blood with power
the sea is another story
the sea is not a question of power   40
I have to learn alone
to turn my body without force
in the deep element.

And now: it is easy to forget
what I came for   45
among so many who have always
lived here
swaying their crenellated fans
between the reefs
and besides   50
you breathe differently down here.

1. Jacques-Yves Cousteau (1910–1997), French underwater explorer and author.

I came to explore the wreck.
The words are purposes.
The words are maps.
I came to see the damage that was done   55
and the treasures that prevail.
I stroke the beam of my lamp
slowly along the flank
of something more permanent
than fish or weed   60

the thing I came for:
the wreck and not the story of the wreck
the thing itself and not the myth
the drowned face[2] always staring
toward the sun   65
the evidence of damage
worn by salt and sway into this threadbare beauty
the ribs of the disaster
curving their assertion
among the tentative haunters.   70

This is the place.
And I am here, the mermaid whose dark hair
streams black, the merman in his armored body
We circle silently
about the wreck   75
we dive into the hold.
I am she: I am he

whose drowned face sleeps with open eyes
whose breasts still bear the stress
whose silver, copper, vermeil cargo lies   80
obscurely inside barrels
half-wedged and left to rot
we are the half-destroyed instruments
that once held to a course
the water-eaten log   85
the fouled compass

We are, I am, you are
by cowardice or courage
the one who find our way
back to this scene   90
carrying a knife, a camera
a book of myths
in which
our names do not appear.

1972   1973

---

2. Referring to the ornamental female figurehead that formed the prow of many old sailing ships.

Power

Living   in the earth-deposits   of our history

Today a backhoe divulged   out of a crumbling flank of earth
one bottle   amber   perfect   a hundred-year-old
cure for fever   or melancholy   a tonic
for living on this earth   in the winters of this climate   5

Today I was reading about Marie Curie:[1]
she must have known she suffered   from radiation sickness
her body bombarded for years   by the element
she had purified
It seems she denied to the end   10
the source of the cataracts on her eyes
the cracked and suppurating[2] skin   of her finger-ends
till she could no longer hold   a test-tube or a pencil

She died   a famous woman   denying
her wounds   15
denying
her wounds   came   from the same source as her power

1974   1978

Transcendental Etude[1]

for Michelle Cliff

This August evening I've been driving
over backroads fringed with queen anne's lace
my car startling young deer in meadows—one
gave a hoarse intake of her breath and all
four fawns sprang after her   5
into the dark maples.
Three months from today they'll be fair game
for the hit-and-run hunters, glorying
in a weekend's destructive power,
triggers fingered by drunken gunmen, sometimes   10
so inept as to leave the shattered animal
stunned in her blood. But this evening deep in summer
the deer are still alive and free,
nibbling apples from early-laden boughs
so weighted, so englobed   15
with already yellowing fruit

---

1. Physical chemist (1867–1934) who with her
husband investigated radioactivity and on her
own discovered polonium and radium; she
received the Nobel Prize in 1911.

2. Discharging pus.

1. "Etude": a piece of music played for the practice of a point of technique or a composition built
on technique but played for its artistic value.

they seem eternal, Hesperidean[2]
in the clear-tuned, cricket-throbbing air.

Later I stood in the dooryard,
my nerves singing the immense   20
fragility of all this sweetness,
this green world already sentimentalized, photographed,
advertised to death. Yet, it persists
stubbornly beyond the fake Vermont
of antique barnboards glazed into discothèques,   25
artificial snow, the sick Vermont of children
conceived in apathy, grown to winters
of rotgut violence,
poverty gnashing its teeth like a blind cat at their lives.
Still, it persists. Turning off onto a dirt road   30
from the raw cuts bulldozed through a quiet village
for the tourist run to Canada,
I've sat on a stone fence above a great, soft, sloping field
of musing heifers, a farmstead
slanting its planes calmly in the calm light,   35
a dead elm raising bleached arms
above a green so dense with life,
minute, momentary life—slugs, moles, pheasants, gnats,
spiders, moths, hummingbirds, groundhogs, butterflies—
a lifetime is too narrow   40
to understand it all, beginning with the huge
rockshelves that underlie all that life.

No one ever told us we had to study our lives,
make of our lives a study, as if learning natural history
or music, that we should begin   45
with the simple exercises first
and slowly go on trying
the hard ones, practicing till strength
and accuracy became one with the daring
to leap into transcendence, take the chance   50
of breaking down in the wild arpeggio
or faulting the full sentence of the fugue.[3]
—And in fact we can't live like that: we take on
everything at once before we've even begun
to read or mark time, we're forced to begin   55
in the midst of the hardest movement,
the one already sounding as we are born.
At most we're allowed a few months
of simply listening to the simple line
of a woman's voice singing a child   60
against her heart. Everything else is too soon,
too sudden, the wrenching-apart, that woman's heartbeat

2. I.e., like the golden apples of the tree guarded by the Hesperides, daughters of Atlas, in Greek mythology.

3. Musical piece characterized by the interweaving of several voices. "Arpeggio": production of a chord's tones in succession.

heard ever after from a distance,
the loss of that ground-note echoing
whenever we are happy, or in despair.   65

Everything else seems beyond us,
we aren't ready for it, nothing that was said
is true for us, caught naked in the argument,
the counterpoint, trying to sightread
what our fingers can't keep up with, learn by heart   70
what we can't even read. And yet
it *is* this we were born to. We aren't virtuosi
or child prodigies, there are no prodigies
in this realm, only a half-blind, stubborn
cleaving to the timbre, the tones of what we are   75
—even when all the texts describe it differently.

And we're not performers, like Liszt,[4] competing
against the world for speed and brilliance
(the 79-year-old pianist said, when I asked her
What makes a virtuoso?—Competitiveness.)
The longer I live the more I mistrust   80
theatricality, the false glamour cast
by performance, the more I know its poverty beside
the truths we are salvaging from
the splitting-open of our lives.   85
The woman who sits watching, listening,
eyes moving in the darkness
in rehearsing in her body, hearing-out in her blood
a score touched off in her perhaps
by some words, a few chords, from the stage: 90
a tale only she can tell.

But there come times—perhaps this is one of them—
when we have to take ourselves more seriously or die;
when we have to pull back from the incantations,
rhythms we've moved to thoughtlessly,   95
and disenthrall ourselves, bestow
ourselves to silence, or a severer listening, cleansed
of oratory, formulas, choruses, laments, static
crowding the wires. We cut the wires,
find ourselves in free-fall, as if   100
our true home were the undimensional
solitudes, the rift
in the Great Nebula.[5]
No one who survives to speak
new language, has avoided this: 105
the cutting-away of an old force that held her
rooted to an old ground

4. Franz Liszt (1811–1886), Hungarian composer
and pianist noted for his virtuoso performances.
5. A nebula is an immense body of rarefied gas
or dust in interstellar space. Rich may be referring to the Great Nebula in the Orion constellation or to a body of dark nebulae, usually called
the "Great Rift," which in photographs appears
to divide the Milky Way.

the pitch of utter loneliness
where she herself and all creation
seem equally dispersed, weightless, her being a cry   110
to which no echo comes or can ever come.

But in fact we were always like this,
rootless, dismembered: knowing it makes the difference.
Birth stripped our birthright from us,
tore us from a woman, from women, from ourselves   115
so early on
and the whole chorus throbbing at our ears
like midges, told us nothing, nothing
of origins, nothing we needed
to know, nothing that could re-member us.   120

Only: that it is unnatural,
the homesickness for a woman, for ourselves,
for that acute joy at the shadow her head and arms
cast on a wall, her heavy or slender
thighs on which we lay, flesh against flesh,   125
eyes steady on the face of love; smell of her milk, her sweat,
terror of her disappearance, all fused in this hunger
for the element they have called most dangerous, to be
lifted breathtaken on her breast, to rock within her
—even if beaten back, stranded against, to apprehend   130
in a sudden brine-clear thought
trembling like the tiny, orbed, endangered
egg-sac of a new world:
This is what she was to me, and this
is how I can love myself—   135
as only a woman can love me.

Homesick for myself, for her—as, after the heatwave
breaks, the clear tones of the world
manifest: cloud, bough, wall, insect, the very soul of light:
homesick as the fluted vault of desire   140
articulates itself: *I am the lover and the loved,*
home and wanderer, she who splits
firewood and she who knocks, a stranger
in the storm, two women, eye to eye
measuring each other's spirit, each other's   145
limitless desire,
                    a whole new poetry beginning here.

Vision begins to happen in such a life
as if a woman quietly walked away
from the argument and jargon in a room   150
and sitting down in the kitchen, began turning in her lap
bits of yarn, calico and velvet scraps,
laying them out absently on the scrubbed boards
in the lamplight, with small rainbow-colored shells
sent in cotton-wool from somewhere far away,   155

and skeins of milkweed from the nearest meadow—
original domestic silk, the finest findings—
and the darkblue petal of the petunia,
and the dry darkbrown lace of seaweed;
not forgotten either, the shed silver   160
whisker of the cat,
the spiral of paper-wasp-nest curling
beside the finch's yellow feather.
Such a composition has nothing to do with eternity,
the striving for greatness, brilliance—   165
only with the musing of a mind
one with her body, experienced fingers quietly pushing
dark against bright, silk against roughness,
pulling the tenets of a life together
with no mere will to mastery,   170
only care for the many-lived, unending
forms in which she finds herself,
becoming now the sherd of broken glass
slicing light in a corner, dangerous
to flesh, now the plentiful, soft leaf   175
that wrapped round the throbbing finger, soothes the wound;
and now the stone foundation, rockshelf further
forming underneath everything that grows.

1977   1978

Shattered Head

A life hauls itself uphill
        through hoar-mist steaming
the sun's tongue licking
        leaf upon leaf into stricken liquid
When? When? cry the soothseekers   5
        but time is a bloodshot eye
seeing its last of beauty its own
        foreclosure
                        a bloodshot mind
finding itself unspeakable   10
        What is the last thought?
Now I will let you know?
        or, Now I know?
(porridge of skull-splinters, brain tissue
        mouth and throat membrane, cranial fluid)   15

Shattered head on the breast
        of a wooded hill
laid down there endlessly so
        tendrils soaked into matted compost
become a root   20
        torqued over the faint springhead

groin whence illegible
    matter leaches: worm-borings, spurts of silt
volumes of sporic changes
    hair long blown into far follicles   25
blasted into a chosen place

Revenge on the head (genitals, breast, untouched)
    revenge on the mouth
packed with its inarticulate confessions
    revenge on the eyes   30
green-gray and restless
    revenge on the big and searching lips
                      the tender tongue
revenge on the sensual, on the nose the
    carrier of history   35
revenge on the life devoured
in another incineration

You can walk by such a place, the earth is made of them
where the stretched tissue of a field or woods is humid
    with belovéd matter   40
the soothseekers have withdrawn
you feel no ghost, only a sporic chorus
when that place utters its worn sigh
    let us have peace

And the shattered head answers back   45
    I believed I was loved, I believed I loved,
       who did this to us?

1996–97   1999

Five O'Clock, January 2003

Tonight as cargoes of my young
fellow countrymen and women are being hauled
into positions aimed at death, positions
they who did not will it suddenly
have to assume   5
I am thinking of Ed Azevedo
half-awake in recovery
if he has his arm whole
and how much pain he must bear
under the drugs   10
On cliffs above a beach
luxuriant in low tide after storms
littered with driftwood hurled and piled and
humanly arranged in fantastic
installations and beyond   15
silk-blue and onion-silver-skinned

Jeffers' "most glorious creature on earth"[1]
we passed, greeting, I saw his arm
bandaged to the elbow
asked and he told me: It was just   20
a small cut, nothing, on the hand he'd
washed in peroxide thinking
that was it until the pain began
traveling up his arm
and then the antibiotics the splint the   25
numbing drugs the sick sensation
and this evening at five o'clock the emergency
surgery and last summer
the train from Czechoslovakia to Spain
with his girl, cheap wine, bread and cheese   30
room with a balcony, ocean like this
nobody asking for pay in advance
kindness of foreigners
in that country, sick sensation now
needing to sit in his brother's truck again   35
even the accident on the motorcycle
was nothing like this
I'll be thinking of you at five
this evening I said
afterward you'll feel better, your body   40
will be clean of this poison
I didn't say Your war is here
but could you have believed
that from a small thing infection
would craw through the blood   45
and the enormous ruffled shine
of an ocean wouldn't tell you.

2003   2004

Wait

In paradise every
the desert wind is rising
third thought
in hell there are no thoughts
is of earth   5
sand screams against your government
issued tent   hell's noise
in your nostrils   crawl
into your ear-shell
wrap ourself in no-thought   10

---

1. See Robinson Jeffers, "Ninth Anniversary," in *The Wild God of the World: An Anthology of Robinson Jeffers*, ed. Albert Gelpi (Stanford, Calif.: Stanford University Press, 2003), p. 52: "there the most gorious / Creature on earth shines in the nights or glitters in the suns, / Or feels of its stone in the blind fog" [Rich's note].

wait   no place for the little lyric
wedding-ring glint the reason why
on earth
they never told you

2003   2004

MARTIN LUTHER KING JR.
1929–1968

On August 28, 1963, the Reverend Dr. Martin Luther King Jr. addressed a massive gathering from the steps of the Lincoln Memorial in Washington, D.C. With listeners standing shoulder to shoulder throughout the full length of the Mall, Dr. King summarized the achievement of the Civil Rights Movement and rallied sentiment for the full achievement of its goals. Battles against segregation had been waged in the courts for more than a decade, and demonstrations—such as lunch-counter sit-ins, bus boycotts, and freedom marches—had become increasingly common occurrences in American life, both in the South, where discrimination remained protected by laws, and in the North, where social conditions had long maintained a de facto separation of the races in matters of education, employment, and commerce. That morning, Dr. King and other leaders had met with President John F. Kennedy to argue for federal civil rights legislation. Achieving it would take until 1964 and the administration of the soon-to-be murdered president's successor, Lyndon B. Johnson. But the presence of such great numbers of Americans at Dr. King's 1963 speech, Americans of all races and political persuasions, was vivid proof that the time for such change was at hand.

The son of a minster, Dr. King was born in Atlanta, Georgia, and received bachelor's degrees in sociology and divinity from Morehouse College and Crozer Theological seminary before earning a doctorate in philosophy from Boston University in 1955, By then he had accepted his first pastorate at the Dexter Avenue Baptist Church in Montgomery, Alabama. It was in this city late in 1955 that a citizen named Rosa Parks, tired after a day's work, had refused to heed the local ordinance restricting African Americans to seats at the rear of city buses. Dr. King and other religious leaders offered support for Mrs. Parks and organized a boycott of Montgomery's public transport system that drew national attention. Although it took a year, this economic pressure and Dr. King's social activism (which led to his arrest and the bombing of his home) prompted federal injunctions that led to the bus system's integration. Dr. King's efforts in this struggle led to his invitation to speak at the annual convention of the National Association for the Advancement of Colored People in San Francisco and to his appearance on the February 18, 1957, cover of *Time* magazine.

For the next decade Martin Luther King Jr. was the most highly visible and politically effective leader of the Civil Rights Movement, thanks to his inspiring speeches, his deeply thoughtful books, and his practical manner of working with pragmatic forces in government. Hands-on experience with the Southern Christian Leadership Conference combined with high-profile visibility (including being named *Time* magazine's Man of the Year in January 1964 and receiving the Nobel Prize for Peace that same year) to make Dr. King a genuine hero of the movement. His talent lay in

August 28, 1963. In "the greatest demonstration for freedom in the history of our nation," Dr. Martin Luther King Jr. is photographed addressing his audience on the Mall in Washington, D.C.

a unique ability to apply relentless pressure for change in a strictly nonviolent manner; for this his acknowledged model was the Indian independence leader Mahatma Gandi. The speech on the Mall concludes with a list of just some of the places across the United States where Dr. King had worked for social justice. In the less than five years of life left to him he would continue his struggles with a voter-registration campaign in Selma, Alabama (featuring a dangerous march from Selma to Montgomery in March 1965), a protest of the Vietnam War in 1966 (for its diversion of economic resources from social needs), and a more generalized program in support of poor people of all races. This last endeavor took him to Memphis. Tennessee, where he supported sanitation workers in their strike for better wages and working conditions. There, on April 4, 1968, he was assassinated by an avowed white supremacist, James Earl Ray, who later died in prison while serving a life sentence for his act. Dr. King's speech on the evening before his death, "I See the Promised Land," concluded with a memorable reference to having "been to the mountaintop" from which a future of justice and equality could be foreseen.

The literary features of Martin Luther King Jr.'s ascent to greatness are examined by Eric Sundquist in *King's Dream* (2008). The speech delivered from the Lincoln Memorial in 1963 draws on key rhetorical features of Dr. King's writing and speaking and pushes them to new heights at the same time that the concision and focus demanded by the occasion made the statements themselves virtually iconic. Dr. King's rhetoric is that of the pulpit, using cadence and exhortation to move listeners to inspired agreement with not just the topic but also the enthusiasm behind it. Here the Bible is ever present as a source for allusion and a confirmation of value. Long familiar to members of African American religious congregations, Dr. King's strongly emotional style of presentation was new to many white listeners. Its effectiveness for a broad audience was proven by Dr. King's success and was applied to politics in coming years by the Reverend Jesse Jackson, whose 1988 campaign in the U.S. presidential primary elections would have the candidate winning the highest raw vote total in Iowa, a state with relatively few African American voters—the same state that in 2008 gave Barack Obama his first campaign victory.

The following text is from *I Have a Dream: Writings and Speeches That Changed the World* (1992).

I Have a Dream

I am happy to join with you today in what will go down in history as the greatest demonstration for freedom in the history of our nation.

Fivescore years ago, a great American, in whose symbolic shadow we stand today, signed the Emancipation Proclamation.[1] This momentous decree came as a great beacon light of hope to millions of Negro slaves who had been seared in the flames of withering injustice. It came as a joyous daybreak to end the long night of their captivity.

But one hundred years later, the Negro still is not free; one hundred years later, the life of the Negro is still sadly crippled by the manacles of segregation and the chains of discrimination; one hundred years later, the Negro lives on a lonely island of poverty in the midst of a vast ocean of material prosperity; one hundred years later, the Negro is still languishing in the corners of American society and finds himself in exile in his own land.

So we've come here today to dramatize a shameful condition. In a sense we've come to our nation's capital to cash a check. When the architects of our republic wrote the magnificent words of the Constitution and the Declaration of Independence, they were signing a promissory note to which every American was to fall heir. This note was the promise that all men, yes, black men as well as white men, would be guaranteed the unalienable rights of life, liberty, and the pursuit of happiness.

It is obvious today that America has defaulted on this promissory note in so far as her citizens of color are concerned. Instead of honoring this sacred obligation, America has given the Negro people a bad check; a check which has come back marked "insufficient funds." We refuse to believe that there are insufficient funds in the great vaults of opportunity of this nation. And so we've come to cash this check, a check that will give us upon demand the riches of freedom and the security of justice.

We have also come to this hallowed spot to remind America of the fierce urgency of now. This is no time to engage in the luxury of cooling off or to take the tranquilizing drug of gradualism. Now is the time to make real the promises of democracy; now is the time to rise from the dark and desolate valley of segregation to the sunlit path of racial justice; now is the time to lift our nation from the quicksands of racial injustice to the solid rock of brotherhood; now is the time to make justice a reality for all God's children. It would be fatal for the nation to overlook the urgency of the moment. This sweltering summer of the Negro's legitimate discontent will not pass until there is an invigorating autumn of freedom and equality.

---

1. Abraham Lincoln (1809–1865), sixteenth president of the United States, signed the Emancipation Proclamation on September 22, 1862, abolishing slavery in all portions of the country, including the Confederacy.

Nineteen sixty-three is not an end, but a beginning. And those who hope that the Negro needed to blow off steam and will now be content, will have a rude awakening if the nation returns to business as usual.

There will be neither rest nor tranquility in America until the Negro is granted his citizenship rights. The whirlwinds of revolt will continue to shake the foundations of our nation until the bright day of justice emerges.

But there is something that I must say to my people who stand on the warm threshold which leads into the palace of justice. In the process of gaining our rightful place we must not be guilty of wrongful deeds.

Let us not seek to satisfy our thirst for freedom by drinking from the cup of bitterness and hatred. We must forever conduct our struggle on the high plane of dignity and discipline. We must not allow our creative protest to degenerate into physical violence. Again and again we must rise to the majestic heights of meeting physical force with soul force.

The marvelous new militancy which has engulfed the Negro community[2] must not lead us to a distrust of all white people, for many of our white brothers, as evidenced by their presence here today, have come to realize that their destiny is tied up with our destiny and they have come to realize that their freedom is inextricably bound to our freedom. This offense we share mounted to storm the battlements of injustice must be carried forth by a biracial army. We cannot walk alone.

And as we walk, we must make the pledge that we shall always march ahead. We cannot turn back. There are those who are asking the devotees of civil rights, "When will you be satisfied?" We can never be satisfied as long as the Negro is the victim of the unspeakable horrors of police brutality.

We can never be satisfied as long as our bodies, heavy with fatigue of travel, cannot gain lodging in the motels of the highways and the hotels of the cities. We cannot be satisfied as long as the Negro's basic mobility is from a smaller ghetto to a larger one.

We can never be satisfied as long as our children are stripped of their self-hood and robbed of their dignity by signs stating "for whites only." We cannot be satisfied as long as a Negro in Mississippi cannot vote and a Negro in New York believes he has nothing for which to vote. No, we are not satisfied, and we will not be satisfied until justice rolls down like waters and righteousness like a mighty stream.

I am not unmindful that some of you come here out of excessive trials and tribulation. Some of you have come fresh from narrow jail cells. Some of you have come from areas where your quest for freedom left you battered by the storms of persecution and staggered by the winds of police brutality. You have been the veterans of creative suffering. Continue to work with the faith that unearned suffering is redemptive.

Go back to Mississippi; go back to Alabama; go back to South Carolina; go back to Georgia; go back to Louisiana; go back to the slums and ghettos of the northern cities, knowing that somehow this situation can, and will be changed. Let us not wallow in the valley of despair.

So I say to you, my friends, that even though we must face the difficulties of today and tomorrow, I still have a dream. It is a dream deeply rooted in the

---

2. The Civil Rights Movement of the 1950s and 1960s was marked by strong activism, which was met at times by violence.

American dream that one day this nation will rise up and live out the true meaning of its creed—we hold these truths to be self-evident, that all men are created equal.

I have a dream that one day on the red hills of Georgia, sons of former slaves and sons of former slave-owners will be able to sit down together at the table of brotherhood.

I have a dream that one day, even the state of Mississippi, a state sweltering with the heat of injustice, sweltering with the heat of oppression, will be transformed into an oasis of freedom and justice.

I have a dream my four little children will one day live in a nation where they will not be judged by the color of their skin but by the content of their character. I have a dream today!

I have a dream that one day, down in Alabama, with its vicious racists, with its governor having his lips dripping with the words of interposition and nullification,[3] that one day, right there in Alabama, little black boys and black girls will be able to join hands with little white boys and white girls as sisters and brothers. I have a dream today!

I have a dream that one day every valley shall be exalted, every hill and mountain shall be made low, the rough places shall be made plain, and the crooked places shall be made straight and the glory of the Lord will be revealed and all flesh shall see it together.

This is our hope. This is the faith that I go back to the South with.

With this faith we will be able to hew out of the mountain of despair a stone of hope. With this faith we will be able to transform the jangling discords of our nation into a beautiful symphony of brotherhood.

With this faith we will be able to work together, to pray together, to struggle together, to go to jail together, to stand up for freedom together, knowing that we will be free one day. This will be the day when all of God's children will be able to sing with new meaning—"my country 'tis of thee; sweet land of liberty; of thee I sing; land where my fathers died, land of the pilgrim's pride; from every mountain side, let freedom ring"—and if America is to be a great nation, this must become true.

So let freedom ring from the prodigious hilltops of New Hampshire.

Let freedom ring from the mighty mountains of New York.

Let freedom ring from the heightening Alleghenies of Pennsylvania.

Let freedom ring from the snow-capped Rockies of Colorado.

Let freedom ring from the curvaceous slopes of California.

But not only that.

Let freedom ring from Stone Mountain of Georgia.

Let freedom ring from Lookout Mountain of Tennessee.

Let freedom ring from every hill and molehill of Mississippi, from every mountainside, let freedom ring.

And when we allow freedom to ring, when we let it ring from every village and hamlet, from every state and city, we will be able to speed up that day when all of God's children—black men and white men, Jews and Gentiles, Catholics and Protestants—will be able to join hands and to sing in the words of the old Negro spiritual, "Free at last, free at last; thank God Almighty, we are free at last."

3. Legal concepts invoked by Alabama's segregationist governor, George Wallace (1919–1998), to challenge the authority of federal antidiscrimination laws.

URSULA K. LE GUIN
b. 1929

Gender, social behavior, and art combine in Ursula K. Le Guin's fiction to create model worlds, all with their own systems of organized belief. In doing so this author inquires more broadly and with more depth than is usual in science fiction. Traditionally, science fiction writers have been at their best when dealing with dystopian worlds, projecting alternative visions in which their satiric powers criticize contemporary tendencies gone bad in a nightmare future; utopias within this subgenre are more often declarative statements of what would be good—and therefore less interesting and less engaging as art. Le Guin distinguishes herself by demonstrating a sincere interest in exploring the legitimacy of other styles of existence—not just what they are but how they work. Her utopian creations are tested against all we know not just about physical and mechanical science but about anthropology in general and gender relationships in particular.

Drawing on what she first learned from Alfred L. and Theodora K. Kroeber, her anthropologist father and folklorist/writer mother, Le Guin has produced science fiction that shifts readers' interests from the pageantry of outer-space discovery and battle to the more subtle dimensions of human identity and communication. Foremost is the power of art. In "A Wizard of Earthsea" (1968) the power of naming something brings it into being; a similar creative effect is apparent in "She Unnames Them" (printed here), in which Eve revises Adam's masculine, typifying style by introducing an ethic representative of woman's feelings. Her novel *The Left Hand of Darkness* (1969) shows a human ethnologist investigating a world in which gender does not shape reality at all. In this society of hermaphrodites who experience sexual distinctions only for a short time during reproduction, such limitations as binary thinking disappear. Yet this is no simple utopia, for the author believes that any reality is a cultural rather than strictly scientific description—and that one description is superior to another only in its functional persuasiveness. Hence even her creatures in *The Left Hand of Darkness* need to overcome the restrictions of their society and develop secure identities capable of sharing love. This same appraisal informs her story "Schrödinger's Cat" (printed here), in which the famous Austrian physicist's great *Gedankenexperiment* (literally "thinking experiment," as opposed to a demonstration with physical matter) is examined in terms of its cultural implications, not its scientific truth. A similarly complex understanding of socioeconomics informs the action of "The Dispossessed" (1974), in which a scientist compares visits to an outworn anarchistic utopia with a younger world whose capitalistic versus communistic rivalries are much like our own. Here, as is usual in her work, Le Guin dresses her thought with rich nuances of character and motivated behavior; the intelligence behind her work is always accessible in human terms—sometimes uncomfortably revealing terms, as apparent in the manner of her narrators in "She Unnames Them" and "Schrödinger's Cat."

Born in Berkeley, California, where her father taught at the University of California, Le Guin was raised in this academic environment before attending Radcliffe College (for an undergraduate degree in French) and Columbia University (for a master's degree in romance languages). Her longtime residence has been in Oregon, and the ecology of the Pacific Northwest figures as an element in her fiction as well as in the amazing amount and variety of her other work. In addition to many novels (often written in trilogies) she has written poetry, essays, children's books, and ecological statements and has collaborated on photographic and cinematic projects. As a science fictionist she is one of the most highly honored writers in her field, a consistent winner of the subgenre's highest awards, including the Hugo and the Nebula several times.

Both of the following texts are from *The Compass Rose* (1982).

Schrödinger's Cat[1]

As things appear to be coming to some sort of climax, I have withdrawn to this place. It is cooler here, and nothing moves fast.

On the way here I met a married couple who were coming apart. She had pretty well gone to pieces, but he seemed, at first glance, quite hearty. While he was telling me that he had no hormones of any kind, she pulled herself together and, by supporting her head in the crook of her right knee and hopping on the toes of the right foot, approached us shouting, "Well what's *wrong* with a person trying to express themselves?" The left leg, the arms, and the trunk, which had remained lying in the heap, twitched and jerked in sympathy. "Great legs," the husband pointed out, looking at the slim ankle. "My wife has great legs."

A cat has arrived, interrupting my narrative. It is a striped yellow tom with white chest and paws. He has long whiskers and yellow eyes. I never noticed before that cats had whiskers above their eyes; is that normal? There is no way to tell. As he has gone to sleep on my knee, I shall proceed.

Where?

Nowhere, evidently. Yet the impulse to narrate remains. Many things are not worth doing, but almost anything is worth telling. In any case, I have a severe congenital case of *Ethica laboris puritanica*,[2] or Adam's Disease. It is incurable except by total decapitation. I even like to dream when asleep, and to try and recall my dreams: it assures me that I haven't wasted seven or eight hours just lying there. Now here I am, lying, here. Hard at it.

Well, the couple I was telling you about finally broke up. The pieces of him trotted around bouncing and cheeping, like little chicks, but she was finally reduced to nothing but a mass of nerves: rather like fine chicken wire, in fact, but hopelessly tangled.

So I came on, placing one foot carefully in front of the other, and grieving. This grief is with me still. I fear it is part of me, like foot or loin or eye, or may even be myself: for I seem to have no other self, nothing further, nothing that lies outside the borders of grief.

Yet I don't know what I grieve for: my wife? my husband? my children, or myself? I can't remember. Most dreams are forgotten, try as one will to remember. Yet later music strikes the note, and the harmonic rings along the mandolin strings of the mind, and we find tears in our eyes. Some note keeps playing that makes me want to cry; but what for? I am not certain.

---

1. The Austrian physicist Erwin Schrödinger (1887–1961) proposed the following thought experiment in 1935: if a cat is sealed in a box such that it will die in the event of a random and unpredictable atomic-level event, then, according to quantum theory, the cat is simulta-neously alive and dead until the box is opened for inspection.

2. Puritan work ethic (Latin); a trait the narrator sees as a necessary consequence of the biblical expulsion from the Garden of Eden ("Adam's Disease").

The yellow cat, who may have belonged to the couple that broke up, is dreaming. His paws twitch now and then, and once he makes a small, suppressed remark with his mouth shut. I wonder what a cat dreams of, and to whom he was speaking just then. Cats seldom waste words. They are quiet beasts. They keep their counsel, they reflect. They reflect all day, and at night their eyes reflect. Overbred Siamese cats may be as noisy as little dogs, and then people say, "They're talking," but the noise is farther from speech than is the deep silence of the hound or the tabby. All this cat can say is meow, but maybe in his silences he will suggest to me what it is that I have lost, what I am grieving for. I have a feeling that he knows. That's why he came here. Cats look out for Number One.

It was getting awfully hot. I mean, you could touch less and less. The stove burners, for instance. Now I know that stove burners always used to get hot; that was their final cause, they existed in order to get hot. But they began to get hot without having been turned on. Electric units or gas rings, there they'd be when you came into the kitchen for breakfast, all four of them glaring away, the air above them shaking like clear jelly with the heat waves. It did no good to turn them off, because they weren't on in the first place. Besides, the knobs and dials were also hot, uncomfortable to the touch.

Some people tried hard to cool them off. The favorite technique was to turn them on. It worked sometimes, but you could not count on it. Others investigated the phenomenon, tried to get at the root of it, the cause. They were probably the most frightened ones, but man is most human at his most frightened. In the face of the hot stove burners they acted with exemplary coolness. They studied, they observed. They were like the fellow in Michelangelo's *Last Judgment*,[3] has clapped his hands over his face in horror as the devils drag him down to Hell—but only over one eye. The other eye is busy looking. It's all he can do, but he does it. He observes. Indeed, one wonders if Hell would exist, if he did not look at it. However, neither he, nor the people I am talking about, had enough time left to do much about it. And then finally of course there were the people who did not try to do or think anything about it at all.

When the water came out of the cold-water taps hot one morning, however, even people who had blamed it all on the Democrats began to feel a more profound unease. Before long, forks and pencils and wrenches were too hot to handle without gloves; and cars were really terrible. It was like opening the door of an oven going full blast, to open the door of your car. And by then, other people almost scorched your fingers off. A kiss was like a branding iron. Your child's hair flowed along your hand like fire.

Here, as I said, it is cooler; and, as a matter of fact, this animal is cool. A real cool cat. No wonder it's pleasant to pet his fur. Also he moves slowly, at least for the most part, which is all the slowness one can reasonably expect of a cat. He hasn't that frenetic quality most creatures acquired—all they did was ZAP and gone. They lacked presence. I suppose birds always tended to be that way, but even the hummingbird used to halt for a second in the very center of his metabolic frenzy, and hang, still as a hub, present, above the fuchsias—then gone again, but you knew something was there besides the blurring brightness. But it got so that even robins and pigeons,

---

3. Monumental fresco by the Italian Renaissance painter Michelangelo Buonarotti (1475–1564).

the heavy impudent birds, were a blur; and as for swallows, they cracked the sound barrier. You knew of swallows only by the small, curved sonic booms that looped about the eaves of old houses in the evening.

Worms shot like subway trains through the dirt of gardens, among the writhing roots of roses.

You could scarcely lay a hand on children, by then: too fast to catch, too hot to hold. They grew up before your eyes.

But then, maybe that's always been true.

I was interrupted by the cat, who woke and said meow once, then jumped down from my lap and leaned against my legs diligently. This is a cat who knows how to get fed. He also knows how to jump. There was a lazy fluidity to his leap, as if gravity affected him less than it does other creatures. As a matter of fact there were some localised cases, just before I left, of the failure of gravity; but this quality in the cat's leap was something quite else. I am not yet in such a state of confusion that I can be alarmed by grace. Indeed, I found it reassuring. While I was opening a can of sardines, a person arrived.

Hearing the knock, I thought it might be the mailman. I miss mail very much, so I hurried to the door and said, "Is it the mail?"

A voice replied, "Yah!" I opened the door. He came in, almost pushing me aside in his haste. He dumped down an enormous knapsack he had been carrying, straightened up, massaged his shoulders, and said, "Wow!"

"How did you get here?"

He stared at me and repeated, "How?"

At this my thoughts concerning human and animal speech recurred to me, and I decided that this was probably not a man, but a small dog. (Large dogs seldom go yah, wow, how, unless it is appropriate to do so.)

"Come on, fella," I coaxed him. "Come, come on, that's a boy, good doggie!" I opened a can of pork and beans for him at once, for he looked half starved. He ate voraciously, gulping and lapping. When it was gone he said "Wow!" several times. I was just about to scratch him behind the ears when he stiffened, his hackles bristling, and growled deep in his throat. He had noticed the cat.

The cat had noticed him some time before, without interest, and was now sitting on a copy of *The Well-Tempered Clavier*[4] washing sardine oil off its whiskers.

"Wow!" the dog, whom I had thought of calling Rover, barked. "Wow! Do you know what that is? *That's Schrödinger's cat!*"

"No it's not, not any more; it's my cat," I said, unreasonably offended.

"Oh, well, Schrödinger's dead, of course, but it's his cat. I've seen hundreds of pictures of it. Erwin Schrödinger, the great physicist, you know. Oh, wow! To think of finding it here!"

The cat looked coldly at him for a moment, and began to wash its left shoulder with negligent energy. An almost religious expression had come into Rover's face. "It was meant," he said in a low, impressive tone. "Yah. It was *meant*. It can't be a mere coincidence. It's too improbable. Me, with the box; you, with the cat; to meet—here—now." He looked up at me, his eyes

---

4. Music by the German Baroque-era composer Johann Sebastian Bach (1685–1750).

shining with happy fervor. "Isn't it wonderful?" he said. "I'll get the box set up right away." And he started to tear open his huge knapsack.

While the cat washed its front paws, Rover unpacked. While the cat washed its tail and belly, regions hard to reach gracefully, Rover put together what he had unpacked, a complex task. When he and the cat finished their operations simultaneously and looked at me, I was impressed. They had come out even, to the very second. Indeed it seemed that something more than chance was involved. I hoped it was not myself.

"What's that?" I asked, pointing to a protuberance on the outside of the box. I did not ask what the box was as it was quite clearly a box.

"The gun," Rover said with excited pride.

"The gun?"

"To shoot the cat."

"To shoot the cat?"

"Or to *not shoot* the cat. Depending on the photon."

"The photon?"

"Yah! It's Schrödinger's great Gedankenexperiment.[5] You see, there's a little emitter here. At Zero Time, five seconds after the lid of the box is closed, it will emit one photon. The photon will strike a half-silvered mirror. The quantum mechanical probability of the photon passing through the mirror is exactly one half, isn't it? So! If the photon passes through, the trigger will be activated and the gun will fire. If the photon is deflected, the trigger will not be activated and the gun will not fire. Now, you put the cat in. The cat is in the box. You close the lid. You go away! You stay away! What happens?" Rover's eyes were bright.

"The cat gets hungry?"

"The cat gets shot—or not shot," he said, seizing my arm, though not, fortunately, in his teeth. "But the gun is silent, perfectly silent. The box is soundproof. There is no way to know whether or not the cat has been shot, until you lift the lid of the box. There is *no* way! Do you see how central this is to the whole of quantum theory? Before Zero Time the whole system, on the quantum level or on our level, is nice and simple. But after Zero Time the whole system can be represented only by a linear combination of two waves. We cannot predict the behavior of the photon, and thus, once it has behaved, we cannot predict the state of the system it has determined. We cannot predict it! God plays dice with the world![6] So it is beautifully demonstrated that if you desire certainty, any certainty, you must create it yourself!"

"How?"

"By lifting the lid of the box, of course," Rover said, looking at me with sudden disappointment, perhaps a touch of suspicion, like a Baptist who finds he has been talking church matters not to another Baptist as he thought, but a Methodist, or even, God forbid, an Episcopalian. "To find out whether the cat is dead or not."

"Do you mean," I said carefully, "that until you lift the lid of the box, the cat has neither been shot nor not been shot?"

---

5. Thought experiment (German, literal trans.); the intellectual demonstration of a theory, often making use of analogy.

6. The German-born American physicist Albert Einstein (1879–1955) stated that God *did not* play dice with the universe.

"Yah!" Rover said, radiant with relief, welcoming me back to the fold. "Or maybe, you know, both."

"But why does opening the box and looking reduce the system back to one probability, either live cat or dead cat? Why don't we get included in the system when we lift the lid of the box?"

There was a pause. "How?" Rover barked, distrustfully.

"Well, we would involve ourselves in the system, you see, the superposition of two waves. There's no reason why it should only exist *inside* an open box, is there? So when we came to look, there we would be, you and I, both looking at a live cat, and both looking at a dead cat. You see?"

A dark cloud lowered on Rover's eyes and brow. He barked twice in a subdued, harsh voice, and walked away. With his back turned to me he said in a firm, sad tone, "You must not complicate the issue. It is complicated enough."

"Are you sure?"

He nodded. Turning, he spoke pleadingly. "Listen. It's all we have—the box. Truly it is. The box. And the cat. And they're here. The box, the cat, at last. Put the cat in the box. Will you? Will you let me put the cat in the box?"

"No," I said, shocked.

"Please. Please. Just for a minute. Just for half a minute! Please let me put the cat in the box!"

"Why?"

"I can't stand this terrible uncertainty," he said, and burst into tears.

I stood some while indecisive. Though I felt sorry for the poor son of a bitch, I was about to tell him, gently, No; when a curious thing happened. The cat walked over to the box, sniffed around it, lifted his tail and sprayed a corner to mark his territory, and then lightly, with that marvellous fluid case, leapt into it. His yellow tail just flicked the edge of the lid as he jumped, and it closed, falling into place with a soft, decisive click.

"The cat is in the box," I said.

"The cat is in the box," Rover repeated in a whisper, falling to his knees. "Oh, wow. Oh, wow. Oh, wow."

There was silence then: deep silence. We both gazed, I afoot, Rover kneeling, at the box. No sound. Nothing happened. Nothing would happen. Nothing would ever happen, until we lifted the lid of the box.

"Like Pandora,"[7] I said in a weak whisper. I could not quite recall Pandora's legend. She had let all the plagues and evils out of the box, of course, but there had been something else, too. After all the devils were let loose, something quite different, quite unexpected, had been left. What had it been? Hope? A dead cat? I could not remember.

Impatience welled up in me. I turned on Rover, glaring. He returned the look with expressive brown eyes. You can't tell me dogs haven't got souls.

"Just exactly what are you trying to prove?" I demanded.

"That the cat will be dead, or not dead," he murmured submissively. "Certainty. All I want is certainty. To know for *sure* that God *does* play dice with the world."

I looked at him for a while with fascinated incredulity. "Whether he does, or doesn't," I said, "do you think he's going to leave you a note about it in the

---

7. In Greek mythology the first mortal woman, who out of curiosity opened a box and released human ills into the world; another version has her losing all human blessings except hope.

box?" I went to the box, and with a rather dramatic gesture, flung the lid back. Rover staggered up from his knees, gasping, to look. The cat was, of course, not there.

Rover neither barked, nor fainted, nor cursed, nor wept. He really took it very well.

"Where is the cat?" he asked at last.

"Where is the box?"

"Here."

"Where's here?"

"Here is now."

"We used to think so," I said, "but really we should use larger boxes."

He gazed about him in mute bewilderment, and did not flinch even when the roof of the house was lifted off just like the lid of a box, letting in the unconscionable, inordinate light of the stars. He had just time to breathe, "Oh, wow!"

I have identified the note that keeps sounding. I checked it on the mandolin before the glue melted. It is the note A, the one that drove the composer Schumann mad.[8] It is a beautiful, clear tone, much clearer now that the stars are visible. I shall miss the cat. I wonder if he found what it was we lost?

1982

She Unnames Them

Most of them accepted namelessness with the perfect indifference with which they had so long accepted and ignored their names. Whales and dolphins, seals and sea otters consented with particular grace and alacrity, sliding into anonymity as into their element. A faction of yaks, however, protested. They said that "yak" sounded right, and that almost everyone who knew they existed called them that. Unlike the ubiquitous creatures such as rats or fleas who had been called by hundreds or thousands of different names since Babel,[1] the yaks could truly say, they said, that they had *a name*. They discussed the matter all summer. The councils of the elderly females finally agreed that though the name might be useful to others, it was so redundant from the yak point of view that they never spoke it themselves, and hence might as well dispense with it. After they presented the argument in this light to their bulls, a full consensus was delayed only by the onset of severe early blizzards. Soon after the beginning of the thaw their agreement was reached and the designation "yak" was returned to the donor.

Among the domestic animals, few horses had cared what anybody called them since the failure of Dean Swift's[2] attempt to name them from their own vocabulary. Cattle, sheep, swine, asses, mules, and goats, along with

---

8. The German Romantic composer and pianist Robert Schumann (1810–1856) died from mental stress that included tinnitus, a persistent ringing in the ears.
1. Biblical city where God determined people wouldn't speak just one language.

2. Anglo-Irish satirist Jonathan Swift (1667–1745), who in book IV of *Gulliver's Travels* (1726) depicts horses who are smarter and more humane than people as a way to mock human pretensions of higher intelligence.

chickens, geese, and turkeys, all agreed enthusiastically to give their names back to the people to whom—as they put it—they belonged.

A couple of problems did come up with pets. The cats of course steadfastly denied ever having had any name other than those self-given, unspoken, effanineffably personal names which, as the poet named Eliot[3] said, they spend long hours daily contemplating—though none of the contemplators has ever admitted that what they contemplate is in fact their name, and some onlookers have wondered if the object of that meditative gaze might not in fact be the Perfect, or Platonic,[4] Mouse. In any case it is a moot point now. It was with the dogs, and with some parrots, lovebirds, ravens, and mynahs that the trouble arose. These verbally talented individuals insisted that their names were important to them, and flatly refused to part with them. But as soon as they understood that the issue was precisely one of individual choice, and that anybody who wanted to be called Rover, or Froufrou, or Polly, or even Birdie in the personal sense, was perfectly free to do so, not one of them had the least objection to parting with the lower case (or, as regards German creatures, uppercase) generic appellations poodle, parrot, dog, or bird, and all the Linnaean[5] qualifiers that had trailed along behind them for two hundred years like tin cans tied to a tail.

The insects parted with their names in vast clouds and swarms of ephemeral syllables buzzing and stinging and humming and flitting and crawling and tunneling away.

As for the fish of the sea, their names dispersed from them in silence throughout the oceans like faint, dark blurs of cuttlefish ink, and drifted off on the currents without a trace.

None were left now to unname, and yet how close I felt to them when I saw one of them swim or fly or trot or crawl across my way or over my skin, or stalk me in the night, or go along beside me for a while in the day. They seemed far closer than when their names had stood between myself and them like a clear barrier: so close that my fear of them and their fear of me became one same fear. And the attraction that many of us felt, the desire to smell one another's smells, feel or rub or caress one another's scales or skin or feathers or fur, taste one another's blood or flesh, keep one another warm,—that attraction was now all one with the fear, and the hunter could not be told from the hunted, nor the eater from the food.

This was more or less the effect I had been after. It was somewhat more powerful than I had anticipated, but I could not now, in all conscience, make an exception for myself. I resolutely put anxiety away, went to Adam, and said, "You and your father lent me this—gave it to me, actually. It's been really useful, but it doesn't exactly seem to fit very well lately. But thanks very much! It's really been very useful."

It is hard to give back a gift without sounding peevish or ungrateful, and I did not want to leave him with that impression of me. He was not paying

---

3. T. S. Eliot (1888–1965), American-born British poet and author of *Old Possum's Practical Book of Cats* (1939).
4. The Greek philosopher Plato (427–347 B.C.E.) posited that perfect archetypal forms underlie the many imperfect manifestations of things in the real world.
5. Swedish botanist Carolus Linnaeus (1707–1778) classified plants and animals by using a double name designating genus and species. "Uppercase": in German, all nouns are capitalized.

much attention, as it happened, and said only, "Put it down over there, OK?" and went on with what he was doing.

One of my reasons for doing what I did was that talk was getting us nowhere; but all the same I felt a little let down. I had been prepared to defend my decision. And I thought that perhaps when he did notice he might be upset and want to talk. I put some things away and fiddled around a little, but he continued to do what he was doing and to take no notice of anything else. At last I said, "Well, goodbye, dear. I hope the garden key turns up."

He was fitting parts together, and said without looking around, "OK, fine, dear. When's dinner?"

"I'm not sure," I said. "I'm going now. With the—" I hesitated, and finally said, "With them, you know," and went on. In fact I had only just then realized how hard it would have been to explain myself. I could not chatter away as I used to do, taking it all for granted. My words now must be as slow, as new, as single, as tentative as the steps I took going down the path away from the house, between the dark-branched, tall dancers motionless against the winter shining.

1982

GARY SNYDER
b. 1930

" I try to hold both history and wildness in my mind, that my poems may approach the true measure of things and stand against the unbalance and ignorance of our time," Gary Snyder has said. Throughout his life Snyder has sought alternatives to this imbalance. His quest has led him to the natural world, to the study of mythology and the discipline of Eastern religions, and to living oral traditions including those of Native American societies. Snyder understands the work of poetry as recovery and healing. Like the shaman-poet of primitive cultures whose power to "heal disease and resist death" is "acquired from dreams" (as he writes in the essay "Poetry and the Primitive"), he seeks to restore contact with a vital universe in which all things are interdependent. The journey of Snyder's life and work has taken him back to what he calls "the most archaic values on earth." His poems are acts of cultural criticism, challenges to the dominant values of the contemporary world.

The American West Coast is Snyder's native landscape; its forests and mountains have always attracted him, and they inspire many of his poems. He was born in San Francisco, grew up in Washington State, and later moved with his family to Portland, Oregon. In 1947 he entered Reed College, where he studied anthropology and developed a special interest in Native American cultures (Northwest Coast Indian myths and tales inform his second book, *Myths and Texts*, 1960). After doing graduate work in linguistics at Indiana University, he returned to the West, where he became associated with Kenneth Rexroth and Philip Whalen as well as Jack Kerouac and Allen Ginsberg, all of whom participated in what came to be called the San Francisco Renaissance. In this period Snyder also studied classical Chinese at the University of California at Berkeley and translated some of the Cold Mountain poems of the Zen poet Han-shan. In the mid-1950s Snyder went to Japan, where he resided, except intermittently, until 1968; in Japan he took formal instruction in Buddhism under Zen masters. The various traditions Snyder has studied come together in his varied vision-quest poems.

Snyder's poems, like his life, combine reading and formal study with physical activity; he has worked as a timber scaler, a forest-fire lookout (one of his lookouts inspired "August on Sourdough"), a logger, and a crewman on a tanker in the South Pacific. "My poems follow the rhythms of the physical work I'm doing and the life I'm leading at any given time," he has remarked. The title of his first book, *Riprap* (1959), is a forester's term for, he explains, "a cobble of stone laid on steep slick rock to make a trail for horses in the mountains." Snyder's poems often follow a trail of ascent or descent, as in "Straight-Creek–Great Burn" from his Pulitzer Prize–winning volume, *Turtle Island* (1975). Hiking with friends, he experiences the world as dynamic and flowing (running water and "changing clouds"), but the journey brings the walkers to a still point; they lie "resting on dry fern and / watching." From such a stillness the central image of a Snyder poem often rises, like the birds who "arch and loop," then "settle down." The achievement of stillness in a universe of change is, for Snyder, pivotal. The mind empties itself, the individual ego is erased, and the local place reveals the universal.

If Snyder's poems contain a Zenlike stillness, they also exhibit an appealing energy, one source of which is his love of wildness. Like the Henry David Thoreau of *Walden*, explicitly evoked in sections of *Myths and Texts*, Snyder finds a tonic wildness in the natural world, but unlike Thoreau he is an unabashed celebrant of erotic experience (his earlier poems show that he also knows its destructive possibilities). He renders one of the various faces of Eros in "Beneath My Hand and Eye the Distant Hills. Your Body" (from *The Back Country*, 1968).

Some of Snyder's numerous essays on politics and ecology are included in his influential *Earth House Hold* (1969), *The Practice of the Wild* (1990), and *A Place in Space: Ethics, Aesthetics, and Watersheds* (1995). His collections *Axe Handles* (1983), *Left Out in the Rain* (1986), and *No Nature: New and Selected Poems* (1992) confirm that his poems are bound up in the same concerns. *Danger on Peaks* (2004) continues Snyder's explorations of landscape and ecology and also registers the upheavals of change in the earth and in the body, including the world-changing events of September 11, 2001, memorialized in "Falling from a Height, Holding Hands." Although his didactic impulse sometimes leads him to oversimplification, Snyder's political vision remains one strength of his poetry. The potential in this vision for self-importance and over-seriousness is tempered by his sense of humor and the conviction, palpable in his best poems, that his experiences are common and shared. Snyder's poems suggest diverse contexts: his belief in the writer as cultural critic links him to Thoreau and Robert Duncan, his rhythms and strong images recall Ezra Pound, his meticulous attention to the natural world reminds us of Robert Frost and A. R. Ammons. Eclectic yet respectful of ancient traditions, Snyder is an American original who sees his own work as part of a "continual creation," one manifestation of the energy that sustains all life.

Milton[1] by Firelight

Piute Creek,[2] August 1955

"O hell, what do mine eyes
        with grief behold?"[3]
Working with an old
Singlejack miner, who can sense
The vein and cleavage   5
In the very guts of rock, can
Blast granite, build
Switchbacks[4] that last for years
Under the beat of snow, thaw, mule-hooves.
What use, Milton, a silly story   10
Of our lost general[5] parents,
        eaters of fruit?

The Indian, the chainsaw boy,
And a string of six mules
Came riding down to camp   15
Hungry for tomatoes and green apples.
Sleeping in saddle blankets
Under a bright night-sky
Han River slantwise by morning.
Jays squall   20
Coffee boils

In ten thousand years the Sierras
Will be dry and dead, home of the scorpion.
Ice-scratched slabs and bent trees.
No paradise, no fall,   25
Only the weathering land
The wheeling sky,
Man, with his Satan
Scouring the chaos of the mind.
Oh Hell!   30

Fire down
Too dark to read, miles from a road
The bell-mare clangs in the meadow
That packed dirt for a fill-in
Scrambling through loose rocks   35
On an old trail
All of a summer's day.[6]

1959

1. John Milton (1608–1674), major English poet and author of *Paradise Lost*, which retells the biblical story of humanity's Fall from Grace.
2. Part of Yosemite National Park, where Snyder served as a fire lookout. The Sierra Nevada mountain range includes Yosemite in its span.
3. Satan's words when he first sees Adam and Eve in the Garden of Eden (*Paradise Lost* 4.358).
4. Roads ascending a steep incline in a zigzag pattern.
5. I.e., shared by all of humankind.
6. Alludes to an epic simile describing Satan's fall: "From morn / to noon he fell, from noon to dewy eve, / A summer's day" (*Paradise Lost* 1.742–44).

Riprap[1]

Lay down these words
Before your mind like rocks.
         placed solid, by hands
In choice of place, set
Before the body of the mind   5
         in space and time:
Solidity of bark, leaf, or wall
         riprap of things:
Cobble of milky way,
         straying planets,   10
These poems, people,
         lost ponies with
Dragging saddles—
         and rocky sure-foot trails.
The worlds like an endless   15
         four-dimensional
Game of *Go*.[2]
         ants and pebbles
In the thin loam, each rock a word
         a creek-washed stone   20
Granite: ingrained
         with torment of fire and weight
Crystal and sediment linked hot
         all change, in thoughts,
As well as things.   25

                  1959

August on Sourdough,[1] A Visit from Dick Brewer

You hitched a thousand miles
         north from San Francisco
Hiked up the mountainside   a mile in the air
The little cabin—one room—
         walled in glass   5
Meadows and snowfields,   hundreds of peaks.
We lay in our sleeping bags
         talking half the night;
Wind in the guy-cables   this summer mountain rain.
Next morning I went with you   10
         as far as the cliffs,

---

1. A cobble of stone laid on steep slick rock to make a trail for horses in the mountains [Snyder's note].
2. An ancient Japanese game played with black and white stones, placed one after the other on a checkered board.
1. Mountain in Washington State, where Snyder worked as a fire-watcher during the summer of 1953.

Loaned you my poncho—   the rain across the shale—
You down the snowfield
                          flapping in the wind
Waving a last goodbye   half hidden in the clouds   15
To go on hitching
                  clear to New York;
Me back to my mountain   and far, far, west.

                                                              1968

Beneath My Hand and Eye the Distant Hills. Your Body

What my hand follows on your body
Is the line. A stream of love
    of heat, of light,   what my
    eye   lascivious
              licks   5
    over, watching
    far snow-dappled Uintah mountains[1]
Is that stream.
Of power.   what my
    hand curves over, following the line.
    "hip" and "groin"   10

Where "I"
    follow by hand and eye
    the swimming limit of your body.
As when vision idly dallies on the hills   15
Loving what it feeds on.
    soft cinder cones and craters;
    —Drum Hadley in the Pinacate[2]
       took ten minutes more to look again—
A leap of power unfurling: 20
       left,   right—right—
My heart beat faster looking
    at the snowy Uintah mountains.

As my hand feeds on you
    runs down your side and curls beneath your hip.   25
    oil pool; stratum; water—

What "is" within   not known
    but feel it
    sinking with a breath
    pusht ruthless, surely, down.   30

---

1. In northeastern Utah.   2. California town.

Beneath this long caress of hand and eye
"we" learn the flower burning,
    outward, from "below".

1968

Straight-Creek—Great Burn[1]

for Tom and Martha Burch

Lightly, in the April mountains—
        Straight Creek,
dry grass freed again of snow
& the chickadees are pecking
last fall's seeds   5
        fluffing tail in chilly wind,

Avalanche piled up cross the creek
        and chunked-froze solid—
water sluicing under; spills out
        rock lip pool, bends over,   10
        braided, white, foaming,
returns to trembling
        deep-dark hole.

Creek boulders show the flow-wear lines
        in shapes the same   15
        as running blood
        carves in the heart's main
            valve,

Early spring dry. Dry snow flurries;
        walk on crusty high snow slopes   20
—grand dead burn pine—
        chartreuse lichen as adornment
        (a dye for wool)
angled tumbled talus rock
of geosyncline[2] warm sea bottom   25
yes, so long ago.
"Once on a time."

Far light on the Bitteroots;[3]
        scrabble down willow slide
changing clouds above,   30

---

1. Scottish dialect word for "brook"; the word may also be used in the sense of a burned area, as from a forest fire.
2. Downward turning of the earth's crust. "Talus": rock debris under a cliff.
3. Range of the Rocky Mountains extending along the Idaho–Montana border.

shapes on glowing sun-ball
writhing,   choosing
            reaching out against eternal
                        azure—

us resting on dry fern and   35
                watching

Shining Heaven
change his feather garments
            overhead.

A whoosh of birds   40
swoops up and round
tilts back
almost always flying all apart
and yet hangs on!
together;   45

never a leader,
all of one swift

empty
dancing   mind.

They arc and loop & then   50
their flight is done.
they settle down.
end of poem.

                                    1974

Ripples on the Surface

"Ripples on the surface of the water
were silver salmon passing under—different
from the sorts of ripples caused by breezes"

A scudding plume on the wave—
a humpback whale is   5
breaking out in air up
gulping herring
      —Nature not a book, but a *performance*, a
high old culture

Ever-fresh events   10
scraped out, rubbed out, and used, used, again—
the braided channels of the rivers
hidden under fields of grass—

The vast wild.
    the house, alone.   15
the little house in the wild,
    the wild in the house.

both forgotten.

No nature.

Both together, one big empty house   20

                                   1993

Falling from a Height, Holding Hands

What was *that?*
storms of flying glass
& billowing flames

a clear day to the far sky—

better than burning,   5
hold hands.

We will be
two   peregrines   diving

all the way down

                                   2004

DONALD BARTHELME
1931–1989

Born in Philadelphia, where his parents were attending college, Donald Barthelme was raised in Houston, Texas, where his father became a prominent architect. The author's collegiate experience as a reporter for and editor of the student newspaper at the University of Houston influenced his career and his literary style. After army service he returned to Houston and worked on the city newspaper, wrote publicity for the university, edited the school's quarterly magazine of the arts, *Forum*, and directed the Contemporary Arts Museum. During these years Barthelme became fascinated with the mechanical workings of language, from the appearance of type on the page to verbal equivalents for nonverbal popular artifacts. When in 1962 he moved to New York to edit *Location*, a short-lived journal of literature and art, and started writing short stories and parodies for *The New Yorker*, Barthelme began to have a unique impact on literature through his recognition that language, rather than what language represents, could be the subject of fiction.

Lives, his narratives show, are influenced by the quality of language within which they are conducted. In today's world a material culture and a communications medium given to advertising and promotion feed each other in a frenzy of consumption; as in a shark's maw, everything is ingested, nothing is digested, with the result that meaning becomes a casualty of process. Danger exists in letting fine-sounding words and phrases pass without questioning the motives that inform them—something that Barthelme's engineers get away with in "Report" (collected in *Unspeakable Practices, Unnatural Acts*, 1968) when they propose to work on "realtime online computer-controlled wish evaporation" (a task they believe necessary in "meeting the rising expectations of the world's peoples, which are as you know rising entirely too fast"). Witty and satirical, Barthelme could be especially adept at making sophisticated philosophical points within mundane situations. "Me and Miss Mandible," from his first collection, *Come Back, Dr. Caligari* (1964), argues a postmodern understanding of semiotics from a sixth-grade classroom to which an adult has been mysteriously returned to suffer, with all his experience, in the company of twelve-year-olds. What he learns, and wishes he could teach the others now struggling through behavior molded by television and movies, is that "signs are signs, and that some of them are lies."

Barthelme's four novels move in the same direction as his ten volumes of short stories. *Snow White* (1967), like his early fiction, uses a preposterous situation—the fairy tale character living with seven small men in a contemporary Greenwich Village apartment—to show how modern life lacks heroism and romance. *The Dead Father* (1975) is more weighted with psychological issues, principally the power of fatherhood and how that power is absurdly clung to. Here the author began relying less on satirical references to current life and more on narrative statement. In the middle to late 1970s Barthelme's fiction also became more comfortable in describing life as lived without the superimposition of defamiliarizing actions; *Paradise* (1986) reads almost conventionally. Yet as had happened so productively in such early work as "The Balloon" (printed here), Barthelme wondered at existence. At his death he had completed a fanciful romance, *The King* (published posthumously in 1990); in it he recasts the situation of Britain in the early years of World War II, applying literally the Arthurian terms to which commentators of the time liked to allude.

The following text is from *Unspeakable Practices, Unnatural Acts* (1968).

The Balloon

The balloon, beginning at a point on Fourteenth Street, the exact location of which I cannot reveal, expanded northward all one night, while people were sleeping, until it reached the Park. There, I stopped it; at dawn the northernmost edges lay over the Plaza,[1] the free-hanging motion was frivolous and gentle. But experiencing a faint irritation at stopping, even to protect the trees, and seeing no reason the balloon should not be allowed to expand upward, over the parts of the city it was already covering, into the "air space" to be found there, I asked the engineers to see to it. This expan-

---

1. Grand Army Plaza, site of the Plaza Hotel (also called the Plaza), at the southeastern corner of Central Park in New York City, approximately 2.5 miles north of Fourteenth Street, the northern boundary of Greenwich Village.

sion took place throughout the morning, soft imperceptible sighing of gas through the valves. The balloon then covered forty-five blocks north-south and an irregular area east-west, as many as six crosstown blocks on either side of the Avenue[2] in some places. That was the situation, then.

But it is wrong to speak of "situations," implying sets of circumstances leading to some resolution, some escape of tension; there were no situations, simply the balloon hanging there—muted heavy grays and browns for the most part, contrasting with walnut and soft yellows. A deliberate lack of finish, enhanced by skillful installation, gave the surface a rough, forgotten quality; sliding weights on the inside, carefully adjusted, anchored the great, vari-shaped mass at a number of points. Now we have had a flood of original ideas in all media, works of singular beauty as well as significant milestones in the history of inflation, but at that moment there was only *this balloon*, concrete particular, hanging there.

There were reactions. Some people found the balloon "interesting." As a response this seemed inadequate to the immensity of the balloon, the suddenness of its appearance over the city; on the other hand, in the absence of hysteria or other societally induced anxiety, it must be judged a calm "mature" one. There was a certain amount of initial argumentation about the "meaning" of the balloon; this subsided, because we have learned not to insist on meanings, and they are rarely even looked for now, except in cases involving the simplest, safest phenomena. It was agreed that since the meaning of the balloon could never be known absolutely, extended discussion was pointless, or at least less purposeful than the activities of those who, for example, hung green and blue paper lanterns from the warm gray underside, in certain streets, or seized the occasion to write messages on the surface, announcing their availability for the performance of unnatural acts, or the availability of acquaintances.

Daring children jumped, especially at those points where the balloon hovered close to a building, so that the gap between balloon and building was a matter of a few inches, or points where the balloon actually made contact, exerting an ever-so-slight pressure against the side of a building, so that balloon and building seemed a unity. The upper surface was so structured that a "landscape" was presented, small valleys as well as slight knolls, or mounds; once atop the balloon, a stroll was possible, or even a trip, from one place to another. There was pleasure in being able to run down an incline, then up the opposing slope, both gently graded, or in making a leap from one side to the other. Bouncing was possible, because of the pneumaticity of the surface, and even falling, if that was your wish. That all these varied motions, as well as others, were within one's possibilities, in experiencing the "up" side of the balloon, was extremely exciting for children, accustomed to the city's flat, hard skin. But the purpose of the balloon was not to amuse children.

Too, the number of people, children and adults, who took advantage of the opportunities described was not so large as it might have been: a certain timidity, lack of trust in the balloon, was seen. There was, furthermore, some hostility. Because we had hidden the pumps, which fed helium to the interior, and because the surface was so vast that the authorities could not determine the point of entry—that is, the point at which the gas was

2. Fifth Avenue.

injected—a degree of frustration was evidenced by those city officers into whose province such manifestations normally fell. The apparent purposelessness of the balloon was vexing (as was the fact that it was "there" at all). Had we painted, in great letters, "LABORATORY TESTS PROVE" OR "18% MORE EFFECTIVE" on the sides of the balloon, this difficulty would have been circumvented. But I could not bear to do so. On the whole, these officers were remarkably tolerant, considering the dimensions of the anomaly, this tolerance being the result of, first, secret tests conducted by night that convinced them that little or nothing could be done in the way of removing or destroying the balloon, and, secondly, a public warmth that arose (not uncolored by touches of the aforementioned hostility) toward the balloon, from ordinary citizens.

As a single balloon must stand for a lifetime of thinking about balloons, so each citizen expressed, in the attitude he chose, a complex of attitudes. One man might consider that the balloon had to do with the notion *sullied*, as in the sentence *The big balloon sullied the otherwise clear and radiant Manhattan sky.* That is, the balloon was, in this man's view, an imposture, something inferior to the sky that had formerly been there, something interposed between the people and their "sky." But in fact it was January, the sky was dark and ugly; it was not a sky you could look up into, lying on your back in the street, with pleasure, unless pleasure, for you, proceeded from having been threatened, from having been misused. And the underside of the balloon was a pleasure to look up into, we had seen to that, muted grays and browns for the most part, contrasted with walnut and soft, forgotten yellows. And so, while this man was thinking *sullied*, still there was an admixture of pleasurable cognition in his thinking, struggling with the original perception.

Another man, on the other hand, might view the balloon as if it were part of a system of unanticipated rewards, as when one's employer walks in and says, "Here, Henry, take this package of money I have wrapped for you, because we have been doing so well in the business here, and I admire the way you bruise the tulips, without which bruising your department would not be a success, or at least not the success that it is." For this man the balloon might be a brilliantly heroic "muscle and pluck" experience, even if an experience poorly understood.

Another man might say, "Without the example of ———, it is doubtful that ——— would exist today in its present form," and find many to agree with him, or to argue with him. Ideas of "bloat" and "float" were introduced, as well as concepts of dream and responsibility. Others engaged in remarkably detailed fantasies having to do with a wish either to lose themselves in the balloon, or to engorge it. The private character of these wishes, of their origins, deeply buried and unknown, was such that they were not much spoken of; yet there is evidence that they were widespread. It was also argued that what was important was what you felt when you stood under the balloon; some people claimed that they felt sheltered, warmed, as never before, while enemies of the balloon felt, or reported feeling, constrained, a "heavy" feeling.

Critical opinion was divided:

"monstrous pourings"

"harp"

XXXXXXX "certain contrasts with darker portions"

"inner joy"

"large, square corners"

"conservative eclecticism that has so far governed modern balloon design"

::::::: "abnormal vigor"

"warm, soft, lazy passages"

"Has unity been sacrificed for a sprawling quality?"

"Quelle catastrophe!"

"munching"

People began, in a curious way, to locate themselves in relation to aspects of the balloon: "I'll be at that place where it dips down into Forty-seventh Street almost to the sidewalk, near the Alamo Chile House," or, "Why don't we go stand on top, and take the air, and maybe walk about a bit, where it forms a tight, curving line with the façade of the Gallery of Modern Art—" Marginal intersections offered entrances within a given time duration, as well as "warm, soft, lazy passages" in which . . . But it is wrong to speak of "marginal intersections," each intersection was crucial, none could be ignored (as if, walking there, you might not find someone capable of turning your attention, in a flash, from old exercises to new exercises, risks and escalations). Each intersection was crucial, meeting of balloon and building, meeting of balloon and man, meeting of balloon and balloon.

It was suggested that what was admired about the balloon was finally this: that it was not limited, or defined. Sometimes a bulge, blister, or subsection would carry all the way east to the river on its own initiative, in the manner of an army's movements on a map, as seen in a headquarters remote from the fighting. Then that part would be, as it were, thrown back again, or would withdraw into new dispositions; the next morning, that part would have made another sortie, or disappeared altogether. This ability of the balloon to shift its shape, to change, was very pleasing, especially to people whose lives were rather rigidly patterned, persons to whom change, although desired, was not available. The balloon, for the twenty-two days of its existence, offered the possibility, in its randomness, of mislocation of the self, in contradistinction to the grid of precise, rectangular pathways under our feet. The amount of specialized training currently needed, and the consequent desirability of long-term commitments, has been occasioned by the steadily growing importance of complex machinery, in virtually all kinds of operations; as this tendency increases, more and more people will turn, in bewildered inadequacy, to solutions for which the balloon may stand as a prototype, or "rough draft."

I met you under the balloon, on the occasion of your return from Norway; you asked if it was mine; I said it was. The balloon, I said, is a spontaneous autobiographical disclosure, having to do with the unease I felt at your absence, and with sexual deprivation, but now that your visit to Bergen has been terminated, it is no longer necessary or appropriate. Removal of the balloon was easy; trailer trucks carried away the depleted fabric, which is now stored in West Virginia, awaiting some other time of unhappiness, sometime, perhaps, when we are angry with one another.

1968

TONI MORRISON
b. 1931

The 1993 Nobel Laureate in literature, Toni Morrison is a novelist of great importance in her own right and has been the central figure in putting fiction by and about African American women at the forefront of the late twentieth-century literary canon. Whereas the legacy of slavery had all but effaced a usable tradition, and critical stereotypes at times restricted such writers' range, Morrison's fiction serves as a model for reconstructing a culturally empowering past. She joins the great American tradition of self-invention: her example and her editorial work have figured importantly in the careers of other writers, such as Toni Cade Bambara (included in this volume) and Gayl Jones.

Morrison was born in Lorain, Ohio, where much of her fiction is set (a departure from earlier African American narratives typically located in the rural South or urban North). Having earned a B.A. from Howard University with a major in English and a minor in classics, and an M.A. from Cornell University (with a thesis on suicide in the novels of Virginia Woolf and William Faulkner), Morrison began a teaching career in 1955 that reached from Texas Southern University back to Howard, where her students included the future activist Stokeley Carmichael and the future critic Houston A. Baker Jr. At this time she married Harold Morrison, a Jamaican architect, with whom she had two children before ending their marriage in 1964. Already writing, she took a job with the publishing firm Random House and eventually settled in New York City, where she worked until 1983. During these same years she held visiting teaching appointments at institutions including Yale University and Bard College.

As a first novel *The Bluest Eye* (1970) is uncommonly mature for its confident use of various narrative voices. Throughout her career Morrison has been dedicated to constructing a practical cultural identity of a race and a gender whose self-images have been obscured or denied by dominating forces, and in *The Bluest Eye* she already shows that narrative strategy is an important element in such construction. A girl's need to be loved generates the novel's action, action that involves displaced and alienated affections (and eventually incestuous rape); the family's inability to produce a style of existence in which love can be born and thrive leads to just such a devastating fate for Morrison's protagonist. Love is also denied in *Sula* (1974), in which relationships extend in two directions: between contemporaries (Sula and her friend Nel) and with previous generations.

With *Song of Solomon* (1977) Morrison seeks a more positive redemption of her characters. Turning away from his parents' loveless marriage, Milkman Dead makes a physical and mental journey to his ancestral roots. Here he discovers a more useful legacy in communal tales about Grandmother and Great-Grandfather, each long dead but infusing the local culture with emotionally sustaining lore. Milkman uses this lore to learn how the spiritual guidance offered by his aunt Pilate eclipses the material concerns of his parents' world.

Allegory becomes an important strategy in *Tar Baby* (1981), drawing on the strong folk culture of Haiti, where two contrasting persons form a troubled relationship based on their distinct searches for and rejections of a heritage. Yet it is in a rebuilding of history, rather than allegory or myth, that Morrison achieves her great strength as a novelist in *Beloved* (1987), the winner of her first major award, the Pulitzer Prize. Set in the middle 1870s, when race relations in America were at their most crucial juncture (slavery having ended and the course of the South's Reconstruction not yet fully determined), this novel shows a mother (Sethe) being haunted and eventually destroyed by the ghost of a daughter (Beloved) whom she had killed eighteen years earlier rather than allow to be taken by a vicious slavemaster. This novel is central to Morrison's canon because it involves so many important themes and techniques, from love and guilt to history's role in clarifying the past's influence on the present, all told in a style of magical realism that transforms (without denying) more mundane facts.

Jazz (1992) finds Morrison modeling her narrative voice on the progression of a jazz solo to demonstrate how improvisation with detail can change the nature of what is expressed. Present and past weave together in her characters' lives as the narrative seeks to understand the jealousies of love and the sometimes macabre manifestations of hatred. *Paradise* (1988) takes a nineteenth-century utopia and reexamines its ideals in the face of 1970s realities—a reminder of how neither past nor present can be insulated from the other. *Love* (2003), with its murder, arson, pedophilia, and several rapes punctuating a narrative in which arguments over a legacy dislodge awkward elements of the past, is a reminder of how disturbing Morrison's fiction can be. *A Mercy* (2008) explores the contradictions between American and pastoral ideals, and the realities of Native American extermination and African American slavery.

Presently serving as the prestigious Golheen Professor of the Humanities at Princeton University, Morrison has moved easily into the role of spokesperson for literary issues. Together with her Nobel lecture, her essays collected as *Playing in the Dark: Whiteness and the Literary Imagination* (1992) challenge stereotypes in white critical thinking about black literature. Her short story "Recitatif," written for *Confirmation,* the 1983 anthology edited by Amiri and Amina Baraka, directly addresses the issues of individual and family, past and present, and race and its effacements that motivate the larger sense of her work. A "recitatif" is a vocal performance in which a narrative is not stated but sung. In her work Morrison's voice sings proudly of a past that in the artistic nature of its reconstruction puts all Americans in touch with a more positively usable heritage.

The following text is from *Confirmation.*

Recitatif

My mother danced all night and Roberta's was sick. That's why we were taken to St. Bonny's. People want to put their arms around you when you tell them you were in a shelter, but it really wasn't bad. No big long room with one hundred beds like Bellevue.[1] There were four to a room, and when Roberta and me came, there was a shortage of state kids, so we were the only ones assigned to 406 and could go from bed to bed if we wanted to. And we

---

1. Bellevue Hospital in New York City is known for its psychiatric ward. St. Bonaventure's offers the services of a youth shelter and school.

wanted to, too. We changed beds every night and for the whole four months we were there we never picked one out as our own permanent bed.

It didn't start out that way. The minute I walked in and the Big Bozo introduced us, I got sick to my stomach. It was one thing to be taken out of your own bed early in the morning—it was something else to be stuck in a strange place with a girl from a whole other race. And Mary, that's my mother, she was right. Every now and then she would stop dancing long enough to tell me something important and one of the things she said was that they never washed their hair and they smelled funny. Roberta sure did. Smell funny, I mean. So when the Big Bozo (nobody ever called her Mrs. Itkin, just like nobody ever said St. Bonaventure)—when she said, "Twyla, this is Roberta. Roberta, this is Twyla. Make each other welcome." I said, "My mother won't like you putting me in here."

"Good," said Bozo. "Maybe then she'll come and take you home."

How's that for mean? If Roberta had laughed I would have killed her, but she didn't. She just walked over to the window and stood with her back to us.

"Turn around," said the Bozo. "Don't be rude. Now Twyla. Roberta. When you hear a loud buzzer, that's the call for dinner. Come down to the first floor. Any fights and no movie." And then, just to make sure we knew what we would be missing, "*The Wizard of Oz.*"[2]

Roberta must have thought I meant that my mother would be mad about my being put in the shelter. Not about rooming with her, because as soon as Bozo left she came over to me and said, "Is your mother sick too?"

"No," I said. "She just likes to dance all night."

"Oh," she nodded her head and I liked the way she understood things so fast. So for the moment it didn't matter that we looked like salt and pepper standing there and that's what the other kids called us sometimes. We were eight years old and got F's all the time. Me because I couldn't remember what I read or what the teacher said. And Roberta because she couldn't read at all and didn't even listen to the teacher. She wasn't good at anything except jacks, at which she was a killer: pow scoop pow scoop pow scoop.

We didn't like each other all that much at first, but nobody else wanted to play with us because we weren't real orphans with beautiful dead parents in the sky. We were dumped. Even the New York City Puerto Ricans and the upstate Indians ignored us. All kinds of kids were in there, black ones, white ones, even two Koreans. The food was good, though. At least I thought so. Roberta hated it and left whole pieces of things on her plate: Spam, Salisbury steak—even jello with fruit cocktail in it, and she didn't care if I ate what she wouldn't. Mary's idea of supper was popcorn and a can of Yoo-Hoo.[3] Hot mashed potatoes and two weenies was like Thanksgiving for me.

It really wasn't bad, St. Bonny's. The big girls on the second floor pushed us around now and then. But that was all. They wore lipstick and eyebrow pencil and wobbled their knees while they watched TV. Fifteen, sixteen, even, some of them were. They were put-out girls, scared runaways most of them. Poor little girls who fought their uncles off but looked tough to us, and mean. God did they look mean. The staff tried to keep them separate from the younger children, but sometimes they caught us watching them in

---

2. The 1939 film based on the 1900 children's book by the American writer L. Frank Baum (1856–1919).

3. A chocolate soft drink.

the orchard where they played radios and danced with each other. They'd light out after us and pull our hair or twist our arms. We were scared of them, Roberta and me, but neither of us wanted the other one to know it. So we got a good list of dirty names we could shout back when we ran from them through the orchard. I used to dream a lot and almost always the orchard was there. Two acres, four maybe, of these little apple trees. Hundreds of them. Empty and crooked like beggar women when I first came to St. Bonny's but fat with flowers when I left. I don't know why I dreamt about that orchard so much. Nothing really happened there. Nothing all that important, I mean. Just the big girls dancing and playing the radio. Roberta and me watching. Maggie fell down there once. The kitchen woman with legs like parentheses. And the big girls laughed at her. We should have helped her up, I know, but we were scared of those girls with lipstick and eyebrow pencil. Maggie couldn't talk. The kids said she had her tongue cut out, but I think she was just born that way: mute. She was old and sandy-colored and she worked in the kitchen. I don't know if she was nice or not. I just remember her legs like parentheses and how she rocked when she walked. She worked from early in the morning till two o'clock, and if she was late, if she had too much cleaning and didn't get out till two-fifteen or so, she'd cut through the orchard so she wouldn't miss her bus and have to wait another hour. She wore this really stupid little hat—a kid's hat with ear flaps—and she wasn't much taller than we were. A really awful little hat. Even for a mute, it was dumb—dressing like a kid and never saying anything at all.

"But what about if somebody tries to kill her?" I used to wonder about that. "Or what if she wants to cry? Can she cry?"

"Sure," Roberta said. "But just tears. No sounds come out."

"She can't scream?"

"Nope. Nothing."

"Can she hear?"

"I guess."

"Let's call her," I said. And we did.

"Dummy! Dummy!" She never turned her head.

"Bow legs! Bow legs!" Nothing. She just rocked on, the chin straps of her baby-boy hat swaying from side to side. I think we were wrong. I think she could hear and didn't let on. And it shames me even now to think there was somebody in there after all who heard us call her those names and couldn't tell on us.

We got along all right, Roberta and me. Changed beds every night, got F's in civics and communication skills and gym. The Bozo was disappointed in us, she said. Out of 130 of us state cases, 90 were under twelve. Almost all were real orphans with beautiful dead parents in the sky. We were the only ones dumped and the only ones with F's in three classes including gym. So we got along—what with her leaving whole pieces of things on her plate and being nice about not asking questions.

I think it was the day before Maggie fell down that we found out our mothers were coming to visit us on the same Sunday. We had been at the shelter twenty-eight days (Roberta twenty-eight and a half) and this was their first visit with us. Our mothers would come at ten o'clock in time for chapel, then lunch with us in the teachers' lounge. I thought if my dancing mother met her sick mother it might be good for her. And Roberta thought her sick mother would get a big bang out of a dancing one. We got excited about it and curled each other's hair. After breakfast we sat on the bed watching the road from the window. Roberta's socks were still wet. She washed them the night before and put them on the radiator to dry. They hadn't, but she put them on anyway because their tops were so pretty—scalloped in pink. Each of us had a purple construction-paper basket that we had made in craft class. Mine had a yellow crayon rabbit on it. Roberta's had eggs with wiggly lines of color. Inside were cellophane grass and just the jelly beans because I'd eaten the two marshmallow eggs they gave us. The Big Bozo came herself to get us. Smiling she told us we looked very nice and to come downstairs. We were so surprised by the smile we'd never seen before, neither of us moved.

"Don't you want to see your mommies?"

I stood up first and spilled the jelly beans all over the floor. Bozo's smile disappeared while we scrambled to get the candy up off the floor and put it back in the grass.

She escorted us downstairs to the first floor, where the other girls were lining up to file into the chapel. A bunch of grown-ups stood to one side. Viewers mostly. The old biddies who wanted servants and the fags who wanted company looking for children they might want to adopt. Once in a while a grandmother. Almost never anybody young or anybody whose face wouldn't scare you in the night. Because if any of the real orphans had young relatives they wouldn't be real orphans. I saw Mary right away. She had on those green slacks I hated and hated even more now because didn't she know we were going to chapel? And that fur jacket with the pocket linings so ripped she had to pull to get her hands out of them. But her face was pretty—like always, and she smiled and waved like she was the little girl looking for her mother—not me.

I walked slowly, trying not to drop the jelly beans and hoping the paper handle would hold. I had to use my last Chiclet because by the time I finished cutting everything out, all the Elmer's was gone. I am left-handed and the scissors never worked for me. It didn't matter, though; I might just as well have chewed the gum. Mary dropped to her knees and grabbed me, mashing the basket, the jelly beans, and the grass into her ratty fur jacket.

"Twyla, baby. Twyla, baby!"

I could have killed her. Already I heard the big girls in the orchard the next time saying, "Twyyyyyyla, baby!" But I couldn't stay mad at Mary while she was smiling and hugging me and smelling of Lady Esther dusting powder. I wanted to stay buried in her fur all day.

To tell the truth I forgot about Roberta. Mary and I got in line for the traipse into chapel and I was feeling proud because she looked so beautiful even in those ugly green slacks that made her behind stick out. A pretty mother on earth is better than a beautiful dead one in the sky even if she did leave you all alone to go dancing.

I felt a tap on my shoulder, turned, and saw Roberta smiling. I smiled back, but not too much lest somebody think this visit was the biggest thing that ever happened in my life. Then Roberta said, "Mother, I want you to meet my roommate, Twyla. And that's Twyla's mother."

I looked up it seemed for miles. She was big. Bigger than any man and on her chest was the biggest cross I'd ever seen. I swear it was six inches long each way. And in the crook of her arm was the biggest Bible ever made.

Mary, simple-minded as ever, grinned and tried to yank her hand out of the pocket with the raggedy lining—to shake hands, I guess. Roberta's mother looked down at me and then looked down at Mary too. She didn't say anything, just grabbed Roberta with her Bible-free hand and stepped out of line, walking quickly to the rear of it. Mary was still grinning because she's not too swift when it comes to what's really going on. Then this light bulb goes off in her head and she says "That bitch!" really loud and us almost in the chapel now. Organ music whining; the Bonny Angels singing sweetly. Everybody in the world turned around to look. And Mary would have kept it up—kept calling names if I hadn't squeezed her hand as hard as I could. That helped a little, but she still twitched and crossed and uncrossed her legs all through service. Even groaned a couple of times. Why did I think she would come there and act right? Slacks. No hat like the grandmothers and viewers, and groaning all the while. When we stood for hymns she kept her mouth shut. Wouldn't even look at the words on the page. She actually reached in her purse for a mirror to check her lipstick. All I could think of was that she really needed to be killed. The sermon lasted a year, and I knew the real orphans were looking smug again.

We were supposed to have lunch in the teachers' lounge, but Mary didn't bring anything, so we picked fur and cellophane grass off the mashed jelly beans and ate them. I could have killed her. I sneaked a look at Roberta. Her mother had brought chicken legs and ham sandwiches and oranges and a whole box of chocolate-covered grahams. Roberta drank milk from a thermos while her mother read the Bible to her.

Things are not right. The wrong food is always with the wrong people. Maybe that's why I got into waitress work later—to match up the right people with the right food. Roberta just let those chicken legs sit there, but she did bring a stack of grahams up to me later when the visit was over. I think she was sorry that her mother would not shake my mother's hand. And I liked that and I liked the fact that she didn't say a word about Mary groaning all the way through the service and not bringing any lunch.

Roberta left in May when the apple trees were heavy and white. On her last day we went to the orchard to watch the big girls smoke and dance by the radio. It didn't matter that they said, "Twyyyyyla, baby." We sat on the ground and breathed. Lady Esther. Apple blossoms. I still go soft when I smell one or the other. Roberta was going home. The big cross and the big Bible was coming to get her and she seemed sort of glad and sort of not. I thought I would die in that room of four beds without her and I knew Bozo had plans to move some other dumped kid in there with me. Roberta promised to write every day, which was really sweet of her because she couldn't read a lick so how could she write anybody. I would have drawn pictures and sent them to her but she never gave me her address. Little by little she faded. Her wet socks with the pink scalloped tops and her big serious-looking eyes—that's all I could catch when I tried to bring her to mind.

I was working behind the counter at the Howard Johnson's on the Thruway just before the Kingston exit. Not a bad job. Kind of a long ride from Newburgh,[4] but okay once I got there. Mine was the second night shift—

4. A community beside the Hudson River, located eighty miles north of New York City.

eleven to seven. Very light until a Greyhound checked in for breakfast around six-thirty. At that hour the sun was all the way clear of the hills behind the restaurant. The place looked better at night—more like shelter— but I loved it when the sun broke in, even if it did show all the cracks in the vinyl and the speckled floor looked dirty no matter what the mop boy did.

It was August and a bus crowd was just unloading. They would stand around a long while: going to the john, and looking at gifts and junk-for-sale machines, reluctant to sit down so soon. Even to eat. I was trying to fill the coffee pots and get them all situated on the electric burners when I saw her. She was sitting in a booth smoking a cigarette with two guys smothered in head and facial hair. Her own hair was so big and wild I could hardly see her face. But the eyes. I would know them anywhere. She had on a powder-blue halter and shorts outfit and earrings the size of bracelets. Talk about lipstick and eyebrow pencil. She made the big girls look like nuns. I couldn't get off the counter until seven o'clock, but I kept watching the booth in case they got up to leave before that. My replacement was on time for a change, so I counted and stacked my receipts as fast as I could and signed off. I walked over to the booth, smiling and wondering if she would remember me. Or even if she wanted to remember me. Maybe she didn't want to be reminded of St. Bonny's or to have anybody know she was ever there. I know I never talked about it to anybody.

I put my hands in my apron pockets and leaned against the back of the booth facing them.

"Roberta? Roberta Fisk?"

She looked up. "Yeah?"

"Twyla."

She squinted for a second and then said, "Wow."

"Remember me?"

"Sure. Hey. Wow."

"It's been a while," I said, and gave a smile to the two hairy guys.

"Yeah. Wow. You work here?"

"Yeah," I said. "I live in Newburgh."

"Newburgh? No kidding?" She laughed then a private laugh that included the guys but only the guys, and they laughed with her. What could I do but laugh too and wonder why I was standing there with my knees showing out from under that uniform. Without looking I could see the blue and white triangle on my head, my hair shapeless in a net, my ankles thick in white oxfords. Nothing could have been less sheer than my stockings. There was this silence that came down right after I laughed. A silence it was her turn to fill up. With introductions, maybe, to her boyfriends or an invitation to sit down and have a Coke. Instead she lit a cigarette off the one she'd just finished and said, "We're on our way to the Coast. He's got an appointment with Hendrix."[5] She gestured casually toward the boy next to her.

"Hendrix? Fantastic," I said. "Really fantastic. What's she doing now?"

Roberta coughed on her cigarette and the two guys rolled their eyes up at the ceiling.

---

5. Jimi Hendrix (1942–1970), African American musician and rock star.

"Hendrix. Jimi Hendrix, asshole. He's only the biggest—Oh, wow. Forget it."

I was dismissed without anyone saying goodbye, so I thought I would do it for her.

"How's your mother?" I asked. Her grin cracked her whole face. She swallowed. "Fine," she said. "How's yours?"

"Pretty as a picture," I said and turned away. The backs of my knees were damp. Howard Johnson's really was a dump in the sunlight.

James is as comfortable as a house slipper. He liked my cooking and I liked his big loud family. They have lived in Newburgh all of their lives and talk about it the way people do who have always known a home. His grandmother is a porch swing older than his father and when they talk about streets and avenues and buildings they call them names they no longer have. They still call the A & P[6] Rico's because it stands on property once a mom and pop store owned by Mr. Rico. And they call the new community college Town Hall because it once was. My mother-in-law puts up jelly and cucumbers and buys butter wrapped in cloth from a dairy. James and his father talk about fishing and baseball and I can see them all together on the Hudson in a raggedy skiff. Half the population of Newburgh is on welfare now, but to my husband's family it was still some upstate paradise of a time long past. A time of ice houses and vegetable wagons, coal furnaces and children weeding gardens. When our son was born my mother-in-law gave me the crib blanket that had been hers.

But the town they remembered had changed. Something quick was in the air. Magnificent old houses, so ruined they had become shelter for squatters and rent risks, were bought and renovated. Smart IBM people[7] moved out of their suburbs back into the city and put shutters up and herb gardens in their backyards. A brochure came in the mail announcing the opening of a Food Emporium. Gourmet food it said—and listed items the rich IBM crowd would want. It was located in a new mall at the edge of town and I drove out to shop there one day—just to see. It was late in June. After the tulips were gone and the Queen Elizabeth roses were open everywhere. I trailed my cart along the aisle tossing in smoked oysters and Robert's sauce and things I knew would sit in my cupboard for years. Only when I found some Klondike ice cream bars did I feel less guilty about spending James's fireman's salary so foolishly. My father-in-law ate them with the same gusto little Joseph did.

Waiting in the check-out line I heard a voice say, "Twyla!"

The classical music piped over the aisles had affected me and the woman leaning toward me was dressed to kill. Diamonds on her hand, a smart white summer dress. "I'm Mrs. Benson," I said.

"Ho. Ho. The Big Bozo," she sang.

For a split second I didn't know what she was talking about. She had a bunch of asparagus and two cartons of fancy water.

"Roberta!"

"Right."

<hr>

6. Supermarket, part of a national chain once called the Great Atlantic and Pacific Tea Company.

7. High-salaried employees of the International Business Machine Corporation, headquartered in the suburbs north of New York City.

"For heaven's sake. Roberta."

"You look great," she said.

"So do you. Where are you? Here? In Newburgh?"

"Yes. Over in Annandale."

I was opening my mouth to say more when the cashier called my attention to her empty counter.

"Meet you outside." Roberta pointed her finger and went into the express line.

I placed the groceries and kept myself from glancing around to check Roberta's progress. I remembered Howard Johnson's and looking for a chance to speak only to be greeted with a stingy "wow." But she was waiting for me and her huge hair was sleek now, smooth around a small, nicely shaped head. Shoes, dress, everything lovely and summery and rich. I was dying to know what happened to her, how she got from Jimi Hendrix to Annandale, a neighborhood full of doctors and IBM executives. Easy, I thought. Everything is so easy for them. They think they own the world.

"How long," I asked her. "How long have you been here?"

"A year. I got married to a man who lives here. And you, you're married too, right? Benson, you said."

"Yeah. James Benson."

"And is he nice?"

"Oh, is he nice?"

"Well, is he?" Roberta's eyes were steady as though she really meant the question and wanted an answer.

"He's wonderful, Roberta. Wonderful."

"So you're happy."

"Very."

"That's good," she said and nodded her head. "I always hoped you'd be happy. Any kids? I know you have kids."

"One. A boy. How about you?"

"Four."

"Four?"

She laughed. "Step kids. He's a widower."

"Oh."

"Got a minute? Let's have a coffee."

I thought about the Klondikes melting and the inconvenience of going all the way to my car and putting the bags in the trunk. Served me right for buying all that stuff I didn't need. Roberta was ahead of me.

"Put them in my car. It's right here."

And then I saw the dark blue limousine.

"You married a Chinaman?"

"No," she laughed. "He's the driver."

"Oh, my. If the Big Bozo could see you now."

We both giggled. Really giggled. Suddenly, in just a pulse beat, twenty years disappeared and all of it came rushing back. The big girls (whom we called gar girls—Roberta's misheard word for the evil stone faces described in a civics class) there dancing in the orchard, the ploppy mashed potatoes, the double weenies, the Spam with pineapple. We went into the coffee shop holding on to one another and I tried to think why we were glad to see each other this time and not before. Once, twelve years ago, we passed like strangers. A black girl and a white girl meeting in a Howard Johnson's on the road and having nothing to say. One in a blue and white triangle wait-ress hat—the other on her way to see Hendrix. Now we were behaving like sisters separated for much too long. Those four short months were nothing in time. Maybe it was the thing itself. Just being there, together. Two little girls who knew what nobody else in the world knew—how not to ask questions. How to believe what had to be believed. There was politeness in that reluctance and generosity as well. Is your mother sick too? No, she dances all night. Oh—and an understanding nod.

We sat in a booth by the window and fell into recollection like veterans.

"Did you ever learn to read?"

"Watch." She picked up the menu. "Special of the day. Cream of corn soup. Entrées. Two dots and a wriggly line. Quiche. Chef salad, scallops . . ."

I was laughing and applauding when the waitress came up.

"Remember the Easter baskets?"

"And how we tried to *introduce* them?"

"Your mother with that cross like two telephone poles."

"And yours with those tight slacks."

We laughed so loudly heads turned and made the laughter harder to suppress.

"What happened to the Jimi Hendrix date?"

Roberta made a blow-out sound with her lips.

"When he died I thought about you."

"Oh, you heard about him finally?"

"Finally. Come on, I was a small-town country waitress."

"And I was a small-town country dropout. God, were we wild. I still don't know how I got out of there alive."

"But you did."

"I did. I really did. Now I'm Mrs. Kenneth Norton."

"Sounds like a mouthful."

"It is."

"Servants and all?"

Roberta held up two fingers.

"Ow! What does he do?"

"Computers and stuff. What do I know?"

"I don't remember a hell of a lot from those days, but Lord, St. Bonny's is as clear as daylight. Remember Maggie? The day she fell down and those gar girls laughed at her?"

Roberta looked up from her salad and stared at me. "Maggie didn't fall," she said.

"Yes, she did. You remember."

"No, Twyla. They knocked her down. Those girls pushed her down and tore her clothes. In the orchard."

"I don't—that's not what happened."

"Sure it is. In the orchard. Remember how scared we were?"

"Wait a minute. I don't remember any of that."

"And Bozo was fired."

"You're crazy. She was there when I left. You left before me."

"I went back. You weren't there when they fired Bozo."

"What?"

"Twice. Once for a year when I was about ten, another for two months when I was fourteen. That's when I ran away."

"You ran away from St. Bonny's?"

"I had to. What do you want? Me dancing in that orchard?"

"Are you sure about Maggie?"

"Of course I'm sure. You've blocked it, Twyla. It happened. Those girls had behavior problems, you know."

"Didn't they, though. But why can't I remember the Maggie thing?"

"Believe me. It happened. And we were there."

"Who did you room with when you went back?" I asked her as if I would know her. The Maggie thing was troubling me.

"Creeps. They tickled themselves in the night."

My ears were itching and I wanted to go home suddenly. This was all very well but she couldn't just comb her hair, wash her face and pretend everything was hunky-dory. After the Howard Johnson's snub. And no apology. Nothing.

"Were you on dope or what that time at Howard Johnson's?" I tried to make my voice sound friendlier than I felt.

"Maybe, a little. I never did drugs much. Why?"

"I don't know; you acted sort of like you didn't want to know me then."

"Oh, Twyla, you know how it was in those days: black—white. You know how everything was."

But I didn't know. I thought it was just the opposite. Busloads of blacks and whites came into Howard Johnson's together. They roamed together then: students, musicians, lovers, protesters. You got to see everything at Howard Johnson's and blacks were very friendly with whites in those days. But sitting there with nothing on my plate but two hard tomato wedges wondering about the melting Klondikes it seemed childish remembering the slight. We went to her car, and with the help of the driver, got my stuff into my station wagon.

"We'll keep in touch this time," she said.

"Sure," I said. "Sure. Give me a call."

"I will," she said, and then just as I was sliding behind the wheel, she leaned into the window. "By the way. Your mother. Did she ever stop dancing?"

I shook my head. "No. Never."

Roberta nodded.

"And yours? Did she ever get well?"

She smiled a tiny sad smile. "No. She never did. Look, call me, okay?"

"Okay," I said, but I knew I wouldn't. Roberta had messed up my past somehow with that business about Maggie. I wouldn't forget a thing like that. Would I?

Strife came to us that fall. At least that's what the paper called it. Strife. Racial strife. The word made me think of a bird—a big shrieking bird out of 1,000,000,000 B.C. Flapping its wings and cawing. Its eye with no lid always bearing down on you. All day it screeched and at night it slept on the rooftops. It woke you in the morning and from the *Today* show to the eleven o'clock news it kept you an awful company. I couldn't figure it out from one day to the next. I knew I was supposed to feel something strong, but I didn't know what, and James wasn't any help. Joseph was on the list of kids to be transferred from the junior high school to another one at some far-out-of-the-way place and I thought it was a good thing until I heard it was a bad thing. I mean I didn't know. All the schools seemed dumps to me, and the fact that one was nicer looking didn't hold much weight. But the papers were full of it and then the kids began to get jumpy. In August, mind you. Schools weren't even open yet. I thought Joseph might be frightened to go over there, but he didn't seem scared so I forgot about it, until I found myself driving along Hudson Street out there by the school they were trying to integrate and saw a line of women marching. And who do you suppose was in line, big as life, holding a sign in front of her bigger than her mother's cross? MOTHERS HAVE RIGHTS TOO! it said.

I drove on, and then changed my mind. I circled the block, slowed down, and honked my horn.

Roberta looked over and when she saw me she waved. I didn't wave back, but I didn't move either. She handed her sign to another woman and came over to where I was parked.

"Hi."

"What are you doing?"

"Picketing. What's it look like?"

"What for?"

"What do you mean 'What for?' They want to take my kids and send them out of the neighborhood. They don't want to go."

"So what if they go to another school? My boy's being bussed too, and I don't mind. Why should you?"

"It's not about us, Twyla. Me and you. It's about our kids."

"What's more us than that?"

"Well, it is a free country."

"Not yet, but it will be."

"What the hell does that mean? I'm not doing anything to you."

"You really think that?"

"I know it."

"I wonder what made me think you were different."

"I wonder what made me think you were different."

"Look at them," I said. "Just look. Who do they think they are? Swarming all over the place like they own it. And now they think they can decide where my child goes to school. Look at them, Roberta. They're Bozos."

Roberta turned around and looked at the women. Almost all of them were standing still now, waiting. Some were even edging toward us. Roberta looked at me out of some refrigerator behind her eyes. "No, they're not. They're just mothers."

"And what am I? Swiss cheese?"

"I used to curl your hair."

"I hated your hands in my hair."

The women were moving. Our faces looked mean to them of course and they looked as though they could not wait to throw themselves in front of a police car, or better yet, into my car and drag me away by my ankles. Now they surrounded my car and gently, gently began to rock it. I swayed back and forth like a sideways yo-yo. Automatically I reached for Roberta, like the old days in the orchard when they saw us watching them and we had to get out of there, and if one of us fell the other pulled her up and if one of us was caught the other stayed to kick and scratch, and neither would leave the other behind. My arm shot out of the car window but no receiving hand was there. Roberta was looking at me sway from side to side in the car and her face was still. My purse slid from the car seat down under the dashboard. The four policemen who had been drinking Tab[8] in their car finally got the message and strolled over, forcing their way through the women. Quietly, firmly they spoke. "Okay, ladies. Back in line or off the streets."

Some of them went away willingly; others had to be urged away from the car doors and the hood. Roberta didn't move. She was looking steadily at me. I was fumbling to turn on the ignition, which wouldn't catch because the gearshift was still in drive. The seats of the car were a mess because the swaying had thrown my grocery coupons all over it and my purse was sprawled on the floor.

"Maybe I am different now, Twyla. But you're not. You're the same little state kid who kicked a poor old black lady when she was down on the ground. You kicked a black lady and you have the nerve to call me a bigot."

The coupons were everywhere and the guts of my purse were bunched under the dashboard. What was she saying? Black? Maggie wasn't black.

"She wasn't black," I said.

"Like hell she wasn't, and you kicked her. We both did. You kicked a black lady who couldn't even scream."

"Liar!"

"You're the liar! Why don't you just go on home and leave us alone, huh?"

She turned away and I skidded away from the curb.

The next morning I went into the garage and cut the side out of the carton our portable TV had come in. It wasn't nearly big enough, but after a while I had a decent sign: red spray-painted letters on a white background—AND SO DO CHILDREN * * * *. I meant just to go down to the school and tack it up somewhere so those cows on the picket line across the street could see it, but when I got there, some ten or so others had already assembled—protesting the cows across the street. Police permits and everything. I got in line and we strutted in time on our side while Roberta's group strutted on theirs. That first day we were all dignified, pretending the other side didn't exist. The second day there was name calling and finger gestures. But that was about all. People changed signs from time to time, but Roberta never did and neither did I. Actually my sign didn't make sense without Roberta's. "And so do children what?" one of the women on my side asked me. Have rights, I said, as though it was obvious.

Roberta didn't acknowledge my presence in any way and I got to thinking maybe she didn't know I was there. I began to pace myself in the line, jostling people one minute and lagging behind the next, so Roberta and I could reach the end of our respective lines at the same time and there would be a moment in our turn when we would face each other. Still, I couldn't tell whether she saw me and knew my sign was for her. The next day I went early before we were scheduled to assemble. I waited until she got there before I exposed my new creation. As soon as she hoisted her MOTHERS HAVE RIGHTS TOO I began to wave my new one, which said, HOW WOULD YOU KNOW? I know

8. A diet soda.

she saw that one, but I had gotten addicted now. My signs got crazier each day, and the women on my side decided that I was a kook. They couldn't make heads or tails out of my brilliant screaming posters.

I brought a painted sign in queenly red with huge black letters that said, IS YOUR MOTHER WELL? Roberta took her lunch break and didn't come back for the rest of the day or any day after. Two days later I stopped going too and couldn't have been missed because nobody understood my signs anyway.

It was a nasty six weeks. Classes were suspended and Joseph didn't go to anybody's school until October. The children—everybody's children—soon got bored with that extended vacation they thought was going to be so great. They looked at TV until their eyes flattened. I spent a couple of mornings tutoring my son, as the other mothers said we should. Twice I opened a text from last year that he had never turned in. Twice he yawned in my face. Other mothers organized living room sessions so the kids would keep up. None of the kids could concentrate so they drifted back to *The Price Is Right* and *The Brady Bunch*.[9] When the school finally opened there were fights once or twice and some sirens roared through the streets every once in a while. There were a lot of photographers from Albany. And just when ABC was about to send up a news crew, the kids settled down like nothing in the world had happened. Joseph hung my HOW WOULD YOU KNOW? sign in his bedroom. I don't know what became of AND SO DO CHILDREN * * * *. I think my father-in-law cleaned some fish on it. He was always puttering around in our garage. Each of his five children lived in Newburgh and he acted as though he had five extra homes.

I couldn't help looking for Roberta when Joseph graduated from high school, but I didn't see her. It didn't trouble me much what she had said to me in the car. I mean the kicking part. I know I didn't do that, I couldn't do that. But I was puzzled by her telling me Maggie was black. When I thought about it I actually couldn't be certain. She wasn't pitch-black, I knew, or I would have remembered that. What I remember was the kiddie hat, and the semicircle legs. I tried to reassure myself about the race thing for a long time until it dawned on me that the truth was already there, and Roberta knew it. I didn't kick her; I didn't join in with the gar girls and kick that lady, but I sure did want to. We watched and never tried to help her and never called for help. Maggie was my dancing mother. Deaf, I thought, and dumb. Nobody inside. Nobody who would hear you if you cried in the night. Nobody who could tell you anything important that you could use. Rocking, dancing, swaying as she walked. And when the gar girls pushed her down, and started roughhousing, I knew she wouldn't scream, couldn't—just like me—and I was glad about that.

We decided not to have a tree, because Christmas would be at my mother-in-law's house, so why have a tree at both places? Joseph was at SUNY New Paltz[1] and we had to economize, we said. But at the last minute, I changed my mind. Nothing could be that bad. So I rushed around town looking for a tree, something small but wide. By the time I found a place, it was snowing and very late. I dawdled like it was the most important purchase in the

---

9. Popular television programs: respectively, a game show and a situation comedy.

1. A campus in the State University of New York system, located 70 miles north of New York City.

world and the tree man was fed up with me. Finally I chose one and had it tied onto the trunk of the car. I drove away slowly because the sand trucks were not out yet and the streets could be murder at the beginning of a snowfall. Downtown the streets were wide and rather empty except for a cluster of people coming out of the Newburgh Hotel. The one hotel in town that wasn't built out of cardboard and Plexiglas. A party, probably. The men huddled in the snow were dressed in tails and the women had on furs. Shiny things glittered from underneath their coats. It made me tired to look at them. Tired, tired, tired. On the next corner was a small diner with loops and loops of paper bells in the window. I stopped the car and went in. Just for a cup of coffee and twenty minutes of peace before I went home and tried to finish everything before Christmas Eve.

"Twyla?"

There she was. In a silvery evening gown and dark fur coat. A man and another woman were with her, the man fumbling for change to put in the cigarette machine. The woman was humming and tapping on the counter with her fingernails. They all looked a little bit drunk.

"Well. It's you."

"How are you?"

I shrugged. "Pretty good. Frazzled. Christmas and all."

"Regular?" called the woman from the counter.

"Fine," Roberta called back and then, "Wait for me in the car."

She slipped into the booth beside me. "I have to tell you something, Twyla. I made up my mind if I ever saw you again, I'd tell you."

"I'd just as soon not hear anything, Roberta. It doesn't matter now, anyway."

"No," she said. "Not about that."

"Don't be long," said the woman. She carried two regulars to go and the man peeled his cigarette pack as they left.

"It's about St. Bonny's and Maggie."

"Oh, please."

"Listen to me. I really did think she was black. I didn't make that up. I really thought so. But now I can't be sure. I just remember her as old, so old. And because she couldn't talk—well, you know, I thought she was crazy. She'd been brought up in an institution like my mother was and like I thought I would be too. And you were right. We didn't kick her. It was the gar girls. Only them. But, well, I wanted to. I really wanted them to hurt her. I said we did it, too. You and me, but that's not true. And I don't want you to carry that around. It was just that I wanted to do it so bad that day— wanting to is doing it."

Her eyes were watery from the drinks she'd had, I guess. I know it's that way with me. One glass of wine and I start bawling over the littlest thing.

"We were kids, Roberta."

"Yeah. Yeah. I know, just kids."

"Eight."

"Eight."

"And lonely."

"Scared, too."

She wiped her cheeks with the heel of her hand and smiled. "Well, that's all I wanted to say."

I nodded and couldn't think of any way to fill the silence that went from the diner past the paper bells on out into the snow. It was heavy now. I thought I'd better wait for the sand trucks before starting home.

"Thanks, Roberta."

"Sure."

"Did I tell you? My mother, she never did stop dancing."

"Yes. You told me. And mine, she never got well." Roberta lifted her hands from the tabletop and covered her face with her palms. When she took them away she really was crying. "Oh shit, Twyla. Shit, shit, shit. What the hell happened to Maggie?"

1983

SYLVIA PLATH
1932–1963

I n an introduction to Sylvia Plath's *Ariel* (1965), published two years after her suicide in London, Robert Lowell wrote: "In these poems . . . Sylvia Plath becomes herself, becomes something imaginary, newly, wildly, and subtly created— . . . one of those super-real, hypnotic great classical heroines." Lowell had first met Plath in 1958, during her regular visits to his poetry seminar at Boston University, where he remembered her "air of maddening docility." Later, writing his introduction, he recognized her astonishing creation of a poetic self. The poems of *Ariel* were written at white heat, two or three a day, in the last months of Plath's life, but there is nothing hurried in their language or structure. When they are taken together with the poems posthumously published in *Crossing the Water* (1971) and *Winter Trees* (1972), a coherent persona emerges: larger than life, operatic in feeling. Although this focus on the self often excludes attention to the larger world, it generates the dynamic energy of her work. Plath appropriates a centrally American tradition, the heroic ego confronting the sublime, but she brilliantly revises this tradition by turning what the American Transcendentalist Ralph Waldo Emerson called the "great and crescive self" into a heroine instead of a hero. Seizing a mythic power, the Plath of the poems transmutes the domestic and the ordinary into the hallucinatory, the utterly strange. Her revision of the romantic ego dramatizes its tendency toward disproportion and excess, and she is fully capable of both using and mocking this heightened sense of self, as she does in her poem "Lady Lazarus."

Plath's well-known autobiographical novel, *The Bell Jar* (1963) has nothing of the brilliance of her poems, but it effectively dramatizes the stereotyping of women's roles in the 1950s and the turmoil of a young woman only partly aware that her gifts and ambitions greatly exceed the options available to her. In the novel Plath uses her experience as a guest editor of a young-women's magazine (in real life, *Mademoiselle*) and then, in an abrupt shift, presents her heroine's attempted suicide and hospitalization. Plath herself had suffered a serious breakdown and attempted suicide between her junior and senior years in college. The popularity of *The Bell Jar* may be one reason why attention to Plath's life has sometimes obscured the accomplishments of her art. While her poems often begin in autobiography, their success depends on Plath's imaginative transformations of experience into myth, as in a number of her poems (such as "Daddy") where the figure of her Prussian father is transformed into an emblem for masculine authority. Otto Plath was an entomologist and the author of a treatise on bumblebees. His death in 1940 from gangrene (the consequence of a diabetic condition he refused to treat), when Plath was eight, was the crucial event of her childhood. After his death her mother, Aurelia, while struggling to support two small children, encouraged her daughter's literary ambitions.

In many ways Plath embodied the bright, young, middle-class woman of the 1950s. She went to Smith College on a scholarship and graduated summa cum laude. On a Fulbright grant she studied in England at Cambridge University, where she met and married the poet Ted Hughes. On the face of it her marriage must have seemed the perfect fate for such a young woman; it combined romance, two poets beginning careers together (Plath's first book, *The Colossus*, appeared in 1960), and two children (Frieda, born in 1960, and Nicholas, born in 1962), with a country house in Devon, England. In her poems, however, we find the strains of such a life; the work is galvanized by suffering, by a terrible constriction against which she unlooses "The lioness, / The shriek in the bath, / The cloak of holes" ("Purdah"). In articulating a dark vision of domestic life Plath adopted the license of Robert Lowell and Anne Sexton, a fellow student in Lowell's poetry seminar, to write about "private and taboo subjects."

While still living in Devon, Plath wrote most of the poems that were to make up *Ariel* (by Christmas, 1962, she had gathered them in a black binder and arranged them in a careful sequence). The marriage broke up in the summer of 1962, and at the beginning of the new year Plath found herself with two small children, living in a London flat during one of the coldest winters in recent British history. There she began new poems, writing furiously until February 1963, when she took her own life. The *Ariel* collection published by Hughes in 1965 does not follow Plath's intended sequence; it omits what Hughes called "some of the more personally aggressive poems from 1962" and includes the dozen or so poems Plath wrote in the months before her death and that she had envisioned as the beginnings of a third book. Nonetheless, the powerful, angry poems of *Ariel*, mining a limited range of deep feeling, are Plath's best-known work. Fueled by an anger toward her husband and her father, she speaks in these poems as one whose feelings are more than her own; it is as if she were the character in George Eliot's *Daniel Deronda* (1876) who appears suddenly before the novel's heroine and says, "I am a woman's life." Other poems, however, demonstrate her ability to render a wider variety of emotion; they include poems about her children (such as "Morning Song," "Child," and "Parliament Hill Fields") and a number of arresting poems about the natural world. In the vastness of natural processes the Romantic ego finds something as large as itself, and Plath's response to nature is intense, often uncanny. Her poems offer an eccentric vision where (as in "Blackberrying") the appearance of the natural world is never separable from the consciousness of the one who sees it.

For all her courting of excess Plath is a remarkably controlled writer; her lucid stanzas, her clear diction, her dazzling alterations of sound display that control. The imaginative intensity of her poems is her own triumphant creation out of the difficult circumstances of her life. She once remarked, "I cannot sympathize with those cries from the heart that are informed by nothing except a needle or a knife. . . . I believe that one should be able to control and manipulate experiences, even the most terrifying . . . with an informed and intelligent mind." The influence of her style, and of the persona she created, continues to be felt in the work of a wide variety of contemporary poets.

Morning Song

Love set you going like a fat gold watch.
The midwife slapped your footsoles, and your bald cry
Took its place among the elements.

Our voices echo, magnifying your arrival. New statue.
In a drafty museum, your nakedness   5
Shadows our safety. We stand round blankly as walls.

I'm no more your mother
Than the cloud that distills a mirror to reflect its own slow
Effacement at the wind's hand.

All night your moth-breath   10
Flickers among the flat pink roses. I wake to listen:
A far sea moves in my ear.

One cry, and I stumble from bed, cow-heavy and floral
In my Victorian nightgown.
Your mouth opens clean as a cat's. The window square   15

Whitens and swallows its dull stars. And now you try
Your handful of notes;
The clear vowels rise like balloons.

1961   1966

Lady Lazarus[1]

I have done it again.
One year in every ten
I manage it—

A sort of walking miracle, my skin
Bright as a Nazi lampshade,[2]   5
My right foot

A paperweight,
My face a featureless, fine
Jew linen.

Peel off the napkin   10
O my enemy.
Do I terrify?——

---

1. Lazarus was raised from the dead by Jesus (John 11.1–45).

2. In the Nazi death camps the victims' skins were sometimes used to make lampshades.

The nose, the eye pits, the full set of teeth?
The sour breath
Will vanish in a day.   15

Soon, soon the flesh
The grave cave ate will be
At home on me

And I a smiling woman.
I am only thirty.   20
And like the cat I have nine times to die.

This is Number Three.
What a trash
To annihilate each decade.

What a million filaments.   25
The peanut-crunching crowd
Shoves in to see

Them unwrap me hand and foot——
The big strip tease.
Gentlemen, ladies   30

These are my hands
My knees.
I may be skin and bone,

Nevertheless, I am the same, identical woman.
The first time it happened I was ten.   35
It was an accident.

The second time I meant
To last it out and not come back at all.
I rocked shut

As a seashell.   40
They had to call and call
And pick the worms off me like sticky pearls.

Dying
Is an art, like everything else.
I do it exceptionally well.   45

I do it so it feels like hell.
I do it so it feels real.
I guess you could say I've a call.

It's easy enough to do it in a cell.
It's easy enough to do it and stay put.   50
It's the theatrical

Comeback in broad day
To the same place, the same face, the same brute
Amused shout:

'A miracle!'   55
That knocks me out.
There is a charge

For the eyeing of my scars, there is a charge
For the hearing of my heart——
It really goes.   60

And there is a charge, a very large charge
For a word or a touch
Or a bit of blood

Or a piece of my hair or my clothes.
So, so, Herr[3] Doktor.   65
So, Herr Enemy.

I am your opus,
I am your valuable,
The pure gold baby

That melts to a shriek.   70
I turn and burn.
Do not think I underestimate your great concern.

Ash, ash——
You poke and stir.
Flesh, bone, there is nothing there——   75

A cake of soap,
A wedding ring,
A gold filling.[4]

Herr God, Herr Lucifer
Beware   80
Beware.

Out of the ash[5]
I rise with my red hair
And I eat men like air.

1962   1966

---

3. Mr. (German).
4. The Nazis used human remains in the making of soap and scavenged corpses for jewelry and gold teeth.

5. An allusion to the phoenix, a mythical bird that dies by fire and is reborn out of its own ashes.

Ariel[1]

Stasis in darkness.
Then the substanceless blue
Pour of tor[2] and distances.

God's lioness,
How one we grow,   5
Pivot of heels and knees!—The furrow

Splits and passes, sister to
The brown arc
Of the neck I cannot catch,

Nigger-eye   10
Berries cast dark
Hooks——

Black sweet blood mouthfuls,
Shadows.
Something else   15

Hauls me through air——
Thighs, hair;
Flakes from my heels.

White
Godiva,[3] I unpeel——   20
Dead hands, dead stringencies.

And now I
Foam to wheat, a glitter of seas.
The child's cry

Melts in the wall.   25
And I
Am the arrow,

The dew that flies
Suicidal, at one with the drive
Into the red   30

Eye, the cauldron of morning.

1962   1966

---

1. The spirit of fire and air in Shakespeare's
Tempest. Ariel was also the name of the horse
Plath rode weekly in 1961–62, when she lived in
Devon, England.

2. A rocky peak.
3. In 1040 Lady Godiva rode naked on horseback
through the streets of Coventry to win a remission of feudal obligations and taxes.

Daddy

You do not do, you do not do
Any more, black shoe
In which I have lived like a foot
For thirty years, poor and white,
Barely daring to breathe or Achoo.   5

Daddy, I have had to kill you.
You died before I had time——
Marble-heavy, a bag full of God,
Ghastly statue with one grey toe[1]
Big as a Frisco seal   10

And a head in the freakish Atlantic
Where it pours bean green over blue
In the waters of beautiful Nauset.[2]
I used to pray to recover you.
Ach, du.[3]   15

In the German tongue, in the Polish town[4]
Scraped flat by the roller
Of wars, wars, wars.
But the name of the town is common.
My Polack friend   20

Says there are a dozen or two.
So I never could tell where you
Put your foot, your root,
I never could talk to you.
The tongue stuck in my jaw.   25

It stuck in a barb wire snare.
Ich,[5] ich, ich, ich,
I could hardly speak.
I thought every German was you.
And the language obscene   30

An engine, an engine
Chuffing me off like a Jew.
A Jew to Dachau, Auschwitz, Belsen.[6]
I began to talk like a Jew.
I think I may well be a Jew.   35

1. Plath's father's toe turned black from gangrene, a complication of diabetes.
2. Massachusetts beach.
3. Ah, you (German): the first of a series of references to her father's German origins.
4. The poet's father, of German descent, was born in Grabow, Poland.
5. I (German).
6. German concentration camps, where millions of Jews were murdered during World War II.

The snows of the Tyrol,[7] the clear beer of Vienna
Are not very pure or true.
With my gypsy ancestress and my weird luck
And my Taroc[8] pack and my Taroc pack
I may be a bit of a Jew.   40

I have always been scared of *you*,
With your Luftwaffe,[9] your gobbledygoo.
And your neat mustache
And your Aryan eye, bright blue.
Panzer[1]-man, panzer-man, O You——   45

Not God but a swastika
So black no sky could squeak through.
Every woman adores a Fascist,
The boot in the face, the brute
Brute heart of a brute like you.   50

You stand at the blackboard, daddy,
In the picture I have of you,
A cleft in your chin instead of your foot
But no less a devil for that, no not
And less the black man who   55

Bit my pretty red heart in two.
I was ten when they buried you.
At twenty I tried to die
And get back, back, back to you.
I thought even the bones would do.   60

But they pulled me out of the sack,
And they stuck me together with glue.[2]
And then I knew what to do.
I made a model of you,
A man in black with a Meinkampf[3] look   65

And a love of the rack and the screw.
And I said I do, I do.
So daddy, I'm finally through.
The black telephone's off at the root,
The voices just can't worm through.   70

If I've killed one man, I've killed two——
The vampire who said he was you
And drank my blood for a year,

7. Austrian Alpine region.
8. Variation of Tarot, ancient fortune-telling cards. Gypsies, like Jews, were objects of Nazi genocidal ambition; many died in the concentration camps.
9. The German air force.
1. Armor (German); refers to the German army's tank corps in World War II. Hitler preached the superiority of the Aryans—people of German stock with blond hair and blue eyes.
2. An allusion to Plath's first suicide attempt.
3. A reference to Hitler's political autobiography, *Mein Kampf* (my struggle), written and published before his rise to power, in which the future dictator outlined his plans for world conquest.

Seven years, if you want to know.
Daddy, you can lie back now.   75

There's a stake in your fat black heart
And the villagers never liked you.
They are dancing and stamping on you.
They always *knew* it was you.
Daddy, daddy, you bastard, I'm through.   80

1962   1966

Words

Axes
After whose stroke the wood rings,
And the echoes!
Echoes traveling
Off from the centre like horses.   5

The sap
Wells like tears, like the
Water striving
To re-establish its mirror
Over the rock   10

That drops and turns,
A white skull,
Eaten by weedy greens.
Years later I
Encounter them on the road——   15

Words dry and riderless,
The indefatigable hoof-taps.
While
From the bottom of the pool, fixed stars
Govern a life.   20

1963   1966

Blackberrying

Nobody in the lane, and nothing, nothing but blackberries,
Blackberries on either side, though on the right mainly,
A blackberry alley, going down in hooks, and a sea
Somewhere at the end of it, heaving. Blackberries
Big as the ball of my thumb, and dumb as eyes   5
Ebon in the hedges, fat
With blue-red juices. These they squander on my fingers.

I had not asked for such a blood sisterhood; they must love me.
They accommodate themselves to my milkbottle, flattening their sides.

Overhead go the choughs[1] in black, cacophonous flocks— 10
Bits of burnt paper wheeling in a blown sky.
Theirs is the only voice, protesting, protesting.
I do not think the sea will appear at all.
The high, green meadows are glowing, as if lit from within.
I come to one bush of berries so ripe it is a bush of flies, 15
Hanging their bluegreen bellies and their wing panes in a Chinese screen.
The honey-feast of the berries has stunned them; they believe in heaven.
One more hook, and the berries and bushes end.

The only thing to come now is the sea.
From between two hills a sudden wind funnels at me, 20
Slapping its phantom laundry in my face.
These hills are too green and sweet to have tasted salt.
I follow the sheep path between them. A last hook brings me
To the hills' northern face, and the face is orange rock
That looks out on nothing, nothing but a great space 25
Of white and pewter lights, and a din like silversmiths
Beating and beating at an intractable metal.

1961   1971

Purdah[1]

Jade—
Stone of the side,
The agonized

Side of green Adam, I
Smile, cross-legged, 5
Enigmatical,

Shifting my clarities.
So valuable!
How the sun polishes this shoulder!

And should 10
The moon, my
Indefatigable cousin

Rise, with her cancerous pallors,
Dragging trees—
Little bushy polyps,[2] 15

---

1. Small, chattering birds of the crow family.
1. Among Muslims and some Hindu sects, seclusion of women from public observation.
2. Animals that have many feet or tentacles, like octopuses, cuttlefish, and smaller coelenterates; also a general term for tumors that have tentacle-like protrusions.

Little nets,
My visibilities hide.
I gleam like a mirror.

At this facet the bridegroom arrives   20
Lord of the mirrors!
It is himself he guides

In among these silk
Screens, these rustling appurtenances.
I breathe, and the mouth

Veil stirs its curtain   25
My eye
Veil is

A concatenation of rainbows.
I am his.
Even in his   30

Absence, I
Revolve in my
Sheath of impossibles,

Priceless and quiet
Among these parakeets, macaws!³   35
O chatterers

Attendants of the eyelash!
I shall unloose
One feather, like the peacock.

Attendants of the lip!   40
I shall unloose
One note

Shattering
The chandelier
Of air that all day flies   45

Its crystals
A million ignorants.
Attendants!

Attendants!
And at his next step   50
I shall unloose

---

3. Two kinds of parrots.

I shall unloose—
From the small jeweled
Doll he guards like a heart—

The lioness,   55
The shriek in the bath,
The cloak of holes.

1962   1972

The Applicant

First, are you our sort of a person?
Do you wear
A glass eye, false teeth or a crutch,
A brace or a hook,
Rubber breasts or a rubber crotch,   5

Stitches to show something's missing? No, no? Then
How can we give you a thing?
Stop crying.
Open your hand.
Empty? Empty. Here is a hand   10

To fill it and willing
To bring teacups and roll away headaches
And do whatever you tell it.
Will you marry it?
It is guaranteed   15

To thumb shut your eyes at the end
And dissolve of sorrow.
We make new stock from the salt.
I notice you are stark naked.
How about this suit——   20

Black and stiff, but not a bad fit.
Will you marry it?
It is waterproof, shatterproof, proof
Against fire and bombs through the roof.
Believe me, they'll bury you in it.   25

Now your head, excuse me, is empty.
I have the ticket for that.
Come here, sweetie, out of the closet.
Well, what do you think of *that*?
Naked as paper to start   30

But in twenty-five years she'll be silver,
In fifty, gold.

A living doll, everywhere you look.
It can sew, it can cook,
It can talk, talk, talk.   35

It works, there is nothing wrong with it.
You have a hole, it's a poultice.
You have an eye, it's an image.
My boy, it's your last resort.
Will you marry it, marry it, marry it.   40

1962   1965

Child

Your clear eye is the one absolutely beautiful thing.
I want to fill it with color and ducks,
The zoo of the new

Whose names you meditate—
April snowdrop, Indian pipe,   5
Little

Stalk without wrinkle,
Pool in which images
Should be grand and classical

Not this troublous   10
Wringing of hands, this dark
Ceiling without a star.

1963   1972

JOHN UPDIKE
1932–2009

"To transcribe middleness with all its grits, bumps and anonymities, in its fullness of satisfaction and mystery: is it possible . . . or worth doing?" John Updike's novels and stories give a positive answer to the question he asks in his early memoir, *The Dogwood Tree: A Boyhood*; for he is arguably the most significant transcriber, or creator rather, of "middleness" in American writing since William Dean Howells (about whom he has written appreciatively) a century earlier. Falling in love in high school, meeting a college roommate, going to the eye doctor or dentist, eating supper on Sunday night, visiting your mother with your wife and son—these activities are made to yield up their possibilities to a writer as responsively curious in imagination and delicately precise in his literary expression as Updike showed himself to be.

Born in Shillington, Pennsylvania, John Updike was an only child. He was gifted at drawing and caricature, and after graduating summa cum laude from Harvard in 1954, he spent a year studying art in England, then returned to America and went to work for *The New Yorker*, where his first stories appeared and to which he contributed regularly for five decades. When later in the 1950s he left the magazine, he also left New York City and with his wife and children settled in Ipswich, Massachusetts. There he pursued "his solitary trade as methodically as the dentist practiced his," resisting the temptations of university teaching as successfully as he did the blandishments of media talk shows. His ample output was achieved through dedicated, steady work; his books are the fruit of patience, leisure, and craft.

Since 1959, when his first novel, *The Poorhouse Fair*, appeared, Updike published not only many novels and stories but also eight books of poetry, a play, and a vast store of book reviews and other prose writings. He is most admired by some readers as the author of the "Olinger" stories (included in *The Early Stories: 1953–1975*, 2003) about life in an imaginary Pennsylvania town that takes on its colors from the real Shillington of his youth. The heroes of these stories are adolescents straining to break out of their fast-perishing environments, as they grow up and as their small town turns into something else. Updike treats them with a blend of affection and ironic humor that is wonderfully assured in its touch, although his sense of place, of growing up during the Depression and the years of World War II, is always vividly present. Like Howells (whose fine memoir of his youthful days in Ohio, *A Boy's Town*, is an ancestor of Updike's *The Dogwood Tree*) he shows how one's spirit takes on its coloration from the material circumstances—houses, clothes, landscape, food, parents—one is bounded by.

This sense of place, which is also a sense of life, is found in the stories and in the novels too, although Updike found it harder to invent convincing forms in which to tell longer tales. His most ambitious novel is probably *The Centaur* (1964), memorable for its portrayal of three days of confusion and error in the life of an American high school teacher seen through his son's eyes, but the book is also burdened with an elaborate set of mythical trappings that seem less than inevitable. *Couples* (1968), a novel that gained him a good deal of notoriety as a chronicler of sexual relationships, marital and adulterous, is jammed with much interesting early 1960s lore about suburban life but seems uncertain whether it is an exercise in realism or a creative fantasy, as does *Marry Me* (1976).

In the four "Rabbit" novels Updike found his most congenial and engaging subject for longer fiction. In each book he had rendered the sense of an era—the 1950s in *Rabbit, Run*; the late 1960s in *Rabbit Redux*; the great gasoline crisis of 1979 in *Rabbit Is Rich*; the end of the Reagan era (and the end of Rabbit) in *Rabbit at Rest* (1990)—through the eyes of a hero who both is and is not like his creator. Harry "Rabbit" Angstrom, ex–high school basketball star, a prey to nostalgia and in love with his own past, perpetually lives in a present he can't abide. *Rabbit, Run* shows him trying to escape from his town, his job, his wife, and his child by a series of disastrously sentimental and humanly irresponsible actions; yet Updike makes us feel Rabbit's yearnings even as we judge the painful consequences of yielding to them. Ten years later the fading basketball star has become a fortyish, dispirited printer with a wayward wife and a country that is both landing on the moon and falling to pieces. *Rabbit Redux* is masterly in presenting a small town rotting away from its past certainties; it also attempts to deal with the Vietnam War and the black revolution. *Rabbit Is Rich* is a gentler, sadder chronicling of the hero's settling into grandfatherhood as he draws ever closer to death; while *Rabbit at Rest*, the longest and richest of the four novels, brings him to a moving conclusion; Rabbit's coda is presented in the reflections of his son and illegitimate daughter in "Rabbit Remembered," collected in *Licks of Love* (2000). In *Roger's Version* (1986) and *S* (1988) Updike adopted—or permitted his protagonists to adopt—a more broadly, sometimes a harsher, satiric view of contemporary religion, computer technology, feminism, and other forms of "liberation." Still, for all his virtuosity as a novelist, his best work may be found in the stories and in his short novel *Of the Farm* (1965). In "Separating" (printed here) the boy from "The Happiest I've Been" (*The Same Door*, 1959) has grown up, married, and fathered children and is now about to leave them as he moves into divorce. It is a beautiful example of Updike's careful, poised sense of how things work, a sense that can also be observed in the poem "Dog's Death" and in his memoir *Self-Consciousness* (1989).

Near the end of "The Dogwood Tree" he summarized his boyish dream of becoming an artist:

> He saw art—between drawing and writing he ignorantly made no distinction—as a method of riding a thin pencil out of Shillington, out of time altogether, into an infinity of unseen and even unborn hearts. He pictured this infinity as radiant. How innocent!

Most writers would name that innocence only to deplore it. Updike maintained instead that, as with the Christian faith he professed, succeeding years gave him no better assumptions with which to replace it. In any case, his fine sense of fact protected him from fashionable extravagances in black humor and experimental narratives, while enabling him to be both a satirist and a celebrator of our social and domestic conditions. In the last decade of his life a fabulative, almost magical atmosphere appeared in some works, as with his 2000 novel, *Gertrude and Claudius*. Yet even here John Updike showed himself to be our era's most sensitive craftsman of personal and societal manners, as he did in the generational family saga based on spiritual perceptions, *In the Beauty of the Lilies* (1996), in *Villages* (2004), a bildungsroman about a protagonist's marriages, careers, and communities, and in the sociopolitical challenge of *Terrorist* (2006).

The following text is from *The New Yorker* (June 23, 1975).

Separating

The day was fair. Brilliant. All that June the weather had mocked the Maples' internal misery with solid sunlight—golden shafts and cascades of green in which their conversations had wormed unseeing, their sad murmuring selves the only stain in Nature. Usually by this time of the year they had acquired tans; but when they met their elder daughter's plane on her return from a year in England they were almost as pale as she, though Judith was too dazzled by the sunny opulent jumble of her native land to notice. They did not spoil her homecoming by telling her immediately. Wait a few days, let her recover from jet lag, had been one of their formulations, in that string of gray dialogues—over coffee, over cocktails, over Cointreau— that had shaped the strategy of their dissolution, while the earth performed its annual stunt of renewal unnoticed beyond their closed windows. Richard had thought to leave at Easter; Joan had insisted they wait until the four children were at last assembled, with all exams passed and ceremonies attended, and the bauble of summer to console them. So he had drudged away, in love, in dread, repairing screens, getting the mowers sharpened, rolling and patching their new tennis court.

The court, clay, had come through its first winter pitted and windswept bare of redcoat. Years ago the Maples had observed how often, among their friends, divorce followed a dramatic home improvement, as if the marriage were making one last twitchy effort to live; their own worst crisis had come amid the plaster dust and exposed plumbing of a kitchen renovation. Yet, a summer ago, as canary-yellow bulldozers gaily churned a grassy, daisy-dotted knoll into a muddy plateau, and a crew of pigtailed young men raked and tamped clay into a plane, this transformation did not strike them as ominous, but festive in its impudence; their marriage could rend the earth for fun. The next spring, waking each day at dawn to a sliding sensation as if the bed were being tipped, Richard found the barren tennis court, its net and tapes still rolled in the barn, an environment congruous with his mood of purposeful desolation, and the crumbling of handfuls of clay into cracks and holes (dogs had frolicked on the court in a thaw; rivulets had evolved trenches) an activity suitably elemental and interminable. In his sealed heart he hoped the day would never come.

Now it was here. A Friday. Judith was reacclimated; all four children were assembled, before jobs and camps and visits again scattered them. Joan thought they should be told one by one. Richard was for making an announcement at the table. She said, "I think just making an announcement is a cop-out. They'll start quarrelling and playing to each other instead of focussing. They're each individuals, you know, not just some corporate obstacle to your freedom."

"O.K., O.K. I agree." Joan's plan was exact. That evening, they were giving Judith a belated welcome-home dinner, of lobster and champagne. Then, the party over, they, the two of them, who nineteen years before would push her in a baby carriage along Tenth Street to Washington Square,[1] were to walk her out of the house, to the bridge across the salt creek, and tell her, swearing her to secrecy. Then Richard Jr., who was going directly from work to a rock concert in Boston, would be told, either late when he returned on the train or early Saturday morning before he went off to his job; he was seventeen and employed as one of a golf-course maintenance crew. Then the two younger children, John and Margaret, could, as the morning wore on, be informed.

"Mopped up, as it were," Richard said.

"Do you have any better plan? That leaves you the rest of Saturday to answer any questions, pack, and make your wonderful departure."

"No," he said, meaning he had no better plan, and agreed to hers, though it had an edge of false order, a plea for control in the semblance of its achievement, like Joan's long chore lists and financial accountings and, in the days when he first knew her, her too copious lecture notes. Her plan turned one hurdle for him into four—four knife-sharp walls, each with a sheer blind drop on the other side.

All spring he had been morbidly conscious of insides and outsides, of barriers and partitions. He and Joan stood as a thin barrier between the children and the truth. Each moment was a partition, with the past on one side and the future on the other, a future containing this unthinkable *now*. Beyond four knifelike walls a new life for him waited vaguely. His skull cupped a secret, a white face, a face both frightened and soothing, both strange and

---

1. In Greenwich Village, an area in lower Manhattan, New York City.

known, that he wanted to shield from tears, which he felt all about him, solid as the sunlight. So haunted, he had become obsessed with battening down the house against his absence, replacing screens and sash cords, hinges and latches—a Houdini[2] making things snug before his escape.

The lock. He had still to replace a lock on one of the doors of the screened porch. The task, like most such, proved more difficult than he had imagined. The old lock, aluminum frozen by corrosion, had been deliberately rendered obsolete by manufacturers. Three hardware stores had nothing that even approximately matched the mortised hole its removal (surprisingly easy) left. Another hole had to be gouged, with bits too small and saws too big, and the old hole fitted with a block of wood—the chisels dull, the saw rusty, his fingers thick with lack of sleep. The sun poured down, beyond the porch, on a world of neglect. The bushes already needed pruning, the windward side of the house was shedding flakes of paint, rain would get in when he was gone, insects, rot, death. His family, all those he would lose, filtered through the edges of his awareness as he struggled with screw holes, splinters, opaque instructions, minutiae of metal.

Judith sat on the porch, a princess returned from exile. She regaled them with stories of fuel shortages, of bomb scares in the Underground, of Pakistani workmen loudly lusting after her as she walked past on her way to dance school. Joan came and went, in and out of the house, calmer than she should have been, praising his struggles with the lock as if this were one more and not the last of their chain of shared chores. The younger of his sons, John, now at fifteen suddenly, unwittingly handsome, for a few minutes held the rickety screen door while his father clumsily hammered and chiselled, each blow a kind of sob in Richard's ears. His younger daughter, having been at a slumber party, slept on the porch hammock through all the noise—heavy and pink, trusting and forsaken. Time, like the sunlight, continued relentlessly; the sunlight slowly slanted. Today was one of the longest days. The lock clicked, worked. He was through. He had a drink; he drank it on the porch, listening to his daughter. "It was so sweet," she was saying, "during the worst of it, how all the butcher's and bakery shops kept open by candlelight. They're all so plucky and cute. From the papers, things sounded so much worse here—people shooting people in gas lines, and everybody freezing."

Richard asked her, "Do you still want to live in England forever?" *Forever*: the concept, now a reality upon him, pressed and scratched at the back of his throat.

"No," Judith confessed, turning her oval face to him, its eyes still childishly far apart, but the lips set as over something succulent and satisfactory. "I was anxious to come home. I'm an American." She was a woman. They had raised her; he and Joan had endured together to raise her, alone of the four. The others had still some raising left in them. Yet it was the thought of telling Judith—the image of her, their first baby, walking between them arm in arm to the bridge—that broke him. The partition between himself

2. Harry Houdini (1874–1926), American magician and escape artist.

and the tears broke. Richard sat down to the celebratory meal with the back of his throat aching; the champagne, the lobster seemed phases of sunshine; he saw them and tasted them through tears. He blinked, swallowed, croakily joked about hay fever. The tears would not stop leaking through; they came not through a hole that could be plugged but through a permeable spot in a membrane, steadily, purely, endlessly, fruitfully. They became, his tears, a shield for himself against these others—their faces, the fact of their assembly, a last time as innocents, at a table where he sat the last time as head. Tears dropped from his nose as he broke the lobster's back; salt flavored his champagne as he sipped it; the raw clench at the back of his throat was delicious. He could not help himself.

His children tried to ignore his tears. Judith on his right, lit a cigarette, gazed upward in the direction of her too energetic, too sophisticated exhalation; on her other side, John earnestly bent his face to the extraction of the last morsels—legs, tail segments—from the scarlet corpse. Joan, at the opposite end of the table, glanced at him surprised, her reproach displaced by a quick grimace, of forgiveness, or of salute to his superior gift of strategy. Between them, Margaret, no longer called Bean, thirteen and large for her age, gazed from the other side of his pane of tears as if into a shopwindow at something she coveted—at her father, a crystalline heap of splinters and memories. It was not she, however, but John who, in the kitchen, as they cleared the plates and carapaces away, asked Joan the question: *"Why is Daddy crying?"*

Richard heard the question but not the murmured answer. Then he heard Bean cry, "Oh, no-oh!"—the faintly dramatized exclamation of one who had long expected it.

John returned to the table carrying a bowl of salad. He nodded tersely at his father and his lips shaped the conspiratorial words "She told."

"Told what?" Richard asked aloud, insanely.

The boy sat down as if to rebuke his father's distraction with the example of his own good manners and said quietly, "The separation."

Joan and Margaret returned; the child, in Richard's twisted vision, seemed diminished in size, and relieved, relieved to have had the boogeyman at last proved real. He called out to her—the distances at the table had grown immense—"You knew, you always knew," but the clenching at the back of his throat prevented him from making sense of it. From afar he heard Joan talking, levelly, sensibly, reciting what they had prepared: it was a separation for the summer, an experiment. She and Daddy both agreed it would be good for them; they needed space and time to think; they liked each other but did not make each other happy enough, somehow.

Judith, imitating her mother's factual tone, but in her youth off-key, too cool, said, "I think it's silly. You should either live together or get divorced."

Richard's crying, like a wave that has crested and crashed, had become tumultuous; but it was overtopped by another tumult, for John, who had been so reserved, now grew larger and larger at the table. Perhaps his younger sister's being credited with knowing set him off. "Why didn't you *tell* us?" he asked, in a large round voice quite unlike his own. "You should have *told* us you weren't getting along."

Richard was startled into attempting to force words through his tears. "We *do* get along, that's the trouble, so it doesn't show even to us—"

"That we do not love each other" was the rest of the sentence; he couldn't finish it.

Joan finished for him, in her style. "And we've always, *especially*, loved our children."

John was not mollified. "What do you care about *us*?" he boomed. "We're just little things you *had*." His sisters' laughing forced a laugh from him, which he turned hard and parodistic: "Ha ha *ha*." Richard and Joan realized simultaneously that the child was drunk, on Judith's homecoming champagne. Feeling bound to keep the center of the stage, John took a cigarette from Judith's pack, poked it into his mouth, let it hang from his lower lip, and squinted like a gangster.

"You're not little things we had," Richard called to him. "You're the whole point. But you're grown. Or almost."

The boy was lighting matches. Instead of holding them to his cigarette (for they had never seen him smoke; being "good" had been his way of setting himself apart), he held them to his mother's face, closer and closer, for her to blow out. Then he lit the whole folder—a hiss and then a torch, held against his mother's face. Prismed by tears, the flame filled Richard's vision; he didn't know how it was extinguished. He heard Margaret say, "Oh stop showing off," and saw John, in response, break the cigarette in two and put the halves entirely into his mouth and chew, sticking out his tongue to display the shreds to his sister.

Joan talked to him, reasoning—a fountain of reason, unintelligible. "Talked about it for years . . . our children must help us . . . Daddy and I both want . . ." As the boy listened, he carefully wadded a paper napkin into the leaves of his salad, fashioned a ball of paper and lettuce, and popped it into his mouth, looking around the table for the expected laughter. None came. Judith said, "Be mature," and dismissed a plume of smoke.

Richard got up from this stifling table and led the boy outside. Though the house was in twilight, the outdoors still brimmed with light, the long waste light of high summer. Both laughing, he supervised John's spitting out the lettuce and paper and tobacco into the pachysandra.[3] He took him by the hand—a square gritty hand, but for its softness a man's. Yet, it held on. They ran together up into the field, past the tennis court. The raw banking left by the bulldozers was dotted with daisies. Past the court and a flat stretch where they used to play family baseball stood a soft green rise glorious in the sun, each weed and species of grass distinct as illumination on parchment. "I'm sorry, so sorry," Richard cried. "You were the only one who ever tried to help me with all the goddam jobs around this place."

Sobbing, safe within his tears and the champagne, John explained, "It's not just the separation, it's the whole crummy year, I *hate* that school, you can't make any friends, the history teacher's a scud."[4]

They sat on the crest of the rise, shaking and warm from their tears but easier in their voices, and Richard tried to focus on the child's sad year— the weekdays long with homework, the weekends spent in his room with model airplanes, while his parents murmured down below, nursing their separation. How selfish, how blind, Richard thought; his eyes felt scoured.

---

3. Green, leafy plant, frequently used as ground cover.
4. Dull, disagreeable, objectionable person.

He told his son, "We'll think about getting you transferred. Life's too short to be miserable."

They had said what they could, but did not want the moment to heal, and talked on, about the school, about the tennis court, whether it would ever again be as good as it had been that first summer. They walked to inspect it and pressed a few more tapes more firmly down. A little stiltedly, perhaps trying to make too much of the moment, to prolong it, Richard led the boy to the spot in the field where the view was best, of the metallic blue river, the emerald marsh, the scattered islands velvet with shadow in the low light, the white bits of beach far away. "See," he said. "It goes on being beautiful. It'll be here tomorrow."

"I know," John answered, impatiently. The moment had closed.

Back in the house, the others had opened some white wine, the champagne being drunk, and still sat at the table, the three females, gossiping. Where Joan sat had become the head. She turned, showing him a tearless face, and asked, "All right?"

"We're fine," he said, resenting it, though relieved, that the party went on without him.

In bed she explained, "I couldn't cry I guess because I cried so much all spring. It really wasn't fair. It's your idea, and you made it look as though I was kicking you out."

"I'm sorry," he said. "I couldn't stop. I wanted to but couldn't."

"You *didn't* want to. You loved it. You were having your way, making a general announcement."

"I love having it over," he admitted. "God, those kids were great. So brave and funny." John, returned to the house, had settled to a model airplane in his room, and kept shouting down to them, "I'm O.K. No sweat." "And the way," Richard went on, cozy in his relief, "they never questioned the reasons we gave. No thought of a third person. Not even Judith."

"That *was* touching," Joan said.

He gave her a hug. "You were great too. Thank you." Guiltily, he realized he did not feel separated.

"You still have Dickie to do," she told him. These words set before him a black mountain in the darkness; its cold breath, its near weight affected his chest. Of the four children Dickie was most nearly his conscience. Joan did not need to add, "That's one piece of your dirty work I won't do for you."

"I know. I'll do it. You go to sleep."

Within minutes, her breathing slowed, became oblivious and deep. It was quarter to midnight. Dickie's train from the concert would come in at one-fourteen. Richard set the alarm for one. He had slept atrociously for weeks. But whenever he closed his lids some glimpse of the last hours scorched them—Judith exhaling toward the ceiling in a kind of aversion, Bean's mute staring, the sunstruck growth of the field where he and John had rested. The mountain before him moved closer, moved within him; he was huge, momentous. The ache at the back of his throat felt stale. His wife slept as if slain beside him. When, exasperated by his hot lids, his crowded heart, he rose from bed and dressed, she awoke enough to turn over. He told her then, "If I could undo it all, I would."

"Where would you begin?" she asked. There was no place. Giving him courage, she was always giving him courage. He put on shoes without socks in the dark. The children were breathing in their rooms, the downstairs was hollow. In their confusion they had left lights burning. He turned off all but one, the kitchen overhead. The car started. He had hoped it wouldn't. He met only moonlight on the road; it seemed a diaphanous companion, flickering in the leaves along the roadside, haunting his rearview mirror like a pursuer, melting under his headlights. The center of town, not quite deserted, was eerie at this hour. A young cop in uniform kept company with a gang of T-shirted kids on the steps of the bank. Across from the railroad station, several bars kept open. Customers, mostly young, passed in and out of the warm night, savoring summer's novelty. Voices shouted from cars as they passed; an immense conversation seemed in progress. Richard parked and in his weariness put his head on the passenger seat, out of the commotion and wheeling lights. It was as when, in the movies, an assassin grimly carries his mission through the jostle of a carnival—except the movies cannot show the precipitous, palpable slope you cling to within. You cannot climb back down; you can only fall. The synthetic fabric of the car seat, warmed by his cheek, confided to him an ancient, distant scent of vanilla.

A train whistle caused him to lift his head. It was on time; he had hoped it would be late. The slender drawgates descended. The bell of approach tingled happily. The great metal body, horizontally fluted, rocked to a stop, and sleepy teen-agers disembarked, his son among them. Dickie did not show surprise that his father was meeting him at this terrible hour. He sauntered to the car with two friends, both taller than he. He said "Hi" to his father and took the passenger's seat with an exhausted promptness that expressed gratitude. The friends got into the back, and Richard was grateful; a few more minutes' postponement would be won by driving them home.

He asked, "How was the concert?"

"Groovy," one boy said from the back seat.

"It bit," the other said.

"It was O.K.," Dickie said, moderate by nature, so reasonable that in his childhood the unreason of the world had given him headaches, stomach aches, nausea. When the second friend had been dropped off at his dark house, the boy blurted, "Dad, my eyes are killing me with hay fever! I'm out there cutting that mothering grass all day!"

"Do we still have those drops?"

"They didn't do any good last summer."

"They might this." Richard swung a U-turn on the empty street. The drive home took a few minutes. The mountain was here, in his throat. "Richard," he said, and felt the boy, slumped and rubbing his eyes, go tense at his tone, "I didn't come to meet you just to make your life easier. I came because your mother and I have some news for you, and you're a hard man to get ahold of these days. It's sad news."

"That's O.K." The reassurance came out soft, but quick, as if released from the tip of a spring.

Richard had feared that his tears would return and choke him, but the boy's manliness set an example, and his voice issued forth steady and dry. "It's sad news, but it needn't be tragic news, at least for you. It should have no practical effect on your life, though it's bound to have an emotional effect. You'll work at your job, and go back to school in September. Your mother and I are really proud of what you're making of your life; we don't want that to change at all."

"Yeah," the boy said lightly, on the intake of his breath, holding himself up. They turned the corner; the church they went to loomed like a gutted fort. The home of the woman Richard hoped to marry stood across the green. Her bedroom light burned.

"Your mother and I," he said, "have decided to separate. For the summer. Nothing legal, no divorce yet. We want to see how it feels. For some years now, we haven't been doing enough for each other, making each other as happy as we should be. Have you sensed that?"

"No," the boy said. It was an honest, unemotional answer: true or false in a quiz.

Glad for the factual basis, Richard pursued, even garrulously, the details. His apartment across town, his utter accessibility, the split vacation arrangements, the advantages to the children, the added mobility and variety of the summer. Dickie listened, absorbing. "Do the others know?"

Richard described how they had been told.

"How did they take it?"

"The girls pretty calmly. John flipped out; he shouted and ate a cigarette and made a salad out of his napkin and told us how much he hated school."

His brother chuckled. "He did?"

"Yeah. The school issue was more upsetting for him than Mom and me. He seemed to feel better for having exploded."

"He did?" The repetition was the first sign that he was stunned.

"Yes. Dickie, I want to tell you something. This last hour, waiting for your train to get in, has been about the worst of my life. I hate this. *Hate* it. My father would have died before doing it to me." He felt immensely lighter, saying this. He had dumped the mountain on the boy. They were home. Moving swiftly as a shadow, Dickie was out of the car, through the bright kitchen. Richard called after him, "Want a glass of milk or anything?"

"No thanks."

"Want us to call the course tomorrow and say you're too sick to work?"

"No, that's all right." The answer was faint, delivered at the door to his room; Richard listened for the slam of a tantrum. The door closed normally. The sound was sickening.

Joan had sunk into that first deep trough of sleep and was slow to awake. Richard had to repeat, "I told him."

"What did he say?"

"Nothing much. Could you go say good night to him? Please."

She left their room, without putting on a bathrobe. He sluggishly changed back into his pajamas and walked down the hall. Dickie was already in bed, Joan was sitting beside him, and the boy's bedside clock radio was murmuring music. When she stood, an inexplicable light—the moon?—outlined her body through the nightie. Richard sat on the warm place she had indented on the child's narrow mattress. He asked him, "Do you want the radio on like that?"

"It always is."

"Doesn't it keep you awake? It would me."

"No."

"Are you sleepy?"

"Yeah."

"Good. Sure you want to get up and go to work? You've had a big night."

"I want to."

Away at school this winter he had learned for the first time that you can go short of sleep and live. As an infant he had slept with an immobile, sweating intensity that had alarmed his babysitters. As the children aged, he became the first to go to bed, earlier for a time than his younger brother and sister. Even now, he would go slack in the middle of a television show, his sprawled legs hairy and brown. "O.K. Good boy. Dickie, listen. I love you so much, I never knew how much until now. No matter how this works out, I'll always be with you. Really."

Richard bent to kiss an averted face but his son, sinewy, turned and with wet cheeks embraced him and gave him a kiss, on the lips, passionate as a woman's. In his father's ear he moaned one word, the crucial, intelligent word: *"Why?"*

Why. It was a whistle of wind in a crack, a knife thrust, a window thrown open on emptiness. The white face was gone, the darkness was featureless. Richard had forgotten why.

1975

PHILIP ROTH
b. 1933

From the moment Philip Roth's collection of stories *Goodbye, Columbus* won the Houghton Mifflin Literary Fellowship for 1959, his career has received the ambiguous reward of much anxious concern, directed at it by critics and centered on whether he would develop the promise displayed in this first book. Ten years later, with *Portnoy's Complaint*, Roth became overnight the famous author of a "dirty" best-seller, yet his success only made his critics more uneasy. Was this gifted portrayer of Jewish middle-class life really more interested in scoring points off caricatures than in creating and exploring characters? Did his very facility with words inhibit the exercise of deeper sympathies and more humanly generous purposes?

Roth grew up in Newark, New Jersey, attended the branch of Rutgers University there, graduated from Bucknell University, took an M.A. in English literature at the University of Chicago, then served in the army. Over the years he has taught at a number of universities while receiving many awards and fellowships. Like John Barth, another "university" writer, Roth is an ironic humorist, although the impulse behind his early stories is darker and less playful. *Goodbye, Columbus* is about Jews on the verge of being or already having been assimilated into the larger American culture, and the stories confidently take the measure of their embattled heroes, as in "The Conversion of the Jews" or "Epstein" or the long title story. "Defender of the Faith" (printed here), arguably the best piece in the collection, is distinguished for the way Roth explores rather than exploits the conflict between personal feelings and religious loyalties as they are felt by Nathan Marx, a U.S. Army sergeant in a Missouri training company near the end of World War II. Throughout *Goodbye, Columbus* the narrator's voice is centrally important: in some stories it is indistinguishable from that of a campus wiseguy; in others it reaches out to a calmer and graver sense of disparities between promises and performance.

Roth's first two novels, *Letting Go* (1962) and *When She Was Good* (1967), markedly extended the territory charted in *Goodbye, Columbus* and showed him eager and equipped to write about people other than Jews. *Letting Go* is conventional in technique and in its subjects—love, marriage, university life—but Roth's easy mastery of the look and feel of places and things is everywhere evident. F. Scott Fitzgerald is the American writer whose presence in these early novels is most strongly felt; in particular, the section from *Letting Go* told in the first person by a graduate student in English betrays its indebtedness to Fitzgerald's Nick Carraway, the narrator of *The Great Gatsby*. This Fitzgeraldian atmosphere, with its nostalgic evocation of adolescence and early romantic visions, is even more evident in *When She Was Good*, which is strong in its rendering of middle-American living rooms and kitchens, the flushed atmosphere of late-night 1950s sex in parked cars, or the lyrics of popular songs—bits of remembered trivia that Roth, like his predecessor, has a genius for bringing to life.

The less-than-overwhelming reception of his second novel probably helped Roth move away from relatively sober realism; certainly *Portnoy's Complaint* (1969) is a louder and more virtuoso performance than the earlier books. Alexander Portnoy's recollections of early childhood miseries are really a pretext for Roth to perform a succession of clever numbers in the inventive mode of a stand-up comic. Memories of growing up in New Jersey, listening to radio programs, playing softball, ogling girls at the ice-skating rink, or (most sensationally) masturbating in outlandish ways add up to an entertaining narrative that is sometimes crude but more often delicate and precise.

After *Portnoy* Roth moved toward fantasy and further showmanly operations: *Our Gang* (1970) attempted to do for Richard Nixon and his associates what actual events were to do one better; *The Breast* (1971) is a rather unamusing fable about a man's metamorphosis into that object; *The Great American Novel* (1973) threatened to sink under its weight of baseball lore dressed up in tall tales and sick jokes. But in *My Life as a Man* (1974) and *The Professor of Desire* (1977) he returned to matters that have traditionally preoccupied the social novelist and that inform his own best work: marriage, divorce, the family, Jewishness, and psychoanalysis—the pressures of civilization and the resultant individual discontents.

His finest work is to be found in the Zuckerman trilogy (*Zuckerman Bound*, 1985) and its successor, *The Counterlife* (1987). In these novels Roth created a hero-as-novelist whose experience parallels in important ways his creator's. A scandalous novel, *Carnovsky*, recalls *Portnoy's Complaint*; a critic named Milton Appel is a stand-in for the real critic Irving Howe, who once subjected Roth's work to hostile criticism. Yet for all the dangers of self-pity or self-absorption such autobiographical reference involves, the novels add up to something much deeper, more comic and touching, than self-advertisement and complaint. Scenes like the death of Zuckerman's father in a Florida hospital and the subsequent return of the son to the vanished Newark where he grew up are moving expressions of the generous purposes and human sympathies we find in Roth's work at its best. And those purposes and sympathies are also evident in his autobiographical writing: in *The Facts* (1988) and especially in *Patrimony* (1991), a poignant memoir of his father.

In the 1990s and into the twenty-first century Roth has developed his art of impersonation into audacious and sometimes excessive forms. *Operation Shylock* (1993) poses a presumably real Philip Roth who encounters an impostor; *Sabbath's Theater* (1995) recasts his typical protagonist as a puppeteer who manipulates women much the same way; *American Pastoral* (1997) brings back Nathan Zuckerman for a high school reunion and the investigation of a "more ordinary" classmate's life. Zuckerman remains on hand for *I Married a Communist* (1998) and *The Human Stain* (2000), while David Kepesh (who had turned into a female breast in the author's much earlier fantasy) reappears as a professor who seduces his students in *The Dying Animal* (2001). Further seduction takes place in *Everyman* (2006), although the author's most disturbing projections are reserved for *The Plot against America* (2004), in which a fictive Charles A. Lindbergh becomes president and initiates repression of American Jews. *Exit Ghost* (2007) has Nathan Zuckerman return to New York City and reencounter characters from previous novels. *Indignation* (2008) set a young man's maturation against the looming threat of military service in the Korean War. *The Humbling* (2009) projects Roth's late-life anxieties as a writer onto the career of an actor in decline. *Nemesis* (2010) expands the author's concerns with human morality (and the role of a God who allows such suffering) to encompass a polio epidemic in the Newark of his childhood. Throughout his work, Roth's emphasis remains on invention, reminding readers that the writerly self is a virtually inexhaustible resource for the imagination.

The following text is from *Goodbye, Columbus* (1959).

Defender of the Faith

In May of 1945, only a few weeks after the fighting had ended in Europe, I was rotated back to the States, where I spent the remainder of the war with a training company at Camp Crowder, Missouri. We had been racing across Germany so swiftly during the late winter and spring that when I boarded the plane that drizzly morning in Berlin, I couldn't believe our destination lay to the west. My mind might inform me otherwise, but there was an inertia of the spirit that told me we were flying to a new front where we would disembark and continue our push eastward—eastward until we'd circled the globe, marching through villages along whose twisting, cobbled streets crowds of the enemy would watch us take possession of what up till then they'd considered their own. I had changed enough in two years not to mind the trembling of the old people, the crying of the very young, the uncertain fear in the eyes of the once-arrogant. After two years I had been fortunate enough to develop an infantryman's heart which, like his feet, at first aches and swells, but finally grows horny enough for him to travel the weirdest paths without feeling a thing.

Captain Paul Barrett was to be my C.O. at Camp Crowder. The day I reported for duty he came out of his office to shake my hand. He was short, gruff, and fiery, and indoors or out he wore his polished helmet liner[1] down on his little eyes. In Europe he had received a battlefield commission and a serious chest wound, and had been returned to the States only a few months before. He spoke easily to me, but was, I thought, unnecessarily abusive towards the troops. At the evening formation, he introduced me.

"Gentlemen," he called. "Sergeant Thurston, as you know, is no longer with this Company. Your new First Sergeant is Sergeant Nathan Marx here. He is a veteran of the European theater and consequently will take no shit."

---

1. Plastic liner worn under a helmet to prevent chafing and bruising.

I sat up late in the orderly room that evening, trying halfheartedly to solve the riddle of duty rosters, personnel forms, and morning reports. The CQ[2] slept with his mouth open on a mattress on the floor. A trainee stood reading the next day's duty roster, which was posted on the bulletin board directly inside the screen door. It was a warm evening and I could hear the men's radios playing dance music over in the barracks.

The trainee, who I knew had been staring at me whenever I looked groggily into the forms, finally took a step in my direction.

"Hey, Sarge—we having a G.I. party tomorrow night?" A G.I. party is a barracks-cleaning.

"You usually have them on Friday nights?"

"Yes," and then he added mysteriously, "that's the whole thing."

"Then you'll have a G.I. party."

He turned away and I heard him mumbling. His shoulders were moving and I wondered if he was crying.

"What's your name, soldier?" I asked.

He turned, not crying at all. Instead his green-speckled eyes, long and narrow, flashed like fish in the sun. He walked over to me and sat on the edge of my desk.

He reached out a hand. "Sheldon," he said.

"Stand on your own two feet, Sheldon."

Climbing off the desk, he said, "Sheldon Grossbart." He smiled wider at the intimacy into which he'd led me.

"You against cleaning the barracks Friday night, Grossbart? Maybe we shouldn't have G.I. parties—maybe we should get a maid." My tone startled me: I felt like a Charlie McCarthy, with every top sergeant I had ever known as my Edgar Bergen.[3]

"No, Sergeant." He grew serious, but with a seriousness that seemed only to be the stifling of a smile. "It's just G.I. parties on Friday night, of all nights . . ."

He slipped up to the corner of the desk again—not quite sitting, but not quite standing either. He looked at me with those speckled eyes flashing and then made a gesture with his hand. It was very slight, no more than a rotation back and forth of the wrist, and yet it managed to exclude from our affairs everything else in the orderly room, to make the two of us the center of the world. It seemed, in fact, to exclude everything about the two of us except our hearts. "Sergeant Thurston was one thing," he whispered, an eye flashing to the sleeping CQ, "but we thought with you here, things might be a little different."

"We?"

"The Jewish personnel."

"Why?" I said, harshly.

He hesitated a moment, and then, uncontrollably, his hand went up to his mouth. "I mean . . ." he said.

"What's on your mind?" Whether I was still angry at the "Sheldon" business or something else, I hadn't a chance to tell—but clearly I was angry.

2. Noncommissioned officer in charge of quarters at night or on weekends.

3. A ventriloquist who, with Charlie McCarthy, his dummy, was a popular radio comedian.

". . . we thought you . . . Marx, you know, like Karl Marx. The Marx brothers. Those guys are all . . . M-A-R-X, isn't that how you spell it, Sergeant?"

"M-A-R-X."

"Fishbein said—" He stopped. "What I mean to say, Sergeant—" His face and neck were red, and his mouth moved but no words came out. In a moment, he raised himself to attention, gazing down at me. It was as though he had suddenly decided he could expect no more sympathy from me than from Thurston, the reason being that I was of Thurston's faith and not his. The young man had managed to confuse himself as to what my faith really was, but I felt no desire to straighten him out. Very simply, I didn't like him.

When I did nothing but return his gaze, he spoke, in an altered tone. "You see, Sergeant," he explained to me, "Friday nights, Jews are supposed to go to services."

"Did Sergeant Thurston tell you you couldn't go to them when there was a G.I. party?"

"No."

"Did he say you had to stay and scrub the floors?"

"No, Sergeant."

"Did the Captain say you had to stay and scrub the floors?"

"That isn't it, Sergeant. It's the other guys in the barracks." He leaned toward me. "They think we're goofing off. But we're not. That's when Jews go to services, Friday night. We have to."

"Then go."

"But the other guys make accusations. They have no right."

"That's not the Army's problem, Grossbart. It's a personal problem you'll have to work out yourself."

"But it's unfair."

I got up to leave. "There's nothing I can do about it," I said.

Grossbart stiffened in front of me. "But this is a matter of *religion*, sir."

"Sergeant."

"I mean 'Sergeant,'" he said, almost snarling.

"Look, go see the chaplain. The I.G.[4] You want to see Captain Barrett, I'll arrange an appointment."

"No, no. I don't want to make trouble, Sergeant. That's the first thing they throw up to you. I just want my rights!"

"Damn it, Grossbart, stop whining. You have your rights. You can stay and scrub floors or you can go to *shul*[5]—"

The smile swam in again. Spittle gleamed at the corners of his mouth. "You mean church, Sergeant."

"I mean *shul*, Grossbart!" I walked past him and outside. Near me I heard the scrunching of a guard's boots on gravel. In the lighted windows of the barracks the young men in T-shirts and fatigue pants were sitting on their bunks, polishing their rifles. Suddenly there was a light rustling behind me. I turned and saw Grossbart's dark frame fleeing back to the barracks, racing to tell his Jewish friends that they were right—that like Karl and Harpo, I was one of them.

---

4. Inspector general, who, apart from the chaplain, provided the only route by which complaints could be registered.

5. Synagogue (Yiddish).

The next morning, while chatting with the Captain, I recounted the incident of the previous evening, as if to unburden myself of it. Somehow in the telling it seemed to the Captain that I was not so much explaining Grossbart's position as defending it.

"Marx, I'd fight side by side with a nigger if the fellow proved to me he was a man. I pride myself," the Captain said looking out the window, "that I've got an open mind. Consequently, Sergeant, nobody gets special treatment here, for the good *or* the bad. All a man's got to do is prove himself. A man fires well on the range, I give him a weekend pass. He scores high in PT, he gets a weekend pass. He *earns* it." He turned from the window and pointed a finger at me. "You're a Jewish fellow, am I right, Marx?"

"Yes, sir."

"And I admire you. I admire you because of the ribbons on your chest, not because you had a hem stitched on your dick before you were old enough to even know you had one. I judge a man by what he shows me on the field of battle, Sergeant. It's what he's got *here*," he said, and then, though I expected he would point to his heart, he jerked a thumb towards the buttons straining to hold his blouse across his belly. "Guts," he said.

"Okay, sir, I only wanted to pass on to you how the men felt."

"Mr. Marx, you're going to be old before your time if you worry about how the men feel. Leave that stuff to the Chaplain—pussy, the clap, church picnics with the little girls from Joplin, that's all his business, not yours. Let's us train these fellas to shoot straight. If the Jewish personnel feels the other men are accusing them of goldbricking . . . well, I just don't know. Seems awful funny how suddenly the Lord is calling so loud in Private Grossman's ear he's just got to run to church."

"Synagogue," I said.

"Synagogue is right, Sergeant. I'll write that down for handy reference. Thank you for stopping by."

That evening, a few minutes before the company gathered outside the orderly room for the chow formation, I called the CQ, Corporal Robert LaHill, in to see me. LaHill was a dark burly fellow whose hair curled out of his clothes wherever it could. He carried a glaze in his eyes that made one think of caves and dinosaurs. "LaHill," I said, "when you take the formation, remind the men that they're free to attend church services *whenever* they are held, provided they report to the orderly room before they leave the area."

LaHill didn't flicker; he scratched his wrist, but gave no indication that he'd heard or understood.

"LaHill," I said, "*church.* You remember? Church, priest, Mass, confession . . ."

He curled one lip into a ghastly smile; I took it for a signal that for a second he had flickered back up into the human race.

"Jewish personnel who want to attend services this evening are to fall out in front of the orderly room at 1900." And then I added, "By order of Captain Barrett."

A little while later, as a twilight softer than any I had seen that year dropped over Camp Crowder, I heard LaHill's thick, inflectionless voice outside my window: "Give me your ears, troopers. Toppie says for me to tell you that at 1900 hours all Jewish personnel is to fall out in front here if they wants to attend the Jewish Mass."

At seven o'clock, I looked out of the orderly-room window and saw three soldiers in starched khakis standing alone on the dusty quadrangle. They looked at their watches, and fidgeted while they whispered back and forth. It was getting darker, and alone on the deserted field they looked tiny. When I walked to the door I heard the noises of the G.I. party coming from the surrounding barracks—bunks being pushed to the wall, faucets pounding water into buckets, brooms whisking at the wooden floors. In the windows big puffs of cloth moved round and round, cleaning the dirt away for Saturday's inspection. I walked outside and the moment my foot hit the ground I thought I heard Grossbart, who was now in the center, call to the other two, "Ten-*hut!*" Or maybe when they all three jumped to attention, I imagined I heard the command.

At my approach, Grossbart stepped forward. "Thank you, sir," he said.

"Sergeant, Grossbart," I reminded him. "You call officers 'Sir.' I'm not an officer. You've been in the Army three weeks—you know that."

He turned his palms out at his sides to indicate that, in truth, he and I lived beyond convention. "Thank you, anyway," he said.

"Yes," the tall boy behind him said. "Thanks a lot."

And the third whispered, "Thank you," but his mouth barely fluttered so that he did not alter by more than a lip's movement, the posture of attention.

"For what?" I said.

Grossbart snorted, happily. "For the announcement before. The Corporal's announcement. It helped. It made it . . ."

"Fancier." It was the tall boy finishing Grossbart's sentence.

Grossbart smiled. "He means formal, sir. Public," he said to me. "Now it won't seem as though we're just taking off, goldbricking, because the work has begun."

"It was by order of Captain Barrett," I said.

"Ahh, but you pull a little weight . . ." Grossbart said. "So we thank you." Then he turned to his companions. "Sergeant Marx, I want you to meet Larry Fishbein."

The tall boy stepped forward and extended his hand. I shook it. "You from New York?" he asked.

"Yes."

"Me too." He had a cadaverous face that collapsed inward from his cheekbone to his jaw, and when he smiled—as he did at the news of our communal, attachment—revealed a mouthful of bad teeth. He blinked his eyes a good deal, as though he were fighting back tears. "What borough?" he asked.

I turned to Grossbart. "It's five after seven. What time are services?"

"*Shul*," he smiled, "is in ten minutes. I want you to meet Mickey Halpern. This is Nathan Marx, our Sergeant."

The third boy hopped forward. "Private Michael Halpern." He saluted.

"Salute officers, Halpern." The boy dropped his hand, and in his nervousness checked to see if his shirt pockets were buttoned on the way down.

"Shall I march them over, sir?" Grossbart asked, "or are you coming along?"

From behind Grossbart, Fishbein piped up. "Afterwards they're having refreshments. A Ladies' Auxiliary from St. Louis, the rabbi told us last week."

"The chaplain," whispered Halpern.

"You're welcome to come along," Grossbart said.

To avoid his plea, I looked away, and saw, in the windows of the barracks, a cloud of faces staring out at the four of us.

"Look, hurry out of here, Grossbart."

"Okay, then," he said. He turned to the others. "Double time, *march!*" and they started off, but ten feet away Grossbart spun about, and running backwards he called to me, "Good *shabus*,[6] sir." And then the three were swallowed into the Missouri dusk.

Even after they'd disappeared over the parade grounds, whose green was now a deep twilight blue, I could hear Grossbart singing the double-time cadence, and as it grew dimmer and dimmer it suddenly touched some deep memory—as did the slant of light—and I was remembering the shrill sounds of a Bronx playground, where years ago, beside the Grand Concourse,[7] I had played on long spring evenings such as this. Those thin fading sounds . . . It was a pleasant memory for a young man so far from peace and home, and it brought so very many recollections with it that I began to grow exceedingly tender about myself. In fact, I indulged myself to a reverie so strong that I felt within as though a hand had opened and was reaching down inside. It had to reach so very far to touch me. It had to reach past those days in the forests of Belgium and the dying I'd refused to weep over; past the nights in those German farmhouses whose books we'd burned to warm us, and which I couldn't bother to mourn; past those endless stretches when I'd shut off all softness I might feel for my fellows, and managed even to deny myself the posture of a conqueror—the swagger that I, as a Jew, might well have worn as my boots whacked against the rubble of Münster, Braunschweig, and finally Berlin.

But now one night noise, one rumor of home and time past, and memory plunged down through all I had anesthetized and came to what I suddenly remembered to be myself. So it was not altogether curious that in search of more of me I found myself following Grossbart's tracks to Chapel No. 3 where the Jewish services were being held.

I took a seat in the last row, which was empty. Two rows in front sat Grossbart, Fishbein, and Halpern, each holding a little white dixie cup. Fishbein was pouring the contents of his cup into Grossbart's, and Grossbart looked mirthful as the liquid drew a purple arc between his hand and Fishbein's. In the glary yellow light, I saw the chaplain on the pulpit chanting the first line of the responsive reading. Grossbart's prayerbook remained closed on his lap; he swished the cup around. Only Halpern responded in prayer. The fingers of his right hand were spread wide across the cover of the book, and his cap was pulled down low onto his brow so that it was round like a *yarmulke*[8] rather than long and pointed. From time to time, Grossbart wet his lips at the cup's edge; Fishbein, his long yellow face, a dying light bulb, looked from here to there, leaning forward at the neck to catch sight of the faces down the row, in front—then behind. He saw me

6. Sabbath (Yiddish).
7. Avenue in the Bronx, New York.

8. Skullcap (Yiddish).

and his eyelids beat a tattoo. His elbow slid into Grossbart's side, his neck inclined towards his friend, and then, when the congregation responded, Grossbart's voice was among them. Fishbein looked into his book now too; his lips, however, didn't move.

Finally it was time to drink the wine. The chaplain smiled down at them as Grossbart swigged in one long gulp, Halpern sipped, meditating, and Fishbein faked devotion with an empty cup.

At last the chaplain spoke: "As I look down amongst the congregation—" he grinned at the word, "this night, I see many new faces, and I want to welcome you to Friday night services here at Camp Crowder. I am Major Leo Ben Ezra, your chaplain . . ." Though an American, the chaplain spoke English very deliberately, syllabically almost, as though to communicate, above all, to the lip-readers in the audience. "I have only a few words to say before we adjourn to the refreshment room where the kind ladies of the Temple Sinai, St. Louis, Missouri, have a nice setting for you."

Applause and whistling broke out. After a momentary grin, the chaplain raised his palms to the congregation, his eyes flicking upward a moment, as if to remind the troops where they were and Who Else might be in attendance. In the sudden silence that followed, I thought I heard Grossbart's cackle—"Let the goyim[9] clean the floors!" Were those the words? I wasn't sure, but Fishbein, grinning, nudged Halpern. Halpern looked dumbly at him, then went back to his prayerbook, which had been occupying him all through the rabbi's talk. One hand tugged at the black kinky hair that stuck out under his cap. His lips moved.

The rabbi continued. "It is about the food that I want to speak to you for a moment. I know, I know, I know," he intoned, wearily, "how in the mouths of most of you the *trafe*[1] food tastes like ashes. I know how you gag, some of you, and how your parents suffer to think of their children eating foods unclean and offensive to the palate. What can I tell you? I can only say close your eyes and swallow as best you can. Eat what you must to live and throw away the rest. I wish I could help more. For those of you who find this impossible, may I ask that you try and try, but then come to see me in private where, if your revulsion is such, we will have to seek aid from those higher up."

A round of chatter rose and subsided; then everyone sang "Ain Keloha-noh," after all those years I discovered I still knew the words.

Suddenly, the service over, Grossbart was upon me. "Higher up? He means the General?"

"Hey, Shelly," Fishbein interrupted, "he means God." He smacked his face and looked at Halpern. "How high can you go!"

"Shhh!" Grossbart said. "What do you think, Sergeant?"

"I don't know. You better ask the chaplain."

"I'm going to. I'm making an appointment to see him in private. So is Mickey."

Halpern shook his head. "No, no, Sheldon . . ."

"You have rights, Mickey. They can't push us around."

"It's okay. It bothers my mother, not me . . ."

9. Gentiles (Yiddish).   1. Unkosher—unfit to eat (Yiddish).

Grossbart looked at me. "Yesterday he threw up. From the hash. It was all ham and God knows what else."

"I have a cold—that was why," Halpern said. He pushed his *yamalkah* back into a cap.

"What about you, Fishbein?" I asked. "You kosher too?"

He flushed, which made the yellow more gray than pink. "A little. But I'll let it ride. I have a very strong stomach. And I don't eat a lot anyway . . ." I continued to look at him, and he held up his wrist to re-enforce what he'd just said. His watch was tightened to the last hole and he pointed that out to me. "So I don't mind."

"But services are important to you?" I asked him.

He looked at Grossbart. "Sure, sir."

"Sergeant."

"Not so much at home," said Grossbart, coming between us, "but away from home it gives one a sense of his Jewishness."

"We have to stick together," Fishbein said.

I started to walk towards the door; Halpern stepped back to make way for me.

"That's what happened in Germany," Grossbart was saying, loud enough for me to hear. "They didn't stick together. They let themselves get pushed around."

I turned. "Look, Grossbart, this is the Army, not summer camp."

He smiled. "So?" Halpern tried to sneak off, but Grossbart held his arm. "So?" he said again.

"Grossbart," I asked, "how old are you?"

"Nineteen."

"And you?" I said to Fishbein.

"The same. The same month even."

"And what about him?" I pointed to Halpern, who'd finally made it safely to the door.

"Eighteen," Grossbart whispered. "But he's like he can't tie his shoes or brush his teeth himself. I feel sorry for him."

"I feel sorry for all of us, Grossbart, but just act like a man. Just don't overdo it."

"Overdo what, sir?"

"The sir business. Don't overdo that," I said, and I left him standing there. I passed by Halpern but he did not look up. Then I was outside, black surrounded me—but behind I heard Grossbart call, "Hey, Mickey, *liebschen*,[2] come on back. Refreshments!"

Liebschen! My grandmother's word for me!

One morning, a week later, while I was working at my desk, Captain Barrett shouted for me to come into his office. When I entered, he had his helmet liner squashed down so that I couldn't even see his eyes. He was on the phone, and when he spoke to me, he cupped one hand over the mouthpiece.

"Who the fuck is Grossbart?"

"Third platoon, Captain," I said. "A trainee."

---

2. Darling (German).

"What's all this stink about food? His mother called a goddam congress-man about the food . . ." He uncovered the mouthpiece and slid his helmet up so I could see the curl of his bottom eyelash. "Yes, sir," he said into the phone. "Yes, sir. I'm still here, sir. I'm asking Marx here right now . . ."

He covered the mouthpiece again and looked back to me. "Lightfoot Harry's on the phone," he said, between his teeth. "This congressman calls General Lyman who calls Colonel Sousa who calls the Major who calls me. They're just dying to stick this thing on me. What's a matter," he shook the phone at me, "I don't feed the troops? What the hell is this?"

"Sir, Grossbart is strange . . ." Barrett greeted that with a mockingly indulgent smile. I altered my approach. "Captain, he's a very orthodox Jew and so he's only allowed to eat certain foods."

"He throws up, the congressman said. Every time he eats something his mother says he throws up!"

"He's accustomed to observing the dietary laws, Captain."

"So why's his old lady have to call the White House!"

"Jewish parents, sir, they're apt to be more protective than you expect. I mean Jews have a very close family life. A boy goes away from home, some-times the mother is liable to get very upset. Probably the boy *mentioned* something in a letter and his mother misinterpreted."

"I'd like to punch him one right in the mouth. There's a goddam war on and he wants a silver platter!"

"I don't think the boy's to blame, sir. I'm sure we can straighten it out by just asking him. Jewish parents worry—"

"*All* parents worry, for Christ sake. But they don't get on their high horse and start pulling strings—"

I interrupted, my voice higher, tighter than before. "The home life, Cap-tain, is so very important . . . but you're right, it may sometimes get out of hand. It's a very wonderful thing, Captain, but because it's so close, this kind of thing—"

He didn't listen any longer to my attempt to present both myself and Lightfoot Harry with an explanation for the letter. He turned back to the phone. "Sir?" he said. "Sir, Marx here tells me Jews have a tendency to be pushy. He says he thinks he can settle it right here in the Company . . . Yes, sir . . . I *will* call back, sir, soon as I can . . ." He hung up. "Where are the men, Sergeant?"

"On the range."

With a whack on the top, he crushed his helmet over his eyes, and charged out of his chair. "We're going for a ride."

The Captain drove and I sat beside him. It was a hot spring day and under my newly starched fatigues it felt as though my armpits were melting down onto my sides and chest. The roads were dry and by the time we reached the firing range, my teeth felt gritty with dust though my mouth had been shut the whole trip. The Captain slammed the brakes on and told me to get the hell out and find Grossbart.

I found him on his belly, firing wildly at the 500 feet target. Waiting their turns behind him were Halpern and Fishbein. Fishbein, wearing a pair of rimless G.I. glasses I hadn't seen on him before, gave the appearance of an old peddler who would gladly have sold you the rifle and cartridges that were slung all over him. I stood back by the ammo boxes, waiting for Grossbart to finish spraying the distant targets. Fishbein straggled back to stand near me.

"Hello, Sergeant Marx."

"How are you?" I mumbled.

"Fine, thank you. Sheldon's really a good shot."

"I didn't notice."

"I'm not so good, but I think I'm getting the hang of it now . . . Sergeant, I don't mean to, you know, ask what I shouldn't . . ." The boy stopped. He was trying to speak intimately but the noise of the shooting necessitated that he shout at me.

"What is it?" I asked. Down the range I saw Captain Barrett standing up in the jeep, scanning the line for me and Grossbart.

"My parents keep asking and asking where we're going. Everybody says the Pacific. I don't care, but my parents . . . If I could relieve their minds I think I could concentrate more on my shooting."

"I don't know where, Fishbein. Try to concentrate anyway."

"Sheldon says you might be able to find out—"

"I don't know a thing, Fishbein. You just take it easy, and don't let Sheldon—"

"*I'm* taking it easy, Sergeant. It's at home—"

Grossbart had just finished on the line and was dusting his fatigues with one hand. I left Fishbein's sentence in the middle.

"Grossbart, the Captain wants to see you."

He came toward us. His eyes blazed and twinkled. "Hi!"

"Don't point that goddam rifle!"

"I wouldn't shoot you, Sarge." He gave me a smile wide as a pumpkin as he turned the barrel aside.

"Damn you, Grossbart—this is no joke! Follow me."

I walked ahead of him and had the awful suspicion that behind me Grossbart was *marching*, his rifle on his shoulder, as though he were a one-man detachment.

At the jeep he gave the Captain a rifle salute. "Private Sheldon Grossbart, sir."

"At ease, Grossman." The Captain slid over to the empty front seat, and crooking a finger, invited Grossbart closer.

"Bart, sir. Sheldon Gross*bart*. It's a common error." Grossbart nodded to me—*I understand*, he indicated. I looked away, just as the mess truck pulled up to the range, disgorging a half dozen K.P.'s with rolled-up sleeves. The mess sergeant screamed at them while they set up the chow line equipment.

"Grossbart, your mama wrote some congressman that we don't feed you right. Do you know that?" the Captain said.

"It was my father, sir. He wrote to Representative Franconi that my religion forbids me to eat certain foods."

"What religion is that, Grossbart?"

"Jewish."

"Jewish, *sir*," I said to Grossbart.

"Excuse me, sir. 'Jewish, sir.'"

"What have you been living on?" the Captain asked. "You've been in the Army a month already. You don't look to me like you're falling to pieces."

"I eat because I have to, sir. But Sergeant Marx will testify to the fact that I don't eat one mouthful more than I need to in order to survive."

"Marx," Barrett asked, "is that so?"

"I've never seen Grossbart eat, sir," I said.

"But you heard the rabbi," Grossbart said. "He told us what to do, and I listened."

The Captain looked at me. "Well, Marx?"

"I still don't know what he eats and doesn't eat, sir."

Grossbart raised his rifle, as though to offer it to me. "But, Sergeant—"

"Look, Grossbart, just answer the Captain's questions!" I said sharply.

Barrett smiled at me and I resented it. "All right, Grossbart," he said, "What is it you want? The little piece of paper? You want out?"

"No, sir. Only to be allowed to live as a Jew. And for the others, too."

"What others?"

"Fishbein, sir, and Halpern."

"They don't like the way we serve either?"

"Halpern throws up, sir. I've seen it."

"I thought *you* threw up."

"Just once, sir. I didn't know the sausage was sausage."

"We'll give menus, Grossbart. We'll show training films about the food, so you can identify when we're trying to poison you."

Grossbart did not answer. Out before me, the men had been organized into two long chow lines. At the tail end of one I spotted Fishbein—or rather, his glasses spotted me. They winked sunlight back at me like a friend. Halpern stood next to him, patting inside his collar with a khaki handkerchief. They moved with the line as it began to edge up towards the food. The mess sergeant was still screaming at the K.P.'s, who stood ready to ladle out the food, bewildered. For a moment I was actually terrorized by the thought that somehow the mess sergeant was going to get involved in Grossbart's problem.

"Come over here, Marx," the Captain said to me. "Marx, you're a Jewish fella, am I right?"

I played straight man. "Yes, sir."

"How long you been in the Army? Tell this boy."

"Three years and two months."

"A year in combat, Grossbart. Twelve goddam months in combat all through Europe. I admire this man," the Captain said, snapping a wrist against my chest. But do you hear him peeping about the food? Do you? I want an answer, Grossbart. Yes or no."

"No, sir."

"And why not? He's a Jewish fella."

"Some things are more important to some Jews than other things to other Jews."

Barrett blew up. "Look, Grossbart, Marx here is a good man, a goddam *hero*. When you were sitting on your sweet ass in high school, Sergeant Marx was killing Germans. Who does more for the Jews, you by throwing up over a lousy piece of sausage, a piece of firstcut meat—or Marx by killing those Nazi bastards? If I was a Jew, Grossbart, I'd kiss this man's feet. He's a goddam hero, you know that? And *he* eats what we give him. Why do you have to cause trouble is what I want to know! What is it you're buckin' for, a discharge?"

"No, sir."

"I'm talking to a *wall!* Sergeant, get him out of my way." Barrett pounced over to the driver's seat. "I'm going to see the chaplain!" The engine roared, the jeep spun around, and then, raising a whirl of dust, the Captain was headed back to camp.

For a moment, Grossbart and I stood side by side, watching the jeep. Then he looked at me and said, "I don't want to start trouble. That's the first thing they toss up to us."

When he spoke I saw that his teeth were white and straight, and the sight of them suddenly made me understand that Grossbart actually did have parents: that once upon a time someone had taken little Sheldon to the dentist. He was someone's son. Despite all the talk about his parents, it was hard to believe in Grossbart as a child, an heir—as related by blood to anyone, mother, father, or, above all, to me. This realization led me to another.

"What does your father do, Grossbart?" I asked, as we started to walk back towards the chow line.

"He's a tailor."

"An American?"

"Now, yes. A son in the Army," he said, jokingly.

"And your mother?" I asked.

He winked. "A *ballabusta*[3]—she practically sleeps with a dustcloth in her hand."

"She's also an immigrant?"

"All she talks is Yiddish, still."

"And your father too?"

"A little English. 'Clean,' 'Press,' 'Take the pants in . . .' That's the extent of it. But they're good to me . . ."

"Then, Grossbart—" I reached out and stopped him. He turned towards me and when our eyes met his seemed to jump back, shiver in their sockets. He looked afraid. "Grossbart, then you were the one who wrote that letter, weren't you?"

It took only a second or two for his eyes to flash happy again. "Yes." He walked on, and I kept pace. "It's what my father *would* have written if he had known how. It was his name, though. *He* signed it. He even mailed it. I sent it home. For the New York postmark."

I was astonished, and he saw it. With complete seriousness, he thrust his right arm in front of me. "Blood is blood, Sergeant," he said, pinching the blue vein in his wrist.

"What the hell *are* you trying to do, Grossbart? I've seen you eat. Do you know that? I told the Captain I don't know what you eat, but I've seen you eat like a hound at chow."

"We work hard, Sergeant. We're in training. For a furnace to work, you've got to feed it coal."

"If you wrote the letter, Grossbart, then why did you say you threw up all the time?"

"I was really talking about Mickey there. But he would never write, Sergeant, though I pleaded with him. He'll waste away to nothing if I don't

3. Good housekeeper (Yiddish).

help. Sergeant, I used my name, my father's name, but it's Mickey and Fishbein too I'm watching out for."

"You're a regular Messiah,[4] aren't you?"

We were at the chow line now.

"That's a good one, Sergeant." He smiled. "But who knows? Who can tell? Maybe you're the Messiah . . . a little bit. What Mickey says is the Messiah is a collective idea. He went to Yeshivah,[5] Mickey, for a while. He says *together* we're the Messiah. Me a little bit, you a little bit . . . You should hear that kid talk, Sergeant, when he gets going."

"Me a little bit, you a little bit. You'd like to believe that, wouldn't you, Grossbart? That makes everything so clean for you."

"It doesn't seem too bad a thing to believe, Sergeant. It only means we should all give a little, is all . . ."

I walked off to eat my rations with the other noncoms.[6]

Two days later a letter addressed to Captain Barrett passed over my desk. It had come through the chain of command—from the office of Congressman Franconi, where it had been received, to General Lyman, to Colonel Sousa, to Major Lamont, to Captain Barrett. I read it over twice while the Captain was at the officers' mess. It was dated May 14th, the day Barrett had spoken with Grossbart on the rifle range.

Dear Congressman:

First let me thank you for your interest in behalf of my son, Private Sheldon Grossbart. Fortunately, I was able to speak with Sheldon on the phone the other night, and I think I've been able to solve our problem. He is, as I mentioned in my last letter, a very religious boy, and it was only with the greatest difficulty that I could persuade him that the religious thing to do— what God Himself would want Sheldon to do—would be to suffer the pangs of religious remorse for the good of his country and all mankind. It took some doing, Congressman, but finally he saw the light. In fact, what he said (and I wrote down the words on a scratch pad so as never to forget), what he said was, "I guess you're right, Dad. So many millions of my fellow Jews gave up their lives to the enemy, the least I can do is live for a while minus a bit of my heritage so as to help end this struggle and regain for all the children of God dignity and humanity." That, Congressman, would make any father proud.

By the way, Sheldon wanted me to know—and to pass on to you—the name of a soldier who helped him reach this decision: SERGEANT NATHAN MARX. Sergeant Marx is a combat veteran who is Sheldon's First Sergeant. This man has helped Sheldon over some of the first hurdles he's had to face in the Army, and is in part responsible for Sheldon's changing his mind about the dietary laws. I know Sheldon would appreciate any recognition Marx could receive.

Thank you and good luck. I look forward to seeing your name on the next election ballot.

Respectfully,
Samuel E. Grossbart

---

4. The deliverer who will rule over the people of Israel at the end of time.

5. Jewish institution of learning.
6. Noncommissioned officers.

Attached to the Grossbart communiqué was a communiqué addressed to General Marshall Lyman, the post commander, and signed by Representative Charles E. Franconi of the House of Representatives. The communiqué informed General Lyman that Sergeant Nathan Marx was a credit to the U.S. Army and the Jewish people.

What was Grossbart's motive in recanting? Did he feel he'd gone too far? Was the letter a strategic retreat—a crafty attempt to strengthen what he considered our alliance? Or had he actually changed his mind, via an imaginary dialogue between Grossbart *père* and *fils*?[7] I was puzzled, but only for a few days—that is, only until I realized that whatever his reasons, he had actually decided to disappear from my life: he was going to allow himself to become just another trainee. I saw him at inspection but he never winked; at chow formations but he never flashed me a sign; on Sundays, with the other trainees, he would sit around watching the noncoms' softball team, for whom I pitched, but not once did he speak an unnecessary or unusual word to me. Fishbein and Halpern retreated from sight too, at Grossbart's command I was sure. Apparently he'd seen that wisdom lay in turning back before he plunged us over into the ugliness of privilege undeserved. Our separation allowed me to forgive him our past encounters, and, finally, to admire him for his good sense.

Meanwhile, free of Grossbart, I grew used to my job and my administrative tasks. I stepped on a scale one day and discovered I had truly become a noncombatant: I had gained seven pounds. I found patience to get past the first three pages of a book. I thought about the future more and more, and wrote letters to girls I'd known before the war—I even got a few answers. I sent away to Columbia for a Law School catalogue. I continued to follow the war in the Pacific, but it was not my war and I read of bombings and battles like a civilian. I thought I could see the end in sight and sometimes at night I dreamed that I was walking on the streets of Manhattan—Broadway, Third Avenue, and 116th Street, where I had lived those three years I'd attended Columbia College. I curled myself around these dreams and I began to be happy.

And then one Saturday when everyone was away and I was alone in the orderly room reading a month-old copy of the *Sporting News*, Grossbart reappeared.

"You a baseball fan, Sergeant?"

I looked up. "How are you?"

"Fine," Grossbart said. "They're making a soldier out of me."

"How are Fishbein and Halpern?"

"Coming along," he said. "We've got no training this afternoon. They're at the movies."

"How come you're not with them?"

"I wanted to come over and say hello."

He smiled—a shy, regular-guy smile, as though he and I well knew that our friendship drew its sustenance from unexpected visits, remembered birthdays, and borrowed lawnmowers. At first it offended me, and then the feeling was swallowed by the general uneasiness I felt at the thought that

7. Father and son (French).

everyone on the post was locked away in a dark movie theater and I was here alone with Grossbart. I folded my paper.

"Sergeant," he said, "I'd like to ask a favor. It is a favor and I'm making no bones about it."

He stopped, allowing me to refuse him a hearing—which, of course, forced me into a courtesy I did not intend. "Go ahead."

"Well, actually it's two favors."

I said nothing.

"The first one's about these rumors. Everybody says we're going to the Pacific."

"As I told your friend Fishbein, I don't know. You'll just have to wait to find out. Like everybody else."

"You think there's a chance of any of us going East?"

"Germany," I said, "maybe."

"I meant New York."

"I don't think so, Grossbart. Offhand."

"Thanks for the information, Sergeant," he said.

"It's not information, Grossbart. Just what I surmise."

"It certainly would be good to be near home. My parents . . . you know." He took a step towards the door and then turned back. "Oh the other thing. May I ask the other?"

"What is it?"

"The other thing is—I've got relatives in St. Louis and they say they'll give me a whole Passover dinner if I can get down there. God, Sergeant, that'd mean an awful lot to me."

I stood up. "No passes during basic, Grossbart."

"But we're off from now till Monday morning, Sergeant. I could leave the post and no one would even know."

"I'd know. You'd know."

"But that's all. Just the two of us. Last night I called my aunt and you should have heard her. 'Come, come,' she said. 'I got gefilte fish, *chrain*,[8] the works!' Just a day, Sergeant, I'd take the blame if anything happened."

"The captain isn't here to sign a pass."

"You could sign."

"Look, Grossbart—"

"Sergeant, for two months practically I've been eating *trafe* till I want to die."

"I thought you'd made up your mind to live with it. To be minus a little bit of heritage."

He pointed a finger at me. "You!" he said. "That wasn't for you to read!"

"I read it. So what."

"That letter was addressed to a congressman."

"Grossbart, don't feed me any crap. You *wanted* me to read it."

"Why are you persecuting me, Sergeant?"

"Are you kidding!"

"I've run into this before," he said, "but never from my own!"

"Get out of here, Grossbart! Get the hell out of my sight!"

---

8. Horseradish.

He did not move. "Ashamed, that's what you are. So you take it out on the rest of us. They say Hitler himself was half a Jew. Seeing this, I wouldn't doubt it!"

"What are you trying to do with me, Grossbart? What are you after? You want me to give you special privileges, to change the food, to find out about your orders, to give you weekend passes."

"You even talk like a goy!" Grossbart shook his fist. "Is this a weekend pass I'm asking for? Is a Seder[9] sacred or not?"

Seder! It suddenly occurred to me that Passover had been celebrated weeks before. I confronted Grossbart with the fact.

"That's right," he said. "Who says no? A month ago, and *I* was in the field eating hash! And now all I ask is a simple favor—a Jewish boy I thought would understand. My aunt's willing to go out of her way—to make a Seder a month later—" He turned to go, mumbling.

"Come back here!" I called. He stopped and looked at me. "Grossbart, why can't you be like the rest? Why do you have to stick out like a sore thumb? Why do you beg for special treatment?"

"Because I'm a Jew, Sergeant. I *am* different. Better, maybe not. But different."

"This is a war, Grossbart. For the time being *be* the same."

"I refuse."

"What?"

"I refuse. I can't stop being me, that's all there is to it." Tears came to his eyes. "It's a hard thing to be a Jew. But now I see what Mickey says—it's a harder thing to stay one." He raised a hand sadly toward me. "Look at you."

"Stop crying!"

"Stop this, stop that, stop the other thing! You stop, Sergeant. Stop closing your heart to your own!" And wiping his face with his sleeve, he ran out the door. "The least we can do for one another . . . the least . . ."

An hour later I saw Grossbart headed across the field. He wore a pair of starched khakis and carried only a little leather ditty bag. I went to the door and from the outside felt the heat of the day. It was quiet—not a soul in sight except over by the mess hall four K.P.'s sitting round a pan, sloped forward from the waists, gabbing and peeling potatoes in the sun.

"Grossbart!" I called.

He looked toward me and continued walking.

"Grossbart, get over here!"

He turned and stepped into his long shadow. Finally he stood before me.

"Where are you going?" I said.

"St. Louis. I don't care."

"You'll get caught without a pass."

"So I'll get caught without a pass."

"You'll go to the stockade."

"I'm in the stockade." He made an about-face and headed off.

I let him go only a step: "Come back here," I said, and he followed me into the office, where I typed out a pass and signed the Captain's name and my own initials after it.

---

9. Ceremonial dinner on the first evening of Passover.

He took the pass from me and then, a moment later, he reached out and grabbed my hand. "Sergeant, you don't know how much this means to me."

"Okay. Don't get in any trouble."

"I wish I could show you how much this means to me."

"Don't do me any favors. Don't write any more congressmen for citations."

Amazingly, he smiled. "You're right. I won't. But let me do something."

"Bring me a piece of that gefilte fish. Just get out of here."

"I will! With a slice of carrot and a little horseradish. I won't forget."

"All right. Just show your pass at the gate. And don't tell *anybody*."

"I won't. It's a month late, but a good Yom Tov[1] to you."

"Good Yom Tov, Grossbart," I said.

"You're a good Jew, Sergeant. You like to think you have a hard heart, but underneath you're a fine decent man. I mean that."

Those last three words touched me more than any words from Grossbart's mouth had the right to. "All right, Grossbart. Now call me 'sir' and get the hell out of here."

He ran out the door and was gone. I felt very pleased with myself—it was a great relief to stop fighting Grossbart. And it had cost me nothing. Barrett would never find out, and if he did, I could manage to invent some excuse. For a while I sat at my desk, comfortable in my decision. Then the screen door flew back and Grossbart burst in again. "Sergeant!" he said. Behind him I saw Fishbein and Halpern, both in starched khakis, both carrying ditty bags exactly like Grossbart's.

"Sergeant, I caught Mickey and Larry coming out of the movies. I almost missed them."

"Grossbart, did I say tell no one?"

"But my aunt said I could bring friends. That I should, in fact."

"I'm the Sergeant, Grossbart—not your aunt!"

Grossbart looked at me in disbelief; he pulled Halpern up by his sleeve. "Mickey, tell the Sergeant what this would mean to you."

"Grossbart, for God's sake, spare us—"

"Tell him what you told me, Mickey. How much it would mean."

Halpern looked at me and, shrugging his shoulders, made his admission. "A lot."

Fishbein stepped forward without prompting. "This would mean a great deal to me and my parents, Sergeant Marx."

"No!" I shouted.

Grossbart was shaking his head. "Sergeant, I could see you denying me, but how you can deny Mickey, a Yeshivah boy, that's beyond me."

"I'm not denying Mickey anything. You just pushed a little too hard, Grossbart. *You* denied him."

"I'll give him my pass, then," Grossbart said. "I'll give him my aunt's address and a little note. At least let him go."

In a second he had crammed the pass into Halpern's pants'pocket. Halpern looked at me, Fishbein too. Grossbart was at the door, pushing it open. "Mickey, bring me a piece of gefilte fish at least." And then he was outside again.

1. Holiday (Yiddish).

The three of us looked at one another and then I said, "Halpern, hand that pass over."

He took it from his pocket and gave it to me. Fishbein had now moved to the doorway, where he lingered. He stood there with his mouth slightly open and then pointed to himself. "And me?" he asked.

His utter ridiculousness exhausted me. I slumped down in my seat and I felt pulses knocking at the back of my eyes. "Fishbein," I said, "you understand I'm not trying to deny you anything, don't you? If it was my Army I'd serve gefilte fish in the mess hall. I'd sell kugel[2] in the PX, honest to God."

Halpern smiled.

"You understand, don't you, Halpern?"

"Yes, Sergeant."

"And you, Fishbein? I don't want enemies. I'm just like you—I want to serve my time and go home. I miss the same things you miss."

"Then, Sergeant," Fishbein interrupted, "Why don't you come too?"

"Where?"

"To St. Louis. To Shelley's aunt. We'll have a regular Seder. Play hide-the-matzah." He gave a broad, black-toothed smile.

I saw Grossbart in the doorway again, on the other side of the screen.

"Pssst!" He waved a piece of paper. "Mickey, here's the address. Tell her I couldn't get away."

Halpern did not move. He looked at me and I saw the shrug moving up his arms into his shoulders again. I took the cover off my typewriter and made out passes for him and Fishbein. "Go," I said, "the three of you."

I thought Halpern was going to kiss my hand.

That afternoon, in a bar in Joplin, I drank beer and listened with half an ear to the Cardinal game. I tried to look squarely at what I'd become involved in, and began to wonder if perhaps the struggle with Grossbart wasn't as much my fault as his. What was I that I had to *muster* generous feelings? Who was I to have been feeling so grudging, so tight-hearted? After all, I wasn't being asked to move the world. Had I a right, then, or a reason, to clamp down on Grossbart, when that meant clamping down on Halpern, too? And Fishbein, that ugly agreeable soul, wouldn't he suffer in the bargain also? Out of the many recollections that had tumbled over me these past few days, I heard from some childhood moment my grandmother's voice: "What are you making a *tsimas*?"[3] It was what she would ask my mother when, say, I had cut myself with a knife and her daughter was busy bawling me out. I would need a hug and a kiss and my mother would moralize! But my grandmother knew—mercy overrides justice. I should have known it, too. Who was Nathan Marx to be such a pennypincher with kindness? Surely, I thought, the Messiah himself—if he should ever come—won't niggle over nickels and dimes. God willing, he'll hug and kiss.

The next day, while we were playing softball over on the Parade Grounds, I decided to ask Bob Wright, who was noncom in charge over at Classification and Assignment, where he thought our trainees would be sent when their cycle ended in two weeks. I asked casually, between innings, and he

---

2. Baked pudding of noodles or potatoes.
3. Fuss (Yiddish, literal trans.); here a side dish made of mixed cooked vegetables and fruit.

said, "They're pushing them all into the Pacific. Shulman cut the orders on your boys the other day."

The news shocked me, as though I were father to Halpern, Fishbein, and Grossbart.

That night I was just sliding into sleep when someone tapped on the door. "What is it?"

"Sheldon."

He opened the door and came in. For a moment I felt his presence without being able to see him. "How was it?" I asked, as though to the darkness.

He popped into sight before me. "Great, Sergeant." I felt my springs sag; Grossbart was sitting on the edge of the bed. I sat up.

"How about you?" he asked. "Have a nice weekend?"

"Yes."

He took a deep paternal breath. "The others went to sleep . . ." We sat silently for a while, as a homey feeling invaded my ugly little cubicle: the door was locked, the cat out, the children safely in bed.

"Sergeant, can I tell you something? Personal?"

I did not answer and he seemed to know why. "Not about me. About Mickey. Sergeant, I never felt for anybody like I feel for him. Last night I heard Mickey in the bed next to me. He was crying so, it could have broken your heart. Real sobs."

"I'm sorry to hear that."

"I had to talk to him to stop him. He held my hand, Sergeant—he wouldn't let it go. He was almost hysterical. He kept saying if he only knew where we were going. Even if he knew it *was* the Pacific, that would be better than nothing. Just to know."

Long ago, someone had taught Grossbart the sad law that only lies can get the truth. Not that I couldn't believe in Halpern's crying—his eyes *always* seemed red-rimmed. But, fact or not, it became a lie when Grossbart uttered it. He was entirely strategic. But then—it came with the force of indictment—so was I! There are strategies of aggression, but there are strategies of retreat, as well. And so, recognizing that I myself, had not been without craft and guile, I told him what I knew. "It is the Pacific."

He let out a small gasp, which was not a lie. "I'll tell him. I wish it was otherwise."

"So do I."

He jumped on my words. "You mean you think you could do something? A change maybe?"

"No, I couldn't do a thing."

"Don't you know anybody over at C & A?"

"Grossbart, there's nothing I can do. If your orders are for the Pacific then it's the Pacific."

"But Mickey."

"Mickey, you, me—everybody, Grossbart. There's nothing to be done. Maybe the war'll end before you go. Pray for a miracle."

"But—"

"Good night, Grossbart." I settled back, and was relieved to feel the springs upbend again as Grossbart rose to leave. I could see him clearly now; his jaw had dropped and he looked like a dazed prizefighter. I noticed for the first time a little paper bag in his hand.

"Grossbart"—I smiled—"my gift?"

"Oh, yes, Sergeant. Here, from all of us." He handed me the bag. "It's egg roll."

"Egg roll?" I accepted the bag and felt a damp grease spot on the bottom. I opened it, sure that Grossbart was joking.

"We thought you'd probably like it. You know, Chinese egg roll. We thought you'd probably have a taste for—"

"Your aunt served egg roll?"

"She wasn't home."

"Grossbart, she invited you. You told me she invited you and your friends."

"I know. I just reread the letter. *Next* week."

I got out of bed and walked to the window. It was black as far off as I could see. "Grossbart," I said. But I was not calling him.

"What?"

"What are you, Grossbart? Honest to God, what are you?"

I think it was the first time I'd asked him a question for which he didn't have an immediate answer.

"How can you do this to people?" I asked.

"Sergeant, the day away did us all a world of good. Fishbein, you should see him, he *loves* Chinese food."

"But the Seder," I said.

"We took second best, Sergeant."

Rage came charging at me. I didn't sidestep—I grabbed it, pulled it in, hugged it to my chest.

"Grossbart, you're a liar! You're a schemer and a crook! You've got no respect for anything! Nothing at all! Not for me, for the truth, not even for poor Halpern! You use us all—"

"Sergeant, Sergeant, I feel for Mickey, honest to God, I do. I *love* Mickey. I try—"

"You try! You feel!" I lurched towards him and grabbed his shirt front. I shook him furiously. "Grossbart, get out. Get out and stay the hell away from me! Because if I see you, I'll make your life miserable. *You understand that?*"

"Yes."

I let him free, and when he walked from the room I wanted to spit on the floor where he had stood. I couldn't stop the fury from rising in my heart. It engulfed me, owned me, till it seemed I could only rid myself of it with tears or an act of violence. I snatched from the bed the bag Grossbart had given me and with all my strength threw it out the window. And the next morning, as the men policed the area around the barracks, I heard a great cry go up from one of the trainees who'd been anticipating only his morning handful of cigarette butts and candy wrappers. "Egg roll!" he shouted. "Holy Christ, Chinese goddam egg roll!"

A week later, when I read the orders that had come down from C & A, I couldn't believe my eyes. Every single trainee was to be shipped to Camp Stoneham, California, and from there to the Pacific. Every trainee but one:

Private Sheldon Grossbart was to be sent to Fort Monmouth, New Jersey. I read the mimeographed sheet several times. Dee, Farrell, Fishbein, Fuselli, Fylypowycz, Glinicki, Gromke, Gucwa, Halpern, Hardy, Helebrandt . . . right down to Anton Zygadlo, all were to be headed West before the month was out. All except Grossbart. He had pulled a string and I wasn't it.

I lifted the phone and called C & A.

The voice on the other end said smartly, "Corporal Shulman, sir."

"Let me speak to Sergeant Wright."

"Who is this calling, sir?"

"Sergeant Marx."

And to my surprise, the voice said, *"Oh."* Then: "Just a minute, Sergeant."

Shulman's *oh* stayed with me while I waited for Wright to come to the phone. Why *oh?* Who was Shulman? And then, so simply, I knew I'd discovered the string Grossbart had pulled. In fact, I could hear Grossbart the day he'd discovered Shulman, in the PX, or the bowling alley, or maybe even at services. "Glad to meet you. Where you from? Bronx? Me too. Do you know so-and-so? And so-and-so? Me too! You work at C & A? Really? Hey, how's chances of getting East? Could you do something? Change something? Swindle, cheat, lie? We gotta help each other, you know . . . if the Jews in Germany . . ."

At the other end Bob Wright answered. "How are you, Nate? How's the pitching arm?"

"Good. Bob, I wonder if you could do me a favor." I heard clearly my own words and they so reminded me of Grossbart that I dropped more easily than I could have imagined into what I had planned. "This may sound crazy, Bob, but I got a kid here on orders to Monmouth who wants them changed. He had a brother killed in Europe and he's hot to go to the Pacific. Says he'd feel like a coward if he wound up stateside. I don't know, Bob, can anything be done? Put somebody else in the Monmouth slot?"

"Who?" he asked cagily.

"Anybody. First guy on the alphabet. I don't care. The kid just asked if something could be done."

"What's his name?"

"Grossbart, Sheldon."

Wright didn't answer.

"Yeah," I said, "he's a Jewish kid, so he thought I could help him out. You know."

"I guess I can do something," he finally said. "The Major hasn't been around here for weeks—TDY[4] to the golf course. I'll try, Nate that's all I can say."

"I'd appreciate it, Bob. See you Sunday," and I hung up, perspiring.

And the following day the corrected orders appeared: Fishbein, Fuselli, Fylypowycz, Glinicki, Grossbart, Gucwa, Halpern, Hardy . . . Lucky Private Harley Alton was to go to Fort Monmouth, New Jersey, where for some reason or other, they wanted an enlisted man with infantry training.

After chow that night I stopped back at the orderly room to straighten out the guard duty roster. Grossbart was waiting for me. He spoke first.

"You son of a bitch!"

4. Temporary Duty, an army orders term used ironically here.

I sat down at my desk and while he glared down at me I began to make the necessary alterations in the duty roster.

"What do you have against me?" he cried. "Against my family? Would it kill you for me to be near my father, God knows how many months he has left to him."

"Why?"

"His heart," Grossbart said. "He hasn't had enough troubles in a lifetime, you've got to add to them. I curse the day I ever met you, Marx! Shulman told me what happened over there. There's no limit to your anti-Semitism, is there! The damage you've done here isn't enough. You have to make a special phone call! You really want me dead!"

I made the last few notations in the duty roster and got up to leave. "Good night, Grossbart."

"You owe me an explanation!" He stood in my path.

"Sheldon, you're the one who owes explanations."

He scowled. "To *you*?"

"To me, I think so, yes. Mostly to Fishbein and Halpern."

"That's right, twist things around. I owe nobody nothing, I've done all I could do for them. Now I think I've got the right to watch out for myself."

"For each other we have to learn to watch out, Sheldon. You told me yourself."

"You call this watching out for me, what you did?"

"No. For all of us."

I pushed him aside and started for the door. I heard his furious breathing behind me, and it sounded like steam rushing from the engine of his terrible strength.

"You'll be all right," I said from the door. And, I thought, so would Fishbein and Halpern be all right, even in the Pacific, if only Grossbart could continue to see in the obsequiousness of the one, the soft spirituality of the other, some profit for himself.

I stood outside the orderly room, and I heard Grossbart weeping behind me. Over in the barracks, in the lighted windows, I could see the boys in their T-shirts sitting on their bunks talking about their orders, as they'd been doing for the past two days. With a kind of quiet nervousness, they polished shoes, shined belt buckles, squared away underwear, trying as best they could to accept their fate. Behind me, Grossbart swallowed hard, accepting his. And then, resisting with all my will an impulse to turn and seek pardon for my vindictiveness, I accepted my own.

1959

1945 to the Present

Autumn Rhythm (Number 30), Jackson Pollock, 1950

With Abstract Expressionism, the style of post–World War II American painting that had international impact, the canvas became less a surface upon which to represent than an arena in which to act. Jackson Pollock (1912–1956) was the most noteworthy of the so-called action painters. One of his favorite methods, working above a canvas stretched on the ground, dancing over and around it, dripping and swirling paint, was dramatic enough to be captured in photographs and film documentaries, just as his emotionally fraught visage found its place on magazine covers and his sometimes violent behavior became as newsworthy as his art.

Guggenheim Museum
Frank Lloyd Wright, 1959

The Solomon R. Guggenheim Museum (commissioned in 1943, completed and opened in 1959) stands on upper Fifth Avenue in New York City as a striking reinvention of not just how art can be exhibited, but how it can be seen. Patrons of the Guggenheim do not stroll through a succession of flat-floored galleries, but instead either work their way up through a large, open-centered spiral or take an elevator to the building's top, then descend at a gentle angle through the spiral. The walls of the spiral display artworks for viewing. Early in his career the museum's architect, Frank Lloyd Wright (1867–1959), had helped end the Victorian era's predilection for boxlike construction. But Wright resisted the stark conceptualism of modern architecture in favor of what he called the "organic." Here, instead of form following function (a premise of modernism), form and function are one.

Blam, Roy Lichtenstein, 1962

Roy Lichtenstein (1923–1997) helped to launch the Pop Art movement. Lichtenstein used bold outlines, vivid colors, and the technique of Benday dots, popular in commercial printing, to simulate with painting the process of mechanical reproduction. This aesthetic clearly defied the expressionist practices of abstract painters like Jackson Pollock. The cartoon style of *Blam* (in fact, Lichtenstein took this image from a comic book) and its onomatopoetic lettering are typical of Lichtenstein's work. The literally explosive image—a fighter plane being blown apart in the air—also suggests the way in which Pop Art sought to explode boundaries between an original and a copy, a unique image and one that is reproduced, and between high and low culture more generally. Fiction writers like Donald Barthelme, poets like John Ashbery, and comic book artists like Art Spiegelman are all indebted in different ways to Pop Art.

Estate, Robert Rauschenberg, 1963

Few artworks reflect the social and aesthetic nature of their times as boldly as do the combines and assemblages of Robert Rauschenberg (b. 1925). Self-consciousness about his medium combines with sociopolitical awareness in works that address both concerns and make them the viewers' own.

Estate employs brushwork, silk-screening, photography, and photocopying to interrogate its audience as well as itself. Most important, every image in this collage remains recognizable, even as the expressive manner of combination (including several brushstrokes and color actions worthy of Abstract Expressionism) emphasizes the artist's creative act.

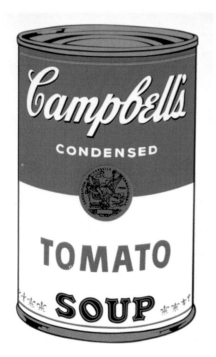

Campbell's Soup 1 (Tomato)
Andy Warhol, 1968

For the Pop artist Andy Warhol (1928–1987), an object as banal as a Campbell's soup can could evoke the spirit of the American 1960s. While both representational and abstract painting had conventionally been dedicated to matters of great importance, whether in the subject portrayed or in the activity of putting paint to canvas, Warhol's soup can undercut the premises of both styles while also commenting on the materialism underlying the whole business of producing and selling art. Creativity was now a matter of selection, in this case of lavishing the artist's considerable talent and technique on (and commanding a high price for) such an everyday object. From this decade onward literary artists would find success by doing much the same thing.

*Earthrise and Lunar Horizon
from* Apollo 8, 1968

The photo of "Earthrise" over the
lunar horizon was taken by the
Apollo 8 crew, astronauts Frank
Borman (b. 1928), James Lovell
(b. 1928), and William Anders (b.
1933), who were the first humans
to leave Earth's orbit, entering
into lunar orbit on Christmas Eve,
1968. The photograph showed the
Earth for the first time as it
appears from deep space. The
philosopher Hannah Arendt, in
her book *The Human Condition*
(1958), anticipated the significance of this image when she
wrote that a shift from seeing men
and women as earthbound creatures to seeing them as dwellers of
the universe would be a radical
change in understanding the
human condition, as revolutionary
as the invention of the telescope.

The American Indian
Fritz Scholder, 1970

The American Indian by Fritz Scholder
(1937–2005), a Luiseño Indian,
belongs to a series of paintings that
blew open the doors of "acceptable"
Indian imagery and undermined
clichés and stereotypes of the stoic
"noble savage." Rather than traditional
Indian regalia, the figure wears a judicial
robe fashioned from the American
flag, as if to suggest that only being
wrapped in the symbol of the colonists
will certify him as "American." But the
whitened face and skeletal rendering
of the figure's mouth suggest what
colonization cost him. The single feather
in his hair, the necklace he wears, and
the tomahawk he holds may suggest
how the expectations of tourists also
shape his depiction.

Untitled, Cindy Sherman, 1981

This photograph by the artist Cindy Sherman (b. 1954) is number 96 of her "Centerfold" series (1981). Like Sherman's earlier, black-and-white "Film Stills," this series consists of "self-portraits" in which the artist explores representations of women by dressing in a variety of costumes and adopting a variety of poses. Sherman's role as both photographer and subject reverses the traditional power of the male gaze, and here she examines and subverts the objectified images of women displayed in magazine centerfolds. Rather than signaling availability, this cropped, color-saturated photograph is enigmatic. Sherman's girlish clothing, evoking the 1950s, conceals more than it reveals, and she holds in her hand a largely unreadable scrap torn from a newspaper. Her gaze, vacant and interior, is also unreadable. Her distinctly unrevealing sweater and the flush on her face become part of the color pattern—oranges and browns forming a series of grids and checks—rather than an erotic sign.

Vietnam Veterans Memorial, Maya Lin, 1982

Located on the mall in Washington, D.C., the Vietnam Veterans Memorial is a 246-foot-long, v-shaped sunken wall of black granite. It is engraved with more than fifty-eight thousand names of those who died in the Vietnam conflict. The names are listed in chronological order, and to locate a particular name a visitor walks along the wall searching for it. The polished surface of the granite reflects the sky, the surrounding landscape, and the visitor. Considerable controversy attended the design, by the Chinese American architect Maya Lin (b. 1959), some objecting to its abstraction in place of the realistic statuary of most war memorials, and some finding it too somber. Lin has said she wanted a structure that would carve out a space for the public display of grief and loss, and the memorial has a powerful elegiac quality. Dedicated on Veterans Day, 1982, it has become the most widely visited monument in Washington.

Sonny's Quilt, Faith Ringgold, 1986

In *Sonny's Quilt*, an acrylic painting on canvas with a pieced fabric border, Faith Ringgold (b. 1930) unites two African American art forms: jazz and the quilt. This quilt painting depicts the jazz saxophonist Theodore Walter "Sonny" Rollins (b. 1930) poised high on the Brooklyn Bridge, the river below him and the skyline above him. To spare his neighbors in Brooklyn, Rollins used to leave his apartment to practice his instrument in public places. The brilliant coloration of the painting recalls the materials of African American quilts, and the girders and wires of the bridge, as well as the repeated squares in the bridge's structure, resemble the designs and borders of quilt patterns. Centered in the painting, Rollins is alone with his music and yet a part of the surrounding city. Ringgold's depiction of the Williamsburg Bridge evokes the iconic status of the nearby Brooklyn Bridge in American painting, photography, and literature, including *The Bridge* (1930) by Hart Crane (1899–1932), a selection from which appears in this anthology.

World Trade Center Burning, Peter Morgan, September 11, 2001

"A screaming comes across the sky." This opening sentence of Thomas Pynchon's 1973 novel *Gravity's Rainbow* had for decades impressed readers with the terrors of modern warfare, in which military technologies at the far edge of human inventiveness were turned against people at home. That Pynchon's scene was London, under attack from German V-2 rockets near the end of World War II, may have allayed readers' most personal fears. Yet on September 11, 2001, another such screaming awoke not just the United States but the whole world to the reality that wholesale destruction was an ever-present possibility. After half a century of Cold War rhetoric that had made such catastrophes unthinkable, the unthinkable happened. Two jet airliners were crashed into the twin towers of New York's World Trade Center in an event witnessed within minutes by television viewers all over the Earth. By the time the buildings collapsed, the whole world was watching. What in normal terms might be a line in a novel or a scene in a movie was now most horribly real.

The Gates, Christo and Jeanne-Claude, 2005

For sixteen days, from February 12 to 27, 2005, New York City's Central Park was transformed by the artists Christo (b. 1935) and Jeanne-Claude (1935–2009) into a series of walkways, extending over twenty-three miles, in which orange-colored fabric panels were suspended from 7,503 vinyl structures or gates. To some who saw them as they stirred in the wind, these panels had a mysterious and dreamlike effect, transforming a familiar landscape and reaffirming the city's beauty after the tragedy of 9/11. Like all of Christo and Jeanne-Claude's creations, *The Gates* was public and temporary. New Yorkers' responses were typically mixed: while some complained about the expense and the hype, many found *The Gates* magical, an experience at once individual and shared by people from all over the country and the world.

AMIRI BARAKA (LEROI JONES)
b. 1934

When in 1967 LeRoi Jones assumed the Bantuized Muslim name Amiri Baraka (meaning Prince, a Blessed One), he was undergoing one of several changes in his progression as a maker of literature. Born Everett Leroy Jones, he was the child of middle-class African American parents in Newark, New Jersey, where his scholastic abilities took him to the best schools available; as Baraka recalls in his autobiography, his classmates were more often white suburbanites than inner-city children of his own race. He restyled his name as "LeRoi" during his under-graduate years at Howard University (a traditionally African American institution), to which he had transferred from the mostly white campus of Rutgers University (where he had won a scholarship). After leaving Howard in 1954 and serving in the U.S. Air Force, from which he was discharged for unapproved political activities, Jones moved to New York City's Greenwich Village and became prominent on the avant-garde poetry scene. His friends were white innovators—Gilbert Sorrentino, Diane DiPrima, and Frank O'Hara among them—with whom he worked on the maga-zine *Kulchur* in addition to editing and publishing his own journal, *Yugen*. Married to Hettie Cohen, he began an interracial family and wrote record reviews for main-stream jazz magazines.

Jones was well established in the more intellectually elite quarters of New York's world of poetry, art, and music. Yet as racial tensions mounted, with the assassina-tion of Medgar Evers; fatal church bombings in Alabama; and the murder of civil rights workers James Chaney, Andrew Goodman, and Michael Schwerner in Missis-sippi, Jones's life underwent major changes as well. In 1965, following the assassi-nation of Malcolm X, he left his wife and children and moved to Harlem, where as a newly declared black cultural nationalist he founded the Black Arts Reper-tory Theater, dedicated to taking socially militant drama directly to the people it represented.

Poetry as a vehicle of popular encouragement remains central to Baraka's belief. He may well have agreed with the judge who once convicted him of incitement to riot that his poems could motivate people to act (whether such culpability had been proven in legal form is another matter, and his incitement conviction was later, overturned on appeal). As opposed to his very first work, which conveyed a personal anguish for which the poet projected no political solution ("I am inside someone / who hates me, I look / out from his eyes") and whose collective title conveys little hope other than in the act of expression (*Preface to a Twenty Volume Suicide Note*, 1961), his later work is replete with exhortations, capitalized imperatives for action, and chantlike repetitions designed to arouse a fury for action and then direct it toward the achievement of specific social goals. Much like his drama, this poetry is overtly presentational, showing what the reader needs to think about and then pro-viding the stimulus to act. Yet all the while the personal nature of Baraka stands behind it, making clear that a deep and complex imagination has been brought to bear on the issues. The range and intensity of Baraka's poetry is evident in his 1995 collection, *Transbluesency: The Selected Poems of Amiri Baraka/LeRoi Jones* (1961–1995). His 2004 collection, *Somebody Blew Up America & Other Poems*, contains Baraka's controversial poem of the same name, written after 9/11, during a period in which he was New Jersey's poet laureate. After the poem's publication, public outcry became so great that the governor of New Jersey took action to abolish the position.

Although Baraka sued, the United States Court of Appeals eventually ruled that state officials were immune from such lawsuits. Baraka has never feared controversy; he remains an influence for many younger writers both as a major poet and as a cultural and political leader.

Since the 1980s Baraka has taught in the African Studies Department at the State University of New York, Stony Brook. In addition to poetry and drama, he continues to write essays on social subjects and on jazz.

An Agony. As Now.

I am inside someone
who hates me. I look
out from his eyes. Smell
what fouled tunes come in
to his breath. Love his   5
wretched women.

Slits in the metal, for sun. Where
my eyes sit turning, at the cool air
the glance of light, or hard flesh
rubbed against me, a woman, a man,   10
without shadow, or voice, or meaning.

This is the enclosure (flesh,
where innocence is a weapon. An
abstraction. Touch. (Not mine,
Or yours, if you are the soul I had   15
and abandoned when I was blind and had
my enemies carry me as a dead man
(if he is beautiful, or pitied.

It can be pain. (As now, as all his
flesh hurts me.) It can be that. Or   20
pain. As when she ran from me into
that forest.
            Or pain, the mind
silver spiraled whirled against the
sun, higher than even old men thought   25
God would be. Or pain. And the other. The
yes. (Inside his books, his fingers. They
are withered yellow flowers and were never
beautiful.) The yes. You will, lost soul, say
'beauty.' Beauty, practiced, as the tree. The   30
slow river. A white sun in its wet sentences.

Or, the cold men in their gale. Ecstasy. Flesh
or soul. The yes. (Their robes blown. Their bowls
empty. They chant at my heels, not at yours.) Flesh
or soul, as corrupt. Where the answer moves too quickly.   35
Where the God is a self, after all.)

Cold air blown through narrow blind eyes. Flesh,
white hot metal. Glows as the day with its sun.
It is a human love, I live inside. A bony skeleton
you recognize as words or simple feeling.   40

But it has no feeling. As the metal, is hot, it is not,
given to love.

It burns the thing
inside it. And that thing
screams.   45

1964

A Poem for Willie Best[1]

I

The face sings, alone
at the top
            of the body. All
flesh, all song, aligned. For hell
is silent, at those cracked lips   5
flakes of skin and mind
twist and whistle softly
as they fall.
            It was your own death
you saw. Your own face, stiff   10
and raw. This
without sound, or
movement. Sweet afton,[2] the
dead beggar bleeds
yet. His blood, for a time   15
alive, and huddled in a door
way, struggling to sing. Rain
washes it into cracks. Pits
whose bottoms are famous. Whose sides
are innocent broadcasts   20
of another life.

II

At this point, neither
front nor back. A point, the
dimensionless line. The top
of a head, seen from Christ's   25
heaven, stripped of history
or desire.

1. Willie Best was a negro character actor whose
Hollywood name was Sleep'n'eat [Baraka's note].
2. "How Gently Sweet Afton," a poem by the
Scottish poet Robert Burns (1759–1796), refers
to the river Afton in Ayrshire, Scotland.

      Fixed, perpendicular
to shadow. (Even speech, vertical,
leaves no trace. Born in to death   30
held fast to it, where
the lover spreads his arms, the line
he makes to threaten Gods with history.
The fingers stretch to emptiness. At
each point, after flesh, even light   35
is speculation. But an end, his end,
failing a beginning.

2

A cross. The gesture, symbol, line
arms held stiff, nailed stiff, with
no sign, of what gave them strength.   40
The point, become a line, a cross, or
the man, and his material, driven in
the ground. If the head rolls back
and the mouth opens, screamed into
existence, there will be perhaps   45
only the slightest hint of movement
a smear; no help will come. No one
will turn to that station again.

III

At a cross roads, sits the
player. No drum, no umbrella, even   50
though it's raining. Again, and we
are somehow less miserable because
here is a hero, used to being wet.
One road is where you are standing now
(reading this, the other, crosses then   55
rushes into a wood.
                      5 lbs neckbones.
                      5 lbs hog innards.
                      10 bottles cheap wine.
                                     (the contents   60
of a paper bag, also shoes, with holes
for the big toe, and several rusted
knives. This is a literature, of
symbols. And it is his gift, as the
bag is.   65
             (The contents
again, holy saviours,
                      300 men on horseback
                      75 bibles
                      the quietness   70
of a field. A rich
man, though wet through
by the rain.

I said,
      47 howitzers[3]   75
      7 polished horse jaws
      a few trees being waved
softly back under
the black night
      All this should be   80
invested.

IV

Where
ever,
      he has gone. Who ever
mourns   85
or sits silent
to remember

There is nothing of pity
here. Nothing
of sympathy.   90

V

This is the dance of the raised
leg. Of the hand on the knee
quickly.
      As a dance it punishes
speech. 'The house burned. The   95
old man killed.'
      As a dance it
is obscure.

VI

This is the song
of the highest C.   100
      The falsetto. An elegance
that punishes silence. This is the song
of the toes pointed inward, the arms swung, the
hips, moved, for fucking, slow, from side
to side. He is quoted   105
saying, "My father was
never a jockey,
      but
    he did teach me
      how to ride."   110

---

3. Short, relatively light cannons for the high-angle firing of shells at a low velocity.

VII

The balance.
        (Rushed in, swarmed of dark, cloaks,
and only red lights pushed a message
to the street. Rub.
             This is the lady,   115
I saw you with.
This is your mother.
This is the lady I wanted
some how to sleep with.
            As a dance, or   120
our elegant song. Sun red and grown
from trees, fences, mud roads in dried out
river beds. This is for me, with no God
but what is given. Give me
               Something more   125
than what is here. I must tell you
my body hurts.

The balance.
         Can you hear? Here
I am again. Your boy, dynamite. Can   130
you hear? My soul is moved. The soul
you gave me. I say, my soul, and it
is moved. That soul
you gave me.
          Yes, I'm sure   135
this is the lady. You
slept with her. Witness, your boy,
here, dynamite. Hear?
          I mean
can you?   140
The balance.
         He was tired of losing. (And
his walking buddies tired
of walking.
         Bent slightly,   145
at the waist. Left hand low, to flick
quick showy jabs ala Sugar.[4] The right
cocked, to complete,
           any combination.
         He was   150
tired of losing, but he was fighting
a big dumb "farmer."
         Such a blue bright
afternoon, and only a few hundred yards
from the beach. He said, I'm tired   155
of losing.
        "I *got* ta cut'cha."

---

4. Sugar Ray Robinson (1921–1989), American boxer.

VIII

A renegade
behind the mask. And even
the mask, a renegade   160
disguise. Black skin
and hanging lip.
             Lazy
             Frightened
             Thieving   165
             Very potent sexually
             Scars
             Generally inferior
                    (but natural
rhythms.   170

His head is
at the window. The only
part
    that sings.
(The word he used   175
        (we are passing St. Mark's place[5]
        and those crazy jews who fuck)
                         to provoke
in neon, still useful
in the rain,   180
        to provoke
some meaning, where before
there was only hell. I said
silence, at his huddled blood.
             It is an obscene invention.   185
             A white sticky discharge.
             "Jism," in white chalk
             on the back of Angel's garage.
             Red jackets with the head of
             Hobbes[6] staring into space. "Jasm"   190
             the name the leader took, had it
             stenciled on his chest.
                        And he sits
wet at the crossroads, remembering distinctly
each weightless face that eases by. (Sun at   195
the back door, and that hideous mindless grin.
                    (Hear?

                                1964

---

5. Street in New York City's East Village.
6. Thomas Hobbes (1588–1679), English philosopher who believed a "social contract" was necessary between rulers and the ruled. Here he represents the Western, white, materialist tradition.

Will They Cry When You're Gone, You Bet

You leave dead friends in
a desert. But they've deserted
you, and them-
selves, and are leaving
themselves,   5
in the foot paths
of madmen and saints
enough sense to get away
from the dryness and uselessness
of such relaxation, dying in the dry   10
light, sand packed in their mouths
eyes burning, white women serenade them
in mystic deviousness, which is another
way of saying they're seeing things, which
are not really there, except for them,   15
never to find an oasis, even bitter water
which we get used to, is better than
white drifting fairies, muses, singing
to us, in calm tones, about how it is better to die
etcetera, than go off from them, how it is better to   20
lie in the cruel sun with your eyes turning to dunes
than leave them alone in that white heat.

1969

N. SCOTT MOMADAY
b. 1934

" I n a certain sense," writes N. Scott Momaday in the nonfiction collection *The
Man Made of Words* (1997), "we are all made of words; . . . our most essential
being consists in language. It is the element in which we think and dream and act,
in which we live our daily lives." Since the publication of his Pulitzer Prize–
winning novel *House Made of Dawn* (1968), Momaday's writing has crossed boundaries of language, form, and genre, thereby creating for Momaday, through will and
imagination, an American Indian identity in words.

Navarre Scott Momaday was born at the Kiowa and Comanche Indian Hospital
in Lawton, Oklahoma, the only child of Al Momaday, a Kiowa, and Natachee Scott,
who was part Cherokee. He spent most of his early years in New Mexico and Arizona, moving in 1946 to Jemez Pueblo in New Mexico's Rio Grande Valley. There
his parents, both artists and teachers, took jobs at a small day school. Growing up
on reservations, including those of the Navajo and the Apache, Momaday experienced the rhythms of traditional tribal life, but saw, too, the changes wrought by
postwar material culture, and their human costs—the alcoholism, unemployment,

and personal disintegration that mark the life of Abel, the returning veteran in *House Made of Dawn*. Early on, Momaday's mother instilled in him the value of a bicultural education that would open the future without closing off his native heritage. Momaday attended reservation, public, and mission schools, then graduated from military high school in Virginia and the University of New Mexico. He received his Ph.D. in 1963 from Stanford University, where his mentor in American and English literature was the poet and critic Yvor Winters. Since then his teaching career has taken him to Santa Barbara, Berkeley, the University of Moscow, Stanford, and the University of Arizona.

What some scholars call the "Native American Renaissance" is usually said to have begun with the publication of *House Made of Dawn* in 1968 and its being awarded the Pulitzer Prize the following year. And, indeed, from 1968 to the present Native American writers have published a substantial body of fine poetry, fiction, and autobiography, gaining considerable notice in the United States and abroad.

Over the decades since the publication of *House Made of Dawn*, Momaday has published two more novels, *The Ancient Child* (1989) and *In the Bear's House* (1999); four volumes of poems, *Angle of Geese and Other Poems* (1974), *Before an Old Painting of the Crucifixion, Carmel Mission, June 1960* (1975), and *The Gourd Dancer* (1976); stories and poems in *In the Presence of the Sun* (1992); and three works of autobiography, *The Journey to Tai-me* (1967, privately published), *The Way to Rainy Mountain* (1969), and *The Names: A Memoir* (1976); as well as critical works. His deliberate engagement with a variety of forms—oral and written poetry, prose fiction and non-fiction, autobiography, legend, history, photography, painting (all "forms of discovery," in Winters's words)—has helped him lay claim to his Kiowa past.

Momaday's idea of the past as a journey is consciously expressed in *The Journey of Tai-me*, which offers his translations of the Kiowa myths he learned as a child from his grandmother, Aho. This work relates the story of the Sun Dance—a ceremony for spiritual guidance and power performed by many Plains Indian groups—to his revelatory memory on journeying to Oklahoma to see the sacred Tai-me bundle: "I became more keenly aware of myself as someone who had walked through time and in whose blood there is something inestimably old and undying. It was as if I had remembered something that happened two hundred years ago. I meant then to seek after the source of my memory and myself." In *The Way to Rainy Mountain* (1969) Momaday undertakes this search, collecting, with his father as translator, Kiowa tales and myths and clustering them with brief, loose historical commentaries and personal family stories. What seem to be fragments come together in a complex structure—twenty-four "quintessential novels," divided into three sections, framed by poems and prose pieces—that follow the Kiowa from emergence through maturity to decline as a Plains Indian culture. Central to *Rainy Mountain* and to all of Momaday's writing is the land—the focal point of memory, the defining place for Kiowa culture. The same rootedness that defines Momaday's ancestors gives his work its conjuring power, a power that comes from distilling in words and pictures, as Momaday writes, "the glare of noon and all the colors of the dawn and dusk."

From The Way to Rainy Mountain

Headwaters

Noon in the intermountain plain:
There is scant telling of the marsh—
A log, hollow and weather-stained,
An insect at the mouth, and moss—
Yet waters rise against the roots,   5

Stand brimming to the stalks. What moves?
What moves on this archaic force
Was wild and welling at the source.

Introduction

A single knoll rises out of the plain in Oklahoma, north and west of the Wichita Range. For my people, the Kiowas,[1] it is an old landmark, and they gave it the name Rainy Mountain. The hardest weather in the world is there. Winter brings blizzards, hot tornadic winds arise in the spring, and in summer the prairie is an anvil's edge. The grass turns brittle and brown, and it cracks beneath your feet. There are green belts along the rivers and creeks, linear groves of hickory and pecan, willow and witch hazel. At a distance in July or August the steaming foliage seems almost to writhe in fire. Great green and yellow grasshoppers are everywhere in the tall grass, popping up like corn to sting the flesh, and tortoises crawl about on the red earth, going nowhere in the plenty of time. Loneliness is an aspect of the land. All things in the plain are isolate; there is no confusion of objects in the eye, but *one* hill or *one* tree or *one* man. To look upon that landscape in the early morning, with the sun at your back, is to lose the sense of proportion. Your imagination comes to life, and this, you think, is where Creation was begun.

I returned to Rainy Mountain in July. My grandmother had died in the spring, and I wanted to be at her grave. She had lived to be very old and at last infirm. Her only living daughter was with her when she died, and I was told that in death her face was that of a child.

I like to think of her as a child. When she was born, the Kiowas were living the last great moment of their history. For more than a hundred years they had controlled the open range from the Smoky Hill River to the Red, from the headwaters of the Canadian to the fork of the Arkansas and Cimarron. In alliance with the Comanches, they had ruled the whole of the southern Plains. War was their sacred business, and they were among the finest horsemen the world has ever known. But warfare for the Kiowas was preeminently a matter of disposition rather than of survival, and they never understood the grim, unrelenting advance of the U.S. Cavalry. When at last, divided and ill-provisioned, they were driven onto the Staked Plains in the cold rains of autumn, they fell into panic. In Palo Duro Canyon[2] they abandoned their crucial stores to pillage and had nothing then but their lives. In order to save themselves, they surrendered to the soldiers at Fort Sill[3] and were imprisoned in the old stone corral that now stands as a military museum. My grandmother was spared the humiliation of those high gray walls by eight or ten years, but she must have known from birth the affliction of defeat, the dark brooding of old warriors.

Her name was Aho, and she belonged to the last culture to evolve in North America. Her forebears came down from the high country in western Montana nearly three centuries ago. They were a mountain people, a mysterious tribe of hunters whose language has never been positively clas-

---

1. The Kiowa were a mobile hunting and gathering people of the Southern Plains.
2. On the Staked Plains, or the Texas Panhandle, that part of the state jutting north between

New Mexico and Oklahoma.
3. U.S. Cavalry fort in Oklahoma and site of the Kiowa-Comanche Agency.

sified in any major group. In the late seventeenth century they began a long migration to the south and east. It was a journey toward the dawn, and it led to a golden age. Along the way the Kiowas were befriended by the Crows, who gave them the culture and religion of the Plains. They acquired horses, and their ancient nomadic spirit was suddenly free of the ground. They acquired Tai-me,[4] the sacred Sun Dance doll, from that moment the object and symbol of their worship, and so shared in the divinity of the sun. Not least, they acquired the sense of destiny, therefore courage and pride. When they entered upon the southern Plains they had been transformed. No longer were they slaves to the simple necessity of survival; they were a lordly and dangerous society of fighters and thieves, hunters and priests of the sun. According to their origin myth, they entered the world through a hollow log. From one point of view, their migration was the fruit of an old prophecy, for indeed they emerged from a sunless world.

Although my grandmother lived out her long life in the shadow of Rainy Mountain, the immense landscape of the continental interior lay like memory in her blood. She could tell of the Crows, whom she had never seen, and of the Black Hills, where she had never been. I wanted to see in reality what she had seen more perfectly in the mind's eye, and traveled fifteen hundred miles to begin my pilgrimage.

Yellowstone, it seemed to me, was the top of the world, a region of deep lakes and dark timber, canyons and waterfalls. But, beautiful as it is, one might have the sense of confinement there. The skyline in all directions is close at hand, the high wall of the woods and deep cleavages of shade. There is a perfect freedom in the mountains, but it belongs to the eagle and the elk, the badger and the bear. The Kiowas reckoned their stature by the distance they could see, and they were bent and blind in the wilderness.

Descending eastward, the highland meadows are a stairway to the plain. In July the inland slope of the Rockies is luxuriant with flax and buckwheat, stonecrop and larkspur. The earth unfolds and the limit of the land recedes. Clusters of trees, and animals grazing far in the distance, cause the vision to reach away and wonder to build upon the mind. The sun follows a longer course in the day, and the sky is immense beyond all comparison. The great billowing clouds that sail upon it are shadows that move upon the grain like water, dividing light. Farther down, in the land of the Crows and Blackfeet, the plain is yellow. Sweet clover takes hold of the hills and bends upon itself to cover and seal the soil. There the Kiowas paused on their way; they had come to the place where they must change their lives. The sun is at home on the plains. Precisely there does it have the certain character of a god. When the Kiowas came to the land of the Crows, they could see the dark lees of the hills at dawn across the Bighorn River, the profusion of light on the grain shelves, the oldest deity ranging after the solstices. Not yet would they veer southward to the caldron of the land that lay below; they must wean their blood from the northern winter and hold the mountains a while longer in their view. They bore Tai-me in procession to the east.

A dark mist lay over the Black Hills, and the land was like iron. At the top of a ridge I caught sight of Devil's Tower upthrust against the gray sky as if

---

4. The sacred being who aids the Kiowa in times of trouble; this being is embodied in the holy doll central to Kiowa ritual.

in the birth of time the core of the earth had broken through its crust and the motion of the world was begun. There are things in nature that engender an awful quiet in the heart of man; Devil's Tower is one of them. Two centuries ago, because they could not do otherwise, the Kiowas made a legend at the base of the rock. My grandmother said:

> Eight children were there at play, seven sisters and their brother. Suddenly the boy was struck dumb; he trembled and began to run upon his hands and feet. His fingers became claws, and his body was covered with fur. Directly there was a bear where the boy had been. The sisters were terrified; they ran, and the bear after them. They came to the stump of a great tree, and the tree spoke to them. It bade them climb upon it, and as they did so it began to rise into the air. The bear came to kill them, but they were just beyond its reach. It reared against the tree and scored the bark all around with its claws. The seven sisters were borne into the sky, and they became the stars of the Big Dipper.

From that moment, and so long as the legend lives, the Kiowas have kinsmen in the night sky. Whatever they were in the mountains, they could be no more. However tenuous their well-being, however much they had suffered and would suffer again, they had found a way out of the wilderness.

My grandmother had a reverence for the sun, a holy regard that now is all but gone out of mankind. There was a wariness in her, and an ancient awe. She was a Christian in her later years, but she had come a long way about, and she never forgot her birthright. As a child she had been to the Sun Dances; she had taken part in those annual rites, and by them she had learned the restoration of her people in the presence of Tai-me. She was about seven when the last Kiowa Sun Dance was held in 1887 on the Washita River above Rainy Mountain Creek. The buffalo were gone. In order to consummate the ancient sacrifice—to impale the head of a buffalo bull upon the medicine tree—a delegation of old men journeyed into Texas, there to beg and barter for an animal from the Goodnight herd. She was ten when the Kiowas came together for the last time as a living Sun Dance culture. They could find no buffalo; they had to hang an old hide from the sacred tree. Before the dance could begin, a company of soldiers rode out from Fort Sill under orders to disperse the tribe. Forbidden without cause the essential act of their faith,[5] having seen the wild herds slaughtered and left to rot upon the ground, the Kiowas backed away forever from the medicine tree. That was July 20, 1890, at the great bend of the Washita. My grandmother was there. Without bitterness, and for as long as she lived, she bore a vision of deicide.

Now that I can have her only in memory, I see my grandmother in the several postures that were peculiar to her: standing at the wood stove on a winter morning and turning meat in a great iron skillet; sitting at the south window, bent above her beadwork, and afterwards, when her vision failed, looking down for a long time into the fold of her hands; going out upon a cane, very slowly as she did when the weight of age came upon her; praying. I remember her most often at prayer. She made long, rambling prayers out of suffering and hope, having seen many things. I was never sure that I had the right to hear, so exclusive were they of all mere custom and company.

---

5. From the 1880s on, the U.S. government sought to ban all "heathenish" practices among Native American peoples in a continuing effort to Christianize and "civilize" them.

The last time I saw her she prayed standing by the side of her bed at night, naked to the waist, the light of a kerosene lamp moving upon her dark skin. Her long, black hair, always drawn and braided in the day, lay upon her shoulders and against her breasts like a shawl. I do not speak Kiowa, and I never understood her prayers, but there was something inherently sad in the sound, some merest hesitation upon the syllables of sorrow. She began in a high and descending pitch, exhausting her breath to silence; then again and again—and always the same intensity of effort, of something that is, and is not, like urgency in the human voice. Transported so in the dancing light among the shadows of her room, she seemed beyond the reach of time. But that was illusion; I think I knew then that I should not see her again.

Houses are like sentinels in the plain, old keepers of the weather watch. There, in a very little while, wood takes on the appearance of great age. All colors wear soon away in the wind and rain, and then the wood is burned gray and the grain appears and the nails turn red with rust. The window-panes are black and opaque; you imagine there is nothing within, and indeed there are many ghosts, bones given up to the land. They stand here and there against the sky, and you approach them for a longer time than you expect. They belong in the distance; it is their domain.

Once there was a lot of sound in my grandmother's house, a lot of coming and going, feasting and talk. The summers there were full of excitement and reunion. The Kiowas are a summer people; they abide the cold and keep to themselves, but when the season turns and the land becomes warm and vital they cannot hold still; an old love of going returns upon them. The aged visitors who came to my grandmother's house when I was a child were made of lean and leather, and they bore themselves upright. They wore great black hats and bright ample shirts that shook in the wind. They rubbed fat upon their hair and wound their braids with strips of colored cloth. Some of them painted their faces and carried the scars of old and cherished enmities. They were an old council of warlords, come to remind and be reminded of who they were. Their wives and daughters served them well. The women might indulge themselves; gossip was at once the mark and compensation of their servitude. They made loud and elaborate talk among themselves, full of jest and gesture, fright and false alarm. They went abroad in fringed and flowered shawls, bright beadwork and German silver. They were at home in the kitchen, and they prepared meals that were banquets.

There were frequent prayer meetings, and great nocturnal feasts. When I was a child I played with my cousins outside, where the lamplight fell upon the ground and the singing of the old people rose up around us and carried away into the darkness. There were a lot of good things to eat, a lot of laughter and surprise. And afterwards, when the quiet returned, I lay down with my grandmother and could hear the frogs away by the river and feel the motion of the air.

Now there is a funeral silence in the rooms, the endless wake of some final word. The walls have closed in upon my grandmother's house. When I returned to it in mourning, I saw for the first time in my life how small it was. It was late at night, and there was a white moon, nearly full. I sat for a long time on the stone steps by the kitchen door. From there I could see out across the land; I could see the long row of trees by the creek, the low light upon the rolling plains, and the stars of the Big Dipper. Once I looked at the moon and caught sight of a strange thing. A cricket had perched upon the handrail, only a few inches away from me. My line of vision was such that the creature filled the moon like a fossil. It had gone there, I thought, to live and die, for there, of all places, was its small definition made whole and eternal. A warm wind rose up and purled like the longing within me.

The next morning I awoke at dawn and went out on the dirt road to Rainy Mountain. It was already hot, and the grasshoppers began to fill the air. Still, it was early in the morning, and the birds sang out of the shadows. The long yellow grass on the mountain shone in the bright light, and a scissortail hied above the land. There, where it ought to be, at the end of a long and legendary way, was my grandmother's grave. Here and there on the dark stones were ancestral names. Looking back once, I saw the mountain and came away.

IV

They lived at first in the mountains. They did not yet know of Tai-me, but this is what they knew: There was a man and his wife. They had a beautiful child, a little girl whom they would not allow to go out of their sight. But one day a friend of the family came and asked if she might take the child outside to play. The mother guessed that would be all right, but she told the friend to leave the child in its cradle and to place the cradle in a tree. While the child was in the tree, a redbird came among the branches. It was not like any bird that you have seen; it was very beautiful, and it did not fly away. It kept still upon a limb, close to the child. After a while the child got out of its cradle and began to climb after the redbird. And at the same time the tree began to grow taller, and the child was borne up into the sky. She was then a woman, and she found herself in a strange place. Instead of a redbird, there was a young man standing before her. The man spoke to her and said: "I have been watching you for a long time, and I knew that I would find a way to bring you here. I have brought you here to be my wife." The woman looked all around; she saw that he was the only living man there. She saw that he was the sun.

There the land itself ascends into the sky. These mountains lie at the top of the continent, and they cast a long rain shadow on the sea of grasses to the east. They arise out of the last North American wilderness, and they have wilderness names: Wasatch, Bitterroot, Bighorn, Wind River.

I have walked in a mountain meadow bright with Indian paintbrush, lupine, and wild buckwheat, and I have seen high in the branches of a lodgepole pine the male pine grosbeak, round and rose-colored, its dark, striped wings nearly invisible in the soft, mottled light. And the uppermost branches of the tree seemed very slowly to ride across the blue sky.

XIII

If an arrow is well made, it will have tooth marks upon it. That is how you know. The Kiowas made fine arrows and straightened them in their teeth. Then they drew them to the bow to see if they were straight. Once there was a man and his wife. They were alone at night in their tipi. By the light of the fire the man was making arrows. After a while he caught sight of something. There was a small opening in the tipi where two hides were sewn together. Someone was there on the outside, looking in. The man went on with his work, but he said to his wife: "Someone is standing outside. Do not be afraid. Let us talk easily, as of ordinary things." He took up an arrow and straightened it in his teeth; then, as it was right for him to do, he drew it to the bow and took aim, first in this direction and then in that. And all the while he was talking, as if to his wife. But this is how he spoke: "I know that you are there on the outside, for I can feel your eyes upon me. If you are a Kiowa, you will understand what I am saying, and you will speak your name." But there was no answer, and the man went on in the same way, pointing the arrow all around. At last his aim fell upon the place where his enemy stood, and he let go of the string. The arrow went straight to the enemy's heart.

The old men were the best arrow-makers, for they could bring time and patience to their craft. The young men—the fighters and hunters—were willing to pay a high price for arrows that were well made.

When my father was a boy, an old man used to come to Mammedaty's[6] house and pay his respects. He was a lean old man in braids and was impressive in his age and bearing. His name was Cheney, and he was an arrowmaker. Every morning, my father tells me, Cheney would paint his wrinkled face, go out, and pray aloud to the rising sun. In my mind I can see that man as if he were there now. I like to watch him as he makes his prayer. I know where he stands and where his voice goes on the rolling grasses and where the sun comes up on the land. There, at dawn, you can feel the silence. It is cold and clear and deep like water. It takes hold of you and will not let you go.

XVII

Bad women are thrown away. Once there was a handsome young man. He was wild and reckless, and the chief talked to the wind about him. After that, the man went hunting. A great whirlwind passed by, and he was blind. The Kiowas have no need

In the Kiowa calendars[7] there is graphic proof that the lives of women were hard, whether they were "bad women" or not. Only the captives, who were slaves, held lower status. During the Sun Dance of 1843, a man stabbed his wife in

6. Momaday's paternal grandfather.
7. The Kiowa recorded their history in pictures that functioned as calendars.

of a blind man; they left him alone with his wife and child. The winter was coming on and food was scarce. In four days the man's wife grew tired of caring for him. A herd of buffalo came near, and the man knew the sound. He asked his wife to hand him a bow and an arrow. "You must tell me," he said, "when the buffalo are directly in front of me." And in that way he killed a bull, but his wife said that he had missed. He asked for another arrow and killed another bull, but again his wife said that he had missed. Now the man was a hunter, and he knew the sound an arrow makes when it strikes home, but he said nothing. Then his wife helped herself to the meat and ran away with her child. The man was blind; he ate grass and kept himself alive. In seven days a band of Kiowas found him and took him to their camp. There in the fire-light a woman was telling a story. She told of how her husband had been killed by enemy warriors. The blind man listened, and he knew her voice. That was a bad woman. At sunrise they threw her away.

XXIV

East of my grandmother's house, south of the pecan grove, there is buried a woman in a beautiful dress. Mammedaty used to know where she is buried, but now no one knows. If you stand on the front porch of the house and look eastward towards Carnegie, you know that the woman is buried somewhere within the range of your vision. But her grave is unmarked. She was buried in a cab-inet, and she wore a beautiful dress.

the breast because she accepted Chief Dohasan's invitation to ride with him in the ceremonial pro-cession. And in the winter of 1851–52, Big Bow stole the wife of a man who was away on a raiding expedi-tion. He brought her to his father's camp and made her wait outside in the bitter cold while he went in to collect his things. But his father knew what was going on, and he held Big Bow and would not let him go. The woman was made to wait in the snow until her feet were frozen.

Mammedaty's grandmother, Kau-au-ointy,[8] was a Mexican captive, taken from her homeland when she was a child of eight or ten years. I never knew her, but I have been to her grave at Rainy Mountain.

KAU-AU-OINTY
BORN 1834
DIED 1929
AT REST

She raised a lot of eyebrows, they say, for she would not play the part of a Kiowa woman. From slavery she rose up to become a figure in the tribe. She owned a great herd of cattle, and she could ride as well as any man. She had blue eyes.

Aho's high moccasins are made of softest, cream-colored skins. On each instep there is a bright disc of bead-work—an eight-pointed star, red and pale blue on a white field—and there are bands of beadwork at the soles and ankles. The flaps of the leggings are wide and richly ornamented with blue and red and green and white and lavender beads.

East of my grandmother's house the sun rises out of the plain. Once in his

---

8. Momaday's great-great-grandmother.

How beautiful it was! It was one of those fine buckskin dresses, and it was decorated with elk's teeth and beadwork. That dress is still there, under the ground.

life a man ought to concentrate his mind upon the remembered earth, I believe. He ought to give himself up to a particular landscape in his experience, to look at it from as many angles as he can, to wonder about it, to dwell upon it. He ought to imagine that he touches it with his hands at every season and listens to the sounds that are made upon it. He ought to imagine the creatures there and all the faintest motions of the wind. He ought to recollect the glare of noon and all the colors of the dawn and dusk.

Epilogue

During the first hours after midnight on the morning of November 13, 1833, it seemed that the world was coming to an end. Suddenly the stillness of the night was broken; there were brilliant flashes of light in the sky, light of such intensity that people were awakened by it. With the speed and density of a driving rain, stars were falling in the universe. Some were brighter than Venus; one was said to be as large as the moon.

That most brilliant shower of Leonid meteors[9] has a special place in the memory of the Kiowa people. It is among the earliest entries in the Kiowa calendars, and it marks the beginning as it were of the historical period in the tribal mind. In the preceding year Tai-me had been stolen by a band of Osages, and although it was later returned, the loss was an almost unimaginable tragedy; and in 1837 the Kiowas made the first of their treaties[1] with the United States. The falling stars seemed to image the sudden and violent disintegration of an old order.

But indeed the golden age of the Kiowas had been short-lived, ninety or a hundred years, say, from about 1740. The culture would persist for a while in decline, until about 1875, but then it would be gone, and there would be very little material evidence that it had ever been. Yet it is within the reach of memory still, though tenuously now, and moreover it is even defined in a remarkably rich and living verbal tradition which demands to be preserved for its own sake. The living memory and the verbal tradition which transcends it were brought together for me once and for all in the person of Ko-sahn.

A hundred-year-old woman came to my grandmother's house one afternoon in July. Aho was dead; Mammedaty had died before I was born. There were very few Kiowas left who could remember the Sun Dances; Ko-sahn was one of them; she was a grown woman when my grandparents came into the world. Her body was twisted and her face deeply lined with age. Her thin white hair was held in place by a cap of black netting, though she wore braids as well, and she had but one eye. She was dressed in the manner of a Kiowa matron, a dark, full-cut dress that reached nearly to the ankles, full, flowing sleeves, and

9. Annual meteor shower that appears to emanate from the constellation Leo; the Leonid shower of 1833 was spectactar to observers in North America east of the Rocky Mountains.
1. This treaty provided for settlers' passage through Kiowa and Comanche lands.

a wide, apron-like sash. She sat on a bench in the arbor so concentrated in her great age that she seemed extraordinarily small. She was quiet for a time—she might almost have been asleep—and then she began to speak and to sing. She spoke of many things, and once she spoke of the Sun Dance:

My sisters and I were very young; that was a long time ago. Early one morning they came to wake us up. They had brought a great buffalo in from the plain. Everyone went out to see and to pray. We heard a great many voices. One man said that the lodge was almost ready. We were told to go there, and someone gave me a piece of cloth. It was very beautiful. Then I asked what I ought to do with it, and they said that I must tie it to the Tai-me tree. There were other pieces of cloth on the tree, and so I put mine there as well.

When the lodge frame was finished, a woman—sometimes a man—began to sing. It was like this:

> Everything is ready.
> Now the four societies must go out.
> They must go out and get the leaves,
>   the branches for the lodge.

And when the branches were tied in place, again there was singing:

> Let the boys go out.
> Come on, boys, now we must get the earth.

The boys began to shout. Now they were not just ordinary boys, not all of them; they were those for whom prayers had been made, and they were dressed in different ways. There was an old, old woman. She had something on her back. The boys went out to see. The old woman had a bag full of earth on her back. It was a certain kind of sandy earth. That is what they must have in the lodge. The dancers must dance upon the sandy earth. The old woman held a digging tool in her hand. She turned towards the south and pointed with her lips. It was like a kiss, and she began to sing:

> We have brought the earth.
> Now it is time to play;
> As old as I am, I still have the feeling of play.

That was the beginning of the Sun Dance. The dancers treated themselves with buffalo medicine, and slowly they began to take their steps. . . . And all the people were around, and they wore splendid things—beautiful buckskin and beads. The chiefs wore necklaces, and their pendants shone like the sun. There were many people, and oh, it was beautiful! That was the beginning of the Sun Dance. It was all for Tai-me, you know, and it was a long time ago.

It was—all of this and more—a quest, a going forth upon the way to Rainy Mountain. Probably Ko-sahn too is dead now. At times, in the quiet of evening, I think she must have wondered, dreaming, who she was. Was she become in her sleep that old purveyor of the sacred earth, perhaps, that ancient one who, old as she was, still had the feeling of play? And in her mind, at times, did she see the falling stars?

Rainy Mountain Cemetery

Most is your name the name of this dark stone.
Deranged in death, the mind to be inheres
Forever in the nominal unknown,
The wake of nothing audible he hears
Who listens here and now to hear your name.   5

The early sun, red as a hunter's moon,
Runs in the plain. The mountain burns and shines;
And silence is the long approach of noon
Upon the shadow that your name defines—
And death this cold, black density of stone.   10

1969

AUDRE LORDE
1934–1992

Audre Lorde's poetry wages what she called "a war against the tyrannies of silence"; it articulates what has been passed over out of fear or discomfort, what has been kept hidden and secret. Reading her we feel the violence inherent in breaking a silence, perhaps most often as she probes the experience of anger—the anger of black toward white or white toward black, a woman's anger at men and other women, and men's anger toward women. "My Black woman's anger," she wrote in her collection of essays, *Sister Outsider*, "is a molten pond at the core of me, my most fiercely guarded secret." Having admitted this secret into her poems, Lorde transforms our expectations of what is a fit subject for the lyric. Her work is often deliberately disturbing, the powerful voice of the poem cutting through denial, politeness, and fear. In developing this voice Lorde drew on African resources, especially the matriarchal mythology and history of West Africa. Her seventh book, *The Black Unicorn* (1978), reflects the time she spent in Africa studying, in particular, Yoruba mythology and reclaiming her connection to the rich African cultures. The African presence is evident in one of her last books, *Our Dead Behind Us* (1986), as well. Lorde's work suggests that she always connected poetry to the speaking voice, but her study of African materials deepened her connection to oral traditions (like the chant or the call) and taught her the power of voice to cut across time and place. From African writers, she said, she learned that "we live in accordance with, in a kind of correspondence with, the rest of the world as a whole." A powerful voice informed by personal and cultural history creates the possibility, for Lorde, of bridging the differences her work does not seek to erase. "It is not difference that immobilizes us," she wrote, "but silence."

Her work celebrates difference and confounds it. In Adrienne Rich's words, Lorde wrote "as a Black woman, a mother, a daughter, a Lesbian, a feminist, a visionary." Her poem "Coal" affirms an *I* that is "the total black, being spoken / from the earth's inside." This total blackness was, for her, also associated with Eros and with creativity; she celebrated this source as what she called "woman's place of power within each of us," which is "neither white nor surface; it is dark, it is ancient; and it is deep." Her best work calls on the deepest places of her own life—on the pain she experienced, on her rage (her second book, in 1972, was titled *Cables to Rage*), on her longing and desire. One of the silences her poems broke concerns love between women, and she wrote a number of poems that are erotic, precise, and true to both the power and delicacy of feeling. Unafraid of anger, she was also capable of tenderness; this is perhaps most clear not only in her love poems but in poems that address a younger generation.

Lorde was born in New York City and lived in New York almost all her life. Her parents were West Indian, and her mother was light skinned. "I grew up in a genuine confusion / between grass and weeds and flowers / and what colored meant," Lorde wrote in her poem "Outside." Part of that confusion was the conflict represented by her father's blackness and her mother's desire for whiteness (in "Black Mother Woman" Lorde speaks of the mother as "split with deceitful longings"). Lorde's understanding of identity forged out of conflict began for her, then, in her own family history with its legacy of "conflicting rebellions" ("Black Mother Woman"). In 1961 she received a B.A. from Hunter College and later a Master's of Library Science from Columbia University. The following year she married and the marriage produced a daughter and a son (she divorced in 1970). In 1968 she became poet-in-residence for a year at Tougaloo College in Mississippi, her first experience in the American South. Thereafter she knew her work to be that of a writer and teacher; she taught at John Jay College of Criminal Justice in New York City and, from 1981, was professor of English at Hunter College. In the last years of her life Lorde traveled extensively, not only to Africa but to Australia (where she met with aborigine women) and Germany. During her last years she lived much of the time in St. Croix.

"I have come to believe over and over again," Lorde said, "that what is most important to me must be spoken, made verbal and shared, even at the risk of having it bruised or misunderstood." (Her essay "Poetry Is Not a Luxury" [1977] makes the case for poetry's essential speaking of what is otherwise unnamed and unthought. A selection from this essay appears in the "Postmodern Manifestos" cluster of this anthology.) The drive toward expression made Lorde a prolific writer and led her to several prose works in which she shared experiences often restricted to privacy: *The Cancer Journals* (1980), an account of her struggle with breast cancer, and *Zami: A New Spelling of My Name* (1982), a "biomythography" of her growing up and her emergent lesbian identity. The urgency Lorde felt to make experience "verbal and shared," however, sometimes overrode a distinction crucial to her work: that between poetry and rhetoric. She preserved this distinction in her best work by listening and responding to other voices in herself and in the world around her. With their combination of pain, anger, and tenderness, her finest poems are poetry as illumination, poetry in which, as she said, "we give name to those ideas which are—until the poem—nameless, formless, about to be birthed, but already felt."

Coal

I
is the total black, being spoken
from the earth's inside.
There are many kinds of open
how a diamond comes into a knot of flame   5
how sound comes into a word, coloured
by who pays what for speaking.

Some words are open like a diamond
on glass windows

singing out within the passing crash of sun   10
Then there are words like stapled wagers
in a perforated book,—buy and sign and tear apart—
and come whatever wills all chances
the stub remains
an ill-pulled tooth with a ragged edge.   15
Some words live in my throat
breeding like adders. Others know sun
seeking like gypsies over my tongue
to explode through my lips
like young sparrows bursting from shell.   20
Some words
bedevil me.

Love is a word, another kind of open.
As the diamond comes into a knot of flame
I am Black because I come from the earth's inside   25
now take my word for jewel in the open light.

                                                              1968

The Woman Thing

The hunters are back from beating the winter's face
in search of a challenge or task
in search of food
making fresh tracks for their children's hunger
they do not watch the sun   5
they cannot wear its heat for a sign
of triumph or freedom;
The hunters are treading heavily homeward
through snow that is marked
with their own bloody footprints.   10
emptyhanded, the hunters return
snow-maddened, sustained by their rages.

In the night after food they may seek
young girls for their amusement. But now
the hunters are coming   15
and the unbaked girls flee from their angers.
All this day I have craved
food for my child's hunger
Emptyhanded the hunters come shouting
injustices drip from their mouths   20
like stale snow melted in sunlight.

Meanwhile
the woman thing my mother taught me
bakes off its covering of snow
like a rising blackening sun.   25

                                                              1968

Black Mother Woman

I cannot recall you gentle
yet through your heavy love
I have become
an image of your once delicate flesh
split with deceitful longings.   5

When strangers come and compliment me
your aged spirit takes a bow
jingling with pride
but once you hid that secret
in the center of furies   10
hanging me
with deep breasts and wiry hair
with your own split flesh
and long suffering eyes
buried in myths of little worth.   15

But I have peeled away your anger
down to the core of love
and look mother
I Am
a dark temple where your true spirit rises   20
beautiful
and tough as chestnut
stanchion[1] against your nightmare of weakness
and if my eyes conceal
a squadron of conflicting rebellions   25
I learned from you
to define myself
through your denials.

                                                        1971

---

1. Upright bar or post (for supporting, e.g., a roof).

CHARLES WRIGHT
b. 1935

"All forms of landscape are autobiographical." This line from Charles Wright's poem "All Landscape Is Abstract, and Tends to Repeat Itself" is a useful gloss on Wright's poetry, in which the poet is a pilgrim who remembers, walks through, and describes the places he has most loved. Among those places are Kingsport, Tennessee, where he grew up; northern Italy, where he was stationed as a young soldier and later lived for some months with his family; Laguna Beach, California; and the Blue Ridge area of Virginia. Wright's landscapes, like his poetry, are a layered mixture of the visible and the invisible; they engage a drama of perception he shares with the painter Paul Cézanne, about whom he has written in homage. This poet walks into his backyard—the landscape of his current home in Charlottesville, Virginia, where he teaches at the University of Virginia—looks at the trees and stars, and each time experiences something that yields a different poem (one such poem is happily titled "Back Yard Boogie Woogie"). The backyard offers him as broad a scope for poetry as the larger landscapes he also renders in his poems because, for Wright, the visible world is always opening up and into a larger, invisible world. The stars that shine above his backyard (and Wright loves the stars) make bounded space part of an infinite cosmos.

Wright belongs to the visionary company of American poetry, but he is also drawn to the visible world and in his poetry the metaphysical is encountered through the physical. An immersion and delight in the visible fills Wright's poems and makes him a poet of impressive descriptive power. What deepens his poems beyond their acute and often startling figurative description is a narrative of spiritual autobiography or what Keats called "soul making." Wright's version of this autobiography is distinctively his and distinctively American—full of discontinuities, laced with a wry sense of humor, and rendered in a language that moves easily in and out of an American vernacular. His selected early poems, *Country Music*, won the National Book Award in 1983, and its title conjures the twang of hillbilly singers and Appalachian mountain hymns, as well as the music of a countryside rendered in the poet's alliterative lines and enjambed rhythms. Like a good country musician, Wright knows how to shift and layer tones in quick and surprising ways. He knows how to be melancholy, lucid, and funny in the same poem. The vocabulary of his poems ranges from the biblical ("mercy and consolation") to the playful exclamation of "hubba-hubba." It's characteristic of Wright to include in a poem about gazing up at the night sky both a line as ornate as "Unhinder my habitat, Starlight, make me insoluble" and a question as casual as "What is it about the stars we can't shake?" ("North American Bear").

"Anyone's autobiography, at least in his own eyes, is made up of a string of luminous moments, numinous moments," Wright said in an interview. Wright's poems are a string of such moments, but the strand is marked by discontinuity. His work is full of juxtapositions that fuse surprising things together ("bandannaed" and "moonlight" in "Star Turn II"), and the movement in his poems from one stanza to the next is often as abrupt as a jump cut, each stanza its own kind of feint and hesitation toward something not quite sayable. The spaces between his stanzas or the space within a line (especially a dropped line) point to "some place beyond the lip of language, / Some silence, some zone of grace" ("Poem Half in the Manner of Li Ho"). The effect is what Wright once called "a kind of American sprawl of a poem." To create this "American sprawl," Wright counts syllables rather than poetic feet. While line length expands or contracts from poem to poem, the seven-syllable line is his base. Whatever the variation in line length, Wright prefers an odd number of syllables, which, he says, lets him retain the ghost of traditional meters without falling into their patterns.

Wright loves and draws on many traditions of poetry. As a young soldier in Italy he was drawn to the work of Ezra Pound, whose emphasis on the image remains an important influence. And, like Pound, Wright often mentions and uses the traditions of ancient Chinese poets (like Tu Fu and Wang Wei and Li Ho). He also loves the Italian poets, among them Eugenio Montale (whose work Wright has translated) and Dante, who is mentioned in "Star Turn II" and whose narrative of spiritual pilgrimage influences many Wright poems, among them "North American Bear." Volumes that bring together Wright's many books of poetry are *Country Music: Selected Early Poems* (1982), *The World of the Ten Thousand Things: Poems 1880–1990* (1990), *Negative Blue: Selected Later Poems* (2000), *Buffalo Yoga* (2005), *Scar Tissue* (2006) *Littlefoot* (2007), and *Sestets* (2009). His collection of essays and interviews, *Halflife: Improvisations and Interviews, 1977–1987* (1988), offers entry into the poet's craft and thought. Wright's work, with its distinctive music and star-tling capacity to fuse the outer world with the inner life of soul making, has estab-lished its own "zone of grace" in contemporary American poetry.

Him

His sorrow hangs like a heart in the star-flowered boundary tree.
It mirrors the endless wind.

He feeds on the lunar differences and flies up at the dawn.

When he lies down, the waters will lie down with him,
And all that walks and all that stands still, and sleep through the thunder.   5

It's for him that the willow bleeds.

Look for him high in the flat black of the northern Pacific sky,
Released in his suit of lights,
                    lifted and laid clear.

                                                                    1977

Two Stories

Tonight, on the deck, the lights
Semaphore up at me through the atmosphere,
Town lights, familiar lights
                    pulsing and slacking off
The way they used to back on the ridge outside of Kingsport[1]   5
Thirty-five years ago,
The moonlight sitting inside my head
Like knives,
            the cold like a drug I knew I'd settle down with.
I used to imagine them shore lights, as these are, then,   10
As something inside me listened with all its weight
For the sea-surge and the sea-change.

There's a soft spot in everything
Our fingers touch,
                    the one place where everything breaks   15
When we press it just right.
The past is like that with its arduous edges and blind sides,
The whorls of our fingerprints
                    embedded along its walls
Like fossils the sea has left behind.   20

----

1. In Tennessee, where the poet grew up.

This is a story I swear is true.

I used to sleepwalk. But only
On camping trips,
              or whenever I slept outside.
One August, when I was eleven, on Mount LeConte in Tennessee,   25
Campfire over, and ghost story over,
Everyone still asleep, apparently I arose
From my sleeping bag,
                opened the tent flap, and started out on the trail
That led to the drop-off, where the mountainside   30
Went straight down for almost a thousand feet.
Half-moon and cloud cover, so some light
As I went on up the path through the rhododendron,
The small pebbles and split roots
                like nothing under my feet.   35
The cliffside was half a mile from the campsite.
As I got closer,
           moving blindly, unerringly,
Deeper in sleep than the shrubs,
I stepped out, it appears,   40
Onto the smooth lip of the rock cape of the cliff,
When my left hand, and then my right hand,
Stopped me as they were stopped
By the breathing side of a bear which woke me
And there we were,   45
           the child and the black bear and the cliff-drop,
And this is the way it went—
                I stepped back, and I turned around,
And I walked down through the rhododendron
And never looked back,   50
           truly awake in the throbbing world,
And I ducked through the low flap
Of the tent, so quietly, and I went to sleep
And never told anyone
Till years later when I thought I knew what it meant,   55
                which now I've forgot.

And this one is questionable,
Though sworn to me by an old friend
Who'd killed a six-foot diamondback about seven o'clock in the morning
(He'd found it coiled in a sunny place)   60
And threw it into a croker sack[2] with its head chopped off,
              and threw the sack in the back of a jeep,
Then left for his day's work
On the farm.
           That evening he started to show the snake   65
To someone, and put his hand in the sack to pull it out.
As he reached in, the snake's stump struck him.

---

2. As used in the South, one of a variety of regional American names for a gunny sack, a large sack
made from loosely woven coarse material.

His wrist was bruised for a week.
It's not age,
                nor time with its gold eyelid and blink,   70
Nor dissolution in all its mimicry
That lifts us and sorts us out.
It's discontinuity
                and all its spangled coming between
That sends us apart and keeps us there in a dread.   75
It's what's in the rearview mirror,
                                smaller and out of sight.

What do you do when the words don't come to you anymore,
And all the embolisms fade in the dirt?
And the ocean sings in its hammock,   80
                                rocking itself back and forth?
And you live at the end of the road where the sky starts its dark decline?

The barking goes on and on
                        from the far hill, constantly
Sticking its noise in my good ear.   85

Goodbye, Miss Sweeney, goodbye.
I'm starting to think about the psychotransference of all things.
It's small bones in the next life.
It's small bones,
                and heel and toe forever and ever.   90

                                                                        1984

From A Journal of the Year of the Ox

12 December 1985

—Late afternoon, blue of the sky blue
As a dove's neck, dove
Color of winter branches among winter branches,
Guttural whistle and up,
                        December violets crooked at my feet,   5
Cloud-wedge starting to slide like a detached retina[1]
Slanting across the blue
                        inaction the dove disappears in.

Mean constellations quip and annoy
                                next night against the same sky   10
As I seek out, unsuccessfully,
In Luke's spyglass Halley's comet[2] and its train of ice:

1. An eye disorder in which the retina, a thin
layer of light-sensitive tissue that translates what
we see into neural impulses, separates from the
inner layer of supportive tissue, affecting the
capacity to see.

2. A periodic comet named for the English
astronomer Edmund Halley (1656–1742), who
observed it in 1682. It was sighted again in 1982,
and it returned to its closest approach to the sun
in late December 1985. Luke is Wright's son.

An ordered and measured affection is virtuous
In its clean cause
     however it comes close in this life.   15
Nothing else moves toward us out of the stars,
         nothing else shines.

         —12 *December 1985*
         1988

Poem Half in the Manner of Li Ho[1]

All things aspire to weightlessness,
     some place beyond the lip of language,
Some silence, some zone of grace,

Sky white as raw silk,
     opening mirror cold-sprung in the west,   5
Sunset like dead grass.

If God hurt the way we hurt,
     he, too, would be heart-sore,
Disconsolate, unappeasable.

—————————

Li Ho, the story goes, would leave home   10
Each day at dawn, riding a colt, a servant boy
     walking behind him,
An antique tapestry bag
Strapped to his back.
     When inspiration struck, Ho would write 15
The lines down and drop them in the bag.
At night he'd go home and work the lines up into a poem,
No matter how disconnected and loose-leafed they were.
His mother once said,
"He won't stop until he has vomited out his heart."   20

And so he did,
   Like John Keats,[2]
He died believing his name would never be written among the Characters.
Without hope, he thought himself—that worst curse—unlucky.
At twenty-seven, at death's line, he saw a man come 25
In purple, driving a red dragon,
A tablet in one hand, who said,
     "I'm here to summon Li Ho."

Ho got from his bed and wept.
Far from the sick room's dragon-dark, snow stormed the passes, 30

—————————

1. Chinese poet (760–816).
2. English Romantic poet (1795–1821) who died of tuberculosis at age twenty-five in Rome, Italy. He asked that his grave bear no name but only the words "Here lies one whose name was writ on water."

Monkeys surfed the bo trees[3]
              and foolish men ate white jade.

How mournful the southern hills are,
              how white their despair
Under December's T'ang blue blank page.   35

What's the use of words—there are no words
For December's chill redaction,
              for the way it makes us feel.

We hang like clouds between heaven and earth,
              between something and nothing,   40
Sometimes with shadows, sometimes without.

                                  1997

Star Turn II

How small the stars are tonight, bandannaed by moonlight,
How few and how far between—
Disordered and drained, like highlights in Dante's[1] death mask.
Or a sequined dress from the forties
                  —hubba-hubba—   5
Some sequins missing, some sequins inalterably in place.

Unlike our lives, which are as they are.
Unlike our imagined selves, which are as we'll never become,
Star-like and shining,
Everyone looking up at, everyone pointing there, O there,   10
Masked and summering in,
              each one a bright point, each one a dodged eclipse.

                                  1998

North American Bear[1]

Early November in the soul,
              a hard rain, and dusky gold
From the trees, late afternoon
Squint-light and heavy heart-weight.
It's always downleaf and dim.   5
A sixty-two-year-old, fallow-voiced, night-leaning man,
I stand at ease on the blank sidewalk.

---

3. Indian fig trees, sacred to Buddhists.
1. Dante Alighieri (1265–1321), Italian poet and author of *The Divine Comedy*, all three sections of which end with the word "stars."

1. The constellation Ursa Major, or Great Bear, was seen as a bear by many cultures, including the Sumerians and the Iroquois Indians. It is also called the Big Dipper.

Unhinder my habitat, starlight, make me insoluble;
Negative in my afterscape,
                    sidle the shadow across my mouth.   10

Random geometry of the stars,
                   random word-strings
As beautiful as the alphabet.
Or so I remember them,
                  North American Bear,   15
Orion, Cassiopeia and the Pleiades,[2]
Stitching their syntax across the deep North Carolina sky
A half-century ago,
The lost language of summer nights, the inarticulate scroll
Of time   20
        pricked on its dark, celestial cylinder.

What is it about the stars we can't shake?
                         What pulse, what tide drop
Pulls us like vertigo upward, what
Height-like reversal urges us toward their clear deeps?   25
Tonight, for instance,
Something is turning behind my eyes,
                    something unwept, something unnamable,
Spinning its line out.
Who is to say the hijacked heart has not returned to its cage?   30
Who is to say some angel has not
                       breathed in my ear?

I walk in the chill of the late autumn night
                     like Orpheus,[3]
Thinking my song, anxious to look back,   35
My vanished life an ornament, a drifting cloud, behind me,
A soft, ashen transcendence
Buried and resurrected once, then time and again.
The sidewalk unrolls like a deep sleep.
Above me the stars, stem stars,   40
Uncover their faces.
            No heartbeat on my heels, no footfall.

The season approaches us, dead leaves and withered grasses
Waxed by the wind wherever you look,
                        the clear night sky   45
Star-struck and star-stung, that constellation, those seven high stars,

---

2. The cluster of six bright stars in the constellation Taurus; in Greek mythology the seven daughters of Atlas and Pleione were placed among the stars (a seventh bright star has apparently faded from view since the original sighting). "Cassiopeia": in Greek mythology, a princess of Ethiopia. She and her husband, Cepheus, became constellations. In Greek mythology Orion, a hunter, was turned at death into a constellation.

3. Poet and musician in Greek mythology who attempted to rescue his wife, Eurydice, from Hades through the power of his music. On the journey back to Earth, he was instructed not to look back at her. He could not resist doing so, and she was returned to the Underworld.

General Ke-Shu[4] lifting his sword, the Chinese say.
Or one of them said,
One at the Western Front as part of his army, without doubt.
I almost can see him myself, 50
                    long-sword over the Bear's neck,
His car wheel-less, darkness sifting away like a sandstorm to the west.

Some of these star fires must surely be ash by now.
I dawdle outside in the back yard,
Humming old songs that no one cares about anymore. 55
The hat of darkness tilts the night sky
Inch by inch, foot by black foot,
                    over the Blue Ridge.[5]
How bright the fire of the world was, I think to myself,
Before white hair and the ash of days. 60
I gaze at the constellations,
                    forgetting whatever it was I had to say.

The sidewalk again, unrolling grey and away. 9 p.m.
A cold wind from the far sky.
There is a final solitude I haven't arrived at yet, 65
Weariness like a dust in my throat.
                    I simmer inside its outline,
However, and feel safe, as the stars spill by, for one more night
Like some medieval journeyman enfrescoed[6] with his poem in his hand,
Heaven remaining my neighborhood. 70
And like him, too, with something red and inviolate
                    under my feet.

2000

4. Officer in the Yuan Dynasty (1279–1368).
5. Eastern range of the Appalachian Mountains extending from South Mountain, Pennsylvania, southward into northern Georgia. The range is visible in Charlottesville, Virginia.
6. Turned into a painting on plaster. An ancient technique, fresco was used by the Romans for decoration and perfected by the masters of the Italian Renaissance.

MARY OLIVER
b. 1935

"[O]f course / loss is the great lesson," Mary Oliver writes in her poem "Poppies." "But also I say this: that light / is an invitation to happiness / and that happiness, when it's done right / is a kind of holiness." What we experience first and most intensely in Mary Oliver's poetry is the earthly delight that constitutes her vision of happiness and holiness. That delight is founded in the world of the alligator, the deer, the bear, the black oak, the trumpet vine, the wild mushroom. This variegated natural world is precisely recorded in Oliver's poetry, from her first book, *No Voyage and Other Poems* (1963), to her collection of prose, prose poems, and poems, *Winter Hours* (2000). But a river of loss runs underground in her poems, whose deeper currents are sometimes an unspoken source propelling the poet out into the natural world; that world restores her to herself; its vitality and beauty open her heart. Yet in Oliver's best work the natural world does more than restore or console; it also teaches the "great lesson" of loving and letting go.

Oliver was born in Maple Heights, Ohio, and attended Vassar College. She lives in Provincetown, Massachusetts, and Bennington, Vermont; not surprisingly, the New England landscape is as central to her work as it is to Robert Frost's. But perhaps the poet she most closely resembles is James Wright (also born in Ohio), to whose memory her Pulitzer Prize–winning *American Primitive* (1983) is dedicated; she shares Wright's capacity for wonder, as well as his movement away from a social world into a natural one. Digging for mussels or spotting bear in the Truro Woods (in poems from *Twelve Moons*, 1979), watching humpback whales or blue herons on the ponds (in *American Primitive*), observing the hummingbird (in *New and Selected Poems*, 1992), Oliver endows her regional landscape with the spaciousness and depth the American Transcendentalist Henry David Thoreau gave to Walden Pond. Indeed, the very title of *American Primitive* suggests her self-conscious participation in an American impulse toward something primary and primal in the self and in the world.

One of the pleasures of reading Oliver's work is the education it provides about plants and animals in its detailed and knowledgeable observation—as when, for example, in "Skunk Cabbage" (*American Primitive*) she sees the "turnip-hearted skunk cabbage / slinging its bunched leaves up / through the chilly mud." The power and precision of her descriptions make it seem that, in lines from her "Alligator Poem" (*New and Selected Poems*), we "saw the world as if for a second time, / the way it really is." But Oliver's poems are as much about transformation as about observation, for in her work—as in "Alligator Poem"—the secret life of the world seems to open itself, for a moment, to human apprehension, transforming the world and the self. For Oliver the natural world casts a spell of amazement over poet and reader (this amazement— the stance of wonder at what is—is frequently registered by Oliver's use of the interrogative). Those moments when she is "washed and washed / in the river / of earthly delight" ("Poppies") restore the poet to her faith in the world that made her. These rapturous antidotes heal night's pain, mitigate loneliness, turn the heaviness of "the great bones of my life" ("Spring Azures") into wings. They are also the antidote to psychic pain, and to a social world with which Mary Oliver's poems want little to do. That world occasionally intrudes into Oliver's poems in the form of disturbing figures, like the woman in the airport restroom in "Singapore," the disfigured boy in "Acid," or, more ominously and persistently, the father who "knocks / wildly at the door" in "A Visitor." These figures unsettle the poet's solitude and threaten a vision of happiness and holiness sometimes too easily affirmed in her work. Though such human and social intrusions are intermittent in Oliver's poems, they seem to gesture toward injuries this poet keeps hidden.

There is such naturalness to Oliver's poems that we may fail to notice their craft. Oliver's language stays close to the spoken American idiom but infuses it with music, and creates, through verbal design, images of startling vividness (in "Alligator Poem" the birds "shook open the snowy pleats of their wings, and drifted away"). In a poetry so attentive to detail, where line breaks focus our attention on particulars—"the line is the device upon which the poem spins itself into being," she has said—there is also extraordinary power. Oliver builds her stanzas so they interlock, one into another, and the reader is pulled through a series of perceptions into the poet's insight. In certain poems the movement of her lines across the page rhythmically enacts the reaching forward and pulling back of the poet's walks into the landscape. Of course, making the design of a poem seem as natural as the hummingbird pausing at the trumpet vine is one sign of how gifted a poet Oliver is.

Her *New and Selected Poems* won the National Book Award in 1992 and includes work from six previous books, including *House of Light* (1990), *Dream Work* (1986), *The Night Traveler* (1978), and *Sleeping in the Forest* (1978). More-recent volumes include *White Pine* (1994), *Thirst* (2006), *Red Bird* (2008), and *Evidence* (2009). She has also published the essay collections *Blue Pastures* (1995) and *Why I Wake Early* (2004); *A Poetry Handbook* (1994); and *Rules for the Dance: A Handbook for Writing and Reading Metrical Verse* (1998).

The Black Snake

When the black snake
flashed onto the morning road,
and the truck could not swerve—
death, that is how it happens.

Now he lies looped and useless   5
as an old bicycle tire.
I stop the car
and carry him into the bushes.

He is as cool and gleaming
as a braided whip, he is as beautiful and quiet   10
as a dead brother.
I leave him under the leaves

and drive on, thinking
about *death*: its suddenness,
its terrible weight,   15
its certain coming. Yet under

reason burns a brighter fire, which the bones
have always preferred.
It is the story of endless good fortune.
It says to oblivion: not me!   20

It is the light at the center of every cell.
It is what sent the snake coiling and flowing forward
happily all spring through the green leaves before
he came to the road.

                                                                      1979

In Blackwater Woods

Look, the trees
are turning
their own bodies
into pillars

of light,   5
are giving off the rich
fragrance of cinnamon
and fulfillment,

the long tapers
of cattails   10
are bursting and floating away over
the blue shoulders

of the ponds,
and every pond,
no matter what its   15
name is, is

nameless now.
Every year
everything
I have ever learned   20

in my lifetime
leads back to this: the fires
and the black river of loss
whose other side

is salvation,   25
whose meaning
none of us will ever know.
To live in this world

you must be able
to do three things: 30
to love what is mortal;
to hold it

against your bones knowing
your own life depends on it;
and, when the time comes to let it go,   35
to let it go.

                                                          1983

Wild Geese

You do not have to be good.
You do not have to walk on your knees
for a hundred miles through the desert, repenting.
You only have to let the soft animal of your body
    love what it loves.   5
Tell me about despair, yours, and I will tell you mine.

Meanwhile the world goes on.
Meanwhile the sun and the dear pebbles of the rain
are moving across the landscapes,
over the prairies and the deep trees,   10
the mountains and the rivers.
Meanwhile the wild geese, high in the clean blue air,
are heading home again.
Whoever you are, no matter how lonely,
the world offers itself to your imagination,   15
calls to you like the wild geese, harsh and exciting—
over and over announcing your place
in the family of things.

                                                        1986

Poppies

The poppies send up their
orange flares; swaying
in the wind, their congregations
are a levitation

of bright dust, of thin   5
and lacy leaves.
There isn't a place
in this world that doesn't

sooner or later drown
in the indigos of darkness,   10
but now, for a while,
the roughage

shines like a miracle
as it floats above everything
with its yellow hair.   15
Of course nothing stops the cold,

black, curved blade
from hooking forward—
of course
loss is the great lesson.   20

But also I say this: that light
is an invitation
to happiness,
and that happiness,

when it's done right,   25
is a kind of holiness,
palpable and redemptive.
Inside the bright fields,

touched by their rough and spongy gold,
I am washed and washed   30
in the river
of earthly delight—

and what are you going to do—
what can you do
about it—   35
deep, blue night?

1991–92   1992

Hummingbird Pauses at the Trumpet Vine

Who doesn't love
roses, and who
doesn't love the lilies
of the black ponds

floating like flocks   5
of tiny swans,
and of course the flaming
trumpet vine

where the hummingbird comes
like a small green angel, to soak   10
his dark tongue
in happiness—

and who doesn't want
to live with the brisk
motor of his heart   15
singing

like a Schubert,[1]
and his eyes
working and working like those days of rapture,
by van Gogh,[2] in Arles?   20

Look! for most of the world
is waiting
or remembering—
most of the world is time

when we're not here,   25
not born yet, or died—
a slow fire
under the earth with all

---

1. Franz Schubert (1797–1828), Austrian composer and proponent of musical Romanticism. 2. Vincent Van Gogh (1853–1890), Dutch Post-impressionist painter.

our dumb wild blind cousins
who also   30
can't even remember anymore
their own happiness—

Look! and then we will be
like the pale cool
stones, that last almost   35
forever.

1991–92   1992

Alligator Poem

I knelt down
at the edge of the water,
and if the white birds standing
in the tops of the trees whistled any warning
I didn't understand,   5
I drank up to the very moment it came
crashing toward me,
its tail flailing
like a bundle of swords,
slashing the grass,   10
and the inside of its cradle-shaped mouth
gaping,
and rimmed with teeth—
and that's how I almost died
of foolishness   15
in beautiful Florida.
But I didn't.
I leaped aside, and fell,
and it streamed past me, crushing everything in its path
as it swept down to the water   20
and threw itself in,
and, in the end,
this isn't a poem about foolishness
but about how I rose from the ground
and saw the world as if for the second time,   25
the way it really is.
The water, that circle of shattered glass,
healed itself with a slow whisper
and lay back
with the back-lit light of polished steel,   30
and the birds, in the endless waterfalls of the trees,
shook open the snowy pleats of their wings, and drifted away,
while, for a keepsake, and to steady myself,
I reached out,
I picked the wild flowers from the grass around me—   35
blue stars

and blood-red trumpets
on long green stems—
for hours in my trembling hands they glittered
like fire.   40

                                                              1992

LUCILLE CLIFTON
b. 1936

Lucille Clifton seems able to lift the poem off the page and return it to the air we breathe. Like the work of Langston Hughes or William Carlos Williams, her poems allow us to hear the language of our daily lives as poetry and to experience the poetry in our ordinary lives. Although a closer look reveals the subtle craft of her poems (for example, the slant rhymes and the carefully paced repetitions), they appear deceptively simple. Their frankness and directness close the distance between poet and reader, especially when these poems are read aloud. Clifton emphasizes the informality in her work through the lowercase letters she prefers and through her frequent omission of titles. The language of her poems reflects her identity; "I am a black woman poet," she has said, "and I sound like one." Grounded in realistic details, her poems do not shy away from what is harsh and painful, including incest, suicide, mental illness, and the effects of poverty and racism. But while Clifton's anger fuels many poems, her imagination finds beauty and humor in unexpected places; indeed, she seems able to make poetry out of anything. In this she resembles the African American quilters who rework the materials of ordinary experience into distinctive and compelling designs. Indeed, she titled one of her books *Quilting* (1991) and borrowed its section headings from the names of traditional quilt patterns.

Born in Depew, New York, to a father who worked in the steel mills and a mother who was a launderer and a homemaker (and who wrote poems but burned them), Clifton was the first person in her family to attend college. "I had a very regular life, the life of a poor black person," Clifton has said; but her background and her gifts sometimes made her feel that "there is no planet stranger / than the one I'm from" ("note, passed to superman"). At sixteen she began her studies at Howard University in Washington, D.C., and she later attended Fredonia State Teachers College in New York State. She went on to work as a claims clerk in the New York State Division of Employment (1958–60) and as a literature assistant at the Office of Education in Washington (1960–71). Clifton never formally studied creative writing, but she wrote poems and thought of herself as a poet from a young age. However, her work did not receive public recognition until she was in her thirties. In 1969 she sent a poem to the poet Robert Hayden at the National Endowment for the Arts. Hayden had left the NEA, but his successor, Carolyn Kizer, read the work and submitted it to the YW-YMHA Poetry Center Discovery Award competition in New York City. Clifton won the competition and at the award ceremony, after she read her poems, an editor from Random House in the audience offered to publish her first book, *Good Times* (1969). *Good Times* appeared when she was thirty-three, a wife and mother with six children under the age of eleven. During these years her method of composition followed those writers, many of them women, who compose lines of poetry in the mind until there is time to write them down.

Clifton comes from a line of African American storytellers extending from her great-grandmother, Caroline Donald, who was born in Dahomey, Africa, sold into slavery, and taken to America. Clifton's memoir, *Generations* (1976), chronicles the history of her family, including the genealogy and the tradition of strong women passed down to Clifton through her father's stories. In much of her work, Clifton consciously seeks to recover an African American past that has too often been omitted from standard histories and to retell history from previously unacknowledged points of view.

In a poem beginning "the light that came to Lucille Clifton," a voice from "the non-dead past" speaks this message to her: "You might as well open the door, my child / for truth is furiously knocking." Throughout her long and productive career as a poet, and as a writer of memoirs and children's books, she has transmitted the voices of a living past. Like Toni Morrison's fiction, Clifton's poems are full of ghosts: her mother and father, her unborn children, her ancestors, and sometimes mythical and biblical figures. These presences in her work bear witness to a legacy of pain, wisdom, and survival. As a writer brave enough to open the door to the truths of her life and her world, Clifton possesses a "gift of understanding" that puts her in touch with the suffering of the "holy lost" ("Wild Blessing"), but the spiritual dimension of her work also reveals the possibility of joy and transformation, evident in "blessing the boats."

Clifton's books include *Good News about the Earth* (1972) and *Two-Headed Woman* (1980), which received the University of Massachusetts Juniper Prize. Both of these volumes were nominated for the Pulitzer Prize. Subsequent collections include *Next* (1987), *The Book of Light* (1993), *Blessing the Boats: New and Selected Poems 1988–2000* (2000), *Mercy* (2004), and *Voices* (2008). Clifton's work for children includes *The Black BCs* (1970), *The Times They Used to Be* (1974), and an award-winning series of books featuring events in the life of Everett Anderson, a young black boy. In 1999 she was elected a chancellor of the Academy of American Poets. She has served as poet laureate for the State of Maryland and is distinguished professor of humanities at St. Mary's College in Maryland.

miss rosie

when i watch you
wrapped up like garbage
sitting, surrounded by the smell
of too old potato peels
or   5
when i watch you
in your old man's shoes
with the little toe cut out
sitting, waiting for your mind
like next week's grocery   10
i say
when i watch you
you wet brown bag of a woman
who used to be the best looking gal in georgia
used to be called the Georgia Rose   15
i stand up

through your destruction
i stand up

1969   1987

the lost baby poem

the time i dropped your almost body down
down to meet the waters under the city
and run one with the sewage to the sea
what did i know about waters rushing back
what did i know about drowning   5
or being drowned

you would have been born into winter
in the year of the disconnected gas
and no car   we would have made the thin
walk over genesee hill[1] into the canada wind   10
to watch you slip like ice into strangers' hands
you would have fallen naked as snow into winter
if you were here i could tell you these
and some other things

if i am ever less than a mountain   15
for your definite brothers and sisters
let the rivers pour over my head
let the sea take me for a spiller
of seas   let black men call me stranger
always   for your never named sake   20

1972

homage to my hips

these hips are big hips
they need space to
move around in.
they don't fit into little
petty places, these hips.   5
are free hips.
they don't like to be held back.
these hips have never been enslaved,
they go where they want to go
they do what they want to do.   10
these hips are mighty hips.
these hips are magic hips.
i have known them
to put a spell on a man and
spin him like a top!   15

1980

1. Genesee County is in northwestern New York State.

wild blessings

licked in the palm of my hand
by an uninvited woman, so i have held
in that hand the hand of a man who
emptied into his daughter, the hand
of a girl who threw herself   5
from a tenement window, the trembling
junkie hand of a priest, of a boy who
shattered across viet nam
someone resembling his mother,
and more, and more.   10
do not ask me to thank the tongue
that circled my fingers
or pride myself on the attentions
of the holy lost.
i am grateful for many blessings   15
but the gift of understanding,
the wild one, maybe not.

1991

wishes for sons

i wish them cramps.
i wish them a strange town
and the last tampon.
i wish them no 7–11.

i wish them one week early   5
and wearing a white skirt.
i wish them one week late.

later i wish them hot flashes
and clots like you
wouldn't believe.   let the   10
flashes come when they
meet someone special.
let the clots come
when they want to.

let them think they have accepted   15
arrogance in the universe,
then bring them to gynecologists
not unlike themselves.

1991

blessing the boats

(at St. Mary's)[1]

may the tide
that is entering even now
the lip of our understanding
carry you out
beyond the face of fear   5
may you kiss
the wind then turn from it
certain that it will
love your back   may you
open your eyes to water   10
water waving forever
and may you in your innocence
sail through this to that

1991

the mississippi river empties into the gulf

and the gulf enters the sea and so forth,
none of them emptying anything,
all of them carrying yesterday
forever on their white tipped backs,
all of them dragging forward tomorrow.   5
it is the great circulation
of the earth's body, like the blood
of the gods, this river in which the past
is always flowing, every water
is the same water coming round.   10
everyday someone is standing on the edge
of this river, staring into time,
whispering mistakenly:
only here, only now.

1996

moonchild[1]

whatever slid into my mother's room that
late June night, tapping her great belly,

---

1. A county in southern Maryland that is a tide-water peninsula bordered by the Chesapeake Bay and three rivers: the Patuxent, the Potomac, and the Wicomico. It is also the location of St. Mary's College, where Clifton teaches.

1. *Moonchild* (1917), a novel by the English occultist Aleister Crowley (1875–1947), involves a magical war between practitioners of white magic and practitioners of black magic over an unborn child.

summoned me out roundheaded and unsmiling.
is this the moon, my father used to grin,
cradling me?   it was the moon   5
but nobody knew it then.

the moon understands dark places.
the moon has secrets of her own.
she holds what light she can.

we girls were ten years old and giggling   10
in our hand-me-downs, we wanted breasts,
pretended that we had them, tissued
our undershirts, jay Johnson is teaching
me to french kiss, ella bragged, who
is teaching you? how do you say; my father?   15

the moon is queen of everything.
she rules the oceans, rivers, rain.
when I am asked whose tears these are
I always blame the moon.

                                                        2000

[oh antic god]

oh antic God
return to me
my mother in her thirties[1]
leaned across the front porch
the huge pillow of her breasts   5
pressing against the rail
summoning me in for bed.

I am almost the dead woman's age times two.

I can barely recall her song
the scent of her hands   10
though her wild hair scratches my dreams
at night.   return to me, oh Lord of then
and now, my mother's calling,
her young voice humming my name.

                                                        2004

---

1. Thelma Moore Sayles, Clifton's mother, died at age forty-four.

STEPHEN DIXON
b. 1936

S tephen Dixon's short stories often begin where narratives by others would end. Consider the opening line of "Mac in Love," the first story in his initial collection, *No Relief* (1976): "She said 'You're crazy, Mac,' and shut the door." Or the opening of "14 Stories," the title work of Dixon's 1980 collection: "Eugene Randall held the gun in front of his mouth and fired." Or later in the same volume, where "The Signing" begins: "My wife dies. Now I'm alone. I kiss her hands and leave the hospital room." Each could be the final line of a traditional short story. But for Dixon such lines are beginnings, a challenge to continue writing just where most narratives would stop.

Others of Dixon's stories are even more minimal. Many start with flat, present-tense statements that are immediately modified or retracted. Occasionally the author begins with the conjunction of just two elements, such as a man walking past a window in which he can see a baby being held, out of which he generates a complete narrative. Or Dixon will eliminate expected material, as in his story "Said" (from his 1989 collection *Love and Will*), where *what* the arguing couple actually said is omitted in favor of an all-too-revealing rhythm of "he saids" and "she saids."

The motive for such writing is evident from literary theory of the time, which suggested that even in its great variety fiction had become exhausted. Dixon's inventions show that something can be made of nothing, or almost nothing, and hence that fiction is inexhaustible. Yet, always, Dixon keeps his action strictly within the bounds of recognizable life, as in "Time to Go" (from his 1984 collection of that title). A parent does not usually accompany a son who is shopping for an engagement present, much less when the engaged couple buys their wedding rings; but what would happen if one did? The presence of the father in this story is typically Dixonesque, for the situation produces inherent complexities far beyond anything extraneous references could add.

Dixon, whose father was a dentist and whose mother worked in interior design, was born and raised in New York City. Unhappy with predental courses at the City College of New York, he switched to a curriculum that prepared him for a reporter's job with a news service in Washington, D.C., where he worked for two years after graduation covering the U.S. Senate and House of Representatives. Returning to New York, he began writing fiction in the early 1960s, taking numerous diverse jobs (technical writing, department store sales, tour leader, waiter, bartender, school bus driver, artist's model, counterman, dishwasher, radio news editor) to support himself. In 1980 he assumed a professorship in the Writing Seminars at Johns Hopkins University, where he continues to teach. With his wife, Anne Frydman (who taught and translated Russian until her death in 2009), and their two daughters, Dixon maintained a home in Baltimore and summered in Maine, but also kept an apartment in New York City; all three settings are prominent in his work.

Dixon's work has been compared to Samuel Beckett's for its spare, ongoing, self-consuming energy. Yet unlike some of Beckett's abstract situations, Dixon's characters and their problems are quite familiar. Not existing to demonstrate universal philosophical absurdities, they simply wish to avoid mistakes and do as well as they can. They struggle with conditions more suitable for closure than for possibility, and many times their sincerity proves their undoing. Yet they all persist, and in that effort they provide narrative motivation.

The following text is from *Long Made Short* (1994).

Flying

She was fooling around with the plane's door handle. I said "Don't touch that, sweetheart, you never know what can happen." Suddenly the door disappeared and she flew out and I yelled "Judith" and saw her looking terrified at me as she was being carried away. I jumped out after her, smiled and held out my arms like wings and yelled "Fly like a bird, my darling, try flying like a bird." She put out her arms, started flying like me and smiled. I flew nearer to her and when she was close enough I pulled her to my body and said "It's not so bad flying like this, is it? It's fun. You hold out one arm and I'll hold out one of mine and we'll see where we can get to." She said "Daddy, you shouldn't have gone after me, you know that," and I said "I wouldn't let you out here all alone. Don't worry, we'll be okay if we keep flying like this and, once we're over land, get ourselves closer and closer to the ground."

The plane by now couldn't be seen. Others could, going different ways, but none seemed to alter their routes for us no matter how much waving I did. It was a clear day, blue sky, no clouds, the sun moving very fast. She said "What's that?" pointing down and I said "Keep your arm up, we have to continue flying." She said "I am, but what's that?" and I said "Looks like a ship but it's probably an illusion." "What's an illusion?" and I said "What a time for word lessons; save them for when we get home. For now just enjoy the flying and hope for no sudden air currents' shifts." My other arm held her tightly and I pressed my face into hers. We flew like that, cheek to cheek, our arms out but not moving. I was worried because I hadn't yet come up with any idea to help us make a safe landing. How do we descend, how do we land smoothly or crash-land without breaking our legs? I'll hold her legs up and just break mine if it has to come to that. She said "I love you, Daddy, I both like you and love you and always will. I'm never going to get married and move away from home." I said "Oh well, one day you might, not that I'll ever really want you to. And me too to you, sweetie, with all that love. I'm glad we're together like this. A little secret though. For the quickest moment in the plane I thought I wouldn't jump out after you, that something would hold me back. Now nothing could make me happier than what I did."

We left the ocean and we were over cliffs and then the wind shifted and we were being carried north along the coast. We'd been up at almost the same distance from water and land for a long time and I still had no idea how to get down. Then along the coastal road I saw my wife driving our car. Daniel was in the front seat, his hand sticking out the window to feel the breeze. The plane must have reported in about the two people sucked out of the plane, and when Sylvia heard about it she immediately got in the car and started looking for us, thinking I'd be able to take care of things in the air and that the wind would carry us east.

"Look at them, sweetheart, Mommy and Daniel. He should stick his arm in; what he's doing is dangerous." She said "There aren't any other cars around, so it can't hurt him." "But it should be a rule he always observes, just in case he forgets and sticks it out on a crowded highway. And a car could suddenly come the other way. People drive like maniacs on these deserted roads and if one got too close to him his arm could be torn off." "But the car would be going the other way—wouldn't it?—so on Mommy's side, not his," and I said "Well, the driver of another car going their way could suddenly lose his head and try and pass on the right and get too close to Daniel's arm. —Daniel," I screamed, "put your arm back right now. This is Daddy talking." His arm went back in. Sylvia stopped the car, got out and looked up and yelled "So there you are. Come back now, my darlings; you'll get yourselves killed." "Look at her worrying about us, Judith—that's nice, right? — Don't worry, Sylvia," I screamed, "we're doing just fine, flying. There's no feeling like it in the world, we're both quite safe, and once I figure out a way to get us down, we will. If we have to crash-land doing it, don't worry about Judith—I'll hold her up and take the whole brunt of it myself. But I think it's going to be some distance from here, inland or on the coast, so you just go home now and maybe we'll see you in time for dinner. But you'll never be able to keep up with us the way this wind's blowing, and I don't know how to make us go slower." "You sure you'll be all right?" she yelled, and I said "I can hardly hear you anymore, but yes, I think I got everything under control."

We flew on, I held her in my arm, kissed her head repeatedly, thinking if anything would stop her from worrying, that would. "You sure there's nothing to worry about, Daddy? I mean about what you said to Mommy," and I said "What are you doing, reading my mind? Yes, everything's okay, I'm positive." We continued flying, each with an arm out, and by the time night came we were still no closer to or farther away from the ground.

1994

RUDOLFO A. ANAYA
b. 1937

L *lano* is a Spanish adjective meaning "plain, simple, even, smooth, level"; as a noun, its feminine form (*llana*) indicates a "mason's trowel," while the masculine, *llano*, signifies an area of plain, flat ground. On the eastern *llanos* of New Mexico, in the village of Pastura, Rudolfo Anaya was born. This high, arid, windy landscape figures in much of Anaya's fiction, suggesting the way that nature's trowel works incessantly to level out human effort. As a Hispanic American, the author can trace his ancestry back through four centuries of activity in this region. As critic Margarite Fernández Olmos notes, Anaya's parents' backgrounds combined both sides of the region's rural life: his mother's family were farmers growing crops and raising pigs, sheep, and cows in the Puerto de Luna valley, while his father was a free-ranging vaquero, a cowboy whose family tradition was to work with cattle herds in the open rather than settling the land. After Anaya's father was killed in an accident, his mother married another vaquero, who helped raise his stepson with an understanding of both farming and ranching lifestyles. When still a small child Anaya moved with his family to the town of Santa Rosa, New

Mexico—"the social hub of the surrounding rural communities," as Olmos describes it, where on busy Highway 66 Anaya could witness the transcontinental link between East Coast and West Coast cultures. Yet the nearby Pecos River and its opportunities for hunting and fishing let the author grow up in close proximity to nature, an experience he would appreciate for its spiritual dimensions. By age fifteen he and his family joined the urban migration that had begun in the years following World War II and moved to a barrio (Hispanic neighborhood) in Albuquerque. Here he learned the ways of big cities, another influence on his subsequent fiction. But an accident more typical of rural life directed his interests to literature: while diving into an irrigation ditch that he and his friends were using as a swimming hole, Anaya fractured two vertebrae in his neck and spent much of his seventeenth year recovering in a world of books and meditation. After a false start in business school he became an English major at the University of New Mexico, where he began writing fiction (for himself) and went on to earn M.A. degrees in English and in counseling, and then found work as a high school teacher and guidance counselor.

Bless Me, Ultima (1972) was Anaya's first novel, published to acclaim within the just-emerging network of the Chicano arts movement that would eventually include recognition of such writers as Rolando Hinojosa, Estella Portillo, Bernice Zamora, and Ricardo Sánchez. As a result of its success Anaya was appointed to a professorship at the University of New Mexico, where he taught until achieving emeritus status in 1993. In the novel, Ultima is a practitioner of folk-healing arts developed by women; she serves as mentor to the boy Antonio, who in the coming-of-age tradition of the *bildungsroman* (think *David Copperfield*, *A Portrait of the Artist as a Young Man*, *The Magic Mountain*) must make the choices that will define his adult life. In Antonio's case these conflicts reflect the alternatives of Anaya's boyhood: farming one's land or wandering as a vaquero, taking one's cultural lead from the Hispanic or the Anglo, and sorting out the gender biases in competing systems of religious belief. *Heart of Aztlán* (1976) and *Tortuga* (1979) complete what critics describe as Anaya's initial Chicano trilogy of novels, as the narrative action shifts from the countryside to the city and then to the experiences of a teenager recovering from a paralyzing accident. In all three works the author blends the modern with the ancient, the formalities of culture with folklorish roots, and the plainly discursive with the richly allegorical, producing narratives that proceed on many different levels all at one time.

"Dos," the second chapter of *Bless Me, Ultima*, displays Anaya's characteristic literary techniques, including the mix of Hispanic and Anglo references that helps create the Chicano experience—a condition of living in the borderland area that until 1848 was part of Mexico and that today retains many aspects of Mexican culture, including the Hispanic, Indian, and mestizo (mixed race). In recent years his writing has expanded from autobiography to a more general social vision of Chicano life. *Alburquque* (1992)—the title reflects the original spelling of the city's name—follows the quest of a young boxer who must look beyond his adoptive family to find his roots. With *Zia Summer* (1995) Anaya writes a full-fledged detective novel, introducing a private eye named Sonny Baca, who seeks the murderer of a prominent politician's wife by sorting through the type of social and ethnic issues the author had treated previously in a more personal manner.

Other Sonny Baca novels have followed, all of them reminders of how far "Alburquque," the largest city in New Mexico, has come from its days as a frontier outpost (while retaining its mix of Spanish, Native American, and mestizo cultures).

The following text is from *Bless Me, Ultima* (1972).

From Bless Me, Ultima

Dos[1]

Ultima slipped easily into the routine of our daily life. The first day she put on her apron and helped my mother with breakfast, later she swept the house and then helped my mother wash our clothes in the old washing machine they pulled outside where it was cooler under the shade of the young elm trees. It was as if she had always been here. My mother was very happy because now she had someone to talk to and she didn't have to wait until Sunday when her women friends from the town came up the dusty path to sit in the sala[2] and visit.

Deborah and Theresa were happy because Ultima did many of the household chores they normally did, and they had more time to spend in the attic and cut out an interminable train of paper dolls which they dressed, gave names to, and most miraculously, made talk.

My father was also pleased. Now he had one more person to tell his dream to. My father's dream was to gather his sons around him and move westward to the land of the setting sun, to the vineyards of California. But the war had taken his three sons and it had made him bitter. He often got drunk on Saturday afternoons and then he would rave against old age, he would rage against the town on the opposite side of the river which drained a man of his freedom, and he would cry because the war had ruined his dream. It was very sad to see my father cry, but I understood it, because sometimes a man has to cry. Even if he is a man.

And I was happy with Ultima. We walked together in the llano[3] and along the river banks to gather herbs and roots for her medicines. She taught me the names of plants and flowers, of trees and bushes, of birds and animals; but most important, I learned from her that there was a beauty in the time of day and in the time of night, and that there was peace in the river and in the hills. She taught me to listen to the mystery of the groaning earth and to feel complete in the fulfillment of its time. My soul grew under her careful guidance.

I had been afraid of the awful *presence* of the river, which was the soul of the river, but through her I learned that my spirit shared in the spirit of all things. But the innocence which our isolation sheltered could not last forever, and the affairs of the town began to reach across our bridge and enter my life. Ultima's owl gave the warning that the time of peace on our hill was drawing to an end.

It was Saturday night. My mother had laid out our clean clothes for Sunday mass, and we had gone to bed early because we always went to early mass. The house was quiet, and I was in the mist of some dream when I heard the owl cry its warning. I was up instantly, looking through the small window at the dark figure that ran madly towards the house. He hurled himself at the door and began pounding.

"¡Márez!" he shouted, "¡Márez! ¡Ándale, hombre!"[4]

I was frightened, but I recognized the voice. It was Jasón's father.

---

1. Two (Spanish).
2. Living room (Spanish).
3. Plain (Spanish).
4. Come on, man (Spanish).

"¡Un momento!" I heard my father call. He fumbled with the farol.[5]

"¡Ándale, hombre, ándale!" Chávez cried pitifully, "mataron a mi hermano—"[6]

"Ya vengo—"[7] My father opened the door and the frightened man burst in. In the kitchen I heard my mother moan, "Ave María Purísima, mis hijos—"[8] She had not heard Chávez' last words, and so she assumed the aviso[9] was one that brought bad news about her sons.

"Chávez, ¿qué pasa?"[1] My father held the trembling man.

"¡Mi hermano, mi hermano!" Chávez sobbed, "He has killed my brother!"

"¿Pero qué dices, hombre?"[2] my father exclaimed. He pulled Chávez into the hall and held up the farol. The light cast by the farol revealed the wild, frightened eyes of Chávez.

"¡Gabriel!" my mother cried and came forward, but my father pushed her back. He did not want her to see the monstrous mask of fear on the man's face.

"It is not our sons, it is something in town—get him some water."

"Lo mató, lo mató—"[3] Chávez repeated.

"Get hold of yourself, hombre, tell me what has happened!" My father shook Chávez and the man's sobbing subsided. He took the glass of water and drank, then he could talk.

"Reynaldo has just brought the news, my brother is dead," he sighed and slumped against the wall. Chávez' brother was the sheriff of the town. The man would have fallen if my father had not held him up.

"¡Madre de Dios![4] Who? How?"

"¡Lupito!" Chávez cried out. His face corded with thick veins. For the first time his left arm came up and I saw the rifle he held.

"Jesús, María y José,"[5] my mother prayed.

My father groaned and slumped against the wall. "Ay que Lupito," he shook his head, "the war[6] made him crazy—"

Chávez regained part of his composure. "Get your rifle, we must go to the bridge—"

"The bridge?"

"Reynaldo said to meet him there—The crazy bastard has taken to the river—"

My father nodded silently. He went to the bedroom and returned with his coat. While he loaded his rifle in the kitchen Chávez related what he knew.

"My brother had just finished his rounds," he gasped, "he was at the bus depot cafe, having coffee, sitting without a care in the world—and the bastard came up to where he sat and without warning shot him in the head—" His body shook as he retold the story.

"Perhaps it is better if you wait here, hombre," my father said with consolation.

"No!" Chávez shouted. "I must go. He was my brother!"

---

5. Lantern (Spanish). "Un momento": Just a minute (Spanish).
6. They killed my brother (Spanish).
7. I'm coming now (Spanish).
8. Hail Virgin Mary, my sons (Spanish).
9. Warning (Spanish).
1. Chávez, what's happening (Spanish).

2. But what are you saying, man (Spanish).
3. He killed him, he killed him (Spanish).
4. Mother of God (Spanish).
5. Jesus, Mary, and Joseph (Spanish).
6. World War II. "Ay que Lupito": Oh, that Lupito (Spanish).

My father nodded. I saw him stand beside Chávez and put his arm around his shoulders. Now he too was armed. I had only seen him shoot the rifle when we slaughtered pigs in the fall. Now they were going armed for a man.

"Gabriel, be careful," my mother called as my father and Chávez slipped out into the dark.

"Sí,"[7] I heard him answer, then the screen door banged. "Keep the doors locked—" My mother went to the door and shut the latch. We never locked our doors, but tonight there was something strange and fearful in the air.

Perhaps this is what drew me out into the night to follow my father and Chávez down to the bridge, or perhaps it was some concern I had for my father. I do not know. I waited until my mother was in the sala then dressed and slipped downstairs. I glanced down the hall and saw candlelight flickering from the sala. That room was never entered unless there were Sunday visitors, or unless my mother took us in to pray novenas and rosaries for my brothers at war. I knew she was kneeling at her altar now, praying. I knew she would pray until my father returned.

I slipped out the kitchen door and into the night. It was cool. I sniffed the air, there was a tinge of autumn in it. I ran up the goat path until I caught sight of two dark shadows ahead of me. Chávez and my father.

We passed Fío's dark house and then the tall juniper tree that stood where the hill sloped down to the bridge. Even from this distance I could hear the commotion on the bridge. As we neared the bridge I was afraid of being discovered as I had no reason for being there. My father would be very angry. To escape detection I cut to the right and was swallowed up by the dark brush of the river. I pushed through the dense bosque[8] until I came to the bank of the river. From where I stood I could look up into the flooding beams of light that were pointed down by the excited men. I could hear them giving frenzied, shouted instructions. I looked to my left where the bridge started and saw my father and Chávez running towards the excitement at the center of the bridge.

My eyes were now accustomed to the dark, but it was a glint of light that made me turn and look at a clump of bullrushes in the sweeping water of the river just a few yards away. What I saw made my blood run cold. Crouched in the reeds and half submerged in the muddy waters lay the figure of Lupito, the man who had killed the sheriff. The glint of light was from the pistol he held in his hand.

It was frightening enough to come upon him so suddenly, but as I dropped to my knees in fright I must have uttered a cry because he turned and looked directly at me. At that same moment a beam of light found him and illuminated a face twisted with madness. I do not know if he saw me, or if the light cut off his vision, but I saw his bitter, contorted grin. As long as I live I will never forget those wild eyes, like the eyes of a trapped, savage animal.

At the same time someone shouted from the bridge, "There!" Then all the lights found the crouched figure. He jumped and I saw him as clear as if it were daylight.

---

7. Yes (Spanish).   8. Wood, forest, (Spanish).

"Ayeeeeee!" He screamed a blood curdling cry that echoed down the river. The men on the bridge didn't know what to do. They stood transfixed, looking down at the mad man waving the pistol in the air. "Ayeeeeeeee!" He cried again. It was a cry of rage and pain, and it made my soul sick. The cry of a tormented man had come to the peaceful green mystery of my river, and the great *presence* of the river watched from the shadows and deep recesses, as I watched from where I crouched at the bank.

"Japanese sol'jer, Japanese sol'jer!" he cried, "I am wounded. Come help me—" he called to the men on the bridge. The rising mist of the river swirled in the beams of spotlights. It was like a horrible nightmare.

Suddenly he leaped up and ran splashing through the water towards me. The lights followed him. He grew bigger, I heard his panting, the water his feet kicked up splashed on my face, and I thought he would run over me. Then as quickly as he had sprinted in my direction he turned and disappeared again into the dark clumps of reeds in the river. The lights moved in all directions, but they couldn't find him. Some of the lights swept over me and I trembled with fear that I would be found out, or worse, that I would be mistaken for Lupito and shot.

"The crazy bastard got away!" someone shouted on the bridge.

"Ayeeeeee!" the scream sounded again. It was a cry that I did not understand, and I am sure the men on the bridge did not either. The man they hunted had slipped away from human understanding; he had become a wild animal, and they were afraid.

"Damn!" I heard them cursing themselves. Then a car with a siren and flashing red light came on the bridge. It was Vigil, the state policeman who patrolled our town.

"Chávez is dead!" I heard him shout. "He never had a chance. His brains blown out—" There was silence.

"We have to kill him!" Jasón's father shouted. His voice was full of anger, rage and desperation.

"I have to deputize you—" Vigil started to say.

"The hell with deputizing!" Chávez shouted. "He killed my brother! ¡Está loco!"[9] The men agreed with their silence.

"Have you spotted him?" Vigil asked.

"Just now we saw him, but we lost him—"

"He's down there," someone added.

"He is an animal! He has to be shot!" Chávez cried out.

"¡Sí!" the men agreed.

"Now wait a moment—" It was my father who spoke. I do not know what he said because of the shouting. In the meantime I searched the dark of the river for Lupito. I finally saw him. He was about forty feet away, crouched in the reeds as before. The muddy waters of the river lapped and gurgled savagely around him. Before the night had been only cool, now it turned cold and I shivered. I was torn between a fear that made my body tremble, and a desire to help the poor man. But I could not move, I could only watch like a chained spectator.

---

9. He's crazy (Spanish).

"Márez is right!" I heard a booming voice on the bridge. In the lights I could make out the figure of Narciso. There was only one man that big and with that voice in town. I knew that Narciso was one of the old people from Las Pasturas, and that he was a good friend to my father. I knew they often drank together on Saturdays, and once or twice he had been to our house.

"¡Por Dios, hombres!"[1] he shouted, "let us act like men! That is not an animal down there, that is a man. Lupito. You all know Lupito. You know that the war made him sick—" But the men would not listen to Narciso. I guess it was because he was the town drunk, and they said he never did anything useful.

"Go back to your drinking and leave this job to men," one of them jeered at him.

"He killed the sheriff in cold blood," another added. I knew that the sheriff had been greatly admired.

"I am not drinking," Narciso persisted, "it is you men who are drunk for blood. You have lost your reason—"

"Reason!" Chávez countered. "What reason did he have for killing my brother. You know," he addressed the men, "my brother did no one harm. Tonight a mad animal crawled behind him and took his life. You call that reason! That animal has to be destroyed!"

"¡Sí! ¡Sí!" the men shouted in unison.

"At least let us try to talk to him," Narciso begged. I knew that it was hard for a man of the llano to beg.

"Yes," Vigil added, "perhaps he will give himself up—"

"Do you think he'll listen to talk!" Chávez jumped forward. "He's down there, and he still has the pistol that killed my brother! Go down and talk to him!" I could see Chávez shouting in Vigil's face, and Vigil said nothing. Chávez laughed. "This is the only talk he will understand—" he turned and fired over the railing of the bridge. His shots roared then whined away down the river. I could hear the bullets make splashing noises in the water.

"Wait!" Narciso shouted. He took Chávez' rifle and with one hand held it up. Chávez struggled against him but Narciso was too big and strong. "I will talk to him," Narciso said. He pushed Chávez back. "I understand your sorrow Chávez," he said, "but one killing is enough for tonight—" The men must have been impressed by his sincerity because they stood back and waited.

Narciso leaned over the concrete railing and shouted down into the darkness. "Hey Lupito! It is me, Narciso. It is me, hombre, your compadre. Listen my friend, a very bad business has happened tonight, but if we act like men we can settle it—Let me come down and talk to you, Lupito. Let me help you—"

I looked at Lupito. He had been watching the action on the bridge, but now as Narciso talked to him I saw his head slump on his chest. He seemed to be thinking. I prayed that he would listen to Narciso and that the angry and frustrated men on the bridge would not commit mortal sin. The night was very quiet. The men on the bridge awaited an answer. Only the lapping water of the river made a sound.

1. By God, men (Spanish).

"¡Amigo!"[2] Narciso shouted, "You know I am your friend, I want to help you, hombre—" He laughed softly. "Hey, Lupito, you remember just a few years ago, before you went to the war, you remember the first time you came into the Eight Ball to gamble a little. Remember how I taught you how Juan Botas marked the aces with a little tobacco juice, and he thought you were green, but you beat him!" He laughed again. "Those were good times, Lupito, before the war came. Now we have this bad business to settle. But we are friends who will help you—"

I saw Lupito's tense body shake. A low, sad mournful cry tore itself from his throat and mixed into the lapping sound of the waters of the river. His head shook slowly, and I guess he must have been thinking and fighting between surrendering or remaining free, and hunted. Then like a coiled spring he jumped up, his pistol aimed straight up. There was a flash of fire and the loud report of the pistol. But he had not fired at Narciso or at any of the men on the bridge! The spotlights found him.

"There's your answer!" Chávez shouted.

"He's firing! He's firing!" Another voice shouted. "He's crazy!"

Lupito's pistol sounded again. Still he was not aiming at the men on the bridge. He was shooting to draw their fire!

"Shoot! Shoot!" someone on the bridge called.

"No, no," I whispered through clenched lips. But it was too late for anything. The frightened men responded by aiming their rifles over the side of the bridge. One single shot sounded then a barrage followed it like the roar of a canon, like the rumble of thunder in a summer thunderstorm.

Many shots found their mark. I saw Lupito lifted off his feet and hurled backward by the bullets. But he got up and ran limping and crying towards the bank where I lay.

"Bless me—" I thought he cried, and the second volley of shots from the bridge sounded, but this time they sounded like a great whirling of wings, like pigeons swirling to roost on the church top. He fell forward then clawed and crawled out of the holy water of the river onto the bank in front of me. I wanted to reach out and help him, but I was frozen by my fear. He looked up at me and his face was bathed in water and flowing, hot blood, but it was also dark and peaceful as it slumped into the sand of the riverbank. He made a strange gurgling sound in his throat, then he was still. Up on the bridge a great shout went up. The men were already running to the end of the bridge to come down and claim the man whose dead hands dug into the soft, wet sand in front of me.

I turned and ran. The dark shadows of the river enveloped me as I raced for the safety of home. Branches whipped at my face and cut it, and vines and tree trunks caught at my feet and tripped me. In my headlong rush I disturbed sleeping birds and their shrill cries and slapping wings hit at my face. The horror of darkness had never been so complete as it was for me that night.

I had started praying to myself from the moment I heard the first shot and I never stopped praying until I reached home. Over and over through my mind ran the words of the Act of Contrition. I had not yet been to catechism nor had I made my first holy communion, but my mother had taught

2. Friend (Spanish).

me the Act of Contrition. It was to be said after one made his confession to the priest, and as the last prayer before death.

Did God listen? Would he hear? Had he seen my father on the bridge? And where was Lupito's soul winging to, or was it washing down the river to the fertile valley of my uncles' farms?

A priest could have saved Lupito. Oh why did my mother dream for me to be a priest! How would I ever wash away the stain of blood from the sweet waters of my river! I think at that time I began to cry because as I left the river brush and headed up the hills I heard my sobs for the first time.

It was also then that I heard the owl. Between my gasps for air and my sobs I stopped and listened for its song. My heart was pounding and my lungs hurt, but a calmness had come over the moonlit night when I heard the hooting of Ultima's owl. I stood still for a long time. I realized that the owl had been with me throughout the night. It had watched over all that had happened on the bridge. Suddenly the terrible, dark fear that had possessed me was gone.

I looked at the house that my father and my brothers had built on the juniper-patched hill; it was quiet and peaceful in the blue night. The sky sparkled with a million stars and the Virgin's horned moon, the moon of my mother's people, the moon of the Lunas.[3] My mother would be praying for the soul of Lupito.

Again the owl sang, Ultima's spirit bathed me with its strong resolution. I turned and looked across the river. Some lights shone in the town. In the moonlight I could make out the tower of the church, the school house top, and way beyond the glistening of the town's water tank. I heard the soft wail of a siren and I knew the men would be pulling Lupito from the river.

The river's brown waters would be stained with blood, forever and ever and ever . . .

In the autumn I would have to go to the school in the town, and in a few years I would go to catechism lessons in the church. I shivered. My body began to hurt from the beating it had taken from the brush of the river. But what hurt more was that I had witnessed for the first time the death of a man.

My father did not like the town or its way. When we had first moved from Las Pasturas we had lived in a rented house in the town. But every evening after work he had looked across the river to these barren, empty hills, and finally he had bought a couple of acres and began building our house. Everyone told him he was crazy, that the rocky, wild hill could sustain no life, and my mother was more than upset. She wanted to buy along the river where the land was fertile and there was water for the plants and trees. But my father won the fight to be close to his llano, because truthfully our hill was the beginning of the llano, from here it stretched away as far as the eye could see, to Las Pasturas and beyond.

The men of the town had murdered Lupito. But he had murdered the sheriff. They said the war had made him crazy. The prayers for Lupito mixed into prayers for my brothers. So many different thoughts raced through my mind that I felt dizzy, and very weary and sick. I ran the last of the way and slipped quietly into the house. I groped for the stair railing in

3. "Luna": moon. "Virgin": Virgin Mary.

the dark and felt a warm hand take mine. Startled, I looked up into Ultima's brown, wrinkled face.

"You knew!" I whispered. I understood that she did not want my mother to hear.

"Sí," she replied.

"And the owl—" I gasped. My mind searched for answers, but my body was so tired that my knees buckled and I fell forward. As small and thin as Ultima was she had the strength to lift me in her arms and carry me into her room. She placed me on her bed and then by the light of a small, flickering candle she mixed one of her herbs in a tin cup, held it over the flame to warm, then gave it to me to drink.

"They killed Lupito," I said as I gulped the medicine.

"I know," she nodded. She prepared a new potion and with this she washed the cuts on my face and feet.

"Will he go to hell?" I asked.

"That is not for us to say, Antonio. The war-sickness was not taken out of him, he did not know what he was doing—"

"And the men on the bridge, my father!"

"Men will do what they must do," she answered. She sat on the bed by my side. Her voice was soothing, and the drink she had given me made me sleepy. The wild, frightening excitement in my body began to die.

"The ways of men are strange, and hard to learn," I heard her say.

"Will I learn them?" I asked. I felt the weight on my eyelids.

"You will learn much, you will see much," I heard her far-away voice. I felt a blanket cover me. I felt safe in the warm sweetness of the room. Outside the owl sang its dark questioning to the night, and I slept.

But even into my deep sleep my dreams came. In my dream I saw my three brothers. I saw them as I remembered them before they went away to war, which seemed so very long ago. They stood by the house that we rented in town and they looked across the river at the hills of the llano.

Father says that the town steals our freedom; he says that we must build a castle across the river, on the lonely hill of the mockingbirds. I think it was León who spoke first, he was the eldest, and his voice always had a sad note to it. But in the dark mist of the dream I could not be sure.

His heart has been heavy since we came to the town, the second figure spoke, his forefathers were men of the sea, the Márez people, they were conquistadores, men whose freedom was unbounded.

It was Andrew who said that! It was Andrew! I was sure because his voice was husky like his thick and sturdy body.

Father says the freedom of the wild horse is in the Márez blood, and his gaze is always westward. His fathers before him were vaqueros,[4] and so he expects us to be men of the llano. I was sure the third voice belonged to Eugene.

I longed to touch them. I was hungry for their company. Instead I spoke.

We must all gather around our father, I heard myself say. His dream is to ride westward in search of new adventure. He builds highways that stretch into the sun, and we must travel that road with him.

My brothers frowned. You are a Luna, they chanted in unison, you are to be a farmer-priest for mother!

---

4. Cowboys (Spanish).

The doves came to drink in the still pooh of the river and their cry was mournful in the darkness of my dream.

My brothers laughed. You are but a baby, Tony, you are our mother's dream. Stay and sleep to the doves cou-rou while we cross the mighty River of the Carp to build our father's castle in the hills.

I must go! I cried to the three dark figures. I must lift the muddy waters of the river in blessing to our new home!

Along the river the tormented cry of a lonely goddess filled the valley. The winding wail made the blood of men run cold.

It is la llorona,[5] my brothers cried in fear, the old witch who cries along the river banks and seeks the blood of boys and men to drink!

La llorona seeks the soul of Antonioooooooooo . . .

It is the soul of Lupito, they cried in fear, doomed to wander the river at night because the waters washed his soul away!

Lupito seeks his blessinggggggggggg . . .

It is neither! I shouted. I swung the dark robe of the priest over my shoulders then lifted my hands in the air. The mist swirled around me and sparks flew when I spoke. It is the presence of the river!

Save us, my brothers cried and cowered at my words.

I spoke to the presence of the river and it allowed my brothers to cross with their carpenter tools to build our castle on the hill.

Behind us I heard my mother moan and cry because with each turning of the sun her son was growing old . . .

1972

5. A ghost (Spanish); in Chicana/o and Mexican lore, a spurned mistress who drowned her children and was fated to eternally seek their recovery.

THOMAS PYNCHON
b. 1937

Thomas Pynchon has remained the most private of contemporary American writers, without so much as a photograph of him in circulation. A few facts are known: born on Long Island, graduated from Cornell University—where he was a student in Vladimir Nabokov's European literature course—in the late 1950s, served a term in the navy, and now lives—it is said—in southern (or is it northern?) California. Beyond that, silence, which has been broken only by seven strange and distinctive novels, plus a few short stories.

"Entropy," one of Pynchon's first publications (1960), is printed here as an introduction to his work. Its thematics of an elusive order within radical disorder anticipates his first novel, *V.* (1963), particularly in its reference to modern physics. That complex novel cannot be understood by reference to convenient fictional signposts. Although it showed an indebtedness to Faulkner and Joyce (an indebtedness shared by most serious American novelists), Pynchon's style was already wholly his own. In writing that was by turns labyrinthine, eloquent, and colloquial, he showed a particular fondness for imitating and parodying various styles. But instead of disparaging or minimizing their subjects, these imitations and parodies radiated a generous exuberance that extended to the many characters who inhabit *V.* and whose individual paranoias—Pynchon's word to characterize attempts to make connections between events—propel them into unbelievably complicated and absurd plots. The interest of *V.* was largely in the inventiveness with which Pynchon developed those plots, which might involve anything from diplomatic spy stories in nineteenth-century Africa to the bombing of Malta during World War II to the surgical reconstruction of a young woman's nose to a hunt for alligators in New York City sewers.

The comic talent shown in various New York episodes from *V.* was also evident in *The Crying of Lot 49* (1966). This short, perfectly controlled novel teases us and itself with questions about the meaning of our American heritage, as embodied in the form of the mysterious legacy left to its heroine, Oedipa Maas. (The jokey yet portentous name exemplifies Pynchon's way of playing at "significance.") What is the connection between this legacy and the mysterious alternative to the U.S. Postal System on which Oedipa believes she has stumbled? Is there a secret network of alienated citizens carrying on their lives outside the ordinary systems and institutions of American life? Or is it all Oedipa's delusion, her private paranoia? These questions are considered through a style that continually surprises and unsettles us, though it is less discontinuous than *V.*'s. In Pynchon's world everything serious has its silly aspects (inspired by the Marx Brothers and countless other comic acts), while bits of trivia and foolery are suddenly elevated, through the style, into objects of sublime contemplation—as at the novel's end, when Oedipa thinks of "squatters" who "slept in junkyards in the stripped shells of wrecked Plymouths, or even, daring, spent the night up some pole in a lineman's tent like caterpillars, swung among a web of telephone wires, living in the very copper rigging and secular miracle of communication, untroubled by the dumb voltages flickering their miles, the night long, in the thousands of unheard messages." Often Pynchon's sentences enact the daring freedom he admires, in contrast to the institutions of a technological society.

Pynchon's longest and most daring and exhaustive effort came with the publication, in 1973, of *Gravity's Rainbow.* This encyclopedic fantasy operates through brilliant improvisations, tall tales, obscene parables, and burlesque stage routines, all of which work together into a story of supersonic capabilities and annihilative retributions. A huge cast of characters, each with a crazy name and a plot to unravel, is located all over the map, but mainly in World War II London and in postwar Germany. As the four main and the countless subsidiary plots take shape, characters—and the reader—attempt to "read" the messages flickering, the dumb intent to communicate, in the most casual as well as the most portentous sign. Pynchon's knowingness and fascination with popular culture are overwhelmingly evident in *Gravity's Rainbow,* as is his preoccupation with the lore of theoretical science, of obscure historical tales, and of contemporary comic books. No one denies the formidably encyclopedic nature of this astonishing effort; the question is, as Warner Berthoff has asked it, whether that effort may not also be "encyclopedically monotonous and static." More readers begin *Gravity's Rainbow* than finish it.

After 1973, except for the publication in 1984 of some of his early stories (in *Slow Learner*), all was silent on the Pynchon front until *Vineland* appeared in 1990, followed by *Mason & Dixon* in 1997 and *Against the Day* in 2006. *Vineland* is wonderful on the California terrain and has much free wheeling and funny inventiveness; at other times Pynchon seems to be flogging his material and repeating himself. *Mason & Dixon*, about the plotters of the line that would differentiate the American North and South, is written in the manner of his more ambitious works, a massive "mega-novel" that by its very excesses of character, plot, and references to history (arcane and otherwise) seeks to overwhelm the reader with its display of authority. *Against the Day* (2006) and *Inherent Vice* (2009) have more conventional subjects—family-revenge drama and crime solving, respectively—yet the author still dotes on fantastic inventions and overwritten prose. But although there is still no consensus on his stature as an enduring American writer, there is general recognition of the quirky, uncanny exactitude of his imagination. Pynchon's theatrical spell-bindings as a man of metaphor, his feats of association (in Robert Frost's phrase), are employed on subjects—like the rocket in *Gravity's Rainbow*—that were thought to be beyond words. For daring, wit, and exuberance, no contemporary writer excels him.

The following text is from *Slow Learner* (1984).

Entropy

> Boris has just given me a summary of his views. He is a weather prophet. The weather will continue bad, he says. There will be more calamities, more death, more despair. Not the slightest indication of a change anywhere. . . . We must get into step, a lockstep toward the prison of death. There is no escape. The weather will not change.
>
> —*Tropic of Cancer*[1]

Downstairs, Meatball Mulligan's lease-breaking party was moving into its 40th hour. On the kitchen floor, amid a litter of empty champagne fifths, were Sandor Rojas and three friends, playing spit in the ocean and staying awake on Heidseck[2] and benzedrine pills. In the living room Duke, Vincent, Krinkles and Paco sat crouched over a 15-inch speaker which had been bolted into the top of a wastepaper basket, listening to 27 watts' worth of *The Heroes' Gate at Kiev*.[3] They all wore hornrimmed sunglasses and rapt expressions, and smoked funny-looking cigarettes which contained not, as you might expect, tobacco, but an adulterated form of *cannabis sativa*.[4] This group was the Duke di Angelis quartet. They recorded for a local label called Tambú and had to their credit one 10' LP entitled *Songs of Outer Space*. From time to time one of them would flick the ashes from his cigarette into the speaker cone to watch them dance around. Meatball himself was sleeping over by the window, holding an empty magnum to his chest as if it were a teddy bear. Several government girls, who worked for people like the State Department and NSA, had passed out on couches, chairs and in one case the bathroom sink.

This was in early February of '57 and back then there were a lot of American expatriates around Washington, D.C., who would talk, every time they met you, about how someday they were going to go over to Europe for real but right now it seemed they were working for the government. Everyone saw a fine irony in this. They would stage, for instance, polyglot parties where the newcomer was sort of ignored if he couldn't carry on simultaneous

---

1. Novel (1934) by the American writer Henry Miller (1891–1980).
2. A very dry champagne.
3. Music by the Russian composer Modest Mus-

sorgsky (1839–1881) from his *Pictures at an Exhibition*.
4. Marijuana.

The Gerry Mulligan Quartet premiered in Los Angeles in 1952 with Mulligan on baritone saxophone, Chet Baker on trumpet, Bob Whitlock on bass, and Chico Hamilton on drums. There was no pianist, an innovation for small ensemble jazz, leaving harmonic silences for the other instruments to fill.

conversations in three or four languages. They would haunt Armenian delicatessens for weeks at a stretch and invite you over for bulghour and lamb in tiny kitchens whose walls were covered with bullfight posters. They would have affairs with sultry girls from Andalucía or the Midi[5] who studied economics at Georgetown. Their Dôme was a collegiate Rathskeller out on Wisconsin Avenue called the Old Heidelberg and they had to settle for cherry blossoms instead of lime trees when spring came, but in its lethargic way their life provided, as they said, kicks.

At the moment, Meatball's party seemed to be gathering its second wind. Outside there was rain. Rain splatted against the tar paper on the roof and was fractured into a fine spray off the noses, eyebrows and lips of wooden gargoyles under the eaves, and ran like drool down the windowpanes. The day before, it had snowed and the day before that there had been winds of gale force and before that the sun had made the city glitter bright as April, though the calendar read early February. It is a curious season in Washington, this false spring. Somewhere in it are Lincoln's Birthday and the Chinese New Year, and a forlornness in the streets because cherry blossoms are weeks away still and, as Sarah Vaughan has put it, spring will be a little late this year. Generally crowds like the one which would gather in the Old Hei-

5. Regions of Spain and France, respectively.

delberg on weekday afternoons to drink Würtzburger and to sing Lili Marlene (not to mention The Sweetheart of Sigma Chi) are inevitably and incorrigibly Romantic. And as every good Romantic knows, the soul (*spiritus, ruach, pneuma*) is nothing, substantially, but air; it is only natural that warpings in the atmosphere should be recapitulated in those who breathe it. So that over and above the public components—holidays, tourist attractions—there are private meanderings, linked to the climate as if this spell were a *stretto* passage in the year's fugue: haphazard weather, aimless loves, unpredicted commitments: months one can easily spend *in* fugue, because oddly enough, later on, winds, rains, passions of February and March are never remembered in that city, it is as if they had never been.

The last bass notes of *The Heroes' Gate* boomed up through the floor and woke Callisto from an uneasy sleep. The first thing he became aware of was a small bird he had been holding gently between his hands, against his body. He turned his head sidewise on the pillow to smile down at it, at its blue hunched-down head and sick, lidded eyes, wondering how many more nights he would have to give it warmth before it was well again. He had been holding the bird like that for three days: it was the only way he knew to restore its health. Next to him the girl stirred and whimpered, her arm thrown across her face. Mingled with the sounds of the rain came the first tentative, querulous morning voices of the other birds, hidden in philodendrons and small fan palms: patches of scarlet, yellow and blue laced through this Rousseau-like[6] fantasy, this hothouse jungle it had taken him seven years to weave together. Hermetically sealed, it was a tiny enclave of regularity in the city's chaos, alien to the vagaries of the weather, of national politics, of any civil disorder. Through trial-and-error Callisto had perfected its ecological balance, with the help of the girl its artistic harmony, so that the swayings of its plant life, the stirrings of its birds and human inhabitants were all as integral as the rhythms of a perfectly-executed mobile. He and the girl could no longer, of course, be omitted from that sanctuary; they had become necessary to its unity. What they needed from outside was delivered. They did not go out.

"Is he all right," she whispered. She lay like a tawny question mark facing him, her eyes suddenly huge and dark and blinking slowly. Callisto ran a finger beneath the feathers at the base of the bird's neck; caressed it gently. "He's going to be well, I think. See: he hears his friends beginning to wake up." The girl had heard the rain and the birds even before she was fully awake. Her name was Aubade: she was part French and part Annamese, and she lived on her own curious and lonely planet, where the clouds and the odor of poincianas, the bitterness of wine and the accidental fingers at the small of her back or feathery against her breasts came to her reduced inevitably to the terms of sound: of music which emerged at intervals from a howling darkness of discordancy. "Aubade," he said, "go see." Obedient, she arose; padded to the window, pulled aside the drapes and after a moment said: "It is 37. Still 37." Callisto frowned. "Since Tuesday, then," he said. "No change." Henry Adams,[7]

---

6. Henri Rousseau (1844–1910), French primitive painter of exotic landscapes.
7. American historian and man of letters (1838–1918) whose writings explore the nature of power, cultural figurations of which ranged from the Virgin Mary to the modern dynamo engine.

three generations before his own, had stared aghast at Power; Callisto found himself now in much the same state over Thermodynamics, the inner life of that power, realizing like his predecessor that the Virgin and the dynamo stand as much for love as for power; that the two are indeed identical; and that love therefore not only makes the world go round but also makes the boccie ball spin, the nebula precess. It was this latter or sidereal element which disturbed him. The cosmologists had predicted an eventual heat-death for the universe (something like Limbo: form and motion abolished, heat-energy identical at every point in it); the meteorologists, day-to-day, staved it off by contradicting with a reassuring array of varied temperatures.

But for three days now, despite the changeful weather, the mercury had stayed at 37 degrees Fahrenheit. Leery at omens of apocalypse, Callisto shifted beneath the covers. His fingers pressed the bird more firmly, as if needing some pulsing or suffering assurance of an early break in the temperature.

It was that last cymbal crash that did it. Meatball was hurled wincing into consciousness as the synchronized wagging of heads over the wastebasket stopped. The final hiss remained for an instant in the room, then melted into the whisper of rain outside. "Aarrgghh," announced Meatball in the silence, looking at the empty magnum. Krinkles, in slow motion, turned, smiled and held out a cigarette. "Tea time, man," he said. "No, no," said Meatball. "How many times I got to tell you guys. Not at my place. You ought to know, Washington is lousy with Feds." Krinkles looked wistful. "Jeez, Meatball," he said, "you don't want to do nothing no more." "Hair of dog," said Meatball. "Only hope. Any juice left?" He began to crawl toward the kitchen. "No champagne, I don't think," Duke said. "Case of tequila behind the icebox." They put on an Earl Bostic[8] side. Meatball paused at the kitchen door, glowering at Sandor Rojas. "Lemons," he said after some thought. He crawled to the refrigerator and got out three lemons and some cubes, found the tequila and set about restoring order to his nervous system. He drew blood once cutting the lemons and had to use two hands squeezing them and his foot to crack the ice tray but after about ten minutes he found himself, through some miracle, beaming down into a monster tequila sour. "That looks yummy," Sandor Rojas said. "How about you make me one." Meatball blinked at him. "Kitchi lofass a shegithe,"[9] he replied automatically, and wandered away into the bathroom. "I say," he called out a moment later to no one in particular. "I say, there seems to be a girl or something sleeping in the sink." He took her by the shoulders and shook. "Wha," she said. "You don't look too comfortable," Meatball said. "Well," she agreed. She stumbled to the shower, turned on the cold water and sat down crosslegged in the spray. "That's better," she smiled.

"Meatball," Sandor Rojas yelled from the kitchen. "Somebody is trying to come in the window. A burglar, I think. A second-story man." "What are you worrying about," Meatball said. "We're on the third floor." He loped back into the kitchen. A shaggy woebegone figure stood out on the fire escape, raking his fingernails down the windowpane. Meatball opened the window. "Saul," he said.

---

8. American jazz musician (1913–1965) who also recorded rhythm-and-blues material.

9. Little horse prick in your asshole (Hungarian).

"Sort of wet out," Saul said. He climbed in, dripping. "You heard, I guess."

"Miriam left you," Meatball said, "or something, is all I heard."

There was a sudden flurry of knocking at the front door. "Do come in," Sandor Rojas called. The door opened and there were three coeds from George Washington, all of whom were majoring in philosophy. They were each holding a gallon of Chianti. Sandor leaped up and dashed into the living room. "We heard there was a party," one blonde said. "Young blood," Sandor shouted. He was an ex-Hungarian freedom fighter who had easily the worst chronic case of what certain critics of the middle class have called Don Giovannism in the District of Columbia. *Purchè porti la gonnella, voi sapete quel che fa.*[1] Like Pavlov's dog: a contralto voice or a whiff of Arpège and Sandor would begin to salivate. Meatball regarded the trio blearily as they filed into the kitchen; he shrugged. "Put the wine in the icebox," he said, "and good morning."

Aubade's neck made a golden bow as she bent over the sheets of foolscap, scribbling away in the green murk of the room. "As a young man at Princeton," Callisto was dictating, nestling the bird against the gray hairs of his chest, "Callisto had learned a mnemonic device for remembering the Laws of Thermodynamics: you can't win, things are going to get worse before they get better, who says they're going to get better. At the age of 54, confronted with Gibbs'[2] notion of the universe, he suddenly realized that undergraduate cant had been oracle, after all. That spindly maze of equations became, for him, a vision of ultimate, cosmic heat-death. He had known all along, of course, that nothing but a theoretical engine or system ever runs at 100% efficiency; and about the theorem of Clausius, which states that the entropy of an isolated system always continually increases. It was not, however, until Gibbs and Boltzmann[3] brought to this principle the methods of statistical mechanics that the horrible significance of it all dawned on him: only then did he realize that the isolated system—galaxy, engine, human being, culture, whatever—must evolve spontaneously toward the Condition of the More Probable. He was forced, therefore, in the sad dying fall of middle age, to a radical reëvaluation of everything he had learned up to then; all the cities and seasons and casual passions of his days had now to be looked at in a new and elusive light. He did not know if he was equal to the task. He was aware of the dangers of the reductive fallacy and, he hoped, strong enough not to drift into the graceful decadence of an enervated fatalism. His had always been a vigorous, Italian sort of pessimism: like Machiavelli, he allowed the forces of *virtù* and *fortuna*[4] to be about 50/50; but the equations now introduced a random factor which pushed the odds to some unutterable and indeterminate ratio which he found himself afraid to calculate." Around him loomed vague hothouse shapes; the pitifully small heart fluttered against his own. Counterpointed against his

1. As long as she wears a skirt, you know what he does (Italian); from Lorenzo da Ponte's libretto to Mozart's opera *Don Giovanni* (1787).
2. Josiah Willard Gibbs (1839–1903), American physicist and chemist, a founder of statistical mechanics.
3. Ludwig Boltzmann (1844–1906), Austrian

physicist who studied how atoms determine visual properties of matter. Rudolf Clausius (1822–1888), German physicist, developer of the science of thermodynamics.
4. Niccolò Machiavelli (1469–1527), Florentine statesman and writer on government, contrasted virtuous behavior (*virtù*) with good luck (*fortuna*).

words the girl heard the chatter of birds and fitful car honkings scattered along the wet morning and Earl Bostic's alto rising in occasional wild peaks through the floor. The architectonic purity of her world was constantly threatened by such hints of anarchy: gaps and excrescences and skew lines, and a shifting or tilting of planes to which she had continually to readjust lest the whole structure shiver into a disarray of discrete and meaningless signals. Callisto had described the process once as a kind of "feedback": she crawled into dreams each night with a sense of exhaustion, and a desperate resolve never to relax that vigilance. Even in the brief periods when Callisto made love to her, soaring above the bowing of taut nerves in haphazard double-stops would be the one singing string of her determination.

"Nevertheless," continued Callisto, "he found in entropy or the measure of disorganization for a closed system an adequate metaphor to apply to certain phenomena in his own world. He saw, for example, the younger generation responding to Madison Avenue with the same spleen his own had once reserved for Wall Street: and in American 'consumerism' discovered a similar tendency from the least to the most probable, from differentiation to sameness, from ordered individuality to a kind of chaos. He found himself, in short, restating Gibbs' prediction in social terms, and envisioned a heat-death for his culture in which ideas, like heat-energy, would no longer be transferred, since each point in it would ultimately have the same quantity of energy; and intellectual motion would, accordingly, cease." He glanced up suddenly. "Check it now," he said. Again she rose and peered out at the thermometer. "37," she said. "The rain has stopped." He bent his head quickly and held his lips against a quivering wing. "Then it will change soon," he said, trying to keep his voice firm.

Sitting on the stove Saul was like any big rag doll that a kid has been taking out some incomprehensible rage on. "What happened," Meatball said. "If you feel like talking, I mean."

"Of course I feel like talking," Saul said. "One thing I did, I slugged her."

"Discipline must be maintained."

"Ha, ha. I wish you'd been there. Oh Meatball, it was a lovely fight. She ended up throwing a *Handbook of Chemistry and Physics* at me, only it missed and went through the window, and when the glass broke I reckon something in her broke too. She stormed out of the house crying, out in the rain. No raincoat or anything."

"She'll be back."

"No."

"Well!" Soon Meatball said: "It was something earthshattering, no doubt. Like who is better, Sal Mineo or Ricky Nelson."[5]

"What it was about," Saul said, "was communication theory. Which of course makes it very hilarious."

"I don't know anything about communication theory."

"Neither does my wife. Come right down to it, who does? That's the joke."

When Meatball saw the kind of smile Saul had on his face he said: "Maybe you would like tequila or something."

5. Contemporary figures from film and television who were icons of bad and good teenage behavior, respectively.

"No. I mean, I'm sorry. It's a field you can go off the deep end in, is all. You get where you're watching all the time for security cops: behind bushes, around corners. MUFFET is top secret."

"Wha."

"Multi-unit factorial field electronic tabulator."

"You were fighting about that."

"Miriam has been reading science fiction again. That and *Scientific American*. It seems she is, as we say, bugged at this idea of computers acting like people. I made the mistake of saying you can just as well turn that around, and talk about human behavior like a program fed into an IBM machine."

"Why not," Meatball said.

"Indeed, why not. In fact it is sort of crucial to communication, not to mention information theory. Only when I said that she hit the roof. Up went the balloon. And I can't figure out *why*. If anybody should know why, I should. I refuse to believe the government is wasting taxpayers' money on me, when it has so many bigger and better things to waste it on."

Meatball made a moue. "Maybe she thought you were acting like a cold, dehumanized amoral scientist type."

"My god," Saul flung up an arm. "Dehumanized. How much more human can I get? I worry, Meatball, I do. There are Europeans wandering around North Africa these days with their tongues torn out of their heads because those tongues have spoken the wrong words. Only the Europeans thought they were the right words."

"Language barrier," Meatball suggested.

Saul jumped down off the stove. "That," he said, angry, "is a good candidate for sick joke of the year. No, ace, it is *not* a barrier. If it is anything it's a kind of leakage. Tell a girl: 'I love you.' No trouble with two-thirds of that, it's a closed circuit. Just you and she. But that nasty four-letter word in the middle, *that's* the one you have to look out for. Ambiguity. Redundance. Irrelevance, even. Leakage. All this is noise. Noise screws up your signal, makes for disorganization in the circuit."

Meatball shuffled around. "Well, now, Saul," he muttered, "you're sort of, I don't know, expecting a lot from people. I mean, you know. What it is is, most of the things we say, I guess, are mostly noise."

"Ha! Half of what you just said, for example."

"Well, you do it too."

"I know." Saul smiled grimly. "It's a bitch, ain't it."

"I bet that's what keeps divorce lawyers in business. Whoops."

"Oh I'm not sensitive. Besides," frowning, "you're right. You find I think that most 'successful' marriages—Miriam and me, up to last night—are sort of founded on compromises. You never run at top efficiency, usually all you have is a minimum basis for a workable thing. I believe the phrase is Togetherness."

"Aarrgghh."

"Exactly. You find that one a bit noisy, don't you. But the noise content is different for each of us because you're a bachelor and I'm not. Or wasn't. The hell with it."

"Well sure," Meatball said, trying to be helpful, "you were using different words. By 'human being' you meant something that you can look at like it was a computer. It helps you think better on the job or something. But Miriam meant something entirely—"

"The hell with it."

Meatball fell silent. "I'll take that drink," Saul said after a while.

The card game had been abandoned and Sandor's friends were slowly getting wasted on tequila. On the living room couch, one of the coeds and Krinkles were engaged in amorous conversation. "No," Krinkles was saying, "no, I can't put Dave *down*. In fact I give Dave a lot of credit, man. Especially considering his accident and all." The girl's smile faded. "How terrible," she said. "What accident?" "Hadn't you heard?" Krinkles said. "When Dave was in the army, just a private E-2, they sent him down to Oak Ridge on special duty. Something to do with the Manhattan Project.[6] He was handling hot stuff one day and got an overdose of radiation. So now he's got to wear lead gloves all the time." She shook her head sympathetically. "What an awful break for a piano player."

Meatball had abandoned Saul to a bottle of tequila and was about to go to sleep in a closet when the front door flew open and the place was invaded by five enlisted personnel of the U.S. Navy, all in varying stages of abomination. "This is the place," shouted a fat, pimply seaman apprentice who had lost his white hat. "This here is the hoorhouse that chief was telling us about." A stringy-looking 3rd class boatswain's mate pushed him aside and cased the living room. "You're right, Slab," he said. "But it don't look like much, even for Stateside. I seen better tail in Naples, Italy." "How much, hey," boomed a large seaman with adenoids, who was holding a Mason jar full of white lightning. "Oh, my god," said Meatball.

Outside the temperature remained constant at 37 degrees Fahrenheit. In the hothouse Aubade stood absently caressing the branches of a young mimosa, hearing a motif of sap-rising, the rough and unresolved anticipatory theme of those fragile pink blossoms which, it is said, insure fertility. That music rose in a tangled tracery: arabesques of order competing fugally with the improvised discords of the party downstairs, which peaked sometimes in cusps and ogees of noise. That precious signal-to-noise ratio, whose delicate balance required every calorie of her strength, seesawed inside the small tenuous skull as she watched Callisto, sheltering the bird. Callisto was trying to confront any idea of the heat-death now, as he nuzzled the feathery lump in his hands. He sought correspondences. Sade, of course. And Temple Drake, gaunt and hopeless in her little park in Paris, at the end of *Sanctuary*.[7] Final equilibrium. *Nightwood*.[8] And the tango. Any tango, but more than any perhaps the sad sick dance in Stravinsky's *L'Histoire du Soldat*.[9] He thought back: what had tango music been for them after the war, what meanings had he missed in all the stately coupled automatons in the *cafés'-dansants*,[1] or in the metronomes which had ticked behind the eyes of his own partners? Not even the clean constant winds of Switzerland could cure the *grippe espagnole*.[2] Stravinsky had had it, they all

6. The research that developed the atomic bomb for use at the end of World War II.
7. Sexually notorious novel published in 1931 by the American writer William Faulkner (1897–1962).
8. Novel published in 1936 by the American

expatriate writer Djuna Barnes (1892–1982).
9. A 1918 work by the Russian composer Igor Stravinsky (1882–1971).
1. Café dancers (French).
2. Spanish flu (French).

had had it. And how many musicians were left after Passchendaele, after the Marne?[3] It came down in this case to seven: violin, double-bass. Clarinet, bassoon. Cornet, trombone. Tympani. Almost as if any tiny troupe of saltimbanques had set about conveying the same information as a full pit-orchestra. There was hardly a full complement left in Europe. Yet with violin and tympani Stravinsky had managed to communicate in that tango the same exhaustion, the same airlessness one saw in the slicked-down youths who were trying to imitate Vernon Castle, and in their mistresses, who simply did not care. *Ma maîtresse*.[4] Celeste. Returning to Nice after the second war he had found that café replaced by a perfume shop which catered to American tourists. And no secret vestige of her in the cobblestones or in the old pension next door; no perfume to match her breath heavy with the sweet Spanish wine she always drank. And so instead he had purchased a Henry Miller novel and left for Paris,[5] and read the book on the train so that when he arrived he had been given at least a little forewarning. And saw that Celeste and the others and even Temple Drake were not all that had changed. "Aubade," he said, "my head aches." The sound of his voice generated in the girl an answering scrap of melody. Her movement toward the kitchen, the towel, the cold water, and his eyes following her formed a weird and intricate canon; as she placed the compress on his forehead his sigh of gratitude seemed to signal a new subject, another series of modulations.

"No," Meatball was still saying, "no, I'm afraid not. This is not a house of ill repute. I'm sorry, really I am." Slab was adamant. "But the chief said," he kept repeating. The seaman offered to swap the moonshine for a good piece. Meatball looked around frantically, as if seeking assistance. In the middle of the room, the Duke di Angelis quartet were engaged in a historic moment. Vincent was seated and the others standing: they were going through the motions of a group having a session, only without instruments. "I say," Meatball said. Duke moved his head a few times, smiled faintly, lit a cigarette, and eventually caught sight of Meatball. "Quiet, man," he whispered. Vincent began to fling his arms around, his fists clenched; then, abruptly, was still, then repeated the performance. This went on for a few minutes while Meatball sipped his drink moodily. The navy had withdrawn to the kitchen. Finally at some invisible signal the group stopped tapping their feet and Duke grinned and said, "At least we ended together."

Meatball glared at him. "I say," he said. "I have this new conception, man," Duke said. "You remember your namesake. You remember Gerry."

"No," said Meatball. "I'll remember April, if that's any help."

"As a matter of fact," Duke said, "it was Love for Sale. Which shows how much you know. The point is, it was Mulligan, Chet Baker[6] and that crew, way back then, out yonder. You dig?"

"Baritone sax," Meatball said. "Something about a baritone sax."

"But no piano, man. No guitar. Or accordion. You know what that means."

3. Battle sites in World War I noted for their extremely high casualties.
4. My mistress (French).
5. Miller was famous for his strongly sexual novels written in Paris during the 1930s.
6. In 1952 the American jazz musicians Gerry Mulligan (1927–1996) and Chet Baker (1929–1988) became famous for their revolutionary pianoless quartet.

"Not exactly," Meatball said.

"Well first let me just say, that I am no Mingus, no John Lewis.[7] Theory was never my strong point. I mean things like reading were always difficult for me and all—"

"I know," Meatball said drily. "You got your card taken away because you changed key on Happy Birthday at a Kiwanis Club picnic."

"Rotarian. But it occurred to me, in one of these flashes of insight, that if that first quartet of Mulligan's had no piano, it could only mean one thing."

"No chords," said Paco, the baby-faced bass.

"What he is trying to say," Duke said, "is no root chords. Nothing to listen to while you blow a horizontal line. What one does in such a case is, one *thinks* the roots."

A horrified awareness was dawning on Meatball. "And the next logical extension," he said.

"Is to think everything," Duke announced with simple dignity. "Roots, line, everything."

Meatball looked at Duke, awed. "But," he said.

"Well," Duke said modestly, "there are a few bugs to work out."

"But," Meatball said.

"Just listen," Duke said. "You'll catch on." And off they went again into orbit, presumably somewhere around the asteroid belt. After a while Krinkles made an embouchure and started moving his fingers and Duke clapped his hand to his forehead. "Oaf!" he roared. "The new head we're using, you remember, I wrote last night?" "Sure," Krinkles said, "the new head. I come in on the bridge. All your heads I come in then." "Right," Duke said. "So why—" "Wha," said Krinkles, "16 bars, I wait, I come in—" "16?" Duke said. "No. No, Krinkles. Eight you waited. You want me to sing it? A cigarette that bears a lipstick's traces, an airline ticket to romantic places." Krinkles scratched his head. "These Foolish Things, you mean." "Yes," Duke said, "yes, Krinkles. Bravo." "Not I'll Remember April," Krinkles said. "*Minghe morte,*"[8] said Duke. "I *figured* we were playing it a little slow," Krinkles said. Meatball chuckled. "Back to the old drawing board," he said. "No, man," Duke said, "back to the airless void." And they took off again, only it seemed Paco was playing in G sharp while the rest were in E flat, so they had to start all over.

In the kitchen two of the girls from George Washington and the sailors were singing Let's All Go Down and Piss on the Forrestal.[9] There was a two-handed, bilingual *morra*[1] game on over by the icebox. Saul had filled several paper bags with water and was sitting on the fire escape, dropping them on passersby in the street. A fat government girl in a Bennington sweatshirt, recently engaged to an ensign attached to the Forrestal, came charging into the kitchen, head lowered, and butted Slab in the stomach. Figuring this was as good an excuse for a fight as any, Slab's buddies piled in. The *morra* players were nose-to-nose, screaming *trois, sette* at the tops of

---

7. Charles Mingus (1922–1979) and John Lewis (1920–2001), American jazz musicians noted for their compositions based in musical theory.
8. Dead prick (Italian).
9. Aircraft carrier in the U.S. Navy.
1. Finger game originally played by Italians. The commands are numbers; below, three (*trois*, French) and seven (*sette*, Italian).

their lungs. From the shower the girl Meatball had taken out of the sink announced that she was drowning. She had apparently sat on the drain and the water was now up to her neck. The noise in Meatball's apartment had reached a sustained, ungodly crescendo.

Meatball stood and watched, scratching his stomach lazily. The way he figured, there were only about two ways he could cope: (a) lock himself in the closet and maybe eventually they would all go away, or (b) try to calm everybody down, one by one. (a) was certainly the more attractive alternative. But then he started thinking about that closet. It was dark and stuffy and he would be alone. He did not feature being alone. And then this crew off the good ship Lollipop[2] or whatever it was might take it upon themselves to kick down the closet door, for a lark. And if that happened he would be, at the very least, embarrassed. The other way was more a pain in the neck, but probably better in the long run.

So he decided to try and keep his lease-breaking party from deteriorating into total chaos: he gave wine to the sailors and separated the *morra* players; he introduced the fat government girl to Sandor Rojas, who would keep her out of trouble; he helped the girl in the shower to dry off and get into bed; he had another talk with Saul; he called a repairman for the refrigerator, which someone had discovered was on the blink. This is what he did until nightfall, when most of the revellers had passed out and the party trembled on the threshold of its third day.

Upstairs Callisto, helpless in the past, did not feel the faint rhythm inside the bird begin to slacken and fail. Aubade was by the window, wandering the ashes of her own lovely world; the temperature held steady, the sky had become a uniform darkening gray. Then something from downstairs—a girl's scream, an overturned chair, a glass dropped on the floor, he would never know what exactly—pierced that private time-warp and he became aware of the faltering, the constriction of muscles, the tiny tossings of the bird's head; and his own pulse began to pound more fiercely, as if trying to compensate. "Aubade," he called weakly, "he's dying." The girl, flowing and rapt, crossed the hothouse to gaze down at Callisto's hands. The two remained like that, poised, for one minute, and two, while the heartbeat ticked a graceful diminuendo down at last into stillness. Callisto raised his head slowly. "I held him," he protested, impotent with the wonder of it, "to give him the warmth of my body. Almost as if I were communicating life to him, or a sense of life. What has happened? Has the transfer of heat ceased to work? Is there no more . . ." He did not finish.

"I was just at the window," she said. He sank back, terrified. She stood a moment more, irresolute; she had sensed his obsession long ago, realized somehow that that constant 37 was now decisive. Suddenly then, as if seeing the single and unavoidable conclusion to all this she moved swiftly to the window before Callisto could speak; tore away the drapes and smashed out the glass with two exquisite hands which came away bleeding and glistening with splinters; and turned to face the man on the bed and wait with him until the moment of equilibrium was reached, when 37 degrees

2. The subject of film and song popularized in the 1930s by the American child actress Shirley Temple.

Fahrenheit should prevail both outside and inside, and forever, and the hovering, curious dominant of their separate lives should resolve into a tonic of darkness and the final absence of all motion.

1984

RAYMOND CARVER
1938–1988

Minimal fiction; designer fiction; even "dirty fiction," a phrase the British magazine *Granta* used to characterize the new style of American writing that was supposedly polluting the realistic short story with unconventional, irrealistic techniques—these terms were tossed around by critics of an abruptly new style of work that at times seemed to dominate the 1980s. Popularized by Bobbie Ann Mason, Ann Beattie, Frederick Barthelme, and Barry Hannah as well, its chief practitioner was a master of fine arts graduate from the University of Iowa's Writers Workshop, Raymond Carver, whose collections *Will You Please Be Quiet, Please?* (1976), *What We Talk About When We Talk About Love* (1981), and *Cathedral* (1983) set the most imitated style of their generation. Moved to put some order to these many definitions, writer John Barth—whose nonrealistic, innovative work had helped characterize the writing of the decades before—coined the term Post-Alcoholic Blue-Collar Minimalist Hyperrealism to describe the school Carver may have inadvertently founded. A recovering alcoholic, Carver had worked as a janitor, sawmill hand, delivery person, and sales representative, suggesting the profile Barth had in mind. But more pertinent to the style of his fiction was his training at Iowa and teaching in creative writing programs at universities around the country. By the time of his death, his became the most accepted style in such academic programs and in the literary magazines they generated.

This style's success is important. With conventions of literary realism having been challenged and theorists questioning all such previously stable assumptions, readers of Barth, Donald Barthelme, Kurt Vonnegut, and other such experimenters may have felt that simple realism was no longer an up-to-date way in which to write. Raymond Carver proved that it was, and that previous challenges to realistic tradition had only made it all the more effective, especially when those challenges are incorporated in the new style. Carver's patient narration does not strive for a reader's suspension of disbelief. Rather, as in the introduction of the bizarre situation experienced in "Cathedral" (printed here), its plain, even flat statement presents matter unadorned by devices meant to persuade or convince. So a blind man wants to learn what the architecture of a cathedral suggests? Here it is, Carver's story says: what you see is what there is; take it or leave it; if you are blind, he will help you feel your way through, but never as a direction to meaning, only to an apprehension of the facts. Carver's characters are usually working-class people somewhat down on their luck. Often, alcohol figures in their lives, less as a stimulant than as a further depressant. Totally unexceptional, their failures, like their hopes, are small, even puny. But from such stripped-down essentials the author is able to write in a plain, simple manner, sticking to the absolute minimum so that no one can accuse him of trying to create illusions.

Much was made of Raymond Carver's alcoholism and recovery. He made no apologies for his hard, sometimes abusive life, the rigors of which contributed to ill health and an early death. His stories and poems have the same quiet toughness to them, not flamboyant in confrontation with life's meanness but dedicated to holding on against time's slowly destructive friction with a grittiness all their own.

The following text is from *Cathedral* (1983).

Cathedral

This blind man, an old friend of my wife's, he was on his way to spend the night. His wife had died. So he was visiting the dead wife's relatives in Connecticut. He called my wife from his in-laws'. Arrangements were made. He would come by train, a five-hour trip, and my wife would meet him at the station. She hadn't seen him since she worked for him one summer in Seattle ten years ago. But she and the blind man had kept in touch. They made tapes and mailed them back and forth. I wasn't enthusiastic about his visit. He was no one I knew. And his being blind bothered me. My idea of blindness came from the movies. In the movies, the blind moved slowly and never laughed. Sometimes they were led by seeing-eye dogs. A blind man in my house was not something I looked forward to.

That summer in Seattle she had needed a job. She didn't have any money. The man she was going to marry at the end of the summer was in officers' training school. He didn't have any money, either. But she was in love with the guy, and he was in love with her, etc. She'd seen something in the paper: HELP WANTED—*Reading to Blind Man*, and a telephone number. She phoned and went over, was hired on the spot. She'd worked with this blind man all summer. She read stuff to him, case studies, reports, that sort of thing. She helped him organize his little office in the county social-service department. They'd become good friends, my wife and the blind man. How do I know these things? She told me. And she told me something else. On her last day in the office, the blind man asked if he could touch her face. She agreed to this. She told me he touched his fingers to every part of her face, her nose—even her neck! She never forgot it. She even tried to write a poem about it. She was always trying to write a poem. She wrote a poem or two every year, usually after something really important had happened to her.

When we first started going out together, she showed me the poem. In the poem, she recalled his fingers and the way they had moved around over her face. In the poem, she talked about what she had felt at the time, about what went through her mind when the blind man touched her nose and lips. I can remember I didn't think much of the poem. Of course, I didn't tell her that. Maybe I just don't understand poetry. I admit it's not the first thing I reach for when I pick up something to read.

Anyway, this man who'd first enjoyed her favors, the officer-to-be, he'd been her childhood sweetheart. So okay. I'm saying that at the end of the summer she let the blind man run his hands over her face, said goodbye to him, married her childhood etc., who was now a commissioned officer, and she moved away from Seattle. But they'd kept in touch, she and the blind man. She made the first contact after a year or so. She called him up one night from an Air Force base in Alabama. She wanted to talk. They talked. He asked her to send him a tape and tell him about her life. She did this. She sent the tape. On the tape, she told the blind man about her husband and about their life together in the military. She told the blind man she loved her husband but she didn't like it where they lived and she didn't like it that he was a part of the military-industrial thing. She told the blind man she'd written a poem and he was in it. She told him that she was writing a poem about what it was like to be an Air Force officer's wife. The poem wasn't finished yet. She was still writing it. The blind man made a tape. He sent her the tape. She made a tape. This went on for years. My wife's officer was posted to one base and then another. She sent tapes from Moody AFB,[1] McGuire, McConnell, and finally Travis, near Sacramento, where one night she got to feeling lonely and cut off from people she kept losing in that moving-around life. She got to feeling she couldn't go it another step. She went in and swallowed all the pills and capsules in the medicine chest and washed them down with a bottle of gin. Then she got into a hot bath and passed out.

But instead of dying, she got sick. She threw up. Her officer—why should he have a name? he was the childhood sweetheart, and what more does he want?—came home from somewhere, found her, and called the ambulance. In time, she put it all on a tape and sent the tape to the blind man. Over the years, she put all kinds of stuff on tapes and sent the tapes off lickety-split. Next to writing a poem every year, I think it was her chief means of recreation. On one tape, she told the blind man she'd decided to live away from her officer for a time. On another tape, she told him about her divorce. She and I began going out, and of course she told her blind man about it. She told him everything, or so it seemed to me. Once she asked me if I'd like to hear the latest tape from the blind man. This was a year ago. I was on the tape, she said. So I said okay, I'd listen to it. I got us drinks and we settled down in the living room. We made ready to listen. First she inserted the tape into the player and adjusted a couple of dials. Then she pushed a lever. The tape squeaked and someone began to talk in this loud voice. She lowered the volume. After a few minutes of harmless chitchat, I heard my own name in the mouth of this stranger, this blind man I didn't even know! And then this: "From all you've said about him, I can only conclude—" But we were interrupted, a knock at the door, something, and we didn't ever get back to the tape. Maybe it was just as well. I'd heard all I wanted to.

Now this same blind man was coming to sleep in my house.

"Maybe I could take him bowling," I said to my wife. She was at the draining board doing scalloped potatoes. She put down the knife she was using and turned around.

"If you love me," she said, "you can do this for me. If you don't love me, okay. But if you had a friend, any friend, and the friend came to visit, I'd make him feel comfortable." She wiped her hands with the dish towel.

"I don't have any blind friends," I said.

"You don't have *any* friends," she said. "Period. Besides," she said, "goddam it, his wife's just died! Don't you understand that? The man's lost his wife!"

---

1. Air force base. Names of other air force bases follow.

I didn't answer. She'd told me a little about the blind man's wife. Her name was Beulah. Beulah! That's a name for a colored woman.

"Was his wife a Negro?" I asked.

"Are you crazy?" my wife said. "Have you just flipped or something?" She picked up a potato. I saw it hit the floor, then roll under the stove. "What's wrong with you?" she said. "Are you drunk?"

"I'm just asking," I said.

Right then my wife filled me in with more detail than I cared to know. I made a drink and sat at the kitchen table to listen. Pieces of the story began to fall into place.

Beulah had gone to work for the blind man the summer after my wife had stopped working for him. Pretty soon Beulah and the blind man had themselves a church wedding. It was a little wedding—who'd want to go to such a wedding in the first place?—just the two of them, plus the minister and the minister's wife. But it was a church wedding just the same. It was what Beulah had wanted, he'd said. But even then Beulah must have been carrying the cancer in her glands. After they had been inseparable for eight years—my wife's word, *inseparable*—Beulah's health went into a rapid decline. She died in a Seattle hospital room, the blind man sitting beside the bed and holding on to her hand. They'd married, lived and worked together, slept together—had sex, sure—and then the blind man had to bury her. All this without his having ever seen what the goddamned woman looked like. It was beyond my understanding. Hearing this, I felt sorry for the blind man for a little bit. And then I found myself thinking what a pitiful life this woman must have led. Imagine a woman who could never see herself as she was seen in the eyes of her loved one. A woman who could go on day after day and never receive the smallest compliment from her beloved. A woman whose husband could never read the expression on her face, be it misery or something better. Someone who could wear makeup or not—what difference to him? She could, if she wanted, wear green eyeshadow around one eye, a straight pin in her nostril, yellow slacks and purple shoes, no matter. And then to slip off into death, the blind man's hand on her hand, his blind eyes streaming tears—I'm imagining now—her last thought maybe this: that he never even knew what she looked like, and she on an express to the grave. Robert was left with a small insurance policy and half of a twenty-peso Mexican coin. The other half of the coin went into the box with her. Pathetic.

So when the time rolled around, my wife went to the depot to pick him up. With nothing to do but wait—sure, I blamed him for that—I was having a drink and watching the TV when I heard the car pull into the drive. I got up from the sofa with my drink and went to the window to have a look.

I saw my wife laughing as she parked the car. I saw her get out of the car and shut the door. She was still wearing a smile. Just amazing. She went around to the other side of the car to where the blind man was already starting to get out. This blind man, feature this, he was wearing a full beard! A beard on a blind man! Too much, I say. The blind man reached into the back seat and dragged out a suitcase. My wife took his arm, shut the car door, and, talking all the way, moved him down the drive and then up the steps to the front porch. I turned off the TV. I finished my drink, rinsed the glass, dried my hands. Then I went to the door.

My wife said, "I want you to meet Robert. Robert, this is my husband. I've told you all about him." She was beaming. She had this blind man by his coat sleeve.

The blind man let go of his suitcase and up came his hand.

I took it. He squeezed hard, held my hand, and then he let it go.

"I feel like we've already met," he boomed.

"Likewise," I said. I didn't know what else to say. Then I said, "Welcome. I've heard a lot about you." We began to move then, a little group, from the porch into the living room, my wife guiding him by the arm. The blind man was carrying his suitcase in his other hand. My wife said things like, "To your left here, Robert. That's right. Now watch it, there's a chair. That's it. Sit down right here. This is the sofa. We just bought this sofa two weeks ago."

I started to say something about the old sofa. I'd liked that old sofa. But I didn't say anything. Then I wanted to say something else, small-talk, about the scenic ride along the Hudson. How going *to* New York, you should sit on the right-hand side of the train, and coming *from* New York, the left-hand side.

"Did you have a good train ride?" I said. "Which side of the train did you sit on, by the way?"

"What a question, which side!" my wife said. "What's it matter which side?" she said.

"I just asked," I said.

"Right side," the blind man said. "I hadn't been on a train in nearly forty years. Not since I was a kid. With my folks. That's been a long time. I'd nearly forgotten the sensation. I have winter in my beard now," he said. "So I've been told, anyway. Do I look distinguished, my dear?" the blind man said to my wife.

"You look distinguished, Robert," she said. "Robert," she said. "Robert, it's just so good to see you."

My wife finally took her eyes off the blind man and looked at me. I had the feeling she didn't like what she saw. I shrugged.

I've never met, or personally known, anyone who was blind. This blind man was late forties, a heavy-set, balding man with stooped shoulders, as if he carried a great weight there. He wore brown slacks, brown shoes, a light-brown shirt, a tie, a sports coat. Spiffy. He also had this full beard. But he didn't use a cane and he didn't wear dark glasses. I'd always thought dark glasses were a must for the blind. Fact was, I wished he had a pair. At first glance, his eyes looked like anyone else's eyes. But if you looked close, there was something different about them. Too much white in the iris, for one thing, and the pupils seemed to move around in the sockets without his knowing it or being able to stop it. Creepy. As I stared at his face, I saw the left pupil turn in toward his nose while the other made an effort to keep in one place. But it was only an effort, for that eye was on the roam without his knowing it or wanting it to be.

I said, "Let me get you a drink. What's your pleasure? We have a little of everything. It's one of our pastimes."

"Bub, I'm a Scotch man myself," he said fast enough in this big voice.

"Right," I said. Bub! "Sure you are. I knew it."

He let his fingers touch his suitcase, which was sitting alongside the sofa. He was taking his bearings. I didn't blame him for that.

"I'll move that up to your room," my wife said.

"No, that's fine," the blind man said loudly. "It can go up when I go up."

"A little water with the Scotch?" I said.

"Very little," he said.

"I knew it," I said.

He said, "Just a tad. The Irish actor, Barry Fitzgerald?[2] I'm like that fellow. When I drink water, Fitzgerald said, I drink water. When I drink whiskey, I drink whiskey." My wife laughed. The blind man brought his hand up under his beard. He lifted his beard slowly and let it drop.

I did the drinks, three big glasses of Scotch with a splash of water in each. Then we made ourselves comfortable and talked about Robert's travels. First the long flight from the West Coast to Connecticut, we covered that. Then from Connecticut up here by train. We had another drink concerning that leg of the trip.

I remembered having read somewhere that the blind didn't smoke because, as speculation had it, they couldn't see the smoke they exhaled. I thought I knew that much and that much only about blind people. But this blind man smoked his cigarette down to the nubbin and then lit another one. This blind man filled his ashtray and my wife emptied it.

When we sat down at the table for dinner, we had another drink. My wife heaped Robert's plate with cube steak, scalloped potatoes, green beans. I buttered him up two slices of bread. I said, "Here's bread and butter for you." I swallowed some of my drink. "Now let us pray," I said, and the blind man lowered his head. My wife looked at me, her mouth agape. "Pray the phone won't ring and the food doesn't get cold," I said.

We dug in. We ate everything there was to eat on the table. We ate like there was no tomorrow. We didn't talk. We ate. We scarfed. We grazed that table. We were into serious eating. The blind man had right away located his foods, he knew just where everything was on his plate. I watched with admiration as he used his knife and fork on the meat. He'd cut two pieces of meat, fork the meat into his mouth, and then go all out for the scalloped potatoes, the beans next, and then he'd tear off a hunk of buttered bread and eat that. He'd follow this up with a big drink of milk. It didn't seem to bother him to use his fingers once in a while, either.

We finished everything, including half a strawberry pie. For a few moments, we sat as if stunned. Sweat beaded on our faces. Finally, we got up from the table and left the dirty plates. We didn't look back. We took ourselves into the living room and sank into our places again. Robert and my wife sat on the sofa. I took the big chair. We had us two or three more drinks while they talked about the major things that had come to pass for them in the past ten years. For the most part, I just listened. Now and then I joined in. I didn't want him to think I'd left the room, and I didn't want her to think I was feeling left out. They talked of things that had happened to them—to them!—these past ten years. I waited in vain to hear my name

2. Noted for his stock characterizations of Irish figures (often priests) in American films of the 1940s and 1950s.

on my wife's sweet lips: "And then my dear husband came into my life"—
something like that. But I heard nothing of the sort. More talk of Robert.
Robert had done a little of everything, it seemed, a regular blind jack-of-all-
trades. But most recently he and his wife had had an Amway[3] distributor-
ship, from which, I gathered, they'd earned their living, such as it was. The
blind man was also a ham radio operator. He talked in his loud voice about
conversations he'd had with fellow operators in Guam, in the Philippines,
in Alaska, and even in Tahiti. He said he'd have a lot of friends there if he
ever wanted to go visit those places. From time to time, he'd turn his blind
face toward me, put his hand under his beard, ask me something. How long
had I been in my present position? (Three years.) Did I like my work? (I
didn't.) Was I going to stay with it? (What were the options?) Finally, when
I thought he was beginning to run down, I got up and turned on the TV.

My wife looked at me with irritation. She was heading toward a boil.
Then she looked at the blind man and said, "Robert, do you have a TV?"

The blind man said, "My dear, I have two TVs. I have a color set and a
black-and-white thing, an old relic. It's funny, but if I turn the TV on, and
I'm always turning it on, I turn on the color set. It's funny, don't you think?"

I didn't know what to say to that. I had absolutely nothing to say to that.
No opinion. So I watched the news program and tried to listen to what the
announcer was saying.

"This is a color TV," the blind man said. "Don't ask me how, but I can tell."

"We traded up a while ago," I said.

The blind man had another taste of his drink. He lifted his beard, sniffed
it, and let it fall. He leaned forward on the sofa. He positioned his ashtray
on the coffee table, then put the lighter to his cigarette. He leaned back on
the sofa and crossed his legs at the ankles.

My wife covered her mouth, and then she yawned. She stretched. She
said, "I think I'll go upstairs and put on my robe. I think I'll change into
something else. Robert, you make yourself comfortable," she said.

"I'm comfortable," the blind man said.

"I want you to feel comfortable in this house," she said.

"I am comfortable," the blind man said.

After she'd left the room, he and I listened to the weather report and then to
the sports roundup. By that time, she'd been gone so long I didn't know if she
was going to come back. I thought she might have gone to bed. I wished she'd
come back downstairs. I didn't want to be left alone with a blind man. I asked
him if he wanted another drink, and he said sure. Then I asked if he wanted
to smoke some dope with me. I said I'd just rolled a number. I hadn't, but I
planned to do so in about two shakes.

"I'll try some with you," he said.

"Damn right," I said. "That's the stuff."

I got our drinks and sat down on the sofa with him. Then I rolled us two
fat numbers. I lit one and passed it. I brought it to his fingers. He took it
and inhaled.

"Hold it as long as you can," I said. I could tell he didn't know the first
thing.

---

3. A retail sales business operated by selling directly to consumers in their homes.

My wife came back downstairs wearing her pink robe and her pink slippers.

"What do I smell?" she said.

"We thought we'd have us some cannabis," I said.

My wife gave me a savage look. Then she looked at the blind man and said, "Robert, I didn't know you smoked."

He said, "I do now, my dear. There's a first time for everything. But I don't feel anything yet."

"This stuff is pretty mellow," I said. "This stuff is mild. It's dope you can reason with," I said. "It doesn't mess you up."

"Not much it doesn't, bub," he said, and laughed.

My wife sat on the sofa between the blind man and me. I passed her the number. She took it and toked and then passed it back to me. "Which way is this going?" she said. Then she said, "I shouldn't be smoking this. I can hardly keep my eyes open as it is. That dinner did me in. I shouldn't have eaten so much."

"It was the strawberry pie," the blind man said. "That's what did it," he said, and he laughed his big laugh. Then he shook his head.

"There's more strawberry pie," I said.

"Do you want some more, Robert?" my wife said.

"Maybe in a little while," he said.

We gave our attention to the TV. My wife yawned again. She said, "Your bed is made up when you feel like going to bed, Robert. I know you must have had a long day. When you're ready to go to bed, say so." She pulled his arm. "Robert?"

He came to and said, "I've had a real nice time. This beats tapes, doesn't it?"

I said, "Coming at you," and I put the number between his fingers. He inhaled, held the smoke, and then let it go. It was like he'd been doing it since he was nine years old.

"Thanks, bub," he said. "But I think this is all for me. I think I'm beginning to feel it," he said. He held the burning roach out for my wife.

"Same here," she said. "Ditto. Me, too." She took the roach and passed it to me. "I may just sit here for a while between you two guys with my eyes closed. But don't let me bother you, okay? Either one of you. If it bothers you, say so. Otherwise, I may just sit here with my eyes closed until you're ready to go to bed," she said. "Your bed's made up, Robert, when you're ready. It's right next to our room at the top of the stairs. We'll show you up when you're ready. You wake me up now, you guys, if I fall asleep." She said that and then she closed her eyes and went to sleep.

The news program ended. I got up and changed the channel. I sat back down on the sofa. I wished my wife hadn't pooped out. Her head lay across the back of the sofa, her mouth open. She'd turned so that her robe had slipped away from her legs, exposing a juicy thigh. I reached to draw her robe back over her, and it was then that I glanced at the blind man. What the hell! I flipped the robe open again.

"You say when you want some strawberry pie," I said.

"I will," he said.

I said, "Are you tired? Do you want me to take you up to your bed? Are you ready to hit the hay?"

"Not yet," he said. "No, I'll stay up with you, bub. If that's all right. I'll stay up until you're ready to turn in. We haven't had a chance to talk. Know what I mean? I feel like me and her monopolized the evening." He lifted his beard and he let it fall. He picked up his cigarettes and his lighter.

"That's all right," I said. Then I said, "I'm glad for the company."

And I guess I was. Every night I smoked dope and stayed up as long as I could before I fell asleep. My wife and I hardly ever went to bed at the same time. When I did go to sleep, I had these dreams. Sometimes I'd wake up from one of them, my heart going crazy.

Something about the church and the Middle Ages was on the TV. Not your run-of-the-mill TV fare. I wanted to watch something else. I turned to the other channels. But there was nothing on them, either. So I turned back to the first channel and apologized.

"Bub, it's all right," the blind man said. "It's fine with me. Whatever you want to watch is okay. I'm always learning something. Learning never ends. It won't hurt me to learn something tonight. I got ears," he said.

We didn't say anything for a time. He was leaning forward with his head turned at me, his right ear aimed in the direction of the set. Very disconcerting. Now and then his eyelids drooped and then they snapped open again. Now and then he put his fingers into his beard and tugged, like he was thinking about something he was hearing on the television.

On the screen, a group of men wearing cowls was being set upon and tormented by men dressed in skeleton costumes and men dressed as devils. The men dressed as devils wore devil masks, horns, and long tails. This pageant was part of a procession. The Englishman who was narrating the thing said it took place in Spain once a year. I tried to explain to the blind man what was happening.

"Skeletons," he said. "I know about skeletons," he said, and he nodded.

The TV showed this one cathedral. Then there was a long, slow look at another one. Finally, the picture switched to the famous one in Paris, with its flying buttresses and its spires reaching up to the clouds. The camera pulled away to show the whole of the cathedral rising above the skyline.

There were times when the Englishman who was telling the thing would shut up, would simply let the camera move around over the cathedrals. Or else the camera would tour the countryside, men in fields walking behind oxen. I waited as long as I could. Then I felt I had to say something. I said, "They're showing the outside of this cathedral now. Gargoyles. Little statues carved to look like monsters. Now I guess they're in Italy. Yeah, they're in Italy. There's paintings on the walls of this one church."

"Are those fresco paintings, bub?" he asked, and he sipped from his drink.

I reached for my glass. But it was empty. I tried to remember what I could remember. "You're asking me are those frescoes?" I said. "That's a good question. I don't know."

The camera moved to a cathedral outside Lisbon. The differences in the Portuguese cathedral compared with the French and Italian were not that great. But they were there. Mostly the interior stuff. Then something occurred to me, and I said, "Something has occurred to me. Do you have any idea what a cathedral is? What they look like, that is? Do you follow me? If somebody says cathedral to you, do you have any notion what they're talking about? Do you know the difference between that and a Baptist church, say?"

He let the smoke dribble from his mouth. "I know they took hundreds of workers fifty or a hundred years to build," he said. "I just heard the man say that, of course. I know generations of the same families worked on a cathedral. I heard him say that, too. The men who began their life's work on them, they never lived to see the completion of their work. In that wise, bub, they're no different from the rest of us, right?" He laughed. Then his eyelids drooped again. His head nodded. He seemed to be snoozing. Maybe he was imagining himself in Portugal. The TV was showing another cathedral now. This one was in Germany. The Englishman's voice droned on. "Cathedrals," the blind man said. He sat up and rolled his head back and forth. "If you want the truth, bub, that's about all I know. What I just said. What I heard him say. But maybe you could describe one to me? I wish you'd do it. I'd like that. If you want to know, I really don't have a good idea."

I stared hard at the shot of the cathedral on the TV. How could I even begin to describe it? But say my life depended on it. Say my life was being threatened by an insane guy who said I had to do it or else.

I stared some more at the cathedral before the picture flipped off into the countryside. There was no use. I turned to the blind man and said, "To begin with, they're very tall." I was looking around the room for clues. "They reach way up. Up and up. Toward the sky. They're so big, some of them, they have to have these supports. To help hold them up, so to speak. These supports are called buttresses. They remind me of viaducts, for some reason. But maybe you don't know viaducts, either? Sometimes the cathedrals have devils and such carved into the front. Sometimes lords and ladies. Don't ask me why this is," I said.

He was nodding. The whole upper part of his body seemed to be moving back and forth.

"I'm not doing so good, am I?" I said.

He stopped nodding and leaned forward on the edge of the sofa. As he listened to me, he was running his fingers through his beard. I wasn't getting through to him, I could see that. But he waited for me to go on just the same. He nodded, like he was trying to encourage me. I tried to think what else to say. "They're really big," I said. "They're massive. They're built of stone. Marble, too, sometimes. In those olden days, when they built cathedrals, men wanted to be close to God. In those olden days, God was an important part of everyone's life. You could tell this from their cathedral-building. I'm sorry," I said, "but it looks like that's the best I can do for you. I'm just no good at it."

"That's all right, bub," the blind man said. "Hey, listen. I hope you don't mind my asking you. Can I ask you something? Let me ask you a simple question, yes or no. I'm just curious and there's no offense. You're my host. But let me ask if you are in any way religious? You don't mind my asking?"

I shook my head. He couldn't see that, though. A wink is the same as a nod to a blind man. "I guess I don't believe in it. In anything. Sometimes it's hard. You know what I'm saying?"

"Sure, I do," he said.

"Right," I said.

The Englishman was still holding forth. My wife sighed in her sleep. She drew a long breath and went on with her sleeping.

"You'll have to forgive me," I said. "But I can't tell you what a cathedral looks like. It just isn't in me to do it. I can't do any more than I've done."

The blind man sat very still, his head down, as he listened to me.

I said, "The truth is, cathedrals don't mean anything special to me. Nothing. Cathedrals. They're something to look at on late-night TV. That's all they are."

It was then that the blind man cleared his throat. He brought something up. He took a handkerchief from his back pocket. Then he said, "I get it, bub. It's okay. It happens. Don't worry about it," he said. "Hey, listen to me. Will you do me a favor? I got an idea. Why don't you find us some heavy paper? And a pen. We'll do something. We'll draw one together. Get us a pen and some heavy paper. Go on, bub, get the stuff," he said.

So I went upstairs. My legs felt like they didn't have any strength in them. They felt like they did after I'd done some running. In my wife's room, I looked around. I found some ballpoints in a little basket on her table. And then I tried to think where to look for the kind of paper he was talking about.

Downstairs, in the kitchen, I found a shopping bag with onion skins in the bottom of the bag. I emptied the bag and shook it. I brought it into the living room and sat down with it near his legs. I moved some things, smoothed the wrinkles from the bag, spread it out on the coffee table.

The blind man got down from the sofa and sat next to me on the carpet.

He ran his fingers over the paper. He went up and down the sides of the paper. The edges, even the edges. He fingered the corners.

"All right," he said. "All right, let's do her."

He found my hand, the hand with the pen. He closed his hand over my hand. "Go ahead, bub, draw," he said. "Draw. You'll see. I'll follow along with you. It'll be okay. Just begin now like I'm telling you. You'll see. Draw," the blind man said.

So I began. First I drew a box that looked like a house. It could have been the house I lived in. Then I put a roof on it. At either end of the roof, I drew spires. Crazy.

"Swell," he said. "Terrific. You're doing fine," he said. "Never thought anything like this could happen in your lifetime, did you, bub? Well, it's a strange life, we all know that. Go on now. Keep it up."

I put in windows with arches. I drew flying buttresses. I hung great doors. I couldn't stop. The TV station went off the air. I put down the pen and closed and opened my fingers. The blind man felt around over the paper. He moved the tips of his fingers over the paper, all over what I had drawn, and he nodded.

"Doing fine," the blind man said.

I took up the pen again, and he found my hand. I kept at it. I'm no artist. But I kept drawing just the same.

My wife opened up her eyes and gazed at us. She sat up on the sofa, her robe hanging open. She said, "What are you doing? Tell me, I want to know."

I didn't answer her.

The blind man said, "We're drawing a cathedral. Me and him are working on it. Press hard," he said to me. "That's right. That's good," he said. "Sure. You got it, bub. I can tell. You didn't think you could. But you can,

can't you? You're cooking with gas now. You know what I'm saying? We're going to really have us something here in a minute. How's the old arm?" he said. "Put some people in there now. What's a cathedral without people?"

My wife said, "What's going on? Robert, what are you doing? What's going on?"

"It's all right," he said to her. "Close your eyes now," the blind man said to me.

I did it. I closed them just like he said.

"Are they closed?" he said. "Don't fudge."

"They're closed," I said.

"Keep them that way," he said. He said, "Don't stop now. Draw."

So we kept on with it. His fingers rode my fingers as my hand went over the paper. It was like nothing else in my life up to now.

Then he said, "I think that's it. I think you got it," he said. "Take a look. What do you think?"

But I had my eyes closed. I thought I'd keep them that way for a little longer. I thought it was something I ought to do.

"Well?" he said. "Are you looking?"

My eyes were still closed. I was in my house. I knew that. But I didn't feel like I was inside anything.

"It's really something," I said.

1983

ISHMAEL REED
b. 1938

Ishmael Reed's love-hate affair with American popular culture has led him to both literary successes and entanglements with sociocultural obstacles. On the positive side his appreciation of America cultural riches, including such American-born art forms as jazz, rhythm and blues, detective novels, comic books, and the rich blend of all the world's cultures and their unique vernaculars, has enabled him to champion a truly native literature apart from the standards imposed (in a colonial manner) from European culture. Perhaps partly in recognition of this versatility, Reed was awarded a MacArthur Foundation "genius" fellowship. Negatively, his unbounded sense of satire has managed to offend almost every interest group in the profession of literature, from feminists to creative-writing-program teachers of poetry. In the chapter from his novel *The Last Days of Louisiana Red* (1974) printed here, Reed humorously critiques a presumed ally, someone who teaches African American literature. The text being taught, Richard Wright's *Native Son* (1940), is one of the most important novels in American literature. Yet Reed objects to the stereotyping that this very success makes possible. So too for his character Minnie the Moocher from this same novel. The satire is especially cutting in naming the novel's chief feminist after a figure in bandleader Cab Calloway's song from the 1940s, an era of popular culture heavy with now-abhorrent sexual caricatures; it is effective, however, because of the way Reed shows how people like Minnie cooperate with their own oppression by maintaining forces of exclusion. It is to Reed's credit that he uses history and folklore to subvert such exclusionary processes, just as his novel employs figures from classic radio comedy such as Amos and Andy and their friend King-fish to undermine ideas that, when stated by others, pass for the logic of a black bourgeoisie.

Reed draws a good picture of himself in the biographical note to his second novel, *Yellow Back Radio Broke-Down* (1969):

> Ishmael Reed was born in Chattanooga, Tennessee, on February 22, 1938. Chattanooga built a monument to every Confederate soldier killed in the Civil War, so Ishmael Reed spent his early years bumping into stone. He grew up in Buffalo, New York, where "polack" is scribbled on the bust of Chopin in Humboldt Park.
>
> Ishmael Reed attended the University of Buffalo and left after receiving rude phone calls from an anti-Gnostic bursar. At 20 he was stranded in North Platte, Nebraska. Buffalo Bill once had a drink there. He has taught American fiction at the University of California at Berkeley, and the University of Washington at Seattle.
>
> He startled the scientific community by making his home in New York City. Ishmael Reed has been buffaloed by many aspects of American society, which makes him uniquely qualified to write about the West.

Yellow Back Radio Broke-Down is indeed about the West, but a West in which a band of cowboy rustlers is confronted by the pope in a helicopter. Similar absurdities and anachronisms distinguish Reed's other novels, including the Egyptology and Haitian Aoodoo of *Mumbo Jumbo* (1972), in which West Indian religion is employed for its imaginative resources, and the Civil War slave narrative of *Flight to Canada* (1976). Subsequent novels lampoon contemporary politics, including political correctness; notable among these are *Reckless Eyeballing* (1986), *Japanese by Spring* (1993), and *Juice!* (2011).

Most of Ishmael Reed's literary methods are evident in *The Last Days of Louisiana Red*. Hoodoo is present in the folklore practices of Papa LaBas and his Solid Gumbo Works, an enterprise that, much like this native religion, draws on the spiritual nature of life, especially in contrast to the materialism of its rivals, Louisiana Red and the Moochers. It is set in a Berkeley, California, rife with early 1970s turbulence, including a university curriculum destabilized by an intellectual who, in the chapter printed here, dreams he has become the character Mary Dalton in Richard Wright's *Native Son*, a novel in which a young, rich white woman is inadvertently killed by her family's physically intimidating black chauffeur, Bigger Thomas. Sexual, racial, intellectual, and religious issues are thrown together in a mixed bag of popular references, all of which Reed shakes up and displays in fresh new postures. Like all good satirists, he exposes his subjects' weaknesses by emphasizing problems in their own terms.

Reed's poetry is an even more direct introduction to his general literary activity, for here is seen the blending of popular forms from many different cultures that to him constitutes truly American expression. His "Neo-HooDoo Manifesto," presented as a poem, is in fact a program for what Reed would write himself and help others publish (via his *Yardbird Reader* series of books and anthologies produced with the Before Columbus Foundation). His message is that a rich culture, an original culture, exists within the very forms older European standards disallow as lowbrow. He catalogs a wide range of popular entertainment figures and devises a poetic language that employs the power of expression so evident in the rhythms of such music. His editing and anthologizing and small-press productions have called on the resources not just of African Americans but of Chinese

Americans, Japanese Americans, white Americans of various ethnic backgrounds, and Native Americans, a blending of influences into non-Eurocentric aesthetic forms that is unique to America.

From The Last Days of Louisiana Red

Chapter 36

[MARY DALTON'S DREAM]

He was a blonde. He lay in the bed, tossing and turning. His room. What was that odor? The pungent odor of middle-class perfume making the air misty. He didn't feel right. His hair. What on earth was the matter with his hair? It was long and was covering the pillow. The pillows? They had a flower print and were pink. Pink? He rose in his bed and his breasts jiggled. BREASTS? THE BREASTS?? He looked back into the mirror next to the bed and his mouth made a black hollow hole of horror. "O MY GOD. MY GOD." He was a woman. You know what he said next, don't you, reader? He's from New York and so . . . you guessed it! "Kafka.[1] Pure Kafka," he said. A feeling crept over him. Tingly. What could he do? He felt like screaming, but he couldn't scream. Was that someone coming down the hall? He ran and jumped back into the bed, pulled the covers up to his neck and pretended to be asleep. Someone *was* coming down the hall. They stood for a moment outside in the hall. And then the knob slowly turned. Someone was now in the room; a dark foreboding shadow crept to the foot of the bed. A giant colored man—an Olmec-headed[2] giant wearing a chauffeur's cap. Max started to really scream this time.

"Please, Ms. Dalton,[3] you will wake the whole house," the figure says. *Look at that white bitch laying there. Sloppy drunk. Probably wants some peter too. That's all they think about anyway. I'll fuck her into a cunt energy crisis she mess with me. That's probably what she wont. Been hittin on me all night. Probably pretending to be drunk. Wonts to see how far I go. I know Jan ain't gettin any. One simple dude. Tried to give me that old PROGRESSIVE LABOR[4] line. Who don't know that? Who don't know that old simple ass mutherfuckin bullshit? Them mens was working at the Ford plant. Had some good jobs too. Then here come this Progressive Labor bullshit and them niggers lost they job after it was over. Ha! When is this bitch going to go to sleep? I wont to take that dark blue Buick with steel spoke wheels over to the South Side. Man, will them mo'fugs be mad when they see. Think I'm a pimp. Then I'll go up to the counter and roll out my 75 dollars. Man, they think I'm one of them pimps. Then I go get me some rangs. Lots of them. Have them all shining on my fingers. Shining. Justa shining. Gee. Bet I could have me plenty ol stankin bitches. Commisstee. That shit ain't nothing but some bunk. Roosia. Shhhhhhit. Started to bust that mo'fug Jan right in the mouf. Must be*

---

1. Franz Kafka (1883–1924), Austrian-Czech author of *The Metamorphosis*, in which the protagonist awakes to find himself turned into a giant insect.
2. Large-headed statues were a cultural characteristic of the Olmec, pre-Aztec Indian peoples

of what is now Tabasco and Veracruz in Mexico.
3. The character murdered by Bigger Thomas in *Native Son* (1940), a novel by the American writer Richard Wright (1908–1960).
4. A Marxist magazine and political party active in the United States beginning in the 1930s.

a sissy. . . . The door opens and in comes a woman tapping a cane. *Ahhhh-shitt. Here come that other old crazy white woman down the hall. Look like Ms. Mary trying to say something. I better do something quick.*

Max finally realized the situation. He made a futile effort to move his lips. "Bigggg. Biggggg." Meanwhile the cane tapping comes closer to the door. Bigger picks up the pillow and starts towards Mary Dalton when—

Max wakes up from the nightmare.

There was some bamming at the door real rough. Bam! Bam! Bam! Bam! Bam, Bam! Max leaped out of his dream and rushed to the door. Who could this be bamming at his door this time of night? The woman, trembling, rushed into the room.

"What do you want? I told you to never come here."

She wriggled out of her raincoat, then nervously wrung out a match after lighting a cigarette. She plopped down in a chair and drew her breath. It was Lisa, stripped of her Nanny's rags, sharp, voluptuous.

"It's LaBas. He called. He wants to talk about Ed's killing. Suppose he starts to ask me a lot of questions? You know I can't stand up under a lot of questions."

"You fool. You come here for that? I told you never to contact me here on this assignment."

"Look, you've only been here for a few years. I've been here more than ten, ever since his wife Ruby left. I've worked on that household and put my conjure all over the place. Then they sent you in to begin this organization to add to Ed's problems. Just as I had worked hard to prepare Minnie to do that. We've done enough damage to that family. When will it end?"

"It will end when Solid Gumbo Works has folded."

"I can't wait any longer. Since Wolf was killed, she's brought those Moochers into the household. I have to shuffle about like Hattie McDaniel[5] to take care of their needs. They write slogans all over the walls and sleep on stained mattresses. They leave rings in the bathtub. They've been up all night with the mimeograph machine, trying to free Kingfish and Andy."[6]

"Yes, I know," Max said. "I wrote the copy."

"I have to fix breakfast and clean up their mess. You know how Moochers are, never clean up after themselves, always expect someone else to do their cleaning for them. I told you not to draw the girl into that organization. I was doing O.K. All I needed was some more time."

"You were taking too long. Besides, the Moochers provided us with the numbers to wear down Solid Gumbo Works."

"Well, I still maintain that if it had been left to me, I would have put her on Ed. I never did go along with his killing."

"It was necessary. You know that. If we hadn't butchered him that night, he would have discovered the cure for heroin addiction. That was the industrial secret you passed on to me; the papers of his you Xeroxed. We

---

5. An actress known for portraying African American maids in American films of the 1930s and 1940s, including *Gone with the Wind* (1939), for which she won the Academy Award for Best Supporting Actress.

6. African American characters in the *Amos 'n' Andy* radio and television comedy show of the 1930s, '40s, and '50s.

had to do it. If he had found a legitimate cure, our quack operation would have shut down: the southern mailhouse empire we built would shut down. Heroin, jukeboxes, our black record company in the east, The House of Cocaine. Everybody would have been asking for Ed's Gumbo. Wasn't it enough that he found a cure for cancer?"

"You thought you'd gotten rid of that threat when you killed that Chinese acupuncturist, but Ed found different means."

"You always respected him a bit, didn't you?"

"He was a man. Ed was a hard-working man. Sometimes I wanted to tell him who I was, where I was from, and what was wrong with me. That I had been sent into his house to train his child to drive him crazy."

"You can't quit. I received orders from Louisiana Red that we have one more job. You think you have problems. Do you think I like posing as a visiting lecturer at the University of California at Berkeley? The way the women in the English Department office whisper about my lack of potency and sometimes refuse to file for my office post box.

"Do you think that I enjoy it when they refuse to mimeograph copies of lecture notes for my students? Why, this campus reminds me of the set of *I Was a Teenage Werewolf.*[7] If Louisiana Red hadn't promised me this one-million-dollar retirement money, I never would have taken care of this assignment. I was doing all right with my New York industrial spy firm. But you, you have to stay until it's over. They have you where they want you."

"I'm leaving."

Max pulls out a sheet of paper from a desk drawer. "You know that Louisiana Red doesn't play. They will get to you through your police record. You are a fugitive from justice, you know, you bag woman. (Reads) 'Real name: The Hammerhead Shark.' The title you picked up in that caper when you hit a man on the head with a hammer, put a hex on a congressman, double-crossed Jack Johnson, stabbed Martin Luther King, brought charges against Father Divine, brought down Sam Cooke in a blaze of gunfire and bad-mouthed Joe Louis.[8] They know your penchant for Coon-Can and about your scar too. Not only are the law enforcement bureaus after you, but you know the consequences of crossing the Louisiana Red Corporation."

"I'm not frightened any more. I've sent a message to the Red Rooster and told him that I want out, Max."

"I've thought about leaving myself."

"You have? Why, Max, we can leave together, go to Reno; why, I can get a job as a waitress, you can deal blackjack."

"But they'll follow us."

"Not if we move fast enough."

"Maybe we ought to. You know how I missed you during those long days. When you couldn't be with me in my arms. How we had to limit ourselves

---

7. Popular American film of the 1950s.
8. Popular figures from African American culture. Johnson (1878–1946), first black heavyweight champion of the world. King (1929–1968),

civil rights leader. Father Divine, born George Baker (1877–1965), American religious leader. Cooke (1935–1964), popular singer. Louis (1914–1981), world heavyweight champion.

to meeting every other Thursday, your day off. There must be thousands of us all over the country, meeting like this out of public view.

"Yes, my dearest, the American underground of Desire, the name of the first American slaver; we know each other on the street and recognize each other's signals. How we pay subscriptions to our propaganda organs which convince the public that it's only the Jim Brown and Racquel Welch[9] bedroom scene that's the problem. We rule America, all of it, my Nanny and me. The 'Every Other Thursday Society.' Yes, I want to leave, Lisa. My cover is getting to me."

"I don't understand."

"That book I'm doing—the one on Richard Wright's book." He rushes to the bar, makes a drink and gulps it down. Then he slams the empty glass on the bar. "It's getting to me. I'm having these dreams. Just before you knocked on the door, I had one. I was the murder victim and this big brute was coming towards me with a pillow."

"That dream will come true if you won't move over to the wall."

The startled couple turned around to see the gunman standing in the doorway.

"Son of a bitch. So you were going to take it on the lam and leave me stranded now that the assignment has heated up."

"T, take it easy, have a drink."

"No thanks, I'm not thirsty. Here I have been playing the fool for these past years, helping you set up Ed Yellings, and now you are going to drop me. Years of swallowing my pride and acting like a kookie rookie when all along you two were carrying on. I'm finished with this assignment. I feel sick about what has happened to Minnie. She wants more power now than Marie Laveau,[1] and you two did it to her. I'm going to call the Director of Louisiana Red Corporation, the Red Rooster, and tell him everything I know about you two. You see, it's all over. That's what I came up here to tell you about."

"What's all over?" Lisa says. "You don't make sense."

"About an hour ago Minnie busted George Kingfish Stevens and Andy Brown out of jail and then commandeered an airplane after miraculously evading San Francisco security, which was as tight as a drum. You don't have anything else to use against Solid Gumbo Works because Minnie has been shot."

"Shot," both Lisa and Max exclaim.

"Yes, she was shot by a passenger. The poor child was rushed to a New York hospital. It sickens me, my part in this whole thing."

He walks over to the telephone and dials.

"Hello, operator, give me Louisiana Red Corporation in New Orleans, person to person to the Red Rooster, the number is area code 504—" but before he could say anything Max lunged for him and with incredible strength wrestled him to the floor. The gun went off, killing T Feeler.

"Max, let's get out of here. We really must go now."

Max slowly looked up from where he knelt over the corpse. "Who you callin Max, bitch? I'll whip you into bad health."

9. Then current film stars, respectively African American and white.   1. Quasi-legendary hoodoo priestess in old New Orleans.

"Max, what's the matter with you? Why are you talking that way?"

"I'm gone fix you good. Killing you won't count. Not even the best critics will notice it. I'm going to kill you." He walks towards her. She screams.

"Max! Stop!"

"Max? Who Max? I'm Bigger," Max growls.

1974

Neo-HooDoo Manifesto[1]

Neo-HooDoo is a "Lost American Church" updated. Neo-HooDoo is the music of James Brown[2] without the lyrics and ads for Black Capitalism. Neo-HooDoo is the 8 basic dances of 19-century New Orleans' *Place Congo*—the Calinda the Bamboula the Chacta the Babouille the Conjaille the Juba the Congo and the VooDoo—modernized into the Philly Dog, the Hully Gully, the Funky Chicken, the Popcorn, the Boogaloo and the dance of great American choreographer Buddy Bradley.

Neo-HooDoos would rather "shake that thing" than be stiff and erect. (There were more people performing a Neo-HooDoo sacred dance, the Boogaloo, at Woodstock than chanting Hare Krishna . . . Hare Hare!) All so-called "Store Front Churches" and "Rock Festivals"[3] receive their matrix in the HooDoo rites of Marie Laveau[4] conducted at New Orleans' Lake Pontchartrain, and Bayou St. John in the 1880's. The power of HooDoo challenged the stability of civil authority in New Orleans and was driven underground where to this day it flourishes in the Black ghettos throughout the country. Thats why in Ralph Ellison's[5] modern novel *Invisible Man* New Orleans is described as "The Home of Mystery." "Everybody from New Orleans got that thing," Louis Armstrong[6] said once.

HooDoo is the strange and beautiful "fits" the Black slave Tituba gave the children of Salem.[7] (Notice the arm waving ecstatic females seemingly possessed at the "Pentecostal," "Baptist," and "Rock Festivals," [all fronts for Neo-HooDoo]). The reason that HooDoo isn't given the credit it deserves in influencing American Culture is because the students of that culture both "overground" and "underground" are uptight closet Jeho-vah revisionists. They would assert the American and East Indian and Chinese thing before they would the Black thing. Their spiritual leaders Ezra Pound and T. S. Eliot[8] hated Africa and "Darkies." In Theodore Roszak's book *The Making of a Counter Culture*[9]—there is barely any mention of the Black influence

1. From *Conjure: Selected Poems, 1963–1970* (1972).
2. African American rhythm-and-blues singer (1933–2006).
3. Massively attended concerts, often outdoors, popular in the 1960s and 1970s; Woodstock was the major one. "Store Front Churches": small churches with improvised sites in neighborhood shops.
4. See n. 1, p. 752.

5. African American writer (1914–1994).
6. American jazz musician and vocalist (1900–1971).
7. A town in Massachusetts that was the site of witchcraft hysteria in 1692.
8. Pound (1885–1972) and Eliot (1888–1965) were modernist American and Anglo-American poets, respectively.
9. A 1969 study of contemporary young people's revolt against establishment codes and traditions.

on this culture even though its members dress like Blacks talk like Blacks
walk like Blacks, gesture like Blacks wear Afros and indulge in Black music
and dance (Neo-HooDoo).

Neo-HooDoo is sexual, sensual and digs the old "heathen" good good loving. An early American HooDoo song says:

> Now lady I ain't no mill man
> Just the mill man's son
> But I can do your grinding
> till the mill man comes

Which doesn't mean that women are treated as "sexual toys" in Neo-HooDoo
or as one slick Jeho-vah Revisionist recently said, "victims of a raging hormone imbalance." Neo-HooDoo claims many women philosophers and theo-
reticians which is more than ugh religions Christianity and its offspring
Islam can claim. When our theoretician Zora Neale Hurston[1] asked a
Mambo (a female priestess in the Haitian VooDoo) a definition of VooDoo
the Mambo lifted her skirts and exhibited her Erzulie Seal, her Isis seal.
Neo-HooDoo identifies with Julia Jackson[2] who stripped HooDoo of its
oppressive Catholic layer—Julia Jackson said when asked the origin of the
amulets and talismans in her studio, "I make all my own stuff. It saves money
and it's as good. People who has to buy their stuff ain't using their heads."

Neo-HooDoo is not a church for egotripping—it takes its "organization"
from Haitian VooDoo of which Milo Rigaud wrote:

Unlike other established religions, there is no hierarchy of bishops, archbish-
ops, cardinals, or a pope in VooDoo. Each oum'phor is a law unto itself, fol-
lowing the traditions of VooDoo but modifying and changing the ceremonies
and rituals in various ways. Secrets of VooDoo.

Neo-HooDoo believes that every man is an artist and every artist a priest.
You can bring your own creative ideas to Neo-HooDoo. Charlie "Yardbird
(Thoth)" Parker[3] is an example of the Neo-HooDoo artist as an innovator
and improvisor.

In Neo-HooDoo, Christ the landlord deity ("render unto Caesar") is on pro-
bation. This includes "The Black Christ" and "The Hippie Christ." Neo-
HooDoo tells Christ to get lost. (Judas Iscariot holds an honorary degree
from Neo-HooDoo.)

Whereas at the center of Christianity lies the graveyard the organ-drone
and the cross, the center of Neo-HooDoo is the drum the anhk and the
Dance. So Fine, Barefootin, Heard it Through the Grapevine,[4] are all
Neo-HooDoos.

---

1. American fiction writer, poet, and folklorist
(1891–1960).
2. American sculptor (b. 1936).
3. American jazz musician (1920–1955), pioneer
of the bebop style of modern jazz.
4. Popular rock 'n' roll and rhythm-and-blues
songs that inspired new dances.

Neo-HooDoo has "seen a lot of things in this old world."

Neo-HooDoo borrows from Ancient Egyptians (ritual accessories of Ancient Egypt are still sold in the House of Candles and Talismans on Stanton Street in New York, the Botanical Gardens in East Harlem, and Min and Mom on Haight Street in San Francisco, examples of underground centers found in ghettos throughout America).

Neo-HooDoo borrows from Haiti Africa and South America. Neo-HooDoo comes in all styles and moods. Louis Jordon Nellie Lutcher John Lee Hooker Ma Rainey Dinah Washington the Temptations Ike and Tina Turner Aretha Franklin Muddy Waters Otis Redding Sly and the Family Stone B. B. King Junior Wells Bessie Smith Jelly Roll Morton Ray Charles Jimi Hendrix Buddy Miles the 5th Dimension the Chambers Brothers Etta James and acolytes Creedence Clearwater Revival the Flaming Embers Procol Harum are all Neo-HooDoos. Neo-HooDoo never turns down pork. In fact Neo-HooDoo is the Bar-B-Cue of Amerika. The Neo-HooDoo cuisine is Geechee Gree Gree Verta Mae's *Vibration Cooking*.[5] (Ortiz Walton's Neo-HooDoo Jass Band performs at the Native Son Restaurant in Berkeley, California. Joe Overstreet's[6] Neo-HooDoo exhibit will happen at the Berkeley Gallery Sept. 1, 1970 in Berkeley.)

Neo-HooDoo ain't Negritude.[7] Neo-HooDoo never been to France. Neo-HooDoo is "your Mama" as Larry Neal[8] said. Neo-HooDoos Little Richard and Chuck Berry nearly succeeded in converting the Beatles.[9] When the Beatles said they were more popular than Christ they seemed astonished at the resulting outcry. This is because although they could feebly through amplification and technological sham "mimic" (as if Little Richard and Chuck Berry were Loa [Spirits] practicing ventriloquism on their "Horses") the Beatles failed to realize that they were conjuring the music and ritual (although imitation) of a Forgotten Faith, a traditional enemy of Christianity which Christianity the Cop Religion has had to drive underground each time they meet. Neo-HooDoo now demands a rematch, the referees were bribed and the adversary had resin on his gloves.

The Vatican Forbids Jazz Masses in Italy
Rome, Aug. 6 (UPI)—The Vatican today barred jazz and popular music from masses in Italian churches and forbade young Roman Catholics to change prayers or readings used on Sundays and holy days.

It said such changes in worship were "eccentric and arbitrary."

A Vatican document distributed to all Italian bishops did not refer to similar experimental masses elsewhere in the world, although Pope Paul VI and

---

5. This paragraph lists a mélange of contemporary popular musicians and musical groups from a wide range of musical styles, including the blues, jazz, rock 'n' roll, and Motown.
6. American painter (b. 1934)
7. A 20th-century literary school of poetry written in French by African authors.

8. Music critic, theoretician of African American literature, and anthologist (1937–1981).
9. British rock group of the 1960s. Little Richard (b. 1935) and Chuck Berry (b. 1926), African American rock 'n' rollers who had a formative influence on the Beatles.

*other high-ranking churchmen are known to dislike the growing tendency to
deviate from the accepted form of the mass.*

*Some Italian churches have permitted jazz masses played by combos while
youthful worshipers sang such songs as "We Shall Overcome."*

Church leaders two years ago rebuked priests who permitted such experiments. The New York Times, August 7, 1970.

Africa is the home of the Ioa (Spirits) of Neo-HooDoo although we are
building our own American "pantheon." Thousands of "Spirits" (Ka) who
would laugh at Jeho-vah's fury concerning "false idols" (translated everybody else's religion) or "fetishes." Moses, Jeho-vah's messenger and zombie
swiped the secrets of VooDoo from old Jethro but nevertheless ended up
with a curse. (Warning, many White "Black delineators" who practiced
HooDoo VooDoo for gain and did not "feed" the Black Spirits of HooDoo
ended up tragically. Bix Beiderbecke and Irene Castle (who exploited Black
Dance in the 1920s and relished in dressing up as a Nun) are examples of
this tragic tendency.

Moses had a near heart attack when he saw his sons dancing nude before
the Black Bull God Apis. They were dancing to a "heathen sound" that
Moses had "heard before in Egypt" (probably a mixture of Sun Ra and
Jimmy Reed[1] played in the nightclub district of ancient Egypt's "The
Domain of Osiris"—named after the god who enjoyed the fancy footwork of
the pigmies).

The continuing war between Moses and his "Sons" was recently acted out
in Chicago in the guise of an American "trial."

I have called Jeho-vah (most likely Set the Egyptian Sat-on [a pun on the
fiend's penalty] Satan) somewhere "a party-pooper and hater of dance."
NeoHooDoos are detectives of the metaphysical about to make a pinch. We
have issued warrants for a god arrest. If Jeho-vah reveals his real name he
will be released on his own recognizance de-horned and put out to
pasture.

A dangerous paranoid pain-in-the-neck a CopGod from the git-go, Jeho-vah
was the successful law and order candidate in the mythological relay of the
4th century A.D. Jeho-vah is the God of punishment. The H-Bomb is a typical Jeho-vah "miracle." Jeho-vah is why we are in Vietnam.[2] He told Moses
to go out and "subdue" the world.

*There has never been in history another such culture as the Western civilization—a culture which has practiced the belief that the physical and social
environment of man is subject to rational manipulation and that history is
subject to the will and action of man; whereas central to the traditional cul-*

---

1. Blues musician (1925–1976) from the 1950s.
Sun Ra (1914–1993), avant-garde jazz musician
of the 1950s.
2. The war in Vietnam was being waged at the
time this essay was written. In 1965 then president Lyndon Johnson delivered a famous speech,
"Why We Are in Vietnam."

tures of the rivals of Western civilization, those of Africa and Asia, is a belief that it is environment that dominates man. The Politics of Hysteria, *Edmund Stillman and William Pfaff.*

"Political leaders" are merely altar boys from Jeho-vah. While the targets of some "revolutionaries" are laundramats and candy stores, Neo-HooDoo targets are TV the museums the symphony halls and churches art music and literature departments in Christianizing (education I think they call it!) universities which propogate the Art of Jeho-vah—much Byzantine Middle Ages Renaissance painting of Jeho-vah's "500 years of civilization" as Nixon[3] put it are Jeho-vah propaganda. Many White revolutionaries can only get together with 3rd world people on the most mundane 'political' level because they are of Jeho-vah's party and don't know it. How much Black music do so-called revolutionary underground radio stations play. On the other hand how much Bach?[4]

Neo-HooDoos are Black Red (Black Hawk an American Indian was an early philosopher of the HooDoo Church) and occasionally White (Mademoiselle Charlotte is a Haitian Loa [Spirit]).

Neo-HooDoo is a litany seeking its text
Neo-HooDoo is a Dance and Music closing in on its words
Neo-HooDoo is a Church finding its lyrics
Cecil Brown Al Young Calvin Hernton
David Henderson Steven Cannon Quincy Troupe
Ted Joans Victor Cruz N. H. Pritchard Ishmael Reed
Lennox Raphael Sarah Fabio Ron Welburn[5] are Neo-
HooDoo's "Manhattan Project"[6] of writing . . .

A Neo-HooDoo celebration will involve the dance music
and poetry of Neo-HooDoo and whatever ideas the
participating artists might add. A Neo-HooDoo seal
is the Face of an Old American Train.
Neo-HooDoo signs are everywhere!
Neo-HooDoo is the Now Locomotive swinging
up the Tracks of the American Soul.

Almost 100 years ago HooDoo was forced to say
Goodbye to America. Now HooDoo is
back as Neo-HooDoo
You can't keep a good church down!

1972

---

3. Richard Nixon (1913–1994) was president of the United States at the time this essay was written.
4. Johann Sebastian Bach (1685–1750), German organist and composer.

5. These lines list contemporary multicultural writers.
6. The research that developed the atomic bomb for use at the end of World War II.

CHARLES SIMIC
b. 1938

C harles Simic came to the United States from Belgrade, Yugoslavia, at the age of sixteen. When in 2007 he was named as poet laureate of the United States for the coming year, he responded that he was "especially touched and honored to be selected because I am an immigrant boy who didn't speak English until I was fifteen." His earliest childhood memories are of bombs dropping, people disappearing, and buildings in ruins. "My own home movie begins with the German bombing of Belgrade on April 6, 1941," he has said, "when a bomb hit the building across the street. I flew out of my bed all the way across the room. I was three years old and more astonished than I actually was frightened by the flames that rose everywhere." The unpredictability of Simic's poetry, with its feeling for the bizarre and irrational quality of ordinary things, may have originated in his childhood. During the German occupation of Yugoslavia a civil war broke out among the partisans; from it the communist Marshal Tito emerged as the Yugoslav leader. In 1944 the American and British forces bombed German-occupied Belgrade, where the Simics continued to live. After the war Tito established a repressive communist regime: "People were being arrested left and right. Everybody was afraid. In school there was indoctrination," Simic writes in his memoir *A Fly in the Soup* (2000). During those years Simic, his mother, and his brother spent time in refugee camps and prisons; they were finally able to leave Yugoslavia for Paris in 1953. A year later they immigrated to the United States, where his father was already living. "After what we had been through," he writes, "the wildest lies seemed plausible and the poems that I was going to write had to take that into account."

Simic's poetry is often full of mysterious fragments, as if some unspecified force has detonated both the larger, cohesive structure of the world and the narrative of the poem. At the same time Simic's stanzas function as regulating and balancing structures in tension with what is incomprehensible and often absurd. This tension, along with Simic's deadpan tone, renders the comic and the frightening qualities of a world where truth and justice are "The Famous No-Shows" and existence is a cosmic joke. It is not surprising that Simic admires the early film comedian Buster Keaton (1895–1966) for his "serenity in the face of chaos." The joke in Simic's poems is also a form of black humor, born of a historical dread Simic attributes to life in the twentieth century. Menace permeates the ordinary and domestic moments in Simic's poems. In "A Book Full of Pictures" a child is reading, a father studying, a mother knitting, but the quiet of the poem is disturbing. A "black raincoat / in the upstairs bedroom" sways from the ceiling. The declarative statements of the poem, like the click of the knitting needles, seem designed to fend off violence within and without the scene.

Simic's years in a Yugoslavia that monitored dissent through a secret police taught him the brutal consequences of a politically repressive conformity, and he has always been attracted to irreverence and unpredictability. As a young man he lived in New York and was drawn to surrealist poetry and to the wild flights of twentieth-century Latin American verse. Impatient with what he saw as the academic conservatism of poetry in the 1950s and early 1960s, he wrote verse that celebrated surreal and associative leaps (exemplified by the "controlled anarchy" of the jazz saxophonist Sonny Rollins, who is depicted in Faith Ringgold's painting *Sonny's Quilt*, reproduced in the color insert in this anthology) and untamable erotic impulses. His work since that period continues to celebrate irreverence and humor. Along with such outward wildness, Simic's poetry is full of secrets, and the presence of something hidden frequently disturbs or haunts a Simic poem. Often the poems read like enigmatic disclosures in the form of riddles or jokes. He loves metaphysical speculation and can suggest philosophical questions through the most particular and even ordinary things, such as a fork or a glove; he has said that he practices "a kind of bedroom and kitchen metaphysics."

Among Simic's many books of poems are *Selected Poems 1963–1983* (1985, revised and expanded 1990), *The Book of Gods and Devils* (1990), *Hotel Insomnia* (1992), *Walking the Black Cat* (1996), *Jackstraws* (1999), *Night Picnic* (2001), *The Voice at 3:00 A.M.: Selected Late and New Poems* (2003), *My Noiseless Entourage* (2005), *That Little Something* (2008), and *The Monster Loves the Labyrinth* (2008). *Master of Disguises* (2010) shows Simic at the height of his powers. In addition he has edited and translated the work of Eastern European poets such as Vasko Popa and Tomaz Salamun. His collections of essays and memoirs include *The Uncertain Certainty* (1985), *Wonderful Words Silent Truth* (1990), and *A Fly in the Soup* (2000). Simic has described his work as a kind of "nonsense made up of fiction, autobiography, the essay, poetry, and, of course, the joke." With their mixture of the comic and the terrible and with their surreal storytelling power, Simic's poems haunt the mind long after one has read them.

Fork

This strange thing must have crept
Right out of hell.
It resembles a bird's foot
Worn around the cannibal's neck.

As you hold it in your hand,   5
As you stab with it into a piece of meat,
It is possible to imagine the rest of the bird:
Its head which like your fist
Is large, bald, beakless and blind.

                                                          1971

Prodigy

I grew up bent over
a chessboard.

I loved the word *endgame*.[1]

All my cousins looked worried.

It was a small house   5
near a Roman graveyard.
Planes and tanks
shook its windowpanes.

---

1. Late stage of a chess game after the major reduction of forces.

A retired professor of astronomy
taught me how to play.   10

That must have been in 1944.

In the set we were using,
the paint had almost chipped off
the black pieces.

The white King was missing   15
and had to be substituted for.

I'm told but do not believe
that that summer I witnessed
men hung from telephone poles.

I remember my mother   20
blindfolding me a lot.
She had a way of tucking my head
suddenly under her overcoat.

In chess, too, the professor told me,
the masters play blindfolded,   25
the great ones on several boards
at the same time.

                                                                    1980

The Devils

You were a "victim of semiromantic anarchism
In its most irrational form."
I was "ill at ease in an ambiguous world

Deserted by Providence." We drank gin
And made love in the afternoon. The neighbors'   5
TV's were tuned to soap operas.

The unhappy couples spoke little.
There were interminable pauses.
Soft organ music. Someone coughing.

"It's like Strindberg's *Dream Play*,"[1] you said.   10
"What is?" I asked and got no reply.
I was watching a spider on the ceiling.

---

1. The play, by the Swedish dramatist and novelist August Strindberg (1849–1912), eschews straight-forward narrative and character, anticipating cubism and surrealism in its use of montage.

It was the kind St. Veronica[2] ate in her martyrdom.
"That woman subsisted on spiders only,"
I told the janitor when he came to fix the faucet.   15

He wore dirty overalls and a derby hat.
Once he had been an inmate of a notorious state institution.
"I'm no longer Jesus," he informed us happily.

He believed only in devils now.
"This building is full of them," he confided.   20
One could see their horns and tails

If one caught them in their baths.
"He's got Dark Ages[3] on his brain," you said.
"Who does?" I asked and got no reply.

The spider had the beginnings of a web   25
Over our heads. The world was quiet
Except when one of us took a sip of gin.

1990

A Book Full of Pictures

Father studied theology through the mail
And this was exam time.
Mother knitted. I sat quietly with a book
Full of pictures. Night fell.
My hands grew cold touching the faces   5
Of dead kings and queens.

There was a black raincoat
      in the upstairs bedroom
Swaying from the ceiling,
But what was it doing there?   10
Mother's long needles made quick crosses.
They were black
Like the inside of my head just then.

The pages I turned sounded like wings.
"The soul is a bird," he once said.   15
In my book full of pictures
A battle raged: lances and swords
Made a kind of wintry forest
With my heart spiked and bleeding in its branches.

1992

2. She is said to have wiped the face of Jesus
when he stumbled under the weight of the Cross
on his way to Calvary. An imprint of his face was
reportedly left on the cloth she used, known
thereafter as the Veil of Veronica.
3. The Early Middle Ages, a period in European
history from the fall of the Western Roman
Empire in the 5th century to the 11th century.

Arriving Celebrities

Tragedy and Comedy
Stepping out of a limousine
In ritzy furs;
Diminutive skirts,
Blowing kisses   5
Left and right.

Bedlam of adoring fans,
Pushing and squeezing,
Hollering for a glimpse,
When—all of a sudden!   10
A hush.
An all-inclusive clam-up.

Is someone, I inquired
Of my neighbors,
Already lying knifed   15
On the dance floor
Mouthing the name
We are all straining to overhear?

The towering bodyguards
With shaved heads   20
And mirror-tinted shades,
Don't hear me right,
Or will not deign
To grant my presence.

                                           1999

In the Street

He was kneeling down to tie his shoes which she
    mistook for a proposal of marriage.
—Arise, arise, sweet man, she said with tears glistening
    in her eyes while people hurried past as if stung by
    bees.   5
—We shall spend the day riding in a balloon, she
    announced happily.
—My ears will pop, he objected.
—We'll throw our clothes overboard as we rise higher
    and higher.   10
—I'll smoke a cigar that may sputter fireworks.
—Don't worry my love, she hugged him. Even where
    the clouds are darkest, I have a secret getaway.

                                           1999

Late September

The mail truck goes down the coast
Carrying a single letter.
At the end of a long pier
The bored seagull lifts a leg now and then
And forgets to put it down.   5
There is a menace in the air
Of tragedies in the making.

Last night you thought you heard television
In the house next door.
You were sure it was some new   10
Horror they were reporting,
So you went out to find out.
Barefoot, wearing just shorts.
It was only the sea sounding weary
After so many lifetimes   15
Of pretending to be rushing off somewhere
And never getting anywhere.

This morning, it felt like Sunday.
The heavens did their part
By casting no shadow along the boardwalk   20
Or the row of vacant cottages,
Among them a small church
With a dozen gray tombstones huddled close
As if they, too, had the shivers.

2001   2003

MICHAEL S. HARPER
b. 1938

" I've been listening to music all my life," Michael S. Harper has said, and his first book of poems, *Dear John, Dear Coltrane* (1970), took its title from his poem to the great American jazz saxophonist. Recalling Coltrane's life in his prose piece "Don't They Speak Jazz," Harper tells this story: "Trane was searching for a particular tone on his horn; he had what we thought was a perfect embouchure, but his teeth hurt constantly, so he searched for the soft reed which would ease the pain. After searching for a year, each session killing his chops, he gave it up completely; there was no easy way to get that sound: play through the pain to *a love supreme.*" Playing through the pain is a part of what Harper brings to his poetry. Like the great blues singers and jazz musicians, his work celebrates life as song, especially as tragic song, full of losses and griefs, but song nevertheless. Sometimes the pain Harper sings through is personal, like the death of one of his sons in "Deathwatch" (he and his wife lost two of their infant sons shortly after birth), sometimes the pain belongs to family history (as in "Grandfather"). Sometimes it is the pain of history more generally, its violence and oppression.

History is Harper's second love as a poet, following right behind music. His poem for Coltrane, while dependent on the techniques of jazz and the blues, reflects Harper's concern with an imaginative recovery of history, especially black history, in an America where (as he once put it) the "amnesia level" is high. "I think the important thing about Americans is that they're not very good historians," Harper has said. "And Americans are really bad historians when it comes to moral ideas because they can't keep them in their heads very long." For Harper, to be a poet is to be a good historian; history identifies and inscribes moral issues that continue to engage us in the present. In college, Harper recalled, he read William Carlos Williams's *In the American Grain* (1925), in which Williams announces that "History for us begins with murder and enslavement, not with discovery." Like Williams, Harper wants to bring his personal imagination in contact with an American history (black and white) essentially tragic, tragic because, he says, "so many possibilities exist and there's been so much waste." This tragic sense informs Harper's work perhaps most clearly in his volume *Nightmare Begins Responsibility* (1975)—the title is a variation on one of the Irish poet William Butler Yeats's epigraphs—where a personal sense of loss is never separable from the sufferings of black history or of human history more generally. His collections *Images of Kin* (1977) and *Healing Song for the Inner Ear* (1985) followed. *Honorable Amendments* appeared in 1995, and *Songlines in Michaeltree: New and Collected Poems* was published in 2000.

Born in Brooklyn, New York, Harper remembers a childhood in which "my parents weren't rich, but they had a good record collection." He grew up hearing the blues and jazz, but also reading the work of Langston Hughes and, later, James Baldwin and Ralph Ellison, and his poetic technique owes something to his literary as well as to his musical sensibility. An additional resource was a family tradition of oral storytelling ("My people were good storytellers," he has said), out of which some of his poems have grown. In fact, the jazz techniques of variation on a theme, of improvisation around an existing form, recall traditions of oral storytelling and both jazz and oral traditions influenced the formal experiments of an Ellison or a Baldwin. After high school Harper took a B.A. and an M.A. at what is now California State University, then went to the University of Iowa for an MFA. His travels abroad, first to Mexico and Europe and later (1977) to South Africa, intensified his historical sense both of his own family roots and of their connection with racial history. Since 1970 he has taught at Brown University, where he is professor of English and director of the writing program.

"Most great art is finally testamental," Harper has written; "its technical brilliance never shadows the content of the song." Harper writes poems to remember and to witness, but at times the urgency of the content overpowers his form, and his language cannot sustain the urgency the poem asserts. This may be the cost for a poet whose engagement with moral issues, whose deep historical sense, and whose rhythmic inventiveness enable him to create powerful and moving poems. His finest work possesses what he admires in Coltrane: "the energy and passion with which he approached his instrument and music," resembling the energy it takes "to break oppressive conditions, oppressive musical structures, and oppressive societal structures." Harper's inclusive sense of history lets him write (in "Blue Ruth: America") that "*history is your own heartbeat*," but also lets him hear his own heart beat in time with those who lived in other times, other places. Responsible to memory, Harper also shares the affirmative impulse he finds in the blues: "The blues say 'Yes' to life no matter what it is. That doesn't mean you're going to survive it. But it means you're going to say yes to it."

Dear John, Dear Coltrane[1]

a love supreme, a love supreme
a love supreme, a love supreme

Sex fingers toes
in the marketplace
near your father's church
in Hamlet, North Carolina[2]—
witness to this love   5
in this calm fallow
of these minds,
there is no substitute for pain:
genitals gone or going,
seed burned out,   10
you tuck the roots in the earth,
turn back, and move
by river through the swamps,
singing: *a love supreme, a love supreme*;
what does it all mean?   15
Loss, so great each black
woman expects your failure
in mute change, the seed gone.
You plod up into the electric city—
your song now crystal and   20
the blues. You pick up the horn
with some will and blow
into the freezing night:
a love supreme, a love supreme—

Dawn comes and you cook   25
up the thick sin 'tween
impotence and death, fuel
the tenor sax cannibal
heart, genitals and sweat
that makes you clean—   30
a love supreme, a love supreme—

Why you so black?
cause I am
why you so funky?
cause I am   35
why you so black?
cause I am
why you so sweet?
cause I am
why you so black?   40
cause I am
a love supreme, a love supreme:

1. John Coltrane (1926–1967), avant-garde jazz
musician. The epigraph is a phrase chanted at
the beginning of his four-part composition *A*
Love Supreme.
2. Coltrane's birthplace.

So sick
you couldn't play *Naima*,[3]
so flat we ached   45
for song you'd concealed
with your own blood,
your diseased liver gave
out its purity,
the inflated heart   50
pumps out, the tenor[4] kiss,
tenor love:
a love supreme, a love supreme—
a love supreme, a love supreme—

                                                    1970

American History

for John Callahan

Those four black girls blown up
in that Alabama church[1]
remind me of five hundred
middle passage blacks,[2]
in a net, under water   5
in Charleston harbor
so redcoats[3] wouldn't find them.
Can't find what you can't see
can you?

                                                    1970

Martin's Blues[1]

He came apart in the open,
the slow motion cameras
falling quickly
neither alive nor kicking;
stone blind dead   5
on the balcony
that old melody
etched his black lips
in a pruned echo:
We shall overcome   10

---

3. One of Coltrane's most famous songs.
4. Perhaps an allusion to the tenor saxophone, Coltrane's instrument.
1. By white racists as a reprisal against civil rights demonstrations.
2. Captured and en route from Africa (along the

"Middle Passage," the usual route for slave ships) to be sold as slaves.
3. I.e., British soldiers.
1. Martin Luther King Jr. (1929–1968), American civil rights leader, was assassinated on a motel balcony in Memphis, Tennessee.

some day—[2]
Yes we did!
Yes we did!

1971

"*Bird Lives*": Charles Parker[1] in St. Louis

Last on legs, last on sax,
last in Indian wars, last on *smack*,
Bird is specious, *Bird* is alive,
horn, unplayable, before, after,
right now: it's heroin time: 5
smack, in the melody a trip;
smack, in the Mississippi;
smack, in the drug merchant trap;
smack, in St. Louis, Missouri.

We knew you were through—   10
trying to get out of town,
unpaid bills, connections
unmet, unwanted, unasked,
Bird's in the last arc
of his own light: *blow Bird!*   15
And you did—
screaming, screaming, baby,
for life, after it, around it,
screaming for life, *blow Bird!*

What is the meaning of music?   20
What is the meaning of war?
What is the meaning of oppression?
Blow Bird! Ripped up and down
into the interior of life, the pain,
Bird, the embraceable you,[2]   25
how many brothers gone,
smacked out: blues and racism,
the hardest, longest penis
in the Mississippi urinal:
Blow Bird!   30

Taught more musicians, then forgot,
space loose, fouling the melodies,
the marching songs, the fine white
geese from the plantations,
syrup in this pork barrel,   35

2. Line from a hymn that became an anthem of the Civil Rights Movement.
1. American jazz musician (1920–1955), known as "Bird"; he was a heroin (smack) addict.
2. Title of a song Parker made famous.

Kansas City, the even teeth
of the mafia, the big band:
Blow Bird! Inside out Charlie's
guts, *Blow Bird!* get yourself killed.

In the first wave, the musicians,   40
out there, alone, in the first wave;
everywhere you went, Massey Hall,
Sweden, New Rochelle, *Birdland,*
nameless bird, Blue Note, Carnegie,[3]
tuxedo junction, out of nowhere,   45
confirmation, confirmation, confirmation:
Bird Lives! Bird Lives! and you do:
Dead—

                                                           1972

Nightmare Begins Responsibility[1]

I place these numbed wrists to the pane
watching white uniforms whisk over
him in the tube-kept
prison
fear what they will do in experiment   5
watch my gloved stickshifting gasolined hands
breathe *boxcar-information-please* infirmary tubes
distrusting white-pink mending paperthin
silkened end hairs, distrusting tubes
shrunk in his *trunk-skincapped*   10
shaven head, in thighs
distrusting-white-hands-picking-baboon-light
on this son who will not make his second night
of this wardstrewn intensive airpocket
where his father's asthmatic   15
hymns of *night-train,* train done gone
his mother can only know that he has flown
up into essential calm unseen corridor
going boxscarred home, *mamaborn, sweetsonchild*
gonedowntown into *researchtestingwarehousebatteryacid*   20
mama-son-done-gone / me telling her 'nother
train tonight, no music, no breathstroked
heartbeat in my infinite distrust of them:

3. Among the places where Parker performed
were Massey Concert Hall in Toronto, Canada;
Malmo, Sweden; New Rochelle, New York; Birdland, the landmark New York City jazz club
named after him; the Blue Note, another New
York City jazz club; and Carnegie Hall, the
famous New York City concert hall.
1. Cf. the title of a book by the American poet
Delmore Schwartz, *In Dreams Begin Responsi-*
bilities (1938); Schwartz took the title from a line
in the Irish poet William Butler Yeats's "Responsibilities" (1913).

and of my distrusting self
white-doctor-who-breathed-for-him-all-night   25
say it for two sons gone,
say nightmare, say it loud
panebreaking heartmadness:
nightmare begins responsibility.

1975

TONI CADE BAMBARA
1939–1995

" H er writing is woven, aware of its music, its overlapping waves of scenic action, so clearly on its way," Toni Morrison wrote about editing the work of her friend Toni Cade Bambara, "like a magnet collecting details in its wake, each of which is essential to the final effect." In her preface to the posthumous collection of fiction, essays, and conversations *Deep Sightings and Rescue Missions* (1996), Morrison describes Bambara as an "ever vocal woman," and the remarkable presence of a living voice distinguishes the stories collected in *Gorilla, My Love* (1972) and *The Sea Birds Are Still Alive* (1977), as well as Bambara's novels, *The Salt Eaters* (1981) and the posthumously published *Those Bones Are Not My Child* (1999).

Born and raised in New York City, Bambara was as much a social activist as a writer. She worked in organizations dedicated to the most practical day-to-day benefits for minority city dwellers and also traveled to Cuba and Vietnam to lobby for reformed national politics. She spent the last fifteen years of her professional life working on television documentaries, including *The Bombing of Orange Avenue* (about the Philadelphia police department's deadly assault on the MOVE organization). Yet she will be remembered for her short stories, particularly the first-person narratives of her women storytellers about their experiences in the black community. Her protagonists are activists in their societies, societies that in their flux demand creative readjustment at every stage. Such is the dynamic of "Medley" (printed here), in which a culture's music indexes the pace and rhythms of its social existence. As in this story, Bambara's plots are always moving, existing in a state of being "on their way" toward an imperatively stated conclusion, as Toni Morrison has said of this writer's prose style.

As her novel *The Salt Eaters* shows, Bambara was sensitive to the role storytelling plays in healthy communities. Here, when an activist is frustrated over divisiveness in the people she wishes to help, a traditional healer comes to the rescue with her tales of folk values. Life is change, Bambara understood; the fluid nature of language teaches that no stable, secure place exists beyond the voice's constant ability to reinvent itself. Hence Bambara meant to be of service in editing *Tales and Stories of Black Folks* (1971), an anthology that provides ample evidence for how African Americans not only created folk legends but adapted European and African materials to their own uniquely American ends. In this writer's fiction readers can see the same process taking place, a joyful embrace of voice as the most personal statement possible in a world dependent on self-invention for survival.

The following text is from *The Sea Birds Are Still Alive* (1977).

Medley

I could tell the minute I got in the door and dropped my bag, I wasn't staying. Dishes piled sky-high in the sink looking like some circus act. Glasses all ghosty on the counter. Busted tea bags, curling canteloupe rinds, white cartons from the Chinamen, green sacks from the deli, and that damn dog creeping up on me for me to wrassle his head or kick him in the ribs one. No, I definitely wasn't staying. Couldn't even figure why I'd come. But picked my way to the hallway anyway till the laundry-stuffed pillowcases stopped me. Larry's bass blocking the view to the bedroom.

"That you, Sweet Pea?"

"No, man, ain't me at all," I say, working my way back to the suitcase and shoving that damn dog out the way. "See ya round," I holler, the door slamming behind me, cutting off the words abrupt.

Quite naturally sitting cross-legged at the club, I embroider a little on the homecoming tale, what with an audience of two crazy women and a fresh bottle of Jack Daniels.[1] Got so I could actually see shonuff toadstools growing in the sink. Canteloupe seeds sprouting in the muck. A goddamn compost heap breeding near the stove, garbage gardens on the grill.

"Sweet Pea, you oughta hush, cause you can't possibly keep on lying so," Pot Limit's screaming, tears popping from her eyes. "Lawd hold my legs, cause this liar bout to kill me off."

"Never mind about Larry's housekeeping, girl," Sylvia's soothing me, sloshing perfectly good bourbon all over the table. "You can come and stay with me till your house comes through. It'll be like old times at Aunt Merriam's."

I ease back into the booth to wait for the next set. The drummer's fooling with the equipment, tapping the mikes, hoping he's watched, so I watch him. But feeling worried in my mind about Larry, cause I've been through days like that myself. Cold cream caked on my face from the day before, hair matted, bathrobe funky, not a clean pair of drawers to my name. Even the emergency ones, the draggy cotton numbers stuffed way in the back of the drawer under the scented paper gone. And no clean silverware in the box and the last of the paper cups gone too. Icebox empty cept for a rock of cheese and the lone water jug that ain't even half full that's how anyhow the thing's gone on. And not a clue as to the next step. But then Pot Limit'll come bamming on the door to say So-and-so's in town and can she have the card table for a game. Or Sylvia'll send a funny card inviting herself to dinner and even giving me the menu. Then I zoom through that house like a manic work brigade till me and the place ready for white-glove inspection. But what if some somebody or other don't intervene for Larry, I'm thinking.

The drummer's messin round on the cymbals, head cocked to the side, rings sparkling. The other dudes are stepping out from behind the curtain. The piano man playing with the wah-wah doing splashy, breathy science fiction stuff. Sylvia checking me out to make sure I ain't too blue. Blue got hold to me, but I lean foward out of the shadows and babble something

---

1. A potent brand of Tennessee sour mash whisky.

about how off the bourbon tastes these days. Hate worryin Sylvia, who is the kind of friend who bleeds at the eyes with your pain. I drain my glass and hum along with the opening riff of the guitar and I keep my eyes strictly off the bass player, whoever he is.

Larry Landers looked more like a bass player than ole Mingus[2] himself. Got these long arms that drape down over the bass like they were grown special for that purpose. Fine, strong hands with long fingers and muscular knuckles, the dimples deep black at the joints. His calluses so other-colored and hard, looked like Larry had swiped his grandmother's tarnished thimbles to play with. He'd move in on that bass like he was going to hump it or something, slide up behind it as he lifted it from the rug, all slinky. He'd become one with the wood. Head dipped down sideways bobbing out the rhythm, feet tapping, legs jiggling, he'd look good. Thing about it, though, ole Larry couldn't play for shit. Couldn't never find the right placement for the notes. Never plucking with enough strength, despite the perfectly capable hands. Either you didn't hear him at all or what you heard was off. The man couldn't play for nuthin is what I'm saying. But Larry Landers was baad in the shower, though.

He'd soap me up and down with them great, fine hands, doing a deep bass walking in the back of his mouth. And I'd just have to sing, though I can't sing to save my life. But we'd have one hellafyin musical time in the shower, lemme tell you. "Green Dolphin Street"[3] never sounded like nuthin till Larry bopped out them changes and actually made me sound good. On "My Funny Valentine"[4] he'd do a whizzing sounding bow thing that made his throat vibrate real sexy and I'd cutesy up the introduction, which is, come to think of it, my favorite part. But the main number when the hot water started running out was "I Feel Like Making Love." That was usually the wind up of our repertoire cause you can imagine what that song can do to you in the shower and all.

Got so we spent a helluva lotta time in the shower. Just as well, cause didn't nobody call Larry for gigs. He a nice man, considerate, generous, baad in the shower, and good taste in music. But he just wasn't nobody's bass player. Knew all the stances, though, the postures, the facial expressions, had the choreography down. And right in the middle of supper he'd get some Ron Carter[5] thing going in his head and hop up from the table to go get the bass. Haul that sucker right in the kitchen and do a number in dumb show, all the playing in his throat, the acting with his hands. But that ain't nuthin. I mean that can't get it. I can impersonate Betty Carter[6] if it comes to that. The arms crooked just so, the fingers popping, the body working, the cap and all, the teeth, authentic. But I got sense enough to know I ain't nobody's singer. Actually, I am a mother, though I'm only just now getting it together. And too, I'm an A-1 manicurist.

Me and my cousin Sinbad come North working our show in cathouses at first. Set up a salon right smack in the middle of Miz Maybry's Saturday traffic. But that wasn't no kind of life to be bringing my daughter into. So I

---

2. Charles Mingus (1922–1979), African American jazz bassist, band leader, and composer.
3. Song made into a modern jazz classic by the Miles Davis Quintet and other groups.

4. Popular 1937 song by Richard Rodgers and Lorenz Hart that has become a jazz standard.
5. Contemporary jazz bassist (b. 1937).
6. Contemporary jazz singer (1929–1998).

parked her at a boarding school till I could make some other kind of life. Wasn't no kind of life for Sinbad either, so we quit.

Our first shop was a three-chair affair on Austin. Had a student barber who could do anything—blow-outs, do's, corn rows, weird cuts, afros, press and curl, whatever you wanted. Plus he din't gab you to death. And he always brought his sides and didn't blast em neither. He went on to New York and opened his own shop. Was a bootblack too then, an old dude named James Noughton, had a crooked back and worked at the post office at night, and knew everything about everything, read all the time.

"Whatcha want to know about Marcus Garvey,[7] Sweet Pea?"

If it wasn't Garvey, it was the rackets or the trucking industry or the flora and fauna of Greenland or the planets or how the special effects in the disaster movies were done. One Saturday I asked him to tell me about the war, cause my nephew'd been drafted and it all seemed so wrong to me, our men over there in Nam fighting folks who fighting for the same things we are, to get that blood-sucker off our backs.

Well, what I say that for. Old dude gave us a deep knee bend, straight up eight-credit dissertation on World Wars I and II—the archduke getting offed, Africa cut up like so much cake, Churchill and his cigars, Gabriel Heatter on the radio, Hitler at the Olympics igging Owens, Red Cross doing Bloods dirty refusing donuts and bandages, A. Philip Randolph scaring the white folks to death, Mary McLeod Bethune[8] at the White House, Liberty Bond drives, the Russian front, frostbite of the feet, the Jew stiffs, the gypsies no one mourned . . . the whole johnson. Talked straight through the day, Miz Mary's fish dinner growing cold on the radiator, his one and only customer walking off with one dull shoe. Fell out exhausted, his shoe rag limp in his lap, one arm draped over the left foot platform, the other clutching his heart. Took Sinbad and our cousin Pepper to get the old man home. I stayed with him all night with the ice pack and a fifth of Old Crow.[9] He liked to die.

After while trade picked up and with a better class of folk too. Then me and Sinbad moved to North and Gaylord and called the shop Chez Sinbad. No more winos stumbling in or deadbeats wasting my time talking raunchy shit. The paperboy, the numbers man, the dudes with classier hot stuff coming in on Tuesday mornings only. We did up the place nice. Light globes from a New Orleans whorehouse, Sinbad likes to lie. Brown-and-black-and-silver-striped wallpaper. Lots of mirrors and hanging plants. Them old barber chairs spruced up and called antiques and damn if someone didn't buy one off us for eight hundred, cracked me up.

I cut my schedule down to ten hours in the shop so I could do private sessions with the gamblers and other business men and women who don't like sitting around the shop even though it's comfy, specially my part. Got me a cigar showcase with a marble top for serving coffee in clear glass mugs with heatproof handles too. My ten hours in the shop are spent leisurely. And my

---

7. American black nationalist leader (1887–1940).
8. American educator and founder of the National Council of Negro Women (1875–1955). Chancellor Adolf Hitler (1889–1945), representing Germany as host of the 1936 Olympic Games, refused to honor the African American track and field star Jessie Owens (1913–1980), who had won four gold medals. Randolph (1889–1979), American labor leader and organizer of the Brotherhood of Sleeping Car Porters.
9. A common brand of whiskey.

twenty hours out are making me a mint. Takes dust to be a mother, don't you know.

It was a perfect schedule once Larry Landers came into my life. He part-timed at a record shop and bartended at Topp's on the days and nights I worked at the shops. That gave us most of Monday and Wednesdays to listen to sides and hit the clubs. Gave me Fridays all to myself to study in the library and wade through them college bulletins and get to the museum and generally chart out a routine for when Debbie and me are a team. Sundays I always drive to Delaware to see her, and Larry detours to D.C. to see his sons. My bankbook started telling me I was soon going to be a full-time mama again and a college girl to boot, if I can ever talk myself into doing a school thing again, old as I am.

Life with Larry was cool. Not just cause he wouldn't hear about me going halves on the bills. But cause he was an easy man to be easy with. He liked talking softly and listening to music. And he liked having folks over for dinner and cards. Larry a real nice man and I liked him a lot. And I liked his friend Hector, who lived in the back of the apartment. Ole moon-face Hector went to school with Larry years ago and is some kind of kin. And they once failed in the funeral business together and I guess those stories of them times kinda keep them friends.

The time they had to put Larry's brother away is their best story, Hector's story really, since Larry got to play a little grief music round the edges. They decided to pass up a church service, since Bam was such a treacherous desperado wouldn't nobody want to preach over his body and wouldn't nobody want to come to hear no lies about the dearly departed untimely ripped or cut down or whatever. So Hector and Larry set up some kind of pop stand awning right at the gravesite, expecting close blood only. But seems the whole town turned out to make sure ole evil, hell-raising Bam was truly dead. Dudes straight from the barber chair, the striped ponchos blowing like wings, fuzz and foam on they face and all, lumbering up the hill to the hole taking bets and talking shit, relating how Ole Crazy Bam had shot up the town, shot up the jail, shot up the hospital pursuing some bootlegger who'd come up one keg short of the order. Women from all around come to demand the lid be lifted so they could check for themselves and be sure that Bam was stone cold. No matter how I tried I couldn't think of nobody bad enough to think on when they told the story of the man I'd never met.

Larry and Hector so bent over laughing bout the funeral, I couldn't hardly put the events in proper sequence. But I could surely picture some neighbor lady calling on Larry and Bam's mama reporting how the whole town had turned out for the burying. And the mama snatching up the first black thing she could find to wrap around herself and make an appearance. No use passing up a scene like that. And Larry prancing round the kitchen being his mama. And I'm too stunned to laugh, not at somebody's mama, and somebody's brother dead. But him and Hector laughing to beat the band and I can't help myself.

Thing about it, though, the funeral business stories are Hector's stories and he's not what you'd call a good storyteller. He never gives you the names, so you got all these he's and she's floating around. And he don't believe in giving details, so you got to scramble to paint your own pictures.

Toward the end of that particular tale of Bam, all I could picture was the townspeople driving a stake through the dead man's heart, then hurling that coffin into the hole right quick. There was also something in that story about the civil rights workers wanting to make a case cause a white cop had cut Bam down. But looked like Hector didn't have a hold to that part of the story, so I just don't know.

Stories are not Hector's long suit. But he is an absolute artist on windows. Ole Moon-Face can wash some windows and make you cry about it too. Makes these smooth little turns out there on that little bitty sill just like he wasn't four stories up without a belt. I'd park myself at the breakfast counter and thread the new curtains on the rods while Hector mixed up the vinegar solution real chef-like. Wring out the rags just so, scrunch up the newspapers into soft wads that make you think of cat's paws. Hector was a cat himself out there on the sill, making these marvelous circles in the glass, rubbing the hardhead spots with a strip of steel wool he had pinned to his overalls.

Hector offered to do my car once. But I put a stop to that after that first time. My windshield so clear and sparkling felt like I was in an accident and heading over the hood, no glass there. But it was a pleasure to have coffee and watch Hector. After while, though, Larry started hinting that the apartment wasn't big enough for four. I agreed, thinking he meant Earl had to go. Come to find Larry meant Hector, which was a real drag. I love to be around people who do whatever it is they do with style and care.

Larry's dog's named Earl P. Jessup Bowers, if you can get ready for that. And I should mention straightaway that I do not like dogs one bit, which is why I was glad when Larry said somebody had to go. Cats are bad enough. Horses are a total drag. By the age of nine I was fed up with all that noble horse this and noble horse that. They got good PR,[1] horses. But I really can't use em. Was a fire once when I was little and some dumb horse almost burnt my daddy up messin around, twisting, snorting, broncing, rearing up, doing everything but comin on out the barn like even the chickens had sense enough to do. I told my daddy to let that horse's ass burn. Horses be as dumb as cows. Cows just don't have good press agents at all.

I used to like cows when I was real little and needed to hug me something bigger than a goldfish. But don't let it rain, the dumbbells'll fall right in a ditch and you break a plow and shout yourself hoarse trying to get them fools to come up out the ditch. Chipmunks I don't mind when I'm at the breakfast counter with my tea and they're on their side of the glass doing Disney things in the yard. Blue jays are law-and-order birds, thoroughly despicable. And there's one prize fool in my Aunt Merriam's yard I will one day surely kill. He tries to "whip whip whippoorwill" like the Indians do in the Fort This or That movies when they're signaling to each other closing in on George Montgomery but don't never get around to wiping that sucker out. But dogs are one of my favorite hatreds. All the time woofing, bolting down their food, slopping water on the newly waxed linoleum, messin with you when you trying to read, chewin on the slippers.

Earl P. Jessup Bowers was an especial drag. But I could put up with Earl when Hector was around. Once Hector was gone and them windows got cloudy and gritty, I was through. Kicked that dog every chance I got. And

1. Public relations; here suggesting a good image, good reputation.

after thinking what it meant, how the deal went down, place too small for four and it was Hector not Earl—I started moving up my calendar so I could get out of there. I ain't the kind of lady to press no ultimatum on no man. Like "Choose, me or the dog." That's unattractive. Kicking Hector out was too. An insult to me, once I got to thinking on it. Especially since I had carefully explained from jump street to Larry that I got one item on my agenda, making a home for me and my kid. So if anybody should've been given walking papers, should've been me.

Anyway. One day Moody comes waltzing into. Chez Sinbad's and tips his hat. He glances at his nails and glances at me. And I figure here is my house in a green corduroy suit. Pot Limit had just read my cards and the jack of diamonds kept coming up on my resource side. Sylvia and me put our heads together and figure it got to be some gambler or hustler who wants his nails done. What other jacks do I know to make my fortune? I'm so positive about Moody, I whip out a postcard from the drawer where I keep the emeries and write my daughter to start packing.

"How much you make a day, Miss Lady?"

"Thursdays are always good for fifty," I lie.

He hands me fifty and glances over at Sinbad, who nods that it's cool. "I'd like my nails done at four-thirty. My place."

"Got a customer at that time, Mr. Moody, and I like to stay reliable. How bout five-twenty?"

He smiles a slow smile and glances at Sinbad, who nods again, everything's cool. "Fine," he says. "And do you think you can manage a shave without cutting a person's throat?"

"Mr. Moody, I don't know you well enough to have just cause. And none of your friends have gotten to me yet with that particular proposition. Can't say what I'm prepared to do in the future, but for now I can surely shave you real careful-like."

Moody smiles again, then turns to Sinbad, who says it's cool and he'll give me the address. This look-nod dialogue burns my ass. That's like when you take a dude to lunch and pay the check and the waiter's standing there with *your* money in his paws asking *the dude* was everything all right and later for *you*. Shit. But I take down Moody's address and let the rest roll off me like so much steaming lava. I start packing up my little alligator case— buffer, batteries, clippers, emeries, massager, sifter, arrowroot and cornstarch, clear sealer, magnifying glass, and my own mixture of green and purple pigments.

"Five-twenty ain't five-twenty-one, is it, Miss Lady?"

"Not in my book," I say, swinging my appointment book around so he can see how full it is and how neatly the times are printed in. Course I always fill in phony names case some creep starts pressing me for a session.

For six Thursdays running and two Monday nights, I'm at Moody's bending over them nails with a miner's light strapped to my forehead, the magnifying glass in its stand, nicking just enough of the nails at the sides, tinting just enough with the color so he can mark them cards as he shuffles. Takes an hour to do it proper. Then I sift my talc concoction and brush his hands till they're smooth. Them cards move around so fast in his hands, he can actually tell me he's about to deal from the bottom in the next three moves and I miss it and I'm not new to this. I been a gambler's manicurist for more years than I care to mention. Ten times he'll cut and each time the same fifteen cards in the top cut and each time in exactly the same order. Incredible.

Now, I've known hands. My first husband, for instance. To see them hands work their show in the grandstands, at a circus, in a parade, the parimutuels—artistry in action. We met on the train. As a matter of fact, he was trying to burgle my bag. Some story to tell the grandchildren, hunh? I had to get him straight about robbing from folks. I don't play that. Ya gonna steal, hell, steal back some of them millions we got in escrow is my opinion. We spent three good years on the circuit. Then credit cards moved in. Then choke-and-grab muggers killed the whole tradition. He was reduced to a mere shell of his former self, as they say, and took to putting them hands on me. I try not to think on when things went sour. Try not to think about them big slapping hands, only of them working hands. Moody's working hands were something like that, but even better. So I'm impressed and he's impressed. And he pays me fifty and tips me fifty and shuts up when I shave him and keeps his hands off my lovely person.

I'm so excited counting up my bread, moving up the calendar, making impulsive calls to Delaware and the two of us squealing over the wire like a coupla fools, that what Larry got to say about all these goings-on just rolls off my back like so much molten lead.

"Well, who be up there while he got his head in your lap and you squeezing his goddamn blackheads?"

"I don't squeeze his goddamn blackheads, Larry, on account of he don't have no goddamn blackheads. I give him a shave, a steam, and an egg-white face mask. And when I'm through, his face is as smooth as his hands."

"I'll bet," Larry says. That makes me mad cause I expect some kind of respect for my work, which is better than just good.

"And he doesn't have his head in my lap. He's got a whole barbershop set up on his solarium."

"His what?" Larry squinting at me, raising the wooden spoon he stirring the spaghetti with, and I raise the knife I'm chopping the onions with. Thing about it, though, he don't laugh. It's funny as hell to me, but Larry got no sense of humor sometimes, which is too bad cause he's a lotta fun when he's laughing and joking.

"It's not a bedroom. He's got this screened-in sun porch where he raises African violets and—"

"Please, Sweet Pea. Why don't you quit? You think I'm dumb?"

"I'm serious. I'm serious and I'm mad cause I ain't got no reason to lie to you whatever was going on, Larry." He turns back to the pot and I continue working on the sauce and I'm pissed off cause this is silly. "He sits in the barber chair and I shave him and give him a manicure."

"What else you be giving him? A man don't be paying a good-looking woman to come to his house and all and don't—"

"Larry, if you had the dough and felt like it, wouldn't you pay Pot Limit to come read your cards? And couldn't you keep your hands to yourself and she a good-looking woman? And couldn't you see yourself paying Sylvia to come and cook for you and no funny stuff, and she's one of the best-looking women in town?"

Larry cooled out fast. My next shot was to bring up the fact that he was insulting my work. Do I go around saying the women who pass up Bill the bartender and come to him are after his joint? No, cause I respect the fact that Larry Landers mixes the best piña coladas this side of Barbados. And he's flashy with the blender and the glasses and the whole show. He's good and I respect that. But he cooled out so fast I didn't have to bring it up. I don't believe in overkill, besides I like to keep some things in reserve. He cooled out so fast I realized he wasn't really jealous. He was just going through one of them obligatory male numbers, all symbolic, no depth.

Like the time this dude came into the shop to talk some trash and Sinbad got his ass on his shoulders, talking about the dude showed no respect for him cause for all he knew I could be Sinbad's woman. And me arguing that since that ain't the case, what's the deal? I mean why get hot over what if if what if ain't. Men are crazy. Now there is Sinbad, my blood cousin who grew up right in the same house like a brother damn near, putting me through simple-ass changes like that. Who's got time for grand opera and comic strips, I'm trying to make a life for me and my kid. But men are like that. Gorillas, if you know what I mean.

Like at Topp's sometimes. I'll drop in to have a drink with Larry when he's on the bar and then I leave. And maybe some dude'll take it in his head to walk me to the car. That's cool. I lay it out right quick that me and Larry are a we and then we take it from there, just two people gassing in the summer breeze and that's just fine. But don't let some other dude holler over something like "Hey, man, can you handle all that? Why don't you step aside, junior, and let a man . . ." and blah-de-da-de-dah. They can be the best of friends or total strangers just kidding around, but right away they two gorillas pounding on their chest, pounding on their chest and talking over my head, yelling over the tops of cars just like I'm not a person with some say-so in the matter. It's a man-to-man ritual that ain't got nothing to do with me. So I just get in my car and take off and leave them to get it on if they've a mind to. They got it.

But if one of the gorillas is a relative, or a friend of mine, or a nice kinda man I got in mind for one of my friends, I will stick around long enough to shout em down and point out that they are some ugly gorillas and are showing no respect for me and therefore owe me an apology. But if they don't fit into one of them categories, I figure it ain't my place to try to develop them so they can make the leap from gorilla to human. If their own mamas and daddies didn't care whether they turned out to be amoebas or catfish or whatever, it ain't my weight. I got my own weight. I'm a mother. So they got it.

Like I use to tell my daughter's daddy, the key to getting along and living with other folks is to keep clear whose weight is whose. His drinking, for instance, was not my weight. And him waking me up in the night for them long, rambling, ninety-proof monologues bout how the whole world's made up of victims, rescuers, and executioners and I'm the dirty bitch cause I ain't rescuing him fast enough to suit him. Then got so I was the executioner, to hear him tell it. I don't say nuthin cause my philosophy of life and death is this—I'll go when the wagon comes, but I ain't going out behind somebody else's shit. I arranged my priorities long ago when I jumped into my woman stride. Some things I'll go off on. Some things I'll hold my silence and wait it out. Some things I just bump off, cause the best solution to some problems is to just abandon them.

But I struggled with Mac, Debbie's daddy. Talked to his family, his church, AA, hid the bottles, threatened the liquor man, left a good job to play nurse, mistress, kitten, buddy. But then he stopped calling me Dahlin and started calling me Mama. I don't play that. I'm my daughter's mama. So I split. Did my best to sweeten them last few months, but I'd been leaving for a long time.

The silliest thing about all of Larry's grumblings back then was Moody had no eyes for me and vice versa. I just like the money. And I like watching him mess around with the cards. He's exquisite, dazzling, stunning shuffling, cutting, marking, dealing from the bottom, the middle, the near top. I ain't never seen nothing like it, and I seen a whole lot. The thing that made me mad, though, and made me know Larry Landers wasn't ready to deal with no woman full grown was the way he kept bringing it up, always talking about what he figured was on Moody's mind, like what's on my mind don't count. So I finally did have to use up my reserves and point out to Larry that he was insulting my work and that I would never dream of accusing him of not being a good bartender, of just being another pretty face, like they say.

"You can't tell me he don't have eyes," he kept saying.

"What about my eyes? Don't my eyes count?" I gave it up after a coupla tries. All I know is, Moody wasn't even thinking about me. I was impressed with his work and needed the trade and vice versa.

One time, for instance, I was doing his hands on the solarium and thought I saw a glint of metal up under his jacket. I rearranged myself in the chair so I could work my elbow in there to see if he was carrying heat. I thought I was being cool about it.

"How bout keeping your tits on your side of the table, Miss Lady."

I would rather he think anything but that. I would rather he think I was clumsy in my work even. "Wasn't about tits, Moody. I was just trying to see if you had a holster on and was too lazy to ask."

"Would have expected you too. You a straight-up, direct kind of person." He opened his jacket away with the heel of his hand, being careful with his nails. I liked that.

"It's not about you," he said quietly, jerking his chin in the direction of the revolver. "Had to transport some money today and forgot to take it off. Sorry."

I gave myself two demerits. One for the tits, the other for setting up a situation where he wound up telling me something about his comings and goings. I'm too old to be making mistakes like that. So I apologized. Then gave myself two stars. He had a good opinion of me and my work. I did an extra-fine job on his hands that day.

Then the house happened. I had been reading the rental ads and For Sale columns for months and looking at some awful, tacky places. Then one Monday me and Sylvia lucked up on this cute little white-brick job up on a hill away from the street. Lots of light and enough room and not too much yard to kill me off. I paid my money down and rushed them papers through. Got back to Larry's place all excited and found him with his mouth all poked out.

Half grumbling, half proposing, he hinted around that we all should live at his place like a family. Only he didn't quite lay it out plain in case of rejection.

And I'll tell you something, I wouldn't want to be no man. Must be hard on the heart always having to get out there, setting yourself up to be possibly shot down, approaching the lady, calling, the invitation, the rap. I don't think I could handle it myself unless everybody was just straight up at all times from day one till the end. I didn't answer Larry's nonproposed proposal cause it didn't come clear to me till after dinner. So I just let my silence carry whatever meaning it will. Ain't nuthin too much changed from the first day he came to get me from my Aunt Merriam's place. My agenda is still to make a home for my girl. Marriage just ain't one of the things on my mind no more, not after two. Got no regrets or bad feelings about them husbands neither. Like the poem says, when you're handed a lemon, make lemonade, honey, make lemonade. That's Gwen Brooks'[2] motto, that's mine too. You get a lemon, well, just make lemonade.

"Going on the road next week," Moody announces one day through the steam towel. "Like you to travel with me, keep my hands in shape. Keep the women off my neck. Check the dudes at my back. Ain't asking you to carry heat or money or put yourself in no danger. But I could use your help." He pauses and I ease my buns into the chair, staring at the steam curling from the towel.

"Wicked schedule though—Mobile, Birmingham, Sarasota Springs, Jacksonville, then Puerto Rico and back. Can pay you two thousand and expenses. You're good, Miss Lady. You're good and you got good sense. And while I don't believe in nothing but my skill and chance, I gotta say you've brought me luck. You a lucky lady, Miss Lady."

He raises his hands and cracks his knuckles and it's like the talking towel has eyes as well cause damn if he ain't checking his cuticles.

"I'll call you later, Moody," I manage to say, mind reeling. With two thousand I can get my stuff out of storage, and buy Debbie a real nice bedroom set, pay tuition at the college too and start my three-credit-at-a-time grind.

Course I never dreamed the week would be so unnerving, exhausting, constantly on my feet, serving drinks, woofing sisters, trying to distract dudes, keeping track of fifty-leven umpteen goings on. Did have to carry the heat on three occasions and had to do a helluva lotta driving. Plus was most of the time holed up in the hotel room close to the phone. I had pictured myself lazying on the beach in Florida dreaming up cruises around the world with two matching steamer trunks with the drawers and hangers and stuff. I'd pictured traipsing through the casinos in Puerto Rico ordering chicken salad and coffee liqueur and tipping the croupiers with blue chips. Shit no. Was work. And I sure as hell learned how Moody got his name. Got so we didn't even speak, but I kept those hands in shape and his face smooth and placid. And whether he won, lost, broke even, or got wiped out, I don't even know. He gave me my money and took off for New Orleans. That trip liked to kill me.

"You never did say nothing interesting about Moody," Pot Limit says insinuatingly, swinging her legs in from the aisle cause ain't nobody there to snatch so she might as well sit comfortable.

"Yeah, she thought she'd put us off the trail with a rip-roaring tale about Larry's housekeeping."

---

2. Gwendolyn Brooks (1917–2000), American poet, novelist, and autobiographer.

They slapping five and hunching each other and making a whole lotta noise, spilling Jack Daniels on my turquoise T-straps from Puerto Rico.

"Come on, fess up, Sweet Pea," they crooning. "Did you give him some?"

"Ahhh, yawl bitches are tiresome, you know that?"

"Naaw, naaw," say Sylvia, grabbing my arm. "You can tell us. We wantta know all about the trip, specially the nights." She winks at Pot Limit.

"Tell us about this Moody man and his wonderful hands one more time, cept we want to hear how the hands feel on the flesh, honey." Pot Limit doing a bump and grind in the chair that almost makes me join in the fun, except I'm worried in my mind about Larry Landers.

Just then the piano player comes by and leans over Sylvia, blowing in her ear. And me and Pot Limit mimic the confectionary goings-on. And just as well, cause there's nothin to tell about Moody. It wasn't a movie after all. And in real life the good-looking gambler's got cards on his mind. Just like I got my child on my mind. Onliest thing to say about the trip is I'm five pounds lighter, not a shade darker, but two thousand closer toward my goal.

"Ease up," Sylvia says, interrupting the piano player to fuss over me. Then the drummer comes by and eases in on Pot Limit. And I ease back into the shadows of the booth to think Larry over.

I'm staring at the entrance half expecting Larry to come into Topps, but it's not his night. Then too, the thing is ended if I'd only know it. Larry the kind of man you're either living with him or you're out. I for one would've liked us to continue, me and Debbie in our place, him and Earl at his. But he got so grumpy the time I said that, I sure wasn't gonna bring it up again. Got grumpy in the shower too, got so he didn't want to wash my back.

But that last night fore I left for Birmingham, we had us one crazy musical time in the shower. I kept trying to lure him into "Maiden Voyage," which I really can't do without back-up, cause I can't sing all them changes. After while he come out from behind his sulk and did a Jon Lucien[3] combination on vocal and bass, alternating the sections, eight bars of singing words, eight bars of singing bass. It was baad. Then he insisted on doing "I Love You More Today Than Yesterday." And we like to break our arches, stomping out the beat against the shower mat.

The bathroom was all steamy and we had the curtains open so we could see the plants and watch the candles burning. I had bought us a big fat cake of sandalwood soap and it was matching them candles scent for scent. Must've been two o'clock in the morning and looked like the hot water would last forever and ever and ever. Larry finally let go of the love songs, which were making me feel kinda funny cause I thought it was understood that I was splitting, just like he'd always made it clear either I was there or nowhere.

Then we hit on a tune I don't even know the name of cept I like to scat and do my thing Larry calls Swahili wailing. He laid down the most intricate weaving, walking, bopping, strutting bottom to my singing I ever heard. It inspired me. Took that melody and went right on out that shower, them candles bout used up, the fatty soap long since abandoned in the dish, our bodies barely visible in the steamed-up mirrors walling his bathroom. Took that melody right on out the room and out of doors and somewhere out this world. Larry changing instruments fast as I'm changing moods, colors. Took an alto

3. Caribbean-born American jazz vocalist and musician (b. 1942).

solo and gave me a rest, worked an intro up on the piano playing the chords across my back, drove me all up into the high register while he weaved in and out around my head on a flute sounding like them chilly pipes of the Andes.[4] And I was Yma Sumac[5] for one minute there, up there breathing some rare air and losing my mind, I was so high on just sheer music. Music and water, the healthiest things in the world. And that hot water pounding like it was part of the group with a union card and all. And I could tell that if that bass could've fit in the tub, Larry would've dragged that bad boy in there and played the hell out of them soggy strings once and for all.

I dipped way down and reached way back for snatches of Jelly Roll Morton's "Deep Creek Blues"[6] and Larry so painful, so stinging on the bass, could make you cry. Then I'm racing fast through Bessie and all the other Smith singers, Mildred Bailey, Billie and imitators, Betty Roche, Nat King Cole vintage 46, a little Joe Carroll, King Pleasure, some Babs.[7] Found myself pulling lines out of songs I don't even like, but ransacked songs just for the meaningful lines or two cause I realized we were doing more than just making music together, and it had to be said just how things stood.

Then I was off again and lost Larry somewhere down there doing scales, sound like. And he went back to that first supporting line that had drove me up into the Andes. And he stayed there waiting for me to return and do some more Swahili wailing. But I was elsewhere and liked it out there and ignored the fact that he was aiming for a wind-up of "I Love You More Today Than Yesterday." I sang myself out till all I could ever have left in life was "Brown Baby" to sing to my little girl. Larry stayed on the ground with the same supporting line, and the hot water started getting funny and I knew my time was up. So I came crashing down, jarring the song out of shape, diving back into the melody line and somehow, not even knowing what song each other was doing, we finished up together just as the water turned cold.

1977

4. Mountain range in South America. "Chilly pipes": i.e., panpipes, common in Chilean folk music.
5. Peruvian singer (b. 1922) popular with Ameri-

can audiences in the 1950s.
6. Dixieland jazz classic of the 1920s.
7. Blues and jazz musicians of the 1920s, 1930s, and 1940s.

THOMAS McGUANE
b. 1939

Traditionally, the novel of manners is associated with the later nineteenth century and themes of developed societies. In America, Nathaniel Hawthorne (1804–1859) wrote a Preface to *The House of the Seven Gables: A Romance* (1851) that voiced his depair over the lack of sufficiently civilized manners in his milieu for such a novel, while a generation later Henry James (1843–1916) either placed his narratives in the sophisticated circles of Boston and New York or looked to

England and Europe for more compelling social contexts. Hence it is noteworthy that after a century and more one of the most distinctive American novelists of manners is a Westerner whose orientation is toward what remains of the frontier.

Thomas McGuane was born in Wyandotte, Michigan, and attended the nearby Cranbrook Academy in Bloomfield Hills, but his delight was working summers on a ranch in Wyoming owned by a friend's father and spending vacations at his family's retreats in coastal Massachusetts and along the Pere Marquette River in the northern reaches of his native state. As a boy he learned the codes of behavior that governed life in these places devoted to riding and fishing, the social manners of which he portrayed in his first novel, *The Sporting Club* (1969). *The Bushwacked Piano* (1971), *Ninety-Two in the Shade* (1973), and *Panama* (1978) follow the adventures of a protagonist sensitive to the varying manners of the rich and the poor across the United States, ending up in the Florida Keys, to which McGuane had been drawn for its fishing. *An Outside Chance: Essays on Sport* (1980) collects his reflections on how such endeavors provide a useful index for understanding traits of characters and expressions of value.

Work as a screenwriter on *Rancho Deluxe* (1975) and *The Missouri Breaks* (1976) took McGuane to Montana, where he had purchased a ranch in 1968 with the advance for his first novel (while maintaining homes in Key West in the meantime). Publication of his novel *Nobody's Angel* (1982) marks his self-definition as a Western writer, now residing mostly on his ranch and placing his work, fiction and nonfiction alike, almost exclusively in the region. His first Montana hero is Patrick Fitzgerald, living on a third-generation family ranch and cognizant that out here "you would have to care about the country. Nobody had been here long enough and the Indians had been very thoroughly kicked out. It would take a shovel to find they'd ever been here." For McGuane the fiction writer, the West is neither a place for romantic visions nor explosive action. Instead, his characters create an existence on the tabula rasa of the High Plains, where beauty is measured in the scores of miles to the ridgeline of distant mountains, while the business of life is worked out in a society stripped down to its basic elements.

McGuane's subsequent Montana canon includes the novels *Something to Be Desired* (1984), *Keep the Change* (1989), *Nothing But Blue Skies* (1992), *The Cadence of Grass* (2002), and *Driving on the Rim* (2010); the short story collections *To Skin a Cat* (1986) and *Gallatin Canyon* (2006); and the nonfiction volumes *An Outside Chance: Classic and New Essays on Sport* (1990), *Some Horses* (1999), and *The Longest Silence: A Life in Fishing* (1999). His literary environment has included part-time Montana residents Richard Brautigan and Jim Harrison, as well as visitors such as Jimmy Buffett. A champion roper, McGuane was inducted into the National Cutting Horse Hall of Fame on his sixty-sixth birthday in 2005.

The following text is the title story from the 2006 collection *Gallatin Canyon*.

Gallatin Canyon

The day we planned the trip, I told Louise that I didn't like going to Idaho via the Gallatin Canyon.[1] It's too narrow, and while trucks don't belong on this road, there they are, lots of them. Tourist pull-offs and wild animals on the highway complete the picture. We could have gone by way of Ennis, but Louise had learned that there were road repairs on Montana Highway 84—twelve miles of torn-up asphalt—in addition to its being rodeo weekend.

---

1. Spectacular canyon in southwestern Montana formed by the Gallatin River, a renowned trout stream.

"Do we have to go to Idaho?" she asked.

I said I thought it was obvious. A lot rode on the success of our little jaunt, which was ostensibly to close the sale of a small car dealership I owned in the sleepy town of Rigby. But, since accepting the offer of a local buyer, I had received a far better one from elsewhere, which, my attorney said, I couldn't take unless my original buyer backed out—and he would only back out if he got sufficiently angry at me. Said my attorney, Make him mad. So I was headed to Rigby, Idaho, expressly to piss off a small-town business-man, who was trying to give me American money for a going concern on the strip east of town, and thereby make room for a rich Atlanta investor, new to our landscape, who needed this dealership as a kind of flagship for his other intentions. The question was how to provoke Rigby without arousing his suspicions, and I might have collected my thoughts a little better had I not had to battle trucks and tourists in the Gallatin Canyon.

Louise and I had spent a lot of time together in recent years, and we were both probably wondering where things would go from here. She had been married, briefly, long ago, and that fact, together with the relatively peaceful intervening years, gave a pleasant detachment to most of her relationships, including the one she had with me. In the past, that would have suited me perfectly; it did not seem to suit me now, and I was so powerfully attached to her it made me uncomfortable that she wasn't interested in discussing our mutual future, though at least she had never suggested that we wouldn't have one. With her thick blond hair pulled back in a barrette, her strong, shapely figure, and the direct fullness of her mouth, she was often noticed by other men. After ten years in Montana, she still had a strong Massachu-setts accent. Louise was a lawyer, specializing in the adjudication of water rights between agricultural and municipal interests. In our rapidly changing world, she was much in demand. Though I wished we could spend more time together, Louise had taught me not to challenge her on this.

No longer the country crossroads of recent memory, Four Corners was filled with dentists' offices, fast-food and espresso shops, and large and somehow foreboding filling stations that looked, at night, like colonies in space; never-theless, the intersection was true to its name, sending you north to a transcon-tinental interstate, east into town, west to the ranches of Madison County, and south, my reluctant choice, up the Gallatin Canyon to Yellowstone and the towns of southeast Idaho, one of which contained property with my name on the deed.

We joined the stream of traffic heading south, the Gallatin River along-side and usually much below the roadway, a dashing high-gradient river with anglers in reflective stillness at the edges of its pools and bright rafts full of delighted tourists in flotation jackets and crash helmets sweeping through its white water. Gradually, the mountains pressed in on all this humanity, and I found myself behind a long line of cars trailing a cattle truck at well below the speed limit. This combination of cumbersome com-mercial traffic and impatient private cars was a lethal mixture that kept our canyon in the papers, as it regularly spat out corpses. In my rearview mir-ror, I could see a line behind me that was just as long as the one ahead, stretching back, thinning, and vanishing around a green bend. There was no passing lane for several miles. A single amorous elk could have turned us all into twisted, smoking metal.

"You might have been right," Louise said. "It doesn't look good."

She almost certainly had better things to do. But, looking down the line of cars, I felt my blood pressure rising. Her hands rested quietly in her lap. I couldn't possibly have rivaled such serenity.

"How do you plan to anger this guy in Rigby?" she asked.

"I'm going to try haughtiness. If I suggest that he bought the dealership cheap, he might tell me to keep the damn thing. The Atlanta guy just wants to start somewhere. All these people have a sort of parlay mentality, and they need to get on the playing field before they can start running it up. I'm a trader. It all happens for me in the transition. The moment of liquidation is the essence of capitalism."

"What about the man in Rigby?"

"He's an end user. He wants to keep it."

I reflected on the pathos of ownership and the way it could bog you down.

"You should be in my world," Louise said. "According to the law, water has no reality except its use. In Montana, water isn't even wet. Every time some misguided soul suggests that fish need it, it ends up in the state supreme court."

Birds were fleeing the advance of automobiles. I was elsewhere, trying to imagine my buyer, red-faced, storming out of the closing. I'd offer to let bygones be bygones, I'd take him to dinner, I'd throw a steak into him, for Christ's sake. In the end, he'd be glad he wasn't stuck with the lot.

Traffic headed toward us, far down the road. We were all packed together to make sure no one tried to pass. The rules had to be enforced. Occasionally, someone drifted out for a better look, but not far enough that someone else could close his space and possibly seal his fate.

This trip had its risks. I had only recently admitted to myself that I would like to make more of my situation with Louise than currently existed. Though ours was hardly a chaste relationship, real intimacy was relatively scarce. People in relationships nowadays seemed to retain their secrets like bank deposits—they always set some aside, in case they might need them to spend on someone new. I found it unpleasant to think that Louise could be withholding anything.

But I thought I was more presentable than I had been. When Louise and I first met, I was just coming off two and a half years of peddling satellite dishes in towns where a couple of dogs doing the wild thing in the middle of the road amounted to the high point of a year, and the highest-grossing business was a methamphetamine tent camp out in the sagebrush. Now I had caught the upswing in our local economy: cars, storage, tool rental, and mortgage discounting. I had a pretty home, debt-free, out on Sourdough. I owned a few things. I could be okay. I asked Louise what she thought of the new prosperity around us. She said wearily, "I'm not sure it's such a good thing, living in a boomtown. It's basically a high-end carny atmosphere."

We were just passing Storm Castle and Garnet Mountain. When I glanced in the mirror, I saw a low red car with a scoop in its hood pull out to pass. I must have reacted somehow, because Louise asked me if I would like her to drive.

"No, that's fine. Things are getting a bit lively back there."

"Drive defensively."

"Not much choice, is there?"

I had been mentally rehearsing the closing in Rigby, and I wasn't getting anywhere. I had this sort of absurd picture of myself strutting into the meeting. I tried again to picture the buyer looking seriously annoyed, but I'd met him before and he seemed pretty levelheaded. I suspected I'd have to be really outlandish to get a rise out of him. He was a fourth-generation resident of Rigby, so I could always urge him to get to know his neighbors, I decided. Or, since he had come up through the service department, I could try emphasizing the need to study how the cars actually ran. I'd use hand signals to fend off objections. I felt more secure.

Some elk had wandered into the parking lot at Buck's T4 and were grazing indifferently as people pulled off the highway to admire them. I don't know if it was the great unmarred blue sky overhead or the balsamic zephyr that poured down the mountainside, but I found myself momentarily buoyed by all this idleness, people out of their cars. I am always encouraged when I see animals doing something other than running for their lives. In any case, the stream of traffic ahead of us had been much reduced by the pedestrian rubbernecking.

"My husband lived here one winter," Louise said. "He sold his pharmacy after we divorced, not that he had to, and set out to change his life. He became a mountain man, wore buckskin clothes. He tried living off the land one day a week, with the idea that he would build up. But then he just stuck with one day a week—he'd shoot a rabbit or something, more of a diet, really. He's a real-estate agent now, at Big Sky. I think he's doing well. At least he's quit killing rabbits."

"Remarried?"

"Yes."

As soon as we hit the open country around West Yellowstone, Louise called her office. When her secretary put her on hold, Louise covered the mouthpiece and said, "He married a super gal. Minnesota, I think. She should be good for Bob, and he's not easy. Bob's from the South. For men, it's a full-time job being Southern. It just wears them out. It wore me out too. I developed doubtful behaviors. I pulled out my eyelashes and ate twenty-eight hundred dollars' worth of macadamia nuts."

Her secretary came back on the line, and Louise began editing her schedule with impressive precision, mouthing the word *sorry* to me when the conversation dragged on. I began musing about my capacity to live successfully with someone as competent as Louise. There was no implied hierarchy of status between us, but I wondered if, in the long run, something would have to give.

West Yellowstone seemed entirely given over to the well-being of the snowmobile, and the billboards dedicated to it were anomalous on a sunny day like today. By winter, schoolchildren would be petitioning futilely to control the noise at night so they could do their schoolwork, and the town would turn a blind eye as a cloud of smoke arose to gas residents, travelers, and park rangers alike. It seemed incredible to me that recreation could acquire this level of social momentum, that it could be seen as an inalienable right.

We came down Targhee Pass to Idaho, into a wasteland of spindly pines that had replaced the former forest, and Louise gave voice to the thoughts she'd been having for the past few miles. "Why don't you just let this deal close? You really have no guarantees from the man from Atlanta. And there's a good-faith issue here too, I think."

"A lawyerly notation."

"So be it, but it's true. Are you trying to get every last cent out of this sale?"

"That's second. The first priority is to be done with it. It was meant to be a passive investment, and it has turned out not to be. I get twenty calls a day from the dealership, most with questions I can't answer. It's turning me into a giant bullshit machine."

"No investments are really passive."

"Mutual funds are close."

"That's why they don't pay."

"Some of them pay, or they would cease to exist."

"You make a poor libertarian, my darling. You sound like that little puke David Stockman."[2]

"Stockman was right about everything. Reagan[3] just didn't have the guts to take his advice."

"Reagan. Give me a break."

I didn't mind equal billing in a relationship, but I did dread the idea of parties speaking strictly from their entitlements across a chasm. Inevitably, sex would make chaos of much of this, but you couldn't, despite Benjamin Franklin's[4] suggestion, "use venery" as a management tool.

Louise adjusted her seat back and folded her arms, gazing at the sunny side of the road. The light through the windshield accentuated the shape of her face, now in repose. I found her beautiful. I adored her when she was a noun and was alarmed when she was a verb, which was usually the case. I understood that this was not the best thing I could say about myself. When her hand drifted over to my leg, I hardly knew what to do with this reference to the other life we led. I knew it was an excellent thing to be reminded of how inconsequential my worldly concerns were, but one warm hand, rested casually, and my interest traveled to the basics of the species.

Ashton, St. Anthony, Sugar City: Mormon hamlets, small farms, and the furious reordering of watersheds into industrial canals. Irrigation haze hung over the valley of the Snake, and the skies were less bright than they had been just a few miles back, in Montana. Many locals had been killed when the Teton Dam burst,[5] and despite that they wanted to build it again: the relationship to water here was like a war, and in war lives are lost. These were the folk to whom I'd sold many a plain car; ostentation was thoroughly unacceptable hereabouts. The four-door sedan with a six-cylinder engine was the desired item, an identical one with a hundred and fifty thousand miles on it generally taken in trade at zero value, thanks to the manipulation of rebates against the manufacturer's suggested retail. Appearances were

2. American politician and businessman who served as Director of the Office of Management and Budget (1981–1985) during the first term of the Reagan Administration. He counseled substantial budget cuts to offset the effects of tax cuts, but his advice was largely ignored as the U.S. debt soared.
3. American film actor, television host, and political leader (1911–2004), thirty-third governor of California and fortieth president of the United States.
4. American author, publisher, and statesman (1706–1790), whose autobiography (begun in 1771 but never finished) counsels: "Rarely use venery but for health or offspring, never to dullness, weakness, or the injury of your own or another's peace or reputation."
5. The collapse of the Teton Dam in Idaho on June 5, 1976, left 11 persons dead and 25,000 homeless.

foremost, and the salesman who could leave a customer's smugness undisturbed flourished in this atmosphere. I had two of them, potato-fattened bland opportunists with nine kids between them. They were the asset I was selling; the rest was little more than bricks and mortar.

We pressed on toward Rexburg, and amid the turnoffs for Wilford, Newdale, Hibbard, and Moody the only thing that had any flavor was Hog Hollow Road, which was a shortcut to France—not the one in Europe but the one just a hop, skip, and a jump south of Squirrel, Idaho. There were license-plate holders with my name on them in Squirrel, and I was oddly vain about that.

"Sure seems lonesome around here," Louise said.

"Oh, boy."

"The houses are like little forts."

"The winters are hard." But it was less that the small neat dwellings around us appeared defensive than that they seemed to be trying to avoid attracting the wrath of some inattentive god.

"It looks like government housing for Eskimos. They just sit inside, waiting for a whale or something."

This banter had the peculiar effect of making me want to cleave to Louise, and desperately, too—to build a warm new civilization, possibly in a foolish house with turrets. The road stretched before me like an arrow. There was only enough of it left before Rigby for me to say, perhaps involuntarily, "I wonder if we shouldn't just get married."

Louise quickly looked away. Her silence conferred a certain seriousness on my question.

But there was Rigby, and, in the parlance of all who have extracted funds from locals, Rigby had been good to me. Main Street was lined with ambitious and beautiful stone buildings, old for this part of the world. Their second and third floors were now affordable housing, and their street levels were occupied by businesses hanging on by their fingernails. You could still detect the hopes of the dead, their dreams, even, though it seemed to be only a matter of time before the wind carried them away, once and for all.

I drove past the car lot at 200 East Fremont without comment and—considering the amount of difficulty it had caused me in the years before I got it stabilized and began to enjoy its very modest yields—without much feeling. I remembered the day, sometime earlier, when I had tried to help park the cars in the front row and got everything so crooked that the salesmen, not concealing their contempt, had to do it all over again. The title company where we were heading was on the same street, and it was a livelier place, from the row of perky evergreens out front to the merry receptionist who greeted us, a handsome young woman, probably a farm girl only moments before, enjoying the clothes, makeup, and perquisites of the new world that her firm was helping to build.

We were shown into a spacious conference room with a long table and chairs, freshly sharpened pencils, and crisp notepads bearing the company letterhead. "Shall I stay?" Louise asked, the first thing she'd said since my earlier inadvertent remark, which I intuited had not been altogether rejected.

"Please," I said, gesturing toward a chair next to the one I meant to take. At that moment, the escrow agent entered and, standing very close to us, introduced himself as Brent Colby. Then he went to the far end of the table, where he spread his documents around in an orderly fan. Colby was around fifty, with iron gray hair and a deeply lined face. He wore pressed jeans, a brilliant white snap-button shirt, cowboy boots, and a belt buckle with a steer head on it. He had thick, hairy hands and a gleaming wedding band. Just as he raised his left wrist to check his watch, the door opened and Oren Johnson, the buyer, entered. He went straight to Louise and, taking her hand in both of his, introduced himself. It occurred to me that, in trying to be suave, Oren Johnson had revealed himself to be a clodhopper, but I was probably just experiencing the mild hostility that emanates from every sale of property. Oren wore a suit, though it suggested less a costume for business than one for church. He had a gold tooth and a cautious pompadour. He too bore an investment-grade wedding band, and I noted that there was plenty of room in his black-laced shoes for his toes. He turned and said it was good to see me again after so long. The time had come for me to go into my act. With grotesque hauteur, I said I didn't realize we had ever met. This was work.

Oren Johnson bustled with inchoate energy; he was the kind of small-town leader who sets an example by silently getting things done. He suggested this just by arranging his pencils and notepad and repositioning his chair with rough precision. Locking eyes with me, he stated that he was a man of his word. I didn't know what he was getting at, but took it to mean that the formalities of a closing were superfluous to the old-time handshake with which Oren Johnson customarily did business. I smiled and quizzically cocked my head as if to say that the newfangled arrangements with well-attested documents promptly conveyed to the courthouse suited me just fine, that deals made on handshakes were strictly for the pious or the picturesque. My message was clear enough that Louise shifted uncomfortably in her chair, and Brent Colby knocked his documents edgewise on the desk to align them. As far as Oren Johnson was concerned, I was beginning to feel that anyone who strayed from the basic patterns of farm life to sell cars bore watching. Like a Method[6] actor, I already believed my part.

"You're an awfully lucky man, Oren Johnson," I said to him, leaning back in my chair. I could see Louise openmouthed two seats away from Brent Colby, and observing myself through her eyes gave me a sudden burst of panic.

"Oh?" Oren Johnson said. "How's that?"

"How's that?" I did a precise job of replicating his inflection. "I am permitting you to purchase my car lot. You've seen the books: how often does a man get a shot at a business where all the work's been done for him?"

Brent Colby was doing an incomplete job of concealing his distaste; he was enough of a tinhorn to clear his throat theatrically. But Oren Johnson treated this as a colossal interruption and cast a firm glance his way.

"It doesn't look all that automatic to me," he said.

"Aw, hell, you're just going to coin it. Pull the lever and relax!"

"What about the illegal oil dump? I wish I had a nickel for every crankcaseful that went into that hole. Then I wouldn't worry about what's going to happen when the D.E.Q.[7] lowers the boom."

---

6. A style of acting, popularized by the Actors Studio in New York City during the 1940s and 1950s, in which the performers create in themselves the psychological state of the character whose role they are playing.

7. Department of Environmental Quality, an agency of state government.

"Maybe you ought to ride your potato harvester another year or two, if you're so risk-averse. Cars are the future. They're not for everybody."

Oren Johnson's face reddened. He pushed his pencils and notepad almost out of reach in the middle of the conference table. He contemplated these supplies a moment before raising his eyes to mine. "I suppose you could put this car lot where the sun don't shine, if that suits you."

Johnson having taken a stand, I immediately felt unsure that I even had another buyer. Had I ever acknowledged how much I longed to get rid of this business and put an end to all those embarrassing phone calls? I wanted to hand the moment off to someone else while I collected my thoughts, but as I looked around the room I found no one who was interested in rescuing me—least of all Louise, who had raised one eyebrow at the vast peculiarity of my performance. Suddenly, I was desperate to keep the deal from falling apart. I gave my head a little twist to free my neck from the constrictions of my collar. I performed this gesture too vigorously, and I had the feeling that it might seem like the first movement of some sort of dance filled with sensual flourishes and bordering on the moronic. I had lost my grip.

"Oren," I said, and the familiarity seemed inappropriate. "I was attached to this little enterprise. I wanted to be sure you valued it."

The deal closed, and I had my check. I tipped back in my chair to think of a few commemorative words for the new owner, but the two men left the room without giving me the chance to speak. I shrugged at Louise and she, too, rose to go, pausing a moment beneath an enormous Kodachrome of a bugling elk. I was aware of her distance, and I sensed that my waffling hadn't gone over particularly well. I concluded that at no time in the future would I act out a role to accomplish anything. This decision quickly evaporated with the realization that that is practically all we do in life. Comedy failed, too. When I told Louise that I had been within an inch of opening a can of whup-ass on the buyer, I barely got a smile. There's nothing more desolating than having a phrase like that die on your lips.

It was dark when we got back to Targhee Pass. Leaving town, we passed the Beehive assisted-living facility and the Riot Zone, a "family fun park." Most of the citizens we spotted there seemed unlikely rioters. I drove past a huge neon steak, its blue T-bone flashing above a restaurant that was closed and dark. There were deer on the road, and once, as we passed through a murky section of forest, we saw the pale faces of children waiting to cross.

"What are they doing out at this hour?"

"I don't know," Louise said.

I made good time on the pine flats north of the Snowmobile Capital of the World, and I wondered what it would be like to live in a town that was the world capital of a mechanical gadget. In Rigby, we had seen a homely museum dedicated to Philo T. Farnsworth,[8] the inventor of television, which featured displays of Farnsworth's funky assemblages of tubes and wire and, apparently, coat hangers—stuff his wife was probably always attempting to throw out, a goal Louise supported. "Too bad Mama Farnsworth didn't take all that stuff to the dump," she said.

---

8. American inventor (1906–1971), born near Beaver Creek, Utah.

We had the highway to ourselves, and clouds of stars seemed to rise up from the wilderness, lighting the treetops in a cool fire. Slowly, the canyon closed in around us, and we entered its dark flowing space.

The idyll ended just past the ranger station at Black Butte, when a car pulled in behind us abruptly enough that I checked my speed to see if I was violating the limit, but I wasn't. When the car was very close, the driver shifted his lights to a high beam so intense that I could see our shadows on the dashboard, my knuckles on the steering wheel glaringly white. I was nearly blinded by my own mirrors, which I hastily adjusted.

I said, "What's with this guy?"

"Just let him pass."

"I don't know that he wants to."

I softened my pressure on the gas pedal. I thought that by easing my already moderate speed I would politely suggest that he might go by me. I even hugged the shoulder, but he remained glued to our bumper. There was something about this that reminded me strongly of my feeling of failure back in Rigby, but I was unable to put my finger on it. Maybe it was the hot light of liquidation, in the glare of which all motives seem laid bare. I slowed down even more without managing to persuade my tormentor to pass. "Jesus," Louise said. "Pull over." In her accent, it came out as "pull ovah."

I moved off to the side of the road slowly and predictably, but although I had stopped, the incandescent globes persisted in our rearview mirror. "This is very strange," Louise said.

"Shall I go back and speak to him?"

After considering for a moment, she said, "No."

"Why?"

"Because this is not normal."

I put the car in gear again and pulled back onto the highway. The last reasonable thought I had was that I would proceed to Bozeman as though nothing were going on; once I was back in civilization my tormentor's behavior would be visible to all, and I could, if necessary, simply drive to the police station with him in tow.

Our blinding, syncopated journey continued another mile before we reached a sweeping eastward bend, closely guarded by the canyon walls. I knew that just beyond the bend there was a scenic pull-off, and that the approaching curve was acute enough for a small lead to put me out of sight. Whether or not this was plausible, I had no idea: I was exhilarated to be taking a firm hand in my own affairs. And a firm foot! As we entered the narrows, I pinned the accelerator, and we shot into the dark. Louise grabbed the front edges of her seat and stared at the road twisting in front of us. She emitted something like a moan, which I had heard before in a very different context. Halfway around the curve, my tormentor vanished behind us, and although my car seemed only marginally under control, the absence of blinding light was a relief as we fled into darkness.

When we emerged and the road straightened, I turned off my lights. I was going so fast I felt light-headed, but the road was visible under the stars, and I was able to brake hard and drop down into the scenic turn-off. Seconds later, our new friend shot past, lights blazing into nowhere. He was clearly determined to catch us; his progress up the canyon was rapid and increasingly erratic. We watched in fascination until the lights suddenly jerked sideways, shining in white cones across the river, turned downward, then disappeared.

I heard Louise say, in a tone of reasonable observation, "He went in."

I had an urgent feeling that took a long time to turn into words. "Did I do that?"

She shook her head, and I pulled out onto the highway, my own headlights on once more. I drove in an odd, measured way, as if bound for an undesired destination, pulled along by something outside myself, thinking: liquidation. We could see where he'd gone through the guardrail. We pulled over and got out. Any hope we might have had for the driver—and we shall be a long time determining if we had any—was gone the minute we looked down from the riverbank. The car was submerged, its lights still burning freakishly, illuminating a bulge of crystalline water, a boulder in the exuberance of a mountain watershed. Presently, the lights sank into blackness, and only the silver sheen of river in starlight remained.

Louise cried, "I wish I could feel something!" And when I reached to comfort her she shoved me away. I had no choice but to climb back up to the roadway.

After that, I could encounter Louise only by telephone. I told her he had a record as long as your arm. "It's not enough!" she said. I called later to say that he was of German and Italian extraction. That proved equally unsatisfactory, and when I called to inform her that he hailed from Wisconsin she just hung up on me, this time for good.

2006

MAXINE HONG KINGSTON
b. 1940

Maxine Hong Kingston was born in Stockton, California, to Chinese immigrant parents. Before they emigrated from China Kingston's father had been a schoolteacher and a poet; her mother had been a rural doctor in a profession consisting almost entirely of men. In America they took on quite different identities: her father, at times unemployed, worked in a gambling house and a laundry; her mother raised six children, of whom Kingston was the eldest.

Kingston graduated from the University of California at Berkeley, studying there in the turbulent middle sixties. Her debut as a writer was auspicious: in 1976, an unknown, she published her first and most widely read book, *The Woman Warrior*, and was catapulted to literary fame. Subtitled "Memoirs of a Girlhood among Ghosts," it combines autobiographical fact with legends, especially Asian ones, to make a distinct imaginative creation. Reviews of the book, almost universally laudatory, emphasized its poetic and lyric beauty. *The Woman Warrior* is about the cultural conflicts Chinese Americans must confront. Still, what remains in the mind is its quality of vivid particularity, as for example at the beginning of "Shaman," the book's third section:

Once in a long while, four times so far for me, my mother brings out the metal tube that holds her medical diploma. On the tube are gold circles crossed with seven red lines each—"joy" ideographs in abstract. There are also little flowers that look like gears for a gold machine. . . . When I open it the smell of China flies out, a thousand-year-old bat flying heavy-handed out of the Chinese caverns where bats are as white as dust, a smell that comes from long ago, far back in my brain.

Although *The Woman Warrior* received the National Book Critics' Circle award for general nonfiction, there is nothing "general" in the richness of its language.

The importance of storytelling to Kingston's enterprise in *The Woman Warrior* and its successor, *China Men* (1980), cannot be overemphasized. In an interview with Bill Moyers on public television, Kingston said that her attempt was to push the account toward "form" by giving it a "redemptive" meaning, making it a "beautiful" story rather than a sordid one. As is typically the case with her practice as a writer, her effort is to mediate between present and past: "I think that my stories have a constant breaking in and out of the present and past. So the reader might be walking along very well in the present, but the past breaks through and changes and enlightens the present and vice versa."

Kingston had originally conceived of *The Woman Warrior* and *China Men* as one long book, but decided to preserve an overall division by gender: *Warrior* is about her female antecedents; while *China Men*, which won the 1980 National Book Award for nonfiction, deals with her relation to her father and complements that relation by providing epiclike biographies of earlier male forebears, especially those Chinese who came to America and worked on building the railroads. In a final section she writes about her brother who served in the U.S. Navy during the Vietnam War. As she discusses in the interview with Moyers, her father annotated both of these memoir-meditations, carrying further the conversation between the generations.

Tripmaster Monkey (1989), presented more deliberately as a novel, is an exercise as excessive as the young fifth-generation American hero, Wittman Ah Sing, who is portrayed there. Subtitled "His Fake Book," the novel is an extended, picaresque account of Wittman's adventures as an aspiring playwright who imagines himself to be an incarnation of the legendary Monkey King—a trickster hero said to have brought the Buddha's teaching to China. Combining magic, realism, and black humor, *Tripmaster Monkey* is about a young man's search for a community in America. Although Kingston's myth-laden narratives have been called "exotic," she dislikes the word, since she has dedicated her art to exploring what it means to be a human being in American society. In fact, she thinks of her books as more American than Chinese, sees the American poet William Carlos Williams's *In the American Grain* as a true prose predecessor, and probably would be happy to think of the hero of *Tripmaster Monkey* as a later, different version of Huck Finn (in Mark Twain's novel) or Augie March (in Saul Bellow's). As the critic Jennie Wang explains in even larger dimensions, Kingston's Wittman Ah Sing, "the maker/magician . . . conceived in the mind's fancy of a metafictionist," joins in his multiculturalism American and postmodern ambitions.

In 2011 Kingston celebrated her sixty-fifth birthday by publishing a memoir, *I Love a Broad Margin to My Life*. Written in verse form, this work engages issues of aging as the writer recalls incidents in her marriage, her career, and her involvement with social causes. She considers imaginative elements as well, including the ultimate fate of her Woman Warrior and the experiences of her protagonist in *Tripmaster Monkey* in a projected visit to China.

The following text is from *The Woman Warrior* (1976).

From The Woman Warrior

No Name Woman

"You must not tell anyone," my mother said, "what I am about to tell you. In China your father had a sister who killed herself. She jumped into the family well. We say that your father has all brothers because it is as if she had never been born.

"In 1924 just a few days after our village celebrated seventeen hurry-up weddings—to make sure that every young man who went 'out on the road' would responsibly come home—your father and his brothers and your grandfather and his brothers and your aunt's new husband sailed for America, the Gold Mountain. It was your grandfather's last trip. Those lucky enough to get contracts waved good-bye from the decks. They fed and guarded the stowaways and helped them off in Cuba, New York, Bali, Hawaii. 'We'll meet in California next year,' they said. All of them sent money home.

"I remember looking at your aunt one day when she and I were dressing; I had not noticed before that she had such a protruding melon of a stomach. But I did not think, 'She's pregnant,' until she began to look like other pregnant women, her shirt pulling and the white tops of her black pants showing. She could not have been pregnant, you see, because her husband had been gone for years. No one said anything. We did not discuss it. In early summer she was ready to have the child, long after the time when it could have been possible.

"The village had also been counting. On the night the baby was to be born the villagers raided our house. Some were crying. Like a great saw, teeth strung with lights, files of people walked zigzag across our land, tearing the rice. Their lanterns doubled in the disturbed black water, which drained away through the broken bunds.[1] As the villagers closed in, we could see that some of them, probably men and women we knew well, wore white masks. The people with long hair hung it over their faces. Women with short hair made it stand up on end. Some had tied white bands around their foreheads, arms, and legs.

"At first they threw mud and rocks at the house. Then they threw eggs and began slaughtering our stock. We could hear the animals scream their deaths—the roosters, the pigs, a last great roar from the ox. Familiar wild heads flared in our night windows; the villagers encircled us. Some of the faces stopped to peer at us, their eyes rushing like searchlights. The hands flattened against the panes, framed heads, and left red prints.

"The villagers broke in the front and the back doors at the same time, even though we had not locked the doors against them. Their knives dripped with the blood of our animals. They smeared blood on the doors and walls. One woman swung a chicken, whose throat she had slit, splattering blood in red arcs about her. We stood together in the middle of our house, in the family hall with the pictures and tables of the ancestors around us, and looked straight ahead.

"At that time the house had only two wings. When the men came back, we would build two more to enclose our courtyard and a third one to begin a

---

1. Embankments built to enclose rice paddies and control the flow of irrigation water.

second courtyard. The villagers pushed through both wings, even your grandparents' rooms, to find your aunt's, which was also mine until the men returned. From this room a new wing for one of the younger families would grow. They ripped up her clothes and shoes and broke her combs, grinding them underfoot. They tore her work from the loom. They scattered the cooking fire and rolled the new weaving in it. We could hear them in the kitchen breaking our bowls and banging the pots. They overturned the great waist-high earthenware jugs; duck eggs, pickled fruits, vegetables burst out and mixed in acrid torrents. The old woman from the next field swept a broom through the air and loosed the spirits-of-the-broom over our heads. 'Pig,' 'Ghost.' 'Pig,' they sobbed and scolded while they ruined our house.

"When they left, they took sugar and oranges to bless themselves. They cut pieces from the dead animals. Some of them took bowls that were not broken and clothes that were not torn. Afterward we swept up the rice and sewed it back up into sacks. But the smells from the spilled preserves lasted. Your aunt gave birth in the pigsty that night. The next morning when I went for the water, I found her and the baby plugging up the family well.

"Don't let your father know that I told you. He denies her. Now that you have started to menstruate, what happened to her could happen to you. Don't humiliate us. You wouldn't like to be forgotten as if you had never been born. The villagers are watchful."

Whenever she had to warn us about life, my mother told stories that ran like this one, a story to grow up on. She tested our strength to establish realities. Those in the emigrant generations who could not reassert brute survival died young and far from home. Those of us in the first American generations have had to figure out how the invisible world the emigrants built around our childhoods fits in solid America.

The immigrants confused the gods by diverting their curses, misleading them with crooked streets and false names. They must try to confuse their offspring as well, who, I suppose, threaten them in similar ways—always trying to get things straight, always trying to name the unspeakable. The Chinese I know hide their names; sojourners take new names when their lives change and guard their real names with silence.

Chinese-Americans, when you try to understand what things in you are Chinese, how do you separate what is peculiar to childhood, to poverty, insanities, one family, your mother who marked your growing with stories, from what is Chinese? What is Chinese tradition and what is the movies?

If I want to learn what clothes my aunt wore, whether flashy or ordinary, I would have to begin. "Remember Father's drowned-in-the-well sister?" I cannot ask that. My mother has told me once and for all the useful parts. She will add nothing unless powered by Necessity, a riverbank that guides her life. She plants vegetable gardens rather than lawns, she carries the odd-shaped tomatoes home from the fields and eats food left for the gods.

Whenever we did frivolous things, we used up energy, we flew high kites. We children came up off the ground over the melting cones our parents brought home from work and the American movie on New Year's Day—Oh, You Beautiful Doll with Betty Grable one year, and She Wore a Yellow Ribbon with John Wayne another year. After the one carnival ride each, we paid in guilt; our tired father counted his change on the dark walk home.

Adultery is extravagance. Could people who hatch their own chicks and eat the embryos and the heads for delicacies and boil the feet in vinegar for party food, leaving only the gravel, eating even the gizzard lining—could such people engender a prodigal aunt? To be a woman, to have a daughter in starvation time was a waste enough. My aunt could not have been the lone romantic who gave up everything for sex. Women in the old China did not choose. Some man had commanded her to lie with him and be his secret evil. I wonder whether he masked himself when he joined the raid on her family.

Perhaps she had encountered him in the fields or on the mountain where the daughters-in-law collected fuel. Or perhaps he first noticed her in the marketplace. He was not a stranger because the village housed no strangers. She had to have dealings with him other than sex. Perhaps he worked an adjoining field, or he sold her the cloth for the dress she sewed and wore. His demand must have surprised, then terrified her. She obeyed him; she always did as she was told.

When the family found a young man in the next village to be her husband, she had stood tractably beside the best rooster, his proxy,[2] and promised before they met that she would be his forever. She was lucky that he was her age and she would be the first wife, an advantage secure now. The night she first saw him, he had sex with her. Then he left for America. She had almost forgotten what he looked like. When she tried to envision him, she only saw the black and white face in the group photograph the men had had taken before leaving.

The other man was not, after all, much different from her husband. They both gave orders: she followed. "If you tell your family, I'll beat you. I'll kill you. Be here again next week." No one talked sex, ever. And she might have separated the rapes from the rest of living if only she did not have to buy her oil from him or gather wood in the same forest. I want her fear to have lasted just as long as rape lasted so that the fear could have been contained. No drawnout fear. But women at sex hazarded birth and hence lifetimes. The fear did not stop but permeated everywhere. She told the man, "I think I'm pregnant." He organized the raid against her.

On nights when my mother and father talked about their life back home, sometimes they mentioned an "outcast table" whose business they still seemed to be settling, their voices tight. In a commensal tradition,[3] where food is precious, the powerful older people made wrongdoers eat alone. Instead of letting them start separate new lives like the Japanese, who could become samurais and geishas,[4] the Chinese family, faces averted but eyes glowering sideways, hung on to the offenders and fed them leftovers. My aunt must have lived in the same house as my parents and eaten at an outcast table. My mother spoke about the raid as if she had seen it, when she and my aunt, a daughter-in-law to a different household, should not have been living together at all. Daughters-in-law lived with their husbands' parents, not their own; a synonym for marriage in Chinese is "taking a daughter-in-law." Her husband's parents could have sold her, mortgaged her, stoned her. But they had sent her back to her own mother and father, a

2. Someone or something that has the power to substitute or act for another.
3. A tradition in which people eat together at the same table.
4. In Japanese society, women trained to entertain men. "Samurai": the Japanese warrior elite.

mysterious act hinting at disgraces not told me. Perhaps they had thrown her out to deflect the avengers.

She was the only daughter; her four brothers went with her father, husband, and uncles "out on the road" and for some years became western men. When the goods were divided among the family, three of the brothers took land, and the youngest, my father, chose an education. After my grandparents gave their daughter away to her husband's family, they had dispensed all the adventure and all the property. They expected her alone to keep the traditional ways, which her brothers, now among the barbarians, could fumble without detection. The heavy, deep-rooted women were to maintain the past against the flood, safe for returning. But the rare urge west had fixed upon our family, and so my aunt crossed boundaries not delineated in space.

The work of preservation demands that the feelings playing about in one's guts not be turned into action. Just watch their passing like cherry blossoms. But perhaps my aunt, my forerunner, caught in a slow life, let dreams grow and fade and after some months or years went toward what persisted. Fear at the enormities of the forbidden kept her desires delicate, wire and bone. She looked at a man because she liked the way the hair was tucked behind his ears, or she liked the question-mark line of a long torso curving at the shoulder and straight at the hip. For warm eyes or a soft voice or a slow walk— that's all—a few hairs, a line, a brightness, a sound, a pace, she gave up family. She offered us up for a charm that vanished with tiredness, a pigtail that didn't toss when the wind died. Why, the wrong lighting could erase the dearest thing about him.

It could very well have been, however, that my aunt did not take subtle enjoyment of her friend, but, a wild woman, kept rollicking company. Imagining her free with sex doesn't fit, though. I don't know any women like that, or men either. Unless I see her life branching into mine, she gives me no ancestral help.

To sustain her being in love, she often worked at herself in the mirror, guessing at the colors and shapes that would interest him, changing them frequently in order to hit on the right combination. She wanted him to look back.

On a farm near the sea, a woman who tended her appearance reaped a reputation for eccentricity. All the married women blunt-cut their hair in flaps about their ears or pulled it back in tight buns. No nonsense. Neither style blew easily into heart-catching tangles. And at their weddings they displayed themselves in their long hair for the last time. "It brushed the backs of my knees," my mother tells me. "It was braided, and even so, it brushed the backs of my knees."

At the mirror my aunt combed individuality into her bob. A bun could have been contrived to escape into black streamers blowing in the wind or in quiet wisps about her face, but only the older women in our picture album wear buns. She brushed her hair back from her forehead, tucking the flaps behind her ears. She looped a piece of thread, knotted into a circle between her index fingers and thumbs, and ran the double strand across her forehead. When she closed her fingers as if she were making a pair of shadow geese bite, the string twisted together catching the little hairs. Then she pulled the thread away from her skin, ripping the hair out neatly, her eyes watering from the needles of pain. Opening her fingers, she cleaned the thread, then rolled it along her hairline and the tops of her eyebrows. My mother did the same to me and my sisters and herself. I used to believe that the expression "caught by the short hairs" meant a captive held with a depilatory string. It especially hurt at the temples, but my mother said we were lucky we didn't have to have our feet bound when we were seven. Sisters used to sit on their beds and cry together, she said, as their mothers or their slave removed the bandages for a few minutes each night and let the blood gush back into their veins. I hope that the man my aunt loved appreciated a smooth brow, that he wasn't just a tits-and-ass man.

Once my aunt found a freckle on her chin, at a spot that the almanac said predestined her for unhappiness. She dug it out with a hot needle and washed the wound with peroxide.

More attention to her looks than these pullings of hairs and pickings at spots would have caused gossip among the villagers. They owned work clothes and good clothes, and they wore good clothes for feasting the new seasons. But since a woman combing her hair hexes beginnings, my aunt rarely found an occasion to look her best. Women looked like great sea snails—the corded wood, babies, and laundry they carried were the whorls on their backs. The Chinese did not admire a bent back; goddesses and warriors stood straight. Still there must have been a marvelous freeing of beauty when a worker laid down her burden and stretched and arched.

Such commonplace loveliness, however, was not enough for my aunt. She dreamed of a lover for the fifteen days of New Year's, the time for families to exchange visits, money, and food. She plied her secret comb. And sure enough she cursed the year, the family, the village, and herself.

Even as her hair lured her imminent lover, many other men looked at her. Uncles, cousins, nephews, brothers would have looked, too, had they been home between journeys. Perhaps they had already been restraining their curiosity, and they left, fearful that their glances, like a field of nesting birds, might be startled and caught. Poverty hurt, and that was their first reason for leaving. But another, final reason for leaving the crowded house was the never-said.

She may have been unusually beloved, the precious only daughter, spoiled and mirror gazing because of the affection the family lavished on her. When her husband left, they welcomed the chance to take her back from the in-laws; she could live like the little daughter for just a while longer. There are stories that my grandfather was different from other people, "crazy ever since the little Jap bayoneted him in the head." He used to put his naked penis on the dinner table, laughing. And one day he brought home a baby girl, wrapped up inside his brown western-style greatcoat.[5] He had traded one of his sons, probably my father, the youngest, for her. My grandmother made him trade back. When he finally got a daughter of his own, he doted on her. They must have all loved her, except perhaps my father, the only brother who never went back to China, having once been traded for a girl.

Brothers and sisters, newly men and women, had to efface their sexual color and present plain miens. Disturbing hair and eyes, a smile like no other, threatened the ideal of five generations living under one roof. To focus blurs, people shouted face to face and yelled from room to room. The immigrants I

---

5. A heavy overcoat.

know have loud voices, unmodulated to American tones even after years away from the village where they called their friendships out across the fields. I have not been able to stop my mother's screams in public libraries or over telephones. Walking erect (knees straight, toes pointed forward, not pigeon-toed, which is Chinese-feminine) and speaking in an inaudible voice, I have tried to turn myself American-feminine. Chinese communication was loud, public. Only sick people had to whisper. But at the dinner table, where the family members came nearest one another, no one could talk, not the outcasts nor any eaters. Every word that falls from the mouth is a coin lost. Silently they gave and accepted food with both hands. A preoccupied child who took his bowl with one hand got a sideways glare. A complete moment of total attention is due everyone alike. Children and lovers have no singularity here, but my aunt used a secret voice, a separate attentiveness.

She kept the man's name to herself throughout her labor and dying; she did not accuse him that he be punished with her. To save her inseminator's name she gave silent birth.

He may have been somebody in her own household, but intercourse with a man outside the family would have been no less abhorrent. All the village were kinsmen, and the titles shouted in loud country voices never let kinship be forgotten. Any man within visiting distance would have been neutralized as a lover—"brother," "younger brother," "older brother"—one hundred and fifteen relationship titles. Parents researched birth charts probably not so much to assure good fortune as to circumvent incest in a population that has but one hundred surnames. Everybody has eight million relatives. How useless then sexual mannerisms, how dangerous.

As if it came from an atavism[6] deeper than fear, I used to add "brother" silently to boys' names. It hexed the boys, who would or would not ask me to dance, and made them less scary and as familiar and deserving of benevolence as girls.

But, of course, I hexed myself also—no dates. I should have stood up, both arms waving, and shouted out across libraries, "Hey, you! Love me back." I had no idea, though, how to make attraction selective, how to control its direction and magnitude. If I made myself American-pretty so that the five or six Chinese boys in the class fell in love with me, everyone else—the Caucasian, Negro, and Japanese boys—would too. Sisterliness, dignified and honorable, made much more sense.

Attraction eludes control so stubbornly that whole societies designed to organize relationships among people cannot keep order, not even when they bind people to one another from childhood and raise them together. Among the very poor and the wealthy, brothers married their adopted sisters, like doves. Our family allowed some romance, paying adult brides' prices and providing dowries so that their sons and daughters could marry strangers. Marriage promises to turn strangers into friendly relatives—a nation of siblings.

In the village structure, spirits shimmered among the live creatures, balanced and held in equilibrium by time and land. But one human being flaring up into violence could open up a black hole; a maelstrom[7] that pulled in the sky. The frightened villagers, who depended on one another to maintain

---

6. A trait with origins further back than the preceding generation; a throwback.

7. A powerful, violent whirlpool.

the real, went to my aunt to show her a personal, physical representation of the break she had made in the "roundness." Misallying couples snapped off the future, which was to be embodied in true offspring. The villagers punished her for acting as if she could have a private life, secret and apart from them.

If my aunt had betrayed the family at a time of large grain yields and peace, when many boys were born, and wings were being built on many houses, perhaps she might have escaped such severe punishment. But the men— hungry, greedy, tired of planting in dry soil—had been forced to leave the village in order to send food-money home. There were ghost plagues, bandit plagues, wars with the Japanese, floods. My Chinese brother and sister had died of an unknown sickness. Adultery, perhaps only a mistake during good times, became a crime when the village needed food.

The round moon cakes and round doorways, the round tables of gradu- ated size that fit one roundness inside another, round windows and rice bowls—these talismans had lost their power to warn this family of the law: a family must be whole, faithfully keeping the descent line by having sons to feed the old and the dead, who in turn look after the family. The villagers came to show my aunt and her lover in hiding a broken house. The villagers were speeding up the circling of events because she was too shortsighted to see that her infidelity had already harmed the village, that waves of conse- quences would return unpredictably, sometimes in disguise, as now, to hurt her. This roundness had to be made coin-sized so that she would see its cir- cumference: punish her at the birth of her baby. Awaken her to the inexorable. People who refused fatalism because they could invent small resources insisted on culpability. Deny accidents and wrest fault from the stars.

After the villagers left, their lanterns now scattering in various directions toward home, the family broke their silence and cursed her. "Aiaa, we're going to die. Death is coming. Death is coming. Look what you've done. You've killed us. Ghost! Dead ghost! Ghost! You've never been born." She ran out into the fields, far enough from the house so that she could no lon- ger hear their voices, and pressed herself against the earth, her own land no more. When she felt the birth coming, she thought that she had been hurt. Her body seized together. "They've hurt me too much," she thought. "This is gall, and it will kill me." With forehead and knees against the earth, her body convulsed and then relaxed. She turned on her back, lay on the ground. The black well of sky and stars went out and out and out forever; her body and her complexity seemed to disappear. She was one of the stars, a bright dot in blackness, without home, without a companion, in eternal cold and silence. An agoraphobia[8] rose in her, speeding higher and higher, bigger and bigger; she would not be able to contain it; there would be no end to fear.

Flayed, unprotected against space, she felt pain return, focusing her body. This pain chilled her—a cold, steady kind of surface pain. Inside, spasmodically, the other pain, the pain of the child, heated her. For hours she lay on the ground, alternately body and space. Sometimes a vision of normal comfort obliterated reality: she saw the family in the evening gam- bling at the dinner table, the young people massaging their elder's backs.

---

8. An abnormal fear of open space.

She saw them congratulating one another, high joy on the mornings the rice shoots came up. When these pictures burst, the stars drew yet further apart. Black space opened.

She got to her feet to fight better and remembered that old-fashioned women gave birth in their pigsties to fool the jealous, pain-dealing gods, who do not snatch piglets. Before the next spasms could stop her, she ran to the pigsty, each step a rushing out into emptiness. She climbed over the fence and knelt in the dirt. It was good to have a fence enclosing her, a tribal person alone.

Laboring, this woman who had carried her child as a foreign growth that sickened her every day, expelled it at last. She reached down to touch the hot, wet, moving mass, surely smaller than anything human, and could feel that it was human after all—fingers, toes, nails, nose. She pulled it up on to her belly, and it lay curled there, but in the air, feet precisely tucked one under the other. She opened her loose shirt and buttoned the child inside. After resting, it squirmed and thrashed and she pushed it up to her breast. It turned its head this way and that until it found her nipple. There, it made little snuffling noises. She clenched her teeth at its preciousness, lovely as a young calf, a piglet, a little dog.

She may have gone to the pigsty as a last act of responsibility: she would protect this child as she had protected its father. It would look after her soul, leaving supplies on her grave. But how would this tiny child without family find her grave when there would be no marker for her anywhere, neither in the earth nor the family hall? No one would give her a family hall name. She had taken the child with her into the wastes. At its birth the two of them had felt the same raw pain of separation, a wound that only the family pressing tight could close. A child with no descent line would not soften her life but only trail after her, ghostlike, begging her to give it purpose. At dawn the villagers on their way to the fields would stand around the fence and look.

Full of milk, the little ghost slept. When it awoke, she hardened her breasts against the milk that crying loosens. Toward morning she picked up the baby and walked to the well.

Carrying the baby to the well shows loving. Otherwise abandon it. Turn its face into the mud. Mothers who love their children take them along. It was probably a girl; there is some hope of forgiveness for boys.

"Don't tell anyone you had an aunt. Your father does not want to hear her name. She has never been born." I have believed that sex was unspeakable and words so strong and fathers so frail that "aunt" would do my father mysterious harm. I have thought that my family, having settled among immigrants who had also been their neighbors in the ancestral land, needed to clean their name, and a wrong word would incite the kinspeople even here. But there is more to this silence: they want me to participate in her punishment. And I have.

In the twenty years since I heard this story I have not asked for details nor said my aunt's name; I do not know it. People who can comfort the dead can also chase after them to hurt them further—a reverse ancestor worship. The real punishment was not the raid swiftly inflicted by the villagers, but the family's deliberately forgetting her. Her betrayal so maddened them, they saw to it that she would suffer forever, even after death. Always hungry, always needing, she would have to beg food from other ghosts, snatch and steal it from those whose living descendants give them gifts. She would have to fight the ghosts massed at crossroads for the buns a few thoughtful citizens leave to decoy her away from village and home so that the ancestral spirits could feast unharassed. At peace, they could act like gods, not ghosts, their descent lines providing them with paper suits and dresses, spirit money, paper houses, paper automobiles, chicken, meat, and rice[9] into eternity—essences delivered up in smoke and flames, steam and incense rising from each rice bowl. In an attempt to make the Chinese care for people outside the family, Chairman Mao[1] encourages us now to give our paper replicas to the spirits of outstanding soldiers and workers, no matter whose ancestors they may be. My aunt remains forever hungry. Goods are not distributed evenly among the dead.

My aunt haunts me—her ghost drawn to me because now, after fifty years of neglect, I alone devote pages of paper to her, though not origamied into houses and clothes. I do not think she always means me well. I am telling on her, and she was a spite suicide, drowning herself in the drinking water. The Chinese are always very frightened of the drowned one, whose weeping ghost, wet hair hanging and skin bloated, waits silently by the water to pull down a substitute.

1976

9. Traditionally, offerings left at the graves of ancestors.
1. Mao Zedong (1893–1976), head of the Chi-nese Communist Party and leader of China from 1949 to 1976.

FANNY HOWE
b. 1940

Fanny Howe's poems are meditations on matter and spirit. A philosophical, religious, and political poet, Howe explores both the mysteries of interior life and the weight of the material world. Like the work of Emily Dickinson, with whom Howe is often compared, her poems are startling and elliptical in their movements, each line ambiguously connected to what follows. The effect can be like that of a riddle. At the heart of poetry, she believes, is bewilderment, a condition of uncertainty and contradiction that extends to the idea of a poetic self—"the strange Whoever who goes under the name of 'I' in my poems" ("Bewilderment"). Calling attention to the ways in which language structures and restricts experience, she seeks to set words loose from their usual moorings so that she can explore the nature of consciousness and track "the nomadic heart" as it wanders in search of meaning.

Howe was born and grew up in Cambridge, Massachusetts, to an artistic and activist family. Her father, Mark DeWolfe, was a distinguished law professor at Harvard and a civil rights activist, and her mother, Mary Manning, an Irish-born playwright and actress, founded the Poets Theater in Cambridge. As a child Howe and her sister (Susan Howe, also a gifted poet) traveled back and forth to Ireland with their mother. Both the musicality of language in Ireland and the sense of mystery in Irish culture are important in all her work, and the Irish landscape she inhabited as a child is especially evident in the series of poems called "O'Clock" (from which "After the girl was grown" is excerpted here).

Some of Howe's many works of fiction are based on her years growing up in Boston and explore that city's social divisions by race, class, and religion. Howe left Boston in 1957 and studied at Stanford University for a number of years. Returning east in the mid-1960s, she volunteered to work with the Boston chapter of the Congress on Racial Equality and met and married Carl Senna, a writer and activist of Mexican and African American parentage. The couple had three children in four years, and Howe later presented some remarkable poems about pregnancy, childbirth, and infancy in the series "The Nursery," which includes "The baby was made in a cell," presented here. Howe lived with her family in a house on Robeson Street in Jamaica Plains (the setting for a series of poems collected in *Robeson Street* [1985]), which became a kind of center for friends and political activists. The late 1960s and the 1970s were a period of racial tension and upheaval in Boston, with special friction around the integration of the public schools. As Howe has written, "Boston, recalcitrant and class divided, was a poor choice of a place to live for a mixed race couple." As the mother of mixed-race children who attended Boston's public schools, Howe came to feel that "my skin is white but my soul is not, and I am in camouflage."

These tensions contributed to her divorce from Senna, after which Howe struggled as a single parent to support her young children, a struggle that gave her an understanding of invisibility in the social order. In these years she often moved from apartment to apartment, sharing space with other single mothers of mixed-race children. Howe explores invisibility as a political condition in *One Crossed Out* (1985), a collection of poems narrated by a homeless woman (the poem "[Nobody wants crossed out girls around]" comes from this series). In the period following her divorce Howe also converted to Catholicism, a religion whose sense of spiritual mystery deepened her inquiry into the invisible.

For almost a decade Howe lectured at MIT, and she later became professor of creative writing and literature at the University of California, San Diego. Although she never seems to have felt at home in California ("my interior landscape was composed of wet, watery images—soggy brick, flowerpots, begonias, big morning glories, sloppy roads and turbulent skies"), she found there a group of poets and writers, among them Lyn Hejinian, Alice Notley, and Michael Palmer, who shared her investigations of poetic language. Since her retirement Howe has returned to the East Coast, although she travels widely and seldom stays in one place long.

For many years Howe's poetry was published only by small presses and had a relatively small readership beyond other poets. This situation changed with the publication by the University of California Press of her *Selected Poems* (2000), which earned the Lenore Marshall Award from the Academy of American Poets and was short-listed for the Griffen Trust for Excellence in Poetry's international prize. Since that time the UC Press has published *Gone* (2003), a collection of new poems, and *The Wedding Dress* (2003), a collection of what Howe calls "meditations on word and life." Howe has also written over ten novels, including ones for young adults, and two short-story collections.

[I'd speak if I wasn't afraid of inhaling]

I'd speak if I wasn't afraid of inhaling
A memory I want to forget
Like I trusted the world which wasn't mine
The hollyhock in the tall vase is wide awake

And feelings are only overcome by fleeing   5
To their opposite. Moisture and dirt
Have entered the space between threshold and floor
A lot is my estimate when I step on it
Sorrow can be a home to stand on so
And see far to: another earth, a place I might know   10

                                                        1985

From The Nursery

The baby
          was made in a cell
in the silver & rose underworld.
Invisibly prisoned
          in vessels & cords, no gold   5
for a baby; instead
eyes, and a sudden soul, twelve weeks
old, which widened its will.

Tucked in the notch of my fossil: bones
          laddered a spine from a cave,   10
the knees & skull
were etched in this cell, no stone, no gold
where no sun brushed its air.

                                                        1986

From O'Clock

After this girl was grown
the tedium of the nursery began.

Either overdressed or a mess
she was a metaphor
for the suffering of the Irish.   5

Seven boys and seven girls, a harnessed pony
and a clay pipe, delinquency laws and bad thin boys.

Out like a scout, she tackled the fields
in her hem or heels.

When she was dragged and staked   10
she called the story of her life
Where My Body Went.

                                                        1995

From One Crossed Out

Nobody wants crossed-out girls around.
Any agreement with them is difficult to achieve.
Hanging in hammocks all day, they only know how to wisecrack.
And with whatever happens to be the meaning of their days—
    they will make a pact.   5
A sneaker hangs in their trees.
They say things like "I'm not who's who in America. Are you?"
No, I'm just here with my corpse.
Double overalls like fences endlessly trespassing and nobody
saying thanks for everything.   10
Were these the pants I kicked in the air? one of them might ask.
To the fish, a person is a fish. But a crossed-out girl is always
    just that.
One has a teddy bear that looks like Ireland on a map.
Others beg a way out of their jobs from the boss.   15
Then one of them suddenly gets up one day and acts.
She will work as a labor union organizer beginning with female
    laundry workers.
Another will make jam when the raspberries strike.
And with her bellows a third will make the flames rise to beat down   20
    the damp
and raise up the poor. A bunch will raise five children who aren't
    white.
I am wishing for this way to happen fast.
Dreams have orientation. Dreams like women who are bad.   25

                        1997

[We moved to be happy]

We moved to be happy

Like a remote sensing tool each body
in the family
adapted to earth's urbanity and travelled

When the water went south for the winter   5

it carried us down like storm-driven gulls
to this crash that we call a city

                        1998

[When I was a child]

When I was a child

I left my body to look for one
whose image nestles in the center of a wide valley

in perfect isolation wild as Eden

till one became many: spirits in presence   5

yes workers and no, workers up on the tops
of the hills in striped overalls

toy capes puffing
and blue veils as yet unrealized in the sky

I made myself homeless   10
on purpose for this shinnying up the silence

murky hand-pulls
Gray the first color
many textured clay beneath my feet

my face shining up I lost faith but once   15

(theology)

2003

Some Day

Some day a sheep with green eyes will meet me
at a door

"Self, come in
and be as vigilant
as the alien you are."   5

I will enter with a book in my hand, I'm sure

2003

[Come back]

Come back
to three lines of light on a little river—
one pink, one green and one aluminum—
come back to being

2003

From Bewilderment

One definition of the lyric might be that it is a method of searching for
something that can't be found. It is an air that blows and buoys and
settles. It says, "Not this, not this," instead of, "I have it."

Sequences of lyrical poems have the heave, thrill, and murmur of
the nomadic heart. Though they may at first look like static, fixed-
place poems with a confessional personal base, they hold the narrator
up as an idea, even an abstract example, of consciousness shifting in
its spatial locations.

2003

ROBERT PINSKY
b. 1940

A poet, critic, and translator, Robert Pinsky is a remarkable and influential figure in contemporary poetry. His appointment in 1997 for a two-year term as
the ninth Poet Laureate of the United States (among his predecessors in this position were Rita Dove, Robert Perm Warren, and Richard Wilbur, also represented in
this anthology) confirms the range and ambition of his work. In his first collection
of poetry, *Sadness and Happiness* (1975), Pinsky staked out a territory neglected by
an image-dominated American poetry in the 1970s: the discursiveness poetry
shares with prose and speech, including declaration, statement, and abstract definition. A year later, his influential book of criticism, *The Situation of Poetry* (1976),
argued for a poetry with the prose virtues of "Clarity, Flexibility, Efficiency, and
Cohesiveness." In Pinsky's hands this "drab, unglamorous group" of virtues produced the winning and pleasurable poems of his first book and two following collections: *An Explanation of America* (1980) and *History of My Heart* (1984). Like
William Carlos Williams and Elizabeth Bishop before him, Pinsky endows his
poems with the casualness of prose inflections; the result is a wonderfully sociable
body of poetry, with a relaxed and familiar sense of middle-class life. Here are
poems of tennis and psychiatrists, baseball and daughters in school, high school
dances, movies, "the small-town main street" ("History of My Heart").

But Pinsky's emphasis on the explanatory and the domestic can obscure his ambition and his formal virtuosity. The long title poem of *An Explanation of America* bespeaks his desire to bring together domestic life (the poem is addressed to his daughter) and the nation, to unite private feeling with "general Happiness and Safety." The poems of *History of My Heart* call on the personal memories at work in his first book but also introduce another sort of music, more mysterious and—what other word?—poetic. The publication of *The Want Bone* in 1990 and a book of new and collected poems, *The Figured Wheel*, in 1996, further demonstrated that the language of Pinsky's best poems is ordinary and yet also mysterious. If one of his strengths is the way he makes poetry a conversation about ideas, increasingly he also summons the power of poetry to sing what is "impossible to say." Pinsky's formal virtuosity lies in his ability to marry variations on traditional poetic rhythms (like the pentameter line at work in "The Want Bone," "At Pleasure Bay," and "Shirt") with American speech rhythms. This ability to shape a poetic line close to ordinary rhythms of speech and prose, and thus to render and deepen the everyday, connects him to Frank Bidart and James McMichael, two contemporary poets he admires. Pinsky is also an American master of the half or slant rhyme (like "twice" and "police" in "At Pleasure Bay" and the alliterative echo, like "bell" and "blue" in "The Want Bone," which gives his work a sense of both formal music and relaxation; there is the repeated echo of sound within and between stanzas, without the closure of full rhyme. The sensuousness of poetry, Pinsky remarks in his collection of essays *Poetry and the World* (1988), gives "elegance and significance to the sounds that breath makes vibrating in the mouth and throat." In "The Want Bone" (the dried jawbone of a shark, which he saw on a friend's mantle) he renders the sound vibrating in "this scalded toothless harp" as song: "my food my parent my child I want you my own/My flower my fin my life my lightness my O." Reading these lines we might easily forget that this poet has argued for poetry's discursive qualities. At the same time Pinsky's work continues to include what is sometimes excluded from American poetry, such as explanation or back-slapping ethnic jokes (in "Impossible to Tell" from *The Figured Wheel*).

Pinsky grew up in what he has called a "nominally orthodox" Jewish family in Long Branch, New Jersey. He later attended Rutgers and then Stanford University (where he studied with Yvor Winters). Though he lived in California for several years and now teaches in the graduate writing program at Boston University, Long Branch is Pinsky's middle America, despite its location at the ocean's edge ("bounded on three sides by similar places/and on one side by vast, uncouth houses/A glum boardwalk and, / as we say, the beach"). In Long Branch are his childhood memories and streets, as well as his sense of ethnic experience. With its fading boardwalk and movie houses, it also exemplifies an American popular culture for which Pinsky has unabashed appreciation. "At Pleasure Bay" (from *The Want Bone*), included here, beautifully commingles childhood memory and a sense of place with a feeling for the larger historical forces shaping the lives of local inhabitants. Though it is unlike Pinsky to move too far afield from everyday life, "At Pleasure Bay" and poems like it reveal the ways that Pinsky's vision extends beyond the personal and local into a deeper past and (in the poem's closing vision) future. The same process of enlarging a sense of community and connection while not straying too far from daily experience unfolds in "Shirt," which works its own variations on the pentameter line and is beautifully shaped by Pinsky's trademark half rhymes, here working within a single line as well as between lines.

The pleasures of Pinsky's poetry are also literary; he is unabashed in his references to literary antecedents but in no sense narrowly academic. Instead his work acknowledges and celebrates the way literature shapes his (and our) sense of life and experience, as well as his (and our) use of language. Pinsky's poetry is so distinctively American in its diction and subjects that his important work as a translator can come as a surprise. Among the poets he has translated are Czeslaw Milosz (the two have worked together on the translations) and Paul Célan. In 1994 Pinsky published *The Inferno of Dante*, recipient of the Academy of American Poets translation award, in which his formal gifts allowed him to re-create an American version of Dante's interlocked rhyme scheme, the terza rima. In a review of this translation in the *New York Times*, Edward Hirsch described the effect of Pinsky's stanzas as "moving through a series of interpenetrating rooms . . . or going down a set of winding stairs." While his sense of literary tradition is deep and wide-ranging, Pinsky is also engaged with new possibilities for literature created by computer technology. In 1985, in collaboration with computer programmers, he created an interactive text adventure game, *Mindwheel*, and he has served as the poetry editor of the weekly online magazine *Slate*. Computer software and poetry, Pinsky has said, "share a great human myth or trope, an image that could be called the secret passage: the discovery of large manifold channels through a small, ordinary-looking or all but invisible aperture. . . . This passage to vast complexities is what writing through the machine might become." Pinsky's volume *Gulf Music* was published to wide acclaim in 2007.

The Figured Wheel

The figured wheel rolls through shopping malls and prisons,
Over farms, small and immense, and the rotten little downtowns.
Covered with symbols, it mills everything alive and grinds
The remains of the dead in the cemeteries, in unmarked graves and oceans.

Sluiced by salt water and fresh, by pure and contaminated rivers,   5
By snow and sand, it separates and recombines all droplets and grains,
Even the infinite sub-atomic particles crushed under the illustrated,
Varying treads of its wide circumferential track.

Spraying flecks of tar and molten rock it rumbles
Through the Antarctic station of American sailors and technicians,   10
And shakes the floors and windows of whorehouses for diggers and
    smelters
From Bethany, Pennsylvania to a practically nameless, semi-penal New
    Town

In the mineral-rich tundra of the Soviet northernmost settlements.
Artists illuminate it with pictures and incised mottoes
Taken from the Ten Thousand Stories and the Register of True Dramas.   15
They hang it with colored ribbons and with bells of many pitches.

With paints and chisels and moving lights they record
On its rotating surface the elegant and terrifying doings
Of the inhabitants of the Hundred Pantheons of major Gods
Disposed in iconographic stations at hub, spoke and concentric bands,   20

And also the grotesque demi-Gods, Hopi gargoyles and Ibo dryads.[1]
They cover it with wind-chimes and electronic instruments
That vibrate as it rolls to make an all-but-unthinkable music,
So that the wheel hums and rings as it turns through the births of stars

---

1. Woodland spirits. "Ibo": a West African tribe, many of whose members were sent as slaves to America.

And through the dead-world of bomb, fireblast and fallout   25
Where only a few doomed races of insects fumble in the smoking grasses.
It is Jesus oblivious to hurt turning to give words to the unrighteous,
And is also Gogol's[2] feeding pig that without knowing it eats a baby chick

And goes on feeding. It is the empty armor of My Cid,[3] clattering
Into the arrows of the credulous unbelievers, a metal suit   30
Like the lost astronaut revolving with his useless umbilicus
Through the cold streams, neither energy nor matter, that agitate

The cold, cyclical dark, turning and returning.
Even in the scorched and frozen world of the dead after the holocaust
The wheel as it turns goes on accreting ornaments.   35
Scientists and artists festoon it from the grave with brilliant

Toys and messages, jokes and zodiacs, tragedies conceived
From among the dreams of the unemployed and the pampered,
The listless and the tortured. It is hung with devices
By dead masters who have survived by reducing themselves magically   40

To tiny organisms, to wisps of matter, crumbs of soil,
Bits of dry skin, microscopic flakes, which is why they are called "great,"
In their humility that goes on celebrating the turning
Of the wheel as it rolls unrelentingly over

A cow plodding through car-traffic on a street in *Iasi*,[4]   45
And over the haunts of Robert Pinsky's mother and father
And wife and children and his sweet self
Which he hereby unwillingly and inexpertly gives up, because it is

There, figured and pre-figured in the nothing-transfiguring wheel.

1984

The Street

   Streaked and fretted with effort, the thick
   Vine of the world, red nervelets
   Coiled at its tips.

   All roads lead from it. All night
   Wainwrights and upholsterers work finishing   5
   The wheeled coffin

   Of the dead favorite of the Emperor,
   The child's corpse propped seated
   On brocade, with yellow

2. Nikolai Gogol (1809–1852), Russian novelist, short-story writer, and playwright.
3. The Castillian epic *Poem of the Cid* (c. 1140) celebrates the legendary Spanish hero, the Cid.
4. City in Moldavia, Romania.

Oiled curls, kohl on the stiff lids.   10
Slaves throw petals on the roadway
For the cortege, white

Languid flowers shooting from dark
Blisters on the vine, ramifying
Into streets. On mine,   15

Rockwell Avenue, it was embarrassing:
Trouble—fights, the police, sickness—
Seemed never to come

For anyone when they were fully dressed.
It was always underwear or dirty pyjamas,   20
Unseemly stretches

Of skin showing through a torn housecoat.
Once a stranger drove off in a car
With somebody's wife,

And he ran after them in his undershirt   25
And threw his shoe at the car. It bounced
Into the street

Harmlessly, and we carried it back to him;
But the man had too much dignity
To put it back on,   30

So he held it and stood crying in the street:
"He's breaking up my home," he said,
"The son of a bitch

Bastard is breaking up my home." The street
Rose undulant in pavement-breaking coils   35
And the man rode it,

Still holding his shoe and stiffly upright
Like a trick rider in the circus parade
That came down the street

Each August. As the powerful dragonlike   40
Hump swelled he rose cursing and ready
To throw his shoe—woven

Angular as a twig into the fabulous
Rug or brocade with crowns and camels,
Leopards and rosettes,   45

All riding the vegetable wave of the street
From the John Flock Mortuary Home
Down to the river.

It was a small place, and off the center,
But so much a place to itself, I felt   50
Like a young prince

Or aspirant squire. I knew that Ivanhoe[1]
Was about race. The Saxons were Jews,
Or even Coloreds,

With their low-ceilinged, unbelievably   55
Sour-smelling houses down by the docks.
Everything was written

Or woven, ivory and pink and emerald—
Nothing was too ugly or petty or terrible
To be weighed in the immense   60

Silver scales of the dead: the looming
Balances set right onto the live, dangerous
Gray bark of the street.

1984

The Want Bone

The tongue of the waves tolled in the earth's bell.
Blue rippled and soaked in the fire of blue.
The dried mouthbones of a shark in the hot swale
Gaped on nothing but sand on either side.

The bone tasted of nothing and smelled of nothing,   5
A scalded toothless harp, uncrushed, unstrung.
The joined arcs made the shape of birth and craving
And the welded-open shape kept mouthing O.

Ossified cords held the corners together
In groined spirals pleated like a summer dress.   10
But where was the limber grin, the gash of pleasure?
Infinitesimal mouths bore it away,

The beach scrubbed and etched and pickled it clean.
But O I love you it sings, my little my country
My food my parent my child I want you my own   15
My flower my fin my life my lightness my O.

1990

---

1. The title and hero of Sir Walter Scott's romance novel (1819), set in 12th-century England, in which the hero wins the Saxon princess Rowena and champions a Jewish woman, Rebecca.

Shirt

The back, the yoke, the yardage. Lapped seams,[1]
The nearly invisible stitches along the collar
Turned in a sweatshop by Koreans or Malaysians

Gossiping over tea and noodles on their break
Or talking money or politics while one fitted   5
This armpiece with its overseam to the band

Of cuff I button at my wrist. The presser, the cutter,
The wringer, the mangle. The needle, the union,
The treadle, the bobbin. The code. The infamous blaze

At the Triangle Factory[2] in nineteen-eleven   10
One hundred and forty-six died in the flames
On the ninth floor, no hydrants, no fire escapes—

The witness in a building across the street
Who watched how a young man helped a girl to step
up to the windowsill, then held her out   15

Away from the masonry wall and let her drop.
And then another. As if he were helping them up
To enter a streetcar, and not eternity.

A third before he dropped her put her arms
Around his neck and kissed him. Then he held   20
Her into space, and dropped her. Almost at once

He stepped to the sill himself, his jacket flared
And fluttered up from his shirt as he came down,
Air filling up the legs of his gray trousers—

Like Hart Crane's Bedlamite,[3] "shrill shirt ballooning."   25
Wonderful how the pattern matches perfectly
Across the placket and over the twin bar-tacked

Corners of both pockets, like a strict rhyme
Or a major chord. Prints, plaids, checks,
Houndstooth, Tattersall, Madras. The clan tartans   30

1. Overlapping seams used to join fabric in interfacings to make them less bulky.
2. In 1911 the Triangle shirtwaist factory in New York City was the scene of a notorious fire in which 146 women who worked in the factory jumped to their deaths to escape the flames. This event marked the beginning of rigorous efforts to enforce workplace safety.
3. A reference to lines from the opening section ("To Brooklyn Bridge") of the American poet Hart Crane's sequence *The Bridge* (1930): "Out of some subway scuttle, cell or loft / A bedlamite speeds to thy parapets." A bedlamite is an inmate of a hospital for the mentally ill.

Invented by mill-owners inspired by the hoax of Ossian,[4]
To control their savage Scottish workers, tamed
By a fabricated heraldry: MacGregor,

Bailey, MacMartin. The kilt, devised for workers
To wear among the dusty clattering looms.   35
Weavers, carders, spinners. The loader,

The docker, the navvy.[5] The planter, the picker, the sorter
Sweating at her machine in a litter of cotton
As slaves in calico headrags sweated in fields:

George Herbert,[6] your descendant is a Black   40
Lady in South Carolina, her name is Irma
And she inspected my shirt. Its color and fit

And feel and its clean smell have satisfied
Both her and me. We have culled its cost and quality
Down to the buttons of simulated bone,   45

The buttonholes, the sizing, the facing, the characters
Printed in black on neckband and tail. The shape,
The label, the labor, the color, the shade. The shirt.

                                                         1990

At Pleasure Bay

In the willows along the river at Pleasure Bay
A catbird singing, never the same phrase twice.
Here under the pines a little off the road
In 1927 the Chief of Police
And Mrs. W. killed themselves together,   5
Sitting in a roadster. Ancient unshaken pilings
And underwater chunks of still-mortared brick
In shapes like bits of puzzle strew the bottom
Where the landing was for Price's Hotel and Theater.
And here's where boats blew two blasts for the keeper   10
To shunt the iron swing-bridge. He leaned on the gears
Like a skipper in the hut that housed the works
And the bridge moaned and turned on its middle pier
To let them through. In the middle of the summer
Two or three cars might wait for the iron trusswork   15
Winching aside, with maybe a child to notice
A name on the stern in black-and-gold on white,

---

4. In 1760 James Macpherson published *Poems
of Ossian*, which falsely claimed to be a translation of a text by the 3rd-century Irish hero of
that name.

5. An unskilled laborer, especially one engaged
in excavating or construction.
6. English poet (1593–1633).

Sandpiper, Patsy Ann, Do Not Disturb,
The Idler. If a boat was running whiskey,
The bridge clanged shut behind it as it passed   20
And opened up again for the Coast Guard cutter
Slowly as a sundial, and always jammed halfway.
The roadbed whole, but opened like a switch,
The river pulling and coursing between the piers.
Never the same phrase twice, the catbird filling   25
The humid August evening near the inlet
With borrowed music that he melds and changes.
Dragonflies and sandflies, frogs in the rushes, two bodies
Not moving in the open car among the pines,
A sliver of story. The tenor at Price's Hotel,   30
In clown costume, unfurls the sorrow gathered
In ruffles at his throat and cuffs, high quavers
That hold like splashes of light on the dark water,
The aria's closing phrases, changed and fading.
And after a gap of quiet, cheers and applause   35
Audible in the houses across the river,
Some in the audience weeping as if they had melted
Inside the music. Never the same. In Berlin
The daughter of an English lord, in love
With Adolf Hitler, whom she has met. She is taking   40
Possession of the apartment of a couple,
Elderly well-off Jews. They survive the war
To settle here in the Bay, the old lady
Teaches piano, but the whole world swivels
And gapes at their feet as the girl and a high-up Nazi   45
Examine the furniture, the glass, the pictures,
The elegant story that was theirs and now
Is a part of hers. A few months later the English
Enter the war and she shoots herself in a park,
An addled, upper-class girl, her life that passes   50
Into the lives of others or into a place.
The taking of lives—the Chief and Mrs. W.
Took theirs to stay together, as local ghosts.
Last flurries of kisses, the revolver's barrel,
Shivers of a story that a child might hear   55
And half remember, voices in the rushes,
A singing in the willows. From across the river,
Faint quavers of music, the same phrase twice and again,
Ranging and building. Over the high new bridge
The flashing of traffic homeward from the racetrack,   60
With one boat chugging under the arches, outward
Unnoticed through Pleasure Bay to the open sea.
Here's where the people stood to watch the theater
Burn on the water. All that night the fireboats
Kept playing their spouts of water into the blaze.   65
In the morning, smoking pilasters and beams.
Black smell of char for weeks, the ruin already
Soaking back into the river. After you die
You hover near the ceiling above your body

And watch the mourners awhile. A few days more 70
You float above the heads of the ones you knew
And watch them through a twilight. As it grows darker
You wander off and find your way to the river
And wade across. On the other side, night air,
Willows, the smell of the river, and a mass 75
Of sleeping bodies all along the bank,
A kind of singing from among the rushes
Calling you further forward in the dark.
You lie down and embrace one body, the limbs
Heavy with sleep reach eagerly up around you 80
And you make love until your soul brims up
And burns free out of you and shifts and spills
Down over into that other body, and you
Forget the life you had and begin again
On the same crossing—maybe as a child who passes 85
Through the same place. But never the same way twice.
Here in the daylight, the catbird in the willows,
The new café, with a terrace and a landing,
Frogs in the cattails where the swing-bridge was—
Here's where you might have slipped across the water 90
When you were only a presence, at Pleasure Bay.

1990

ROBERT HASS
b. 1941

Robert Hass was born in San Francisco and grew up in California, where he lives and teaches. He was influenced by West Coast writers like Robinson Jeffers, Kenneth Rexroth, and Gary Snyder, sharing with them a feeling for the natural world and humans' place within it. Hass's first book was *Field Guide* (1973), and the title suggests the way his poems map out the particulars of landscape and place, often making use of the names of native creatures, trees and plants—for example, "little orange-silver fish / called *pumpkinseed*" ("Meditation at Lagunitas") or "madrone bark / cracking and curling" ("Faint Music"). The title of his second collection, *Praise* (1979), signals one of this poet's chief characteristics and attractions: his sense of wonder and pleasure in the world. Yet it is the function of art, as Hass has said, both "to praise or dispraise, enchant or disenchant" and "you have to include a lot of the one if you're going to do the other." Thus the music of his poems frequently hums with the "thin wire of grief" ("Mediation at Lagunitas"), and the inclusive structure of a typical Hass poem is a collage, incorporating natural description, metaphysics, anecdote, history, botany, myth, and autobiography. Binding together these various elements is the poet's meditative voice, so remarkably natural in sound that we feel we are overhearing his conversations with himself.

Hass's poetic line, which doesn't settle into traditional forms, enacts the process of discovering interrelatedness. Each discovered connection brings about a shift in feeling or thought; for example, in "Dragonflies Mating" his delight in the Channelleño creation story modulates into a memory of the devastation wrought by disease on California's Native peoples and then ("in the same thought," he says) to himself as a child on "the free throw line," dreading the arrival of his alcoholic mother. Hass can no more separate the layers of experience—self and world, sensation and thought, the particular and the general, the private and the social—than the "insect lovers" in "Dragonflies Mating" can separate their quivering bodies.

Frequently cast as parts of several stories, his poems resist the sense of a revealing ending, the moment when the story teller declares, "And then I realized"—a moment Hass calls "the part of stories one never quite believes" ("Faint Music"). So, for example, in "Dragonflies Mating," when he includes the Channel Island Indian people's creation story in his poem, he emphasizes the humorous way the story leaves a central question unresolved: "how come Coyote was worried about people when he had to pee and there were no people?" As the story migrates into the poem, it moves between native and nonnative culture and between generations, maintaining its irresolution. The only "answer" to the question posed is the Channel Island Indian storyteller's: "when I was a kid, I wondered about that."

After attending St Mary's College in Moraga, California, Robert Hass received both an M.A. and a Ph.D. in English from Stanford University. Since 1989 he has been a professor of English at the University of California, Berkeley. Among his many collections of poetry are *The Apple Trees at Olema: New and Selected Poems* (2010), his National Book Award–winning volume *Time and Materials* (2007), *Sun Under Wood* (1996), and *Human Wishes* (1989). Hass is also a notable critic and translator; besides his translations of the Japanese haiku masters Basho, Buson, and Issa, he also translated over many years the work of his UC Berkeley colleague, the Polish poet Czeslaw Milosz (1911—2004). Perhaps Hass's love for the sound of poetry comes, in part, from this work as a translator. When, in 1995, Hass became for two years the Poet Laureate Consultant in Poetry to the Library of Congress, he postponed his writing life for what he has called an "act of citizenship," and served as a tireless and creative spokesman for the place and pleasure of poetry.

Measure

Recurrences.
Coppery light hesitates
again in the small-leaved

Japanese plum. Summer
and sunset, the peace   5
of the writing desk

and the habitual peace
of writing, these things
form an order I only

belong to in the idleness   10
of attention. Last light
rims the blue mountain

and I almost glimpse
what I was born to,
not so much in the sunlight   15

or the plum tree
as in the pulse
that forms these lines.

1973

Meditation at Lagunitas

All the new thinking is about loss.
In this it resembles all the old thinking.
The idea, for example, that each particular erases
the luminous clarity of a general idea. That the clown-
faced woodpecker probing the dead sculpted trunk   5
of that black birch is, by his presence,
some tragic falling off from a first world
of undivided light. Or the other notion that,
because there is in this world no one thing
to which the bramble of *blackberry* corresponds,   10
a word is elegy to what it signifies.
We talked about it late last night and in the voice
of my friend, there was a thin wire of grief, a tone
almost querulous. After a while I understood that,
talking this way, everything dissolves: *justice,*   15
pine, hair, woman, you and *I.* There was a woman
I made love to and I remembered how, holding
her small shoulders in my hands sometimes,
I felt a violent wonder at her presence
like a thirst for salt, for my childhood river   20
with its island willows, silly music from the pleasure boat,
muddy places where we caught the little orange-silver fish
called *pumpkinseed.*[1] It hardly had to do with her.
Longing, we say, because desire is full
of endless distances. I must have been the same to her.   25
But I remember so much, the way her hands dismantled bread,
the thing her father said that hurt her, what
she dreamed. There are moments when the body is as numinous
as words, days that are the good flesh continuing.
Such tenderness, those afternoons and evenings,   30
saying *blackberry, blackberry, blackberry.*

1979

---

1. A colorful freshwater sunfish native to northeastern North America whose compressed, oval body
shape resembles the seed of a pumpkin.

Dragonflies Mating

1.

The people who lived here before us
also loved these high mountain meadows on summer mornings.
They made their way up here in easy stages
when heat began to dry the valleys out,
following the berry harvest probably and the pine buds: 5
climbing and making camp and gathering,
then breaking camp and climbing and making camp and gathering.
A few miles a day. They sent out the children
to dig up bulbs of the mariposa lilies[1] that they liked to roast
at night by the fire where they sat talking about how this year   10
was different from last year. Told stories,
knew where they were on earth from the names,
owl moon, bear moon, gooseberry moon.[2]

2.

Jaime de Angulo[3] (1934) was talking to a Channel Island Indian[4]
in a Santa Barbara bar. You tell me how your people said   15
the world was made. Well, the guy said, Coyote[5] was on the mountain
and he had to pee. Wait a minute, Jaime said,
I was talking to a Pomo[6] the other day and he said
Red Fox[7] made the world. They say Red Fox, the guy shrugged,
we say Coyote. So, he had to pee   20
and he didn't want to drown anybody, so he turned toward the place
where the ocean would be. Wait a minute, Jaime said,
if there were no people yet, how could he drown anybody?
The Channelleño[8] got a funny look on his face. You know,
he said, when I was a kid, I wondered about that,   25
and I asked my father. We were living up toward Santa Ynez.[9]
He was sitting on a bench in the yard shaving down fence posts
with an ax, and I said, how come Coyote was worried about people
when he had to pee and there were no people? The guy laughed.
And my old man looked up at me with this funny smile   30
and said, You know, when I was a kid, I wondered about that.

---

1. A tall bulbous plant, native to California and the Pacific Northwest, with wedge-shaped petals and markings inside the flower that resemble a butterfly; its name is Spanish for butterfly. The bulbs of many such species were eaten by Native Americans.
2. Rather than the names of months, many Native American peoples gave each full moon a name, reflecting various seasons, activities, and the presence of particular animals. These names vary from tribe to tribe and by region.
3. Jaime de Angulo (1887–1950) was a linguist, novelist, and ethnomusicologist in the western United States, who contributed to knowledge of certain North American Indian languages.

4. Member of the primarily Chumash populations of the Channel Islands, a chain of eight islands located in the Pacific Ocean off the coast of Southern California.
5. A mythological character common to many Native American cultures, often referred to as Trickster.
6. Native American tribe that lives along the Northern California coast.
7. Figure in Pomo mythology comparable to the Coyote Trickster of other indigenous traditions.
8. A Channel Island (Chumash) Indian.
9. Town in the Santa Ynez Valley in Southern California.

3.

Thinking about that story just now, early morning heat,
first day in the mountains, I remembered stories about sick Indians
and—in the same thought—standing on the free throw line.

St. Raphael's[1] parish, where the northern-most of the missions   35
had been, was founded as a hospital, was named for the angel
in the scriptures who healed the blind man with a fish[2]

he laid across his eyes.—I wouldn't mind being that age again,
hearing those stories, eyes turned upward toward the young nun
in her white, fresh-smelling, immaculately laundered robes.—   40

The Franciscan priests[3] who brought their faith in God
across the Atlantic, brought with the baroque[4] statues and metalwork
    crosses
and elaborately embroidered cloaks, influenza and syphilis and the
coughing disease.[5]

Which is why we settled an almost empty California.
There were drawings in the mission museum of the long, dark wards   45
full of small brown people, wasted, coughing into blankets,

the saintly Franciscan fathers moving patiently among them.
It would, Sister Marietta said, have broken your hearts to see it.
They meant so well, she said, and such a terrible thing

came here with their love. And I remembered how I hated it   50
after school—because I loved basketball practice more than
    anything
on earth—that I never knew if my mother was going to show up

well into one of those weeks of drinking she disappeared into,
and humiliate me in front of my classmates with her bright, confident
    eyes,
and slurred, though carefully pronounced words, and the appalling   55

impromptu sets of mismatched clothes she was given to
when she had the dim idea of making a good impression in that state.
Sometimes from the gym floor with its sweet, heady smell of varnish

---

1. A California Mission, established as a medical sub-mission in 1817 to treat sick Native Americans of the Bay Area; granted full mission status in 1822.
2. St. Raphael, one of the three archangels, was a divine healer who resorted to human form in order to heal the blindness of Tobias, a devout and elderly follower, by using the gall of a fish.
3. Members of Catholic religious orders founded by Saint Francis of Assisi, who seek to follow most directly the manner of life led by Francis.
Franciscans established missions to spread the Christian faith among local Native Americans in California between 1769 and 1823.
4. Artistic style of the late 16th to early 18th centuries in Europe characterized by dynamic movement, overt emotion, and self-confident rhetoric, and encouraged by the Roman Catholic Church.
5. Three of many infectious diseases brought by European settlers that devastated indigenous populations.

I'd see her in the entryway looking for me, and I'd bounce
the ball two or three times, study the orange rim as if it were,   60
which it was, the true level of the world, the one sure thing

the power in my hands could summon. I'd bounce the ball
once more, feel the grain of the leather in my fingertips and shoot.
It was a perfect thing; it was almost like killing her.

4.

When we say "mother" in poems,   65
we usually mean some woman in her late twenties
or early thirties trying to raise a child.

We use this particular noun
to secure the pathos of the child's point of view
and to hold her responsible.   70

5.

If you're afraid now?
Fear is a teacher.
Sometimes you thought that
Nothing could reach her,
Nothing can reach you.   75
Wouldn't you rather
Sit by the river, sit
On the dead bank,
Deader than winter,
Where all the roots gape?   80

6.

This morning in the early sun,
steam rising from the pond the color of smoky topaz,
a pair of delicate, copper-red, needle-fine insects
are mating in the unopened crown of a Shasta daisy[6]
just outside your door. The green flowerheads look like wombs   85
or the upright, supplicant bulbs of a vegetal pre-erection.
The insect lovers seem to be transferring the cosmos into each other
by attaching at the tail, holding utterly still, and quivering intently.

I think (on what evidence?) that they are different from us.
That they mate and are done with mating.   90
They don't carry all this half-mated longing up out of childhood
and then go looking for it everywhere.
And so, I think, they can't wound each other the way we do.
They don't go through life dizzy or groggy with their hunger,
kill with it, smear it on everything, though it is perhaps also true   95
that nothing happens to them quite like what happens to us

6. Commonly grown, hardy perennial plant with white-petal flowers and golden yellow centers.

when the blue-backed swallow dips swiftly toward the green pond
and the pond's green-and-blue reflected swallow marries it a moment
in the reflected sky and the heart goes out to the end of the rope
it has been throwing into abyss after abyss, and a singing shimmers   100
from every color the morning has risen into.

My insect instructors have stilled, they are probably stuck together
in some bliss and minute pulse of after-longing
evolution worked out to suck the last juice of the world
into the receiver body. They can't separate probably   105
until it is done.

1996

Faint Music

Maybe you need to write a poem about grace.

When everything broken is broken,
and everything dead is dead,
and the hero has looked into the mirror with complete contempt,
and the heroine has studied her face and its defects   5
remorselessly, and the pain they thought might,
as a token of their earnestness, release them from themselves
has lost its novelty and not released them,
and they have begun to think, kindly and distantly,
watching the others go about their days—   10
likes and dislikes, reasons, habits, fears—
that self-love is the one weedy stalk
of every human blossoming, and understood,
therefore, why they had been, all their lives,
in such a fury to defend it, and that no one—   15
except some almost inconceivable saint in his pool
of poverty and silence—can escape this violent, automatic
life's companion ever, maybe then, ordinary light,
faint music under things, a hovering like grace appears.

As in the story a friend told once about the time   20
he tried to kill himself. His girl had left him.
Bees in the heart, then scorpions, maggots, and then ash.
He climbed onto the jumping girder of the bridge,
the bay side, a blue, lucid afternoon.
And in the salt air he thought about the word "seafood,"   25
that there was something faintly ridiculous about it.
No one said "landfood." He thought it was degrading to the
    rainbow perch
he'd reeled in gleaming from the cliffs, the black rockbass,
scales like polished carbon, in beds of kelp
along the coast—and he realized that the reason for the word   30
was crabs, or mussels, clams. Otherwise

the restaurants could just put "fish" up on their signs,
and when he woke—he'd slept for hours, curled up
on the girder like a child—the sun was going down
and he felt a little better, and afraid. He put on the jacket   35
he'd used for a pillow, climbed over the railing
carefully, and drove home to an empty house.

There was a pair of her lemon yellow panties
hanging on a doorknob. He studied them. Much-washed.
A faint russet in the crotch that made him sick   40
with rage and grief. He knew more or less
where she was. A flat somewhere on Russian Hill.[1]
They'd have just finished making love. She'd have tears
in her eyes and touch his jawbone gratefully. "God,"
she'd say, "you are so good for me." Winking lights,   45
a foggy view downhill toward the harbor and the bay.
"You're sad," he'd say. "Yes." "Thinking about Nick?"
"Yes," she'd say and cry. "I tried so hard," sobbing now,
"I really tried so hard." And then he'd hold her for a while—
Guatemalan weavings from his fieldwork on the wall—   50
and then they'd fuck again, and she would cry some more,
and go to sleep.
             And he, he would play that scene
once only, once and a half, and tell himself
that he was going to carry it for a very long time
and that there was nothing he could do   55
but carry it. He went out onto the porch, and listened
to the forest in the summer dark, madrone bark[2]
cracking and curling as the cold came up.

It's not the story though, not the friend
leaning toward you, saying "And then I realized—,"   60
which is the part of stories one never quite believes.
I had the idea that the world's so full of pain
it must sometimes make a kind of singing.
And that the sequence helps, as much as order helps—
First an ego, and then pain, and then the singing.   65

                                                                          1996

---

1. A residential neighborhood in San Francisco, California, named for a small Russian graveyard found at its crest by Gold Rush–era settlers.

2. The rich, orange-red bark of the madrone, a broadleaf evergreen tree, which peels away to leave a smooth, silver-green sheen.

SIMON J. ORTIZ
b. 1941

I n his poem "A Designated National Park," Simon J. Ortiz tells of visiting Monte-
zuma Castle in Verde Valley, Arizona, where he experiences as present in himself
the life of the people there: "Hear / in my cave, sacred song. / Morning feeling,
sacred song. / We shall plant today." His connection to that landscape, however, is
complicated by the fact that it is now a "DESIGNATED FEDERAL RECREATION
FEE AREA": "This morning / I have to buy a permit to get back home." Ortiz's treatment of Verde Valley is characteristic of the way he inhabits a conflicted landscape.
He was born and raised in the Acoma Pueblo Community in Albuquerque, New
Mexico. One meaning of the name *Acoma* is "the place that always was," and in this
sense it transcends the poet's place of origin and represents for him the Native
American way of life. Ortiz continually returns to this abiding sense of origin after
traveling great distances from it. Often his poems enact a journey, and as Joseph
Bruhac reminds us, in American Indian cultures the theme of traveling implicitly
recalls the "tragic epic movements of Native American nations." Many of Ortiz's
poems dramatize his disorientation as he moves within an America where Indian
names are reduced to billboard signs, where rivers burn from industrial wastes and
construction fills up the spaces of the earth. His sense of contemporary life, especially its absurdities, is acute.

But the America he travels conceals within it an older landscape animated by
spirit, where the earth is alive with "wind visions" and "The Mountains dream /
about pine brothers and friends" ("Vision Shadows"); to travel it is to seek "the center
of the center" ("Between Albuquerque and Santa Fe"), the place where the spirits
enter the world. Asked in an interview, "Why do you write?" Ortiz once responded,
"Because Indians always tell a story. . . . The only way to continue is to tell a story
and there is no other way. Your children will not survive unless you tell something
about them—how they were born, how they came to this certain place, how they
continued." Tellingly, Ortiz chose to reprint these comments at the beginning of his
collection *A Good Journey* (1977). The stories his poems narrate are evidence that
the Native American way of life is continuous, despite all the forces that attempt to
eradicate it. But his work also tells of the painful costs involved in survival.

After receiving his early education at a Bureau of Indian Affairs school on the
Acoma Reservation, Ortiz later attended the University of New Mexico and the
University of Iowa. He has since taught at San Diego State University and the University of New Mexico. "I never decided to become a poet," Ortiz has said, suggesting that his relatives transmitted to him the power of words. "An old-man relative
with a humpback used to come to our home when I was a child, and he would carry
me on his back. He told me stories. . . . That contact must have contributed the
language of myself." His father, a stonemason, carpenter, and woodcarver, would
talk and sing as he worked. In "A Story of How a Wall Stands," he remembers his
father saying "Underneath / what looks like loose stone, / there is stone woven
together." This sense of underlying connection is true of Ortiz's poetry as well,
often at its finest when revealing how a moment or event fits into the ongoing cycles
celebrated by ritual. His best poems are sometimes surprising in the way the apparently loose details suddenly blaze into an arrangement. Characteristically, this happens through powerful repetitions culminating in the last movements of a poem, a
technique that depends on rereading. Ortiz's collection *Going for Rain* appeared in

1976; its poems sometimes show a writer whose strong feelings have not yet found a distinctive language or rhythm. His next book, *The Good Journey*, is more assured and its range significantly broader. His work also includes *From Sand Creek*, which won the 1982 Pushcart Prize; *A Poem Is a Journey* (1981); and an edition that collects earlier volumes together with new work, *Woven Stone* (1992). *After and Before the Lightning* was published in 1994; his short stories were collected in *Men on the Moon* (1999). Ortiz's mission—continuance and preservation—sometimes allows a didactic impulse to shape his work too rigidly. But his finest poems have a richness of experience and a vital, imaginative sense of the earth that refuses any single conceptual or moral frame.

A recurring image in several Ortiz poems is the "Wisconsin horse" he once saw standing "within a fence // silent in the hot afternoon" while one mile away new construction was going on: "I tell the horse, / 'That's America building something'" ("The Wisconsin Horse"). The spirit of the horse, restrained by the chainlink fence and threatened by the approaching construction, suggests Ortiz's sense of constriction in the VA hospitals (his experience in one of these prompted his sequence *Poems from the Veterans Hospital*), as well as in small-town bars, in the Salvation Army store, or in the boundaries of the designated National Parks. Something threatens to break loose in these poems; feelings precariously held in check shake the formal structures. Other poems, like "Earth and Rain, the Plants & Sun," have the freedom and buoyancy of the hawk's flight; the words move in a space that seems immense. Instead of explosive anger or despair, the tone of the poem is close to song or prayer. What is so moving in Ortiz's work is that these voices are both his; together they suggest the fracture of identity and the possibility of reintegration.

Passing through Little Rock

The old Indian ghosts—
                    "Quapaw"
"Waccamaw"[1]—
                    are just billboard words
in this crummy town.   5

"You know, I'm worrying a lot lately,"
he says in the old hotel bar.

"You're getting older and scared ain't you?"

I just want to cross the next hill,
through that clump of trees   10
and come out the other side

and see a clean river,
the whole earth new
and hear the noise it makes
at birth.   15

                                                              1976

---

1. Names of Native American tribes formerly living in Arkansas.

Earth and Rain, the Plants & Sun

Once near San Ysidro
on the way to Colorado,
I stopped and looked.
The sound of a meadowlark
through smell of fresh cut alfalfa.   5

Raho would say,
"Look, Dad." A hawk

sweeping
          its wings

clear through   10
          the blue
of whole and pure
          the wind
                    the sky.

It is writhing   15
overhead.
Hear. The Bringer.
          The Thunderer.

Sunlight falls
through cloud curtains,   20
a straight bright shaft.

It falls,
          it falls,
     down
          to earth,   25
a green plant.

Today, the Katzina[1] come.
The dancing prayers.

Many times, the Katzina.
The dancing prayers.   30
It shall not end,
son, it will not end,
this love.

Again and again,
the earth is new again.   35

---

1. Or Kachina; spirits of the invisible life forces
of the Pueblo Indians of North America. The
Kachinas are impersonated by elaborately cos-
tumed masked men and boys of the tribes who
visit Pueblo villages the first half of the year.
Although not worshiped as gods, Kachinas are
greatly revered; one of their main purposes is to
bring rain for the spring crops.

They come, listen, listen.
Hold on to your mother's hand.
They come

O great joy, they come.
The plants with bells.   40
The stones with voices.
Listen, son, hold my hand.

                                                                1977

Vision Shadows

Wind visions are honest.
Eagles clearly soar
to the craggy peaks
of the mind.
The mind is full   5
of sunprayer
and childlaughter.

The Mountains dream
about pine brothers and friends,
the mystic realm of boulders   10
which shelter
rabbits, squirrels, wrens.
They believe in the power.
They also believe
in quick eagle death.   15

The eagle loops
into the wind power.
He can see a million miles
and more because of it.

All believe things   20
of origin and solitude.

            But what has happened
(I hear strange news from Wyoming
of thallium sulphate.[1] Ranchers
bearing arms in helicopters.)   25
to these visions?
I hear foreign tremors.
Breath comes thin and shredded.
I hear the scabs of strange deaths
falling off.   30

---

1. A chemical used by farmers as a rat poison.

Snake hurries through the grass.
Coyote is befuddled by his own tricks.
And Bear whimpers pain into the wind.

Poisonous fumes cross our sacred paths.
The wind is still.   35
O Blue Sky, O Mountain, O Spirit, O
what has stopped?

Eagles tumble dumbly into shadows
that swallow them with dull thuds.
The sage can't breathe.   40
Jackrabbit is lonely and alone
with eagle gone.

It is painful, aiiee, without visions
to soothe dry whimpers
or repair the flight of eagle, our own brother.   45

                                                                    1977

From Poems from the Veterans Hospital

Travelling

A man has been in the VAH Library all day long,
looking at the maps, the atlas, and the globe,
finding places.
        Acapulco, the Bay of Bengal,
Antarctica, Madagascar, Rome, Luxembourg,   5
places.

He writes their names on a letter pad, hurries
to another source, asks the librarian for a book
but it is out and he looks hurt and then he rushes
back to the globe, turns it a few times and finds   10
Yokohama and then the Aleutian Islands.

Later on, he studies Cape Cod for a moment,
a faraway glee on his face, in his eyes.
He is Gauguin, he is Coyote,[1] he is who he is,
travelling the known and unknown places,   15
travelling, travelling.

                                                                    1977

1. The trickster figure in southwestern and other Native American tales. The French painter Paul Gauguin (1848–1903) left his home in France for Tahiti and the Marquesas Islands.

From From Sand Creek

At the Salvation Army
a clerk
caught me
wandering
among old spoons   5
            and knives,
                        sweaters and shoes.

I couldn't have stolen anything;
my life was stolen already.

In protest though,   10
I should have stolen.
My life. My life.

She caught me;
Carson[1] caught Indians,
secured them with his lies.   15
Bound them with his belief.

After winter,
our own lives fled.

I reassured her
what she believed.   20
Bought a sweater.

And fled.

I should have stolen.
My life. My life.

                                            1981

---

1. Christopher ("Kit") Carson (1809–1868), trapper, scout, Indian agent, and soldier, was hired by the government to help control the Navajo. Beginning in 1863 he waged a brutal economic war against the tribe, marching through the heart of their territory to destroy their crops, orchards, and livestock. In 1864 most Navajo surrendered to Carson, who forced nearly eight thousand Navajo men, women, and children to take what came to be called the "Long Walk" of three hundred miles from Arizona to Fort Sumner, New Mexico, where they remained in disease-ridden confinement until 1868.

BILLY COLLINS
b. 1941

The voice in a Billy Collins poem is so intimate and immediate that we feel we are in the same room with the poet. Collins imagines poet and reader sitting together at a breakfast table: "I will lean forward, / elbows on the table, / with something to tell you / and you will look up, as always, / your spoon dripping with milk, ready to listen" ("A Portrait of the Reader with a Bowl of Cereal"). The colloquial voice in his poems charms us with its air of spontaneous expression, its modesty, its humor. If some of his poems coast on charm alone, Collins's best work takes us on a surprising ride: its strange and unexpected associations deepen the familiar into the mysterious or make the mysterious familiar.

Describing the structures of his poetry, Collins says, "We are attempting, all the time, to create a logical, rational path through the day. To the left and right there are an amazing set of distractions that we can't afford to follow. But the poet is willing to stop anywhere." His poems often proceed as accounts of a day and its distractions, as in "Tuesday, June 4, 1991." At the same time the formal shapeliness of Collins's work endows ordinary activity with a strange and pleasing formality and turns it, line by measured line and stanza by stanza, into a ritual including both the pleasures and the pathos of life. These poems present a humorous self-awareness about the speaker's dramatizing and obsessive love of distraction—anything, no matter how insignificant, can carry off his attention—and one thing that is so welcome about Collins's poems is that they are funny. Only on later readings do we realize that they are also sad. When he looks over the edges of domestic life there is blankness; unlike the work of a Jorie Graham or a Charles Wright, a Collins poem evokes no metaphysical structures that might sustain this fragile world. Yet (in the Irish poet William Butler Yeats's phrase) Collins loves "what vanishes"—the day in June, the good meal, even one's memories. This knowledge of how things large and small disappear is a great equalizer. The humor in Collins's poetry puts this equalizing principle to work; he deflates the grandiose and subjects large statements of truth to the test of the particular. Collins's titles, imaginative and playful, suggest the way he alights on small, usually trivial instances in which life's strangeness and mystery flash out: "Weighing the Dog," "I Chop Some Parsley While Listening to Art Blakey's Version of 'Three Blind Mice.'" Other titles signal the way he grounds the improbable within the everyday: "Taking Off Emily Dickinson's Clothes," "Shoveling Snow with Buddha."

Collins's collections of poems include *Questions about Angels* (1977), *The Art of Drowning* (1995), *Picnic, Lightning* (1998), *Sailing Alone Around the World: New and Selected Poems* (2001), *Nine Horses* (2003), *The Trouble with Poetry and Other Poems* (2005), *Ballistics* (2008), and *Horoscopes for the Dead* (2011). He served as poet laureate of the United States from 2001 to 2003. Born in New York City (in a hospital where, as he likes to note, William Carlos Williams worked as a pediatric resident), Collins teaches at Lehman College of the City University. Walking the city streets animates him and inflects some of his poems in a way that recalls the work of Frank O'Hara, with whom Collins shares an idiomatic American voice, colloquial and understated, shaped by jazz and the blues. Collins's work often plays with the melody of a pentameter line as a jazz musician plays on and off the melody of a song; the pentameter is an undertone from which a more idiosyncratic rhythm moves around and away. While the rhythms of Collins's poetry often enforce a slowing-down, a tender lingering over everyday life, their breezy tone and quick humor seem to suggest that nothing too serious is going on. It is as if Collins were fending off the large, prophetic claims made by visionary poets (early in his career he earned a Ph.D. at the University of California at Riverside, specializing in the Romantic period), even as some of his poems are riffs on the Romantic tradition. Such Collins poems as "Keats's Handwriting" and "Lines Composed Over Three Thousand Miles from Tintern Abbey" deflate the romantic sublime and substitute for it a vision self-deprecating and humorous. Thus when we hear nightingales in a Collins poem, they're a group singing on the gospel radio station ("Sunday Morning with the Sensational Nightingales").

Collins's modest claims for poetry and the fact that his work is so appealing and accessible can lead us to underestimate the necessity and reward of rereading him. The best of his poems open up a moment like a series of nested boxes; if we read too quickly, we miss the pleasure and surprise of intricate connections and deepening discoveries. A Collins poem has a spontaneity that yields immediate pleasure, but only when we listen again more attentively do we recognize the art that makes itself look easy.

Forgetfulness

The name of the author is the first to go
followed obediently by the title, the plot,
the heartbreaking conclusion, the entire novel
which suddenly becomes one you have never read, never even heard of,

as if, one by one, the memories you used to harbor   5
decided to retire to the southern hemisphere of the brain,
to a little fishing village where there are no phones.

Long ago you kissed the names of the nine Muses goodbye,
and watched the quadratic equation pack its bag,
and even now as you memorize the order of the planets,   10

something else is slipping away, a state flower perhaps,
the address of an uncle, the capital of Paraguay.

Whatever it is you are struggling to remember
it is not poised on the tip of your tongue,
not even lurking in some obscure corner of your spleen.   15

It has floated away down a dark mythological river
whose name begins with an *L* as far as you can recall,
well on your own way to oblivion where you will join those
who have even forgotten how to swim and how to ride a bicycle.

No wonder you rise in the middle of the night   20
to look up the date of a famous battle in a book on war.
No wonder the moon in the window seems to have drifted
out of a love poem that you used to know by heart.

1991

Osso Buco[1]

I love the sound of the bone against the plate
and the fortress-like look of it
lying before me in a moat of risotto,[2]
the meat soft as the leg of an angel
who has lived a purely airborne existence.   5
And best of all, the secret marrow,
the invaded privacy of the animal
prized out with a knife and swallowed down
with cold, exhilarating wine.

I am swaying now in the hour after dinner,   10
a citizen tilted back on his chair,
a creature with a full stomach—
something you don't hear much about in poetry,
that sanctuary of hunger and deprivation.
You know: the driving rain, the boots by the door,   15
small birds searching for berries in winter.

But tonight, the lion of contentment
has placed a warm, heavy paw on my chest,
and I can only close my eyes and listen
to the drums of woe throbbing in the distance   20
and the sound of my wife's laughter
on the telephone in the next room,
the woman who cooked the savory osso buco,
who pointed to show the butcher the ones she wanted.
She who talks to her faraway friend   25
while I linger here at the table
with a hot, companionable cup of tea,
feeling like one of the friendly natives,
a reliable guide, maybe even the chief's favorite son.

Somewhere, a man is crawling up a rocky hillside   30
on bleeding knees and palms, an Irish penitent
carrying the stone of the world in his stomach;
and elsewhere people of all nations stare
at one another across a long, empty table.

But here, the candles give off their warm glow,   35
the same light that Shakespeare and Izaac Walton[3] wrote by,
the light that lit and shadowed the faces of history.
Only now it plays on the blue plates,
the crumpled napkins, the crossed knife and fork.

In a while, one of us will go up to bed   40
and the other one will follow.

1. An Italian dish made with veal shanks.
2. An Italian rice dish.
3. English writer (1593–1683), author of *The*

Compleat Angler, a treatise on fishing and a picture of peace and simple virtues; it is among the most republished books in English literature.

Then we will slip below the surface of the night
into miles of water, drifting down and down
to the dark, soundless bottom
until the weight of dreams pulls us lower still,   45
below the shale and layered rock,
beneath the strata of hunger and pleasure,
into the broken bones of the earth itself,
into the marrow of the only place we know.

1995

Tuesday, June 4, 1991

By the time I get myself out of bed, my wife has left
the house to take her botany final and the painter
has arrived in his van and is already painting
the columns of the front porch white and the decking gray.

It is early June, a breezy and sun-riddled Tuesday   5
that would quickly be forgotten were it not for my
writing these few things down as I sit here empty-headed
at the typewriter with a cup of coffee, light and sweet.

I feel like the secretary to the morning whose only
responsibility is to take down its bright, airy dictation   10
until it's time to go to lunch with the other girls,
all of us ordering the cottage cheese with half a pear.

This is what stenographers do in courtrooms, too,
alert at their miniature machines taking down every word.
When there is a silence they sit still as I do, waiting   15
and listening, fingers resting lightly on the keys.

This is also what Samuel Pepys[1] did, jotting down in
private ciphers minor events that would have otherwise
slipped into the dark amnesiac waters of the Thames.
His vigilance finally paid off when London caught fire   20

as mine does when the painter comes in for coffee
and says how much he likes this slow vocal rendition
of "You Don't Know What Love Is"[2] and I figure I will
make him a tape when he goes back to his brushes and pails.

Under the music I can hear the rush of cars and trucks   25
on the highway and every so often the new kitten, Felix,
hops into my lap and watches my fingers drumming out
a running record of this particular June Tuesday

---

1. English writer (1633–1703), known primarily
for his diaries.

2. A song from the jazz repertoire, written by
Gene de Paul in 1941.

as it unrolls before my eyes, a long intricate carpet
that I am walking on slowly with my head bowed 30
knowing that it is leading me to the quiet shrine
of the afternoon and the melancholy candles of evening.

If I look up, I see out the window the white stars
of clematis climbing a ladder of strings, a woodpile,
a stack of faded bricks, a small green garden of herbs, 35
things you would expect to find outside a window,

all written down now and placed in the setting
of a stanza as unalterably as they are seated
in their chairs in the ontological[3] rooms of the world.
Yes, this is the kind of job I could succeed in, 40

an unpaid but contented amanuensis[4] whose hands
are two birds fluttering on the lettered keys,
whose eyes see sunlight splashing through the leaves,
and the bright pink asterisks of honeysuckle

and the piano at the other end of this room with 45
its small vase of faded flowers and its empty bench.
So convinced am I that I have found my vocation,
tomorrow I will begin my chronicling earlier, at dawn,

a time when hangmen and farmers are up and doing,
when men holding pistols stand in a field back to back. 50
It is the time the ancients imagined in robes, as Eos
or Aurora,[5] who would leave her sleeping husband in bed,

not to take her botany final, but to pull the sun,
her brother, over the horizon's brilliant rim,
her four-horse chariot aimed at the zenith of the sky, 55
But tomorrow, dawn will come the way I picture her,

barefoot and disheveled, standing outside my window
in one of the fragile cotton dresses of the poor.
She will look in at me with her thin arms extended,
offering a handful of birdsong and a small cup of light. 60

1995

I Chop Some Parsley While Listening to Art Blakey's[1] Version of "Three Blind Mice"

And I start wondering how they came to be blind.
If it was congenital, they could be brothers and sisters,

---

3. Having to do with the branch of metaphysics that deals with the nature of being.
4. One employed to write from dictation or to copy manuscripts.
5. The Greek and Roman goddesses of dawn.
1. Jazz drummer and bandleader (1919–1990).

Art Blakey on the drums.

and I think of the poor mother
brooding over her sightless young triplets.

Or was it a common accident, all three caught   5
in a searing explosion, a fireworks perhaps?
If not,
if each came to his or her blindness separately,

how did they ever manage to find one another?
Would it not be difficult for a blind mouse   10
to locate even one fellow mouse with vision
let alone two other blind ones?

And how, in their tiny darkness,
could they possibly have run after a farmer's wife
or anyone else's wife for that matter?   15
Not to mention why.

Just so she could cut off their tails
with a carving knife, is the cynic's answer,
but the thought of them without eyes
and now without tails to trail through the moist grass   20

or slip around the corner of a baseboard
has the cynic who always lounges within me

up off his couch and at the window
trying to hide the rising softness that he feels.

By now I am on to dicing an onion   25
which might account for the wet stinging
in my own eyes, though Freddie Hubbard's
mournful trumpet on "Blue Moon,"

which happens to be the next cut,[2]
cannot be said to be making matters any better.   30

1998

The Night House

Every day the body works in the fields of the world
mending a stone wall
or swinging a sickle through the tall grass—
the grass of civics, the grass of money—
and every night the body curls around itself   5
and listens for the soft bells of sleep.

But the heart is restless and rises
from the body in the middle of the night,
leaves the trapezoidal bedroom
with its thick, pictureless walls   10
to sit by herself at the kitchen table
and heat some milk in a pan.

And the mind gets up too, puts on a robe
and goes downstairs, lights a cigarette,
and opens a book on engineering.   15
Even the conscience awakens
and roams from room to room in the dark,
darting away from every mirror like a strange fish.

And the soul is up on the roof
in her nightdress, straddling the ridge,   20
singing a song about the wildness of the sea
until the first rip of pink appears in the sky.
Then, they all will return to the sleeping body
the way a flock of birds settles back into a tree,

resuming their daily colloquy,   25
talking to each other or themselves
even through the heat of the long afternoons.
Which is why the body—that house of voices—

---

2. The next song on *Three Blind Mice, Vol. 1*, a 1962 live recording by Art Blakey's Jazz Messengers,
which included Freddie Hubbard (1938–2008).

sometimes puts down its metal tongs, its needle, or its pen
to stare into the distance,   30

to listen to all its names being called
before bending again to its labor.

1998

Litany

You are the bread and the knife,
The crystal goblet and the wine.

Jacques Crickillon

You are the bread and the knife,
the crystal goblet and the wine.
You are the dew on the morning grass,
and the burning wheel of the sun.
You are the white apron of the baker   5
and the marsh birds suddenly in flight.

However, you are not the wind in the orchard,
the plums on the counter,
or the house of cards.
And you are certainly not the pine-scented air.   10
There is no way you are the pine-scented air.

It is possible that you are the fish under the bridge,
maybe even the pigeon on the general's head,
but you are not even close
to being the field of cornflowers at dusk.   15

And a quick look in the mirror will show
that you are neither the boots in the corner
nor the boat asleep in its boathouse.

It might interest you to know,
speaking of the plentiful imagery of the world,   20
that I am the sound of rain on the roof.

I also happen to be the shooting star,
the evening paper blowing down an alley,
and the basket of chestnuts on the kitchen table.

I am also the moon in the trees   25
and the blind woman's teacup.
But don't worry, I am not the bread and the knife.
You are still the bread and the knife.
You will always be the bread and the knife,
not to mention the crystal goblet and—somehow—the wine.   30

2002

Sonnet

All we need is fourteen lines,[1] well, thirteen now,
and after this one just a dozen
to launch a little ship on love's storm-tossed seas,
then only ten more left like rows of beans.
How easily it goes unless you get Elizabethan[2]   5
and insist the iambic[3] bongos must be played
and rhymes positioned at the ends of lines,
one for every station of the cross.
But hang on here while we make the turn[4]
into the final six where all will be resolved,   10
where longing and heartache will find an end,
where Laura will tell Petrarch[5] to put down his pen,
take off those crazy medieval tights,
blow out the lights, and come at last to bed.

2001

1. The line count typical of a sonnet.
2. A sonnet composed of three quatrains and a terminal couplet, in iambic pentameter, with the rhyme pattern abab cdcd efef gg (also called Shakespearean).
3. A metrical foot consisting of one unstressed syllable followed by one stressed syllable.

4. In an Elizabethan sonnet, the turn is the ninth line, often marked by a change in tone or mood.
5. The sight of a woman named "Laura" spurred Francesco Petrarch (1304–1374), an Italian scholar, poet, and Renaissance humanist, to write a collection mostly of sonnets entitled *Il Canzoniere*.

GLORIA ANZALDÚA
1942–2004

The term "Chicano" was originally pejorative, used on both sides of the border to identify Mexican Americans of the lowest social class. Just as the once demeaning label "black" was appropriated and revalued by African Americans during the civil rights, black power, and black arts movements of the 1960s, so "Chicano" was embraced by Hispanic activists as a badge of pride, especially among university students and farm workers. By 1987, when the first edition of Gloria Anzaldúa's *Borderlands / La Frontera: The New Mestiza* appeared, two more politically sensitive terms had been added to the sociocultural lexicon: "Chicana," specifically identifying Mexican American women, particularly in light of their announced aims and the general interests of the Chicano movement, and "mestiza," describing Chicana women who are especially concerned with a heritage that is both Chicana and Native American. Together with Cherríe Moraga, her coeditor on *This Bridge Called My Back: Writings by Radical Women of Color* (1981), Anzaldúa emerged as a pioneer in both the writing and the study of Chicana literature.

The daughter of ranchers in Jesus Maria of the Valley, Texas, Anzaldúa labored as a migrant fieldworker before earning a B.A. from Pan American University (1969) and an M.A. from the University of Texas at Austin (1973); she did further graduate study at the University of California at Santa Cruz. She taught creative writing, Chicano studies, and feminist studies at major universities from Texas to California. She published the novel *La Prieta* (Spanish for "the dark one," 1997), other anthologies, and a series of children's books, the most notable of which—*Prietita and the Ghost Woman / Prietita y La Llorona* (1996)—introduces young readers to an important figure in Chicana culture.

La Llorona is one of the three principal representations of women in Mexican culture: *La Virgen de Guadalupe*, a vision of the Virgin Mary who appeared to an Indian, Juan Diego, in 1531 on a hillside outside Mexico City that was sacred to the worship of Tonantzín, the Indian "Mother of Heaven"; *La Chingada*, incorrectly translated as "The Raped One" but whom Anzaldúa insists be accurately identified as "The Fucked One," the deposed Aztec princess (also known as La Malinche, Doña Marina, and Malintzín Tenepal) who served the Spanish military leader Hernan Cortés as translator and lover during his consolidation of colonial power between 1519 and 1522; and *La Llorona*, "The Woman Who Cries," a spurned mistress of Mexican legend who drowned her children and was fated to eternally seek their recovery. Each of these representations metaphorically controls a narrow realm of possibility for Chicanas. At the core of Anzaldúa's work is the belief that because metaphors structure the way we think, the metaphorical influences of these types of women must be reshaped so that Chicanas can escape the binary constraint of being judged as either a virgin or a whore (and nothing else). *Borderlands/La Frontera* is Anzaldúa's most comprehensive effort toward that restructuring.

Although written mainly in English, the personal essays and narrative poem printed here reflect another key part of Anzaldúa's art: not only did she wish to write in Spanish from time to time but she did not always translate that Spanish into English. When she did not provide such a translation in a piece that is primarily in English, she wanted to speak directly to those who either could not or chose not to communicate in English. This practice, much like her blending of fiction, poetry, social commentary, and personal memoir, helps create the narrative richness that characterizes her work.

The following texts are from the second edition of *Borderlands/La Frontera* (1999).

La conciencia de la mestiza/Towards a New Consciousness

> *Por la mujer de mi raza*
> *hablará el espíritu.*[1]

José Vasconcelos, Mexican philosopher, envisaged *una raza mestiza, una mezcla de razas afines, una raza de color—la primera raza síntesis del globo.* He called it a cosmic race, *la raza cósmica,* a fifth race embracing the four major races of the world.[2] Opposite to the theory of the pure Aryan,[3] and to the policy of racial purity that white America practices, his theory is one of inclusivity. At the confluence of two or more genetic streams, with chromosomes constantly "crossing over," this mixture of races, rather than resulting in an inferior being, provides hybrid progeny, a mutable, more malleable species with a rich gene pool. From this racial, ideological, cultural and biological cross-pollinization, an "alien" consciousness is presently in the

1. "This is my own 'take off' on Jose Vasconcelos' idea. José Vasconcelos, *La Raza Cósmica: Misión de la Raza Ibero-Americana* (México: Aguilar S.A. de Ediciones, 1961)" [Anzaldúa's note]. José Vas-

concelos (1882–1959) was a Mexican philosopher.
2. Vasconcelos [Anzaldúa's note].
3. Nazi misnomer for Caucasians of non-Jewish descent.

making—a new *mestiza* consciousness, *una conciencia de mujer*. It is a consciousness of the Borderlands.

Una lucha de fronteras/A Struggle of Borders

Because I, a *mestiza*,
continually walk out of one culture
and into another,
because I am in all cultures at the same time,
alma entre dos mundos, tres, cuatro,
me zumba la cabeza con lo contradictorio.
Estoy norteada por todas las voces que me hablan
simultáneamente.

The ambivalence from the clash of voices results in mental and emotional states of perplexity. Internal strife results in insecurity and indecisiveness. The *mestiza's* dual or multiple personality is plagued by psychic restlessness.

In a constant state of mental nepantilism, an Aztec[4] word meaning torn between ways, *la mestiza* is a product of the transfer of the cultural and spiritual values of one group to another. Being tricultural, monolingual, bilingual, or multilingual, speaking a patois, and in a state of perpetual transition, the *mestiza* faces the dilemma of the mixed breed: which collectivity does the daughter of a darkskinned mother listen to?

El choque de un alma atrapado entire el mundo del espíritu y el mundo de la técnica a veces la deja entullada. Cradled in one culture, sandwiched between two cultures, straddling all three cultures and their value systems, *la mestiza* undergoes a struggle of flesh, a struggle of borders, an inner war. Like all people, we perceive the version of reality that our culture communicates. Like others having or living in more than one culture, we get multiple, often opposing messages. The coming together of two self-consistent but habitually incompatible frames of reference[5] causes *un choque*, a cultural collision.

Within us and within *la cultura chicana*, commonly held beliefs of the white culture attack commonly held beliefs of the Mexican culture, and both attack commonly held beliefs of the indigenous culture. Subconsciously, we see an attack on ourselves and our beliefs as a threat and we attempt to block with a counterstance.

But it is not enough to stand on the opposite river bank, shouting questions, challenging patriarchal, white conventions. A counterstance locks one into a duel of oppressor and oppressed; locked in mortal combat, like the cop and the criminal, both are reduced to a common denominator of violence. The counterstance refutes the dominant culture's views and beliefs, and, for this, it is proudly defiant. All reaction is limited by, and dependent on, what it is reacting against. Because the counterstance stems from a problem with authority—outer as well as inner—it's a step towards liberation from cultural domination. But it is not a way of life. At some point, on our way to a new consciousness, we will have to leave the opposite

---

4. A precolonial people of Mexico with a highly developed civilization.
5. Arthur Koestler [(1905–1983), Hungarian-born writer active in Germany and Britain] termed this term "bisociation." Albert Rothenberg, *The Creative Process in Art, Science, and Other Fields* (Chicago, IL: University of Chicago Press, 1979), 12 [Anzaldúa's note].

bank, the split between the two mortal combatants somehow healed so that we are on both shores at once and, at once, see through serpent and eagle[6] eyes. Or perhaps we will decide to disengage from the dominant culture, write it off altogether as a lost cause, and cross the border into a wholly new and separate territory. Or we might go another route. The possibilities are numerous once we decide to act and not react.

A Tolerance for Ambiguity

These numerous possibilities leave *la mestiza* floundering in uncharted seas. In perceiving conflicting information and points of view, she is subjected to a swamping of her psychological borders. She has discovered that she can't hold concepts or ideas in rigid boundaries. The borders and walls that are supposed to keep the undesirable ideas out are entrenched habits and patterns of behavior; these habits and patterns are the enemy within. Rigidity means death. Only by remaining flexible is she able to stretch the psyche horizontally and vertically. *La mestiza* constantly has to shift out of habitual formations; from convergent thinking, analytical reasoning that tends to use rationality to move toward a single goal (a Western mode), to divergent think-ing,[7] characterized by movement away from set patterns and goals and toward a more whole perspective, one that includes rather than excludes.

The new *mestiza* copes by developing a tolerance for contradictions, a toler-ance for ambiguity. She learns to be an Indian in Mexican culture, to be Mexican from an Anglo point of view. She learns to juggle cultures. She has a plural personality, she operates in a pluralistic mode—nothing is thrust out, the good the bad and the ugly, nothing rejected, nothing abandoned. Not only does she sustain contradictions, she turns the ambivalence into some-thing else.

She can be jarred out of ambivalence by an intense, and often painful, emotional event which inverts or resolves the ambivalence. I'm not sure exactly how. The work takes place underground—subconsciously. It is work that the soul performs. That focal point or fulcrum, that juncture where the *mestiza* stands, is where phenomena tend to collide. It is where the possibil-ity of uniting all that is separate occurs. This assembly is not one where severed or separated pieces merely come together. Nor is it a balancing of opposing powers. In attempting to work out a synthesis, the self has added a third element which is greater than the sum of its severed parts. That third element is a new consciousness—a *mestiza* consciousness—and though it is a source of intense pain, its energy comes from continual creative motion that keeps breaking down the unitary aspect of each new paradigm.

En unas pocas centurias, the future will belong to the *mestiza*. Because the future depends on the breaking down of paradigms, it depends on the straddling of two or more cultures. By creating a new mythos—that is, a change in the way we perceive reality, the way we see ourselves, and the ways we behave—*la mestiza* creates a new consciousness.

The work of *mestiza* consciousness is to break down the subject-object duality that keeps her a prisoner and to show in the flesh and through the

---

6. Female and male, respectively; a binarism in traditional Mexican culture.
7. In part, I derive my definitions for "conver- gent" and "divergent" thinking from Rothen-berg, 12–13 [Anzaldúa's note].

images in her work how duality is transcended. The answer to the problem between the white race and the colored, between males and females, lies in healing the split that originates in the very foundation of our lives, our culture, our languages, our thoughts. A massive uprooting of dualistic thinking in the individual and collective consciousness is the beginning of a long struggle, but one that could, in our best hopes, bring us to the end of rape, of violence, of war.

La encrucijada/The Crossroads

A chicken is being sacrificed
   at a crossroads, a simple mound of earth
a mud shrine for *Eshu*,
   Yoruba[8] god of indeterminacy,
who blesses her choice of path.
She begins her journey.

Su cuerpo es una bocacalle. La mestiza has gone from being the sacrificial goat to becoming the officiating priestess at the crossroads.

As a *mestiza* I have no country, my homeland cast me out; yet all countries are mine because I am every woman's sister or potential lover. (As a lesbian I have no race, my own people disclaim me; but I am all races because there is the queer of me in all races.) I am cultureless because, as a feminist, I challenge the collective cultural/religious male-derived beliefs of Indo-Hispanics and Anglos; yet I am cultured because I am participating in the creation of yet another culture, a new story to explain the world and our participation in it, a new value system with images and symbols that connect us to each other and to the planet. *Soy un amasamiento*, I am an act of kneading, of uniting and joining that not only has produced both a creature of darkness and a creature of light, but also a creature that questions the definitions of light and dark and gives them new meanings.

We are the people who leap in the dark, we are the people on the knees of the gods. In our very flesh, (r)evolution works out the clash of cultures. It makes us crazy constantly, but if the center holds, we've made some kind of evolutionary step forward. *Nuestra alma el trabajo*, the opus, the great alchemical work; spiritual *mestizaje*, a "morphogenesis,"[9] an inevitable unfolding. We have become the quickening serpent movement.

Indigenous like corn, like corn, the *mestiza* is a product of crossbreeding, designed for preservation under a variety of conditions. Like an ear of corn—a female seed-bearing organ—the *mestiza* is tenacious, tightly wrapped in the husks of her culture. Like kernels she clings to the cob; with thick stalks and strong brace roots, she holds tight to the earth—she will survive the crossroads.

8. Large ethnic group of southwest Nigeria and southeast Benin, in Africa.
9. "To borrow from chemist Ilya Prigogine's theory of 'dissipative structures.' Prigogine discovered that substances interact not in predictable ways as it was taught in science, but in different and fluctuating ways to produce new and more complex structures, a kind of birth he called 'morphogenesis,' which created unpredictable innovations. Harold Gilliam, 'Searching for a New World View,' *This World* (January, 1981), 23" [Anzaldúa's note]. Ilya Prigogine (1917–2003), Russian-born Belgian physical chemist active in the United States.

Lavando y remojando el maíz en agua de cal, despojando el pellejo. Moliendo, mixteando, amasando, haciendo tortillas de masa.[1] She steeps the corn in lime, it swells, softens. With stone roller on *metate*, she grinds the corn, then grinds again. She kneads and moulds the dough, pats the round balls into *tortillas*.

> We are the porous rock in the stone *metate*
> squatting on the ground.
> We are the rolling pin, *el maíz y agua,*
> la masa harina. Somos el amasijo.
> Somos lo molido en el metate.
> We are the *comal* sizzling hot,
> the hot *tortilla*, the hungry mouth.
> We are the coarse rock.
> We are the grinding motion,
> the mixed potion, *somos el molcajete.*
> We are the pestle, the *comino, ajo, pimienta,*
> We are the *chile colorado,*
> the green shoot that cracks the rock.
> We will abide.

El camino de la mestiza/The Mestiza Way

Caught between the sudden contraction, the breath sucked in and the endless space, the brown woman stands still, looks at the sky. She decides to go down, digging her way along the roots of trees. Sifting through the bones, she shakes them to see if there is any marrow in them. Then, touching the dirt to her forehead, to her tongue, she takes a few bones, leaves the rest in their burial place.

She goes through her backpack, keeps her journal and address book, throws away the muni-bart metromaps. The coins are heavy and they go next, then the greenbacks flutter through the air. She keeps her knife, can opener and eyebrow pencil. She puts bones, pieces of bark, *hierbas*, eagle feather, snakeskin, tape recorder, the rattle and drum in her pack and she sets out to become the complete *tolteca.*[2]

Her first step is to take inventory. *Despojando, desgranando, quitando paja.* Just what did she inherit from her ancestors? This weight on her back—which is the baggage from the Indian mother, which the baggage from the Spanish father, which the baggage from the Anglo?

Pero es difícil differentiating between *lo heredado, lo adquirido, lo impuesto.* She puts history through a sieve, winnows out the lies, looks at the forces that we as a race, as women, have been a part of. *Luego bota lo que no vale, los desmientos, los desencuentos, el embrutecimiento. Aguarda el juicio, hondo y enraízado, de la gente antigua.* This step is a conscious rupture with all oppressive traditions of all cultures and religions. She communicates that rupture, documents the struggle. She reinterprets history and, using new symbols, she

---

1. *Tortillas de masa harina:* corn tortillas are of two types, the smooth uniform ones made in a tortilla press and usually bought at a tortilla factory or supermarket, and *gorditas*, made by mixing *masa* with lard or shortening or butter (my mother sometimes puts in bits of bacon or chicharones [Anzaldúa's note].

2. Female member of the ancient Toltec group of Nahuatl Indians who lived in Mexico before the Aztecs.

shapes new myths. She adopts new perspectives toward the darkskinned, women and queers. She strengthens her tolerance (and intolerance) for ambiguity. She is willing to share, to make herself vulnerable to foreign ways of seeing and thinking. She surrenders all notions of safety of the familiar. Deconstruct, construct. She becomes a *nahual*, able to transform herself into a tree, a coyote, into another person. She learns to transform the small "I" into the total Self. *Se hace moldeadora de su alma. Según la concepción que tiene de sí misma, así será.*

Que no se nos olviden los hombres

> *"Tú no sirves pa'nada—*
> you're good for nothing.
> *Eres pura vieja."*

"You're nothing but a woman" means you are defective. Its opposite is to be *un macho*. The modern meaning of the word "machismo," as well as the concept, is actually an Anglo invention. For men like my father, being "macho" meant being strong enough to protect and support my mother and us, yet being able to show love. Today's macho has doubts about his ability to feed and protect his family. His "machismo" is an adaptation to oppression and poverty and low self-esteem. It is the result of hierarchical male dominance. The Anglo, feeling inadequate and inferior and powerless, displaces or transfers these feelings to the Chicano by shaming him. In the Gringo world, the Chicano suffers from excessive humility and self-effacement, shame of self and self-deprecation. Around Latinos he suffers from a sense of language inadequacy and its accompanying discomfort; with Native Americans he suffers from a racial amnesia which ignores our common blood, and from guilt because the Spanish part of him took their land and oppressed them. He has an excessive compensatory hubris when around Mexicans from the other side. It overlays a deep sense of racial shame.

The loss of a sense of dignity and respect in the macho breeds a false machismo which leads him to put down women and even to brutalize them. Coexisting with his sexist behavior is a love for the mother which takes precedence over that of all others. Devoted son, macho pig. To wash down the shame of his acts, of his very being, and to handle the brute in the mirror, he takes to the bottle, the snort, the needle, and the fist.

Though we "understand" the root causes of male hatred and fear, and the subsequent wounding of women, we do not excuse, we do not condone, and we will no longer put up with it. From the men of our race, we demand the admission/acknowledgment/disclosure/testimony that they wound us, violate us, are afraid of us and of our power. We need them to say they will begin to eliminate their hurtful put-down ways. But more than the words, we demand acts. We say to them: We will develop equal power with you and those who have shamed us.

It is imperative that *mestizas* support each other in changing the sexist elements in the Mexican-Indian culture. As long as woman is put down, the Indian and the Black in all of us is put down. The struggle of the *mestiza* is above all a feminist one. As long as *los hombres* think they have to *chingar mujeres* and each other to be men, as long as men are taught that they are superior and therefore culturally favored over *la mujer,* as long as to be a *vieja* is a thing of derision, there can be no real healing of our psyches. We're halfway there—we have such love of the Mother, the good mother. The first step is to unlearn the *puta/virgen* dichotomy and to see *Coatlalopeuh-Coatlicue* in the Mother, *Guadalupe.*[3]

Tenderness, a sign of vulnerability, is so feared that it is showered on women with verbal abuse and blows. Men, even more than women, are fettered to gender roles. Women at least have had the guts to break out of bondage. Only gay men have had the courage to expose themselves to the woman inside them and to challenge the current masculinity. I've encountered a few scattered and isolated gentle straight men, the beginnings of a new breed, but they are confused, and entangled with sexist behaviors that they have not been able to eradicate. We need a new masculinity and the new man needs a movement.

Lumping the males who deviate from the general norm with man, the oppressor, is a gross injustice. *Asombra pensar que nos hemos quedado en ese pozo oscuro donde el mundo encierra a las lesbianas. Asombra pensar que hemos, como femenistas y lesbianas, cerrado nuestros corazónes a los hombres, a nuestros hermanos los jotos, desheredados y marginales como nosotros.* Being the supreme crossers of cultures, homosexuals have strong bonds with the queer white, Black, Asian, Native American, Latino, and with the queer in Italy, Australia and the rest of the planet. We come from all colors, all classes, all races, all time periods. Our role is to link people with each other—the Blacks with Jews with Indians with Asians with whites with extraterrestrials. It is to transfer ideas and information from one culture to another. Colored homosexuals have more knowledge of other cultures; have always been at the forefront (although sometimes in the closet) of all liberation struggles in this country; have suffered more injustices and have survived them despite all odds. Chicanos need to acknowledge the political and artistic contributions of their queer. People, listen to what your *jotería* is saying.

The *mestizo* and the queer exist at this time and point on the evolutionary continuum for a purpose. We are a blending that proves that all blood is intricately woven together, and that we are spawned out of similar souls.

Somos una gente

> *Hay tantísimas fronteras*
> *que dividen a la gente,*
> *pero por cada frontera*
> *existe también un puente.*
> —Gina Valdés[4]

<u>Divided Loyalties</u>. Many women and men of color do not want to have any dealings with white people. It takes too much time and energy to

---

3. The Virgin of Guadalupe, patron saint of Mexico. In matriarchal Olmec culture Coatl was a figuration of the sacred womb from which all things were born and to which they returned. Coatlicue is the Meso-American serpent that is half male, half female.

4. Gina Valdés, *Puentes y Fronteras: Coplas Chicanas* (Los Angeles, CA: Castle Lithograph, 1982), 2 [Anzaldúa's note].

explain to the downwardly mobile, white middle-class women that it's okay for us to want to own "possessions," never having had any nice furniture on our dirt floors or "luxuries" like washing machines. Many feel that whites should help their own people rid themselves of race hatred and fear first. I, for one, choose to use some of my energy to serve as mediator. I think we need to allow whites to be our allies. Through our literature, art, *corridos*, and folktales we must share our history with them so when they set up committees to help Big Mountain *Navajos* or the Chicano farmworkers or *los Nicaragüenses*[5] they won't turn people away because of their racial fears and ignorances. They will come to see that they are not helping us but following our lead.

Individually, but also as a racial entity, we need to voice our needs. We need to say to white society: We need you to accept the fact that Chicanos are different, to acknowledge your rejection and negation of us. We need you to own the fact that you looked upon us as less than human, that you stole our lands, our personhood, our self-respect. We need you to make public restitution: to say that, to compensate for your own sense of defectiveness, you strive for power over us, you erase our history and our experience because it makes you feel guilty—you'd rather forget your brutish acts. To say you've split yourself from minority groups, that you disown us, that your dual consciousness splits off parts of yourself, transferring the "negative" parts onto us. (Where there is persecution of minorities, there is shadow projection. Where there is violence and war, there is repression of shadow.) To say that you are afraid of us, that to put distance between us, you wear the mask of contempt. Admit that Mexico is your double, that she exists in the shadow of this country, that we are irrevocably tied to her. Gringo, accept the doppelganger[6] in your psyche. By taking back your collective shadow the intracultural split will heal. And finally, tell us what you need from us.

By Your True Faces We Will Know You

I am visible—see this Indian face—yet I am invisible. I both blind them with my beak nose and am their blind spot. But I exist, we exist. They'd like to think I have melted in the pot. But I haven't, we haven't.

The dominant white culture is killing us slowly with its ignorance. By taking away our self-determination, it has made us weak and empty. As a people we have resisted and we have taken expedient positions, but we have never been allowed to develop unencumbered—we have never been allowed to be fully ourselves. The whites in power want us people of color to barricade ourselves behind our separate tribal walls so they can pick us off one at a time with their hidden weapons; so they can whitewash and distort history. Ignorance splits people, creates prejudices. A misinformed people is a subjugated people.

---

5. Nicaraguans; here a reference to the Sandinista government, which was opposed covertly by the United States in the 1980s. "Big Mountain *Navajos*": Dineh people of Big Mountain, Arizona, forcibly removed in a land dispute with energy companies in 1997. "Farmworkers": members of the United Farm Workers, a union founded in 1962.
6. Literally, "double-goer" (German); an alter ego or the ghost of a living person.

Before the Chicano and the undocumented worker and the Mexican from the other side can come together, before the Chicano can have unity with Native Americans and other groups, we need to know the history of their struggle and they need to know ours. Our mothers, our sisters and brothers, the guys who hang out on street corners, the children in the playgrounds, each of us must know our Indian lineage, our afro-*mestizaje*, our history of resistance.

To the immigrant *mexicano* and the recent arrivals we must teach our history. The 80 million *mexicanos* and the Latinos from Central and South America must know of our struggles. Each one of us must know basic facts about Nicaragua, Chile and the rest of Latin America. The Latinoist movement (Chicanos, Puerto Ricans, Cubans and other Spanish-speaking people working together to combat racial discrimination in the marketplace) is good but it is not enough. Other than a common culture we will have nothing to hold us together. We need to meet on a broader communal ground.

The struggle is inner: Chicano, *indio*, American Indian, *mojado*, *mexicano*, immigrant Latino, Anglo in power, working class Anglo, Black, Asian—our psyches resemble the bordertowns and are populated by the same people. The struggle has always been inner, and is played out in the outer terrains. Awareness of our situation must come before inner changes, which in turn come before changes in society. Nothing happens in the "real" world unless it first happens in the images in our heads.

El día de la Chicana

I will not be shamed again
Nor will I shame myself.

I am possessed by a vision: that we Chicanas and Chicanos have taken back or uncovered our true faces, our dignity and self-respect. It's a validation vision.

Seeing the Chicana anew in light of her history. I seek an exoneration, a seeing through the fictions of white supremacy, a seeing of ourselves in our true guises and not as the false racial personality that has been given to us and that we have given to ourselves. I seek our woman's face, our true features, the positive and the negative seen clearly, free of the tainted biases of male dominance. I seek new images of identity, new beliefs about ourselves, our humanity and worth no longer in question.

Estamos viviendo en la noche de la Raza, un tiempo cuando el trabajo se hace a lo quieto, en lo oscuro. El día cuando aceptamos tal y como somos y para donde vamos y porque—ese día será el día de la Raza. Yo tengo el conpromiso de expresar mi visión, mi sensibilidad, mi percepción de la revalidación de la gente mexicana, su mérito, estimación, honra, aprecio, y validez.

On December 2nd when my sun goes into my first house, I celebrate *el día de la Chicana y el Chicano*: On that day I clean my altars, light my *Coatlalo-*

peuh candle, burn sage and copal,[7] take *el baño para espantar basura*; sweep my house. On that day I bare my soul, make myself vulnerable to friends and family by expressing my feelings. On that day I affirm who we are.

On that day I look inside our conflicts and our basic introverted racial temperament. I identify our needs, voice them. I acknowledge that the self and the race have been wounded. I recognize the need to take care of our personhood, of our racial self. On that day I gather the splintered and disowned parts of *la gente mexicana* and hold them in my arms. *Todas las partes de nosotros valen.*

On that day I say, "Yes, all you people wound us when you reject us. Rejection strips us of self-worth; our vulnerability exposes us to shame. It is our innate identity you find wanting. We are ashamed that we need your good opinion, that we need your acceptance. We can no longer camouflage our needs, can no longer let defenses and fences sprout around us. We can no longer withdraw. To rage and look upon you with contempt is to rage and be contemptuous of ourselves. We can no longer blame you, nor disown the white parts, the male parts, the pathological parts, the queer parts, the vulnerable parts. Here we are weaponless with open arms, with only our magic. Let's try it our way, the *mestiza* way, the Chicana way, the woman way."

On that day, I search for our essential dignity as a people, a people with a sense of purpose—to belong and contribute to something greater than our *pueblo*. On that day I seek to recover and reshape my spiritual identity. *¡Anímate! Raza, a celebrar el día de la Chicana.*

El retorno

> All movements are accomplished in six stages,
> and the seventh brings return.
> —I Ching[8]

> *Tanto tiempo sin verte casa mía,*
> *mi cuna, mi hondo nido de la huerta.*
> —"Soledad"[9]

I stand at the river, watch the curving, twisting serpent, a serpent nailed to the fence where the mouth of the Rio Grande empties into the Gulf.

I have come back. *Tanto dolor me costó el alejamiento.* I shade my eyes and look up. The bone beak of a hawk slowly circling over me, checking me out as potential carrion. In its wake a little bird flickering its wings, swimming sporadically like a fish. In the distance the expressway and the slough of traffic like an irritated sow. The sudden pull in my gut, *la tierra, los aguaceros.* My land, *el viento soplando la arena, el lagartijo debajo de un nopalito. Me acuerdo como era antes. Una región desértica de vasta llanuras, costeras de baja altura, de escasa lluvia, de chaparrales formados por mesquites y huizaches.* If I look real hard I can almost see the Spanish fathers who were

---

7. Amber fossilized resin from tropical trees.
8. "Richard Wilhelm, *The I Ching or Book of Changes*, trans. Cary F. Baynes (Princeton: Princeton University Press, 1950), 98" [Anzaldúa's

note]. Central text of Confucianism dating from the first millennium B.C.E.
9. *Soledad* is sung by the group Haciendo Punto en Otro Son [Anzaldúa's note].

called "the cavalry of Christ" enter this valley riding their *burros*, see the clash of cultures commence.

Tierra natal. This is home, the small towns in the Valley, *los pueblitos* with chicken pens and goats picketed to mesquite shrubs. *En las colonias* on the other side of the tracks, junk cars line the front yards of hot pink and lavender-trimmed houses—Chicano architecture we call it, self-consciously. I have missed the TV shows where hosts speak in half and half, and where awards are given in the category of Tex-Mex music. I have missed the Mexican cemeteries blooming with artificial flowers, the fields of aloe vera and red pepper, rows of sugar cane, of corn hanging on the stalks, the cloud of *polvareda* in the dirt roads behind a speeding pickup truck, *el sabor de tamales de rez y venado* I have missed *la yegua colorada* gnawing the wooden gate of her stall, the smell of horse flesh from Carito's corrals. *Hecho menos las noches calientes sin aire, noches de linternas y lechuzas* making holes in the night.

I still feel the old despair when I look at the unpainted, dilapidated, scrap lumber houses consisting mostly of corrugated aluminum. Some of the poorest people in the U.S. live in the Lower Rio Grande Valley, and arid and semiarid land of irrigated farming, intense sunlight and heat, citrus groves next to chaparral and cactus. I walk through the elementary school I attended so long ago, that remained segregated until recently. I remember how the white teachers used to punish us for being Mexican.

How I love this tragic valley of South Texas, as Ricardo Sánchez calls it; this borderland between the Nueces and the Rio Grande.[1] This land has survived possession and ill-use by five countries: Spain, Mexico, the Republic of Texas, the U.S., the Confederacy,[2] and the U.S. again. It has survived Anglo-Mexican blood feuds, lynchings, burnings, rapes, pillage.

Today I see the Valley still struggling to survive. Whether it does or not, it will never be as I remember it. The borderlands depression that was set off by the 1982 peso devaluation in Mexico resulted in the closure of hundreds of Valley businesses. Many people lost their homes, cars, land. Prior to 1982, U.S. store owners thrived on retail sales to Mexicans who came across the border for groceries and clothes and appliances. While goods on the U.S. side have become 10, 100, 1000 times more expensive for Mexican buyers, goods on the Mexican side have become 10, 100, 1000 times cheaper for Americans. Because the Valley is heavily dependent on agriculture and Mexican retail trade, it has the highest unemployment rates along the entire border region; it is the Valley that has been hardest hit.[3]

"It's been a bad year for corn," my brother, Nune, says. As he talks, I remember my father scanning the sky for a rain that would end the drought, looking up into the sky, day after day, while the corn withered on its stalk. My father has

---

1. Rivers in southern Texas. Sánchez (1941–1995), Chicano poet, educator, and activist.

2. I.e., the Confederate States of America, made up of eleven southern states (including Texas) that seceded from the Union at the start of the U.S. Civil War (1861–65). After it won independence from Mexico (1836) and before it was admitted as a state to the United States (1845), Texas was a republic.

3. Out of the twenty-two border counties in the four border states, Hidalgo County (named for Father Hidalgo who was shot in 1810 after instigating Mexico's revolt against Spanish rule under the banner of *la Virgen de Guadalupe*) is the most poverty-stricken county in the nation as well as the largest home base (along with Imperial in California) for migrant farmworkers. It was here I was born and raised. I am amazed that both it and I have survived [Anzaldúa's note].

been dead for 29 years, having worked himself to death. The life span of a Mexican farm laborer is 56—he lived to be 38. It shocks me that I am older than he. I, too, search the sky for rain. Like the ancients, I worship the rain god and the maize goddess, but unlike my father I have recovered their names. Now for rain (irrigation) one offers not a sacrifice of blood, but of money.

"Farming is in a bad way," my brother says. "Two to three thousand small and big farmers went bankrupt in this country last year. Six years ago the price of corn was $8.00 per hundred pounds," he goes on. "This year it is $3.90 per hundred pounds." And, I think to myself, after taking inflation into account, not planting anything puts you ahead.

I walk out to the back yard, stare at *los rosales de mamá*. She wants me to help her prune the rose bushes, dig out the carpet grass that is choking them. *Mamagrande Ramona también tenía rosales.* Here every Mexican grows flowers. If they don't have a piece of dirt, they use car tires, jars, cans, shoe boxes. Roses are the Mexican's favorite flower. I think, how symbolic—thorns and all.

Yes, the Chicano and Chicana have always taken care of growing things and the land. Again I see the four of us kids getting off the school bus, changing into our work clothes, walking into the field with Papi and Mami, all six of us bending to the ground. Below our feet, under the earth lie the watermelon seeds. We cover them with paper plates, putting *terremotes* on top of the plates to keep them from being blown away by the wind. The paper plates keep the freeze away. Next day or the next, we remove the plates, bare the tiny green shoots to the elements. They survive and grow, give fruit hundreds of times the size of the seed. We water them and hoe them. We harvest them. The vines dry, rot, are plowed under. Growth, death, decay, birth. The soil prepared again and again, impregnated, worked on. A constant changing of forms, *renacimientos de la tierra madre.*

<blockquote>
This land was Mexican once
was Indian always
and is.
And will be again.
</blockquote>

1987

How to Tame a Wild Tongue

"We're going to have to control your tongue," the dentist says, pulling out all the metal from my mouth. Silver bits plop and tinkle into the basin. My mouth is a motherlode.

The dentist is cleaning out my roots. I get a whiff of the-stench when I gasp. "I can't cap that tooth yet, you're still draining," he says.

"We're going to have to do something about your tongue," I hear the anger rising in his voice. My tongue keeps pushing out the wads of cotton, pushing back the drills, the long thin needles. "I've never seen anything as strong or as stubborn," he says. And I think, how do you tame a wild tongue, train it to be quiet, how do you bridle and saddle it? How do you make it lie down?

> "Who is to say that robbing a people of
> its language is less violent than war?"
> —Ray Gwyn Smith[1]

I remember being caught speaking Spanish at recess—that was good for three licks on the knuckles with a sharp ruler. I remember being sent to the corner of the classroom for "talking back" to the Anglo teacher when all I was trying to do was tell her how to pronounce my name. "If you want to be American, speak 'American.' If you don't like it, go back to Mexico where you belong."

"I want you to speak English. *Pa'hallar buen trabajo tienes que saber hablar el inglés bien. Qué vale toda tu educación si todavía hablas inglés con un 'accent,'*" my mother would say, mortified that I spoke English like a Mexican. At Pan American University, I, and all Chicano students were required to take two speech classes. Their purpose: to get rid of our accents.

Attacks on one's form of expression with the intent to censor are a violation of the First Amendment. *El Anglo con cara de inocente nos arrancó la lengua.* Wild tongues can't be tamed, they can only be cut out.

Overcoming the Tradition of Silence

Ahogadas, escupimos el oscuro.
Peleando con nuestra propia sombra
el silencio nos sepulta.

En boca cerrada no entran moscas. "Flies don't enter a closed mouth" is a saying I kept hearing when I was a child. *Ser habladora* was to be a gossip and a liar, to talk too much. *Muchachitas bien criadas*, well-bred girls don't answer back. *Es una falta de respeto* to talk back to one's mother or father. I remember one of the sins I'd recite to the priest in the confession box the few times I went to confession: talking back to my mother, *hablar pa' 'trás, repelar. Hocicona, repelona, chismosa*, having a big mouth, questioning, carrying tales are all signs of being *mal criada*. In my culture they are all words that are derogatory if applied to women—I've never heard them applied to men.

The first time I heard two women, a Puerto Rican and a Cuban, say the word *"nosotras,"* I was shocked. I had not known the word existed. Chicanas use *nosotros* whether we're male or female. We are robbed of our female being by the masculine plural. Language is a male discourse.

> And our tongues have become
> dry   the wilderness has
> dried out our tongues   and
> we have forgotten speech.
> —Irena Klepfisz[2]

---

1. Ray Gwyn Smith [(b. 1944), Welsh painter and art educator active in the United States], *Moorland Is Cold Country*, unpublished book [Anzaldúa's note].
2. Irena Klepfisz [(b. 1941), North American critic], *"Di rayze aheym / The Journey Home,"* in *The Tribe of Dina: A Jewish Women's Anthology*, Melanie Kaye/Kantrowitz and Irena Klepfisz, eds. (Montpelier, VT: Sinister Wisdom Books, 1986), 49 [Anzaldúa's note].

Even our own people, other Spanish speakers *nos quieren poner candados en la boca*. They would hold us back with their bag of *reglas de academia*.

Oyé como ladra: el lenguaje de la frontera

Quien tiene boca se equivoca.
—Mexican saying

"*Pocho,*[3] cultural traitor, you're speaking the oppressor's language by speaking English, you're ruining the Spanish language," I have been accused by various Latinos and Latinas. Chicano Spanish is considered by the purist and by most Latinos deficient, a mutilation of Spanish.

But Chicano Spanish is a border tongue which developed naturally. Change, *evolución, enriquecimiento de palabras nuevas por invención o adopción* have created variants of Chicano Spanish, *un nuevo lenguaje. Un lenguaje que corresponde a un modo de vivir*. Chicano Spanish is not incorrect, it is a living language.

For a people who are neither Spanish nor live in a country in which Spanish is the first language; for a people who live in a country in which English is the reigning tongue but who are not Anglo; for a people who cannot entirely identify with either standard (formal, Castillian) Spanish nor standard English, what recourse is left to them but to create their own language? A language which they can connect their identity to, one capable of communicating the realities and values true to themselves—a language with terms that are neither *español ni inglés*, but both. We speak a patois, a forked tongue, a variation of two languages.

Chicano Spanish sprang out of the Chicanos' need to identify ourselves as a distinct people. We needed a language with which we could communicate with ourselves, a secret language. For some of us, language is a homeland closer than the Southwest—for many Chicanos today live in the Midwest and the East. And because we are a complex, heterogeneous people, we speak many languages. Some of the languages we speak are:

1. Standard English
2. Working class and slang English
3. Standard Spanish
4. Standard Mexican Spanish
5. North Mexican Spanish dialect
6. Chicano Spanish (Texas, New Mexico, Arizona and California have regional variations)
7. Tex-Mex
8. *Pachuco* (called *caló*)

My "home" tongues are the languages I speak with my sister and brothers, with my friends. They are the last five listed, with 6 and 7 being closest to my heart. From school, the media and job situations, I've picked up standard and working class English. From Mamagrande Locha and from reading Spanish and Mexican literature, I've picked up Standard Spanish and Standard Mexican Spanish. From *los recién llegados*, Mexican immigrants, and *braceros*, I

---

3. An anglicized Mexican or American of Mexican origin who speaks Spanish with an accent characteristic of North Americans and who dis- torts and reconstructs the language according to the influence of English. Anzaldúa offers a definition later in this selection.

learned the North Mexican dialect. With Mexicans I'll try to speak either Standard Mexican Spanish or the North Mexican dialect. From my parents and Chicanos living in the Valley,[4] I picked up Chicano Texas Spanish, and I speak it with my mom; younger brother (who married a Mexican and who rarely mixes Spanish with English), aunts and older relatives.

With Chicanas from *Nuevo México* or *Arizona* I will speak Chicano Spanish a little, but often they don't understand what I'm saying. With most California Chicanas I speak entirely in English (unless I forget). When I first moved to San Francisco, I'd rattle off something in Spanish, unintentionally embarrassing them. Often it is only with another Chicana *tejana* that I can talk freely.

Words distorted by English are known as anglicisms or *pochismos*. The *pocho* is an anglicized Mexican or American of Mexican origin who speaks Spanish with an accent characteristic of North Americans and who distorts and reconstructs the language according to the influence of English.[5] Tex-Mex, or Spanglish, comes most naturally to me. I may switch back and forth from English to Spanish in the same sentence or in the same word. With my sister and my brother Nune and with Chicano *tejano* contemporaries I speak in Tex-Mex.

From kids and people my own age I picked up *Pachuco*. Pachuco (the language of the zoot suiters) is a language of rebellion, both against Standard Spanish and Standard English. It is a secret language. Adults of the culture and outsiders cannot understand it. It is made up of slang words from both English and Spanish. *Ruca* means girl or woman, *vato* means guy or dude, *chale* means no, *simón* means yes, *churo* is sure, talk is *periquiar*, *pigionear* means petting, *que gacho* means how nerdy, *ponte águila* means watch out, death is called *la pelona*. Through lack of practice and not having others who can speak it, I've lost most of the *Pachuco* tongue.

Chicano Spanish

Chicanos, after 250 years of Spanish/Anglo colonization have developed significant differences in the Spanish we speak. We collapse two adjacent vowels into a single syllable and sometimes shift the stress in certain words such as *maíz / maiz, cohete / cuete*. We leave out certain consonants when they appear between vowels: *lado/lao, mojado/mojao*. Chicanos from South Texas pronounced *f* as *j* as in *jue* (*fue*). Chicanos use "archaisms," words that are no longer in the Spanish language, words that have been evolved out. We say *semos, truje, haiga, ansina*, and *naiden*. We retain the "archaic" *j*, as in *jalar*, that derives from an earlier *h*, (the French *halar* or the Germanic *halon* which was lost to standard Spanish in the 16th century), but which is still found in several regional dialects such as the one spoken in South Texas. (Due to geography, Chicanos from the Valley of South Texas were cut off linguistically from other Spanish speakers. We tend to use words that the Spaniards brought over from Medieval Spain. The majority of the Spanish colonizers in Mexico and the Southwest came from Extremadura—Hernán

4. I.e., of the Rio Grande River in southern Texas, bordering Mexico.
5. R. C. Ortega, *Dialectología Del Barrio*, trans. Hortencia S. Alwan (Los Angeles, CA: R. C. Ortega Publisher & Bookseller, 1977), 132 [Anzaldúa's note].

Cortés was one of them—and Andalucía.[6] Andalucians pronounce *ll* like a *y*, and their *d*'s tend to be absorbed by adjacent vowels: *tirado* becomes *tirao*. They brought *el lenguaje popular, dialectos y regionalismos*.)[7]

Chicanos and other Spanish speakers also shift *ll* to *y* and *z* to *s*.[8] We leave out initial syllables, saying *tar* for *estar, toy* for *estoy; hora* for *ahora* (*cubanos* and *puertorriqueños* also leave out initial letters of some words.) We also leave out the final syllable such as *pa* for *para*. The intervocalic *y*, the *ll* as in *tortilla, ella, botella*, gets replaced by *tortia* or *tortiya, ea, botea*. We add an additional syllable at the beginning of certain words: *atocar* for *tocar, agastar* for *gastar*. Sometimes we'll say *lavaste las vacijas*, other times *lavates* (substituting the *ates* verb endings for the *aste*).

We use anglicisms, words borrowed from English: *bola* from ball, *carpeta* from carpet, *máchina de lavar* (instead of *lavadora*) from washing machine. Tex-Mex argot, created by adding a Spanish sound at the beginning or end of an English word such as *cookiar* for cook, *watchar* for watch, *parkiar* for park, and *rapiar* for rape, is the result of the pressures on Spanish speakers to adapt to English.

We don't use the word *vosotros/as* or its accompanying verb form. We don't say *claro* (to mean yes), *imagínate*, or *me emociona*, unless we picked up Spanish from Latinas, out of a book, or in a classroom. Other Spanish-speaking groups are going through the same, or similar, development in their Spanish.

Linguistic Terrorism

Deslenguadas. Somos los del español deficiente. We are your linguistic nightmare, your linguistic aberration, your linguistic *mestizaje*, the subject of your *burla*. Because we speak with tongues of fire we are culturally crucified. Racially, culturally and linguistically *somos huérfanos*—we speak an orphan tongue.

Chicanas who grew up speaking Chicano Spanish have internalized the belief that we speak poor Spanish. It is illegitimate, a bastard language. And because we internalize how our language has been used against us by the dominant culture, we use our language differences against each other.

Chicana feminists often skirt around each other with suspicion and hesitation. For the longest time I couldn't figure it out. Then it dawned on me. To be close to another Chicana is like looking into the mirror. We are afraid of what we'll see there. *Pena*. Shame. Low estimation of self. In childhood we are told that our language is wrong. Repeated attacks on our native tongue diminish our sense of self. The attacks continue throughout our lives.

Chicanas feel uncomfortable talking in Spanish to Latinas, afraid of their censure. Their language was not outlawed in their countries. They had a whole lifetime of being immersed in their native tongue; generations, centuries in which Spanish was a first language, taught in school, heard on radio and TV, and read in the newspaper.

6. Region in southern Spain. Extremadura is a city in central Spain. Cortés (1485–1547), Spanish soldier and explorer who conquered the Aztecs and claimed Mexico for Spain.
7. Eduardo Hernandéz-Chávez, Andrew D. Cohen, and Anthony F. Beltramo, *El Lenguaje de*

los Chicanos: Regional and Social Characteristics of Language Used by Mexican Americans (Arlington, VA: Center for Applied Linguistics, 1975), 39 [Anzaldúa's note].
8. Hernandéz-Chávez, xvii [Anzaldúa's note].

If a person, Chicana or Latina, has a low estimation of my native tongue, she also has a low estimation of me. Often with *mexicanas y latinas* we'll speak English as a neutral language. Even among Chicanas we tend to speak English at parties or conferences. Yet, at the same time, we're afraid the other will think we're *agringadas* because we don't speak Chicano Spanish. We oppress each other trying to out-Chicano each other, vying to be the "real" Chicanas, to speak like Chicanos. There is no one Chicano language just as there is no one Chicano experience. A monolingual Chicana whose first language is English or Spanish is just as much a Chicana as one who speaks several variants of Spanish. A Chicana from Michigan or Chicago or Detroit is just as much a Chicana as one from the Southwest. Chicano Spanish is as diverse linguistically as it is regionally.

By the end of this century, Spanish speakers will comprise the biggest minority group in the U.S., a country where students in high schools and colleges are encouraged to take French classes because French is considered more "cultured." But for a language to remain alive it must be used.[9] By the end of this century English, and not Spanish, will be the mother tongue of most Chicanos and Latinos.

So, if you want to really hurt me, talk badly about my language. Ethnic identity is twin skin to linguistic identity—I am my language. Until I can take pride in my language, I cannot take pride in myself. Until I can accept as legitimate Chicano Texas Spanish, Tex-Mex and all the other languages I speak, I cannot accept the legitimacy of myself. Until I am free to write bilingually and to switch codes without having always to translate, while I still have to speak English or Spanish when I would rather speak Spanglish, and as long as I have to accommodate the English speakers rather than having them accommodate me, my tongue will be illegitimate.

I will no longer be made to feel ashamed of existing. I will have my voice: Indian, Spanish, white. I will have my serpent's tongue—my woman's voice, my sexual voice, my poet's voice. I will overcome the tradition of silence.

> My fingers
> move sly against your palm
> Like women everywhere, we speak in code. . . .
>
>   —Melanie Kaye/Kantrowitz[1]

"Vistas," corridos, y comida: My Native Tongue

In the 1960s, I read my first Chicano novel. It was *City of Night* by John Rechy[2] a gay Texan, son of a Scottish father and a Mexican mother. For days I walked around in stunned amazement that a Chicano could write and could get published. When I read *I Am Joaquín*[3] I was surprised to see a bilingual book by a Chicano in print. When I saw poetry written in Tex-Mex

9. Irena Klepfisz, "Secular Jewish Identity: Yidishkayt in America," in *The Tribe of Dina*, Kaye/Kantrowitz, eds., 43 [Anzaldúa's note].
1. Melanie Kaye/Kantrowitz, "Sign," in *We Speak in Code: Poems and Other Writings* (Pittsburgh, PA: Motheroot Publications, Inc., 1980), 85 [Anzaldúa's note].

2. American novelist (b. 1934). The book was published in 1963.
3. Rodolfo Gonzales [(b. 1928), Chicano novelist], *I Am Joaquín Yo Soy Joaquín* (New York, NY: Bantam Books, 1972). It was first published in 1967 [Anzaldúa's note].

for the first time, a feeling of pure joy flashed through me. I felt like we really existed as a people. In 1971, when I started teaching High School English to Chicano students, I tried to supplement the required texts with works by Chicanos, only to be reprimanded and forbidden to do so by the principal. He claimed that I was supposed to teach "American" and English literature. At the risk of being fired, I swore my students to secrecy and slipped in Chicano short stories, poems, a play. In graduate school, while working toward a Ph.D., I had to "argue" with one advisor after the other, semester after semester, before I was allowed to make Chicano literature an area of focus.

Even before I read books by Chicanos or Mexicans, it was the Mexican movies I saw at the drive-in—the Thursday night special of $1.00 a carload—that gave me a sense of belonging. *"Vámonos a las vistas,"* my mother would call out and we'd all—grandmother, brothers, sister and cousins—squeeze into the car. We'd wolf down cheese and bologna white bread sandwiches while watching Pedro Infante in melodramatic tear-jerkers like *Nosotros los pobres,*[4] the first "real" Mexican movie (that was not an imitation of European movies). I remember seeing *Cuando los hijos se van*[5] and surmising that all Mexican movies played up the love a mother has for her children and what ungrateful sons and daughters suffer when they are not devoted to their mothers. I remember the singing-type "westerns" of Jorge Negrete and Miguel Aceves Mejía.[6] When watching Mexican movies, I felt a sense of homecoming as well as alienation. People who were to amount to something didn't go to Mexican movies, or *bailes* or tune their radios to *bolero, rancherita,* and *corrido* music.

The whole time I was growing up, there was *norteño* music sometimes called North Mexican border music, or Tex-Mex music, or Chicano music, or *cantina* (bar) music. I grew up listening to *conjuntos,* three- or four-piece bands made up of folk musicians playing guitar, *bajo sexto,*[7] drums and button accordion, which Chicanos had borrowed from the German immigrants who had come to Central Texas and Mexico to farm and build breweries. In the Rio Grande Valley, Steve Jordan and Little Joe Hernández were popular, and Flaco Jiménez[8] was the accordion king. The rhythms of Tex-Mex music are those of the polka, also adapted from the Germans, who in turn had borrowed the polka from the Czechs and Bohemians.

I remember the hot, sultry evenings when *corridos*—songs of love and death on the Texas-Mexican borderlands—reverberated out of cheap amplifiers from the local *cantinas* and wafted in through my bedroom window.

Corridos first became widely used along the South Texas / Mexican border during the early conflict between Chicanos and Anglos. The *corridos* are usually about Mexican heroes who do valiant deeds against the Anglo oppressors. Pancho Villa's song, *"La cucaracha,"* is the most famous one. *Corridos* of John F. Kennedy[9] and his death are still very popular in the

---

4. A 1947 film. Infante (1917–1957), Mexican film actor and singer.
5. A 1941 film.
6. Mexican singer and film actor (b. 1916). Negrete (1911–1953), Mexican singing actor.
7. Twelve-string guitar tuned one octave lower than normal.

8. Mexican American musicians. Esteban Jordán (1939–2010). José María De Leon Hérnandez (b. 1940), Leonardo "Flaco" Jiménez (b. 1939).
9. Thirty-fifth U.S. president (1917–1963), assassinated in Dallas, Texas. Villa (ca. 1877–1923), born Doroteo Arango, Mexican revolutionary leader.

Valley. Older Chicanos remember Lydia Mendoza,[1] one of the great border *corrido* singers who was called *la Gloria de Tejas*. Her *"El tango negre,"* sung during the Great Depression, made her a singer of the people. The everpresent *corridos* narrated one hundred years of border history, bringing news of events as well as entertaining. These folk musicians and folk songs are our chief cultural mythmakers, and they made our hard lives seem bearable.

I grew up feeling ambivalent about our music. Country-western and rock-and-roll had more status. In the 50s and 60s, for the slightly educated and *agringado* Chicanos, there existed a sense of shame at being caught listening to our music. Yet I couldn't stop my feet from thumping to the music, could not stop humming the words, nor hide from myself the exhilaration I felt when I heard it.

There are more subtle ways that we internalize identification, especially in the forms of images and emotions. For me food and certain smells are tied to my identity, to my homeland. Woodsmoke curling up to an immense blue sky; woodsmoke perfuming my grandmother's clothes, her skin. The stench of cow manure and the yellow patches on the ground; the crack of a .22 rifle and the reek of cordite. Homemade white cheese sizzling in a pan, melting inside a folded *tortilla*. My sister Hilda's hot, spicy *menudo*[2] *chile colorado* making it deep red, pieces of *panza* and hominy floating on top. My brother Carito barbecuing *fajitas* in the backyard. Even now and 3,000 miles away, I can see my mother spicing the ground beef, pork and venison with *chile*. My mouth salivates at the thought of the hot steaming *tamales* I would be eating if I were home.

> *Si le preguntas a mi mamá, "¿Qué eres?"*

> "Identity is the essential core of who
> we are as individuals, the conscious
> experience of the self inside."
> —Kaufman[3]

Nosotros los Chicanos straddle the borderlands. On one side of us, we are constantly exposed to the Spanish of the Mexicans, on the other side we hear the Anglos' incessant clamoring so that we forget our language. Among ourselves we don't say *nosotros los americanos, o nosotros los españoles, o nosotros los hispanos*. We say *nosotros los mexicanos* (by *mexicanos* we do not mean citizens of Mexico; we do not mean a national identity, but a racial one). We distinguish between *mexicanos del otro lado* and *mexicanos de este lado*. Deep in our hearts we believe that being Mexican has nothing to do with which country one lives in. Being Mexican is a state of soul—not one of mind, not one of citizenship. Neither eagle nor serpent,[4] but both. And like the ocean, neither animal respects borders.

---

1. Mexican American singer, songwriter, and musician (b. 1916).
2. Mexican soup made of simmered tripe, onion, garlic, chili, and hominy.
3. Gershen Kaufman [(b. 1943), American psychologist], *Shame: The Power of Caring* (Cam-
bridge: Schenkman Books, Inc. 1980), 68. This book was instrumental in my understanding of shame [from Anzaldúa's note].
4. Respectively, male and female cultural figurations.

Dime con quien andas y te diré quien eres.
(Tell me who your friends are and I'll tell you who
you are.)
—Mexican saying

Si le preguntas a mi mamá, "¿Qué eres?" te dirá, "Soy mexicana." My
brothers and sister say the same. I sometimes will answer *"soy mexicana"*
and at others will say *"soy Chicana" o "soy tejana."* But I identified as *"Raza"*
before I ever identified as *"mexicana"* or "Chicana."

As a culture, we call ourselves Spanish when referring to ourselves as a
linguistic group and when copping out. It is then that we forget our pre-
dominant Indian genes. We are 70 to 80 percent Indian.[5] We call ourselves
Hispanic[6] or Spanish-American or Latin American or Latin when linking
ourselves to other Spanish-speaking peoples of the Western hemisphere
and when copping out. We call ourselves Mexican-American[7] to signify we
are neither Mexican nor American, but more the noun "American" than the
adjective "Mexican" (and when copping out).

Chicanos and other people of color suffer economically for not accultur-
ating. This voluntary (yet forced) alienation makes for psychological conflict, a kind of dual identity—we don't identify with the Anglo-American
cultural values and we don't totally identify with the Mexican cultural values. We are a synergy of two cultures with various degrees of Mexicanness
or Angloness. I have so internalized the borderland conflict that sometimes
I feel like one cancels out the other and we are zero, nothing, no one. *A
veces no soy nada ni nadie. Pero hasta cuando no lo soy, lo soy.*

When not copping out, when we know we are more than nothing, we call
ourselves Mexican, referring to race and ancestry; *mestizo* when affirming
both our Indian and Spanish (but we hardly ever own our Black ancestry);
Chicano when referring to a politically aware people born and/or raised in
the U.S.; *Raza* when referring to Chicanos; *tejanos* when we are Chicanos
from Texas.

Chicanos did not know we were a people until 1965 when Cesar Chavez[8]
and the farmworkers united and *I Am Joaquín* was published and *la Raza
Unida* party[9] was formed in Texas. With that recognition, we became a distinct people. Something momentous happened to the Chicano soul—we
became aware of our reality and acquired a name and a language (Chicano
Spanish) that reflected that reality. Now that we had a name, some of the
fragmented pieces began to fall together—who we were, what we were, how
we had evolved. We began to get glimpses of what we might eventually
become.

Yet the struggle of identities continues, the struggle of borders is our reality still. One day the inner struggle will cease and a true integration take
place. In the meantime, *tenemos que hacerla lucha. ¿Quién está protegiendo
los ranchos de mi gente? ¿Quién está tratando de cerrar la fisura entre la india*

5. John R. Chávez [(b. 1949), American scholar and educator], *The Lost Land: The Chicano Images of the Southwest* (Albuquerque, NM: University of New Mexico Press, 1984), 88–90 [from Anzaldúa's note].
6. "Hispanic" is derived from Hispanis (*España*, a name given to the Iberian Peninsula in ancient times when it was a part of the Roman Empire)

and is a term designated by the U.S. government to make it easier to handle us on paper [Anzaldúa's note].
7. The Treaty of Guadalupe Hidalgo created the Mexican-American in 1848 [Anzaldúa's note].
8. Chicano union organizer (1927–1993).
9. Known in America as the United Farm Workers; founded in 1962.

y el bianco en nuestra sangre? El Chicano, sí, el Chicano que anda como un ladrón en su propia casa.[1]

Los Chicanos, how patient we seem, how very patient. There is the quiet of the Indian about us. We know how to survive. When other races have given up their tongue, we've kept ours. We know what it is to live under the hammer blow of the dominant *norteamericano* culture. But more than we count the blows, we count the days the weeks the years the centuries the eons until the white laws and commerce and customs will rot in the deserts they've created, lie bleached. *Humildes* yet proud, *quietos* yet wild, *nosotros los mexicanos* Chicanos will walk by the crumbling ashes as we go about our business. Stubborn, persevering, impenetrable as stone, yet possessing a malleability that renders us unbreakable, we, the *mestizas* and *mestizos*, will remain.

1987

El sonavabitche

(for Aishe Berger)

Car flowing down a lava of highway
just happened to glance out the window
in time to see brown faces bent backs
like prehistoric boulders in a field
so common a sight no one   5
notices
blood rushes to my face
twelve years I'd sat on the memory
the anger scorching me
my throat so tight I can   10
barely get the words out.

I got to the farm
in time to hear the shots
ricochet off barn,
spit into the sand,   15
in time to see tall men in uniforms
thumping fists on doors
metallic voices yelling Halt!
their hawk eyes constantly shifting.

When I hear the words, *"Corran muchachos"*[1]   20
I run back to the car, ducking,
see the glistening faces, arms outflung,
of the *mexicanos* running headlong
through the fields
kicking up clouds of dirt   25

1. Anglos, in order to alleviate their guilt for dispossessing the Chicano, stressed the Spanish part of us and perpetrated the myth of the Spanish Southwest. We have accepted the fiction that we are Hispanic, that is Spanish, in order to accommodate ourselves to the dominant culture and its abhorrence of Indians. Chávez, 88–91 [Anzaldúa's note].

1. Run boys [Anzaldúa's note].

see them reach the tree line
foliage opening, swishing closed behind them.
I hear the tussling of bodies, grunts, panting
squeak of leather squawk of walkie-talkies
sun reflecting off gunbarrels   30
    the world a blinding light
    a great buzzing in my ears
    my knees like aspens in the wind.
    I see that wide cavernous look of the hunted
    the look of hares   35
    thick limp blue-black hair
    The bare heads humbly bent
    of those who do not speak
    the ember in their eyes extinguished.

I lean on the shanty wall of that migrant camp   40
north of Muncie, Indiana.
Wets, a voice says.
I turn to see a Chicano pushing
the head of his *muchachita*[2]
back into the *naguas*[3] of the mother   45
a tin plate face down on the floor
tortillas scattered around them.
His other hand signals me over.
He too is from *el valle de Tejas*[4]
I had been his kid's teacher.   50
I'd come to get the grower
to fill up the sewage ditch near the huts
saying it wouldn't do for the children
to play in it.
    Smoke from a cooking fire and   55
    shirtless *niños* gather around us.

    Mojados[5] he says again,
leaning on his chipped Chevy station wagon
Been here two weeks
about a dozen of them.   60
The *sonavabitche* works them
from sunup to dark—15 hours sometimes.
Como mulcts los trabaja[6]
no saben como hacer la perra.[7]
Last Sunday they asked for a day off   65
wanted to pray and rest,
write letters to their *familias.*
¿Y sabes lo que hizo el sonavabitche?[8]
He turns away and spits.

2. Little girl [Anzaldúa's note].
3. Skirt [Anzaldúa's note].
4. Rio Grande Valley in Texas [Anzaldúa's note].
5. Wetbacks, undocumented workers, illegal immigrants from Mexico and parts south [Anzaldúa's note].

6. He works them like mules [Anzaldúa's note].
7. They don't know how to make the work easier for themselves [Anzaldúa's note].
8. And you know what the son of a bitch did? [Anzaldúa's note].

Says he has to hold back half their wages   70
that they'd eaten the other half:
sack of beans, sack of rice, sack of flour.
Frijoleros sí lo son[9] but no way
could they have eaten that many *frijoles.*
I nod.   75

Como le dije, son doce[1]—started out 13
five days packed in the back of a pickup
boarded up tight
fast cross-country run no stops
except to change drivers, to gas up   80
no food they pissed into their shoes—
those that had *guaraches*[2]
slept slumped against each other
sabe Dios[3] where they shit.
One smothered to death on the way here   85

Miss, you should've seen them when they
stumbled out.
First thing the *sonavabitche* did was clamp
a handkerchief over his nose
then ordered them stripped   90
hosed them down himself
in front of everybody.
They hobbled about
learning to walk all over again.
Flacos con caras de viejos[4]   95
aunque la mita'eran jóvenes.[5]

Como le estaba diciendo[6]
today was payday.
You saw them, *la migra*[7] came busting in
waving their *pinche pistolas.*[8]   100
Said someone made a call,
what you call it? Anonymous.
Guess who? That *sonavabitche*, who else?
Done this three times since we've been coming here
Sepa Dios how many times in between.   105
Wets, free labor, *esclavos.*[9]
Pobres jijos de la Chingada.[1]
This the last time we work for him
no matter how *fregados*[2] we are
he said, shaking his head,   110

9. Bean eaters they are [Anzaldúa's note].
1. Like I told you, they're 12 [Anzaldúa's note].
2. Sandals [Anzaldúa's note].
3. God knows [Anzaldúa's note].
4. Skinny with old faces [Anzaldúa's note].
5. Though half were youths [Anzaldúa's note].
6. As I was telling you [Anzaldúa's note].
7. Slang for immigration officials [Anzaldúa's note].
8. Guns [Anzaldúa's note].

9. Slaves [Anzaldúa's note].
1. "Poor sons of the fucked one" [Anzaldúa's note]. *La Chingada* is the preferred Chicana term for *La Malinche* or *Malintzin*, the deposed Aztec princess who served Hernan Cortés as translator and became his lover during the Spanish Conquest of Mexico (1519–22).
2. Poor, beaten, downtrodden, in need [Anzaldúa's note].

spitting at the ground.
Vámonos, mujer, empaca el mugrero.[3]

He hands me a cup of coffee,
half of it sugar, half of it milk
my throat so dry I even down the dregs.   115
It has to be done.
Steeling myself
I take that walk to the big house.

Finally the big man lets me in.
How about a drink? I shake my head.   120
He looks me over, opens his eyes wide
and smiles, says how sorry he is immigration[4]
is getting so tough
a poor Mexican can't make a living
and they sure do need the work.   125
My throat so thick the words stick.
He studies me, then says,
Well, what can I do you for?
I want two weeks wages
including two Saturdays and Sundays,   130
minimum wage, 15 hours a day.
I'm more startled than he.
Whoa there, sinorita,
wets work for whatever you give them
the season hasn't been good.   135
Besides most are halfway to Mexico by now.
Two weeks wages, I say,
the words swelling in my throat.

Miss uh what did you say your name was?
I fumble for my card.   140
You can't do this,
I haven't broken no law,
his lidded eyes darken, I step back.
I'm leaving in two minutes and I want cash
the whole amount right here in my purse   145
when I walk out.
No hoarseness, no trembling.
It startled both of us.

You want me telling every single one
of your neighbors what you've been doing   150
all these years? The mayor, too?
Maybe make a call to Washington?
Slitted eyes studied the card again.
They had no cards, no papers.
I'd seen it over and over.   155
Work them, then turn them in before paying them.

---

3. Let's go, woman, pack our junk [Anzaldúa's note].

4. The U.S. Immigration and Naturalization Service.

Well, now, he was saying,
I know we can work something out,
a sweet young thang like yourself.
Cash, I said. I didn't know anyone in D.C.   160
now I didn't have to.
You want to keep it for yourself?
That it? His eyes were pin pricks.
Sweat money, Mister, blood money,
not my sweat, but same blood.   165
Yeah, but who's to say you won't abscond with it?
If I ever hear that you got illegals on your land
even a single one, I'm going to come here
in broad daylight and have you
hung by your balls.   170
He walks slowly to his desk.
Knees shaking, I count every bill
taking my time.

                                                        1987

SHARON OLDS
b. 1942

Like Whitman, Sharon Olds celebrates the body and writes about it without shame.
And like Whitman, her candor arouses a mixed response in contemporary readers.
Some find Olds's poems, with their close observations about sexuality, family life, and
family pathology, disturbingly graphic, while many others find them moving and
brave. Nonetheless, her second book, *The Dead and the Living* (1984), won the
National Book Award and has gone on to become one of the best-selling volumes in
contemporary poetry. The fact that Olds is a woman who writes about desire and
sexual pleasure, or who describes her father's genitals ("My Father Speaks to Me
from the Dead"), may intensify reader response. We are far more accustomed to male
writers exploring the sexual and bodily terrain. In her poems Olds lays out the domestic territory of erotic life, which extends to motherhood ("First Weeks"), daughter-
hood, and the body's life of sensation. She is unabashed about the ways in which
pleasure can be entangled with pain, especially in her numerous poems about parents and parental cruelty. In "I Go Back to May 1937" the speaker warns younger
versions of her parents, about to get married, "you are going to do things / you cannot
imagine you would ever do, / you are going to do bad things to children."

Olds's examination of intimate subjects has a distinctive quality of fascination and
even tenderness. As she writes in "Little Things": "I am doing something I learned
early to do, I am / paying attention to the small beauties, / whatever I have—as if it
were our duty / to find things to love, to bind ourselves to this world." These lines
articulate a central strategy in Olds's work: paying attention to what otherwise might
be overlooked, finding beauty in surprising places. They also provide an example of
how carefully her poems are shaped. Working from the base of an iambic pentameter

line, Olds fashions a freer, more conversational style and binds the lines together with a series of subtle rhymes, or half rhymes, several of them internal to the line ("do/beauties/duty"; "find/bind"). Olds has a particular gift for metaphor that transfigures the ordinary without forsaking its ordinariness. Metaphor renders the "small beauties" she discovers even in embarrassing or painful experience: applying spermicide to a slippery diaphragm ("I'd decorate it / like a cake" in "Adolescence") or imagining the parents as paper dolls from which she "strikes sparks" ("I go Back to May 1937"), or seeing the navel as "thistle/seed fossil" ("My Father Speaks to Me from the Dead"). Because so many of Olds's poems focus on intimate experience, it is perhaps too easy to assume that the work is simply autobiographical or confessional (a description Olds herself rejects; she calls the work "apparently very personal"). The candor in these poems is an imaginative creation; it is not make-believe but, in the critic Elaine Scarry's phrase, "made-real."

Sharon Olds grew up in Berkeley, California, and attended Stanford University, then earned her Ph.D. at Columbia. She published her first book of poems, *Satan Says* (1980), when she was 37 years old. Since then she has published nine additional volumes besides *The Dead and The Living*, among them *The Gold Cell* (1987), *The Father* (1992), *Blood, Tin, Straw* (1999), and *Strike Sparks: Selected Poems* 1980–2002 (2002). In 1984 she started a poetry workshop at Goldwater Hospital for the severely disabled on Roosevelt Island, and since 1992 has taught in the Graduate Creative Writing Program at NYU.

Sex Without Love

How do they do it, the ones who make love
without love? Formal as dancers,
gliding over each other like ice-skaters
over the ice, fingers hooked
inside each other's bodies, faces   5
red as steak, wine, wet as the
children at birth whose mothers are going to
give them away. How do they come to the
come to the   come to the   God   come to the
still waters, and not love   10
the one who came there with them, heat
rising slowly as steam off their joined
skin? I guess they are the true religious,
the purists, the pros, the ones who will not
accept a false Messiah, love the   15
priest instead of the God. They do not
mistake the partner for their own pleasure,
they are like great runners: they know they are alone
with the road surface, the cold, the wind,
the fit of their shoes, their overall cardio-   20
vascular health—just factors, like the other
in the bed, and not their truth, which is
the single body alone in the universe
against its own best time.

1984

I Go Back to May 1937

I see them standing at the formal gates of their colleges,
I see my father strolling out
under the ochre sandstone arch, the
red tiles glinting like bent
plates of blood behind his head, I   5
see my mother with a few light books at her hip
standing at the pillar made of tiny bricks,
the wrought-iron gate still open behind her, its
sword-tips aglow in the May air,
they are about to graduate, they are about to get married,   10
they are kids, they are dumb, all they know is they are
innocent, they would never hurt anybody.
I want to go up to them and say Stop,
don't do it—she's the wrong woman,
he's the wrong man, you are going to do things   15
you cannot imagine you would ever do,
you are going to do bad things to children,
you are going to suffer in ways you have not heard of,
you are going to want to die. I want to go
up to them there in the late May sunlight and say it,   20
her hungry pretty face turning to me,
her pitiful beautiful untouched body,
his arrogant handsome face turning to me,
his pitiful beautiful untouched body,
but I don't do it I want to live. I   25
take them up like the male and female
paper dolls and bang them together
at the hips, like chips of flint, as if to
strike sparks from them, I say
Do what you are going to do, and I will tell about it.   30

1987

Little Things

After she's gone to camp, in the early
evening I clear our girl's breakfast dishes
from the rosewood table, and find a dinky
crystallized pool of maple syrup, the
grains standing there, round, in the night, I   5
rub it with my fingertip
as if I could read it, this raised dot of
amber sugar, and this time,
when I think of my father, I wonder why
I think of my father, of the Vulcan[1] blood-red   10
glass in his hand, or his black hair gleaming like a

1. The ancient Roman mythological god of fire and metal working.

broken-open coal. I think I learned
to love the little things about him
because of all the big things
I could not love, no one could, it would be wrong to.   15
So when I fix on this image of resin,
or sweep together with the heel of my hand a
pile of my son's sunburn peels like
insect wings, where I peeled his back the night before camp,
I am doing something I learned early to do, I am   20
paying attention to small beauties,
whatever I have—as if it were our duty
to find things to love, to bind ourselves to this world.

                                                  1987

My Father Speaks to Me from the Dead

I seem to have woken up in a pot-shed,
on clay, on shards, the glitter paths
of slugs kiss-crossing my body. I don't know
where to start, with this grime on me.
I take the spider glue-net, plug   5
of the dead, out of my mouth, let's see
if where I have been I can do this.
I love your feet. I love your knees,
I love your our my legs, they are so
long because they are yours and mine   10
both. I love your—what can I call it,
between your legs, we never named it, the
glint and purity of its curls. I love
your rear end, I changed you once,
washed the detritus off your tiny   15
bottom, with my finger rubbed
the oil on you; when I touched your little
anus I crossed wires with God for a moment.
I never hated your shit—that was
your mother. I love your navel, thistle   20
seed fossil, even though
it's her print on you. Of course I love
your breasts—did you see me looking up
from within your daughter's face, as she nursed?
I love your bony shoulders and you know I   25
love your hair, thick and live
as earth. And I never hated your face,
I hated its eruptions. You know what I love?
I love your brain, its halves and silvery
folds, like a woman's labia.   30
I love in you
even what comes
from deep in your mother—your heart, that hard worker,

and your womb, it is a heaven to me,
I lie on its gentle hills and gaze up   35
at its rosy vault.
I have been in a body without breath,
I have been in the morgue, in fire, in the slagged
chimney, in the air over the earth,
and buried in the earth, and pulled down   40
into the ocean—where I have been
I understand this life, I am matter,
your father, I made you, when I say now that I love you
I mean look down at your hand, move it,
that action is matter's love, for human   45
love go elsewhere.

                                                                        1992

Adolescence

When I think of my adolescence, I think
of the bathroom of that seedy hotel
in San Francisco, where my boyfriend would take me.
I had never seen a bathroom like that—
no curtains, no towels, no mirror, just   5
a sink green with grime and a toilet
yellow and rust-colored—like something in a science experiment,
growing the plague in bowls.
Sex was still a crime, then,
I'd sign out of my college dorm   10
to a false destination, sign into
the flophouse under a false name,
go down the hall to the one bathroom
and lock myself in. And I could not learn to get that
diaphragm in, I'd decorate it   15
like a cake, with glistening spermicide,
and lean over, and it would leap from my fingers
and sail, into a corner, to land
in a concave depression like a rat's nest,
I'd bend and pluck it out and wash it   20
and wash it down to that fragile dome,
I'd frost it again till it was shimmering
and bend it into its tensile arc and it would
fly through the air, rim humming
like Saturn's ring,[1] I would bow down and crawl to retrieve it.   25
When I think of being eighteen,
that's what I see, that brimmed disc
floating through the air and descending, I see myself
kneeling and reaching, reaching for my own life.

                                                                        1996

1. Also the name of a contraceptive vaginal ring.

The Talkers

All week, we talked. We talked
in the morning on the porch, when I combed my hair
and flung the comb-hair out into the air,
it floated down the slope, toward the valley.
We talked while walking to the car, talked   5
over its mild, belled roof,
while opening the doors, then ducked down
and there we were, bent toward the interior, talking.
Meeting, in the middle of the day,
the first thing when we saw each other   10
we opened our mouths. All day,
we sang to each other the level music
of spoken language. Even while we ate
we did not pause, I'd speak to him through
the broken body of the butter cookie,   15
gently spraying him with crumbs. We talked
and walked, we leaned against the opposite sides of the
car and talked in the parking lot
until everyone else had driven off, we clung to its
dark cold raft and started a new subject.   20
We did not talk about his wife, much,
or my husband, but to everything else
we turned the workings of our lips and tongues
—up to our necks in the hot tub, or
walking up the steep road,   25
stepping into the hot dust as if
down into the ions of a wing, and on the
sand, next to each other, as we turned
the turns that upon each other would be the
turnings of joy—even under   30
water there trailed from our mouths the delicate
chains of our sentences. But mostly at night, and
far into the night, we talked until we
dropped, as if, stopping for an instant, we might
move right toward each other. Today,   35
he said he felt he could talk to me forever,
it must be the way the angels live,
sitting across from each other, deep
in the bliss of their shared spirit. My God,
they are not going to touch each other.   40

1999

First Weeks

Those first weeks, I don't know if I knew
how to love our daughter. Her face looked crushed,
crumpled with worry—and not even
despair, but just depression, a look of
endurance. The skin of her face was finely   5
wrinkled, there were wisps of hair on her ears,
she looked a little like a squirrel, suspicious,
tranced. And smallish, 6.13,
wizened—she looked as if she were wincing
away from me without moving. The first   10
moment I had seen her, my glasses off,
in the delivery room, a blur of blood,
and blue skin, and limbs, I had known her,
upside down, and they righted her, and there
came that faint, almost sexual, wail, and her   15
whole body flushed rose.
When I saw her next, she was bound in cotton,
someone else had cleaned her, wiped
the inside of my body off her
and combed her hair in narrow scary   20
plough-lines. She was ten days early,
sleepy, the breast so engorged it stood out nearly
even with the nipple, her lips would so much as
approach it, it would hiss and spray.
In two days we took her home, she shrieked   25
and whimpered, like a dream of a burn victim,
and when she was quiet, she would lie there and peer, not quite
anxiously. I didn't blame her,
she'd been born to my mother's daughter. I would kneel
and gaze at her, and pity her.   30
All day I nursed her, all night I walked her,
and napped, and nursed, and walked her. And then,
one day, she looked at me, as if
she knew me. She lay along my forearm, fed, and
gazed at me as if remembering me,   35
as if she had known me, and liked me, and was getting
her memory back. When she smiled at me,
delicate rictus like a birth-pain coming,
I fell in love, I became human.

2002

The Unswept

Broken bay leaf. Olive pit.
Crab leg. Claw. Crayfish armor.
Whelk shell. Mussel shell. Dogwinkle.[1] Snail.
Wishbone tossed unwished on. Test
of sea urchin. Chicken foot.   5
Wrasse[2] skeleton. Hen head,
eye shut, beak open as if
singing in the dark. Laid down in tiny
tiles, by the rhyparographer,[3]
each scrap has a shadow—each shadow cast   10
by a different light. Permanently fresh
husks of the feast! When the guest has gone,
the morsels dropped on the floor are left
as food for the dead—O my characters,
my imagined, here are some fancies of crumbs   15
from under love's table.

2002

1. Mollusk also known as dog whelk. (Whelk is a common name used for some sea snails.)
2. Bony, thick-lipped marine fish.

3. A person who paints or writes about distasteful or sordid subject matter.

SAM SHEPARD
b. 1943

Assessing Sam Shepard's importance, the critic Richard Gilman finds the key in his fascination with rootlessness. In this quality are his works' greatest difficulties and their deepest appeal, a dramaturgy famous for what Gilman describes as "the frantic efforts of so many of his characters to make themselves felt, often by violence (or cartoon violence—blows without injuries, bullets without death: dream or make-believe, something filmed), of the great strand in his work of the ego run wild, of the craving for altered states of being and the power to transcend physical or moral limitations." Whether monologues or dialogues, his actors' lines are more than contributions to plot and action—they are "outcries of characters craving to be known."

Because of his success as an actor in a score of major motion pictures, including *The Right Stuff* (1983), *Steel Magnolias* (1989), and *Black Hawk Down* (2002), Shepard is one of America's most recognizable contemporary dramatists. His image is a strongly self-created one, as he transformed himself from Samuel Shepard Rogers III (called "Steve" at home, the son of career-military parents who later became ranchers in rural California) into Sam Shepard, underground rock musician and experimental Off-Broadway playwright. Doing this meant abandoning studies he had begun at an agricultural college and giving up work as a horseman and ranch hand. Arriving in New York City as a nineteen-year-old, he found work as a waiter at The Village Gate, Greenwich

Village's top jazz club at the time, where he met musicians, actors and actresses, and most helpfully Ralph Cook, founder and director of Theater Genesis (whose company included actress O-Lan Johnson, later to be Shepard's wife) His one-act plays were first presented by the Theater Genesis ensemble at St. Mark's-in-the-Bowery in 1964, beginning a prolific Off-Broadway career that would win him eleven Obie awards. By 1979 he had won a Pulitzer Prize as well (for his three-act play *Buried Child*). Also a short-story writer and essayist, Shepard was invited by the German filmmaker Wim Wenders to adapt some of this nontheatrical material for the motion picture *Paris, Texas*, which won the Palm d'Or award when it premiered at the Cannes Film Festival in 1984. By then his marriage with O-Lan Johnson had ended; a long-term relationship with the film actress Jessica Lange followed. *Far North* (1988) displays Shepard's skills as a cinematic director, and his playwriting career has continued with such works as *Eyes for Consuela* (1998), *The Late Henry Moss* (2002), and *The God of Hell* (2004).

True West (1980) finds Shephard expanding his dramaturgy from the one-act vignette to a more conventional running time, channeling his earlier penchant for symbolic abstraction into the suggestions (if not always the practicalities) of realism. As in many of his plays the American West, past and present, shares attention with family concerns, as an undercurrent of violence sets the deliberately uneasy tone. In a style that draws from the works of Samuel Beckett and Edward Albee, *True West* is starkly minimal, putting just four characters in a single set, here a familiar kitchen-dinette scene. The play's general aura is what Shepard scholars have called "frontier gothic," in which themes from the American West of pioneer days (independence, isolation, a climate of physical violence) appear in contemporary life, especially within familial and social relationships.

The text is from *Seven Plays* (1981).

True West

CHARACTERS

AUSTIN: *early thirties, light blue sports shirt, light tan cardigan sweater, clean blue jeans, white tennis shoes*

LEE: *his older brother, early forties, filthy white t-shirt, tattered brown overcoat covered with dust, dark blue baggy suit pants from the Salvation Army, pink suede belt, pointed black forties dress shoes scuffed up, holes in the soles, no socks, no hat, long pronounced sideburns, "Gene Vincent" hairdo,*[1] *two days' growth of beard, bad teeth*

SAUL KIMMER: *late forties, Hollywood producer, pink and white flower print sports shirt, white sports coat with matching polyester slacks, black and white loafers*

MOM: *early sixties, mother of the brothers, small woman, conservative white skirt and matching jacket, red shoulder bag, two pieces of matching red luggage*

True West was first performed at the Magic Theatre in San Francisco on July 10, 1980. The director was Robert Woodruff, and the cast was as follows:

AUSTIN	Peter Coyote
LEE	Jim Haynie
SAUL KIMMER	Tom Dahlgren
MOM	Carol McElheney

---

1. Style favored by some American rock 'n' roll musicians of the late 1950s.

SCENE: *All nine scenes take place on the same set; a kitchen and adjoining alcove of an older home in a Southern California suburb, about 40 miles east of Los Angeles. The kitchen takes up most of the playing area to stage left. The kitchen consists of a sink, upstage center, surrounded by counter space, a wall telephone, cupboards, and a small window just above it bordered by neat yellow curtains. Stage left of sink is a stove. Stage right, a refrigerator. The alcove adjoins the kitchen to stage right. There is no wall division or door to the alcove. It is open and easily accessible from the kitchen and defined only by the objects in it: a small round glass breakfast table mounted on white iron legs, two matching white iron chairs set across from each other. The two exterior walls of the alcove which prescribe a corner in the upstage right are composed of many small windows, beginning from a solid wall about three feet high and extending to the ceiling. The windows look out to bushes and citrus trees. The alcove is filled with all sorts of house plants in various pots, mostly Boston ferns hanging in planters at different levels. The floor of the alcove, is composed of green synthetic grass.*

All entrances and exits are made stage left from the kitchen. There is no door. The actors simply go off and come onto the playing area.

NOTE ON SET AND COSTUME: *The set should be constructed realistically with no attempt to distort its dimensions, shapes, objects, or colors. No objects should be introduced which might draw special attention to themselves other than the props demanded by the script. If a stylistic "concept" is grafted onto the set design it will only serve to confuse the evolution of the characters' situation, which is the most important focus of the play.*

Likewise, the costumes should be exactly representative of who the characters are and not added onto for the sake of making a point to the audience.

NOTE ON SOUND: *The Coyote of Southern California has a distinct yapping, dog-like bark, similar to a Hyena. This yapping grows more intense and maniacal as the pack grows in numbers, which is usually the case when they lure and kill pets from suburban yards. The sense of growing frenzy in the pack should be felt in the background, particularly in Scenes 7 and 8. In any case, these Coyotes never make the long, mournful, solitary howl of the Hollywood stereotype.*

The sound of Crickets can speak for itself.

These sounds should also be treated realistically even though they sometimes grow in volume and numbers.

Act One

SCENE 1

Night. Sound of crickets in dark. Candlelight appears in alcove, illuminating AUSTIN, *seated at glass table hunched over a writing notebook, pen in hand, cigarette burning in ashtray, cup of coffee, typewriter on table, stacks of paper, candle burning on table.*

Soft moonlight fills kitchen illuminating LEE, *beer in hand, six-pack on counter behind him. He's leaning against the sink, mildly drunk; takes a slug of beer.*

LEE So, Mom took off for Alaska, huh?
AUSTIN Yeah.
LEE Sorta' left you in charge.
AUSTIN Well, she knew I was coming down here so she offered me the place.

LEE You keepin' the plants watered?

AUSTIN Yeah.

LEE Keepin' the sink clean? She don't like even a single tea leaf in the sink ya' know.

AUSTIN [*trying to concentrate on writing*] Yeah, I know.
    [*Pause.*]

LEE She gonna' be up there a long time?

AUSTIN I don't know.

LEE Kinda' nice for you, huh? Whole place to yourself.

AUSTIN Yeah, it's great.

LEE Ya' got crickets anyway. Tons a' crickets out there. [*looks around kitchen*] Ya' got groceries? Coffee?

AUSTIN [*looking up from writing*] What?

LEE You got coffee?

AUSTIN Yeah.

LEE At's good, [*short pause*] Real coffee? From the bean?

AUSTIN Yeah. You want some?

LEE Naw. I brought some uh—[*motions to beer*]

AUSTIN Help yourself to whatever's—[*motions to refrigerator*]

LEE I will. Don't worry about me. I'm not the one to worry about. I mean I can uh—[*pause*] You always work by candlelight?

AUSTIN No—uh—Not always.

LEE Just sometimes?

AUSTIN [*puts pen down, rubs his eyes*] Yeah. Sometimes it's soothing.

LEE Isn't that what the old guys did?

AUSTIN What old guys?

LEE The Forefathers.[2] You know.

AUSTIN Forefathers?

LEE Isn't that what they did? Candlelight burning into the night? Cabins in the wilderness.

AUSTIN [*rubs hand through his hair*] I suppose.

LEE I'm not botherin' you am I? I mean I don't wanna break into yer uh—concentration or nothin'.

AUSTIN No, it's all right.

LEE That's good. I mean I realize that yer line a' work demands a lota' concentration.

AUSTIN It's okay.

LEE You probably think that I'm not fully able to comprehend somethin' like that, huh?

AUSTIN Like what?

LEE That stuff yer doin'. That art. You know. Whatever you call it.

AUSTIN It's just a little research.

LEE You may not know it but I did a little art myself once.

AUSTIN You did?

LEE Yeah! I did some a' that. I fooled around with it. No future in it.

AUSTIN What'd you do?

LEE Never mind what I did! Just never mind about that. [*pause*] It was ahead of its time.

---

2. Common phrase for the founders of the United States.

[*Pause.*]

AUSTIN   So, you went out to see the old man, huh?

LEE   Yeah, I seen him.

AUSTIN   How's he doing?

LEE   Same. He's doin' just about the same.

AUSTIN   I was down there too, you know.

LEE   What d'ya' want, an award? You want some kinda' medal? You were down there. He told me all about you.

AUSTIN   What'd he say?

LEE   He told me. Don't worry.

[*Pause.*]

AUSTIN   Well—

LEE   You don't have to say nothin'.

AUSTIN   I wasn't.

LEE   Yeah, you were gonna' make somethin' up. Somethin' brilliant.

[*Pause.*]

AUSTIN   You going to be down here very long, Lee?

LEE   Might be. Depends on a few things.

AUSTIN   You got some friends down here?

LEE   [*laughs*]   I know a few people. Yeah.

AUSTIN   Well, you can stay here as long as I'm here.

LEE   I don't need your permission do I?

AUSTIN   No.

LEE   I mean she's my mother too, right?

AUSTIN   Right.

LEE   She might've just as easily asked me to take care of her place as you.

AUSTIN   That's right.

LEE   I mean I know how to water plants.

[*Long pause.*]

AUSTIN   So you don't know how long you'll be staying then?

LEE   Depends mostly on houses, ya' know.

AUSTIN   Houses?

LEE   Yeah. Houses. Electric devices. Stuff like that. I gotta' make a little tour first.

[*Short pause.*]

AUSTIN   Lee, why don't you just try another neighborhood, all right?

LEE   [*laughs.*]   What'sa' matter with this neighborhood? This is a great neighborhood. Lush. Good class a' people. Not many dogs.

AUSTIN   Well, our uh—Our mother just happens to live here. That's all.

LEE   Nobody's gonna' know. All they know is somethin's missing. That's all. She'll never even hear about it. Nobody's gonna' know.

AUSTIN   You're going to get picked up if you start walking around here at night.

LEE   Me? I'm gonna' git picked up? What about you? You stick out like a sore thumb. Look at you. You think yer regular lookin'?

AUSTIN   I've got too much to deal with here to be worrying about—

LEE   Yer not gonna' have to worry about me! I've been doin' all right without you. I haven't been anywhere near you for five years! Now isn't that true?

AUSTIN   Yeah.

LEE   So you don't have to worry about me. I'm a free agent.

AUSTIN   All right.

LEE   Now all I wanna' do is borrow yer car.

AUSTIN   No!

LEE   Just fer a day. One day.

AUSTIN   No!

LEE   I won't take it outside a twenty mile radius. I promise ya'. You can check the speedometer.

AUSTIN   You're not borrowing my car! That's all there is to it.
        [*Pause.*]

LEE   Then I'll just take the damn thing.

AUSTIN   Lee, look—I don't want any trouble, all right?

LEE   That's a dumb line. That is a dumb fuckin' line. You git paid fer dreamin' up a line like that?

AUSTIN   Look, I can give you some money if you need money.
        [LEE *suddenly lunges at* AUSTIN, *grabs him violently by the shirt and shakes him with tremendous power.*]

LEE   Don't you say that to me! Don't you ever say that to me! [*just as suddenly he turns him loose, pushes him away and backs off*] You may be able to git away with that with the Old Man. Git him tanked up for a week! Buy him off with yer Hollywood blood money, but not me! I can git my own money my own way. Big money!

AUSTIN   I was just making an offer.

LEE   Yeah, well keep it to yourself!
        [*Long pause.*]
   Those are the most monotonous fuckin' crickets I ever heard in my life.

AUSTIN   I kinda' like the sound.

LEE   Yeah. Supposed to be able to tell the temperature by the number a' pulses. You believe that?

AUSTIN   The temperature?

LEE   Yeah. The air. How hot it is.

AUSTIN   How do you do that?

LEE   I don't know. Some woman told me that. She was a Botanist. So I believed her.

AUSTIN   Where'd you meet her?

LEE   What?

AUSTIN   The woman Botanist?

LEE   I met her on the desert. I been spendin' a lota' time on the desert.

AUSTIN   What were you doing out there?

LEE   [*pause, stares in space*]   I forgit. Had me a Pit Bull there for a while but I lost him.

AUSTIN   Pit Bull?

LEE   Fightin' dog. Damn I made some good money off that little dog. Real good money.
        [*Pause.*]

AUSTIN   You could come up north with me, you know.

LEE   What's up there?

AUSTIN   My family.

LEE   Oh, that's right, you got the wife and kiddies now don't ya'. The house, the car, the whole slam. That's right.

AUSTIN You could spend a couple days. See how you like it. I've got an extra room.

LEE Too cold up there.
> [*Pause.*]

AUSTIN You want to sleep for a while?

LEE [*pause, stares at* AUSTIN] I don't sleep.
> [*Lights to black.*]

SCENE 2

Morning. AUSTIN *is watering plants with a vaporizer,* LEE *sits at glass table in alcove drinking beer.*

LEE I never realized the old lady was so security-minded.

AUSTIN How do you mean?

LEE Made a little tour this morning. She's got locks on everything. Locks and double-locks and chain locks and—What's she got that's so valuable?

AUSTIN Antiques I guess. I don't know.

LEE Antiques? Brought everything with her from the old place, huh. Just the same crap we always had around. Plates and spoons.

AUSTIN I guess they have personal value to her.

LEE Personal value. Yeah. Just a lota' junk. Most of it's phony anyway. Idaho decals. Now who in the hell wants to eat offa' plate with the State of Idaho starin' ya' in the face. Every time ya' take a bite ya' get to see a little bit more.

AUSTIN Well it must mean something to her or she wouldn't save it.

LEE Yeah, well personally I don't wann' be invaded by Idaho when I'm eatin'. When I'm eatin' I'm home. Ya' know what I'm sayin'? I'm not driftin', I'm home. I don't need my thoughts swept off to Idaho. I don't need that!
> [*Pause.*]

AUSTIN Did you go out last night?

LEE Why?

AUSTIN I thought I heard you go out.

LEE Yeah, I went out. What about it?

AUSTIN Just wondered.

LEE Damn coyotes kept me awake.

AUSTIN Oh yeah, I heard them. They must've killed somebody's dog or something.

LEE Yappin' their fool heads off. They don't yap like that on the desert. They howl. These are city coyotes here.

AUSTIN Well, you don't sleep anyway do you?
> [*Pause,* LEE *stares at him.*]

LEE You're pretty smart aren't ya?

AUSTIN How do you mean?

LEE I mean you never had any more on the ball than I did. But here you are gettin' invited into prominent people's houses. Sittin' around talkin' like you know somethin'.

AUSTIN They're not so prominent.

LEE They're a helluva' lot more prominent than the houses I get invited into.

AUSTIN   Well you invite yourself.

LEE   That's right. I do. In fact I probably got a wider range a' choices than you do, come to think of it.

AUSTIN   I wouldn't doubt it.

LEE   In fact I been inside some pretty classy places in my time. And I never even went to an Ivy League school either.

AUSTIN   You want some breakfast or something?

LEE   Breakfast?

AUSTIN   Yeah. Don't you eat breakfast?

LEE   Look, don't worry about me pal. I can take care a' myself. You just go ahead as though I wasn't even here, all right?

[AUSTIN *goes into kitchen, makes coffee.*]

AUSTIN   Where'd you walk to last night?

[*Pause.*]

LEE   I went up in the foothills there. Up in the San Gabriels.[3] Heat was drivin' me crazy.

AUSTIN   Well, wasn't it hot out on the desert?

LEE   Different kinda' heat. Out there it's clean. Cools off at night. There's a nice little breeze.

AUSTIN   Where were you, the Mojave?

LEE   Yeah. The Mojave. That's right.

AUSTIN   I haven't been out there in years.

LEE   Out past Needles there.

AUSTIN   Oh yeah.

LEE   Up here it's different. This country's real different.

AUSTIN   Well, it's been built up.

LEE   Built up? Wiped out is more like it. I don't even hardly recognize it.

AUSTIN   Yeah. Foothills are the same though, aren't they?

LEE   Pretty much. It's funny goin' up in there. The smells and everything. Used to catch snakes up there, remember?

AUSTIN   You caught snakes.

LEE   Yeah. And you'd pretend you were Geronimo or some damn thing. You used to go right out to lunch.

AUSTIN   I enjoyed my imagination.

LEE   That what you call it? Looks like yer still enjoyin' it.

AUSTIN   So you just wandered around up there, huh?

LEE   Yeah. With a purpose.

AUSTIN   See any houses?

[*Pause.*]

LEE   Couple. Couple a' real nice ones. One of 'em didn't even have a dog. Walked right up and stuck my head in the window. Not a peep. Just a sweet kinda' surburban silence.

AUSTIN   What kind of a place was it?

LEE   Like a paradise. Kinda' place that sorta' kills ya' inside. Warm yellow lights. Mexican tile all around. Copper pots hangin' over the stove. Ya' know like they got in the magazines. Blonde people movin' in and outa'

---

3. Mountains between Los Angeles and the Mojave Desert in Southern California; the Mojave Desert stretches from this mountain barrier east of Los Angeles to Arizona and Nevada; Needles, mentioned below, is a city in California on the Colorado River in the Mojave Valley, which straddles the California-Arizona border.

the rooms, talkin' to each other. [*pause*] Kinda' place you wish you sorta' grew up in, ya' know.

AUSTIN That's the kind of place you wish you'd grown up in?

LEE Yeah, why not?

AUSTIN I thought you hated that kind of stuff.

LEE Yeah, well you never knew too much about me did ya'?
[*Pause.*]

AUSTIN Why'd you go out to the desert in the first place?

LEE I was on my way to see the old man.

AUSTIN You mean you just passed through there?

LEE Yeah. That's right. Three months of passin' through.

AUSTIN Three months?

LEE Somethin' like that. Maybe more. Why?

AUSTIN You lived on the Mojave for three months?

LEE Yeah. What'sa' matter with that?

AUSTIN By yourself?

LEE Mostly. Had a couple a' visitors. Had that dog for a while.

AUSTIN Didn't you miss people?

LEE [*laughs*] People?

AUSTIN Yeah. I mean I go crazy if I have to spend three nights in a motel by myself.

LEE Yer not in a motel now.

AUSTIN No, I know. But sometimes I have to stay in motels.

LEE Well, they got people in motels don't they?

AUSTIN Strangers.

LEE Yer friendly aren't ya'? Aren't you the friendly type?
[*Pause.*]

AUSTIN I'm going to have somebody coming by here later, Lee.

LEE Ah! Lady friend?

AUSTIN No, a producer.

LEE Aha! What's he produce?

AUSTIN Film. Movies. You know.

LEE Oh, movies. Motion Pictures! A Big Wig huh?

AUSTIN Yeah.

LEE What's he comin' by here for?

AUSTIN We have to talk about a project.

LEE Whadya' mean, "a project"? What's "a project"?

AUSTIN A script.

LEE Oh. That's what yer doin' with all these papers?

AUSTIN Yeah.

LEE Well, what's the project about?

AUSTIN We're uh—it's a period piece.

LEE What's "a period piece"?

AUSTIN Look, it doesn't matter. The main thing is we need to discuss this alone. I mean—

LEE Oh, I get it. You want me outa' the picture.

AUSTIN Not exactly. I just need to be alone with him for a couple of hours. So we can talk.

LEE Yer afraid I'll embarrass ya' huh?

AUSTIN I'm not afraid you'll embarrass me!

LEE Well, I tell ya' what—Why don't you just gimme the keys to yer car and I'll be back here around six o'clock or so. That give ya' enough time?

AUSTIN I'm not loaning you my car, Lee.

LEE You want me to just git lost huh? Take a hike? Is that it? Pound the pavement for a few hours while you bullshit yer way into a million bucks.

AUSTIN Look, it's going to be hard enough for me to face this character on my own without—

LEE You don't know this guy?

AUSTIN No I don't know—He's a producer. I mean I've been meeting with him for months but you never get to know a producer.

LEE Yer tryin' to hustle him? Is that it?

AUSTIN I'm not trying to hustle him! I'm trying to work out a deal! It's not easy.

LEE What kinda' deal?

AUSTIN Convince him it's a worthwhile story.

LEE He's not convinced? How come he's comin' over here if he's not convinced? I'll convince him for ya'.

AUSTIN You don't understand the way things work down here.

LEE How do things work down here?
      [Pause.]

AUSTIN Look, if I loan you my car will you have it back here by six?

LEE On the button. With a full tank a' gas.

AUSTIN [digging in his pocket for keys] Forget about the gas.

LEE Hey, these days gas is gold, old buddy.
      [AUSTIN hands the keys to LEE.]
   You remember that car I used to loan you?

AUSTIN Yeah.

LEE Forty Ford. Flathead.[4]

AUSTIN Yeah.

LEE Sucker hauled ass didn't it?

AUSTIN Lee, it's not that I don't want to loan you my car—

LEE You are loanin' me yer car.
      [LEE gives AUSTIN a pat on the shoulder, pause.]

AUSTIN I know. I just wish—

LEE What? You wish what?

AUSTIN I don't know. I wish I wasn't—I wish I didn't have to be doing business down here. I'd like to just spend some time with you.

LEE I thought it was "Art" you were doin'.
      [LEE moves across kitchen toward exit, tosses keys in his hand.]

AUSTIN Try to get it back here by six, okay?

LEE No sweat. Hey, ya' know, if that uh—story of yours doesn't go over with the guy—tell him I got a couple a' "projects" he might be interested in. Real commercial. Full a' suspense. True-to-life stuff.
      [LEE exits, AUSTIN stares after LEE then turns, goes to papers at table, leafs through pages, lights fade to black.]

---

4. Type of internal combustion engine, here used in a Ford automobile of 1940, at this time popular as a hotrod.

SCENE 3

Afternoon. Alcove, SAUL KIMMER *and* AUSTIN *seated across from each other at table.*

SAUL Well, to tell you the truth Austin, I have never felt so confident about a project in quite a long time.

AUSTIN Well, that's good to hear, Saul.

SAUL I am absolutely convinced we can get this thing off the ground. I mean we'll have to make a sale to television and that means getting a major star. Somebody bankable. But I think we can do it. I really do.

AUSTIN Don't you think we need a first draft before we approach a star?

SAUL No, no, not at all. I don't think it's necessary. Maybe a brief synopsis. I don't want you to touch the typewriter until we have some seed money.

AUSTIN That's fine with me.

SAUL I mean it's a great story. Just the story alone. You've really managed to capture something this time.

AUSTIN I'm glad you like it, Saul.
  [LEE *enters abruptly into kitchen carrying a stolen television set, short pause.*]

LEE Aw shit, I'm sorry about that. I am really sorry Austin.

AUSTIN [*standing*] That's all right.

LEE [*moving toward them*] I mean I thought it was way past six already. You said to have it back here by six.

AUSTIN We were just finishing up. [*to Saul*]. This is my, uh—brother, Lee.

SAUL [*standing*] Oh, I'm very happy to meet you.
  [LEE *sets T.V. on sink counter, shakes hands with* SAUL.]

LEE I can't tell ya' how happy I am to meet you sir.

SAUL Saul Kimmer.

LEE Mr. Kipper.

SAUL Kimmer.

AUSTIN Lee's been living out on the desert and he just uh—

SAUL Oh, that's terrific! [*to* LEE] Palm Springs?[5]

LEE Yeah. Yeah, right. Right around in that area. Near uh—Bob Hope[6] Drive there.

SAUL Oh I love it out there. I just love it. The air is wonderful.

LEE Yeah. Sure is. Healthy.

SAUL And the golf. I don't know if you play golf, but the golf is just about the best.

LEE I play a lota' golf.

SAUL Is that right?

LEE Yeah. In fact I was hoping I'd run into somebody out here who played a little golf. I've been lookin' for a partner.

SAUL Well, I uh—

AUSTIN Lee's just down for a visit while our mother's in Alaska.

---

5. City in south-central California where streets are named for stars in the Hollywood entertainment industry.

6. British-born American film comedian (1903–2003).

SAUL Oh, your mother's in Alaska?

AUSTIN Yes. She went up there on a little vacation. This is her place.

SAUL I see. Well isn't that something. Alaska.

LEE What kinda' handicap do ya' have, Mr. Kimmer?

SAUL Oh I'm just a Sunday duffer really. You know.

LEE That's good 'cause I haven't swung a club in months.

SAUL Well we ought to get together sometime and have a little game. Austin, do you play?

[SAUL *mimes a Johnny Carson golf swing for* AUSTIN.]

AUSTIN No. I don't uh—I've watched it on TV.

LEE [*to* SAUL] How 'bout tomorrow morning? Bright and early. We could get out there and put in eighteen holes before breakfast.

SAUL Well, I've got uh—I have several appointments—

LEE No, I mean real early. Crack a'dawn. While the dew's still thick on the fairway.

SAUL Sounds really great.

LEE Austin could be our caddie.

SAUL Now that's an idea. [*laughs*]

AUSTIN I don't know the first thing about golf.

LEE There's nothin' to it. Isn't that right, Saul? He'd pick it up in fifteen minutes.

SAUL Sure. Doesn't take long. 'Course you have to play for years to find your true form. [*chuckles*]

LEE [*to* AUSTIN] We'll give ya' a quick run-down on the club faces. The irons, the woods. Show ya' a couple pointers on the basic swing. Might even let ya' hit the ball a couple times. Whadya' think, Saul?

SAUL Why not. I think it'd be great. I haven't had any exercise in weeks.

LEE 'At's the spirit! We'll have a little orange juice right afterwards.

[*Pause.*]

SAUL Orange juice?

LEE Yeah! Vitamin C! Nothin' like a shot a' orange juice after a round a' golf. Hot shower. Snappin' towels at each others' privates. Real sense a' fraternity.

SAUL [*smiles at* AUSTIN] Well, you make it sound very inviting, I must say. It really does sound great.

LEE Then it's a date.

SAUL Well, I'll call the country club and see if I can arrange something.

LEE Great! Boy, I sure am sorry that I busted in on ya' all in the middle of yer meeting.

SAUL Oh that's quite all right. We were just about finished anyway.

LEE I can wait out in the other room if you want.

SAUL No really—

LEE Just got Austin's color TV. back from the shop. I can watch a little amateur boxing now.

[LEE *and* AUSTIN *exchange looks.*]

SAUL Oh—Yes.

LEE You don't fool around in Television, do you Saul?

SAUL Uh—I have in the past. Produced some TV. Specials. Network stuff. But it's mainly features now.

LEE That's where the big money is, huh?

SAUL   Yes. That's right.

AUSTIN   Why don't I call you tomorrow, Saul and we'll get together. We can have lunch or something.

SAUL   That'd be terrific.

LEE   Right after the golf.
　　　[*Pause.*]

SAUL   What?

LEE   You can have lunch right after the golf.

SAUL   Oh, right.

LEE   Austin was tellin' me that yer interested in stories.

SAUL   Well, we develop certain projects that we feel have commercial potential.

LEE   What kinda' stuff do ya' go in for?

SAUL   Oh, the usual. You know. Good love interest. Lots of action. [*chuckles at* AUSTIN]

LEE   Westerns?

SAUL   Sometimes.

AUSTIN   I'll give you a ring, Saul.
　　　[AUSTIN *tries to move* SAUL *across the kitchen but* LEE *blocks their way.*]

LEE   I got a Western that'd knock yer lights out.

SAUL   Oh really?

LEE   Yeah. Contemporary Western. Based on a true story. 'Course I'm not a writer like my brother here. I'm not a man of the pen.

SAUL   Well—

LEE   I mean I can tell ya' a story off the tongue but I can't put it down on paper. That don't make any difference though does it?

SAUL   No, not really.

LEE   I mean plenty a' guys have stories don't they? True-life stories. Musta' been a lota' movies made from real life.

SAUL   Yes. I suppose so.

LEE   I haven't seen a good Western since "Lonely Are the Brave."[7] You remember that movie?

SAUL   No, I'm afraid I—

LEE   Kirk Douglas. Helluva' movie. You remember that movie, Austin?

AUSTIN   Yes.

LEE [*to* SAUL]   The man dies for the love of a horse.

SAUL   Is that right.

LEE   Yeah. Ya' hear the horse screamin' at the end of it. Rain's comin' down. Horse is screamin'. Then there's a shot. BLAM! Just a single shot like that. Then nothin' but the sound of rain. And Kirk Douglas is ridin' in the ambulance. Ridin' away from the scene of the accident. And when he hears that shot he knows that his horse has died. He knows. And you see his eyes. And his eyes die. Right inside his face. And then his eyes close. And you know that he's died too. You know that Kirk Douglas has died from the death of his horse.

SAUL [*eyes* AUSTIN *nervously*]   Well, it sounds like a great movie. I'm sorry I missed it.

---

7. Film (1962) directed by David Miller, starring the American film actor Kirk Douglas (b. 1916).

LEE   Yeah, you shouldn't a' missed that one.

SAUL   I'll have to try to catch it some time. Arrange a screening or something. Well, Austin, I'll have to hit the freeway before rush hour.

AUSTIN [*ushers him toward exit*]   It's good seeing you, Saul.
[AUSTIN *and* SAUL *shake hands.*]

LEE   So ya' think there's room for a real Western these days? A true-to-life Western?

SAUL   Well, I don't see why not. Why don't you uh—tell the story to Austin and have him write a little outline.

LEE   You'd take a look at it then?

SAUL   Yes. Sure. I'll give it a read-through. Always eager for new material.
[*smiles at* AUSTIN]

LEE   That's great! You'd really read it then huh?

SAUL   It would just be my opinion of course.

LEE   That's all I want. Just an opinion. I happen to think it has a lota' possibilities.

SAUL   Well, it was great meeting you and I'll—
[SAUL *and* LEE *shake.*]

LEE   I'll call you tomorrow about the golf.

SAUL   Oh. Yes, right.

LEE   Austin's got your number, right?

SAUL   Yes.

LEE   So long Saul. [*gives* SAUL *a pat on the back*]
[SAUL *exits,* AUSTIN *turns to* LEE, *looks at T.V. then back to* LEE.]

AUSTIN   Give me the keys.
[AUSTIN *extends his hand toward* LEE, LEE *doesn't move, just stares at* AUSTIN, *smiles, lights to black.*]

SCENE 4

Night. Coyotes in distance, fade, sound of typewriter in dark, crickets, candlelight in alcove, dim light in kitchen, lights reveal AUSTIN *at glass table typing,* LEE *sits across from him, foot on table, drinking beer and whiskey, the T.V. is still on sink counter,* AUSTIN *types for a while, then stops.*

LEE   All right, now read it back to me.

AUSTIN   I'm not reading it back to you, Lee. You can read it when we're finished. I can't spend all night on this.

LEE   You got better things to do?

AUSTIN   Let's just go ahead. Now what happens when he leaves Texas?

LEE   Is he ready to leave Texas yet? I didn't know we were that far along. He's not ready to leave Texas.

AUSTIN   He's right at the border.

LEE [*sitting up*]   No, see this is one a' the crucial parts. Right here. [*taps paper with beer can*] We can't rush through this. He's not right at the border. He's a good fifty miles from the border. A lot can happen in fifty miles.

AUSTIN   It's only an outline. We're not writing an entire script now.

LEE   Well ya' can't leave things out even if it is an outline. It's one a' the most important parts. Ya' can't go leavin' it out.

AUSTIN   Okay, okay. Let's just—get it done.

LEE   All right. Now. He's in the truck and he's got his horse trailer and his horse.

AUSTIN   We've already established that.

LEE   And he sees this other guy comin' up behind him in another truck. And that truck is pullin' a gooseneck.

AUSTIN   What's a gooseneck?

LEE   Cattle trailer. You know the kind with a gooseneck, goes right down in the bed a' the pick-up.

AUSTIN   Oh. All right. [*types*]

LEE   It's important.

AUSTIN   Okay. I got it.

LEE   All these details are important.
  [AUSTIN *types as they talk.*]

AUSTIN   I've got it.

LEE   And this other guy's got his horse all saddled up in the back a' the gooseneck.

AUSTIN   Right.

LEE   So both these guys have got their horses right along with 'em, see.

AUSTIN   I understand.

LEE   Then this first guy suddenly realizes two things.

AUSTIN   The guy in front?

LEE   Right. The guy in front realizes two things almost at the same time. Simultaneous.

AUSTIN   What were the two things?

LEE   Number one, he realizes that the guy behind him is the husband of the woman he's been—
  [LEE *makes gesture of screwing by pumping his arm.*]

AUSTIN   [*sees* LEE's *gesture*]   Oh. Yeah.

LEE   And number two, he realizes he's in the middle of Tornado Country.

AUSTIN   What's "Tornado Country"?

LEE   Panhandle.[8]

AUSTIN   Panhandle?

LEE   Sweetwater.[9] Around in that area. Nothin'. Nowhere. And number three—

AUSTIN   I thought there was only two.

LEE   There's three. There's a third unforeseen realization.

AUSTIN   And what's that?

LEE   That he's runnin' outa' gas.

AUSTIN   [*stops typing*]   Come on, Lee.
  [AUSTIN *gets up, moves to kitchen, gets a glass of water.*]

LEE   Whadya' mean, "come on"? That's what it is. Write it down! He's runnin' outa' gas.

AUSTIN   It's too—

LEE   What? It's too what? It's too real! That's what ya' mean isn't it? It's too much like real life!

---

8. Northern extension of Texas or western extension of Oklahoma.

9. City at the southern extreme of the Texas Panhandle.

AUSTIN It's not like real life! It's not enough like real life. Things don't happen like that.

LEE What! Men don't fuck other men's women?

AUSTIN Yes. But they don't end up chasing each other across the Panhandle. Through "Tornado Country."

LEE They do in this movie!

AUSTIN And they don't have horses conveniently along with them when they run out of gas! And they don't run out of gas either!

LEE These guys run outa' gas! This is my story and one a' these guys runs outa' gas!

AUSTIN It's just a dumb excuse to get them into a chase scene. It's contrived.

LEE It is a chase scene! It's already a chase scene. They been chasin' each other fer days.

AUSTIN So now they're supposed to abandon their trucks, climb on their horses and chase each other into the mountains?

LEE [*standing suddenly*] There aren't any mountains in the Panhandle! It's flat!

> [LEE *turns violently toward windows in alcove and throws beer can at them.*]

LEE Goddamn these crickets! [*yells at crickets*] Shut up out there! [*pause, turns back toward table*] This place is like a fuckin' rest home here. How're you supposed to think!

AUSTIN You wanna' take a break?

LEE No, I don't wanna' take a break! I wanna' get this done! This is my last chance to get this done.

AUSTIN [*moves back into alcove*] All right. Take it easy.

LEE I'm gonna' be leavin' this area. I don't have time to mess around here.

AUSTIN Where are you going?

LEE Never mind where I'm goin'! That's got nothin' to do with you. I just gotta' get this done. I'm not like you. Hangin' around bein' a parasite offa' other fools. I gotta' do this thing and get out.

> [*Pause.*]

AUSTIN A parasite? Me?

LEE Yeah, you!

AUSTIN After you break into people's houses and take their televisions?

LEE They don't need their televisions! I'm doin' them a service.

AUSTIN Give me back my keys, Lee.

LEE Not until you write this thing! You're gonna' write this outline thing for me or that car's gonna' wind up in Arizona with a different paint job.

AUSTIN You think you can force me to write this? I was doing you a favor.

LEE Git off yer high horse will ya'! Favor! Big favor. Handin' down favors from the mountain top.

AUSTIN Let's just write it, okay? Let's sit down and not get upset and see if we can just get through this.

> [AUSTIN *sits at typewriter.*]
> [*Long pause.*]

LEE Yer not gonna' even show it to him, are ya'?

AUSTIN   What?

LEE   This outline. You got no intention of showin' it to him. Yer just doin' this 'cause yer afraid a' me.

AUSTIN   You can show it to him yourself.

LEE   I will, boy! I'm gonna' read it to him on the golf course.

AUSTIN   And I'm not afraid of you either.

LEE   Then how come yer doin' it?

AUSTIN   [pause]   So I can get my keys back.
[Pause as LEE takes keys out of his pocket slowly and throws them on table, long pause, AUSTIN stares at keys.]

LEE   There. Now you got yer keys back.
[AUSTIN looks up at LEE but doesn't take keys.]

LEE   Go ahead. There's yer keys.
[AUSTIN slowly takes keys off table and puts them back in his own pocket.]
Now what're you gonna' do? Kick me out?

AUSTIN   I'm not going to kick you out, Lee.

LEE   You couldn't kick me out, boy.

AUSTIN   I know.

LEE   So you can't even consider that one. [pause] You could call the police. That'd be the obvious thing.

AUSTIN   You're my brother.

LEE   That don't mean a thing. You go down to the L.A. Police Department there and ask them what kinda' people kill each other the most. What do you think they'd say?

AUSTIN   Who said anything about killing?

LEE   Family people. Brothers. Brothers-in-law. Cousins. Real American-type people. They kill each other in the heat mostly. In the Smog-Alerts. In the Brush Fire Season. Right about this time a' year.

AUSTIN   This isn't the same.

LEE   Oh no? What makes it different?

AUSTIN   We're not insane. We're not driven to acts of violence like that. Not over a dumb movie script. Now sit down.
[Long pause, LEE considers which way to go with it.]

LEE   Maybe not. [he sits back down at table across from AUSTIN] Maybe you're right. Maybe we're too intelligent, huh? [pause] We got our heads on our shoulders. One of us has even got a Ivy League diploma. Now that means somethin' don't it? Doesn't that mean somethin'?

AUSTIN   Look, I'll write this thing for you, Lee. I don't mind writing it. I just don't want to get all worked up about it. It's not worth it. Now, come on. Let's just get through it, okay?

LEE   Nah. I think there's easier money. Lotsa' places I could pick up thousands. Maybe millions. I don't need this shit. I could go up to Sacramento Valley and steal me a diesel. Ten thousand a week dismantling one a' those suckers. Ten thousand a week!
[LEE opens another beer, puts his foot back up on table.]

AUSTIN   No, really, look, I'll write it out for you. I think it's a great idea.

LEE   Nah, you got yer own work to do. I don't wanna' interfere with yer life.

AUSTIN   I mean it'd be really fantastic if you could sell this. Turn it into a movie. I mean it.

[*Pause.*]

LEE Ya' think so huh?

AUSTIN Absolutely. You could really turn your life around, you know. Change things.

LEE I could get me a house maybe.

AUSTIN Sure you could get a house. You could get a whole ranch if you wanted to.

LEE [*laughs*] A ranch? I could get a ranch?

AUSTIN 'Course you could. You know what a screenplay sells for these days?

LEE No. What's it sell for?

AUSTIN A lot. A whole lot of money.

LEE Thousands?

AUSTIN Yeah. Thousands.

LEE Millions?

AUSTIN Well—

LEE We could get the old man outa' hock then.

AUSTIN Maybe.

LEE Maybe? Whadya' mean, maybe?

AUSTIN I mean it might take more than money.

LEE You were just tellin' me it'd change my whole life around. Why wouldn't it change his?

AUSTIN He's different.

LEE Oh, he's of a different ilk huh?

AUSTIN He's not gonna' change. Let's leave the old man out of it.

LEE That's right. He's not gonna' change but I will. I'll just turn myself right inside out. I could be just like you then, huh? Sittin' around dreamin' stuff up. Gettin' paid to dream. Ridin' back and forth on the freeway just dreamin' my fool head off.

AUSTIN It's not all that easy.

LEE It's not, huh?

AUSTIN No. There's a lot of work involved.

LEE What's the toughest part? Deciding whether to jog or play tennis?
[*Long pause.*]

AUSTIN Well, look. You can stay here—do whatever you want to. Borrow the car. Come in and out. Doesn't matter to me. It's not my house. I'll help you write this thing or—not. Just let me know what you want. You tell me.

LEE Oh. So now suddenly you're at my service. Is that it?

AUSTIN What do you want to do Lee?
[*Long pause,* LEE *stares at him then turns and dreams at windows.*]

LEE I tell ya' what I'd do if I still had that dog. Ya' wanna' know what I'd do?

AUSTIN What?

LEE Head out to Ventura. Cook up a little match. God that little dog could bear down. Lota' money in dog fightin'. Big money.
[*Pause.*]

AUSTIN Why don't we try to see this through, Lee. Just for the hell of it. Maybe you've really got something here. What do you think?
[*Pause,* LEE *considers.*]

LEE   Maybe so. No harm in tryin' I guess. You think it's such a hot idea. Besides, I always wondered what'd be like to be you.

AUSTIN   You did?

LEE   Yeah, sure. I used to picture you walkin' around some campus with yer arms fulla' books. Blondes chasin' after ya'.

AUSTIN   Blondes? That's funny.

LEE   What's funny about it?

AUSTIN   Because I always used to picture you somewhere.

LEE   Where'd you picture me?

AUSTIN   Oh, I don't know. Different places. Adventures. You were always on some adventure.

LEE   Yeah.

AUSTIN   And I used to say to myself, "Lee's got the right idea. He's out there in the world and here I am. What am I doing?"

LEE   Well you were settin' yourself up for somethin'.

AUSTIN   I guess.

LEE   We better get started on this thing then.

AUSTIN   Okay.

[AUSTIN *sits up at typewriter, puts new paper in.*]

LEE   Oh. Can I get the keys back before I forget?

[AUSTIN *hesitates.*]

You said I could borrow the car if I wanted, right? Isn't that what you said?

AUSTIN   Yeah. Right.

[AUSTIN *takes keys out of his pocket, sets them on table,* LEE *takes keys slowly, plays with them in his hand.*]

LEE   I could get a ranch, huh?

AUSTIN   Yeah. We have to write it first though.

LEE   Okay. Let's write it.

[*Lights start dimming slowly to end of scene as* AUSTIN *types,* LEE *speaks.*]
So they take off after each other straight into an endless black prairie. The sun is just comin' down and they can feel the night on their backs. What they don't know is that each one of 'em is afraid, see. Each one separately thinks that he's the only one that's afraid. And they keep ridin' like that straight into the night. Not knowing. And the one who's chasin' doesn't know where the other one is taking him. And the one who's being chased doesn't know where he's going.

[*Lights to black, typing stops in the dark, crickets fade.*]

Act Two

SCENE 5

Morning. LEE *at the table in alcove with a set of golf clubs in a fancy leather bag,* AUSTIN *at sink washing a few dishes.*

AUSTIN   He really liked it, huh?

LEE   He wouldn't a' gave me these clubs if he didn't like it.

AUSTIN   He gave you the clubs?

LEE   Yeah. I told ya' he gave me the clubs. The bag too.

AUSTIN I thought he just loaned them to you.

LEE He said it was part a' the advance. A little gift like. Gesture of his good faith.

AUSTIN He's giving you an advance?

LEE Now what's so amazing about that? I told ya' it was a good story. You even said it was a good story.

AUSTIN Well that is really incredible Lee. You know how many guys spend their whole lives down here trying to break into this business? Just trying to get in the door?

LEE [pulling clubs out of bag, testing them] I got no idea. How many?
  [Pause.]

AUSTIN How much of an advance is he giving you?

LEE Plenty. We were talkin' big money out there. Ninth hole is where I sealed the deal.

AUSTIN He made a firm commitment?

LEE Absolutely.

AUSTIN Well, I know Saul and he doesn't fool around when he says he likes something.

LEE I thought you said you didn't know him.

AUSTIN Well, I'm familiar with his tastes.

LEE I let him get two up on me goin' into the back nine. He was sure he had me cold. You shoulda' seen his face when I pulled out the old pitching wedge and plopped it pin-high, two feet from the cup. He 'bout shit his pants. "Where'd a guy like you ever learn how to play golf like that?" he says.
  [LEE laughs, AUSTIN stares at him.]

AUSTIN 'Course there's no contract yet. Nothing's final until it's on paper.

LEE It's final, all right. There's no way he's gonna' back out of it now. We gambled for it.

AUSTIN Saul, gambled?

LEE Yeah, sure. I mean he liked the outline already so he wasn't risking that much. I just guaranteed it with my short game.
  [Pause.]

AUSTIN Well, we should celebrate or something. I think Mom left a bottle of champagne in the refrigerator. We should have a little toast.
  [AUSTIN gets glasses from cupboard, goes to refrigerator, pulls out bottle of champagne.]

LEE You shouldn't oughta' take her champagne, Austin. She's gonna' miss that.

AUSTIN Oh, she's not going to mind. She'd be glad we put it to good use. I'll get her another bottle. Besides, it's perfect for the occasion.
  [Pause.]

LEE Yer gonna' get a nice fee fer writin' the script a' course. Straight fee.
  [AUSTIN stops, stares at LEE, puts glasses and bottle on table, pause.]

AUSTIN I'm writing the script?

LEE That's what he said. Said we couldn't hire a better screenwriter in the whole town.

AUSTIN But I'm already working on a script. I've got my own project. I don't have time to write two scripts.

LEE No, he said he was gonna' drop that other one.

[*Pause.*]

AUSTIN What? You mean mine? He's going to drop mine and do yours instead?

LEE [*Smiles*] Now look, Austin, it's jest beginner's luck ya' know. I mean I sank a fifty foot putt for this deal. No hard feelings.
[AUSTIN *goes to phone on wall, grabs it, starts dialing.*] He's not gonna' be in, Austin. Told me he wouldn't be in 'till late this afternoon.

AUSTIN [*stays on phone, dialing, listens*] I can't believe this. I just can't believe it. Are you sure he said that? Why would he drop mine?

LEE That's what he told me.

AUSTIN He can't do that without telling me first. Without talking to me at least. He wouldn't just make a decision like that without talking to me!

LEE Well I was kinda' surprised myself. But he was real enthusiastic about my story.
[AUSTIN *hangs up phone violently, paces.*]

AUSTIN What'd he say! Tell me everything he said!

LEE I been tellin' ya'! He said he liked the story a whole lot. It was the first authentic Western to come along in a decade.

AUSTIN He liked that story! Your story?

LEE Yeah! What's so surprisin' about that?

AUSTIN It's stupid! It's the dumbest story I ever heard in my life.

LEE Hey, hold on! That's my story yer talkin' about!

AUSTIN It's a bullshit story! It's idiotic. Two lamebrains chasing each other across Texas! Are you kidding? Who do you think's going to go see a film like that?

LEE It's not a film! It's a movie. There's a big difference. That's somethin' Saul told me.

AUSTIN Oh he did, huh?

LEE Yeah, he said, "In this business we make movies, American movies. Leave the films to the French."

AUSTIN So you got real intimate with old Saul huh? He started pouring forth his vast knowledge of Cinema.

LEE I think he liked me a lot, to tell ya' the truth. I think he felt I was somebody he could confide in.

AUSTIN What'd you do, beat him up or something?

LEE [*stands fast*] Hey, I've about had it with the insults buddy! You think yer the only one in the brain department here? Yer the only one that can sit around and cook things up? There's other people got ideas too, ya' know!

AUSTIN You must've done something. Threatened him or something. Now what'd you do Lee?

LEE I convinced him!
[LEE *makes sudden menacing lunge toward* AUSTIN, *wielding golf club above his head, stops himself, frozen moment, long pause,* LEE *lowers club.*]

AUSTIN Oh, Jesus. You didn't hurt him did you?
[*Long silence,* LEE *sits back down at table.*]
Lee! Did you hurt him?

LEE I didn't do nothin' to him! He liked my story. Pure and simple. He said it was the best story he's come across in a long, long time.

AUSTIN   That's what he told me about my story! That's the same thing he said to me.

LEE   Well, he musta' been lyin'. He musta' been lyin' to one of us anyway.

AUSTIN   You can't come into this town and start pushing people around. They're gonna' put you away!

LEE   I never pushed anybody around! I beat him fair and square. [*pause*] They can't touch me anyway. They can't put a finger on me. I'm gone. I can come in through the window and go out through the door. They never knew what hit 'em. You, yer stuck. Yer the one that's stuck. Not me. So don't be warnin' me what to do in this town.

[*Pause,* AUSTIN *crosses to table, sits at typewriter, rests.*]

AUSTIN   Lee, come on, level with me will you? It doesn't make any sense that suddenly he'd throw my idea out the window. I've been talking to him for months. I've got too much at stake. Everything's riding on this project.

LEE   What's yer idea?

AUSTIN   It's just a simple love story.

LEE   What kinda' love story?

AUSTIN [*stands, crosses into kitchen*]   I'm not telling you!

LEE   Ha! 'Fraid I'll steal it huh? Competition's gettin' kinda' close to home isn't it?

AUSTIN   Where did Saul say he was going?

LEE   He was gonna' take my story to a couple studios.

AUSTIN   That's *my* outline you know! I wrote that outline! You've got no right to be peddling it around.

LEE   You weren't ready to take credit for it last night.

AUSTIN   Give me my keys!

LEE   What?

AUSTIN   The keys! I want my keys back!

LEE   Where you goin'?

AUSTIN   Just give me my keys! I gotta' take a drive. I gotta' get out of here for a while.

LEE   Where you gonna' go, Austin?

AUSTIN [*pause*]   I might just drive out to the desert for a while. I gotta' think.

LEE   You can think here just as good. This is the perfect setup for thinkin'. We got some writin' to do here, boy. Now let's just have us a little toast. Relax. We're partners now.

[LEE *pops the cork of the champagne bottle, pours two drinks as the lights fade to black.*]

SCENE 6

Afternoon. LEE *and* SAUL *in kitchen,* AUSTIN *in alcove.*

LEE   Now you tell him. You tell him, Mr. Kipper.

SAUL   Kimmer.

LEE   Kimmer. You tell him what you told me. He don't believe me.

AUSTIN   I don't want to hear it.

SAUL   It's really not a big issue, Austin. I was simply amazed by your brother's story and—

AUSTIN   Amazed? You lost a bet! You gambled with my material!

SAUL   That's really beside the point, Austin. I'm ready to go all the way with your brother's story. I think it has a great deal of merit.

AUSTIN   I don't want to hear about it, okay? Go tell it to the executives! Tell it to somebody who's going to turn it into a package deal or something. A TV. series. Don't tell it to me.

SAUL   But I want to continue with your project too, Austin. It's not as though we can't do both. We're big enough for that aren't we?

AUSTIN   "We"? *I* can't do both! I don't know about "we."

LEE [*to* SAUL]   See, what'd I tell ya'. He's totally unsympathetic.

SAUL   Austin, there's no point in our going to another screenwriter for this. It just doesn't make sense. You're brothers. You know each other. There's a familiarity with the material that just wouldn't be possible otherwise.

AUSTIN   There's no familiarity with the material! None! I don't know what "Tornado Country" is. I don't know what a "gooseneck" is. And I don't want to know! [*pointing to* LEE] He's a hustler! He's a bigger hustler than you are! If you can't see that, then—

LEE [*to* AUSTIN]   Hey, now hold on. I didn't have to bring this bone back to you, boy. I persuaded Saul here that you were the right man for the job. You don't have to go throwin' up favors in my face.

AUSTIN   Favors! I'm the one who wrote the fuckin' outline! You can't even spell.

SAUL [*to* AUSTIN]   Your brother told me about the situation with your father. [*Pause.*]

AUSTIN   What? [*looks at* LEE]

SAUL   That's right. Now we have a clear-cut deal here, Austin. We have big studio money standing behind this thing. Just on the basis of your outline.

AUSTIN [*to* SAUL]   What'd he tell you about my father?

SAUL   Well—that he's destitute. He needs money.

LEE   That's right. He does.

[AUSTIN *shakes his head, stares at them both.*]

AUSTIN [*to* LEE]   And this little assignment is supposed to go toward the old man? A charity project? Is that what this is? Did you cook this up on the ninth green too?

SAUL   It's a big slice, Austin.

AUSTIN [*to* LEE]   I gave him money! I already gave him money. You know that. He drank it all up!

LEE   This is a different deal here.

SAUL   We can set up a trust for your father. A large sum of money. It can be doled out to him in parcels so he can't misuse it.

AUSTIN   Yeah, and who's doing the doling?

SAUL   Your brother volunteered.

[AUSTIN *laughs.*]

LEE   That's right. I'll make sure he uses it for groceries.

AUSTIN [*to* SAUL]   I'm not doing this script! I'm not writing this crap for you or anybody else. You can't blackmail me into it. You can't threaten me into it. There's no way I'm doing it. So just give it up. Both of you. [*Long pause.*]

SAUL Well, that's it then. I mean this is an easy three hundred grand. Just for a first draft. It's incredible, Austin. We've got three different studios all trying to cut each other's throats to get this material. In one morning. That's how hot it is.

AUSTIN Yeah, well you can afford to give me a percentage on the outline then. And you better get the genius here an agent before he gets burned.

LEE Saul's gonna' be my agent. Isn't that right, Saul?

SAUL That's right, [to AUSTIN] Your brother has really got something, Austin. I've been around too long not to recognize it. Raw talent.

AUSTIN He's got a lota' balls is what he's got. He's taking you right down the river.

SAUL Three hundred thousand, Austin. Just for a first draft. Now you've never been offered that kind of money before.

AUSTIN I'm not writing it.
[Pause.]

SAUL I see. Well—

LEE We'll just go to another writer then. Right, Saul? Just hire us somebody with some enthusiasm. Somebody who can recognize the value of a good story.

SAUL I'm sorry about this, Austin.

AUSTIN Yeah.

SAUL I mean I was hoping we could continue both things but now I don't see how it's possible.

AUSTIN So you're dropping my idea altogether. Is that it? Just trade horses in midstream? After all these months of meetings.

SAUL I wish there was another way.

AUSTIN I've got everything riding on this, Saul. You know that. It's my only shot. If this falls through—

SAUL I have to go with what my instincts tell me—

AUSTIN Your instincts!

SAUL My gut reaction.

AUSTIN You lost! That's your gut reaction. You lost a gamble. Now you're trying to tell me you like his story? How could you possibly fall for that story? It's as phony as Hoppalong Cassidy.[1] What do you see in it? I'm curious.

SAUL It has the ring of truth, Austin.

AUSTIN [Laughs] Truth?

LEE It is true.

SAUL Something about the real West.

AUSTIN Why? Because it's got horses? Because it's got grown men acting like little boys?

SAUL Something about the land. Your brother is speaking from experience.

AUSTIN So am I!

SAUL But nobody's interested in love these days, Austin. Let's face it.

LEE That's right.

---

1. Popular television western in the early 1950s, based on the central character from motion pictures, mostly serials, produced between 1935 and 1948.

AUSTIN [*to* SAUL]   He's been camped out on the desert for three months. Talking to cactus. What's he know about what people wanna' see on the screen! I drive on the freeway every day. I swallow the smog. I watch the news in color. I shop in the Safeway.[2] I'm the one who's in touch! Not him!

SAUL   I have to go now, Austin.
[SAUL *starts to leave.*]

AUSTIN   There's no such thing as the West anymore! It's a dead issue! It's dried up, Saul, and so are you.
[SAUL *stops and turns to* AUSTIN.]

SAUL   Maybe you're right. But I have to take the gamble, don't I?

AUSTIN   You're a fool to do this, Saul.

SAUL   I've always gone on my hunches. Always. And I've never been wrong. [*to* LEE] I'll talk to you tomorrow, Lee.

LEE   All right, Mr. Kimmer.

SAUL   Maybe we could have some lunch.

LEE   Fine with me. [*smiles at* AUSTIN]

SAUL   I'll give you a ring.
[SAUL *exits, lights to black as brothers look at each other from a distance.*]

SCENE 7

Night. Coyotes, crickets, sound of typewriter in dark, candlelight up on LEE *at typewriter struggling to type with one finger system,* AUSTIN *sits sprawled out on kitchen floor with whiskey bottle, drunk.*

AUSTIN [*singing, from floor*]
"Red sails in the sunset
Way out on the blue
Please carry my loved one
Home safely to me

Red sails in the sunset—"[3]

LEE [*slams fist on table*]   Hey! Knock it off will ya'! I'm tryin' to concentrate here.

AUSTIN [*laughs*]   You're tryin' to concentrate?

LEE   Yeah. That's right.

AUSTIN   Now you're tryin' to concentrate.

LEE   Between you, the coyotes and the crickets a thought don't have much of a chance.

AUSTIN   "Between me, the coyotes and the crickets." What a great title.

LEE   I don't need a title! I need a thought.

AUSTIN [*laughs*]   A thought! Here's a thought for ya'—

LEE   I'm not askin' fer yer thoughts! I got my own. I can do this thing on my own.

AUSTIN   You're going to write an entire script on your own?

LEE   That's right.
[*Pause.*]

AUSTIN   Here's a thought. Saul Kimmer—

---

2. Major grocery store chain, mainly in California and other Western and central states.
3. From "Red Sails in the Sunset," American song
by Hugh Williams and Jimmy Kennedy published in 1935 and popularly revived in 1951 by Nat King Cole.

LEE Shut up will ya'!

AUSTIN He thinks we're the same person.

LEE Don't get cute.

AUSTIN He does! He's lost his mind. Poor old Saul. [*giggles*] Thinks we're one and the same.

LEE Why don't you ease up on that champagne.

AUSTIN [*holding up bottle*] This isn't champagne anymore. We went through the champagne a long time ago. This is serious stuff. The days of champagne are long gone.

LEE Well, go outside and drink it.

AUSTIN I'm enjoying your company, Lee. For the first time since your arrival I am finally enjoying your company. And now you want me to go outside and drink alone?

LEE That's right.
[LEE *reads through paper in typewriter, makes an erasure.*]

AUSTIN You think you'll make more progress if you're alone? You might drive yourself crazy.

LEE I could have this thing done in a night if I had a little silence.

AUSTIN Well you'd still have the crickets to contend with. The coyotes. The sounds of the Police Helicopters prowling above the neighborhood. Slashing their searchlights down through the streets. Hunting for the likes of you.

LEE I'm a screenwriter now! I'm legitimate.

AUSTIN [*laughing*] A screenwriter!

LEE That's right. I'm on salary. That's more'n I can say for you. I got an advance coming.

AUSTIN This is true. This is very true. An advance. [*pause*] Well, maybe I oughta' go out and try my hand at your trade. Since you're doing so good at mine.

LEE Ha!
[LEE *attempts to type some more but gets the ribbon tangled up, starts trying to re-thread it as they continue talking.*]

AUSTIN Well why not? You don't think I've got what it takes to sneak into people's houses and steal their T.V.s?

LEE You couldn't steal a toaster without losin' yer lunch.
[AUSTIN *stands with a struggle, supports himself by the sink.*]

AUSTIN You don't think I could sneak into somebody's house and steal a toaster?

LEE Go take a shower or somethin' will ya!
[LEE *gets more tangled up with the typewriter ribbon, pulling it out of the machine as though it was fishing line.*]

AUSTIN You really don't think I could steal a crumby toaster? How much you wanna' bet I can't steal a toaster! How much? Go ahead! You're a gambler aren't you? Tell me how much yer willing to put on the line. Some part of your big advance? Oh, you haven't got that yet have you. I forgot.

LEE All right. I'll bet you your car that you can't steal a toaster without gettin' busted.

AUSTIN You already got my car!

LEE Okay, your house then.

AUSTIN What're you gonna' give me! I'm not talkin' about my house and my car, I'm talkin' about what are you gonna' give me. You don't have nothin' to give me.

LEE I'll give you—shared screen credit. How 'bout that? I'll have it put in the contract that this was written by the both of us.

AUSTIN I don't want my name on that piece of shit! I want something of value. You got anything of value? You got any tidbits from the desert? Any Rattlesnake bones? I'm not a greedy man. Any little personal treasure will suffice.

LEE I'm gonna' just kick yer ass out in a minute.

AUSTIN Oh, so now you're gonna' kick me out! Now I'm the intruder. I'm the one who's invading your precious privacy.

LEE I'm trying to do some screenwriting here!!
      [LEE *stands, picks up typewriter, slams it down hard on table, pause, silence except for crickets.*]

AUSTIN Well, you got everything you need. You got plenty a' coffee? Groceries. You got a car. A contract. [*pause*] Might need a new typewriter ribbon but other than that you're pretty well fixed. I'll just leave ya' alone for a while.
      [AUSTIN *tries to steady himself to leave,* LEE *makes a move toward him.*]

LEE Where you goin'?

AUSTIN Don't worry about me. I'm not the one to worry about.
      [AUSTIN *weaves toward exit, stops.*]

LEE What're you gonna' do? Just go wander out into the night?

AUSTIN I'm gonna' make a little tour.

LEE Why don't ya' just go to bed for Christ's sake. Yer makin' me sick.

AUSTIN I can take care a' myself. Don't worry about me.
      [AUSTIN *weaves badly in another attempt to exit, he crashes to the floor,* LEE *goes to him but remains standing.*]

LEE You want me to call your wife for ya' or something?

AUSTIN [*from floor*] My wife?

LEE Yeah. I mean maybe she can help ya' out. Talk to ya' or somethin'.

AUSTIN [*struggles to stand again*] She's five hundred miles away. North. North of here. Up in the North country where things are calm. I don't need any help. I'm gonna' go outside and I'm gonna' steal a toaster. I'm gonna' steal some other stuff too. I might even commit bigger crimes. Bigger than you ever dreamed of. Crimes beyond the imagination!
      [AUSTIN *manages to get himself vertical, tries to head for exit again.*]

LEE Just hang on a minute, Austin.

AUSTIN Why? What for? You don't need my help, right? You got a handle on the project. Besides, I'm lookin' forward to the smell of the night. The bushes. Orange blossoms. Dust in the driveways. Rain bird sprinklers. Lights in people's houses. You're right about the lights, Lee. Everybody else is livin' the life. Indoors. Safe. This is a Paradise down here. You know that? We're livin' in a Paradise. We've forgotten about that.

LEE You sound just like the old man now.

AUSTIN Yeah, well we all sound alike when we're sloshed. We just sorta' echo each other.

LEE Maybe if we could work on this together we could bring him back out here. Get him settled down some place.

[AUSTIN *turns violently toward* LEE, *takes a swing at him, misses and crashes to the floor again,* LEE *stays standing.*]

AUSTIN   I don't want him out here! I've had it with him! I went all the way out there! I went out of my way. I gave him money and all he did was play Al Jolson[4] records and spit at me! I gave him money!
[*Pause.*]

LEE   Just help me a little with the characters, all right? You know how to do it, Austin.

AUSTIN [*on floor, laughs*]   The characters!

LEE   Yeah. You know. The way they talk and stuff. I can hear it in my head but I can't get it down on paper.

AUSTIN   What characters?

LEE   The guys. The guys in the story.

AUSTIN   Those aren't characters.

LEE   Whatever you call 'em then. I need to write somethin' out.

AUSTIN   Those are illusions of characters.

LEE   I don't give a damn what ya' call 'em! You know what I'm talkin' about!

AUSTIN   Those are fantasies of a long lost boyhood.

LEE   I gotta' write somethin' out on paper!!
[*Pause.*]

AUSTIN   What for? Saul's gonna' get you a fancy screenwriter isn't he?

LEE   I wanna' do it myself!

AUSTIN   Then do it! Yer on your own now, old buddy. You bulldogged yer way into contention. Now you gotta' carry it through.

LEE   I will but I need some advice. Just a couple a' things. Come on, Austin. Just help me get 'em talkin' right. It won't take much.

AUSTIN   Oh, now you're having a little doubt huh? What happened? The pressure's on, boy. This is it. You gotta' come up with it now. You don't come up with a winner on your first time out they just cut your head off. They don't give you a second chance ya' know.

LEE   I got a good story! I know it's a good story. I just need a little help is all.

AUSTIN   Not from me. Not from yer little old brother. I'm retired.

LEE   You could save this thing for me, Austin. I'd give ya' half the money. I would. I only need half anyway. With this kinda' money I could be a long time down the road. I'd never bother ya' again. I promise. You'd never even see me again.

AUSTIN [*still on floor*]   You'd disappear?

LEE   I would for sure.

AUSTIN   Where would you disappear to?

LEE   That don't matter. I got plenty a' places.

AUSTIN   Nobody can disappear. The old man tried that. Look where it got him. He lost his teeth.

LEE   He never had any money.

AUSTIN   I don't mean that. I mean his teeth! His real teeth. First he lost his real teeth, then he lost his false teeth. You never knew that did ya'? He never confided in you.

LEE   Nah, I never knew that.

4. Lithuanian-born American popular singer (1886–1950), depicted in blackface makeup on his record-album covers and in films; a purveyor of songs in the minstrel manner.

AUSTIN   You wanna' drink?

[AUSTIN *offers bottle to* LEE, LEE *takes it, sits down on kitchen floor with* AUSTIN, *they share the bottle.*]

Yeah, he lost his real teeth one at a time. Woke up every morning with another tooth lying on the mattress. Finally, he decides he's gotta' get 'em all pulled out but he doesn't have any money. Middle of Arizona with no money and no insurance and every morning another tooth is lying on the mattress. [*takes a drink*] So what does he do?

LEE   I dunno'. I never knew about that.

AUSTIN   He begs the government. G.I. Bill[5] or some damn thing. Some pension plan he remembers in the back of his head. And they send him out the money.

LEE   They did?

[*They keep trading the bottle between them, taking drinks.*]

AUSTIN   Yeah. They send him the money but it's not enough money. Costs a lot to have all yer teeth yanked. They charge by the individual tooth, ya' know. I mean one tooth isn't equal to another tooth. Some are more expensive. Like the big ones in the back—

LEE   So what happened?

AUSTIN   So he locates a Mexican dentist in Juarez[6] who'll do the whole thing for a song. And he takes off hitchhiking to the border.

LEE   Hitchhiking?

AUSTIN   Yeah. So how long you think it takes him to get to the border? A man his age.

LEE   I dunno.

AUSTIN   Eight days it takes him. Eight days in the rain and the sun and every day he's droppin' teeth on the blacktop and nobody'll pick him up 'cause his mouth's full a' blood.

[*Pause, they drink.*]

So finally he stumbles into the dentist. Dentist takes all his money and all his teeth. And there he is, in Mexico, with his gums sewed up and his pockets empty.

[*Long silence,* AUSTIN *drinks.*]

LEE   That's it?

AUSTIN   Then I go out to see him, see. I go out there and I take him out for a nice Chinese dinner. But he doesn't eat. All he wants to do is drink Martinis outa' plastic cups. And he takes his teeth out and lays 'em on the table 'cause he can't stand the feel of 'em. And we ask the waitress for one a' those doggie bags to take the Chop Suey home in. So he drops his teeth in the doggie bag along with the Chop Suey. And then we go out to hit all the bars up and down the highway. Says he wants to introduce me to all his buddies. And in one a' those bars, in one a' those bars up and down the highway, he left that doggie bag with his teeth laying in the Chop Suey.

LEE   You never found it?

AUSTIN   We went back but we never did find it. [*pause*] Now that's a true story. True to life.

[*They drink as lights fade to black.*]

---

5. Post-World War II legislation according housing and educational benefits to military veterans.

6. Mexican city immediately across the Rio Grande from El Paso, Texas.

SCENE 8

Very early morning, between night and day. No crickets, coyotes yapping fever-
ishly in distance before light comes up, a small fire blazes up in the dark from
alcove area, sound of LEE *smashing typewriter with a golf club, lights coming*
up, LEE *seen smashing typewriter methodically then dropping pages of his script*
into a burning bowl set on the floor of alcove, flames leap up, AUSTIN *has a whole*
bunch of stolen toasters lined up on the sink counter along with LEE's *stolen T.V.,*
the toasters are of a wide variety of models, mostly chrome, AUSTIN *goes up and*
down the line of toasters, breathing on them and polishing them with a dish
towel, both men are drunk, empty whiskey bottles and beer cans litter floor of
kitchen, they share a half empty bottle on one of the chairs in the alcove, LEE
keeps periodically taking deliberate ax-chops at the typewriter using a nine-iron
as AUSTIN *speaks, all of their mother's house plants are dead and drooping.*

AUSTIN [*polishing toasters*]   There's gonna' be a general lack of toast in the
   neighborhood this morning. Many, many unhappy, bewildered breakfast faces. I guess it's best not to even think of the victims. Not to even
   entertain it. Is that the right psychology?
LEE [*pause*]   What?
AUSTIN   Is that the correct criminal psychology? Not to think of the vic-
   tims?
LEE   What victims?
      [LEE *takes another swipe at typewriter with nine-iron, adds pages to the*
      fire.]
AUSTIN   The victims of crime. Of breaking and entering. I mean is it a
   prerequisite for a criminal not to have a conscience?
LEE   Ask a criminal.
      [*Pause,* LEE *stares at* AUSTIN.]
   What're you gonna' do with all those toasters? That's the dumbest thing
   I ever saw in my life.
AUSTIN   I've got hundreds of dollars worth of household appliances here.
   You may not realize that.
LEE   Yeah, and how many hundreds of dollars did you walk right past?
AUSTIN   It was toasters you challenged me to. Only toasters. I ignored
   every other temptation.
LEE   I never challenged you! That's no challenge. Anybody can steal a
   toaster.
      [LEE *smashes typewriter again.*]
AUSTIN   You don't have to take it out on my typewriter ya' know. It's not
   the machine's fault that you can't write. It's a sin to do that to a good
   machine.
LEE   A sin?
AUSTIN   When you consider all the writers who never even had a machine.
   Who would have given an eyeball for a good typewriter. Any typewriter.
      [LEE *smashes typewriter again.*]
AUSTIN [*polishing toaster*]   All the ones who wrote on matchbook covers.
   Paper bags. Toilet paper. Who had their writing destroyed by their jailers.
   Who persisted beyond all odds. Those writers would find it hard to
   understand your actions.

[LEE *comes down on typewriter with one final crushing blow of the nine-iron then collapses in one of the chairs, takes a drink from bottle, pause.*]

AUSTIN [*after pause*]   Not to mention demolishing a perfectly good golf club. What about all the struggling golfers? What about Lee Trevino?[7] What do you think he would've said when he was batting balls around with broomsticks at the age of nine. Impoverished.

[*Pause.*]

LEE   What time is it anyway?

AUSTIN   No idea. Time stands still when you're havin' fun.

LEE   Is it too late to call a woman? You know any women?

AUSTIN   I'm a married man.

LEE   I mean a local woman.

[AUSTIN *looks out at light through window above sink.*]

AUSTIN   It's either too late or too early. You're the nature enthusiast. Can't you tell the time by the light in the sky? Orient yourself around the North Star or something?

LEE   I can't tell anything.

AUSTIN   Maybe you need a little breakfast. Some toast! How 'bout some toast?

[AUSTIN *goes to cupboard, pulls out loaf of bread and starts dropping slices into every toaster,* LEE *stays sitting, drinks, watches* AUSTIN.]

LEE   I don't need toast. I need a woman.

AUSTIN   A woman isn't the answer. Never was.

LEE   I'm not talkin' about permanent. I'm talkin' about temporary.

AUSTIN [*putting toast in toasters*]   We'll just test the merits of these little demons. See which brands have a tendency to burn. See which one can produce a perfectly golden piece of fluffy toast.

LEE   How much gas you got in yer car?

AUSTIN   I haven't driven my car for days now. So I haven't had an opportunity to look at the gas gauge.

LEE   Take a guess. You think there's enough to get me to Bakersfield?[8]

AUSTIN   Bakersfield? What's in Bakersfield?

LEE   Just never mind what's in Bakersfield! You think there's enough goddamn gas in the car!

AUSTIN   Sure.

LEE   Sure. You could care less, right. Let me run outa' gas on the Grapevine.[9] You could give a shit.

AUSTIN   I'd say there was enough gas to get you just about anywhere, Lee. With your determination and guts.

LEE   What the hell time is it anyway?

[LEE *pulls out his wallet, starts going through dozens of small pieces of paper with phone numbers written on them, drops some on the floor, drops others in the fire.*]

AUSTIN   Very early. This is the time of morning when the coyotes kill people's cocker spaniels. Did you hear them? That's what they were doing out there. Luring innocent pets away from their homes.

---

7. American golf champion (b. 1939).
8. City in Kern County, California, about 115 miles north-northwest of Los Angeles.

9. Steep, winding section of the Ridge Route, the highway linking Los Angeles and Bakersfield.

LEE [*searching through his papers*]   What's the area code for Bakersfield? You know?

AUSTIN   You could always call the operator.

LEE   I can't stand that voice they give ya'.

AUSTIN   What voice?

LEE   That voice that warns you that if you'd only tried harder to find the number in the phone book you wouldn't have to be calling the operator to begin with.

> [LEE *gets up, holding a slip of paper from his wallet, stumbles toward phone on wall, yanks receiver, starts dialing.*]

AUSTIN   Well I don't understand why you'd want to talk to anybody else anyway. I mean you can talk to me. I'm your brother.

LEE [*dialing*]   I wanna' talk to a woman. I haven't heard a woman's voice in a long time.

AUSTIN   Not since the Botanist?

LEE   What?

AUSTIN   Nothing. [*starts singing as he tends toast*]
"Red sails in the sunset
Way out on the blue
Please carry my loved one
Home safely to me"

LEE   Hey, knock it off will ya'! This is long distance here.

AUSTIN   Bakersfield?

LEE   Yeah, Bakersfield. It's Kern County.

AUSTIN   Well, what County are *we* in?

LEE   You better get yourself a 7-Up, boy.

AUSTIN   One County's as good as another.

> [AUSTIN *hums "Red Sails" softly as* LEE *talks on phone.*]

LEE [*to phone*]   Yeah, operator look—first off I wanna' know the area code for Bakersfield. Right. Bakersfield! Okay. Good. Now I wanna' know if you can help me track somebody down. [*pause*] No, no I mean a phone number. Just a phone number. Okay. [*holds a piece of paper up and reads it*] Okay, the name is Melly Ferguson. Melly. [*pause*] I dunno'. Melly. Maybe. Yeah. Maybe Melanie. Yeah. Melanie Ferguson. Okay. [*pause*] What? I can't hear ya' so good. Sounds like yer under the ocean. [*pause*] You got ten Melanie Fergusons? How could that be? Ten Melanie Fergusons in Bakersfield? Well gimme all of 'em then. [*pause*] What d'ya' mean? Gimmie all ten Melanie Fergusons! That's right. Just a second. [*to* AUSTIN] Gimme a pen.

AUSTIN   I don't have a pen.

LEE   Gimme a pencil then!

AUSTIN   I don't have a pencil.

LEE [*to phone*]   Just a second, operator. [*to* AUSTIN] Yer a writer and ya' don't have a pen or a pencil!

AUSTIN   I'm not a writer. You're a writer.

LEE   I'm on the phone here! Get me a pen or a pencil.

AUSTIN   I gotta' watch the toast.

LEE [*to phone*]   Hang on a second, operator.

> [LEE *lets the phone drop then starts pulling all the drawers in the kitchen out on the floor and dumping the contents, searching for a pencil,* AUSTIN *watches him casually.*]

LEE [*crashing through drawers, throwing contents around kitchen*] This is the last time I try to live with people, boy! I can't believe it. Here I am! Here I am again in a desperate situation! This would never happen out on the desert. I would never be in this kinda' situation out on the desert. Isn't there a pen or a pencil in this house! Who lives in this house anyway!

AUSTIN Our mother.

LEE How come she don't have a pen or a pencil! She's a social person isn't she? Doesn't she have to make shopping lists? She's gotta' have a pencil. [*finds a pencil*] Aaha! [*he rushes back to phone, picks up receiver*] All right operator. Operator? Hey! Operator! Goddamnit!
[LEE *rips the phone off the wall and throws it down, goes back to chair and falls into it, drinks, long pause.*]

AUSTIN She hung up?

LEE Yeah, she hung up. I knew she was gonna' hang up. I could hear it in her voice.
[LEE *starts going through his slips of paper again.*]

AUSTIN Well, you're probably better off staying here with me anyway. I'll take care of you.

LEE I don't need takin' care of! Not by you anyway.

AUSTIN Toast is almost ready.
[AUSTIN *starts buttering all the toast as it pops up.*]

LEE I don't want any toast!
[*Long pause.*]

AUSTIN You gotta' eat something. Can't just drink. How long have we been drinking, anyway?

LEE [*looking through slips of paper*] Maybe it was Fresno.[1] What's the area code for Fresno? How could I have lost that number! She was beautiful.
[*Pause.*]

AUSTIN Why don't you just forget about that, Lee. Forget about the woman.

LEE She had green eyes. You know what green eyes do to me?

AUSTIN I know but you're not gonna' get it on with her now anyway. It's dawn already. She's in Bakersfield for Christ's sake.
[*Long pause,* LEE *considers the situation.*]

LEE Yeah, [*looks at windows*] It's dawn?

AUSTIN Let's just have some toast and—

LEE What is this bullshit with the toast anyway! You make it sound like salvation or something. I don't want any goddamn toast! How many times I gotta' tell ya'! [LEE *gets up, crosses upstage to windows in alcove, looks out,* AUSTIN *butters toast*]

AUSTIN Well it is like salvation sort of. I mean the smell. I love the smell of toast. And the sun's coming up. It makes me feel like anything's possible. Ya' know?

LEE [*back to* AUSTIN, *facing windows upstage*] So go to church why don't ya'.

AUSTIN Like a beginning. I love beginnings.

LEE Oh yeah. I've always been kinda' partial to endings myself.

AUSTIN What if I come with you, Lee?

LEE [*pause as* LEE *turns toward* AUSTIN] What?

AUSTIN What if I come with you out to the desert?

LEE Are you kiddin'?

1. City in central California.

AUSTIN   No. I'd just like to see what it's like.

LEE   You wouldn't last a day out there pal.

AUSTIN   That's what you said about the toasters. You said I couldn't steal a toaster either.

LEE   A toaster's got nothin' to do with the desert.

AUSTIN   I could make it, Lee. I'm not that helpless. I can cook.

LEE   Cook?

AUSTIN   I can.

LEE   So what! You can cook. Toast.

AUSTIN   I can make fires. I know how to get fresh water from condensation.

[AUSTIN *stacks buttered toast up in a tall stack on plate.*]
[LEE *slams table.*]

LEE   It's not somethin' you learn out of a Boy Scout handbook!

AUSTIN   Well how do you learn it then! How're you supposed to learn it!
[*Pause.*]

LEE   Ya' just learn it, that's all. Ya' learn it 'cause ya' have to learn it. You don't *have* to learn it.

AUSTIN   You could teach me.

LEE   [*stands*]   What're you, crazy or somethin'? You went to college. Here, you are down here, rollin' in bucks. Floatin' up and down in elevators. And you wanna' learn how to live on the desert!

AUSTIN   I do, Lee. I really do. There's nothin' down here for me. There never was. When we were kids here it was different. There was a life here then. But now—I keep comin' down here thinkin' it's the fifties or somethin'. I keep finding myself getting off the freeway at familiar landmarks that turn out to be unfamiliar. On the way to appointments. Wandering down streets I thought I recognized that turn out to be replicas of streets I remember. Streets I misremember. Streets I can't tell if I lived on or saw in a postcard. Fields that don't even exist anymore.

LEE   There's no point cryin' about that now.

AUSTIN   There's nothin' real down here, Lee! Least of all me!

LEE   Well I can't save you from that!

AUSTIN   You can let me come with you.

LEE   No dice, pal.

AUSTIN   You could let me come with you, Lee!

LEE   Hey, do you actually think I chose to live out in the middle a' nowhere? Do ya'? Ya' think it's some kinda' philosophical decision I took or somethin'? I'm livin' out there 'cause I can't make it here! And yer bitchin' to me about all yer success!

AUSTIN   I'd cash it all in in a second. That's the truth.

LEE   [*Pause, shakes his head*]   I can't believe this.

AUSTIN   Let me go with you.

LEE   Stop sayin' that will ya'! Yer worse than a dog.

[AUSTIN *offers out the plate of neatly stacked toast to* LEE.]

AUSTIN   You want some toast?

[LEE *suddenly explodes and knocks the plate out of* AUSTIN'S *hand, toast goes flying, long frozen moment where it appears* LEE *might go all the way this time when* AUSTIN *breaks it by slowly lowering himself to his knees and begins gathering the scattered toast from the floor and stacking it back on the plate,* LEE *begins to circle* AUSTIN *in a slow, predatory way, crushing pieces of toast in his wake, no words for a while,* AUSTIN *keeps gathering toast, even the crushed pieces.*]

LEE   Tell ya' what I'll do, little brother. I might just consider makin' you a deal. Little trade, [AUSTIN *continues gathering toast as* LEE *circles him through this*] You write me up this screenplay thing just like I tell ya'. I mean you can use all yer usual tricks and stuff. Yer fancy language. Yer artistic hocus pocus. But ya' gotta' write everything like I say. Every move. Every time they run outa' gas, they run outa' gas. Every time they wanna' jump on a horse, they do just that. If they wanna' stay in Texas, by God they'll stay in Texas! [*Keeps circling*] And you finish the whole thing up for me. Top to bottom. And you put my name on it. And I own all the rights. And every dime goes in my pocket. You do that and I'll sure enough take ya' with me to the desert, [LEE *stops, pause, looks down at* AUSTIN] How's that sound?
      [*Pause as* AUSTIN *stands slowly holding plate of demolished toast, their faces are very close, pause.*]

AUSTIN   It's a deal.
      [LEE *stares straight into* AUSTIN's *eyes, then he slowly takes a piece of toast off the plate, raises it to his mouth and takes a huge crushing bite never taking his eyes off* AUSTIN's, *as* LEE *crunches into the toast the lights black out.*]

SCENE 9

Mid-day. No sound, blazing heat, the stage is ravaged; bottles, toasters, smashed typewriter, ripped out telephone, etc. All the debris from previous scene is now starkly visible in intense yellow light, the effect should be like a desert junkyard at high noon, the coolness of the preceding scenes is totally obliterated. AUSTIN *is seated at table in alcove, shirt open, pouring with sweat, hunched over a writing notebook, scribbling notes desperately with a ballpoint pen.* LEE *with no shirt, beer in hand, sweat pouring down his chest, is walking a slow circle around the table, picking his way through the objects, sometimes kicking them aside.*

LEE [*as he walks*]   All right, read it back to me. Read it back to me!
AUSTIN [*scribbling at top speed*]   Just a second.
LEE   Come on, come on! Just read what ya' got.
AUSTIN   I can't keep up! It's not the same as if I had a typewriter.
LEE   Just read what we got so far. Forget about the rest.
AUSTIN   All right. Let's see—okay—[*wipes sweat from his face, reads as* LEE *circles*] Luke says uh—
LEE   Luke?
AUSTIN   Yeah.
LEE   His name's Luke? All right, all right—we can change the names later. What's he say? Come on, come on.
AUSTIN   He says uh—[*reading*] "I told ya' you were a fool to follow me in here. I know this prairie like the back a' my hand."
LEE   No, no, no! That's not what I said. I never said that.
AUSTIN   That's what I wrote.
LEE   It's not what I said. I never said "like the back a' my hand." That's stupid. That's one a' those—whadya' call it? Whadya' call that?

AUSTIN What?

LEE Whadya' call it when somethin's been said a thousand times before. Whadya' call that?

AUSTIN Um—a cliché?

LEE Yeah. That's right. Cliché. That's what that is. A cliché. "The back a' my hand." That's stupid.

AUSTIN That's what you said.

LEE I never said that! And even if I did, that's where yer supposed to come in. That's where yer supposed to change it to somethin' better.

AUSTIN Well how am I supposed to do that and write down what you say at the same time?

LEE Ya' just do, that's all! You hear a stupid line you change it. That's yer job.

AUSTIN All right, [*makes more notes*]

LEE What're you changin' it to?

AUSTIN I'm not changing it. I'm just trying to catch up.

LEE Well change it! We gotta' change that, we can't leave that in there like that. ". . . the back a' my hand." That's dumb.

AUSTIN [*stops writing, sits back*] All right.

LEE [*pacing*] So what'll we change it to?

AUSTIN Um—How 'bout—"I'm on intimate terms with this prairie."

LEE [*to himself considering line as he walks*] "I'm on intimate terms with this prairie." Intimate terms, intimate terms. Intimate—that means like uh—sexual right?

AUSTIN Well—yeah—or—

LEE He's on sexual terms with the prairie? How dya' figure that?

AUSTIN Well it doesn't necessarily have to mean sexual.

LEE What's it mean then?

AUSTIN It means uh—close—personal—

LEE All right. How's it sound? Put it into the uh—the line there. Read it back. Let's see how it sounds. [*to himself*]. "Intimate terms."

AUSTIN [*scribbles in notebook*] Okay. It'd go something like this: [*reads*] "I told ya' you were a fool to follow me in here. I'm on intimate terms with this prairie."

LEE That's good. I like that. That's real good.

AUSTIN You do?

LEE Yeah. Don't you?

AUSTIN Sure.

LEE Sounds original now. "Intimate terms." That's good. Okay. Now we're cookin! That has a real ring to it.

> [AUSTIN *makes more notes,* LEE *walks around, pours beer on his arms and rubs it over his chest feeling good about the new progress, as he does this* MOM *enters unobtrusively down left with her luggage, she stops and stares at the scene still holding luggage as the two men continue, unaware of her presence,* AUSTIN *absorbed in his writing,* LEE *cooling himself off with beer.*]

LEE [*continues*] "He's on intimate terms with this prairie." Sounds real mysterious and kinda' threatening at the same time.

AUSTIN [*writing rapidly*] Good.

LEE Now—[LEE *turns and suddenly sees* MOM, *he stares at her for a while, she stares back,* AUSTIN *keeps writing feverishly, not noticing,* LEE *walks slowly over to* MOM *and takes a closer look, long pause.*]

LEE Mom?
> [AUSTIN *looks up suddenly from his writing, sees* MOM, *stands quickly, long pause,* MOM *surveys the damage.*]

AUSTIN Mom. What're you doing back?

MOM I'm back.

LEE Here, lemme take those for ya.
> [LEE *sets beer on counter then takes both her bags but doesn't know where to set them down in the sea of junk so he just keeps holding them.*]

AUSTIN I wasn't expecting you back so soon. I thought uh—How was Alaska?

MOM Fine.

LEE See any igloos?

MOM No. Just glaciers.

AUSTIN Cold huh?

MOM What?

AUSTIN It must've been cold up there?

MOM Not really.

LEE Musta' been colder than this here. I mean we're havin' a real scorcher here.

MOM Oh? [*she looks at damage*]

LEE Yeah. Must be in the hundreds.

AUSTIN You wanna' take your coat off, Mom?

MOM No. [*pause, she surveys space*] What happened in here?

AUSTIN Oh um—Me and Lee were just sort of celebrating and uh—

MOM Celebrating?

AUSTIN Yeah. Uh—Lee sold a screenplay. A story, I mean.

MOM Lee did?

AUSTIN Yeah.

MOM Not you?

AUSTIN No. Him.

MOM [*to* LEE] You sold a screenplay?

LEE Yeah. That's right. We're just sorta' finishing it up right now. That's what we're doing here.

AUSTIN Me and Lee are going out to the desert to live.

MOM You and Lee?

AUSTIN Yeah. I'm taking off with Lee.

MOM [*she looks back and forth at each of them, pause*] You gonna go live with your father?

AUSTIN No. We're going to a different desert Mom.

MOM I see. Well, you'll probably wind up on the same desert sooner or later. What're all these toasters doing here?

AUSTIN Well—we had kind of a contest.

MOM Contest?

LEE Yeah.

AUSTIN Lee won.

MOM Did you win a lot of money, Lee?

LEE   Well not yet. It's comin' in any day now.

MOM *[to* LEE*]*   What happened to your shirt?

LEE   Oh. I was sweatin' like a pig and I took it off.

> [AUSTIN *grabs* LEE*'s shirt off the table and tosses it to him,* LEE *sets down suitcases and puts his shirt on.*]

MOM   Well it's one hell of a mess in here isn't it?

AUSTIN   Yeah, I'll clean it up for you, Mom. I just didn't know you were coming back so soon.

MOM   I didn't either.

AUSTIN   What happened?

MOM   Nothing. I just started missing all my plants.

> [*She notices dead plants.*]

AUSTIN   Oh.

MOM   Oh, they're all dead aren't they, [*she crosses toward them, examines them closely*] You didn't get a chance to water I guess.

AUSTIN   I was doing it and then Lee came and—

LEE   Yeah I just distracted him a whole lot here, Mom. It's not his fault.

> [*Pause, as* MOM *stares at plants.*]

MOM   Oh well, one less thing to take care of I guess, [*turns toward brothers*] Oh, that reminds me—You boys will probably never guess who's in town. Try and guess.

> [*Long pause, brothers stare at her.*]

AUSTIN   Whadya' mean, Mom?

MOM   Take a guess. Somebody very important has come to town. I read it, coming down on the Greyhound.

LEE   Somebody very important?

MOM   See if you can guess. You'll never guess.

AUSTIN   Mom—we're trying to uh—[*points to writing pad*]

MOM   Picasso.[1] [*pause*] Picasso's in town. Isn't that incredible? Right now.

> [*Pause.*]

AUSTIN   Picasso's dead, Mom.

MOM   No, he's not dead. He's visiting the museum. I read it on the bus. We have to go down there and see him.

AUSTIN   Mom—

MOM   This is the chance of a lifetime. Can you imagine? We could all go down and meet him. All three of us.

LEE   Uh—I don't think I'm really up fer meetin' anybody right now. I'm uh—What's his name?

MOM   Picasso! Picasso! You've never heard of Picasso? Austin, you've heard of Picasso.

AUSTIN   Mom, we're not going to have time.

MOM   It won't take long. We'll just hop in the car and go down there. An opportunity like this doesn't come along every day.

AUSTIN   We're gonna' be leavin' here, Mom!

> [*Pause.*]

MOM   Oh.

LEE   Yeah.

> [*Pause.*]

---

1. Pablo Picasso (1881–1973), Spanish-born modernist painter active in France.

MOM   You're both leaving?

LEE [*looks at* AUSTIN]   Well we were thinkin' about that before but now I—

AUSTIN   No, we are! We're both leaving. We've got it all planned.

MOM [*to* AUSTIN]   Well you can't leave. You have a family.

AUSTIN   I'm leaving. I'm getting out of here.

LEE [*to* MOM]   I don't really think Austin's cut out for the desert do you?

MOM   No. He's not.

AUSTIN   I'm going with you, Lee!

MOM   He's too thin.

LEE   Yeah, he'd just burn up out there.

AUSTIN [*to* LEE]   We just gotta' finish this screenplay and then we're gonna' take off. That's the plan. That's what you said. Come on, let's get back to work, Lee.

LEE   I can't work under these conditions here. It's too hot.

AUSTIN   Then we'll do it on the desert.

LEE   Don't be tellin' me what we're gonna do!

MOM   Don't shout in the house.

LEE   We're just gonna' have to postpone the whole deal.

AUSTIN   I can't postpone it! It's gone past postponing! I'm doing everything you said. I'm writing down exactly what you tell me.

LEE   Yeah, but you were right all along see. It is a dumb story. "Two lamebrains chasin' each other across Texas." That's what you said, right?

AUSTIN   I never said that.

[LEE *sneers in* AUSTIN's *face then turns to* MOM.]

LEE   I'm gonna' just borrow some a' your antiques, Mom. You don't mind do ya'? Just a few plates and things. Silverware.

[LEE *starts going through all the cupboards in kitchen pulling out plates and stacking them on counter as* MOM *and* AUSTIN *watch*.]

MOM   You don't have any utensils on the desert?

LEE   Nah, I'm fresh out.

AUSTIN [*to* LEE]   What're you doing?

MOM   Well some of those are very old. Bone China.

LEE   I'm tired of eatin' outa' my bare hands, ya' know. It's not civilized.

AUSTIN [*to* LEE]   What're you doing? We made a deal!

MOM   Couldn't you borrow the plastic ones instead? I have plenty of plastic ones.

LEE [*as he stacks plates*]   It's not the same. Plastic's not the same at all. What I need is somethin' authentic. Somethin' to keep me in touch. It's easy to get outa' touch out there. Don't worry I'll get 'em back to ya'.

[AUSTIN *rushes up to* LEE, *grabs him by shoulders*.]

AUSTIN   You can't just drop the whole thing, Lee!

[LEE *turns, pushes* AUSTIN *in the chest knocking him backwards into the alcove*, MOM *watches numbly*, LEE *returns to collecting the plates, silverware, etc.*]

MOM   You boys shouldn't fight in the house. Go outside and fight.

LEE   I'm not fightin'. I'm leavin'.

MOM   There's been enough damage done already.

LEE [*his back to* AUSTIN *and* MOM, *stacking dishes on counter*]   I'm clearin' outa' here once and for all. All this town does is drive a man insane. Look what it's done to Austin there. I'm not lettin' that happen to me.

Sell myself down the river. No sir. I'd rather be a hundred miles from nowhere than let that happen to me.

[*During this* AUSTIN *has picked up the ripped-out phone from the floor and wrapped the cord tightly around both his hands, he lunges at* LEE *whose back is still to him, wraps the cord around* LEE's *neck, plants a foot in* LEE's *back and pulls back on the cord, tightening it,* LEE *chokes desperately, can't speak and can't reach* AUSTIN *with his arms,* AUSTIN *keeps applying pressure on* LEE's *back with his foot, bending him into the sink,* MOM *watches.*]

AUSTIN [*tightening cord*] You're not goin' anywhere! You're not takin' anything with you. You're not takin' my car! You're not takin' the dishes! You're not takin' anything! You're stayin' right here!

MOM You'll have to stop fighting in the house. There's plenty of room outside to fight. You've got the whole outdoors to fight in.

[LEE *tries to tear himself away, he crashes across the stage like an enraged bull dragging* AUSTIN *with him, he snorts and bellows but* AUSTIN *hangs on and manages to keep clear of* LEE's *attempts to grab him, they crash into the table, to the floor,* LEE *is face down thrashing wildly and choking,* AUSTIN *pulls cord tighter, stands with one foot planted on* LEE's *back and the cord stretched taut.*]

AUSTIN [*holding cord*] Gimme back my keys, Lee! Take the keys out! Take 'em out!

[LEE *desperately tries to dig in his pockets, searching for the car keys,* MOM *moves closer.*]

MOM [*calmly to* AUSTIN.] You're not killing him are you?

AUSTIN I don't know. I don't know if I'm killing him. I'm stopping him. That's all. I'm just stopping him.

[LEE *thrashes but* AUSTIN *is relentless.*]

MOM You oughta' let him breathe a little bit.

AUSTIN Throw the keys out, Lee!

[LEE *finally gets keys out and throws them on floor but out of* AUSTIN's *reach,* AUSTIN *keeps pressure on cord, pulling* LEE's *neck back,* LEE *gets one hand to the cord but can't relieve the pressure.*]

Reach me those keys would ya', Mom.

MOM [*not moving*] Why are you doing this to him?

AUSTIN Reach me the keys!

MOM Not until you stop choking him.

AUSTIN I can't stop choking him! He'll kill me if I stop choking him!

MOM He won't kill you. He's your brother.

AUSTIN Just get me the keys would ya'!

[*Pause* MOM *picks keys up off floor, hands them to* AUSTIN.]

AUSTIN [*to* MOM] Thanks.

MOM Will you let him go now?

AUSTIN I don't know. He's not gonna' let me get outa' here.

MOM Well you can't kill him.

AUSTIN I can kill him! I can easily kill him. Right now. Right here. All I gotta' do is just tighten up. See? [*he tightens cord,* LEE *thrashes wildly,* AUSTIN *releases pressure a little, maintaining control*] Ya' see that?

MOM That's a savage thing to do.

AUSTIN Yeah well don't tell me I can't kill him because I can. I can just twist. I can just keep twisting. [AUSTIN *twists the cord tighter,* LEE *weakens, his breathing changes to a short rasp*]

MOM   Austin!
    [AUSTIN *relieves pressure*, LEE *breathes easier but* AUSTIN *keeps him under control.*]
AUSTIN   [*eyes on* LEE, *holding cord*]   I'm goin' to the desert. There's nothing stopping me. I'm going by myself to the desert.
    [MOM *moving toward her luggage.*]
MOM   Well, I'm going to go check into a motel. I can't stand this anymore.
AUSTIN   Don't go yet!
    [MOM *pauses.*]
MOM   I can't stay here. This is worse than being homeless.
AUSTIN   I'll get everything fixed up for you, Mom. I promise. Just stay for a while.
MOM   [*picking up luggage*]   You're going to the desert.
AUSTIN   Just wait!
    [LEE *thrashes*, AUSTIN *subdues him*, MOM *watches holding luggage, pause.*]
MOM   It was the worst feeling being up there. In Alaska. Staring out a window. I never felt so desperate before. That's why when I saw that article on Picasso I thought—
AUSTIN   Stay here, Mom. This is where you live.
    [*She looks around the stage.*]
MOM   I don't recognize it at all.
    [*She exits with luggage*, AUSTIN *makes a move toward her but* LEE *starts to struggle and* AUSTIN *subdues him again with cord, pause.*]
AUSTIN   [*holding cord*]   Lee? I'll make ya' a deal. You let me get outa' here. Just let me get to my car. All right, Lee? Gimme a little headstart and I'll turn you loose. Just gimme a little headstart. All right?
    [LEE *makes no response*, AUSTIN *slowly releases tension cord, still nothing from* LEE.]
AUSTIN   Lee?
    [LEE *is motionless*, AUSTIN *very slowly begins to stand, still keeping a tenuous hold on the cord and his eyes riveted to* LEE *for any sign of movement*, AUSTIN *slowly drops the cord and stands, he stares down at* LEE *who appears to be dead.*]
AUSTIN   [*whispers*]   Lee?
    [*Pause*, AUSTIN *considers, looks toward exit, back to* LEE, *then makes a small movement as if to leave. Instantly* LEE *is on his feet and moves toward exit, blocking* AUSTIN's *escape. They square off to each other, keeping a distance between them. Pause, a single coyote heard in distance, lights fade softly into moonlight, the figures of the brothers now appear to be caught in a vast desert-like landscape, they are very still but watchful for the next move, lights go slowly to black as the afterimage of the brothers pulses in the dark, coyote fades.*]

1980

LOUISE GLÜCK
b. 1943

" I was born to a vocation: / to bear witness / to the great mysteries," Louise Glück writes in "Parados." Apparently, she took the vocation of poet seriously from a young age. As a child, asked by a friend's mother to recite a poem she had written for an assignment, Glück readily complied: "My special triumph with this poem," she recounts in her essay "The Education of the Poet," "had involved a metrical inversion in the last line (not that I called it that), an omission of the final rhyme: to my ear it was exhilarating, a kind of explosion of form." The friend's mother congratulated her: "'a very good poem,' she said, 'right until the last line,' which she then proceeded to rearrange aloud into the order I had explicitly intended to violate. 'You see,' she told me, 'all that was missing was that last rhyme.' I was furious" (*Proofs and Theories*, 1994). In part this portrait of a superior, knowing child anticipates the oracular, prophetic tone we sometimes hear in Glück's work. As with the declaration "I was born to a vocation," the poet seems elevated from the ordinary world and set apart by her knowledge. At the same time Glück's childhood memory suggests what she has elsewhere called "the mandarin in my nature which would have to be checked," which is to say, her exceptional intelligence had to be schooled in common experience; she had to learn to identify with rather than to separate herself from others. The lesson of such schooling, enacted in some of Glück's best poems, such as the sequence "October," is this: what makes the poet exceptional is her ability to render the representative experience she also recognizes as her own.

Glück's work illuminates with particular power the mysteries of those utterly common experiences, pain and loss. The title of Glück's first collection of poetry, *Firstborn* (1968), refers to two firstborn children: a sister who died as an infant before Glück was born, and the poet, the older of two surviving sisters. "I have always been, in one way or another, obsessed with sisters, the dead and the living both," she writes in "Death and Absences." Glück saw herself as the dead sister's substitute; at the same time, she says, "I took on the guilty responsibility of the survivor." Although in her early volumes—*Firstborn, The House on Marshland* (1975), *Descending Figure* (1980), and *The Triumph of Achilles* (1985)—the traces of autobiography are distanced and mythic, much of Glück's work revisits the lost sister and explores the poet's feelings of grief and insufficiency. Few contemporary poets have registered so powerfully the self's compulsive efforts, inevitably failing, to become invulnerable to loss and absence, though her mythic transformations of biography can be compared to the work of Sylvia Plath and the early Stanley Kunitz, and her articulation of pain has an affinity with the poems of Frank Bidart.

Nevertheless, Glück has always refused any easy equation of art with personal experience (one of her essays is titled "Against Sincerity"), and it is therefore striking that in an essay on her education as a poet she gives a remarkably acute account of her struggle with anorexia, which came to a crisis when she was sixteen. This struggle, she writes, was shaped by a terror of "incompleteness and ravenous need" and by the concomitant desire to appear "completely free of all forms of dependency, to appear complete, self-contained." She was saved from dying, she believes, by psychoanalysis ("analysis taught me to think") and by her experience at the School of General Studies at Columbia, which she entered at eighteen. Her teachers, Leonie Adams and Stanley Kunitz, provided her work with "the steady application of scrutiny." Glück's poetry demonstrates that she took the lesson of this scrutiny and trained it on herself and her world. The intensity of perception in her poems—whether of an infant son, a father's gesture of good-bye, or her own childhood portrait—can be startling.

Her poetry is often impatient with the transitory and hungry for the unchanging—the "blue and permanent" water of "The Drowned Children," the eternal world that stands in implicit contrast to earthly loss and change (the blighted tomato plants in "Vespers"). In this regard she shares the "religious mind" she describes in her essay on T. S. Eliot, the mind that craves "what is final, immutable" and "cannot sustain itself on matter and process." But the impulse of "repulsion" toward the physical world F. R. Leavis once noted in Eliot is countered in Glück by an engagement with complex family relations and with the beauty of the natural world. Her collection *The Wild Iris* (1992), a series of flower poems spoken to and by a divinity, expresses the longing for what is eternal and an arresting sense of the earth's transient loveliness. In *The Meadowlands* (1996) the warring parties in an unraveling marriage (they are modeled on characters in the *Odyssey*) are depicted in wickedly comic tones.

Glück has sought to vary her stylistic habits and preoccupations from one book to another ("Each book I've written has culminated in a conscious diagnostic act, a swearing off"). Clearly the child exulting in a metrical inversion anticipates Glück's lifelong attention to and experiment with form. While her work provides some haunting and resonant images, the resources of syntax generate much of her poems' power. Glück's sentences are muscles of perception, capable of complex extension and retraction, at times unwinding in a stanza to bring together opposing forces or experiences (like authority and woundedness, or the timeless and the transient). Her work moves, in varying degrees from poem to poem, between syntactical control and giving way (what she has called "abandon"). Sometimes her complex sentences spill forward from one clause into another, but line breaks or the beginning of a new sentence midline interrupt this motion, giving her work the consistent sense of something incomplete, clipped off, unsaid (she shares this quality with her predecessors George Oppen and Emily Dickinson). At other times, as in parts of her sequence "October," Glück's equation of the sentence with the line ("It does me no good; violence has changed me") has an authoritative tone and declarative control simultaneously undermined by the way one sentence is laid against another without transition or copula. Characteristically for this poet, the pressure of what is unsaid fills the spaces between sentences, between lines, and between stanzas. The distinctive voice we hear in Glück—part oracle, part acute observer, part hapless participant in the rush of feeling and experience—often arises from the way her poems (like certain of Dickinson's) move between statement and mystery, between words and silences. Her response to the events of September 11, 2001, in "October," displays all of these qualities.

Glück teaches at Williams College in Massachusetts. She received the 1993 Pulitzer Prize for *The Wild Iris* and the PEN Award for her indispensible collection of essays on poetic vocation, *Proofs and Theories* (1994). More recent volumes include *Vita Nova* (1999), *The Seven Ages* (2001) *Averno* (2006), and *A Village Life* (2009). Glück received the Bollingen Prize for poetry in 2001.

The Drowned Children

You see, they have no judgment.
So it is natural that they should drown,
first the ice taking them in
and then, all winter, their wool scarves
floating behind them as they sink
until at last they are quiet.
And the pond lifts them in its manifold dark arms.

5

But death must come to them differently,
so close to the beginning.
As though they had always been   10
blind and weightless. Therefore
the rest is dreamed, the lamp,
the good white cloth that covered the table,
their bodies.

And yet they hear the names they used   15
like lures slipping over the pond:
What are you waiting for
come home, come home, lost
in the waters, blue and permanent.

1980

From Descending Figure[1]

2 *The Sick Child*

—Rijksmuseum[2]

A small child
is ill, has wakened.
It is winter, past midnight   20
in Antwerp.[3] Above a wooden chest,
the stars shine.
And the child
relaxes in her mother's arms.
The mother does not sleep;   25
she stares
fixedly into the bright museum.
By spring the child will die.
Then it is wrong, wrong
to hold her—   30
Let her be alone,
without memory, as the others wake
terrified, scraping the dark
paint from their faces.

3 *For My Sister*

Far away my sister is moving in her crib.   35
The dead ones are like that,
always the last to quiet.

Because, however long they lie in the earth,
they will not learn to speak

1. Printed here are parts 2 and 3 of the three-part sequence.
2. The national museum of the Netherlands, in Amsterdam.
3. A city in Belgium.

but remain uncertainly pressing against the wooden bars,   40
so small the leaves hold them down.

Now, if she had a voice,
the cries of hunger would be beginning.
I should go to her;
perhaps if I sang very softly,   45
her skin so white,
her head covered with black feathers. . . .

          1980

Appearances

When we were children, my parents had our portraits painted,
then hung them side by side, over the mantel,
where we couldn't fight.
I'm the dark one, the older one. My sister's blond,
the one who looks angry because she can't talk.   5

It never bothered me, not talking.
That hasn't changed much. My sister's still blond, not different
from the portrait. Except we're adults now, we've been analyzed:
we understand our expressions.

My mother tried to love us equally,   10
dressed us in the same dresses; she wanted us
perceived as sisters.
That's what she wanted from the portraits:
you need to see them hanging together, facing one another—
separated, they don't make the same statement.   15
You wouldn't know what the eyes were fixed on;
they'd seem to be staring into space.

This was the summer we went to Paris, the summer I was seven.
Every morning, we went to the convent.
Every afternoon, we sat still, having the portraits painted,   20
wearing green cotton dresses, the square neck marked with a ruffle.
Monsieur Davanzo added the flesh tones: my sister's ruddy; mine, faintly
    bluish.
To amuse us, Madame Davanzo hung cherries over our ears.

It was something I was good at: sitting still, not moving.
I did it to be good, to please my mother, to distract her from the child that
    died.   25
I wanted to be child enough. I'm still the same,
like a toy that can stop and go, but not change direction.

Anyone can love a dead child, love an absence.
My mother's strong; she doesn't do what's easy.

She's like her mother: she believes in family, in order.　　　　　30
She doesn't change her house, just freshens the paint occasionally.
Sometimes something breaks, gets thrown away, but that's all.
She likes to sit there, on the blue couch, looking up at her daughters,
at the two who lived. She can't remember how it really was,
how anytime she ministered to one child, loved that child,　　　　35
she damaged the other. You could say
she's like an artist with a dream, a vision.
Without that, she'd have been torn apart.
We were like the portraits, always together: you had to shut out one child
　　　to see the other.　　　　40
That's why only the painter noticed: a face already so controlled, so
　　　withdrawn,
and too obedient, the clear eyes saying
If you want me to be a nun, I'll be a nun.

　　　　　　　　　　　　　　　　　　　　　1990

Vespers[1]

In your extended absence, you permit me
use of earth, anticipating
some return on investment. I must report
failure in my assignment, principally
regarding the tomato plants.　　　　　　5
I think I should not be encouraged to grow
tomatoes. Or, if I am, you should withhold
the heavy rains, the cold nights that come
so often here, while other regions get
twelve weeks of summer. All this　　　　10
belongs to you: on the other hand,
I planted the seeds, I watched the first shoots
like wings tearing the soil, and it was my heart
broken by the blight, the black spot so quickly
multiplying in the rows. I doubt　　　　15
you have a heart, in our understanding of
that term. You who do not discriminate
between the dead and the living, who are, in consequence,
immune to foreshadowing, you may not know
how much terror we bear, the spotted leaf,　　　　20
the red leaves of the maple falling
even in August, in early darkness: I am responsible
for these vines.

　　　　　　　　　　　　　　　　　　　　　1992

---

1. Evening prayers. Also, the sixth and next to last of the canonical hours, whose office of prayer services is said before nightfall in, e.g., a Roman Catholic monastery.

October

1

Is it winter again, is it cold again,
didn't Frank just slip on the ice,
didn't he heal, weren't the spring seeds planted

didn't the night end,
didn't the melting ice
flood the narrow gutters   5

wasn't my body
rescued, wasn't it safe

didn't the scar form, invisible
above the injury   10

terror and cold,
didn't they just end, wasn't the back garden
harrowed and planted—

I remember how the earth felt, red and dense,
in stiff rows, weren't the seeds planted,   15
didn't vines climb the south wall

I can't hear your voice
for the wind's cries, whistling over the bare ground

I no longer care
what sound it makes   20

when was I silenced, when did it first seem
pointless to describe that sound

what it sounds like can't change what it is—

didn't the night end, wasn't the earth
safe when it was planted   25

didn't we plant the seeds,
weren't we necessary to the earth,

the vines, were they harvested?

2

Summer after summer has ended,
balm after violence: 30
it does me no good
to be good to me now;
violence has changed me.

Daybreak. The low hills shine
ochre and fire, even the fields shine.   35
I know what I see; sun that could be
the August sun, returning
everything that was taken away—

You hear this voice? This is my mind's voice;
you can't touch my body now.   40
It has changed once, it has hardened,
don't ask it to respond again.

A day like a day in summer.
Exceptionally still. The long shadows of the maples
nearly mauve on the gravel paths.   45
And in the evening, warmth. Night like a night in summer.

It does me no good; violence has changed me.
My body has grown cold like the stripped fields;
now there is only my mind, cautious and wary,
with the sense it is being tested.   50

Once more, the sun rises as it rose in summer;
bounty, balm after violence.
Balm after the leaves have changed, after the fields
have been harvested and turned.

Tell me this is the future,   55
I won't believe you.
Tell me I'm living,
I won't believe you.

                                       3

Snow had fallen. I remember
music from an open window.   60

Come to me, said the world.
This is not to say
it spoke in exact sentences
but that I perceived beauty in this manner.

Sunrise. A film of moisture   65
on each living thing. Pools of cold light
formed in the gutters.

I stood
at the doorway,
ridiculous as it now seems.   70

What others found in art,
I found in nature. What others found

in human love, I found in nature.
Very simple. But there was no voice there.

Winter was over. In the thawed dirt,   75
bits of green were showing.

Come to me, said the world. I was standing
in my wool coat at a kind of bright portal—
I can finally say
long age; it gives me considerable pleasure. Beauty   80
the healer, the teacher—

death cannot harm me
more than you have harmed me,
my beloved life.

4

The light has changed;   85
middle C^1 is tuned darker now.
And the songs of morning sound over-rehearsed.

This is the light of autumn, not the light of spring.
The light of autumn: *you will not be spared.*

The songs have changed; the unspeakable   90
has entered them.

This is the light of autumn, not the light that says
I am reborn.

Not the spring dawn: *I strained, I suffered, I was delivered.*
This is the present, an allegory of waste.   95

So much has changed. And still, you are fortunate:
the ideal burns in you like a fever.
Or not like a fever, like a second heart.

The songs have changed, but really they are still quite beautiful.
They have been concentrated in a smaller space, the space of the mind. 100
They are dark, now, with desolation and anguish.

And yet the notes recur. They hover oddly
in anticipation of silence.
The ear gets used to them.
The eye gets used to them.   105
The eye gets used to disappearances.

---

1. A tone represented by the note "C," located on the grand staff between the bass and treble clefs, the middle of the piano keyboard; the piano key used as a reference for all other notes.

You will not be spared, nor will what you love be spared.

A wind has come and gone, taking apart the mind;
it has left in its wake a strange lucidity.

How privileged you are, to be still passionately   110
clinging to what you love;
the forfeit of hope has not destroyed you.

Maestoso, doloroso:[2]

This is the light of autumn; it has turned on us.
Surely it is a privilege to approach the end   115
still believing in something.

5

It is true there is not enough beauty in the world.
It is also true that I am not competent to restore it.
Neither is there candor, and here I may be of some use.

I am   120
at work, though I am silent.

The bland

misery of the world
bounds us on either side, an alley

lined with trees, we are   125

companions here, not speaking,
each with his own thoughts;

behind the trees, iron
gates of private houses,
the shuttered rooms   130

somehow deserted, abandoned,

as though it were the artist's
duty to create
hope, but out of what? what?

the word itself   135
false, a device to refute
perception—At the intersection,

2. Italian musical terms, directing the play of the music to have grand, dignified, majestic phrasing, and to carry a sorrowful, melancholy, plaintive tone.

ornamental lights of the season.

I was young here. Riding
the subway with my small book   140
as though to defend myself against

this same world:

you are not alone,
the poem said,
in the dark tunnel.   145

6

The brightness of the day becomes
the brightness of the night;
the fire becomes the mirror.

My friend the earth is bitter; I think
sunlight has failed her.   150
Bitter or weary, it is hard to say.

Between herself and the sun,
something has ended.
She wants, now, to be left alone;
I think we must give up   155
turning to her for affirmation.

Above the fields,
above the roofs of the village houses,
the brilliance that made all life possible
becomes the cold stars.   160

Lie still and watch:
they give nothing but ask nothing.

From within the earth's
bitter disgrace, coldness and barrenness

my friend the moon rises: 165
she is beautiful tonight, but when is she not beautiful?

2006

ALICE WALKER
b. 1944

O f the two daughters at odds over family heirlooms in the story "Everyday Use" (printed here), Alice Walker resembles each one. Like the burned Maggie, she spent a childhood even more limited than her family's rural poverty dictated, for as a little girl she was shot in the eye with a BB gun; the disfigurement plagued her until it was corrected during her college years. Like Dee, she was able to attend college—first Spelman College and then Sarah Lawrence College on a scholarship—and acquire urban sophistications from the North. Many of Walker's characters become adept in the new cultural language of Black Arts and black power to which the author contributed as a young writer—and all of them are subjected to the same dismay Dee's mother feels at having to rule against this daughter's wishes. Like the mother, therefore, Walker is given to seeing both sides of a situation; and when it comes to choosing between her characters' opposing positions, she tends to be critical of her own personality first and extremely sparing in her judgment of others.

From her native Eatonton, Georgia, Walker gained an understanding of the rural South. In her essay "Beyond the Peacock," Walker evaluates both the older white writer Flannery O'Connor, who lived in nearby Milledgeville, and the perspectives from which readers see the region and its heritage. Visitors to O'Connor's home, for example, often romanticize the house's handmade bricks; Walker points out that the slaves who made those bricks surely suffered in the process. As the educated child of sharecroppers, Walker can critically reexamine the myths in and around O'Connor's life while doing justice to the complexity of O'Connor's work.

After college Walker returned to the South, first to work in the Civil Rights Movement against segregation and then to teach at Jackson State College in Mississippi. Her first novel, *The Third Life of Grange Copeland* (1970), follows its protagonist through three generations of domestic experience. In *Meridian* (1976) Walker presents fragmentary recollections of the 1960s among characters trying to make sense of their recent past. This novel reflects many of the topics treated in the author's short-story collection, *In Love & Trouble* (1973), in which a range of African American women almost always have unhappy relationships with men. Walker's third novel, *The Color Purple* (1982), makes her strongest narrative statement, formulated from what she calls a "womanist" (as opposed to strictly feminist) perspective. This approach draws on the black folk expression "womanish," which in a mother-to-daughter context signifies a call to adult, mature, responsible (and courageous) behavior. Such behavior benefits women and men and is necessary, Walker argues, for the survival of all African Americans by keeping creativity alive. The plot and the style of *The Color Purple* show how this happens, as the young black woman Celie draws on her sister's letters (written from Africa) for her own letters to God. Though Celie's life by any other terms could be considered disastrous (including rape, incest, and the killing of her babies by her father, and both physical and psychological abuse by her husband), her actions and her ability to express herself give her status as an individual. To everyone who will listen, Celie says: "I am here."

Walker has continued to publish novels, short stories, poetry, and essays. In *The Same River Twice* (1996) she writes about how the filming of *The Color Purple* challenged and changed her life. As a sociocultural critic she has examined the atrocity of female genital mutilation in parts of Africa, also incorporating her conclusions in her novel *Possessing the Secret of Joy* (1992), and as a literary critic she has spoken for a richer and more complete understanding of Zora Neale Hurston, whose employment of folk materials in narrative anticipates Walker's. Throughout her career she has spoken about the need for strength from African American women, and her writing seeks workable models for such strength.

The following text is from *In Love & Trouble* (1973).

Everyday Use

For Your Grandmama

I will wait for her in the yard that Maggie and I made so clean and wavy yesterday afternoon. A yard like this is more comfortable than most people know. It is not just a yard. It is like an extended living room. When the hard clay is swept clean as a floor and the fine sand around the edges lined with tiny, irregular grooves, anyone can come and sit and look up into the elm tree and wait for the breezes that never come inside the house.

Maggie will be nervous until after her sister goes: she will stand hopelessly in corners, homely and ashamed of the burn scars down her arms and legs, eyeing her sister with a mixture of envy and awe. She thinks her sister has held life always in the palm of one hand, that "no" is a word the world never learned to say to her.

You've no doubt seen those TV shows where the child who has "made it" is confronted, as a surprise, by her own mother and father, tottering in weakly from backstage. (A pleasant surprise, of course: What would they do if parent and child came on the show only to curse out and insult each other?) On TV mother and child embrace and smile into each other's faces. Sometimes the mother and father weep, the child wraps them in her arms and leans across the table to tell how she would not have made it without their help. I have seen these programs.

Sometimes I dream a dream in which Dee and I are suddenly brought together on a TV program of this sort. Out of a dark and soft-seated limousine I am ushered into a bright room filled with many people. There I meet a smiling, gray, sporty man like Johnny Carson who shakes my hand and tells me what a fine girl I have. Then we are on the stage and Dee is embracing me with tears in her eyes. She pins on my dress a large orchid, even though she has told me once that she thinks orchids are tacky flowers.

In real life I am a large, big-boned woman with rough, man-working hands. In the winter I wear flannel nightgowns to bed and overalls during the day. I can kill and clean a hog as mercilessly as a man. My fat keeps me hot in zero weather. I can work outside all day, breaking ice to get water for washing; I can eat pork liver cooked over the open fire minutes after it comes steaming from the hog. One winter I knocked a bull calf straight in the brain between the eyes with a sledge hammer and had the meat hung up to chill before nightfall. But of course all this does not show on television. I am the way my daughter would want me to be: a hundred pounds lighter, my skin like an uncooked barley pancake. My hair glistens in the hot bright lights. Johnny Carson has much to do to keep up with my quick and witty tongue.

But that is a mistake. I know even before I wake up. Who ever knew a Johnson with a quick tongue? Who can even imagine me looking a strange white man in the eye? It seems to me I have talked to them always with one foot raised in flight, with my head turned in whichever way is farthest from them. Dee, though. She would always look anyone in the eye. Hesitation was no part of her nature.

"How do I look, Mama?" Maggie says, showing just enough of her thin body enveloped in pink skirt and red blouse for me to know she's there, almost hidden by the door.

"Come out into the yard," I say.

Have you ever seen a lame animal, perhaps a dog run over by some careless person rich enough to own a car, sidle up to someone who is ignorant enough to be kind to them? That is the way my Maggie walks. She has been like this, chin on chest, eyes on ground, feet in shuffle, ever since the fire that burned the other house to the ground.

Dee is lighter than Maggie, with nicer hair and a fuller figure. She's a woman now, though sometimes I forget. How long ago was it that the other house burned? Ten, twelve years? Sometimes I can still hear the flames and feel Maggie's arms sticking to me, her hair smoking and her dress falling off her in little black papery flakes. Her eyes seemed stretched open, blazed open by the flames reflected in them. And Dee. I see her standing off under the sweet gum tree she used to dig gum out of; a look of concentration on her face as she watched the last dingy gray board of the house fall in toward the red-hot brick chimney. Why don't you do a dance around the ashes? I'd wanted to ask her. She had hated the house that much.

I used to think she hated Maggie, too. But that was before we raised the money, the church and me, to send her to Augusta to school. She used to read to us without pity; forcing words, lies, other folks' habits, whole lives upon us two, sitting trapped and ignorant underneath her voice. She washed us in a river of make-believe, burned us with a lot of knowledge we didn't necessarily need to know. Pressed us to her with the serious way she read, to shove us away at just the moment, like dimwits, we seemed about to understand.

Dee wanted nice things. A yellow organdy dress to wear to her graduation from high school; black pumps to match a green suit she'd made from an old suit somebody gave me. She was determined to stare down any disaster in her efforts. Her eyelids would not flicker for minutes at a time. Often I fought off the temptation to shake her. At sixteen she had a style of her own: and knew what style was.

I never had an education myself. After second grade the school was closed down. Don't ask me why: in 1927 colored asked fewer questions than they do now. Sometimes Maggie reads to me. She stumbles along good-naturedly but can't see well. She knows she is not bright. Like good looks and money, quickness passed her by. She will marry John Thomas (who has mossy teeth in an earnest face) and then I'll be free to sit here and I guess just sing church songs to myself. Although I never was a good singer. Never could carry a tune. I was always better at a man's job. I used to love to milk till I was hooked in the side in '49. Cows are soothing and slow and don't bother you, unless you try to milk them the wrong way.

I have deliberately turned my back on the house. It is three rooms, just like the one that burned, except the roof is tin; they don't make shingle roofs any more. There are no real windows, just some holes cut in the sides, like the portholes in a ship, but not round and not square, with rawhide holding the shutters up on the outside. This house is in a pasture, too, like the other one. No doubt when Dee sees it she will want to tear it down. She wrote me once that no matter where we "choose" to live, she will manage to come see us. But she will never bring her friends. Maggie and I thought about this and Maggie asked me, "Mama, when did Dee ever *have* any friends?"

She had a few. Furtive boys in pink shirts hanging about on washday after school. Nervous girls who never laughed. Impressed with her they worshiped the well-turned phrase, the cute shape, the scalding humor that erupted like bubbles in lye. She read to them.

When she was courting Jimmy T she didn't have much time to pay to us, but turned all her faultfinding power on him. He *flew* to marry a cheap city girl from a family of ignorant flashy people. She hardly had time to recompose herself.

When she comes I will meet—but there they are!

Maggie attempts to make a dash for the house, in her shuffling way, but I stay her with my hand. "Come back here," I say. And she stops and tries to dig a well in the sand with her toe.

It is hard to see them clearly through the strong sun. But even the first glimpse of leg out of the car tells me it is Dee. Her feet were always neat-looking, as if God himself had shaped them with a certain style. From the other side of the car comes a short, stocky man. Hair is all over his head a foot long and hanging from his chin like a kinky mule tail. I hear Maggie suck in her breath. "Uhnnnh," is what it sounds like. Like when you see the wriggling end of a snake just in front of your foot on the road. "Uhnnnh."

Dee next. A dress down to the ground, in this hot weather. A dress so loud it hurts my eyes. There are yellows and oranges enough to throw back the light of the sun. I feel my whole face warming from the heat waves it throws out. Earrings gold, too, and hanging down to her shoulders. Bracelets dangling and making noises when she moves her arm up to shake the folds of the dress out of her armpits. The dress is loose and flows, and as she walks closer, I like it. I hear Maggie go "Uhnnnh" again. It is her sister's hair. It stands straight up like the wool on a sheep. It is black as night and around the edges are two long pigtails that rope about like small lizards disappearing behind her ears.

"Wa-su-zo-Tean-o!" she says, coming on in that gliding way the dress makes her move. The short stocky fellow with the hair to his navel is all grinning and he follows up with "Asalamalakim, my mother and sister!" He moves to hug Maggie but she falls back, right up against the back of my chair. I feel her trembling there and when I look up I see the perspiration falling off her chin.

"Don't get up," says Dee. Since I am stout it takes something of a push. You can see me trying to move a second or two before I make it. She turns, showing white heels through her sandals, and goes back to the car. Out she peeks next with a Polaroid. She stoops down quickly and lines up picture after picture of me sitting there in front of the house with Maggie cowering behind me. She never takes a shot without making sure the house is included. When a cow comes nibbling around the edge of the yard she snaps it and me and Maggie *and* the house. Then she puts the Polaroid in the back seat of the car, and comes up and kisses me on the forehead.

Meanwhile Asalamalakim is going through motions with Maggie's hand. Maggie's hand is as limp as a fish, and probably as cold, despite the sweat, and she keeps trying to pull it back. It looks like Asalamalakim wants to shake hands but wants to do it fancy. Or maybe he don't know how people shake hands. Anyhow, he soon gives up on Maggie.

"Well," I say. "Dee."

"No, Mama," she says. "Not 'Dee,' Wangero Leewanika Kemanjo!"

"What happened to 'Dee'?" I wanted to know.

"She's dead," Wangero said. "I couldn't bear it any longer, being named after the people who oppress me."

"You know as well as me you was named after your aunt Dicie," I said. Dicie is my sister. She named Dee. We called her "Big Dee" after Dee was born.

"But who was *she* named after?" asked Wangero.

"I guess after Grandma Dee," I said.

"And who was she named after?" asked Wangero.

"Her mother," I said, and saw Wangero was getting tired. "That's about as far back as I can trace it," I said. Though, in fact, I probably could have carried it back beyond the Civil War through the branches.

"Well," said Asalamalakim, "there you are."

"Uhnnnh," I heard Maggie say.

"There I was not," I said, "before 'Dicie' cropped up in our family, so why should I try to trace it that far back?"

He just stood there grinning, looking down on me like somebody inspecting a Model A car.[1] Every once in a while he and Wangero sent eye signals over my head.

"How do you pronounce this name?" I asked.

"You don't have to call me by it if you don't want to," said Wangero.

"Why shouldn't I?" I asked. "If that's what you want us to call you, we'll call you."

"I know it might sound awkward at first," said Wangero.

"I'll get used to it," I said. "Ream it out again."

Well, soon we got the name out of the way. Asalamalakim had a name twice as long and three times as hard. After I tripped over it two or three times he told me to just call him Hakim-a-barber. I wanted to ask him was he a barber, but I didn't really think he was, so I didn't ask.

"You must belong to those beef-cattle peoples down the road," I said. They said "Asalamalakim" when they met you, too, but they didn't shake hands. Always too busy: feeding the cattle, fixing the fences, putting up salt-lick shelters, throwing down hay. When the white folks poisoned some of the herd the men stayed up all night with rifles in their hands. I walked a mile and a half just to see the sight.

Hakim-a-barber said, "I accept some of their doctrines, but farming and raising cattle is not my style." (They didn't tell me, and I didn't ask, whether Wangero (Dee) had really gone and married him.)

---

1. Popular model of Ford automobile introduced in 1928.

We sat down to eat and right away he said he didn't eat collards and pork was unclean. Wangero, though, went on through the chitlins and corn bread, the greens and everything else. She talked a blue streak over the sweet potatoes. Everything delighted her. Even the fact that we still used the benches her daddy made for the table when we couldn't afford to buy chairs.

"Oh, Mama!" she cried. Then turned to Hakim-a-barber. "I never knew how lovely these benches are. You can feel the rump prints," she said, running her hands underneath her and along the bench. Then she gave a sigh and her hand closed over Grandma Dee's butter dish. "That's it!" she said. "I knew there was something I wanted to ask you if I could have." She jumped up from the table and went over in the corner where the churn stood, the milk in it clabber by now. She looked at the churn and looked at it.

"This churn top is what I need," she said. "Didn't Uncle Buddy whittle it out of a tree you all used to have?"

"Yes," I said.

"Uh huh," she said happily. "And I want the dasher, too."

"Uncle Buddy whittle that, too?" asked the barber.

Dee (Wangero) looked up at me.

"Aunt Dee's first husband whittled the dash," said Maggie so low you almost couldn't hear her. "His name was Henry, but they called him Stash."

"Maggie's brain is like an elephant's," Wangero said, laughing. "I can use the churn top as a centerpiece for the alcove table," she said, sliding a plate over the churn, "and I'll think of something artistic to do with the dasher."

When she finished wrapping the dasher the handle stuck out. I took it for a moment in my hands. You didn't even have to look close to see where hands pushing the dasher up and down to make butter had left a kind of sink in the wood. In fact, there were a lot of small sinks; you could see where thumbs and fingers had sunk into the wood. It was beautiful light yellow wood, from a tree that grew in the yard where Big Dee and Stash had lived.

After dinner Dee (Wangero) went to the trunk at the foot of my bed and started rifling through it. Maggie hung back in the kitchen over the dishpan. Out came Wangero with two quilts. They had been pieced by Grandma Dee and then Big Dee and me had hung them on the quilt frames on the front porch and quilted them. One was in the Lone Star pattern. The other was Walk Around the Mountain. In both of them were scraps of dresses Grandma Dee had worn fifty and more years ago. Bits and pieces of Grandpa Jarrell's Paisley shirts. And one teeny faded blue piece, about the size of a penny matchbox, that was from Great Grandpa Ezra's uniform that he wore in the Civil War.

"Mama," Wangero said sweet as a bird. "Can I have these old quilts?"

I heard something fall in the kitchen, and a minute later the kitchen door slammed.

"Why don't you take one or two of the others?" I asked. "These old things was just done by me and Big Dee from some tops your grandma pieced before she died."

"No," said Wangero. "I don't want those. They are stitched around the borders by machine."

"That'll make them last better," I said.

"That's not the point," said Wangero. "These are all pieces of dresses Grandma used to wear. She did all this stitching by hand. Imagine!" She held the quilts securely in her arms, stroking them.

"Some of the pieces, like those lavender ones, come from old clothes her mother handed down to her," I said, moving up to touch the quilts. Dee (Wangero) moved back just enough so that I couldn't reach the quilts. They already belonged to her.

"Imagine!" she breathed again, clutching them closely to her bosom.

"The truth is," I said, "I promised to give them quilts to Maggie, for when she marries John Thomas."

She gasped like a bee had stung her.

"Maggie can't appreciate these quilts!" she said. "She'd probably be backward enough to put them to everyday use."

"I reckon she would," I said. "God knows I been saving 'em for long enough with nobody using 'em. I hope she will!" I didn't want to bring up how I had offered Dee (Wangero) a quilt when she went away to college. Then she had told me they were old-fashioned, out of style.

"But they're *priceless!*" she was saying now, furiously; for she has a temper. "Maggie would put them on the bed and in five years they'd be in rags. Less than that!"

"She can always make some more," I said. "Maggie knows how to quilt."

Dee (Wangero) looked at me with hatred. "You just will not understand. The point is these quilts, *these* quilts!"

"Well," I said, stumped. "What would *you* do with them?"

"Hang them," she said. As if that was the only thing you *could* do with quilts.

Maggie by now was standing in the door. I could almost hear the sound her feet made as they scraped over each other.

"She can have them, Mama," she said, like somebody used to never winning anything, or having anything reserved for her. "I can 'member Grandma Dee without the quilts."

I looked at her hard. She had filled her bottom lip with checkerberry snuff and it gave her face a kind of dopey, hangdog look. It was Grandma Dee and Big Dee who taught her how to quilt herself. She stood there with her scarred hands hidden in the folds of her skirt. She looked at her sister with something like fear but she wasn't mad at her. This was Maggie's portion. This was the way she knew God to work.

When I looked at her like that something hit me in the top of my head and ran down to the soles of my feet. Just like when I'm in church and the spirit of God touches me and I get happy and shout. I did something I never had done before: hugged Maggie to me, then dragged her on into the room, snatched the quilts out of Miss Wangero's hands and dumped them into Maggie's lap. Maggie just sat there on my bed with her mouth open.

"Take one or two of the others," I said to Dee.

But she turned without a word and went out to Hakim-a-barber.

"You just don't understand," she said, as Maggie and I came out to the car. "What don't I understand?" I wanted to know.

"Your heritage," she said. And then she turned to Maggie, kissed her, and said, "You ought to try to make something of yourself, too, Maggie. It's really a new day for us. But from the way you and Mama still live you'd never know it."

She put on some sunglasses that hid everything above the tip of her nose and her chin.

Maggie smiled; maybe at the sunglasses. But a real smile, not scared. After we watched the car dust settle I asked Maggie to bring me a dip of snuff. And then the two of us sat there just enjoying, until it was time to go in the house and go to bed.

1973

AUGUST WILSON
1945–2005

In a preface to a collection of three August Wilson plays, their creator noted that "writing a play is for me like walking down the landscape of the self, unattended, unadorned, exploring what D. H. Lawrence called 'the dark forest of the soul.'" The evident sincerity, even solemnity, of this pronouncement indicates the heroic intensity with which Wilson conceived his artistic mission. That mission was nothing less than to provide a collective history of African American experience in the twentieth century. By centering his plays in different decades Wilson hoped to use them as chronicles on an epic scale of the conflicts, joys, and sufferings of black people—"Put them all together and you have a history," he said about his plays. His first successful one, *Ma Rainey's Black Bottom* (1984), is set in 1920s Chicago and deals with black jazz musicians, their relations with one another and between themselves and their white employers. *Fences* (1985), its successor, is set in Pittsburgh in 1957, where the tensions of a black family play themselves out in various disruptions on a smaller but no less intense scale than would be ushered in, the following decade, by what Wilson calls (referring to the civil rights activism of those years) "the hot winds of change." Subsequent plays explored other decades, but most of them are situated in Wilson's native Pittsburgh in a black section called The Hill.

Wilson dropped out of school in ninth grade and, therefore, conducted his own education, reading widely—especially African-American writers—and being particularly touched by Ralph Ellison and Langston Hughes. He founded a community theater called Black Horizon on the Hill and later began to write plays for another black theater in St. Paul, Minnesota. It was *Ma Rainey* that drew the attention of the director of Yale's Repertory Theater, Lloyd Richards, who produced it at Yale, then took it to Broadway. Richards henceforth became the director of Wilson's plays, first through staged readings at the Playwright's Conference, then through performances in New Haven and on Broadway. Wilson has written that one night in 1965 (he was twenty years old) he put on a Bessie Smith record and discovered the blues: at that moment, "the universe stuttered and everything fell to a new place." Like Bessie Smith, Ma Rainey was a legendary African-American singer, often regarded as the mother of the blues, and Wilson's play, set in a recording studio where the white producers and the black musicians are waiting for Ma to show up, explores tensions of race and sexuality. Like all his plays, it unfolds leisurely through characters who do little more than talk to each other. But out of this talk is eventually generated a moment of violent action, in the case of *Ma Rainey* the fatal stabbing of one of the musicians by his enraged cohort.

In response to the criticism that his plays are "talky," Wilson pointed out that an oral culture is central to the people he writes about, thus "the talk is the whole point." Most certainly, the talk is liveliest in Wilson when it is laced with humor and with the animus one character displays toward another. At times, in dramatizing a number of competing voices raised in harmony or disharmony, Wilson achieved something like an operatic feel to the conversation as the voices—instinct with the rhythms and language of black culture and black music—play against each other in satisfying orchestration (George Bernard Shaw was a master of such operatic effects).

Speaking of *Ma Rainey* and *Fences*, Wilson said that he was concerned in them with the idea of missed possibilities: "Music and sports were the traditional inroads for blacks," and for the protagonist in each play "even those inroads fail." The hero of *Fences*, perhaps Wilson's most engaging although least experimental play, is Troy Maxson whose color denied him a career in Major League Baseball (in Troy's prime as a player, baseball was still segregated). His stubborn dramatization of himself as a man who missed out on greatness puts him in conflict with both his wife and his son Cory, since Troy tries to repress Cory's potential career as a football star, believing that things haven't improved for black athletes. At certain moments in the play Troy rises to expressive arias in praise of himself as a heroic loser:

> Woman . . . I do the best I can do. I come in here every Friday. I carry a sack of potatoes and a bucket of lard. You all line up at the door with your hands out. I give you the lint from my pockets. I give you my sweat and blood. I ain't got no tears. I don't spend them. We go upstairs in that room at night . . . and I fall down on you and try to blast a hole into forever. I get up Monday morning . . . find my lunch on the table. I go out. Make my way. Find my strength to carry me through the next Friday.

One understands why *Fences* has been compared with Arthur Miller's *Death of a Salesman*. Both plays risk sentimentality in their underlining of the hero's plangent complaints, but at their best those complaints have idiomatic force and resonate with a true voice of feeling.

Wilson went on to write probably his most ambitious and difficult play, *Joe Turner's Come and Gone*, in which the occupants of a Pittsburgh boardinghouse in 1911 rehearse their individual stories, mainly ones of migrating from the South to the North. The most eloquently dark of these stories is that of Herald Loomis, who spent seven years in bondage to the bounty hunter Joe Turner. *Joe Turner* is usually called Wilson's most "poetic" drama, and the critic Frank Rich accurately pointed out that it was a "mixture of the well-made naturalistic boardinghouse drama and the mystical, non-Western theater of ritual and metaphor." The play is about secrets, about the tension between what can be expressed in words and what lies beyond them, inexpressible. In any case, the persistent presence of the vernacular, of folktales and dream visions, takes *Joe Turner* into a different realm from the naturalism of *Fences*. In Wilson's later plays he continued to experiment with this realm and to challenge his audience and his critics.

Fences[1]

CHARACTERS

TROY MAXSON

JIM BONO, TROY's friend

ROSE, TROY's wife

LYONS, TROY's oldest son by previous
marriage

GABRIEL, TROY's brother

CORY, TROY and ROSE's son

RAYNELL, TROY's daughter

Setting

The setting is the yard which fronts the only entrance to the MAXSON household, an ancient two-story brick house set back off a small alley in a big-city neighborhood. The entrance to the house is gained by two or three steps leading to a wooden porch badly in need of paint.

A relatively recent addition to the house and running its full width, the porch lacks congruence. It is a sturdy porch with a flat roof. One or two chairs of dubious value sit at one end where the kitchen window opens onto the porch. An old-fashioned icebox stands silent guard at the opposite end.

The yard is a small dirt yard, partially fenced, except for the last scene, with a wooden sawhorse, a pile of lumber, and other fence-building equipment set off to the side. Opposite is a tree from which hangs a ball made of rags. A baseball bat leans against the tree. Two oil drums serve as garbage receptacles and sit near the house at right to complete the setting.

The Play

Near the turn of the century, the destitute of Europe sprang on the city with tenacious claws and an honest and solid dream. The city devoured them. They swelled its belly until it burst into a thousand furnaces and sewing machines, a thousand butcher shops and bakers' ovens, a thousand churches and hospitals and funeral parlors and money-lenders. The city grew. It nourished itself and offered each man a partnership limited only by his talent, his guile, and his willingness and capacity for hard work. For the immigrants of Europe, a dream dared and won true.

The descendants of African slaves were offered no such welcome or participation. They came from places called the Carolinas and the Virginias, Georgia, Alabama, Mississippi, and Tennessee. They came strong, eager, searching. The city rejected them and they fled and settled along the riverbanks and under bridges in shallow, ramshackle houses made of sticks and tar-paper. They collected rags and wood. They sold the use of their muscles and their bodies. They cleaned houses and washed clothes, they shined shoes, and in quiet desperation and vengeful pride, they stole, and lived in pursuit of their own dream. That they could breathe free, finally, and stand to meet life with the force of dignity and whatever eloquence the heart could call upon.

By 1957, the hard-won victories of the European immigrants had solidified the industrial might of America. War had been confronted and won with new energies that used loyalty and patriotism as its fuel. Life was rich, full, and flourishing. The Milwaukee Braves won the World Series, and the hot winds of

1. The text is from the 4th printing of the NAL edition of the play (1994).

change that would make the sixties a turbulent, racing, dangerous, and pro-
vocative decade had not yet begun to blow full.

Act 1

SCENE 1

It is 1957. TROY *and* BONO *enter the yard, engaged in conversation.* TROY *is fifty-*
three years old, a large man with thick, heavy hands; it is this largeness that he
strives to fill out and make an accommodation with. Together with his blackness,
his largeness informs his sensibilities and the choices he has made in his life.

Of the two men, BONO *is obviously the follower. His commitment to their*
friendship of thirty-odd years is rooted in his admiration of troy's *honesty, capac-*
ity for hard work, and his strength, which BONO *seeks to emulate.*

It is Friday night, payday, and the one night of the week the two men engage in
a ritual of talk and drink. TROY *is usually the most talkative and at times he can*
be crude and almost vulgar, though he is capable of rising to profound heights of
expression. The men carry lunch buckets and wear or carry burlap aprons and
are dressed in clothes suitable to their jobs as garbage collectors.

BONO Troy, you ought to stop that lying!
TROY I ain't lying! The nigger had a watermelon this big. [*He indicates with*
  his hands.] Talking about . . . "What watermelon, Mr. Rand?" I liked to fell
  out! "What watermelon, Mr. Rand?" . . . And it sitting there big as life.
BONO What did Mr. Rand say?
TROY Ain't said nothing. Figure if the nigger too dumb to know he carrying a watermelon, he wasn't gonna get much sense out of him. Trying to
  hide that great big old watermelon under his coat. Afraid to let the
  white man see him carry it home.
BONO I'm like you . . . I ain't got no time for them kind of people.
TROY Now what he look like getting mad cause he see the man from the
  union talking to Mr. Rand?
BONO He come to me talking about . . . "Maxson gonna get us fired." I
  told him to get away from me with that. He walked away from me calling you a troublemaker. What Mr. Rand say?
TROY Ain't said nothing. He told me to go down the Commissioner's
  office next Friday. They called me down there to see them.
BONO Well, as long as you got your complaint filed, they can't fire you.
  That's what one of them white fellows tell me.
TROY I ain't worried about them firing me. They gonna fire me cause I
  asked a question? That's all I did. I went to Mr. Rand and asked him,
  "Why? Why you got the white mens driving and the colored lifting?"
  Told him, "what's the matter, don't I count? You think only white fellows
  got sense enough to drive a truck. That ain't no paper job! Hell, anybody
  can drive a truck. How come you got all whites driving and the colored
  lifting?" He told me "take it to the union." Well, hell, that's what I done!
  Now they wanna come up with this pack of lies.
BONO I told Brownie if the man come and ask him any questions . . . just
  tell the truth! It ain't nothing but something they done trumped up on
  you cause you filed a complaint on them.

TROY   Brownie don't understand nothing. All I want them to do is change the job description. Give everybody a chance to drive the truck. Brownie can't see that. He ain't got that much sense.

BONO   How you figure he be making out with that gal be up at Taylors' all the time . . . that Alberta gal?

TROY   Same as you and me. Getting just as much as we is. Which is to say nothing.

BONO   It is, huh? I figure you doing a little better than me . . . and I ain't saying what I'm doing.

TROY   Aw, nigger, look here . . . I know you. If you had got anywhere near that gal, twenty minutes later you be looking to tell somebody. And the first one you gonna tell . . . that you gonna want to brag to . . . is gonna be me.

BONO   I ain't saying that. I see where you be eyeing her.

TROY   I eye all the women. I don't miss nothing. Don't never let nobody tell you Troy Maxson don't eye the women.

BONO   You been doing more than eyeing her. You done bought her a drink or two.

TROY   Hell yeah, I bought her a drink! What that mean? I bought you one, too. What that mean cause I buy her a drink? I'm just being polite.

BONO   It's alright to buy her one drink. That's what you call being polite. But when you wanna be buying two or three . . . that's what you call eyeing her.

TROY   Look here, as long as you known me . . . you ever known me to chase after women?

BONO   Hell yeah! Long as I done known you. You forgetting I knew you when.

TROY   Naw, I'm talking about since I been married to Rose?

BONO   Oh, not since you been married to Rose. Now, that's the truth, there. I can say that.

TROY   Alright then! Case closed.

BONO   I see you be walking up around Alberta's house. You supposed to be at Taylors' and you be walking around there.

TROY   What you watching where I'm walking for? I ain't watching after you.

BONO   I seen you walking around there more than once.

TROY   Hell, you liable to see me walking anywhere! That don't mean nothing cause you see me walking around there.

BONO   Where she come from anyway? She just kinda showed up one day.

TROY   Tallahassee. You can look at her and tell she one of them Florida gals. They got some big healthy women down there. Grow them right up out the ground. Got a little bit of Indian in her. Most of them niggers down in Florida got some Indian in them.

BONO   I don't know about that Indian part. But she damn sure big and healthy. Woman wear some big stockings. Got them great big old legs and hips as wide as the Mississippi River.

TROY   Legs don't mean nothing. You don't do nothing but push them out of the way. But them hips cushion the ride!

BONO   Troy, you ain't got no sense.

TROY   It's the truth! Like you riding on Goodyears!

[ROSE *enters from the house. She is ten years younger than* TROY, *her devotion to him stems from her recognition of the possibilities of her life without him: a succession of abusive men and their babies, a life of partying and running the streets, the Church, or aloneness with its attendant pain and frustration. She recognizes* TROY's *spirit as a fine and illuminating one and she either ignores or forgives his faults, only some of which she recognizes. Though she doesn't drink, her presence is an integral part of the Friday night rituals. She alternates between the porch and the kitchen, where supper preparations are under way.*]

ROSE   What you all out here getting into?

TROY   What you worried about what we getting into for? This is men talk, woman.

ROSE   What I care what you all talking about? Bono, you gonna stay for supper?

BONO   No, I thank you, Rose. But Lucille say she cooking up a pot of pig-feet.

TROY   Pigfeet! Hell, I'm going home with you! Might even stay the night if you got some pigfeet. You got something in there to top them pigfeet, Rose?

ROSE   I'm cooking up some chicken. I got some chicken and collard greens.

TROY   Well, go on back in the house and let me and Bono finish what we was talking about. This is men talk. I got some talk for you later. You know what kind of talk I mean. You go on and powder it up.

ROSE   Troy Maxson, don't you start that now!

TROY   [*puts his arm around her*]   Aw, woman . . . come here. Look here, Bono . . . when I met this woman . . . I got out that place, say, "Hitch up my pony, saddle up my mare . . . there's a woman out there for me somewhere. I looked here. Looked there. Saw Rose and latched on to her." I latched on to her and told her—I'm gonna tell you the truth—I told her, "Baby, I don't wanna marry, I just wanna be your man." Rose told me . . . tell him what you told me, Rose.

ROSE   I told him if he wasn't the marrying kind, then move out the way so the marrying kind could find me.

TROY   That's what she told me. "Nigger, you in my way. You blocking the view! Move out the way so I can find me a husband." I thought it over two or three days. Come back—

ROSE   Ain't no two or three days nothing. You was back the same night.

TROY   Come back, told her . . . "Okay, baby . . . but I'm gonna buy me a banty rooster and put him out there in the backyard . . . and when he see a stranger come, he'll flap his wings and crow . . ." Look here, Bono, I could watch the front door by myself . . . it was that back door I was worried about.

ROSE   Troy, you ought not talk like that. Troy ain't doing nothing but tell-ing a lie.

TROY   Only thing is . . . when we first got married . . . forget the rooster . . . we ain't had no yard!

BONO   I hear you tell it. Me and Lucille was staying down there on Logan Street. Had two rooms with the outhouse in the back. I ain't mind the outhouse none. But when that goddamn wind blow through there in the winter . . . that's what I'm talking about! To this day I wonder why in the hell I ever stayed down there for six long years. But see, I didn't know I could do no better. I thought only white folks had inside toilets and things.

ROSE There's a lot of people don't know they can do no better than they doing now. That's just something you got to learn. A lot of folks still shop at Bella's.

TROY Ain't nothing wrong with shopping at Bella's. She got fresh food.

ROSE I ain't said nothing about if she got fresh food. I'm talking about what she charge. She charge ten cents more than the A&P.

TROY The A&P ain't never done nothing for me. I spends my money where I'm treated right. I go down to Bella, say, "I need a loaf of bread, I'll pay you on Friday." She give it to me. What sense that make when I got money to go and spend it somewhere else and ignore the person who done right by me? That ain't in the Bible.

ROSE We ain't talking about what's in the Bible. What sense it make to shop there when she overcharge?

TROY You shop where you want to. I'll do my shopping where the people been good to me.

ROSE Well, I don't think it's right for her to overcharge. That's all I was saying.

BONO Look here . . . I got to get on. Lucille going be raising all kind of hell.

TROY Where you going, nigger? We ain't finished this pint. Come here, finish this pint.

BONO Well, hell, I am . . . if you ever turn the bottle loose.

TROY [hands him the bottle] The only thing I say about the A&P is I'm glad Cory got that job down there. Help him take care of his school clothes and things. Gabe done moved out and things getting tight around here. He got that job. . . . He can start to look out for himself.

ROSE Cory done went and got recruited by a college football team.

TROY I told that boy about that football stuff. The white man ain't gonna let him get nowhere with that football. I told him when he first come to me with it. Now you come telling me he done went and got more tied up in it. He ought to go and get recruited in how to fix cars or something where he can make a living.

ROSE He ain't talking about making no living playing football. It's just something the boys in school do. They gonna send a recruiter by to talk to you. He'll tell you he ain't talking about making no living playing football. It's a honor to be recruited.

TROY It ain't gonna get him nowhere. Bono'll tell you that.

BONO If he be like you in the sports . . . he's gonna be alright. Ain't but two men ever played baseball as good as you. That's Babe Ruth and Josh Gibson. Them's the only two men ever hit more home runs than you.

TROY What it ever get me? Ain't got a pot to piss in or a window to throw it out of.

ROSE Times have changed since you was playing baseball, Troy. That was before the war. Times have changed a lot since then.

TROY How in hell they done changed?

ROSE They got lots of colored boys playing ball now. Baseball and football.

BONO You right about that, Rose. Times have changed, Troy. You just come along too early.

TROY There ought not never have been no time called too early! Now you take that fellow . . . what's that fellow they had playing right field for the Yankees back then? You know who I'm talking about, Bono. Used to play right field for the Yankees?

ROSE Selkirk?

TROY Selkirk! That's it! Man batting .269, understand? .269. What kind of sense that make? I was hitting .432 with thirty-seven home runs! Man batting .269 and playing right field for the Yankees! I saw Josh Gibson's daughter yesterday. She walking around with raggedy shoes on her feet. Now I bet you Selkirk's daughter ain't walking around with raggedy shoes on her feet. I bet you that!

ROSE They got a lot of colored baseball players now. Jackie Robinson was the first. Folks had to wait for Jackie Robinson.

TROY I done seen a hundred niggers play baseball better than Jackie Robinson. Hell, I know some teams Jackie Robinson couldn't even make! What you talking about Jackie Robinson. Jackie Robinson wasn't nobody. I'm talking about if you could play ball then they ought to have let you play. Don't care what color you were. Come telling me I come along too early. If you could play . . . then they ought to have let you play. [TROY *takes a long drink from the bottle.*]

ROSE You gonna drink yourself to death. You don't need to be drinking like that.

TROY Death ain't nothing. I done seen him. Done wrassled with him. You can't tell me nothing about death. Death ain't nothing but a fastball on the outside corner. And you know what I'll do to that! Lookee here, Bono . . . am I lying? You get one of them fastballs, about waist high, over the outside corner of the plate where you can get the meat of the bat on it . . . and good god! You can kiss it goodbye. Now, am I lying?

BONO Naw, you telling the truth there. I seen you do it.

TROY If I'm lying . . . that 450 feet worth of lying! [*Pause.*] That's all death is to me. A fastball on the outside corner.

ROSE I don't know why you want to get on talking about death.

TROY Ain't nothing wrong with talking about death. That's part of life. Everybody gonna die. You gonna die, I'm gonna die. Bono's gonna die. Hell, we all gonna die.

ROSE But you ain't got to talk about it. I don't like to talk about it.

TROY You the one brought it up. Me and Bono was talking about baseball . . . you tell me I'm gonna drink myself to death. Ain't that right, Bono? You know I don't drink this but one night out of the week. That's Friday night. I'm gonna drink just enough to where I can handle it. Then I cuts it loose. I leave it alone. So don't you worry about me drinking myself to death. 'Cause I ain't worried about Death. I done seen him. I done wrestled with him. Look here, Bono . . . I looked up one day and Death was marching straight at me. Like Soldiers on Parade! The Army of Death marching straight at me. The middle of July, 1941. It got real cold just like it be winter. It seem like Death himself reached out and touched me on the shoulder. He touch me just like I touch you. I got cold as ice and Death standing there grinning at me.

ROSE Troy, why don't you hush that talk.

TROY I say . . . "What you want, Mr. Death? You be wanting me? You done brought your army to be getting me?" I looked him dead in the eye. I wasn't fearing nothing. I was ready to tangle. Just like I'm ready to tangle now. The Bible say be ever vigilant. That's why I don't get but so drunk. I got to keep watch.

ROSE Troy was right down there in Mercy Hospital. You remember he had pneumonia? Laying there with a fever talking plumb out of his head.

TROY Death standing there staring at me . . . carrying that sickle in his hand. Finally he say, "You want bound over for another year?" See, just like that . . . "You want bound over for another year?" I told him, "Bound over hell! Let's settle this now!" It seem like he kinda fell back when I said that, and all the cold went out of me. I reached down and grabbed that sickle and threw it just as far as I could throw it . . . and me and him commenced to wrestling. We wrestled for three days and three nights. I can't say where I found the strength from. Every time it seemed like he was gonna get the best of me, I'd reach way down deep inside myself and find the strength to do him one better.

ROSE Every time Troy tell that story he find different ways to tell it. Different things to make up about it.

TROY I ain't making up nothing. I'm telling you the facts of what happened. I wrestled with Death for three days and three nights and I'm standing here to tell you about it. [Pause.] Alright. At the end of the third night we done weakened each other to where we can't hardly move. Death stood up, throwed on his robe . . . had him a white robe with a hood on it. He throwed on that robe and went off to look for his sickle. Say, "I'll be back." Just like that. "I'll be back." I told him, say, "Yeah, but . . . you gonna have to find me!" I wasn't no fool. I wasn't going looking for him. Death ain't nothing to play with. And I know he's gonna get me. I know I got to join his army . . . his camp followers. But as long as I keep my strength and see him coming . . . as long as I keep up my vigilance . . . he's gonna have to fight to get me. I ain't going easy.

BONO Well, look here, since you got to keep up your vigilance . . . let me have the bottle.

TROY Aw hell, I shouldn't have told you that part. I should have left out that part.

ROSE Troy be talking that stuff and half the time don't even know what he be talking about.

TROY Bono know me better than that.

BONO That's right. I know you. I know you got some Uncle Remus[2] in your blood. You got more stories than the devil got sinners.

TROY Aw hell, I done seen him too! Done talked with the devil.

ROSE Troy, don't nobody wanna be hearing all that stuff.

[LYONS *enters the yard from the street. Thirty-four years old,* TROY's *son by a previous marriage, he sports a neatly trimmed goatee, sport coat, white shirt, tieless and buttoned at the collar. Though he fancies himself*

---

2. Old slave and folk philosopher whose proverbs and stories were recorded by Joel Chandler Harris (1848–1908).

a musician, he is more caught up in the rituals and "idea" of being a musician than in the actual practice of the music. He has come to borrow money from TROY, and while he knows he will be successful, he is uncertain as to what extent his lifestyle will be held up to scrutiny and ridicule.]

LYONS   Hey, Pop.

TROY   What you come "Hey, Popping" me for?

LYONS   How you doing, Rose? [*He kisses her.*] Mr. Bono, how you doing?

BONO   Hey, Lyons . . . how you been?

TROY   He must have been doing alright. I ain't seen him around here last week.

ROSE   Troy, leave your boy alone. He come by to see you and you wanna start all that nonsense.

TROY   I ain't bothering Lyons. [*Offers him the bottle.*] Here . . . get you a drink. We got an understanding. I know why he come by to see me and he know I know.

LYONS   Come on, Pop . . . I just stopped by to say hi . . . see how you was doing.

TROY   You ain't stopped by yesterday.

ROSE   You gonna stay for supper, Lyons? I got some chicken cooking in the oven.

LYONS   No, Rose . . . thanks. I was just in the neighborhood and thought I'd stop by for a minute.

TROY   You was in the neighborhood alright, nigger. You telling the truth there. You was in the neighborhood cause it's my payday.

LYONS   Well, hell, since you mentioned it . . . let me have ten dollars.

TROY   I'll be damned! I'll die and go to hell and play blackjack with the devil before I give you ten dollars.

BONO   That's what I wanna know about . . . that devil you done seen.

LYONS   What . . . Pop done seen the devil? You too much, Pops.

TROY   Yeah, I done seen him. Talked to him too!

ROSE   You ain't seen no devil. I done told you that man ain't had nothing to do with the devil. Anything you can't understand, you want to call it the devil.

TROY   Look here, Bono . . . I went down to see Hertzberger about some furniture. Got three rooms for two-ninety-eight. That what it say on the radio. "Three rooms . . . two-ninety-eight." Even made up a little song about it. Go down there . . . man tell me I can't get no credit. I'm working every day and can't get no credit. What to do? I got an empty house with some raggedy furniture in it. Cory ain't got no bed. He's sleeping on a pile of rags on the floor. Working every day and can't get no credit. Come back here—Rose'll tell you—madder than hell. Sit down . . . try to figure what I'm gonna do. Come a knock on the door. Ain't been living here but three days. Who know I'm here? Open the door . . . devil standing there bigger than life. White fellow . . . got on good clothes and everything. Standing there with a clipboard in his hand. I ain't had to say nothing. First words come out of his mouth was . . . "I understand you need some furniture and can't get no credit." I liked to fell over. He say "I'll give you all the credit you want, but you got to pay the interest on it." I told him, "Give me three rooms worth and charge whatever you want." Next day a truck pulled up here and two men unloaded them three rooms. Man what drove the truck give me a book. Say send ten dollars, first of every month to the address in the book and everything will be alright. Say if I miss a payment the devil was coming back and it'll be hell to pay. That was fifteen years ago. To this day . . . the first of the month I send my ten dollars, Rose'll tell you.

ROSE Troy lying.

TROY I ain't never seen that man since. Now you tell me who else that could have been but the devil? I ain't sold my soul or nothing like that, you understand. Naw, I wouldn't have truck with the devil about nothing like that. I got my furniture and pays my ten dollars the first of the month just like clockwork.

BONO How long you say you been paying this ten dollars a month?

TROY Fifteen years!

BONO Hell, ain't you finished paying for it yet? How much the man done charged you.

TROY Aw hell, I done paid for it. I done paid for it ten times over! The fact is I'm scared to stop paying it.

ROSE Troy lying. We got that furniture from Mr. Glickman. He ain't paying no ten dollars a month to nobody.

TROY Aw hell, woman. Bono know I ain't that big a fool.

LYONS I was just getting ready to say . . . I know where there's a bridge for sale.

TROY Look here, I'll tell you this . . . it don't matter to me if he was the devil. It don't matter if the devil give credit. Somebody has got to give it.

ROSE It ought to matter. You going around talking about having truck with the devil . . . God's the one you gonna have to answer to. He's the one gonna be at the Judgment.

LYONS Yeah, well, look here, Pop . . . let me have that ten dollars. I'll give it back to you. Bonnie got a job working at the hospital.

TROY What I tell you, Bono? The only time I see this nigger is when he wants something. That's the only time I see him.

LYONS Come on, Pop, Mr. Bono don't want to hear all that. Let me have the ten dollars. I told you Bonnie working.

TROY What that mean to me? "Bonnie working." I don't care if she working. Go ask her for the ten dollars if she working. Talking about "Bonnie working." Why ain't you working?

LYONS Aw, Pop, you know I can't find no decent job. Where am I gonna get a job at? You know I can't get no job.

TROY I told you I know some people down there. I can get you on the rubbish if you want to work. I told you that the last time you came by here asking me for something.

LYONS Naw, Pop . . . thanks. That ain't for me. I don't wanna be carrying nobody's rubbish. I don't wanna be punching nobody's time clock.

TROY What's the matter, you too good to carry people's rubbish? Where you think that ten dollars you talking about come from? I'm just supposed to haul people's rubbish and give my money to you cause you too lazy to work. You too lazy to work and wanna know why you ain't got what I got.

ROSE What hospital Bonnie working at? Mercy?

LYONS She's down at Passavant working in the laundry.

TROY   I ain't got nothing as it is. I give you that ten dollars and I got to eat beans the rest of the week. Naw . . . you ain't getting no ten dollars here.

LYONS   You ain't got to be eating no beans. I don't know why you wanna say that.

TROY   I ain't got no extra money. Gabe done moved over to Miss Pearl's paying her the rent and things done got tight around here. I can't afford to be giving you every payday.

LYONS   I ain't asked you to give me nothing. I asked you to loan me ten dollars. I know you got ten dollars.

TROY   Yeah, I got it. You know why I got it? Cause I don't throw my money away out there in the streets. You living the fast life . . . wanna be a musician . . . running around in them clubs and things . . . then, you learn to take care of yourself. You ain't gonna find me going and asking nobody for nothing. I done spent too many years without.

LYONS   You and me is two different people, Pop.

TROY   I done learned my mistake and learned to do what's right by it. You still trying to get something for nothing. Life don't owe you nothing. You owe it to yourself. Ask Bono. He'll tell you I'm right.

LYONS   You got your way of dealing with the world . . . I got mine. The only thing that matters to me is the music.

TROY   Yeah, I can see that! It don't matter how you gonna eat . . . where your next dollar is coming from. You telling the truth there.

LYONS   I know I got to eat. But I got to live too. I need something that gonna help me to get out of the bed in the morning. Make me feel like I belong in the world. I don't bother nobody. I just stay with my music cause that's the only way I can find to live in the world. Otherwise there ain't no telling what I might do. Now I don't come criticizing you and how you live. I just come by to ask you for ten dollars. I don't wanna hear all that about how I live.

TROY   Boy, your mama did a hell of a job raising you.

LYONS   You can't change me, Pop. I'm thirty-four years old. If you wanted to change me, you should have been there when I was growing up. I come by to see you . . . ask for ten dollars and you want to talk about how I was raised. You don't know nothing about how I was raised.

ROSE   Let the boy have ten dollars, Troy.

TROY   [to LYONS]   What the hell you looking at me for? I ain't got no ten dollars. You know what I do with my money. [to ROSE.] Give him ten dollars if you want him to have it.

ROSE   I will. Just as soon as you turn it loose.

TROY   [handing ROSE the money]   There it is. Seventy-six dollars and forty-two cents. You see this, Bono? Now, I ain't gonna get but six of that back.

ROSE   You ought to stop telling that lie. Here, Lyons. [She hands him the money.]

LYONS   Thanks, Rose. Look . . . I got to run . . . I'll see you later.

TROY   Wait a minute. You gonna say, "thanks, Rose" and ain't gonna look to see where she got that ten dollars from? See how they do me, Bono?

LYONS   I know she got it from you, Pop. Thanks. I'll give it back to you.

TROY   There he go telling another lie. Time I see that ten dollars . . . he'll be owing me thirty more.

LYONS   See you, Mr. Bono.

BONO   Take care, Lyons!

LYONS   Thanks, Pop. I'll see you again. [LYONS *exits the yard.*]

TROY   I don't know why he don't go and get him a decent job and take care of that woman he got.

BONO   He'll be alright, Troy. The boy is still young.

TROY   The *boy* is thirty-four years old.

ROSE   Let's not get off into all that.

BONO   Look here . . . I got to be going. I got to be getting on. Lucille gonna be waiting.

TROY   [*puts his arm around* ROSE]   See this woman, Bono? I love this woman. I love this woman so much it hurts. I love her so much . . . I done run out of ways of loving her. So I got to go back to basics. Don't you come by my house Monday morning talking about time to go to work . . . 'cause I'm still gonna be stroking!

ROSE   Troy! Stop it now!

BONO   I ain't paying him no mind, Rose. That ain't nothing but gin-talk. Go on, Troy. I'll see you Monday.

TROY   Don't you come by my house, nigger! I done told you what I'm gonna be doing.

[*The lights go down to black.*]

SCENE 2

The lights come up on ROSE *hanging up clothes. She hums and sings softly to herself. It is the following morning.*

> [ROSE *sings*]
> Jesus, be a fence all around me every day
> Jesus, I want you to protect me as I travel on my way.
> Jesus, be a fence all around me every day.
> [TROY *enters from the house.*]
> [ROSE *(continued)*]
> Jesus, I want you to protect me
> As I travel on my way.
> [*To* TROY]

'Morning. You ready for breakfast? I can fix it soon as I finish hanging up these clothes?

TROY   I got the coffee on. That'll be alright. I'll just drink some of that this morning.

ROSE   That 651 hit yesterday. That's the second time this month. Miss Pearl hit for a dollar . . . seem like those that need the least always get lucky. Poor folks can't get nothing.

TROY   Them numbers don't know nobody. I don't know why you fool with them. You and Lyons both.

ROSE   It's something to do.

TROY   You ain't doing nothing but throwing your money away.

ROSE   Troy, you know I don't play foolishly. I just play a nickel here and a nickel there.

TROY   That's two nickels you done thrown away.

ROSE   Now I hit sometimes . . . that makes up for it. It always comes in handy when I do hit. I don't hear you complaining then.

TROY   I ain't complaining now. I just say it's foolish. Trying to guess out of six hundred ways which way the number gonna come. If I had all the money niggers, these Negroes, throw away on numbers for one week— just one week—I'd be a rich man.

ROSE   Well, you wishing and calling it foolish ain't gonna stop folks from playing numbers. That's one thing for sure. Besides . . . some good things come from playing numbers. Look where Pope done bought him that restaurant off of numbers.

TROY   I can't stand niggers like that. Man ain't had two dimes to rub together. He walking around with his shoes all run over bumming money for cigarettes. Alright. Got lucky there and hit the numbers . . .

ROSE   Troy, I know all about it.

TROY   Had good sense, I'll say that for him. He ain't throwed his money away. I seen niggers hit the numbers and go through two thousand dollars in four days. Man brought him that restaurant down there . . . fixed it up real nice . . . and then didn't want nobody to come in it! A Negro go in there and can't get no kind of service. I seen a white fellow come in there and order a bowl of stew. Pope picked all the meat out the pot for him. Man ain't had nothing but a bowl of meat! Negro come behind him and ain't got nothing but the potatoes and carrots. Talking about what numbers do for people, you picked a wrong example. Ain't done nothing but make a worser fool out of him than he was before.

ROSE   Troy, you ought to stop worrying about what happened at work yesterday.

TROY   I ain't worried. Just told me to be down there at the Commissioner's office on Friday. Everybody think they gonna fire me. I ain't worried about them firing me. You ain't got to worry about that [*Pause.*] Where's Cory? Cory in the house? [*Calls*] Cory?

ROSE   He gone out.

TROY   Out, huh? He gone out 'cause he know I want him to help me with this fence. I know how he is. That boy scared of work.

        [GABRIEL *enters. He comes halfway down the alley and, hearing* TROY's *voice, stops.*]

TROY [*continues*]   He ain't done a lick of work in his life.

ROSE   He had to go to football practice. Coach wanted them to get in a little extra practice before the season start.

TROY   I got his practice . . . running out of here before he get his chores done.

ROSE   Troy, what is wrong with you this morning? Don't nothing set right with you. Go on back in there and go to bed . . . get up on the other side.

TROY   Why something got to be wrong with me? I ain't said nothing wrong with me.

ROSE   You got something to say about everything. First it's the numbers . . . then it's the way the man runs his restaurant . . . then you done got on Cory. What's it gonna be next? Take a look up there and see if the weather suits you . . . or is it gonna be how you gonna put up the fence with the clothes hanging in the yard.

TROY   You hit the nail on the head then.

ROSE I know you like I know the back of my hand. Go on in there and get you some coffee . . . see if that straighten you up. 'Cause you ain't right this morning.

[TROY *starts into the house and sees* GABRIEL. GABRIEL *starts singing.* TROY's *brother, he is seven years younger than* TROY. *Injured in World War II, he has a metal plate in his head. He carries an old trumpet tied around his waist and believes with every fiber of his being that he is the Archangel Gabriel. He carries a chipped basket with an assortment of discarded fruits and vegetables he has picked up in the strip district and which he attempts to sell.*]

[GABRIEL *singing.*]

Yes ma'am, I got plums
You ask me how I sell them
Oh ten cents apiece
Three for a quarter
Come and buy now
'Cause I'm here today
And tomorrow I'll be gone

[GABRIEL *enters.*]

GABRIEL Hey, Rose!

ROSE How you doing, Gabe?

GABRIEL There's Troy . . . Hey, Troy!

TROY Hey, Gabe. [*Exit into kitchen.*]

ROSE [*to* GABRIEL] What you got there?

GABRIEL You know what I got, Rose. I got fruits and vegetables.

ROSE [*looking in basket*] Where's all these plums you talking about?

GABRIEL I ain't got no plums today, Rose. I was just singing that. Have some tomorrow. Put me in a big order for plums. Have enough plums tomorrow for St. Peter and everybody. [TROY *re-enters from kitchen, crosses to steps. To* ROSE.] Troy's mad at me.

TROY I ain't mad at you. What I got to be mad at you about? You ain't done nothing to me.

GABRIEL I just moved over to Miss Pearl's to keep out from in your way. I ain't mean no harm by it.

TROY Who said anything about that? I ain't said anything about that.

GABRIEL You ain't mad at me, is you?

TROY Naw . . . I ain't mad at you, Gabe. If I was mad at you I'd tell you about it.

GABRIEL Got me two rooms. In the basement. Got my own door too. Wanna see my key? [*He holds up a key.*] That's my own key! Ain't nobody else got a key like that. That's my key! My two rooms!

TROY Well, that's good, Gabe. You got your own key . . . that's good.

ROSE You hungry, Gabe? I was just fixing to cook Troy his breakfast.

GABRIEL I'll take some biscuits. You got some biscuits? Did you know when I was in heaven . . . every morning me and St. Peter would sit down by the gate and eat some big fat biscuits? Oh, yeah! We had us a good time. We'd sit there and eat us them biscuits and then St. Peter would go off to sleep and tell me to wake him up when it's time to open the gates for the judgment.

942 | AUGUST WILSON

ROSE   Well, come on . . . I'll make up a batch of biscuits. [ROSE *exits into the house.*]

GABRIEL   Troy . . . St. Peter got your name in the book. I seen it. It say . . . Troy Maxson. I say . . . I know him! He got the same name like what I got. That's my brother!

TROY   How many times you gonna tell me that, Gabe?

GABRIEL   Ain't got my name in the book. Don't have to have my name. I done died and went to heaven. He got your name though. One morning St. Peter was looking at his book . . . marking it up for the judgment . . . and he let me see your name. Got it in there under M. Got Rose's name . . . I ain't seen it like I seen yours . . . but I know it's in there. He got a great big book. Got everybody's name what was ever been born. That's what he told me. But I seen your name. Seen it with my own eyes.

TROY   Go on in the house there. Rose going to fix you something to eat.

GABRIEL   Oh, I ain't hungry. I done had breakfast with Aunt Jemimah. She come by and cooked me up a whole mess of flapjacks. Remember how we used to eat them flapjacks?

TROY   Go on in the house and get you something to eat now.

GABRIEL   I got to go sell my plums. I done sold some tomatoes. Got me two quarters. Wanna see? [*He shows* TROY *his quarters.*] I'm gonna save them and buy me a new horn so St. Peter can hear me when it's time to open the gates. [GABRIEL *stops suddenly. Listens.*] Hear that? That's the hell-hounds. I got to chase them out of here. Go on get out of here! Get out!

[GABRIEL *exits singing.*]

Better get ready for the judgment
Better get ready for the judgment
My lord is coming down

[ROSE *enters from the house.*]

TROY   He gone off somewhere.

GABRIEL [*offstage*]

Better get ready for the judgment
Better get ready for the judgment morning
Better get ready for the judgment
My God is coming down.

ROSE   He ain't eating right. Miss Pearl say she can't get him to eat nothing.

TROY   What you want me to do about it, Rose? I done did everything I can for the man. I can't make him get well. Man got half his head blown away . . . what you expect?

ROSE   Seem like something ought to be done to help him.

TROY   Man don't bother nobody. He just mixed up from that metal plate he got in his head. Ain't no sense for him to go back into the hospital.

ROSE   Least he be eating right. They can help him take care of himself.

TROY   Don't nobody wanna be locked up, Rose. What you wanna lock him up for? Man go over there and fight the war . . . messin' around with them Japs, get half his head blown off . . . and they give him a lousy three thousand dollars. And I had to swoop down on that.

ROSE   Is you fixing to go into that again?

TROY   That's the only way I got a roof over my head . . . cause of that metal plate.

ROSE Ain't no sense you blaming yourself for nothing. Gabe wasn't in no condition to manage that money. You done what was right by him. Can't nobody say you ain't done what was right by him. Look how long you took care of him . . . till he wanted to have his own place and moved over there with Miss Pearl.

TROY That ain't what I'm saying, woman! I'm just stating the facts. If my brother didn't have that metal plate in his head . . . I wouldn't have a pot to piss in or a window to throw it out of. And I'm fifty-three years old. Now see if you can understand that! [TROY *gets up from the porch and starts to exit the yard.*]

ROSE Where you going off to? You been running out of here every Saturday for weeks. I thought you was gonna work on this fence?

TROY I'm gonna walk down to Taylors'. Listen to the ball game. I'll be back in a bit. I'll work on it when I get back.
[*He exits the yard. The lights go to black.*]

SCENE 3

The lights come up on the yard. It is four hours later. ROSE *is taking down the clothes from the line.* CORY *enters carrying his football equipment.*

ROSE Your daddy liked to had a fit with you running out of here this morning without doing your chores.

CORY I told you I had to go to practice.

ROSE He say you were supposed to help him with this fence.

CORY He been saying that the last four or five Saturdays, and then he don't never do nothing, but go down to Taylors'. Did you tell him about the recruiter?

ROSE Yeah, I told him.

CORY What he say?

ROSE He ain't said nothing too much. You get in there and get started on your chores before he gets back. Go on and scrub down them steps before he gets back here hollering and carrying on.

CORY I'm hungry. What you got to eat, Mama?

ROSE Go on and get started on your chores. I got some meat loaf in there. Go on and make you a sandwich . . . and don't leave no mess in there. [CORY *exits into the house.* ROSE *continues to take down the clothes.* TROY *enters the yard and sneaks up and grabs her from behind.*] Troy! Go on, now. You liked to scared me to death. What was the score of the game? Lucille had me on the phone and I couldn't keep up with it.

TROY What I care about the game? Come here, woman. [*He tries to kiss her.*]

ROSE I thought you went down Taylors' to listen to the game. Go on, Troy! You supposed to be putting up this fence.

TROY [*attempting to kiss her again*] I'll put it up when I finish with what is at hand.

ROSE Go on, Troy. I ain't studying you.

TROY [*chasing after her*] I'm studying you . . . fixing to do my homework!

ROSE Troy, you better leave me alone.

TROY Where's Cory? That boy brought his butt home yet?

ROSE He's in the house doing his chores.

TROY [*calling*]   Cory! Get your butt out here, boy! [ROSE *exits into the house with the laundry.* TROY *goes over to the pile of wood, picks up a board, and starts sawing.* CORY *enters from the house.*] You just now coming in here from leaving this morning?

CORY   Yeah, I had to go to football practice.

TROY   Yeah, what?

CORY   Yessir.

TROY   I ain't but two seconds off you noway. The garbage sitting in there overflowing . . . you ain't done none of your chores . . . and you come in here talking about, "Yeah."

CORY   I was just getting ready to do my chores now, Pop . . .

TROY   Your first chore is to help me with this fence on Saturday. Everything else come after that. Now get that saw and cut them boards.
[CORY *takes the saw and begins cutting the boards.* TROY *continues working. There is a long pause.*]

CORY   Hey, Pop . . . why don't you buy a TV?

TROY   What I want with a TV? What I want one of them for?

CORY   Everybody got one. Earl, Ba Bra . . . Jesse!

TROY   I ain't asked you who had one. I say what I want with one?

CORY   So you can watch it. They got lots of things on TV. Baseball games and everything. We could watch the World Series.

TROY   Yeah . . . and how much this TV cost?

CORY   I don't know. They got them on sale for around two hundred dollars.

TROY   Two hundred dollars, huh?

CORY   That ain't that much, Pop.

TROY   Naw, it's just two hundred dollars. See that roof you got over your head at night? Let me tell you something about that roof. It's been over ten years since that roof was last tarred. See now . . . the snow come this winter and sit up there on that roof like it is . . . and it's gonna seep inside. It's just gonna be a little bit . . . ain't gonna hardly notice it. Then the next thing you know, it's gonna be leaking all over the house. Then the wood rot from all that water and you gonna need a whole new roof. Now, how much you think it cost to get that roof tarred?

CORY   I don't know.

TROY   Two hundred and sixty-four dollars . . . cash money. While you thinking about a TV, I got to be thinking about the roof . . . and whatever else go wrong around here. Now if you had two hundred dollars, what would you do . . . fix the roof or buy a TV?

CORY   I'd buy a TV. Then when the roof started to leak . . . when it needed fixing . . . I'd fix it.

TROY   Where you gonna get the money from? You done spent it for a TV. You gonna sit up and watch the water run all over your brand new TV.

CORY   Aw, Pop. You got money. I know you do.

TROY   Where I got it at, huh?

CORY   You got it in the bank.

TROY   You wanna see my bankbook? You wanna see that seventy-three dollars and twenty-two cents I got sitting up in there.

CORY   You ain't got to pay for it all at one time. You can put a down payment on it and carry it on home with you.

TROY Not me. I ain't gonna owe nobody nothing if I can help it. Miss a payment and they come and snatch it right out your house. Then what you got? Now, soon as I get two hundred dollars clear, then I'll buy a TV. Right now, as soon as I get two hundred and sixty-four dollars, I'm gonna have this roof tarred.

CORY Aw . . . Pop!

TROY You go on and get you two hundred dollars and buy one if ya want it. I got better things to do with my money.

CORY I can't get no two hundred dollars. I ain't never seen two hundred dollars.

TROY I'll tell you what . . . you get you a hundred dollars and I'll put the other hundred with it.

CORY Alright, I'm gonna show you.

TROY You gonna show me how you can cut them boards right now.
[CORY *begins to cut the boards. There is a long pause.*]

CORY The Pirates won today. That makes five in a row.

TROY I ain't thinking about the Pirates. Got an all-white team. Got that boy . . . that Puerto Rican boy . . . Clemente. Don't even half-play him. That boy could be something if they give him a chance. Play him one day and sit him on the bench the next.

CORY He gets a lot of chances to play.

TROY I'm talking about playing regular. Playing every day so you can get your timing. That's what I'm talking about.

CORY They got some white guys on the team that don't play every day. You can't play everybody at the same time.

TROY If they got a white fellow sitting on the bench . . . you can bet your last dollar he can't play! The colored guy got to be twice as good before he get on the team. That's why I don't want you to get all tied up in them sports. Man on the team and what it get him? They got colored on the team and don't use them. Same as not having them. All them teams the same.

CORY The Braves got Hank Aaron and Wes Covington. Hank Aaron hit two home runs today. That makes forty-three.

TROY Hank Aaron ain't nobody. That's what you supposed to do. That's how you supposed to play the game. Ain't nothing to it. It's just a matter of timing . . . getting the right follow-through. Hell, I can hit forty-three home runs right now!

CORY Not off no major-league pitching, you couldn't.

TROY We had better pitching in the Negro leagues. I hit seven home runs off of Satchel Paige. You can't get no better than that!

CORY Sandy Koufax. He's leading the league in strikeouts.

TROY I ain't thinking of no Sandy Koufax.

CORY You got Warren Spahn and Lew Burdette. I bet you couldn't hit no home runs off of Warren Spahn.

TROY I'm through with it now. You go on and cut them boards. [*Pause.*] Your mama tells me you got recruited by a college football team? Is that right?

CORY Yeah. Coach Zellman say the recruiter gonna be coming by to talk to you. Get you to sign the permission papers.

TROY I thought you supposed to be working down there at the A&P. Ain't you suppose to be working down there after school?

CORY Mr. Stawicki say he gonna hold my job for me until after the football season. Say starting next week I can work weekends.

TROY I thought we had an understanding about this football stuff? You suppose to keep up with your chores and hold that job down at the A&P. Ain't been around here all day on a Saturday. Ain't none of your chores done . . . and now you telling me you done quit your job.

CORY I'm gonna be working weekends.

TROY You damn right you are! And ain't no need for nobody coming around here to talk to me about signing nothing.

CORY Hey, Pop . . . you can't do that. He's coming all the way from North Carolina.

TROY I don't care where he coming from. The white man ain't gonna let you get nowhere with that football noway. You go on and get your booklearning so you can work yourself up in that A&P or learn how to fix cars or build houses or something, get you a trade. That way you can have something can't nobody take away from you. You go on and learn how to put your hands to some good use. Besides hauling people's garbage.

CORY I get good grades, Pop. That's why the recruiter wants to talk with you. You got to keep up your grades to get recruited. This way I'll be going to college. I'll get a chance . . .

TROY First, you gonna get your butt down there to the A&P and get your job back.

CORY Mr. Stawicki done already hired somebody else 'cause I told him I was playing football.

TROY You a bigger fool than I thought . . . to let somebody take away your job so you can play some football. Where you gonna get your money to take out your girlfriend and whatnot? What kind of foolishness is that to let somebody take away your job?

CORY I'm still gonna be working weekends.

TROY Naw . . . naw. You getting your butt out of here and finding you another job.

CORY Come on, Pop! I got to practice. I can't work after school and play football too. The team needs me. That's what Coach Zellman say . . .

TROY I don't care what nobody else say. I'm the boss . . . you understand? I'm the boss around here. I do the only saying what counts.

CORY Come on, Pop!

TROY I asked you . . . Did you understand?

CORY Yeah . . .

TROY What!

CORY Yessir.

TROY You go down there to that A&P and see if you can get your job back. If you can't do both . . . then you quit the football team. You've got to take the crookeds with the straights.

CORY Yessir. [*Pause.*] Can I ask you a question?

TROY What the hell you wanna ask me? Mr. Stawicki the one you got the questions for.

CORY How come you ain't never liked me?

TROY Liked you? Who the hell say I got to like you? What law is there say I got to like you? Wanna stand up in my face and ask a damn fool-ass question like that. Talking about liking somebody. Come here, boy, when

I talk to you. [CORY *comes over to where* TROY *is working. He stands slouched over and* TROY *shoves him on his shoulder.*] Straighten up, god-dammit! I asked you a question . . . what law is there say I got to like you?

CORY None.

TROY Well, alright then! Don't you eat every day? [*Pause.*] Answer me when I talk to you! Don't you eat every day?

CORY Yeah.

TROY Nigger, as long as you in my house, you put that sir on the end of it when you talk to me!

CORY Yes . . . sir.

TROY You eat every day.

CORY Yessir!

TROY Got a roof over your head.

CORY Yessir!

TROY Got clothes on your back.

CORY Yessir.

TROY Why you think that is?

CORY Cause of you.

TROY Aw, hell I know it's 'cause of me . . . but why do you think that is?

CORY [*hesitant*] Cause you like me.

TROY Like you? I go out of here every morning . . . bust my butt . . . putting up with them crackers every day . . . cause I like you? You about the big-gest fool I ever saw. [*Pause.*] It's my job. It's my responsibility! You under-stand that? A man got to take care of his family. You live in my house . . . sleep you behind on my bedclothes . . . fill you belly up with my food . . . cause you my son. You my flesh and blood. Not 'cause I like you! 'Cause it's my duty to take care of you. I owe a responsibility to you! Let's get this straight right here . . . before it go along any further . . . I ain't got to like you. Mr. Rand don't give me my money come payday cause he likes me. He gives me cause he owe me. I done give you everything I had to give you. I gave you your life! Me and your mama worked that out between us. And liking your black ass wasn't part of the bargain. Don't you try and go through life worrying about if somebody like you or not. You best be mak-ing sure they doing right by you. You understand what I'm saying, boy?

CORY Yessir.

TROY Then get the hell out of my face, and get on down to that A&P.
    [ROSE *has been standing behind the screen door for much of the scene. She enters as* CORY *exits.*]

ROSE Why don't you let the boy go ahead and play football, Troy? Ain't no harm in that. He's just trying to be like you with the sports.

TROY I don't want him to be like me! I want him to move as far away from my life as he can get. You the only decent thing that ever happened to me. I wish him that. But I don't wish him a thing else from my life. I decided seventeen years ago that boy wasn't getting involved in no sports. Not after what they did to me in the sports.

ROSE Troy, why don't you admit you was too old to play in the major leagues? For once . . . why don't you admit that?

TROY What do you mean too old? Don't come telling me I was too old. I just wasn't the right color. Hell, I'm fifty-three years old and I can do better than Selkirk's .269 right now!

ROSE How's was you gonna play ball when you were over forty? Sometimes I can't get no sense out of you.

TROY I got good sense, woman. I got sense enough not to let my boy get hurt over playing no sports. You been mothering that boy too much. Worried about if people like him.

ROSE Everything that boy do . . . he do for you. He wants you to say "Good job, son." That's all.

TROY Rose, I ain't got time for that. He's alive. He's healthy. He's got to make his own way. I made mine. Ain't nobody gonna hold his hand when he get out there in that world.

ROSE Times have changed from when you was young, Troy. People change. The world's changing around you and you can't even see it.

TROY [slow, methodical] Woman . . . I do the best I can do. I come in here every Friday. I carry a sack of potatoes and a bucket of lard. You all line up at the door with your hands out. I give you the lint from my pockets. I give you my sweat and my blood. I ain't got no tears. I done spent them. We go upstairs in that room at night . . . and I fall down on you and try to blast a hole into forever. I get up Monday morning . . . find my lunch on the table. I go out. Make my way. Find my strength to carry me through to the next Friday. [Pause.] That's all I got, Rose. That's all I got to give. I can't give nothing else.

[TROY exits into the house. The lights go down to black.]

SCENE 4

It is Friday. Two weeks later. CORY starts out of the house with his football equipment. The phone rings.

CORY [calling] I got it! [He answers the phone and stands in the screen door talking.] Hello? Hey, Jesse. Naw . . . I was just getting ready to leave now.

ROSE [calling] Cory!

CORY I told you, man, them spikes is all tore up. You can use them if you want, but they ain't no good. Earl got some spikes.

ROSE [calling] Cory!

CORY [calling to ROSE] Mam? I'm talking to Jesse. [Into phone.] When she say that? [Pause.] Aw, you lying, man. I'm gonna tell her you said that.

ROSE [calling] Cory, don't you go nowhere!

CORY I got to go to the game, Ma! [Into the phone.] Yeah, hey, look, I'll talk to you later. Yeah, I'll meet you over Earl's house. Later. Bye, Ma!

[CORY exits the house and starts out the yard.]

ROSE Cory, where you going off to? You got that stuff all pulled out and thrown all over your room.

CORY [in the yard] I was looking for my spikes. Jesse wanted to borrow my spikes.

ROSE Get up there and get that cleaned up before your daddy gets back in here.

CORY I got to go to the game! I'll clean it up when I get back. [CORY exits.]

ROSE That's all he need to do is see that room all messed up.

[ROSE exits into the house. TROY and BONO enter the yard. TROY is dressed in clothes other than his work clothes.]

BONO He told him the same thing he told you. Take it to the union.

TROY   Brownie ain't got that much sense. Man wasn't thinking about nothing. He wait until I confront them on it . . . then he wanna come crying seniority. [*Calls.*] Hey, Rose!

BONO   I wish I could have seen Mr. Rand's face when he told you.

TROY   He couldn't get it out of his mouth! Liked to bit his tongue! When they called me down there to the Commissioner's office . . . he thought they was gonna fire me. Like everybody else.

BONO   I didn't think they was gonna fire you. I thought they was gonna put you on the warning paper.

TROY   Hey, Rose! [*To* BONO.] Yeah, Mr. Rand like to bit his tongue. [TROY *breaks the seal on the bottle, takes a drink, and hands it to* BONO.]

BONO   I see you ran right down to Taylors' and told that Alberta gal.

TROY   [*calling*]   Hey Rose! [*To* BONO] I told everybody. Hey Rose! I went down there to cash my cheek.

ROSE   [*entering from the house*]   Hush all that hollering, man! I know you out here. What they say down there at the Commissioner's office?

TROY   You supposed to come when I call you, woman. Bono'll tell you that. [*To* BONO.] Don't Lucille come when you call her?

ROSE   Man, hush your mouth. I ain't no dog . . . talk about "come when you call me."

TROY   [*puts his arm around* ROSE]   You hear this, Bono? I had me an old dog used to get uppity like that. You say, "C'mere, Blue!" . . . and he just lay there and look at you. End up getting a stick and chasing him away trying to make him come.

ROSE   I ain't studying you and your dog. I remember you used to sing that old song.

TROY   [*He sings.*]   Hear it ring! Hear it ring! I had a dog his name was Blue.

ROSE   Don't nobody wanna hear you sing that old song.

TROY   [*sings*]   You know Blue was mighty true.

ROSE   Used to have Cory running around here singing that song.

BONO   Hell, I remember that song myself.

TROY   [*sings*]

You know Blue was a good old dog.
Blue treed a possum in a hollow log.

That was my daddy's song. My daddy made up that song.

ROSE   I don't care who made it up. Don't nobody wanna hear you sing it.

TROY   [*makes a song like calling a dog*]   Come here, woman.

ROSE   You come in here carrying on, I reckon they ain't fired you. What they say down there at the Commissioner's office?

TROY   Look here, Rose . . . Mr. Rand called me into his office today when I got back from talking to them people down there . . . it come from up top . . . he called me in and told me they was making me a driver.

ROSE   Troy, you kidding!

TROY   No I ain't. Ask Bono.

ROSE   Well, that's great, Troy. Now you don't have to hassle them people no more.

[LYONS *enters from the street.*]

TROY   Aw hell, I wasn't looking to see you today. I thought you was in jail. Got it all over the front page of the *Courier* about them raiding Sefus' place . . . where you be hanging out with all them thugs.

LYONS   Hey, Pop . . . that ain't got nothing to do with me. I don't go down there gambling. I go down there to sit in with the band. I ain't got nothing to do with the gambling part. They got some good music down there.

TROY   They got some rogues . . . is what they got.

LYONS   How you been, Mr. Bono? Hi, Rose.

BONO   I see where you playing down at the Crawford Grill tonight.

ROSE   How come you ain't brought Bonnie like I told you. You should have brought Bonnie with you, she ain't been over in a month of Sundays.

LYONS   I was just in the neighborhood . . . thought I'd stop by.

TROY   Here he come . . .

BONO   Your daddy got a promotion on the rubbish. He's gonna be the first colored driver. Ain't got to do nothing but sit up there and read the paper like them white fellows.

LYONS   Hey, Pop . . . if you knew how to read you'd be alright.

BONO   Naw . . . naw . . . you mean if the nigger knew how to *drive* he'd be all right Been fighting with them people about driving and ain't even got a license. Mr. Rand know you ain't got no driver's license?

TROY   Driving ain't nothing. All you do is point the truck where you want it to go. Driving ain't nothing.

BONO   Do Mr. Rand know you ain't got no driver's license? That's what I'm talking about. I ain't asked if driving was easy. I asked if Mr. Rand know you ain't got no driver's license.

TROY   He ain't got to know. The man ain't got to know my business. Time he find out, I have two or three driver's licenses.

LYONS   [*going into his pocket*]   Say, look here, Pop . . .

TROY   I knew it was coming. Didn't I tell you, Bono? I know what kind of "Look here, Pop" that was. The nigger fixing to ask me for some money. It's Friday night. It's my payday. All them rogues down there on the avenue . . . the ones that ain't in jail . . . and Lyons is hopping in his shoes to get down there with them.

LYONS   See, Pop . . . if you give somebody else a chance to talk sometime, you'd see that I was fixing to pay you back your ten dollars like I told you. Here . . . I told you I'd pay you when Bonnie got paid.

TROY   Naw . . . you go ahead and keep that ten dollars. Put it in the bank. The next time you feel like you wanna come by here and ask me for something . . . you go on down there and get that.

LYONS   Here's your ten dollars, Pop. I told you I don't want you to give me nothing. I just wanted to borrow ten dollars.

TROY   Naw . . . go on and keep that for the next time you want to ask me.

LYONS   Come on, Pop . . . here go your ten dollars.

ROSE   Why don't you go on and let the boy pay you back, Troy?

LYONS   Here you go, Rose. If you don't take it I'm gonna have to hear about it for the next six months. [*He hands her the money.*]

ROSE   You can hand yours over here too, Troy.

TROY   You see this, Bono. You see how they do me.

BONO   Yeah, Lucille do me the same way.

[GABRIEL *is heard singing offstage. He enters.*]

GABRIEL   Better get ready for the Judgment! Better get ready for . . . Hey! . . . Hey! . . . There's Troy's boy!

LYONS   How you doing, Uncle Gabe?

GABRIEL   Lyons . . . the King of the Jungle! Rose . . . hey, Rose. Got a flower for you. [*He takes a rose from his pocket.*] Picked it myself. That's the same rose like you is!

ROSE   That's right nice of you, Gabe.

LYONS   What you been doing, Uncle Gabe?

GABRIEL   Oh, I been chasing hellhounds and waiting on the time to tell St. Peter to open the gates.

LYONS   You been chasing hellhounds, huh? Well . . . you doing the right thing, Uncle Gabe. Somebody got to chase them.

GABRIEL   Oh, yeah . . . I know it. The devil's strong. The devil ain't no pushover. Hellhounds snipping at everybody's heels. But I got my trumpet waiting on the judgment time.

LYONS   Waiting on the Battle of Armageddon, huh?

GABRIEL   Ain't gonna be too much of a battle when God get to waving that Judgment sword. But the peoples gonna have a hell of a time trying to get into heaven if them gates ain't open.

LYONS   [*putting his arm around* GABRIEL]   You hear this, Pop. Uncle Gabe, you alright!

GABRIEL   [*laughing with* LYONS]   Lyons! King of the Jungle.

ROSE   You gonna stay for supper, Gabe. Want me to fix you a plate?

GABRIEL   I'll take a sandwich, Rose. Don't want no plate. Just wanna eat with my hands. I'll take a sandwich.

ROSE   How about you, Lyons? You staying? Got some short ribs cooking.

LYONS   Naw, I won't eat nothing till after we finished playing. [*Pause.*] You ought to come down and listen to me play, Pop.

TROY   I don't like that Chinese music. All that noise.

ROSE   Go on in the house and wash up, Gabe . . . I'll fix you a sandwich.

GABRIEL   [*to* LYONS, *as he exits*]   Troy's mad at me.

LYONS   What you mad at Uncle Gabe for, Pop.

ROSE   He thinks Troy's mad at him cause he moved over to Miss Pearl's.

TROY   I ain't mad at the man. He can live where he want to live at.

LYONS   What he move over there for? Miss Pearl don't like nobody.

ROSE   She don't mind him none. She treats him real nice. She just don't allow all that singing.

TROY   She don't mind that rent he be paying . . . that's what she don't mind.

ROSE   Troy, I ain't going through that with you no more. He's over there cause he want to have his own place. He can come and go as he please.

TROY   Hell, he could come and go as he please here. I wasn't stopping him. I ain't put no rules on him.

ROSE   It ain't the same thing, Troy. And you know it. [GABRIEL *comes to the door.*] Now, that's the last I wanna hear about that. I don't wanna hear nothing else about Gabe and Miss Pearl. And next week . . .

GABRIEL   I'm ready for my sandwich, Rose.

ROSE   And next week . . . when that recruiter come from that school . . . I want you to sign that paper and go on and let Cory play football. Then that'll be the last I have to hear about that.

TROY   [*to* ROSE *as she exits into the house*]   I ain't thinking about Cory nothing.

LYONS   What . . . Cory got recruited? What school he going to?

TROY   That boy walking around here smelling his piss . . . thinking he's grown. Thinking he's gonna do what he want, irrespective of what I say. Look here, Bono . . . I left the Commissioner's office and went down to the A&P . . . that boy ain't working down there. He lying to me. Telling me he got his job back . . . telling me he working weekends . . . telling me he working after school . . . Mr. Stawicki tell me he ain't working down there at all!

LYONS   Cory just growing up. He's just busting at the seams trying to fill out your shoes.

TROY   I don't care what he's doing. When he get to the point where he wanna disobey me . . . then it's time for him to move on. Bono'll tell you that. I bet he ain't never disobeyed his daddy without paying the consequences.

BONO   I ain't never had a chance. My daddy came on through . . . but I ain't never knew him to see him . . . or what he had on his mind or where he went. Just moving on through. Searching out the New Land. That's what the old folks used to call it. See a fellow moving around from place to place . . . woman to woman . . . called it searching out the New Land. I can't say if he ever found it. I come along, didn't want no kids. Didn't know if I was gonna be in one place long enough to fix on them right as their daddy. I figured I was going searching too. As it turned out I been hooked up with Lucille near about as long as your daddy been with Rose. Going on sixteen years.

TROY   Sometimes I wish I hadn't known my daddy. My daddy ain't cared nothing about no kids. A kid to him wasn't nothing. All he wanted was for you to learn how to walk so he could start you to working. When it come time for eating . . . he ate first. If there was anything left over, that's what you got. Man would sit down and eat two chickens and give you the wing.

LYONS   You ought to stop that, Pop. Everybody feed their kids. No matter how hard times is . . . everybody care about their kids. Make sure they have something to eat.

TROY   The only thing my daddy cared about was getting them bales of cotton in to Mr. Lubin. That's the only thing that mattered to him. Sometimes I used to wonder why he was living. Wonder why the devil hadn't come and got him. "Get them bales of cotton in to Mr. Lubin" and find out he owe him money . . .

LYONS   He should have just went on and left when he saw he couldn't get nowhere. That's what I would have done.

TROY   How he gonna leave with eleven kids? And where he gonna go? He ain't knew how to do nothing but farm. No, he was trapped and I think he knew it. But I'll say this for him . . . he felt a responsibility toward us. Maybe he ain't treated us the way I felt he should have . . . but without that responsibility he could have walked off and left us . . . made his own way.

BONO   A lot of them did. Back in those days what you talking about . . . they walk out their front door and just take on down one road or another and keep on walking.

LYONS   There you go! That's what I'm talking about.

BONO   Just keep on walking till you come to something else. Ain't you never heard of nobody having the walking blues? Well, that's what you call it when you just take off like that.

TROY   My daddy ain't had them walking blues! What you talking about? He stayed right there with his family. But he was just as evil as he could be. My mama couldn't stand him. Couldn't stand that evilness. She run off when I was about eight. She sneaked off one night after he had gone to sleep. Told me she was coming back for me. I ain't never seen her no more. All his women run off and left him. He wasn't good for nobody. When my turn come to head out, I was fourteen and got to sniffing around Joe Canewell's daughter. Had us an old mule we called Greyboy. My daddy sent me out to do some plowing and I tied up Greyboy and went to fooling around with Joe Canewell's daughter. We done found us a nice little spot, got real cozy with each other. She about thirteen and we done figured we was grown anyway . . . so we down there enjoying ourselves . . . ain't thinking about nothing. We didn't know Greyboy had got loose and wandered back to the house and my daddy was looking for me. We down there by the creek enjoying ourselves when my daddy come up on us. Surprised us. He had them leather straps off the mule and commenced to whupping me like there was no tomorrow. I jumped up, mad and embarrassed. I was scared of my daddy. When he commenced to whupping on me . . . quite naturally I run to get out of the way. [*Pause.*] Now I thought he was mad cause I ain't done my work. But I see where he was chasing me off so he could have the gal for himself. When I see what the matter of it was, I lost all fear of my daddy. Right there is where I become a man . . . at fourteen years of age. [*Pause.*] Now it was my turn to run him off. I picked up them same reins that he had used on me. I picked up them reins and commenced to whupping on him. The gal jumped up and run off . . . and when my daddy turned to face me, I could see why the devil had never come to get him . . . cause he was the devil himself. I don't know what happened. When I woke up, I was laying right there by the creek, and Blue . . . this old dog we had . . . was licking my face. I thought I was blind. I couldn't see nothing. Both my eyes were swollen shut. I layed there and cried. I didn't know what I was gonna do. The only thing I knew was the time had come for me to leave my daddy's house. And right there the world suddenly got big. And it was a long time before I could cut it down to where I could handle it. Part of that cutting down was when I got to the place where I could feel him kicking in my blood and knew that the only thing that separated us was the matter of a few years.

   [GABRIEL *enters from the house with a sandwich.*]

LYONS   What you got there, Uncle Gabe?

GABRIEL   Got me a ham sandwich. Rose gave me a ham sandwich.

TROY   I don't know what happened to him. I done lost touch with everybody except Gabriel. But I hope he's dead. I hope he found some peace.

LYONS   That's a heavy story, Pop. I didn't know you left home when you was fourteen.

TROY   And didn't know nothing. The only part of the world I knew was the forty-two acres of Mr. Lubin's land. That's all I knew about life.

LYONS Fourteen's kinda young to be out on your own. [*Phone rings.*] I don't even think I was ready to be out on my own at fourteen. I don't know what I would have done.

TROY I got up from the creek and walked on down to Mobile. I was through with farming. Figured I could do better in the city. So I walked the two hundred miles to Mobile.

LYONS Wait a minute . . . you ain't walked no two hundred miles, Pop. Ain't nobody gonna walk no two hundred miles. You talking about some walking there.

BONO That's the only way you got anywhere back in them days.

LYONS Shhh. Damn if I wouldn't have hitched a ride with somebody!

TROY Who you gonna hitch it with? They ain't had no cars and things like they got now. We talking about 1918.

ROSE [*entering*] What you all out here getting into?

TROY [*to* ROSE] I'm telling Lyons how good he got it. He don't know nothing about this I'm talking.

ROSE Lyons, that was Bonnie on the phone. She say you supposed to pick her up.

LYONS Yeah, okay, Rose.

TROY I walked on down to Mobile and hitched up with some of them fellows that was heading this way. Got up here and found out . . . not only couldn't you get a job . . . you couldn't find no place to live. I thought I was in freedom. Shhh. Colored folks living down there on the riverbanks in whatever kind of shelter they could find for themselves. Right down there under the Brady Street Bridge. Living in shacks made of sticks and tarpaper. Messed around there and went from bad to worse. Started stealing. First it was food. Then I figured, hell, if I steal money I can buy me some food. Buy me some shoes too! One thing led to another. Met your mama. I was young and anxious to be a man. Met your mama and had you. What I do that for? Now I got to worry about feeding you and her. Got to steal three times as much. Went out one day looking for somebody to rob . . . that's what I was, a robber. I'll tell you the truth. I'm ashamed of it today. But it's the truth. Went to rob this fellow . . . pulled out my knife . . . and he pulled out a gun. Shot me in the chest. It felt just like somebody had taken a hot branding iron and laid it on me. When he shot me I jumped at him with my knife. They tell me I killed him and they put me in the penitentiary and locked me up for fifteen years. That's where I met Bono. That's where I learned how to play baseball. Got out that place and your mama had taken you and went on to make life without me. Fifteen years was a long time for her to wait. But that fifteen years cured me of that robbing stuff. Rose'll tell you. She asked me when I met her if I had gotten all that foolishness out of my system. And I told her, "Baby, it's you and baseball all what count with me." You hear me, Bono? I meant it too. She say, "Which one comes first?" I told her, "Baby, there ain't no doubt it's baseball . . . but you stick and get old with me and we'll both outlive this baseball." Am I right, Rose? And it's true.

ROSE Man, hush your mouth. You ain't said no such thing. Talking about, "Baby, you know you'll always be number one with me." That's what you was talking.

TROY You hear that, Bono? That's why I love her.

BONO Rose'll keep you straight. You get off the track, she'll straighten you up.

ROSE Lyons, you better get on up and get Bonnie. She waiting on you.

LYONS [*gets up to go*] Hey, Pop, why don't you come down to the Grill and hear me play?

TROY I ain't going down there. I'm too old to be sitting around in them clubs.

BONO You got to be good to play down at the Grill.

LYONS Come on, Pop . . .

TROY I got to get up in the morning.

LYONS You ain't got to stay long.

TROY Naw, I'm gonna get my supper and go on to bed.

LYONS Well, I got to go. I'll see you again.

TROY Don't you come around my house on my payday!

ROSE Pick up the phone and let somebody know you coming. And bring Bonnie with you. You know I'm always glad to see her.

LYONS Yeah, I'll do that, Rose. You take care now. See you, Pop. See you, Mr. Bono. See you, Uncle Gabe.

GABRIEL Lyons! King of the Jungle!

[LYONS *exits.*]

TROY Is supper ready, woman? Me and you got some business to take care of. I'm gonna tear it up too!

ROSE Troy, I done told you now!

TROY [*puts his arm around* BONO] Aw hell, woman . . . this is Bono. Bono like family. I done known this nigger since . . . how long I done know you?

BONO It's been a long time.

TROY I done known this nigger since Skippy was a pup. Me and him done been through some times.

BONO You sure right about that.

TROY Hell, I done know him longer than I known you. And we still standing shoulder to shoulder. Hey, look here, Bono . . . a man can't ask for no more than that. [*Drinks to him.*] I love you, nigger.

BONO Hell, I love you too . . . but I got to get home see my woman. You got yours in hand. I got to go get mine.

[BONO *starts to exit as* CORY *enters the yard, dressed in his football uniform. He gives* TROY *a hard, uncompromising look.*]

CORY What you do that for, Pop? [*He throws his helmet down in the direction of* TROY.]

ROSE What's the matter? Cory . . . what's the matter?

CORY Papa done went up to the school and told Coach Zellman I can't play football no more. Wouldn't even let me play the game. Told him to tell the recruiter not to come.

ROSE Troy . . .

TROY What you Troying me for. Yeah, I did it. And the boy know why I did it.

CORY Why you wanna do that to me? That was the one chance I had.

ROSE Ain't nothing wrong with Cory playing football, Troy.

TROY The boy lied to me. I told the nigger if he wanna play football . . . to keep up his chores and hold down that job at the A&P. That was the conditions. Stopped down there to see Mr. Stawicki . . .

CORY I can't work after school during the football season, Pop! I tried to tell you that Mr. Stawicki's holding my job for me. You don't never want to listen to nobody. And then you wanna go and do this to me!

TROY I ain't done nothing to you. You done it to yourself.

CORY Just cause you didn't have a chance! You just scared I'm gonna be better than you, that's all.

TROY Come here.

ROSE Troy . . .

[CORY *reluctantly crosses over to* TROY.]

TROY Alright! See. You done made a mistake.

CORY I didn't even do nothing!

TROY I'm gonna tell you what your mistake was. See . . . you swung at the ball and didn't hit it. That's strike one. See, you in the batter's box now. You swung and you missed. That's strike one. Don't you strike out!

[*Lights fade to black.*]

Act 2

SCENE 1

The following morning. CORY *is at the tree hitting the ball with the bat. He tries to mimic* TROY, *but his swing is awkward, less sure.* ROSE *enters from the house.*

ROSE Cory, I want you to help me with this cupboard.

CORY I ain't quitting the team. I don't care what Poppa say.

ROSE I'll talk to him when he gets back. He had to go see about your Uncle Gabe. The police done arrested him. Say he was disturbing the peace. He'll be back directly. Come on in here and help me clean out the top of this cupboard. [CORY *exits into the house.* ROSE *sees* TROY *and* BONO *coming down the alley.*] Troy . . . what they say down there?

TROY Ain't said nothing. I give them fifty dollars and they let him go. I'll talk to you about it. Where's Cory?

ROSE He's in there helping me clean out these cupboards.

TROY Tell him to get his butt out here.

[TROY *and* BONO *go over to the pile of wood.* BONO *picks up the saw and begins sawing.*]

TROY [*to* BONO] All they want is the money. That makes six or seven times I done went down there and got him. See me coming they stick out their *hands.*

BONO Yeah, I know what you mean. That's all they care about . . . that money. They don't care about what's right. [*Pause.*] Nigger, why you got to go and get some hard wood? You ain't doing nothing but building a little old fence. Get you some soft pine wood. That's all you need.

TROY I know what I'm doing. This is outside wood. You put pine wood inside the house. Pine wood is inside wood. This here is outside wood. Now you tell me where the fence is gonna be?

BONO You don't need this wood. You can put it up with pine wood and it'll stand as long as you gonna be here looking at it.

TROY How you know how long I'm gonna be here, nigger? Hell, I might just live forever. Live longer than old man Horsely.

BONO   That's what Magee used to say.

TROY   Magee's a damn fool. Now you tell me who you ever heard of gonna pull their own teeth with a pair of rusty pliers?

BONO   The old folks . . . my granddaddy used to pull his teeth with pliers. They ain't had no dentists for the colored folks back then.

TROY   Get clean pliers! You understand? Clean pliers! Sterilize them! Besides we ain't living back then. All Magee had to do was walk over to Doc Goldblums.

BONO   I see where you and that Tallahassee gal . . . that Alberta . . . I see where you all done got tight.

TROY   What you mean "got tight"?

BONO   I see where you be laughing and joking with her all the time.

TROY   I laughs and jokes with all of them, Bono. You know me.

BONO   That ain't the kind of laughing and joking I'm talking about.
[CORY *enters from the house.*]

CORY   How you doing, Mr. Bono?

TROY   Cory? Get that saw from Bono and cut some wood. He talking about the wood's too hard to cut. Stand back there, Jim, and let that young boy show you how it's done.

BONO   He's sure welcome to it. [CORY *takes the saw and begins to cut the wood.*] Whew-e-e Look at that. Big old strong boy. Look like Joe Louis.[3] Hell, must be getting old the way I'm watching that boy whip through that wood.

CORY   I don't see why Mama want a fence around the yard noways.

TROY   Damn if I know either. What the hell she keeping out with it? She ain't got nothing nobody want.

BONO   Some people build fences to keep people out . . . and other people build fences to keep people in. Rose wants to hold on to you all. She loves you.

TROY   Hell, nigger, I don't need nobody to tell me my wife loves me, Cory . . . go on in the house and see if you can find that other saw.

CORY   Where's it at?

TROY   I said find it! Look for it till you find it! [CORY *exits into the house.*] What's that supposed to mean? Wanna keep us in?

BONO   Troy . . . I done known you seem like damn near my whole life. You and Rose both. I done know both of you all for a long time. I remember when you met Rose. When you was hitting them baseball out the park. A lot of them old gals was after you then. You had the pick of the litter. When you picked Rose, I was happy for you. That was the first time I knew you had any sense. I said . . . My man Troy knows what he's doing . . . I'm gonna follow this nigger . . . he might take me somewhere. I been following you too. I done learned a whole heap of things about life watching you. I done learned how to tell where the shit lies. How to tell it from the alfalfa. You done learned me a lot of things. You showed me how to not make the same mistakes . . . to take life as it comes along and keep putting one foot in front of the other. [*Pause.*] Rose a good woman, Troy.

3. Boxer (1914–1981), heavyweight champion from 1937 to 1949.

TROY Hell, nigger, I know she a good woman. I been married to her for eighteen years. What you got on your mind, Bono?

BONO I just say she a good woman. Just like I say anything. I ain't got to have nothing on my mind.

TROY You just gonna say she a good woman and leave it hanging out there like that? Why you telling me she a good woman?

BONO She loves you, Troy. Rose loves you.

TROY You saying I don't measure up. That's what you trying to say. I don't measure up cause I'm seeing this other gal. I know what you trying to say.

BONO I know what Rose means to you, Troy. I'm just trying to say I don't want to see you mess up.

TROY Yeah, I appreciate that, Bono. If you was messing around on Lucille I'd be telling you the same thing.

BONO Well, that's all I got to say. I just say that because I love you both.

TROY Hell, you know me . . . I wasn't out there looking for nothing. You can't find a better woman than Rose. I know that. But seems like this woman just stuck onto me where I can't shake her loose. I done wrestled with it, tried to throw her off me . . . but she just stuck on tighter. Now she's stuck on for good.

BONO You's in control . . . that's what you tell me all the time. You responsible for what you do.

TROY I ain't ducking the responsibility of it. As long as it sets right in my heart . . . then I'm okay. Cause that's all I listen to. It'll tell me right from wrong every time. And I ain't talking about doing Rose no bad turn. I love Rose. She done carried me a long ways and I love and respect her for that.

BONO I know you do. That's why I don't want to see you hurt her. But what you gonna do when she find out? What you got then? If you try and juggle both of them . . . sooner or later you gonna drop one of them. That's common sense.

TROY Yeah, I hear what you saying, Bono. I been trying to figure a way to work it out.

BONO Work it out right, Troy. I don't want to be getting all up between you and Rose's business . . . but work it so it come out right.

TROY Aw hell, I get all up between you and Lucille's business. When you gonna get that woman that refrigerator she been wanting? Don't tell me you ain't got no money now. I know who your banker is. Mellon don't need that money bad as Lucille want that refrigerator. I'll tell you that.

BONO Tell you what I'll do . . . when you finish building this fence for Rose . . . I'll buy Lucille that refrigerator.

TROY You done stuck your foot in your mouth now! [TROY *grabs up a board and begins to saw.* BONO *starts to walk out the yard.*] Hey, nigger . . . where you going?

BONO I'm going home. I know you don't expect me to help you now. I'm protecting my money. I wanna see you put that fence up by yourself. That's what I want to see. You'll be here another six months without me.

TROY Nigger, you ain't right.

BONO When it comes to my money . . . I'm right as fireworks on the Fourth of July.

TROY Alright, we gonna see now. You better get out your bankbook.

[BONO *exits, and* TROY *continues to work.* ROSE *enters from the house.*]

ROSE What they say down there? What's happening with Gabe?

TROY I went down there and got him out. Cost me fifty dollars. Say he was disturbing the peace. Judge set up a hearing for him in three weeks. Say to show cause why he shouldn't be re-committed.

ROSE What was he doing that cause them to arrest him?

TROY Some kids was teasing him and he run them off home. Say he was howling and carrying on. Some folks seen him and called the police. That's all it was.

ROSE Well, what's you say? What'd you tell the judge?

TROY Told him I'd look after him. It didn't make no sense to recommit the man. He stuck out his big greasy palm and told me to give him fifty dollars and take him on home.

ROSE Where's he at now? Where'd he go off to?

TROY He's gone on about his business. He don't need nobody to hold his hand.

ROSE Well, I don't know. Seem like that would be the best place for him if they did put him into the hospital. I know what you're gonna say. But that's what I think would be best.

TROY The man done had his life ruined fighting for what? And they wanna take and lock him up. Let him be free. He don't bother nobody.

ROSE Well, everybody got their own way of looking at it I guess. Come on and get your lunch. I got a bowl of lima beans and some cornbread in the oven. Come on get something to eat. Ain't no sense you fretting over Gabe. [ROSE *turns to go into the house.*]

TROY Rose . . . got something to tell you.

ROSE Well, come on . . . wait till I get this food on the table.

TROY Rose! [*She stops and turns around.*] I don't know how to say this. [*Pause.*] I can't explain it none. It just sort of grows on you till it gets out of hand. It starts out like a little bush . . . and the next thing you know it's a whole forest.

ROSE Troy . . . what are you talking about?

TROY I'm talking, woman, let me talk. I'm trying to find a way to tell you . . . I'm gonna be a daddy. I'm gonna be somebody's daddy.

ROSE Troy . . . you're not telling me this? You're gonna be . . . what?

TROY Rose . . . now . . . see . . .

ROSE You telling me you gonna be somebody's daddy? You telling your *wife* this?

[GABRIEL *enters from the street. He carries a rose in his hand.*]

GABRIEL Hey, Troy! Hey, Rose!

ROSE I have to wait eighteen years to hear something like this.

GABRIEL Hey, Rose . . . I got a flower for you. [*He hands it to her.*] That's a rose. Same rose like you is.

ROSE Thanks, Gabe.

GABRIEL Troy, you ain't mad at me is you? Them bad mens come and put me away. You ain't mad at me is you?

TROY Naw, Gabe, I ain't mad at you.

ROSE Eighteen years and you wanna come with this.

GABRIEL [*takes a quarter out of his pocket*] See what I got? Got a brand new quarter.

TROY Rose . . . it's just . . .

ROSE Ain't nothing you can say, Troy. Ain't no way of explaining that.

GABRIEL Fellow that give me this quarter had a whole mess of them. I'm gonna keep this quarter till it stop shining.

ROSE Gabe, go on in the house there. I got some watermelon in the frigidaire. Go on and get you a piece.

GABRIEL Say, Rose . . . you know I was chasing hellhounds and them bad mens come and get me and take me away. Troy helped me. He come down there and told them they better let me go before he beat them up. Yeah, he did!

ROSE You go on and get you a piece of watermelon, Gabe. Them bad mens is gone now.

GABRIEL Okay, Rose . . . gonna get me some watermelon. The kind with the stripes on it. [GABRIEL *exits into the house.*]

ROSE Why, Troy? Why? After all these years to come dragging this in to me now. It don't make no sense at your age. I could have expected this ten or fifteen years ago, but not now.

TROY Age ain't got nothing to do with it, Rose.

ROSE I done tried to be everything a wife should be. Everything a wife could be. Been married eighteen years and I got to live to see the day you tell me you been seeing another woman and done fathered a child by her. And you know I ain't never wanted no half nothing in my family. My whole family is half. Everybody got different fathers and mothers . . . my two sisters and my brother. Can't hardly tell who's who. Can't never sit down and talk about Papa and Mama. It's your papa and your mama and my papa and my mama . . .

TROY Rose . . . stop it now.

ROSE I ain't never wanted that for none of my children. And now you wanna drag your behind in here and tell me something like this.

TROY You ought to know. It's time for you to know.

ROSE Well, I don't want to know, goddamn it!

TROY I can't just make it go away. It's done now. I can't wish the circumstance of the thing away.

ROSE And you don't want to either. Maybe you want to wish me and my boy away. Maybe that's what you want? Well, you can't wish us away. I've got eighteen years of my life invested in you. You ought to have stayed upstairs in my bed where you belong.

TROY Rose . . . now listen to me . . . we can get a handle on this thing. We can talk this out . . . come to an understanding.

ROSE All of a sudden it's "we." Where was "we" at when you was down there rolling around with some godforsaken woman? "We" should have come to an understanding before you started making a damn fool of yourself. You're a day late and a dollar short when it comes to an understanding with me.

TROY It's just . . . She gives me a different idea . . . a different understanding about myself. I can step out of this house and get away from the pressures and problems . . . be a different man. I ain't got to wonder how I'm gonna pay the bills or get the roof fixed. I can just be a part of myself that I ain't never been.

ROSE What I want to know . . . is do you plan to continue seeing her? That's all you can say to me.

TROY   I can sit up in her house and laugh. Do you understand what I'm saying. I can laugh out loud . . . and it feels good. It reaches all the way down to the bottom of my shoes. [*Pause.*] Rose, I can't give that up.

ROSE   Maybe you ought to go on and stay down there with her . . . if she a better woman than me.

TROY   It ain't about nobody being a better woman or nothing. Rose, you ain't the blame. A man couldn't ask for no woman to be a better wife than you've been. I'm responsible for it. I done locked myself into a pattern trying to take care of you all that I forgot about myself.

ROSE   What the hell was I there for? That was my job, not somebody else's.

TROY   Rose, I done tried all my life to live decent . . . to live a clean . . . hard . . . useful life. I tried to be a good husband to you. In every way I knew how. Maybe I come into the world backwards, I don't know. But . . . you born with two strikes on you before you come to the plate. You got to guard it closely . . . always looking for the curve-ball on the inside corner. You can't afford to let none get past you. You can't afford a call strike. If you going down . . . you going down swinging. Everything lined up against you. What you gonna do. I fooled them, Rose. I bunted. When I found you and Cory and a halfway decent job . . . I was safe. Couldn't nothing touch me. I wasn't gonna strike out no more. I wasn't going back to the penitentiary. I wasn't gonna lay in the streets with a bottle of wine. I was safe. I had me a family. A job. I wasn't gonna get that last strike. I was on first looking for one of them boys to knock me in. To get me home.

ROSE   You should have stayed in my bed, Troy.

TROY   Then, when I saw that gal . . . she firmed up my backbone. And I got to thinking that if I tried . . . I just might be able to steal second. Do you understand after eighteen years I wanted to steal second.

ROSE   You should have held me tight. You should have grabbed me and held on.

TROY   I stood on first base for eighteen years and I thought . . . well, goddamn it . . . go on for it!

ROSE   We're not talking about baseball! We're talking about you going off to lay in bed with another woman . . . and then bring it home to me. That's what we're talking about. We ain't talking about no baseball.

TROY   Rose, you're not listening to me. I'm trying the best I can to explain it to you. It's not easy for me to admit that I been standing in the same place for eighteen years.

ROSE   I been standing with you! I been right here with you, Troy. I got a life too. I gave eighteen years of my life to stand in the same spot with you. Don't you think I ever wanted other things? Don't you think I had dreams and hopes? What about my life? What about me? Don't you think it ever crossed my mind to want to know other men? That I wanted to lay up somewhere and forget about my responsibilities? That I wanted someone to make me laugh so I could feel good? You not the only one who's got wants and needs. But I held on to you, Troy. I took all my feelings, my wants and needs, my dreams . . . and I buried them inside you. I planted a seed and watched and prayed over it. I planted myself inside you and waited to bloom. And it didn't take me no eighteen years to find out the soil was hard and rocky and it wasn't never gonna bloom. But I held on to you, Troy. I held you tighter. You was my husband. I owed you everything I had. Every part of me I could find to give you. And upstairs in that room . . . with the darkness falling in on me . . . I gave everything I had to try and erase the doubt that you wasn't the finest man in the world. And wherever you was going . . . I wanted to be there with you. Cause you was my husband. Cause that's the only way I was gonna survive as your wife. You always talking about what you give . . . and what you don't have to give. But you take too. You take . . . and don't even know nobody's giving!

[ROSE *turns to exit into the house;* TROY *grabs her arm.*]

TROY   You say I take and don't give!

ROSE   Troy! You're hurting me!

TROY   You say I take and don't give!

ROSE   Troy . . . you're hurting my arm! Let go!

TROY   I done give you everything I got. Don't you tell that lie on me.

ROSE   Troy!

TROY   Don't you tell that lie on me!

[CORY *enters from the house.*]

CORY   Mama!

ROSE   Troy, you're hurting me.

TROY   Don't you tell me about no taking and giving.

[CORY *comes up behind* TROY *and grabs him.* TROY, *surprised, is thrown off balance just as* CORY *throws a glancing blow that catches him on the chest and knocks him down.* TROY *is stunned, as is* CORY.]

ROSE   Troy. Troy. No! [TROY *gets to his feet and starts at* CORY.] Troy no. Please! Troy!

[ROSE *pulls on* TROY *to hold him back.* TROY *stops himself.*]

TROY [*to* CORY]   Alright. That's strike two. You stay away from around me, boy. Don't you strike out. You living with a full count.[4] Don't you strike out.

[TROY *exits out the yard as the lights go down.*]

SCENE 2

It is six months later, early afternoon. TROY *enters from the house and starts to exit the yard.* ROSE *enters from the house.*

ROSE   Troy, I want to talk to you.

TROY   All of a sudden, after all this time, you want to talk to me, huh? You ain't wanted to talk to me for months. You ain't wanted to talk to me last night. You ain't wanted no part of me then. What you wanna talk to me about now?

ROSE   Tomorrow's Friday.

TROY   I know what day tomorrow is. You think I don't know tomorrow's Friday? My whole life I ain't done nothing but look to see Friday coming and you got to tell me it's Friday.

ROSE   I want to know if you're coming home.

TROY   I always come home, Rose. You know that. There ain't never been a night I ain't come home.

---

4. In baseball, a count of three balls and two strikes; one more ball will result in a walk; one more strike will put the batter out.

ROSE That ain't what I mean . . . and you know it. I want to know if you're coming straight home after work.

TROY I figure I'd cash my check . . . hang out at Taylors' with the boys . . . maybe play a game of checkers . . .

ROSE Troy, I can't live like this. I won't live like this. You livin' on borrowed time with me. It's been going on six months now you ain't been coming home.

TROY I be here every night. Every night of the year. That's 365 days.

ROSE I want you to come home tomorrow after work.

TROY Rose . . . I don't mess up my pay. You know that now. I take my pay and I give it to you. I don't have no money but what you give me back. I just want to have a little time to myself . . . a little time to enjoy life.

ROSE What about me? When's my time to enjoy life?

TROY I don't know what to tell you, Rose. I'm doing the best I can.

ROSE You ain't been home from work but time enough to change your clothes and run out . . . and you wanna call that the best you can do?

TROY I'm going over to the hospital to see Alberta. She went into the hospital this afternoon. Look like she might have the baby early. I won't be gone long.

ROSE Well, you ought to know. They went over to Miss Pearl's and got Gabe today. She said you told them to go ahead and lock him up.

TROY I ain't said no such thing. Whoever told you that telling a lie. Pearl ain't doing nothing but telling a big fat lie.

ROSE She ain't had to tell me. I read it on the papers.

TROY I ain't told them nothing of the kind.

ROSE I saw it right there on the papers.

TROY What it say, huh?

ROSE It said you told them to take him.

TROY Then they screwed that up, just the way they screw up everything. I ain't worried about what they got on the paper.

ROSE Say the government send part of his check to the hospital and the other part to you.

TROY I ain't got nothing to do with that if that's the way it works. I ain't made up the rules about how it work.

ROSE You did Gabe just like you did Cory. You wouldn't sign the paper for Cory . . . but you signed for Gabe. You signed that paper.

[*The telephone is heard ringing inside the house.*]

TROY I told you I ain't signed nothing, woman! The only thing I signed was the release form. Hell, I can't read, I don't know what they had on the paper! I ain't signed nothing about sending Gabe away.

ROSE I said send him to the hospital . . . you said let him be free . . . now you done went down there and signed him to the hospital for half his money. You went back on yourself, Troy. You gonna have to answer for that.

TROY See now . . . you been over there talking to Miss Pearl. She done got mad cause she ain't getting Gabe's rent money. That's all it is. She's liable to say anything.

ROSE Troy, I seen where you signed the paper.

TROY You ain't seen nothing I signed. What she doing got papers on my brother anyway? Miss Pearl telling a big fat lie. And I'm gonna tell her about it too! You ain't seen nothing I signed. Say . . . you ain't seen nothing I signed.

[ROSE *exits into the house to answer the telephone. Presently she returns.*]

ROSE Troy . . . that was the hospital. Alberta had the baby.

TROY What she have? What is it?

ROSE It's a girl.

TROY I better get on down to the hospital to see her.

ROSE Troy . . .

TROY Rose . . . I got to go see her now. That's only right . . . what's the matter . . . the baby's alright, ain't it?

ROSE Alberta died having the baby.

TROY Died . . . you say she's dead? Alberta's dead?

ROSE They said they done all they could. They couldn't do nothing for her.

TROY The baby? How's the baby?

ROSE They say it's healthy. I wonder who's gonna bury her.

TROY She had family, Rose. She wasn't living in the world by herself.

ROSE I know she wasn't living in the world by herself.

TROY Next thing you gonna want to know if she had any insurance.

ROSE Troy, you ain't got to talk like that.

TROY That's the first thing that jumped out your mouth. "Who's gonna bury her?" Like I'm fixing to take on that task for myself.

ROSE I am your wife. Don't push me away.

TROY I ain't pushing nobody away. Just give me some space. That's all. Just give me some room to breathe.

[ROSE *exits into the house.* TROY *walks about the yard.*]

TROY [*with a quiet rage that threatens to consume him*] Alright . . . Mr. Death. See now . . . I'm gonna tell you what I'm gonna do. I'm gonna take and build me a fence around this yard. See? I'm gonna build me a fence around what belongs to me. And then I want you to stay on the other side. See? You stay over there until you're ready for me. Then you come on. Bring your army. Bring your sickle. Bring your wrestling clothes. I ain't gonna fall down on my vigilance this time. You ain't gonna sneak up on me no more. When you ready for me . . . when the top of your list say Troy Maxson . . . that's when you come around here. You come up and knock on the front door. Ain't nobody else got nothing to do with this. This is between you and me. Man to man. You stay on the other side of that fence until you ready for me. Then you come up and knock on the front door. Anytime you want. I'll be ready for you.

[*The lights go down to black.*]

SCENE 3

The lights come up on the porch. It is late evening three days later. ROSE *sits listening to the ball game waiting for* TROY. *The final out of the game is made and* ROSE *switches off the radio.* TROY *enters the yard carrying an infant wrapped in blankets. He stands back from the house and calls.*

[ROSE *enters and stands on the porch. There is a long, awkward silence, the weight of which grows heavier with each passing second.*]

TROY   Rose . . . I'm standing here with my daughter in my arms. She ain't
but a wee bittie little old thing. She don't know nothing about grownups'
business. She innocent . . . and she ain't got no mama.
ROSE   What you telling me for, Troy? [*She turns and exits into the house.*]
TROY   Well . . . I guess we'll just sit out here on the porch. [*He sits down on
the porch. There is an awkward indelicateness about the way he handles the
baby. His largeness engulfs and seems to swallow it. He speaks loud enough
for* ROSE *to hear.*] A man's got to do what's right for him. I ain't sorry for
nothing I done. It felt right in my heart. [*To the baby.*] What you smiling at?
Your daddy's a big man. Got these great big old hands. But sometimes he's
scared. And right now your daddy's scared cause we sitting out here and
ain't got no home. Oh, I been homeless before. I ain't had no little baby
with me. But I been homeless. You just be out on the road by your lonesome
and you see one of them trains coming and you just kinda go like this . . .
[*He sings as a lullaby.*]
Please, Mr. Engineer let a man ride the line
Please, Mr. Engineer let a man ride the line
I ain't got no ticket please let me ride the blinds
[ROSE *enters from the house.* TROY *hearing her steps behind him, stands
and faces her.*]
She's my daughter, Rose. My own flesh and blood. I can't deny her no
more than I can deny them boys. [*Pause.*] You and them boys is my fam-
ily. You and them and this child is all I got in the world. So I guess what
I'm saying is . . . I'd appreciate it if you'd help me take care of her.
ROSE   Okay, Troy . . . you're right. I'll take care of your baby for you . . .
cause . . . like you say . . . she's innocent . . . and you can't visit the sins
of the father upon the child. A motherless child has got a hard time.
[*She takes the baby from him.*] From right now . . . this child got a
mother. But you a womanless man.
[ROSE *turns and exits into the house with the baby. Lights go down to
black.*]

SCENE 4

It is two months later. LYONS *enters from the street. He knocks on the door and
calls.*

LYONS   Hey, Rose! [*Pause.*] Rose!
ROSE [*from inside the house*]   Stop that yelling. You gonna wake up Raynell.
I just got her to sleep.
LYONS   I just stopped by to pay Papa this twenty dollars I owe him. Where's
Papa at?
ROSE   He should be here in a minute. I'm getting ready to go down to the
church. Sit down and wait on him.
LYONS   I got to go pick up Bonnie over her mother's house.
ROSE   Well, sit it down there on the table. He'll get it.
LYONS [*enters the house and sets the money on the table*]   Tell Papa I said
thanks. I'll see you again.
ROSE   Alright, Lyons. We'll see you.
[LYONS *starts to exit as* CORY *enters.*]

CORY   Hey, Lyons.

LYONS   What's happening, Cory. Say man, I'm sorry I missed your graduation. You know I had a gig and couldn't get away. Otherwise, I would have been there. So what you doing?

CORY   I'm trying to find a job.

LYONS   Yeah, I know how that go, man. It's rough out here. Jobs are scarce.

CORY   Yeah, I know.

LYONS   Look here, I got to run. Talk to Papa . . . he know some people. He'll be able to help get you a job. Talk to him . . . see what he say.

CORY   Yeah . . . alright, Lyons.

LYONS   You take care. I'll talk to you soon. We'll find some time to talk.

[LYONS *exits the yard.* CORY *wanders over to the tree, picks up the bat and assumes a batting stance. He studies an imaginary pitcher and swings. Dissatisfied with the result, he tries again.* TROY *enters. They eye each other for a beat.* CORY *puts the bat down and exits the yard.* TROY *starts into the house as* ROSE *exits with* RAYNELL. *She is carrying a cake.*]

TROY   I'm coming in and everybody's going out.

ROSE   I'm taking this cake down to the church for the bakesale. Lyons was by to see you. He stopped by to pay you your twenty dollars. It's laying in there on the table.

TROY [*going into his pocket*]   Well . . . here go this money.

ROSE   Put it in there on the table, Troy. I'll get it.

TROY   What time you coming back?

ROSE   Ain't no use in you studying me. It don't matter what time I come back.

TROY   I just asked you a question, woman. What's the matter . . . can't I ask you a question?

ROSE   Troy, I don't want to go into it. Your dinner's in there on the stove. All you got to do is heat it up. And don't you be eating the rest of them cakes in there. I'm coming back for them. We having a bakesale at the church tomorrow.

[ROSE *exits the yard.* TROY *sits down on the steps, takes a pint bottle from his pocket, opens it, and drinks. He begins to sing.*]

[TROY]

Hear it ring! Hear it ring!
Had an old dog his name was Blue
You know Blue was mighty true
You know Blue as a good old dog
Blue trees a possum in a hollow log
You know from that he was a good old dog

[BONO *enters the yard.*]

BONO   Hey, Troy.

TROY   Hey, what's happening, Bono?

BONO   I just thought I'd stop by to see you.

TROY   What you stop by and see me for? You ain't stopped by in a month of Sundays. Hell, I must owe you money or something.

BONO   Since you got your promotion I can't keep up with you. Used to see you everyday. Now I don't even know what route you working.

TROY   They keep switching me around. Got me out in Greentree now . . . hauling white folks' garbage.

BONO Greentree, huh? You lucky, at least you ain't got to be lifting them barrels. Damn if they ain't getting heavier. I'm gonna put in my two years and call it quits.

TROY I'm thinking about retiring myself. How's Lucille?

BONO You got it easy. You can *drive* for another five years.

TROY It ain't the same, Bono. It ain't like working the back of the truck. Ain't got nobody to talk to . . . feel like you working by yourself. Naw, I'm thinking about retiring. How's Lucille?

BONO She alright. Her arthritis get to acting up on her sometime. Saw Rose on my way in. She going down to the church, huh?

TROY Yeah, she took up going down there. All them preachers looking for somebody to fatten their pockets. [*Pause.*] Got some gin here.

BONO Naw, thanks. I just stopped by to say hello.

TROY Hell, nigger . . . you can take a drink. I ain't never known you to say no to a drink. You ain't got to work tomorrow.

BONO I just stopped by. I'm fixing to go over to Skinner's. We got us a domino game going over his house every Friday.

TROY Nigger, you can't play no dominoes. I used to whup you four games out of five.

BONO Well, that learned me. I'm getting better.

TROY Yeah? Well, that's alright.

BONO Look here . . . I got to be getting on. Stop by sometime, huh?

TROY Yeah, I'll do that, Bono. Lucille told Rose you bought her a new refrigerator.

BONO Yeah, Rose told Lucille you had finally built your fence . . . so I figured we'd call it even.

TROY I knew you would.

BONO Yeah . . . okay. I'll be talking to you.

TROY Yeah, take care, Bono. Good to see you. I'm gonna stop over.

BONO Yeah. Okay, Troy.

[BONO *exits.* TROY *drinks from the bottle.*]

TROY

        Old Blue died and I dig his grave
        Let him down with a golden chain
        Every night when I hear old Blue bark
        I know Blue treed a possum in Noah's Ark.
        Hear it ring! Hear it ring!

[CORY *enters the yard. They eye each other for a beat.* TROY *is sitting in the middle of the steps.* CORY *walks over.*]

CORY I got to get by.

TROY Say what? What's you say?

CORY You in my way. I got to get by.

TROY You got to get by where? This is my house. Bought and paid for. In full. Took me fifteen years. And if you wanna go in my house and I'm sitting on the steps . . . you say excuse me. Like your mama taught you.

CORY Come on, Pop . . . I got to get by.

[CORY *starts to maneuver his way past* TROY. TROY *grabs his leg and shoves him back.*]

TROY You just gonna walk over top of me?

CORY   I live here too!

TROY [*advancing toward him*]   You just gonna walk over top of me in my own house?

CORY   I ain't scared of you.

TROY   I ain't asked if you was scared of me. I asked you if you was fixing to walk over top of me in my own house? That's the question. You ain't gonna say excuse me? You just gonna walk over top of me?

CORY   If you wanna put it like that.

TROY   How else am I gonna put it?

CORY   I was walking by you to go into the house cause you sitting on the steps drunk, singing to yourself. You can put it like that.

TROY   Without saying excuse me?? [CORY *doesn't respond.*] I asked you a question. Without saying excuse me??

CORY   I ain't got to say excuse me to you. You don't count around here no more.

TROY   Oh, I see . . . I don't count around here no more. You ain't got to say excuse me to your daddy. All of a sudden you done got so grown that your daddy don't count around here no more . . . Around here in his own house and yard that he done paid for with the sweat of his brow. You done got so grown to where you gonna take over. You gonna take over my house. Is that right? You gonna wear my pants. You gonna go in there and stretch out on my bed. You ain't got to say excuse me cause I don't count around here no more. Is that right?

CORY   That's right. You always talking this dumb stuff. Now, why don't you just get out my way.

TROY   I guess you got someplace to sleep and something to put in your belly. You got that, huh? You got that? That's what you need. You got that, huh?

CORY   You don't know what I got. You ain't got to worry about what I got.

TROY   You right! You one hundred percent right! I done spent the last seventeen years worrying about what you got. Now it's your turn, see? I'll tell you what you do. You grown . . . we done established that. You a man. Now, let's see you act like one. Turn your behind around and walk out this yard. And when you get out there in the alley . . . you can forget about this house. See? Cause this is my house. You go on and be a man and get your own house. You can forget about this. 'Cause this is mine. You go on and get yours cause I'm through with doing for you.

CORY   You talking about what you did for me . . . what'd you ever give me?

TROY   Them feet and bones! That pumping heart nigger! I give you more than anybody else is ever gonna give you.

CORY   You ain't never gave me nothing! You ain't never done nothing but hold me back. Afraid I was gonna be better than you. All you ever did was try and make me scared of you. I used to tremble every time you called my name. Every time I heard your footsteps in the house. Wondering all the time . . . what's Papa gonna say if I do this? . . . What's he gonna say if I do that? . . . what's Papa gonna say if I turn on the radio? And Mama, too . . . she tries . . . but she's scared of you.

TROY   You leave your mama out of this. She ain't got nothing to do with this.

CORY   I don't know how she stand you . . . after what you did to her.

TROY   I told you to leave your mama out of this! [*He advances toward* CORY.]

CORY   What you gonna do . . . give me a whupping? You can't whup me no more. You're too old. You just an old man.

TROY   [*shoves him on his shoulder*]   Nigger! That's what you are. You just another nigger on the street to me!

CORY   You crazy! You know that?

TROY   Go on now! You got the devil in you. Get on away from me!

CORY   You just a crazy old man . . . talking about I got the devil in me.

TROY   Yeah, I'm crazy! If you don't get on the other side of that yard . . . I'm gonna show you how crazy I am! Go on . . . get the hell out of my yard.

CORY   It ain't your yard. You took Uncle Gabe's money he got from the army to buy this house and then you put him out.

TROY   [TROY *advances on* CORY.]   Get your black ass out of my yard!
    [TROY's *advance backs* CORY *up against the tree.* CORY *grabs up the bat.*]

CORY   I ain't going nowhere! Come on . . . put me out! I ain't scared of you.

TROY   That's my bat!

CORY   Come on!

TROY   Put my bat down!

CORY   Come on, put me out. [CORY *swings at* TROY, *who backs across the yard.*] What's the matter? You so bad . . . put me out!
    [TROY *advances toward* CORY.]

CORY   [*backing up*]   Come on! Come on!

TROY   You're gonna have to use it! You wanna draw that bat back on me . . . you're gonna have to use it.

CORY   Come on! . . . Come on!
    [CORY *swings the bat at* TROY *a second time. He misses.* TROY *continues to advance toward him.*]

TROY   You're gonna have to kill me! You wanna draw that bat back on me. You're gonna have to kill me.
    [CORY, *backed up against the tree, can go no farther.* TROY *taunts him. He sticks out his head and offers him a target.*]

Come on! Come on!
    [CORY *is unable to swing the bat.* TROY *grabs it.*]

TROY   Then I'll show you.
    [CORY *and* TROY *struggle over the bat. The struggle is fierce and fully engaged.* TROY *ultimately is the stronger, and takes the bat from* CORY *and stands over him ready to swing. He stops himself.*]

Go on and get away from around my house.
    [CORY, *stung by his defeat, picks himself up, walks slowly out of the yard and up the alley.*]

CORY   Tell Mama I'll be back for my things.

TROY   They'll be on the other side of that fence.
    [CORY *exits.*]

TROY   I can't taste nothing. Helluljah! I can't taste nothing no more. [TROY *assumes a batting posture and begins to taunt Death, the fastball in the outside corner.*] Come on! It's between you and me now! Come on! Anytime you want! Come on! I be ready for you . . . but I ain't gonna be easy.
    [*The lights go down on the scene.*]

SCENE 5

The time is 1965. The lights come up in the yard. It is the morning of TROY'S *funeral. A funeral plaque with a light hangs beside the door. There is a small garden plot off to the side. There is noise and activity in the house as* ROSE, LYONS *and* BONO *have gathered. The door opens and* RAYNELL, *seven years old, enters dressed in a flannel nightgown. She crosses to the garden and pokes around with a stick.* ROSE *calls from the house.*

ROSE Raynell!

RAYNELL Mam?

ROSE What you doing out there?

RAYNELL Nothing.

[ROSE *comes to the door.*]

ROSE Girl, get in here and get dressed. What you doing?

RAYNELL Seeing if my garden growed.

ROSE I told you it ain't gonna grow overnight. You got to wait.

RAYNELL It don't look like it never gonna grow. Dag!

ROSE I told you a watched pot never boils. Get in here and get dressed.

RAYNELL This ain't even no pot, Mama.

ROSE You just have to give it a chance. It'll grow. Now you come on and do what I told you. We got to be getting ready. This ain't no morning to be playing around. You hear me?

RAYNELL Yes, mam.

[ROSE *exits into the house.* RAYNELL *continues to poke at her garden with a stick.* CORY *enters. He is dressed in a Marine corporal's uniform, and carries a duffel bag. His posture is that of a military man, and his speech has a clipped sternness.*]

CORY [*to* RAYNELL] Hi. [*Pause.*] I bet your name is Raynell.

RAYNELL Uh huh.

CORY Is your mama home?

[RAYNELL *runs up on the porch and calls through the screendoor.*]

RAYNELL Mama . . . there's some man out here. Mama?

[ROSE *comes to the door.*]

ROSE Cory? Lord have mercy! Look here, you all! [ROSE *and* CORY *embrace in a tearful reunion as* BONO *and* LYONS *enter from the house dressed in funeral clothes.*]

BONO Aw, looka here . . .

ROSE Done got all grown up!

CORY Don't cry, Mama. What you crying about?

ROSE I'm just so glad you made it.

CORY Hey Lyons. How you doing, Mr. Bono.

[LYON *goes to embrace* CORY.]

LYONS Look at you, man. Look at you. Don't he look good, Rose. Got them Corporal stripes.

ROSE What took you so long.

CORY You know how the Marines are, Mama. They got to get all their paperwork straight before they let you do anything.

ROSE Well, I'm sure glad you made it. They let Lyons come. Your Uncle Gabe's still in the hospital. They don't know if they gonna let him out or not. I just talked to them a little while ago.

LYONS   A Corporal in the United States Marines.

BONO   Your daddy knew you had it in you. He used to tell me all the time.

LYONS   Don't he look good, Mr. Bono?

BONO   Yeah, he remind me of Troy when I first met him. [*Pause.*] Say, Rose, Lucille's down at the church with the choir. I'm gonna go down and get the pallbearers lined up. I'll be back to get you all.

ROSE   Thanks, Jim.

CORY   See you, Mr. Bono.

LYONS   [*With his arm around* RAYNELL]   Cory . . . look at Raynell. Ain't she precious? She gonna break a whole lot of hearts.

ROSE   Raynell, come and say hello to your brother. This is your brother, Cory. You remember Cory.

RAYNELL   No, Mam.

CORY   She don't remember me, Mama.

ROSE   Well, we talk about you. She heard us talk about you. [*To* RAYNELL.] This is your brother, Cory. Come on and say hello.

RAYNELL   Hi.

CORY   Hi. So you're Raynell. Mama told me a lot about you.

ROSE   You all come on into the house and let me fix you some breakfast. Keep up your strength.

CORY   I ain't hungry, Mama.

LYONS   You can fix me something, Rose. I'll be in there in a minute.

ROSE   Cory, you sure you don't want nothing. I know they ain't feeding you right.

CORY   No, Mama . . . thanks. I don't feel like eating. I'll get something later.

ROSE   Raynell . . . get on upstairs and get that dress on like I told you.
[ROSE *and* RAYNELL *exit into the house.*]

LYONS   So . . . I hear you thinking about getting married.

CORY   Yeah, I done found the right one, Lyons. It's about time.

LYONS   Me and Bonnie been split up about four years now. About the time Papa retired. I guess she just got tired of all them changes I was putting her through. [*Pause.*] I always knew you was gonna make something out yourself. Your head was always in the right direction. So . . . you gonna stay in . . . make it a career . . . put in your twenty years?

CORY   I don't know. I got six already, I think that's enough.

LYONS   Stick with Uncle Sam and retire early. Ain't nothing out here. I guess Rose told you what happened with me. They got me down the workhouse. I thought I was being slick cashing other people's checks.

CORY   How much time you doing?

LYONS   They give me three years. I got that beat now. I ain't got but nine more months. It ain't so bad. You learn to deal with it like anything else. You got to take the crookeds with the straights. That's what Papa used to say. He used to say that when he struck out. I seen him strike out three times in a row . . . and the next time up he hit the ball over the grandstand. Right out there in Homestead Field. He wasn't satisfied hitting in the seats . . . he want to hit it over everything! After the game he had two hundred people standing around waiting to shake his hand. You got to take the crookeds with the straights. Yeah, Papa was something else.

CORY   You still playing?

LYONS   Cory . . . you know I'm gonna do that. There's some fellows down there we got us a band . . . we gonna try and stay together when we get out . . . but yeah, I'm still playing. It still helps me to get out of bed in the morning. As long as it do that I'm gonna be right there playing and trying to make some sense out of it.

ROSE [*calling*]   Lyons, I got these eggs in the pan.

LYONS   Let me go on and get these eggs, man. Get ready to go bury Papa. [*Pause.*] How you doing? You doing alright?

> [CORY *nods.* LYONS *touches him on the shoulder and they share a moment of silent grief.* LYONS *exits into the house.* CORY *wanders about the yard.* RAYNELL *enters.*]

RAYNELL   Hi.

CORY   Hi.

RAYNELL   Did you used to sleep in my room?

CORY   Yeah . . . that used to be my room.

RAYNELL   That's what Papa call it. "Cory's room." It got your football in the closet.

> [ROSE *comes to the door.*]

ROSE   Raynell, get in there and get them good shoes on.

RAYNELL   Mama, can't I wear these. Them other one hurt my feet.

ROSE   Well, they just gonna have to hurt your feet for a while. You ain't said they hurt your feet when you went down to the store and got them.

RAYNELL   They didn't hurt then. My feet done got bigger.

ROSE   Don't you give me no backtalk now. You get in there and get them shoes on. [RAYNELL *exits into the house.*] Ain't too much changed. He still got that piece of rag tied to that tree. He was out here swinging that bat. I was just ready to go back in the house. He swung that bat and then he just fell over. Seem like he swung it and stood there with this grin on his face . . . and then he just fell over. They carried him on down to the hospital, but I knew there wasn't no need . . . why don't you come on in the house?

CORY   Mama . . . I got something to tell you. I don't know how to tell you this . . . but I've got to tell you . . . I'm not going to Papa's funeral.

ROSE   Boy, hush your mouth. That's your daddy you talking about. I don't want hear that kind of talk this morning. I done raised you to come to this? You standing there all healthy and grown talking about you ain't going to your daddy's funeral?

CORY   Mama . . . listen . . .

ROSE   I don't want to hear it, Cory. You just get that thought out of your head.

CORY   I can't drag Papa with me everywhere I go. I've got to say no to him. One time in my life I've got to say no.

ROSE   Don't nobody have to listen to nothing like that. I know you and your daddy ain't seen eye to eye, but I ain't got to listen to that kind of talk this morning. Whatever was between you and your daddy . . . the time has come to put it aside. Just take it and set it over there on the shelf and forget about it. Disrespecting your daddy ain't gonna make you a man, Cory. You got to find a way to come to that on your own. Not going to your daddy's funeral ain't gonna make you a man.

CORY The whole time I was growing up . . . living in his house . . . Papa was like a shadow that followed you everywhere. It weighed on you and sunk into your flesh. It would wrap around you and lay there until you couldn't tell which one was you anymore. That shadow digging in your flesh. Trying to crawl in. Trying to live through you. Everywhere I looked, Troy Maxson was staring back at me . . . hiding under the bed . . . in the closet. I'm just saying I've got to find a way to get rid of that shadow, Mama.

ROSE You just like him. You got him in you good.

CORY Don't tell me that, Mama.

ROSE You Troy Maxson all over again.

CORY I don't want to be Troy Maxson. I want to be me.

ROSE You can't be nobody but who you are, Cory. That shadow wasn't nothing but you growing into yourself. You either got to grow into it or cut it down to fit you. But that's all you got to make life with. That's all you got to measure yourself against that world out there. Your daddy wanted you to be everything he wasn't . . . and at the same time he tried to make you into everything he was. I don't know if he was right or wrong . . . but I do know he meant to do more good than he meant to do harm. He wasn't always right. Sometimes when he touched he bruised. And sometimes when he took me in his arms he cut. When I first met your daddy I thought . . . Here is a man I can lay down with and make a baby. That's the first thing I thought when I seen him. I was thirty years old and had done seen my share of men. But when he walked up to me and said, "I can dance a waltz that'll make you dizzy," I thought, Rose Lee, here is a man that you can open yourself up to and be filled to bursting. Here is a man that can fill all them empty spaces you been tipping around the edges of. One of them empty spaces was being somebody's mother. I married your daddy and settled down to cooking his supper and keeping clean sheets on the bed. When your daddy walked through the house he was so big he filled it up. That was my first mistake. Not to make him leave some room for me. For my part in the matter. But at that time I wanted that. I wanted a house that I could sing in. And that's what your daddy gave me. I didn't know to keep up his strength I had to give up little pieces of mine. I did that. I took on his life as mine and mixed up the pieces so that you couldn't hardly tell which was which anymore. It was my choice. It was my life and I didn't have to live it like that. But that's what life offered me in the way of being a woman, and I took it. I grabbed hold of it with both hands. By the time Raynell came into the house, me and your daddy had done lost touch with one another. I didn't want to make my blessing off of nobody's misfortune . . . but I took on to Raynell like she was all them babies I had wanted and never had. [*The phone rings.*] Like I'd been blessed to relive a part of my life. And if the Lord see fit to keep up my strength . . . I'm gonna do her just like your daddy did you . . . I'm gonna give her the best of what's in me.

RAYNELL [*entering, still with her old shoes*] Mama . . . Reverend Tollivier on the phone.

[ROSE *exits into the house.*]

RAYNELL Hi.

CORY Hi.

RAYNELL   You in the Army or the Marines?
CORY   Marines.
RAYNELL   Papa said it was the Army. Did you know Blue?
CORY   Blue? Who's Blue?
RAYNELL   Papa's dog what he sing about all the time.

> [CORY *singing.*]
> Hear it ring! hear it ring!
> I had a dog his name was Blue
> You know Blue was mighty true
> You know Blue was a good old dog
> Blue treed a possum in a hollow log
> You know from that he was a good old dog.
> Hear it ring! Hear it ring!

[RAYNELL *joins in singing.*]

> [CORY *and* RAYNELL]
> Blue treed a possum out on a limb
> Blue looked at me and I looked at him
> Grabbed that possum and put him in a sack
> Blue stayed there till I came back
> Old Blue's feets was big and round
> Never allowed a possum to touch the ground.
>
> Old Blue died and I dug his grave
> I dug his grave with a silver spade
> Let him down with a golden chain
> And every night I call his name
> Go on Blue, you good dog you
> Go on Blue, you good dog you
> [RAYNELL]
> Blue laid down and died like a man
> Blue laid down and died . . .
> [BOTH]
> Blue laid down and died like a man
> Now he's treeing possums in the Promised Land
> I'm gonna tell you this to let you know
> Blue's gone where the good dogs go
> When I hear old Blue bark
> When I heard old Blue bark
> Blue treed a possum in Noah's Ark
> Blue treed a possum in Noah's Ark.

[ROSE *comes to the screen door.*]

ROSE   Cory, we gonna be ready to go in a minute.
CORY   [*to* RAYNELL]   You go on in the house and change them shoes like Mama told you so we can go to papa's funeral.
RAYNELL   Okay, I'll be right back.

> [RAYNELL *exits into the house.* CORY *gets up and crosses over to the tree.* ROSE *stands in the screen door watching him.* GABRIEL *enters from the alley.*]

GABRIEL   [*calling*]   Hey, Rose!
ROSE   Gabe?
GABRIEL   I'm here, Rose. Hey Rose, I'm here!

[ROSE *enters from the house.*]

ROSE Lord . . . Look here, Lyons!

LYONS See, I told you, Rose . . . I told you they'd let him come.

CORY How you doing, Uncle Gabe?

LYONS How you doing, Uncle Gabe?

GABRIEL Hey, Rose. It's time. It's time to tell St. Peter to open the gates. Troy, you ready? You ready, Troy. I'm gonna tell St. Peter to open the gates. You get ready now.

> [GABRIEL, *with great fanfare, braces himself to blow. The trumpet is without a mouthpiece. He puts the end of it into his mouth and blows with great force, like a man who has been waiting some twenty-odd years for this single moment. No sound comes out of the trumpet. He braces himself and blows again with the same result. A third time he blows. There is a weight of impossible description that falls away and leaves him bare and exposed to a frightful realization. It is a trauma that a sane and normal mind would be unable to withstand. He begins to dance. A slow, strange dance, eerie and life-giving. A dance of atavistic signature and ritual.* LYONS *attempts to embrace him.* GABRIEL *pushes* LYONS *away. He begins to howl in what is an attempt at song, or perhaps a song turning back into itself in an attempt at speech. He finishes his dance and the gates of heaven stand open as wide as God's closet.*]

That's the way that go!

[*BLACKOUT.*]

ANNIE DILLARD
b. 1945

Annie Dillard was born in Pittsburgh, Pennsylvania; was educated at Hollins College, Virginia; and has taught creative writing at Western Washington University and Wesleyan University. She has lived in the Blue Ridge Mountains of the Appalachian chain and among the Cascades of the Pacific Northwest; it is the solitude and close attention to nature and one's own thoughts prompted by rural life in these regions that motivate her writing, which among her generation is stylistically unique. She is deeply meditative, even spiritual, yet she can express herself in a swinging rhythm that sweeps up poetic insight and religious references with the same joyful ease of describing nature at play. *Pilgrim at Tinker Creek* (1974) follows the progress of the seasons as the author lives a quiet, closely observant life in the seclusion of Virginia's Roanoke Valley. Nature is studied, but so are books of a widely ranging theological, philosophical, and scientific nature. The author's subject is nothing less than cosmic, a search for understanding how beauty and violence form necessary parts of the world as we know it. Nature, like human life, is generously productive and violently destructive, equally inclusive and isolative. These tensions reinforce the thoughts Dillard examines: her own, and also those of writers who have formed our intellectual heritage. In this way her work resembles that of the American Transcendentalist Henry David Thoreau in *Walden*, particularly in its appreciation of nature's cyclic patterns. More like Thoreau's friend

Ralph Waldo Emerson, however, Dillard directs her thoughts to metaphysical ends, joining a tradition reaching back to Puritan poetry and sermons. "Seeing," excerpted here, helps establish a rhythm important to all of *Pilgrim at Tinker Creek*, that of paging through nature as though it is a book while reading commentaries by critics as though they are signs of nature. As the critic Wendy Lesser noted about the author's essay "For the Time Being" (1999), Dillard excels with "the conjunction of seemingly disparate facts that eventually add up to a complex whole."

Elsewhere in Dillard's canon are lighter subjects, such as the status of the contemporary novel (*Living by Fiction*, 1982) and accounts of picturesque travel (*Teaching a Stone to Talk*, 1982). The author has written about meeting Chinese writers, reminisced about her childhood, and studied her writing processes. In 1992 she published *The Living*, a historical novel set in the Pacific Northwest that is as much about the landscape as about its inhabitants. A second novel, *The Maytrees* (2007), is very much a product of a writerly mind, in which the progress of a long marriage allows ample time for meditation. As the critic Ihab Hassan has said of Dillard's "Holy the Firm" (1977): "Her language is as textured as her perception, an Orphic poetry with terrors small and near at hand; her path is that of the solitary wanderer, in the wilderness of the Cascades or Blue Ridge Mountains, living in a rough cabin to 'study hard things.'"

The following text is from *Pilgrim at Tinker Creek* (1974).

From Pilgrim at Tinker Creek

Seeing

When I was six or seven years old, growing up in Pittsburgh, I used to take a precious penny of my own and hide it for someone else to find. It was a curious compulsion; sadly, I've never been seized by it since. For some reason I always "hid" the penny along the same stretch of sidewalk up the street. I would cradle it at the roots of a sycamore, say, or in a hole left by a chipped-off piece of sidewalk. Then I would take a piece of chalk, and, starting at either end of the block, draw huge arrows leading up to the penny from both directions. After I learned to write I labeled the arrows: SURPRISE AHEAD or MONEY THIS WAY. I was greatly excited, during all this arrow-drawing, at the thought of the first lucky passer-by who would receive in this way, regardless of merit, a free gift from the universe. But I never lurked about. I would go straight home and not give the matter another thought, until, some months later, I would be gripped again by the impulse to hide another penny.

It is still the first week in January, and I've got great plans. I've been thinking about seeing. There are lots of things to see, unwrapped gifts and free surprises. The world is fairly studded and strewn with pennies cast broadside from a generous hand. But—and this is the point—who gets excited by a mere penny? If you follow one arrow, if you crouch motionless on a bank to watch a tremulous ripple thrill on the water and are rewarded by the sight of a muskrat kit paddling from its den, will you count that sight a chip of copper only, and go your rueful way? It is dire poverty indeed when a man is so malnourished and fatigued that he won't stoop to pick up a penny. But if you cultivate a healthy poverty and simplicity, so that finding a penny will literally make your day, then, since the world is in fact planted in pennies, you have with your poverty bought a lifetime of days. It is that simple. What you see is what you get.

I used to be able to see flying insects in the air. I'd look ahead and see, not the row of hemlocks across the road, but the air in front of it. My eyes would focus along that column of air, picking out flying insects. But I lost interest, I guess, for I dropped the habit. Now I can see birds. Probably some people can look at the grass at their feet and discover all the crawling creatures. I would like to know grasses and sedges—and care. Then my least journey into the world would be a field trip, a series of happy recognitions. Thoreau,[1] in an expansive mood, exulted, "What a rich book might be made about buds, including, perhaps, sprouts!" It would be nice to think so. I cherish mental images I have of three perfectly happy people. One collects stones. Another—an Englishman, say—watches clouds. The third lives on a coast and collects drops of seawater which he examines microscopically and mounts. But I don't see what the specialist sees, and so I cut myself off, not only from the total picture, but from the various forms of happiness.

Unfortunately, nature is very much a now-you-see-it, now-you-don't affair. A fish flashes, then dissolves in the water before my eyes like so much salt. Deer apparently ascend bodily into heaven; the brightest oriole fades into leaves. These disappearances stun me into stillness and concentration; they say of nature that it conceals with a grand nonchalance, and they say of vision that it is a deliberate gift, the revelation of a dancer who for my eyes only flings away her seven veils. For nature does reveal as well as conceal: now-you-don't-see-it, now-you-do. For a week last September migrating red-winged blackbirds were feeding heavily down by the creek at the back of the house. One day I went out to investigate the racket; I walked up to a tree, an Osage orange,[2] and a hundred birds flew away. They simply materialized out of the tree. I saw a tree, then a whisk of color, then a tree again. I walked closer and another hundred blackbirds took flight. Not a branch, not a twig budged: the birds were apparently weightless as well as invisible. Or, it was as if the leaves of the Osage orange had been freed from a spell in the form of red-winged blackbirds; they flew from the tree, caught my eye in the sky, and vanished. When I looked again at the tree the leaves had reassembled as if nothing had happened. Finally I walked directly to the trunk of the tree and a final hundred, the real diehards, appeared, spread, and vanished. How could so many hide in the tree without my seeing them? The Osage orange, unruffled, looked just as it had looked from the house, when three hundred red-winged blackbirds cried from its crown. I looked downstream where they flew, and they were gone. Searching, I couldn't spot one. I wandered downstream to force them to play their hand, but they'd crossed the creek and scattered. One show to a customer. These appearances catch at my throat; they are the free gifts, the bright coppers at the roots of trees.

It's all a matter of keeping my eyes open. Nature is like one of those line drawings of a tree that are puzzles for children: Can you find hidden in the

---

1. Henry David Thoreau (1817–1862), American writer and naturalist associated with the Transcendentalist movement.

2. Hardwood tree of the mulberry family, sometimes called the mock orange.

leaves a duck, a house, a boy, a bucket, a zebra, and a boot? Specialists can find the most incredibly well-hidden things. A book I read when I was young recommended an easy way to find caterpillars to rear: you simply find some fresh caterpillar droppings, look up, and there's your caterpillar. More recently an author advised me to set my mind at ease about those piles of cut stems on the ground in grassy fields. Field mice make them; they cut the grass down by degrees to reach the seeds at the head. It seems that when the grass is tightly packed, as in a field of ripe grain, the blade won't topple at a single cut through the stem; instead, the cut stem simply drops vertically, held in the crush of grain. The mouse severs the bottom again and again, the stem keeps dropping an inch at a time, and finally the head is low enough for the mouse to reach the seeds. Meanwhile, the mouse is positively littering the field with its little piles of cut stems into which, presumably, the author of the book is constantly stumbling.

If I can't see these minutiae, I still try to keep my eyes open. I'm always on the lookout for antlion traps in sandy soil, monarch pupae near milkweed, skipper larvae in locust leaves. These things are utterly common, and I've not seen one. I bang on hollow trees near water, but so far no flying squirrels have appeared. In flat country I watch every sunset in hopes of seeing the green ray. The green ray is a seldom-seen streak of light that rises from the sun like a spurting fountain at the moment of sunset; it throbs into the sky for two seconds and disappears. One more reason to keep my eyes open. A photography professor at the University of Florida just happened to see a bird die in mid-flight; it jerked, died, dropped, and smashed on the ground. I squint at the wind because I read Stewart Edward White.[3] "I have always maintained that if you looked closely enough you could *see* the wind—the dim, hardly-made-out, fine débris fleeing high in the air." White was an excellent observer, and devoted an entire chapter of *The Mountains*[4] to the subject of seeing deer: "As soon as you can forget the naturally obvious and construct an artificial obvious, then you too will see deer."

But the artificial obvious is hard to see. My eyes account for less than one percent of the weight of my head; I'm bony and dense; I see what I expect. I once spent a full three minutes looking at a bullfrog that was so unexpectedly large I couldn't see it even though a dozen enthusiastic campers were shouting directions. Finally I asked, "What color am I looking for?" and a fellow said, "Green." When at last I picked out the frog, I saw what painters are up against: the thing wasn't green at all, but the color of wet hickory bark.

The lover can see, and the knowledgeable. I visited an aunt and uncle at a quarter-horse ranch in Cody, Wyoming.[5] I couldn't do much of anything useful, but I could, I thought, draw. So, as we all sat around the kitchen table after supper, I produced a sheet of paper and drew a horse. "That's one lame horse," my aunt volunteered. The rest of the family joined in: "Only place to saddle that one is his neck"; "Looks like we better shoot the poor thing, on account of those terrible growths." Meekly, I slid the pencil and paper down the table. Everyone in that family, including my three young cousins, could draw a horse. Beautifully. When the paper came back

3. American spiritualist writer (1873–1946).
4. Published in 1904.
5. City in the northwestern section of the state.

"Quarter horse": type of small horse bred for strength, speed, and endurance.

it looked as though five shining, real quarter horses had been corraled by mistake with a papier-mâché moose; the real horses seemed to gaze at the monster with a steady, puzzled air. I stay away from horses now, but I can do a creditable goldfish. The point is that I just don't know what the lover knows; I just can't see the artificial obvious that those in the know construct. The herpetologist asks the native, "Are there snakes in that ravine?" "Nosir." And the herpetologist comes home with, yessir, three bags full. Are there butterflies on that mountain? Are the bluets in bloom, are there arrowheads here, or fossil shells in the shale?

Peeping through my keyhole I see within the range of only about thirty percent of the light that comes from the sun; the rest is infrared and some little ultraviolet, perfectly apparent to many animals, but invisible to me. A nightmare network of ganglia, charged and firing without my knowledge, cuts and splices what I do see, editing it for my brain. Donald E. Carr[6] points out that the sense impressions of one-celled animals are *not* edited for the brain: "This is philosophically interesting in a rather mournful way, since it means that only the simplest animals perceive the universe as it is."

A fog that won't burn away drifts and flows across my field of vision. When you see fog move against a backdrop of deep pines, you don't see the fog itself, but streaks of clearness floating across the air in dark shreds. So I see only tatters of clearness through a pervading obscurity. I can't distinguish the fog from the overcast sky; I can't be sure if the light is direct or reflected. Everywhere darkness and the presence of the unseen appalls. We estimate now that only one atom dances alone in every cubic meter of intergalactic space. I blink and squint. What planet or power yanks Halley's Comet[7] out of orbit? We haven't seen that force yet; it's a question of distance, density, and the pallor of reflected light. We rock, cradled in the swaddling band of darkness. Even the simple darkness of night whispers suggestions to the mind. Last summer, in August, I stayed at the creek too late.

Where Tinker Creek flows under the sycamore log bridge to the tear-shaped island, it is slow and shallow, fringed thinly in cattail marsh. At this spot an astonishing bloom of life supports vast breeding populations of insects, fish, reptiles, birds, and mammals. On windless summer evenings I stalk along the creek bank or straddle the sycamore log in absolute stillness, watching for muskrats. The night I stayed too late I was hunched on the log staring spellbound at spreading, reflected stains of lilac on the water. A cloud in the sky suddenly lighted as if turned on by a switch; its reflection just as suddenly materialized on the water upstream, flat and floating, so that I couldn't see the creek bottom, or life in the water under the cloud. Downstream, away from the cloud on the water, water turtles smooth as beans were gliding down with the current in a series of easy, weightless push-offs, as men bound on the moon. I didn't know whether to trace the progress of one turtle I was sure of, risking sticking my face in one of the bridge's spider webs made invisible by the gathering dark, or take a chance on seeing the carp, or scan the mudbank in hope of seeing a muskrat, or

6. American environmentalist and writer (1903–1986).
7. Observed by the English astronomer Edmond Halley (1656–1742), who predicted that its orbit would return the comet to earthly view every seventy-six years.

follow the last of the swallows who caught at my heart and trailed it after them like streamers as they appeared from directly below, under the log, flying upstream with their tails forked, so fast.

But shadows spread, and deepened, and stayed. After thousands of years we're still strangers to darkness, fearful aliens in an enemy camp with our arms crossed over our chests. I stirred. A land turtle on the bank, startled, hissed the air from its lungs and withdrew into its shell. An uneasy pink here, an unfathomable blue there, gave great suggestion of lurking beings. Things were going on. I couldn't see whether that sere rustle I heard was a distant rattlesnake, slit-eyed, or a nearby sparrow kicking in the dry flood debris slung at the foot of a willow. Tremendous action roiled the water everywhere I looked, big action, inexplicable. A tremor welled up beside a gaping muskrat burrow in the bank and I caught my breath, but no muskrat appeared. The ripples continued to fan upstream with a steady, powerful thrust. Night was knitting over my face an eyeless mask, and I still sat transfixed. A distant airplane, a delta wing out of nightmare, made a gliding shadow on the creek's bottom that looked like a stingray cruising upstream. At once a black fin slit the pink cloud on the water, shearing it in two. The two halves merged together and seemed to dissolve before my eyes. Darkness pooled in the cleft of the creek and rose, as water collects in a well. Untamed, dreaming lights flickered over the sky. I saw hints of hulking underwater shadows, two pale splashes out of the water, and round ripples rolling close together from a blackened center.

At last I stared upstream where only the deepest violet remained of the cloud, a cloud so high its underbelly still glowed feeble color reflected from a hidden sky lighted in turn by a sun halfway to China. And out of that violet, a sudden enormous black body arced over the water. I saw only a cylindrical sleekness. Head and tail, if there was a head and tail, were both submerged in cloud. I saw only one ebony fling, a headlong dive to darkness; then the waters closed, and the lights went out.

I walked home in a shivering daze, up hill and down. Later I lay open-mouthed in bed, my arms flung wide at my sides to steady the whirling darkness. At this latitude I'm spinning 836 miles an hour round the earth's axis; I often fancy I feel my sweeping fall as a breakneck arc like the dive of dolphins, and the hollow rushing of wind raises hair on my neck and the side of my face. In orbit around the sun I'm moving 64,800 miles an hour. The solar system as a whole, like a merry-go-round unhinged, spins, bobs, and blinks at the speed of 43,200 miles an hour along a course set east of Hercules.[8] Someone has piped, and we are dancing a tarantella until the sweat pours. I open my eyes and I see dark, muscled forms curl out of water, with flapping gills and flattened eyes. I close my eyes and I see stars, deep stars giving way to deeper stars, deeper stars bowing to deepest stars at the crown of an infinite cone.

"Still," wrote van Gogh[9] in a letter, "a great deal of light falls on everything." If we are blinded by darkness, we are also blinded by light. When too much light falls on everything, a special terror results. Peter Freuchen[1]

---

8. A large northern constellation, named after the Greek and Roman god.
9. Vincent van Gogh (1853–1890), Dutch Post-

impressionist painter.
1. Danish writer, explorer, and authority on Greenland (1886–1957).

describes the notorious kayak sickness to which Greenland Eskimos are prone. "The Greenland fjords are peculiar for the spells of completely quiet weather, when there is not enough wind to blow out a match and the water is like a sheet of glass. The kayak hunter must sit in his boat without stirring a finger so as not to scare the shy seals away. . . . The sun, low in the sky, sends a glare into his eyes, and the landscape around moves into the realm of the unreal. The reflex from the mirrorlike water hypnotizes him, he seems to be unable to move, and all of a sudden it is as if he were floating in a bottomless void, sinking, sinking, and sinking. . . . Horror-stricken, he tries to stir, to cry out, but he cannot, he is completely paralyzed, he just falls and falls." Some hunters are especially cursed with this panic, and bring ruin and sometimes starvation to their families.

Sometimes here in Virginia at sunset low clouds on the southern or northern horizon are completely invisible in the lighted sky. I only know one is there because I can see its reflection in still water. The first time I discovered this mystery I looked from cloud to no-cloud in bewilderment, checking my bearings over and over, thinking maybe the ark of the covenant[2] was just passing by south of Dead Man Mountain. Only much later did I read the explanation: polarized light from the sky is very much weakened by reflection, but the light in clouds isn't polarized. So invisible clouds pass among visible clouds, till all slide over the mountains; so a greater light extinguishes a lesser as though it didn't exist.

In the great meteor shower of August, the Perseid, I wail all day for the shooting stars I miss. They're out there showering down, committing hara-kiri in a flame of fatal attraction, and hissing perhaps at last into the ocean. But at dawn what looks like a blue dome clamps down over me like a lid on a pot. The stars and planets could smash and I'd never know. Only a piece of ashen moon occasionally climbs up or down the inside of the dome, and our local star without surcease explodes on our heads. We have really only that one light, one source for all power, and yet we must turn away from it by universal decree. Nobody here on the planet seems aware of this strange, powerful taboo, that we all walk about carefully averting our faces, this way and that, lest our eyes be blasted forever.

Darkness appalls and light dazzles; the scrap of visible light that doesn't hurt my eyes hurts my brain. What I see sets me swaying. Size and distance and the sudden swelling of meanings confuse me, bowl me over. I straddle the sycamore log bridge over Tinker Creek in the summer. I look at the lighted creek bottom: snail tracks tunnel the mud in quavering curves. A crayfish jerks, but by the time I absorb what has happened, he's gone in a billowing smokescreen of silt. I look at the water: minnows and shiners. If I'm thinking minnows, a carp will fill my brain till I scream. I look at the water's surface: skaters, bubbles, and leaves sliding down. Suddenly, my own face, reflected, startles me witless. Those snails have been tracking my face! Finally, with a shuddering wrench of the will, I see clouds, cirrus clouds. I'm dizzy, I fall in. This looking business is risky.

Once I stood on a humped rock on nearby Purgatory Mountain, watching through binoculars the great autumn hawk migration below, until I

2. In ancient Israel a chest containing two stone tablets of the Ten Commandments, seen as a symbol of God's presence.

discovered that I was in danger of joining the hawks on a vertical migration of my own. I was used to binoculars, but not, apparently, to balancing on humped rocks while looking through them. I staggered. Everything advanced and receded by turns; the world was full of unexplained fore-shortenings and depths. A distant huge tan object, a hawk the size of an elephant, turned out to be the browned bough of a nearby loblolly pine. I followed a sharp-shinned hawk against a featureless sky, rotating my head unawares as it flew, and when I lowered the glass a glimpse of my own looming shoulder sent me staggering. What prevents the men on Palomar[3] from falling, voiceless and blinded, from their tiny, vaulted chairs?

I reel in confusion; I don't understand what I see. With the naked eye I can see two million light-years to the Andromeda galaxy. Often I slop some creek water in a jar and when I get home I dump it in a white china bowl. After the silt settles I return and see tracings of minute snails on the bottom, a planarian or two winding round the rim of water, roundworms shimmying frantically, and finally, when my eyes have adjusted to these dimensions, amoebae. At first the amoebae look like muscae volitantes, those curled moving spots you seem to see in your eyes when you stare at a distant wall. Then I see the amoebae as drops of water congealed, bluish, translucent, like chips of sky in the bowl. At length I choose one individual and give myself over to its idea of an evening. I see it dribble a grainy foot before it on its wet, unfathomable way. Do its unedited sense impressions include the fierce focus of my eyes? Shall I take it outside and show it Andromeda, and blow its little endoplasm? I stir the water with a finger, in case it's running out of oxygen. Maybe I should get a tropical aquarium with motorized bubblers and lights, and keep this one for a pet. Yes, it would tell its fissioned descendants, the universe is two feet by five, and if you listen closely you can hear the buzzing music of the spheres.

Oh, it's mysterious lamplit evenings, here in the galaxy, one after the other. It's one of those nights when I wander from window to window, looking for a sign. But I can't see. Terror and a beauty insoluble are a ribband of blue woven into the fringes of garments of things both great and small. No culture explains, no bivouac offers real haven or rest. But it could be that we are not seeing something. Galileo[4] thought comets were an optical illusion. This is fertile ground: since we are certain that they're not, we can look at what our scientists have been saying with fresh hope. What if there are *really* gleaming, castellated cities hung upside-down over the desert sand? What limpid lakes and cool date palms have our caravans always passed untried? Until, one by one, by the blindest of leaps, we light on the road to these places, we must stumble in darkness and hunger. I turn from the window. I'm blind as a bat, sensing only from every direction the echo of my own thin cries.

I chanced on a wonderful book by Marius von Senden, called *Space and Sight.*[5] When Western surgeons discovered how to perform safe cataract

---

3. I.e., in the Palomar Observatory, on Palomar Mountain, in San Diego County, California.
4. Galileo Galilei (1564–1642), Italian astromer and physicist.

5. Written by the 20th-century German physician and published in German in 1932; English translation, 1960.

operations, they ranged across Europe and America operating on dozens of men and women of all ages who had been blinded by cataracts since birth. Von Senden collected accounts of such cases; the histories are fascinating. Many doctors had tested their patients' sense perceptions and ideas of space both before and after the operations. The vast majority of patients, of both sexes and all ages, had, in von Senden's opinion, no idea of space whatsoever. Form, distance, and size were so many meaningless syllables. A patient "had no idea of depth, confusing it with roundness." Before the operation a doctor would give a blind patient a cube and a sphere; the patient would tongue it or feel it with his hands, and name it correctly. After the operation the doctor would show the same objects to the patient without letting him touch them; now he had no clue whatsoever what he was seeing. One patient called lemonade "square" because it pricked on his tongue as a square shape pricked on the touch of his hands. Of another postoperative patient, the doctor writes, "I have found in her no notion of size, for example, not even within the narrow limits which she might have encompassed with the aid of touch. Thus when I asked her to show me how big her mother was, she did not stretch out her hands, but set her two index-fingers a few inches apart." Other doctors reported their patients' own statements to similar effect. "The room he was in . . . he knew to be but part of the house, yet he could not conceive that the whole house could look bigger"; "Those who are blind from birth . . . have no real conception of height or distance. A house that is a mile away is thought of as nearby, but requiring the taking of a lot of steps. . . . The elevator that whizzes him up and down gives no more sense of vertical distance than does the train of horizontal."

For the newly sighted, vision is pure sensation unencumbered by meaning: "The girl went through the experience that we all go through and forget, the moment we are born. She saw, but it did not mean anything but a lot of different kinds of brightness." Again, "I asked the patient what he could see; he answered that he saw an extensive field of light, in which everything appeared dull, confused, and in motion. He could not distinguish objects." Another patient saw "nothing but a confusion of forms and colours." When a newly sighted girl saw photographs and paintings, she asked, "'Why do they put those dark marks all over them?' 'Those aren't dark marks,' her mother explained, 'those are shadows. That is one of the ways the eye knows that things have shape. If it were not for shadows many things would look flat.' 'Well, that's how things do look,' Joan answered. 'Everything looks flat with dark patches.'"

But it is the patients' concepts of space that are most revealing. One patient, according to his doctor, "practiced his vision in a strange fashion; thus he takes off one of his boots, throws it some way off in front of him, and then attempts to gauge the distance at which it lies; he takes a few steps towards the boot and tries to grasp it; on failing to reach it, he moves on a step or two and gropes for the boot until he finally gets hold of it." "But even at this stage, after three weeks' experience of seeing," von Senden goes on, "'space,' as he conceives it, ends with visual space, i.e. with colour-patches that happen to bound his view. He does not yet have the notion that a larger object (a chair) can mask a smaller one (a dog), or that the latter can still be present even though it is not directly seen."

In general the newly sighted see the world as a dazzle of color-patches. They are pleased by the sensation of color, and learn quickly to name the colors, but the rest of seeing is tormentingly difficult. Soon after his operation a patient "generally bumps into one of these colour-patches and observes them to be substantial, since they resist him as tactual objects do. In walking about it also strikes him—or can if he pays attention—that he is continually passing in between the colours he sees, that he can go past a visual object, that a part of it then steadily disappears from view; and that in spite of this, however he twists and turns—whether entering the room from the door, for example, or returning back to it—he always has a visual space in front of him. Thus he gradually comes to realize that there is also a space behind him, which he does not see."

The mental effort involved in these reasonings proves overwhelming for many patients. It oppresses them to realize, if they ever do at all, the tremendous size of the world, which they had previously conceived of as something touchingly manageable. It oppresses them to realize that they have been visible to people all along, perhaps unattractively so, without their knowledge or consent. A disheartening number of them refuse to use their new vision, continuing to go over objects with their tongues, and lapsing into apathy and despair. "The child can see, but will not make use of his sight. Only when pressed can he with difficulty be brought to look at objects in his neighbourhood; but more than a foot away it is impossible to bestir him to the necessary effort." Of a twenty-one-year-old girl, the doctor relates, "Her unfortunate father, who had hoped for so much from this operation, wrote that his daughter carefully shuts her eyes whenever she wishes to go about the house, especially when she comes to a staircase, and that she is never happier or more at ease than when, by closing her eyelids, she relapses into her former state of total blindness." A fifteen-year-old boy, who was also in love with a girl at the asylum for the blind, finally blurted out, "No, really, I can't stand it any more; I want to be sent back to the asylum again. If things aren't altered, I'll tear my eyes out."

Some do learn to see, especially the young ones. But it changes their lives. One doctor comments on "the rapid and complete loss of that striking and wonderful serenity which is characteristic only of those who have never yet seen." A blind man who learns to see is ashamed of his old habits. He dresses up, grooms himself, and tries to make a good impression. While he was blind he was indifferent to objects unless they were edible; now, "a sifting of values sets in . . . his thoughts and wishes are mightily stirred and some few of the patients are thereby led into dissimulation, envy, theft and fraud."

On the other hand, many newly sighted people speak well of the world, and teach us how dull is our own vision. To one patient, a human hand, unrecognized, is "something bright and then holes." Shown a bunch of grapes, a boy calls out, "It is dark, blue and shiny. . . . It isn't smooth, it has bumps and hollows." A little girl visits a garden. "She is greatly astonished, and can scarcely be persuaded to answer, stands speechless in front of the tree, which she only names on taking hold of it, and then as 'the tree with the lights in it.'" Some delight in their sight and give themselves over to the visual world. Of a patient just after her bandages were removed, her doctor writes, "The first things to attract her attention were her own hands; she looked at them very closely, moved them repeatedly to and fro, bent and stretched the fingers, and seemed greatly astonished at the sight." One girl was eager to tell her blind friend that "men do not really look like trees at all," and astounded to discover that her every visitor had an utterly different face. Finally, a twenty-two-old girl was dazzled by the world's brightness and kept her eyes shut for two weeks. When at the end of that time she opened her eyes again, she did not recognize any objects, but, "the more she now directed her gaze upon everything about her, the more it could be seen how an expression of gratification and astonishment overspread her features; she repeatedly exclaimed: 'Oh God! How beautiful!'"

I saw color-patches for weeks after I read this wonderful book. It was summer; the peaches were ripe in the valley orchards. When I woke in the morning, color-patches wrapped round my eyes, intricately, leaving not one unfilled spot. All day long I walked among shifting color-patches that parted before me like the Red Sea and closed again in silence, transfigured, wherever I looked back. Some patches swelled and loomed, while others vanished utterly, and dark marks flitted at random over the whole dazzling sweep. But I couldn't sustain the illusion of flatness. I've been around for too long. Form is condemned to an eternal danse macabre with meaning: I couldn't unpeach the peaches. Nor can I remember ever having seen without understanding; the color-patches of infancy are lost. My brain then must have been smooth as any balloon. I'm told I reached for the moon; many babies do. But the color-patches of infancy swelled as meaning filled them; they arrayed themselves in solemn ranks down distance which unrolled and stretched before me like a plain. The moon rocketed away. I live now in a world of shadows that shape and distance color, a world where space makes a kind of terrible sense. What gnosticism is this, and what physics? The fluttering patch I saw in my nursery window—silver and green and shape-shifting blue—is gone; a row of Lombardy poplars takes its place, mute, across the distant lawn. That humming oblong creature pale as light that stole along the walls of my room at night, stretching exhilaratingly around the corners, is gone, too, gone the night I ate of the bittersweet fruit, put two and two together and puckered forever my brain. Martin Buber[6] tells this tale: "Rabbi Mendel once boasted to his teacher Rabbi Elimelekh that evenings he saw the angel who rolls away the light before the darkness, and mornings the angel who rolls away the darkness before the light. 'Yes,' said Rabbi Elimelekh, 'in my youth I saw that too. Later on you don't see these things any more.'"

Why didn't someone hand those newly sighted people paints and brushes from the start, when they still didn't know what anything was? Then maybe we all could see color-patches too, the world unraveled from reason, Eden before Adam gave names. The scales would drop from my eyes; I'd see trees like men walking; I'd run down the road against all orders, hallooing and leaping.

Seeing is of course very much a matter of verbalization. Unless I call my attention to what passes before my eyes, I simply won't see it. It is, as

---

6. Austrian-born Jewish philosopher (1878–1965) active in Germany and Israel.

Ruskin[7] says, "not merely unnoticed, but in the full, clear sense of the word, unseen." My eyes alone can't solve analogy tests using figures, the ones which show, with increasing elaborations, a big square, then a small square in a big square, then a big triangle, and expect me to find a small triangle in a big triangle. I have to say the words, describe what I'm seeing. If Tinker Mountain erupted, I'd be likely to notice. But if I want to notice the lesser cataclysms of valley life, I have to maintain in my head a running description of the present. It's not that I'm observant; it's just that I talk too much. Otherwise, especially in a strange place, I'll never know what's happening. Like a blind man at the ball game, I need a radio.

When I see this way I analyze and pry. I hurl over logs and roll away stones; I study the bank a square foot at a time, probing and tilting my head. Some days when a mist covers the mountains, when the muskrats won't show and the microscope's mirror shatters, I want to climb up the blank blue dome as a man would storm the inside of a circus tent, wildly, dangling, and with a steel knife claw a rent in the top, peep, and, if I must, fall.

But there is another kind of seeing that involves a letting go. When I see this way I sway transfixed and emptied. The difference between the two ways of seeing is the difference between walking with and without a camera. When I walk with a camera I walk from shot to shot, reading the light on a calibrated meter. When I walk without a camera, my own shutter opens, and the moment's light prints on my own silver gut. When I see this second way I am above all an unscrupulous observer.

It was sunny one evening last summer at Tinker Creek; the sun was low in the sky, upstream. I was sitting on the sycamore log bridge with the sunset at my back, watching the shiners the size of minnows who were feeding over the muddy sand in skittery schools. Again and again, one fish, then another, turned for a split second across the current and flash! the sun shot out from its silver side. I couldn't watch for it. It was always just happening somewhere else, and it drew my vision just as it disappeared: flash, like a sudden dazzle of the thinnest blade, a sparking over a dun and olive ground at chance intervals from every direction. Then I noticed white specks, some sort of pale petals, small, floating from under my feet on the creek's surface, very slow and steady. So I blurred my eyes and gazed towards the brim of my hat and saw a new world. I saw the pale white circles roll up, roll up, like the world's turning, mute and perfect, and I saw the linear flashes, gleaming silver, like stars being born at random down a rolling scroll of time. Something broke and something opened. I filled up like a new wineskin. I breathed an air like light; I saw a light like water. I was the lip of a fountain the creek filled forever; I was ether, the leaf in the zephyr; I was flesh-flake, feather, bone.

When I see this way I see truly. As Thoreau says, I return to my senses. I am the man who watches the baseball game in silence in an empty stadium. I see the game purely; I'm abstracted and dazed. When it's all over and the white-suited players lope off the green field to their shadowed dugouts, I leap to my feet; I cheer and cheer.

---

7. John Ruskin (1819–1900), English art critic and social observer.

But I can't go out and try to see this way. I'll fail, I'll go mad. All I can do is try to gag the commentator, to hush the noise of useless interior babble that keeps me from seeing just as surely as a newspaper dangled before my eyes. The effort is really a discipline requiring a lifetime of dedicated struggle; it marks the literature of saints and monks of every order East and West, under every rule and no rule, discalced and shod. The world's spiritual geniuses seem to discover universally that the mind's muddy river, this ceaseless flow of trivia and trash, cannot be dammed, and that trying to dam it is a waste of effort that might lead to madness. Instead you must allow the muddy river to flow unheeded in the dim channels of consciousness; you raise your sights; you look along it, mildly, acknowledging its presence without interest and gazing beyond it into the realm of the real where subjects and objects act and rest purely, without utterance. "Launch into the deep," says Jacques Ellul,[8] "and you shall see."

The secret of seeing is, then, the pearl of great price. If I thought he could teach me to find it and keep it forever I would stagger barefoot across a hundred deserts after any lunatic at all. But although the pearl may be found, it may not be sought. The literature of illumination reveals this above all: although it comes to those who wait for it, it is always, even to the most practiced and adept, a gift and a total surprise. I return from one walk knowing where the killdeer nests in the field by the creek and the hour the laurel blooms. I return from the same walk a day later scarcely knowing my own name. Litanies hum in my ears; my tongue flaps in my mouth Ailinon, alleluia![9] I cannot cause light; the most I can do is try to put myself in the path of its beam. It is possible, in deep space, to sail on solar wind. Light, be it particle or wave, has force: you rig a giant sail and go. The secret of seeing is to sail on solar wind. Hone and spread your spirit till you yourself are a sail, whetted, translucent, broadside to the merest puff.

When her doctor took her bandages off and led her into the garden, the girl who was no longer blind saw "the tree with the lights in it." It was for this tree I searched through the peach orchards of summer, in the forests of fall and down winter and spring for years. Then one day I was walking along Tinker Creek thinking of nothing at all and I saw the tree with the lights in it. I saw the backyard cedar where the mourning doves roost charged and transfigured, each cell buzzing with flame. I stood on the grass with the lights in it, grass that was wholly fire, utterly focused and utterly dreamed. It was less like seeing than like being for the first time seen, knocked breathless by a powerful glance. The flood of fire abated, but I'm still spending the power. Gradually the lights went out in the cedar, the colors died, the cells unflamed and disappeared. I was still ringing. I had been my whole life a bell, and never knew it until at that moment I was lifted and struck. I have since only very rarely seen the tree with the lights in it. The vision comes and goes, mostly goes, but I live for it, for the moment when the mountains open and a new light roars in spate through the crack, and the mountains slam.

1974

---

8. French sociologist, theologian, historian, philosopher, and critic of technology (1912–1994).
9. In Greek a representation of a woeful, plaintive dirge.

KAY RYAN
b. 1945

Although she loves the work of Emily Dickinson, Robert Frost, and William Carlos Williams, Kay Ryan's poems don't really sound like those of anyone else. Instead they make us rethink some of our conventional ideas about poetry. Most of her poems are short, accessible, frequently funny (as well as scary), and contain very few first-person pronouns. She loves playing with verbal material many poets disdain: puns, common idioms (see "Starblock"), clichés (see "Say Uncle" and "Home to Roost"), and she "is crazy about malapropisms" (words used mistakenly, and often quite humorously, for similar-sounding words). Perhaps her unconventional style has its origins in her background and her apprenticeship to poetry. Ryan grew up in Rosamond, California, a small and isolated town in the Mojave desert; her father was an oil driller and the family never had much money. She attended a community college close to home soon after her father died; at nineteen she transferred to UCLA, where she earned her B.A. and MFA. She subsequently entered, and later dropped out of, the Ph.D. program at UC Irvine (she couldn't stand the idea of being "a doctor of something I couldn't fix"). An ardent cyclist, during a 4,000-mile bicycle trip across the country in 1976 she realized that writing gave her "pleasure like nothing else," and she decided to become a poet. But she had no idea of how to go about it, so she turned to surprising sources for inspiration: *Ripley's Believe It or Not*, which deals in bizarre events so strange readers might question their truth, and Tarot cards. Each day she would turn one card over—"Love" it might say, or "Death"—and then write a poem on that subject. Seven years later she published her first collection, *Dragon Acts to Dragon Ends* (1983). She didn't imagine, in those days, that her work would be included in "The Best American Poetry" collection four times and she would be the recipient of numerous awards; in 2008 she was appointed the Poet Laureate Consultant in Poetry to the Library of Congress.

Unusual among contemporary poets who often discard the use of rhyme, Ryan makes extravagant and witty use of rhyme, often in unexpected places like the front

The Boondocks, by Aaron McGruder.

or middle of the line. She calls this strategy of rhyming "recombinant," appropriating a term from genetics in a characteristically surprising, smart, and fanciful way. Not only are Ryan's poems short, her lines are also short, and reading her work can be like encountering a series of sharp, unexpected turns or even like coming to the edge of a cliff; you look down at the next line and everything shifts. "[E]dges are the most powerful parts of a poem," Ryan has said, and her poems often explore the way the comic teeters on the brink of the serious. Humor, or what she calls "this cartoonish thing," is central to her poetry. Despite her penchant for brevity, she "cartoonishly" blows up the size of things in order to get them into "the visible range," and, like the best cartoons, what's comic contains an aftershock. When she reads her work aloud, audiences often laugh, but she warns them that "things will turn scary when they get home."

So perhaps it isn't so surprising that one Sunday she discovered her poem "Patience" quoted in Aaron McGruder's comic strip *Boondocks*—and reacted with delight. Readers who come to Ryan's poetry open to having their expectations about poems overturned will also experience a sense of delight. Her collections include *Flamingo Watching* (1994), which was a finalist for both the Lamont Poetry Selection and the Lenore Marshall Prize; *Elephant Rocks* (1996); *Say Uncle* (2000); *The Niagara River* (2005); and *The Best of It: New and Selected Poems* (2010). For more than thirty years Kay Ryan taught English part-time at the College of Marin at Kentfield, in Marin County, California. During her term as poet laureate she used her position to highlight community colleges as vital educational institutions.

Say Uncle[1]

Every day
you say,
*Just one
more try.*
Then another   5
irrecoverable
day slips by.
You will
say *ankle*,
you will   10
say *knuckle*;
why won't
you why
won't you
say *uncle*?   15

2000

---

1. An idiomatic informal expression demanding submission or an admission of defeat.

Star Block

There is no such thing
as *star block*.
We do not think of
locking out the light
of other galaxies.   5
It is light
so rinsed of impurities
(heat, for instance)
that it excites
no antibodies in us.   10
Yet people are
curiously soluble
in starlight.
Bathed in its
absence of insistence   15
their substance
loosens willingly,
their bright
designs dissolve.
Not proximity   20
but distance
burns us with love.

2000

Failure 2

There could be nutrients
in failure—
deep amendments
to the shallow soil
of wishes.   5
Think of the
dark and bitter
flavors of
black ales
and peasant loaves.[1]   10
Think of licorices.[2]
Think about
the tales of how
Indians put fishes
under corn plants.[3]   15

---

1. Rustic, hearty breads.
2. A type of plant root used medicinally or as a flavor in candy, commonly sold in black sticks.
3. Native Americans are said to have taught Plymouth settlers how to use fish as a fertilizer.

Next time hope
relinquishes a form,
think about that.

2000

The Material

*The ratio between the material Cornell[1] collected and the
material that ended up in his boxes was probably a thousand to one.*
—Deborah Solomon, Utopia Parkway

Whatever is done
leaves a hole in the
possible, a snip in
the gauze, a marble
and thimble missing   5
from the immaterial.
The laws are cruel
on this point. The
undone can't be
patched or stretched.   10
The wounds last.
The bundles of
nothing that are
our gift at birth, the
lavish trains we   15
trail into our span
like vans of seamless
promise, like fresh
sheets in baskets,
are our stock. We   20
must extract parts
to do work. As
time passes, the
promise is tattered
like a battle flag   25
above a war we
hope mattered.

2005

Carrying a Ladder

We are always
really carrying
a ladder, but it's
invisible. We

1. The American artist Joseph Cornell (1903–1972) is best known for his display boxes containing assemblages of found objects.

only know   5
something's
the matter:
something precious
crashes; easy doors
prove impassable.   10
Or, in the body,
there's too much
swing or off-
center gravity.
And, in the mind,   15
a drunken capacity,
access to out-of-range
apples. As though
one had a way to climb
out of the damage   20
and apology.

                                          2005

Lighthouse Keeping

Seas pleat
winds keen
fogs deepen
ships lean no
doubt, and   5
the lighthouse
keeper keeps
a light for
those left out.
It is intimate   10
and remote both
for the keeper
and those afloat.

                                          2005

The Niagara River[1]

As though
the river were
a floor, we position
our table and chairs
upon it, eat, and   5
have conversation.
As it moves along,

---

1. A river flowing about 35 miles in a northerly direction from Lake Erie to Lake Ontario, forming part of the border between Ontario and New York State, and including Niagara Falls in its course.

we notice—as
calmly as though
dining room paintings   10
were being replaced—
the changing scenes
along the shore. We
do know, we do
know this is the   15
Niagara River, but
it is hard to remember
what that means.

2005

Home to Roost

The chickens
are circling and
blotting out the
day. The sun is
bright, but the   5
chickens are in
the way. Yes,
the sky is dark
with chickens,
dense with them.   10
They turn and
then they turn
again. These
are the chickens
you let loose   15
one at a time
and small—
various breeds.
Now they have
come home   20
to roost—all
the same kind
at the same speed.

2005

Things Shouldn't Be So Hard

A life should leave
deep tracks:
ruts where she
went out and back
to get the mail   5
or move the hose
around the yard;

where she used to
stand before the sink,
a worn-out place;   10
beneath her hand
the china knobs
rubbed down to
white pastilles;
the switch she   15
used to feel for
in the dark
almost erased.
Her things should
keep her marks.   20
The passage
of a life should show;
it should abrade.
And when life stops,
a certain space—   25
however small—
should be left scarred
by the grand and
damaging parade.
Things shouldn't   30
be so hard.

2005

ANN BEATTIE
b. 1947

I f one writer has been held responsible for chronicling the fortunes of young people
from the American 1960s as they grew up, got married and divorced, worked at different jobs, and went to the same parties, Ann Beattie, who graduated from high
school in 1965, is that writer; indeed she has picked up some of the mythical reputation that adheres to the film *The Big Chill* (1983) as somehow "representative" in its
representation of late-sixties idealism and conviction gone flat or sour. Yet to stress
Beattie's importance as portraitist of a generation may be to do her a disservice, since
she is above all else a *fiction* writer, often a comic one, with an unrepresentative, even
idiosyncratic, style. Her stories and novels should be taken not merely as vehicles for
displaying social attitudes and manners, but as mannerist compositions that need to
be both looked at and listened to. Her style is too pronounced, too carefully contrived,
to be treated as a transparent medium through which "reality" is given us directly.

On its surface her life has been relatively uneventful, from growing up in a middle-
class suburb of Washington, D.C. (she was "an artsy little thing . . . painting pictures, writing," as she put it), taking her undergraduate degree at American
University, then going on to graduate study for a time at the University of Connecti-

cut. She soon began to send stories to the *New Yorker* and after the usual spate of rejections had one accepted, then others. By her mid-twenties she was contributing regularly to that most sought-after magazine, and in 1976, on the verge of her thirtieth birthday, she brought out simultaneously a collection of her stories, *Distortions*, and her first novel, *Chilly Scenes of Winter*.

The stories—some of them more experimental in style than her more recent work—are about transient, usually unsatisfactory relationships between people, married and single, male and female. Her characters' work provides them with little pleasure or fulfillment; almost anything threatens to become "just a job." What these people do best, and incessantly, is talk to each other about themselves, how they feel about their lives. In fact such talk is the essential ingredient in her fiction. As one of her more severe critics, Joseph Epstein, has pointed out, Beattie strives for not "development of character, accounts of motivation or moral resolution" but rather "states of feeling." In stories from her second collection, *Secrets and Surprises* (1978), such as "A Reasonable Man," "Lawn Party," and "Weekend," feelings are talked around, hinted at, never quite said, but are the only "things" that happen in the story. In "Weekend" (printed here) the force of that happening is cumulative and disturbing.

Like many fiction writers, Beattie acknowledges the influence of Hemingway ("I sound like someone talking in *The Sun Also Rises*," says a character in "The Lawn Party"), but her kinship with him is especially strong in that each uses language, exchanges between characters, to suggest—by all that is left unsaid in the spare, often dull sentences, the platitudinous conversations—that something interesting lies behind the words, that conversation. Hemingway manages in his best stories to make us feel the presence of something powerful behind the conventional words. Beattie's characters, decades later, yearn for there to be something real or interesting behind their banal words, but her work's poignancy lies in the hint that, as the characters themselves half guess, there may be nothing much behind them. Something important got lost, back there in the sixties.

Of her seven novels the most ambitious is *Falling in Place* (1980), which spreads the usual urban and suburban anomie over the usual Beattie cast of dispirited seekers after a better than usual day. But the book comes to life when it focuses on a fifteen-year-old girl, whose favorite characterizing response to things is "Suck-O," and her younger brother, a compulsive eater who loves violent comics but little else. This twosome, who could give the most obnoxious of Flannery O'Connor's fictional children a run for their money, is observed with satiric verve, and the book includes a number of brilliant parts. Beattie is essentially a writer of scenes rather than a contriver of extended sequences, just as the people she writes about can deal with life only—and just barely—a moment at a time.

Like her contemporary the short-fiction writer Raymond Carver, Beattie has many imitators, "minimalists" who try to prove that less is more and most often make the attempt with less than maximum talents. In fact, like all distinctive stylists, she cannot be imitated, only travestied. Her sharp, idiomatic humor, often operating so quietly the reader almost misses it, insures against airlessness in her fiction. Now that she has fully developed her distinctive style, the question is whether she can avoid further bureaucratizing of it—continuing efficiently to turn out the same product— and move instead in new and surprising directions.

The following text is from *Secrets and Surprises* (1978).

Weekend

On Saturday morning Lenore is up before the others. She carries her baby into the living room and puts him in George's favorite chair, which tilts because its back legs are missing, and covers him with a blanket. Then she lights a fire in the fireplace, putting fresh logs on a few embers that are still glowing from the night before. She sits down on the floor beside the chair and checks the baby, who has already gone back to sleep—a good thing, because there are guests in the house. George, the man she lives with, is very hospitable and impetuous; he extends invitations whenever old friends call, urging them to come spend the weekend. Most of the callers are his former students—he used to be an English professor—and when they come it seems to make things much worse. It makes *him* much worse, because he falls into smoking too much and drinking and not eating, and then his ulcer bothers him. When the guests leave, when the weekend is over, she has to cook bland food: applesauce, oatmeal, puddings. And his drinking does not taper off easily anymore; in the past he would stop cold when the guests left, but lately he only tapers down from Scotch to wine, and drinks wine well into the week—a lot of wine, perhaps a whole bottle with his meal—until his stomach is much worse. He is hard to live with. Once when a former student, a woman named Ruth, visited them—a lover, she suspected—she overheard George talking to her in his study, where he had taken her to see a photograph of their house before he began repairing it. George had told Ruth that she, Lenore, stayed with him because she was simple. It hurt her badly, made her actually dizzy with surprise and shame, and since then, no matter who the guests are, she never feels quite at ease on the weekends. In the past she enjoyed some of the things she and George did with their guests, but since overhearing what he said to Ruth she feels that all their visitors have been secretly told the same thing about her. To her, though, George is usually kind. But she is sure that is the reason he has not married her, and when he recently remarked on their daughter's intelligence (she is five years old, a girl named Maria) she found that she could no longer respond with simple pride; now she feels spite as well, feels that Maria exists as proof of her own good genes. She has begun to expect perfection of the child. She knows this is wrong, and she has tried hard not to communicate her anxiety to Maria, who is already, as her kindergarten teacher says, "untypical."

At first Lenore loved George because he was untypical, although after she had moved in with him and lived with him for a while she began to see that he was not exceptional but a variation on a type. She is proud of observing that, and she harbors the discovery—her silent response to his low opinion of her. She does not know why he found her attractive—in the beginning he did—because she does not resemble the pretty, articulate young women he likes to invite, with their lovers or girl friends, to their house for the weekend. None of these young women have husbands; when they bring a man with them at all they bring a lover, and they seem happy not to be married. Lenore, too, is happy to be single—not out of conviction that marriage is wrong but because she knows that it would be wrong to be married to George if he thinks she is simple. She thought at first to confront him with what she had overheard, to demand an explanation. But he can weasel out of any corner. At best, she can mildly fluster him, and later he will only blame it on Scotch. Of course she might ask why he has all these women come to visit, why he devotes so little time to her or the children. To that he would say that it was the quality of the time they spent together that mattered, not the quantity. He has already said that, in fact, without being asked. He says things over and over so that she will accept them as truths. And eventually she does. She does not like to think long and hard, and when there is an answer—even his answer—it is usually easier to accept it and go on with things. She goes on with what she has always done: tending the house and the children and George, when he needs her. She likes to bake and she collects art postcards. She is proud of their house, which was bought cheaply and improved by George when he was still interested in that kind of work, and she is happy to have visitors come there, even if she does not admire them or even like them.

Except for teaching a night course in photography at a junior college once a week, George has not worked since he left the university two years ago, after he was denied tenure. She cannot really tell if he is unhappy working so little, because he keeps busy in other ways. He listens to classical music in the morning, slowly sipping herbal teas, and on fair afternoons he lies outdoors in the sun, no matter how cold the day. He takes photographs, and walks alone in the woods. He does errands for her if they need to be done. Sometimes at night he goes to the library or goes to visit friends; he tells her that these people often ask her to come too, but he says she would not like them. This is true—she would not like them. Recently he has done some late-night cooking. He has always kept a journal, and he is a great letter writer. An aunt left him most of her estate, ten thousand dollars, and said in her will that he was the only one who really cared, who took the time, again and again, to write. He had not seen his aunt for five years before she died, but he wrote regularly. Sometimes Lenore finds notes that he has left for her. Once, on the refrigerator, there was a long note suggesting clever Christmas presents for her family that he had thought of while she was out. Last week he scotch-taped a slip of paper to a casserole dish that contained leftover veal stew, saying "This was delicious." He does not compliment her verbally, but he likes to let her know that he is pleased.

A few nights ago—the same night they got a call from Julie and Sarah, saying they were coming for a visit—she told him that she wished he would talk more, that he would confide in her.

"Confide what?" he said.

"You always take that attitude," she said. "You pretend that you have no thoughts. Why does there have to be so much silence?"

"I'm not a professor anymore," he said. "I don't have to spend every minute *thinking*."

But he loves to talk to the young women. He will talk to them on the phone for as much as an hour; he walks with them through the woods for most of the day when they visit. The lovers the young women bring with them always seem to fall behind; they give up and return to the house to sit and talk to her, or to help with the preparation of the meal, or to play with the children. The young woman and George come back refreshed, ready for another round of conversation at dinner.

A few weeks ago one of the young men said to her, "Why do you let it go on?" They had been talking lightly before that—about the weather, the children—and then, in the kitchen, where he was sitting shelling peas, he put his head on the table and said, barely audibly, "Why do you let it go on?" He did not raise his head, and she stared at him, thinking that she must have imagined his speaking. She was surprised—surprised to have heard it, and surprised that he had said nothing after that, which made her doubt that he had spoken.

"Why do I let what go on?" she said.

There was a long silence. "Whatever this sick game is, I don't want to get involved in it," he said at last. "It was none of my business to ask. I understand that you don't want to talk about it."

"But it's really cold out there," she said. "What could happen when it's freezing out?"

He shook his head, the way George did, to indicate that she was beyond understanding. But she wasn't stupid, and she knew what might be going on. She had said the right thing, had been on the right track, but she had to say what she felt, which was that nothing very serious could be happening at that moment because they were walking in the woods. There wasn't even a barn on the property. She knew perfectly well that they were talking.

When George and the young woman had come back, he fixed hot apple juice, into which he trickled rum. Lenore was pleasant, because she was sure of what had not happened; the young man was not, because he did not think as she did. Still at the kitchen table, he ran his thumb across a pea pod as though it were a knife.

This weekend Sarah and Julie are visiting. They came on Friday evening. Sarah was one of George's students—the one who led the fight to have him rehired. She does not look like a troublemaker; she is pale and pretty, with freckles on her cheeks. She talks too much about the past, and this upsets him, disrupts the peace he has made with himself. She tells him that they fired him because he was "in touch" with everything, that they were afraid of him because he was so in touch. The more she tells him the more he remembers, and then it is necessary for Sarah to say the same things again and again; once she reminds him, he seems to need reassurance—needs to have her voice, to hear her bitterness against the members of the tenure committee. By evening they will both be drunk. Sarah will seem both agitating and consoling, Lenore and Julie and the children will be upstairs, in bed. Lenore suspects that she will not be the only one awake listening to them. She thinks that in spite of Julie's glazed look she is really very attentive. The night before, when they were all sitting around the fireplace talking, Sarah made a gesture and almost upset her wineglass, but Julie reached for it and stopped it from toppling over. George and Sarah were talking so energetically that they did not notice. Lenore's eyes met Julie's as Julie's hand shot out. Lenore feels that she is like Julie: Julie's face doesn't betray emotion, even when she is interested, even when she cares deeply. Being the same kind of person, Lenore can recognize this.

Before Sarah and Julie arrived Friday evening, Lenore asked George if Sarah was his lover.

"Don't be ridiculous," he said. "You think every student is my lover? Is Julie my lover?"

She said, "That wasn't what I said."

"Well, if you're going to be preposterous, go ahead and say that," he said. "If you think about it long enough, it would make a lot of sense, wouldn't it?"

He would not answer her question about Sarah. He kept throwing Julie's name into it. Some other woman might then think that he was protesting too strongly—that Julie really was his lover. She thought no such thing. She also stopped suspecting Sarah, because he wanted that, and it was her habit to oblige him.

He is twenty-one years older than Lenore. On his last birthday he was fifty-five. His daughter from his first marriage (his *only* marriage; she keeps reminding herself that they are not married, because it often seems that they might as well be) sent him an Irish country hat. The present made him irritable. He kept putting it on and pulling it down hard on his head. "She wants to make me a laughable old man," he said. "She wants me to put this on and go around like a fool." He wore the hat all morning, complaining about it, frightening the children. Eventually, to calm him, she said, "She intended *nothing*." She said it with finality, her tone so insistent that he listened to her. But having lost his reason for bitterness, he said, "Just because you don't think doesn't mean others don't think." Is he getting old? She does not want to think of him getting old. In spite of his ulcer, his body is hard. He is tall and handsome, with a thick mustache and a thin black goatee, and there is very little gray in his kinky black hair. He dresses in tight-fitting blue jeans and black turtleneck sweaters in the winter, and old white shirts with the sleeves rolled up in the summer. He pretends not to care about his looks, but he does. He shaves carefully, scraping slowly down each side of his goatee. He orders his soft leather shoes from a store in California. After taking one of his long walks—even if he does it twice a day—he invariably takes a shower. He always looks refreshed, and very rarely admits any insecurity. A few times, at night in bed, he has asked, "Am I still the man of your dreams?" And when she says yes he always laughs, turning it into a joke, as if he didn't care. She knows he does. He pretends to have no feeling for clothing, but actually he cares so strongly about his turtlenecks and shirts (a few are Italian silk) and shoes that he will have no others. She has noticed that the young women who visit are always vain. When Sarah arrived, she was wearing a beautiful silk scarf, pale as conch shells.

Sitting on the floor on Saturday morning, Lenore watches the fire she has just lit. The baby, tucked in George's chair, smiles in his sleep, and Lenore thinks what a good companion he would be if only he were an adult. She gets up and goes into the kitchen and tears open a package of yeast and dissolves it, with sugar and salt, in hot water, slushing her fingers through it and shivering because it is so cold in the kitchen. She will bake bread for dinner—there is always a big meal in the early evening when they have guests. But what will she do for the rest of the day? George told the girls the night before that on Saturday they would walk in the woods, but she does not really enjoy hiking, and George will be irritated because of the discussion the night before, and she does not want to aggravate him. "You are unwilling to challenge anyone," her brother wrote her in a letter that came a few days ago. He has written her for years—all the years she has been with George—asking when she is going to end the relationship. She rarely writes back because she knows that her answers sound too simple. She has a comfortable house. She cooks. She keeps busy and she loves her two children. "It seems unkind to say *but*," her brother writes, "but . . ." It is true; she likes simple things. Her brother, who is a lawyer in Cambridge, cannot understand that.

Lenore rubs her hand down the side of her face and says good morning to Julie and Sarah, who have come downstairs. Sarah does not want orange juice; she already looks refreshed and ready for the day. Lenore pours a glass for Julie. George calls from the hallway, "Ready to roll?" Lenore is surprised that he wants to leave so early. She goes into the living room. George is wearing a denim jacket, his hands in the pockets.

"Morning," he says to Lenore. "You're not up for a hike, are you?"

Lenore looks at him, but does not answer. As she stands there, Sarah walks around her and joins George in the hallway and he holds the door open for her. "Let's walk to the store and get Hershey bars to give us energy for a long hike," George says to Sarah. They are gone. Lenore finds Julie still in the kitchen, waiting for the water to boil. Julie says that she had a bad night and she is happy not to be going with George and Sarah. Lenore fixes tea for them. Maria sits next to her on the sofa, sipping orange juice. The baby likes company, but Maria is a very private child; she would rather that she and her mother were always alone. She has given up being possessive about her father. Now she gets out a cardboard box and takes out her mother's collection of postcards, which she arranges on the floor in careful groups. Whenever she looks up, Julie smiles nervously at her; Maria does not smile, and Lenore doesn't prod her. Lenore goes into the kitchen to punch down the bread, and Maria follows. Maria has recently gotten over chicken pox, and there is a small new scar in the center of her forehead. Instead of looking at Maria's blue eyes, Lenore lately has found herself focusing on the imperfection.

As Lenore is stretching the loaves onto the cornmeal-covered baking sheet, she hears the rain start. It hits hard on the garage roof.

After a few minutes Julie comes into the kitchen. "They're caught in this downpour," Julie says. "If Sarah had left the car keys, I could go get them."

"Take my car and pick them up," Lenore says, pointing with her elbow to the keys hanging on a nail near the door.

"But I don't know where the store is."

"You must have passed it driving to our house last night. Just go out of the driveway and turn right. It's along the main road."

Julie gets her purple sweater and takes the car keys. "I'll be right back," she says.

Lenore can sense that she is glad to escape from the house, that she is happy the rain began.

In the living room Lenore turns the pages of a magazine, and Maria mutters a refrain of "Blue, blue, dark blue, green blue," noticing the color every time it appears. Lenore sips her tea. She puts a Michael Hurley record on George's stereo. Michael Hurley is good rainy-day music. George has hundreds of records. His students used to love to paw through them. Cleverly, he has never made any attempt to keep up with what is currently popular. Everything is jazz or eclectic: Michael Hurley, Keith Jarrett, Ry Cooder.[1]

Julie comes back. "I couldn't find them," she says. She looks as if she expects to be punished.

Lenore is surprised. She is about to say something like "You certainly didn't look very hard, did you?" but she catches Julie's eye. She looks young and afraid, and perhaps even a little crazy.

---

1. Musical performers who combine elements of folk, jazz, and rock.

"Well, we tried," Lenore says.

Julie stands in front of the fire, with her back to Lenore. Lenore knows she is thinking that she is dense—that she does not recognize the implications.

"They might have walked through the woods instead of along the road," Lenore says. "That's possible."

"But they would have gone out to the road to thumb when the rain began, wouldn't they?"

Perhaps she misunderstood what Julie was thinking. Perhaps it has never occurred to Julie until now what might be going on.

"Maybe they got lost," Julie says. "Maybe something happened to them."

"Nothing happened to them," Lenore says. Julie turns around and Lenore catches that small point of light in her eye again. "Maybe they took shelter under a tree," she says. "Maybe they're screwing. How should I know?"

It is not a word Lenore often uses. She usually tries not to think about that at all, but she can sense that Julie is very upset.

"Really?" Julie says. "Don't you care, Mrs. Anderson?"

Lenore is amused. There's a switch. All the students call her husband George and her Lenore; now one of them wants to think there's a real adult here to explain all this to her.

"What am I going to do?" Lenore says. She shrugs.

Julie does not answer.

"Would you like me to pour you tea?" Lenore asks.

"Yes," Julie says. "Please."

George and Sarah return in the middle of the afternoon. George says that they decided to go on a spree to the big city—it is really a small town he is talking about, but calling it the big city gives him an opportunity to speak ironically. They sat in a restaurant bar, waiting for the rain to stop, George says, and then they thumbed a ride home. "But I'm completely sober," George says, turning for the first time to Sarah. "What about you?" He is all smiles. Sarah lets him down. She looks embarrassed. Her eyes meet Lenore's quickly, and jump to Julie. The two girls stare at each other, and Lenore, left with only George to look at, looks at the fire and then gets up to pile on another log.

Gradually it becomes clear that they are trapped together by the rain. Maria undresses her paper doll and deliberately rips a feather off its hat. Then she takes the pieces to Lenore, almost in tears. The baby cries, and Lenore takes him off the sofa, where he has been sleeping under his yellow blanket, and props him in the space between her legs as she leans back on her elbows to watch the fire. It's her fire, and she has the excuse of presiding over it.

"How's my boy?" George says. The baby looks, and looks away.

It gets dark early, because of the rain. At four-thirty George uncorks a bottle of Beaujolais and brings it into the living room, with four glasses pressed against his chest with his free arm. Julie rises nervously to extract the glasses, thanking him too profusely for the wine. She gives a glass to Sarah without looking at her.

They sit in a semicircle in front of the fire and drink the wine. Julie leafs through magazines—*New Times, National Geographic*—and Sarah holds a small white dish painted with gray-green leaves that she has taken from the coffee table; the dish contains a few shells and some acorn caps, a polished stone or two, and Sarah lets these objects run through her fingers. There are several such dishes in the house, assembled by George. He and Lenore gathered the shells long ago, the first time they went away together, at a beach in North Carolina. But the acorn caps, the shiny turquoise and amethyst stones—those are there, she knows, because George likes the effect they have on visitors; it is an expected unconventionality, really. He has also acquired a few small framed pictures, which he points out to guests who are more important than worshipful students—tiny oil paintings of fruit, prints with small details from the unicorn tapestries. He pretends to like small, elegant things. Actually, when they visit museums in New York he goes first to El Grecos and big Mark Rothko canvases. She could never get him to admit that what he said or did was sometimes false. Once, long ago, when he asked if he was still the man of her dreams, she said, "We don't get along well anymore." "Don't talk about it," he said—no denial, no protest. At best, she could say things and get away with them; she could never get him to continue such a conversation.

At the dinner table, lit with white candles burning in empty wine bottles, they eat off his grandmother's small flowery plates. Lenore looks out a window and sees, very faintly in the dark, their huge oak tree. The rain has stopped. A few stars have come out, and there are glints on the wet branches. The oak tree grows very close to the window. George loved it when her brother once suggested that some of the bushes and trees should be pruned away from the house so it would not always be so dark inside; it gave him a chance to rave about the beauty of nature, to say that he would never tamper with it. "It's like a tomb in here all day," her brother had said. Since moving here, George has learned the names of almost all the things growing on the land: he can point out abelia bushes, spirea, laurels. He subscribes to *National Geographic* (although she rarely sees him looking at it). He is at last in touch, he says, being in the country puts him in touch. He is saying it now to Sarah, who has put down her ivory-handled fork to listen to him. He gets up to change the record. Side two of the Telemann[2] record begins softly.

Sarah is still very much on guard with Lenore; she makes polite conversation with her quickly when George is out of the room. "You people are so wonderful," she says. "I wish my parents could be like you."

"George would be pleased to hear that," Lenore says, lifting a small piece of pasta to her lips.

When George is seated again, Sarah, anxious to please, tells him, "If only my father could be like you."

"Your father," George says. "I won't have that analogy." He says it pleasantly, but barely disguises his dismay at the comparison.

"I mean, he cares about nothing but business," the girl stumbles on.

The music, in contrast, grows lovelier.

Lenore goes into the kitchen to get the salad and hears George say, "I simply won't let you girls leave. Nobody leaves on a Saturday."

2. Georg Philipp Telemann (1681–1767), German composer.

There are polite protests, there are compliments to Lenore on the meal—there is too much talk. Lenore has trouble caring about what's going on. The food is warm and delicious. She pours more wine and lets them talk.

"Godard, yes, I know . . . panning that row of honking cars *so* slowly, that long line of cars stretching on and on."[3]

She has picked up the end of George's conversation. His arm slowly waves out over the table, indicating the line of motionless cars in the movie.

"That's a lovely plant," Julie says to Lenore.

"It's Peruvian ivy," Lenore says. She smiles. She is supposed to smile. She will not offer to hack shoots off her plant for these girls.

Sarah asks for a Dylan record when the Telemann finishes playing. White wax drips onto the wood table. George waits for it to solidify slightly, then scrapes up the little circles and with thumb and index finger flicks them gently toward Sarah. He explains (although she asked for no particular Dylan record) that he has only Dylan before he went electric. And "Planet Waves"—"because it's so romantic. That's silly of me, but true."[4] Sarah smiles at him. Julie smiles at Lenore. Julie is being polite, taking her cues from Sarah, really not understanding what's going on. Lenore does not smile back. She has done enough to put them at ease. She is tired now, brought down by the music, a full stomach, and again the sounds of rain outside. For dessert there is homemade vanilla ice cream, made by George, with small black vanilla-bean flecks in it. He is still drinking wine, though; another bottle has been opened. He sips wine and then taps his spoon on his ice cream, looking at Sarah. Sarah smiles, letting them all see the smile, then sucks the ice cream off her spoon. Julie is missing more and more of what's going on. Lenore watches as Julie strokes her hand absently on her napkin. She is wearing a thin silver choker and—Lenore notices for the first time—a thin silver ring on the third finger of her hand.

"It's just terrible about Anna," George says, finishing his wine, his ice cream melting, looking at no one in particular, although Sarah was the one who brought up Anna the night before, when they had been in the house only a short time—Anna dead, hit by a car, hardly an accident at all. Anna was also a student of his. The driver of the car was drunk, but for some reason charges were not pressed. (Sarah and George have talked about this before, but Lenore blocks it out. What can she do about it? She met Anna once: a beautiful girl, with tiny, childlike hands, her hair thin and curly—wary, as beautiful people are wary.) Now the driver has been flipping out, Julie says, and calling Anna's parents, wanting to talk to them to find out why it has happened.

The baby begins to cry. Lenore goes upstairs, pulls up more covers, talks to him for a minute. He settles for this. She goes downstairs. The wine must have affected her more than she realizes; otherwise, why is she counting the number of steps?

3. A famous scene from Jean-Luc Godard's film *Weekend* (1969).
4. The American singer, musician, and composer Bob Dylan (b. 1941 as Robert Zimmerman) combined electric rock with acoustic folk in 1965. He released the *Planet Waves* album in 1974.

1004 | ANN BEATTIE

In the candlelit dining room, Julie sits alone at the table. The girl has been left alone again; George and Sarah took the umbrellas, decided to go for a walk in the rain.

It is eight o'clock. Since helping Lenore load the dishes into the dishwasher, when she said what a beautiful house Lenore had, Julie has said very little. Lenore is tired, and does not want to make conversation. They sit in the living room and drink wine.

"Sarah is my best friend," Julie says. She seems apologetic about it. "I was so out of it when I came back to college. I was in Italy, with my husband, and suddenly I was back in the States. I couldn't make friends. But Sarah wasn't like the other people. She cared enough to be nice to me."

"How long have you been friends?"

"For two years. She's really the best friend I've ever had. We understand things—we don't always have to talk about them."

"Like her relationship with George," Lenore says.

Too direct. Too unexpected. Julie has no answer.

"You act as if you're to blame," Lenore says.

"I feel strange because you're such a nice lady."

A nice lady! What an odd way to speak. Has she been reading Henry James? Lenore has never known what to think of herself, but she certainly thinks of herself as being more complicated than a "lady."

"Why do you look that way?" Julie asks. "You *are* nice. I think you've been very nice to us. You've given up your whole weekend."

"I always give up my weekends. Weekends are the only time we socialize, really. In a way, it's good to have something to do."

"But to have it turn out like this . . ." Julie says. "I think I feel so strange because when my own marriage broke up I didn't even suspect. I mean, I couldn't act the way you do, anyway, but I—"

"For all I know, nothing's going on," Lenore says. "For all I know, your friend is flattering herself, and George is trying to make me jealous." She puts two more logs on the fire. When these are gone, she will either have to walk to the woodshed or give up and go to bed. "Is there something . . . *major* going on?" she asks.

Julie is sitting on the rug, by the fire, twirling her hair with her finger. "I didn't know it when I came out here," she says. "Sarah's put me in a very awkward position."

"But do you know how far it has gone?" Lenore asks, genuinely curious now.

"No," Julie says.

No way to know if she's telling the truth. Would Julie speak the truth to a lady? Probably not.

"Anyway," Lenore says with a shrug, "I don't want to think about it all the time."

"I'd never have the courage to live with a man and not marry," Julie says. "I mean, I wish I had, that we hadn't gotten married, but I just don't have that kind of . . . I'm not secure enough."

"You have to live somewhere," Lenore says.

Julie is looking at her as if she does not believe that she is sincere. Am I? Lenore wonders. She has lived with George for six years, and sometimes she thinks she has caught his way of playing games, along with his colds, his bad moods.

"I'll show you something," Lenore says. She gets up, and Julie follows. Lenore puts on the light in George's study, and they walk through it to a bathroom he has converted to a darkroom. Under a table, in a box behind another box, there is a stack of pictures. Lenore takes them out and hands them to Julie. They are pictures that Lenore found in his darkroom last summer; they were left out by mistake, no doubt, and she found them when she went in with some contact prints he had left in their bedroom. They are high-contrast photographs of George's face. In all of them he looks very serious and very sad; in some of them his eyes seem to be narrowed in pain. In one, his mouth is open. It is an excellent photograph of a man in agony, a man about to scream.

"What are they?" Julie whispers.

"Pictures he took of himself," Lenore says. She shrugs. "So I stay," she says.

Julie nods. Lenore nods, taking the pictures back. Lenore has not thought until this minute that this may be why she stays. In fact, it is not the only reason. It is just a very demonstrable, impressive reason. When she first saw the pictures, her own face had become as distorted as George's. She had simply not known what to do. She had been frightened and ashamed. Finally she put them in an empty box, and put the box behind another box. She did not even want him to see the horrible pictures again. She does not know if he has ever found them, pushed back against the wall in that other box. As George says, there can be too much communication between people.

Later, Sarah and George come back to the house. It is still raining. It turns out that they took a bottle of brandy with them, and they are both drenched and drunk. He holds Sarah's finger with one of his. Sarah, seeing Lenore, lets his finger go. But then he turns—they have not even said hello yet—and grabs her up, spins her around, stumbling into the living room, and says, "I am in love."

Julie and Lenore watch them in silence.

"See no evil," George says, gesturing with the empty brandy bottle to Julie. "Hear no evil," George says, pointing to Lenore. He hugs Sarah closer. "I speak no evil. I speak the truth. I am in love!"

Sarah squirms away from him, runs from the room and up the stairs in the dark.

George looks blankly after her, then sinks to the floor and smiles. He is going to pass it off as a joke. Julie looks at him in horror, and from upstairs Sarah can be heard sobbing. Her crying awakens the baby.

"Excuse me," Lenore says. She climbs the stairs and goes into her son's room, and picks him up. She talks gently to him, soothing him with lies. He is too sleepy to be alarmed for long. In a few minutes he is asleep again, and she puts him back in his crib. In the next room Sarah is crying more quietly now. Her crying is so awful that Lenore almost joins in, but instead she pats her son. She stands in the dark by the crib and then at last goes out and down the hallway to her bedroom. She takes off her clothes and gets into the cold bed. She concentrates on breathing normally. With the door closed and Sarah's door closed, she can hardly hear her. Someone taps lightly on her door.

"Mrs. Anderson," Julie whispers. "Is this your room?"

"Yes," Lenore says. She does not ask her in.

"We're going to leave. I'm going to get Sarah and leave. I didn't want to just walk out without saying anything."

Lenore just cannot think how to respond. It was really very kind of Julie to say something. She is very close to tears, so she says nothing.

"Okay," Julie says, to reassure herself. "Good night. We're going."

There is no more crying. Footsteps. Miraculously, the baby does not wake up again, and Maria has slept through all of it. She has always slept well. Lenore herself sleeps worse and worse, and she knows that George walks much of the night, most nights. She hasn't said anything about it. If he thinks she's simple, what good would her simple wisdom do him?

The oak tree scrapes against the window in the wind and rain. Here on the second floor, under the roof, the tinny tapping is very loud. If Sarah and Julie say anything to George before they leave, she doesn't hear them. She hears the car start, then die out. It starts again—she is praying for the car to go—and after conking out once more it rolls slowly away, crunching gravel. The bed is no warmer; she shivers. She tries hard to fall asleep. The effort keeps her awake. She squints her eyes in concentration instead of closing them. The only sound in the house is the electric clock, humming by her bed. It is not even midnight.

She gets up, and without turning on the light, walks downstairs. George is still in the living room. The fire is nothing but ashes and glowing bits of wood. It is as cold there as it was in the bed.

"That damn bitch," George says. "I should have known she was a stupid little girl."

"You went too far," Lenore says. "I'm the only one you can go too far with."

"Damn it," he says and pokes the fire. A few sparks shoot up. "Damn it," he repeats under his breath.

His sweater is still wet. His shoes are muddy and ruined. Sitting on the floor by the fire, his hair matted down on his head, he looks ugly, older, unfamiliar.

She thinks of another time, when it was warm. They were walking on the beach together, shortly after they met, gathering shells. Little waves were rolling in. The sun went behind the clouds and there was a momentary illusion that the clouds were still and the sun was racing ahead of them. "Catch me," he said, breaking away from her. They had been talking quietly, gathering shells. She was so surprised at him for breaking away that she ran with all her energy and did catch him, putting her hand out and taking hold of the band of his swimming trunks as he veered into the water. If she hadn't stopped him, would he really have run far out into the water, until she couldn't follow anymore? He turned on her, just as abruptly as he had run away, and grabbed her and hugged her hard, lifted her high. She had clung to him, held him close. He had tried the same thing when he came back from the walk with Sarah, and it hadn't worked.

"I wouldn't care if their car went off the road," he says bitterly.

"Don't say that," she says.

They sit in silence, listening to the rain. She slides over closer to him, puts her hand on his shoulder and leans her head there, as if he could protect her from the awful things he has wished into being.

1978

YUSEF KOMUNYAKAA
b. 1947

The excavation of lost names is one of the driving impulses of Yusef Komunyakaa's work. His poems recover and reanimate figures from history such as the African American elevator operator, Thomas McKeller, who appears in a stunning portrait by John Singer Sargent ("Nude Study"). In researching the portrait, Komunyakaa learned that it had been "unearthed in Sargent's studio after his death" and that "McKeller's image had been cannibalized to depict [the ancient Greek and Roman god] Apollo and a bas-relief of [the ancient Greek poet and musician] Arion—other heads and lines grafted onto his classical physique." Komunyakaa's work continually questions and revises both the cultural contradictions projected onto the black body and the erasure of black presence from history and culture. Significantly, he adopted the lost surname of a Trinidadian grandfather who came to the United States as a child, "smuggled in like a sack of papaya / On a banana boat." As the poet recounts in "Mismatched Shoes," his grandfather's "true name" disappeared in the process of assimilation. After his death his grandson "slipped into his skin" and took back the name "Komunyakaa," in what the poet calls "an affirmation of my heritage and its ambiguity."

Komunyakaa was born in Bogalusa, Louisiana, seventy miles northeast of New Orleans. Bogalusa means "Magic City" (a phrase that became the title of his 1992 collection of poems), and a lush, semitropical landscape informs many of his poems. But as the oldest of six children, and as the son of a carpenter who could write only his name, Komunyakaa grew up in an impoverished neighborhood and experienced a racial inequity that coexisted with natural beauty. At a young age, he has said, he decided that "imagination could serve as a choice of weapons."

Because the military seemed to offer a way into a larger world, Komunyakaa enlisted in the army and was sent to Vietnam, where he served as a war correspondent and editor of the military newspaper, writing accounts of what he witnessed in combat. For his work he was awarded the Bronze Star. While in Vietnam he carried with him several anthologies of poetry, but only after his military service ended did he begin to write poems, studying at the University of Colorado and then at the University of California at Irvine, where his teachers included Charles Wright and C. K. Williams. In 1984, fourteen years after his tour of duty ended, Komunyakaa began to write poems about his war experience. From his father he had learned to build and renovate houses; as he works, he has said, he keeps a pad of paper close by. While renovating a house in New Orleans he began to write down images and lines about Vietnam and so began the first in what became a series of poems about his Vietnam experience. These were collected in *Dien Cai Dau* (1988), whose tide (meaning "crazy") is a Vietnamese phrase used to describe American soldiers. In one of these poems, "Facing It," he sees his own "clouded reflection" in the "black granite" of the Vietnam War Memorial designed by Maya Lin, an image of which appears in the color insert of this anthology.

To write about his surreal wartime experiences Komunyakaa drew on the work of surrealists like the French poet and critic André Breton. Komunyakaa shares with these writers and artists an emphasis on the image as linked to the unconscious, and his poems often work through a series of short lines whose quick, associative images bypass logic. A surrealist impulse to distort the familiar and juxtapose beauty and violence appears in Komunyakaa's Vietnam poems and in the racial and erotic tensions of poems like "Jasmine" (from *The Pleasure Dome*, 2001). An emphasis on the dreamlike, irrational, and fantastic was already apparent in his first two books, *Copacetic* (1984) and *I Apologize for the Eyes in My Head* (1986), both of which also reflect the musical influences of his native Louisiana.

Growing up so close to New Orleans brought Komunyakaa in early contact with jazz and the blues. The title of his first book, *Copacetic*, is a term adapted by jazz musicians from the African American tap dancer Bill "Bojangles" Robinson; in jazz it refers to especially pleasing and mellow music. Like Langston Hughes, Komunyakaa explores throughout his work the power of music—blues, jazz, and poetry—to address and, in part, to heal the pain of living in a racially divided society. The rapid energy of poems like "Facing It" and "Slam, Dunk, & Hook" belong to what the poet calls a "felt and lived syncopation," a rhythm of shifting beats that bears the influence of musicians like Charlie Parker, John Coltrane, and Miles Davis. Komunyakaa also works in tighter formal structures, whose exactness and precision suggest the careful measuring and fitting of carpentry. The quatrains of *Talking Dirty to the Gods* (2000) and the three-line stanzas of *Taboo* (2004) provide what the poet calls "an illusion of control" over volatile and complicated social and psychic material. They reflect Komunyakaa's preferred poetic strategy of "insinuation and nuance." Although his work often looks unflinchingly at what otherwise is hidden or denied, the social, racial, or erotic context of a poem often emerges in details or images, rather than in direct description. *Warhorses* (2008) continues this poet's ongoing investigation of war and violence.

Komunyakaa coedited with J. A. Sascha Feinstein a two-volume collection, *The Jazz Poetry Anthology* (1991) and *Second Set* (1996), and has also been extensively involved in collaborations with jazz musicians and vocalists. His poetry has received numerous awards, among them both the Pulitzer Prize and the Kingsley Tuft Poetry Award for *Neon Vernacular: New and Selected Poems 1977–1989* (1994). He is a professor in the Council of Humanities and Creative Writing Program at Princeton University.

Facing It

My black face fades,
hiding inside the black granite.
I said I wouldn't
dammit: No tears.
I'm stone. I'm flesh.   5
My clouded reflection eyes me
like a bird of prey, the profile of night
slanted against morning. I turn
this way—the stone lets me go.
I turn that way—I'm inside   10

the Vietnam Veterans Memorial[1]
again, depending on the light
to make a difference.
I go down the 58,022 names,
half-expecting to find   15
my own in letters like smoke.
I touch the name Andrew Johnson;
I see the booby trap's white flash.
Names shimmer on a woman's blouse
but when she walks away   20
the names stay on the wall.
Brushstrokes flash, a red bird's
wings cutting across my stare.
The sky. A plane in the sky.
A white vet's image floats   25
closer to me, then his pale eyes
look through mine. I'm a window.
He's lost his right arm
inside the stone. In the black mirror
a woman's trying to erase names: 30
No, she's brushing a boy's hair.

                                                        1988

My Father's Love Letters

On Fridays he'd open a can of Jax[1]
After coming home from the mill,
& ask me to write a letter to my mother
Who sent postcards of desert flowers
Taller than men. He would beg,   5
Promising to never beat her
Again. Somehow I was happy
She had gone, & sometimes wanted
To slip in a reminder, how Mary Lou
Williams' "Polka Dots & Moonbeams"[2]   10
Never made the swelling go down.
His carpenter's apron always bulged
With old nails, a claw hammer
Looped at his side & extension cords
Coiled around his feet.   15
Words rolled from under the pressure
Of my ballpoint: Love,
Baby, Honey, Please.

1. An image of the Vietnam War Memorial in Washington, D.C., designed by the architect Maya Lin and dedicated in 1982, appears in the color insert of this anthology.
1. A beer originally brewed in New Orleans, Louisiana.
2. The American jazz pianist Mary Lou Williams (1910–1981) performed with and composed for many of the great jazz artists of the 1940s and 1950s. The song "Polka Dots and Moonbeams" (1940) was composed by Jimmy Van Heusen (1913–1990) and Johnny Burke (1908–1964).

We sat in the quiet brutality
Of voltage meters & pipe threaders,   20
Lost between sentences . . .
The gleam of a five-pound wedge
On the concrete floor
Pulled a sunset
Through the doorway of his toolshed.   25
I wondered if she laughed
& held them over a gas burner.
My father could only sign
His name, but he'd look at blueprints
& say how many bricks   30
Formed each wall. This man,
Who stole roses & hyacinth
For his yard, would stand there
With eyes closed & fists balled,
Laboring over a simple word, almost   35
Redeemed by what he tried to say.

                                                        1992

Slam, Dunk, & Hook

Fast breaks. Lay ups. With Mercury's
Insignia[1] on our sneakers,
We outmaneuvered to footwork
Of bad angels. Nothing but a hot
Swish of strings like silk   5
Ten feet out. In the roundhouse
Labyrinth our bodies
Created, we could almost
Last forever, poised in midair
Like storybook sea monsters.   10
A high note hung there
A long second. Off
The rim. We'd corkscrew
Up & dunk balls that exploded
The skullcap of hope & good   15
Intention. Lanky, all hands
& feet . . . sprung rhythm.[2]
We were metaphysical when girls
Cheered on the sidelines.
Tangled up in a falling,   20
Muscles were a bright motor
Double-flashing to the metal hoop
Nailed to our oak.
When Sonny Boy's mama died

---

1. Mercury, the messenger of the ancient Greek gods, is depicted wearing winged sandals.
2. "Sprung rhythm" is a term used by the English poet Gerard Manley Hopkins (1844–1889) to describe a poetic meter with a variable rather than fixed number of syllables in each poetic foot.

He played nonstop all day, so hard   25
Our backboard splintered.
Glistening with sweat,
We rolled the ball off
Our fingertips. Trouble
Was there slapping a blackjack[3]   30
Against an open palm.
Dribble, drive to the inside,
& glide like a sparrow hawk.[4]
Lay ups. Fast breaks.
We had moves we didn't know   35
We had. Our bodies spun
On swivels of bone & faith,
Through a lyric slipknot
Of joy, & we knew we were
Beautiful & dangerous.   40

1992

From Song for My Father

[*Sometimes you could be*]

Sometimes you could be
That man on a red bicycle,
With me on the handlebars,
Just rolling along a country road
On the edge of July, honeysuckle   5
Lit with mosquito hawks.[1]
We rode from under the shady
Overhang, back into sunlight.
The day bounced off car hoods
As the heat & stinking exhaust   10
Brushed against us like a dragon's
Roar, nudging the bike with a tremor,
But you steered us through the flowering
Dogwood like a thread of blood.

1993

When Dusk Weighs Daybreak

I want Catullus[1]
In every line, a barb
The sun plays for good
Luck. I need to know if iron

---

3. A small leather-covered bludgeon.
4. One of the best-known, handsomest, and smallest North American hawks.
1. In the American South, a term for dragonflies, which eat mosquitos and other small insects.
1. Gaius Valerius Catullus (c. 86–c. 54 B.C.E.), Roman poet who wittily expressed love and hate in some of the finest lyric poetry of his time.

Tastes like laudanum[2]   5
Or a woman. I already sense
What sleeps in the same flesh,
Ariadne & her half brother[3]

Caught in the other's dream.
I want each question to fit me   10
Like a shiny hook, a lure
In the gullet. What it is

To look & know how much muscle
It takes to lift a green slab.
I need a Son House blues[4]   15
To wear out my tongue.

                                                    2000

Jasmine

I sit beside two women, kitty-corner
to the stage, as Elvin's[1] sticks blur
the club into a blue fantasia.
I thought my body had forgotten the Deep
South, how I'd cross the street   5
if a woman like these two walked
towards me, as if a cat traversed
my path beneath the evening star.
Which one is wearing jasmine?
If my grandmothers saw me now   10
they'd say, Boy, the devil never sleeps.
My mind is lost among November
cotton flowers, a soft rain on my face
as Richard Davis[2] plucks the fat notes
of chance on his upright   15
leaning into the future.
The blonde, the brunette—
which one is scented with jasmine?
I can hear Duke in the right hand
& Basie in the left[3]   20
as the young piano player
nudges us into the past.

2. An opium-based painkiller.
3. In Greek mythology Ariadne was the daughter of Pasiphaë and the Cretan king, Minos. She fell in love with the Athenian hero Theseus and helped him escape the Labyrinth after he slew her half-brother, the Minotaur, a beast half bull and half man.
4. Eddie James House Jr. (1902–1988), better known as "Son," American blues singer and guitarist regarded as an epitome of the Delta blues tradition.

1. Elvin Jones (1927–2004), American jazz drummer and bandleader.
2. American bassist (b. 1930) known for his jazz sessions in an all-star small group at New York City's Village Vanguard under the rubric "Jazz for a Sunday Afternoon."
3. Duke Ellington (1899–1974), American pianist and bandleader who was also one of the greatest jazz composers. Count Basie (1904–1984), American jazz pianist and bandleader.

The trumpet's almost kissed
by enough pain. Give him a few more years,
a few more ghosts to embrace—Clifford's[4]   25
shadow on the edge of the stage.
The sign says, *No Talking.*
Elvin's guardian angel lingers
at the top of the stairs,
counting each drop of sweat   30
paid in tribute. The blonde
has her eyes closed, & the brunette
is looking at me. Our bodies
sway to each riff, the jasmine
rising from a valley somewhere   35
in Egypt, a white moon
opening countless false mouths
of laughter. The midnight
gatherers are boys & girls
with the headlights of trucks   40
aimed at their backs, because
their small hands refuse to wound
the knowing scent hidden in each bloom.

2001

Nude Study[1]

Someone lightly brushed the penis
   alive. Belief is almost
      flesh. Wings beat,

dust trying to breathe, as if the figure
   might rise from the oils   5
      & flee the dead

artist's studio. For years
   this piece of work was there
      like a golden struggle

shadowing Thomas McKeller, a black   10
   elevator operator at the Boston
      Copley Plaza Hotel, a friend

of John Singer Sargent—hidden
   among sketches & drawings, a model
      for Apollo & a bas-relief   15

4. Clifford Brown (1930–1956), American jazz trumpeter noted for his graceful technique.
1. *Nude Study of Thomas E. McKeller* (1917–20?), a portrait by the American painter John Singer Sargent (1856–1925), hangs in the Museum of Fine Arts, Boston. McKeller was an African American elevator operator. The portrait was found in Sargent's studio after his death.

of Arion.[2] So much taken
for granted & denied, only
grace & mutability

can complete this face belonging
to Greek bodies castrated   20
with a veil of dust.

2004

2. Ancient Greek poet and musician. "Apollo": the sun god in ancient Greek and Roman mythology.

LESLIE MARMON SILKO
b. 1948

Born in Albuquerque, New Mexico, Leslie Marmon Silko was raised in Old Laguna, a village fifty miles west of Albuquerque. The Spaniards had founded a mission there early in the eighteenth century, but Old Laguna had been formed centuries earlier by cattle-keeping Pueblos who successfully repelled raids on them by the Navajos and the Apaches. Writing of the unchanging character of Pueblo religious practices over the centuries, the historian Joe S. Sando notes that "the tradition of religious beliefs permeates every aspect of the people's life; it determines man's relation with the natural world and with his fellow man. Its basic concern is continuity of a harmonious relationship with the world in which man lives."

Silko's work addresses such matters. Her own heritage is complicated in that her great-grandfather Robert Marmon was white, whereas her mother was a mixed-blood Plains Indian who kept her daughter on the traditional cradle board during her first year of infancy. (Her ancestry also includes some Mexican blood.) Silko has made this heritage a source of strength. She writes: "I suppose at the core of my writing is the attempt to identify what it is to be a half-breed or mixed blooded person; what it is to grow up neither white nor fully traditional Indian." At the same time she insists that "what I know is Laguna. This place I am from is everything I am as a writer and human being." An active child, Silko had a horse of her own by age eight, and by thirteen she owned a rifle, with which she took part in deer hunts. Commuting to Albuquerque, she attended Catholic schools, earned a B.A. at the University of New Mexico, then began law school under a special program for Native Americans, though she soon gave it up to become a writer and teacher.

Her first published story, "The Man to Send Rain Clouds" (1969), came out of a writing assignment in college. She had heard, in Laguna, of an old man who died in a sheep camp and was given a traditional native burial—a fact resented by the Catholic priest who was not called in. The story she wrote about this situation, published in the *New Mexico Quarterly*, put her on the road to success as a writer. In 1974 a selection of her poems was published in the volume *Laguna Woman*, and in 1977 her novel *Ceremony* brought her recognition as a leading voice among Native American writers. *Ceremony* shows the dark aspects of modern American Indian life, focusing on a World War II veteran who is in acute physical and emotional straits as the novel begins, but who manages to survive by reestablishing contact with his native roots. Silko has insisted that the book is not just or even mainly about characters: "This novel is essentially about the powers inherent in the process of storytelling. . . . The chanting or telling of ancient stories to effect certain cures or protect from illness and harm have always been a part of the Pueblo's curing ceremonies." So this story of a family represents an attempt "to search for a ceremony to deal with despair"—the despair that has led to the "suicide, the alcoholism, and the violence which occur in so many Indian communities today."

Thus a strong moral connection exists between Silko's purely aesthetic delight in the writing of a story and the therapeutic, functional uses she hopes the story will play in the Native American community. In *Ceremony* and the aptly titled 1981 collection *Storyteller* of 1981 (which also contains poems and photographs), Silko's prose is an expressive, active presence, sympathetically creating landscape as well as animals and human beings. Plants assume narrative status in her third novel, *Gardens in the Dunes* (1999), which looks back to late-nineteenth-century events to underscore a basic theme: that myth and history do not coincide.

The following text is from *Storyteller* (1981).

Lullaby

The sun had gone down but the snow in the wind gave off its own light. It came in thick tufts like new wool—washed before the weaver spins it. Ayah reached out for it like her own babies had, and she smiled when she remembered how she had laughed at them. She was an old woman now, and her life had become memories. She sat down with her back against the wide cottonwood tree, feeling the rough bark on her back bones; she faced east and listened to the wind and snow sing a high-pitched Yeibechei[1] song. Out of the wind she felt warmer, and she could watch the wide fluffy snow fill in her tracks, steadily, until the direction she had come from was gone. By the light of the snow she could see the dark outline of the big arroyo[2] a few feet away. She was sitting on the edge of Cebolleta Creek, where in the springtime the thin cows would graze on grass already chewed flat to the ground. In the wide deep creek bed where only a trickle of water flowed in the summer, the skinny cows would wander, looking for new grass along winding paths splashed with manure.

Ayah pulled the old Army blanket over her head like a shawl. Jimmie's blanket—the one he had sent to her. That was a long time ago and the green wool was faded, and it was unraveling on the edges. She did not want to think about Jimmie. So she thought about the weaving and the way her mother had done it. On the wall wooden loom set into the sand under a tamarack tree for shade. She could see it clearly. She had been only a little girl when her grandma gave her the wooden combs to pull the twigs and burrs from the raw, freshly washed wool. And while she combed the wool, her grandma sat beside her, spinning a silvery strand of yarn around the smooth cedar spindle. Her mother worked at the loom with yarns dyed bright yellow and red and gold. She watched them dye the yarn in boiling black pots full of beeweed petals, juniper berries, and sage. The blankets her mother made were soft and woven so tight that rain rolled off them like birds' feathers. Ayah

---

1. Navajo dance.   2. Gully carved by water.

remembered sleeping warm on cold windy nights, wrapped in her mother's blankets on the hogan's[3] sandy floor.

The snow drifted now, with the northwest wind hurling it in gusts. It drifted up around her black overshoes—old ones with little metal buckles. She smiled at the snow which was trying to cover her little by little. She could remember when they had no black rubber overshoes; only the high buckskin leggings that they wrapped over their elkhide moccasins. If the snow was dry or frozen, a person could walk all day and not get wet; and in the evenings the beams of the ceiling would hang with lengths of pale buckskin leggings, drying out slowly.

She felt peaceful remembering. She didn't feel cold any more. Jimmie's blanket seemed warmer than it had ever been. And she could remember the morning he was born. She could remember whispering to her mother, who was sleeping on the other side of the hogan, to tell her it was time now. She did not want to wake the others. The second time she called to her, her mother stood up and pulled on her shoes; she knew. They walked to the old stone hogan together, Ayah walking a step behind her mother. She waited alone, learning the rhythms of the pains while her mother went to call the old woman to help them. The morning was already warm even before dawn and Ayah smelled the bee flowers blooming and the young willow growing at the springs. She could remember that so clearly, but his birth merged into the births of the other children and to her it became all the same birth. They named him for the summer morning and in English they called him Jimmie.

It wasn't like Jimmie died. He just never came back, and one day a dark blue sedan with white writing on its doors pulled up in front of the boxcar shack where the rancher let the Indians live. A man in a khaki uniform trimmed in gold gave them a yellow piece of paper and told them that Jimmie was dead. He said the Army would try to get the body back and then it would be shipped to them; but it wasn't likely because the helicopter had burned after it crashed. All of this was told to Chato because he could understand English. She stood inside the doorway holding the baby while Chato listened. Chato spoke English like a white man and he spoke Spanish too. He was taller than the white man and he stood straighter too. Chato didn't explain why; he just told the military man they could keep the body if they found it. The white man looked bewildered; he nodded his head and he left. Then Chato looked at her and shook his head, and then he told her, "Jimmie isn't coming home anymore," and when he spoke, he used the words to speak of the dead. She didn't cry then, but she hurt inside with anger. And she mourned him as the years passed, when a horse fell with Chato and broke his leg, and the white rancher told them he wouldn't pay Chato until he could work again. She mourned Jimmie because he would have worked for his father then; he would have saddled the big bay horse and ridden the fence lines each day, with wire cutters and heavy gloves, fixing the breaks in the barbed wire and putting the stray cattle back inside again.

She mourned him after the white doctors came to take Danny and Ella away. She was at the shack alone that day they came. It was back in the days before they hired Navajo women to go with them as interpreters. She recog-

---

3. Navajo dwelling usually made of logs and mud.

nized one of the doctors. She had seen him at the children's clinic at Cañ-oncito about a month ago. They were wearing khaki uniforms and they waved papers at her and a black ball-point pen, trying to make her understand their English words. She was frightened by the way they looked at the children, like the lizard watches the fly. Danny was swinging on the tire swing on the elm tree behind the rancher's house, and Ella was toddling around the front door, dragging the broomstick horse Chato made for her. Ayah could see they wanted her to sign the papers, and Chato had taught her to sign her name. It was something she was proud of. She only wanted them to go, and to take their eyes away from her children.

She took the pen from the man without looking at his face and she signed the papers in three different places he pointed to. She stared at the ground by their feet and waited for them to leave. But they stood there and began to point and gesture at the children. Danny stopped swinging. Ayah could see his fear. She moved suddenly and grabbed Ella into her arms; the child squirmed, trying to get back to her toys. Ayah ran with the baby toward Danny; she screamed for him to run and then she grabbed him around his chest and carried him too. She ran south into the foothills of juniper trees and black lava rock. Behind her she heard the doctors running, but they had been taken by surprise, and as the hills became steeper and the cholla cactus were thicker, they stopped. When she reached the top of the hill, she stopped to listen in case they were circling around her. But in a few minutes she heard a car engine start and they drove away. The children had been too surprised to cry while she ran with them. Danny was shaking and Ella's little fingers were gripping Ayah's blouse.

She stayed up in the hills for the rest of the day, sitting on a black lava boulder in the sunshine where she could see for miles all around her. The sky was light blue and cloudless, and it was warm for late April. The sun warmth relaxed her and took the fear and anger away. She lay back on the rock and watched the sky. It seemed to her that she could walk into the sky, stepping through clouds endlessly. Danny played with little pebbles and stones, pretending they were birds eggs and then little rabbits. Ella sat at her feet and dropped fistfuls of dirt into the breeze, watching the dust and particles of sand intently. Ayah watched a hawk soar high above them, dark wings gliding; hunting or only watching, she did not know. The hawk was patient and he circled all afternoon before he disappeared around the high volcanic peak the Mexicans called Guadalupe.

Late in the afternoon, Ayah looked down at the gray boxcar shack with the paint all peeled from the wood; the stove pipe on the roof was rusted and crooked. The fire she had built that morning in the oil drum stove had burned out. Ella was asleep in her lap now and Danny sat close to her, complaining that he was hungry; he asked when they would go to the house. "We will stay up here until your father comes," she told him, "because those white men were chasing us." The boy remembered then and he nodded at her silently.

If Jimmie had been there he could have read those papers and explained to her what they said. Ayah would have known then, never to sign them. The doctors came back the next day and they brought a BIA[4] policeman with

---

4. Bureau of Indian Affairs, an agency of the U.S. government charged with assisting the tribal authorities of reservations.

them. They told Chato they had her signature and that was all they needed. Except for the kids. She listened to Chato sullenly; she hated him when he told her it was the old woman who died in the winter, spitting blood; it was her old grandma who had given the children this disease. "They don't spit blood," she said coldly. "The whites lie." She held Ella and Danny close to her, ready to run to the hills again. "I want a medicine man first," she said to Chato, not looking at him. He shook his head. "It's too late now. The policeman is with them. You signed the paper." His voice was gentle.

It was worse than if they had died: to lose the children and to know that somewhere, in a place called Colorado, in a place full of sick and dying strangers, her children were without her. There had been babies that died soon after they were born, and one that died before he could walk. She had carried them herself, up to the boulders and great pieces of the cliff that long ago crashed down from Long Mesa; she laid them in the crevices of sandstone and buried them in fine brown sand with round quartz pebbles that washed down the hills in the rain. She had endured it because they had been with her. But she could not bear this pain. She did not sleep for a long time after they took her children. She stayed on the hill where they had fled the first time, and she slept rolled up in the blanket Jimmie had sent her. She carried the pain in her belly and it was fed by everything she saw: the blue sky of their last day together and the dust and pebbles they played with; the swing in the elm tree and broomstick horse choked life from her. The pain filled her stomach and there was no room for food or for her lungs to fill with air. The air and the food would have been theirs.

She hated Chato, not because he let the policeman and doctors put the screaming children in the government car, but because he had taught her to sign her name. Because it was like the old ones always told her about learning their language or any of their ways: it endangered you. She slept alone on the hill until the middle of November when the first snows came. Then she made a bed for herself where the children had slept. She did not lie down beside Chato again until many years later, when he was sick and shivering and only her body could keep him warm. The illness came after the white rancher told Chato he was too old to work for him anymore, and Chato and his old woman should be out of the shack by the next afternoon because the rancher had hired new people to work there. That had satisfied her. To see how the white man repaid Chato's years of loyalty and work. All of Chato's fine-sounding English talk didn't change things.

It snowed steadily and the luminous light from the snow gradually diminished into the darkness. Somewhere in Cebolleta a dog barked and other village dogs joined with it. Ayah looked in the direction she had come, from the bar where Chato was buying the wine. Sometimes he told her to go on ahead and wait; and then he never came. And when she finally went back looking for him, she would find him passed out at the bottom of the wooden steps to Azzie's Bar. All the wine would be gone and most of the money too, from the pale blue check that came to them once a month in a government envelope. It was then that she would look at his face and his hands, scarred by ropes and the barbed wire of all those years, and she would think, this man is a stranger; for forty years she had smiled at him and cooked his food, but he remained a stranger. She stood up again, with the snow almost to her knees, and she walked back to find Chato.

It was hard to walk in the deep snow and she felt the air burn in her lungs. She stopped a short distance from the bar to rest and readjust the blanket. But this time he wasn't waiting for her on the bottom step with his old Stetson hat pulled down and his shoulders hunched up in his long wool overcoat.

She was careful not to slip on the wooden steps. When she pushed the door open, warm air and cigarette smoke hit her face. She looked around slowly and deliberately, in every corner, in every dark place that the old man might find to sleep. The bar owner didn't like Indians in there, especially Navajos, but he let Chato come in because he could talk Spanish like he was one of them. The men at the bar stared at her, and the bartender saw that she left the door open wide. Snowflakes were flying inside like moths and melting into a puddle on the oiled wood floor. He motioned to her to close the door, but she did not see him. She held herself straight and walked across the room slowly, searching the room with every step. The snow in her hair melted and she could feel it on her forehead. At the far corner of the room, she saw red flames at the mica window of the old stove door; she looked behind the stove just to make sure. The bar got quiet except for the Spanish polka music playing on the jukebox. She stood by the stove and shook the snow from her blanket and held it near the stove to dry. The wet wool smell reminded her of new-born goats in early March, brought inside to warm near the fire. She felt calm.

In past years they would have told her to get out. But her hair was white now and her face was wrinkled. They looked at her like she was a spider crawling slowly across the room. They were afraid; she could feel the fear. She looked at their faces steadily. They reminded her of the first time the white people brought her children back to her that winter. Danny had been shy and hid behind the thin white woman who brought them. And the baby had not known her until Ayah took her into her arms, and then Ella had nuzzled close to her as she had when she was nursing. The blonde woman was nervous and kept looking at a dainty gold watch on her wrist. She sat on the bench near the small window and watched the dark snow clouds gather around the mountains; she was worrying about the unpaved road. She was frightened by what she saw inside too: the strips of venison drying on a rope across the ceiling and the children jabbering excitedly in a language she did not know. So they stayed for only a few hours. Ayah watched the government car disappear down the road and she knew they were already being weaned from these lava hills and from this sky. The last time they came was in early June, and Ella stared at her the way the men in the bar were now staring. Ayah did not try to pick her up; she smiled at her instead and spoke cheerfully to Danny. When he tried to answer her, he could not seem to remember and he spoke English words with the Navajo. But he gave her a scrap of paper that he had found somewhere and carried in his pocket; it was folded in half, and he shyly looked up at her and said it was a bird. She asked Chato if they were home for good this time. He spoke to the white woman and she shook her head. "How much longer?" he asked, and she said she didn't know; but Chato saw how she stared at the boxcar shack. Ayah turned away then. She did not say good-bye.

She felt satisfied that the men in the bar feared her. Maybe it was her face and the way she held her mouth with teeth clenched tight, like there was nothing anyone could do to her now. She walked north down the road, searching for the old man. She did this because she had the blanket, and there would be no place for him except with her and the blanket in the old adobe barn near the arroyo. They always slept there when they came to Cebolleta. If the money and the wine were gone, she would be relieved because then they could go home again; back to the old hogan with a dirt roof and rock walls where she herself had been born. And the next day the old man could go back to the few sheep they still had, to follow along behind them, guiding them, into dry sandy arroyos where sparse grass grew. She knew he did not like walking behind old ewes when for so many years he rode big quarter horses and worked with cattle. But she wasn't sorry for him; he should have known all along what would happen.

There had not been enough rain for their garden in five years; and that was when Chato finally hitched a ride into the town and brought back brown boxes of rice and sugar and big tin cans of welfare peaches. After that, at the first of the month they went to Cebolleta to ask the postmaster for the check; and then Chato would go to the bar and cash it. They did this as they planted the garden every May, not because anything would survive the summer dust, but because it was time to do this. The journey passed the days that smelled silent and dry like the caves above the canyon with yellow painted buffaloes on their walls.

He was walking along the pavement when she found him. He did not stop or turn around when he heard her behind him. She walked beside him and she noticed how slowly he moved now. He smelled strongly of woodsmoke and urine. Lately he had been forgetting. Sometimes he called her by his sister's name and she had been gone for a long time. Once she had found him wandering on the road to the white man's ranch, and she asked him why he was going that way; he laughed at her and said, "You know they can't run that ranch without me," and he walked on determined, limping on the leg that had been crushed many years before. Now he looked at her curiously, as if for the first time, but he kept shuffling along, moving slowly along the side of the highway. His gray hair had grown long and spread out on the shoulders of the long overcoat. He wore the old felt hat pulled down over his ears. His boots were worn out at the toes and he had stuffed pieces of an old red shirt in the holes. The rags made his feet look like little animals up to their ears in snow. She laughed at his feet; the snow muffled the sound of her laugh. He stopped and looked at her again. The wind had quit blowing and the snow was falling straight down; the southeast sky was beginning to clear and Ayah could see a star.

"Let's rest awhile," she said to him. They walked away from the road and up the slope to the giant boulders that had tumbled down from the red sandrock mesa throughout the centuries of rainstorms and earth tremors. In a place where the boulders shut out the wind, they sat down with their backs against the rock. She offered half of the blanket to him and they sat wrapped together.

The storm passed swiftly. The clouds moved east. They were massive and full, crowding together across the sky. She watched them with the feeling of horses—steely blue-gray horses startled across the sky. The powerful haunches pushed into the distances and the tail hairs streamed white mist behind them. The sky cleared. Ayah saw that there was nothing between her and the stars. The light was crystalline. There was no shimmer, no distortion through earth haze. She breathed the clarity of the night sky; she smelled the purity of the half moon and the stars. He was lying on his side with his knees pulled up near his belly for warmth. His eyes were closed now, and in the light from the stars and the moon, he looked young again.

She could see it descend out of the night sky: an icy stillness from the edge of the thin moon. She recognized the freezing. It came gradually, sinking snowflake by snowflake until the crust was heavy and deep. It had the strength of the stars in Orion, and its journey was endless. Ayah knew that with the wine he would sleep. He would not feel it. She tucked the blanket around him, remembering how it was when Ella had been with her; and she felt the rush so big inside her heart for the babies. And she sang the only song she knew to sing for babies. She could not remember if she had ever sung it to her children, but she knew that her grandmother had sung it and her mother had sung it:

> *The earth is your mother,*
> *she holds you.*
> *The sky is your father,*
> *he protects you.*
> *Sleep,*
> *sleep.*
> *Rainbow is your sister,*
> *she loves you.*
> *The winds are your brothers,*
> *they sing to you.*
> *Sleep,*
> *sleep.*
> *We are together always*
> *We are together always*
> *There never was a time*
> *when this*
> *was not so.*

1981

ART SPIEGELMAN
b. 1948

Comic panels have existed since the end of the nineteeth century, beginning with Richard F. Outcault's *The Yellow Kid* in 1895. By the 1920s panels had evolved into strips—George Herriman's *Krazy Kat* was the most famous—and by the end of the 1930s these strips had grown into comic books, most successfully with the *Superman* series produced by Jerry Siegel and Joe Schuster. It would take the cultural transformations of the 1960s, however, for this trend of interweaving visual elements with an expanding sense of narrative to achieve literary form. As opposed to simple entertainment, literature involves, on a genuinely cultural level, both expression and reflection, comprising the beliefs and practices of a people. In the 1960s, as beliefs and practices were challenged and to some extent changed, comic-book art found itself uniquely positioned as an underground form ready to disrupt a traditional, more conservative order.

How underground comics became graphic novels is apparent from Art Spiegelman's career. A college dropout, Spiegelman found his first work in the most elemental form of cartoon humor, the illustrations for cards and stickers packaged with bubblegum and marketed as Wacky Packages and Garbage Pail Kids, a basely satirical form of 1960s counterculture created in the New York design studios of Topps and other novelty companies. When in 1970 Spiegelman moved from New York to San Francisco, his work progressed from novelty to subversion—of the comic-strip form and of larger cultural themes. Cartoonist R. Crumb had recently developed *Zap Comix* as a way of replacing convention with creation, both in the way comics were drawn and in the subjects they treated. Spiegelman's affinity was with the second wave of this movement, including the Zippy comics drawn by Bill Griffin, in which sequential art pushed common limits to be boldly experimental. Here older practices were turned against themselves, with action breaking out of frames, narratives interrogating themselves, and characters challenging all standards of social acceptability.

Spiegelman's return to New York prompted the key development in his work and emergence as a graphic novelist. Married to the artist and designer Françoise Mouly in 1977 and beginning a family, Spiegelman paid new attention to his father's stories about the signal event in the elder Spiegelmans' lives, the Holocaust. As Polish Jews who had been persecuted and imprisoned at Auschwitz, where their first son died, the Spiegelmans had emigrated first to Sweden (where Art was born three years after the war's end) and then to the United States, settling in the Rego Park neighborhood of Queens, New York City, and becoming naturalized American citizens. His parents' cultural transformation was greater than any Spiegelman had experienced in the 1960s, and he sought the artistic tools to represent it. In 1978 Will Eisner had taken comic books to a new level of expression by arguing theological matters in *A Contract with God*—the type of work that could be sold in bookstores rather than just on newsstands. But by applying his cartoonist's serial-narrative skills to his father's experiences, Siegelman gave the graphic novel literary importance.

Maus I (1986) and *Maus II* (1991) are complex creations, enfolding not just the father's tale but also his act of telling it, both of which are measured by the son's reception. Their handling of the Holocaust, a subject of countless previous treatments and certain to endure as one of humanity's major stories, as a cartoon adds great imaginative dimension. Thanks to suggestive set of references, with Jews as mice (victims of prey), Germans as cats (predators of mice), French as frogs (a reminder of the self-conscious vulgarity of older comic strips), and Poles as pigs (a dietary contrast with Jews, but also a calculated insult), graphic representation gives new facets to a familiar story. Cartooning by nature involves a great amount of artistic license. Parameters of taste are much more elastic than those for fiction, poetry, and all but the most performative of drama, while the form's roots in popular culture continue to show despite the bleachings of high taste.

Even in becoming a countercultural icon, Spiegelman has maintained a sense of humor about himself. No matter how serious his subject matter (including his 2004 treatment of the 9/11 attacks, *In the Shadow of No Towers*), the cartoonist is always the fall guy, enduring his father's occasional impatience and the terrors of life. In this sense Spiegelman's mature works echo the sentiments of his first publications, *The Complete Mr. Infinity* (1970) and *The Viper Vicar of Vice, Villany, and Vickedness*

(1972), both expressive of the 1960s counterculture and older comic book tradition that a new generation of readers would accept as illustrative of their own sensibilities.

The following text is from *Maus I and II* (1997).

From Maus

C H A P T E R   S I X

I WALKED SLOW....

CLIK CLIK

BEHIND ME ALSO WALKED SLOW.

IF I WALKED *FAST*...

BEHIND ME ALSO WALKED FAST.

WE WERE ALONE. HE SPOKE...

AMCHA?

IN HEBREW HE SAID TO ME, "OUR NATION?"

HAD I TO ANSWER HIM, OR NO?

A-AMCHA.

I *THOUGHT* YOU WERE A JEW.

...I'M JEWISH TOO! THERE ARE VERY FEW OF US LEFT...

...MY WIFE AND I HAVE BEEN HIDING IN SOSNOWIEC FOR OVER A YEAR.

I'M WITH MY WIFE TOO. WE'RE HUNGRY AND WE NEED A PLACE TO HIDE!

GO TO THE BLACK MARKET ON DE-KERTA STREET, NUMBER 8.

SO I LEFT HIM AND WENT RIGHT AWAY TO DEKERTA 8. THERE IT WAS A BIG COURTYARD...

?

ALL AROUND I LOOKED, BUT IT WAS NOBODY.

PSSST!

!

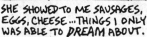

WANNA BUY SOME FOOD WITHOUT COUPONS, MISTER?

SHE SHOWED TO ME SAUSAGES, EGGS, CHEESE...THINGS I ONLY WAS ABLE TO *DREAM* ABOUT.

I BOUGHT AND WENT QUICK BACK TO ANJA.

GOOD MORNING.

VLADEK! YOU WERE GONE SO LONG.

I HAD TO GET BREAKFAST!... WANT SOME SAUSAGES? ...OR EGGS?..OR WOULD YOU PREFER CHOCOLATE?

WHAT?

IT'S A *MIRACLE!* HOW DID YOU MANAGE IT?

I'M A MAGICIAN! HAVE SOME MILK.

I WENT AGAIN BACK TO DEKERTA. THERE I COULD CHANGE JEWELRY FOR MARKS-AND MARKS FOR FOOD, OR A PLACE TO STAY.

THIS TIME IT WAS MORE PEOPLE...THERE EVEN, I SAW SOME JEWISH BOYS I KNEW FROM BEFORE THE WAR.

VLADEK SPIEGELMAN?! I HARDLY RECOGNIZED YOU. SO YOU'RE STILL ALIVE, EH?

LEO? YES. I'M WITH ANJA.

WE NEED A HIDING PLACE.

HOW ABOUT MRS. KAWKA?

SHE HAS A SMALL FARM ON THE OUTSKIRTS OF TOWN...

SHE MIGHT TAKE YOU IN, IF YOU CAN PAY.

IT WAS NOT SO FAR TO GO TO KAWKA'S FARM...

ALRIGHT THEN, MR. SPIEGELMAN. YOU AND YOUR WIFE CAN STAY IN MY BARN.

WE'LL COME LATE TONIGHT.

BUT, REMEMBER-IF YOU'RE FOUND THERE, I DON'T KNOW YOU! ... YOU MUST SAY THAT THE BARN DOOR WAS OPEN AND YOU JUST SNEAKED IN.

DON'T WORRY...WE WON'T BETRAY YOU!

AND SO WE CAME THERE TO LIVE WITH KAWKA'S COW.

IT'S ALMOST DAWN—WHEN MRS KAWKA COMES TO MILK HER COW, SHE'LL BRING YOU SOME COFFEE.

WHERE ARE YOU GOING?

TO DEKERTA.

DON'T LEAVE ME ALONE AGAIN. I'M TERRIFIED WHILE YOU'RE GONE.

DON'T WORRY, ANJA. I'LL BE SAFE. IF I DIDN'T GO OUT WE WOULDN'T HAVE FOOD...WE WOULDN'T HAVE THIS PLACE!...

AND WE'VE GOT TO FIND A WARMER PLACE FOR THE WINTER...AWAY FROM SOSNOWIEC IF POSSIBLE...

I-I'LL BE OKAY. COME BACK QUICK.

I TRAVELED OFTEN WITH THE STREETCAR TO TOWN.

IT WAS TWO CARS. ONE WAS ONLY GERMANS AND OFFICIALS. THE SECOND, IT WAS ONLY THE POLES.

ALWAYS I WENT STRAIGHT IN THE OFFICIAL CAR...

HEIL HITLER.

THE GERMANS PAID NO ATTENTION OF ME...IN THE POLISH CAR THEY COULD SMELL IF A POLISH JEW CAME IN.

AT THE BLACK MARKET I SAW SEVERAL TIMES A NICE WOMAN, WHAT I MADE A LITTLE FRIENDS WITH HER...

GOOD MORNING, MR. SPIEGELMAN.

HOW DO YOU DO, MRS. MOTONOWA! WHAT DO YOU HAVE IN YOUR BASKET TODAY?

HOW ABOUT A LOAF OF FRESH BREAD?

FINE, FINE.

OH. I'M SORRY. I DON'T HAVE ANY CHANGE.

IT'S OKAY... KEEP IT FOR YOUR LITTLE BOY.

ARE YOU AND YOUR WIFE STILL LIVING IN A BARN?

WE HAVEN'T FOUND ANYTHING BETTER.

I'VE BEEN THINKING ABOUT IT... WHY DON'T YOU BOTH MOVE IN WITH MY SON AND ME?

WHAT ABOUT YOUR HUSBAND?

HE WORKS IN GERMANY, AND ONLY COMES HOME FOR 10 DAYS EVERY 3 MONTHS... I'LL KEEP YOU HIDDEN IN THE CELLAR WHEN HE'S AROUND.

IT SOUNDS GOOD TO ME, BUT IT'S OVER 20 KILOMETERS TO YOUR HOUSE IN SZOPIENICE. MY WIFE WILL BE AFRAID TO GO!

DON'T WORRY. I'LL ES-COAT YOU!

THE NEXT EVENING SHE CAME WITH HER 7-YEARS-OLD BOY TO KAWKA'S FARMHOUSE...

I WALKED WITH MOTONOWA AS IF *SHE* WAS MY WIFE.

AND ANJA, LIKE A GOVERNESS, WENT WITH THE LITTLE BOY BEHIND. AND NOBODY EVEN *LOOKED* ON US.

WE HAD HERE A LITTLE COMFORTABLE... WE HAD WHERE TO SIT.

REMEMBER, LITTLE ONE — NEVER TELL ANYBODY THERE ARE JEWS HERE. THEY'LL SHOOT US ALL!

YES, AUNT ANJA.

THE LITTLE BOY WAS VERY SMART AND HE LOVED VERY MUCH ANJA.

YOU HAD TO PAY MRS. MOTO-NOWA TO KEEP YOU, RIGHT?

OF COURSE I PAID... AND WELL I PAID.

...WHAT YOU THINK? SOMEONE WILL RISK THEIR LIFE FOR NOTHING?

...I PAID ALSO FOR THE FOOD WHAT SHE GAVE TO US FROM HER SMUGGLING BUSINESS.

BUT, ONE TIME I MISSED A FEW COINS TO THE BREAD...

I'LL PAY YOU THE REST TOMORROW, AFTER I GO OUT AND CASH SOME VALUABLES.

SORRY... I WASN'T ABLE TO FIND ANY BREAD TODAY.

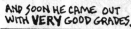

ALWAYS SHE GOT BREAD, SO I DIDN'T BELIEVE... BUT, STILL, SHE WAS A GOOD WOMAN.

IN HIS SCHOOL THE BOY WAS VERY BAD IN GERMAN. SO ANJA TUTORED TO HIM.

ICH BIN... DU BIST... ER IST...

SHE KNEW GERMAN LIKE AN EXPERT.

AND SOON HE CAME OUT WITH VERY GOOD GRADES.

MY TEACHER ASKED ME HOW I IMPROVED SO MUCH...

SO I TOLD HIM MY MOTHER WAS HELPING ME.

WHEW

HE WAS REALLY A CLEVER BOY.

BUT IT WAS A FEW THINGS HERE NOT SO GOOD... HER HOME WAS VERY SMALL AND IT WAS ON THE GROUND FLOOR...

BE SURE TO KEEP AWAY FROM THE WINDOW—YOU MIGHT BE SEEN!

ONE MINUTE!

(QUICK—GET IN THE CLOSET!)

NOK NOK

IF SOMEBODY CAME, WE HAD FAST TO HIDE.

A LETTER FROM YOUR HUSBAND, MRS. MOTONOWA.

THANKS.

BUT I HAD SOME-THING ALLERGIC IN THE CLOSET...

AAH·

OR MAYBE IT WAS A COLD—I CAN'T REMEMBER...

·CHMF

BUT ALWAYS I HAD TO SNEEZE.

STILL, EVERYTHING HERE WAS FINE, UNTIL ONE SATURDAY MOTONOWA RAN VERY EARLY BACK FROM HER BLACK MARKET WORK...

THIS IS TERRIBLE!

THE GESTAPO JUST SEARCHED ME.—THEY TOOK MY GOODS!

THEY MAY COME SEARCH HERE ANY MINUTE! YOU'VE GOT TO LEAVE!

WHAT?

BUT WHERE CAN WE GO?

I DON'T KNOW. BUT YOU MUST GET OUT NOW!

OH MY GOD...THIS IS THE END!

ANJA STARTED TO CRY... BUT WE HAD NOT A CHOICE.

WE'LL WALK TOWARD SOS-NOWIEC—AT LEAST WE'LL KNOW OUR WAY AROUND.

ANJA WAS SO AFRAID SHE WAS SHAKING.

STAY CALM—WALK AS IF WE'RE JUST STROLLING...AND SPEAK GERMAN.

FOR HOURS WE WALKED.

B-BESUCHEN WIR DOCH FRAU KAWKA.

GUTE IDEE.

VLADEK—WE'RE BEING FOLLOWED.

RELAX.

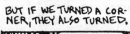

BUT IF WE TURNED A COR-NER, THEY ALSO TURNED.

ES IST KALT.

JA. JA.

OF COURSE I WAS RIGHT—THEY DIDN'T MEAN ANYTHING ON US.

WOOSH

THEY JUST WERE WALKING.

STAYING ON THE STREET ALL NIGHT IS TOO DANGEROUS... MAYBE WE CAN HIDE IN THAT CONSTRUCTION SITE.

GOOD—I'M EXHAUSTED.

HERE WAS A FOUNDATION MADE VERY DEEP DOWN IN THE GROUND...

BE CAREFUL!

I JUMPED FIRST IN, AND I PULLED OVER BRICKS FOR ANJA TO STEP DOWN.

AND HERE WE WAITED A COLD FEW HOURS FOR THE DAY.

IT STARTED TO BE LIGHT...

COME. WE WON'T BE NOTICED IF WE MIX WITH PEOPLE OUT ON THE STREET.

I'M SO TIRED AND COLD...

WE CAN REST NOW.

WE CAME FINALLY AGAIN TO THIS PLACE WITH THE COW AND WENT INSIDE.

LATER, KAWKA CAME IN...

W-WHO'S IN HERE?

THE SPIEGEL-MANS... WE HAD NOWHERE ELSE TO GO.

WELL... I GUESS YOU CAN STAY. BUT, REMEMBER: I DON'T KNOW YOU'RE HERE!

WHY, MRS. SPIEGELMAN, YOU'RE SHIVERING!

YOU CAN COME INTO MY HOUSE FOR AN HOUR OR SO, 'TIL YOU WARM UP.

SHE TOOK ANJA INSIDE AND BROUGHT TO ME SOME FOOD...IN THOSE DAYS I WAS SO STRONG I COULD SIT EVEN IN THE SNOW ALL NIGHT...

THINGS CAN'T BE THIS BAD EVERYWHERE! I'D GIVE ANYTHING TO GET OUT OF POLAND!

YOU KNOW, BEFORE I TOOK YOU IN, I HAD A YOUNG MAN AND HIS SON HERE...

TWO PEOPLE I KNOW SMUG-GLED THEM INTO HUNGARY. I HEARD HE AND HIS BOY WERE DOING WELL THERE.

HUNGARY! REALLY?! I'D LIKE TO MEET THOSE SMUGGLERS!

SHE TOLD ME THESE TWO ACQUAINTANCES VISITED OFTEN TO HER ON THURSDAY EVENINGS... TODAY WAS MAYBE A MONDAY...

I DON'T GET IT... WASN'T HUNGARY AS DANGEROUS AS POLAND?

NO. FOR A LONGER TIME IT WAS *BETTER* THERE IN HUNGARY FOR THE JEWS... BUT THEN, NEAR THE VERY FINISH OF THE WAR, THEY ALL GOT PUT *ALSO* TO AUSCHWITZ.

I WAS THERE, AND I SAW IT. THOUSANDS - HUNDREDS OF THOUSANDS OF JEWS FROM HUNGARY...

SO MANY, IT WASN'T EVEN ROOM ENOUGH TO BURY THEM ALL IN THE OVENS.

BUT AT THAT TIME, WHEN I WAS THERE WITH KAWKA, WE COULDN'T *KNOW* THEN.

SO... I WENT NEXT DAY TO DEKERTA STREET TO BUY FOOD...

OH GOD! OH GOD! MR. SPIEGELMAN, YOU'RE ALIVE! I'M SO GLAD TO SEE YOU!

MRS. MOTONOWA!

I WANTED TO FIND A NEW CONNECTION TO HIDE US. BUT *REALLY* I DIDN'T THINK TO FIND AGAIN *HER*.

PRAISE MARY, YOU'RE SAFE! I COULDN'T *SLEEP*, I FELT SO GUILTY ABOUT CHASING YOU AND YOUR WIFE OUT.

THE GESTAPO NEVER EVEN CAME TO MY HOUSE. I JUST PANICKED FOR NOTHING.

PLEASE COME BACK AGAIN.

ANJA WAS GLAD OF GOING BACK. AND MOTONOWA ALSO... ALWAYS I PAID HER NICELY.

AND THAT SAME NIGHT WE SAID GOODBYE TO KAWKA AND WENT AGAIN TO SZOPIENICE.

AFTER WE WERE BACK ONLY A SHORT TIME...

WELL, MY HUSBAND WRITES THAT HE'S COMING HOME FOR HIS 10-DAY VACATION.

IF HE KNEW YOU WERE HERE HE'D THROW US ALL OUT. BUT, DON'T WORRY... YOU'LL BE ALL RIGHT IN MY CELLAR.

...I SET UP A MATTRESS... I'LL COME DOWN WHENEVER I CAN.

SO EACH DAY AND NIGHT WE SAT IN SUCH A STORAGE LOCKER...

IN THE DAYS WE WERE AFRAID TO BREATHE— PEOPLE CAME DOWN OFTEN TO *THEIR* LOCKERS.

AT NIGHT WE COULD MOVE AROUND A LITTLE, BUT IT WAS SOMETHING ELSE DOWN THERE...

AIEEE!

WH-WHAT IS IT?

TH-THERE ARE **RATS** DOWN HERE!

SHH- CALM DOWN, STOP SCREAMING.

THOSE AREN'T RATS. THEY'RE VERY SMALL. ONE RAN OVER MY HAND BEFORE. THEY'RE JUST **MICE!**

OF COURSE, IT **WAS** REALLY RATS. BUT I WANTED ANJA TO FEEL MORE EASY.

BUT, THEN, MOTONOWA STOPPED TO COME DOWN.

ALSO, HERE WE HAD NO PLACE WHERE TO WASH, SO ANJA GOT ON ALL HER SKIN A TERRIBLE RASH.

IT'S BEEN 3 DAYS SINCE SHE BROUGHT ANY FOOD.

HERE...HAVE ANOTHER CANDY...

I HAD STILL CANDIES I ORGANIZED ON DEKERTA. ONLY *THIS* WE HAD TO EAT.

I DON'T KNOW WHAT'S WORSE—THE HUNGER OR THE ITCHING.

DON'T SCRATCH! IT ONLY—SHH!

KLIK

THE DOOR.

I'M SORRY I COULDN'T GET DOWN BEFORE—MY HUSBAND IS GETTING SUSPICIOUS.

HE ASKED WHY I GO TO THE CELLAR SO OFTEN. HE EVEN ASKED IF I WAS HIDING JEWS HERE! ...HE WAS JOKING, BUT STILL...

ARE YOU ALL RIGHT HERE?

THERE ARE *RATS*, GIANT RATS! THEY'RE HORRIBLE!

WELL—YOU'RE BETTER OFF WITH THE RATS THAN WITH THE GESTAPO... AT LEAST THE RATS WON'T *KILL* YOU!

MMM...

AND SHE WAS RIGHT. WE WERE HAPPY EVEN TO HAVE *THESE* CONDITIONS.

AFTER THE TEN DAYS HER HUSBAND LEFT, AND SHE TOOK US BACK.

IT'S GOOD TO BE "HOME," EH, VLADEK?

IT'S A LOT NICER THAN THAT CELLAR.

BUT I DIDN'T FEEL SAFE HERE. IT WAS TOO MANY WAYS SOMEBODY COULD FIND US OUT. I WANTED TO GO BETTER TO HUNGARY.

SO, WHEN IT CAME THURSDAY, I WENT IN THE DIRECTION TO TAKE A STREETCAR TO SEE KAWKA IN SOSNOWIEC.

LOOK!

I HAD TO PASS WHERE SOME CHILDREN WERE PLAYING.

A JEW! A JEW!

THEY RAN SCREAMING HOME.

HELP! MOMMY! A JEW!!

A JEW!

QUICK, THE MOTHERS CAME OUTSIDE TO SEE WHAT WAS!

THE MOTHERS ALWAYS TOLD SO: "BE CARE-FUL! A JEW WILL CATCH YOU TO A BAG AND EAT YOU!"... SO THEY TAUGHT TO THEIR CHILDREN.

I APPROACHED OVER TO THEM...

HEIL HITLER.

IF I RAN AWAY THEY, WOULD SEE: "YES, IT IS A JEW HERE."

DON'T BE AFRAID, LITTLE ONES. I'M NOT A JEW. I WON'T HURT YOU.

SORRY, MISTER. YOU KNOW HOW KIDS ARE... HEIL HITLER.

SO I CAME OUT WELL FROM THIS...

BUT THE EXPERIENCE COST ME REALLY A LOT OF HAIRS.

1986

JULIA ALVAREZ
b. 1950

anguage, culture, politics, and region are customarily subjects for serious study, but in the work of Julia Alvarez they become the impetus for great creativity, even festivity. This is because many of Alvarez's characters share a background like her own, in which these elements are anything but stable. Born in New York City, raised in the Dominican Republic, and returned to Brooklyn when her father's political activities put him in danger from the dictator Rafael Trujillo, Alvarez faced the same prospect as her most typical protagonist: that of improvising a sense of self. Such improvisation typifies young Yolanda in Alvarez's first novel, *How the García Girls Lost Their Accents* (1991), and the sixteen members of Yolanda's immediate and extended family react to that improvisation in its sequel, *¡Yo!* (1997). If Yolanda, nicknamed "Yo" (meaning "I" in Spanish), can invent herself, so can her parents, siblings, cousins, aunts, and close friends judge her approximation of reality against theirs—and how many there are! The result is a carnival of language and language's many contexts, in which humor and the self-conscious joy of storytelling create a virtual conversation with the reader.

As a writer Alvarez has explored the double identities she shared as a young girl negotiating her way on Brooklyn playgrounds, no longer a citizen of the Dominican Republic but not yet accepted as an American. After doing graduate work at Syracuse University and publishing a book of poems, *Homecoming* (1984), she turned to the multiform saga of the García girls as a way of exploring the more playful aspects of language, a style of heteroglossia advocated by the Russian literary theorist M. M. Bakhtin. *How the García Girls Lost Their Accents* uses interrelated narratives of the four sisters to contrast their hard-won American identities with the different styles of life they had led as youngsters, first in the Dominican Republic and then as immigrants to fast-paced New York. A third novel (more loosely a sequel than is *¡Yo!*), *In the Time of the Butterflies* (1994), takes the historical event of three sisters' murder by Trujillo's secret police and retells it from a fictional perspective, that of a fourth, surviving sibling. Here are the more sober aspects of language, culture, politics, and region that are presented more happily in *¡Yo!*

In recent years Alvarez, like other Latina writers, has focused on the writer's role in fashioning a voice, particularly as that voice undertakes what critic Kelli Lyon Johnson calls "generic transgressions" in which fiction, poetry, autobiography, history, children's literature, and even literary theory intermix. *In the Name of Salomé* (2000) is presented as a novel, although its protagonists are historical figures prominent as a poet in the Dominican Republic (the mother) and a scholar in the United States (her daughter). Alvarez has taught for many years at Vermont's Middlebury College, where she is writer-in-residence between regular visits to the Dominican Republic.

The following text is from *¡Yo!* (1997).

From ¡Yo!

The Mother

To tell you the truth, the hardest thing coming to this country wasn't the winter everyone warned me about—it was the language. If you had to choose the most tongue-twisting way of saying you love somebody or how much a pound for the ground round, then say it in English. For the longest time I thought Americans must be smarter than us Latins—because how else could they speak such a difficult language. After a while, it struck me the other way. Given the choice of languages, only a fool would choose to speak English on purpose.

I guess for each one in the family it was different what was the hardest thing. For Carlos, it was having to start all over again at forty-five, getting a license, setting up a practice. My eldest Carla just couldn't bear that she wasn't the know-it-all anymore. Of course, the Americans knew their country better than she did. Sandi got more complicated, prettier, and I suppose that made it hard on her, discovering she was a princess just as she had lost her island kingdom. Baby Fifi took to this place like china in a china shop, so if anything, the hardest thing for her was hearing the rest of us moan and complain. As for Yo, I'd have to say the hardest thing about this country was being thrown together in such close proximity with me.

Back on the island[1] we lived as a clan, not as what is called here *the nuclear family*,[2] which already the name should be a hint that you're asking for trouble cooping up related tempers in the small explosive chambers of each other's attention. The girls used to run with their gang of cousins, supervised—if you can call it that—by a whole bunch of aunts and nanny-maids who had wiped our bottoms when *we* were babies and now were wiping the drool of the old people who had hired them half a century ago. There was never any reason to clash with anyone. You didn't get along with your mother? You had two sisters, one brother-in-law, three brothers and their wives, thirteen nieces and nephews, a husband, your own kids, two great-aunts, your father, a bachelor uncle, a deaf poor relation, and a small army of housemaids to mediate and appease—so that if you muttered under your breath, "You bitch!" by the time it got to your mother it would sound something like, "Pass the mango dish, please."

And this was true for Yo and me.

Back there, that one was mostly raised by the maids. She seemed to like to hang around them more than she did her own kin, so that if she had been darker, I would have thought she was a changeling that got switched with my own flesh and blood. True, from time to time we did have our run-downs—not even three, four dozen people could always block the clashing of our two strong wills.

But I had a trick that I played back then, not just on her, but on all my girls, to make them behave. I called it putting on the bear. Of course, by the time we left the island, it no longer worked there, and it was only by mistake that it worked once here.

---

1. The Dominican Republic, a Caribbean nation that shares the island of Hispaniola with Haiti.

2. A family consisting of a father, mother, and a small number of children, closely spaced in age.

It started innocently enough. My mother had given me a mink coat she used to wear when she and my father were traveling a lot to New York for vacations away from the dictatorship.[3] I kept it at the back of the walk-in closet, thinking maybe someday we would escape the hell we were living in, and I'd get to wear that coat into freedom. Often I thought about selling it. I hadn't married a rich man and we were always short on money.

But every time I got ready to sell it, I don't know. I'd bury my nose in that tickling fur that still held the smell of my mother's perfume. I'd imagine myself walking down Fifth Avenue with lights twinkling in the shop windows and snowflakes coming down so pretty, and I just couldn't bear to part with the coat. I'd slip the plastic cover back over it and think, I'll hold on to it a while longer.

Then one Christmas, I thought it'd be kind of neat to dress up for all the kids. So I draped this coat over my head with a bit of my face poking out, and the rest of the fur falling all the way down to my calves. I had some story worked out that Santa Claus couldn't make it down from the North Pole, so he had sent one of his bears instead.

My girls and their cousins took one look at me and it was like sheets hitting a fan. They screamed and ran. No one could be coaxed to come forward for a present. Finally, Carlos pantomined chasing me off with a broom, and as I hurried away, I dropped my pillowcase of goodies. Minutes later, when I walked back in, dressed in my red organdy, the girls ran to me, "Mami! Mami! El cuco[4] was here!" El cuco was the Haitian boogeyman I had told them would come and steal them away if they didn't behave.

"Really?" I said, miming surprise. "What did you do?"

The girls looked at each other, big-eyed. What could they have done but avoid being mouthfuls for a monster with an appetite for their toys. But Yo piped up, "I beat him and chased him away!"

Here was a little problem that was not going to go away by itself. Often, I put Tabasco in that mouth hoping to burn away the lies that seemed to spring from her lips. For Yo, talking was like an exercise in what you could make up. But that night was Christmas Eve, and the dictatorship seemed far away in some storybook about cucos, and Carlos looked so handsome in his white guayabera,[5] like a rich plantation owner in an American ad for coffee beans or cigars. Besides I felt pleased with my little trick.

From then on, especially when I heard them fighting, I threw that coat over my head and went hooting down the hall. I'd burst into their room, swinging my arms, calling out their names, and they'd scream, holding on to each other, whatever fight they had been in the middle of forgotten. Step by step, I approached, until they were at the edge of hysterics, their little faces pale and their eyes wide with terror. Then I flung the coat off and threw out my arms, "It's me, Mami!"

For a minute, even though they could see it was me, they hung back, unconvinced.

Maybe it was a mean thing to do, I don't know. After a few times, what I was really trying to do was see if my girls had any sense at all. I thought for

3. Of Rafael Trujillo (1891–1961), president of the Dominican Republic (1930–38, 1942–52) and always in ultimate control thanks to the support of the army, until a military coup led to his assassination.
4. The cuckoo (Spanish), by implication shrewd, crafty, and sly.
5. Light, blousy shirt.

sure they would catch on. But no, each time, I fooled them. And I began to feel angry at them for being so slow.

Yo figured it out, finally. Maybe she was five, six—I don't know. All those years have mixed together like an old puzzle whose box top is lost. (I don't even know anymore what picture all those little pieces make.) As usual, I went howling into the girls' bedroom. But this time, Yo broke loose, came right up to me, and yanked that coat off my head. "See," she said, turning to the others. "It *is* just Mami like I told you."

It was no surprise to me that she was the one who caught on.

Back in my room, I was returning the coat when I noticed someone had been poking around in the closet. My shoes were scattered every which way, a hat box knocked over. That closet wasn't just any walk-in closet. It had once been a hallway between the master bedroom and Carlos's study, but we had closed it off on both sides in order to make a closet you could enter from either room. It was almost always locked on account of we kept everything valuable there. I suppose at the back of our minds, Carlos and I always knew that one day we would have to leave the island in a hurry and that it would be handy to have our cash and valuables on hand. And so, I was fit to be fried seeing signs that someone had been rifling through our hiding place.

Then it came to me who our intruder had been—Yo! Earlier, I had seen her in Carlos's study, looking over the medical books her father let her play with. She must have gone in our closet, and that's how she had figured out the fur was just a fur. I was ready to call her in and give her a large serving of my right hand when I saw that the floorboards close to the study side had been pried open and not exactly wedged back in place. I crawled in under the clothes with a flashlight and lifted one of those boards. It was my turn to go pale—stashed inside and wrapped in one of my good towels was a serious-looking gun.

You can bet when Carlos came home, I threatened to leave him right then and there if he didn't tell me what he was up to. I found out more than I wanted to know.

"No harm done," Carlos kept saying. "I'll just move it to another location tonight." And he did, wrapping it inside my fur coat and laying the bundle on the back seat of the Buick like he was going off to sell that coat after all. He came back late that night, the coat over his arm, and it wasn't until the next morning as I was hanging it up that I found the oil stains on the lining. They looked just like dried blood.

After that, I was a case all right. Nights, I was up to four sleeping pills to numb myself into a few hours of the skimpiest sleep. Days I took Valium[6] to ease that jumpy feeling. It was hell on the wheels of our marriage having me down so much of the time. Worst were the migraines I got practically every afternoon. I'd have to lie down in that small, hot bedroom with the jalousies angled shut and a wet towel on my face. Far off, I could hear the kids yelling in their bedroom, and I'd wish I could squeeze that bear trick one more time to terrify them into silence.

Lots of worries went through my pounding head those afternoons. One of them that kept hammering away was that Yo had been snooping around in that closet. If she had seen that hidden gun, it was just a matter of time

6. Anti-anxiety prescription drug.

before she'd tell someone about it. Already I could see the SIM[7] coming to the door to drag us away. One afternoon when I just couldn't stand it anymore, I leapt out of my bed and called down the hall for her to come to my room this instant.

She must have thought she was going to get it about all the loud bickering coming from their bedroom. She hurried down the hall already defending herself that she had plucked off Fifi's baby doll's head only because Fifi had asked her to. "Hush now," I said, "it's not about that!" That stopped her short. She hung back at the door, looking around my bedroom like maybe she wasn't so sure the bear was nothing but her mother in a fur coat after all.

I gave her a little pep talk in a soft voice—the way you talk to babies as you stroke them till their eyes drift shut. I told her Papá Dios in heaven could see into every one of our souls. He knew when we were good and when we were bad. When we lied and when we told the truth. That He could have asked us to do whatever He wanted, but out of all the hundred million things, He had only chosen ten holy commandments for us to obey. And one of those ten was honor thy father and mother which meant you shouldn't lie to them.

"So always, always, you must tell your mami the truth." I served her a big smile of which she only returned a little slice back. She knew something else was coming. She sat on the bed, watching me. Just as she had seen through the fur to her mother, now she was looking through her mother to the scared woman inside. I let out a long sigh, and said, "Now, cuca darling, Mami wants you to tell her what things you saw when you went looking in the closet the other day."

"You mean the big closet?" she said, pointing down the passageway that led from the master bedroom to the walk-in closet and right through to her father's study.

"That very one," I said. The migraine was hammering away inside my head, building its big house of pain.

She looked at me like she knew that admitting she had been snooping would get her into a closet full of trouble. So, I promised her that telling the truth this time would make her my and God's little darling.

"I saw your coat," she said.

"That's very good," I said. "That's what I mean. What else did you see in Mami's closet?"

"Your funny shoes," she remarked. She meant the heels with little holes pockmarked in the leather.

"Excellent!" I said. "Mami's darling. What else?"

She went through that whole closet with the full inventory of practically every piece of clothing I owned. My God, I thought, give her another decade and *she* could work for the SIM. I lay there, listening because what else could I do? If she hadn't really seen anything, I didn't want to put any ideas in her head. That one had a mouth from here to China going the long way like Columbus's ships.

"How about the floor?" I asked stupidly. "Did you see anything *in* the floor?"

She shook her head in a way that didn't convince me. I went back over the ten commandments and not lying to thy mother, and still I couldn't flush any

<hr>

7. Servicio de Inteligencia Militar (Spanish for "Military Intelligence Service"), Trujillo's dreaded secret police.

more information from her except my monogrammed hankies and, oh yes, my nylons in a pleated plastic case. I finally made her promise that if she remembered anything else, she should come and tell Mami directly and no one else. "It will be our little secret," I whispered to her.

Just as she was slipping out the door, she turned around and said a curious thing. "Mami, the bear won't be coming anymore." It was as if she were stating her part of our bargain. "Honey cuca," I said. "Remember, Mami was the one playing the bear. It was just a silly joke. But no," I promised her, "that bear's gone for good. Okay?" She nodded her approval.

As soon as the door latched shut I cried into my pillow. My head was hurting so much. I missed not having nice things, money and freedom. I hated being at the mercy of my own child, but in that house we were all at the mercy of her silence from that day on.

Isn't a story a charm? All you have to say is, *And then we came to the United States*, and with that *and then*, you skip over four more years of disappearing friends, sleepless nights, house arrest, narrow escape, *and then*, you've got two adults and four wired-up kids in a small, dark apartment near Columbia University. Yo must have kept her mouth shut or no charm would have worked to get us free of the torture chambers we kept telling the immigration people about so they wouldn't send us back.

Not being one hundred percent sure we would get to stay—that was the hardest thing at the beginning. Even the problem with the English language seemed like a drop in a leaky bucket then. It was later that I got to thinking English was the hardest thing of all for me. But believe me, back then at the beginning, I had my hands too full to be making choices among our difficulties.

Carlos was morose. All he could think about was the compañeros he had left behind. I kept asking him what else he could have done but stay to die with them. He was studying like cats and dogs for his license exam. We were living on the low end of the hog off what little savings we had left, and there was no money coming in. I was worried how I was going to pay for the warm clothes my kids would be needing once the cold weather set in.

The last thing I needed was their whining and fighting. Every day it was the same question, "When are we going to go back?" Now that we were far away and I wasn't afraid of their blurting things out, I tried to explain. But it was as if they thought I was lying to them with a story to make them behave. They'd listen, but as soon as I was done, they'd start in again. They wanted to go back to their cousins and uncles and aunts and the maids. I thought they would feel more at home once school began. But September, October, November, December passed by, and they were still having nightmares and nagging me all the long days that they wanted to go back. Go back. Go back. Go back.

I resorted to locking them in closets. That old-fashioned apartment was full of them, deep closets with glass knobs and those keyholes like in cartoons for detectives to look through and big iron keys with the handle part shaped like a fleur-de-lis. I always used the same four closets, a small one in the girls' bedroom and the big one in mine, the broom closet in the hall, and finally the coat closet in the living room. Which child went into which depended on who I grabbed first where.

I wouldn't leave them in there for long. Believe me. I'd go from door to door, like a priest taking confession, promising to let them out the minute they calmed down and agreed to live in peace. I don't know how it happened that Yo never got the coat closet until that one time that I lived to regret.

I had shut them all up and gone round, letting out the baby first, then the oldest, who was always so outraged. Then the two middle kids, first Sandi. When I got to Yo's door, I didn't get an answer. That scared me, and I opened that door quick. There she stood, pale with fright. And, ay, I felt so terrible!— she had gone in her pants.

That damn mink coat was in that closet, way to one side, but of course, being Yo, she'd gone poking around in the dark. She must have touched the fur and lost her bananas. I don't understand because it had seemed she knew the fur was just a coat. Maybe she associated me being under that coat, and here I was on one side of the door, and there she was alone on the other side with a monster she was sure we had left behind in the Dominican Republic.

I pulled her out and into the bathroom. She didn't cry. No—just that low moan kids do when they go deep inside themselves looking for the mother you haven't turned out to be for them. All she said that whole time I was trying to clean her up was, "You promised that bear was gone for good."

I got weepy myself. "You girls are the bears! And here I thought all our troubles would end when we got here." I laid down my head on my arms on the side of the bathtub, and I started bawling. "Ay, Mami, ay," the other three joined in. They had come to the door of the bathroom to see what was going on. "We promise we'll be good."

Not Yo. She stood up in the water and grabbed a towel, then stomped out of the tub. When she was out of my reach, she cried, "I don't want to be in this crazy family!"

Even back then, she always had to have the last word.

Not a week later a social worker at the school, Sally O'Brien, calls up and asks to make a house visit. The minute I get off the phone, I interrogate my girls about what they might have said to this lady. But they all swear that they have nothing to confess. I warn them if this lady gives us a bad report we'll be sent back, and if we are sent back, cucos and bears are going to be stuffed animals compared to the SIM fieras[8] that will tear us apart there. I send them off to put on their matching polka dot dresses I made them for coming to the United States. And then I do what I haven't done in our six months here. I take a Valium to give this lady a good impression.

In she comes, a tall lady in flat black shoes with straps and a blond braid down her back like a schoolgirl dressed in an old lady's suit. She has a pleasant, un-made-up face and eyes so blue and sincere you know they've yet to see the worst things in the world. She carries a satchel with little hearts painted on it. Out of it she pulls a long yellow tablet with our name already written on it. "Is it all right if I take some notes?"

"Of course, Mrs. O'Brien." I don't know if she is a married woman but I've decided to compliment her with a husband even if she doesn't have one.

"Will your husband be joining us?" she asks, looking around the room. I follow her glance since I am sure she is checking out whether the place looks

8. Wild beasts (Spanish).

clean and adequate for raising four girls. The coat closet I forgot to shut looms like a torture chamber.

"My husband just received his medical license. So he has been working like a god every day, even Sunday," I add, which she writes down in her notepad. "We have been through hard times." I've already decided that I won't try to pretend that we're having a ball in America, though believe it or not, that was my original plan on how to handle this visit. I thought it would sound more patriotic.

"That must be a relief!" she says, nodding her head and looking at me. Everything she says it's like she just put the rattle in the baby's hand and is waiting to see what the baby is going to do with it.

I shake it, good and hard. "We are free at last," I tell her. "Thanks to this great country which has offered us the green cards. We cannot go back," I add. "It would be certain death."

Her eyes blink at this, and she makes a note. "I read things in the paper," she says, bringing her braid from behind to fall down the front of her suit. She doesn't seem the nervous type, but the way she keeps minding that braid it's like she is getting paid to keep it occupied. "But are things really that bad?"

And right then and there in my broken English that usually cuts my ideas down to the wrong size, I fill her two ears full with what is happening back on the island—homes raided, people hauled off, torture chambers, electric prods, attacks by dogs, fingernails pulled out. I get a little carried away and invent a few tortures of my own—nothing the SIM hadn't thought up, I'm sure. As I talk, she keeps wincing until her hands go up to her forehead like she has caught one of my migraines. In a whisper she says, "This is truly awful. You must be so worried about the rest of your family."

I can't trust my voice to say so. I give her a little nod.

"But what I don't get is how the girls keep saying they want to go back. That things were better there."

"They are sick of home—" I explain, but that doesn't sound right.

"Homesick, yes," she says.

I nod. "They are children. They do not see the forest or the trees."

"I understand." She says it so nicely that I am convinced that even with those untried blue eyes, she does understand. "They can't know the horror you and your husband have lived through."

I try to keep the tears back, but of course they come. What this lady can't know is that I'm not just crying about leaving home or about everything we've lost, but about what's to come. It's not really until now with the whole clan pulled away like the foundation under a house that I wonder if the six of us will stand together.

"I understand, I understand," she keeps saying until I get control of myself. "We're just concerned because the girls seem so anxious. Especially Yolanda."

I knew it! "Has she been telling stories?"

The lady nods slowly. "Her teacher says she loves stories. But some of the ones she tells, well—" She lets out a sigh. She tosses her braid behind her back like she doesn't want it to hear this. "Frankly, they are a little disturbing."

"Disturbing?" I ask. Even though I know what the word means, it sounds worse coming out of this woman's mouth.

"Oh, she's been mentioning things . . ." The lady waves her hand vaguely. "Things like what you were describing. Kids locked in closets and their mouths burned with lye. Bears mauling little children." She stops a moment, maybe because of the shocked look on my face.

"It doesn't surprise me," the woman explains. "In fact, I'm glad she's getting it all out."

"Yes," I say. And suddenly, I am feeling such envy for my daughter, who is able to speak of what terrifies her. I myself can't find the words in English—or Spanish. Only the howling of the bear I used to impersonate captures some of what I feel.

"Yo has always been full of stories." I say it like an accusation.

"Oh, but you should be proud of her," the lady says, bringing her braid forward like she is going to defend Yo with it.

"Proud?" I say in disbelief, ready to give her all the puzzle pieces of my mind so she gets the full picture. But then, I realize it is no use. How can this lady with her child's eyes and her sweet smile understand who I am and what I have been through? And maybe this is a blessing after all. That people only know the parts we want to tell about ourselves. Look at her. Inside that middle-aged woman is a nervous girl playing with her braid. But how that girl got stuck in there, and where the key is to let her out, maybe not even she can tell?

"Who knows where Yo got that need to invent," I finally say because I don't know what else to say.

"This has been very helpful, Laura," she says, standing up to go. "And I want you to know if there's anything we can do to help you all in settling in, please don't hesitate to call." She hands me a little card, not like our calling cards back home with all your important family names in fancy gold lettering. This one shows her name and title and the name of the school and her phone number in black print.

"Let me call the girls to say goodbye."

She smiles when they come out in their pretty, ironed dresses, curtsying like I taught them. And as she bends to shake each one's hand, I glance down at her pad on the coffee table and read the notes she has jotted: *Trauma/dictatorship/family bonds strong/mother devoted.*

For a moment I feel redeemed as if everything we are suffering and everything we will suffer is the fault of the dictatorship. I know this will be the story I tell in the future about those hard years—how we lived in terror, how the girls were traumatized by the experience, how many nights I got up to check on their blankets and they screamed if I touched them.

But never mind. Within a year of all this, the dictator will be shot dead by some of the very men who were in the underground with my husband. The girls will be jabbering away in English like they were born to it. As for the mink, I will exchange it at the secondhand shop on Fifth Avenue for four little-girl coats. If nothing else, my children will be warm that first winter everyone warned would be the hardest thing about coming to this country.

1997

JORIE GRAHAM
b. 1950

Jorie Graham's ability to render the disjunctive activity of modern thought, without abandoning the sensuousness of perception, has made her a prominent contemporary poet. Her poems are sites of self-questioning thinking—about metaphysics, epistemology, or the nature of language. As her imagination moves between polarities, she explores the tensions between spirit and matter, thought and sensation, formlessness and form. Rather than resolve these tensions, her poems examine the dependence of each term on the other, as well as the gap between them. This gap is sometimes figured as a literal blank ("_____"), a space language cannot fill. At other times it appears as the moment when things "scatter, blow away, scatter, recollect" ("The Dream of the Unified Field"), a moment in which form and the undoing of form coexist. Graham's poems often work in liminal spaces between the visible and the invisible, like the scene of the souls at Judgment hurrying to reenter the flesh in "At Luca Signorelli's Resurrection of the Body": "there is no / entrance, / only entering." She has called poetic form "a vessel for active tension," and the rapid shifts in Graham's poems from past to present, from abstract to particular, make the surface of her work appear to be eddied by verbal and intellectual turbulence. No wonder "roil" is one of her favorite verbs.

Graham was born in New York, but when she was a child her father, a *Newsweek* correspondent, and her mother, a sculptor, moved to Italy, where Graham grew up in the neighborhood of Trastevere, the old part of Rome. She lived surrounded by Italian churches full of frescoes, and references to Italian art inform many of her poems, among them "San Sepolcro" and "At Luca Signorelli's Resurrection of the Body." In Italy Graham attended a French lycée, and at seventeen she went to Paris to study at the Sorbonne, where she became involved in the student uprisings of 1968. In 1969 she returned to the United States and enrolled in film school at New York University (where she remembers hearing poetry read aloud in English for the first time), and from the start her poetry has been influenced by cinema. She went on to earn an MFA from the University of Iowa Writers Workshop, where she later taught for a number of years; currently she is on the faculty at Harvard University. The range of reference in Graham's work is wide and suggests her European background and especially her French education, with its emphasis on philosophy. But she is equally preoccupied with American history and the nature of American life, a preoccupation evident in "The Dream of the Unified Field," which closes with her revision of entries from Christopher Columbus's journals.

What Graham calls "the calm assurance of the standard English line" has "interested and troubled" her. Although her poems often move in and out of an iambic measure (as in the openings of "The Geese" and "The Dream of the Unified Field"), like many poets she believes contemporary experience requires a more unpredictable music. The poems of her first book, *Hybrids of Plants and of Ghosts* (1980; the title is taken from the German philosopher Friedrich Nietzsche), were mostly constructed of short, tightly controlled lines. But in subsequent works her verse has loosened (a second volume is called *Erosion*, 1983) and her line grown longer. Many of the poems from *The End of Beauty* (1987), *The Region of Unlikeness* (1991), *Materialism* (1993), *The Errancy* (1994), *Swarm* (2000), and *Overlord* (2005) hurtle across and down the page, sometimes without punctuation. Because she shares a contemporary skepticism of any version of reality that claims to be total, her work characteristically undercuts what it asserts. She works best in a form that supports the pull of coexisting and unreconciled tensions; for example, the short, enjambed lines of "At Luca Signorelli's Resurrection of the Body" separate each distinct detail and gesture while also tugging one perception into the next. The rhythmic structure of that poem holds apart and, at the same time, overlaps the visible and the invisible; the poem ends without resolving or unifying this opposition.

When Graham tries to imagine a unity that includes polarities (as in "The Dream of the Unified Field"), that unity is a "dream" because she is aware that the drive for order and closure (what she calls "the silky swerve into shapelessness / and then the click shut" in "Region of Unlikeness") risks narrowness and exclusion. Therefore Graham's work exposes the fractures in experience and in the self (fractures often gendered as male and female). But her poems also work to uncover, through a series of associations, the connections between daily experience (looking up at a flock of geese, bringing her daughter a leotard she had forgotten) and the larger frameworks of history, metaphysics, and myth. At times her drive to find or make analogies between a particular experience and its larger historical contexts can feel false or strained. But, resolutely self-interrogating, Graham sees each new book as a critique of her previous work. She is willing to risk failure in pursuit of a poetry that renders the drama of consciousness unfolding in language and the world; in this she is the heir of Wallace Stevens, with his vision of "the poem of the mind in the act of finding / What will suffice." If the life of thought makes her poems abstract (one is titled "What Is Called Thinking"), the activity of perception, registered sometimes in almost microscopic detail (as in "Opulence"), makes them concrete. Her best and most challenging work combines these two modes in a series of rapid-moving procedures. "The Dream of the Unified Field," for example, explores memory and possession by building layers of association through shifting concrete images. The poem begins with thoughts of a daughter—"On my way to bringing you the leotard / you forgot to include in your overnight bag"—and shifts to a snowstorm, then to a vision of starlings "swarming / then settling," then to the leaves of a tree scattering and recollecting, until the poet returns to the thought of her daughter dancing. When the memory of the poet's childhood ballet teacher surfaces, and then dissolves into the historical memory of Columbus's voyage of discovery, we experience an unexpected break in focus, a gap in thought marked out by a series of interruptive dashes.

Graham's poems characteristically include the gaps in thought. Her work is also riddled with questions that implicitly or explicitly address the reader: "Do you think these words are still enough?" and "Are you listening?" ("Manifest Destiny"). Describing her poetic strategies, Graham says she imagines a reader "who has heard it all before" (her poem "Imperialism" names this reader: "dear are-you-there"), one who distrusts language as a medium for truth. The difficult surfaces of Graham's poems try to wake us into full attention, so that we may confront, together with the poet, the question of what language can and cannot say.

The Geese

Today as I hang out the wash I see them again, a code
as urgent as elegant,
tapering with goals.
For days they have been crossing. We live beneath these geese

as if beneath the passage of time, or a most perfect heading.   5
Sometimes I fear their relevance.

Closest at hand,
between the lines,

the spiders imitate the paths the geese won't stray from,
imitate them endlessly to no avail: 10
things will not remain connected,
will not heal,

and the world thickens with texture instead of history,
texture instead of place.
Yet the small fear of the spiders   15
binds and binds

the pins to the lines, the lines to the eaves, to the pincushion bush,
as if, at any time, things could fall further apart
and nothing could help them
recover their meaning. And if these spiders had their way,   20

chainlink over the visible world,
would we be in or out? I turn to go back in.
There is a feeling the body gives the mind
of having missed something, a bedrock poverty, like falling

without the sense that you are passing through one world,   25
that you could reach another
anytime. Instead the real
is crossing you,

your body an arrival
you know is false but can't outrun. And somewhere in between   30
these geese forever entering and
these spiders turning back,

this astonishing delay, the everyday, takes place.

                                                              1980

At Luca Signorelli's[1] Resurrection of the Body

See how they hurry
    to enter
their bodies,
    these spirits,
Is it better, flesh,   5
    that they

1. Italian painter (1450–1523) of the Umbrian
school, associated with a region in central Italy
distinguished in the Renaissance by the achieve-
ments of its painters. His series on the Last Judgment decorates the Cappella Nuova in the gothic
cathedral in Orvieto, Italy, a town in the Umbrian
region. One of the sections of this series is titled
Resurrection of the Flesh.

should hurry so?
From above
the green-winged angels
blare down   10
trumpets and light. But
they don't care,

they hurry to congregate,
they hurry
into speech, until   15
it's a marketplace,
it is humanity. But still
we wonder

in the chancel[2]
of the dark cathedral,   20
is it better, back?
The artist
has tried to make it so: each tendon
they press

to re-enter   25
is perfect. But is it
perfection
they're after,
pulling themselves up
through the soil   30

into the weightedness, the color,
into the eye
of the painter? Outside
it is 1500,
all round the cathedral   35
streets hurry to open

through the wild
silver grasses. . . .
The men and women
on the cathedral wall   40
do not know how,
having come this far,

to stop their
hurrying. They amble off
in groups, in   45
couples. Soon
some are clothed, there is
distance, there is

perspective. Standing below them
in the church   50

---

2. Space around a church altar, often enclosed by lattice or railing.

in Orvieto, how can we
    tell them
to be stern and brazen
    and slow,

that there is no   55
    entrance,
only entering. They keep on
    arriving,
wanting names,
    wanting   60

happiness. In his studio
    Luca Signorelli
in the name of God
    and Science
and the believable   65
    broke into the body

studying arrival.
    But the wall
of the flesh
    opens endlessly,   70
its vanishing point so deep
    and receding

we have yet to find it,
    to have it
stop us. So he cut   75
    deeper,
graduating slowly
    from the symbolic

to the beautiful. How far
    is true?   80
When his one son
    died violently,
he had the body brought to him
    and laid it

on the drawing-table,   85
    and stood
at a certain distance
    awaiting the best
possible light, the best depth
    of day,   90

then with beauty and care
    and technique
and judgment, cut into
    shadow, cut
into bone and sinew and every   95
    pocket

in which the cold light
    pooled.
It took him days,
    that deep   100
caress, cutting,
    unfastening,

until his mind
    could climb into
the open flesh and   105
    mend itself.

                                    1983

The Dream of the Unified Field[1]

1

On my way to bringing you the leotard
you forgot to include in your overnight bag,
the snow started coming down harder.
I watched each gathering of leafy flakes
melt round my footfall.   5
I looked up into it—late afternoon but bright.
Nothing true or false in itself. Just motion. Many strips of
motion. Filaments of falling marked by the tiny certainties
of flakes. Never blurring yet themselves a cloud. Me in it
                and yet   10
moving easily through it, black Lycra leotard balled into
                my pocket,
your tiny dream in it, my left hand on it or in it
             to keep
warm. Praise this. Praise that. Flash a glance up and try   15
             to see
the arabesques and runnels,[2] gathering and loosening, as they
define, as a voice would, the passaging through from
                the-other-than-
human. Gone as they hit the earth. But embellishing.   20
Flourishing. The road with me on it going on through. Inscribed with the present. As if it really
were possible to exist, and exist, never to be pulled back
in, given and given never to be received. The music
of the footfalls doesn't stop, doesn't   25
mean. *Here are your things,* I said.

---

1. In physics, unified field is a set of theories that seeks to relate all the known, basic forces that exist in nature, especially those that operate at a subatomic level.

2. Rivulets or brooks. "Arabesques": ballet positions in which the dancer stands on one leg with the other extended in the back.

2

Starting home I heard—bothering, lifting, then
                              bothering again—
the huge flock of starlings massed over our
                              neighborhood   30
these days; heard them lift and
swim overhead through the falling snow
as though the austerity of a true, cold thing, a verity,
the black bits of their thousands of bodies swarming
                              then settling   35
overhead. I stopped. All up and down the empty oak
they stilled. Every limb sprouting. Every leafy backlit
                              body
filling its part of the empty crown. I tried to count—
then tried to estimate—   40
but the leaves of this wet black tree at the heart of
                              the storm—shiny—
river through limbs, back onto limbs,
scatter, blow away, scatter, recollect—
undoing again and again the tree without it ever ceasing to be   45
                              full.
Foliage of the tree of the world's waiting.
Of having waited a long time and
                              still having
to wait. Of trailing and screaming.   50
Of engulfed readjustments. Of blackness redisappearing
                              into
downdrafts of snow. Of indifference. Of indifferent
                              reappearings.
          I think of you   55
back of me now in the bright house of
          your friend
twirling in the living room in the shiny leotard
                              you love.
I had looked—as I was leaving—through the window   60

to see you, slick in your magic,
pulling away from the wall—

I watch the head explode then recollect, explode, recollect.

3

Then I heard it, inside the swarm, the single cry

of the crow. One syllable—one—inside the screeching and the   65
                              skittering,
inside the constant repatterning of a thing not nervous yet
                              not ever

still—but not uncertain—without obedience

yet not without law—one syllable—   70
black, shiny, twirling on its single stem,
rooting, one foot on the earth,
twisting and twisting—

and then again—a little further off this time—*down the*
ravine, voice inside a head, filling a head. . . .   75

See, my pocket is empty now. I let my hand
open and shut in there. I do it again. Two now, skull and
                                    pocket
with their terrified inhabitants.

       You turn the music up. The window nothing to you, liquid, dark,   80
where now your mother has come back to watch.

                                    4

Closeup, he's blue—streaked iris blue, india-ink blue—and
black—an oily, fiery set of blacks—none of them
true—as where hate and order touch—something that cannot
become known. Stages of black but without   85
graduation. So there is no direction.
All of this happened, yes. Then disappeared
into the body of the crow, chorus of meanings,
layers of blacks, then just the crow, plain, big,
lifting his claws to walk thrustingly   90
forward and back—indigo, cyanine, beryl, grape, steel . . . Then
       suddenly he
wings and—braking as he lifts
the chest in which an eye-sized heart now beats—
—he's up—a blunt clean stroke—
one ink-streak on the early evening snowlit scene—   95
See the gesture of the painter?—Recall the
crow?—Place him quickly on his limb as he comes sheering in,
close to the trunk, to land—Is he now
disappeared again?

                                    5

. . . . *long neck, up, up with the head,*   100
eyes on the fingertips, bent leg, shift of
the weight—*turn*—No, no, begin again . . .
What had she seen, Madame Sakaroff, at Stalingrad,[3] now in
her room of mirrors tapping her cane
as the piano player begins the interrupted Minuet[4] again   105
and we line up right foot extended, right
                            hand extended, the Bach[5] mid-phrase—

---

3. Russian city, site of one of the bloodiest battles in World War II.
4. Music accompanying a slow, stately dance

pattern in 3/4 time.
5. Johann Sebastian Bach (1685–1750), German composer of the Baroque period.

Europe? The dream of Europe?—midwinter afternoon,
rain at the windowpane, ceilings at thirty feet and coffered
floating over the wide interior spaces . . .   110
No one must believe in God again I heard her say
one time when I had come to class too soon
and had been sent to change. The visitor had left,
kissing her hand, small bow, and I had seen her (from the curtain)
(having forgotten I was there)   115
turn from the huge pearl-inlaid doors she had just closed,
one hand still on the massive, gold, bird-headed knob,
and see—a hundred feet away—herself—a woman in black in
                              a mirrored room—
saw her not shift her gaze but bring her pallid tensile hand—   120
as if it were not part of her—slowly down from
the ridged, cold, feathered knob and, recollected, fixed upon
                              that other woman, emigrée,[6]
begin to move in stiffly towards her . . . You out there
                              now,   125
you in here with me—I watched the two of them,
black and black, in the gigantic light,
glide at each other, heads raised, necks long—
me wanting to cry out—where were the others?—wasn't it late?
the two of her like huge black hands—   130
clap once and once only and the signal is given—
out to what?—regarding what?—till closer-in I saw
                              more suddenly
how her eyes eyed themselves: no wavering:
like a vast silver page burning: the black hole   135
                              expanding:
like a meaning coming up quick from inside that page—
coming up quick to seize the reading face—
each face wanting the other to *take* it—
but where? and *from* where?—I was eight—   140
I saw the different weights of things,
saw the vivid performance of the present,
saw the light rippling almost shuddering where her body finally
                              touched
the image, the silver film between them like something that would   145
                              have shed itself in nature now
but wouldn't, couldn't, here, on tight,
between, not thinning, not slipping off to let some
                              seed-down
through, no signal in it, no information . . . Child,   150
                              what should I know
to save you that I do not know, hands on this windowpane?—

---

6. The feminine version of a French noun for a person who has left her native country, especially for political reasons.

6

The storm: I close my eyes and,
standing in it, try to make it *mine*. An inside
thing. Once I was . . . once, once.   155
It settles, in my head, the wavering white
sleep, the instances—they stick, accrue,
grip up, connect, they do not melt,
I will not let them melt, they build, cloud and cloud,
I feel myself weak, I feel the thinking muscle-up—   160
outside, the talk-talk of the birds—outside,
strings and their roots, leaves inside the limbs,
in some spots the skin breaking—
but inside, no more exploding, no more smoldering, no more,
inside, a splinter colony, new world, possession   165
gripping down to form,
wilderness brought deep into my clearing,
out of the ooze of night,
limbed, shouldered, necked, visaged, the white—
now the clouds coming in (don't look up),   170
now the Age behind the clouds, The Great Heights,
all in there, reclining, eyes closed, huge,
centuries and centuries long and wide,
and underneath, barely attached but attached,
like a runner, my body, my tiny piece of   175
the century—minutes, houses going by—The Great
                                            Heights—
anchored by these footsteps, now and now,
the footstepping—now and now—carrying its vast
white sleeping geography—mapped—   180
not a lease—*possession*—"At the hour of vespers[7]
in a sudden blinding snow,
they entered the harbor and he named it Puerto[8] de

7

San Nicolas and at its entrance he imagined he
                                            could see   185
its beauty and goodness, *sand right up to the land
where you can put the side of a ship.* He thought
                                            he saw
Indians fleeing through the white before
the ship . . . As for him, he did not believe what his   190
                                            crew
told him, nor did he understand them well, nor they
him. In the white swirl, he placed a large cross
                        at the western side of

---

7. The passages which make up the final gesture
[of the poem] are rewritten sections from the
*Diario of Christopher Columbus. First Voyages to
America, 1492–93*, abstracted by Fray Bartolome
de La Casas (translated by Oliver Dunn and
James E. Kelley Jr.) [Graham's note]. "Vespers":
the evening prayer service in the Roman Catholic Church. From the Latin *vesper*, meaning
"evening."
8. Port (Spanish).

the harbor, on a conspicuous height,   195
as a sign that Your Highness claim the land as
Your own. After the cross was set up,
three sailors went into the bush (immediately erased
from sight by the fast snow) to see what kinds of
trees. They captured three very black Indian   200
women—one who was young and pretty.
The Admiral ordered her clothed and returned to
                              her land
courteously. There her people told
that she had not wanted to leave the ship,   205
but wished to stay on it. The snow was wild.
Inside it, though, you could see
this woman was wearing a little piece of
gold on her nose, which was a sign there was
                              gold   210
on that land"—

                                                                              1995

JOY HARJO
b. 1951

J oy Harjo was born in Tulsa, Oklahoma, to a mother of mixed Cherokee, French,
  and Irish blood. She has described her father's family, members of the Creek
(also known as Muskogee) tribe, as "rebels and speakers," among them a Baptist
minister (Harjo's paternal grandfather), two painters (her grandmother and aunt),
and a great-great-grandfather who in 1832 led a Creek rebellion against their forced
removal from Alabama into Oklahoma. As the critic Laura Coltelli has pointed out,
the work of many contemporary Native American writers (a large number of whom
are of mixed blood) enacts a quest to reenvision identity by confronting the historical, cultural, and political realities that shape lives experienced between different
worlds. Drawing on a family tradition of powerful speaking, Harjo participates in a
search to reimagine and repair painful fractures in contemporary experience:
between past and present, between person and landscape, and between parts of the
self. Thus traveling is a mythic activity in her poems, enacting this search for community and historical connectedness. As in the work of James Welch, Simon J.
Ortiz, and Leslie Marmon Silko, the theme of traveling in Harjo's poems resonates
with the historical displacements and migrations of native peoples (especially the
forced removal of the Creeks). She has called herself the wanderer in her family, and
her poems often map her journeys, whether on foot, by car, or in a plane. Perhaps
Harjo thinks of herself as the family wanderer because she left Oklahoma to attend
high school at the Institute of American Indian Arts in Santa Fe, New Mexico ("in a
way it saved my life," she has said). Since receiving a B.A. from the University of
New Mexico in 1976 and an MFA from the University of Iowa, she has taught at the
Institute of American Indian Arts, Arizona State University, the University of Colorado, the University of Arizona, and the University of New Mexico.

Harjo's vision of the interrelatedness of all things is common to Native American storytelling. The ethic that emerges from this worldview stresses reciprocity between people and various sources of power, including tradition and the natural world. Harjo's poems bring together mythic, feminist, and cultural perspectives and also unite contemporary urban experience with Native American myth and legend. In her collection *She Had Some Horses* (1983) this integration seeks to assuage the loneliness and desperation of those on the margin who populate much of the volume: a woman raising her mixed-blood children alone, a friend who threatens suicide, a woman who threatens to drop from a thirteenth-story window. The collection *In Mad Love and War* (1990) exhibits anger at the separations caused by dispossession and violence, as in an elegy for Anna Mae Pictou Aquash, a young Micmac woman shot dead on the Pine Ridge Reservation. Poems such as this recall the passion for social justice in the works of James Wright, Audre Lorde, and Leslie Marmon Silko; indeed, the spirit of Harjo's rebel great-great-grandfather is never far from her work.

Harjo has been a leading figure in the adaptation of oral traditions into written forms, consciously using the written word in her poems in a way that duplicates certain oral and ceremonial techniques. Her poems extensively and emphatically use repetition, of both words and units of thought, as mnemonic and structuring devices. For example, her poem "When the World As We Knew It Ended," written in response to the events of September 11, 2001, begins a series of stanzas with the repetition and variation of "We saw it," "We heard it," "We knew it. . . ." Reflecting the understanding that Native American tradition is not fixed but evolves and changes, Harjo has fearlessly experimented, adapting new musical and poetic forms to Native American traditions. She has long drawn on reggae, rock, Creek Stomp Dance songs, country, and African music and has integrated performance and dance into her poetry. A musician and songwriter, she has released three CD collections: *Letter from the End of the Twentieth Century* (1997), *Native Joy for Real* (2005), and a musical version of her recently republished *She Had Some Horses* (2006). Harjo plays the saxophone, which is not a traditional Native American instrument, but, she has said, "Someday it may be."

Metamorphosis, common in Native American storytelling, is central to Harjo's vision, where the world is constituted by change and constancy. Her collection *The Woman Who Fell from the Sky* (1994) embodies metamorphosis in its structure—the retelling of contemporary experience through traditional myths—and metamorphosis recurs in its stories. Various Native American traditions tell the story of a sky woman who falls through the void of space and creates the human universe. In the title poem of this volume, a group of women ("angry at their inattentive husbands") run off with stars; one of these women dares to look back at Earth and falls from the sky. In Harjo's hands this myth becomes the story of two lovers, who were children together at an Indian boarding school. Adrift in an urban landscape, they are reunited, their narrative characterized by fracture and repair. In the same collection "Flood" renders a young girl's sexuality and imaginative power through the myth of the water monster. The prose poems that form much of this book remind us that Native American storytelling, an oral tradition, does not distinguish between poetry and prose. For all Harjo's anguished sense of the warring factions in our world and our selves, her works consistently engage in a process of healing and regeneration, themes that continue in her collection *A Map to the Next World* (2000). Like the kitchen table in her poem "Perhaps the World Ends Here," Harjo's poems are a space where "we sing with joy, with sorrow. We pray of suffering and remorse. We give thanks."

Harjo has also written screenplays and the text for Stephen Strom's photographs of the Southwestern landscape, *Secrets from the Center of the World* (1989), and she has edited an anthology of tribal women's writings from around the world. A collection of interviews, *The Spiral of Memory* (1996), edited by Laura Coltelli, is a valuable accompaniment to her poems. *How We Became Human* (2003) presents a selection from Harjo's earlier work, including poems from hard-to-find chapbooks, as well as new work.

Call It Fear

There is this edge where shadows
and bones of some of us walk
             backwards.
Talk backwards. There is this edge
call it an ocean of fear of the dark. Or   5
name it with other songs. Under our ribs
our hearts are bloody stars. Shine on
shine on, and horses in their galloping flight
strike the curve of ribs.
                    Heartbeat   10
and breathe back sharply. Breathe
                    backwards.
There is this edge within me
                  I saw it once
an August Sunday morning when the heat hadn't   15
left this earth. And Goodluck
sat sleeping next to me in the truck.
We had never broken through the edge of the
singing at four a.m.
                  We had only wanted to talk, to hear   20
any other voice to stay alive with.
                  And there was this edge—
not the drop of sandy rock cliff
bones of volcanic earth into
                  Albuquerque.   25
Not that,
           but a string of shadow horses kicking
and pulling me out of my belly,
              not into the Rio Grande[1] but into the music
barely coming through   30
                  Sunday church singing
from the radio. Battery worn-down but the voices
talking backwards.

                                      1983

White Bear

She begins to board the flight
    to Albuquerque. Late night.

---

1. River flowing from southern Colorado through New Mexico and then forming the boundary between Texas and Mexico.

But stops in the corrugated tunnel,
    a space between leaving and staying,
where the night sky catches   5

            her whole life

she has felt like a woman
    balancing on a wooden nickle heart
approaching herself from here to
    there, Tulsa or New York   10
with knives or corn meal.

The last flight someone talked
    about how coming from Seattle
the pilot flew a circle
    over Mt. St. Helens,[1] she sat   15
quiet. (But had seen the eruption
    as the earth beginning
to come apart, as in birth
    out of violence.)

She watches the yellow lights   20
    of towns below the airplane flicker,
fade and fall backwards. Somewhere,
    she dreamed, there is the white bear
moving down from the north, motioning her paws
    like a long arctic night, that kind   25
of circle and the whole world balanced in
    between carved of ebony and ice

            oh so hard

the clear black nights
    like her daughter's eyes, and the white   30
bear moon, cupped like an ivory rocking
cradle, tipping back it could go
either way
            all darkness
                        is open to all light.   35

                                                    1983

Summer Night

The moon is nearly full,
                    the humid air sweet like melon.
Flowers that have cupped the sun all day
                        dream of iridescent wings

1. A volcanic peak in Washington State; it erupted in 1980.

under the long dark sleep.   5
                  Children's invisible voices call out
in the glimmering moonlight.
                  Their parents play worn-out records
of the cumbia.[1] Behind the screen door
                  their soft laughter swells   10
into the rhythm of a smooth guitar.
                  I watch the world shimmer
inside this globe of a summer night,
                  listen to the wobble of her
spin and dive. It happens all the time, waiting for you   15
                  to come home.
There is an ache that begins
                  in the sound of an old blues song.
It becomes a house where all the lights have gone out
                  but one.   20
And it burns and burns
                  until there is only the blue smoke of dawn
and everyone is sleeping in someone's arms
                  even the flowers
even the sound of a thousand silences.   25
                  And the arms of night
in the arms of day.
                  Everyone except me.
But then the smell of damp honeysuckle twisted on the vine.
And the turn of the shoulder   30
                  of the ordinary spirit who keeps watch
over this ordinary street.
                  And there you are, the secret
of your own flower of light
                  blooming in the miraculous dark.   35

                          1990

The Flood

It had been years since I'd seen the watermonster, the snake who lived at the bottom of the lake. He had disappeared in the age of reason, as a mystery that never happened.

For in the muggy lake was the girl I could have been at sixteen, wrested from the torment of exaggerated fools, one version anyway, though the   5
story at the surface would say car accident, or drowning while drinking, all of it eventually accidental.

This story is not an accident, nor is the existence of the watersnake in the memory of the people as they carried the burden of the myth from

---

1. A Latin American dance.

Alabama to Oklahoma.[1] Each reluctant step pounded memory into the   10
broken heart and no one will ever forget it.

When I walk the stairway of water into the abyss, I return as the wife
of the watermonster, in a blanket of time decorated with swatches of
cloth and feathers from our favorite clothes.

The stories of the battles of the watersnake are forever ongoing, and those   15
stories soaked into my blood since infancy like deer gravy, so how could
I resist the watersnake, who appeared as the most handsome man in the
tribe, or any band whose visits I'd been witness to since childhood?

This had been going on for centuries: the first time he appeared I carried
my baby sister on my back as I went to get water. She laughed at a wood-   20
pecker flitting like a small sun above us and before I could deter the
symbol we were in it.

My body was already on fire with the explosion of womanhood as if
I were flint, hot stone, and when he stepped out of the water he was the
first myth I had ever seen uncovered. I had surprised him in a human   25
moment. I looked aside but I could not discount what I had seen.

My baby sister's cry pinched reality, the woodpecker a warning of a
disjuncture in the brimming sky, and then a man who was not a man
but a myth.

What I had seen there were no words for except in the sacred language   30
of the most holy recounting, so when I ran back to the village, drenched
in salt, how could I explain the water jar left empty by the river to my
mother who deciphered my burning lips as shame?

My imagination swallowed me like a mica sky, but I had seen the water
monster in the fight of lightning storms, breaking trees, stirring up kill-   35
ing winds, and had lost my favorite brother to a spear of the sacred
flame, so certainly I would know my beloved if he were hidden in the
blushing skin of the suddenly vulnerable.

I was taken with a fever and nothing cured it until I dreamed my fiery
body dipped in the river where it fed into the lake. My father carried me   40
as if I were newborn, as if he were presenting me once more to the
world, and when he dipped me I was quenched, pronounced healed.

My parents immediately made plans to marry me to an important man
who was years older but would provide me with everything I needed to
survive in this world, a world I could no longer perceive, as I had been   45
blinded with a ring of water when I was most in need of a drink by a
snake who was not a snake, and how did he know my absolute secrets,
those created at the brink of acquired language?

---

1. In 1832 the Muskogee (also known as Creek) tribe was forcibly relocated by the United States government from Alabama to Oklahoma.

When I disappeared it was in a storm that destroyed the houses of my
relatives; my baby sister was found sucking on her hand in the crook of   50
an oak.

And though it may have appeared otherwise, I did not go willingly.
That night I had seen my face strung on the shell belt of my ancestors,
and I was standing next to a man who could not look me in the eye.

The oldest woman in the tribe wanted to remember me as a symbol in   55
the story of a girl who disobeyed, who gave in to her desires before
marriage and was destroyed by the monster disguised as the seductive
warrior.

Others saw the car I was driving as it drove into the lake early one morning, the time the carriers of tradition wake up, before the sun or the   60
approach of woodpeckers, and found the emptied six-pack on the sandy
shores of the lake.

The power of the victim is a power that will always be reckoned with,
one way or the other. When the proverbial sixteen-year-old woman
walked down to the lake within her were all sixteen-year-old women who   65
had questioned their power from time immemorial.

Her imagination was larger than the small frame house at the north
edge of town, with the broken cars surrounding it like a necklace of
futility, larger than the town itself leaning into the lake. Nothing could
stop it, just as no one could stop the bearing-down thunderheads as they   70
gathered overhead in the war of opposites.

Years later when she walked out of the lake and headed for town, no one
recognized her, or themselves, in the drench of fire and rain. The watersnake was a story no one told anymore. They'd entered a drought that no
one recognized as drought, the convenience store a signal of temporary   75
amnesia.

I had gone out to get bread, eggs and the newspaper before breakfast
and hurried the cashier for my change as the crazy woman walked in, for
I could not see myself as I had abandoned her some twenty years ago in
a blue windbreaker at the edge of the man-made lake as everyone dove   80
naked and drunk off the sheer cliff, as if we had nothing to live for, not
then or ever.

It was beginning to rain in Oklahoma, the rain that would flood the
world.[2]

1994

---

2. Embedded in Muscogee tribal memory is the
creature known as the tie snake, a huge monster
who lives in waterways and will do what he can to
take us with him. He represents the power of the
underworld.

He is still present today in the lakes and rivers
of Oklahoma and Alabama, a force we reckon
with despite the proliferation of inventions that
keep us from ourselves [Harjo's note].

When the World As We Knew It Ended—

We were dreaming on an occupied island at the farthest edge
of a trembling nation when it went down.

Two towers rose up from the east island of commerce and touched
the sky. Men walked on the moon. Oil was sucked dry
by two brothers. Then it went down. Swallowed   5
by a fire dragon, by oil and fear.
Eaten whole.

It was coming.

We had been watching since the eve of the missionaries in their long and
solemn clothes, to see what would happen.   10

We saw it
from the kitchen window over the sink
as we made coffee, cooked rice and
potatoes, enough for an army.

We saw it all, as we changed diapers and fed   15
the babies. We saw it,
through the branches
of the knowledgeable tree
through the snags of stars, through
the sun and storms from our knees   20
as we bathed and washed
the floors.

The conference of the birds warned us, as they flew over
destroyers in the harbor, parked there since the first takeover.
It was by their song and talk we knew when to rise   25
when to look out the window
to the commotion going on—
the magnetic field thrown off by grief.

We heard it.
The racket in every corner of the world. As   30
the hunger for war rose up in those who would steal to be president
to be king or emperor, to own the trees, stones, and everything
else that moved about the earth, inside the earth
and above it.

We knew it was coming, tasted the winds who gathered intelligence   35
from each leaf and flower, from every mountain, sea
and desert, from every prayer and song all over this tiny universe
floating in the skies of infinite
being.

And then it was over, this world we had grown to love   40
for its sweet grasses, for the many-colored horses
and fishes, for the shimmering possibilities
while dreaming.

But then there were the seeds to plant and the babies
who needed milk and comforting, and someone   45
picked up a guitar or ukelele from the rubble
and began to sing about the light flutter
the kick beneath the skin of the earth
we felt there, beneath us

a warm animal   50
a song being born between the legs of her,
a poem.

2003

RITA DOVE
b. 1952

What she has called the "friction" between the beauty of a poetic form and a difficult or painful subject appeals to Rita Dove. Her own formal control and discipline create a beautiful design and a haunting music in "Parsley," a poem based on a murderous event: in 1957 the dictator of the Dominican Republic, Rafael Trujillo, ordered twenty thousand black Haitians killed because they could not pronounce the letter "r" in the Spanish word for parsley. What compels Dove in this poem is the way a "single, beautiful word" has the power of life and death. More astonishing is that she writes from the perspectives of both the Haitians in the cane fields and General Trujillo in his palace. When asked in an interview about her capacity to imagine Trujillo, Dove responded, "I frankly don't believe anyone who says they've never felt any evil, that they cannot understand that process of evil. It was important to me to try to understand that arbitrary quality of his cruelty. . . . Making us get into his head may shock us all into seeing what the human being is capable of, because if we can go that far into his head, we're halfway there ourselves." An ability to enter into different points of view in a single poem is characteristic of Dove's disinterested imagination. Her method is to avoid commentary, to let the imagined person or object, the suggestive detail, speak for itself. Often her work suggests what the English poet John Keats called "negative capability," the gift of the poet to become what he or she is not.

Born in Akron, Dove attended Miami University of Ohio and, after her graduation, studied modern European literature as a Fulbright/Hays fellow at the University of Tübingen in Germany. When she returned from Europe she earned an MFA at the University of Iowa (in 1977). Later she taught creative writing at Arizona State University before joining the University of Virginia, where she is now Commonwealth

Professor of English. Since her Fulbright year she has repeatedly chosen to live abroad, in Ireland, Israel, France, and especially Germany. Her travel in Europe and elsewhere suggests part of the imperative she feels as a poet: to range widely through fields of experience, to cross boundaries of space as well as time. Her first book, *The Yellow House on the Corner* (1980), is notable for its intense poems about adolescence; her second book, *Museum* (1983), dramatically extends the range of her work. "When I started *Museum*," she has said, "I was in Europe, and I had a way of looking back on America and distancing myself from my experience." As well as for several fine poems about her father (a subject that may also have needed distance), the book is remarkable for the way distance allowed Dove to move out of her immediate experience, freed her to imagine widely different lives.

As if to show that it is also possible to travel widely while staying at home, Dove's *Thomas and Beulah* (1986) is an extended sequence based on her grandparents' lives. Her continuing fascination with imagining different perspectives on the same event is evident in this sequence. Dove has described the book's origins this way:

> My grandmother had told me a story that had happened to my grandfather when he was young, coming up on a riverboat to Akron, Ohio, my hometown. But that was all I had basically. And the story so fascinated me that I tried to write about it. I started off writing stories about my grandfather and soon, because I ran out of real fact, in order to keep going, I made up facts for this character, Thomas. . . . then this poem "Dusting" appeared, really out of nowhere. I didn't realize this was Thomas's wife saying, "I want to talk. And you can't do his side without my side. . . ."

This is the story, in part, of a marriage and of a black couple's life in the industrial Midwest in the period from 1900 to 1960. Thomas's point of view controls the poems of the book's first section, while the second part imagines his wife's. The larger framework of the sequence links family history to social history. Thomas's journey from the rural South to the industrial city of Akron (where he finds employment in the Goodyear Zeppelin factory until the Depression puts him out of work) is part of the larger social movement of African Americans from the South into Northern industrial cities in the first part of this century. The individual lyrics of Dove's sequence create and sustain the story through distinct and often ordinary moments in which each life is vividly portrayed. It is part of Dove's gift that she can render the apparently unimportant moments that inform a life and set them against a background of larger historical forces, as do Robert Hayden in *Elegies for Paradise Valley* and Robert Lowell in *Notebook*.

Many of the figures in Dove's poems are displaced, on the border between different worlds: for example, Thomas and Beulah, and the biracial violin prodigy, George Bridgetower (1780–1860), who is the focus of her volume *Sonata Mulattica* (2009). The experience of displacement, of what she has called living in "two different worlds, seeing things with double vision," consistently compels this poet's imagination. It takes both detachment and control to maintain (and to live with) such doubleness. This may be why Dove's rich sense of language and her love of sound are joined to a disciplined formal sense. The forms of her poems often hold in place difficult or ambiguous feelings and keep the expression of feeling understated. While restraint is one strength of Dove's poems, her work can sometimes seem austere. Such careful control recalls Elizabeth Bishop's early work, also highly controlled and even, at times, guarded. As Bishop grew to relax her restraints, to open into an extraordinary expressiveness, so Dove's career shows a similar growth. Her collections *Grace Notes* (1989), *Mother Love* (1995), and *American Smooth* (2004) suggest just such a relaxing of the poet's guard, while *On the Bus with Rosa Parks* (2000) demonstrates an ongoing ability to unite social conscience with a transformative sense of language and form. With each book she asks something more from herself, and she has now become one of our indispensable poets. Dove was poet laureate of the United States from 1993 to 1995.

Geometry

I prove a theorem and the house expands:
the windows jerk free to hover near the ceiling,
the ceiling floats away with a sigh.

As the walls clear themselves of everything
but transparency, the scent of carnations   5
leaves with them. I am out in the open

and above the windows have hinged into butterflies,
sunlight glinting where they've intersected.
They are going to some point true and unproven.

                                                        1980

Adolescence—I

In water-heavy nights behind grandmother's porch
We knelt in the tickling grasses and whispered:
Linda's face hung before us, pale as a pecan,
And it grew wise as she said:
        "A boy's lips are soft,   5
        As soft as baby's skin."
The air closed over her words.
A firefly whirred near my ear, and in the distance
I could hear streetlamps ping
Into miniature suns   10
Against a feathery sky.

                                                        1980

Adolescence—II

Although it is night, I sit in the bathroom, waiting.
Sweat prickles behind my knees, the baby-breasts are alert.
Venetian blinds slice up the moon; the tiles quiver in pale strips.

Then they come, the three seal men with eyes as round
As dinner plates and eyelashes like sharpened tines.   5
They bring the scent of licorice. One sits in the washbowl,

One on the bathtub edge; one leans against the door.
"Can you feel it yet?" they whisper.
I don't know what to say, again. They chuckle,

Patting their sleek bodies with their hands.   10
"Well, maybe next time." And they rise,
Glittering like pools of ink under moonlight,

And vanish. I clutch at the ragged holes
They leave behind, here at the edge of darkness.
Night rests like a ball of fur on my tongue.   15

1980

Adolescence—III

With Dad gone, Mom and I worked
The dusky rows of tomatoes.
As they glowed orange in sunlight
And rotted in shadow, I too
Grew orange and softer, swelling out   5
Starched cotton slips.

The texture of twilight made me think of
Lengths of Dotted Swiss. In my room
I wrapped scarred knees in dresses
That once went to big-band dances;   10
I baptized my earlobes with rosewater.
Along the window-sill, the lipstick stubs
Glittered in their steel shells.

Looking out at the rows of clay
And chicken manure, I dreamed how it would happen: 15
He would meet me by the blue spruce,
A carnation over his heart, saying,
"I have come for you, Madam;
I have loved you in my dreams."
At his touch, the scabs would fall away.   20
Over his shoulder, I see my father coming toward us:
He carries his tears in a bowl,
And blood hangs in the pine-soaked air.

1980

Parsley[1]

1. The Cane[2] Fields

There is a parrot imitating spring
in the palace, its feathers parsley green.
Out of the swamp the cane appears

to haunt us, and we cut it down. El General
searches for a word; he is all the world   5
there is. Like a parrot imitating spring,

we lie down screaming as rain punches through
and we come up green. We cannot speak an R—
out of the swamp, the cane appears

and then the mountain we call in whispers *Katalina*.[3]   10
The children gnaw their teeth to arrowheads.
There is a parrot imitating spring.

El General has found his word: *perejil*.
Who says it, lives. He laughs, teeth shining
out of the swamp. The cane appears   15

in our dreams, lashed by wind and streaming.
And we lie down. For every drop of blood
there is a parrot imitating spring.
Out of the swamp the cane appears.

2. The Palace

The word the general's chosen is parsley.   20
It is fall, when thoughts turn
to love and death; the general thinks
of his mother, how she died in the fall
and he planted her walking cane at the grave
and it flowered, each spring stolidly forming   25
four-star blossoms. The general

pulls on his boots, he stomps to
her room in the palace, the one without
curtains, the one with a parrot
in a brass ring. As he paces he wonders   30
Who can I kill today. And for a moment
the little knot of screams
is still. The parrot, who has traveled

---

1. On October 2, 1937, Rafael Trujillo (1891–1961), dictator of the Dominican Republic, ordered 20,000 blacks killed because they could not pronounce the letter "r" in *perejil*, the Spanish word for parsley [Dove's note].
2. I.e., sugar cane.
3. Katarina (because "we cannot speak an R").

all the way from Australia in an ivory
cage, is, coy as a widow, practising   35
spring. Ever since the morning
his mother collapsed in the kitchen
while baking skull-shaped candies
for the Day of the Dead,[4] the general
has hated sweets. He orders pastries   40
brought up for the bird; they arrive

dusted with sugar on a bed of lace.
The knot in his throat starts to twitch;
he sees his boots the first day in battle
splashed with mud and urine   45
as a soldier falls at his feet amazed—
how stupid he looked!—at the sound
of artillery. *I never thought it would sing*
the soldier said, and died. Now

the general sees the fields of sugar   50
cane, lashed by rain and streaming.
He sees his mother's smile, the teeth
gnawed to arrowheads. He hears
the Haitians sing without R's
as they swing the great machetes: 55
Katalina, they sing, *Katalina*,

mi madle, mi amol en muelte.[5] God knows
his mother was no stupid woman; she
could roll an R like a queen. Even
a parrot can roll an R! In the bare room   60
the bright feathers arch in a parody
of greenery, as the last pale crumbs
disappear under the blackened tongue. Someone

calls out his name in a voice
so like his mother's, a startled tear   65
splashes the tip of his right boot.
My mother, my love in death.
The general remembers the tiny green sprigs
men of his village wore in their capes
to honor the birth of a son. He will   70
order many, this time, to be killed

for a single, beautiful word.

1983

---

4. All Soul's Day, November 2. An Aztec festival
for the spirits of the dead that coincides with the
Catholic calendar. In Latin America and the
Caribbean, people move in processions to cemeteries, bearing candles, flowers, and food, all of
which may be shaped to resemble symbols of
death, such as skulls or coffins.
5. I.e., *mi madre, mi amor en muerte*—"my
mother, my love in death."

FROM THOMAS AND BEULAH[1]

The Event

Ever since they'd left the Tennessee ridge
with nothing to boast of
but good looks and a mandolin,

the two Negroes leaning
on the rail of a riverboat   5
were inseparable: Lem plucked

to Thomas' silver falsetto.
But the night was hot and they were drunk.
They spat where the wheel

churned mud and moonlight,   10
they called to the tarantulas
down among the bananas

to come out and dance.
You're so fine and mighty; let's see
what you can do, said Thomas, pointing   15

to a tree-capped island.
Lem stripped, spoke easy: *Them's chestnuts,*
I believe. Dove

quick as a gasp. Thomas, dry
on deck, saw the green crown shake   20
as the island slipped

under, dissolved
in the thickening stream.
At his feet

a stinking circle of rags,   25
the half-shell mandolin.
Where the wheel turned the water

gently shirred.[2]

1986

---

1. The story in this sequence of poems begins
with Thomas as he makes his way north to Akron,
Ohio. He loses his best friend, who, on a drunken
dare from Thomas, drowns, leaving his mandolin
behind. Thomas carries the mandolin with him
and eventually hangs it on his parlor wall. He and
Beulah marry when he is twenty-four and she is
twenty; they have four daughters. Thomas works
at the Goodyear Zeppelin factory (a zeppelin is a
cylindrical airship kept aloft by helium). The
Depression puts him out of work, so he sweeps
offices for a living until Goodyear rehires him at
the advent of World War II. Beulah works in a
dress shop and later makes hats. Thomas dies at
sixty-three from his second heart attack; Beulah
dies six years later.
2. Drew together.

The Zeppelin Factory

The zeppelin factory
needed workers, all right—
but, standing in the cage
of the whale's belly, sparks
flying off the joints   5
and noise thundering,
Thomas wanted to sit
right down and cry.

That spring the third
largest airship was dubbed   10
the biggest joke
in town, though they all
turned out for the launch.
Wind caught,
"The Akron" floated   15
out of control,

three men in tow—
one dropped
to safety, one
hung on but the third,
muscles and adrenalin   20
failing, fell
clawing
six hundred feet.

Thomas at night   25
in the vacant lot:
        Here I am, intact
        and faint-hearted.

Thomas hiding
his heart with his hat   30
at the football game, eyeing
the Goodyear blimp overhead:
        Big boy I know
        you're in there.

                                            1986

Dusting

Every day a wilderness—no
shade in sight. Beulah[1]

---

1. Hebrew for "married one" or "possessed." In the Bible it refers to the Promised Land.

patient among knicknacks,
the solarium a rage
of light, a grainstorm 5
as her gray cloth brings
dark wood to life.

Under her hand scrolls
and crests gleam
darker still. What 10
was his name, that
silly boy at the fair with
the rifle booth? And his kiss and
the clear bowl with one bright
fish, rippling 15
wound!

Not Michael—
something finer. Each dust
stroke a deep breath and
the canary in bloom. 20
Wavery memory: home
from a dance, the front door
blown open and the parlor
in snow, she rushed
the bowl to the stove, watched 25
as the locket of ice
dissolved and he
swam free.

That was years before
Father gave her up 30
with her name, years before
her name grew to mean
Promise, then
Desert-in-Peace.
Long before the shadow and 35
sun's accomplice, the tree.

Maurice.

1986

Poem in Which I Refuse Contemplation

A letter from my mother was waiting:
read in standing, one a.m.,
just arrived at my German mother-in-law

six hours from Paris by car.
Our daughter hops on Oma's bed, 5
happy to be back in a language

she knows. *Hello, all! Your postcard*
came on the nineth—familiar misspelled
words, exclamations. I wish my body

wouldn't cramp and leak; I want to—   10
as my daughter says, pretending to be
"Papa"—pull on boots and go for a long walk

alone. *Your cousin Ronnie in D.C.—*
remember him?—he was the one
a few months younger than you—   15

was strangulated at some chili joint,
your Aunt May is beside herself!
Mom slaps to the garden which is

producing—onions, swiss chard,
lettuce, lettuce, lettuce, turnip greens and more lettuce   20
so far! The roses are flurishing.

Haven't I always hated gardening? And German,
with its patient, grunting building blocks,
and for that matter, English, too,

Americanese's chewy twang? *Raccoons*   25
have taken up residence
we were ten *in the crawl space*

but I can't feel his hand *who knows*
anymore *how we'll get them out?*
I'm still standing. Bags to unpack.   30

That's all for now. Take care.

                                          1989

Missing

I am the daughter who went out with the girls,
never checked back in and nothing marked my "last
known whereabouts," not a single glistening petal.

Horror is partial; it keeps you going. A lost
child is a fact hardening around its absence,   5
a knot in the breast purring *Touch, and I will*

come true. I was "returned," I watched her
watch as I babbled *It could have been worse. . . .*
Who can tell
what penetrates? Pity is the brutal   10

discipline. Now I understand she can never
die, just as nothing can bring me back—

I am the one who comes and goes;
I am the footfall that hovers.

1995

Rosa[1]

How she sat there,
the time right inside a place
so wrong it was ready.

That trim name with
its dream of a bench   5
to rest on. Her sensible coat.

Doing nothing was the doing:
the clean flame of her gaze
carved by a camera flash.

How she stood up   10
when they bent down to retrieve
her purse. That courtesy.

2000

Fox Trot Fridays

Thank the stars there's a day
each week to tuck in

the grief, lift your pearls, and
stride brush stride

quick-quick with a   5
heel-ball-toe. Smooth

as Nat King Cole's[1]
slow satin smile,

1. Rosa Parks (1913–2005). From a series of poems titled *On the Bus with Rosa Parks*. On December 1, 1955, in Montgomery, Alabama, Parks, an African American seamstress and secretary of the local National Association for the Advancement of Colored People (NAACP), was arrested and taken to jail for refusing to yield her seat on a bus to a white passenger. Her arrest prompted a boycott of the city bus system and inspired the Civil Rights Movement in the late 1950s and the 1960s.
1. Popular African American jazz singer, songwriter, and pianist (1919–1965).

easy as taking
one day at a time: 10

one man and
one woman,

rib to rib,
with no heartbreak in sight—

just the sweep of Paradise   15
and the space of a song

to count all the wonders in it.

2004

ALBERTO RÍOS
b. 1952

The poet Rita Dove once recalled in an interview W. E. B. Du Bois's remark on the "second sight that comes from having to live in two different cultures." As a Latino whose heritage includes Spanish and English, Alberto Ríos often writes poems possessed of literal second sight. His work gives us magical and poetic ways of understanding the world, like the account of his grandmother as a young woman in "Refugio's Hair." A knowledge inaccessible in books is transmitted through stories: "In the old days of our family," the poem begins. In Ríos's best poems we feel both that anything can happen and that everything has happened before; we hear a particular voice whose rhythms recall stories passed from generation to generation.

Ríos has said of his background, "My father, born in southern Mexico, and my mother, born in England, gave me a language-rich, story-fat upbringing." He was born in Nogales, Arizona (on the border of Mexico), and earned an MFA at the University of Arizona. He has worked on the Arizona Commission on the Arts and presently is on the faculty of Arizona State University in Tempe. His first book, *Whispering to Fool the Wind* (1982), won the Walt Whitman Award. He has since published *Five Indiscretions* (1985), *The Lime Orchard Women* (1989), *Teodora Luna's Two Kisses* (1990), *The Smallest Muscle in the Human Body* (2002), *The Theater of Night* (2006), and *The Dangerous Shirt* (2009). He has also published volumes of fiction—*The Iguana Killer: Twelve Stories of the Heart* (1984) and *The Curtain of Trees* (1999)—and *Capirotada* (1999), a memoir of growing up on the Arizona-Mexico border. Ríos is a talented storyteller whose poems often suggest oral traditions, including Spanish ballads. For him, stories are forms of remembering and means of understanding; they honor the claims of dream and fact, past and present. Whether he is writing with humorous self-awareness about a childhood visit to a fortune-teller ("Madre Sofía") or rendering the unbearable reality behind the newspaper accounts of those among the "disappeared" (in "Taking Away the Name of a Nephew"), the details of his poems accumulate to reveal a startling sense of the world. At times, however, the story the poem tells must overcome too-predictable uses of the line. If Ríos's magical sense of the world sometimes yields too easily to the surreal, the pleasures of his poems often lie in a fluid movement between layers of reality, a deft integration of the factual and fantastic. Given Ríos's sense of the possibilities in language, the epigraph for his first book, taken from the Chilean poet Pablo Neruda, is especially fitting: "You see there are in our countries rivers which have no names, trees which nobody knows, and birds which nobody has described. . . . Our duty, then, as we understand it, is to express what is unheard of." Flavored with the music of Spanish and English, Ríos's poems create a new landscape: a contemporary America beneath which lives both an older way of life and the country of the imagination.

Madre Sofía[1]

My mother took me because she couldn't
wait the second ten years to know.
This was the lady rumored to have been
responsible for the box-wrapped baby
among the presents at that wedding,   5
but we went in, anyway, through the curtains.
Loose jar-top, half turned
and not caught properly in the threads
her head sat mimicking its original intention
like the smile of a child hitting himself.   10
Central in that head grew unfamiliar poppies
from a face mahogany, eyes half yellow
half gray at the same time, goat and fog,
slit eyes of the devil, his tweed suit, red
lips, and she smelled of smoke, cigarettes,   15
but a diamond smoke, somehow; I inhaled
sparkles, I could feel them, throat, stomach.
She did not speak, and as a child
I could only answer, so that together
we were silent, cold and wet, dry and hard: 20
from behind my mother pushed me forward.
The lady put her hand on the face
of a thin animal wrap, tossing that head
behind her to be pressed incredibly
as she sat back in the huge chair and leaned.   25
And then I saw the breasts as large as her
head, folded together, coming out of her dress
as if it didn't fit, not like my mother's.
I could see them, how she kept them
penned up, leisurely, in maroon feed bags,   30
horse nuzzles of her wide body,
but exquisitely penned up
circled by pearl reins and red scarves.
She lifted her arm, but only with the tips
of her fingers motioned me to sit opposite.   35
She looked at me but spoke to my mother

---

1. Mother Sofía (Spanish). "Sofía" derives from the Greek word meaning "wisdom."

words dark, smoky like the small room,
words coming like red ants stepping occasionally
from a hole on a summer day in the valley,
red ants from her mouth, her nose, her ears,   40
tears from the comers of her cinched eyes.
And suddenly she put her hand full on my head
pinching tight again with those finger tips
like a television healer, young Oral Roberts[2]
half standing, quickly, half leaning   45
those breasts swinging toward me
so that I reach with both my hands to my lap
protecting instinctively whatever it is
that needs protection when a baseball is thrown
and you're not looking but someone yells,   50
the hand, then those breasts coming toward me
like the quarter-arms of the amputee Joaquín
who came back from the war to sit
in the park, reaching always for children
until one day he had to be held back.   55
I sat there, no breath, and could see only
hair around her left nipple, like a man.
Her clothes were old.
Accented, in a language whose spine had been
snapped, she whispered the words of a city   60
witch, and made me happy, alive like a man:
The future will make you tall.

                                                                    1982

Wet Camp

We have been here before, but we are lost.
The earth is black and the trees are bent
and broken and piled as if the game
of pick-up-sticks were ready and the children
hiding, waiting their useless turns.   5
The west bank of the river is burned
and the Santa Cruz[1] has poured onto it.
The grit brown ponds
sit like dirty lilies in the black.
The afternoon is gone grazing   10
over the thin mountains.
The night is colder here without leaves.
Nothing holds up the sky.

                                                                    1982

2. American televangelist (1918–2009) and leader of a Christian charismatic movement.
1. River in southern Arizona.

Taking Away the Name of a Nephew

One of the disappeared[1] looks like this:
One shirt, reasonable shoes, no laces, no face
Recognizable even to the mother of this thing.
Lump. Dropped egg, bag of old potatoes
Too old and without moisture, a hundred eyes   5
Sprouted out and gone wild into forest
Food for the maggot flies and small monsters.
Bag. Pulled by the tiestring
The laces around his ankles have become.
A crisp bag of seventeen birthdays   10
Six parties with piñatas and the particular
Memory of a thick hugging
His Tía[2] Susí gave him with the strong arms
Her breasts were, how they had held him
Around his just-tall-enough throat and had reached   15
To touch each other behind his neck.

His memory of Susí was better than how the soldier held him
She hoped this out of all things.
That she had made him warm.
In that body the three soldiers were fooled, tricked   20
A good hundred strings of wool put over their eyes:
They did not take away the boy.
They took away his set of hands and his spine
Which in weeks would look like railroad tracks
Along the side of any young mountain.   25
One of the disappeared looks like this
The newspaper said. She had seen
The photograph which looked like all
Newspaper photographs,
Had thought it does not say *looked* like this,   30
But *looks* like this, still; had thought
What is being said here is that he did not die.
It was not death that took him.

She thinks about things like this, this way:
Here is the new mathematics made simple   35
Here is the algebra I once did not understand.
She sets for herself the tasks of a student,
Making clear the equations
Breathing the air that Einstein[3] breathed.
She looks in her purse and pulls out three coins.   40
This much for one dozen corn tortillas. Easy.
A paper cut, small slice, magnified three times:

---

1. Between 1975 and 1983 approximately thirty thousand Argentinians "disappeared" as a result of the military dictatorship's regime of terror, in which anyone viewed as a threat to the state was liable to abduction, torture, and murder.

2. Aunt (Spanish).
3. Albert Einstein (1879–1955), U.S. physicist and mathematician who formulated, among other things, the theory of relativity.

PC × 3 =
This is what a very small Newberry's letter opener—
A gift from her cousin in the United States—   45
Held as a knife at the stomach of a man
Then pushed in, this is what it might feel like.
Stomachache from a winter's flu, the rocking kind
During which one must hold and bite a towel
Or those first days womanhood finds its way   50
Shaking her with pains, magnified three times, also:
This must be what the beginnings of a cancer
Feel like, how one's hands can do nothing
More than rub, or clean, or stroke the forehead,
Cannot in a last, most desperate attempt   55
Go out into the alley behind the bar like the men
and try to beat it up.

She thinks about this like this:
Then she stops, because she can
Understand a paper cut and stomach flu   60
As she understands salt and bread,
Can imagine them even together, and eating them.

She stops because understanding the blossom
Pain must be, or more,
That pain is a blossom snapped off   65
That moment and the pungent smell
A long *o* sound makes in the mouth
On a face not big enough—
All this disallows the thinking of a thing for too long
Because one understands.   70
All this stops the reading of newspapers.
But some nights she cannot do otherwise, as tonight:
She begins to add up, again, to put numbers
In the equation of how many cuts and glowing scrapes
One more thing or another adds up to,   75
What it must feel like,
How many paper cuts might roughly equal
The breaking neck of a favorite nephew.

                                                                    1985

Seniors

William cut a hole in his Levi's pocket
so he could flop himself out in class
behind the girls so the other guys
could see and shit what guts we all said.
All Konga wanted to do over and over   5
was the rubber band trick, but he showed

everyone how, so nobody wanted to see
anymore and one day he cried, just cried
until his parents took him away forever.
Maya had a Hotpoint refrigerator standing   10
in his living room, just for his family to show
anybody who came that they could afford it.

Me, I got a French kiss, finally, in the catholic
darkness, my tongue's farthest half vacationing
loudly in another mouth like a man in Bermudas,   15
and my body jumped against a flagstone wall,
I could feel it through her thin, almost
nonexistent body: I had, at that moment, that moment,
a hot girl on a summer night, the best of all
the things we tried to do. Well, she   20
let me kiss her, anyway, all over.

Or it was just a flagstone wall
with a flaw in the stone, an understanding cavity
for burning young men with smooth dreams—
the true circumstance is gone, the true   25
circumstances about us all then
are gone. But when I kissed her, all water,
she would close her eyes, and they into somewhere
would disappear. Whether she was there
or not, I remember her, clearly, and she moves   30
around the room, sometimes, until I sleep.

I have lain on the desert in watch
low in the back of a pick-up truck
for nothing in particular, for stars, for
the things behind stars, and nothing comes   35
more than the moment: always now, here in a truck,
the moment again to dream of making love and sweat,
this time to a woman, or even to all of them
in some allowable way, to those boys, then,
who couldn't cry, to the girls before they were   40
women, to friends, me on my back, the sky over me
pressing its simple weight into her body
on me, into the bodies of them all, on me.

                                                       1985

Refugio's Hair

In the old days of our family,
My grandmother was a young woman
Whose hair was as long as the river.
She lived with her sisters on the ranch

La Calera—The Land of the Lime—   5
And her days were happy.

But her uncle Carlos lived there too,
Carlos whose soul had the edge of a knife.
One day, to teach her to ride a horse,
He made her climb on the fastest one,   10
Bareback, and sit there
As he held its long face in his arms.

And then he did the unspeakable deed
For which he would always be remembered:
He called for the handsome baby Pirrín   15
And he placed the child in her arms.
With that picture of a Madonna on horseback
He slapped the shank of the horse's rear leg.

The horse did what a horse must,
Racing full toward the bright horizon.   20
But first he ran under the *álamo*[1] trees
To rid his back of this unfair weight:
This woman full of tears
And this baby full of love.

When they reached the trees and went under,   25
Her hair, which had trailed her,
Equal in its magnificence to the tail of the horse,
That hair rose up and flew into the branches
As if it were a thousand arms,
All of them trying to save her.   30

The horse ran off and left her,
The baby still in her arms,
The two of them hanging from her hair.
The baby looked only at her
And did not cry, so steady was her cradle.   35
Her sisters came running to save them.

But the hair would not let go.
From its fear it held on and had to be cut,
All of it, from her head.
From that day on, my grandmother   40
Wore her hair short like a scream,
But it was long like a river in her sleep.

                                                          2002

---

1. Popular or aspen.

The Chair She Sits In[1]

I've heard this thing where, when someone dies,
People close up all the holes around the house—

The keyholes, the chimney, the windows,
Even the mouths of the animals, the dogs and the pigs.

It's so the soul won't be confused, or tempted.   5
It's so when the soul comes out of the body it's been in

But that doesn't work anymore,
It won't simply go into another one

And try to make itself at home,
Pretending as if nothing happened.   10

There's no mystery—it's too much work to move on.
It isn't anybody's fault. A soul is like any of us.

It gets used to things, especially after a long life.
The way I sit in my living-room chair,

The indentation I have put in it now   15
After so many years—that's how I understand.

It's my chair,
And I know how to sit in it.

2005

1. Refers to the first line of the second section ("A Game of Chess") of T. S. Eliot's poem *The Waste Land* (1922), "The chair she sat in, like a burnished throne," which itself refers to a line from Shakespeare's *Antony and Cleopatra* (written between 1603 and 1607) regarding the queen. "The barge she sat in, like a burnish'd throne" (2.2. 190).

AMY TAN
b. 1952

Born in Oakland, California, to parents who had only recently immigrated from China, Amy Tan emerged as a novelist just when American readers were focusing on multiculturalism, mother-daughter relations, and contrasts between old-country and new-world generations—three important factors in Tan's own experience. Her first novel, *The Joy Luck Club* (1989), addresses precisely these issues, drawing its energy from the transitional forces at work on its characters' multiple cultures. Four sets of mothers and daughters feature in the book, and each pair's story is a personal narrative that juxtaposes different perspectives and radically different values. The daughters find their mothers' values alien and threatening, for example, until they learn to understand what their mothers are saying and grasp how a new generation's life can draw meaning from that of the old. Hence the novel delivers a series of conversations, the dynamics of which express the vital nature of each person.

The historical events behind *The Joy Luck Club* inform the pasts of many Chinese families whose older members immigrated to the United States soon after World War II. From missionary activities going back to the nineteenth century to a wartime alliance with Chiang Kai-shek's Nationalist government (which was even then being challenged by the Communist forces of Mao Tse-tung), American interests were involved with China. In China Amy Tan's father, John, worked as a Chinese citizen for the United States Information Service, and in the turbulence leading up to Mao's victory in 1949 he left for a career with the Baptist ministry in the U.S. Her mother's early life was less kind, fraught with atrocities not uncommon to those of an old order falling violently to a new one, involving concubinage (the fate of Amy's grandmother, who eventually killed herself), orphanhood, and an arranged marriage that ended in divorce. After emigrating from China to the U.S., she met John Tan and began the marriage that produced two sons plus a daughter who resisted assimilation into the more superficial and materialistic aspects of American culture.

Amy Tan's American childhood took an international turn at age fifteen, when following her father's and older brother's deaths her mother moved the remainder of the family to Switzerland. After graduation Tan returned to the San Francisco Bay Area for college and graduate school, earning a B.A. in English and an M.A. in linguistics. Marriage followed, and some uncompleted doctoral studies led to work as a language-development specialist for disabled children and then as a medical writer. Wanting an outlet from the demands of her professional schedule, she began writing fiction, becoming an immediate success with stories that were later incorporated into *The Joy Luck Club*. In this novel and in a second, *The Kitchen God's Wife* (1991), Tan addressed the daughterly relationship that gave her not only material for fruitful complaint but also grounds for reconciliation, based on her better understanding of her mother's past, a story she had turned a deaf ear to as a rebellious teenager. Sections of this second novel, for example, move back and forth between the mother's narrative and the daughter's, each character fully endowed with a persuasive voice that defines the nature of her being, different as the two experiences are.

Tan has since published other novels and two works for children. She moved toward light-hearted satire in her 2005 novel, *Saving Fish from Drowning*, a chronicle of the adventures and misadventures of some second-generation Chinese Americans who have embarked on a trip to discover the art and culture of ancient China and ancient Burma.

"Two Kinds" first appeared as a short story in the *Atlantic Monthly*. The following text is from *The Joy Luck Club* (1989).

From The Joy Luck Club

Two Kinds

My mother believed you could be anything you wanted to be in America. You could open a restaurant. You could work for the government and get good retirement. You could buy a house with almost no money down. You could become rich. You could become instantly famous.

"Of course you can be prodigy, too," my mother told me when I was nine. "You can be best anything. What does Auntie Lindo know? Her daughter, she is only best tricky."

America was where all my mother's hopes lay. She had come here in 1949 after losing everything in China.[1] Her mother and father, her family home, her first husband, and two daughters, twin baby girls. But she never looked back with regret. There were so many ways for things to get better.

We didn't immediately pick the right kind of prodigy. At first my mother thought I could be a Chinese Shirley Temple.[2] We'd watch Shirley's old movies on TV as though they were training films. My mother would poke my arm and say, "Ni kan"—You watch. And I would see Shirley tapping her feet, or singing a sailor song, or pursing her lips into a very round O while saying, "Oh my goodness."

"Ni kan," said my mother as Shirley's eyes flooded with tears. "You already know how. Don't need talent for crying!"

Soon after my mother got this idea about Shirley Temple, she took me to a beauty training school in the Mission district[3] and put me in the hands of a student who could barely hold the scissors without shaking. Instead of getting big fat curls, I emerged with an uneven mass of crinkly black fuzz. My mother dragged me off to the bathroom and tried to wet down my hair.

"You look like Negro Chinese," she lamented, as if I had done this on purpose.

The instructor of the beauty training school had to lop off these soggy clumps to make my hair even again. "Peter Pan[4] is very popular these days," the instructor assured my mother. I now had hair the length of a boy's, with straight-across bangs that hung at a slant two inches above my eyebrows. I liked the haircut and it made me actually look forward to my future fame.

In fact, in the beginning, I was just as excited as my mother, maybe even more so. I pictured this prodigy part of me as many different images, trying each one on for size. I was a dainty ballerina girl standing by the curtains, waiting to hear the right music that would send me floating on my tiptoes. I was like the Christ child lifted out of the straw manger, crying with holy indignity. I was Cinderella[5] stepping from her pumpkin carriage with sparkly cartoon music filling the air.

In all of my imaginings, I was filled with a sense that I would soon become *perfect*. My mother and father would adore me. I would be beyond reproach. I would never feel the need to sulk for anything.

But sometimes the prodigy in me became impatient. "If you don't hurry up and get me out of here, I'm disappearing for good," it warned. "And then you'll always be nothing."

Every night after dinner, my mother and I would sit at the Formica[6] kitchen table. She would present new tests, taking her examples from stories of amazing children she had read in *Ripley's Believe It or Not*, or *Good Housekeeping*,

1. The People's Republic of China was proclaimed on October 10, 1949, as the climactic act of the Chinese Communist Revolution. The Nationalist government then relocated to the island of Taiwan.
2. American film actress (b. 1928), a child star.
3. Multicultural neighborhood in San Francisco.
4. Children's play (1904) by the Scottish playwright and novelist James M. Barrie (1860–1937),

basis for a feature cartoon and Broadway musical in the 1950s, in which the protagonist (a boy) wears his hair in a pixielike cut soon favored by girls.
5. Stepsister-turned-princess in a Walt Disney animated musical (1950) based on a folktale dating from 16th-century Europe.
6. Trademark for a laminated-plastic kitchen-countertop covering popular in the 1950s.

Reader's Digest,[7] and a dozen other magazines she kept in a pile in our bathroom. My mother got these magazines from people whose houses she cleaned. And since she cleaned many houses each week, we had a great assortment. She would look through them all, searching for stories about remarkable children.

The first night she brought out a story about a three-year-old boy who knew the capitals of all the states and even most of the European countries. A teacher was quoted as saying the little boy could also pronounce the names of the foreign cities correctly.

"What's the capital of Finland?" my mother asked me, looking at the magazine story.

All I knew was the capital of California, because Sacramento was the name of the street we lived on in Chinatown. "Nairobi!" I guessed, saying the most foreign word I could think of. She checked to see if that was possibly one way to pronounce "Helsinki"[8] before showing me the answer.

The tests got harder—multiplying numbers in my head, finding the queen of hearts in a deck of cards, trying to stand on my head without using my hands, predicting the daily temperatures in Los Angeles, New York, and London.

One night I had to look at a page from the Bible for three minutes and then report everything I could remember. "Now Jehoshaphat had riches and honor in abundance and[9] . . . that's all I remember, Ma," I said.

And after seeing my mother's disappointed face once again, something inside of me began to die. I hated the tests, the raised hopes and failed expectations. Before going to bed that night, I looked in the mirror above the bathroom sink and when I saw only my face staring back—and that it would always be this ordinary face—I began to cry. Such a sad, ugly girl! I made high-pitched noises like a crazed animal, trying to scratch out the face in the mirror.

And then I saw what seemed to be the prodigy side of me—because I had never seen that face before. I looked at my reflection, blinking so I could see more clearly. The girl staring back at me was angry, powerful. This girl and I were the same. I had new thoughts, willful thoughts, or rather thoughts filled with lots of won'ts. I won't let her change me, I promised myself. I won't be what I'm not.

So now on nights when my mother presented her tests, I performed listlessly, my head propped on one arm. I pretended to be bored. And I was. I got so bored I started counting the bellows of the foghorns out on the bay[1] while my mother drilled me in other areas. The sound was comforting and reminded me of the cow jumping over the moon.[2] And the next day, I played a game with myself, seeing if my mother would give up on me before eight bellows. After a while I usually counted only one, maybe two bellows at most. At last she was beginning to give up hope.

---

7. Popular middle-class American magazines of the era.
8. Capital of Finland, in northern Europe. "Chinatown": ethnic Chinese neighborhood in San Francisco. "Nairobi": capital of Kenya, in Africa.
9. 2 Chronicles 17.5: "Therefore the Lord established the kingdom in his hand, and all Judah brought tribute to Jehosaphat; and he had great riches and honor."
1. San Francisco Bay.
2. A Mother Goose rhyme.

Two or three months had gone by without any mention of my being a prodigy again. And then one day my mother was watching *The Ed Sullivan Show*[3] on TV. The TV was old and the sound kept shorting out. Every time my mother got halfway up from the sofa to adjust the set, the sound would go back on and Ed would be talking. As soon as she sat down, Ed would go silent again. She got up, the TV broke into loud piano music. She sat down. Silence. Up and down, back and forth, quiet and loud. It was like a stiff embraceless dance between her and the TV set. Finally she stood by the set with her hand on the sound dial.

She seemed entranced by the music, a little frenzied piano piece with this mesmerizing quality, sort of quick passages and then teasing lilting ones before it returned to the quick playful parts.

"*Ni kan*," my mother said, calling me over with hurried hand gestures, "Look here."

I could see why my mother was fascinated by the music. It was being pounded out by a little Chinese girl, about nine years old, with a Peter Pan haircut. The girl had the sauciness of a Shirley Temple. She was proudly modest like a proper Chinese child. And she also did this fancy sweep of a curtsy, so that the fluffy skirt of her white dress cascaded slowly to the floor like the petals of a large carnation.

In spite of these warning signs, I wasn't worried. Our family had no piano and we couldn't afford to buy one, let alone reams of sheet music and piano lessons. So I could be generous in my comments when my mother bad-mouthed the little girl on TV.

"Play note right, but doesn't sound good! No singing sound," complained my mother.

"What are you picking on her for?" I said carelessly. "She's pretty good. Maybe she's not the best, but she's trying hard." I knew almost immediately I would be sorry I said that.

"Just like you," she said. "Not the best. Because you not trying." She gave a little huff as she let go of the sound dial and sat down on the sofa.

The little Chinese girl sat down also to play an encore of "Anitra's Dance" by Grieg.[4] I remember the song, because later on I had to learn how to play it.

Three days after watching *The Ed Sullivan Show*, my mother told me what my schedule would be for piano lessons and piano practice. She had talked to Mr. Chong, who lived on the first floor of our apartment building. Mr. Chong was a retired piano teacher and my mother had traded housecleaning services for weekly lessons and a piano for me to practice on every day, two hours a day, from four until six.

When my mother told me this, I felt as though I had been sent to hell. I whined and then kicked my foot a little when I couldn't stand it anymore.

"Why don't you like me the way I am? I'm *not* a genius! I can't play the piano. And even if I could, I wouldn't go on TV if you paid me a million dollars!" I cried.

---

3. Longest-running variety series (1948–71) in American television history, hosted by New York newspaper society and entertainment columnist Ed Sullivan (1902–1974).
4. From the *Peer Gynt Suite* (1874–75), by the Norwegian composer Edvard Grieg (1843–1907).

My mother slapped me. "Who ask you be genius?" she shouted. "Only ask you be your best. For you sake. You think I want you be genius? Hnnh! What for! Who ask you!"

"So ungrateful," I heard her mutter in Chinese. "If she had as much talent as she has temper, she would be famous now."

Mr. Chong, whom I secretly nicknamed Old Chong, was very strange, always tapping his fingers to the silent music of an invisible orchestra. He looked ancient in my eyes. He had lost most of the hair on top of his head and he wore thick glasses and had eyes that always looked tired and sleepy. But he must have been younger than I thought, since he lived with his mother and was not yet married.

I met Old Lady Chong once and that was enough. She had this peculiar smell like a baby that had done something in its pants. And her fingers felt like a dead person's, like an old peach I once found in the back of the refrigerator; the skin just slid off the meat when I picked it up.

I soon found out why Old Chong had retired from teaching piano. He was deaf. "Like Beethoven!"[5] he shouted to me. "We're both listening only in our head!" And he would start to conduct his frantic silent sonatas.

Our lessons went like this. He would open the book and point to different things, explaining their purpose: "Key! Treble! Bass! No sharps or flats! So this is C major! Listen now and play after me!"

And then he would play the C scale a few times, a simple chord, and then, as if inspired by an old, unreachable itch, he gradually added more notes and running trills and a pounding bass until the music was really something quite grand.

I would play after him, the simple scale, the simple chord, and then I just played some nonsense that sounded like a cat running up and down on top of garbage cans. Old Chong smiled and applauded and then said, "Very good! But now you must learn to keep time!"

So that's how I discovered that Old Chong's eyes were too slow to keep up with the wrong notes I was playing. He went through the motions in half-time. To help me keep rhythm, he stood behind me, pushing down on my right shoulder for every beat. He balanced pennies on top of my wrists so I would keep them still as I slowly played scales and arpeggios. He had me curve my hand around an apple and keep that shape when playing chords. He marched stiffly to show me how to make each finger dance up and down, staccato like an obedient little soldier.

He taught me all these things, and that was how I also learned I could be lazy and get away with mistakes, lots of mistakes. If I hit the wrong notes because I hadn't practiced enough, I never corrected myself. I just kept playing in rhythm. And Old Chong kept conducting his own private reverie.

So maybe I never really gave myself a fair chance. I did pick up the basics pretty quickly, and I might have become a good pianist at that young age. But I was so determined not to try, not to be anybody different that I learned to play only the most ear-splitting preludes, the most discordant hymns.

Over the next year, I practiced like this, dutifully in my own way. And then one day I heard my mother and her friend Lindo Jong both talking in a

5. Ludwig van Beethoven (1770–1827), German composer who began losing his hearing in 1801 and was totally deaf by 1817, yet who continued to compose monumental works.

loud bragging tone of voice so others could hear. It was after church, and I was leaning against the brick wall wearing a dress with stiff white petti-coats. Auntie Lindo's daughter, Waverly,[6] who was about my age, was stand-ing farther down the wall about five feet away. We had grown up together and shared all the closeness of two sisters squabbling over crayons and dolls. In other words, for the most part, we hated each other. I thought she was snotty. Waverly Jong had gained a certain amount of fame as "Chinatown's Littlest Chinese Chess Champion."

"She bring home too many trophy," lamented Auntie Lindo that Sunday. "All day she play chess. All day I have no time do nothing but dust off her winnings." She threw a scolding look at Waverly, who pretended not to see her.

"You lucky you don't have this problem," said Auntie Lindo with a sigh to my mother.

And my mother squared her shoulders and bragged: "Our problem worser than yours. If we ask Jing-mei wash dish, she hear nothing but music. It's like you can't stop this natural talent."

And right then, I was determined to put a stop to her foolish pride.

A few weeks later, Old Chong and my mother conspired to have me play in a talent show which would be held in the church hall. By then, my parents had saved up enough to buy me a secondhand piano, a black Wurlitzer[7] spinet with a scarred bench. It was the showpiece of our living room.

For the talent show, I was to play a piece called "Pleading Child" from Schumann's *Scenes from Childhood*.[8] It was a simple, moody piece that sounded more difficult than it was. I was supposed to memorize the whole thing, playing the repeat parts twice to make the piece sound longer. But I dawdled over it, playing a few bars and then cheating, looking up to see what notes followed. I never really listened to what I was playing. I daydreamed about being somewhere else, about being someone else.

The part I liked to practice best was the fancy curtsy: right foot out, touch the rose on the carpet with a pointed foot, sweep to the side, left leg bends, look up and smile.

My parents invited all the couples from the Joy Luck Club[9] to witness my debut. Auntie Lindo and Uncle Tin were there. Waverly and her two older brothers had also come. The first two rows were filled with children both younger and older than I was. The littlest ones got to go first. They recited simple nursery rhymes, squawked out tunes on miniature violins, twirled Hula Hoops;[1] pranced in pink ballet tutus, and when they bowed or curtsied, the audience would sigh in unison, "Awww," and then clap enthusiastically.

When my turn came, I was very confident. I remember my childish excitement. It was as if I knew, without a doubt, that the prodigy side of me really did exist. I had no fear whatsoever, no nervousness. I remember

---

6. *Waverley* (1814) is the first of the Waverley novels, by the Scottish novelist Sir Walter Scott (1771–1832), whose works were a staple of middle-class American education in the first half of the 20th century.
7. The Wurlitzer Company, manufacturer of pianos, organs, and jukeboxes.
8. Properly *Kinderszenen* (1838), a set of piano pieces by the German composer Robert Alexan-der Schumann (1810–1856).
9. In Tan's novel, a four-member club formed to play mah-jong (a table game popular in its present form since 1920) and continued as a social unit.
1. Exercise toy popular as a novelty item in the 1950s.

thinking to myself, This is it! This is it! I looked out over the audience, at my mother's blank face, my father's yawn, Auntie Lindo's stiff-lipped smile, Waverly's sulky expression. I had on a white dress layered with sheets of lace, and a pink bow in my Peter Pan haircut. As I sat down I envisioned people jumping to their feet and Ed Sullivan rushing up to introduce me to everyone on TV.

And I started to play. It was so beautiful. I was so caught up in how lovely I looked that at first I didn't worry how I would sound. So it was a surprise to me when I hit the first wrong note and I realized something didn't sound quite right. And then I hit another and another followed that. A chill started at the top of my head and began to trickle down. Yet I couldn't stop playing, as though my hands were bewitched. I kept thinking my fingers would adjust themselves back, like a train switching to the right track. I played this strange jumble through two repeats, the sour notes staying with me all the way to the end.

When I stood up, I discovered my legs were shaking. Maybe I had just been nervous and the audience, like Old Chong, had seen me go through the right motions and had not heard anything wrong at all. I swept my right foot out, went down on my knee, looked up and smiled. The room was quiet, except for Old Chong, who was beaming and shouting, "Bravo! Bravo! Well done!" But then I saw my mother's face, her stricken face. The audience clapped weakly, and as I walked back to my chair, with my whole face quivering as I tried not to cry, I heard a little boy whisper loudly to his mother, "That was awful," and the mother whispered back, "Well, she certainly tried."

And now I realized how many people were in the audience, the whole world it seemed. I was aware of eyes burning into my back. I felt the shame of my mother and father as they sat stiffly throughout the rest of the show.

We could have escaped during intermission. Pride and some strange sense of honor must have anchored my parents to their chairs. And so we watched it all: the eighteen-year-old boy with a fake mustache who did a magic show and juggled flaming hoops while riding a unicycle. The breasted girl with white makeup who sang from *Madama Butterfly*[2] and got honorable mention. And the eleven-year-old boy who won first prize playing a tricky violin song that sounded like a busy bee.

After the show, the Hsus, the Jongs, and the St. Clairs from the Joy Luck Club came up to my mother and father.

"Lots of talented kids," Auntie Lindo said vaguely, smiling broadly.

"That was somethin' else," said my father, and I wondered if he was referring to me in a humorous way, or whether he even remembered what I had done.

Waverly looked at me and shrugged her shoulders. "You aren't a genius like me," she said matter-of-factly. And if I hadn't felt so bad, I would have pulled her braids and punched her stomach.

But my mother's expression was what devastated me: a quiet, blank look that said she had lost everything. I felt the same way, and it seemed as if everybody were now coming up, like gawkers at the scene of an accident, to see what parts were actually missing. When we got on the bus to go home, my

---

2. Opera (1904), set in Japan, by the Italian composer Giacomo Puccini (1858–1924).

father was humming the busy-bee tune and my mother was silent. I kept thinking she wanted to wait until we got home before shouting at me. But when my father unlocked the door to our apartment, my mother walked in and then went to the back, into the bedroom. No accusations. No blame. And in a way, I felt disappointed. I had been waiting for her to start shouting, so I could shout back and cry and blame her for all my misery.

I assumed my talent-show fiasco meant I never had to play the piano again. But two days later, after school, my mother came out of the kitchen and saw me watching TV.

"Four clock," she reminded me as if it were any other day. I was stunned, as though she were asking me to go through the talent-show torture again. I wedged myself more tightly in front of the TV.

"Turn off TV," she called from the kitchen five minutes later.

I didn't budge. And then I decided. I didn't have to do what my mother said anymore. I wasn't her slave. This wasn't China. I had listened to her before and look what happened. She was the stupid one.

She came out from the kitchen and stood in the arched entryway of the living room. "Four clock," she said once again, louder.

"I'm not going to play anymore," I said nonchalantly. "Why should I? I'm not a genius."

She walked over and stood in front of the TV. I saw her chest was heaving up and down in an angry way.

"No!" I said, and I now felt stronger, as if my true self had finally emerged. So this was what had been inside me all along.

"No! I won't!" I screamed.

She yanked me by the arm, pulled me off the floor, snapped off the TV. She was frighteningly strong, half pulling, half carrying me toward the piano as I kicked the throw rugs under my feet. She lifted me up and onto the hard bench. I was sobbing by now, looking at her bitterly. Her chest was heaving even more and her mouth was open, smiling crazily as if she were pleased I was crying.

"You want me to be someone that I'm not!" I sobbed. "I'll never be the kind of daughter you want me to be!"

"Only two kinds of daughters," she shouted in Chinese. "Those who are obedient and those who follow their own mind! Only one kind of daughter can live in this house. Obedient daughter!"

"Then I wish I wasn't your daughter. I wish you weren't my mother," I shouted. As I said these things I got scared. It felt like worms and toads and slimy things crawling out of my chest, but it also felt good, as if this awful side of me had surfaced, at last.

"Too late change this," said my mother shrilly.

And I could sense her anger rising to its breaking point. I wanted to see it spill over. And that's when I remembered the babies she had lost in China, the ones we never talked about. "Then I wish I'd never been born!" I shouted. "I wish I were dead! Like them."

It was as if I had said the magic words. Alakazam![3]—and her face went blank, her mouth closed, her arms went slack, and she backed out of the

3. A magical incantation (slang).

room, stunned, as if she were blowing away like a small brown leaf, thin, brittle, lifeless.

It was not the only disappointment my mother felt in me. In the years that followed, I failed her so many times, each time asserting my own will, my right to fall short of expectations. I didn't get straight As. I didn't become class president. I didn't get into Stanford.[4] I dropped out of college.

For unlike my mother, I did not believe I could be anything I wanted to be. I could only be me.

And for all those years, we never talked about the disaster at the recital or my terrible accusations afterward at the piano bench. All that remained unchecked, like a betrayal that was now unspeakable. So I never found a way to ask her why she had hoped for something so large that failure was inevitable.

And even worse, I never asked her what frightened me the most: Why had she given up hope?

For after our struggle at the piano, she never mentioned my playing again. The lessons stopped. The lid to the piano was closed, shutting out the dust, my misery, and her dreams.

So she surprised me. A few years ago, she offered to give me the piano, for my thirtieth birthday. I had not played in all those years. I saw the offer as a sign of forgiveness, a tremendous burden removed.

"Are you sure?" I asked shyly. "I mean, won't you and Dad miss it?"

"No, this your piano," she said firmly. "Always your piano. You only one can play."

"Well, I probably can't play anymore," I said. "It's been years."

"You pick up fast," said my mother, as if she knew this was certain. "You have natural talent. You could been genius if you want to."

"No I couldn't."

"You just not trying," said my mother. And she was neither angry nor sad. She said it as if to announce a fact that could never be disproved. "Take it," she said.

But I didn't at first. It was enough that she had offered it to me. And after that, every time I saw it in my parents' living room, standing in front of the bay windows, it made me feel proud, as if it were a shiny trophy I had won back.

Last week I sent a tuner over to my parents' apartment and had the piano reconditioned, for purely sentimental reasons. My mother had died a few months before and I had been getting things in order for my father, a little bit at a time. I put the jewelry in special silk pouches. The sweaters she had knitted in yellow, pink, bright orange—all the colors I hated—I put those in mothproof boxes. I found some old Chinese silk dresses, the kind with little slits up the sides. I rubbed the old silk against my skin, then wrapped them in tissue and decided to take them home with me.

After I had the piano tuned, I opened the lid and touched the keys. It sounded even richer than I remembered. Really, it was a very good piano. Inside the bench were the same exercise notes with handwritten scales, the

---

4. Prestigious private university in Palo Alto California, south of San Francisco Bay.

same secondhand music books with their covers held together with yellow tape.

I opened up the Schumann book to the dark little piece I had played at the recital. It was on the left-hand side of the page, "Pleading Child." It looked more difficult than I remembered. I played a few bars, surprised at how easily the notes came back to me.

And for the first time, or so it seemed, I noticed the piece on the right-hand side. It was called "Perfectly Contented." I tried to play this one as well. It had a lighter melody but the same flowing rhythm and turned out to be quite easy. "Pleading Child" was shorter but slower; "Perfectly Contented" was longer, but faster. And after I played them both a few times, I realized they were two halves of the same song.

1989

SANDRA CISNEROS
b. 1954

Sandra Cisneros began writing at age ten, much like the young Chicana narrator of *The House on Mango Street* (1984), the volume of interrelated vignettes from a child's perspective that brought Cisneros her first major attention. In brief, sharply drawn, but quietly expressed segments, the narrator, Esperanza, conveys the ambience of growing up in Chicago's Mexican American community. The social bond of this neighborhood eases the contrast between Esperanza's nurturing family and the more hostile forces of poverty and racism. Cisneros cultivates a sense of warmth and naive humor for her protagonists, qualities that are evident in introductory parts to *Woman Hollering Creek* (1991), a short-story collection that also deals with more troublesome aspects of young women's facing hostile forces. Without sentimentalizing or idealizing her narrator's perspective, Cisneros presents glimpses of a world full of adult challenges and multicultural complexities. Sex is a topic in all Cisneros's work, including her poetry collected as *My Wicked Wicked Ways* (1987) and *Loose Woman* (1994)—sometimes gentle and even silly, other times brutally assaultive. What remains constant is the author's view that by romanticizing sexual relations women cooperate with a male view that can be oppressive, even physically destructive. As is said of the protagonist of her 2002 novel, *Caramelo*, Cisneros is "caught between here and there." Yet "here" and "there" are not as dichotomous as young versus old, female versus male, or Mexico versus the United States. Instead, the flow of experience between these poles yields her work's subject: people finding their own lifestyles in the space between fixed boundaries. Because this intervening space is so rich in creative potential, Cisneros can balance unhappiness with humor and find personal victories where others might see social defeat.

Born in Chicago, the child of a Mexican father and a Mexican American mother, Cisneros spent parts of her childhood in Texas and Mexico as well. Her Catholic-school background led to a B.A. degree from Chicago's Loyola University, after which she earned a graduate degree in creative writing from the University of Iowa's Writers Workshop. Teaching in San Antonio, Texas, she has used her position as a writer and an educator to champion Chicana feminism, especially as this movement combines cultural issues with women's concerns. In raising controversy by having her house painted very brightly, she openly questioned monocultural "historical districts" and "community covenants." *Whose* history? Cisneros asked; *which* community sets standards? (Through research she established that her decorating style was in accordance with her home's background and that the standards used to dispute her choice were arbitrary.) A dissatisfaction with the politics of publishing has made her an advocate of small-press dissemination. Most of all, as in the story reprinted here, she is eager to show the rich dynamics of characters existing in the blend of Mexican and American cultures that begins with speaking two languages and extends to almost every aspect of life. Spanish words, Mexican holidays, ethnic foods, and localized religious practices punctuate her narratives; her characters have a facility with cultural play that reflects what for others would be an anthropologically enhanced understanding.

The following text is from *Woman Hollering Creek* (1991).

Woman Hollering Creek

The day Don Serafín gave Juan Pedro Martínez Sánchez permission to take Cleófilas Enriqueta DeLeón Hernández as his bride, across her father's threshold, over several miles of dirt road and several miles of paved, over one border and beyond to a town *en el otro lado*—on the other side—already did he divine the morning his daughter would raise her hand over her eyes, look south, and dream of returning to the chores that never ended, six good-for-nothing brothers, and one old man's complaints.

He had said, after all, in the hubbub of parting: I am your father, I will never abandon you. He *had* said that, hadn't he, when he hugged and then let her go. But at the moment Cleófilas was busy looking for Chela, her maid of honor, to fulfill their bouquet conspiracy. She would not remember her father's parting words until later. *I am your father, I will never abandon you.*

Only now as a mother did she remember. Now, when she and Juan Pedrito sat by the creek's edge. How when a man and a woman love each other, sometimes that love sours. But a parent's love for a child, a child's for its parents, is another thing entirely.

This is what Cleófilas thought evenings when Juan Pedro did not come home, and she lay on her side of the bed listening to the hollow roar of the interstate, a distant dog barking, the pecan trees rustling like ladies in stiff petticoats—*shh-shh-shh, shh-shh-shh*—soothing her to sleep.

In the town where she grew up, there isn't very much to do except accompany the aunts and godmothers to the house of one or the other to play cards. Or walk to the cinema to see this week's film again, speckled and with one hair quivering annoyingly on the screen. Or to the center of town to order a milk shake that will appear in a day and a half as a pimple on her backside. Or to the girlfriend's house to watch the latest *telenovela*[1] episode and try to copy the way the women comb their hair, wear their makeup.

But what Cleófilas has been waiting for, has been whispering and sighing and giggling for, has been anticipating since she was old enough to lean

1. Serialized TV melodrama (Spanish).

against the window displays of gauze and butterflies and lace, is passion. Not the kind on the cover of the *¡Alarma!*[2] magazines, mind you, where the lover is photographed with the bloody fork she used to salvage her good name. But passion in its purest crystalline essence. The kind the books and songs and *telenovelas* describe when one finds, finally, the great love of one's life, and does whatever one can, must do, at whatever the cost.

Tú o Nadie. "You or No One." The title of the current favorite *telenovela.* The beautiful Lucía Méndez having to put up with all kinds of hardships of the heart, separation and betrayal, and loving, always loving no matter what, because *that* is the most important thing, and did you see Lucía Méndez on the Bayer aspirin commercials—wasn't she lovely? Does she dye her hair do you think? Cleófilas is going to go to the *farmacía*[3] and buy a hair rinse; her girlfriend Chela will apply it—it's not that difficult at all.

Because you didn't watch last night's episode when Lucía confessed she loved him more than anyone in her life. In her life! And she sings the song "You or No One" in the beginning and end of the show. *Tú o Nadie.* Somehow one ought to live one's life like that, don't you think? You or no one. Because to suffer for love is good. The pain all sweet somehow. In the end.

Seguín. She had liked the sound of it. Far away and lovely. Not like *Monclova. Coahuia.*[4] Ugly.

Seguín, Tejas. A nice sterling ring to it. The tinkle of money. She would get to wear outfits like the women on the *tele*, like Lucía Méndez. And have a lovely house, and wouldn't Chela be jealous.

And yes, they will drive all the way to Laredo[5] get her wedding dress. That's what they say. Because Juan Pedro wants to get married right away, without a long engagement since he can't take off too much time from work. He has a very important position in Seguin with, with . . . a beer company, I think. Or was it tires? Yes, he has to be back. So they will get married in the spring when he can take off work, and then they will drive off in his new pickup—did you see it?—to their new home in Seguin. Well, not exactly new, but they're going to repaint the house. You know newlyweds. New paint and new furniture. Why not? He can afford it. And later on add maybe a room or two for the children. May they be blessed with many.

Well, you'll see. Cleófilas has always been so good with her sewing machine. A little *rrrr, rrrr, rrrr* of the machine and *¡zas!* Miracles. She's always been so clever, that girl. Poor thing. And without even a mama to advise her on things like her wedding night. Well, may God help her. What with a father with a head like a burro, and those six clumsy brothers. Well, what do you think! Yes, I'm going to the wedding. Of course! The dress I want to wear just needs to be altered a teensy bit to bring it up to date. See, I saw a new style last night that I thought would suit me. Did you watch last night's episode of *The Rich Also Cry?*[6] Well, did you notice the dress the mother was wearing?

---

2. Graphic, sensationalistic Mexican magazine published since 1963.
3. Pharmacy, drugstore (Spanish).
4. Respectively a town and state in Mexico, the latter bordering Texas. "Seguín": city in Guadalupe County, south-central Texas.

5. City in southwestern Texas, on the Mexican border.
6. First global soap opera (production beginning in Mexico in 1979), exported to Russia, China, the United States, and other countries.

La Gritona.[7] Such a funny name for such a lovely *arroyo*.[8] But that's what they called the creek that ran behind the house. Though no one could say whether the woman had hollered from anger or pain. The natives only knew the *arroyo* one crossed on the way to San Antonio, and then once again on the way back, was called Woman Hollering, a name no one from these parts questioned, little less understood. *Pues, allá de los indios, quién sabe*[9]—who knows, the townspeople shrugged, because it was of no concern to their lives how this trickle of water received its curious name.

"What do you want to know for?" Trini the laundromat attendant asked in the same gruff Spanish she always used whenever she gave Cleófilas change or yelled at her for something. First for putting too much soap in the machines. Later, for sitting on a washer. And still later, after Juan Pedrito was born, for not understanding that in this country you cannot let your baby walk around with no diaper and his pee-pee hanging out, it wasn't nice, *¿entiendes?Pues*.[1]

How could Cleófilas explain to a woman like this why the name Woman Hollering fascinated her. Well, there was no sense talking to Trini.

On the other hand there were the neighbor ladies, one on either side of the house they rented near the *arroyo*. The woman Soledad on the left, the woman Dolores on the right.

The neighbor lady Soledad liked to call herself a widow, though how she came to be one was a mystery. Her husband had either died, or run away with an ice-house[2] floozie, or simply gone out for cigarettes one afternoon and never came back. It was hard to say which since Soledad, as a rule, didn't mention him.

In the other house lived *la señora*[3] Dolores, land and very sweet, but her house smelled too much of incense and candles from the altars that burned continuously in memory of two sons who had died in the last war and one husband who had died shortly after from grief. The neighbor lady Dolores divided her time between the memory of these men and her garden, famous for its sunflowers—so tall they had to be supported with broom handles and old boards; red red cockscombs, fringed and bleeding a thick menstrual color; and, especially, roses whose sad scent reminded Cleófilas of the dead. Each Sunday *la señora* Dolores clipped the most beautiful of these flowers and arranged them on three modest headstones at the Seguin cemetery.

The neighbor ladies, Soledad, Dolores, they might've known once the name of the *arroyo* before it turned English but they did not know now. They were too busy remembering the men who had left through either choice or circumstance and would never come back.

Pain or rage, Cleófilas wondered when she drove over the bridge the first time as a newlywed and Juan Pedro had pointed it out. *La Gritona*, he had said, and she had laughed. Such a funny name for a creek so pretty and full of happily ever after.

7. The Shouter, Yeller, Hollerer (Spanish).
8. Stream (Spanish).
9. Well, beyond the Indians, who knows (Spanish).

1. Do you understand? Well (Spanish).
2. Tavern.
3. The lady (Spanish).

The first time she had been so surprised she didn't cry out or try to defend herself. She had always said she would strike back if a man, any man, were to strike her.

But when the moment came, and he slapped her once, and then again, and again; until the lip split and bled an orchid of blood, she didn't fight back, she didn't break into tears, she didn't run away as she imagined she might when she saw such things in the *telenovelas*.

In her own home her parents had never raised a hand to each other or to their children. Although she admitted she may have been brought up a little leniently as an only daughter—*la consentida*,[4] the princess—there were some things she would never tolerate. Ever.

Instead, when it happened the first time, when they were barely man and wife, she had been so stunned, it left her speechless, motionless, numb. She had done nothing but reach up to the heat on her mouth and stare at the blood on her hand as if even then she didn't understand.

She could think of nothing to say, said nothing. Just stroked the dark curls of the man who wept and would weep like a child, his tears of repentance and shame, this time and each.

The men at the ice house. From what she can tell, from the times during her first year when still a newlywed she is invited and accompanies her husband, sits mute beside their conversation, waits and sips a beer until it grows warm, twists a paper napkin into a knot, then another into a fan, one into a rose, nods her head, smiles, yawns, politely grins, laughs at the appropriate moments, leans against her husband's sleeve, tugs at his elbow, and finally becomes good at predicting where the talk will lead, from this Cleófilas concludes each is nightly trying to find the truth lying at the bottom of the bottle like a gold doubloon on the sea floor.

They want to tell each other what they want to tell themselves. But what is bumping like a helium balloon at the ceiling of the brain never finds its way out. It bubbles and rises, it gurgles in the throat, it rolls across the surface of the tongue, and erupts from the lips—a belch.

If they are lucky, there are tears at the end of the long night. At any given moment, the fists try to speak. They are dogs chasing their own tails before lying down to sleep, trying to find a way, a route, an out, and—finally—get some peace.

In the morning sometimes before he opens his eyes. Or after they have finished loving. Or at times when he is simply across from her at the table putting pieces of food into his mouth and chewing. Cleófilas thinks, This is the man I have waited my whole life for.

Not that he isn't a good man. She has to remind herself why she loves him when she changes the baby's Pampers, or when she mops the bathroom floor, or tries to make the curtains for the doorways without doors, or whiten the linen. Or wonder a little when he kicks the refrigerator and says he hates this shitty house and is going out where he won't be bothered with the baby's howling and her suspicious questions, and her requests to fix this and this

---

4. The spoiled one (Spanish).

and this because if she had any brains in her head she'd realize he's been up before the rooster earning his living to pay for the food in her belly and the roof over her head and would have to wake up again early the next day so why can't you just leave me in peace, woman.

He is not very tall, no, and he doesn't look like the men on the *telenovelas*. His face still scarred from acne. And he has a bit of a belly from all the beer he drinks. Well, he's always been husky.

This man who farts and belches and snores as well as laughs and kisses and holds her. Somehow this husband whose whiskers she finds each morning in the sink, whose shoes she must air each evening on the porch, this husband who cuts his fingernails in public, laughs loudly, curses like a man, and demands each course of dinner be served on a separate plate like at his mother's, as soon as he gets home, on time or late, and who doesn't care at all for music or *telenovelas* or romance or roses or the moon floating pearly over the *arroyo*, or through the bedroom window for that matter, shut the blinds and go back to sleep, this man, this father, this rival, this keeper, this lord, this master, this husband till kingdom come.

A doubt. Slender as a hair. A washed cup set back on the shelf wrong-side-up. Her lipstick, and body talc, and hairbrush all arranged in the bathroom a different way.

No. Her imagination. The house the same as always. Nothing.

Coming home from the hospital with her new son, her husband. Something comforting in discovering her house slippers beneath the bed, the faded housecoat where she left it on the bathroom hook. Her pillow. Their bed.

Sweet sweet homecoming. Sweet as the scent of face powder in the air, jasmine, sticky liquor.

Smudged fingerprint on the door. Crushed cigarette in a glass. Wrinkle in the brain crumpling to a crease.

Sometimes she thinks of her father's house. But how could she go back there? What a disgrace. What would the neighbors say? Coming home like that with one baby on her hip and one in the oven. Where's your husband?

The town of gossips. The town of dust and despair. Which she has traded for this town of gossips. This town of dust, despair. Houses farther apart perhaps, though no more privacy because of it. No leafy *zócalo*[5] in the center of the town, though the murmur of talk is clear enough all the same. No huddled whispering on the church steps each Sunday. Because here the whispering begins at sunset at the ice house instead.

This town with its silly pride for a bronze pecan the size of a baby carriage in front of the city hall. TV repair shop, drugstore, hardware, dry cleaner's, chiropractor's, liquor store, bail bonds, empty storefront, and nothing, nothing, nothing of interest. Nothing one could walk to, at any rate. Because the towns here are built so that you have to depend on husbands. Or you stay home. Or you drive. If you're rich enough to own, allowed to drive, your own car.

_____

5. Town square (Spanish).

There is no place to go. Unless one counts the neighbor ladies. Soledad on one side, Dolores on the other. Or the creek.

Don't go out there after dark, *mi'jita*.[6] Stay near the house. *No es bueno para la salud*.[7] Mala suerte. Bad luck. *Mal aire*.[8] You'll get sick and the baby too. You'll catch a fright wandering about in the dark, and then you'll see how right we were.

The stream sometimes only a muddy puddle in the summer, though now in the springtime, because of the rains, a good-size alive thing, a thing with a voice all its own, all day and all night calling in its high, silver voice. Is it La Llorona,[9] the weeping woman? La Llorona, who drowned her own children. Perhaps La Llorona is the one they named the creek after, she thinks, remembering all the stories she learned as a child.

La Llorona calling to her. She is sure of it. Cleófilas sets the baby's Donald Duck blanket on the grass. Listens. The day sky turning to night. The baby pulling up fistfuls of grass and laughing. La Llorona. Wonders if something as quiet as this drives a woman to the darkness under the trees.

What she needs is . . . and made a gesture as if to yank a woman's buttocks to his groin. Maximiliano, the foul-smelling fool from across the road, said this and set the men laughing, but Cleófilas just muttered. *Grosera*,[1] and went on washing dishes.

She knew he said it not because it was true, but more because it was he who needed to sleep with a woman, instead of drinking each night at the ice house and stumbling home alone.

Maximiliano who was said to have killed his wife in an ice-house brawl when she came at him with a mop. I had to shoot, he had said—she was armed.

Their laughter outside the kitchen window. Her husband's, his friends'. Manolo, Beto, Efraín, el Perico.[2] Maximiliano.

Was Cleófilas just exaggerating as her husband always said? It seemed the newspapers were full of such stories. This woman found on the side of the interstate. This one pushed from a moving car. This one's cadaver, this one unconscious, this one beaten blue. Her ex-husband, her husband, her lover, her father, her brother, her uncle, her friend, her co-worker. Always. The same grisly news in the pages of the dailies. She dunked a glass under the soapy water for a moment—shivered.

He had thrown a book. Hers. From across the room. A hot welt across the cheek. She could forgive that. But what stung more was the fact it was *her* book, a love story by Corín Tellado,[3] what she loved most now that she lived in the U.S., without a television set, without the *telenovelas*.

Except now and again when her husband was away and she could manage it, the few episodes glimpsed at the neighbor lady Soledad's house because Dolores didn't care for that sort of thing, though Soledad was often

6. My daughter (Spanish).
7. It's not good for one's health (Spanish).
8. Bad air (Spanish).
9. The Woman Who Cries (Spanish), a spurned mistress of Mexican legend who drowned her children and was fated to eternally seek their recovery.
1. Vulgar, crude (Spanish).
2. The Parakeet (Spanish).
3. Pseudonym of María del Socorro Tellado López (1927–2009), Spanish novelist.

kind enough to retell what had happened on what episode of *María de Nadie*,[4] the poor Argentine country girl who had the ill fortune of falling in love with the beautiful son of the Arrocha family, the very family she worked for, whose roof she slept under and whose floors she vacuumed, while in that same house, with the dust brooms and floor cleaners as witnesses, the square-jawed Juan Carlos Arrocha had uttered words of love, I love you, María, listen to me, *mi querida*,[5] but it was she who had to say No, no, we are not of the same class, and remind him it was not his place nor hers to fall in love, while all the while her heart was breaking, can you imagine.

Cleófilas thought her life would have to be like that, like a *telenovela*, only now the episodes got sadder and sadder. And there were no commercials in between for comic relief. And no happy ending in sight. She thought this when she sat with the baby out by the creek behind the house. Celófilas de . . . ? But somehow she would have to change her name to Topazio, or Yesenia, Cristal, Adriana, Stefania, Andrea, something more poetic than Cleófilas. Everything happened to women with names like jewels. But what happened to a Cleófilas? Nothing. But a crack in the face.

Because the doctor has said so. She has to go. To make sure the new baby is all right, so there won't be any problems when he's born, and the appointment card says next Tuesday. Could he please take her. And that's all.

No, she won't mention it. She promises. If the doctor asks she can say she fell down the front steps or slipped when she was out in the backyard, slipped out back, she could tell him that. She has to go back next Tuesday, Juan Pedro, please, for the new baby. For their child.

She could write to her father and ask maybe for money, just a loan, for the new baby's medical expenses. Well then if he'd rather she didn't. All right, she won't. Please don't anymore. Please don't. She knows it's difficult saving money with all the bills they have, but how else are they going to get out of debt with the truck payments? And after the rent and the food and the electricity and the gas and the water and the who-knows-what, well, there's hardly anything left. But please, at least for the doctor visit. She won't ask for anything else. She has to. Why is she so anxious? Because.

Because she is going to make sure the baby is not turned around backward this time to split her down the center. Yes. Next Tuesday at five-thirty. I'll have Juan Pedrito dressed and ready. But those are the only shoes he has. I'll polish them, and we'll be ready. As soon as you come from work. We won't make you ashamed.

Felice? It's me, Graciela.

No, I can't talk louder. I'm at work.

Look, I need kind of a favor. There's a patient, a lady here who's got a problem.

Well, wait a minute. Are you listening to me or what?

I can't talk real loud 'cause her husband's in the next room.

Well, would you just listen?

4. *María of No One* (Spanish), television series produced in Argentina.   5. My love (Spanish).

I was going to do this sonogram on her—she's pregnant, right?—and she just starts crying on me. *Híjole*,[6] Felice! This poor lady's got black-and-blue marks all over. I'm not kidding.

From her husband. Who else? Another one of those brides from across the border. And her family's all in Mexico.

Shit. You think they're going to help her? Give me a break. This lady doesn't even speak English. She hasn't been allowed to call home or write or nothing. That's why I'm calling you.

She needs a ride.

Not to Mexico, you goof. Just to the Greyhound.[7] In San Anto.

No, just a ride. She's got her own money. All you'd have to do is drop her off in San Antonio on your way home. Come on, Felice. Please? If we don't help her, who will? I'd drive her myself, but she needs to be on that bus before her husband gets home from work. What do you say?

I don't know. Wait.

Right away, tomorrow even.

Well, if tomorrow's no good for you . . .

It's a date, Felice. Thursday. At the Cash N Carry[8] off I-10. Noon. She'll be ready.

Oh, and her name's Cleófilas.

I don't know. One of those Mexican saints, I guess. A martyr or something.

Cleófilas. C-L-E-O-F-I-L-A-S. Cle. O. Fi. Las. Write it down.

Thanks, Felice. When her kid's born she'll have to name her after us, right?

Yeah, you got it. A regular soap opera sometimes. *Qué vida, comadre. Bueno*[9] bye.

All morning that flutter of half-fear, half-doubt. At any moment Juan Pedro might appear in the doorway. On the street. At the Cash N Carry. Like in the dreams she dreamed.

There was that to think about, yes, until the woman in the pickup drove up. Then there wasn't time to think about anything but the pickup pointed toward San Antonio. Put your bags in the back and get in.

But when they drove across the *arroyo*, the driver opened her mouth and let out a yell as loud as any mariachi. Which startled not only Cleófilas, but Juan Pedrito as well.

Pues,[1] look how cute. I scared you two, right? Sorry. Should've warned you. Every time I cross that bridge I do that. Because of the name, you know. Woman Hollering. *Pues*, I holler. She said this in a Spanish pocked with English and laughed. Did you ever notice, Felice continued, how nothing around here is named after a woman? Really. Unless she's the Virgin. I guess you're only famous if you're a virgin. She was laughing again.

That's why I like the name of that *arroyo*. Makes you want to holler like Tarzan, right?

Everything about this woman, this Felice, amazed Cleófilas. The fact that she drove a pickup. A pickup, mind you, but when Cleófilas asked if it was her

6. Shoot! or Gee! (Spanish).
7. Long-distance bus line.
8. Retail store.

9. What a life, girlfriend, well (Spanish).
1. Well (Spanish).

husband's, she said she didn't have a husband. The pickup was hers. She herself had chosen it. She herself was paying for it.

I used to have a Pontiac Sunbird.[2] But those cars are for *viejas*.[3] Pussy cars. Now this here is a *real* car.

What kind of talk was that coming from a woman? Cleófilas thought. But then again, Felice was like no woman she'd ever met. Can you imagine, when we crossed the *arroyo* she just started yelling like a crazy, she would say later to her father and brothers. Just like that. Who would've thought?

Who would've? Pain or rage, perhaps, but not a hoot like the one Felice had just let go. Makes you want to holler like Tarzan, Felice had said.

Then Felice began laughing again, but it wasn't Felice laughing. It was gurgling out of her own throat, a long ribbon of laughter, like water.

1991

2. Compact American automobile.   3. Old ladies (Spanish).

LOUISE ERDRICH
b. 1954

Louise Erdrich grew up in the small town of Wahpeton, North Dakota, on the Minnesota border. Her mother was French Chippewa, her maternal grandmother was tribal chairman on the Turtle Mountain Reservation, and both of her parents worked in the Bureau of Indian Affairs boarding school in Wahpeton. She wrote stories as a child, encouraged by her father, who paid her a nickel for each one, but Erdrich's growing up was not marked by a special awareness of her Chippewa background. She has said that she never thought about "what was Native American and what wasn't. . . . There wasn't a political climate at the time about Indian rights." The eldest of seven children, she "grew up just taking it all in as something that was part of me."

In 1972 she entered Dartmouth College, participating in a Native American studies program run by Michael Dorris—himself part American Indian and a writer—whom eventually she would marry (a relationship ending with their separation and his suicide in 1997). In her undergraduate years she won prizes for poetry and fiction and worked at a variety of jobs, such as teaching poetry in prisons, editing a Boston Indian Council newspaper, and flag-signaling on a construction site. After deciding on a career as a writer, she earned an MFA degree at Johns Hopkins, for which degree she submitted a number of poems—later to appear in her collection *Jacklight* (1984)—and part of a novel. There followed the usual sending out of poems and stories, the rejection slips, eventually the acceptances.

Her first novel, *Love Medicine*, which won the National Book Critics Circle award for 1984, began as a short story. Collaborating with her husband, she not only expanded the story but planned the resulting novel as the first of a tetralogy, ranging over different periods of time and focusing on the lives of two Chippewa families. Her interest in the interaction of quirky, passionate, complex individuals—Native American, mixed blood, German American, or Anglo—lies at the center of her fiction.

Successive chapters of *Love Medicine* jump from 1981 to 1934 to 1948, each chapter told through a particular character's point of view (sometimes we see the same event from succeeding points of view). But each individual chapter is more a discrete whole than is the case with a traditional novel, a technique Erdrich uses in many of her novels, including *Tracks* (1988), the second chapter of which was published as the story "Fleur" (printed here). Like many of Erdrich's narratives, *Tracks* draws context from High Plains Dakotas town life, where Anglo and Native American cultures meet (if not mix).

Erdrich's style is easy, offhand, quietly unostentatious, but her language often has an unpredictability and sense of surprise, as in the first paragraph of "The Red Convertible," whose protagonist, Lyman Lamartine, tells us:

> I was the first one to drive a convertible on my reservation. And of course, it was red, a red Olds. I owned that car along with my brother Henry Junior. We owned it together until his boots filled with water on a windy night and he bought out my share. Now Henry owns the whole car, and his younger brother (that's myself) Lyman walks everywhere he goes.

Such clarity and directness are only part of the story, however, since her style also calls upon lyric resources, notable in the following sentence from her second novel, *The Beet Queen*: "After the miraculous sheets of black ice came the floods, stranding boards and snaky knots of debris high in the branches, leaving brown leeches to dry like raisins on the sidewalks when the water receded, and leaving the smell of river mud, a rotten sweetness, in the backyards and gutters."

Native American oral expression does not distinguish between prose and poetry, and like many Native American writers Erdrich works in several forms. "I began as a poet, writing poetry," she has said. "I began to tell stories in poems." The lyrical descriptions in her fiction resemble the language of her poems, and the characterizations and narratives in her poetry resemble those of her fiction. Her most recent poetry collection, *Original Fire* (2003), presents new poems together with work from two earlier collections, *Jacklight* and *Baptism of Fire* (1989). Among the previously published poems are "The Butcher's Wife," which has close affinities in setting and character to her novels, and "The Potchikoo Stories," a group of prose poems about the mythical Potchikoo's life and afterlife. "Grief," a new poem, suggests the traditions of imagist poetry. But in the end such generic distinctions run counter to Erdrich's fusion of storytelling modes.

Like her fiction, Erdrich's poetry sometimes offers realistic accounts of small-town life and sometimes retells mythical stories. "I was Sleeping Where the Black Oaks Move" exemplifies her lyrical description and her mythical imagination. Many of the poems also reflect Erdrich's awareness of the historical and ongoing devastations of Native American life, what she calls in the poem "Dear John Wayne" "the history that brought us all here." Whatever forms her storytelling takes, its linguistic resources and mixture of grief, humor, anger, and tenderness deepen our understanding of the complexities of experience.

Dear John Wayne[1]

August and the drive-in picture is packed.
We lounge on the hood of the Pontiac

---

1. American movie actor (1907–1979) who embodied the image of the strong, taciturn cowboy or soldier, and who in many ways personified the dominant American values of his era. He died of cancer.

surrounded by the slow-burning spirals they sell
at the window, to vanquish the hordes of mosquitoes.
Nothing works. They break through the smoke screen for blood.   5

Always the lookout spots the Indians first,
spread north to south, barring progress.
The Sioux or some other Plains bunch[2]
in spectacular columns, ICBM missiles,[3]
feathers bristling in the meaningful sunset.   10

The drum breaks. There will be no parlance.
Only the arrows whining, a death-cloud of nerves
swarming down on the settlers
who die beautifully, tumbling like dust weeds
into the history that brought us all here   15
together: this wide screen beneath the sign of the bear.

The sky fills, acres of blue squint and eye
that the crowd cheers. His face moves over us,
a thick cloud of vengeance, pitted
like the land that was once flesh. Each rut,   20
each scar makes a promise: *It is
not over, this fight, not as long as you resist.*

Everything we see belongs to us.

A few laughing Indians fall over the hood
slipping in the hot spilled butter.   25
The eye sees a lot, John, but the heart is so blind.
Death makes us owners of nothing.
He smiles, a horizon of teeth
the credits reel over, and then the white fields

again blowing in the true-to-life dark.   30
The dark films over everything.
We get into the car
scratching our mosquito bites, speechless and small
as people are when the movie is done.
We are back in our skins.   35

How can we help but keep hearing his voice,
the flip side of the sound track, still playing:
Come on, boys, we got them
where we want them, drunk, running.
They'll give us what we want, what we need.   40
Even his disease was the idea of taking everything.
Those cells, burning, doubling, splitting out of their skins.

1984

2. The Sioux are a North American Plains Indian people.

3. Intercontinental Ballistic Missiles, developed starting in 1971.

I Was Sleeping Where the Black Oaks Move

We watched from the house
as the river grew, helpless
and terrible in its unfamiliar body.
Wrestling everything into it,
the water wrapped around trees   5
until their life-hold was broken.
They went down, one by one,
and the river dragged off their covering.

Nests of the herons, roots washed to bones,
snags of soaked bark on the shoreline: 10
a whole forest pulled through the teeth
of the spillway. Trees surfacing
singly, where the river poured off
into arteries for fields below the reservation.

When at last it was over, the long removal,   15
they had all become the same dry wood.
We walked among them, the branches
whitening in the raw sun.
Above us drifted herons,
alone, hoarse-voiced, broken,   20
settling their beaks among the hollows.

Grandpa said, *These are the ghosts of the tree people,*
moving above us, unable to take their rest.

Sometimes now, we dream our way back to the heron dance.
Their long wings are bending the air   25
into circles through which they fall.
They rise again in shifting wheels.
How long must we live in the broken figures
their necks make, narrowing the sky.

                                                          1984

Grief

Sometimes you have to take your own hand
as though you were a lost child
and bring yourself stumbling
home over twisted ice.

Whiteness drifts over your house.   5
A page of warm light
falls steady from the open door.

Here is your bed, folded open.
Lie down, lie down, let the blue snow cover you.

2003

Fleur[1]

The first time she drowned in the cold and glassy waters of Lake Turcot, Fleur Pillager was only a girl. Two men saw the boat tip, saw her struggle in the waves. They rowed over to the place she went down, and jumped in. When they dragged her over the gunwales, she was cold to the touch and stiff, so they slapped her face, shook her by the heels, worked her arms back and forth, and pounded her back until she coughed up lake water. She shivered all over like a dog, then took a breath. But it wasn't long afterward that those two men disappeared. The first wandered off and the other, Jean Hat, got himself run over by a cart.

It went to show, my grandma said. It figured to her, all right. By saving Fleur Pillager, those two men had lost themselves.

The next time she fell in the lake, Fleur Pillager was twenty years old and no one touched her. She washed onshore, her skin a dull dead gray, but when George Many Women bent to look closer, he saw her chest move. Then her eyes spun open, sharp black riprock, and she looked at him. "You'll take my place," she hissed. Everybody scattered and left her there, so no one knows how she dragged herself home. Soon after that we noticed Many Women changed, grew afraid, wouldn't leave his house, and would not be forced to go near water. For his caution, he lived until the day that his sons brought him a new tin bathtub. Then the first time he used the tub he slipped, got knocked out, and breathed water while his wife stood in the other room frying breakfast.

Men stayed clear of Fleur Pillager after the second drowning. Even though she was good-looking, nobody dared to court her because it was clear that Misshepeshu, the waterman, the monster, wanted her for himself. He's a devil, that one, love-hungry with desire and maddened for the touch of young girls, the strong and daring especially, the ones like Fleur.

Our mothers warn us that we'll think he's handsome, for he appears with green eyes, copper skin, a mouth tender as a child's. But if you fall into his arms, he sprouts horns, fangs, claws, fins. His feet are joined as one and his skin, brass scales, rings to the touch. You're fascinated, cannot move. He casts a shell necklace at your feet, weeps gleaming chips that harden into mica on your breasts. He holds you under. Then he takes the body of a lion or a fat brown worm. He's made of gold. He's made of beach moss. He's a thing of dry foam, a thing of death by drowning, the death a Chippewa cannot survive.

Unless you are Fleur Pillager. We all knew she couldn't swim. After the first time, we thought she'd never go back to Lake Turcot. We thought she'd keep to herself, live quiet, stop killing men off by drowning in the lake.

1. First published in *Esquire* magazine, August 1986.

After the first time, we thought she'd keep the good ways. But then, after the second drowning, we knew that we were dealing with something much more serious. She was haywire, out of control. She messed with evil, laughed at the old women's advice, and dressed like a man. She got herself into some half-forgotten medicine, studied ways we shouldn't talk about. Some say she kept the finger of a child in her pocket and a powder of unborn rabbits in a leather thong around her neck. She laid the heart of an owl on her tongue so she could see at night, and went out, hunting, not even in her own body. We know for sure because the next morning, in the snow or dust, we followed the tracks of her bare feet and saw where they changed, where the claws sprang out, the pad broadened and pressed into the dirt. By night we heard her chuffing cough, the bear cough. By day her silence and the wide grin she threw to bring down our guard made us frightened. Some thought that Fleur Pillager should be driven off the reservation, but not a single person who spoke like this had the nerve. And finally, when people were just about to get together and throw her out, she left on her own and didn't come back all summer. That's what this story is about.

During that summer, when she lived a few miles south in Argus, things happened. She almost destroyed that town.

When she got down to Argus in the year of 1920, it was just a small grid of six streets on either side of the railroad depot. There were two elevators, one central, the other a few miles west. Two stores competed for the trade of the three hundred citizens, and three churches quarreled with one another for their souls. There was a frame building for Lutherans, a heavy brick one for Episcopalians, and a long narrow shingled Catholic church. This last had a tall slender steeple, twice as high as any building or tree.

No doubt, across the low, flat wheat, watching from the road as she came near Argus on foot, Fleur saw that steeple rise, a shadow thin as a needle. Maybe in that raw space it drew her the way a lone tree draws lightning. Maybe, in the end, the Catholics are to blame. For if she hadn't seen that sign of pride, that slim prayer, that marker, maybe she would have kept walking.

But Fleur Pillager turned, and the first place she went once she came into town was to the back door of the priest's residence attached to the landmark church. She didn't go there for a handout, although she got that, but to ask for work. She got that too, or the town got her. It's hard to tell which came out worse, her or the men or the town, although the upshot of it all was that Fleur lived.

The four men who worked at the butcher's had carved up about a thousand carcasses between them, maybe half of that steers and the other half pigs, sheep, and game animals like deer, elk, and bear. That's not even mentioning the chickens, which were beyond counting. Pete Kozka owned the place, and employed Lily Veddar, Tor Grunewald, and my stepfather, Dutch James, who had brought my mother down from the reservation the year before she disappointed him by dying. Dutch took me out of school to take her place. I kept house half the time and worked the other in the butcher shop, sweeping floors, putting sawdust down, running a hambone across the street to a customer's bean pot or a package of sausage to the corner. I was a good one to have around because until they needed me, I was invisible. I blended into the stained brown walls, a skinny, big-nosed girl with staring eyes. Because I could fade into a corner or squeeze beneath a shelf, I knew everything, what the men said when no one was around, and what they did to Fleur.

Kozka's Meats served farmers for a fifty-mile area, both to slaughter, for it had a stock pen and chute, and to cure the meat by smoking it or spicing it in sausage. The storage locker was a marvel, made of many thicknesses of brick, earth insulation, and Minnesota timber, lined inside with sawdust and vast blocks of ice cut from Lake Turcot, hauled down from home each winter by horse and sledge.

A ramshackle board building, part slaughterhouse, part store, was fixed to the low, thick square of the lockers. That's where Fleur worked. Kozka hired her for her strength. She could lift a haunch or carry a pole of sausages without stumbling, and she soon learned cutting from Pete's wife, a string-thin blonde who chain-smoked and handled the razor-edged knives with nerveless precision, slicing close to her stained fingers. Fleur and Fritzie Kozka worked afternoons, wrapping their cuts in paper, and Fleur hauled the packages to the lockers. The meat was left outside the heavy oak doors that were only opened at 5:00 each afternoon, before the men ate supper.

Sometimes Dutch, Tor, and Lily stayed at the lockers, and when they did I stayed too, cleaned floors, restoked the fires in the front smokehouses, while the men sat around the squat cast-iron stove spearing slats of herring onto hardtack bread. They played long games of poker or cribbage on a board made from the planed end of a salt crate. They talked and I listened, although there wasn't much to hear since almost nothing ever happened in Argus. Tor was married, Dutch had lost my mother, and Lily read circulars. They mainly discussed about the auctions to come, equipment, or women.

Every so often, Pete Kozka came out front to make a whist, leaving Fritzie to smoke cigarettes and fry raised doughnuts in the back room. He sat and played a few rounds but kept his thoughts to himself. Fritzie did not tolerate him talking behind her back, and the one book he read was the New Testament. If he said something, it concerned weather or a surplus of sheep stomachs, a ham that smoked green or the markets for corn and wheat. He had a good-luck talisman, the opal-white lens of a cow's eye. Playing cards, he rubbed it between his fingers. That soft sound and the slap of cards was about the only conversation.

Fleur finally gave them a subject.

Her cheeks were wide and flat, her hands large, chapped, muscular. Fleur's shoulders were broad as beams, her hips fishlike, slippery, narrow. An old green dress clung to her waist, worn thin where she sat. Her braids were thick like the tails of animals, and swung against her when she moved, deliberately, slowly in her work, held in and half-tamed, but only half. I could tell, but the others never saw. They never looked into her sly brown eyes or noticed her teeth, strong and sharp and very white. Her legs were bare, and since she padded in beadworked moccasins they never saw that her fifth toes were missing. They never knew she'd drowned. They were blinded, they were stupid, they only saw her in the flesh.

And yet it wasn't just that she was a Chippewa, or even that she was a woman, it wasn't that she was good-looking or even that she was alone that made their brains hum. It was how she played cards.

Women didn't usually play with men, so the evening that Fleur drew a chair to the men's table without being so much as asked, there was a shock of surprise.

"What's this," said Lily. He was fat, with a snake's cold pale eyes and precious skin, smooth and lily-white, which is how he got his name. Lily had a dog, a stumpy mean little bull of a thing with a belly drum-tight from eating pork rinds. The dog liked to play cards just like Lily, and straddled his barrel thighs through games of stud, rum poker, vingt-un.[2] The dog snapped at Fleur's arm that first night, but cringed back, its snarl frozen, when she took her place.

"I thought," she said, her voice soft and stroking, "you might deal me in."

There was a space between the heavy bin of spiced flour and the wall where I just fit. I hunkered down there, kept my eyes open, saw her black hair swing over the chair, her feet solid on the wood floor. I couldn't see up on the table where the cards slapped down, so after they were deep in their game I raised myself up in the shadows, and crouched on a sill of wood.

I watched Fleur's hands stack and ruffle, divide the cards, spill them to each player in a blur, rake them up and shuffle again. Tor, short and scrappy, shut one eye and squinted the other at Fleur. Dutch screwed his lips around a wet cigar.

"Gotta see a man," he mumbled, getting up to go out back to the privy. The others broke, put their cards down, and Fleur sat alone in the lamplight that glowed in a sheen across the push of her breasts. I watched her closely, then she paid me a beam of notice for the first time. She turned, looked straight at me, and grinned the white wolf grin a Pillager turns on its victims, except that she wasn't after me.

"Pauline there," she said. "How much money you got?"

We had all been paid for the week that day. Eight cents was in my pocket.

"Stake me," she said, holding out her long fingers. I put the coins in her palm and then I melted back to nothing, part of the walls and tables. It was a long time before I understood that the men would not have seen me no matter what I did, how I moved. I wasn't anything like Fleur. My dress hung loose and my back was already curved, an old woman's. Work had roughened me, reading made my eyes sore, caring for my mother before she died had hardened my face. I was not much to look at, so they never saw me.

When the men came back and sat around the table, they had drawn together. They shot each other small glances, stuck their tongues in their cheeks, burst out laughing at odd moments, to rattle Fleur. But she never minded. They played their vingt-un, staying even as Fleur slowly gained. Those pennies I had given her drew nickels and attracted dimes until there was a small pile in front of her.

Then she hooked them with five card draw, nothing wild. She dealt, discarded, drew, and then she sighed and her cards gave a little shiver. Tor's eye gleamed, and Dutch straightened in his seat.

"I'll pay to see that hand," said Lily Veddar.

Fleur showed, and she had nothing there, nothing at all.

Tor's thin smile cracked open, and he threw his hand in too.

---

2. Twenty-one (French); a card game.

"Well, we know one thing," he said, leaning back in his chair, "the squaw can't bluff."

With that I lowered myself into a mound of swept sawdust and slept. I woke up during the night, but none of them had moved yet, so I couldn't either. Still later, the men must have gone out again, or Fritzie come out to break the game, because I was lifted, soothed, cradled in a woman's arms and rocked so quiet that I kept my eyes shut while Fleur rolled me into a closet of grimy ledgers, oiled paper, balls of string, and thick files that fit beneath me like a mattress.

The game went on after work the next evening. I got my eight cents back five times over, and Fleur kept the rest of the dollar she'd won for a stake. This time they didn't play so late, but they played regular, and then kept going at it night after night. They played poker now, or variations, for one week straight, and each time Fleur won exactly one dollar, no more and no less, too consistent for luck.

By this time, Lily and the other men were so lit with suspense that they got Pete to join the game with them. They concentrated, the fat dog sitting tense in Lily Veddar's lap, Tor suspicious, Dutch stroking his huge square brow, Pete steady. It wasn't that Fleur won that hooked them in so, because she lost hands too. It was rather that she never had a freak hand or even anything above a straight. She only took on her low cards, which didn't sit right. By chance, Fleur should have gotten a full or a flush by now. The irritating thing was she beat with pairs and never bluffed, because she couldn't, and still she ended each night with exactly one dollar. Lily couldn't believe, first of all, that a woman could be smart enough to play cards, but even if she was, that she would then be stupid enough to cheat for a dollar a night. By day I watched him turn the problem over, his hard white face dull, small fingers probing at his knuckles, until he finally thought he had Fleur figured as a bit-time player, caution her game. Raising the stakes would throw her.

More than anything now, he wanted Fleur to come away with something but a dollar. Two bits less or ten more, the sum didn't matter, just so he broke her streak.

Night after night she played, won her dollar, and left to stay in a place that just Fritzie and I knew about. Fleur bathed in the slaughtering tub, then slept in the unused brick smokehouse behind the lockers, a windowless place tarred on the inside with scorched fats. When I brushed against her skin I noticed that she smelled of the walls, rich and woody, slightly burnt. Since that night she put me in the closet I was no longer afraid of her, but followed her close, stayed with her, became her moving shadow that the men never noticed, the shadow that could have saved her.

August, the month that bears fruit, closed around the shop, and Pete and Fritzie left for Minnesota to escape the heat. Night by night, running, Fleur had won thirty dollars, and only Pete's presence had kept Lily at bay. But Pete was gone now, and one payday, with the heat so bad no one could move but Fleur, the men sat and played and waited while she finished work. The cards sweat, limp in their fingers, the table was slick with grease, and even the walls were warm to the touch. The air was motionless. Fleur was in the next room boiling heads.

Her green dress, drenched, wrapped her like a transparent sheet. A skin of lakeweed. Black snarls of veining clung to her arms. Her braids were loose, half unraveled, tied behind her neck in a thick loop. She stood in steam, turning skulls through a vat with a wooden paddle. When scraps boiled to the surface, she bent with a round tin sieve and scooped them out. She'd filled two dishpans.

"Ain't that enough now?" called Lily. "We're waiting." The stump of a dog trembled in his lap, alive with rage. It never smelled me or noticed me above Fleur's smoky skin. The air was heavy in my corner, and pressed me down. Fleur sat with them.

"Now what do you say?" Lily asked the dog. It barked. That was the signal for the real game to start.

"Let's up the ante," said Lily, who had been stalking this night all month. He had a roll of money in his pocket. Fleur had five bills in her dress. The men had each saved their full pay.

"Ante a dollar then," said Fleur, and pitched hers in. She lost, but they let her scrape along, cent by cent. And then she won some. She played unevenly, as if chance were all she had. She reeled them in. The game went on. The dog was stiff now, poised on Lily's knees, a ball of vicious muscle with its yellow eyes slit in concentration. It gave advice, seemed to sniff the lay of Fleur's cards, twitched and nudged. Fleur was up, then down, saved by a scratch. Tor dealt seven cards, three down. The pot grew, round by round, until it held all the money. Nobody folded. Then it all rode on one last card and they went silent. Fleur picked hers up and drew a long breath. The heat lowered like a bell. Her card shook, but she stayed in.

Lily smiled and took the dog's head tenderly between his palms. "Say Fatso," he said, crooning the words. "You reckon that girl's bluffing?"

The dog whined and Lily laughed. "Me too," he said, "let's show." He swept his bills and coins into the pot and then they turned their cards over.

Lily looked once, looked again, then he squeezed the dog like a fist of dough and slammed it on the table.

Fleur threw out her arms and drew the money over, grinning that same wolf grin that she'd used on me, the grin that had them. She jammed the bills in her dress, scooped the coins up in waxed white paper that she tied with string.

"Let's go another round," said Lily, his voice choked with burrs. But Fleur opened her mouth and yawned, then walked out back to gather slops for the one big hog that was waiting in the stock pen to be killed.

The men sat still as rocks, their hands spread on the oiled wood table. Dutch had chewed his cigar to damp shreds, Tor's eye was dull. Lily's gaze was the only one to follow Fleur. I didn't move. I felt them gathering, saw my stepfather's veins, the ones in his forehead that stood out in anger. The dog rolled off the table and curled in a knot below the counter, where none of the men could touch it.

Lily rose and stepped out back to the closet of ledgers where Pete kept his private stock. He brought back a bottle, uncorked and tipped it between his fingers. The lump in his throat moved, then he passed it on. They drank, quickly felt the whiskey's fire, and planned with their eyes things they couldn't say aloud.

When they left, I followed. I hid out back in the clutter of broken boards and chicken crates beside the stock pen, where they waited. Fleur could not be seen at first, and then the moon broke and showed her, slipping cautiously along the rough board chute with a bucket in her hand. Her hair fell, wild and coarse, to her waist, and her dress was a floating patch in the dark. She made a pig-calling sound, rang the tin pail lightly against the wood, froze suspiciously. But too late. In the sound of the ring Lily moved, fat and nimble, stepped right behind Fleur and put out his creamy hands. At his first touch, she whirled and doused him with the bucket of sour slops. He pushed her against the big fence and the package of coins split, went clinking and jumping, winked against the wood. Fleur rolled over once and vanished into the yard.

The moon fell behind a curtain of ragged clouds, and Lily followed into the dark muck. But he tripped, pitched over the huge flank of the pig, who lay mired to the snout, heavily snoring. I sprang out of the weeds and climbed the side of the pen, stuck like glue. I saw the sow rise to her neat, knobby knees, gain her balance and sway, curious, as Lily stumbled forward. Fleur had backed into the angle of rough wood just beyond, and when Lily tried to jostle past, the sow tipped up on her hind legs and struck, quick and hard as a snake. She plunged her head into Lily's thick side and snatched a mouthful of his shirt. She lunged again, caught him lower, so that he grunted in pained surprise. He seemed to ponder, breathing deep. Then he launched his huge body in a swimmer's dive.

The sow screamed as his body smacked over hers. She rolled, striking out with her knife-sharp hooves, and Lily gathered himself upon her, took her foot-long face by the ears and scraped her snout and cheeks against the trestles of the pen. He hurled the sow's tight skull against an iron post, but instead of knocking her dead, he merely woke her from her dream.

She reared, shrieked, drew him with her so that they posed standing upright. They bowed jerkily to each other, as if to begin. Then his arms swung and flailed. She sank her black fangs into his shoulder, clasping him, dancing him forward and backward through the pen. Their steps picked up pace, went wild. The two dipped as one, box-stepped, tripped one another. She ran her split foot through his hair. He grabbed her kinked tail. They went down and came up, the same shape and then the same color until the men couldn't tell one from the other in that light and Fleur was able to launch herself over the gates, swing down, hit gravel.

The men saw, yelled, and chased her at a dead run to the smokehouse. And Lily too, once the sow gave up in disgust and freed him. That is where I should have gone to Fleur, saved her, thrown myself on Dutch. But I went stiff with fear and couldn't unlatch myself from the trestles or move at all. I closed my eyes and put my head in my arms, tried to hide, so there is nothing to describe but what I couldn't block out, Fleur's hoarse breath, so loud it filled me, her cry in the old language, and my name repeated over and over among the words.

The heat was still dense the next morning when I came back to work. Fleur was gone but the men were there, slack-faced, hung over. Lily was paler and softer than ever, as if his flesh had steamed on his bones. They smoked, took pulls off a bottle. It wasn't noon yet. I worked awhile, waiting shop and sharp-ening steel. But I was sick, I was smothered, I was sweating so hard that my hands slipped on the knives, and I wiped my fingers clean of the greasy touch of the customers' coins. Lily opened his mouth and roared once, not in anger. There was no meaning to the sound. His boxer dog, sprawled limp beside his foot, never lifted its head. Nor did the other men.

They didn't notice when I stepped outside, hoping for a clear breath. And then I forgot them because I knew that we were all balanced, ready to tip, to fly, to be crushed as soon as the weather broke. The sky was so low that I felt the weight of it like a yoke. Clouds hung down, witch teats, a tornado's green-brown cones, and as I watched one flicked out and became a delicate probing thumb. Even as I picked up my heels and ran back inside, the wind blew suddenly, cold, and then came rain.

Inside, the men had disappeared already and the whole place was trembling as if a huge hand was pinched at the rafters, shaking it. I ran straight through, screaming for Dutch or for any of them, and then I stopped at the heavy doors of the lockers, where they had surely taken shelter. I stood there a moment. Everything went still. Then I heard a cry building in the wind, faint at first, a whistle and then a shrill scream that tore through the walls and gathered around me, spoke plain so I understood that I should move, put my arms out, and slam down the great iron bar that fit across the hasp and lock.

Outside, the wind was stronger, like a hand held against me. I struggled forward. The bushes tossed, the awnings flapped off storefronts, the rails of porches rattled. The odd cloud became a fat snout that nosed along the earth and sniffled, jabbed, picked at things, sucked them up, blew them apart, rooted around as if it was following a certain scent, then stopped behind me at the butcher shop and bored down like a drill.

I went flying, landed somewhere in a ball. When I opened my eyes and looked, stranger things were happening.

A herd of cattle flew through the air like giant birds, dropping dung, their mouths opened in stunned bellows. A candle, still lighted, blew past, and tables, napkins, garden tools, a whole school of drifting eyeglasses, jackets on hangers, hams, a checkerboard, a lampshade, and at last the sow from behind the lockers, on the run, her hooves a blur, set free, swooping, diving, screaming as everything in Argus fell apart and got turned upside down, smashed, and thoroughly wrecked.

Days passed before the town went looking for the men. They were bache-lors, after all, except for Tor, whose wife had suffered a blow to the head that made her forgetful. Everyone was occupied with digging out, in high relief because even though the Catholic steeple had been torn off like a peaked cap and sent across five fields, those huddled in the cellar were unhurt. Walls had fallen, windows were demolished, but the stores were intact and so were the bankers and shop owners who had taken refuge in their safes or beneath their cash registers. It was a fair-minded disaster, no one could be said to have suffered much more than the next, at least not until Pete and Fritzie came home.

Of all the businesses in Argus, Kozka's Meats had suffered worst. The boards of the front building had been split to kindling, piled in a huge pyramid, and the shop equipment was blasted far and wide. Pete paced off the distance the iron bathtub had been flung—a hundred feet. The glass candy case went fifty, and landed without so much as a cracked pane. There were other surprises as well, for the back rooms where Fritzie and Pete lived were undisturbed. Fritzie said the dust still coated her china figures, and upon her kitchen table, in the ashtray, perched the last cigarette she'd put out in haste. She lit and finished it, looking through the window. From there, she could see that the old smokehouse Fleur had slept in was crushed to a reddish sand and the stockpens were completely torn apart, the rails stacked helter-skelter. Fritzie asked for Fleur. People shrugged. Then she asked about the others and, suddenly, the town understood that three men were missing.

There was a rally of help, a gathering of shovels and volunteers. We passed boards from hand to hand, stacked them, uncovered what lay beneath the pile of jagged splinters. The lockers, full of meat that was Pete and Fritzie's investment, slowly came into sight, still intact. When enough room was made for a man to stand on the roof, there were calls, a general urge to hack through and see what lay below. But Fritzie shouted that she wouldn't allow it because the meat would spoil. And so the work continued, board by board, until at last the heavy oak doors of the freezer were revealed and people pressed to the entry. Everyone wanted to be the first, but since it was my stepfather lost, I was let go in when Pete and Fritzie wedged through into the sudden icy air.

Pete scraped a match on his boot, lit the lamp Fritzie held, and then the three of us stood still in its circle. Light glared off the skinned and hanging carcasses, the crates of wrapped sausages, the bright and cloudy blocks of lake ice, pure as winter. The cold bit into us, pleasant at first, then numbing. We must have stood there a couple of minutes before we saw the men, or more rightly, the humps of fur, the iced and shaggy hides they wore, the bearskins they had taken down and wrapped about themselves. We stepped closer and Fritzie tilted the lantern beneath the flaps of fur into their faces. The dog was there, perched among them, heavy as a doorstop. The three had hunched around a barrel where the game was still laid out, and a dead lantern and an empty bottle too. But they had thrown down their last hands and hunkered tight, clutching one another, knuckles raw from beating at the door they had also attacked with hooks. Frost stars gleamed off their eyelashes and the stubble of their beards. Their faces were set in concentration, mouths open as if to speak some careful thought, some agreement they'd come to in each other's arms.

Power travels in the bloodlines, handed out before birth. It comes down through the hands, which in the Pillagers were strong and knotted, big, spidery, and rough, with sensitive fingertips good at dealing cards. It comes through the eyes, too, belligerent, darkest brown, the eyes of those in the bear clan, impolite as they gaze directly at a person.

In my dreams, I look straight back at Fleur, at the men. I am no longer the watcher on the dark sill, the skinny girl.

The blood draws us back, as if it runs through a vein of earth. I've come home and, except for talking to my cousins, live a quiet life. Fleur lives quiet too, down on Lake Turcot with her boat. Some say she's married to the waterman, Misshepeshu, or that she's living in shame with white men or windigos, or that she's killed them all. I'm about the only one here who ever goes to visit her. Last winter, I went to help out in her cabin when she bore the child, whose green eyes and skin the color of an old penny made more talk, as no one could decide if the child was mixed blood or what, fathered in a smokehouse, or by a man with brass scales, or by the lake. The girl is bold, smiling in her sleep, as if she knows what people wonder, as if she hears the old men talk, turning the story over. It comes up different every time and has no ending, no beginning. They get the middle wrong too. They only know they don't know anything.

1988

LORNA DEE CERVANTES
b. 1954

In "Visions of Mexico While at a Writing Symposium in Port Townsend, Washington" Lorna Dee Cervantes imagines herself in transit, like the seabirds in her poem who "elbow their wings / in migratory ways" between north and south, Washington and Mexico. The image of migration appears frequently in her book *Emplumada* (1981), where it suggests the larger social patterns that characterize Latino history. But Cervantes's identification with the "migratory ways" of birds is also personal. "At heart I'm a hoverer," she writes in "Como lo Siento," and her poems often hover in the space between worlds, in the gap between her sense of social need and her own desires. In *Emplumada* (the title is derived from the Spanish word that means both "feathered" and "made by the stroke of a pen"), the poet confronts and sometimes bridges divisions in herself and in her landscape, her native California crisscrossed by the freeway. Her second book, *From the Cables of Genocide* (1991), extends that landscape to the nation at large and has an angry energy animated by "love and hunger," in a phrase from the book's subtitle. In 2006 she published an ambitious new collection, *Drive: The First Quartet (New Poems 1980–2005)*, inspired by T. S. Eliot's exploration of time in "Burnt Norton," the first of his *Four Quartets* (1943).

In her self-defined role as "scribe" in her "woman family" ("Beneath the Shadow of the Freeway"), Cervantes mediates a written tradition largely male and North American ("books, those staunch, upright men") and the Mexican oral traditions embodied by her grandmother. Transcribing the oral into the written, Cervantes negotiates forms of understanding: the ring around the moon in her poem "The Body as Braille" is both what her grandmother calls "'A witch's moon,' / dijo mi abuela" and what the schools define as "a reflection of ice crystals." Experiencing these separate forms of perception, she fuses them in her own powerful metaphor: "It's a storm brewing in the cauldron / of the sky."

Cervantes was born in San Francisco and has lived in California most of her life. She graduated from San José State University and has studied at the University of California at Santa Cruz. For several years she edited and published *Mango*, a small-press journal in which the work of Latino poets (many of whom identified themselves socially and politically with the Chicano movement) appeared, and she served as coeditor of *Red Dirt*, a cross-cultural poetry journal. She wrote a number of the poems in *Emplumada* while she was a fellow in poetry at the Fine Arts Work Center in Provincetown, Massachusetts. Like several other important Latino poets (Alberto Ríos, Ricardo Sanchez, Bernice Zamora) she employs Spanish phrases and lines in her poems to represent her double heritage and to underscore the difficulty of rendering the experiences of one cultural tradition in the language of another. Words are her craft and her weapon as well, as the epigraph from Antonio Porchia, which opens the second section of her first book, suggests: "This world understands nothing but words / and you have come into it with almost none." Although the ambiguous tone in some of her poems suggests an uncertain degree of distance from her experience, the intensity of feeling in her work is undeniable.

Uncle's First Rabbit

He was a good boy
making his way through
the Santa Barbara[1] pines,
sighting the blast of fluff
as he leveled the rifle,   5
and the terrible singing began.
He was ten years old,
hunting my grandpa's supper.
He had dreamed of running,
shouldering the rifle to town,   10
selling it, and taking the next
train out.
      Fifty years
have passed and he still hears
that rabbit "just like a baby."   15
He remembers how the rabbit
stopped keening under the butt
of his rifle, how he brought
it home with tears streaming
down his blood soaked jacket.   20
"That bastard. That bastard."
He cried all night and the week
after, remembering that voice
like his dead baby sister's,
remembering his father's drunken   25
kicking that had pushed her
into birth. She had a voice
like that, growing faint
at its end; his mother rocking,
softly, keening. He dreamed   30
of running, running
the bastard out of his life.
He would forget them, run down
the hill, leave his mother's
silent waters, and the sounds   35
of beating night after night.

1. City and county in southern California.

When war came,
he took the man's vow. He was
finally leaving and taking
the bastard's last bloodline   40
with him. At war's end, he could
still hear her, her soft
body stiffening under water
like a shark's. The color
of the water, darkening, soaking,   45
as he clung to what was left
of a ship's gun. Ten long hours
off the coast of Okinawa,[2] he sang
so he wouldn't hear them.
He pounded their voices out   50
of his head, and awakened
to find himself slugging the bloodied
face of his wife.
           Fifty years
have passed and he has not run   55
the way he dreamed. The Paradise
pines shadow the bleak hills
to his home. His hunting hounds,
dead now. His father, long dead.
His wife, dying, hacking in the bed   60
she has not let him enter for the last
thirty years. He stands looking,
he mouths the words, "Die you bitch.
I'll live to watch you die." He turns,
entering their moss-soft livingroom.   65
He watches out the picture window
and remembers running: how he'll
take the new pickup to town, sell it,
and get the next train out.

                            1981

For Virginia Chavez

It was never in the planning,
in the life we thought
we'd live together, two fast
women living cheek to cheek,
still tasting the dog's   5
breath of boys in our testy
new awakening.
We were never the way
they had it planned.

---

2. One of the southernmost islands of Japan, scene of fierce World War II fighting between the United States and Japan in the spring of 1945.

Their wordless tongues we stole   10
and tasted the power
that comes of that.
We were never what they wanted
but we were bold. We could take
something of life and not   15
give it back. We could utter
the rules, mark the lines
and cross them ourselves—we two
women using our fists, we thought,
our wits, our tunnels. They were such   20
dumb hunks of warm fish
swimming inside us,
but this was love,
we knew, love, and that was all
we were ever offered.   25

You were always alone
so *another lonely life*
wouldn't matter.
In the still house
your mother left you,   30
when the men were gone
and the television droned
into test patterns, with our cups
of your mother's whiskey
balanced between the brown thighs   35
creeping out of our shorts, I read
you the poems of Lord Byron, Donne,
the Brownings:[1] all about love,
explaining the words
before realizing that you knew   40
all that the kicks in your belly
had to teach you. You were proud
of the woman blooming out of your
fourteen lonely years, but you cried
when you read that poem I wrote you,   45
something about our "waning moons"
and the child in me
I let die that summer.

In the years that separate,
in the tongues that divide   50
and conquer, in the love
that was a language
in itself, you never spoke,
never regret. Even
that last morning   55
I saw you with blood

---

1. George Gordon, Lord Byron (1788–1824); John Donne (1572–1631); Elizabeth Barrett Browning (1806–1861) and Robert Browning (1812–1899)—English poets famed for writing about love.

in your eyes, blood
on your mouth, the blood
pushing out of you
in purple blossoms.   60

He did this.
When I woke, the kids
were gone. They told me
I'd never get them back.

With our arms holding   65
each other's waists, we walked
the waking streets
back to your empty flat,
ignoring the horns and catcalls
behind us, ignoring what   70
the years had brought between us:
my diploma and the bare bulb
that always lit your bookless room.

                                                      1981

Visions of Mexico While at a Writing Symposium in Port Townsend, Washington

México

When I'm that far south, the old words
molt off my skin, the feathers
of all my nervousness.
My own words somersault naturally as my name,
joyous among all those meadows: Michoacán,   5
Vera Cruz, Tenochtitlán, Oaxaca[1] . . .
Pueblos green on the low hills
where men slap handballs below acres of maíz.[2]
I watch and understand.
My frail body has never packed mud   10
or gathered in the full weight of the harvest.
Alone with the women in the adobe,[3] I watch men,
their taut faces holding in all their youth.
This far south we are governed by the law
of the next whole meal. We work   15
and watch seabirds elbow their wings
in migratory ways, those mispronouncing gulls
coming south
to refuge or gameland.

1. Mexican states, except for Tenochtitlán, which is the ancient name for Mexico City.
2. "Corn" [Cervantes's note]. "Pueblos": commu-nal dwellings.
3. I.e., in a house made of sun-dried earth and straw.

I don't want to pretend I know more   20
and can speak all the names. I can't.
My sense of this land can only ripple through my veins
like the chant of an epic corrido.[4]
I come from a long line of eloquent illiterates
whose history reveals what words don't say.   25
Our anger is our way of speaking,
the gesture is an utterance more pure than word.
We are not animals
but our senses are keen and our reflexes,
accurate punctuation.   30
All the knifings in a single night, low-voiced
scufflings, sirens, gunnings . . .
We hear them
and the poet within us bays.

Washington

I don't belong this far north.   35
The uncomfortable birds gawk at me.
They hem and haw from their borders in the sky.
I heard them say: México is a stumbling comedy.
A loose-legged Cantinflas woman
acting with Pancho Villa[5] drunkenness.   40
Last night at the tavern
this was all confirmed
in a painting of a woman: her glowing
silk skin, a halo
extending from her golden coiffure   45
while around her, dark-skinned men with Jap slant eyes
were drooling in a caricature of machismo.[6]
Below it, at the bar, two Chicanas
hung at their beers. They had painted black
birds that dipped beneath their eyelids.   50
They were still as foam while the men
fiddled with their asses, absently;
the bubbles of their teased hair snapped
open in the forced wind of the beating fan.
There are songs in my head I could sing you   55
songs that could drone away
all the Mariachi bands[7] you thought you ever heard
songs that could tell you what I know
or have learned from my people
but for that   I need words   60
simple black nymphs between white sheets of paper
obedient words   obligatory words   words I steal
in the dark when no one can hear me

---

4. An epic Mexican ballad [Cervantes's note].
5. A Mexican bandit and revolutionary leader (1878–1923). "Cantinflas—a Mexican comedian similar to Charlie Chaplin" [Cervantes's note].
6. Masculinity; macho [Cervantes's note].
7. Traditional Mexican street bands.

as pain sends seabirds south from the cold
I come north   65
to gather my feathers
for quills

1981

The Body as Braille

He tells me "Your back
is so beautiful." He traces
my spine with his hand.

I'm burning like the white ring
around the moon. "A witch's moon,"   5
dijo mi abuela.[1] The schools call it

"a reflection of ice crystals."
It's a storm brewing in the cauldron
of the sky. I'm in love

but won't tell him   10
if it's omens
or ice.

1981

1. My grandmother told me [Cervantes's note].

CATHY SONG
b. 1955

In many of Cathy Song's poems a particular moment or event becomes a window
through which we enter a field of vision. "What frames the view," she has written, "is the mind in the diamond pinpoint light of concentration tunneling into
memory, released by the imagination." As the title of her second book, *Frameless
Windows, Squares of Light*, suggests, Song's poems capture the way a warm afternoon, a childhood Easter, a picnic in the park is an opening for memory and reflection. The visual quality of her poems can suggest a photograph or painting, and Song
feels a connection between her work and those of the Japanese printmaker Kitagawa
Utamaro and the American painter Georgia O'Keeffe. Song's first book, *Picture
Bride* (1983), contains a number of poems inspired by the work of these artists. Writing, in "Beauty and Sadness," of the way Utamaro's prints rendered "Teahouse waitresses, actresses, / geishas, courtesans and maids" in "their fleeting loveliness," Song

suggests that the artist and poet capture the moment, knowing that it is always dissolving.

Picture Bride was chosen by the poet Richard Hugo for the Yale Younger Poets series. In the title poem Song comes as close as imagination allows to the experience of her grandmother, who, the poem implies, was chosen as a bride from a photograph and summoned from Korea to Hawaii. But Song is also aware of the limits of imaginative identification and the difficulty of knowing the full truth of the past. She respects the mystery of another's identity. The grandmother in "Picture Bride," the woman in "Lost Sister," the mother in "Humble Jar," and the geishas painted by Utamaro possess a privacy that the poet discloses but cannot fully enter. Song's tactful sense of both the power and the limits of imagination is one of her distinctive marks as a poet.

She was born in Honolulu, Hawaii, and grew up in Wahiawa, a small town on the island of Oahu. The setting of sugar-cane fields, of island life where "the sound of the ocean / could be heard through the ironwoods" ("Waialaua"), and of the rain that comes "even when the sun was shining" ("A Pale Arrangement of Hands") is central to her work. That landscape belongs to her present but also evokes her childhood and the memory of another, more distant landscape—the Asia of her ancestors. Many of Song's poems render the mysteries of what she has called "familial and personal ties; lives overlapping," and her sense of these ties extends backward to her Chinese and Korean ancestors as well as forward to her children. She began her college education at the University of Hawaii and then attended Wellesley College. After her graduation from Wellesley, she received an M.A. in creative writing from Boston University and has since taught creative writing at a number of colleges and universities. Her third collection of poems, *School Figures*, appeared in 1994 followed by *The Land of Bliss* (2001) and *Cloud-Moving Hands* (2007).

Song's ability to write about her own or another's experience as an acute observer may have to do with her multicultural background, which often places her on the boundary of what she sees. Her capacity to let the power of observation give rise to feeling recalls at times the work of Elizabeth Bishop and also suggests Song's resemblance to the Utamaro of her poem "Beauty and Sadness," whose "invisible presence / one feels in these prints." At other times Song writes about herself more directly. She has, for example, deftly rendered the erotic nature of her own experience: "But there is this slow arousal. / The small buttons / of my cotton blouse / are pulling away from my body" ("The White Porch"). The careful composition of her poems, with their vivid detail, blend the accidental and spontaneous quality of life with the design of art. Although her work can sometimes seem too composed, too removed from the sharp impact of experience, her strongest poems balance a sense of tradition with a feel for contemporary life and catch in the patterns of art the transient instant: "the flicker of a dragonfly's delicate wing."

The White Porch

I wrap the blue towel
after washing,
around the damp
weight of hair, bulky
as a sleeping cat,   5
and sit out on the porch.
Still dripping water,
it'll be dry by supper,
by the time the dust
settles off your shoes,   10

though it's only five
past noon. Think
of the luxury: how to use
the afternoon like the stretch
of lawn spread before me.   15
There's the laundry,
sun-warm clothes at twilight,
and the mountain of beans
in my lap. Each one,
I'll break and snap   20
thoughtfully in half.

But there is this slow arousal.
The small buttons
of my cotton blouse
are pulling away from my body.   25
I feel the strain of threads,
the swollen magnolias
heavy as a flock of birds
in the tree. Already,
the orange sponge cake   30
is rising in the oven.
I know you'll say it makes
your mouth dry
and I'll watch you
drench your slice of it   35
in canned peaches
and lick the plate clean.

So much hair, my mother
used to say, grabbing
the thick braided rope   40
in her hands while we washed
the breakfast dishes, discussing
dresses and pastries.
My mind often elsewhere
as we did the morning chores together.   45
Sometimes, a few strands
would catch in her gold ring.
I worked hard then,
anticipating the hour
when I would let the rope down   50
at night, strips of sheets,
knotted and tied,
while she slept in tight blankets.
My hair, freshly washed
like a measure of wealth,   55
like a bridal veil.
Crouching in the grass,
you would wait for the signal,
for the movement of curtains
before releasing yourself   60

from the shadow of moths.
Cloth, hair and hands,
smuggling you in.

1983

Beauty and Sadness

for Kitagawa Utamaro[1]

He drew hundreds of women
in studies unfolding
like flowers from a fan.
Teahouse waitresses, actresses,
geishas,[2] courtesans and maids.   5
They arranged themselves
before this quick, nimble man
whose invisible presence
one feels in these prints
is as delicate   10
as the skinlike paper
he used to transfer
and retain their fleeting loveliness.

Crouching like cats,
they purred amid the layers of kimono[3]   15
swirling around them
as though they were bathing
in a mountain pool with irises
growing in the silken sunlit water.
Or poised like porcelain vases,   20
slender, erect and tall; their heavy
brocaded hair was piled high
with sandalwood combs and blossom sprigs
poking out like antennae.
They resembled beautiful iridescent insects,   25
creatures from a floating world.[4]

Utamaro absorbed these women of Edo[5]
in their moments of melancholy
as well as of beauty.
He captured the wisp of shadows,   30
the half-draped body
emerging from a bath; whatever

1. Japanese artist (1753–1806) who specialized
in studies of sensual and beautiful women.
2. Women trained to provide entertaining, light-
hearted company for men.
3. Traditional Japanese robe with long sleeves.

4. The pictures "were called 'pictures of the
floating world' because of their preoccupation
with the pleasures of the moment" [Song's note].
5. Present-day Tokyo [Song's note].

skin was exposed
was powdered white as snow.
A private space disclosed.   35
Portraying another girl
catching a glimpse of her own vulnerable
face in the mirror, he transposed
the trembling plum lips
like a drop of blood   40
soaking up the white expanse of paper.

At times, indifferent to his inconsolable
eye, the women drifted
through the soft gray feathered light,
maintaining stillness, the moments in between.   45
Like the dusty ash-winged moths
that cling to the screens in summer
and that the Japanese venerate
as ancestors reincarnated;
Utamaro graced these women with immortality   50
in the thousand sheaves of prints
fluttering into the reverent hands of keepers:
the dwarfed and bespectacled painter
holding up to a square of sunlight
what he had carried home beneath his coat   55
one afternoon in winter.

                                                                 1983

Lost Sister

1

In China,
even the peasants
named their first daughters
Jade—
the stone that in the far fields   5
could moisten the dry season,
could make men move mountains
for the healing green of the inner hills
glistening like slices of winter melon.

And the daughters were grateful: 10
they never left home.
To move freely was a luxury
stolen from them at birth.
Instead, they gathered patience,
learning to walk in shoes   15
the size of teacups,
without breaking—

the arc of their movements
as dormant as the rooted willow,
as redundant as the farmyard hens.
But they traveled far   20
in surviving,
learning to stretch the family rice,
to quiet the demons,
the noisy stomachs.   25

2

There is a sister
across the ocean,
who relinquished her name,
diluting jade green
with the blue of the Pacific.   30
Rising with a tide of locusts,
she swarmed with others
to inundate another shore.
In America,
there are many roads   35
and women can stride along with men.

But in another wilderness,
the possibilities,
the loneliness,
can strangulate like jungle vines.   40
The meager provisions and sentiments
of once belonging—
fermented roots, Mah-Jongg[1] tiles and firecrackers—
set but a flimsy household
in a forest of nightless cities.   45
A giant snake rattles above,
spewing black clouds into your kitchen.
Dough-faced landlords
slip in and out of your keyholes,
making claims you don't understand,   50
tapping into your communication systems
of laundry lines and restaurant chains.

You find you need China:
your one fragile identification,
a jade link   55
handcuffed to your wrist.
You remember your mother
who walked for centuries,
footless—
and like her,   60
you have left no footprints,

---

1. A board game of Chinese origin.

but only because
there is an ocean in between,
the unremitting space of your rebellion.

1983

Heaven

He thinks when we die we'll go to China.
Think of it—a Chinese heaven
where, except for his blond hair,
the part that belongs to his father,
everyone will look like him.   5
China, that blue flower on the map,
bluer than the sea
his hand must span like a bridge
to reach it.
An octave away.   10

I've never seen it.
It's as if I can't sing that far.
But look—
on the map, this black dot.
Here is where we live,   15
on the pancake plains
just east of the Rockies,
on the other side of the clouds.
A mile above the sea,
the air is so thin, you can starve on it.   20
No bamboo trees
but the alpine equivalent,
reedy aspen with light, fluttering leaves.
Did a boy in Guangzhou[1] dream of this
as his last stop?   25

I've heard the trains at night
whistling past our yards,
what we've come to own,
the broken fences, the whiny dog, the rattletrap cars.
It's still the wild west,   30
mean and grubby,
the shootouts and fistfights in the back alley.
With my son the dreamer
and my daughter, who is too young to walk,
I've sat in this spot   35
and wondered why here?
Why in this short life,
this town, this creek they call a river?

---

1. Or Canton, seaport city in southeastern China.

He had never planned to stay,
the boy who helped to build
the railroads for a dollar a day.[2]
He had always meant to go back.
When did he finally know
that each mile of track led him further away,
that he would die in his sleep,
dispossessed,
having seen Gold Mountain,[3]
the icy wind tunneling through it,
these landlocked, makeshift ghost towns?

It must be in the blood,
this notion of returning.
It skipped two generations, lay fallow,
the garden an unmarked grave.
On a spring sweater day
it's as if we remember him.
I call to the children.
We can see the mountains
shimmering blue above the air.
If you look really hard
says my son the dreamer,
leaning out from the laundry's rigging,
the work shirts fluttering like sails,
you can see all the way to heaven.

1988

2. The Chinese provided much of the cheap labor that laid the tracks of the transcontinental railroads in the 19th century.
3. In China in the 1840s and 1850s, the U.S. state of California was known as "Gold Mountain." Many Chinese emigrated to California to search for gold, only to discover that mining was uncertain, unreliable, and dangerous.

LI-YOUNG LEE
b. 1957

In his poem "Persimmons" Li-Young Lee remembers his father saying, "Some things never leave a person." Many of the poems in Lee's books—*Rose* (1986), *The City in Which I Love You* (1990), *Book of My Nights* (2001), and *Behind My Eyes* (2008)—testify to a sense of the past, especially his father's past, which never leaves Lee. The father in Lee's poems is personal and mythic; he instructs the poet-son in "the art of memory." Lee's father, born in China, served as a personal physician to Mao Zedong. He later was jailed for nineteen months, a political prisoner of the Indonesian dictator Sukarno. Lee was born in Jakarta, Indonesia. In 1959 the family fled Indonesia and traveled in the Far East (Hong Kong, Macao, and Japan), finally arriving in America, where Lee's father became a Presbyterian minister in a small town in western

Pennsylvania. Many of Lee's poems seek to remember and understand his father's life and to come to terms with Lee's differences from that powerful figure.

Lee's work reminds us about the ancient connections between memory and poetry. In his work memory is often sweet; it draws the poet to the past even when, as in "Eating Alone," that sweetness is as dizzying as the juice of a rotten pear in which a hornet spins. But memory can also be a burden, and its pull is countered in Lee's work by a sensuous apprehension of the present. As in his poem "This Room and Everything in It," the erotic immediacy of the moment can disrupt any effort to fix that moment in the orders of memory. Everywhere in Lee's work is the evidence of hearing, taste, smell, and touch as well as sight. If the poet's bodily presence in the world recalls his great American precursor Walt Whitman, Lee's fluid motion between the physical world and the domain of memory, dream, or vision also carries out Whitman's visionary strain and links Lee to the work of Theodore Roethke, James Wright, and Denise Levertov, among others. The intensity of Lee's poems, however, is often leavened by a subtle and winning humor and playfulness; such qualities are especially valuable in a poet at times too easily seduced by beauty.

Lee studied at the University of Pittsburgh (where one of his teachers was the poet Gerald Stern), the University of Arizona, and the State University of New York College at Brockport. He has since taught at various universities. In 1995 he published a prose memoir, *The Winged Seed: A Remembrance*. His prose, like his poetry, is characterized by his deep sense of connection between an individual life and a powerful past, mediated by his ability to move between plain speech and a lushness evocative of biblical language.

The Gift

To pull the metal splinter from my palm
my father recited a story in a low voice.
I watched his lovely face and not the blade.
Before the story ended, he'd removed
the iron sliver I thought I'd die from.   5

I can't remember the tale,
but hear his voice still, a well
of dark water, a prayer.
And I recall his hands,
two measures of tenderness   10
he laid against my face,
the flames of discipline
he raised above my head.

Had you entered that afternoon
you would have thought you saw a man   15
planting something in a boy's palm,
a silver tear, a tiny flame.
Had you followed that boy
you would have arrived here,
where I bend over my wife's right hand.   20

Look how I shave her thumbnail down
so carefully she feels no pain.

Watch as I lift the splinter out.
I was seven when my father
took my hand like this,   25
and I did not hold that shard
between my fingers and think,
Metal that will bury me,
christen it Little Assassin,
Ore Going Deep for My Heart.   30
And I did not lift up my wound and cry,
Death visited here!
I did what a child does
when he's given something to keep.
I kissed my father.   35

1986

Persimmons

In sixth grade Mrs. Walker
slapped the back of my head
and made me stand in the corner
for not knowing the difference
between *persimmon* and *precision*.   5
How to choose

persimmons. This is precision.
Ripe ones are soft and brown-spotted.
Sniff the bottoms. The sweet one
will be fragrant. How to eat: 10
put the knife away, lay down newspaper.
Peel the skin tenderly, not to tear the meat.
Chew the skin, suck it,
and swallow. Now, eat
the meat of the fruit,   15
so sweet,
all of it, to the heart.

Donna undresses, her stomach is white.
In the yard, dewy and shivering
with crickets, we lie naked,   20
face-up, face-down.
I teach her Chinese.
Crickets: *chiu chiu.* Dew: I've forgotten.
Naked: I've forgotten.
Ni, wo: you and me.   25
I part her legs,
remember to tell her
she is beautiful as the moon.

Other words
that got me into trouble were   30

fight and *fright*, *wren* and *yarn*.
Fight was what I did when I was frightened,
fright was what I felt when I was fighting.
Wrens are small, plain birds,
yarn is what one knits with.   35
Wrens are soft as yarn.
My mother made birds out of yarn.
I loved to watch her tie the stuff;
a bird, a rabbit, a wee man.

Mrs. Walker brought a persimmon to class   40
and cut it up
so everyone could taste
a *Chinese apple.* Knowing
it wasn't ripe or sweet, I didn't eat
but I watched the other faces.   45

My mother said every persimmon has a sun
inside, something golden, glowing,
warm as my face.

Once, in the cellar, I found two wrapped in newspaper,
forgotten and not yet ripe.   50
I took them and set both on my bedroom windowsill,
where each morning a cardinal
sang, *The sun, the sun.*

Finally understanding
he was going blind,   55
my father sat up all one night
waiting for a song, a ghost.
I gave him the persimmons,
swelled, heavy as sadness,
and sweet as love.   60

This year, in the muddy lighting
of my parents' cellar, I rummage, looking
for something I lost.
My father sits on the tired, wooden stairs,
black cane between his knees,   65
hand over hand, gripping the handle.

He's so happy that I've come home.
I ask how his eyes are, a stupid question.
All gone, he answers.

Under some blankets, I find a box.   70
Inside the box I find three scrolls.
I sit beside him and untie
three paintings by my father:
Hibiscus leaf and a white flower.

Two cats preening. 75
Two persimmons, so full they want to drop from the cloth.

He raises both hands to touch the cloth,
asks, *Which is this?*

This is persimmons, Father.

Oh, the feel of the wolftail on the silk, 80
the strength, the tense
precision in the wrist.
I painted them hundreds of times
eyes closed. These I painted blind.
Some things never leave a person: 85
scent of the hair of one you love,
the texture of persimmons,
in your palm, the ripe weight.

1986

Eating Alone

I've pulled the last of the year's young onions.
The garden is bare now. The ground is cold,
brown and old. What is left of the day flames
in the maples at the corner of my
eye. I turn, a cardinal vanishes. 5
By the cellar door, I wash the onions,
then drink from the icy metal spigot.

Once, years back, I walked beside my father
among the windfall pears. I can't recall
our words. We may have strolled in silence. But 10
I still see him bend, that way—left hand braced
on knee, creaky—to lift and hold to my
eye a rotten pear. In it, a hornet
spun crazily, glazed in slow, glistening juice.

It was my father I saw this morning 15
waving to me from the trees. I almost
called to him, until I came close enough
to see the shovel, leaning where I had
left it, in the flickering, deep green shade.

White rice steaming, almost done. Sweet green peas 20
fried in onions. Shrimp braised in sesame
oil and garlic. And my own loneliness.
What more could I, a young man, want.

1986

Eating Together

In the steamer is the trout
seasoned with slivers of ginger,
two sprigs of green onion, and sesame oil.
We shall eat it with rice for lunch,
brothers, sister, my mother who will   5
taste the sweetest meat of the head,
holding it between her fingers
deftly, the way my father did
weeks ago. Then he lay down
to sleep like a snow-covered road   10
winding through pines older than him,
without any travelers, and lonely for no one.

1986

This Room and Everything in It

Lie still now
while I prepare For my future,
certain hard days ahead,
when I'll need what I know so clearly this moment.

I am making use   5
of the one thing I learned
of all the things my father tried to teach me:
the art of memory.

I am letting this room
and everything in it   10
stand for my ideas about love
and its difficulties.

I'll let your love-cries,
those spacious notes
of a moment ago,   15
stand for distance.

Your scent,
that scent
of spice and a wound,
I'll let stand for mystery.   20

Your sunken belly
is the daily cup
of milk I drank
as a boy before morning prayer.

The sun on the face   25
of the wall
is God, the face
I can't see, my soul,

and so on, each thing
standing for a separate idea,   30
and those ideas forming the constellation
of my greater idea.
And one day, when I need
to tell myself something intelligent
about love,   35

I'll close my eyes
and recall this room and everything in it:
My body is estrangement.
This desire, perfection.
Your closed eyes my extinction.   40
Now I've forgotten my
idea. The book
on the windowsill, riffled by wind . . .
the even-numbered pages are
the past, the odd-   45
numbered pages, the future.
The sun is
God, your body is milk . . .

useless, useless . . .
your cries are song, my body's not me . . .   50
no good . . . my idea
has evaporated . . . your hair is time, your thighs are song . . .
it had something to do
with death . . . it had something
to do with love.   55

1990

Nativity

In the dark, a child might ask, *What is the world?*
just to hear his sister
promise, *An unfinished wing of heaven,*
just to hear his brother say,
A house inside a house,   5
but most of all to bear his mother answer,
One more song, then you go to sleep.

How could anyone in that bed guess
the question finds its beginning
in the answer long growing   10

inside the one who asked, that restless boy,
the night's darling?

Later, a man lying awake,
he might ask it again,
just to hear the silence   15
charge him, *This night*
arching over your sleepless wondering,

this night, the near ground
every reaching-out-to overreaches,

just to remind himself   20
out of what little earth and duration,
out of what immense good-bye,

each must make a safe place of his heart,
before so strange and wild a guest
as God approaches.   25

Creative Nonfiction

"Creative nonfiction" is a relatively new term—it first appeared officially in 1983 as a category for creative writing fellowships in the National Endowment of the Arts—but examples of the form appear much earlier in American literature. If Thoreau and Emerson were publishing their personal essays today their work would probably be called examples of creative nonfiction, as might much of the travel and nature writing long a part of American literature. The term is fluid, suggesting a hybrid that involves facts, research, and information while using the resources and strategies of fiction, poetry, and autobiography, biography in shaping its material.

The term is closely allied with what was, in the 1970s, called "The New Journalism" (the writer Tom Wolfe published a book with that title in 1973), in which, instead of simply reporting the event, the writer reports on himself or herself within the event, either as a participant or an observer (or both). Examples of the "The New Journalism" include Truman Capote's *In Cold Blood* (1966), Norman Mailer's *Armies of the Night* (1968), Joan Didion's *Slouching Towards Bethlehem* (1968), Hunter Thompson's *Fear and Loathing in Las Vegas* (1972), and Wolfe's own *The Right Stuff* (1979). This approach to journalism addressed the problem of what the physicist Werner Heisenberg called "the uncertainty principle" (a theory the novelist Thomas Pynchon frequently invokes in his work), which asserts that the observer's presence alters the phenomenon being observed. "The New Journalism" sought to reveal the writer observing the event and thus make us aware of the lens through which we see. The term now seems specific to a particular cultural moment and group of writers; creative nonfiction is more flexible and expansive, both in terms of the kinds of writing it describes and the range of authors affiliated with it. Ultimately, though, the point is that no direct duplication of reality is possible in language, that all writing is affected by the author's point of view. Creative nonfiction is open in its aim of merging invention with fidelity to fact.

As with all hybrids, the distinctions between it and other forms are slippery. Most memoirs, personal essays, and environmental writing are considered to be creative nonfiction, but the writers in this cluster provide especially innovative examples of these forms. Edwidge Danticat mingles autobiography, political analysis, and biography; Joan Didion's memoir includes clinical observation and medical research. John Crawford's account of his experience as an Iraq war veteran and Dorothy Allison's description of the effects of social class on herself and her family make their works more than the stories of individuals. The environmental writing of Edward Abbey and Barry Lopez combines carefully observed, factual description of landscapes and natural creatures with an equal focus on the writer's feelings and reflections. It is easy to understand why many examples of the form slip back and forth between a variety of categories: among the selections here, Jamaica Kincaid's "Girl" appeared in a book collection advertised as "Stories," but many critics and reviewers have called the work a poem or autobiography.

The term "Creative Nonfiction" is fully at ease with such slippage, and happily embraces work that mixes elements of many different genres; whatever the mixture, it's the quality of writing and the use of various techniques that establish the work as "creative." In the twenty-first century hybridity is a significant cultural modality, and much of contemporary writing is self-consciously hybrid. Mixing poetry and essay, personal reflection and journalism, nature writing and myth, or inventing other combinations, some of the best American writing is now, and always has been, creative nonfiction.

EDWARD ABBEY

A prolific writer, Edward Abbey (1927–1989) was the author of many novels but he is most famous for his personal essays, which have become classics of environmental writing. Born and raised in Pennsylvania, he went west in his teens, and late in the 1950s he worked at Arches National Monument (now Arches National Park) near Moab in eastern Utah, as a seasonal ranger. In the spirit of Thoreau's residence at Walden Pond and Gary Snyder's summers as a fire lookout in Washington State's North Cascades, Abbey said he sought solitude in an effort to "confront, immediately and directly if possible, the bare bones of existence." His most famous book, *Desert Solitaire* (1968), came out of his journals from this period; the book is a compilation of description, natural history, tall tales, and polemical environmentalism.

One of the most gripping chapters in *Desert Solitaire* focuses on Abbey's time in Havasu, at the base of the Grand Canyon. As he tells it, during a stop at the Grand Canyon with friends en route to Los Angeles he decided on the spur of the moment to descend to the canyon floor ("fourteen miles by trail") to take a look at Havasu Canyon in Arizona, the homeland of the Havasupai Native people. Five weeks later, he emerged to find that his friends had sensibly gone on without him. During the weeks he spent there, Abbey camped and explored the surrounding landscape alone. This selection focuses on one such day of exploration, when, looking for a shortcut back to his camp, he made a series of potentially fatal decisions.

Havasu

Most of my wandering in the desert I've done alone. Not so much from choice as from necessity—I generally prefer to go into places where no one else wants to go. I find that in contemplating the natural world my pleasure is greater if there are not too many others contemplating it with me, at the same time. However, there are special hazards in traveling alone. Your chances of dying, in case of sickness or accident, are much improved, simply because there is no one around to go for help.

Exploring a side canyon off Havasu Canyon[1] one day, I was unable to resist the temptation to climb up out of it onto what corresponds in that region to the Tonto Bench.[2] Late in the afternoon I realized that I would not have

---

1. A canyon with waterfall, forming a side branch of the Grand Canyon, that was once the home of a prehistoric people and has been occupied by the Havasupai, "people of the blue-green waters," for the last 800 years.

2. The long, narrow strip of relatively level land located in the Grand Canyon, separating the inner gorge from the upper canyon and following the course of the Colorado River.

enough time to get back to my camp before dark, unless I could find a much shorter route than the one by which I had come. I looked for a shortcut.

Nearby was another little side canyon which appeared to lead down into Havasu Canyon. It was a steep, shadowy, extremely narrow defile with the usual meandering course and overhanging walls; from where I stood, near its head, I could not tell if the route was feasible all the way down to the floor of the main canyon. I had no rope with me—only my walking stick. But I was hungry and thirsty, as always. I started down.

For a while everything went well. The floor of the little canyon began as a bed of dry sand, scattered with rocks. Farther down a few boulders were wedged between the walls; I climbed over and under them. Then the canyon took on the slickrock[3] character—smooth, sheer, slippery sandstone carved by erosion into a series of scoops and potholes which got bigger as I descended. In some of these basins there was a little water left over from the last flood, warm and fetid water under an oily-looking scum, condensed by prolonged evaporation to a sort of broth, rich in dead and dying organisms. My canteen was empty and I was very thirsty but I felt that I could wait.

I came to a lip on the canyon floor which overhung by twelve feet the largest so far of these stagnant pools. On each side rose the canyon walls, roughly perpendicular. There was no way to continue except by dropping into the pool. I hesitated. Beyond this point there could hardly be any returning, yet the main canyon was still not visible below. Obviously the only sensible thing to do was to turn back. I edged over the lip of stone and dropped feet first into the water.

Deeper than I expected. The warm, thick fluid came up and closed over my head as my feet touched the muck at the bottom. I had to swim to the farther side. And here I found myself on the verge of another drop-off, with one more huge bowl of green soup below.

This drop-off was about the same height as the one before, but not over-hanging. It resembled a children's playground slide, concave and S-curved, only steeper, wider, with a vertical pitch in the middle. It did not lead directly into the water but ended in a series of steplike ledges above the pool. Beyond the pool lay another edge, another drop-off into an unknown depth. Again I paused, and for a much longer time. But I no longer had the option of turning around and going back. I eased myself into the chute[4] and let go of everything—except my faithful stick.

I hit rock bottom hard, but without any physical injury. I swam the stink-ing pond dog-paddle[5] style, pushing the heavy scum away from my face, and crawled out on the far side to see what my fate was going to be.

Fatal. Death by starvation, slow and tedious. For I was looking straight down an overhanging cliff to a rubble pile of broken rocks eighty feet below.

After the first wave of utter panic had passed I began to try to think. First of all I was not going to die immediately, unless another flash flood came down the gorge; there was the pond of stagnant water on hand to save me from thirst and a man can live, they say, for thirty days or more without food. My sun-bleached bones, dramatically sprawled at the bottom of the chasm,

---

3. A term used in the Southwest to refer to smooth, consolidated, and hardened sand dunes.
4. A waterfall or steep descent in a river.

5. A simple swimming style, often used by children.

would provide the diversion of the picturesque for future wanderers—if any man ever came this way again.

My second thought was to scream for help, although I knew very well there could be no other human being within miles. I even tried it but the sound of that anxious shout, cut short in the dead air within the canyon walls, was so inhuman, so detached as it seemed from myself, that it terrified me and I didn't attempt it again.

I thought of tearing my clothes into strips and plaiting a rope. But what was I wearing?—boots, socks, a pair of old and ragged blue jeans, a flimsy T-shirt, an ancient and rotten sombrero[6] of straw. Not a chance of weaving such a wardrobe into a rope eighty feet long, or even twenty feet long.

How about a signal fire? There was nothing to burn but my clothes; not a tree, not a shrub, not even a weed grew in this stony cul-de-sac. Even if I burned my clothing the chances of the smoke being seen by some Hualapai Indian[7] high on the south rim were very small; and if he did see the smoke, what then? He'd shrug his shoulders, sigh, and take another pull from his Tokay[8] bottle. Furthermore, without clothes, the sun would soon bake me to death.

There was only one thing I could do. I had a tiny notebook in my hip pocket and a stub of pencil. When these dried out I could at least record my final thoughts. I would have plenty of time to write not only my epitaph but my own elegy.[9]

But not yet.

There were a few loose stones scattered about the edge of the pool. Taking the biggest first, I swam with it back to the foot of the slickrock chute and placed it there. One by one I brought the others and made a shaky little pile about two feet high leaning against the chute. Hopeless, of course, but there was nothing else to do. I stood on the top of the pile and stretched upward, straining my arms to their utmost limit and groped with fingers and fingernails for a hold on something firm. There was nothing. I crept back down. I began to cry. It was easy. AH alone, I didn't have to be brave.

Through the tears I noticed my old walking stick lying nearby. I took it and stood it on the most solid stone in the pile, behind the two topmost stones. I took off my boots, tied them together and hung them around my neck, on my back. I got up on the little pile again and lifted one leg and set my big toe on the top of the stick. This could never work. Slowly and painfully, leaning as much of my weight as I could against the sandstone slide, I applied more and more pressure to the stick, pushing my body upward until I was again stretched out full length above it. Again I felt about for a fingerhold. There was none. The chute was smooth as polished marble.

No, not quite that smooth. This was sandstone, soft and porous, not marble, and between it and my wet body and wet clothing a certain friction was created. In addition, the stick had enabled me to reach a higher section of the S-curved chute, where the angle was more favorable. I discovered

6. A broad-brimmed hat common in Spain and Spanish America.
7. "People of the tall pine," the Hualapai are a Native American people living along the pine-clad southern side of the Grand Canyon.
8. Tokay is a sweet wine, often available in cheap or inexpensive forms.
9. An epitaph is a short text inscribed on a tombstone, honoring a deceased person an elegy is a mournful poem, especially a funeral song or a lament for the dead.

that I could move upward, inch by inch, through adhesion and with the help of the leveling tendency of the curve. I gave an extra little push with my big toe—the stones collapsed below, the stick clattered down—and crawled rather like a snail or slug, oozing slime, up over the rounded summit of the slide.

The next obstacle, the overhanging spout twelve feet above a deep plunge pool, looked impossible. It *was* impossible, but with the blind faith of despair I slogged into the water and swam underneath the drop-off and floundered around for a while, scrabbling at the slippery rock until my nerves and tiring muscles convinced my numbed brain that *this was not the way*. I swam back to solid ground and lay down to rest and die in comfort.

Far above I could see the sky, an irregular strip of blue between the dark, hard-edged canyon walls that seemed to lean toward each other as they towered above me. Across that narrow opening a small white cloud was passing, so lovely and precious and delicate and forever inaccessible that it broke the heart and made me weep like a woman, like a child. In all my life I had never seen anything so beautiful.

The walls that rose on either side of the drop-off were literally perpendicular. Eroded by weathering, however, and not by the corrasion[1] of rushing floodwater, they had a rough surface, chipped, broken, cracked. Where the walls joined the face of the overhang they formed almost a square corner, with a number of minute crevices and inch-wide shelves on either side. It might, after all, be possible. What did I have to lose?

When I had regained some measure of nerve and steadiness I got up off my back and tried the wall beside the pond, clinging to the rock with bare toes and fingertips and inching my way crabwise toward the corner. The watersoaked, heavy boots dangling from my neck, swinging back and forth with my every movement, threw me off balance and I fell into the pool. I swam out to the bank, unslung the boots and threw them up over the drop-off, out of sight. They'd be there if I ever needed them again. Once more I attached myself to the wall, tenderly, sensitively, like a limpet,[2] and very slowly, very cautiously, worked my way into the corner. Here I was able to climb upward, a few centimeters at a time, by bracing myself against the opposite sides and finding sufficient niches for fingers and toes. As I neared the top and the overhang became noticeable I prepared for a slip, planning to push myself away from the rock so as to fall into the center of the pool where the water was deepest. But it wasn't necessary. Somehow, with a skill and tenacity I could never have found in myself under ordinary circumstances, I managed to creep straight up that gloomy cliff and over the brink of the drop-off and into the flower of safety. My boots were floating under the surface of the little puddle above. As I poured the stinking water out of them and pulled them on and laced them up I discovered myself bawling again for the third time in three hours, the hot delicious tears of victory. And up above the clouds replied—thunder.

I emerged from that treacherous little canyon at sundown, with an enormous fire in the western sky and lightning overhead. Through sweet twilight and the sudden dazzling flare of lightning a I hiked back along the

1. The wearing away of rock by the constant flow of water.
2. Common name for numerous kinds of saltwater and freshwater snails.

Tonto Bench, bellowing the *Ode to Joy*.[3] Long before I reached the place where I could descend safely to the main canyon and my camp, however, darkness set in, the clouds opened their bays and the rain poured down. I took shelter under a ledge in a shallow cave about three feet high—hardly room to sit up in. Others had been here before: the dusty floor of the little hole was littered with the droppings of birds, rats, jackrabbits, and coyotes. There were also a few long gray pieces of scat with a curious twist at one tip—cougar? I didn't care. I had some matches with me, sealed in paraffin (the prudent explorer); I scraped together the handiest twigs and animal droppings and built a little fire and waited for the rain to stop.

It didn't stop. The rain came down for hours in alternate waves of storm and drizzle and I very soon had burnt up all the fuel within reach. No matter. I stretched out in the coyote den, pillowed my head on my arm and suffered through the long long night, wet, cold, aching, hungry, wretched, dreaming claustrophobic nightmares. It was one of the happiest nights of my life.

1968

3. A famous theme in the final movement of German composer and pianist Ludwig van Beethoven's (1770–1827) Ninth Symphony (1824).

BARRY LOPEZ

Barry Lopez's "The Raven" is a difficult piece of writing to categorize. In its specific attention to details of the desert landscape and creatures, it belongs to the genre of nature writing for which Lopez (b. 1945) is so well known (for example, his award winning books *Arctic Dreams*, 1986, and *Of Wolves and Men*, 2004). But like much of Lopez's writing, "The Raven" is clearly not a simple factual description of ravens. Embedded in the piece are what we might call "raven tales"—fables or stories about the life and behaviors of a bird whose symbolic importance in indigenous cultures is widespread. And, in fact, the book in which this piece first appeared, *Desert Notes: Reflections in the Eye of a Raven* (1976), bore the subtitle "Short Stories." But as Lopez himself has pointed out, "the distinction between fiction and nonfiction, though logical and even useful, is not as important as the distinction between an authentic and an inauthentic story." "The Raven" is authentic story about the desert landscape and its inhabitants and, equally important, a story that creates in the writer and the reader an authentic sense of wonder. In its presentation of a natural world deeply connected to myth and story telling there are clear affinities between this piece and the work of Native American writers like Louise Erdrich and Sherman Alexie.

Lopez is an intimate observer of the landscape he writes about in "The Raven." Born in 1945, he grew up in rural Southern California and as a child spent time in the Mojave desert. His interest in the relationships between landscapes and human culture has taken him on travels to both remote and populated parts of the world.

The Raven

I am going to have to start at the other end by telling you this: there are no crows in the desert. What appear to be crows are ravens. You must examine the crow, however, before you can understand the raven. To forget the crow completely, as some have tried to do, would be like trying to understand the one who stayed without talking to the one who left. It is important to make note of who has left the desert.

To begin with, the crow does nothing alone. He cannot abide silence and he is prone to stealing things, twigs and bits of straw, from the nests of his neighbors. It is a game with him. He enjoys tricks. If he cannot make up his mind the crow will take two or three wives, but this is not a game. The crow is very accommodating and he admires compulsiveness.

Crows will live in street trees in the residential areas of great cities. They will walk at night on the roofs of parked cars and peck at the grit; they will scrape the pinpoints of their talons across the steel and, with their necks outthrust, watch for frightened children listening in their beds.

Put all this to the raven: he will open his mouth as if to say something. Then he will look the other way and say nothing. Later, when you have forgotten, he will tell you he admires the crow.

The raven is larger than the crow and has a beard of black feathers at his throat. He is careful to kill only what he needs. Crows, on the other hand, will search out the great horned owl, kick and punch him awake, and then, for roosting too close to their nests, they will kill him. They will come out of the sky on a fat, hot afternoon and slam into the head of a dozing rabbit and go away laughing. They will tear out a whole row of planted corn and eat only a few kernels. They will defecate on scarecrows and go home and sleep with 200,000 of their friends in an atmosphere of congratulation. Again, it is only a game; this should not be taken to mean that they are evil.

There is however this: when too many crows come together on a roost there is a lot of shoving and noise and a white film begins to descend over the crows' eyes and they go blind. They fall from their perches and lie on the ground and starve to death. When confronted with this information, crows will look past you and warn you vacantly that it is easy to be misled.

The crow flies like a pigeon. The raven flies like a hawk He is seen only at a great distance and then not very clearly. This is true of the crow too, but if you are very clever you can trap the crow. The only way to be sure what you have seen is a raven is to follow him until he dies of old age, and then examine the body.

Once there were many crows in the desert. I am told it was like this: you could sit back in the rocks and watch a pack of crows working over the carcass of a coyote. Some would eat, the others would try to squeeze out the vultures. The raven would never be seen. He would be at a distance, alone, perhaps eating a scorpion.

There was, at this time, a small alkaline water hole at the desert's edge. Its waters were bitter. No one but crows would drink there, although they drank sparingly, just one or two sips at a time. One day a raven warned someone about the dangers of drinking the bitter water and was overheard by a crow. When word of this passed among the crows they felt insulted.

They jeered and raised insulting gestures to the ravens. They bullied each other into drinking the alkaline water until they had drunk the hole dry and gone blind.

The crows flew into canyon walls and dove straight into the ground at forty miles an hour and broke their necks. The worst of it was their cartwheeling across the desert floor, stiff wings outstretched, beaks agape, white eyes ballooning, surprising rattlesnakes hidden under sage bushes out of the noonday sun. The snakes awoke, struck and held. The wheeling birds strew them across the desert like sprung traps.

When all the crows were finally dead, the desert bacteria and fungi bored into them, burrowed through bone and muscle, through aqueous humor[1] and feathers until they had reduced the stiff limbs of soft black to blue dust.

After that, there were no more crows in the desert. The few who watched from a distance took it as a sign and moved away.

Finally there is this: one morning four ravens sat at the edge of the desert waiting for the sun to rise. They had been there all night and the dew was like beads of quicksilver on their wings. Their eyes were closed and they were as still as the cracks in the desert floor.

The wind came off the snow-capped peaks to the north and ruffled their breath feathers. Their talons arched in the white earth and they smoothed their wings with sleek, dark bills. At first light their bodies swelled and their eyes flashed purple. When the dew dried on their wings they lifted off from the desert floor and flew away in four directions. Crows would never have had the patience for this.

If you want to know more about the raven: bury yourself in the desert so that you have a commanding view of the high basalt[2] cliffs where he lives. Let only your eyes protrude. Do not blink—the movement will alert the raven to your continued presence. Wait until a generation of ravens has passed away. Of the new generation there will be at least one bird who will find you. He will see your eyes staring up out of the desert floor. The raven is cautious, but he is thorough. He will sense your peaceful intentions. Let him have the first word. Be careful: he will tell you he knows nothing.

If you do not have the time for this, scour the weathered desert shacks for some sign of the raven's body. Look under old mattresses and beneath loose floorboards. Look behind the walls. Sooner or later you will find a severed foot. It will be his and it will be well preserved.

Take it out in the sunlight and examine it closely. Notice that there are three fingers that face forward, and a fourth, the longest and like a thumb, that faces to the rear. The instrument will be black but no longer shiny, the back of it sheathed in armor plate and the underside padded like a wolf's foot.

At the end of each digit you will find a black, curved talon. You will see that the talons are not as sharp as you might have suspected. They are made to grasp and hold fast, not to puncture. They are more like the jaws of a trap than a fistful of ice picks. The subtle difference serves the raven well in the desert. He can weather a storm on a barren juniper limb; he can pick up and examine the crow's eye without breaking it.

1976

1. The thick watery substance filling the space between the lens and the cornea of the eye.

2. A common volcanic rock, usually fine-grained due to the rapid cooling of lava.

JAMAICA KINCAID

Jamaica Kincaid was born on the island of Antigua in the West Indies in 1949; at seventeen she felt she had to "rescue herself" from an oppressive cultural and family situation and came to New York as an *au pair* (she calls herself "a servant"). Writing, she has said, was for her "a matter of saving my life." In 1973 she had changed her birth name of Elaine Cynthia Potter Richardson to Jamaica Kincaid, because, she said, her family disapproved of her writing. After she left Antigua she did not see her mother again for twenty years. When she began a career as a writer she became a regular contributor to the *New Yorker* magazine. Her first book, *Annie John* (1983), is an autobiographical coming-of-age novel, as is *Lucy* (1990), a fictional version of her coming to New York. Her other work includes a book about Antigua (*A Small Place*, 1988), a memoir (*My Brother*, 1998), and two books on gardening, one of her passions.

"Girl," which first appeared in the *New Yorker* in 1978, is one all-but-uninterrupted sentence in which a West Indian mother instructs her daughter on how to be the "proper" young woman she is certain her daughter is not. Although the daughter twice tries to interject, she's unable to change what is essentially monologue into dialogue. Kincaid has said that the voice in the story is "my mother's voice exactly over many years" and that, as a child, "a powerless person," she spoke infrequently. Like the other pieces collected in *At the Bottom of the River* (1983), "Girl" resists classification. Its implicit narrative makes it story; its strong rhythm and vivid images make it poetry. Simultaneously, like an essay it documents issues of gender and power. And, like much of this writer's work, it is rooted in autobiography. "I am so happy to write that I don't care what you call it," she has said. The mother/daughter relationship in "Girl" is one of Kincaid's earliest explorations of her ongoing and self-proclaimed "obsessive theme" as a writer: "the relationship between the powerful and the powerless."

Girl

Wash the white clothes on Monday and put them on the stone heap; wash the color clothes on Tuesday and put them on the clothesline to dry; don't walk barehead in the hot sun; cook pumpkin fritters[1] in very hot sweet oil; soak your little cloths right after you take them off; when buying cotton to make yourself a nice blouse, be sure that it doesn't have gum[2] on it, because that way it won't hold up well after a wash; soak salt fish[3] overnight before you cook it; is it true that you sing benna[4] in Sunday school?; always eat your food in such a way that it won't turn someone else's stomach; on Sundays try to walk like a lady and not like the slut you are so bent on becoming; don't sing

1. A Caribbean dish made from fried calabaza, or West Indian pumpkin.
2. A naturally occurring, viscous resin found in the woody parts of plants.
3. A popular West Indian dish of dried and salted codfish sautéed with spices.

4. A calypso-like music characterized by a call-and-response format; it was used as a form of folk communication to spread gossip and other local news across the islands of the British West Indies in the early 20th century.

benna in Sunday school; you mustn't speak to wharf-rat[5] boys, not even to give directions; don't eat fruits on the street—flies will follow you; *but I don't sing benna on Sundays at all and never in Sunday school?*; this is how to sew on a button; this is how to make a buttonhole for the button you have just sewed on; this is how to hem a dress when you see the hem coming down and so to prevent yourself from looking like the slut I know you are so bent on becoming; this is how you iron your father's khaki shirt so that it doesn't have a crease; this is how you iron your father's khaki pants so that they don't have a crease; this is how you grow okra[6]—far from the house, because okra tree harbors red ants; when you are growing dasheen,[7] make sure it gets plenty of water or else it makes your throat itch when you are eating it; this is how you sweep a corner; this is how you sweep a whole house; this is how you sweep a yard; this is how you smile to someone you don't like too much; this is how you smile to someone you don't like at all; this is how you smile to someone you like completely; this is how you set a table for tea; this is how you set a table for dinner; this is how you set a table for dinner with an important guest; this is how you set a table for lunch; this is how you set a table for breakfast; this is how to behave in the presence of men who don't know you very well, and this way they won't recognize immediately the slut I have warned you against becoming; be sure to wash every day, even if it is with your own spit; don't squat down to play marbles—you are not a boy, you know; don't pick people's flowers—you might catch something; don't throw stones at blackbirds; because it might not be a blackbird at all; this is how to make a bread pudding;[8] this is how to make doukona;[9] this is how to make pepper pot;[1] this is how to make a good medicine for a cold; this is how to make a good medicine to throw away a child before it even becomes a child; this is how to catch a fish; this is how to throw back a fish you don't like, and that way something bad won't fall on you; this is how to bully a man; this is how a man bullies you; this is how to love a man, and if this doesn't work there are other ways, and if they don't work don't feel too bad about giving up; this is how to spit up in the air if you feel like it, and this is how to move quick so that it doesn't fall on you; this is how to make ends meet; always squeeze bread to make sure it's fresh; *but what if the baker won't let me feel the bread?*; you mean to say that after all you are really going to be the kind of woman who the baker won't let near the bread?

1978, 1983

---

5. Regarding an individual who lives by stealing from ships or warehouses near wharves.
6. Vegetable thought to be of African origin, grown in tropical and warm temperate climates, often cooked in soups and stews or served raw.
7. The edible, starchy, tuberous root of taro, a tropical plant.
8. A dessert made from leftover bread.
9. A Caribbean pudding made from plantain and wrapped in a plantain leaf.
1. A Caribbean meat stew, strongly flavored with cinnamon, hot peppers, and cassareep, a special sauce made from the cassava root.

DOROTHY ALLISON

The central fact of my life," Dorothy Allison writes, "is that I was born in 1949 in Greenville, South Carolina, the bastard daughter of a white woman from a desperately poor family." The title of her first book, *Trash* (1988), a collection of short stories, deliberately appropriates the contemptuous slur directed toward her family and all those whose poverty is seen, she writes, as "somehow oddly deserved." Her novel *Bastard Out of Carolina* (1989), a fictional account of her experience as the first child of a fifteen-year-old unwed mother who worked as a waitress, is a fierce and passionate articulation of the devastating effects of social class and its link to sexual abuse and violence. An activist on feminist and gay/lesbian issues, Allison has been writer-in-residence at Emory University in Atlanta, Georgia, as well as Davidson College in Davidson, North Carolina, and Columbia College in Chicago.

The selection below comes from "Stubborn Girls and Mean Stories," Allison's introduction to a second edition of *Trash* (2002). In this piece "mean" and "stubborn" are terms of praise implying survival and resilience. "'Now that's mean,'" her mama says with a smile after Allison has sent her one of her stories. "I want it mean," Allison replies. Writing for Allison becomes an act of setting "moment to moment a small piece of stubbornness against an ocean of ignorance and obliteration." "Stubborn Girls and Mean Stories" takes its place beside classic documents of the devastating effects of poverty such as James Agee and Walker Evans's *Let Us Now Praise Famous Men* (1941) as well as accounts (such as Eudora Welty's) in which a writer describes how and why she came to be a writer.

From Stubborn Girls and Mean Stories

Introduction

The central fact of my life is that I was born in 1949 in Greenville, South Carolina,[1] the bastard daughter of a white woman from a desperately poor family, a girl who had left the seventh grade the year before, worked as a waitress, and was just a month past fifteen when she birthed me. That fact, the inescapable impact of being born in a condition of poverty that this society finds shameful, contemptible, and somehow oddly deserved, has had dominion over me to such an extent that I have spent my life trying to overcome or deny it. My family's lives were not on television, not in books, not even comic books. There was a myth of the poor in this country, but it did not include us, no matter how I tried to squeeze us in. There was this concept of the "good" poor, and that fantasy had little to do with the everyday lives my family had survived. The good poor were hardworking, ragged but clean, and intrinsically honorable. We were the bad poor. We were men who drank and couldn't keep a job; women, invariably pregnant before marriage, who quickly became worn, fat, and old from working too many hours and bearing too many children; and children with runny noses, watery eyes, and the wrong attitudes. My cousins quit school, stole cars, used drugs, and took

1. South Carolina's sixth largest city, located upstate in the foothills of the Appalachian Mountains.

dead-end jobs pumping gas or waiting tables. I worked after school in a job provided by Lyndon Johnson's War on Poverty,[2] stole books I could not afford. We were not noble, not grateful, not even hopeful. We knew ourselves despised. What was there to work for, to save money for, to fight for or struggle against? We had generations before us to teach us that nothing ever changed, and that those who did try to escape failed.

Everything I write comes out of that very ordinary American history. There is no story in which my family is not background, even as I have moved very far from both Greenville, South Carolina, and the poverty to which I was born. I remain my mother's bastard girl, a woman who treasures her handmade family, my own adopted bastard child and the lover/partner who has nurtured and provoked me for more than fifteen years. We become what we did not intend, and still the one thing I know for sure is that only my sense of humor will sustain me.

Stories I began as a girl seem different to me when I read them now. It is almost as if I did not write them, as if that writer were another person— which of course she is. Twenty and twenty-five years ago when I first began to publish stories, I was a different person—not just younger but more girlish than it is easy for me to admit today. I grew up writing these stories. I made peace with my family. I forgave myself and some of the people I had held in such contempt—most of all those I loved. That forgiveness took place in large part through the writing of these stories, in a process of making peace with the violence of my childhood, in owning up to it and finding a way to talk about it that did not make me more ashamed of myself or those I loved.

* * *

Before I published any of my own stories, I read a great many stories by people just as passionate about writing as I was, and I learned something from everyone I read—sometimes most important what I should not try to write. I began in the tradition of Muriel Rukeyser,[3] aching to break the world open with what I had to say on the page. There were specific feelings I wanted the stories to create, realizations I wanted people to experience. Sometimes it was grief I wanted to provoke, sometimes anger, almost always a spur to action, to change. I wanted the world to be different in my lifetime, and I truly believed that stories were one way to help that happen. I did not begin with craft, I began with strong feelings and worked toward craft. I wanted to be good and I wanted to be effective, and these are not always the same thing. Sometimes I was trying to write a poem, but the thing would not pare down enough to anything less than narrative. Sometimes I was so angry, I wrote to stop my own rage. Mostly I was angry, and drunk on words, the sound of words more than the way they looked on the page. It is quite literally the case that I wrote out loud, reading the stories out loud over and over until they were closer to what I wanted.

2. The "War on Poverty" is a phrase used by President Lyndon B. Johnson (1908–1973), during his 1964 State of the Union address in response to a rising national poverty rate, which led to the establishment of the Office of Economic Opportunity to administer the local application of federal funds targeting poverty.

3. American poet and political activist (1913–1980), known for her poems about equality, feminism, social justice, and Judaism.

"If I die tomorrow, I want to have gotten this down."

That is how many of these stories started. Once in a while, I had read someone else's story and put it down in rage, beginning my own to refuse the one that had so confounded me. Going back into these stories, I remember those moments even when I no longer remember the actual stories I was refuting. Taylor Caldwell stories,[4] called them in an early journal—stories in which poor Southern characters were framed as if they were brain-damaged, or morally insufficient, or just damn stupid.

"We are not stupid. We do pretty well with what we have." I'd set out to put that on the page—but often I would go south. By that I mean I would not wind up where I intended. I started "Meanest Woman Ever Left Tennessee" to work out in my own mind what it must have been like to have been my grandmother—and her mother, my great-grandma about whom I knew almost nothing, except that her children hated her and that she had lived a long time. How'd that work? I wondered, and made up a fictional Mattie Lee, a pretend Shirley. I gave the children names that actually figured in my grandmother's conversations—names of cousins, second cousins, and lost uncles. I worked it out as if it were a movie, or the kind of story people in my family simply would not tell. Contrary to the myth of Southern families passing stories along on the porch, people in my family kept secrets and only hinted at what might have happened. Some days I think the way to make a storyteller is to refuse to tell her what happened—as my mama and aunts did with me. I had to make up my great-grandmother, and I did it in a story that was originally to be about her daughter—a story I started when I was still in college, and my mother told me my grandmother had died—but three months after the funeral was past, and long past any hope I might have had of going to Greenville, attending the funeral or learning anything about how she had died.

"In a ditch," my Uncle Jack told me a decade later. "Had a stroke halfway between our house and your Uncle Bo's. Just lay down and died."

"Oh." I just stood there.

"Oh." I was living in Tallahassee then, in a feminist collective household,[5] and fiercely determined to learn more about my grandmother, my aunts, even legendary Great-grandma Shirley. But my uncle's brutal comment was all I gathered in that visit, and almost as soon as I asked about it, one of my aunts denied that was how it happened.

"She didn't die down there. She died in the hospital two whole days later. She just fell in that ditch and lay there awhile before we went out and found her."

Maybe that was the story I should have written, but it was not. By the time I got back to my big complicated household, I was working on the story of what Grandma Mattie Lee might have been like as a girl. What if? And I was in it, watching Shirley beat on the steps with that broom handle. Would I have made Mattie Lee so heroic if my own mother had not hidden

---

4. One of the pen names of Janet Miriam Holland (1900–1985), an Anglo-American novelist and prolific author of popular fiction

5. A group of individuals who are motivated by a common interest (feminism, in this case), work together on specific projects to further this common objective, and tend to make decisions on an egalitarian basis.

her death from me, if my uncle had not spoken so brutally? Maybe. Still, what I wrote felt right on the page, and from this distance that seems the primary fact. I did a lot of things because it felt right on the page, or sounded right when read out loud in an empty room. I did not finish that story in Tallahassee. I did not finish that story till Brooklyn; fully fifteen years after my grandmother's death. Even then, I think I finished it because I fell in love with that teenage girl, her month full of white and her eyes full of fire. It worked well enough that it was another of the stories my mama would never talk to me about. "Now that's mean," my mama said about one of the stories I sent her. She smiled and gave a little shudder when she said it. That is what I intended, I told her. I want it mean. I did not say that I also wanted the story to be about love and compassion. For that sometimes I had to dig deeper, into the muscle of character. Still, I think you can tell that I loved my impossible grandmother with my whole heart, her black brows and wide face, her bulldog glare and frank inclination to tell me things my mother never intended me to learn. I knew she worked her children the way her mother had worked her, putting them out to pick strawberries for neighboring farmers and pocketing the money to buy snuff. I knew she was quick to slap and full of desperation, but I knew also that in the context of how she had been raised and what she had survived, she was almost gentle, almost sweet-tempered. But not quite. I had sweet-tempered cousins and I saw them get ground down. I had gentle aunts and it seemed they almost disappeared out of their own lives. Is it any wonder that when I set out to write stories, I made up women like my grandmother, like my great-grandmother? Troublesome, angry, complicated women with secretive, unpredictable natures—that is who you will find in my stories—and little girls who were not me. What are these stories about? Shame and outrage, pride and stubbornness, and the vital necessity of a sense of humor. I wrote to release indignation and refuse humiliation, to admit fault and to glorify the people I loved who were never celebrated. I wrote to celebrate. I wrote to take a little revenge, and sometimes to make clear that revenge was not what I was doing. Always, I tried not to use the flat metallic language of politics and preaching, but sometimes I knew no other way to frame what I had to say.

*　*　*

Now for a word on "trash." I originally claimed the label "trash" in self-defense. The phrase had been applied to me and to my family in crude and hateful ways. I took it on deliberately, as I had "dyke"[6]—though I have to acknowledge that what I heard as a child was more often the phrase "white trash." As an adult I saw all too clearly the look that would cross the face of any black woman in the room when that particular term was spoken. It was like a splash of cold water, and I saw the other side of the hatefulness in the words. It took me right back to being a girl and hearing the uncles I so admired spew racist bile and callous homophobic insults. Some phrases cannot be reclaimed. I gave that one up and took up the simpler honorific.

---

6. Slang term referring to a lesbian regardless of the individual's actual sexual identity; originally a derogatory label for a masculine woman.

By my twenties, that was what I heard most often anyway. Even rednecks get sensitized to insults, abandon some and cultivate others. I have not been called white trash in two decades, but only a couple years ago, I heard myself referred to as "that trash" in a motel corridor in the central valley in California.

In 1988, I titled this short story collection *Trash* to confront the term and to claim it honorific. In 2002, Trash still suits me, even though I live over here in California among people who are almost postconscious. In Sonoma County it makes more sense to call myself a Zen redneck, or just a dyke mama. What it comes down to is that I use "trash" to raise the issue of who the term glorifies as well as who it disdains. There are not simple or direct answers on any of these questions, and it is far harder to be sure your audience understands the textured lay of what you are doing—specially if you are in Northern California rather than Louisiana, and in 2002 rather than 1988. And of course these days I feel like there is a nation of us—displaced Southerners and children of the working class. We listen to Steve Earle, Mary J. Blige, and k.d. lang.[7] We devour paperback novels and tell evil mean stories, value stubbornness above patience and a sense of humor more than a college education. We claim our heritage with a full appreciation of how often it has been disdained.

And let me promise you, you do not want to make us angry.

2002

---

7. Steve Earle (b. 1955), American singer-songwriter known for his rock and country music as well as his political activism; Mary J. Blige (b. 1971), American singer, producer, songwriter, actress, and rapper; k.d. lang (b. 1961), Canadian pop and country singer-songwriter also known as an activist for animal rights, gay rights, and Tibetan human rights.

JOHN CRAWFORD

*T*he *Last True Story I'll Ever Tell* (2006) is, like many war stories, a narrative that speaks for itself. Its author restricts information about himself to the tale. Biographical data that others might find interesting are withheld; the author's date of birth, for instance, is undisclosed. Only the facts relating to his service in Iraq and its aftermath are revealed: in 2002, one semester shy of graduating with a college degree financed by his service in the Florida National Guard, John Crawford was called to active duty and readied for combat. His truthful account cannot help but recall earlier fictional models, from the Civil War (Ambrose Bierce's "Occurrence at Owl Creek Bridge") to Vietnam (Tim O'Brien's *Going after Cacciato*), a reminder that the horrors of warfare stretch even nonfictive prose to its creative limits. Reprinted here is the last chapter from Crawford's book.

The Last True Story I'll Ever Tell

There were trees everywhere. That's all I remember thinking: towering green giants smiling down on the world. My foot slid down a little farther on the gas pedal and my dad's old truck responded in turn, roaring up to eighty-five. The windows were up and the air conditioner blew civilization into my face. On the radio was some new band I hadn't even heard of, but it didn't matter. The old paved road I drove on was full of potholes that threatened to sack me in, but that didn't matter either. Everything important was self-contained. My life was complete, better than it had ever been before, and I couldn't even begin to ruin it by putting it into words.

My wife sat next to me, red hair cradling her doll face as her lips mouthed the words to a song I hadn't heard before. She looked at me, and her eyes twinkled. They were hazel today; yesterday I had thought they were green; it all depended on her mood, I guess. She smiled and put her hand on top of mine. The vibration of the gearshift coursed like an electrical current between us when we touched, and it made my heart tingle.

"God, I missed you so much," I whispered barely audibly over the other noises that cycloned around us.

"I know, baby, I missed you too." My wife put her arm under mine and pulled herself close, her head resting warmly on my shoulder. Her eyes looked through the bug-covered windshield at the road ahead as she wondered where we were going. My own were clouded by tears of happiness. When I was a boy I wasn't allowed to cry, but I guess crying from sheer joy is acceptable.

Stephanie may have wondered where we were going on this windy stretch of blacktop. I had driven this road a thousand times in my childhood and had dreamed of it a thousand more while I was in Iraq. I was home.

We were going into my hometown, a tiny speck of a city south of Jacksonville. Our only claim to fame was the annual Blue Crab Festival. Every Memorial Day, hundreds of thousands of tourists flock to Palatka for the fresh seafood, entertainment, and most important, the beer tent. Tourists, stomachs full from too many crustaceans and arms tired from carrying pieces of carved driftwood and homemade jam, would stop by for one drink and spend the rest of the evening and their wallets there.

Parking was hard to find that time of year, but locals always have tricks, and I was no different. I pulled into the darkened parking lot of Saint Monica's Catholic Church. The engine sputtered to a stop, an occasional clanking continuing as we gathered our effects and stepped out into the shadows behind old Father Joe's house. No tow truck would venture here unless he wanted an earful from the elderly Irish priest.

I reached out in the darkness and found a loving hand. Together we ventured out into the bustling avenue. The craft stores that ventured for a mile in either direction were mostly closed. It was near ten at night, and the remaining food for sale had been swimming in grease all day like tadpoles in a mud puddle. Next to the mural of Billy Graham[1] we turned east toward

---

1. American Christian evangelist (b. 1918).

the riverfront. As we walked, I saw familiar faces. We smiled and nodded to each other—some kid I rode a bus with, another who had suffered through high school trigonometry with me. There was no reason to say hi. Nothing ever changed in my hometown; there was nothing new to talk about.

My wife was from the North. Well, not strictly. Most people don't consider DC to be particularly up there, but when you grow up in Florida, if it snows, it's the North. I looked over at my angel and saw she was gawking, mouth half open, at my battered town and its residents. Most of the tourists go home fairly early, and the locals who spend their days hiding in shantytowns come out like roaches. It wasn't her first visit to Palatka, but it was her first Blue Crab Festival, and that takes some getting used to. People staggered by with no teeth. A man with a hunchback talked to his one-armed girlfriend. A policeman sat sipping a beer and flirted with a seventeen-year-old dropout. I couldn't help broadening my smile and taking a deep breath of stale beer and fried food. For a second I watched it all fade away into the slums, tans, and reek of Baghdad. Smoke and rotten meat tickled my nose. I shook my head. That couldn't happen; I was home.

"John Fucking Crawford!" I swiveled around on my heels and into a bear hug from Kris.

"Kris, what's up?"

He gave Stephanie a hug too. They had met at the wedding, although I wasn't sure that she approved of my Palatka friends. They were all hard-partying guys, and Kris stood out among them, as I had once.

"Where's everyone at?"

"In the beer tent. C'mon, we saved you a seat."

The beer tent was the unequivocal center of the world during Blue Crab. In reality, the whole festival was an excuse to erect a circus tent full of beer-dispensing vixens and tired bands playing tired songs.

The night felt different, though—everything was more colorful and alive. Kris led me to the table where Quint and Joe sat with their wives. They both laughed out loud and gave me hugs when I approached. I laughed, uncomfortable with all the attention, but it sure was good to see them. Quint had been the popular one in school and all the girls had craved his attention. His wife, Amanda, perched on his shoulder and fed off his smile. She scarcely acknowledged the rest of us. If I was unsure how Stephanie felt about my friends, there was no doubt how Amanda viewed Quint's friends.

Next to them were Joe and Jamila. The three of us were closer than the rest because we had gone to Florida State at the same time. Joe was the smartest of us, but still managed to pull off hanging with us. He met Jamila at a bar in Tallahassee; I had been there when they met. Joe had told me to stay away, that she was his the moment they met, and a few years later they were married and Joe was still entranced with her.

There were plenty of hugs and smiles around, and a scantily clad blonde with a soft keg attached to her back came around and filled all our beers for a dollar.

"So I hear you guys just got back from Europe?" I started to say, provoking a long, partially boring tale of exotic cities and cultures. I wanted to catch up on a year and a half's worth of gossip, but the rest of the table was more interested in watching Tony's band play. I hadn't heard them in years, and they had gotten really good.

The beer kept coming like a horror-movie villain, always right behind you. Life was good, my friends were there, my wife sat next to me, her hand resting on my thigh under the table as we smiled at everyone and laughed. We downed drink after drink and talked about the time I nearly flipped my first truck not twenty minutes after it was bought.

We decided to go to Quint's farm the next day and do some shooting, sans the women. Tony's band was kicking, and people were getting up to dance or crowd the stage. The place was full of gleeful noises, young girls giggled and flirted, and old men told fish stories. Lovers whispered and laughed around us. I looked around and felt like pumping my fist in the air. I was home.

"So . . . we spent the last summer in Europe and we told you about that. Tell us about your summer, John?" Joe asked, his eyes on mine, trying to read me.

"Summer, my ass. It fucking sucked."

"Yeah, whatever. C'mon, man, what was it like?" Kris jumped in.

"Tell us a war story." Quint threw in. "Did you shoot anyone?" The rest of the table cheered in agreement and leaned forward over their plastic cups in anticipation. Even my wife looked at me expectantly. I had always been a storyteller, and they were excited to hear what yarn I would give them about this one.

"You guys don't want to hear a war story. None of them make any fucking sense. I'll tell you guys all you want tomorrow." But they wouldn't give up. They badgered, pestered, and hounded me until they saw me breaking.

I leaned over and took a cigarette from Quint's pack, which rested in the center of the table.

"Lemme get a cigarette."

"I suppose you want a light too? Next you'll be taking the fillings outta my fucking teeth." Everyone laughed at Quint's joke except me.

I arrived in An Nasiriyah[2] on March 22. Third Infantry Division had come through an hour earlier and smoldering bodies blackened the sides of the road. In their rush north, the invaders had simply blown through whatever opposition they had met, but bypassed much of the city. We came in with the First Marine Expeditionary Force and were immediately bogged down by heavy fighting. The marines were taking heavy casualties inside the city, while my platoon sat just outside city limits guarding an ammunition supply point that had previously belonged to the Eleventh Iraqi Infantry Division. They had popped smoke at the first sign of American armor. The eggs and flour were still damp on the kitchen counter. Human shit crawled out of the corners to get underneath your boots. No one really noticed it very much, though; we were all preoccupied with staring open-mouthed at the cache of weapons we had found. There were warehouses literally full of rifles, grenades, missiles, mortars, and rocket-propelled grenades. It was one of those sights that overwhelm the mind by just going on as far as the eye can see.

The area we had to secure was too big for one platoon, and we spent most of the time as a quick reactionary force speeding down dusty roads after looters or guerrilla soldiers sneaking in for resupply. We did this for about a

---

2. City in Iraq on the Euphrates River 225 miles southeast of Baghdad.

week, just high-speed chases through the desert after rag-clad hajjis.[3] The modern buildings of Nasiriyah loomed on one horizon, while Abraham's temple reached toward the sky in the other direction. We were in the biblical city of Ur,[4] and I remember being impressed with that. It was still very early in the war.

The place was a slum, though. Bedouins herded goats past us, paying no more attention to us than we did them. Mudbrick houses broke up the skyline. Donkey carts and starving people milled about, rummaging through the belongings of the dead. It was a sight one would expect to find after stepping out of a time machine. Aside from the very occasional beat-up taxicab, it was like looking at a portrait from five thousand years ago. The smell was what I remember most. Burned human flesh combined with diesel and shit. There were bodies all over the place, and although we ran into a few live ones, most of the combatants had long ago left. Some of the guys took pictures, but that wasn't for me. I had no urge to reminisce later over photos of meat on the ground.

We were smack dab in the center of the fertile crescent,[5] except it wasn't nearly as fertile as I had imagined. On one side of the road there were fields of super-green crops, and then, like a dog at the end of its leash, they would stop and turn into lifeless desert. There was no happy reception from the Iraqis. We were greeted with indifference. No one clapped or waved flags. They just stared at us and waited for us to leave. We raided nearby houses and buildings looking for soldiers hiding there. We were excited, ready to get things over with and go home. We were itching. It had been more than two months since any of us had talked to loved ones or received any mail. We were on two meals a day plus water ration, and on top of that we were eating sand, drinking sand. Sand was in every orifice of our bodies. At some point, you begin to imagine that you're made of sand. It gets into you, the desert, not physically, but really into your soul until you're just pissed off.

There was a complex of bunkers to our north, and my squad moved out one morning to clear them. They were empty, but in one room we came upon a large map overlay. Twice as tall as me and from one corner of the room to the other, it marked every Iraqi unit position south of the Tigris River. We called it in, and the commander told us to take it and Charlie Mike[6]— continue mission.

There was nothing else of interest, and before long we returned, drenched in sweat, to the perimeter. The company commander took one look at that map and decided that it needed to be taken to the division headquarters in what is now Tallil Air Force Base. Back then it was just a mechanized battalion, some Special Forces guys, and a few rear-echelon motherfuckers. Regardless, our company commander thought he would get all sorts of kudos for the map *he* had found, so he loaded up in another Humvee[7] with a goofy first lieutenant who looked like he couldn't run a Boy Scout troop,

3. Specifically, a Muslim who has made the pilgrimage to Mecca; U.S. soldiers in Iraq used the term to refer to any Iraqi, especially a combatant.
4. Ancient Sumerian capital and religious center, presently known as Muqayyar; the Bible names Ur as the birthplace and early home of Abraham.
5. The region stretching from Egypt's Nile Valley northward to the Levant (modern-day Israel, Lebanon, and Syria) and then southeastward to include Mesopotamia (modern-day Iraq); the Fertile Crescent is thought to be the birthplace of agricultural and civilization.
6. Military jargon for the letters C and M, respectively.
7. Military slang for HMMWV, the High Mobility, Multipurpose Wheeled Vehicle.

and together we went toward Tallil. They were moving ahead of us, and the sun was slowly painting the desert red as it set.

Staff Sergeant Connel was driving, Specialist Ramirez was in the back with a 240 golf machine gun, and I rode in the passenger seat with my M-249 squad automatic weapon as flank security. The Humvees we drove in were unarmored. You could throw a rock through them if you had a good enough arm, and hell, we didn't even have doors on. There we were, driving thirty-five miles an hour through an area that later that night would be nicknamed Ambush Alley because a young maintenance female got taken prisoner. Best way to earn medals in the army, after all—get lost or be an officer. Do both at the same time and you might even get a high school named after you.

On the right side of the road was the desert. The huts and hovels had sheets flapping in front of the door, light from kerosene lanterns peeking out. Chickens and goats ran free, while young girls and old ladies tried to finish up the daily chores before darkness fell. They stepped mindlessly over the bodies, washing clothes and maintaining the facade that they lived in complete normalcy.

The men, meanwhile, were content to sit on their stoops smoking cigarettes and drinking beer. The little boys emulated them by taking it easy as well. They frolicked about, skipping among the stones. There was no danger in the air, so it was with a total lack of fear that I noticed a group of little boys playing on the left side of the road. There were three, all about eight or nine years old. They stood knee deep in crops, their ragged clothes blowing in the wind around their emaciated bodies. I was about to wave cordially when the center one reached up and pointed his finger at the commander's Humvee in front of us. The sun was setting behind them, and as we rolled up, that finger became the front sight post of an AK-47.[8] Anyone who has ever seen one knows there's nothing else to mistake it for with its thick metal triangle; there's no other rifle in the world that looks like that.

"Fuck!" I yelled to no one.

"He's got a fucking AK!" I yelled again.

It was on the opposite side of the vehicle from me, so there was little I could do except shout a warning. Sergeant Connel slammed on the brakes. The tires squealed and struggled against the pavement, and our screeching halt came with a black rubbery smell catching up with us. Ramirez, on the machine gun in the back, never even got to point in that direction. The sudden stop caused him to fly forward halfway over the cab, his gun banging noisily on the hood.

Connel's rifle sling was snagged on something in the vehicle, and despite his tugs and frantic curses he couldn't free it. Without doors or seat belts, I slid easily out of the Humvee and had my feet in the dirt before the stop was even complete. I slammed my saw onto the hood with a clank. The bipod legs on my weapon were still up and in the locked position, but the boys weren't very far away, so accuracy wasn't too much of a problem.

Our sudden stop had caused quite a commotion, and all three boys were looking at us now. Their eyes wide with wonder. The one holding the rifle slowly turned it toward me. It seemed so slow the way he moved, but I sup-

8. Assault rifle first manufactured for the Soviet military in the late 1940s and now used throughout the world.

pose that was just the way I remember everything happening. My safety was already off, and I had him in the middle of my sight picture.

Why don't they run? Most likely they didn't realize that in a tenth of a second their bodies would be ripped apart, shredded by a hundred bullets manufactured a world away in Cleveland or somewhere. They couldn't have known that that very night the dogs that scavenged the desert would be tearing out their entrails and that they would be unrecognizable to the morning.

I held my breath and steadied on the hood of that vehicle as best I could. They were silhouetted black against the sunset, and I could clearly see the entire barrel assembly of the rifle with a thirty-round magazine locked into the bottom. The muzzle was almost on me, and I had already hesitated too long. While they stood on the swelling bloody sun, I applied pressure to the trigger.

I don't know if that was before or after I realized that the rest of the rifle was missing. The trigger was gone, as was the buttstock and bolt. Someone had killed a hajji there the day before and just run over his rifle with their track, rendering it useless. That kid couldn't have shot spitballs through it even if he had wanted to.

No one at the table said a word; our circle had become a pool of awkward silence. Stephanie squeezed my leg under the table in support, but I didn't move.

"It's no big deal, man, you can just tell us a story some other time," Joe said reassuringly. The table began to resurrect; cups were refilled, cigarettes lit. Tony's band had stopped playing and they were now introducing all the members. The chattering in the background was coming back, growling into a great screeching howl. I wanted to stay and talk, but couldn't. After a few more halfhearted attempts to laugh, we left.

My wife and I were silent as we passed the church on our way back to the car. I remembered being an altar boy when I was, as Father Joe described me, "a wee lad." He used to place this oversized Bible on my head and read from it to the congregation as if I were some form of human lectern. The churchgoers would snicker, incensing me, but I was just a little boy then. I was a man now, and I was fairly sure that book wouldn't fit on my head anymore. What did it matter, though? I was home.

A crashing boom broke the night air and I jumped up on my cot with a start. It took me a moment to realize where I was. Pearson and Hightower were already up, throwing on body armor and grabbing weapons to defend the perimeter. I wiped sleep from my eyes. I had been dreaming, nothing more. It was just a vision of what home could or should be.

What I'm about to write is true. Utterly true. The first thing I wrote for this book was a fiction short story I wrote while still in Iraq. It was all about returning home and finding myself in a world where no one understood my experience, but they were all there to support me. My wife was on my arm, telling me that no matter what she loved me. We would have children soon, and the rest of my life would be wonderful I was wiser in that story than I am now. Like Joseph Campbell's[9] hero with a thousand faces, I returned victorious. I told tales of my exploits and people listened. They cared.

---

9. American scholar and writer (1904–1987), best known for his work in comparative mythology beginning with his first book, *The Hero with a Thousand Faces* (1949).

It wasn't until I got back that truth engulfed me like a storm cloud. Dreams and truth are never intertwined.

I spent a few months drifting around friends' houses, from one couch to the next. When I finally got enough money to get an apartment again, I kept getting kicked out.

I was evicted from one place I was renting because I have a dog, a big one. He sleeps with me at night when I'm drunk and can't understand why I'm alone. Dogs don't turn their backs on you, that's another truth. I moved five times in five months.

Most days I was sick. It was a lingering, wasting sickness that comes only when you have nothing left. There are people out there who really don't know why they get up in the morning; it's sad, and that's how you know it's true.

In my dream, my wife never told me that things would have been better off if I had just never come home. In reality, I agree with her.

This is a true story. You can tell because it makes your stomach turn. I am home now, and I will never again write a true story.

JOAN DIDION

J oan Didion's collection of essays on the 1960s counterculture, *Slouching Toward Bethlehem* (1968), made her famous and established her as a practitioner of "The New Journalism." Her second essay collection *The White Album* (1979), mixes autobiography with cultural events in Los Angeles in the 1960s (the book's title refers to the 1968 double album by the Beatles, which had no graphics or text other than the band's name). These widely influential books confirmed Didion's reputation as a shrewd and edgy cultural observer and literary stylist. She has also published several novels, including *Play It As It Lays* (1970) and *Democracy* (1984).

A native Californian, Joan Didion (b. 1934) moved to New York as a young woman, where she worked for *Vogue* magazine and, in 1964, married the novelist John Gregory Dunne. In the mid-1960s the couple moved to Los Angeles, where they spent the next 20 years. They collaborated on several screenplays and became a glamorous couple whose talents were sought after in Hollywood. In the 1980s they moved back to New York, where Didion continued her work as a screenwriter, novelist, and nonfiction writer.

The Year of Magical Thinking (2005) is Didion's account of the year following the sudden death from cardiac arrest of her husband of forty years. In this book Didion makes herself and her experience of grief the factual center of the book; in a sense she makes herself a case study for the craziness of grief, for the "magical thinking" that assumes, for example, that if you don't let someone tell you a person is dead, then he isn't really dead. The precision of the book's analysis, with its extensive display of medical research, makes *The Year of Magical Thinking* an autobiographical account unlike most others.

Five days before her husband's death, their daughter, Quintana Roo, whom they adopted in 1966, was hospitalized for pneumonia and fell into septic shock and then a coma (two months before the publication of *The Year of Magical Thinking*, Quintana Roo died of pancreatitis). In the selection that appears below, Didion provides an account of the evening of her husband's death precise enough to be

Quintana Roo Dunne, John Gregory Dunne, and Joan Didion at home in Malibu in 1976.

called, at first, clinical. However, the restrained, minimalist style in which she delivers her acute observation can be read as her way of controlling and holding off potentially overwhelming feelings. "We tell stories in order to live," *The White Album* begins. In this excerpt from *The Year of Magical Thinking* we experience the writer using all of the tools at her disposal to make sense of an experience that, as she writes, changed everything.

From The Year of Magical Thinking

December 30, 2003, a Tuesday.

We had seen Quintana in the sixth-floor ICU at Beth Israel North.[1]

We had come home.

We had discussed whether to go out for dinner or eat in.

I said I would build a fire, we could eat in.

I built the fire, I started dinner, I asked John[2] if he wanted a drink.

I got him a Scotch and gave it to him in the living room, where he was reading in the chair by the fire where he habitually sat.

The book he was reading was by David Fromkin, a bound galley of *Europe's Last Summer: Who Started the Great War in 1914?*[3]

I finished getting dinner, I set the table in the living room where, when we were home alone, we could eat within sight of the fire. I find myself stressing

---

1. New York City hospital located on Manhattan's Upper East Side. "ICU": The Intensive Care Unit is a specialized department in many hospitals that provides life support or organ support systems in patients who are critically ill and require intensive monitoring.
2. John Gregory Dunne, American novelist,

screenwriter, and literary critic (1932–2003), was Joan Didion's husband from 1964 until his death in 2003.
3. An account of the underpinnings of World War I by David Fromkin, a noted author, lawyer, and historian.

the fire because fires were important to us. I grew up in California, John and I lived there together for twenty-four years, in California we heated our houses by building fires. We built fires even on summer evenings, because the fog came in. Fires said we were home, we had drawn the circle, we were safe through the night. I lit the candles. John asked for a second drink before sitting down. I gave it to him. We sat down. My attention was on mixing the salad.

John was talking, then he wasn't.

At one point in the seconds or minute before he stopped talking he had asked me if I had used single-malt Scotch[4] for his second drink. I had said no, I used the same Scotch I had used for his first drink. "Good," he had said. "I don't know why but I don't think you should mix them." At another point in those seconds or that minute he had been talking about why World War One was the critical event from which the entire rest of the twentieth century flowed.

I have no idea which subject we were on, the Scotch or World War One, at the instant he stopped talking.

I only remember looking up. His left hand was raised and he was slumped motionless. At first I thought he was making a failed joke, an attempt to make the difficulty of the day seem manageable.

I remember saying *Don't do that.*

When he did not respond my first thought was that he had started to eat and choked. I remember trying to lift him far enough from the back of the chair to give him the Heimlich.[5] I remember the sense of his weight as he fell forward, first against the table, then to the floor. In the kitchen by the telephone I had taped a card with the New York–Presbyterian[6] ambulance numbers. I had not taped the numbers by the telephone because I anticipated a moment like this. I had taped the numbers by the telephone in case someone in the building needed an ambulance.

Someone else.

I called one of the numbers. A dispatcher asked if he was breathing. I said *Just come.* When the paramedics came I tried to tell them what had happened but before I could finish they had transformed the part of the living room where John lay into an emergency department. One of them (there were three, maybe four, even an hour later I could not have said) was talking to the hospital about the electrocardiogram[7] they seemed already to be transmitting. Another was opening the first or second of what would be many syringes for injection. (Epinephrine? Lidocaine? Procainamide?[8] The names came to mind but I had no idea from where.) I remember saying that he might have choked. This was dismissed with a finger swipe: the airway was clear. They seemed now to be using defibrillating paddles,[9] an attempt to restore a rhythm. They got something that could have been a

---

4. High-quality, unblended whiskey distilled in Scotland, using malted barley as the only grain ingredient.
5. A series of abdominal thrusts to help a person choking on a foreign object clear the blocked airway by forcing air from the lungs to create an artificial cough in order to expel the obstruction.
6. Hospital in New York City, considered among the best in the world.
7. A noninvasive test using skin electrodes to for problems with the electrical activity of your heart.

8. Procainamide A pharmaceutical agent used to suppress fast rhythms of the heart (cardiac arrhythmias). "Epinephrine": also, adrenaline; a hormone and neurotransmitter which increases the heart rate, contracts blood vessels, and dilates air passages. "Lidocaine": common local anesthetic and anti-arrhythmic drug.
9. Paddles which, when placed on a patient's chest, deliver a therapeutic surge of electricity to restore normal electrical activity in the heart.

normal heartbeat (or I thought they did, we had all been silent, there was a sharp jump), then lost it, and started again.

"He's still fibbing," I remember the one on the telephone saying.

"V-fibbing,"[1] John's cardiologist said the next morning when he called from Nantucket. "They would have said 'V-fibbing.' V for ventricular."

Maybe they said "V-fibbing" and maybe they did not. Atrial fibrillation[2] did not immediately or necessarily cause cardiac arrest. Ventricular did. Maybe ventricular was the given.

I remember trying to straighten out in my mind what would happen next. Since there was an ambulance crew in the living room, the next logical step would be going to the hospital. It occurred to me that the crew could decide very suddenly to go to the hospital and I would not be ready. I would not have in hand what I needed to take. I would waste time, get left behind. I found my handbag and a set of keys and a summary John's doctor had made of his medical history. When I got back to the living room the paramedics were watching the computer monitor they had set up on the floor. I could not see the monitor so I watched their faces. I remember one glancing at the others. When the decision was made to move it happened very fast. I followed them to the elevator and asked if I could go with them. They said they were taking the gurney down first, I could go in the second ambulance. One of them waited with me for the elevator to come back up. By the time he and I got into the second ambulance the ambulance carrying the gurney was pulling away from the front of the building. The distance from our building to the part of New York–Presbyterian that used to be New York Hospital is six crosstown blocks. I have no memory of sirens. I have no memory of traffic. When we arrived at the emergency entrance to the hospital the gurney was already disappearing into the building. A man was waiting in the driveway. Everyone else in sight was wearing scrubs. He was not. "Is this the wife," he said to the driver, then turned to me. "I'm your social worker," he said, and I guess that is when I must have known.

"I opened the door and I seen the man in the dress greens and I knew. I immediately knew." This was what the mother of a nineteen-year-old killed by a bomb in Kirkuk said on an HBO documentary quoted by Bob Herbert[3] in the New York Times on the morning of November 12, 2004. "But I thought that if, as long as I didn't let him in, he couldn't tell me. And then it—none of that would've happened. So he kept saying, 'Ma'am, I need to come in.' And I kept telling him, 'I'm sorry, but you can't come in.'"

When I read this at breakfast almost eleven months after the night with the ambulance and the social worker I recognized the thinking as my own.

2005

---

1. Ventricular fibrillation, a condition in which there is uncoordinated contraction of the cardiac muscle of the ventricles in the heart.
2. The most common of abnormal heart rhythms, involving the uncoordinated quivering of the heart muscles of the two upper chambers, or atria, of the heart.

3. American journalist and op-ed columnist for the New York Times (b. 1945) who frequently writes about poverty, the Iraq war, racism, and political apathy toward racial issues. "Kirkuk": city in Iraq, invaded by American and British military forces in March 2003. "HBO": Home Box Office, a cable television network.

EDWIDGE DANTICAT

E dwidge Danticat was born in Port-au-Prince, the capital of Haiti, in 1969. Her novels *Breath, Eyes, Memory* (1994) and *The Farming of Bones* (1998), as well as her collection of stories, *Krik? Krak!* (1995—the title comes from a Haitian chant), draw on her experiences as a Haitian American. Danticat was two years old when her father left Haiti to make a better life for the family in the United States; two years later, her mother left to join him. For the next eight years Danticat and her brother remained in Haiti under the care of their uncle Joseph, a Baptist minister who founded his own church and school in Port-au-Prince. She then emigrated to the United States to be reunited with her parents. In 2004, after violence destroyed her uncle's church and put his life in jeopardy, Joseph entered the United States asking for temporary asylum but was detained in Miami by Department of Homeland Security officials suspicious of his plea. During questioning, Joseph collapsed but was refused treatment at the time. The next day he was taken to a Florida hospital where he died. In October 2007 Danticat testified on this issue before the House Judiciary Subcommittee on Immigration, Citizenship Refuges, Border Security, and International Law. Like many creative nonfiction writers, Danticat uses personal narrative to illuminate larger issues: the political and economic situation in Haiti, the challenges facing immigrants to the United States, and the need to reform the practices of immigration detainee medical care.

Brother, I'm Dying is a memoir partly of the writer's childhood in Haiti and, more particularly, of the interconnected lives of her uncle and father, who, after leaving Haiti, ran a car-service business in New York and died from pulmonary fibrosis soon after his brother's death. When the adult Danticat, now pregnant with her first child, listens to her gravely ill father respond to the question "Have you enjoyed your life?" by speaking of his children and family, she recalls living as a child with her uncle when the family would regularly receive letters from her father in the United States. This selection captures Danticat's exploration of what words can and cannot say, a question at the heart of this writer's work.

From Brother, I'm Dying

Listening to my father, I remembered a time when I used to dream of smuggling him words. I was eight years old and Bob and I were living in Haiti with his oldest brother, my uncle Joseph, and his wife. And since they didn't have a telephone at home—few Haitian families did then—and access to the call centers was costly, we had no choice but to write letters. Every other month, my father would mail a half-page, three-paragraph missive addressed to my uncle. Scribbled in his minuscule scrawl, sometimes on plain white paper, other times on lined, hole-punched notebook pages still showing bits of fringe from the spiral binding, my father's letters were composed in stilted French,[1] with the first paragraph offering news of his and my mother's health, the second detailing how to spend the money they had wired for food, lodging, and

---

1. That is, the formal French taught in Haitian schools, rather than the vernacular Creole of everyday life in Haiti.

school expenses for Bob and myself, the third section concluding abruptly after reassuring us that we'd be hearing from him again before long.

Later I would discover in a first-year college composition class that his letters had been written in a diamond sequence, the Aristotelian *Poetics*[2] correspondence, requiring an opening greeting, a middle detail or request, and a brief farewell at the end. The letter-writing process had been such an agonizing chore for my father, one that he'd hurried through while assembling our survival money, that this specific epistolary formula, which he followed unconsciously, had offered him a comforting way of disciplining his emotions.

"I was no writer," he later told me. "What I wanted to tell you and your brother was too big for any piece of paper and a small envelope."

Whatever restraint my father showed in his letters was easily compensated for by Uncle Joseph's reactions to them. First there was the public reading in my uncle's sparsely furnished pink living room, in front of Tante[3] Denise, Bob and me. This was done so there would be no misunderstanding as to how the money my parents sent for me and my brother would be spent. Usually my uncle would read the letters out loud, pausing now and then to ask my help with my father's penmanship, a kindness, I thought, a way to include me a step further. It soon became obvious, however, that my father's handwriting was as clear to me as my own, so I eventually acquired the job of deciphering his letters.

Along with this task came a few minutes of preparation for the reading and thus a few intimate moments with my father's letters, not only the words, and phrases, which did not vary greatly from month to month, but the vowels and syllables, their tilts and slants, which did. Because he wrote so little, I would try to guess his thoughts and moods from the dotting of his *i*'s and the crossing of his *t*'s, from whether there were actual periods at the ends of his sentences or just faint dots where the tip of his pen had simply landed. Did commas split his streamlined phrases, or were they staccato,[4] like someone speaking too rapidly, out of breath?

For the family readings, I recited my father's letters in a monotone, honoring what I interpreted as a secret between us, that the impersonal style of his letters was due as much to his lack of faith in words and their ability to accurately reproduce his emotions as to his caution with Bob's and my feelings, avoiding too-happy news that might add to the anguish of separation, too-sad news that might worry us, and any hint of judgment or disapproval for my aunt and uncle, which they could have interpreted as suggestions that they were mistreating us. The dispassionate letters were his way of avoiding a minefield, one he could have set off from a distance without being able to comfort the victims.

Given all this anxiety, I'm amazed my father wrote at all. The regularity, the consistency of his correspondence now feels like an act of valor. In contrast, my replies, though less routine—Uncle Joseph did most of the writing— were both painstakingly upbeat and suppliant. In my letters, I bragged about my good grades and requested, as a reward for them, an American doll at

---

2. The earliest surviving work of dramatic and literary theory, written by Aristotle (384–322 B.C.E.), which analyzes poetry prescriptively in terms of its essential elements.

3. Aunt (French).
4. A form of musical articulation, signifying an unconnected note, short and detached.

Christmas, a typewriter or sewing machine for my birthday, a pair of "real" gold earrings for Easter. But the things I truly wanted I was afraid to ask for, like when I would finally see him and my mother again. However, since my uncle read and corrected all my letters for faulty grammar and spelling, I wrote for his eyes more than my father's, hoping that even after the vigorous editing, my father would still decode the longing in my childish cursive slopes and arches, which were so much like his own.

The words that both my father and I wanted to exchange we never did. These letters were not approved, in his case by him, in my case by my uncle. No matter what the reason, we have always been equally paralyzed by the fear of breaking each other's heart. This is why I could never ask the question Bob did. I also could never tell my father that I'd learned from the doctor that he was dying. Even when they mattered less, there were things he and I were too afraid to say.

2007

RICHARD POWERS
b. 1957

I n his second novel, *Prisoner's Dilemma* (1988), Richard Powers presents a theory of order his characters experience as the "Butterfly Effect, that model of random motion describing how a butterfly flapping its wings in Peking propagates an unpredictable chain reaction of air currents, ultimately altering tomorrow's weather in Duluth." The human capacity to imagine and understand the real world (poetry) and the human ability to construct technologies capable of measuring it (science) combine in the sense of scientific wonder that typifies his fifth and most popular novel, *Galatea 2.2*. How people and the forces that influence their lives keep pace with each other is the substance of Powers's work.

Powers is one of several contemporaries (including Kathryn Kramer, William T. Vollmann, and David Foster Wallace) who write as the generational successors to Thomas Pynchon, whose novels, particularly *V.* (1963) and *Gravity's Rainbow* (1973), challenged readers to comprehend worlds that were virtually encyclopediac in range yet containable—barely—within the limits of printed novels. As the critic Tom LeClair has noted, Powers and his cohort, the ideal youthful readers of Pynchon, have adapted that author's intellectual overkill and applied it to conditions more typical of late-twentieth-century and early-twenty-first-century America. What was in Pynchon's 1960s a paranoia about government secrecy and terroristic subversion had become, by the millennium's end, literal facts of life, creating an even larger challenge to the novelistic intelligence that would contain them all. To balance the increase of technological capability with the limits of the mind to comprehend things, Powers favors double plots that reflect microcosmic versions of the same theme. In his first novel, *Three Farmers on Their Way to a Dance* (1985), World War I and its global reorderings are related to the three young Dutchmen of the title. *Prisoner's Dilemma* tells the story of the world's emergence into the atomic age with ongoing references to the fate of one small family involuntarily caught in the process. This strategy of intersecting plots continues through an eighth novel, *The Time of Our Singing* (2003), which pairs a brilliant, mixed-race vocalist's struggle to sing the music of his choice with his parents' earlier struggle to raise their three children in a world free from history's racial constraints. A ninth novel, *The Echo Maker* (2006), a winner of the National Book Award, explores memory, the homing instinct, and other brain function as they relate to one family member's caring for another. The novel follows characters in a Nebraska town including a brother who, badly injured in an automobile accident, suffers from a rare brain disorder (Capgras Syndrome) in which he thinks everyone he encounters is an imposter; his sister, who tries to help him recover even though he doubts her identity; and a distinguished neurologist to whom she writes and who comes to investigate this case firsthand. These human stories mesh with an account of the magnificent sandhill cranes, whose migratory behavior might be a possible tourist attraction for the town. In the novel's opening pages, reprinted here, Powers pairs the sister's quest and the cranes' flight as examples of deeply instinctive family behavior. People and nature, people and science, history and music often intersect in diverse ways within most Powers novels, from *The Goldbug Variations* (1991) on through his tenth novel, *Generosity: An Enhancement* (2009) about the commercialization of science in the case of a possible "happiness gene."

Powers was born in Evanston, Illinois, and raised on the far north side of Chicago, in the suburb of Lincolnwood, where his father was a school principal. When Powers was eleven his father accepted an appointment as principal of a school in Bangkok, and the family moved to Thailand for a five-year stint, not returning to the United States until 1974. After earning bachelor's and master's degrees (with initial concentrations on physics and mathematics and ending in English) at the University of Illinois, he worked as a computer-code writer in Boston. The publication of his first novel led to his being awarded a MacArthur fellowship, after which for several years he lived in the Netherlands. In 1992 he returned to the University of Illinois as an artist-in-residence; since 1996 he has held the Swanlund Chair as a professor of English, and he is formally affiliated with programs in the sciences and fine arts.

The following text is from *The Echo Maker* (2006).

From The Echo Maker

Cranes keep landing as night falls. Ribbons of them roll down, slack against the sky. They float in from all compass points, in kettles of a dozen, dropping with the dusk. Scores of *Grus canadensis*[1] settle on the thawing river. They gather on the island flats, grazing, beating their wings, trumpeting: the advance wave of a mass evacuation. More birds land by the minute, the air red with calls.

A neck stretches long; legs drape behind. Wings curl forward, the length of a man. Spread like fingers, primaries tip the bird into the wind's plane. The blood-red head bows and the wings sweep together, a cloaked priest giving benediction. Tail cups and belly buckles, surprised by the upsurge of ground. Legs kick out, their backward knees flapping like broken landing gear. Another bird plummets and stumbles forward, fighting for a spot in the packed staging ground along those few miles of water still clear and wide enough to pass as safe.

1. Sandhill Crane (Latin classification).

Twilight comes early, as it will for a few more weeks. The sky, ice blue through the encroaching willows and cottonwoods, flares up, a brief rose, before collapsing to indigo. Late February on the Platte,[2] and the night's chill haze hangs over this river, frosting the stubble from last fall that still fills the bordering fields. The nervous birds, tall as children, crowd together wing by wing on this stretch of river, one that they've learned to find by memory.

They converge on the river at winter's end as they have for eons, carpeting the wetlands. In this light, something saurian still clings to them: the oldest flying things on earth, one stutter-step away from pterodactyls. As darkness falls for real, it's a beginner's world again, the same evening as that day sixty million years ago when this migration began.

Half a million birds—four-fifths of all the sandhill cranes on earth—home in on this river. They trace the Central Flyway, an hourglass laid over the continent. They push up from New Mexico, Texas, and Mexico, hundreds of miles each day, with thousands more ahead before they reach their remembered nests. For a few weeks, this stretch of river shelters the miles-long flock. Then, by the start of spring, they'll rise and head away, feeling their way up to Saskatchewan, Alaska, or beyond.

This year's flight has always been. Something in the birds retraces a route laid down centuries before their parents showed it to them. And each crane recalls the route still to come.

Tonight's cranes mill again on the braided water. For another hour, their massed calls carry on the emptying air. The birds flap and fidget, edgy with migration. Some tear up frosty twigs and toss them in the air. Their jitters spill over into combat. At last the sandhills settle down into wary, stilt-legged sleep, most standing in the water, a few farther up in the stubbled fields.

A squeal of brakes, the crunch of metal on asphalt, one broken scream and then another rouse the flock. The truck arcs through the air, corkscrewing into the field. A plume shoots through the birds. They lurch off the ground, wings beating. The panicked carpet lifts, circles, and falls again. Calls that seem to come from creatures twice their size carry miles before fading.

By morning, that sound never happened. Again there is only here, now, the river's braid, a feast of waste grain that will carry these flocks north, beyond the Arctic Circle. As first light breaks, the fossils return to life, testing their legs, tasting the frozen air, leaping free, bills skyward and throats open. And then, as if the night took nothing, forgetting everything but this moment, the dawn sandhills start to dance. Dance as they have since before this river started.

Her brother needed her. The thought protected Karin through the alien night. She drove in a trance, keeping to the long dogleg, south down Nebraska 77 from Siouxland, then west on 30, tracking the Platte. The back roads were impossible, in her condition. Still shattered from the telephone's stab at two a.m.: *Karin Schluter? This is Good Samaritan Hospital in Kearney. Your brother has had an accident.*

The aide wouldn't say anything over the phone. Just that Mark had flipped over on the shoulder of North Line Road and had lain pinned in his cab,

2. River crossing the breadth of Nebraska.

almost frozen by the time the paramedics found and freed him. For a long time after hanging up, she couldn't feel her fingers until she found them pressed into her cheeks. Her face was numb, as if *she* had been the one lying out there, in the freezing February night.

Her hands, stiff and blue, clawed the wheel as she slipped through the reservations. First the Winnebago, then the rolling Omaha. The scrub trees along the patchy road bowed under tufts of snow. Winnebago Junction, the Pow Wow grounds, the tribal court and volunteer fire department, the station where she bought her tax-free gas, the hand-painted wooden shingle reading "Native Arts Gift Shop," the high school—*Home of the Indians*—where she'd volunteer-tutored until despair drove her off: the scene turned away from her, hostile. On the long, empty stretch east of Rosalie, a lone male her brother's age in a too-light coat and hat—*Go Big Red*[3] tracked through the roadside drift. He turned and snarled as she passed, repelling the intrusion.

The suture of the centerline drew her downward into the snowy black. It made no sense: Mark, a near-professional driver, rolling off an arrow-straight country road that was as familiar to him as breathing. Driving off the road, in central Nebraska—like falling off a wooden hone. She toyed with the date: 02/20/02. Did it mean anything? Her palms butted the wheel, and the car shook. *Your brother has had an accident.* In fact, he'd long ago taken every wrong turn you could take in life, and from the wrong lane. Telephone calls coming in at awful hours, as far back as she could remember. But never one like this.

She used the radio to keep herself awake. She tuned in to a crackpot talk-radio show about the best way to protect your pets from waterborne terrorist poisonings. All the deranged, static voices in the dark seeped into her, whispering what she was: alone on a deserted road, half a mile from her own disaster.

What a loving child Mark had been, staffing his earthworm hospital, selling his toys to stave off the farm foreclosure, throwing his eight-year-old body between their parents that hideous night nineteen years ago when Cappy took a loop of power cord to Joan. That was how she pictured her brother, as she fell headlong into the dark. The root of all his accidents: too caring by half.

Outside Grand Island, two hundred miles down from Sioux, as the day broke and the sky went peach, she glimpsed the Platte. First light glinted off its muddy brown, calming her. Something caught her eye, bobbing pearl waves flecked with red. Even she thought highway hypnosis, at first. A carpet of four-foot birds spread as far as the distant tree line. She'd seen them every spring for more than thirty years, and still the dancing mass made her jerk the wheel, almost following her brother.

He'd waited until the birds returned to spin out. He'd been a mess already, back in October, when she drove this same route for their mother's wake. Camping out with his beef-packing friends in the ninth circle of Nintendo hell, starting in on the six-packs for liquid brunch, fully loaded by the time he headed in to work on the swing shift. *Traditions to protect, Rabbit; family honor.* She hadn't had the will then, to talk sense to him. He wouldn't have heard her, if she had. But he'd made it through the winter, even pulled himself together a little. Only for this.

---

3. Fans' cheer for the University of Nebraska athletic teams.

Kearney rose up: the scattered outskirts, the newly extruded superstore strip, the fast-food grease trough along Second, the old main drag. The whole town suddenly struck her as a glorified I-80 exit ramp. Familiarity filled her with a weird, inappropriate calm. Home.

She found Good Samaritan the way the birds found the Platte. She spoke to the trauma doctor, working hard to follow him. He kept saying *moderate severity, stable,* and *lucky.* He looked young enough to have been out partying with Mark earlier that night. She wanted to ask to see his med school diploma. Instead she asked what "moderate severity" meant, and nodded politely at the opaque answer. She asked about "lucky," and the trauma doctor explained: "Lucky to be alive."

Firemen had cut him out of his cab with an acetylene torch. He might have lain there all night, coffined against the windshield, freezing and bleeding to death, just off the shoulder of the country road, except for the anonymous call from a gas station on the edge of town.

They let her into the unit to see him. A nurse tried to prepare her, but Karin heard nothing. She stood in front of a nest of cables and monitors. On the bed lay a lump of white wrapping. A face cradled inside the tangle of tubes, swollen and rainbowed, coated in abrasions. His bloody lips and cheeks were flecked with embedded gravel. The matted hair gave way to a patch of bare skull sprouting wires. The forehead had been pressed to a hot grill. In a flimsy robin's-egg gown, her brother struggled to inhale.

She heard herself call him, from a distance. "Mark?" The eyes opened at the sound, like the hard plastic eyes of her girlhood dolls. Nothing moved, not even his eyelids. Nothing, until his mouth pumped, without sound. She leaned down into the equipment. Air hissed through his lips, above the hum of the monitors. Wind through a field of ready wheat.

His face knew her. But nothing came out of his mouth except a trickle of saliva. His eyes pleaded, terrified. He needed something from her, life or death. "It's okay; I'm here," she said. But assurance only made him worse. She was exciting him, exactly what the nurses had forbidden. She looked away, anywhere but at his animal eyes. The room burned into her memory: the drawn curtain, the two racks of threatening electronic equipment, the lime sherbet-colored wall, the rolling table alongside his bed.

She tried again. "Markie, it's Karin. You're going to be all right." Saying it made a kind of truth. A groan escaped his sealed mouth. His hand, stuck with an IV tube, reached up and grabbed her wrist. His aim stunned her. The grip was feeble but deadly, drawing her down into the mesh of tubes. His fingers feathered at her, frantic, as if, in this split second, she might still keep his truck from wiping out.

The nurse made her leave. Karin Schluter sat in the trauma waiting room, a glass terrarium at the end of a long corridor smelling of antiseptics, dread, and ancient health magazines. Rows of head-bowed farmers and their wives, in dark sweatshirts and overalls, sat in the squared-off, padded apricot chairs alongside her. She figured them: *Father heart attack; husband hunting accident; child overdose.* Off in the corner, a muted television beamed images of a mountain wasteland scattered with guerrillas. Afghanistan, winter, 2002.[4]

4. Following the 9/11 attacks in 2001, the United States invaded Afghanistan in pursuit of al-Qaeda forces sheltered by the Islamic funda-mentalist Afghan government and presumed to be responsible for the attacks.

After a while, she noticed a thread of blood wicking down her right index finger, where she'd bitten through her cuticle. She found herself rising and drifting to the restroom, where she vomited.

Later, she ate, something warm and sticky from the hospital cafeteria. At one point, she stood in one of those half-finished stairwells of poured concrete meant to be seen only when the building was on fire, calling back to Sioux City, the massive computer and home electronics company where she worked in consumer relations. She stood smoothing her rumpled bouclé[5] skirt as if her supervisor could see her over the line. She told her boss, as vaguely as she could, about the accident. A remarkably level account: thirty years of practice hiding Schluter truths. She asked for two days off. He offered her three. She started to protest, but switched at once to grateful acceptance.

Back in the waiting room, she witnessed eight middle-aged men in flannel standing in a ring, their slow eyes scanning the floor. A murmur issued from them, wind teasing the lonely screens of a farmhouse. The sound rose and fell in waves. It took her a moment to realize: a prayer circle, for another victim who'd come in just after Mark. A makeshift Pentecostal service, covering anything that scalpels, drugs, and lasers couldn't. The gift of tongues descended on the circle of men, like small talk at a family reunion. Home was the place you never escape, even in nightmare.

Stable. Lucky. The words got Karin through to midday. But when the trauma doctor next talked to her, the words had become *cerebral edema*. Something had spiked the pressure inside her brother's skull. Nurses tried cooling his body. The doctor mentioned a ventilator and ventricular drain. Luck and stability were gone.

When they let her see Mark again, she no longer knew him. The person they took her to the second time lay comatose, his face collapsed into some stranger's. His eyes wouldn't open when she called his name. His arms hung still, even when she squeezed them.

Hospital personnel came to talk to her. They spoke to her as if she were brain-damaged. She pumped them for information. Mark's blood alcohol content had been just under the Nebraska limit—three or four beers in the hours before rolling his truck. Nothing else noticeable in his system. His truck was destroyed.

Two policemen took her aside in the corridor and asked her questions. She answered what she knew, which was nothing. An hour later, she wondered if she'd imagined the conversation. Late that afternoon, a man of fifty in a blue work shirt sat down next to her where she waited. She managed to turn and blink. Not possible, not even in this town: hit on, in the trauma-unit waiting room.

"You should get a lawyer," the man said.

She blinked again and shook her head. Sleep deprivation.

"You're with the fellow who rolled his truck? Read about him in the *Telegraph*. You should definitely get a lawyer."

Her head would not stop shaking. "Are you one?"

The man jerked back. "Good God, no. Just neighborly advice."

5. Literally, "knotted" (French); knitted fabric with a surface of tiny loops and curls.

She hunted down the newspaper and read the flimsy accident account until it crumbled. She sat in the glass terrarium as long as she could, then circled the ward, then sat again. Every hour, she begged to see him. Each time, they denied her. She dozed for five minutes at a shot, propped in the sculpted apricot chair. Mark rose up in her dreams, like buffalo grass after a prairie fire. A child who, out of pity, always picked the worst players for his team. An adult who called only when weepy drunk. Her eyes stung and her mouth thickened with scum. She checked the mirror in the floor's bathroom: blotchy and teetering, her fall of red hair a tangled bead-curtain. But still presentable, given everything.

"There has been some reversal," the doctor explained. He spoke in B waves and millimeters of mercury, lobes and ventricles and hematomas. Karin finally understood. Mark would need surgery.

They slit his throat and put a bolt into his skull. The nurses stopped answering Karin's questions. Hours later, in her best consumer-relations voice, she asked again to see him. They said he was too weakened by the procedures. The nurses offered to get something for her, and Karin only slowly realized they meant medication.

"Oh, no thanks," she said. "I'm good."

"Go home for a while," the trauma doctor advised. "Doctor's orders. You need some rest."

"Other people are sleeping on the floor of the waiting room. I can get a sleeping bag and be right back."

"There's nothing you can do right now," the doctor claimed. But that couldn't be; not in the world she came from.

She promised to go rest if they let her see Mark, just for a moment. They did. His eyes were still closed, and he responded to nothing.

Then she saw the note. It lay on the bed stand, waiting. No one could tell her when it had appeared. Some messenger had slipped into the room unseen, even while Karin was shut out. The writing was spidery, ethereal: immigrant scrawl from a century ago.

> I am No One
> but Tonight on North Line Road
> GOD led me to you
> so You could Live
> and bring back someone else.

A flock of birds, each one burning. Stars swoop down to bullets. Hot red specks take flesh, nest there, a body part, part body.

Lasts forever: no change to measure.

Flock of fiery cinders. When gray pain of them thins, then always water. Flattest width so slow it fails as liquid. Nothing in the end but flow. Nextless stream, lowest thing above knowing. A thing itself the cold and so can't feel it.

Body flat water, falling an inch a mile. Torso long as the world. Frozen run all the way from open to close. Great oxbows, age bends, lazy delayed S, switch current to still as long as possible the one long drop it already finishes.

Not even river, not even *wet brown slow west*, no now or then except in now and then rising. Face forcing up into soundless scream. White column, lit in a river of light Then pure terror, pealing into air, flipping and falling, anything but hit target.

One sound gets not a word but still says: *come*. Come with. Try death.

At last only water. Flat water spreading to its level. Water that is nothing but into nothing falls.

2006

SHERMAN ALEXIE
b. 1966

Except for one great-grandparent, Sherman Alexie's lineage is Native American: Coeur d'Alene on his father's side; Colville, Flathead, and Spokane on his mother's. The cities of Coeur d'Alene (Idaho) and Spokane (Washington) mark the interior northwest corner of the contiguous forty-eight states, the place where Alexie's poetry, fiction, and cinematic work is sometimes set. Yet his interest in Native American culture ranges widely, to include other tribes such as the Navajo and regions throughout the West and Southwest. Raised on the Spokane reservation at Wellpinit, Washington, Alexie thrived in the cultural immersion that secondary education at Reardan High School, some distance from home, provided—especially the popular culture that would later infuse his work. Hence both words in the designation "Native American" figure prominently in how he sees himself as a writer.

Equal doses of trouble and humor characterize Alexie's work. Having survived hydrocephalus (a cerebrospinal abnormality) as a child and alcoholism as a young adult, he drew on his college experience as an undergraduate at Gonzaga University in Spokane and Washington State University in Pullman to find a literary voice, drawing on inspirations as diverse as John Steinbeck's fiction and the Native American poetry collected by Joseph Bruchac in the anthology *Songs from This Earth on Turtle's Back* (1983). In 1992 he published his own first work, *The Business of Fancydancing: Stories and Poems*, with one of America's most prominent small presses. Hanging Loose (Brooklyn, New York). When *The Business of Fancydancing* was published, a review in the *New York Times* called Alexie "one of the major lyric voices of our time." "I was a 25-year-old Spokane Indian guy working as a secretary at a high school exchange program," he has written. "I thought 'Great! Where do I go from here?'"

Alexie has continued telling stories through poetry, fiction, and screenwriting. *Reservation Blues* (1994) was his first novel, followed by *Indian Killer* in 1996. *Flight* (2007) shows the influence of Kurt Vannegut, from its device of time travel to its reinvention of history from a comparative point of view. Presented broadly, even comically, his stories often draw on simple incidents, as in the story reprinted here. His storytelling offers a tragicomic vision of contemporary Native American life, notably in his National Book Award–winning novel *The Absolutely True Diary of a*

Part-Time Indian (2007) and in the stories of his several collections. College educated and street-smart ("I'm a rez kid who's gone urban"), irreverent and also dead serious, Alexie resembles the trickster figure of Crow in his poem "Crow Testament."

The narrative power of his poems has a furious energy. Although some of his work, like the villanelle "Sister Fire, Brother Smoke," takes traditional forms, most of his poems are open and improvisational, frequently and effectively using repetition and parallelism. The title of Alexie's 2000 collection, *One Stick Song*, offers an apt image for his work; it refers to a gambling game in which sticks function like chips. When down to one stick, he explains, "You're desperate," and a "One Stick Song" is "a desperate celebration, a desperate attempt to save yourself, putting everything you have into one song." The best of Alexie's poems, like "The Exaggeration of Despair," make facing up to grief and anger an act of survival. The intensity of this effort is especially evident when he reads from or recites his work. A brilliant performer, sliding between humor, anger, and pain, he makes a poetry reading a dynamic event. It is no wonder that his interest in performance has turned him to stand-up comedy as well.

Popular audiences know Alexie from the 2002 film he wrote and directed, *The Business of Fancydancing*, and especially his 1998 film *Smoke Signal*, a major Hollywood production he scripted from material in his story collection *The Lone Ranger and Tonto Fistfight in Heaven* (1993). These stories and the movies drawn from them cover the range of contemporary Native American experiences. As one of his characters says, Native Americans have "a way of surviving. But it's almost like Indians can easily survive the big stuff. Mass murder, loss of language and land rights. It's the small things that hurt the most. The white waitress who wouldn't take an order, Tonto, the Washington Redskins." "This Is What It Means to Say Phoenix, Arizona" (reprinted here) is typical of both the collection's and the movie's sometimes raucous blending of the sentimental and the ridiculous. Family structures have been set askew by the imposition of a Reservation system, a system all the more confining in the social conditions of current times. Can tribal structures ameliorate these problems? In this story and elsewhere, Alexie's answers vary from comic to tragic.

Married with two children living in Seattle, Alexie has used his work to address issues from national politics to family crises: one of the latter, handled with seriousness and humor, features in "This Is What It Means to Say Phoenix, Arizona."

The text of the story is from The Lone Ranger and Tonto Fistfight in Heaven (1993).

At Navajo Monument Valley Tribal School

from the photograph
by Skeet McAuley

the football field rises
to meet the mesa. Indian boys
gallop across the grass, against

the beginning of their body.
On those Saturday afternoons,   5
unbroken horses gather to watch

their sons growing larger
in the small parts of the world.
Everyone is the quarterback.

Navajo Monument Valley playing field, where "the football field
rises / to meet the mesa." Photograph by Skeet McAuley.

There is no thin man in a big hat   10
writing down all the names
in two columns: winners and losers.

This is the eternal football game,
Indians versus Indians. All the Skins
in the wooden bleachers fancydancing,   15

stomping red dust straight down
into nothing. Before the game is over,
the eighth-grade girls' track team

comes running, circling the field,
their thin and brown legs echoing   20
wild horses, wild horses, wild horses.

                                                    1992

Pawn Shop

I walk into the bar, after being gone for a while, and it's empty. The
Bartender tells me all the Indians are gone, do I know where they went?
I tell him I don't know, and I don't know, so he gives me a beer just for
being Indian, small favors, and I wonder where all the Skins disappeared
to, and after a while, I leave, searching the streets, searching storefronts,   5
until I walk into a pawn shop, find a single heart beating under glass, and
I know who it used to belong to, I know all of them.

                                                    1992

Sister Fire, Brother Smoke

Have I become an accomplished liar,
a man who believes in his inventions?
When I see my sister in every fire,

is it me who sets her in those pyres
and burns her repeatedly? Should I mention   5
I may have become an accomplished liar,

a man who was absent when his sister died,
but still feeds those flames in the present tense?
When I see my sister in every fire,

am I seeing the shadow that survived her   10
conflagration? Because of my obsession
have I become an accomplished liar,

who strikes a match, then creates a choir
of burning matches, with the intention
of seeing my sister in every fire?   15

Is she the whisper of ash floating high
above me? I offer these charred questions.
Have I become an accomplished liar
if I see my sister in every fire?

                                                            1996

From Tourists

3. *Marilyn Monroe*[1]

drives herself to the reservation. Tired and cold,
she asks the Indian women for help.
Marilyn cannot explain what she needs
but the Indian women notice the needle tracks
on her arms and lead her to the sweat lodge   5
where every woman, young and old, disrobes
and leaves her clothes behind
when she enters the dark of the lodge.
Marilyn's prayers may or may not be answered here
but they are kept sacred by Indian women.   10
Cold water is splashed on hot rocks
and steam fills the lodge. There is no place like this.
At first, Marilyn is self-conscious, aware

---

1. American actress and sex symbol (1926–1962).

of her body and face, the tremendous heat, her thirst,
and the brown bodies circled around her.   15
But the Indian women do not stare. It is dark
inside the lodge. The hot rocks glow red
and the songs begin. Marilyn has never heard
these songs before, but she soon sings along.
Marilyn is not Indian, Marilyn will never be Indian   20
but the Indian women sing about her courage.
The Indian women sing for her health.
The Indian women sing for Marilyn.
Finally, she is no more naked than anyone else.

                                                            1996

The Exaggeration of Despair

I open the door

(this Indian girl writes that her brother tried to hang himself
with a belt just two weeks after her other brother did hang himself

and this Indian man tells us that, back in boarding school,
five priests took him into a back room and raped him repeatedly   5

and this homeless Indian woman begs for quarters, and when I ask
her about her tribe, she says she's horny and bends over in front of me

and this homeless Indian man is the uncle of an Indian man
who writes for a large metropolitan newspaper, and so now I know them
     both

and this Indian child cries when he sits to eat at our table   10
because he had never known his own family to sit at the same table

and this Indian woman was born to an Indian woman
who sold her for a six-pack and a carton of cigarettes

and this Indian poet shivers beneath the freeway
and begs for enough quarters to buy pencil and paper   15

and this fancydancer passes out at the powwow
and wakes up naked, with no memory of the evening, all of his regalia
     gone)

I open the door

(and this is my sister, who waits years for a dead eagle from the Park
     Service, receives it
and stores it with our cousins, who then tell her it has disappeared 20

though the feathers reappear in the regalia of another cousin
who is dancing for the very first time

and this is my father, whose own father died on Okinawa,[1] shot
by a Japanese soldier who must have looked so much like him

and this is my father, whose mother died of tuberculosis   25
not long after he was born, and so my father must hear coughing ghosts

and this is my grandmother who saw, before the white men came,
three ravens with white necks, and knew our God was going to change)

I open the door
and invite the wind inside.   30

1996

Crow Testament[1]

1.

Cain lifts Crow, that heavy black bird
and strikes down Abel.[2]

Damn, says Crow, I guess
this is just the beginning.

2.

The white man, disguised   5
as a falcon, swoops in
and yet again steals a salmon
from Crow's talons.

Damn, says Crow, if I could swim
I would have fled this country years ago.   10

3.

The Crow God as depicted
in all of the reliable Crow bibles
looks exactly like a Crow.

Damn, says Crow, this makes it
so much easier to worship myself.   15

1. Japanese island, site of a major battle during World War II.
1. Crow, like Raven, is a trickster figure in many Native American cultures.
2. In Genesis, Cain kills his brother, Abel. They are the sons of Adam and Eve.

4.

Among the ashes of Jericho,[3]
Crow sacrifices his firstborn son.

Damn, says Crow, a million nests
are soaked with blood.

5.

When Crows fight Crows   20
the sky fills with beaks and talons.

Damn, says Crow, it's raining feathers.

6

Crow flies around the reservation
and collects empty beer bottles

but they are so heavy   25
he can carry only one at a time.

So, one by one, he returns them
but gets only five cents a bottle.

Damn, says Crow, redemption
is not easy.   30

7.

Crow rides a pale horse
into a crowded powwow
but none of the Indians panic.

Damn, says Crow, I guess
they already live near the end of the world.   35

2000

This Is What It Means to Say Phoenix, Arizona

Just after Victor lost his job at the BIA,[1] he also found out that his father had
died of a heart attack in Phoenix, Arizona. Victor hadn't seen his father in a
few years, only talked to him on the telephone once or twice, but there still

---

3. This biblical city, famous for its great walls,
was the first town attacked by the Israelites under
Joshua, after they crossed the Jordan River.

1. Bureau of Indian Affairs, an agency of the
U.S. Government that assists tribal officials in
the administration of Indian reservations.

was a genetic pain, which was soon to be pain as real and immediate as a broken bone.

Victor didn't have any money. Who does have money on a reservation, except the cigarette and fireworks salespeople? His father had a savings account waiting to be claimed, but Victor needed to find a way to get to Phoenix. Victor's mother was just as poor as he was, and the rest of his family didn't have any use at all for him. So Victor called the Tribal Council.

"Listen," Victor said. "My father just died. I need some money to get to Phoenix to make arrangements."

"Now, Victor," the council said. "You know we're having a difficult time financially."

"But I thought the council had special funds set aside for stuff like this."

"Now, Victor, we do have some money available for the proper return of tribal members' bodies. But I don't think we have enough to bring your father all the way back from Phoenix."

"Well," Victor said. "It ain't going to cost all that much. He had to be cremated. Things were kind of ugly. He died of a heart attack in his trailer and nobody found him for a week. It was really hot, too. You get the picture."

"Now, Victor, we're sorry for your loss and the circumstances. But we can really only afford to give you one hundred dollars."

"That's not even enough for a plane ticket."

"Well, you might consider driving down to Phoenix."

"I don't have a car. Besides, I was going to drive my father's pickup back up here."

"Now, Victor," the council said. "We're sure there is somebody who could drive you to Phoenix. Or is there somebody who could lend you the rest of the money?"

"You know there ain't nobody around with that kind of money."

"Well, we're sorry, Victor, but that's the best we can do."

Victor accepted the Tribal Council's offer. What else could he do? So he signed the proper papers, picked up his check, and walked over to the Trading Post to cash it.

While Victor stood in line, he watched Thomas Builds-the-Fire standing near the magazine rack, talking to himself. Like he always did. Thomas was a storyteller that nobody wanted to listen to. That's like being a dentist in a town where everybody has false teeth.

Victor and Thomas Builds-the-Fire were the same age, had grown up and played in the dirt together. Ever since Victor could remember, it was Thomas who always had something to say.

Once, when they were seven years old, when Victor's father still lived with the family, Thomas closed his eyes and told Victor this story: "Your father's heart is weak. He is afraid of his own family. He is afraid of you. Late at night he sits in the dark. Watches the television until there's nothing but that white noise. Sometimes he feels like he wants to buy a motorcycle and ride away. He wants to run and hide. He doesn't want to be found."

Thomas Builds-the-Fire had known that Victor's father was going to leave, knew it before anyone. Now Victor stood in the Trading Post with a one-hundred-dollar check in his hand, wondering if Thomas knew that Victor's father was dead, if he knew what was going to happen next.

Just then Thomas looked at Victor, smiled, and walked over to him.

"Victor, I'm sorry about your father," Thomas said.

"How did you know about it?" Victor asked.

"I heard it on the wind. I heard it from the birds. I felt it in the sunlight. Also, your mother was just in here crying."

"Oh," Victor said and looked around the Trading Post. All the other Indians stared, surprised that Victor was even talking to Thomas. Nobody talked to Thomas anymore because he told the same damn stories over and over again. Victor was embarrassed, but he thought that Thomas might be able to help him. Victor felt a sudden need for tradition.

"I can lend you the money you need," Thomas said suddenly. "But you have to take me with you."

"I can't take your money," Victor said. "I mean, I haven't hardly talked to you in years. We're not really friends anymore."

"I didn't say we were friends. I said you had to take me with you."

"Let me think about it."

Victor went home with his one hundred dollars and sat at the kitchen table. He held his head in his hands and thought about Thomas Builds-the-Fire, remembered little details, tears and scars, the bicycle they shared for a summer, so many stories.

Thomas Builds-the-Fire sat on the bicycle, waited in Victor's yard. He was ten years old and skinny. His hair was dirty because it was the Fourth of July.

"Victor," Thomas yelled. "Hurry up. We're going to miss the fireworks."

After a few minutes, Victor ran out of his house, jumped the porch railing, and landed gracefully on the sidewalk.

"And the judges award him a 9.95, the highest score of the summer," Thomas said, clapped, laughed.

"That was perfect, cousin," Victor said. "And it's my turn to ride the bike."

Thomas gave up the bike and they headed for the fair-grounds. It was nearly dark and the fireworks were about to start.

"You know," Thomas said. "It's strange how us Indians celebrate the Fourth of July. It ain't like it was *our* independence everybody was fighting for."

"You think about things too much," Victor said. "It's just supposed to be fun. Maybe Junior will be there."

"Which Junior? Everybody on this reservation is named Junior."

And they both laughed.

The fireworks were small, hardly more than a few bottle rockets and a fountain. But it was enough for two Indian boys. Years later, they would need much more.

Afterwards, sitting in the dark, fighting off mosquitoes, Victor turned to Thomas Builds-the-Fire.

"Hey," Victor said. "Tell me a story."

Thomas closed his eyes and told this story: "There were these two Indian boys who wanted to be warriors. But it was too late to be warriors in the old way. All the horses were gone. So the two Indian boys stole a car and drove to the city. They parked the stolen car in front of the police station and then hitchhiked back home to the reservation. When they got back, all their friends cheered and their parents' eyes shone with pride. *You were very brave,* everybody said to the two Indian boys. *Very brave.*"

"Ya-hey,"[2] Victor said. "That's a good one. I wish I could be a warrior."

"Me, too," Thomas said.

They went home together in the dark, Thomas on the bike now, Victor on foot. They walked through shadows and light from streetlamps.

"We've come a long ways," Thomas said. "We have outdoor lighting."

"All I need is the stars," Victor said. "And besides, you still think about things too much."

They separated then, each headed for home, both laughing all the way.

Victor sat at his kitchen table. He counted his one hundred dollars again and again. He knew he needed more to make it to Phoenix and back. He knew he needed Thomas Builds-the-Fire. So he put his money in his wallet and opened the front door to find Thomas on the porch.

"Ya-hey, Victor," Thomas said. "I knew you'd call me."

Thomas walked into the living room and sat down on Victor's favorite chair.

"I've got some money saved up," Thomas said. "It's enough to get us down there, but you have to get us back."

"I've got this hundred dollars," Victor said. "And my dad had a savings account I'm going to claim."

"How much in your dad's account?"

"Enough. A few hundred."

"Sounds good. When we leaving?"

When they were fifteen and had long since stopped being friends, Victor and Thomas got into a fistfight. That is, Victor was really drunk and beat Thomas up for no reason at all. All the other Indian boys stood around and watched it happen. Junior was there and so were Lester, Seymour, and a lot of others. The beating might have gone on until Thomas was dead if Norma Many Horses hadn't come along and stopped it.

"Hey, you boys," Norma yelled and jumped out of her car. "Leave him alone."

If it had been someone else, even another man, the Indian boys would've just ignored the warnings. But Norma was a warrior. She was powerful. She could have picked up any two of the boys and smashed their skulls together. But worse than that, she would have dragged them all over to some tipi and made them listen to some elder tell a dusty old story.

The Indian boys scattered, and Norma walked over to Thomas and picked him up.

"Hey, little man, are you okay?" she asked.

Thomas gave her a thumbs up.

"Why they always picking on you?"

Thomas shook his head, closed his eyes, but no stories came to him, no words or music. He just wanted to go home, to lie in his bed and let his dreams tell his stories for him.

Thomas Builds-the-Fire and Victor sat next to each other in the airplane, coach section. A tiny white woman had the window seat. She was busy twisting her body into pretzels. She was flexible.

---

2. Invented reservation slang for "yes" or "hello."

"I have to ask," Thomas said, and Victor closed his eyes in embarrassment.

"Don't," Victor said.

"Excuse me, miss," Thomas asked. "Are you a gymnast or something?"

"There's no something about it," she said. "I was first alternate on the 1980 Olympic team."

"Really?" Thomas asked.

"Really."

"I mean, you used to be a world-class athlete?" Thomas asked.

"My husband still thinks I am."

Thomas Builds-the-Fire smiled. She was a mental gymnast, too. She pulled her leg straight up against her body so that she could've kissed her kneecap.

"I wish I could do that," Thomas said.

Victor was ready to jump out of the plane. Thomas, that crazy Indian storyteller with ratty old braids and broken teeth, was flirting with a beautiful Olympic gymnast. Nobody back home on the reservation would ever believe it.

"Well," the gymnast said. "It's easy. Try it."

Thomas grabbed at his leg and tried to pull it up into the same position as the gymnast. He couldn't even come close, which made Victor and the gymnast laugh.

"Hey," she asked. "You two are Indian, right?"

"Full-blood," Victor said.

"Not me," Thomas said "I'm half magician on my mother's side and half clown on my father's."

They all laughed.

"What are your names?" she asked.

"Victor and Thomas."

"Mine is Cathy. Pleased to meet you all."

The three of them talked for the duration of the flight. Cathy the gymnast complained about the government, how they screwed the 1980 Olympic team by boycotting.[3]

"Sounds like you all got a lot in common with Indians," Thomas said.

Nobody laughed.

After the plane landed in Phoenix and they had all found their way to the terminal, Cathy the gymnast smiled and waved good-bye.

"She was really nice," Thomas said.

"Yeah, but everybody talks to everybody on airplanes," Victor said. "It's too bad we can't always be that way."

"You always used to tell me I think too much," Thomas said. "Now it sounds like you do."

"Maybe I caught it from you."

"Yeah."

Thomas and Victor rode in a taxi to the trailer where Victor's father died.

"Listen," Victor said as they stopped in front of the trailer. "I never told you I was sorry for beating you up that time."

"Oh, it was nothing. We were just kids and you were drunk."

"Yeah, but I'm still sorry."

---

3. The United States boycotted the 1980 Summer Olympics, held in Moscow, because of the Soviet Union's 1979 invasion of Afghanistan.

"That's all right."

Victor paid for the taxi and the two of them stood in the hot Phoenix summer. They could smell the trailer.

"This ain't going to be nice," Victor said. "You don't have to go in."

"You're going to need help."

Victor walked to the front door and opened it. The stink rolled out and made them both gag. Victor's father had lain in that trailer for a week in hundred-degree temperatures before anyone found him. And the only reason anyone found him was because of the smell. They needed dental records to identify him. That's exactly what the coroner said. They needed dental records.

"Oh, man," Victor said. "I don't know if I can do this."

"Well, then don't."

"But there might be something valuable in there."

"I thought his money was in the bank."

"It is. I was talking about pictures and letters and stuff like that."

"Oh," Thomas said as he held his breath and followed Victor into the trailer.

When Victor was twelve, he stepped into an underground wasp nest. His foot was caught in the hole, and no matter how hard he struggled, Victor couldn't pull free. He might have died there, stung a thousand times, if Thomas Builds-the-Fire had not come by.

"Run," Thomas yelled and pulled Victor's foot from the hole. They ran then, hard as they ever had, faster than Billy Mills, faster than Jim Thorpe,[4] faster than the wasps could fly.

Victor and Thomas ran until they couldn't breathe, ran until it was cold and dark outside, ran until they were lost and it took hours to find their way home. All the way back, Victor counted his stings.

"Seven," Victor said. "My lucky number."

Victor didn't find much to keep in the trailer. Only a photo album and a stereo. Everything else had that smell stuck in it or was useless anyway.

"I guess this is all," Victor said. "It ain't much."

"Better than nothing," Thomas said.

"Yeah, and I do have the pickup."

"Yeah," Thomas said. "It's in good shape."

"Dad was good about that stuff."

"Yeah, I remember your dad."

"Really?" Victor asked. "What do you remember?"

Thomas Builds-the-Fire closed his eyes and told this story: "I remember when I had this dream that told me to go to Spokane, to stand by the Falls in the middle of the city and wait for a sign. I knew I had to go there but I didn't have a car. Didn't have a license. I was only thirteen. So I walked all the way,

4. William Mervin "Billy" Mills (b. 1938), Native American (Ogalala Lakota) Gold Medalist for the United States at the 1964 Olympics, where he won the 10,000 meter run in a stunning upset of the favorite, Australian Ron Clarke, a feat celebrated in the 1984 film *Running Brave*. James Francis "Jim" Thorpe (1888–1953), American athlete of Native American, Irish, and French descent, Gold Medalist for the United States at the 1912 Olympics, where he won the decathalon and the penthalon, only to be stripped of his awards in 1913 because of his status as a professional; he subsequently played professional baseball and football, and at the time of his death was hailed as the greatest athlete of the first half of the Twentieth Century.

took me all day, and I finally made it to the Falls. I stood there for an hour waiting. Then your dad came walking up. *What the hell are you doing here?* he asked me. I said, *Waiting for a vision.* Then your father said, *All you're going to get here is mugged.* So he drove me over to Denny's, bought me dinner, and then drove me home to the reservation. For a long time I was mad because I thought my dreams had lied to me. But they didn't. Your dad was my vision. *Take care of each other* is what my dreams were saying. *Take care of each other.*"

Victor was quiet for a long time. He searched his mind for memories of his father, found the good ones, found a few bad ones, added it all up, and smiled.

"My father never told me about finding you in Spokane," Victor said.

"He said he wouldn't tell anybody. Didn't want me to get in trouble. But he said I had to watch out for you as part of the deal."

"Really?"

"Really. Your father said you would need the help. He was right."

"That's why you came down here with me, isn't it?" Victor asked.

"I came because of your father."

Victor and Thomas climbed into the pickup, drove over to the bank, and claimed the three hundred dollars in the savings account.

Thomas Builds-the-Fire could fly.

Once, he jumped off the roof of the tribal school and flapped his arms like a crazy eagle. And he flew. For a second, he hovered, suspended above all the other Indian boys who were too smart or too scared to jump.

"He's flying," Junior yelled, and Seymour was busy looking for the trick wires or mirrors. But it was real. As real as the dirt when Thomas lost altitude and crashed to the ground.

He broke his arm in two places.

"He broke his wing," Victor chanted, and the other Indian boys joined in, made it a tribal song.

"He broke his wing, he broke his wing, he broke his wing," all the Indian boys chanted as they ran off, flapping their wings, wishing they could fly, too. They hated Thomas for his courage, his brief moment as a bird. Everybody has dreams about flying. Thomas flew.

One of his dreams came true for just a second, just enough to make it real.

Victor's father, his ashes, fit in one wooden box with enough left over to fill a cardboard box.

"He always was a big man," Thomas said.

Victor carried part of his father and Thomas carried the rest out to the pickup. They set him down carefully behind the seats, put a cowboy hat on the wooden box and a Dodgers cap on the cardboard box. That's the way it was supposed to be.

"Ready to head back home," Victor asked.

"It's going to be a long drive."

"Yeah, take a couple days, maybe."

"We can take turns," Thomas said.

"Okay," Victor said, but they didn't take turns. Victor drove for sixteen hours straight north, made it halfway up Nevada toward home before he finally pulled over.

"Hey, Thomas," Victor said. "You got to drive for a while."

"Okay."

Thomas Builds-the-Fire slid behind the wheel and started off down the road. All through Nevada, Thomas and Victor had been amazed at the lack of animal life, at the absence of water, of movement.

"Where is everything?" Victor had asked more than once.

Now when Thomas was finally driving they saw the first animal, maybe the only animal in Nevada. It was a long-eared jackrabbit.

"Look," Victor yelled. "It's alive."

Thomas and Victor were busy congratulating themselves on their discovery when the jackrabbit darted out into the road and under the wheels of the pickup.

"Stop the goddamn car," Victor yelled, and Thomas did stop, backed the pickup to the dead jackrabbit.

"Oh, man, he's dead," Victor said as he looked at the squashed animal. "Really dead."

"The only thing alive in this whole state and we just killed it."

"I don't know," Thomas said. "I think it was suicide."

Victor looked around the desert, sniffed the air, felt the emptiness and loneliness, and nodded his head.

"Yeah," Victor said. "It had to be suicide."

"I can't believe this," Thomas said. "You drive for a thousand miles and there ain't even any bugs smashed on the windshield. I drive for ten seconds and kill the only living thing in Nevada."

"Yeah," Victor said. "Maybe I should drive."

"Maybe you should."

Thomas Builds-the-Fire walked through the corridors of the tribal school by himself. Nobody wanted to be anywhere near him because of all those stories. Story after story.

Thomas closed his eyes and this story came to him: "We are all given one thing by which our lives are measured, one determination. Mine are the stories which can change or not change the world. It doesn't matter which as long as I continue to tell the stories. My father, he died on Okinawa[5] in World War II, died fighting for this country, which had tried to kill him for years. My mother, she died giving birth to me, died while I was still inside her. She pushed me out into the world with her last breath. I have no brothers or sisters. I have only my stories which came to me before I even had the words to speak. I learned a thousand stories before I took my first thousand steps. They are all I have. It's all I can do."

Thomas Builds-the-Fire told his stories to all those who would stop and listen. He kept telling them long after people had stopped listening.

Victor and Thomas made it back to the reservation just as the sun was rising. It was the beginning of a new day on earth, but the same old shit on the reservation.

---

5. Largest of Japan's Ryukyu Islands in the Western Pacific Ocean, site in 1945 of a crucial American victory near the end of World War II that had proceeded from the victory on Iwo Jima in the Japanese Volcano Islands chain, where Ira Hayes (1923–1955), a Native American (Pima) achieved fame among the Marines raising the U.S. flag atop Mount Suribachi on February 23, 1945; "The Ballad of Ira Hayes" (by Peter LaFarge) was popularized by Bob Dylan in the 1960s as a folk song.

"Good morning," Thomas said.

"Good morning."

The tribe was waking up, ready for work, eating breakfast, reading the newspaper, just like everybody else does. Willene LeBret was out in her garden wearing a bathrobe. She waved when Thomas and Victor drove by.

"Crazy Indians made it," she said to herself and went back to her roses.

Victor stopped the pickup in front of Thomas Builds-the-Fire's HUD[6] house. They both yawned, stretched a little, shook dust from their bodies.

"I'm tired," Victor said.

"Of everything," Thomas added.

They both searched for words to end the journey. Victor needed to thank Thomas for his help, for the money, and make the promise to pay it all back.

"Don't worry about the money," Thomas said. "It don't make any difference anyhow."

"Probably not, enit?"[7]

"Nope."

Victor knew that Thomas would remain the crazy storyteller who talked to dogs and cars, who listened to the wind and pine trees. Victor knew that he couldn't really be friends with Thomas, even after all that had happened. It was cruel but it was real. As real as the ashes, as Victor's father, sitting behind the seats.

"I know how it is," Thomas said. "I know you ain't going to treat me any better than you did before. I know your friends would give you too much shit about it."

Victor was ashamed of himself. Whatever happened to the tribal ties, the sense of community? The only real thing he shared with anybody was a bottle and broken dreams. He owed Thomas something, anything.

"Listen," Victor said and handed Thomas the cardboard box which contained half of his father. "I want you to have this."

Thomas took the ashes and smiled, closed his eyes, and told this story: "I'm going to travel to Spokane Falls one last time and toss these ashes into the water. And your father will rise like a salmon, leap over the bridge, over me, and find his way home. It will be beautiful. His teeth will shine like silver, like a rainbow. He will rise, Victor, he will rise."

Victor smiled.

"I was planning on doing the same thing with my half," Victor said. "But I didn't imagine my father looking anything like a salmon. I thought it'd be like cleaning the attic or something. Like letting things go after they've stopped having any use."

"Nothing stops, cousin," Thomas said. "Nothing stops."

Thomas Builds-the-Fire got out of the pickup and walked up his driveway. Victor started the pickup and began the drive home.

"Wait," Thomas yelled suddenly from his porch. "I just got to ask one favor."

Victor stopped the pickup, leaned out the window, and shouted back. "What do you want?"

"Just one time when I'm telling a story somewhere, why don't you stop and listen?" Thomas asked.

---

6. Department of Housing and Urban Development, part of the U.S. Government.
7. That is, "isn't it?"

"Just once?"

"Just once."

Victor waved his arms to let Thomas know that the deal was good. It was a fair trade, and that was all Victor had ever wanted from his whole life. So Victor drove his father's pickup toward home while Thomas went into his house, closed the door behind him, and heard a new story come to him in the silence afterwards.

1993

Survivorman

Here's a fact: Some people want to live more
Than others do. Some can withstand any horror

While others will easily surrender
To thirst, hunger, and extremes of weather.

In Utah, one man carried another
Man on his back like a conjoined brother

And crossed twenty-five miles of desert
To safety. Can you imagine the hurt?

Do you think you could be that good and strong?
Yes, yes, you think, but you're probably wrong.

2009

JHUMPA LAHIRI
b. 1967

When Jhumpa Lahiri writes, her setting is quite literally the world—focused sometimes here and sometimes there, but always with global implications. This orientation is a factor of her times. Unlike children of earlier immigrant generations, Lahiri did not face the pressures of assimilating into an American society apart from and in some cases above other cultures. Instead, international trade, travel, and communications have made global culture a practical reality. In "Sexy," one of Lahiri's most wide-ranging yet deeply penetrating stories, her protagonist listens to a sad tale about a friend's "cousin's husband." The bad news, "a wife's worst nightmare," is being conveyed in Boston, where the friends live, but it involves a flight from Delhi to Montreal stopping at Heathrow Airport outside London. Four locations in two hemispheres an ocean and a continent apart indicate the world that people with family backgrounds in India share when they become Americans. Geographical barriers become much more easily manageable thanks to cell phones and e-mail. Education, employment, friendships, and romantic relationships span the world. Films from India are viewed with American pop songs in mind and Chinese cuisine in the stomach, all, flavorful as they are, seeming as natural as the lives being lived among such givens.

The flavor of Lahiri's fiction defies categorization, other than being dependent on no single national ingredient. A visit to Boston's Mapparium (a giant globe viewed from inside) or Museum of Fine Arts is less a field trip through region and history than a comfortable part of her characters' way of living, a reminder of the larger culture they share.

The author's Bengali parents parted from their large extended family when they moved from Calcutta to London, where Lahiri was born. Following a normal progression in the former British Commonwealth, Lahiri's parents then relocated to the United States, where they worked as educators in Rhode Island while she studied at Barnard College and Boston University, concentrating on literature and creative writing and ending with a Ph.D. Her first stories reflect how much of her family's past had to be conveyed to her via storytelling, such as in "When Mr. Pirzada Came to Dine," where a ten-year-old in America learns about political troubles in India from a visiting family friend. To the youngster, it sounds exotic, but no more so than the situation experienced by a pair of Indian newlyweds, in "This Blessed House," who are alternately intrigued and mystified by fundamentalist Christian curios left behind by the previous tenants of their new home. Much of Lahiri's work, first collected in *Interpreter of Maladies* (1999) and extended in *Unaccustomed Earth* (2008), involves discoveries of this nature, in which she is particularly adept at portraying the learning process of someone acting without monocultural constraint. The curiosity of children or young adults is a hallmark of her style.

In 2003, having married, become a mother, and settled in the Park Slope area of Brooklyn, New York, a neighborhood popular with writers, Lahiri published her novel *The Namesake*. Like her earlier work, it contrasts cultural assimilation with curiosity about the values, beliefs, and practices of a preceding generation. But here a certain amount of anger and confusion come into play, as the protagonist, Gogol Ganguli, is uncomfortable with how the private first name his parents have used for him at home has become his public name as well, all without his understanding its personal (much less literary) significance. Lahiri had been saddled with "Jhumpa" as a first name by her teachers, who found it easier to pronounce than her other two given names, either of which would have been more appropriate for formal use. But while Lahiri's enforced assimilation didn't bother her, Ganguli's does. Although much of his discomfort is comic, such as when he assumes that sociologist's anagrammatical reference to "ABCDs" means not "multiculturals" but "American-born confused deshi" (India countrymen). In fact, Ganguli doesn't even know what "deshi" properly means, just that his parents customarily refer to India as "desh." He "never thinks of India as desh. He thinks of it as Americans do, as India." Other contrasts, such as arranged marriages versus modern ones, are handled with more gravity. But this too helps the protagonist in his process of understanding who he is, something not possible until he comprehends who his parents are.

The following text is from *Interpreter of Maladies* (1999).

Sexy

It was a wife's worst nightmare. After nine years of marriage, Laxmi told Miranda, her cousin's husband had fallen in love with another woman. He sat next to her on a plane, on a flight from Delhi to Montreal, and instead of flying home to his wife and son, he got off with the woman at Heathrow.[1] He called his wife, and told her he'd had a conversation that had changed his life, and that he needed time to figure things out. Laxmi's cousin had taken to her bed.

"Not that I blame her," Laxmi said. She reached for the Hot Mix she munched throughout the day, which looked to Miranda like dusty orange cereal. "Imagine. An English girl, half his age." Laxmi was only a few years older than Miranda, but she was already married, and kept a photo of herself and her husband, seated on a white stone bench in front of the Taj Mahal,[2] tacked to the inside of her cubicle, which was next to Miranda's. Laxmi had been on the phone for at least an hour, trying to calm her cousin down. No one noticed; they worked for a public radio station,[3] in the fundraising department, and were surrounded by people who spent all day on the phone, soliciting pledges.

"I feel worst for the boy," Laxmi added. "He's been at home for days. My cousin said she can't even take him to school."

"It sounds awful," Miranda said. Normally Laxmi's phone conversations—mainly to her husband, about what to cook for dinner—distracted Miranda as she typed letters, asking members of the radio station to increase their annual pledge in exchange for a tote bag or an umbrella. She could hear Laxmi clearly, her sentences peppered every now and then with an Indian word, through the laminated wall between their desks. But that afternoon Miranda hadn't been listening. She'd been on the phone herself, with Dev, deciding where to meet later that evening.

"Then again, a few days at home won't hurt him." Laxmi ate some more Hot Mix, then put it away in a drawer. "He's something of a genius. He has a Punjabi mother and a Bengali[4] father, and because he learns French and English at school he already speaks four languages. I think he skipped two grades."

Dev was Bengali, too. At first Miranda thought it was a religion. But then he pointed it out to her, a place in India called Bengal, in a map printed in an issue of *The Economist*.[5] He had brought the magazine specially to her apartment, for she did not own an atlas, or any other books with maps in them. He'd pointed to the city where he'd been born, and another city where his father had been born. One of the cities had a box around it, intended to attract the reader's eye. When Miranda asked what the box indicated, Dev rolled up the magazine, and said, "Nothing you'll ever need to worry about," and he tapped her playfully on the head.

Before leaving her apartment he'd tossed the magazine in the garbage, along with the ends of the three cigarettes he always smoked in the course of his visits. But after she watched his car disappear down Commonwealth Avenue,[6] back to his house in the suburbs, where he lived with his wife, Miranda retrieved it, and brushed the ashes off the cover, and rolled it in the

---

1. International airport near London.
2. Muslim mausoleum near Agra, India, built on a monumental scale in the mid-seventeenth century by Emperor Shah Jahan for his favorite wife, Mumtaz Mahal.
3. Noncommercial, listener-supported, often oriented toward arts and culture in its broadcasting.

4. Punjab, state in northern India; Bengal, former province of India, now a region that includes Bengal State and East Bengal, the latter part of Bangladesh.
5. Weekly British magazine of news and commentary.
6. Major thoroughfare in Boston.

opposite direction to get it to lie flat. She got into bed, still rumpled from their lovemaking, and studied the borders of Bengal. There was a bay below and mountains above. The map was connected to an article about something called the Gramin Bank.[7] She turned the page, hoping for a photograph of the city where Dev was born, but all she found were graphs and grids. Still, she stared at them, thinking the whole while about Dev, about how only fifteen minutes ago he'd propped her feet on top of his shoulders, and pressed her knees to her chest, and told her that he couldn't get enough of her.

She'd met him a week ago, at Filene's.[8] She was there on her lunch break, buying discounted pantyhose in the Basement. Afterward she took the escalator to the main part of the store, to the cosmetics department, where soaps and creams were displayed like jewels, and eye shadows and powders shimmered like butterflies pinned behind protective glass. Though Miranda had never bought anything other than a lipstick, she liked walking through the cramped, confined maze, which was familiar to her in a way the rest of Boston still was not. She liked negotiating her way past the women planted at every turn, who sprayed cards with perfume and waved them in the air; sometimes she would find a card days afterward, folded in her coat pocket, and the rich aroma, still faintly preserved, would warm her as she waited on cold mornings for the T.[9]

That day, stopping to smell one of the more pleasing cards, Miranda noticed a man standing at one of the counters. He held a slip of paper covered in a precise, feminine hand. A saleswoman took one look at the paper and began to open drawers. She produced an oblong cake of soap in a black case, a hydrating mask, a vial of cell renewal drops, and two tubes of face cream. The man was tanned, with black hair that was visible on his knuckles. He wore a flamingo pink shirt, a navy blue suit, a camel overcoat with gleaming leather buttons. In order to pay he had taken off pigskin gloves. Crisp bills emerged from a burgundy wallet. He didn't wear a wedding ring.

"What can I get you, honey?" the saleswoman asked Miranda. She looked over the tops of her tortoiseshell glasses, assessing Miranda's complexion.

Miranda didn't know what she wanted. All she knew was that she didn't want the man to walk away. He seemed to be lingering, waiting, along with the saleswoman, for her to say something. She stared at some bottles, some short, others tall, arranged on an oval tray, like a family posing for a photograph.

"A cream," Miranda said eventually.

"How old are you?"

"Twenty-two."

The saleswoman nodded, opening a frosted bottle. "This may seem a bit heavier than what you're used to, but I'd start now. All your wrinkles are going to form by twenty-five. After that they just start showing."

While the saleswoman dabbed the cream on Miranda's face, the man stood and watched. While Miranda was told the proper way to apply it, in swift upward strokes beginning at the base of her throat, he spun the lipstick

---

7. Properly the Grameen Bank, which provides credit to the poorest classes in rural Bangladesh as a means of fighting poverty and promoting social economic development.

8. A department store. Filene's Basement, downstairs, is a renowned discount store.

9. Metropolitan Transit Authority (MTA), Boston's subway system.

carousel. He pressed a pump that dispensed cellulite gel and massaged it into the back of his ungloved hand. He opened a jar, leaned over, and drew so close that a drop of cream flecked his nose.

Miranda smiled, but her mouth was obscured by a large brush that the saleswoman was sweeping over her face. "This is blusher Number Two," the woman said. "Gives you some color."

Miranda nodded, glancing at her reflection in one of the angled mirrors that lined the counter. She had silver eyes and skin as pale as paper, and the contrast with her hair, as dark and glossy as an espresso bean, caused people to describe her as striking, if not pretty. She had a narrow, egg-shaped head that rose to a prominent point. Her features, too, were narrow, with nostrils so slim that they appeared to have been pinched with a clothespin. Now her face glowed, rosy at the cheeks, smoky below the brow bone. Her lips glistened.

The man was glancing in a mirror, too, quickly wiping the cream from his nose. Miranda wondered where he was from. She thought he might be Spanish, or Lebanese. When he opened another jar, and said, to no one in particular, "This one smells like pineapple," she detected only the hint of an accent.

"Anything else for you today?" the saleswoman asked, accepting Miranda's credit card.

"No thanks."

The woman wrapped the cream in several layers of red tissue. "You'll be very happy with this product." Miranda's hand was unsteady as she signed the receipt. The man hadn't budged.

"I threw in a sample of our new eye gel," the saleswoman added, handing Miranda a small shopping bag. She looked at Miranda's credit card before sliding it across the counter. "Bye-bye, Miranda."

Miranda began walking. At first she sped up. Then, noticing the doors that led to Downtown Crossing,[1] she slowed down.

"Part of your name is Indian," the man said, pacing his steps with hers.

She stopped, as did he, at a circular table piled with sweaters, flanked with pinecones and velvet bows. "Miranda?"

"Mira. I have an aunt named Mira."

His name was Dev. He worked in an investment bank back that way he said, tilting his head in the direction of South Station.[2] He was the first man with a mustache, Miranda decided, she found handsome.

They walked together toward Park Street station,[3] past the kiosks that sold cheap belts and handbags. A fierce January wind spoiled the part in her hair. As she fished for a token in her coat pocket, her eyes fell to his shopping bag. "And those are for her?"

"Who?"

"Your Aunt Mira."

"They're for my wife." He uttered the words slowly, holding Miranda's gaze. "She's going to India for a few weeks." He rolled his eyes. "She's addicted to this stuff."

Somehow, without the wife there, it didn't seem so wrong. At first Miranda and Dev spent every night together, almost. He explained that he couldn't

---

1. Major interchange of MTA subway lines.
2. MTA commuter hub for lines from the south
suburbs.
3. MTA stop in the business district.

spend the whole night at her place, because his wife called every day at six in the morning, from India, where it was four in the afternoon. And so he left her apartment at two, three, often as late as four in the morning, driving back to his house in the suburbs. During the day he called her every hour, it seemed, from work, or from his cell phone. Once he learned Miranda's schedule he left her a message each evening at five-thirty, when she was on the T coming back to her apartment, just so, he said, she could hear his voice as soon as she walked through the door. "I'm thinking about you," he'd say on the tape. "I can't wait to see you." He told her he liked spending time in her apartment, with its kitchen counter no wider than a breadbox, and scratchy floors that sloped, and a buzzer in the lobby that always made a slightly embarrassing sound when he pressed it. He said he admired her for moving to Boston, where she knew no one, instead of remaining in Michigan, where she'd grown up and gone to college. When Miranda told him it was nothing to admire, that she'd moved to Boston precisely for that reason, he shook his head. "I know what it's like to be lonely," he said, suddenly serious, and at that moment Miranda felt that he understood her—understood how she felt some nights on the T, after seeing a movie on her own, or going to a bookstore to read magazines, or having drinks with Laxmi, who always had to meet her husband at Alewife station[4] in an hour or two. In less serious moments Dev said he liked that her legs were longer than her torso, something he'd observed the first time she walked across a room naked. "You're the first," he told her, admiring her from the bed. "The first woman I've known with legs this long."

Dev was the first to tell her that. Unlike the boys she dated in college, who were simply taller, heavier versions of the ones she dated in high school, Dev was the first always to pay for things, and hold doors open, and reach across a table in a restaurant to kiss her hand. He was the first to bring her a bouquet of flowers so immense she'd had to split it up into all six of her drinking glasses, and the first to whisper her name again and again when they made love. Within days of meeting him, when she was at work, Miranda began to wish that there were a picture of her and Dev tacked to the inside of her cubicle, like the one of Laxmi and her husband in front of the Taj Mahal. She didn't tell Laxmi about Dev. She didn't tell anyone. Part of her wanted to tell Laxmi, if only because Laxmi was Indian, too. But Laxmi was always on the phone with her cousin these days, who was still in bed, whose husband was still in London, and whose son still wasn't going to school. "You must eat something," Laxmi would urge. "You mustn't lose your health." When she wasn't speaking to her cousin, she spoke to her husband, shorter conversations, in which she ended up arguing about whether to have chicken or lamb for dinner. "I'm sorry," Miranda heard her apologize at one point. "This whole thing just makes me a little paranoid."

Miranda and Dev didn't argue. They went to movies at the Nickelodeon and kissed the whole time. They ate pulled pork and cornbread in Davis Square,[5] a paper napkin tucked like a cravat into the collar of Dev's shirt. They sipped sangria at the bar of a Spanish restaurant, a grinning pig's head presiding over their conversation. They went to the MFA[6] and picked

4. MTA stop in Cambridge, Massachusetts, across the Charles River from Boston.
5. MTA stop near Tufts University in a formerly working-class, now upscale neighborhood.
6. Museum of Fine Arts (Boston).

out a poster of water lilies for her bedroom. One Saturday, following an afternoon concert at Symphony Hall, he showed her his favorite place in the city, the Mapparium[7] at the Christian Science center, where they stood inside a room made of glowing stained-glass panels, which was shaped like the inside of a globe, but looked like the outside of one. In the middle of the room was a transparent bridge, so that they felt as if they were standing in the center of the world. Dev pointed to India, which was red, and far more detailed than the map in *The Economist*. He explained that many of the countries, like Siam and Italian Somaliland,[8] no longer existed in the same way; the names had changed by now. The ocean, as blue as a peacock's breast, appeared in two shades, depending on the depth of the water. He showed her the deepest spot on earth, seven miles deep, above the Mariana Islands.[9] They peered over the bridge and saw the Antarctic archipelago[1] at their feet, craned their necks and saw a giant metal star overhead. As Dev spoke, his voice bounced wildly off the glass, sometimes loud, sometimes soft, sometimes seeming to land in Miranda's chest, sometimes eluding her ear altogether. When a group of tourists walked onto the bridge, she could hear them clearing their throats, as if through microphones. Dev explained that it was because of the acoustics.

Miranda found London, where Laxmi's cousin's husband was, with the woman he'd met on the plane. She wondered which of the cities in India Dev's wife was in. The farthest Miranda had ever been was to the Bahamas once when she was a child. She searched but couldn't find it on the glass panels. When the tourists left and she and Dev were alone again, he told her to stand at one end of the bridge. Even though they were thirty feet apart, Dev said, they'd be able to hear each other whisper.

"I don't believe you," Miranda said. It was the first time she'd spoken since they'd entered. She felt as if speakers were embedded in her ears.

"Go ahead," he urged, walking backward to his end of the bridge. His voice dropped to a whisper. "Say something." She watched his lips forming the words; at the same time she heard them so clearly that she felt them under her skin, under her winter coat, so near and full of warmth that she felt herself go hot.

"Hi," she whispered, unsure of what else to say.

"You're sexy," he whispered back.

At work the following week, Laxmi told Miranda that it wasn't the first time her cousin's husband had had an affair. "She's decided to let him come to his senses," Laxmi said one evening as they were getting ready to leave the office. "She says it's for the boy. She's willing to forgive him for the boy." Miranda waited as Laxmi shut off her computer. "He'll come crawling back, and she'll let him," Laxmi said, shaking her head. "Not me. If my husband so much as looked at another woman I'd change the locks." She studied the picture tacked to her cubicle. Laxmi's husband had his arm draped over her shoulder, his knees leaning in toward her on the bench. She turned to Miranda. "Wouldn't you?"

7. Large walk-through globe that maps the earth as stars and planets would be seen in a planetarium.
8. Presently Thailand and Somalia.
9. Island chain in the western Pacific Ocean.
1. Group of islands northwest of the Antarctic Peninsula.

She nodded. Dev's wife was coming back from India the next day. That afternoon he'd called Miranda at work, to say he had to go to the airport to pick her up. He promised he'd call as soon as he could.

"What's the Taj Mahal like?" she asked Laxmi.

"The most romantic spot on earth." Laxmi's face brightened at the memory. "An everlasting monument to love."

While Dev was at the airport, Miranda went to Filene's Basement to buy herself things she thought a mistress should have. She found a pair of black high heels with buckles smaller than a baby's teeth. She found a satin slip with scalloped edges and a knee-length silk robe. Instead of the pantyhose she normally wore to work, she found sheer stockings with a seam. She searched through piles and wandered through racks, pressing back hanger after hanger, until she found a cocktail dress made of a slinky silvery material that matched her eyes, with little chains for straps. As she shopped she thought about Dev, and about what he'd told her in the Mapparium. It was the first time a man had called her sexy, and when she closed her eyes she could still feel his whisper drifting through her body, under her skin. In the fitting room, which was just one big room with mirrors on the walls, she found a spot next to an older woman with a shiny face and coarse frosted hair. The woman stood barefoot in her underwear, pulling the black net of a body stocking taut between her fingers.

"Always check for snags," the woman advised.

Miranda pulled out the satin slip with scalloped edges. She held it to her chest.

The woman nodded with approval. "Oh yes."

"And this?" She held up the silver cocktail dress.

"Absolutely," the woman said. "He'll want to rip it right off you."

Miranda pictured the two of them at a restaurant in the South End[2] they'd been to, where Dev had ordered foie gras and a soup made with champagne and raspberries. She pictured herself in the cocktail dress, and Dev in one of his suits, kissing her hand across the table. Only the next time Dev came to visit her, on a Sunday afternoon several days since the last time they'd seen each other, he was in gym clothes. After his wife came back, that was his excuse: on Sundays he drove into Boston and went running along the Charles. The first Sunday she opened the door in the knee-length robe, but Dev didn't even notice it; he carried her over to the bed, wearing sweatpants and sneakers, and entered her without a word. Later, she slipped on the robe when she walked across the room to get him a saucer for his cigarette ashes, but he complained that she was depriving him of the sight of her long legs, and demanded that she remove it. So the next Sunday she didn't bother. She wore jeans. She kept the lingerie at the back of a drawer, behind her socks and everyday underwear. The silver cocktail dress hung in her closet, the tag dangling from the seam. Often, in the morning, the dress would be in a heap on the floor; the chain straps always slipped off the metal hanger.

Still, Miranda looked forward to Sundays. In the mornings she went to a deli and bought a baguette and little containers of things Dev liked to eat,

2. Trendy Boston neighborhood.

like pickled herring, and potato salad, and tortes of pesto and mascarpone cheese. They ate in bed, picking up the herring with their fingers and ripping the baguette with their hands. Dev told her stories about his childhood, when he would come home from school and drink mango juice served to him on a tray, and then play cricket by a lake, dressed all in white. He told her about how, at eighteen, he'd been sent to a college in upstate New York during something called the Emergency,[3] and about how it took him years to be able to follow American accents in movies, in spite of the fact that he'd had an English-medium education. As he talked he smoked three cigarettes, crushing them in a saucer by the side of her bed. Sometimes he asked her questions, like how many lovers she'd had (three) and how old she'd been the first time (nineteen). After lunch they made love, on sheets covered with crumbs, and then Dev took a nap for twelve minutes. Miranda had never known an adult who took naps, but Dev said it was something he'd grown up doing in India, where it was so hot that people didn't leave their homes until the sun went down. "Plus it allows us to sleep together," he murmured mischievously, curving his arm like a big bracelet around her body.

Only Miranda never slept. She watched the clock on her bedside table, or pressed her face against Dev's fingers, intertwined with hers, each with its half-dozen hairs at the knuckle. After six minutes she turned to face him, sighing and stretching, to test if he was really sleeping. He always was. His ribs were visible through his skin as he breathed, and yet he was beginning to develop a paunch. He complained about the hair on his shoulders, but Miranda thought him perfect, and refused to imagine him any other way.

At the end of twelve minutes Dev would open his eyes as if he'd been awake all along, smiling at her, full of a contentment she wished she felt herself. "The best twelve minutes of the week." He'd sigh, running a hand along the backs of her calves. Then he'd spring out of bed, pulling on his sweatpants and lacing up his sneakers. He would go to the bathroom and brush his teeth with his index finger, something he told her all Indians knew how to do, to get rid of the smoke in his mouth. When she kissed him good-bye she smelled herself sometimes in his hair. But she knew that his excuse, that he'd spent the afternoon jogging, allowed him to take a shower when he got home, first thing.

Apart from Laxmi and Dev, the only Indians whom Miranda had known were a family in the neighborhood where she'd grown up, named the Dixits. Much to the amusement of the neighborhood children, including Miranda, but not including the Dixit children, Mr. Dixit would jog each evening along the flat winding streets of their development in his everyday shirt and trousers, his only concession to athletic apparel a pair of cheap Keds. Every weekend, the family—mother, father, two boys, and a girl—piled into their car and went away, to where nobody knew. The fathers complained that Mr. Dixit did not fertilize his lawn properly, did not rake his leaves on time, and agreed that the Dixits' house, the only one with vinyl siding, detracted from the neighborhood's charm. The mothers never invited Mrs. Dixit to join them around the Armstrongs' swimming pool. Waiting for the school bus

---

3. State of internal emergency declared in 1975 by Indira Gandhi (1917–1984), prime minister of India, that allowed her to rule by decree until 1977, when she was defeated in an election.

with the Dixit children standing to one side, the other children would say "The Dixits dig shit," under their breath, and then burst into laughter.

One year, all the neighborhood children were invited to the birthday party of the Dixit girl. Miranda remembered a heavy aroma of incense and onions in the house, and a pile of shoes heaped by the front door. But most of all she remembered a piece of fabric, about the size of a pillowcase, which hung from a wooden dowel at the bottom of the stairs. It was a painting of a naked woman with a red face shaped like a knight's shield. She had enormous white eyes that tilted toward her temples, and mere dots for pupils. Two circles, with the same dots at their centers, indicated her breasts. In one hand she brandished a dagger. With one foot she crushed a struggling man on the ground. Around her body was a necklace composed of bleeding heads, strung together like a popcorn chain. She stuck her tongue out at Miranda.

"It is the goddess Kali,"[4] Mrs. Dixit explained brightly, shifting the dowel slightly in order to straighten the image. Mrs. Dixit's hands were painted with henna, an intricate pattern of zigzags and stars. "Come please, time for cake."

Miranda, then nine years old, had been too frightened to eat the cake. For months afterward she'd been too frightened even to walk on the same side of the street as the Dixits' house, which she had to pass twice daily, once to get to the bus stop, and once again to come home. For a while she even held her breath until she reached the next lawn, just as she did when the school bus passed a cemetery.

It shamed her now. Now, when she and Dev made love, Miranda closed her eyes and saw deserts and elephants, and marble pavilions floating on lakes beneath a full moon. One Saturday, having nothing else to do, she walked all the way to Central Square,[5] to an Indian restaurant, and ordered a plate of tandoori chicken. As she ate she tried to memorize phrases printed at the bottom of the menu, for things like "delicious" and "water" and "check, please." The phrases didn't stick in her mind, and so she began to stop from time to time in the foreign-language section of a bookstore in Kenmore Square,[6] where she studied the Bengali alphabet in the Teach Yourself series. Once she went so far as to try to transcribe the Indian part of her name, "Mira," into her Filofax,[7] her hand moving in unfamiliar directions, stopping and turning and picking up her pen when she least expected to. Following the arrows in the book, she drew a bar from left to right from which the letters hung; one looked more like a number than a letter, another looked like a triangle on its side. It had taken her several tries to get the letters of her name to resemble the sample letters in the book, and even then she wasn't sure if she'd written Mira or Mara. It was a scribble to her, but somewhere in the world, she realized with a shock, it meant something.

During the week it wasn't so bad. Work kept her busy, and she and Laxmi had begun having lunch together at a new Indian restaurant around the corner, during which Laxmi reported the latest status of her cousin's marriage. Sometimes Miranda tried to change the topic; it made her feel the way

4. Hindu goddess of destruction.
5. In Cambridge.
6. In Boston.

7. Loose-leaf personal organizer, manufactured by the Filofax Company in England.

she once felt in college, when she and her boyfriend at the time had walked away from a crowded house of pancakes without paying for their food, just to see if they could get away with it. But Laxmi spoke of nothing else. "If I were her I'd fly straight to London and shoot them both," she announced one day. She snapped a papadum in half and dipped it into chutney.[8] "I don't know how she can just wait this way."

Miranda knew how to wait. In the evenings she sat at her dining table and coated her nails with clear nail polish, and ate salad straight from the salad bowl, and watched television, and waited for Sunday. Saturdays were the worst because by Saturday it seemed that Sunday would never come. One Saturday when Dev called, late at night, she heard people laughing and talking in the background, so many that she asked him if he was at a concert hall. But he was only calling from his house in the suburbs. "I can't hear you that well," he said. "We have guests. Miss me?" She looked at the television screen, a sitcom that she'd muted with the remote control when the phone rang. She pictured him whispering into his cell phone, in a room upstairs, a hand on the doorknob, the hallway filled with guests. "Miranda, do you miss me?" he asked again. She told him that she did.

The next day, when Dev came to visit, Miranda asked him what his wife looked like. She was nervous to ask, waiting until he'd smoked the last of his cigarettes, crushing it with a firm twist into the saucer. She wondered if they'd quarrel. But Dev wasn't surprised by the question. He told her, spreading some smoked whitefish on a cracker, that his wife resembled an actress in Bombay named Madhuri Dixit.[9]

For an instant Miranda's heart stopped. But no, the Dixit girl had been named something else, something that began with P. Still, she wondered if the actress and the Dixit girl were related. She'd been plain, wearing her hair in two braids all through high school.

A few days later Miranda went to an Indian grocery in Central Square which also rented videos. The door opened to a complicated tinkling of bells. It was dinnertime, and she was the only customer. A video was playing on a television hooked up in a corner of the store: a row of young women in harem pants were thrusting their hips in synchrony on a beach.

"Can I help you?" the man standing at the cash register asked. He was eating a samosa,[1] dipping it into some dark brown sauce on a paper plate. Below the glass counter at his waist were trays of more plump samosas, and what looked like pale, diamond-shaped pieces of fudge covered with foil, and some bright orange pastries floating in syrup. "You like some video?"

Miranda opened up her Filofax, where she had written "Mottery Dixit." She looked up at the videos on the shelves behind the counter. She saw women wearing skirts that sat low on the hips and tops that tied like bandannas between their breasts. Some leaned back against a stone wall, or a tree. They were beautiful, the way the women dancing on the beach were beautiful, with kohl-rimmed eyes and long black hair. She knew then that Madhuri Dixit was beautiful, too.

8. Thick, sweet, spicy sauce used as a condiment. "Papadum": crisp lentil wafer.
9. Indian film actress (b. 1967) renowned for her beauty.
1. Deep-fried turnover filled with vegetables or ground meat.

"We have subtitled versions, miss," the man continued. He wiped his fingertips quickly on his shirt and pulled out three titles.

"No," Miranda said. "Thank you, no." She wandered through the store, studying shelves lined with unlabeled packets and tins. The freezer case was stuffed with bags of pita bread and vegetables she didn't recognize. The only thing she recognized was a rack lined with bags and bags of the Hot Mix that Laxmi was always eating. She thought about buying some for Laxmi, then hesitated, wondering how to explain what she'd been doing in an Indian grocery.

"Very spicy," the man said, shaking his head, his eyes traveling across Miranda's body. "Too spicy for you."

By February, Laxmi's cousin's husband still hadn't come to his senses. He had returned to Montreal, argued bitterly with his wife for two weeks, packed two suitcases, and flown back to London. He wanted a divorce.

Miranda sat in her cubicle and listened as Laxmi kept telling her cousin that there were better men in the world, just waiting to come out of the wood-work. The next day the cousin said she and her son were going to her parents' house in California, to try to recuperate. Laxmi convinced her to arrange a weekend layover in Boston. "A quick change of place will do you good," Laxmi insisted gently, "besides which, I haven't seen you in years."

Miranda stared at her own phone, wishing Dev would call. It had been four days since their last conversation. She heard Laxmi dialing directory assistance, asking for the number of a beauty salon. "Something soothing," Laxmi requested. She scheduled massages, facials, manicures, and pedi-cures. Then she reserved a table for lunch at the Four Seasons. In her deter-mination to cheer up her cousin, Laxmi had forgotten about the boy. She rapped her knuckles on the laminated wall.

"Are you busy Saturday?"

The boy was thin. He wore a yellow knapsack strapped across his back, gray herringbone trousers, a red V-necked sweater, and black leather shoes. His hair was cut in a thick fringe over his eyes, which had dark circles under them. They were the first thing Miranda noticed. They made him look hag-gard, as if he smoked a great deal and slept very little, in spite of the fact that he was only seven years old. He clasped a large sketch pad with a spiral binding. His name was Rohin.

"Ask me a capital," he said, staring up at Miranda.

She stared back at him. It was eight-thirty on a Saturday morning. She took a sip of coffee. "A what?"

"It's a game he's been playing," Laxmi's cousin explained. She was thin like her son, with a long face and the same dark circles under her eyes. A rust-colored coat hung heavy on her shoulders. Her black hair, with a few strands of gray at the temples, was pulled back like a ballerina's. "You ask him a country and he tells you the capital."

"You should have heard him in the car," Laxmi said. "He's already memo-rized all of Europe."

"It's not a game," Rohin said. "I'm having a competition with a boy at school. We're competing to memorize all the capitals. I'm going to beat him."

Miranda nodded. "Okay. What's the capital of India?"

"That's no good." He marched away, his arms swinging like a toy soldier. Then he marched back to Laxmi's cousin and tugged at a pocket of her overcoat. "Ask me a hard one."

"Senegal," she said.

"Dakar!" Rohin exclaimed triumphantly, and began running in larger and larger circles. Eventually he ran into the kitchen. Miranda could hear him opening and closing the fridge.

"Rohin, don't touch without asking," Laxmi's cousin called out wearily. She managed a smile for Miranda. "Don't worry, he'll fall asleep in a few hours. And thanks for watching him."

"Back at three," Laxmi said, disappearing with her cousin down the hallway. "We're double-parked."

Miranda fastened the chain on the door. She went to the kitchen to find Rohin, but he was now in the living room, at the dining table, kneeling on one of the director's chairs. He unzipped his knapsack, pushed Miranda's basket of manicure supplies to one side of the table, and spread his crayons over the surface. Miranda stood over his shoulder. She watched as he gripped a blue crayon and drew the outline of an airplane.

"It's lovely," she said. When he didn't reply, she went to the kitchen to pour herself more coffee.

"Some for me, please," Rohin called out.

She returned to the living room. "Some what?"

"Some coffee. There's enough in the pot. I saw."

She walked over to the table and sat opposite him. At times he nearly stood up to reach for a new crayon. He barely made a dent in the director's chair.

"You're too young for coffee."

Rohin leaned over the sketch pad, so that his tiny chest and shoulders almost touched it, his head tilted to one side. "The stewardess let me have coffee," he said. "She made it with milk and lots of sugar." He straightened, revealing a woman's face beside the plane, with long wavy hair and eyes like asterisks. "Her hair was more shiny," he decided, adding, "My father met a pretty woman on a plane, too." He looked at Miranda. His face darkened as he watched her sip. "Can't I have just a little coffee? Please?"

She wondered, in spite of his composed, brooding expression, if he were the type to throw a tantrum. She imagined his kicking her with his leather shoes, screaming for coffee, screaming and crying until his mother and Laxmi came back to fetch him. She went to the kitchen and prepared a cup for him as he'd requested. She selected a mug she didn't care for, in case he dropped it.

"Thank you," he said when she put it on the table. He took short sips, holding the mug securely with both hands.

Miranda sat with him while he drew, but when she attempted to put a coat of clear polish on her nails he protested. Instead he pulled out a paperback world almanac from his knapsack and asked her to quiz him. The countries were arranged by continent, six to a page, with the capitals in boldface, followed by a short entry on the population, government, and other statistics. Miranda turned to a page in the Africa section and went down the list.

"Mali," she asked him.

"Bamako," he replied instantly.

"Malawi."

"Lilongwe."

She remembered looking at Africa in the Mapparium. She remembered the fat part of it was green.

"Go on," Rohin said.

"Mauritania."

"Nouakchott."

"Mauritius."

He paused, squeezed his eyes shut, then opened them, defeated. "I can't remember."

"Port Louis," she told him.

"Port Louis." He began to say it again and again, like a chant under his breath.

When they reached the last of the countries in Africa, Rohin said he wanted to watch cartoons, telling Miranda to watch them with him. When the cartoons ended, he followed her to the kitchen, and stood by her side as she made more coffee. He didn't follow her when she went to the bathroom a few minutes later, but when she opened the door she was startled to find him standing outside.

"Do you need to go?"

He shook his head but walked into the bathroom anyway. He put the cover of the toilet down, climbed on top of it, and surveyed the narrow glass shelf over the sink which held Miranda's toothbrush and makeup.

"What's this for?" he asked, picking up the sample of eye gel she'd gotten the day she met Dev.

"Puffiness."

"What's puffiness?"

"Here," she explained, pointing.

"After you've been crying?"

"I guess so."

Rohin opened the tube and smelled it. He squeezed a drop of it onto a finger, then rubbed it on his hand. "It stings." He inspected the back of his hand closely, as if expecting it to change color. "My mother has puffiness. She says it's a cold, but really she cries, sometimes for hours. Sometimes straight through dinner. Sometimes she cries so hard her eyes puff up like bullfrogs."

Miranda wondered if she ought to feed him. In the kitchen she discovered a bag of rice cakes and some lettuce. She offered to go out, to buy something from the deli, but Rohin said he wasn't very hungry, and accepted one of the rice cakes. "You eat one too," he said. They sat at the table, the rice cakes between them. He turned to a fresh page in his sketch pad. "You draw."

She selected a blue crayon. "What should I draw?"

He thought for a moment. "I know," he said. He asked her to draw things in the living room: the sofa, the director's chairs, the television, the telephone. "This way I can memorize it."

"Memorize what?"

"Our day together." He reached for another rice cake.

"Why do you want to memorize it?"

"Because we're never going to see each other, ever again."

The precision of the phrase startled her. She looked at him, feeling slightly depressed. Rohin didn't look depressed. He tapped the page. "Go on."

And so she drew the items as best as she could—the sofa, the director's chairs, the television, the telephone. He sidled up to her, so close that it was sometimes difficult to see what she was doing. He put his small brown hand over hers. "Now me."

She handed him the crayon.

He shook his head. "No, now draw me."

"I can't," she said. "It won't look like you."

The brooding look began to spread across Rohin's face again, just as it had when she'd refused him coffee. "Please?"

She drew his face, outlining his head and the thick fringe of hair. He sat perfectly still, with a formal, melancholy expression, his gaze fixed to one side. Miranda wished she could draw a good likeness. Her hand moved in conjunction with her eyes, in unknown ways, just as it had that day in the bookstore when she'd transcribed her name in Bengali letters. It looked nothing like him. She was in the middle of drawing his nose when he wriggled away from the table.

"I'm bored," he announced, heading toward her bedroom. She heard him opening the door, opening the drawers of her bureau and closing them.

When she joined him he was inside the closet. After a moment he emerged, his hair disheveled, holding the silver cocktail dress. "This was on the floor."

"It falls off the hanger."

Rohin looked at the dress and then at Miranda's body. "Put it on."

"Excuse me?"

"Put it on."

There was no reason to put it on. Apart from in the fitting room at Filene's she had never worn it, and as long as she was with Dev she knew she never would. She knew they would never go to restaurants, where he would reach across a table and kiss her hand. They would meet in her apartment, on Sundays, he in his sweatpants, she in her jeans. She took the dress from Rohin and shook it out, even though the slinky fabric never wrinkled. She reached into the closet for a free hanger.

"Please put it on," Rohin asked, suddenly standing behind her. He pressed his face against her, clasping her waist with both his thin arms. "Please?"

"All right," she said, surprised by the strength of his grip.

He smiled, satisfied, and sat on the edge of her bed.

"You have to wait out there," she said, pointing to the door. "I'll come out when I'm ready."

"But my mother always takes her clothes off in front of me."

"She does?"

Rohin nodded. "She doesn't even pick them up afterward. She leaves them all on the floor by the bed, all tangled.

"One day she slept in my room," he continued. "She said it felt better than her bed, now that my father's gone."

"I'm not your mother," Miranda said, lifting him by the armpits off her bed. When he refused to stand, she picked him up. He was heavier than she expected, and he clung to her, his legs wrapped firmly around her hips, his head resting against her chest. She set him down in the hallway and shut the door. As an extra precaution she fastened the latch. She changed into the dress, glancing into the full-length mirror nailed to the back of the door. Her ankle socks looked silly, and so she opened a drawer and found the stockings. She searched through the back of the closet and slipped on the high heels with the tiny buckles. The chain straps of the dress were as light as paper clips against her collarbone. It was a bit loose on her. She could not zip it herself.

Rohin began knocking. "May I come in now?"

She opened the door. Rohin was holding his almanac in his hands, muttering something under his breath. His eyes opened wide at the sight of her. "I need help with the zipper," she said. She sat on the edge of the bed.

Rohin fastened the zipper to the top, and then Miranda stood up and twirled. Rohin put down the almanac. "You're sexy," he declared.

"What did you say?"

"You're sexy."

Miranda sat down again. Though she knew it meant nothing, her heart skipped a beat. Rohin probably referred to all women as sexy. He'd probably heard the word on television, or seen it on the cover of a magazine. She remembered the day in the Mapparium, standing across the bridge from Dev. At the time she thought she knew what his words meant. At the time they'd made sense.

Miranda folded her arms across her chest and looked Rohin in the eyes. "Tell me something."

He was silent.

"What does it mean?"

"What?"

"That word. 'Sexy.' What does it mean?"

He looked down, suddenly shy. "I can't tell you."

"Why not?"

"It's a secret." He pressed his lips together, so hard that a bit of them went white.

"Tell me the secret. I want to know."

Rohin sat on the bed beside Miranda and began to kick the edge of the mattress with the backs of his shoes. He giggled nervously, his thin body flinching as if it were being tickled.

"Tell me," Miranda demanded. She leaned over and gripped his ankles, holding his feet still.

Rohin looked at her, his eyes like slits. He struggled to kick the mattress again, but Miranda pressed against him. He fell back on the bed, his back straight as a board. He cupped his hands around his mouth, and then he whispered, "It means loving someone you don't know."

Miranda felt Rohin's words under her skin, the same way she'd felt Dev's. But instead of going hot she felt numb. It reminded her of the way she'd felt at the Indian grocery, the moment she knew, without even looking at a picture, that Madhuri Dixit, whom Dev's wife resembled, was beautiful.

"That's what my father did," Rohin continued. "He sat next to someone he didn't know, someone sexy, and now he loves her instead of my mother."

He took off his shoes and placed them side by side on the floor. Then he peeled back the comforter and crawled into Miranda's bed with the almanac. A minute later the book dropped from his hands, and he closed his eyes. Miranda watched him sleep, the comforter rising and falling as he breathed. He didn't wake up after twelve minutes like Dev, or even twenty. He didn't open his eyes as she stepped out of the silver cocktail dress and back into her jeans, and put the high-heeled shoes in the back of the closet, and rolled up the stockings and put them back in her drawer.

When she had put everything away she sat on the bed. She leaned toward him, close enough to see some white powder from the rice cakes stuck to the corners of his mouth, and picked up the almanac. As she turned the pages she imagined the quarrels Rohin had overheard in his house in Montreal. "Is she pretty?" his mother would have asked his father, wearing the same bathrobe she'd worn for weeks, her own pretty face turning spiteful. "Is she sexy?" His father would deny it at first, try to change the subject. "Tell me," Rohin's mother would shriek, "tell me if she's sexy." In the end his father would admit that she was, and his mother would cry and cry, in a bed surrounded by a tangle of clothes, her eyes puffing up like bullfrogs. "How could you," she'd ask, sobbing, "how could you love a woman you don't even know?"

As Miranda imagined the scene she began to cry a little herself. In the Mapparium that day, all the countries had seemed close enough to touch, and Dev's voice had bounced wildly off the glass. From across the bridge, thirty feet away, his words had reached her ears, so near and full of warmth that they'd drifted for days under her skin. Miranda cried harder, unable to stop. But Rohin still slept. She guessed that he was used to it now, to the sound of a woman crying.

On Sunday, Dev called to tell Miranda he was on his way. "I'm almost ready. I'll be there at two."

She was watching a cooking show on television. A woman pointed to a row of apples, explaining which were best for baking. "You shouldn't come today."

"Why not?"

"I have a cold," she lied. It wasn't far from the truth; crying had left her congested. "I've been in bed all morning."

"You do sound stuffed up." There was a pause. "Do you need anything?"

"I'm all set."

"Drink lots of fluids."

"Dev?"

"Yes, Miranda?"

"Do you remember that day we went to the Mapparium?"

"Of course."

"Do you remember how we whispered to each other?"

"I remember," Dev whispered playfully.

"Do you remember what you said?"

There was a pause. "'Let's go back to your place.'" He laughed quietly. "Next Sunday, then?"

The day before, as she'd cried, Miranda had believed she would never forget anything—not even the way her name looked written in Bengali. She'd fallen asleep beside Rohin and when she woke up he was drawing an airplane on the copy of *The Economist* she'd saved, hidden under the bed. "Who's Devajit Mitra?" he had asked, looking at the address label.

Miranda pictured Dev, in his sweatpants and sneakers, laughing into the phone. In a moment he'd join his wife downstairs, and tell her he wasn't going jogging. He'd pulled a muscle while stretching, he'd say, settling down to read the paper. In spite of herself, she longed for him. She would see him one more Sunday, she decided, perhaps two. Then she would tell him the things she had known all along: that it wasn't fair to her, or to his wife, that they both deserved better, that there was no point in it dragging on.

But the next Sunday it snowed, so much so that Dev couldn't tell his wife he was going running along the Charles. The Sunday after that, the snow had melted, but Miranda made plans to go to the movies with Laxmi, and when she told Dev this over the phone, he didn't ask her to cancel them. The third Sunday she got up early and went out for a walk. It was cold but sunny, and so she walked all the way down Commonwealth Avenue, past the restaurants where Dev had kissed her, and then she walked all the way to the Christian Science center. The Mapparium was closed, but she bought a cup of coffee nearby and sat on one of the benches in the plaza outside the church, gazing at its giant pillars and its massive dome, and at the clear-blue sky spread over the city.

1999

JUNOT DÍAZ
b. 1968

The people of two neighborhoods inspire most of Junot Díaz's fiction: those living in Villa Juana, a district of Santo Domingo in the Dominican Republic, and others residing in the London Terrace area of Palin, New Jersey. Born on the last day of 1968, Diaz lived in Villa Juana for his first five years, a time when his father was away working in the United States. Just before his fifth birthday he joined his father in New Jersey. Becoming an American did not mark a division in his life, nor would it as a source for his writing. Instead, Díaz appreciates the rich duality of any immigrant's experience. Narratives set in the Dominican Republic show characters ever mindful of what is happening among their relations on the North American mainland, and the young people in his New Jersey stories speak an English heavily laced with Dominican slang and live in a manner still marked by their Caribbean heritage. Not so much people of two worlds, Díaz's characters are creatures of a new world fashioned by multicultural factors and ultimately shaped by their own ingenuity.

The stories collected in *Drown* (1996) show the influence of two authors whose work Díaz read in college, Sandra Cisneros and Toni Morrison. Majoring in English at Kean College and Rutgers University, Díaz profited from a "living-and-learning" residence hall program that provided an immersion in both creative writing and literary studies. From Cisneros's fiction he learned how a neighborhood, such as the one she depicted in *The House on Mango Street* (1984), can be as vital and vibrant a creation as any character—how the neighborhood itself can be a character in the writer's imagination, a technique Díaz would later develop in his own manner. Morrison's novels popular during Díaz's undergraduate years (1988–92) are especially strong in privileging the novelist as creator of an otherwise unwritten minority history, a theme the younger writer would extend to the immigrant's experience of living in two worlds, neither of which conform to dominant cultural models. At the same time Díaz was paying for his education by working numerous part-time jobs that he recalls as roles customarily reserved for adult Latinos recently arrived in the United States, such as in the service industries (washing dishes, delivering pool tables) and in a steel plant. An MFA in creative writing from Cornell University followed in 1995, by which time Díaz had published many of the stories collected in *Drown*, including several in such presigious venues as the *New Yorker* and the *Paris Review*. Díaz lives in New York City, where he remains active in the Dominican community; at the Massachusetts Institute of Technology he teaches creative writing in the Program in Writing and Humanistic Studies.

The fact that Díaz's novel, *The Brief Wondrous Life of Oscar Wao* (2007), appeared eleven years after *Drown* is indicative of his painstaking writing method. A winner of both the 2008 Pulitzer Prize for fiction and the National Book Critics Circle Award for the best novel of 2007, *The Brief Wondrous Life of Oscar Wao* presents a character who fulfills Díaz's professed goal of challenging "the type of protagonist that many of the young male Latino writers I knew were writing," as the author told Meghan O'Rourke of *Slate* in the wake of his awards. In a similar discussion with Jaime Perales Contreras of the bilingual *Literal* magazine, Díaz explained that his title character's name was prompted by a young Mexican literature student's pronunciation of Oscar Wilde's name. "Spanglish" is the slang term for such colorful mixtures of Spanish and English, and as a poetry of sorts it contributes to the texture and rhythm of Díaz's narration. As Meghan O'Rourke puts it, his fiction "is propelled by its attention to the energetic hybridity of American life," stretching from the questions of identity and inclusion dealt with in the stories of *Drown* to the complexities of a multicultural boyhood depicted in the novel. Throughout Díaz's work "authority" is an ever-present concern, from the memories of Oscar Wao's family suffering under the Trujillo dictatorship in the Dominican Republic to the contested nature of various narrative accounts with which young Oscar struggles in his American high school.

The following text is the title story from the 1996 collection *Drown*.

Drown

My mother tells me Beto's home, waits for me to say something, but I keep watching the TV. Only when she's in bed do I put on my jacket and swing through the neighborhood to see. He's a pato[1] now but two years ago we were friends and he would walk into the apartment without knocking, his heavy voice rousing my mother from the Spanish of her room and drawing me up from the basement, a voice that crackled and made you think of uncles or grandfathers.

We were raging then, crazy the way we stole, broke windows, the way we pissed on people's steps and then challenged them to come out and stop us. Beto was leaving for college at the end of the summer and was delirious from the thought of it—he hated everything about the neighborhood, the break-apart buildings, the little strips of grass, the piles of garbage around the cans, and the dump, especially the dump.

I don't know how you can do it, he said to me. I would just find me a job anywhere and go.

Yeah, I said. I wasn't like him. I had another year to go in high school, no promises elsewhere.

---

1. Dominican slang (pejorative) for a gay man (literally, "duck" in Spanish).

Days we spent in the mall or out in the parking lot playing stickball, but nights were what we waited for. The heat in the apartments was like something heavy that had come inside to die. Families arranged on their porches, the glow from their TVs washing blue against the brick. From my family apartment you could smell the pear trees that had been planted years ago, four to a court, probably to save us all from asphyxiation. Nothing moved fast, even the daylight was slow to fade, but as soon as night settled Beto and I headed down to the community center and sprang the fence into the pool. We were never alone, every kid with legs was there. We lunged from the boards and swam out of the deep end, wrestling and farting around. At around midnight abuelas,[2] with their night hair swirled around spiky rollers, shouted at us from their apartment windows. ¡Sinvergüenzas![3] Go home!

I pass his apartment but the windows are dark; I put my ear to the busted-up door and hear only the familiar hum of the air conditioner. I haven't decided yet if I'll talk to him. I can go back to my dinner and two years will become three.

Even from four blocks off I can hear the racket from the pool—radios too—and wonder if we were ever that loud. Little has changed, not the stink of chlorine, not the bottles exploding against the lifeguard station. I hook my fingers through the plastic-coated hurricane fence. Something tells me that he will be here; I hop the fence, feeling stupid when I sprawl on the dandelions and the grass.

Nice one, somebody calls out.

Fuck me, I say. I'm not the oldest motherfucker in the place, but it's close. I take off my shirt and my shoes and then knife in. Many of the kids here are younger brothers of the people I used to go to school with. Two of them swim past, black and Latino, and they pause when they see me, recognizing the guy who sells them their shitty dope. The crackheads have their own man, Lucero, and some other guy who drives in from Paterson,[4] the only full-time commuter in the area.

The water feels good. Starting at the deep end I glide over the slick-tiled bottom without kicking up a spume or making a splash. Sometimes another swimmer churns past me, more a disturbance of water than a body. I can still go far without coming up. While everything above is loud and bright, everything below is whispers. And always the risk of coming up to find the cops stabbing their searchlights out across the water. And then everyone running, wet feet slapping against the concrete, yelling, Fuck you, officers, you puto sucios,[5] fuck you.

When I'm tired I wade through to the shallow end, past some kid who's kissing his girlfriend, watching me as though I'm going to try to cut in, and I sit near the sign that runs the pool during the day. *No Horseplay, No Running, No Defecating, No Urinating, No Expectorating.* At the bottom someone has scrawled in *No Whites, No Fat Chiks* and someone else has provided the missing *c.* I laugh. Beto hadn't known what expectorating meant though he was the one leaving for college. I told him, spitting a greener by the side of the pool.

Shit, he said. Where did you learn that?

---

2. Grandmothers (Spanish).
3. Shameless, brazen ones (Spanish).
4. City in northern New Jersey.
5. Dirty whores (Spanish).

I shrugged.

Tell me. He hated when I knew something he didn't. He put his hands on my shoulders and pushed me under. He was wearing a cross and cutoff jeans. He was stronger than me and held me down until water flooded my nose and throat. Even then I didn't tell him; he thought I didn't read, not even dictionaries.

We live alone. My mother has enough for the rent and groceries and I cover the phone bill, sometimes the cable. She's so quiet that most of the time I'm startled to find her in the apartment. I'll enter a room and she'll stir, detaching herself from the cracking plaster walls, from the stained cabinets, and fright will pass through me like a wire. She has discovered the secret to silence: pouring café without a splash, walking between rooms as if gliding on a cushion of felt, crying without a sound. You have traveled to the East and learned many secret things, I've told her. You're like a shadow warrior.

And you're like a crazy, she says. Like a big crazy.

When I come in she's still awake, her hands picking clots of lint from her skirt. I put a towel down on the sofa and we watch television together. We settle on the Spanish-language news: drama for her, violence for me. Today a child has survived a seven-story fall, busting nothing but his diaper. The hysterical baby-sitter, about three hundred pounds of her, is head-butting the microphone.

It's a goddamn miraclevilla,[6] she cries.

My mother asks me if I found Beto. I tell her that I didn't look.

That's too bad. He was telling me that he might be starting at a school for business.

So what?

She's never understood why we don't speak anymore. I've tried to explain, all wise-like, that everything changes, but she thinks that sort of saying is only around so you can prove it wrong.

He asked me what you were doing.

What did you say?

I told him you were fine.

You should have told him I moved.

And what if he ran into you?

I'm not allowed to visit my mother?

She notices the tightening of my arms. You should be more like me and your father.

Can't you see I'm watching television?

I was angry at him, wasn't I? But now we can talk to each other.

Am I watching television here or what?

Saturdays she asks me to take her to the mall. As a son I feel I owe her that much, even though neither of us has a car and we have to walk two miles through redneck territory to catch the M15.[7]

Before we head out she drags us through the apartment to make sure the windows are locked. She can't reach the latches so she has me test them.

6. Slang term for "miraculous" in "Spanglish," an amalgamation of Spanish and English as spoken in some Hispanic communities.

7. Bus route in the New Brunswick area of New Jersey.

With the air conditioner on we never open windows but I go through the routine anyway. Putting my hand on the latch is not enough—she wants to hear it rattle. This place just isn't safe, she tells me. Lorena got lazy and look what they did to her. They punched her and kept her locked up in her place. Those morenos[8] ate all her food and even made phone calls. Phone calls!

That's why we don't have long-distance, I tell her but she shakes her head. That's not funny, she says.

She doesn't go out much, so when she does it's a big deal. She dresses up, even puts on makeup. Which is why I don't give her lip about taking her to the mall even though I usually make a fortune on Saturdays, selling to those kids going down to Belmar or out to Spruce Run.

I recognize like half the kids on the bus. I keep my head buried in my cap, praying that nobody tries to score. She watches the traffic, her hands somewhere inside her purse, doesn't say a word.

When we arrive at the mall I give her fifty dollars. Buy something, I say, hating the image I have of her, picking through the sale bins, wrinkling everything. Back in the day, my father would give her a hundred dollars at the end of each summer for my new clothes and she would take nearly a week to spend it, even though it never amounted to more than a couple of t-shirts and two pairs of jeans. She folds the bills into a square. I'll see you at three, she says.

I wander through the stores, staying in sight of the cashiers so they won't have reason to follow me. The circuit I make has not changed since my looting days. Bookstore, record store, comic-book shop, Macy's. Me and Beto used to steal like mad from these places, two, three hundred dollars of shit in an outing. Our system was simple—we walked into a store with a shopping bag and came out loaded. Back then security wasn't tight. The only trick was in the exit. We stopped right at the entrance of the store and checked out some worthless piece of junk to stop people from getting suspicious. What do you think? we asked each other. Would she like it? Both of us had seen bad shoplifters at work. All grab and run, nothing smooth about them. Not us. We idled out of the stores slow, like a fat seventies car. At this, Beto was the best. He even talked to mall security, asked them for directions, his bag all loaded up, and me, standing ten feet away, shitting my pants. When he finished he smiled, swinging his shopping bag up to hit me.

You got to stop that messing around, I told him. I'm not going to jail for bullshit like that.

You don't go to jail for shoplifting. They just turn you over to your old man.

I don't know about you, but my pops hits like a motherfucker.

He laughed. You know my dad. He flexed his hands. The nigger's got arthritis.

My mother never suspected, even when my clothes couldn't all fit in my closet, but my father wasn't that easy. He knew what things cost and knew that I didn't have a regular job.

You're going to get caught, he told me one day. Just you wait. When you do I'll show them everything you've taken and then they'll throw your stupid ass away like a bad piece of meat.

---

8. Dark-skinned persons (Spanish).

He was a charmer, my pop, a real asshole, but he was right. Nobody can stay smooth forever, especially kids like us. One day at the bookstore, we didn't even hide the drops. Four issues of the same *Playboy* for kicks, enough audio books to start our own library. No last-minute juke either. The lady who stepped in front of us didn't look old, even with her white hair. Her silk shirt was half unbuttoned and a silver horn necklace sat on the freckled top of her chest. I'm sorry fellows, but I have to check your bag, she said. I kept moving, and looked back all annoyed, like she was asking us for a quarter or something. Beto got polite and stopped. No problem, he said, slamming the heavy bag into her face. She hit the cold tile with a squawk, her palms slapping the ground. There you go, Beto said.

Security found us across from the bus stop, under a Jeep Cherokee. A bus had come and gone, both of us too scared to take it, imagining a plainclothes waiting to clap the cuffs on. I remember that when the rent-a-cop tapped his nightstick against the fender and said, You little shits better come out here real slow, I started to cry. Beto didn't say a word, his face stretched out and gray, his hand squeezing mine, the bones in our fingers pressing together.

Nights I drink with Alex and Danny. The Malibou Bar is no good, just washouts and the sucias[9] we can con into joining us. We drink too much, roar at each other and make the skinny bartender move closer to the phone. On the wall hangs a cork dartboard and a Brunswick Gold Crown[1] blocks the bathroom, its bumpers squashed, the felt pulled like old skin.

When the bar begins to shake back and forth like a rumba, I call it a night and go home, through the fields that surround the apartments. In the distance you can see the Raritan,[2] as shiny as an earthworm, the same river my homeboy goes to school on. The dump has long since shut down, and grass has spread over it like a sickly fuzz, and from where I stand, my right hand directing a colorless stream of piss downward, the landfill might be the top of a blond head, square and old.

In the mornings I run. My mother is already up, dressing for her housecleaning job. She says nothing to me, would rather point to the mangu[3] she has prepared than speak.

I run three miles easily, could have pushed a fourth if I were in the mood. I keep an eye out for the recruiter who prowls around our neighborhood in his dark K-car.[4] We've spoken before. He was out of uniform and called me over, jovial, and I thought I was helping some white dude with directions. Would you mind if I asked you a question?

No.

Do you have a job?

Not right now.

Would you like one? A real career, more than you'll get around here?

I remember stepping back. Depends on what it is, I said.

Son, I know somebody who's hiring. It's the United States government.

Well. Sorry, but I ain't Army material.

---

9. Sluts (Spanish).
1. Pool table.
2. River in New Jersey.
3. Dominican dish made from plantains with butter, salt, pepper, and water.
4. A Chrysler Corporation automobile popular as a fleet vehicle.

That's exactly what I used to think, he said, his ten piggy fingers buried in his carpeted steering wheel. But now I have a house, a car, a gun and a wife. Discipline. Loyalty. Can you say that you have those things? Even one?

He's a southerner, red-haired, his drawl so out of place that the people around here laugh just hearing him. I take to the bushes when I see his car on the road. These days my guts feel loose and cold and I want to be away from here. He won't have to show me his Desert Eagle[5] or flash the photos of the skinny Filipino girls sucking dick. He'll only have to smile and name the places and I'll listen.

When I reach the apartment, I lean against my door, waiting for my heart to slow, for the pain to lose its edge. I hear my mother's voice, a whisper from the kitchen. She sounds hurt or nervous, maybe both. At first I'm terrified that Beto's inside with her but then I look and see the phone cord, swinging lazily. She's talking to my father, something she knows I disapprove of. He's in Florida now, a sad guy who calls her and begs for money. He swears that if she moves down there he'll leave the woman he's living with. These are lies, I've told her, but she still calls him. His words coil inside of her, wrecking her sleep for days. She opens the refrigerator door slightly so that the whir of the compressor masks their conversation. I walk in on her and hang up the phone. That's enough, I say.

She's startled, her hand squeezing the loose folds of her neck. That was him, she says quietly.

On school days Beto and I chilled at the stop together but as soon as that bus came over the Parkwood hill I got to thinking about how I was failing gym and screwing up math and how I hated every single living teacher on the planet.

I'll see *you* in the p.m., I said.

He was already standing on line. I just stood back and grinned, my hands in my pockets. With our bus drivers you didn't have to hide. Two of them didn't give a rat fuck and the third one, the Brazilian preacher, was too busy talking Bible to notice anything but the traffic in front of him.

Being truant without a car was no easy job but I managed. I watched a lot of TV and when it got boring I trooped down to the mall or the Sayreville library, where you could watch old documentaries for free. I always came back to the neighborhood late, so the bus wouldn't pass me on Ernston and nobody could yell Asshole! out the windows. Beto would usually be home or down by the swings, but other times he wouldn't be around at all. Out visiting other neighborhoods. He knew a lot of folks I didn't—a messed-up black kid from Madison Park, two brothers who were into that N.Y. club scene, who spent money on platform shoes and leather backpacks. I'd leave a message with his parents and then watch some more TV. The next day he'd be out at the bus stop, too busy smoking a cigarette to say much about the day before.

You need to learn how to walk the world, he told me. There's a lot out there.

5. A semi-automatic military pistol.

Some nights me and the boys drive to New Brunswick. A nice city, the Raritan so low and silty that you don't have to be Jesus to walk over it. We hit the Melody and the Roxy, stare at the college girls. We drink a lot and then spin out onto the dance floor. None of the chicas[6] ever dance with us, but a glance or a touch can keep us talking shit for hours.

Once the clubs close we go to the Franklin Diner, gorge ourselves on pancakes, and then, after we've smoked our pack, head home. Danny passes out in the back seat and Alex cranks the window down to keep the wind in his eyes. He's fallen asleep in the past, wrecked two cars before this one. The streets have been picked clean of students and townies and we blow through every light, red or green. At the Old Bridge Turnpike we pass the fag bar, which never seems to close. Patos are all over the parking lot, drinking and talking.

Sometimes Alex will stop by the side of the road and say, Excuse me. When somebody comes over from the bar he'll point his plastic pistol at them, just to see if they'll run or shit their pants. Tonight he just puts his head out the window. Fuck you! he shouts and then settles back in his seat, laughing.

That's original, I say.

He puts his head out the window again. Eat me, then!

Yeah, Danny mumbles from the back. Eat me.

Twice. That's it.

The first time was at the end of that summer. We had just come back from the pool and were watching a porn video at his parents' apartment. His father was a nut for these tapes, ordering them from wholesalers in California and Grand Rapids. Beto used to tell me how his pop would watch them in the middle of the day, not caring a lick about his moms, who spent the time in the kitchen, taking hours to cook a pot of rice and gandules.[7] Beto would sit down with his pop and neither of them would say a word, except to laugh when somebody caught it in the eye or the face.

We were an hour into the new movie, some vaina[8] that looked like it had been filmed in the apartment next door, when he reached into my shorts. What the fuck are you doing? I asked, but he didn't stop. His hand was dry. I kept my eyes on the television, too scared to watch. I came right away, smearing the plastic sofa covers. My legs started shaking and suddenly I wanted out. He didn't say anything to me as I left, just sat there watching the screen.

The next day he called and when I heard his voice I was cool but I wouldn't go to the mall or anywhere else. My mother sensed that something was wrong and pestered me about it, but I told her to leave me the fuck alone, and my pops, who was home on a visit, stirred himself from the couch to slap me down. Mostly I stayed in the basement, terrified that I would end up abnormal, a fucking pato, but he was my best friend and back then that mattered to me more than anything. This alone got me out of the apartment and over to the pool that night. He was already there, his body pale and flabby under the water. Hey, he said. I was beginning to worry about you.

Nothing to worry about, I said.

6. Girls (Spanish).
7. Pigeon peas (Spanish).

8. Dominican slang for "stuff" (Spanish).

We swam and didn't talk much and later we watched a Skytop crew pull a bikini top from a girl stupid enough to hang out alone. Give it, she said, covering herself, but these kids howled, holding it up over her head, the shiny laces flopping just out of reach. When they began to pluck at her arms, she walked away, leaving them to try the top on over their flat pecs.

He put his hand on my shoulder, my pulse a code under his palm. Let's go, he said. Unless of course you're not feeling good.

I'm feeling fine, I said.

Since his parents worked nights we pretty much owned the place until six the next morning. We sat in front of his television, in our towels, his hands bracing against my abdomen and thighs. I'll stop if you want, he said and I didn't respond. After I was done, he laid his head in my lap. I wasn't asleep or awake, but caught somewhere in between, rocked slowly back and forth the way surf holds junk against the shore, rolling it over and over. In three weeks he was leaving. Nobody can touch me, he kept saying. We'd visited the school and I'd seen how beautiful the campus was, with all the students drifting from dorm to class. I thought of how in high school our teachers loved to crowd us into their lounge every time a space shuttle took off from Florida. One teacher, whose family had two grammar schools named after it, compared us to the shuttles. A few of you are going to make it. Those are the orbiters. But the majority of you are just going to burn out. Going nowhere. He dropped his hand onto his desk. I could already see myself losing altitude, fading, the earth spread out beneath me, hard and bright.

I had my eyes closed and the television was on and when the hallway door crashed open, he jumped up and I nearly cut my dick off struggling with my shorts. It's just the neighbor, he said, laughing. He was laughing, but I was saying, Fuck this, and getting my clothes on.

I believe I see him in his father's bottomed-out Cadillac, heading towards the turnpike, but I can't be sure. He's probably back in school already. I deal close to home, trooping up and down the same dead-end street where the kids drink and smoke. These punks joke with me, pat me down for taps, sometimes too hard. Now that strip malls line Route 9, a lot of folks have part-time jobs; the kids stand around smoking in their aprons, name tags dangling heavily from pockets.

When I get home, my sneakers are filthy so I take an old toothbrush to their soles, scraping the crap into the tub. My mother has thrown open the windows and propped open the door. It's cool enough, she explains. She has prepared dinner—rice and beans, fried cheese, tostones.[9] Look what I bought, she says, showing me two blue t-shirts. They were two for one so I bought you one. Try it on.

It fits tight but I don't mind. She cranks up the television. A movie dubbed into Spanish, a classic, one that everyone knows. The actors throw themselves around, passionate, but their words are plain and deliberate. It's hard to imagine anybody going through life this way. I pull out the plug of bills from my pockets. She takes it from me, her fingers soothing the creases. A man who treats his plata[1] like this doesn't deserve to spend it, she says.

---

9. Flattened fried plantains, a side dish in the Dominican Republic.
1. Slang term for money (literally, "silver" in Spanish).

We watch the movie and the two hours together makes us friendly. She puts her hand on mine. Near the end of the film, just as our heroes are about to fall apart under a hail of bullets, she takes off her glasses and kneads her temples, the light of the television flickering across her face. She watches another minute and then her chin lists to her chest. Almost immediately her eyelashes begin to tremble, a quiet semaphore. She is dreaming, dreaming of Boca Raton, of strolling under the jacarandas[2] with my father. You can't be anywhere forever, was what Beto used to say, what he said to me the day I went to see him off. He handed me a gift, a book, and after he was gone I threw it away, didn't even bother to open it and read what he'd written.

I let her sleep until the end of the movie and when I wake her she shakes her head, grimacing. You better check those windows, she says. I promise her I will.

---

2. Flowering trees native to the tropics.

Selected Bibliographies

Reference Works and Histories

James L. Harner's *Literary Research Guide* (1993, updated online) is a valuable resource. James D. Hart's *Oxford Companion to American Literature*, 5th ed. (1983), Jack Saltzman's *The Cambridge Handbook of American Literature* (1986), and the annual volumes of *American Literary Scholarship* (currently edited by David J. Nordloh and Gary Scharnhorst) identify authors and trends. Of broader scope are editor Emory Elliott's *The Columbia Literary History of the United States* (1988) and *The Columbia History of the American Novel* (1991), together with editor Jay Parini's *The Columbia History of American Poetry* (1993). Sacvan Bercovitch is general editor of the multivolume, ongoing *Cambridge History of American Literature*. Don B. Wilmeth has edited the *Cambridge Guide to American Theatre* (1996). The vast *Dictionary of Literary Biography*, under the supervision of Matthew J. Bruccoli, the Scribners *American Writers* series, edited by Jay Parini, and vol. 2 of David Perkins's *History of Modern Poetry* (1976) offer wide coverage of specific authors. An indispensable reference guide for poetry is *Contemporary Poets*, 7th ed. (2000), edited by Thomas Riggs. Specific areas are treated by editors Joel Shatzky and Michael Taub's *Contemporary Jewish-American Novelists: A Bio-Critical Sourcebook* (1997), Darryl Dickson-Carr's *The Columbia Guide to Contemporary African American Fiction* (2005), editor Eric Cheyfitz's *The Columbia Guide to American Indian Literatures of the United States since 1945* (2006), and José F. Aranda Jr.'s *When We Arrive: A New Literary History of Mexican America* (2003). Steven Conner's *The Cambridge Companion to Postmodernism* (2004) provides a guide to the cultural contexts of the period. Useful introductory series are the University of South Carolina Press's *Understanding . . .* volumes, the Twayne United States Authors series, Methuen's Contemporary Writers, the University Press of Mississippi's *Conversations with . . .* , the *Critical Essays* books from G. K. Hall Publishers, the Greenwood Press *Critical Response* series, and the *Modern Critical Views* collections edited by Harold Bloom. The University of Michigan's *Poets on Poetry* series offers volumes in which poets comment on their own and others' work.

Literary Theory and Criticism

Theoretical overviews are provided by Christian Moraru in *Memorious Discourse: Reprise and Representation in Postmodernism* (2005) and Stacey Olster in *The Trash Phenomenon: Contemporary Literature, Popular Culture, and the Making of the American Century* (2003). The critic and theorist Marjorie Perloff has written, a series of books that provide theoretical overviews and studies of the poetry of the period: *The Poetics of Indeterminacy* (1981), *The Dance of the Intellect* (1985), *Radical Artifice: Writing in the Age of Media* (1991), and *21st-century Modernism: The New Poetics* (2001). Playwrights and their work are studied by Sanford Sternlicht in *A Reader's Guide to Modern American Drama* (2002), Thomas S. Hischak in *American Theatre: A Chronicle of Comedy and Drama, 1969–2000* (2001), Christopher Bigsby in *Contemporary American Playwrights* (1999), and Herbert Blau in *The Dubious Spectacle: Extremities of the Theater, 1976–2000* (2002). Histories of specific movements in poetry are explored in Michael Palmer's *The San Francisco Renaissance* (1991) and David Lehmann's *The Last Avant-Garde: The Making of the New York School of Poets* (1998). A more general history appears in Robert von Hallberg's *American Poetry and Culture 1945–1980* (1985). The history of poetry may also be traced through statements on poetics: *Poetics of the New American Poetry* (1973), edited by Donald Allen, was groundbreaking, and *Twentieth-Century American Poetry* (2004), edited by Dana Gioia, David Mason, and Meg Schoerke, gathers statements on poetics from throughout the period. Fiction's development is traced in detail in Kathryn Hume's *American Dream, American Nightmare: Fiction since 1960* (2000) and Marc Chénetier's *Beyond Suspicion: New American Fiction since 1960* (1996). Mark McGurl traces the impact of creative writing programs on fiction in *The Program Era* (2009), while Samuel Cohen focuses on a key decade in *After the End of History: American Fiction in the 1990s* (2009). The development of poetry in the period is examined in Dana Gioia's *Disappearing Ink: Poetry at the End of Print Culture* (2004), Christopher MacGowan's *Twentieth-Century American Poetry* (2004), Stephen Fredman's *A Concise Companion to Twentieth-Century American Poetry* (2005), Jennifer Ashton's *From Modernism to Postmodernism: American Poetry and Theory in the Twentieth Century* (2006), and Charles Altieri's *The Art of Twentieth-Century American Poetry: Modernism and After* (2006). Among the useful collections of literary criticism that focus on poetry of the period are Sherman Paul's *The Lost America of Love* (1981), J. D. McClatchy's *White Paper* (1990), Helen Vendler's *The Music of What Happens* (1988) and *Soul Says* (1995), Lynn Keller's *Re-Making It New* (1987), Vernon Shelley's *After the Death of Poetry* (1993), Peter Stitt's *Uncertainty and Plenitude: Five Contemporary Poets* (1997), Charles Altieri's *Postmodernisms Now* (1998), Thomas Travisano's *Mid-Century Quartet* (1999), and Adam Kirsch's *The Wounded Surgeon: Confession and Transformation in Six American Poets* (2005). Political implications are examined by Alan Nadel in *Containment Culture: American Narratives, Postmodernism, and the Atomic Age* (1995), while Wendy Steiner exlores the controversy over sexual elements in *The Scandal of Pleasure* (1995). Politics in poetry is explored in Mutlu Konuk's *Politics and Form in Postmodern Poetry* (1995), Tim

Wood's *The Poetics of the Limit: Ethics and Politics in Modern and Contemporary American Poetry* (2002), and Walter Kalaidjian's *The Edge of Modernism: American Poetry and the Traumatic Past* (2006).

Two important studies from a feminist perspective are Nancy J. Peterson's *Against Amnesia: Contemporary Women Writers and the Crisis of Historical Memory* (2001) and Linda S. Kauffman's *Bad Girls and Sick Boys: Fantasies in Contemporary Art and Culture* (1998). A feminist approach to the study of poetry can be found in *Gendered Modernisms: American Women Poets and Their Readers* (1996), edited by Margaret Dickie and Thomas Travisano. Jean Wyatt considers social issues in *Risking Difference: Identification, Race, and Community in Contemporary Fiction and Feminism* (2004). Multiculturalism concerns Martha J. Cutter in *Lost and Found in Translation: Contemporary Ethnic American Writing and the Politics of Language Diversity* (2005), Paula M. L. Moya in *Learning from Experience: Minority Identities, Multicultural Struggles* (2002), Robert Jackson in *Seeking the Region in American Literature and Culture* (2005), and A. Robert Lee in *Multicultural American Literature: Comparative Black, Native, Latino/a and Asian American Fictions* (2003). Multiculturalism in poetry is the subject of Satya Mohanty's *Literary Theory and the Claims of History: Postmodernism, Objectivity and Multicultural Politics* (1997). Cassie Premo Steele's *We Heal from Memory: Sexton, Lorde, Anzaldúa, and the Poetry of Witness* (2000) treats women poets across the divisions of ethnicity. African American writing is the focus in Bernard W. Bell's *The Contemporary African American Novel: Its Folk Roots and Modern Literary Branches* (2004), Cheryl A. Wall's *Worrying the Line: Black Women Writers, Lineage, and Literary Tradition* (2005), Suzanne W. Jones's *Race Mixing: Southern Fiction since the Sixties* (2004), and James W. Coleman's *Faithful Vision: Treatments of the Sacred, Spiritual, and Supernatural in Twentieth-Century African American Fiction* (2006). *Black Women Writers (1950–1980): A Critical Evaluation,* edited by Mari Evans, explores African American novelists and poets from a feminist perspective. *African American Theater: A cultural companion* (2008) by Gloria Dickerson covers the subject in a narrative manner. African American poetry is examined in Joanne Gabbin's *The Furious Flowering of African American Poetry* (1999) and Alden Lynn Nielsen's *Black Chant: Languages of African-American Postmodernism* (1992). Chicano/a work is treated by Charles M. Tatum in *Chicano Popular Culture* (2001), Mary Pat Brady in *Extinct Lands, Temporal Geographies: Chicana Literature and the Urgency of Space* (2002), Elisabeth Mermann-Jozwiak in *Postmodern Vernaculars: Chicana Literature and Postmodern Rhetoric* (2005), Tey Diana Rebolledo in *The Chronicles of Panchita Villa and Other Guerrilleras* (2005), Ramon Saldívar in *Chicano Narrative* (1990), and Ellie D. Hernandez in *Postnationalism in Chicana/o Literature and Culture* (2009). Deborah L. Madsen's *Understanding Contemporary Chicana Literature* (2000) examines the work of women poets.

Transnational Asian American Literature: Sites and Transits (2006), edited by Shirley Geok-lin Lim, et al., includes essays covering issues from immigration to feminism and globalism. More general concerns occupy David Leiwei Li in *Imagining the Nation: Asian American Literature and Cultural Consent* (1998). Jinqui Ling reconciles conflicting approaches of cultural study and nationalist impulses in *Narrating Nationalisms: Ideology and*

Form in Asian American Literature (1998). Xiaojing Zhou studies Asian American poetry in *The Ethics of Poetics of Alterity in Asian American Poetry* (2006), and Guiyou Huang has edited a resource guide to poets, *Asian American Poets: A Bio-Bibliographical Critical Sourcebook* (2002). Arnold Krupat's *Red Matters: Native American Studies* (2002) looks beyond nationalism, indigenism, and cosmopolitanism to gauge Native American literature's importance to the ethical and intellectual heritage of the West. Catherine Rainwater's *Dreams of Fiery Stars: The Transformation of Native American Fiction* (1999) offers strong artistic analysis. John Lloyd Purdy's *Writing Indian, Native Conversations* (2009) combines criticism and dialogue. Kenneth Lincoln's *Sing with the Heart of a Bear: Fusions of Native and American Poetry, 1890–1999* (1999) stresses poetry's flexible and adaptable nature rather than its conformity to rigid ethnic and literary categories. Robin Riley First's *The Heart Is a Drum: Continuance and Resistance in American Indian Poetry* (2000) provides cultural and historical readings of a wide range of poems.

Especially useful for understanding how and why contemporary writers produce their work is the critical interview, the exploratory technique for which was pioneered by Joe David Bellamy in his *The New New Fiction: Interviews with Innovative American Writers* (1974) and which has been perfected by Larry McCaffery, who with various coeditors has produced a series of extensive, insightful, and critically developed dialogues with important authors of the past four decades: *Anything Can Happen* (1983), *Alive and Writing* (1987), *Across the Wounded Galaxies* (1990), and *Some Other Frequency* (1996). Over the years the *Paris Review* has conducted a series of interviews, "Writers at Work," that includes some of the most important writers of this period. These interviews are now available on the *Paris Review* website. The University of Michigan series, *Poets on Poetry*, includes interviews as well as essays (for individual volumes, consult the bibliographies of specific poets). Other valuable sources for interviews with poets are *Black Women Writers at Work* (1988), edited by Claudia Tate, *Survival This Way: Interviews with American Indian Poets* (1987), edited by Joseph Bruchac, and *Truthtellers of the Time: Interviews with Contemporary Women Poets* (1998), edited by Janet Palmer Mullaney.

The rapidly expanding genre of creative nonfiction has produced a variety of collections that suggest the characteristics and range of the form, including John D'Agata's *The Next American Essay* (2002) and Lee Gutman's series, *The Best Creative Nonfiction* (2010, 2008, 2007), as well as his preceding collection, *In Fact* (2004). David Shields's provocative book, *Reality Hunger* (2010), offers a version of a manifesto for a wide range of work by creative nonfiction writers. A considerable amount of material, some of it useful, can be found on the Internet, including websites that offer audio versions of writers reading from their work. The Academy of American Poets' poets.org is the best general site for poetry and includes an audio component and links to other resources. The Internet Public Library offers "Native American Authors" at www.ipl.org/div/natam/.

AMERICAN LITERATURE SINCE 1945

Edward Abbey

A prolific writer, Abbey published numerous nonfiction works of environmental writing as well as eight novels. Among his nonfiction works are *Desert Solitaire: A Season in the Wilderness* (1968), *Slickrock: The Canyon Country of Southeast Utah* (1971), *Cactus Country* (1973), *The Journey Home* (1977), *The Hidden Canyon: A River Journey* (1977), *Abbey's Road* (1979), *Desert Images* (1979), *Down the River* (1982), and *Beyond the Wall: Essays from Outside* (1984). Two volumes with selections from Abbey's journals are *A Voice Crying in the Wilderness: Notes from a Secret Journal* (1989) and *Confessions of a Barbarian: Selections from the Journals of Edward Abbey, 1951–1989* (1995). Abbey's best-known work of fiction is his novel *The Monkey Wrench Gang* (1975). An anthology, *The Best of Edward Abbey*, appeared in 1988. His poetry is collected in *Earth Apples: The Poetry of Edward Abbey* (1994). *Edward Abbey: A Voice in the Wilderness* (1993), produced and directed by Eric Temple, is a documentary film about Abbey's life. Among the critical discussions of Abbey's work are Anne Ronald's *The New West of Edward Abbey* (1982), John Cooley's edited collection, *Earthly Words: Essays on Contemporary American Nature and Environmental Writers* (1994), James I. McClintock's *Nature's Kindred Spirits: Aldo Leopold, Joseph Wood Krutch, Edward Abbey, Annie Dillard, and Gary Snyder* (1994), Peter Quigley's *Coyote in the Maze: Tracking Edward Abbey in a World of Words* (1998), and John M. Cahalan's important biography, *Edward Abbey: A Life* (2001).

Sherman Alexie

Alexie's novels are *Reservation Blues* (1995), *Indian Killer* (1996), and *The Absolutely True Diary of a Part-Time Indian* (2007). His story collections are *The Lone Ranger and Tonto Fistfight in Heaven* (1993, adapted as a film script for *Smoke Signals* in 1998). *The Toughest Indian in the World* (2000), *Ten Little Indians* (2003), and *War Dances* (2007). His poetry collections are *The Business of Fancydancing* (1992), *I Would Steal Horses* (1992), *First Indian on the Moon* (1993), *Old Shirts and New Skins* (1993), *Seven Mourning Songs for the Cedar Flute I Have Yet to Learn to Play* (1994), *Water Flowing Home* (1996), *The Man Who Loves Salmon* (1998), *One Stick Song* (2000), *Il powwow della fine del mondo* (2005), *Dangerous Astronomy* (2005), and *Face* (2009). He wrote and directed the movie *The Business of Fancydancing* (2000).

Daniel Grassian provides critical analysis in *Understanding Sherman Alexie* (2005).

Dorothy Allison

Allison's fiction includes *Trash: Short Stories* (1988), *Bastard Out of Carolina* (1992), *Two or Three Things I Know for Sure* (1995). A nonfiction collection, *Skin: Talking About Sex, Class, and Literature*, appeared in 1994. Allison has also published a collection of poems, *The Women Who Hate Me: Poetry 1980–1990* (1991). Two valuable pieces are "Moving toward Truth: An Interview with Dorothy Allison," *The Kenyon Review* 16.4 (Autumn 1994): 71–83, and an interview in the online journal *Salon* (1998), at www.salon.com. Kathleen Wilkinson's "Dorothy Allison: The Value of Redemption" is a critical discussion that appears in *Curve* magazine (2009).

Julia Alvarez

Alvarez's novels are *How the García Girls Lost Their Accents* (1991), *In the Time of the Butterflies* (1994), *¡Yo!* (1997), *In the Name of Salomé* (2000), *Saving the World* (2006), and *Return to Sender* (2009). Her poetry collections are *The Housekeeping Book* (1984), *Homecoming* (1984, revised 1996), *The Other Side / El Otro Lado* (1995), *Seven Trees* (1998), and *The Woman I Kept to Myself* (2004). *Something to Declare* (1998) gathers her essays. *Once Upon a Quinceañera: Coming of Age in the USA* (2007) is nonfiction. *How Tía Lola Came to Stay* (2001), *A Cafecito Story* (2002), *Before We Were Free* (2002), and *A Gift of Gracias* (2005) are books for children and young adults.

Kelli Lyon Johnson presents a critical analysis in *Julia Alvarez: Writing a New Place on the Map* (2005).

A. R. Ammons

Collections of Ammons's poetry include a reissue of his *Collected Poems 1951–1971* (2001), *Really Short Poems of A. R. Ammons* (1991), and *Selected Longer Poems* (1980). His individual volumes include *Sphere: The Form of a Motion* (1974), *Diversifications* (1975), *Snow Poems* (1977), *A Coast of Trees* (1981), *Lake Effect Country* (1983), *Sumerian Vistas* (1987), *Garbage* (1993), *Brink Road* (1996), *Garbage: A Poem* (2001), *Bosh and Flapdoodle* (2005), *A. R. Ammons: Selected Poems* (2006), and *ommateum; with Doxology* (2006). A collection of Ammons's essays and interviews, *Set in Motion*, also appeared in 1996.

There are useful critical discussions of his work in Helen Vendler's *The Music of What Happens* (1988), Robert Kirschten's edited *Critical Essays on A. R. Ammons* (1997), Steven P. Schneider's edited *Complexities of Motion: New Essays on A. R. Ammons' Long Poems* (1999), and Roger Gilbert and David Borak's edited *Considering the Radiance: Essays on the Poetry of A. R. Ammons* (2005). An interview with Ammons appear in the *Paris Review* of Spring 1996.

Rudolfo A. Anaya

Anaya's novels are *Bless Me, Ultima* (1972), *Heart of Aztlán* (1976), *Tortuga* (1979), *The Legend of La Llorona* (1984), *Lord of the Dawn* (1987), *Alburquerque* (1992), *Zia Summer* (1995), *Jalamanta* (1996), *Rio Grande Fall* (1996), *Shaman Winter* (1999), *Serifina's Stories* (2004), *Jemez Spring* (2005), and *Rio Grande Fall* (2008). *The Silence of the Llano* (1982), and *The Man Who Could Fly* (2006) are short stories; *The Adventures of Juan Chicapatas* (1985) is poetry; *The Santero's Miracle, Curse of the ChupaCabra* (2006), *The First Tortilla* (2007), and *ChupaCabra and the Rosewell UFO* (2008) are stories for children and young adult readers.

Margarite Fernández Olmos provides a comprehensive study in *Rudolfo A. Anaya: A Critical Companion* (1999). Cesar A. Gonzales has prepared *A Sense of Place: Rudolfo A. Anaya, An Annotated Bio-Bibliography* (1999). The author's crime novels are studied by Ralph C. Rodriguez in *Brown Gumshoes: Detective Fiction and the Search for Chicano Identity* (2005).

Gloria Anzaldúa

Borderlands/La Frontera (1987) includes memoir, historical analysis, and narrative poetry. Anzaldúa has also written several novels: *La Prieta* ("The Dark One") (1997), and (for children) *Prietita Has a Friend—Prietita Tiene un Amigo* (1991), *Friends from the Other Side—Amigos del Otra Lado* (1993), and *Prietita and the Ghost Woman—Prietita y La Llorona* (1996). She is the editor of *Making Face, Making Soul / Haciendo Caras: Creative and Critical Perspectives by Feminists of Color* (1990), and (with Cherríe Moraga) coedited *This Bridge Called My Back: Writings by Radical Women of Color* (1981). In 2002 she coedited, with Analouise Keating, *This Bridge We Call Home: Radical Visions for Transformation*.

Anzaldúa's work is studied by Deborah L. Madsen in *Understanding Contemporary Chicana Literature* (2000). Sonia Sandívar-Hull in *Feminism on the Border: Chicana Politics and Literature* (2000), Paula M. L. Moya in *Learning from Experience: Minority Identities, Multicultural Struggles* (2002), Catrióna Rueda Esquibel in *With Her Machete in Her Hand: Reading Chicana Lesbians* (2006), and Ana Louise Keating in *Extremundos Between Worlds* (2008).

John Ashbery

Ashbery's volumes of poetry include *Some Trees* (1956), *The Tennis Court Oath* (1962), *Rivers and Mountains* (1966), *The Double Dream of Spring* (1970), *Three Poems* (1972), *Self-Portrait in a Convex Mirror* (1975), *Houseboat Days* (1977), *As We Know* (1979), *Shadow Train* (1981), *A Wave* (1984), *Selected Poems* (1985), *April Galleons* (1988), *Flow Chart* (1991), *And the Stars Were Shining* (1994), *Can You Hear, Bird* (1995), *Girls on the Run* (1999), *Your Name Here* (2000), *Chinese Whispers* (2002), *Where Shall I Wander* (2005), and *A Worldly Country* (2007). *Notes From the Air* (2007) is a selection of his later poems. Ashbery is now represented in the Library of America series by *John Ashbery: Collected Poems 1956–87* (2008). Ashbery's Charles Eliot Norton Lectures on Poetry appear in *Other Traditions* (2000), and he has also published *Selected Prose* (2004).

Among useful critical essays are David Kalstone's *Five Temperaments* (1977) and John Shoptaw's book-length study of Ashbery's poetry, *On the Outside Looking Out* (1994). David K. Kermani's *John Ashbery: A Comprehensive Bibliography* (1975) is indispensable and amusing. See also *Beyond Amazement: New Essays on John Ashbery* (1980), edited by David Lehman, Charles Altieri's *Postmodernisms Now* (1998), and John Emil Vincent's *John Ashbery and You: His Later Books* (2007).

James Baldwin

Baldwin's novels are *Go Tell It on the Mountain* (1953), *Giovanni's Room* (1956), *Another Country* (1962), *Tell Me How Long the Train's Been Gone* (1968), *If Beale Street Could Talk* (1974), and *Just Above My Head* (1979). His other books are a collection of short stories, *Going to Meet the Man* (1965); a volume of nonfiction prose, *The Price of the Ticket* (1985); and two plays, *Blues for Mr. Charlie* (1964) and *The Amen Corner* (1968).

James Campbell's *Talking at the Gates: A Life of James Baldwin* (1991) is a biographical study. Critical interpretations include Lynn Orilla Scott's *James Baldwin's Later Fiction: Witness to the Journey* (2002) and Clarence E. Hardy III's *James Baldwin's God: Sex, Hope and Crisis in Black Holiness Culture* (2003). Further essays are found in editor D. Quentin Miller's *Reviewing James Baldwin: Things Not Seen* (2000). Baldwin's nonfiction has been gathered as *Collected Essays* (1998) and *The Cross of Redemption* (2010).

Toni Cade Bambara

Gorilla, My Love (1972) and *The Sea Birds Are Still Alive* (1977) are collections of Bambara's stories; a posthumous volume, *Deep Sightings and Rescue Missions: Fiction, Essays, and Conversations* (1996), gathers her other short work. Her novel *The Salt Eaters* was published in 1980; another novel, *Those Bones Are Not My*

Child (1999), was published posthumously. Numerous screenplays by Bambara were produced in the 1970s and 1980s, including an adaption of Toni Morrison's *The Tar Baby* (1984) and a treatment of writer Zora Neale Hurston, *Zora* (1971). She edited the anthologies *The Black Woman* (1970), *Tales and Stories for Black Folks* (1971, for children), and (with Leah Wise) *Southern Black Utterances Today* (1975). *Deep Sightings and Rescue Missions: Fiction, Essays, and Conversations* (1996) is a posthumous collection of Bambara's later work, edited by Toni Morrison.

Critical analyses of Bambara's work are found in Philip Page's *Reclaiming Community in Contemporary African American Fiction* (1999), Elliott Butler-Evans's *Race, Gender and Desire: Narrative Strategies in the Fiction of Toni Cade Bambara, Toni Morrison, and Alice Walker* (1989), and Robert H. Cataliotti's *The Songs Became the Stories: The Music in African American Fiction 1970–2005* (2007).

Amiri Baraka (LeRoi Jones)

Poetry volumes include *Preface to a Twenty Volume Suicide Note* (1961), *The Dead Lecturer* (1964), *Black Magic* (1969), *Hard Facts* (1975), *Transbluesency* (1995), *Funk Lore* (1996), and *Somebody Blew Up America* (2003). *Eulogies* (1996) uses poetry and prose to memorialize friends. Baraka has authored four books on music: *Blues People* (1963), *Black Music* (1968), and *The Music: Reflections on Jazz and Blues* (1987), and *Digging: The Afro-American Soul of American Classical Music* (2009). His essays are collected in *Home* (1966), *Raise Race Rays Raze* (1971), and *Selected Plays and Prose of Amiri Baraka / LeRoi Jones* (1979). Baraka has produced three important anthologies: *The Moderns* (1963), *Black Fire* (1968, with Larry Neal), and *Confirmation: An Anthology of African American Women* (1983), with Amina Baraka. In 1984 he published *The Autobiography of LeRoi Jones / Amiri Baraka*. Baraka is also a dramatist. His play *Dutchman and the Slave* (1964) was published as a combined edition, as was *The Baptism & The Toilet* (1967). *Four Black Revolutionary Plays* (1969) includes *Experimental Death Unit #1, A Black Mass, Great Goodness of Life*, and *Madheart*. *The Motion of History and Other Plays* (1978) gathers the title work with *Slave Ship* and *S-1*. *The System of Dante's Hell* (1965) is a novel; *Tales* (1967) is a collection of short stories, as is *Tales of the Out & the Gone* (2006).

Early but still useful studies are *Baraka: The Renegade and the Mask* (1976) by Kimberly W. Benston and *Amiri Baraka / LeRoi Jones: The Quest for a "Populist Modernism"* (1978) by Werner Sollors. William J. Harris has written *The Poetry and Poetics of Amiri Baraka: The*

Jazz Aesthetic (1985) and edited *The LeRoi Jones / Amiri Baraka Reader* (1991), supplying introductory literary history and a bibliography. Ross Posnock's *Color and Culture* (1998) locates the author's thought; Jerry Gafio Watt's *Amiri Baraka: The Politics and Art of a Black Intellectual* (2001) is comprehensive. Baraka's first wife, Hettie Cohen, has authored a memoir, *How I Became Hettie Jones* (1990).

Donald Barthelme

Barthelme published three novels during his lifetime: *Snow White* (1967), *The Dead Father* (1975), and *Paradise* (1986). A fourth, *The King*, appeared in 1990, the year after he died. His story collections are *Come Back, Dr. Caligari* (1964), *Unspeakable Practices, Unnatural Acts* (1968), *City Life* (1970), *Sadness* (1972), *Guilty Pleasures* (1974), *Amateurs* (1976), *Great Days* (1979), *Sixty Stories* (1981), *Overnight to Many Distant Cities* (1983), and *Forty Stories* (1987). *The Slightly Irregular Fire Engine* (1971) is a work for children, whereas *Sam's Bar* (1987) provides a narrative for adult cartoons by Seymour Chwast. Kim Hertinger edited *The Teachings of Don B.: Satires, Parodies, Fables, Illustrated Stories, and Plays of Donald Barthelme* (1992), many of which were omitted from Barthelme's own collections, and *Not Knowing: The Essays and Interviews of Donald Barthelme* (1997).

Stanley Trachtenberg's *Understanding Donald Barthelme* (1990) is a sound introduction, while Maurice Couturier and Régis Durand's *Donald Barthelme* (1982) offers a superb explication of Barthelme's literary theory. Jerome Klinkowitz examines the author's entire canon in *Donald Barthelme: An Exhibition* (1991) and provides a primary and secondary bibliography. Tracey Daugherty's *Hiding Man: A Biography of Donald Barthelme* (2009) is historically comprehensive and critically acute.

Ann Beattie

Beattie's novels are *Chilly Scenes of Winter* (1976), *Falling in Place* (1981), *Love Always* (1985), *Picturing Will* (1989), *Another You* (1995), *My Life, Starring Dara Falcon* (1997), and *The Doctor's House* (2002). *Walks with Men* (2010) is a novella. Her story collections are *Distortions* (1976), *Secrets and Surprises* (1978), *The Burning House* (1982), *Where You'll Find Me* (1986), *Park City* (1998), *Perfect Recall* (2001), *Follies* (2005) and *The New Yorker Stories* (2010). She also wrote a critical study of the painter Alex Katz (1987) and collaborated with the photographer Bob Adelman on *Americana* (1992). Her *Spectacles* (1985) is for children.

Barbara Ann Schapiro studies Beattie's fiction in the company of work by John Updike and Toni Morrison in *Literature and the*

Representational Self (1994). A broad sampling of critical opinion distinguishes Jaye Berman Montressor's *The Critical Reaction to Ann Beattie* (1993).

Saul Bellow

Bellow is the author of fourteen novels and novellas: *Dangling Man* (1944), *The Victim* (1947), *The Adventures of Augie March* (1953), *Seize the Day* (1956), *Henderson the Rain King* (1959), *Herzog* (1964), *Mr. Sammler's Planet* (1970), *Humboldt's Gift* (1975), *The Dean's December* (1982), *More Die of Heartbreak* (1987), *A Theft* (1989), *The Bellarosa Connection* (1989), *The Actual* (1997), and *Ravelstein* (2000). His short stories appear in three collections: *Mosby's Memoirs* (1968), *Him with His Foot in His Mouth* (1984), and *Something to Remember Me By* (1991), and are joined by an additional story in *Collected Stories* (2001). A play, *The Last Analysis*, was produced in New York in 1964 and published the following year. *To Jerusalem and Back* (1976) is a personal account of his activities in Israel. *It All Adds Up* (1994) draws on Bellow's essays dating back to 1948. In 2010 Bellow's *Letters* appeared, edited by Benjamin Taylor.

James Atlas's *Bellow: A Biography* (2000) is exhaustive yet critically focused. Malcolm Bradbury provides the best concise introduction to this author's major work in *Saul Bellow* (1982), while in *Saul Bellow: Drumlin Woodchuck* (1980) fellow writer Mark Harris offers an insightful portrait of Bellow as a professional figure. John J. Clayton's *Saul Bellow: In Defense of Man* (1979) celebrates the author's stressfully tested humanism, while Ellen Pifer's *Saul Bellow: Against the Grain* (1990) argues for his culturally atypical belief in the transcendent soul, as does M. A. Quayum's *Saul Bellow and American Trancendentalism* (2004). Gender is Gloria L. Cronin's focus in *A Room of His Own: In Search of the Feminine in the Novels of Saul* Bellow (2001). In *Saul Bellow: Vision and Revision* (1984) Daniel Fuchs examines manuscripts and letters to establish Bellow's Dostoyevskian engagement with issues of character. Julia Eichelberger sums up his work in *Prophets of Recognition* (1999).

John Berryman

Berryman's *Collected Poems: 1937–1971* appeared in 1991; *John Berryman: Selected Poems*, in 2004. *Homage to Mistress Bradstreet* (1956) and a selection of his *Short Poems* (1948) were issued together as a paperback in 1968. His other volumes of poetry include *77 Dream Songs* (1964); *Berryman's Sonnets* (1967); *His Toy, His Dream, His Rest* (1968); *Love and Fame* (1970; rev. 1972); *Delusions, Etc.* (1972); and a posthumous volume, *Henry's Fate* (1977). Berryman's critical biography,

Stephen Crane, appeared in 1950, and a collection of his short fiction and literary essays was issued under the title *The Freedom of the Poet* (1976). Berryman's unfinished novel about his alcoholism, *Recovery*, appeared in 1973.

Valuable critical introductions to Berryman's poetry can be found in Helen Vendler's *The Given and the Made* (1995) and Thomas Travisano's *Midcentury Quartet* (1999). Paul Mariani's *Dream Song: The Life of John Berryman* (1996) and Eileen Simpson's *Poets in Their Youth* (1982) are useful biographical studies.

Elizabeth Bishop

Bishop's poems are available in *The Complete Poems 1927–1979* (1983). *The Collected Prose* (1984) includes memoirs and stories, especially the memory-based story "In the Village," invaluable for a reading of her poems. A remarkable selection of Bishop's correspondence, *One Art* (1994), was edited by her friend and publisher, Robert Giroux, and *Words in the Air: The Complete Correspondence between Elizabeth Bishop and Robert Lowell*, edited by Thomas Travisano and Saskia Hamilton, documents one of the great literary friendships in twentieth century poetry. Reproductions of Bishop's watercolor paintings appear in *Exchanging Hats* (1996). Alice Quinn edited *Edgar Allan Poe & The Juke-Box: Uncollected Poems, Drafts, and Fragments* (2006). Bishop also translated from the Portuguese *The Diary of Helena Morley* (1957, 1977, 1991), an enchanting memoir of provincial life in Brazil.

Useful critical essays on Bishop appear in Seamus Heaney's *The Redress of Poetry* (1995), Lorrie Glodensohn's *Elizabeth Bishop: The Biography of a Poetry* (1992), and David Kalstone's *Becoming a Poet* (1989). *Elizabeth Bishop and Her Art*, edited by Lloyd Schwartz and Sybil P. Estess (1983), includes two interviews as well as essays. A provocative essay on Bishop appears in Adrienne Rich's *Blood, Bread and Poetry* (1986). Among the most valuable of the many critical studies are Brett C. Miller's important biography, *Elizabeth Bishop: Life and the Memory of It* (1993); *Elizabeth Bishop: The Geography of Gender* (1993), a collection of essays edited by Marilyn Lombardi; *Conversations with Elizabeth Bishop* (1996), edited by George Monteiro; and Thomas Travisano's *Midcentury Quartet* (1999). Candace MacMahon's *Elizabeth Bishop: A Bibliography* (1980) is indispensable.

Gwendolyn Brooks

Brooks's volumes of poetry include *A Street in Bronzeville* (1945), *Annie Allen* (1949), *In the Time of Detachment, In the Time of Cold*

(1965), *In the Mecca* (1968), *Riot* (1969), *Family Pictures* (1970), *Aloneness* (1972), *Aurora* (1972), *Beckonings* (1975), *To Disembark* (1981), *Winnie* (1989), and *Children Coming Home* (1991). Many of her poems are collected in *Selected Poems* (1999), *The Essential Gwendolyn Brooks* (2005), and the *Gwendolyn Brooks CD Poetry Collection* (2005). She has also written prose autobiographies, *Report from Part One* (1972) and *Report from Part Two* (1996).

Other useful biographical material appears in *A Life Distilled*, edited by M. K. Mootry and others. Valuable discussions of Brooks's poetry appear in *Black Women Writers (1950–1980)*, edited by Mari Evans (1984). Stephen Wright's *On Gwendolyn Brooks: Reliant Contemplation* (1996), Harold Bloom's *Gwendolyn Brooks* (2000), and Martha E. Rhynes's *Gwendolyn Brooks: Poet from Chicago* (2003) are recent critical studies. An interview with Brooks appears in Janet Mullaney's *Truthtellers of the Times: Interviews with Contemporary Women Poets* (1998). Brooks and Gloria Jean Wade Gayles published *Conversations with Gwendolyn Brooks* (2002).

Raymond Carver

Principal collections of Carver's extensive short fiction are *Put Yourself in My Shoes* (1974), *Will You Please Be Quiet, Please?* (1976), *Furious Seasons* (1977), *What We Talk About When We Talk About Love* (1981), *The Pheasant* (1982), *Cathedral* (1983), and *Where I'm Calling From* (1988). *Fires* (1983) is a sampling of essays, poems, and narratives. Carver's uncollected work has been edited by William L. Stull as *No Heroics, Please* (1991), expanded as *Call If You Need Me* (2000). The Library of America's *Collected Stories* (2009), edited by William L. Stull and Maureen P. Carroll, includes drafts of stories before changes were introduced by Gordon Lish. Throughout his career Carver published poetry as well, the bulk of which appears in several volumes from *Near Klamath* (1968) to *A New Path to the Waterfall* (1989); *All of Us* (1998) collects all his poems.

Arthur M. Saltzman's *Understanding Raymond Carver* (1988) looks beyond the author's apparent realism, as does Randolph Runyon's *Reading Raymond Carver* (1992). Carver's return to traditionalism is celebrated by Kirk Nesset in *The Stories of Raymond Carver* (1995). Editors Sandra Lee Kleppe and Robert Miltner present a wide variety of critical commentaries in *New Paths to Raymond Carver* (2008). Sam Halpert sifts through comments by Carver's associates in *Raymond Carver: An Oral Biography* (1995). The standard biography is *Raymond Carver: A Writer's Life* (2009) by Carol Sklenicka.

Lorna Dee Cervantes

Emplumada was published in 1981, *Cables of Genocide* in 1991, and *Drive: The First Quartet* in 2005.

A discussion of Cervantes's work, and of Chicana poetry more generally, appears in Deborah Madsen's *Understanding Contemporary Chicana Literature* (2000). An interview with Cervantes can be found in Bill Moyers's *Fooling with Words* (2000).

John Cheever

Cheever's seven volumes of short stories, which appeared between 1943 and 1973, are assembled in *The Stories of John Cheever* (1978); *The Uncollected Stories of John Cheever* appeared posthumously in 1988. His novels are *The Wapshot Chronicle* (1957), *The Wapshot Scandal* (1964), *Bullet Park* (1969), *Falconer* (1977), and *Oh What a Paradise It Seems* (1982). *The Letters of John Cheever*, edited by his son, Benjamin Cheever, was published in 1988. *The Journals of John Cheever* (1991) was edited by Robert Gottlieb.

Scott Donaldson's *John Cheever* (1988) is a full-length biography. *Home before Dark* (1984), by his daughter, Susan Cheever, is a personal memoir. Francis J. Bosha has edited *The Critical Response to John Cheever* (1994). Samuel Chase Coale provides an overview in *John Cheever* (1977), while George W. Hunt explores religious dimensions in *John Cheever: The Hobgoblin Company of Love* (1983). The stories are given close study by James Eugene O'Hara in *John Cheever: A Study of the Short Fiction* (1989).

Sandra Cisneros

The House on Mango Street (1984) has been described as both interrelated short stories and a novel, whereas *Woman Hollering Creek* (1991) collects more evidently independent short stories. *Caramello* (2002) is a novel. Cisneros has published two major collections of poetry, *My Wicked Wicked Ways* (1987) and *Loose Woman* (1994). Her *Hairs/Pelitos* (1994), written in English and accompanied by a Spanish text translated by Liliana Valenzuela, is a narrative for children.

Jean Wyatt's *Risking Difference* (2004) focuses on *Women Hollering Creek*. Ramón Saldíva discusses Cisneros's fiction in *Chicano Narrative* (1990), as do Tey Diana Rebolledo in *Women Singing in the Snow* (1995) and Sonia Saldívar-Hull in *Feminism on the Border* (2000). An extensive dialogue with her appears in *Interviews with Writers of the Post-Colonial World* (1992), edited by Feroza Jussawalla and Reed Way Dasenbrock.

Lucille Clifton

Clifton's volumes of poetry are *Good Times* (1969), *Good News About the Earth* (1972), *An Ordinary Woman* (1974), *Two-Headed Woman* (1980), *Good Woman: Poems and a Memoir 1969–1980* (1987), *Next: New Poems* (1987), *Quilting: Poems 1987–1990* (1991), *The Book of Light* (1993), *The Terrible Stories: Poems* (1995), *Blessing the Boats: New and Selected Poems, 1988–2000* (2000), *Mercy* (2004) and *Voices* (2008). Her memoir, *Generations* (1976), provides a valuable context for her work. Clifton's books for children include *The Black BC's* (1970), *Some of the Days of Everett Anderson* (1970), *The Boy Who Didn't Believe in Spring* (1973), *Don't You Remember* (1973), *All Us Come Cross the Water* (1973), *Good, Says Jerome* (1973), *Everett Anderson's Year* (1974; illustrated by Ann Grifalconi), *The Times They Used to Be* (1974), *My Brother Fine With Me* (1975), *Amifika* (1978), *The Lucky Stone* (1979), *My Friend Jacob* (1980), *Sonora Beautiful* (1981), *Everett Anderson's Goodbye* (1983), *Some of the Days of Everett Anderson* (1987), *Everett Anderson's Nine Month Long* (1987), *Everett Anderson's Christmas Coming* (1991; illustrated by Jan Spivey Gilchrist), *Everett Anderson's Friend* (1992), *Everett Anderson's 1-2-3* (1992; illustrated by Ann Grifalconi), *Three Wishes* (1994), *El Nino Que No Creia En La Primavera* (1996), and *Dear Creator: A Week of Poems for Young People and Their Teachers* (1997).

Critical discussions of her work include Hilary Holiday's *Wild Blessings: The Poetry of Lucille Clifton* (2004). Mary Jane Lupton has published *Lucille Clifton: Her Life and Letters* (2006).

Billy Collins

Collections of Collins's poetry include *The Apple That Astonished Paris* (1988), *Questions about Angels* (1991), *The Art of Drowning* (1995), *Picnic, Lightning* (1998), *Sailing Alone Around the World: New and Selected Poems* (2001), *Nine Horses* (2002), and *The Trouble with Poetry, and Other Poems* (2005). *The Best Cigarette* (1997), an audiobook, provides a chance to hear Collins reading thirty-three of his poems. He selected and introduced the anthologies *Poetry 180: A Turning Back to Poetry* (2003) and *180 More: Extraordinary Poems for Everyday Life* (2005).

Critical discussion of Collins's work appears in David Baker's *Heresy and the Ideal: On Contemporary Poetry* (2000).

Robert Creeley

The Collected Poems of Robert Creeley 1945–1975 appeared in 1982, and *The Selected Poems of Robert Creeley, 1975–2005* in 2006. *The Collected Prose* appeared in 1988 and *The*

Collected Essays in 1989. Creeley's many volumes of poetry include *The Whip* (1957), *A Form of Women* (1959), *For Love* (1962), *A Day Book* (1970, 1972), *Away* (1976), *Selected Poems* (1976), *Later* (1978), *Echoes* (1982), *Memories* (1984), *Memory Gardens* (1986), *The Company* (1988), *Echoes* (1994), *Life & Death* (1998), *If I Were Writing This* (2003), and *On Earth: Last Poems and an Essay* (2006). Creeley has also written fiction, including *The Gold Diggers* (1954) and *The Island* (1963). *Contexts of Poetry: Interviews 1961–1971*, edited by Donald Allen (1973), is engaging and valuable, and a new selection of interviews, *Tales Out of School*, appeared in 1993. Many of the essays in Creeley's *Collected Essays* illuminate Creeley's work; the collection also includes important commentary on the work of other poets. The nine volumes of *Charles Olson and Robert Creeley: The Complete Correspondence*, edited and published by George Butterick in 1950–52, constitute a remarkable glimpse into the history of contemporary poetry.

An important critical discussion of Creeley's poetry appears in Sherman Paul, *The Lost America of Love* (1971). Robert von Hallberg, *American Poetry and Culture, 1945–1980* (1985), includes a discussion of Creeley, as does Libbie Rifkin's *Career Moves: Olson, Creeley, Zukofsky, Berrigan, and the American Avant-garde* (2000).

Edwidge Danticat

Danticat has published both fiction and nonfiction. Her nonfiction works include *After the Dance: A Walk Through Carnival in Jacmel, Haiti* (2002) and *Brother, I'm Dying* (2007). She also edited *The Butterfly's Way: Voices from the Haitian Dyaspora in the United States* (2003). Her fiction includes *Krik? Krak!* (1996), *The Farming of Bones* (1998), and *The Dew Breaker* (1994), as well as the young adult novels *Breath, Eyes, Memory* (1994), *Behind the Mountains* (2002), and *Anacaona: Golden Flower, Haiti, 1490* (2005). A video, audio, and print transcript of her 2011 interview on Democracy Now, "The Immigrant Artist at Work," can be found on the program's website www.democracynow.org. Critical discussion of Danticat's work can be found in Meredith M. Gadsby's *Sucking Salt: Caribbean Women Writers, Migration, and Survival* (2006).

Junot Díaz

Drown (1996) collects Díaz's short stories; *The Brief Wondrous Life of Oscar Wao* (2007) is his novel.

Jacquelyn Loss studies Díaz's fiction in *Latino and Latina Writers* (2003), edited by Alan West–Durán, as do Raphael Dalleo and Elena Machado Sáez in *The Latino/a Canon and the Emergence of a Post-Sixties Literature*

(2007). Díaz's cultural context is examined by Lucia Suarez in *The Tears of Hispaniola: Haitian and Dominican Diaspora Memory* (2006).

James Dickey

Dickey's *Poems 1957–1967* includes selections from *Into the Stone* (1957), *Drowning with Others* (1962), *Helmets* (1964), *Two Poems of the Air* (1964), and *Buckdancer's Choice* (1965). More-recent gatherings of work from several volumes appeared as *The Central Motion: Poems 1968–1979* (1983), *The Whole Motion: Collected Poems 1949–1992* (1992), and *The Selected* Poems (1998). Individual collections also include *The Eye-Beaters, Blood, Victory, Madness, Buckhead and Mercy* (1970), *The Zodiac* (1976), *Falling, May Day Sermon, and Other Poems* (1981), *The Early Motion* (1981), *Puella* (1982), and *The Eagle's Mile* (1990).

Dickey's literary criticism and autobiographical collections include *The Suspect in Poetry* (1964), *Babel to Byzantium* (1968), *Self-Interviews* (1970), *Sorties: Journals and New Essays* (1971), and *The Poet Turns on Himself* (1982). *A James Dickey Reader* appeared in 1999. His novels *Deliverance* and *Alnilam* were published in 1970 and 1987, respectively. *The Imagination as Glory* (1984), edited by Bruce Weigl and T. R. Hummer, is a collection of critical essays on Dickey's work. Other critical work on Dickey's poetry includes Robert Kirschten's *Struggling for Wings: The Art of James Dickey* (1997) and Henry Hart's *James Dickey: The World as Lie* (2000). Gordon Van Ness edited *The One Voice of James Dickey: His Letters and Life, 1942–1969* (2003).

Joan Didion

Didion's long and varied career as a writer includes works of both fiction and nonfiction as well as multiple screenplays. Among her nonfiction volumes are *We Tell Ourselves Stories in Order to Live: Collected Nonfiction* (2006), which includes work from *The White Album* (1979), *Salvador* (1983), *Miami* (1987), *After Henry* (1992), *Political Fictions* (2001), *Where I Was From* (2003), *Fixed Ideas: America Since 9.11* (2003). Another collection of her work, *Vintage Didion*, appeared in 2004. Her creative nonfiction memoir, *The Year of Magical Thinking*, appeared in 2005. Didion's novels include *Run, River* (1963), *Play It As It Lays* (1970), *A Book of Common Prayer* (1977), *Democracy* (1984), and *The Last Thing He Wanted* (1996). Among her screenplays are *The Panic in Needle Park* (1971), *Play It As It Lays* (1972), *A Star Is Born* (1976), *True Confessions* (1981), and *Up Close and Personal* (1996). Two interviews with Didion have appeared in the *Paris Review*, one in 1978; a second, "The Art of Nonfiction" (2006), is available online at www.parisreview.org. Critical discussion of Didion's work can be found in James N. Still's "The Minimal Self: Joan Didion's Journalism of Survival" in *Literary Selves: Autobiography and Contemporary American Nonfiction* (1993) and Doug Underwood's *Journalism and the Novel: Truth and Fiction, 1700–2000* (2008).

Annie Dillard

Dillard's nonfiction ranges from autobiography and meditations on nature and philosophy to literary criticism and anecdotes about other writers; published volumes are *Pilgrim at Tinker Creek* (1974), *Holy the Firm* (1977), *Teaching a Stone to Talk* (1982), *Living by Fiction* (1982), *Encounters with Chinese Writers* (1984), *Writing Life* (1989), *An American Childhood* (1987), and *For the Time Being* (1999). *The Living* (1992) and *The Maytrees* (2007) are novels, while *Tickets for a Prayerwheel* (1974) collects her early poetry. *Mornings Like This* (1995) gathers new poems.

Nancy C. Parrish provides a critical biography in *Lee Smith, Annie Dillard, and The Hollins Group* (1998). Still important for its insights on Dillard's first major books is Sandra Humble Johnson's *The Space Between: Literary Epiphany in the Works of Annie Dillard* (1982). Dillard's position in literary history is assessed by Sue Yore in *The Mystic Way in Postmodernity* (2009).

Stephen Dixon

Selections from Dixon's first thirty years of writing appear in *The Stories of Stephen Dixon* (1994); individual short story collections are *No Relief* (1976), *Quite Contrary* (1979), *14 Stories* (1980), *Movies* (1983), *Time to Go* (1984), *Love and Will* (1989), *The Play* (1989), *All Gone* (1990), *Friends* (1990), *Long Made Short* (1993), *Man on Stage* (1996), and *Sleep* (1999). Previously uncollected stories have been published as *What Is All this?* (2010). *Frog* (1991) is a multilayered fiction encompassing eighteen stories, two novellas, a novel, and an assemblage of fragments, all of which are thematically related. *Gould* (1996) combines a historically segmented novel with a more unified novella. Dixon's independently standing novels are *Work* (1977), *Too Late* (1978), *Fall & Rise* (1985), *Garbage* (1988), *Interstate* (1995), *30* (1999), *Tisch* (1999), *Old Friends* (2001), *I.* (2002), *Phone Rings* (2005), *End of I.* (2006), and *Meyer* (2007).

Dixon's work is located in the larger stream of contemporary fiction by Arthur M. Saltzman's *The Novel in the Balance* (1993); Marc Chénetier's *Beyond Suspicion: New American Fiction Since 1960* (1996); and Jerome Klinkowitz's *The Self-Apparent Word* (1984), *Structuring the Void* (1992), and *You've Got to Be Carefully Taught* (2001).

Rita Dove

Dove has published eight volumes of poetry: *The Yellow House on the Corner* (1980), *Museum* (1983), *Thomas and Beulah* (1986), *Grace Notes* (1989), *Selected Poems* (1993), *Mother Love* (1995), *On the Bus with Rosa Parks* (1999), *American Smooth* (2004), and *Sonata Mulattica* (2009). She has also published a collection of fiction; *Fifth Sunday* (1985); a novel, *Through the Ivory Gate* (1992); and a valuable collection of essays, *The Poet's World* (1995). *Conversations with Rita Dove*, edited by Earl G. Ingersol, appeared in 2003.

Therese Steffen's critical study *Crossing Color: Transcultural Space and Place in Rita Dove's Poetry, Fiction, and Drama* appeared in 2001; Malin Pereira's *Rita Dove's Cosmopolitanism*, in 2003; and Pat Righelato's *Understanding Rita Dove*, in 2006.

Robert Duncan

Duncan's poems have not been collected in a single volume, but a number of books gather poems from his many fugitive pamphlet publications. Robert J. Bertholf's edition of Duncan's *Selected Poems* appeared in 1997; Duncan's own volumes of selected work include *The Years as Catches, First Poems 1939–1941* (1966), *Selected Poems 1942–1950* (1959), *The First Decade: Selected Poems, Vol. 1* (1968), and *Derivations: Selected Poems, 1950–1956* (1968). Duncan's final two volumes of poetry, *Ground Work: Before the War* (1984) and *Ground Work II: In the Dark* (1987), contain many major poems written over fifteen years; both volumes are gathered in *Groundwork* (2005). Other important books of his poetry are *The Opening of the Field* (1960), *Roots and Branches* (1964), and *Bending the Bow* (1968). Duncan's prose collection, *Fictive Certainties* (1979), is invaluable to a reader of his poems. *A Selected Prose*, edited by Robert J. Bertholf, appeared in 1995; *The Letters of Robert Duncan and Denise Levertov*, also edited by Bertholf, in 2003.

Robert Duncan: Scales of the Marvelous (1979) collects essays on Duncan's work from a range of poets and critics. Also important are the discussions of Duncan in Sherman Paul's *The Lost America of Love* (1981) and Robert K. Martin's *The Homosexual Tradition in American Poetry* (1998). Robert J. Bertholf's *Robert Duncan: A Descriptive Bibliography* (1986) is a necessary guide to Duncan's many uncollected writings.

Ralph Ellison

In his lifetime Ellison published three books: a novel, *Invisible Man* (1952), and two volumes of essays, *Shadow and Act* (1964) and *Going to the Territory* (1986). The latter materials are combined with other nonfiction in *The Collected Essays of Ralph Ellison* (1995), edited by John F. Callahan with a preface by Saul Bellow. Fragments of his novel in progress are noted in the bibliography to Mark Busby's *Ralph Ellison* (1991) in the Twayne United States Authors series; *Flying Home and Other Stories* (1997) gathers thirteen short stories written between 1937 and 1954, six of which were previously unpublished. In 1999 Callahan, as Ellison's literary executor, drew on manuscripts to assemble *Juneteenth* as a posthumous novel, a fuller version of which is presented by Callahan and editor Adam Bradley as *Three Days Before the Shooting . . .* (2010). Robert G. O'Meally edited *Living with Music: Ralph Ellison's Jazz Writings* (2001). *Trading Twelves: The Selected Letters of Ralph Ellison and Albert Murray*, edited by Murray and Callahan, appeared in 2000.

The centrality of Ellison's first novel to his other work is explained by Edith Shor in *Visible Ellison: A Study of Ralph Ellison's Fiction* (1993). Political interests shape the critical essays collected by Lucas E. Morel in *Ralph Ellison and the Raft of Hope* (2004), as does music in Horace A. Porter's *Jazz Country: Ralph Ellison in America* (2001). Julia Eichelberger's *Prophets of Recognition* (1999) considers his larger impact. *Jazz Country: Ralph Ellison's America* (2001) by Horace A. Porter relates the author's jazz background to his novels and essays. *Ulysses in Black* (2008) by Patrice D. Rankin considers Ellison's debts to the classics. Political influences are studied by Barbara Foley in *Wrestling with the Left: The Making of Ralph Ellison's* Invisible Man (2010). Arnold Rampersand's *Ralph Ellison* (2007) is a comprehensive biography. The author's lifelong growth is measured by Adam Bradley in *Ralph Eilison's Progress* (2010).

Louise Erdrich

Erdrich's novels are *Love Medicine* (1984), *The Beet Queen* (1986), *Tracks* (1988), *The Bingo Palace* (1994), *Tales of Burning Love* (1996), *The Antelope Wife* (1998), *The Last Report on the Miracles at Little No Horse* (2001), *The Master Butcher's Singing Club* (2003), *Four Souls* (2004), *The Painted Drum* (2005), *The Plague of Doves* (2008), and *Shadow Tag* (2010). *The Red Convertible* (2009) collects her short stories. For children she has written *Grandmother's Pigeon* (1996), *The Birchbark House* (1999), *The Game of Silence* (2005), and *The Porcupine Years* (2008). *The Blue Jay's Dance: A Birth Year* (1995) is her account of becoming a mother, *Birds and Islands in Ojibwe Country* (2003) is a memoir. With Michael Dorris she coauthored *The Crown of Columbus* (1991), a novel. Her poetry collections are *Jacklight* (1984), *Baptism of Desire* (1989), and *Original Fire* (2003).

Erdrich's fiction is treated by Louis Owens in *Other Destinies: Understanding the American Indian Novel* (1992), in the essays edited by Allan Chavkin in *The Chippewa Landscape of Louise Erdrich* (1999), and Peter G. Beidler and Gay Barton in *A Reader's Guide to the Novels of Louise Erdrich* (2006).

Allen Ginsberg

Ginsberg's *Collected Poems, 1947–1980* appeared in 1984, *White Shroud: Poems, 1980–1985* in 1986, and *Death and Fame: Poems 1993–1997* in 1999. His individual volumes, with the exception of *Empty Mirror* (early poems collected in 1961), have been issued in the now unmistakable City Lights paperbacks. They include *Howl and Other Poems* (1956), *Kaddish and Other Poems, 1958–1960* (1961), *Reality Sandwiches* (1963), *Planet News, 1961–1967* (1968), *The Fall of America, Poems of These States, 1965–1971* (1973), and *Mind Breaths, Poems 1972–1977* (1977). *Cosmopolitan Greetings* appeared in 1995 and *Selected Poems 1947–1995* in 1996. *Deliberate Prose: Selected Essays, 1952–1995* (2000) is a useful complement to the poetry. Ginsberg published a great number of pages from his journals, dealing with his travels, such as the *Indian Journals* (1970). *Allen Verbatim* (1974) includes transcripts of some of his lectures on poetry. In 1977 he published *Letters: Early Fifties Early Sixties* and in 1980 *Composed on the Tongue: Literary Conversations 1967–1977*, edited by Donald Allen. Ginsberg's interviews are collected in *Spontaneous Mind: Selected Interviews, 1958–1996* (2001).

Jane Kramer's *Allen Ginsberg in America* (1969) is a brilliant documentary piece on Ginsberg in the 1960s. *On the Poetry of Allen Ginsberg*, edited by Lewis Hyde (1980), is a collection of essays by different hands. Michelle Kraus has published *Allen Ginsberg: An Annotated Bibliography, 1969–1977* (1980). Bill Morgan has published *The Works of Allen Ginsberg 1941–1994: A Descriptive Bibliography* (1995) and *The Response to Allen Ginsberg 1926–1994: A Bibliography of Secondary Sources* (1996).

Louise Glück

Glück's *The First Four Books of Poems* (1995) includes all the work from her earlier collections: *First Born* (1969), *The House on Marshland* (1976), *Descending Figure* (1980), and *The Triumph of Achilles* (1985). Later individual volumes are *Ararat* (1990), *The Wild Iris* (1992), *Meadowlands* (1996), *Vita Nova* (1999), *The Seven Ages* (2001), *October* (2004), *Averno* (2006), and *A Village Life* (2009). Her collection of essays, *Proofs and Theories* (1994), is an indispensable companion to her work, both for its discussions of poetic vocation and for its description of the autobiographical contexts of specific poems.

Critical discussion of Glück's poetry can be found in Upton Lee's *The Muse of Abandonment* (1998) and Joanne Diehl's *On Louise Glück: Change What You See* (2005). Helen Vendler's collection of essays on poetry, *Soul Says* (1995), includes commentary-reviews of Glück's work. Elizabeth Dodd's *The Veiled Mirror and The Woman Poet: H. D., Louise Bogan, Elizabeth Bishop, and Louise Glück* (1992) contains a chapter on Glück.

Jorie Graham

The Dream of the Unified Field: Selected Poems 1974–1994 (1995) brings together poems from *Hybrids of Plants and of Ghosts* (1980), *Erosion* (1983), *The End of Beauty* (1987), *Region of Unlikeness* (1991), and *Materialism* (1993). Graham's more recent collections include *The Errancy* (1997), *Swarm* (2000), and *Overlord* (2005) and *Sea Change* (2008). She edited *Earth Took of Earth: 100 Great Poems of the English Language* (1996).

Critical discussion of Graham's work can be found in Helen Vendler's *The Given and the Made* (1995) and *Soul Says* (1995), James Longenbach's *Modern Poetry after Modernism* (1997), and Thomas Gardner's *Regions of Unlikeness: Explaining Contemporary Poetry* (1999). Gardiner also edited the collection *Jorie Graham: Essays on the Poetry* (2004). An extremely useful interview with Graham appears in *Denver Quarterly* (1992).

Joy Harjo

Harjo's collections of poetry include two chap-books, *The Last Song* (1975) and *What Moon Drove Me to This* (1979), and the volumes *She Had Some Horses* (1983), *In Mad Love and War* (1990), *The Woman Who Fell from the Sky* (1996), *A Map to the Next World* (2000), and *How We Became Human: New and Selected Poems 1975–2001* (2002). In *Secrets from the Center of the World* (1989) she wrote the text to accompany Steven Strom's photographs of the particulars of the southwestern landscape. She has also edited an anthology of Native American women's writing, *Reinventing the Enemy's Language: Contemporary Native Women's Writing of North America* (1997).

Laura Coltelli has edited a valuable collection of interviews with Harjo, *The Spiral of Memory* (1990). Commentary on the contexts of Harjo's work appears in Paula Gunn Allen's *The Sacred Hoop: Recovering the Feminine in American Indian Traditions* (1986) and Norma Wilson's *The Nature of Native American Poetry* (2001).

Michael S. Harper

Harper's poems appear in *Dear John, Dear Coltrane* (1970), *History Is Your Own Heartbeat* (1971), *Photographs: Negatives: History as Apple Tree* (1972), *Song: I Want a Witness* (1972), *Nightmare Begins Responsibility* (1974), *Images of Kin: New and Selected Poems* (1977), *Healing Song for the Inner Ear* (1984), and *Honorable Amendments* (1995). An edition of new and collected poems, *Songlines in Michaeltre*, appeared in 2000. Harper also edited (with Robert Stepto) a collection of African American literature, art, and scholarship, *Chants of Saints* (1976), and he edited *The Vintage Book of African American Poetry* (2000).

A conversation about Harper's work can be found in Joanne Gabbin's edited *The Furious Flowering of African American Poetry* (1999).

Robert Hass

Hass's books of verse include *Field Guide* (1973), *Praise* (1979), *Human Wishes* (1989), *Sun Under Wood* (1996), and *Time and Materials: Poems 1997–2005* (2007). *The Apple Trees at Olema: New and Selected Poems* (2010) brings together poems from earlier collections. Hass has published a collection of criticism, *Twentieth Century Pleasures: Prose on Poetry* (1984); a gathering of his musings in the "Poet's Choice" column appeared in *Now and Then: The Poet's Choice Columns, 1997–2000* (2007). He has co-translated several volumes of poetry with Czeslaw Milosz, most recently *The Second Space* (2002), and has edited *The Essential Haiku: Versions of Basho, Buson, and Issa* (1994). Hass has given many informative interviews that have appeared in publication form, among them "A Conversation with Robert Hass," *Chicago Review* 32.4 (Spring 1981): 17–26, "An Informal Occasion with Robert Hass," *The Iowa Review* 21.3 (Fall 1991): 126–45, and "Robert Hass: An Interview," *American Poetry Review* (Mar/Apr 1997). Alexander Neubauer's *Poetry in Person: Twenty-Five years of Conversation with America's Poets* includes a conversation with Hass.

Robert Hayden

Hayden's *Collected Poems* appeared in 1985; his *Collected Prose* appeared the previous year. Both were edited by Frederick Glaysher. Fred M. Fetrow's *Robert Hayden* (1984) is a critical study of Hayden's work. Essays on Hayden's work appear in the journals *Antioch Review* (1997) and *MELUS* (1998) and in Harold Bloom's edited volume *Robert Hayden* (2005).

Fanny Howe

Howe's poetry appears in *Eggs* (1970), *The Meaning of Life* (1984), *Introduction to the World* (1986), *The End* (1992), *O'clock* (1995), *One Crossed Out* (1997), *Q* (1998), *Forged* (1999), *Selected Poems* (2000), *Gone* (2003), and *On the Ground* (2004). Her collection of literary essays, *The Wedding Dress: Meditations on Word and Life* (2003), provides an illuminating context for her work. *Radical Love* (2006) collects five of her many novels: *The Deep North* (1988), *Famous Questions* (1989), *Saving History* (1993), *Nod* (1998), and *Invisible* (2000). She has also written numerous books for young adults. She is an experimental writer, and her work often defies generic classification, as is the case with her prose collection *Lives of the Spirit/Glasstown: Where Something Got Broken* (2005).

Randall Jarrell

Jarrell's *Complete Poems* was published in 1969, and a *Selected Poems* appeared in 1991. A selection of Jarrell's brilliant critical essays is available in *No Other Book* (1999), edited by Brad Leithauser. His novel satirizing American academic life, *Pictures from an Institution*, appeared in 1954.

Some of the most valuable commentary on Jarrell's life and work is to be found in a memorial volume of essays edited by Robert Lowell, Peter Taylor, and Robert Penn Warren, *Randall Jarrell, 1914–1965* (1967). William Pritchard's fine *Randall Jarrell: A Literary Life* (1990) illumines Jarrell's life and work, as does Mary Randall's *Remembering Randall* (1999). Critical discussion of Jarrell's work appears in Thomas Travisano's *Midcentury Quartet* (1999).

Jack Kerouac

Kerouac's novels are *The Town and the City* (1950), *On the Road* (1957), *The Subterraneans* (1958), *The Dharma Bums* (1958), *Doctor Sax* (1959), *Maggie Cassidy* (1959), *Tristessa* (1960), *Big Sur* (1962), *Visions of Gerard* (1963), *Desolation Angels* (1965), *Vanity of Duluoz* (1968), *Pic* (1971), and *Visions of Cody* (1972). His works of nonfiction are *The Scripture of the Golden Eternity* (1960), *Lonesome Traveler* (1960), *Book of Dreams* (1960), and *Satori in Paris* (1966). An important first draft has been restored by editor Howard Cunnell in *On the Road: The Original Scroll* (2007). His poems are collected in *Mexico City Blues* (1959), *Scattered Poems* (1971), *Heaven & Other Poems* (1977), and *San Francisco Blues* (1983). In 2004 Douglas Brinkley edited *Windblown World: The Journals of Jack Kerouac, 1947–1954.*

John Tytell's *Naked Angels: The Lives and Literature of the Beat Generation* (1983) includes Kerouac in his historical and critical context. Stylistic analyses are undertaken by Regina Weinrich in *The Spontaneous Prose of*

Jack Kerouac (1987) and Michael Hrebeniak in *Action Writing: Jack Kerouac's Wild Form* (2006). More specifically thematic is James T. Jones's *Jack Kerouac's Duluoz Legend: The Mythic Form of an Autobiographical Fiction* (1999). Kerouac's friend Carolyn Cassady has written a memoir, *Off the Road* (1990), as has Edie Kerouac-Parker, *You'll Be Okay: My Life with Jack Kerouac* (2007). Biographies include Barry Gifford and Lawrence Lee's *Jack's Book: Jack Kerouac in the Lives and Words of His Friends* (1978), Tom Clark's *Jack Kerouac* (1984), Gerald Nicosia's *Memory Babe* (1983), and Ann Charter's *Jack Kerouac* (1987). Charters also prepared *A Bibliography of Works by Jack Kerouac* (1975). Kerouac's papers are housed in the Berg Collection of the New York Public Library.

Martin Luther King Jr.
Dr. King's published writings, sermons, speeches, unpublished writings, and most significant correspondence have been collected by editor Clayborne Carson in *The Papers of Martin Luther King, Jr.* (1985). The originals of these and other materials are housed in the Martin Luther King Jr. Research and Education Institute at Stanford University, which also maintains the King Document Search Access (OKRA) database.

Roger Bruns has authored *Martin Luther King, Jr.: A Biography* (2006). Taylor Branch studies Dr. King's social and political context in *At Canaan's Edge: America in the King Years, 1965–68* (2006). Eric J. Sundquist offers specific analysis in *King's Dream: The Legacy of Martin Luther King's "I Have a Dream" Speech* (2009).

Maxine Hong Kingston
The Woman Warrior (1976) and *China Men* (1980) were first received as autobiography, though Kingston scholars now recognize important fictive elements. *Tripmaster Monkey: His Fake Book* (1989) is more obviously a novel. Essays Kingston wrote in 1978 appear as *Hawai'i One Summer* (1999). *The Fifth Book of Peace* (2003) incorporates remembered pages of a lost novel with sections of conventional memoir. *I Love a Broad Margin to My Life* (2011) is an autobiography that uses poetry to address concerns of the author's aging.

Shirley Geok-Lim edited *Approaches to Teaching Kingston's "The Woman Warrior"* (1991); also helpful is Sidonie Smith's *A Poetics of Women's Autobiography: Marginality and the Fictions of Self-Representation* (1987). More cognizant of fiction's role in Kingston's writing is *Articulate Silences: Hisaye Yamamoto, Maxine Hong Kingston, and Joy Kogawa* (1993) by King-Kok Cheung and *Writing Tricksters* (1997) by Jeanne Rosier Smith.

Cultural identity features in Martha J. Cutter's *Lost and Found in Translation* (2005).

Jamaica Kincaid
Kincaid has published both fiction and nonfiction, including memoirs and gardening books. Her books include a collection of short pieces variously categorized as stories, prose poems, or memoirs, *At the Bottom of the River* (1984), and the novels, *Annie John* (1985), *Lucy* (1990), and *Mr. Potter* (2002), as well as the fictional memoir *The Autobiography of My Mother* (1995). *My Brother* (1997) is a searing account of her brother's death from AIDS. Kincaid is a passionate gardener; she is the editor of *My Favorite Plant: Writers and Gardeners on the Plants They Love* (editor; 1998) and the author of *My Garden* (1999) and *Among Flowers: A Walk in the Himalayas* (2005). Her essay, "On Seeing England for the First Time" (*Harper's* magazine, August 1991) is a brilliant postcolonial document. An interview in the online journal *Salon* can be found at www.salon.com. Critical discussion of Kincaid's work includes Moira Ferguson's *Jamaica Kincaid: Where the Land Meets the Body* (1994), Lisa Paravisini-Gebert's *Jamaica Kincaid: A Critical Companion* (1999), Justin D. Edwards's *Understanding Jamaica Kincaid* (2007), and Mary Ellen Snodgrass's *Jamaica Kincaid: A Literary Companion* (2008).

Galway Kinnell
Kinnell's *A New Selected Poems* appeared in 2000. Earlier collected volumes of his work were *First Poems 1946–1954* (1970), *The Avenue Bearing the Initial of Christ into the New World: Poems, 1946–1964* (1974), and *Selected Poems* (1982). Important individual volumes of Kinnell's poetry are *What a Kingdom It Was* (1960), *The Book of Nightmares* (1971), *Mortal Acts, Mortal Words* (1980), *The Past* (1985), *When One Has Lived a Long Time Alone* (1990), *Imperfect Thirst* (1994), and *Strong Is Your Hold* (2006). He has also published a collection of criticism, *The Poetics of the Physical World* (1969), and selected interviews, *Walking Down the Stairs*, edited by Donald Hall (1978).

Critical Essays on Galway Kinnell (1996), edited by Nancy Tuten, and David Baker's *Heresy and the Ideal: On Contemporary Poetry* (2000) contain useful critical discussions.

Yusef Komunyakaa
Komunyakaa's poetry appears in *Lost in the Bonewheel Factory* (1979), *Copacetic* (1984), *I Apologize for the Eyes in My Head* (1986), *Dien Cai Dau* (1987), *Magic City* (1992), *Neon Vernacular: New and Selected Poems* (1993), *Thieves of Paradise* (1998), *Talking Dirty to the Gods* (2000), *Pleasure Dome* (2001), *Taboo:*

The Wishbone Trilogy, Part I (2004), and *Warhorses* (2008). With Martha Collins he has translated Nguyen Quang Thieu's *The Insomnia of Fire* (1992). With Sascha Feinstein he has edited *The Jazz Poetry Anthology* (1991) and *The Second Set: The Jazz Poetry Anthology, Volume 2* (1996). In 2000 he published *Blue Notes: Essays, Interviews, and Commentaries.*

Critical discussions of his work include Angela M. Salas's *Flashback Through the Heart: The Poetry of Yusef Komunyakaa* (2004).

Stanley Kunitz

Kunitz's *Collected Poems* (2000) gathers work from *Passing Through: The Later Poems, New and Selected* (1995), *Next-to-Last Things: New Poems and Essays* (1985), *The Poems of Stanley Kunitz, 1928–1978* (1979), *The Testing Tree* (1971), *Selected Poems, 1928–1958* (1958), *Passport to War* (1940), and *Intellectual Things* (1930). *A Kind of Order, A Kind of Folly* (1975) collects Kunitz's essays and interviews. An important example of his translations is *Poems of Akhmatova* (1973). *The Wild Braid: A Poet Reflects on a Century in the Garden* (2005) is nonfiction by Kunitz and Genine Lentine, with photographs by Marnie Crawford Samuelson.

Gregory Orr's *Stanley Kunitz: An Introduction to the Poetry* (1985) and *A Celebration for Stanley Kunitz on His Eightieth Birthday* (1986), a gathering of essays by various hands, offer critical discussion of Kunitz's work.

Jhumpa Lahiri

Lahiri's collections of stories are *Interpreter of Maladies* (1999) and *Unaccustomed Earth* (2008); her first novel is *The Namesake* (2003).

Criticism of her fiction is found in *Transnational Asian American Literature: Sites and Transits* (2006), edited by Shirley Geok-lin Lim, et al., and in *Literary Gestures: The Aesthetic in Asian American Writers* (2007), edited by Rocío G. Davis and Sue-Im Lee.

Li-Young Lee

Lee's volumes of poetry are *Rose* (1986), *The City in Which I Love You* (1990), *A Book of My Nights* (2001), and *Behind My Eyes* (2008). A memoir, *The Winged Seed*, appeared in 1995.

Gerald Stern's foreword to *Rose* provides useful biographical material about Lee's family. Available on videotape, as part of the series *The Power of the Word*, is "Voices of Memory," in which Bill Moyers conducts a valuable interview with Lee. An interview with Lee appears in *Words Matter: Conversations with Asian American Writers* (2000), edited by King-Kok Cheung. *Breaking the Alabaster Jar: Conversation with Li-Young Lee*, edited by

Earl G. Ingersol (2006), is a collection of interviews.

Ursula K. Le Guin

Le Guin's novels include *Rocannon's World* (1966), *Planet of Exile* (1966), *City of Illusions* (1967), *A Wizard of Earthsea* (1968), *The Left Hand of Darkness* (1969), *The Tombs of Atuan* (1971), *The Lathe of Heaven* (1971), *The Farthest Shore* (1972), *The Dispossessed* (1974), *The Word for World Is Forest* (1976), *Malafrena* (1979), *The Eye of the Heron* (1983), *Always Coming Home* (1985), *Tehanu: The Last Book of Earthsea* (1990), *Buffalo Gals, Won't You Come Out Tonight* (1994), *Four Ways to Forgiveness* (1995), *The Telling* (2000), *The Other Wind* (2001), *Gifts* (2004), *Voices* (2006), *Powers* (2007), and *Lavinia* (2008). Her short-story collections are *The Wind's Twelve Quarters* (1975), *The Water Is Wide* (1976), *Orsinian Tales* (1976), *The Compass Rose* (1982), *The Visionary* (1984), *Buffalo Gals and Other Animal Presences* (1987), *Searoad* (1992), *A Fisherman of the Inland Series* (1994) *Worlds of Exile and Illusion* (1996), *The Birthday of the World and Other Stories* (2002), and *Changing Planes* (2004). *Tales from Earthsea* (2001) presents a novella and new short stories. She also wrote fourteen books for children, ten poetry collections, two plays, and several volumes of nonfiction, including *The Language of Night: Essays on Fantasy and Science Fiction* (1979, 1989), *Dancing at the Edge of the World: Thoughts on Words, Women, Places* (1989), *The Wave in the Mind: Talks and Essays on the Writer, the Reader, and the Imagination* (2004) and *Cheek by Jowl: Talks and Essays on How Fantasy Matters* (2009).

Understanding Ursula K. Le Guin (1990) by Elizabeth Cummins Cogell is a good introduction; more critically sophisticated are James Bittner's *Approaches to the Fiction of Ursula K. Le Guin* (1984) and Bernard Selinger's *Le Guin and Identity in Contemporary Fiction* (1988). Le Guin's importance is measured by Darren Harris-Fain in *Understanding Contemporary Science Fiction: The Age of Maturity, 1970–2000* (2005).

Denise Levertov

Some of Levertov's poems have been gathered in *Collected Earlier Poems 1940–1960* (1979). *The Selected Poems of Denise Levertov* appeared in 2002. Her individual volumes include *The Double Image* (1946), *Here and Now* (1957), *Overland to the Islands* (1958), *With Eyes at the Back of Our Heads* (1960), *The Jacob's Ladder* (1962), *O Taste and See* (1964), *The Sorrow Dance* (1967), *Relearning the Alphabet* (1970), *To Stay Alive* (1971), *Footprints* (1972), *The Freedom of the Dust* (1973), *Life in the Forest* (1978), *Candles in Babylon*

(1982), *Oblique Prayers* (1984), *Breathing the Water* (1987), *A Door in the Hive* (1989), *Evening Train* (1992), *Tesserae* (1995), and *The Great Unknowing: Last Poems* (1999). *Making Peace* (2005) is a posthumous collection edited by Peggy Rosenthal. *The Poet in the World* (1973) and *Light Up the Cave* (1981) include essays on her own work, memoirs, reviews of other poets, and some theoretical essays. *New and Selected Essays* appeared in 1992.

Conversations with Denise Levertov (1998) is a collection of interviews. James E. Breslin's *From Modern to Contemporary: American Poetry 1945–1965* (1984) contains a discussion of Levertov. Linda Wagner-Martin edited *Critical Essays on Denise Levertov* (1990), and Anne Little edited *Denise Levertov: New Perspectives* (2000).

Philip Levine
Levine's *New Selected Poems* (1991) gathers work from many of his volumes of poetry, including *Not This Pig* (1968), *Pili's Wall* (1971), *They Feed They Lion* (1972), *1933* (1974), *The Names of the Lost* (1976), *7 Years from Somewhere* (1979), *Ashes: Poems New and Old* (1979), *One for the Rose* (1981), *Sweet Will* (1985), and *A Walk with Tom Jefferson* (1988). He has also published *What Work Is* (1991), *The Simple Truth* (1994), *The Mercy* (1999), *Breath* (2004), and *News of the World* (2009). A memoir, *The Bread to Time: Toward an Autobiography*, appeared in 1994. His translations from the Spanish are available in *Tarumba: The Selected Poems of Jaime Sabines* (with Ernest Trejo, 1979) and *Off the Map: Selected Writings of Gloria Fuertes* (with Ada Long, 1984). A collection of Levine's interviews, *Don't Ask*, appeared in 1981. Another collection of essays and interviews, *So Ask*, appeared in 2002.

Christopher Buckley's *On the Poetry of Philip Levine* appeared in 1991, and Edward Hirsch's "The Visionary Poetics of Philip Levine and Charles Wright" appears in *The Columbia History of American Poetry* (1993). David St. John's *Where Angels Come Toward Us* (1995) contains discussion of Levine's work.

Barry Lopez
Lopez is a prolific writer and has published numerous works of fiction and nonfiction; as is the case with many creative nonfiction writers, his work often combines these genres. Among his environmental and travel writings are *Of Wolves and Men* (1978), the award-winning *Arctic Dreams: Imagination and Desire in a Northern Landscape* (1986), *Crossing Open Ground* (1988), *The Rediscovery of North America* (1991), *About This Life: Journeys on the Threshold of Memory* (1998), and *Home Ground: Language for an American*

Landscape (2010). He mixes fact and fictional techniques in *Desert Notes: Reflections in the Eye of a Raven* (1976), *River Notes: The Dance of Herons* (1979), *Crow and Weasel* (1990), *Field Notes: The Grace Note of the Canyon Wren* (1994), and *Lessons from the Wolverine* (1997). *Winter Count* (1981) is a collection of stories and *Resistance* (2004) is a novel. Useful interviews with Lopez can be found in Christian Martin's "On Resistance: An Interview with Barry Lopez" in *The Georgia Review* (Spring 2006) and Mike Newell's *No Bottom: In Conversation with Barry Lopez* (2008). Critical discussion of Lopez's work includes Scot Slovic's *Seeking Awareness in American Nature Writing: Henry Thoreau, Annie Dillard, Edward Abbey, Wendell Berry, and Barry Lopez* (1992) and William H. Rueckert's essay, "Barry Lopez and the Search for a Dignified and Honorable Relationship with Nature," in *Earthly Words: Essays on Contemporary American Nature and Environmental Writers*, edited by John Cooley (1994).

Audre Lorde
The Collected Poems of Audre Lorde (1997) brings together Lorde's poetry from *Cables to Rage* (1970), *New York Head Shop and Museum* (1975), *The Black Unicorn* (1978), and *Our Dead behind Us* (1986). A collection of essays and speeches, *Sister Outsider* (1984), provides a powerful context for reading her work. Her autobiographical writing includes *The Cancer Journals* (1980) and *Zami: A New Spelling of My Name* (1982).

Critical studies of Lorde's work appear in *Black Women Writers*, edited by Mari Evans (1984), and Cassie Steele's *We Heal From Memory: Sexton, Lorde, Anzaldúa, and the Poetry of Witness* (2000). An interview with Lorde appears in *Women Writers at Work* (1998), edited by George Plimpton.

Robert Lowell
Lowell's books of verse include *Lord Weary's Castle* (1946), *The Mills of the Kavanaughs* (1951), *Life Studies* (1959), *Imitations* (1961), *For the Union Dead* (1964), *Near the Ocean* (1967), *Notebook* (1969; rev. and exp. 1970), *The Dolphin* (1973), *For Lizzie and Harriet* (1973), and *History* (1973). For the stage Lowell adapted Racine's *Phaedra* (1961) and Aeschylus's *Prometheus Bound* (1969) as well as versions of Hawthorne and Melville stories grouped under the title *The Old Glory* (1965). His *Collected Prose* (1987) is an indispensable companion to Lowell's poetry and contains valuable essays on the work of other writers.

Among the many useful critical works on Lowell are Stephen Yenser's *Circle to Circle* (1975), Steven Axelrod's *Robert Lowell: Life and Art* (1978), and Thomas Travisano's

Midcentury Quartet (1999). *Robert Lowell: A Collection of Critical Essays* (1968), edited by Thomas Parkinson, includes an important interview with the poet, and *The Critical Response to Robert Lowell* (1999), edited by Steven Gould Axelrod, provides an overview of criticism on the work. A partial bibliography of Lowell's work can be found in Jerome Mazzaro's *The Achievement of Robert Lowell, 1939–1959* (1960). Ian Hamilton's biography, *Robert Lowell*, appeared in 1982. An edition of Lowell's letters, edited by Saskia Hamilton, appeared in 2005 and provides a valuable context for his work. *Words in the Air: The Complete Correspondence Between Elizabeth Bishop and Robert Lowell*, edited by Thomas Travisano and Saskia Hamilton (2008), documents one of the great literary friendships in twentieth century poetry.

Bernard Malamud
Malamud's short-story collections are *The Magic Barrel* (1958), *Idiots First* (1963), *Rembrandt's Hat* (1973), and *The Stories of Bernard Malamud* (1983). His novels are *The Natural* (1952), *The Assistant* (1957), *A New Life* (1961), *The Fixer* (1966), *Pictures of Fidelman* (1969), *The Tenants* (1971), *Dubin's Lives* (1979), and *God's Grace* (1982). Robert Giroux has edited his unfinished novel and a number of short fictions (*The People and Uncollected Stories*, 1990), together with *The Complete Stories* (1997). Alan Cheuse and Nicholas Delbanco edited *Talking Horse: Bernard Malamud on Life and Work* (1996).

A comprehensive overview of Malamud's works and their place in the American tradition is provided by Edward A. Abramson in *Bernard Malamud Revisited* (1993). Sanford Pinsker's *Jewish-American Fiction, 1917–1987* (1992) examines the author's specifically Jewish-American contribution. Editor Evelyn Avery's *The Magic Worlds of Bernard Malamud* (2001) presents seventeen critical essays. Janice Malamud has written *My Father Is a Book: A Memoir of Bernard Malamud* (2006), and Donald Weber has authored a comprehensive bibliography, *Bernard Malamud: A Writer's Life* (2007). Rita N. Kosofsky has compiled *Bernard Malamud: A Descriptive Bibliography* (1991).

Thomas McGuane
The Sporting Club (1969), *The Bushwacked Piano* (1971), *Ninety-Two in the Shade* (1973), *Panama* (1978), *Nobody's Angel* (1982), *Something to Be Desired* (1984), *Keep the Change* (1989), *Nothing But Blue Skies* (1992), *The Cadence of Grass* (2002), and *Driving on the Rim* (2010) are novels. *To Skin a Cat* (1986) and *Gallatin Canyon* (2006) are short-story

collections. McGuane's essays appear in *An Outside Chance* (1980, expanded in 1990), *Some Horses* (1999), and *The Longest Silence: A Life in Fiction* (1999).

Jerome Klinkowitz studies McGuane's fiction in *The New American Novel of Manners: The Fiction of Richard Yates, Dan Wakefield, and Thomas McGuane* (1986). Beef Torrey collects a wide range of interviews in *Conversations with Thomas McGuane* (2007).

James Merrill
An edition of Merrill's *Collected Poems* (2001), edited by J. D. McClatchy and Stephen Yenser, brings together the poems from all of Merrill's books, with the exception of his book-length epic, *The Changing Light at Sandover* (1982). Merrill also published a prose collection, *Recitative* (1986); a charming memoir, *A Different Person* (1993); two novels, *The Seraglio* (1957) and *The (Diblos) Notebook* (1965); and three plays: *The Immortal Husband* (1956), *The Bait* (1960), and *The Image Maker* (1986).

Useful critical essays appear in David Kalstone's *Five Temperaments* (1977), *James Merrill: Essays in Criticism* (1983), edited by Lehman and Berger, and *Critical Essays on James Merrill* (1996), edited by Guy Rotella. Stephen Yenser's book-length study of Merrill's work, *The Consuming Myth* (1987), is invaluable. More recent critical work includes Timothy Materer's *James Merrill's Apocalypse* (2000) and Rachel Hadas's *Merrill, Cavafy, Poems, and Dreams* (2000).

W. S. Merwin
Merwin's *Collected Poems* appeared in 1988, as did his volume *The Rain in the Trees*. *Collected Poems* gathers work from many important volumes, including *The Drunk in the Furnace* (1960), *The Moving Target* (1963), *The Lice* (1967), *The Carrier of Ladders* (1970), *Writings to an Unfinished Accompaniment* (1974), and *The Compass Flower* (1977). *The First Four Books of Poems* appeared in 2000. *The Miner's Pale Children* (1970) is an important prose collection. Merwin's more recent collections of poems are *Travels* (1992), *The Vixen* (1997), *The River Sound* (1999), *The Pupil* (2001), *Migration* (2005), *Present Company* (2005), and *The Shadow of Sirius*. Merwin also published an autobiographical prose collection, *Unframed Original* (1982), and *Regions of Memory* (1987), which combines memoir and commentary on the work of poetry. The book-length poem *Folding Cliffs: A Narrative* (1988) is a chronicle of nineteenth-century Hawaii.

Various critical essays on Merwin's work are gathered in *W. S. Merwin: Essays on the Poetry* (1987), edited by Cary Nelson and Ed

Folsom. A valuable book-length study of Merwin's poetry is Edward J. Brunner's *Poetry as Labor and as Privilege* (1991). Also useful is Jane Frazier's *From Origin to Ecology: Nature and the Poetry of W. S. Merwin* (1999).

Arthur Miller

Miller's earlier plays—*All My Sons, Death of a Salesman, The Crucible, A Memory of Two Mornings,* and *A View from the Bridge*—are brought together in Arthur Miller's *Collected Plays* (1957), which also includes a lengthy and useful introduction. Later dramas are available in *Collected Plays, 1957–1981* (1981) and thereafter separately, including *Danger, Memory!* (1987), *The Archbishop's Ceiling: The American Clock* (1989), *The Ride Down Mt. Morgan* (1992), *Broken Glass* (1994), *The Last Yankee* (1994), and *The Price* (2002). *Focus* (1945) is a novel; short fiction is collected in *The Misfits and Other Stories* (1987), *Homely Girl, a Life, and Other Stories* (1997), and *Presence* (2007); *The Misfits* (1961) is a screenplay. *Echoes Down the Corridor: Collected Essays, 1944–2000* appeared in 2000. Harold Clurman edited *The Portable Arthur Miller* in 1971, and Robert A. Martin edited *The Theater Essays of Arthur Miller* in 1978. Miller published an account of the production of *Death of a Salesman* in China in 1984 and an autobiography, *Timebends: A Life,* in 1987.

Martin Gottfried's *Arthur Miller: His Life and Work* (2003) is the major biography. The best recent analysis of Miller's work is found in Christopher Bigsby's *Arthur Miller, 1915–1962* (2010), supplemented by Bigsby's *Arthur Miller: A Critical Study* (2005) and his edited *The Cambridge Companion to Arthur Miller* (1997). Also helpful are the materials commissioned by Steven R. Centola for the edited volume *The Achievement of Arthur Miller: New Essays* (1995). Specifics are handled by Brenda Murphy in *Miller: Death of a Salesman* (1995), by Matthew C. Rodané in *Approaches to Teaching Miller's* Death of a Salesman (1995), and in the materials edited by Eric J. Sterling for *Arthur Miller's* Death of a Salesman (2008).

N. Scott Momaday

Momaday's autobiographical works begin with *The Journey to Tai-me* (1967) and continue with *The Way to Rainy Mountain* (1969) and *The Names: A Memoir* (1976), supplemented by *The Man Made of Words: Essays, Stories, Passages* (1997). *House Made of Dawn* (1968), *The Ancient Child* (1989), and *In the Bear's House* (1999) are novels. In 1999 he published *Circle of Wonder: A Native American Christmas Story.* His poems appear in *Angle of Geese* (1974), *Before an Old Painting of the Crucifixion, Carmel Mission, June 1960* (1975), and *The Gourd Dancer* (1976). *In the Presence of the Sun: Stories and Poems 1961–1991* was published in 1992 with illustrations by the author. *Three Plays: The Indolent Boys, Children of the Sun, The Moon in Two Windows* appeared in 2008. Momaday has also written books for children, edited editions of writers, and written the commentary for photographer David Muench's *Colorado: Summer, Fall, Winter, Spring* (1973).

Book-length studies of Momaday include *N. Scott Momaday: The Cultural and Literary Background* (1985) by Matthias Schubnell and *Reading, Learning, and Teaching N. Scott Momaday* (2007) by Jim Charles. Of the many interviews with Momaday, early and worthy is Joseph Bruchac's "The Magic of Words: An Interview with N. Scott Momaday," in *Survival This Way: Interviews with American Indian Poets* (1987), edited by Bruchac. Louis Owens's "N. Scott Momaday," in *This Is about Vision: Interviews with Southwestern Writers* (1990), edited by William Balassi, John F. Crawford, and Annie O. Eysturoy, also offers quite a good interview. Kenneth M. Roemer edited *Approaches to Teaching Momaday's "The Way to Rainy Mountain"* (1988), which is useful. Arnold Krupat's *The Voice in the Margin: Native American Literature and the Canon* (1989) compares autobiographical writing of Momaday and Leslie Marmon Silko. Susan Scarberry-Garcia's *Landmarks of Healing: A Study of "House Made of Dawn"* (1990,) fills in some of the multitribal mythic context. Gerald Vizenor edited *Narrative Chance: Postmodern Discourse on Native American Indian Literatures* (1989), with three articles on Momaday. A fine account, focused on *House Made of Dawn,* is in Louis Owens's *Other Destinies: Understanding the American Indian Novel* (1992), supplemented by Scott B. Vickers's work in *Native American Identities* (1998).

Toni Morrison

Morrison's novels are *The Bluest Eye* (1970), *Sula* (1974), *Song of Solomon* (1977), *Tar Baby* (1981), *Beloved* (1987), *Jazz* (1992), *Paradise* (1998), *Love* (2003), and *A Mercy* (2008). A play, *Dreaming Emmett,* was produced in 1986. Morrison is the author of *Playing in the Dark: Whiteness and the Literary Imagination* (1992) and editor of *Raceing Justice, Engendering Power: Essays on Anita Hill, Clarence Thomas, and the Construction of Social Reality* (1992). Her *Lecture and Speech of Acceptance upon the Award of the Nobel Prize for Literature* was published in 1994.

Book-length studies include Trudier Harris's *Fictions and Folklore: The Novels of Toni Morrison* (1991), Denise Heinze's *The Dilemma of*

"Double-Consciousness": Toni Morrison's Novels (1993), Gurleen Grewal's Circles of Sorrow, Lines of Struggle (1998), John N. Duvall's The Identifying Fictions of Toni Morrison (2000), J. Brooks Bouson's Quiet As It's Kept (2000), Andrea Reilly's Toni Morrison and Motherhood (2004). Susan Neal Mayberry's Can't Love What I Criticize: The Masculine and Morrison (2007), Karen F. Stein's Reading, Learning, Teaching Toni Morrison (2009), K. Zauditu-Salassie's African Spiritual Traditions in the Novels of Toni Morrison (2009), and Evelyn Jaffe Schreiber's Race, Trauma, and Home in the Novels of Toni Morrison (2010). In Deans and Truants: Race and Realism in African American Literature (2007) Gene Andrew Jarrett pays close attention to "Recitatif." Henry Louis Gates Jr. and K. A. Appiah have edited Toni Morrison: Critical Perspectives Past and Present (1993). Toni Morrison: An Annotated Bibliography (1987) has been compiled by David L. Middleton.

Flannery O'Connor

O'Connor's novels and stories (edited by Sally Fitzgerald) are a volume in the Library of America series (1988). Her novels are Wise Blood (1952) and The Violent Bear It Away (1960). Two collections of stories, A Good Man Is Hard to Find (1955) and Everything That Rises Must Converge (1965), are included with earlier uncollected stories in Complete Stories (1971). Her letters are collected in The Habit of Being: The Letters of Flannery O'Connor (1979). The Presence of Grace, and Other Book Reviews (1983) collects some of her critical prose, as does Mystery and Manners (1969), edited by Sally Fitzgerald and Robert Fitzgerald.

Jean W. Cash provides a biography in Flannery O'Connor: A Life (2003), as does Brad Gooch in Flannery (2009). Studies of O'Connor's fiction include Jon Lance Bacon's Flannery O'Connor and Cold War Culture (1993), Lorine M. Gertz's Flannery O'Connor, Literary Theologian (2000), Richard Giannone's Flannery O'Connor, Hermit Novelist (2000), Sarah Gordon's Flannery O'Connor: The Obedient Imagination (2000), Flannery O'Connor's Radical Reality (2006), edited by Jan Nordby Grettund and Karl-Heinz Westarp, and Donald E. Hardy's The Body in Flannery O'Connor's Fiction (2007). Flannery O'Connor: A Descriptive Bibliography (1981) was compiled by David Farmer.

Frank O'Hara

The Collected Poems of Frank O'Hara was published in 1971. It has since been supplemented by Early Poems (1977) and Poems Retrieved (1977), O'Hara's critical articles and other prose can be found in Art Chronicles 1954–1966 (1975), Standing Still and Walking in New York (1975), and In Memory of My Feelings: Frank O'Hara on American Art (1999), edited by Russell Ferguson.

David Lehman's The Last Avant-Garde: The Making of the New York School of Poets (1998) provides valuable contexts for O'Hara's work. An informative critical study is Marjorie Perloff's Frank O'Hara: Poet among Painters (1977). Also useful is Mutlu Konuk Biasing's Politics and Form in Postmodern Poetry (1995).

Sharon Olds

Olds's poetry collections include One Secret Thing (2008) and Strike Sparks: Selected Poems 1980–2002 (2004), which brings together work from Satan Says (1980), The Dead and the Living (1984), The Gold Cell (1987), The Father (1993), The Wellspring (1996), Blood, Tin, Straw (1999), and The Unswept Room (2002). Olds is a gifted teacher and her Judith Stonach Memorial Lecture on the Teaching of Poetry, What Does an Elegy Do?, was published in book form in 2010. An informative interview with Olds appears in the online journal Salon (1999) at www.salon.com. Alicia Ostriker discusses Olds's erotic discourse in Dancing at the Devil's Party: Essays on Poetry, Politics, and the Erotic (2000).

Mary Oliver

Volumes 1 (2004) and 2 (2005) of New and Selected Poems contain selections from No Voyage and Other Poems (1963 and 1965), The River Styx, Ohio, and Other Poems (1972), Sleeping in the Forest and The Night Traveler (both 1978), Twelve Moons (1979), American Primitive (1983), Dream Work (1986), House of Light (1990), and later collections including White Pine: Poems and Prose Poems (1994), Blue Pastures (1995), West Wind (1997), Winter Hours: Prose, Prose Poems, and Poems (1999), The Leaf and the Cloud (2000), Why I Wake Early (2004), Thirst (2006), Red Bird (2008), and Evidence (2009). Oliver also wrote a guide to poetry, A Poetry Handbook (1994), and a collection Long Life: Essays and Other Writings (2004).

Critical discussion of Oliver's work appears in Christina Hendricks's Language and Liberation (1999).

Charles Olson

The best single introduction to Olson is Robert Creeley's Selected Writings of Charles Olson (1967). A complete edition of The Maximus Poems, edited by George F. Butterick, appeared in 1983. The Collected Poems, edited by George Butterick, appeared in 1987. Among Olson's many prose works are his study of Melville, Call Me Ishmael (1947); Mayan Letters (1953); and a two-volume collection of his lectures and interviews, *Mathologos* (1976–79), edited by George F. Butterick. An edition of Olson's *Collected Prose*, edited by Donald Allen, appeared in 1997. The seven volumes of *Charles Olson and Robert Creeley: The Complete Correspondence* (1980–86), edited by Butterick, provide as extensive a discussion of life and poetry as we are ever likely to see.

Among the critical studies of Olson's poetry, some of the most useful are Ed Dorn's *What I See in the Maximus Poems* (1960), Sherman Paul's *Olson's Push* (1978), Robert von Hallberg's *Charles Olson: The Scholar's Art* (1978), and Stephen Fredman's *The Grounding of American Poetry: Charles Olson and the Emersonian Tradition* (1993). For any reader of the *Maximus Poems*, Butterick's *A Guide to the Maximus Poems* (1981) is indispensable. Various "Charles Olson Issues" appeared in the journal *Boundary* 2 (1973–74).

Simon J. Ortiz

Ortiz's collections are *Naked in the Wind* (1970), *Going for Rain* (1976), *A Good Journey* (1977), *Song, Poetry, Language* (1978), *From Sand Creek: Rising in This Heart Which Is Our America* (1981), *A Poem Is a Journey* (1981), and *After and before Lightning* (1994). His work has been gathered in the volume *Woven Stone* (1992). His short-story collections are *Howbah Indians* (1978), *Fightin': New and Collected Stories* (1983), and *Men on the Moon: Collected Short Stories* (1999). He also edited two collections, *These Hearts, These Poems* (1984) and *Speaking for the Generations: Native Writers on Writing* (1998).

A discussion of Ortiz's poetry appears in Kenneth Lincoln's *Native American Renaissance* (1983) and in Lucy Maddox's "Native American Poetry" in *The Columbia History of American Poetry* (1993).

Grace Paley

The Collected Stories (1994) draw on Paley's three major volumes of short fiction: *The Little Disturbances of Man* (1959), *Enormous Changes at the Last Minute* (1974), and *Later the Same Day* (1985). Other stories and poems appear (with paintings by Vera B. Williams) in *Long Walks and Intimate Talks* (1991) *Begin Again: Collected Poems* (2000) brings together the work from Paley's two earlier volumes, *Leaning Forward* (1885) and *New and Collected Poems* (1992). *Just As I Thought* (1998) collects Paley's essays. With Robert Nichols she published *Here and Somewhere Else: Stories and Poems* (2007). *Fidelity* (2008) was her last volume of poetry.

The three major studies of Paley's fiction are *Grace Paley's Life Stories: A Literary Biography* (1993) by Judith Arcana, *Grace Paley: A Study of the Short Fiction* (1990) by Neil D. Isaacs, and *Grace Paley: Illuminating the Dark Lives* (1990) by Jacqueline Taylor.

Robert Pinsky

Pinsky's *The Figured Wheel: New and Collected Poems 1966–1996* (1996) gathers work from *Sadness and Happiness* (1975), *An Explanation of America* (1980), *History of My Heart* (1984), and *The Want Bone* (1990), as well as presenting new poems and selections from his translations. His collections *Jersey Rain* appeared in 2000 and *Gulf Rain* in 2007. He has published two book-length translations the prize-winning *The Inferno of Dante: A New Verse Translation* (1994) and, together with Robert Hass, a translation of the Polish poet Czeslaw Milosz's *The Separate Notebook* (1984). Pinsky's two volumes of criticism, *The Situation of Poetry: Contemporary Poetry and Its Traditions* (1975) and *Poetry and the World* (1988), illuminate his work as well as that of the writers he discusses. He is also the author of *The Sounds of Poetry* (1998) and *Democracy, Culture, and the Voice of Poetry* (2002). Pinsky edited the collection *America's Favorite Poems* (1999).

Sylvia Plath

Plath's books of poetry include *The Colossus and Other Poems* (1962), *Ariel* (1966), *Crossing the Water* (1971), and *Winter Trees* (1972). Her novel *The Bell Jar* was first published in England in 1963. Plath's mother, Aurelia Schober Plath, selected and edited the useful *Letters Home: Correspondence 1950–63* (1975). Karen Kukil edited *The Unabridged Journals of Sylvia Plath, 1950–1962* (2000). Among the biographical and critical studies of Plath's work are Judith Kroll's *Chapters in a Mythology* (1976), Anne Stevenson's *Bitter Fame: The Undiscovered Life of Sylvia Plath* (1988), Linda Wagner-Martin's *Sylvia Plath: A Biography* (1987), Jacqueline Rose's *The Haunting of Sylvia Plath* (1993), Diane Middlebrook's *Sylvia Plath* (1998), and Christina Britzolakis's *Sylvia Plath and the Theatre of Mourning* (1999). *The Cambridge Introduction to Sylvia Plath*, by Jo Gill, appeared in 2008.

Richard Powers

Powers has published ten novels: *Three Farmers on Their Way to a Dance* (1985), *Prisoner's Dilemma* (1988), *The Gold Bug Variations* (1991), *Operation Wandering Soul* (1993), *Galatea 2.2* (1995), *Gain* (1998), *Plowing the Dark* (2000), *In the Time of Our Singing* (2003), *The Echo Maker* (2006), and *Generosity* (2009).

A special issue of the *Review of Contemporary Fiction* (Fall 1998) is devoted to the study of Powers's work. Joseph Dewey's *Understanding Richard Powers* (2002) is comprehensive, while an extensive discussion of *Galatea 2.2* forms part of Arthur Saltzman's *This Mad "Instead": Governing Metaphors in Contemporary American Fiction* (2000). Stephen J. Burn has edited *Intersections: Essays on Richard Powers* (2008).

Thomas Pynchon

Pynchon's novels are *V.* (1963), *The Crying of Lot 49* (1966), *Gravity's Rainbow* (1973), *Vineland* (1990), *Mason & Dixon* (1997), *Against the Day* (2006) and *Inherent Vice* (2009). *Slow Learner* (1984) collects early stories.

Book-length studies are William M. Plater's *The Grim Phoenix: Reconstructing Thomas Pynchon* (1978), Thomas H. Schaub's *Pynchon, The Voice of Ambiguity* (1981), and David Seed's *The Fictional Labyrinths of Thomas Pynchon* (1988). Alan N. Brownlie studies the author's first three novels in *Thomas Pynchon's Narratives: Subjectivity and the Problems of Knowing* (2000), while the fourth and fifth novels are analyzed in Geoffrey Green, Donald J. Greiner, and Larry McCaffery's edited *The Vineland Papers* (1993) and Brooke Horvath and Irving Malin's edited *Pynchon and Mason & Dixon* (2000), respectively. New critical essays are collected by Niran Abbas in *Thomas Pynchon: Reading from The Margins* (2003) and Ian D. Copestake in *American Postmodernity: Essays on the Recent Fiction of Thomas Pynchon* (2003). The author's work is integrated with the canon by John A. McClure in *Partial Faiths: Postmodern Fiction in the Age of Pynchon and Morrison* (2007).

Ishmael Reed

Reed's novels are *The Free-Lance Pallbearers* (1967), *Yellow Back Radio Broke-Down* (1969), *Mumbo Jumbo* (1972), *The Last Days of Louisiana Red* (1974), *Flight to Canada* (1976), *The Terrible Twos* (1982), *Reckless Eyeballing* (1986), *The Terrible Threes* (1989), *Japanese by Spring* (1993), and *Juice!* (2011). His poetry collections are *catechism of d neoamerican hoodoo church* (1970), *Conjure: Selected Poems, 1963–1970* (1972), *Chattanooga* (1973), *A Secretary to the Spirits* (1978), and *New and Collected Poems* (2006). Reed's essays are gathered in *Shrovetide in Old New Orleans* (1978), *God Made Alaska for the Indians* (1982), *Writin' Is Fightin'* (1988), *Airing Dirty Laundry* (1993), *Another Day at the Front: Dispatches from the Race War* (2003), *Mixing It Up* (2008), and *Barack Obama and the Jim Crow Media* (2010). The narrative Reed defines as a fetish was published in 1986 as *Cab Calloway Stands In for the Moon*. He has edited several anthologies, among them *19 Necromancers from Now* (1980), *Yardbird Lives!* (1978), and *The Before Columbus Foundation Fiction and Poetry Anthologies* (1992).

Jay Boyer's booklet *Ishmael Reed* (1993) is a good introduction; Patrick McGhee's *Ishmael Reed and the Ends of Race* (1997) is focused on matters of gender and race. More theoretically inclined is *Ishmael Reed and the New Black Aesthetic* (1988) by Reginald Martin. Reed's position as a polemicist is studied by Jerome Klinkowitz in *Literary Subversions* (1985). Reed's spiritualism and innovations are explored by Pierre-Damien Myuyekure in *The "Dark Heathenism" of the American Novelist Ismael Reed: African Voodoo as American Literary HooDoo* (2007). Elizabeth A. Settle and Thomas A. Settle have compiled *Ishmael Reed: A Primary and Secondary Bibliography* (1982).

Adrienne Rich

The Fact of a Doorframe: Poems 1950–2001 (2002) draws from *A Change of World* (1951), *The Diamond Cutters* (1955), *Snapshots of a Daughter-in-Law* (1963), *Necessities of Life* (1966), *Leaflets* (1969), *The Will to Change* (1971), *Diving into the Wreck* (1973), *The Dream of a Common Language* (1978), *A Wild Patience Has Taken Me This Far* (1981), *Your Native Land, Your Life* (1986), *Time's Power: Poems 1985–1988* (1989), *An Atlas of the Difficult World: Poems 1988–1991* (1991), *Dark Fields of the Republic: Poems 1991–1995* (1995), *Midnight Salvage: Poems 1995–1998* (1999), *Fox: Poems 1998–2000* (2001), *The School among the Ruins: 2000–2004* (2004), and *Telephone Ringing in the Labyrinth: Poems 2004–2006* (2007). Four valuable collections gather Rich's essays, lectures, and speeches: *On Lies, Secrets, and Silence* (1979), *Blood, Bread, and Poetry* (1986), *What Is Found There?: Notebooks on Poetry and Politics* (1993), *Arts of the Possible* (2001), *Poetry and Commitment: An Essay* (2007), and *A Human Eye: Essays in Art in Society* (2009). Rich is also the author of an important study, *Of Woman Born: Motherhood as Experience and Institution* (1976).

Valuable critical essays and an interview appear in *Adrienne Rich's Poetry* (1975), edited by Barbara Charlesworth Gelpi and Albert Gelpi. Other studies are *Reading Adrienne Rich* (1984), edited by Jane Roberta Cooper; Paula Bennett's *My Life, a Loaded Gun: Female Creativity and Feminist Poetics* (1986); Margaret Dickie's *Stein, Bishop, & Rich: Lyrics of Love, War, & Place* (1997); and Molly McQuade's *By Herself: Women Reclaim Poetry* (2000).

Alberto Ríos

Ríos's poetry collections are *Whispering to Fool the Wind* (1982), *Five Indiscretions* (1985), *The Dime Orchard Woman* (1988), *Teodora Luna's Two Kisses* (1992), *The Small-*

est *Muscle in the Human Body* (2002), *The Theater of Night* (2006), and *The Dangerous Shirt* (2009). His short-story collections are *The Iguana Killer* (1984) and *The Curtain of Trees* (1999). His memoir, *Capirodata: A Nogales Memoir*, appeared in 1999.

A discussion of Ríos's work and the larger contexts of Latino poetry appears in Cordelia Candelaria, *Chicano Poetry: A Critical Introduction* (1986). An interview with Ríos can be found in *Americas Review* (1996).

Theodore Roethke

The Collected Poems of Theodore Roethke was published in 1966. *Dirty Dinkey and Other Creatures: Poems for Children*; edited by B. Roethke and Stephen Lushington, appeared in 1973. Useful comments on poetic tradition and his own poetic practice are to be found in several collections of Roethke's prose: *On the Poet and His Craft: Selected Prose of Theodore Roethke* (1965), edited by Ralph J. Mills Jr.; *Straw for the Fire: From the Notebooks of Theodore Roethke, 1948–63* (1972), edited by David Wagoner; and *The Selected Letters of Theodore Roethke* (1970), edited by Mills.

Among the useful studies of Roethke's work are *Theodore Roethke: Essays on the Poetry* (1965), edited by Arnold Stein, and Laurence Lieberman's *Beyond the Muse of Memory: Essays on Contemporary Poets* (1995). Allan Seager's *The Glass House* (1968) contains useful biographical material.

Philip Roth

Roth's fiction consists of *Goodbye, Columbus* (1959)—a novella and five short stories—and the following novels: *Letting Go* (1962), *When She Was Good* (1967), *Portnoy's Complaint* (1969), *Our Gang* (1971), *The Breast* (1972), *The Great American Novel* (1973), *My Life as a Man* (1974), *The Professor of Desire* (1977), *The Ghost Writer* (1979), *Zuckerman Unbound* (1981), *The Anatomy Lesson* (1983), *The Counterlife* (1987), *Deception* (1990), *Operation Shylock* (1993), *Sabbath's Theater* (1995), *American Pastoral* (1997), *I Married a Communist* (1998), *The Human Stain* (2000), *The Dying Animal* (2001), *The Plot against America* (2004), *Everyman* (2006) *Exit Ghost* (2007), *Indignation* (2008), *The Humbling* (2009), and *Nemesis* (2010). *Reading Myself and Others* (1975) is a collection of essays and interviews. *The Facts: A Novelist's Autobiography* (1988) is Roth's memoir. A memoir of his father, *Patrimony*, was published in 1991.

Philip Roth (1982) by Hermione Lee is an excellent introduction, as is *Understanding Philip Roth* (1990) by Murray Baumgarten and Barbara Gottfried. *Philip Roth and the Jews* (1996) by Alan Cooper considers religious and cultural dimensions of the author's work. The broad sweep of Roth's career is covered by James D. Bloom in *The Literary Bent* (1997), by Mark Shechner in *Up Society's Ass, Copper: Reading Philip Roth* (2003), and by Deborah Shostak in *Philip Roth—Countertexts, Counterhues* (2004). Elaine B. Safer's *Mocking the Age: The Later Novels of Philip Roth* (2006) discusses his experiments in narrative, while Ross Posnock handles controversy in *Philip Roth's Rude Truth* (2005). David Bramer provides an overview in *Philip Roth* (2007).

Kay Ryan

Ryan's collection of verse include *Dragon Acts to Dragon Ends* (1983), *Strangely Marked Metal* (1985), *Flamingo Watching* (1994), *Elephant Rocks* (1996), *Say Uncle* (2000), *The Niagara River* (2005), *Jam Jar Lifeboat & Other Novelties Exposed: Second Edition*, with illustrations by Carl Dern (2008). A collection of new and selected poems, *The Best of It*, appeared in 2010. An extremely useful interview appears in "The Art of Poetry No. 94: Kay Ryan," *The Paris Review* (Winter 2008), available online at www.theparisreview.org. Dana Gioia's "Discovering Kay Ryan" appeared in *The Dark Horse* 7 (Winter 1998–99).

Anne Sexton

Sexton's books of poems include *To Bedlam and Part Way Back* (1960), *All My Pretty Ones* (1962), *Live or Die* (1966), *Love Poems* (1969), *Transformations* (1971), *The Book of Folly* (1973), *The Death Notebooks* (1974), and *The Awful Rowing toward God* (1975). *Complete Poems* appeared in 1981.

Diane Wood Middlebrook's biography, *Anne Sexton* (1991), and Sexton's *A Self-Portrait in Letters* (1977) give useful biographical material. Important interviews and critical essays are to be found in J. D. McClatchy's *Anne Sexton: The Artist and Her Critics* (1978) and Diane Hume George's *Sexton: Selected Criticism* (1988). An interview with Sexton appears in *Women Writers at Work* (1998), edited by George Plimpton.

Sam Shepard

Shepard's major plays are *Cowboys* (1964), *The Rock Garden* (1964), *4-H Club* (1965), *Up to Thursday* (1965), *Dog* (1965), *Chicago* (1965), *Icarus's Mother* (1965), *Fourteen Hundred Thousand* (1966), *Red Cross* (1966), *La Turista* (1967), *The Unseen Hand* (1969), *Holy Ghost* (1970), *Operation Sidewinder* (1970), *The Tooth of Crime* (1972), *Curse of the Starving Class* (1978), *Buried Child* (1979), *True West* (1980), *Fool for Love* (1983), *A Lie of the Mind* (1985), *States of Shock* (1991), *Simpatico* (1995), *Eyes for Consuela* (1998), *The Late Henry Moss* (2002), and *The God of Hell* (2004). His major film scripts are *Zabriskie*

Point (1970), *Paris, Texas* (1984), *Fool for Love* (1985), *Far North* (1988), and *Don't Come Knocking* (2005). *Hawk Moon: A Book of Short Stories, Poems, and Monologues* (1973), *Rolling Thunder Logbook* (1977), *Motel Chronicles* (1982), *Cruising Paradise: Tales* (1996), *Great Dream of Heaven: Stories* (2002), and *Day Out of Days: Stories* (2010). are important nondramatic additions to his canon.

Shepard's place in theatrical history is assessed by Robert J. Andreach in *Creating the Self in the Contemporary American Theatre* (1998). Richard Gilman provides a helpful analysis of the playwright's career in his introduction to Shepard's *Seven Plays* (1981). Also helpful are Doris Auerbach's *Sam Shepard, Arthur Kopit, and the Off Broadway Theater* (1982), Laura Graham's *Sam Shepard: Theme, Image, and the Director* (1995), Lynda Hart's *Sam Shepard's Metaphorical Stages* (1987), Kimball King's *Sam Shepard: A Casebook* (1988), and Ron Mottram's *Inner Landscapes: The Theater of Sam Shepard* (1984).

Leslie Marmon Silko

Silko's novels are *Ceremony* (1977), *Almanac of the Dead* (1991), and *Gardens in the Dunes* (1999). *Storyteller* (1981) includes prose poems and related short stories. *Laguna Woman* (1974), *Voices Under One Sky* (1994), and *Rain* (1996) are books of poetry. *Yellow Woman and a Beauty of the Spirit* (1996) consists of Silko's essays on contemporary Native American life. *Lullaby*, coauthored with Frank Chin, was dramatically adapted and produced in San Francisco in 1976. *The Delicacy and Strength of Lace*, a collection of letters between Silko and the poet James Wright, edited by Anne Wright, was published in 1985. Silko's work also appeared in *Yellow Woman* (1993), edited by Melody Graulich.

Leslie Mormon Silko (1980) by Per Seyersted is an introduction to her work. *Four American Indian Literary Masters* (1982) by Alan R. Veile is also relevant, as are Louise K. Barnett and James L. Thorson's edited *Leslie Marmon Silko* (1999), Catherine Rainwater's *Dreams of Fiery Stars* (1999), Rosemary A. King's *Border Influences from the Mexican War to the Present* (2001), and Claudia Sadowsky-Smith's *Border Fictions* (2008).

Charles Simic

Simic's collections include *My Noiseless Entourage* (2005), *Selected Poems: 1963–2003* (2004), *The Voice at 3:00 A.M.: Selected Late and New Poems* (2003), *Night Picnic* (2001), *Jackstraws* (1999), *Walking the Black Cat* (1996), *A Wedding in Hell* (1994), *Hotel Insomnia* (1992), *The Book of Gods and Devils* (1990), and *Unending Blues* (1986). *Selected Poems 1963–1983* (1990) gathers much of his

earlier work. A book of prose poems, *The World Doesn't End*, appeared in 1990; another one, *Dimestore Alchemy: The Art of Joseph Cornell*, in 1992. He has published several volumes of essays and memoirs, which provide valuable contexts for reading his poetry; among these are *A Fly in the Soup: Memoirs* (2001), *The Orphan Factory: Essays and Memoirs* (1998), *The Unemployed Fortune Teller: Essays and Memoirs* (1994), *Wonderful Words, Silent Truths: Essays* (1990), and *The Uncertain Certainty: Interviews, Essays and Notes on Poetry* (1985). An example of Simic's work as a translator is Vasko Popa's *Homage to the Lame Wolf: Selected Poems 1956–1975* (1979). Critical discussions of Simic's poetry can be found in Bruce Weigl's *Charles Simic: Essays on the Poetry* (1996) and Peter Stitt's *Uncertainty and Plentitude: Five Contemporary Poets* (1997).

Gary Snyder

Snyder's poems have been published by several different presses, often with duplication of poems. *Riprap*, originally published in 1959, is most easily obtained in *Riprap and Cold Mountain Poems* (1965, 1991). *Myths and Texts* first appeared in 1960. *The Blue Sky* first appeared in 1969 and reappeared in *Six Sections of Mountains and Rivers without End plus One* (1970). Other volumes include *The Back Country* (1968), *Regarding Wave* (1970), *Turtle Island* (1974), *Axe Handles* (1983), *Left Out in the Rain: New Poems 1947–1985* (1986), *No Nature: New and Selected Poems* (1992), and *Danger on Peaks* (2004). In 1996 Snyder published the completion of *Mountains and Rivers without End*. He has also published important prose collections dealing with ecology, such as *Earth House Hold* (1969) and *A Place in Space: Ethics, Aesthetics, and Watersheds* (1995). A gathering of Snyder's prose and poetry appears in *The Gary Snyder Reader* (1999). *The Real Work: Interviews and Talks 1964–1979*, edited by William Scott McLean, appeared in 1980. Another essay collection, *Back on Fire*, appeared in 2007.

Helpful critical discussion of Snyder's work can be found in Sherman Paul's *In Search of the Primitive* (1986) and Patrick Murphy's *A Place for Wayfaring: The Poetry and Prose of Gary Snyder* (2000). An interview with Snyder appears in the *Paris Review* 141 (1996).

Cathy Song

Song's poetry collections are *Picture Bride* (1983), *Frameless Windows, Squares of Light* (1988), *School Figures* (1994), *The Land of Bliss* (2000), and *Cloud Moving Hands* (2007).

Discussion of Song's work appears in *Conversations and Contestations* (2000), edited by Ruth Hsu and Cynthia Franklin.

Art Spiegelman

Spiegelman's books include *The Complete Mr. Infinity* (1970), *The Viper Vicar of Vice, Villany, and Vickedness* (1972), *Zip-a-Tune and More Melodies* (1972), *Ace Hole, Midget Detective* (1974), *Every Day Has Its Dog* (1979), *Work and Turn* (1979), *Two-Fisted Painters* (1980), *Maus, A Survivor's Tale: My Father Bleeds History* (1986), *Maus II, A Survivor's Tale: And Here My Troubles Began* (1991), *Open Me . . . I'm a Dog!* (1997), *In the Shadow of No Towers* (2004), and *Breakdowns* (2008).

Comic Books as History: The Narrative Art of Jack Jackson, Art Spiegelman, and Harvey Pekar (1989) by Joseph Witek locates Spiegelman's importance in the evolution of underground comics and the graphic novel. A broader view is found in Charles Hatfield's *Alternative Comics: An Emerging Literature* (2005). Alan Rosen analyzes *Maus* in *Sounds of Defiance: The Holocaust, Multilingualism, and the Problem of English* (2005), as do contributors to Jeet Heer and Kent Worcester's *A Comic Studies Reader* (2009).

Amy Tan

Tan's novels are *The Joy Luck Club* (1989), *The Kitchen God's Wife* (1991), *The Hundred Secret Senses* (1995), *The Bonesetter's Daughter* (2001), and *Saving Fish from Drowning* (2005). For children are her *The Moon Lady* (1992) and *The Chinese Siamese Cat* (1994). *Opposite of Fate: A Book of Musings* (2003) is nonfiction.

Critical overviews of Tan and her work are found in E. D. Huntley's *Amy Tan: A Critical Companion* (1998) and Amy Ling's *Between Worlds: Women Writers of Chinese Ancestry* (1990). James Nagel studies *The Joy Luck Club* in *The Contemporary American Short-Story Cycle* (2001), as does Magali Cornier Michael in *New Visions of Community in Contemporary American Fiction* (2006).

John Updike

Updike's novels are *The Poorhouse Fair* (1959), *Rabbit, Run* (1960), *The Centaur* (1963), *Of the Farm* (1965), *Couples* (1968), *Rabbit Redux* (1971), *A Month of Sundays* (1975), *Marry Me* (1976), *The Coup* (1978), *Rabbit Is Rich* (1981), *The Witches of Eastwick* (1984), *Roger's Version* (1986), *S.* (1988), *Rabbit at Rest* (1990), *Memories of the Ford Administration* (1992), *Brazil* (1994), *In the Beauty of the Lilies* (1996), *Toward the End of Time* (1997), *Gertrude and Claudius* (2000), *Seek My Face* (2002), *Villages* (2004), *Terrorist* (2006), and *The Widows of Eastwick* (2008). Collections of short fiction are *The Same Door* (1959), *Pigeon Feathers* (1962), *Olinger Stories: A Selection* (1964), *The Music School* (1966), *Bech: A Book* (1970), *Museums and Women* (1972), *Too Far to Go:*

The Maples Stories (1979), *Problems* (1979), *Bech Is Back* (1982), *Trust Me* (1987), *The Afterlife* (1994), *Bech at Bay* (1998), *Licks of Love* (2000), and *My Father's Tears* (2009). Stories from 1953 to 1975 are presented thematically in *The Early Stories* (2003). Updike's poems are gathered in *Collected Poems 1953–1993* (1993), drawing on the individual volumes *The Carpentered Hen* (1958), *Telephone Poles* (1963), *Midpoint* (1969), *Tossing and Turning* (1977), and *Facing Nature* (1985); *Americana: and Other Poems* (2001) and *Endpoint* (2009) are newer work. Reviews and literary essays appear in *Assorted Prose* (1965, *Picked-Up Pieces* (1975), *Hugging the Shore* (1983), *Odd Jobs* (1991), *More Matter* (1999), and *Due Considerations* (2007). *Self-Consciousness* (1989) is a memoir, *Just Looking* (1989) and *Still Looking* (2005) are art criticism, and *Golf Dreams* (1996) collects the author's essays on his favorite sport. *Buchanan Dying* (1974) is a play meant for reading rather than for stage production. Updike has authored five books for children: *The Magic Flute* (1962), *The Ring* (1964), *A Child's Calendar* (1965), *Bottom's Dream* (1969), and *A Helpful Alphabet of Friendly Objects* (1995).

Donald J. Greiner's thorough examination of the early canon appears in his *John Updike's Novels* (1984) and *The Other John Updike: Poems/Short Stories/Prose/Plays* (1981). Longer views are taken by James A. Schiff in *John Updike Revisited* (1998) and by William Pritchard in *Updike: America's Man of Letters* (2000). Peter J. Bailey pursues theological matters in *Rabbit (Un)Redeemed: The Drama of Belief in John Updike's Fiction* (2006). Jack De Bellis has prepared *The John Updike Encyclopedia* (2007) and (with Michael Broomfield) *John Updike: A Bibliography* (2007). Updike's papers have been deposited in The Houghton Library at Haward University.

Kurt Vonnegut

Vonnegut's novels are *Player Piano* (1952), *The Sirens of Titan* (1959), *Mother Night* (1961), *Cat's Cradle* (1963), *God Bless You, Mr. Rosewater* (1965), *Slaughterhouse-Five* (1969), *Breakfast of Champions* (1973), *Slapstick* (1976) *Jailbird* (1969), *Deadeye Dick* (1982), *Galápagos* (1985), *Bluebeard* (1987), *Hocus Pocus* (1990), and *Timequake* (1997). His short stories are collected in *Canary in a Cat House* (1961), *Welcome to the Monkey House* (1968), and *Bagombo Snuff Box* (1999). His essays fill four volumes: *Wampeters, Foma & Granfalloons* (1974), *Palm Sunday* (1981), *Fates Worse Than Death* (1991), and *A Man Without a Country* (2005). *Happy Birthday, Wanda June* (1971) is a play, while *Between Time and Timbuktu* (1972) is a television script, prefaced by Vonnegut, drawing on his fiction. *Sun/Moon/*

Star (1980), with illustrations by Ivan Chermayeff, is a book for children. *God Bless You, Dr. Kevorkian* (1999) collects Vonnegut's radio satires; *Like Shaking Hands with God* (1999) is his dialogue with social activist Lee Stringer. Noncanonical rejected stories from the early 1950s have been published posthumously as *Armageddon in Retrospect* (2008), *Look at the Birdie* (2009), and *While Mortals Sleep* (2010).

Jerome Klinkowitz surveys Vonnegut's career in *The Vonnegut Effect* (2004), studies his essays in *Vonnegut in Fact* (1998), and undertakes cultural analysis in *Kurt Vonnegut's America* (2009) Specific theses are argued by Leonard Mustazza in *Forever Pursuing Genesis: The Myth of Eden in the Novels of Kurt Vonnegut* (1990), Leonard Broer in *Sanity Plea: Schizophrenia in the Novels of Kurt Vonnegut* (1989, revised 1994), and Todd Davis in *Kurt Vonnegut's Crusade* (2006). A broad sample of criticism is made by editor Leonard Mustazza in *The Critical Response to Kurt Vonnegut* (1994), while Vonnegut's later work (including his public spokesmanship) are examined in *The Vonnegut Chronicles* (1996), edited by Peter J. Reed and Marc Leeds. Loree Rackstraw's *Love As Always, Kurt* (2009) is a memoir. Asa B. Pieratt Jr., Julie Huffman-Klinkowitz, and Jerome Klinkowitz have compiled *Kurt Vonnegut: A Comprehensive Bibliography* (1987).

Alice Walker

Walker's novels are *The Third Life of Grange Copeland* (1970), *Meridian* (1976), *The Color Purple* (1982), *The Temple of My Familiar* (1989), *Possessing the Secret of Joy* (1992), *By the Light of My Father's Smile* (1998), and *Now Is the Time to Open Your Heart* (2004). Her short-story collections are *In Love and Trouble* (1973), *You Can't Keep a Good Woman Down* (1981), and *The Way Forward Is with a Broken Heart* (2000). Poetry collections are *Once* (1986), *Five Poems* (1972), *Revolutionary Petunias* (1973), *Good Night, Willie Lee, I'll See You in the Morning* (1969), *Horses Make a Landscape Look More Beautiful* (1984), *Her Blue Body Everything We Know* (1991), *Absolute Trust in the Goodness of the Earth* (2003), and *A Poem Traveled Down My Arm* (2003). Her *Collected Poems* appeared in 2005. Walker's literary essays are collected in *In Search of Our Mothers' Gardens* (1983), *Living by the Word* (1988), and *Anything We Love Can Be Saved* (2000); she has also written *Warrior Marks: Female Genital Mutilation and the Sexual Blinding of Women* (1987, with Pratibha Parmar), *The Same River Twice: Honoring the Difficult: A Meditation on Life, Spirit, Art, and the Making of the Film* The Color Purple *Ten Years Later* (1996), *We Are the Ones We Have Been Waiting For* (2006), and *Overcoming Speechlessness: A Poet Encounters the Horror in*

Rwanda, Eastern Congo, and Palestine/Israel (2010). Her books for children include an illustrated version of *To Hell with Dying* (1988), *Finding the Green Stone* (1991), and a biography, *Langston Hughes, American Poet* (1974).

Evelyn C. White's *Alice Walker: A Life* (2004) is a comprehensive biography. Good samplings of scholarship on Walker fill two volumes: editors Henry Louis Gates Jr. and K. Anthony Appiah's *Alice Walker: Critical Perspectives Past and Present* (1993) and editor Lillie P. Howard's *Alice Walker and Zora Neale Hurston: The Common Bond* (1993). *Alice Walker* (2000) is Maria Lauret's book-length study.

Robert Penn Warren

An edition of Warren's *Collected Poems*, edited by John Burt, appeared in 1998. It includes work from Warren's volumes *Incarnations* (1968), *Audubon: A Vision* (1969), *Or Else: Poems 1968–1974* (1974), *Now and Then* (1978), *Being Here* (1980), *Rumor Verified* (1981), *Chief Joseph of the Nez Perce* (1983), and *New and Selected Poems 1925–1985* (1985). Burt has also edited a volume of Warren's *Selected Poems* (2001). Warren's best-known novels are *All the King's Men* (1946) and *World Enough and Time* (1950). His Thomas Jefferson Lectures, *Democracy and Poetry*, appeared in 1975. Also available is a collection of interviews, *Robert Penn Warren Talking* (1980), edited by Floyd Watkins and John Tiers.

The best critical studies of Warren's poetry are Calvin Bedient's *In the Heart's Last Kingdom* (1986), James H. Justus's *The Achievement of Robert Penn Warren* (1981), and Victor Stranberg's *The Poetic Vision of Robert Penn Warren*. More-recent critical studies include Lesa Carnes Corrigan's *Poem of Pure Imagination: Robert Penn Warren and the Romantic Tradition* (1999) and *The Legacy of Robert Penn Warren* (2000), edited by David Madden, which gathers essays from various hands.

Eudora Welty

Welty's novels are *The Robber Bridegroom* (1942), *Delta Wedding* (1947), *The Ponder Heart* (1954), *Losing Battles* (1970), and *The Optimist's Daughter* (1972). Her *Collected Stories* (1980) draws from the volumes *A Curtain of Green* (1941), *The Wide Net* (1943), *Music from Spain* (1948), *The Golden Apples* (1949), *The Bride of Innisfallen* (1955), and *Thirteen Stories* (1965). Later volumes are *Moon Lake* (1980) and *Retreat* (1981). *A Flock of Guinea Hens Seen from a Car* (1970) is poetry; among Welty's many volumes of nonfiction prose are *The Eye of the Story: Selected Essays and Reviews* (1978), *One Writer's Beginnings* (1984), and *A Writer's Eye: Collected Book*

Reviews (1994).

Ann Waldron published *Eudora: A Writer's Life* in 1998. Susan Marrs completes the picture in *Eudora Welty: A Biography* (2005) and *One Writer's Imagination: The Fiction of Eudora Welty* (2002). Good introductions are available in Gail Mortimer's *Daughter of the Swan: Love and Knowledge in Eudora Welty's Fiction* (1994), *Eudora Welty's Aesthetics of Place* (1994) by Jan Nordby Gretlund, and Ruth D. Weston's *Gothic Traditions and Narrative Techniques in the Fiction of Eudora Welty* (1994). *Eudora Welty: A Bibliography* by Noel Polk appeared in 1994.

Richard Wilbur

Wilbur's *Collected Poems 1943–2004* (2004) draws from *The Beautiful Changes* (1947), *Ceremony and Other Poems* (1950), *Things of This World* (1956), *Advice to a Prophet* (1961), *Walking to Sleep* (1969), *The Mind-Reader* (1976), and *Mayflies* (2000). His collection *Opposites, More Opposites, and a Few Differences* appeared in 2006. His translations from Molière include *The Misanthrope* (1955), *Tartuffe* (1963), and *Molière: Four Comedies* (1982). He has also published *Responses* (1976) and *The Catbird's Song* (1997), a collection of prose pieces.

Critical discussion of his work can be found in *Richard Wilbur's Creation* (1983), edited by Wendy Salinger, and *Ecstasy Within Discipline: The Poetry of Richard Wilbur* (1995), by John B. Hougen. An essay on Wilbur's new work, by Lee Oser, appears in the journal *Literary Imagination* (2000). A collection of interviews, *Conversations with Richard Wilbur*, edited by William Butts, appeared in 1990.

Tennessee Williams

Most of Williams's plays are collected in the seven-volume *The Theatre of Tennessee Williams* (1971–81). Some later dramas are available in separate editions; a few others are still to be published. Other writings include a novel, *The Roman Spring of Mrs. Stone* (1950); short stories printed in several volumes and finally brought together in *Collected Stories* (1986), edited by Gore Vidal; a volume of screenplays, *Stopped Rocking* (1984); and poems collected as *In the Winter of Cities* (1964) and *Androgyne, Mon Amour* (1977). *Where I Live: Selected Essays*, edited by Christine R. Day and Bob Woods, appeared in 1978.

Williams's *Memoirs* (1975) is interestingly revelatory but is not a reliable biographical guide; neither is Dotson Rader's *Tennessee: Cry of the Heart* (1985). Donald Spoto's *A Kindness of Strangers: The Life of Tennessee Williams* (1985) is workmanlike; a historically sound treatment is *Tennessee Williams: Everyone Else Is an Audience* (1993) by Ronald Hayman. More theoretically inclined is Nicholas Pagan's *Rethinking Literary Biography: A Postmodern Approach* (1993). Judith J. Thompson provides a Jungian analysis of the plays and identifies structural patterns in *Tennessee Williams' Plays: Memory, Myth, and Symbol* (1987, rev. 2002). Time relationships are explored by Patricia Schroeder in *The Presence of the Past in Modern American Drama* (1989). Philip G. Kolin edited *Tennessee Williams: A Guide to Research and Performance* (1998); Matthew C. Rodané prepared *The Cambridge Companion to Tennessee Williams*. George E. Crandell compiled *Tennessee Williams: A Descriptive Bibliography* (1995). *The Selected Letters of Tennessee Williams, Volume I, 1920–1945* (2000) was edited by Albert J. Devlin and Nancy M. Tischler. Margaret Bradham Thornton has edited Williams's *Notebooks* (2007).

August Wilson

Wilson's principal plays are *Ma Rainey's Black Bottom* (1985), *Fences* (1985), *Joe Turner's Come and Gone* (1986). *The Piano Lesson* (1987), *Two Trains Running* (1992), *Jitney* (2004), *Seven Guitars* (1996), *King Hedley II* (2000), *Gem of the Ocean* (2003), and *Radio Golf* (2005). The first three of these have been collected with a preface by Wilson (*Three Plays*, 1991).

August Wilson: Completing the Twentieth-Century Cycle (2010), edited by Alan Nadel, presents essays by various critics covering the breadth of Wilson's cycle of ten plays.

Charles Wright

Negative Blue: Selected Later Poems (2000) brings together Wright's work from *Appalachia* (1998), *Black Zodiac* (1997), and *Chickamauga* (1996). *The World of the Ten Thousand Things: Poems 1980–1990* (1990) includes work from *The Southern Cross* (1981), *The Other Side of the River* (1984), *Zone Journals* (1988), and *Xionia* (1990). *Country Music: Selected Early Poems* (1982, rev. 1991) includes poems from *China Trace* (1977), *Bloodlines* (1975), *Hard Freight* (1973), and *The Grave of the Right Hand* (1970). Recent volumes include *Buffalo Yoga* (2005), *Scar Tissue* (2006), *Littlefoot* (2007), and *Sestets* (2009). Wright's translation of Eugenio Montale's *The Storm and Other Poems* appeared in 1978. Wright's collection *The Wrong End of the Rainbow* appeared in 2005. Some of Wright's essays and interviews are gathered in *Quarter Notes* (1995) and *Halflife* (1988). *The Point Where All Things Meet: Essays on Charles Wright* (1995), edited by Tom Andrews, offers a variety of valuable perspectives on Wright's work. An interview with Wright appears in the journal *Literary Imagination* (2000).

James Wright

Above the River (1990) collects the work in Wright's individual volumes: *The Green Wall* (1956), *Saint Judas* (1963), *Shall We Gather at the River* (1968), *Moments of the Italian Summer* (1976), *To a Blossoming Pear Tree* (1977), and *This Journey* (1982). An edition of his *Collected Prose*, edited by Anne Wright, appeared in 1983. Some of Wright's translations from the Spanish and German are available in *Twenty Poems of Georg Trakl* (1963), *Twenty Poems of Cesar Vallejo* (1964), and *Twenty Poems of Pablo Neruda* (with Robert Bly, 1968).

The best critical discussions of Wright's work appear in the essays collected in *The Pure Clear Word: Essays on the Poetry of James Wright* (1982), edited by Dave Smith, and in Laurence Lieberman's *Beyond the Muse of Memory* (1995). *A Wild Perfection: The Selected Letters of James Wright*, edited by Annie Wright and Saundra Rose Maley, appeared in 2005.

PERMISSIONS ACKNOWLEDGMENTS

IMAGE CREDITS

P. 2: Jackson Pollock, *Autumn Rhythm (Number 30)*; The Metropolitan Museum of Art, George A. Hearn Fund, 1957(57.92) Photograph © 1998 The Metropolitan Museum of Art (c) 2006 The Pollock-Krasner Foundation/Artists Rights Society (ARS), New York; p. 5: Keystone-France/Gamma-Keystone/Getty Images; p. 6: Bettmann/Corbis; p. 8: (SAT EVENING POST) p. 10: Allen Ginsberg/Corbis; p. 14: Christopher Felver/Corbis; p. 51: Courtesy of Eudora Welty, LLC; p. 92: AP Photo; p. 175: Lisa Larsen/Time Life Pictures/Getty Images; p. 207: Yale Collection of American Literature, Beinecke Rare Book and Manuscript Library; p. 237: W. Eugene Smith/Time Life Pictures/Getty Images; p. 373: (left): Richard Petersen/Getty Images; (right): Popperfoto/Getty Images; p. 413: Courtesy of Vassar College Library; p. 491: Jack Manning/The New York Times/Redux; p. 583: AFP/Getty Images; p. 726: © Roy Harte Jazz Archives/CTSIMAGES; p. 834: (c) Mosaic Records; p. 989: THE BOONDOCKS © 2000 Aaron McGruder. Dist. By UNIVERSAL UCLICK. Reprinted with permission. All rights reserved; p. 1195: John Bryson/Sygma/Corbis; p. 1209: Skeet McAuley.

COLOR INSERT CREDITS

C1: Jackson Pollock, *Autumn Rhythm (Number 30)*; The Metropolitan Museum of Art, George A. Hearn Fund, 1957 (57.92) Photograph © 1998 The Metropolitan Museum of Art (c) 2006 The Pollock-Krasner Foundation/Artists Rights Society (ARS), New York; C2: Jeff Albertson/Corbis; C3: Roy Lichtenstein, *Blam*; Yale University Art Gallery, Gift of Richard Brown Baker, BA. 1935, (1995.32.9) (c) 2007 Estate of Roy Lichtenstein; C4: Robert Rauschenberg, Estate Philadelphia Museum of Art/Corbis (c) Robert Rauschenberg/Licensed by VAGA, New York, NY; C5: Andy Warhol, *Campbell's Soup I (Tomato)* 1968; © 2006 Andy Warhol Foundation for the Visual Arts/ARS, New York. Photo: Art Resource, NY; C6: Corbis; C7: Fritz Scholder, *The American Indian* 1970; Indian Arts and Crafts Board Collection, Department of the Interior, Smithsonian National Museum of the American Indian, Washington, DC. Photo by Walter Larrimore; C8: Courtesy of the artist and Metro Pictures; C9: James P. Blair/Corbis; C10: Faith Ringgold (c) 1986; C11: Reuters/Corbis; C12: Christo and Jeanne-Claude The Gates New York City 1979–2005; Photo: Wolfgang Volz (c) Christo 2005 Central Park, New York USA 14.02.2005.

TEXT CREDITS

Edward Abbey: "Havasu" from DESERT SOLITAIRE is reprinted by permission of Don Congdon Associates, Inc. Copyright © 1968 by Edward Abbey, renewed 1996 by Clarke Abbey.

Sherman Alexie: "Crow Testament" from ONE STICK SONG, © 2000 by Sherman Alexie. "Sister Fire, Brother Smoke," #3 from "Tourists," and "The Exaggeration of Despair" from THE SUMMER OF BLACK WIDOWS, © 1996 by Sherman Alexie. "At Navajo Monument Valley Tribal School" and "Pawn Shop" from THE BUSINESS OF FANCY, © 1992 by Sherman Alexie. Used by permission of Hanging Loose Press. "This Is What It Means to Say Phoenix, Arizona" from THE LONE RANGER AND TONTO FISTFIGHT IN HEAVEN, copyright © 1993 by Sherman Alexie. Used by permission of Grove/Atlantic, Inc. and the author. "Survivorman," copyright © 2009 by Sherman Alexie. Used by permission of the author. All rights reserved.

Dorothy Allison: "Introduction: Stubborn Girls and Mean Stories," copyright © 2002 by Dorothy Allison, from TRASH by Dorothy Allison. Copyright © 1988 Dorothy Allison. Reprinted by permission of Plume, an imprint of Penguin Group (USA), Inc., and The Frances Goldin Literary Agency.

Julia Alvarez: Excerpt from ¡Yo! Copyright © 1997 by Julia Alvarez. Published by Plume, an imprint of Penguin Group (USA). Originally published by Algonquin Books of Chapel Hill. Reprinted by permission of Susan Bergholz Literary Services, New York, NY, and Lamy, NM. All rights reserved.

A. R. Ammons: "Corsons Inlet," copyright © 1963 by A. R. Ammons; "Easter Morning," copyright © 1979 by A. R. Ammons; "Singing and Doubling Together," copyright © 1983 by A. R. Ammons from THE SELECTED POEMS, EXPANDED EDITION by A. R. Ammons. "Part 2" from GARBAGE by A. R. Ammons. Copyright © 1993 by A. R. Ammons. "So I Said I Am Ezra," copyright © 1955 by A. R. Ammons, from COLLECTED POEMS 1951–1971 by A. R. Ammons. Used by permission of W. W. Norton & Company, Inc. From "A Poem Is a Walk" by A. R. Ammons, first published in *Epoch*, vol. 18, Fall 1968. All rights reserved. Reprinted by permission of the Estate of A. R. Ammons, c/o Writers Representatives LLC, New York, NY 10011. All rights reserved.

Rudolfo A. Anaya: From BLESS ME, ULTIMA. Copyright © Rudolfo Anaya 1974. Published in hardcover and mass market paperback by Warner Books Inc. 1994; originally published by TQS Publications. Reprinted by permission of Susan Bergholz Literary Services, New York, NY, and Lamy, NM. All rights reserved.

Gloria Anzaldúa: "La concienca de la mestiza/Towards A New Consciousness," "How to Tame a Wild Tongue," and "El sonavabitche" from BORDERLANDS/LA FRONTERA: THE NEW MESTIZA. Copyright © 1987, 1999, 2007 by Gloria Anzaldúa. Reprinted by permission of Aunt Lute Books.

John Ashbery: "Illustration" from SOME TREES by John Ashbery. Copyright © 1956 by John Ashbery. "Soonest Mended" from THE DOUBLE DREAM OF SPRING by John Ashbery. Copyright © 1966, 1970 by John Ashbery. "Myrtle" from AND THE STARS WERE SHINING by John Ashbery. Copyright © 1994 by John Ashbery. Reprinted by permission of Georges Borchardt, Inc. and Carcanet Press Ltd. "Self-Portrait in a Convex Mirror," copyright © 1974 by John Ashbery from SELF-PORTRAIT IN A CONVEX MIRROR by John Ashbery. Used by permission of Viking Penguin, a division of Penguin Group (USA), Inc., and Carcanet Press Ltd.

James Baldwin: "Going to Meet the Man" is collected in GOING TO MEET THE MAN by James Baldwin, published by Vintage Books. Copyright © 1965 by James Baldwin. Copyright renewed. Used by arrangement with the James Baldwin Estate.

Joan Didion: From THE YEAR OF MAGICAL THINKING by Joan Didion, copyright © 2005 by Joan Didion. Used by permission of Alfred A. Knopf, a division of Random House, Inc., and HarperCollins Publishers Ltd.

Annie Dillard: "Seeing" from PILGRIM AT TINKER CREEK by Annie Dillard. Copyright © 1974 by Annie Dillard. Reprinted by permission of HarperCollins Publishers and Russell & Volkening as agents for the author.

Stephen Dixon: "Flying" from LONG MADE SHORT, pp. 32–34. Copyright © 1994 Stephen Dixon. Reprinted with permission of The Johns Hopkins University Press.

Rita Dove: "Geometry," "Adolescence I, II, III" from THE YELLOW HOUSE ON THE CORNER © 1980 by Rita Dove. "The Event," "The Zeppelin Factory," "Dusting," from THOMAS AND BEULAH, © 1986 by Rita Dove. "Parsley" from MUSEUM © 1983 by Rita Dove. All originally published by Carnegie-Mellon University Press and reprinted by permission of the author. "Poem in Which I Refuse Contemplation" from GRACE NOTES by Rita Dove. Copyright © 1989 by Rita Dove. "Missing" from MOTHER LOVE by Rita Dove. Copyright © 1995 by Rita Dove. "Rosa" from ON THE BUS WITH ROSA PARKS by Rita Dove. Copyright © 1999 by Rita Dove. "Fox Trot Fridays" from AMERICAN SMOOTH by Rita Dove. Copyright © 2004 by Rita Dove. Used by permission of the author and W. W. Norton & Company, Inc.

Robert Duncan: "Often I Am Permitted to Return to a Meadow" and "A Poem Beginning with a Line by Pindar" from THE OPENING OF THE FIELD by Robert Duncan. Copyright © 1960 by Robert Duncan. "Interrupted Forms" from GROUND WORK: BEFORE THE WAR by Robert Duncan. Copyright © 1984 by Robert Duncan. Reprinted by permission of New Directions Publishing Corp.

Ralph Ellison: "Battle Royal," copyright 1948 by Ralph Ellison, "Prologue," copyright 1952 by Ralph Ellison, from INVISIBLE MAN by Ralph Ellison. Used by permission of Random House, Inc.

Louise Erdrich: "Dear John Wayne," "I Was Sleeping Where the Black Oaks Move" from JACKLIGHT © 1984 by Louise Erdrich and "Fleur" © 1986 by Louise Erdrich. Reprinted with permission of The Wylie Agency, LLC. "Grief" from ORIGINAL FIRE: SELECTED AND NEW POEMS by Louise Erdrich. Copyright © 2003 by Louise Erdrich. Reprinted by permission of HarperCollins Publishers.

William H. Gass: From FICTION AND THE FIGURES OF LIFE by William H. Gass. Reprinted by permission of David R. Godine, Publisher, Inc. Copyright © 1971 by William H. Gass.

Allen Ginsberg: "Howl," copyright © 1955 by Allen Ginsberg. "A Supermarket in California" copyright © 1955 by Allen Ginsberg. "Sunflower Sutra" copyright © 1955 by Allen Ginsberg. "To Aunt Rose" copyright © 1958 by Allen Ginsberg. "On Burrough's Work" copyright © 1954 by Allen Ginsberg. "Ego Confession" copyright © 1974 by Allen Ginsberg. "Footnote to Howl," copyright © 1955 by Allen Ginsberg. From COLLECTED POEMS 1947–1980 by Allen Ginsberg. Reprinted by permission of HarperCollins Publishers and The Wylie Agency (UK) Ltd.

Louise Glück: "The Drowned Children," and "The Sick Child" and "For My Sister" in "Descending Figure" from THE FIRST FOUR BOOKS OF POEMS by Louise Glück. Copyright © 1968, 1971, 1972, 1973, 1974, 1975, 1976, 1977, 1978, 1979, 1980, 1985, 1995 by Louise Glück. "Appearances" from ARARAT by Louise Glück. Copyright © 1990 by Louise Glück. "Vespers" from THE WILD IRIS by Louise Glück. Copyright © 1992 by Louise Glück. Reprinted by permission of HarperCollins Publishers and Carcanet Press Ltd. "October" by Louise Glück. Copyright © 2004 by Louise Glück. Reprinted with the permission of Sarabande Books, Inc. www.sarabandebooks.org.

Jorie Graham: "The Dream of the Unified Field," "At Luca Signorelli's Resurrection of the Body," and "The Geese" from THE DREAM OF THE UNIFIED FIELD: POEMS 1974–1994 by Jorie Graham. Copyright © 1995 by Jorie Graham. Reprinted by permission of HarperCollins Publishers and Carcanet Press Limited.

Joy Harjo: "Call It Fear" and "White Bear" from SHE HAD SOME HORSES by Joy Harjo, copyright © 1983 by Joy Harjo. Used by permission of W. W. Norton & Company, Inc. "Summer Night" from IN MAD LOVE AND WAR. Copyright © 1990 by Joy Harjo. Reprinted by permission of Wesleyan University Press. "The Flood" from THE WOMAN WHO FELL FROM THE SKY by Joy Harjo. Copyright © 1994 by Joy Harjo. Reprinted by permission of W. W. Norton & Company, Inc., and the author. "When the World As We Knew It Ended" from HOW WE BECAME HUMAN: NEW AND SELECTED POEMS 1975–2001 by Joy Harjo. Copyright © 2002 by Joy Harjo. Used by permission of W. W. Norton & Company, Inc.

Michael S. Harper: "Martin's Blues," "Nightmare Begins Responsibility" "Dear John, Dear Coltrane," "American History," "*Bird Lives*: Charles Parker in St. Louis." Used with permission of the poet and the University of Illinois Press, from SONGLINES IN MICHAELTREE: NEW AND COLLECTED POEMS by Michael S. Harper. Copyright © 2000 by Michael S. Harper.

Robert Hass: "Faint Music" and "Dragonfiles Mating" from SUN UNDER WOOD: NEW POEMS by Robert Hass. Copyright © 1996 by Robert Hass. Reprinted by permission of HarperCollins Publishers. "Meditation at Lagunitas" from PRAISE by Robert Hass. Copyright © 1979 by Robert Hass. Reprinted by permission of HarperCollins Publishers and Bloodaxe Books. "Measure" from FIELD GUIDE by Robert Hass. Copyright © 1973 by Robert Hass. Reprinted by permission of Yale University Press.

Robert Hayden: "Middle Passage," copyright © 1966 by Robert Hayden, "Homage to the Empress of the Blues," copyright © 1966 by Robert Hayden, "Those Winter Sundays," copyright © 1966 by Robert Hayden, "Free Fantasia: Tiger Flowers," copyright © 1975 by Robert Hayden, from COLLECTED POEMS OF ROBERT HAYDEN by Robert Hayden, ed. by Frederick Glaysher. Copyright © 1985 by Emma Hayden. Used by permission of Liveright Publishing Corporation.

Fanny Howe: From THE WEDDING DRESS by Fanny Howe, copyright © 2003 by The Regents of the University of California. From GONE by Fanny Howe copyright © 2003 by The Regents of the University of California. From SELECTED POEMS by Fanny Howe, copyright © 2000 by The Regents of the University of California. Reprinted by permission of The University of California Press. "[Nobody wants crossed-out girls around]" reprinted from ONE CROSSED OUT. Copyright © 1997 by Fanny Howe. Reprinted with the permission of Graywolf Press, Minneapolis, Minn.,www.graywolfpress.org.

Randall Jarrell: "90 North," "The Death of the Ball Turret Gunner," "Second Air Force," "Next Day," "Well Water," and "Thinking of the Lost World" from THE COMPLETE POEMS by Randall Jarrell. Copyright © 1969; renewed 1997 by Mary von S. Jarrell. Reprinted by permission of Farrar, Straus and Giroux, LLC, and Faber and Faber Ltd.

Jack Kerouac: From BIG SUR, copyright © by Jack Kerouac, reprinted by permission of SLL/Sterling Lord Literistic, Inc.

Index

American Literature since 1945

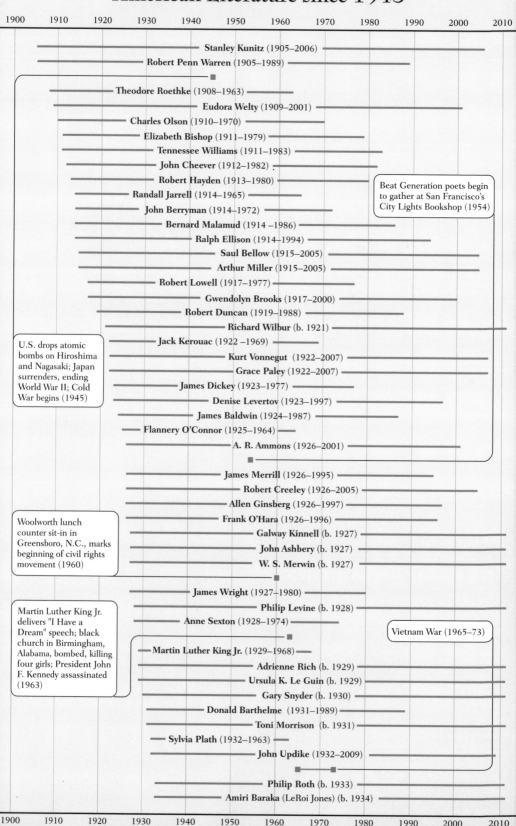

1900 1910 1920 1930 1940 1950 1960 1970 1980 1990 2000 2010

Stanley Kunitz (1905–2006)
Robert Penn Warren (1905–1989)
Theodore Roethke (1908–1963)
Eudora Welty (1909–2001)
Charles Olson (1910–1970)
Elizabeth Bishop (1911–1979)
Tennessee Williams (1911–1983)
John Cheever (1912–1982)
Robert Hayden (1913–1980)
Randall Jarrell (1914–1965)
John Berryman (1914–1972)
Bernard Malamud (1914–1986)
Ralph Ellison (1914–1994)
Saul Bellow (1915–2005)
Arthur Miller (1915–2005)
Robert Lowell (1917–1977)
Gwendolyn Brooks (1917–2000)
Robert Duncan (1919–1988)
Richard Wilbur (b. 1921)
Jack Kerouac (1922–1969)
Kurt Vonnegut (1922–2007)
Grace Paley (1922–2007)
James Dickey (1923–1977)
Denise Levertov (1923–1997)
James Baldwin (1924–1987)
Flannery O'Connor (1925–1964)
A. R. Ammons (1926–2001)
James Merrill (1926–1995)
Robert Creeley (1926–2005)
Allen Ginsberg (1926–1997)
Frank O'Hara (1926–1996)
Galway Kinnell (b. 1927)
John Ashbery (b. 1927)
W. S. Merwin (b. 1927)
James Wright (1927–1980)
Philip Levine (b. 1928)
Anne Sexton (1928–1974)
Martin Luther King Jr. (1929–1968)
Adrienne Rich (b. 1929)
Ursula K. Le Guin (b. 1929)
Gary Snyder (b. 1930)
Donald Barthelme (1931–1989)
Toni Morrison (b. 1931)
Sylvia Plath (1932–1963)
John Updike (1932–2009)
Philip Roth (b. 1933)
Amiri Baraka (LeRoi Jones) (b. 1934)

Beat Generation poets begin to gather at San Francisco's City Lights Bookshop (1954)

U.S. drops atomic bombs on Hiroshima and Nagasaki; Japan surrenders, ending World War II; Cold War begins (1945)

Woolworth lunch counter sit-in in Greensboro, N.C., marks beginning of civil rights movement (1960)

Martin Luther King Jr. delivers "I Have a Dream" speech; black church in Birmingham, Alabama, bombed, killing four girls; President John F. Kennedy assassinated (1963)

Vietnam War (1965–73)

1900 1910 1920 1930 1940 1950 1960 1970 1980 1990 2000 2010

| 1900 | 1910 | 1920 | 1930 | 1940 | 1950 | 1960 | 1970 | 1980 | 1990 | 2000 | 2010 |

N. Scott Momaday (b. 1934)
Audre Lorde (1934–1992)
Charles Wright (b. 1935)
Mary Oliver (b. 1935)

King assassinated;
Senator Robert F.
Kennedy assassinated
(1968)

Lucille Clifton (1936–2010)
Stephen Dixon (b. 1937)
Rudolfo A. Anaya (b. 1937)
Thomas Pynchon (b. 1937)
Raymond Carver (1938–1988)
Ishmael Reed (b. 1938)
Charles Simic (b. 1938)
Michael S. Harper (b. 1938)
Toni Cade Bambara (1939–1995)
Thomas McGuane (b. 1939)
Maxine Hong Kingston (b. 1940)
Fanny Howe (b. 1940)
Robert Pinsky (b. 1940)

U.S. astronauts land on the moon;
Stonewall riots in New York City
initiate gay liberation movement;
Woodstock Festival held near
Bethel, New York (1969)

Robert Haas (b. 1941)
Simon J. Ortiz (b. 1941)
Billy Collins (b. 1941)
Sharon Olds (b. 1942)
Gloria Anzaldúa (1942–2004)
Sam Shepard (b. 1943)
Louise Glück (b. 1943)

Roe v. Wade legalizes abortion;
American Indian Movement
members occupy Wounded Knee
(1973)

Alice Walker (b. 1944)
August Wilson (1945–2005)
Annie Dillard (b. 1945)
Kay Ryan (b. 1945)
Ann Beattie (b. 1947)
David Mamet (b. 1947)
Yusef Komunyakaa (b. 1947)
Leslie Marmon Silko (b. 1948)
Art Spiegelman (b. 1948)
Julia Alvarez (b. 1950)
Jorie Graham (b. 1950)
Joy Harjo (b. 1951)
Rita Dove (b. 1952)
Alberto Ríos (b. 1952)
Amy Tan (b. 1952)

Equal Rights Amendment
defeated; antinuclear movement
protests manufacture of nuclear
weapons; AIDS officially
identified in the United States
(1982)

Soviet Union
collapses; Cold War
ends (1989)

Sandra Cisneros (b. 1954)
Louise Erdrich (b. 1954)
Lorna Dee Cervantes (b. 1954)
Cathy Song (b. 1955)
Li-Young Lee (b. 1957)
Richard Powers (b. 1957)

September 11 terrorist attacks
on Pentagon and World Trade
Center (2001)

United States and
Great Britain
invade Iraq (2003)

Sherman Alexie (b. 1966)
Jhumpa Lahiri (b. 1967)
Junot Díaz (b. 1968)

Advent of the worst economic
recession since the Great
Depression (2007)

| 1900 | 1910 | 1920 | 1930 | 1940 | 1950 | 1960 | 1970 | 1980 | 1990 | 2000 | 2010 |